SIPRI Yearbook 2021
Armaments, Disarmament and International Security

www.sipriyearbook.org

SIPRI Yearbook 2021

Armaments, Disarmament and International Security

**STOCKHOLM INTERNATIONAL
PEACE RESEARCH INSTITUTE**

OXFORD UNIVERSITY PRESS
2021

OXFORD
UNIVERSITY PRESS

Great Clarendon Street, Oxford OX2 6DP,
United Kingdom

Oxford University Press is a department of the University of Oxford.
It furthers the University's objective of excellence in research, scholarship,
and education by publishing worldwide. Oxford is a registered trade mark of
Oxford University Press in the UK and in certain other countries

Published in the United States of America by Oxford University Press
198 Madison Avenue, New York, NY 10016, United States of America

British Library Cataloguing in Publication Data
Data available

Library of Congress Cataloging in Publication Data
Data available

ISBN 978-0-19-284757-7

Typeset and originated by SIPRI
Printed in Great Britain by
Bell & Bain Ltd., Glasgow

Credit: Figures 4.1, 5.1. 6.1, 6.2, 7.1 and 7.2
by Hugo Ahlenius, Nordipil, <https://nordpil.se/>

SIPRI Yearbook 2021 is also published online at
<http://www.sipriyearbook.org>

Contents

3. Armed conflict and peace processes in the Americas   71

Overview
MARINA CAPARINI

    I. *Key general developments in the region*   73
MARINA CAPARINI

Developments in specific countries

   II. *Armed conflict and the peace process in Colombia*   80
MARINA CAPARINI

Non-international armed conflicts between the government and
non-state armed groups—Violence against civilians—The border
conflict between Colombia and Venezuela

 III. *Armed conflict in Mexico*   85
MARINA CAPARINI

4. Armed conflict and peace processes in Asia and Oceania   89

Overview
IAN DAVIS

    I. *Key general developments in the region*   91
IAN DAVIS

Growing geopolitical tensions in East Asia—The impact of
Covid-19

Part II. Military spending and armaments, 2020

Part III. Non-proliferation, arms control and disarmament, 2020

Annexes

Preface

The Covid-19 pandemic is a globally shared human experience. It has brought individuals face to face with mortality and societies face to face with their vulnerability. It has had multiple, far-reaching effects on the global economy and international politics, although many of its ramifications are yet to be determined. Unsurprisingly, it features strongly in this, the 52nd edition of the SIPRI Yearbook, since it forms an essential part of the narrative when reflecting on challenges to human security and international stability in 2020.

The Covid-19 crisis has resulted in the spread of misinformation and conspiracy theories—labelled an 'infodemic' by the World Health Organization. States and non-state actors alike have circulated rumour, half-truth and fake facts about the scale of the pandemic and its origin, prevention, diagnosis and treatment. This experience has confirmed, if confirmation were needed, the risks that are posed by disinformation and a casual attitude to facts and the truth. The SIPRI Yearbook's focus on compiling, authenticating and disseminating the facts is vital in countering misinformation and for mapping cooperative approaches for both responding to and recovering from the pandemic.

The introduction (chapter 1) reflects on a year in which the balance sheet of security and risk remained largely unchanged. In a year dominated by the Covid-19 pandemic, that conclusion might seem overly optimistic, but it is supported by the evidence in the following chapters. The political disputes that festered throughout 2020 about responsibility for the origin of Covid-19 were symptoms of an ailing international body politic. Despite such vicissitudes, many institutions of international cooperation remained vibrant, but simply required greater care and attention. As with the more traditional security challenges discussed in this Yearbook, the pandemic requires multilateral solutions and instruments, and leaders will need to strengthen and re-energize routines of international cooperation.

Part I of the Yearbook covers armed conflicts and conflict management in 2020. It aims to catch key moments and trends in conflict escalation and peacebuilding. Chapter 2 focuses on armed conflicts and peace processes, looking at the multifaceted root causes of both and summarizing their latest developments. Multilateral peace operations feature prominently. Active armed conflicts occurred in at least 39 states in 2020 (chapters 3–7). Nevertheless, the reduction in the severity of several armed conflicts in 2020 led to a further reduction in conflict fatalities, continuing a recent downward trend.

Parts II and III focus on armament and disarmament. The Institute's work in these areas is based on original, rigorous data collection, which forms the foundation of SIPRI's databases. Part II is devoted to military spending and armaments, including comprehensive assessments of recent trends in military expenditure (chapter 8), international arms transfers and arms production (chapter 9), and world nuclear forces, including the current nuclear modernization programmes (chapter 10). Global military spending continued to rise in 2020, but the volume of global arms transfers remained roughly stable.

Part III covers non-proliferation, arms control and disarmament. In it, chapter 11 looks at developments in Russian–US nuclear arms control and Iran's implementation of the Joint Comprehensive Plan of Action to limit its nuclear programme. Nuclear arms control continued to stagnate in 2020 and the USA withdrew from the Open Skies Treaty, but the Treaty on the Prohibition of Nuclear Weapons received sufficient support to enter into force in January 2021. Chapter 12 covers chemical and biological weapons (CBW). It discusses the Covid-19 pandemic and the highly politicized nature of the international effort to identify the source of the disease. The chapter also explores allegations of chemical weapons use and other developments in CBW risks. Chapter 13 includes a round-up of the global instruments for controlling conventional weapons in 2020, while chapter 14 reports on efforts to strengthen controls on the trade in conventional arms and dual-use items.

Taken together, this compendium addresses some of the most urgent matters that confronted humanity in 2020. SIPRI continues to look for ways to make best use of the Yearbook and its contents as a tool of transparency and accountability. To that end, the Yearbook has been translated for many years into Arabic, Chinese, Russian and Ukrainian.

SIPRI, of course, was not immune from the challenges of the pandemic and the majority of staff have worked remotely during the production of this Yearbook. This year's edition features contributions from 34 authors. Its content is refereed extensively, and a dedicated editorial team ensures that it conforms to the highest publishing standards. The communications, library, operations and IT staff at SIPRI all contribute in different ways to the Yearbook's production and distribution. I would like to take this opportunity to express my gratitude to everybody involved, within SIPRI and beyond—and especially our external reviewers, whose insights and suggestions always lead to material improvements in the chapters that are eventually published.

When 'facts' are only a click away, SIPRI's commitment to authenticating the facts means that the volume remains an indispensable global public good. This will continue to be the case as the Institute helps to chart a course for emerging from the Covid-19 with more equitable, resilient and sustainable societies.

Dan Smith
Director, SIPRI
Stockholm, May 2021

Abbreviations and conventions

ABM	Anti-ballistic missile	CWC	Chemical Weapons Convention
ACLED	Armed Conflict Location & Event Data Project	DDR	Disarmament, demobilization and reintegration
AG	Australia Group		
ALCM	Air-launched cruise missile	DPRK	Democratic People's Republic of Korea (North Korea)
APC	Armoured personnel carrier		
APM	Anti-personnel mine		
ASAT	Anti-satellite	DRC	Democratic Republic of the Congo
ASEAN	Association of Southeast Asian Nations	ECOWAS	Economic Community of West African States
ATT	Arms Trade Treaty		
AU	African Union	ERW	Explosive remnants of war
BCC	Bilateral Consultative Commission (of the Russian–US New START treaty)	EU	European Union
		EWIPA	Explosive weapons in populated areas
		FFM	Fact-finding mission
BWC	Biological and Toxin Weapons Convention	FMCT	Fissile material cut-off treaty
CAR	Central African Republic	FY	Financial year
CBM	Confidence-building measure	G7	Group of Seven (industrialized states)
CBW	Chemical and biological weapon/warfare	GDP	Gross domestic product
CCM	Convention on Cluster Munitions	GGE	Group of government experts
CCW	Certain Conventional Weapons (Convention)	GLCM	Ground-launched cruise missile
CD	Conference on Disarmament	HCOC	Hague Code of Conduct
CFSP	Common Foreign and Security Policy (of the EU)	HEU	Highly enriched uranium
		IAEA	International Atomic Energy Agency
CSBM	Confidence- and security-building measure	ICBM	Intercontinental ballistic missile
CSDP	Common Security and Defence Policy (of the EU)	ICC	International Criminal Court
CSP	Conference of States Parties	ICJ	International Court of Justice
CSTO	Collective Security Treaty Organization	IED	Improvised explosive device
CTBT	Comprehensive Nuclear-Test-Ban Treaty	IGAD	Intergovernmental Authority on Development
CTBTO	Comprehensive Nuclear-Test-Ban Treaty Organization	IHL	International humanitarian law
CW	Chemical weapon/warfare	INF	Intermediate-range Nuclear Forces (Treaty)

ISAF	International Security Assistance Force	P5	Five permanent members of the UN Security Council
ISU	Implementation Support Unit	PAROS	Prevention of an arms race in outer space
JCPOA	Joint Comprehensive Plan of Action	POA	Programme of Action to Prevent, Combat and Eradicate the Illicit Trade in Small Arms and Light Weapons in All its Aspects (UN)
LAWS	Lethal autonomous weapon systems		
LEU	Low-enriched uranium		
MENA	Middle East and North Africa	R&D	Research and development
MIRV	Multiple independently targetable re-entry vehicle	SADC	Southern African Development Community
MRBM	Medium-range ballistic missile	SALW	Small arms and light weapons
MTCR	Missile Technology Control Regime	SAM	Surface-to-air missile
NAM	Non-Aligned Movement	SLBM	Submarine-launched ballistic missile
NATO	North Atlantic Treaty Organization	SLCM	Sea-launched cruise missile
NGO	Non-governmental organization	SORT	Strategic Offensive Reductions Treaty
NNWS	Non-nuclear weapon state	SRBM	Short-range ballistic missile
NPT	Non-Proliferation Treaty	START	Strategic Arms Reduction Treaty
NSG	Nuclear Suppliers Group	TPNW	Treaty on the Prohibition of Nuclear Weapons
NWS	Nuclear weapon state		
OAS	Organization of American States	UAE	United Arab Emirates
OECD	Organisation for Economic Co-operation and Development	UAV	Unmanned aerial vehicle
		UN	United Nations
		UNHCR	UN High Commissioner for Refugees
OEWG	Open-ended working group	UNODA	UN Office for Disarmament Affairs
OHCHR	Office of the UN High Commissioner for Human Rights	UNROCA	UN Register of Conventional Arms
OPCW	Organisation for the Prohibition of Chemical Weapons	UNSC	UN Security Council
		WA	Wassenaar Arrangement
		WHO	World Health Organization
OSCC	Open Skies Consultative Commission	WMD	Weapon(s) of mass destruction
OSCE	Organization for Security and Co-operation in Europe		

Conventions

..	Data not available or not applicable
–	Nil or a negligible figure
( )	Uncertain data
b.	Billion (thousand million)
kg	Kilogram
km	Kilometre (1000 metres)
m.	Million
th.	Thousand
tr.	Trillion (million million)
$	US dollars
€	Euros

Geographical regions and subregions

Africa	Consisting of North Africa (Algeria, Libya, Morocco and Tunisia, but excluding Egypt) and sub-Saharan Africa
Americas	Consisting of North America (Canada and the USA), Central America and the Caribbean (including Mexico), and South America
Asia and Oceania	Consisting of Central Asia, East Asia, Oceania, South Asia (including Afghanistan) and South East Asia
Europe	Consisting of Eastern Europe (Armenia, Azerbaijan, Belarus, Georgia, Moldova, Russia and Ukraine) and Western and Central Europe (with South Eastern Europe)
Middle East	Consisting of Egypt, Iran, Iraq, Israel, Jordan, Kuwait, Lebanon, Syria, Turkey and the states of the Arabian peninsula

Note: The boundaries, names and designations used in the maps in this volume do not imply any endorsement or acceptance by SIPRI of claims or stances in disputes over specific territories.

SIPRI Yearbook online

www.sipriyearbook.org

The full content of the SIPRI Yearbook is also available online. With the SIPRI Yearbook online you can

- access the complete SIPRI Yearbook on your desktop or handheld device for research on the go
- navigate easily through content using advanced search and browse functionality
- find content easily: search through the whole SIPRI Yearbook and within your results
- save valuable time: use your personal profile to return to saved searches and content again and again
- share content with colleagues and students easily via email and social networking tools
- enhance your research by following clearly linked references and web resources

How to access the SIPRI Yearbook online

Institutional access

The SIPRI Yearbook online is available to institutions worldwide for a one-time fee or by annual subscription. Librarians and central resource coordinators can contact Oxford University Press to receive a price quotation using the details below or register for a free trial at <http://www.oxford online.com/freetrials/>.

Individuals can recommend this resource to their librarians at <http://www.oup.com/library-recommend/>.

Individual subscriptions

The SIPRI Yearbook online is available to individuals worldwide on a 12-month subscription basis. Purchase details can be found at <http://www.oup.com/>.

Contact information

Customers within the Americas

Email: oxfordonline@oup.com
Telephone: +1 (800) 624 0153
Fax: +1 (919) 677 8877

Customers outside the Americas

Email: institutionalsales@oup.com
Telephone: +44 (0) 1865 353705
Fax: +44 (0) 1865 353308

Introduction

Chapter 1. Introduction: International stability and human security in 2020

1. Introduction: International stability and human security in 2020

DAN SMITH

The histories that have yet to be written of 2020 seem likely to be dominated by the Covid-19 pandemic and the United States presidential election.[1] Neither is a security event or issue as traditionally understood but both have important implications for international stability and human security.

This is the 52nd edition of the SIPRI Yearbook. Recent editions have registered the deteriorating international security environment. Over the last half decade, there have been more armed conflicts, higher military spending, an expanding volume of international arms transfers and a crisis in nuclear arms control. Over the same period, the impact of climate change and other kinds of environmental degradation on human society has intensified, and climate change has combined with armed conflict to drive a rise in world hunger.[2] There have been regional flashpoints and confrontation in almost every region except the Americas and an increasingly sour tone in global geopolitics. This is the international background against which the Covid-19 pandemic took hold and the US presidential election happened.

One reading of the overall situation in international security is to be found in the 'Doomsday Clock' of the journal *Bulletin of the Atomic Scientists*.[3] Metaphorically fixing the hour of the apocalypse at midnight, the clock is 'set' each January. Like any broad assessment of security, this one contains elements of subjective judgement, but it is evidence-based, clearly argued and consistent in its approach. In December 1991 at the end of the cold war, the clock showed 17 minutes to midnight; in 2010, it stood at 10 minutes to midnight; and in 2015 at 3 minutes to. Step by step it has moved closer to midnight until in January 2020 it was set at 100 seconds

---

[1] See e.g. 'A review of 2020 through *Nature*'s editorials', *Nature*, 22 Dec. 2020; Blake, P. and Wadhwa, D., '2020 year in review: The impact of Covid-19 in 12 charts', World Bank Blog, 14 Dec. 2020; and Page, S. and Bravo, V., 'The year that was: A global pandemic, racial protests, a president-elect. Oh, and impeachment', *USA Today*, 29 Dec. 2020.

[2] Food and Agriculture Organization of the United Nations (FAO) et al., *The State of Food Security and Nutrition in the World: Transforming Food Systems for Affordable Healthy Diets* (FAO, International Fund for Agriculture Development, UNICEF, World Food Programme, World Health Organization: Rome, 2020).

[3] 'The Doomsday Clock: A timeline of conflict, culture, and change', *Bulletin of the Atomic Scientists*, [n.d.].

before the apocalypse, the closest it has ever been.[4] Awareness of the steadily intensifying twin risks of climate change and nuclear war were the primary foundations of this judgement. At the start of 2021, based on events in 2020, the clock remained at 100 seconds to midnight. The situation was not better than a year before but, on balance, at least it was no worse.

That may sound like optimistically grasping at straws but the deterioration in global stability and security during the last decade has been extraordinarily sharp. That has hindered cooperation to bring armed conflicts to an end, leaving the global system of conflict management weaker than at any time since 1990.[5] An interruption of that deterioration is both significant and welcome. The deficiencies in international cooperation that have emerged in the last decade apply not only to conflict management but also to other aspects of global risk.

This introductory chapter explores the intersections of the security, environmental, health and political challenges of 2020. It offers a global overview with the core message that the balance sheet of insecurity and security largely remained unchanged in 2020, neither worsening nor improving. The first section looks in turn at trends in military spending, the arms trade and conflicts; arms control; regional hotspots and potential flashpoints; and the relationship between climate change and insecurity. The second section explores the ramifications of the Covid-19 crisis and the third section considers the meaning of the 2020 US presidential election. The chapter finishes with a scan of some aspects of international cooperation. Further detail on many of the issues covered in the chapter is to be found in other chapters of this edition of the SIPRI Yearbook.

I. Security issues in 2020: A global overview

Broad trends

SIPRI's data on arms transfers comparing the five years 2016–20 with the preceding five-year period, 2011–15, indicates that the volume of international transfers of major weapons was approximately stable.[6] Whether that marks a turn towards a downward trend, or is merely a pause in growth, cannot be determined yet. Global military spending, in contrast, increased in 2020, as it had in previous years, imposing a heavier burden on national economies that in most cases shrank during the year under the impact of

---

[4] 'Closer than ever: It is 100 seconds to midnight', 2020 Doomsday Clock Statement, *Bulletin of the Atomic Scientists*, 23 Jan. 2020.

[5] Smith, D., 'Introduction: International stability and human security in 2019', *SIPRI Yearbook 2020*, pp. 5–10.

[6] See chapter 9 in this volume. SIPRI uses a 5-year average as the basis for comparison because annual figures often show fluctuations that are irrelevant and misleading as to the medium- to long-term trends. The 0.5% decline from 2011–15 to 2016–20 is statistically insignificant.

the Covid-19 pandemic.[7] It is possible that, in the wake of the pandemic and its economic effects, coming years will see lower military spending, as happened after the global financial and economic crisis of 2008–2009. This is not inevitable, however; many major military spenders perceive reasons, including anxiety about the security context, to devote more resources to military preparations.

The number of armed conflicts increased again in 2020 but the global total of fatalities in war has fallen well below the level experienced when the Syrian war was at its height some five to six years ago.[8] The overall statistics mask some significant variations. War deaths in sub-Saharan Africa increased by about 40 per cent in 2020 compared to 2019.[9] The war in Yemen remained the source of a major humanitarian disaster throughout 2020 and showed no signs of finding a conclusion either through negotiation or on the battlefield itself.[10] There were hints of frustration and fatigue on the part of one of the governments intervening in the conflict, the United Arab Emirates (UAE), but Saudi Arabia, the main external power in the war, retained US support throughout 2020 and seemed to see little incentive to seek an urgent exit. There was an explosion of combat in the long-simmering conflict between Armenia and Azerbaijan over Nagorno-Karabakh, an ethnic Armenian enclave within Azerbaijan. The latter took a decisive advantage on the battlefield and took back control of territory lying between Nagorno-Karabakh and Armenia itself that Armenia had occupied since the first major war between the two countries ended in 1994.[11] In late 2020, a major new war began in Ethiopia in Tigray province. The large numbers of people fleeing and reports of atrocities by both Ethiopian forces and troops from neighbouring Eritrea became the focus of international concern.[12]

SIPRI's review of armed conflicts in 2020 found limited signs that the Covid-19 pandemic materially affected armed conflicts during the year. Some conflicts eased somewhat but others became more intense.[13] In an attempt to turn a health crisis into a peace opportunity, United Nations Secretary-General António Guterres issued a global ceasefire call on 23 March, calling

---

[7] See chapter 8 in this volume.

[8] Uppsala Conflict Data Program, University of Uppsala, [n.d.]; see also chapter 2, section I, in this volume.

[9] See chapter 7, section I, in this volume.

[10] See chapter 6, section V, in this volume.

[11] See chapter 5, section II, in this volume.

[12] Getachew, S., 'Ethiopia's Tigray conflict sees hundreds dead, thousands flee to Sudan', *New Humanitarian*, 10 Nov. 2020; Akinwotu, E., '"I saw people dying on the road": Tigray's traumatised war refugees', *The Guardian*, 2 Dec. 2020; 'Tigray: Hundreds of civilians reported killed in artillery strikes, warns UN rights chief', *UN News*, 22 Dec. 2020; and AP News, 'I would never go back': Accounts of atrocities grow in Ethiopia's Tigray conflict', *Los Angeles Times*, 28 Dec. 2020. For detail see chapter 7, section IV, in this volume.

[13] See chapter 2, section I, in this volume; and Ide, T., 'Covid-19 and armed conflict', *World Development*, vol. 140 (Apr. 2021).

on all parties to stop fighting and take on the superordinate challenge of the pandemic.[14] There was a supportive response from many quarters, including from some parties actively engaged in armed conflict.[15] In the end, however, the impact was limited. Conflict participants—both governments and non-state armed groups—initiated some 17 ceasefires in response to the call but only 6 clearly lasted beyond a month.[16] The situation was not made more conducive to serious implementation of the ceasefire when the UN Security Council, instead of immediately and loudly supporting the secretary-general's call, became embroiled in an argument between China and the USA about whether an endorsement of his appeal should include reference to the World Health Organization (WHO).[17] The UN Security Council resolution supporting the call for a ceasefire was finally passed on 1 July 2020.[18]

That a straightforward appeal to support a humanitarian goal amid a global health emergency should get caught up in bickering between two great powers was an unfortunate indication of the limits of international cooperation at the time. In 2021, a new, similar effort resulted rather more quickly in a UN Security Council resolution calling for a humanitarian pause so vaccinations against the coronavirus causing Covid-19 could proceed worldwide. It passed unanimously in late February 2021 with none of the previous attempt's bad feeling.[19] This was, perhaps, a welcome sign that the global environment was starting to improve—or, at least, in the vocabulary used above, was no longer deteriorating.

Arms control

Nuclear arms control continued to stagnate in 2020, continuing a process that started almost a decade before. It was in 2013 that the USA, then under the Obama administration, accused Russia of non-compliance with the 1987 Treaty on the Elimination of Intermediate-Range and Shorter-Range Missiles (INF Treaty).[20] The Trump administration's decision to withdraw the USA from the INF Treaty, announced in 2018, was a landmark moment in the crumbling of the treaty-based architecture of US–Russian nuclear arms control. It also appeared to be representative of a profound distaste for arms

---

[14] United Nations, Global Ceasefire, 'Now is the time for a collective new push for peace and reconciliation', [n.d.].

[15] UN Secretary-General, 'Update on the secretary-general's appeal for a global ceasefire', 2 Apr. 2020.

[16] See chapter 2, section I, table 2.3, in this volume.

[17] Gowan, R., 'What's happened to the UN secretary-general's Covid-19 ceasefire call?', Speech, International Crisis Group, 16 June 2020.

[18] UN Security Council Resolution 2532, 1 July 2020.

[19] UN Security Council Resolution 2565, 26 Feb. 2021.

[20] Arms Control Association, 'The Intermediate-Range Nuclear Forces (INF) Treaty at a glance', Fact sheet, Aug. 2019. For a summary of the INF Treaty see annex A, section III, in this volume.

control on the part of the Trump administration. The only exception was the rather short-lived nuclear diplomacy with the Democratic People's Republic of Korea (DPRK, North Korea) from May 2018 until October 2019.[21] As well as withdrawing from the INF Treaty, the Trump administration ended US adherence to the Iran nuclear deal (formally, the Joint Comprehensive Plan of Action, JCPOA) in 2018 and, in 2020, it withdrew from the Open Skies Treaty of 2002.[22] The latter is not directly an arms control agreement but offers an important measure of transparency as a means of building confidence between states. The Trump administration also appeared indifferent to the potential demise in February 2021 of the 2010 New START treaty with Russia on strategic nuclear weapons.[23] The treaty has a clause permitting its extension for five years by mutual agreement; until a late change of approach, the Trump administration opposed extending the treaty and insisted China came into trilateral negotiations on a new treaty.[24] China refused, arguing that it has far fewer nuclear warheads than either the USA or Russia.[25] It offered to join trilateral talks when their numbers come down.[26] More than anything, the US position looked like an excuse for not agreeing to extend. That impression was only strengthened when, in a strange stunt, US negotiators about to meet with Russian representatives to discuss possible extension of the treaty, arranged—and tweeted photos of—empty chairs and a Chinese flag at the negotiating table.[27]

Of particular concern was that neglecting to extend New START could have a negative effect on the deferred five-year review conference (RevCon) of the Nuclear Non-Proliferation Treaty (NPT).[28] The RevCon was scheduled for 2020 but was postponed because of the Covid-19 pandemic to January 2021, before being put off again until August 2021.[29] The NPT is designed both to limit the spread of nuclear weapons to non-nuclear weapons states (NNWS) and to lead to their elimination by the nuclear weapons states (NWS).

[21] On US diplomacy with North Korea including the Singapore summit in June 2018, the Hanoi summit in Feb. 2019, the brief summit in the Korean Demilitarized Zone in June 2019, and the unsuccessful working level meeting in Stockholm in Oct. 2019, see Kile, S. N., 'North Korean–United States nuclear diplomacy', *SIPRI Yearbook 2019*, pp. 361–68, and *SIPRI Yearbook 2020*, pp. 410–17.

[22] On the Open Skies Treaty see chapter 13, section V, and annex A, section II, in this volume. See also Arms Control Association, 'The Open Skies Treaty at a glance', Fact sheet, Nov. 2020.

[23] Arms Control Association, 'New START at a glance', Fact sheet, Feb. 2021. See also chapter 11, section I, in this volume.

[24] Gordon, M. R., 'Trump administration shifts course on Russian Arms talks, easing insistence China join now', *Wall Street Journal*, 18 Aug. 2020.

[25] Quinn, L., 'China's stance on nuclear arms control and New START', Arms Control Now blog, Arms Control Association, 23 Aug. 2019.

[26] AFP–JIJI, 'China says would join nuclear talks if US reduces arsenal', *Japan Times*, 8 July 2020.

[27] Meyer, H. and Wadhams, N., 'Russia, China lash out at US over flag stunt at nuclear talks', Bloomberg, 22 June 2020.

[28] Arms Control Association, 'The Nuclear Nonproliferation Treaty (NPT) at a glance', Fact sheet, Mar. 2020.

[29] United Nations, Review Conference of the Parties to the Treaty on the Non-Proliferation of Nuclear Weapons (NPT), [n.d.].

It is thus a treaty of both arms control and disarmament. When the NPT came into force in 1970, there were five known NWS—the five permanent members of the UN Security Council. Israel already had nuclear weapons but secretly. SIPRI's 1972 Yearbook identified a further 15 states with 'near nuclear' status.[30] This was the proliferation risk as seen at the time. Since then, India, Pakistan and North Korea have developed nuclear weapons. On the other side of the balance sheet, South Africa gave up its nuclear weapon programme when apartheid was overthrown, while Belarus, Kazakhstan and Ukraine all gave up nuclear weapons they could have kept as successor states to the Soviet Union (USSR). Seen in this light, the non-proliferation regime—the NPT plus the International Atomic Energy Agency's system of safeguards and monitoring—has been an imperfect but important measure of arms control.

However, the disarmament aspect of the NPT—the commitment in Article VI to 'pursue negotiations in good faith on effective measures relating to cessation of the nuclear arms race at an early date and to nuclear disarmament'—generates less satisfaction and more controversy. Russia and the USA can point to a significant reduction in their total stockpiles of nuclear warheads from some 70 000 in the mid 1980s to some 11 800 at the start of 2021.[31] For many NNWS, this reduction is not enough: the estimated global total of approximately 13 000 nuclear warheads is more than sufficient for global destruction.[32] Further, the nuclear doctrines and strategic planning of both Russia and the USA appear to many commentators to reveal increasing focus on the use of nuclear weapons in wartime, rather than a sole focus on strategic deterrence. This is because of their investment in low-yield nuclear weapons that in some eyes are 'usable'. The other three NWS are also upgrading their nuclear arsenals.

Impatience with what was seen as slow progress on Article VI brought the Treaty on the Prohibition of Nuclear Weapons (TPNW) into being in 2017.[33] The number of states parties to the TPNW reached 50 in October 2020, which meant it would enter into force in January 2021.[34]

All these factors taken together could mean that a very difficult NPT RevCon was in store, especially if New START were no longer to be in force at the time. The five-yearly RevCons have often seen clashes between NWS and NNWS over Article VI and other issues. A scan of SIPRI's successive

---

[30] SIPRI, *World Armaments and Disarmament: SIPRI Yearbook 1972* (Almqvist & Wiksell: Stockholm, 1972), chapter 9.

[31] See chapter 10 in this volume for details on nuclear stockpiles.

[32] See e.g. International Campaign to Abolish Nuclear Weapons, 'Catastrophic harm', [n.d.]. See also Ellsberg, D., *The Doomsday Machine* (Bloomsbury Press: London, 2017).

[33] United Nations, Office for Disarmament Affairs, 'Treaty on the prohibition of nuclear weapons', [n.d.]. For analysis of the origins and impact of the TPNW see Kile, S. N., 'Treaty on the Prohibition of Nuclear Weapons', *SIPRI Yearbook 2018*, pp. 307–18. See also chapter 11, section III, in this volume.

[34] United Nations (note 33).

assessments is instructive in this regard. In 1990, the RevCon 'failed to issue a Final Document', while in 2005, there was no final report with any substantive decisions, and in 2015, 'After 20 working days, which witnessed heated discussions . . . , the conference ended without any agreement on a concluding document or recommendations'.[35] Against a background of collapsing bilateral US–Russian arms control and enhanced NWS nuclear arsenals, a large number of RevCon participants would likely be highly critical of the NWS stance. It is not impossible that one or more states parties to the NPT would announce they were thinking about withdrawing from it. The result would be a much weaker and less credible architecture of non-proliferation. How these issues and disputes are handled in 2021 and thereafter will be a major test of international leadership.

Further items on the arms control agenda also pose problems. The continuing forward march of technology offers opportunities for military exploitation and sets multiple challenges for security policy and international law. These include the possibility of conflict in both cyber space and outer space; increased feasibility of autonomy in weapon systems; and disruptive effects on the strategic balance with hypersonic weapons, machine learning and advances in ballistic missile defence.[36] One response to technological innovation in the security realm is countervailing innovation, leading perhaps to a form of arms race; the other obvious option is to manage the risks through diplomacy, by regulating innovation in the form of agreements on arms control, if not the more ambitious and definitive form of disarmament measures. One problem here is that the political and diplomatic agenda is already full with the tasks of ensuring a reasonably successful NPT RevCon and, for Russia and the USA, re-energizing their bilateral arms control diplomacy. Though there are some indications of growing interest in possible regulation of military use of the newer technologies, it is unclear how much bandwidth will be left for that demanding task.[37] Here lies a significant challenge for international leadership in 2021 and beyond.

[35] Fischer, D. and Müller, H., 'The fourth review of the Non-Proliferation Treaty', *SIPRI Yearbook 1991*, p. 555; Kile, S. N., 'Nuclear arms control and non-proliferation', *SIPRI Yearbook 2006*, p. 607; and Rauf, T., 'Nuclear arms control and non-proliferation', *SIPRI Yearbook 2016*, p. 689.

[36] Mazarr, M. J. et al., *The Emerging Risk of Virtual Societal Warfare: Social Manipulation in a Changing Information Environment* (RAND Corporation: Santa Monica, CA, 2019); Boulanin, V. et al., *Limits on Autonomy in Weapon Systems: Identifying Practical Elements of Human Control* (SIPRI and the International Committee of the Red Cross: Stockholm and Geneva, 2020); Sayler, K. M. and Woolf, A. F., 'Defense primer: Hypersonic boost-glide weapons', In Focus no. IF11459, US Congress, Congressional Research Service (CRS), 1 Dec. 2020; and Boulanin, V. et al., *Artificial Intelligence, Strategic Stability and Nuclear Risk* (SIPRI: Stockholm, 2020).

[37] On efforts to regulate lethal autonomous weapons see chapter 13, section II, in this volume.

Continuing confrontation and incidents

Events in 2020 marked out two geopolitical dyads, India–Pakistan and Iran–Saudi Arabia, as major causes for concern, as they had been in 2019, adding to them a potential third in China–India. In some respects, relations did not deteriorate as significantly as had been expected, though they did not show notable improvement either. For example, at the end of 2019, some readings of the tense relationship, confrontation and clashes between India and Pakistan over Jammu and Kashmir foresaw escalating violence and danger in 2020.[38] There were frequent clashes, with both military and civilian deaths on both sides, but these did not escalate into combat outside of the immediate region of confrontation, even though trade was disrupted, transport links severed and diplomatic representation in the respective capitals reduced.[39]

In neighbouring Ladakh, at the Line of Actual Control with Aksai Chin, India's long-lasting border dispute with China turned violent during 2020 for the first time in several decades. Large-scale brawls took place between Chinese and Indian troops, reportedly resulting in four fatalities in February 2020 and more than twenty in June.[40] What sparked the clashes remains unclear. There was a degree of disengagement mid-year when both sides withdrew troops from frontline border positions.[41] Talks between military officials on how to handle the border issues were under way at the turn of the year but tensions remained high.[42]

Rivalry between Iran and Saudi Arabia, each with their regional and global allies, has been intense in recent years. The roots of their antagonism are often traced to the 1978–79 revolution that changed Iran from a monarchy into the Islamic Republic. But even during the 1970s before the revolution, there was rivalry between them with accompanying tensions, if no clashes or dangerous incidents.[43] Though religious difference between Shia Iran and Wahhabi Sunni Saudi Arabia is part of their antagonism, the rivalry

---

[38] See e.g. Kugelman, M., 'India and Pakistan are edging closer to war in 2020', *Foreign Policy*, 31 Dec. 2019. On events in Jammu and Kashmir in 2020 see chapter 4, section II, in this volume.

[39] Press Trust of India, 'India–Pakistan relations plumb new depths in 2020', *Economic Times*, 23 Dec. 2020.

[40] The Feb. 2020 fatalities were only revealed by China in Feb. 2021 in an announcement posthumously honouring four soldiers. See 'Ladakh: China reveals soldier deaths in India border clash', BBC News, 19 Feb. 2021. On the June violence see e.g. 'India–China clash: 20 Indian troops killed in Ladakh fighting', BBC News, 16 June 2020. For more detail see chapter 4, section II, in this volume.

[41] Sharma, A., 'Indian, Chinese soldiers disengaging after deadly clash in Ladakh', The Diplomat, 17 July 2020.

[42] Parohit, K. and Zheng, S., 'China–India border dispute: Troops saw "minor" clash amid ninth round of talks to resolve row', *South China Morning Post*, 25 Jan. 2021; and Madhavendra, R., 'Indian Army apprehends Chinese soldier near disputed Himalayan border', CNN, 10 Jan. 2021.

[43] Chubin, S. and Tripp, C., *Iran–Saudi Arabia Relations and Regional Order*, Adelphi Papers, vol. 36, no. 304 (International Institute of Strategic Studies: London, 1996), pp. 9, 71.

also derives from the competing national interests of two regional powers. In some ways, the national interest basis of the two states' rivalry comes into clearer focus when looking at the diplomatic normalization between Israel and two of Saudi Arabia's close allies—Bahrain and the UAE—in the US-brokered agreements known as the Abraham Accords.[44] There are contending views as to whether the accords usher in a more peaceful era in the Middle East.[45] There is little doubt, however, that they bring a group of states that share antipathy to Iran and its regional ambitions into a closer relationship with each other.

In 2019, the Gulf region witnessed missile strikes, proxy attacks and challenges to freedom of navigation, as well as regional involvement in wars in Iraq, Syria and Yemen.[46] At the start of 2020, a US missile strike killed Iranian general Qasem Soleimani, commander of the Quds Force, a division of the Iranian Revolutionary Guards Corps.[47] He was a key strategic leader of Iranian policy in Iraq and beyond. Iran retaliated with a missile attack on two Iraqi military bases that hosted US forces. This was interpreted by some analysts, reportedly including US officials, as a moderate response that indicated Iran did not seek escalation.[48] This relative restraint in the dynamics of confrontation persisted throughout the year.

There were renewed fears of escalation in March when a pro-Iran militia killed US and British soldiers in Iraq and, reportedly, the US Department of Defense ordered plans to be drawn up for a major campaign to destroy the group. These plans were controversial within the US military and were not implemented.[49]

The assassination of Iran's most senior nuclear scientist, Dr Mohsen Fakrizadeh, in November 2020 presented another moment for potential escalation. It came near the end of a year that had been punctuated by a series of explosions and fires at various places in Iran. Locations of incidents included the Natanz nuclear site where uranium enrichment is carried out, a missile production facility in the western outskirts of Tehran, and other sites including a factory, a petrochemical plant, a military base and power

---

[44] The Abraham Accords comprise the general declaration (Abraham Accords Declaration), the Bahrain–Israel agreement, the Israel–Morocco agreement and the Israel–UAE agreement. See US Department of State, 'The Abraham Accords Declaration', [n.d.]; see also chapter 6, section III, in this volume.

[45] Goldberg, J., 'Iran and the Palestinians lose out in the Abraham Accords', *The Atlantic*, 16 Sep. 2020; and Egel, D., Efron, S. and Robinson, L., 'Abraham Accords offer historic opportunity to spur Mideast growth', RAND Blog, 25 Mar. 2021.

[46] For an overview of events in 2019 see Smith (note 5), pp. 5–8.

[47] Crowley, M., Hassan, F. and Schmitt, E., 'US strike in Iraq kills Qassim Suleimani, commander of Iranian forces', *New York Times*, 2 Jan. 2020; and Black, I., 'General Qassem Suleimani obituary', *The Guardian*, 5 Jan. 2020.

[48] Leary, A., Youssef, N. A. and Rasmussen, S. E., 'US and Iran back away from open conflict', *Wall Street Journal*, 9 Jan. 2020. For more detail see chapter 6, section I, in this volume.

[49] Mazetti, M. and Schmitt, E., 'Pentagon order to plan for escalation in Iraq meets warning from top commander', *New York Times*, 27 Mar. 2020.

plants.[50] It is not clear whether these were accidents or acts of sabotage. Iran, however, was quick to accuse Israel of responsibility for the murder of Dr Fakrizadeh, just as it had accused Israel of involvement in killing four Iranian nuclear scientists from 2010 to 2012.[51] Dr Fakrizadeh's importance in Iran's nuclear research was well known, having been highlighted by Israeli Prime Minister Benjamin Netanyahu in a high-profile and contentious presentation about Iran's nuclear programme in April 2018.[52]

Despite this range of incidents throughout 2020, there was no broader escalation of the conflict in any part of the region where Iranian forces or influence were active. It was of particular concern that the USA was so closely involved, and likewise Israel, at least in being named as complicit. However, it was noteworthy in 2020 that Saudi Arabia was not such an active protagonist in the regional political reverberations around these various incidents. This relative disengagement of Saudi Arabia possibly implied there was not much appetite there for taking confrontation further than the tense status quo made up of proxy wars, the competition for regional influence and the always heated war of words.[53]

This ambiguous balance between potential escalation and restraint was also seen in North East Asia. Almost seven decades of post-truce military confrontation on the Korean peninsula since 1953 have produced intermittent violent incidents. Against that backdrop the nuclear weapons programme of North Korea has caused major international concern, as recorded and analysed in successive editions of this Yearbook. In 2018, after a year of particularly heated rhetoric between North Korea and the USA with mutual insults traded between the respective leaders, a dual process of inter-Korean détente and North Korean–US diplomacy got under way. As part of this process, a Joint Liaison Office (JLO) was opened in Kaesong, not far north of the demilitarized zone between the two Koreas, housed in a refurbished four-storey building first constructed in 2005 as part of an earlier enhancement of inter-Korean communication and cooperation.[54] The JLO was a way of facilitating discussions and speeding up decisions

---

[50] Fazeli, Y., 'Timeline: A look back at recent explosions and fires across Iran', Alarabiya News, 8 July 2020; Hamill-Stewart, C., 'Explosions in Iran: Isolated incidents or acts of sabotage?', *Arab News*, 10 July 2020; and 'Iran explosions: Officials deny reports of fresh blast', BBC News, 10 July 2020.

[51] 'Mohsen Fakhrizadeh, Iran's top nuclear scientist, assassinated near Tehran', BBC News, 27 Nov. 2020.

[52] 'Full text of Netanyahu on Iran deal: "100,000 files right here prove they lied"', *Times of Israel*, 30 Apr. 2018.

[53] For a similar line of analysis see Alaaldin, R., 'Iran will lose the battle, but win the war', Brookings Blog, 1 Dec. 2020; and Wintour, P., 'Nervous Saudis try to ease Middle East tensions', *The Guardian*, 9 Jan. 2020.

[54] Lee, J., 'Hopes rise as two Koreas open liaison office on North's side of border', Reuters, 14 Sep. 2018.

and handling of contentious issues. It replaced the previous practice of communicating by fax and special telephone lines.

One problem with the fax and telephone communication the JLO replaced was that lines were often cut when relations soured. In June 2020, the equivalent of cutting the lines happened when North Korea blew up the building housing the JLO.[55] The office had not been staffed for several months because of the Covid-19 pandemic. External commentators offered little by way of clear interpretation of North Korea's motives, except for noting its irritation at leaflets and chocolate biscuits being sent on balloons floating northwards across the border from the Republic of Korea (South Korea), allegedly by defectors from North Korea.[56] The JLO's destruction had little prospect of putting pressure either on South Korean President Moon Jae-in or US President Trump to provide economic aid or concessions in negotiations that had long since stalled, if it were indeed intended for that purpose. It did seem, however, a clear rejection of dialogue. There were some concerns that this was a step toward manufacturing a crisis that would lead to further deterioration of the inter-Korean and the North Korean–US relationships with possible risks of violent clashes. Yet in September when North Korean troops shot and killed a South Korean official who had crossed into North Korean waters, Supreme Leader Kim Jong Un issued a formal apology to the South Korean Government.[57] Though the hopes generated by the initial 2018 improvement in North Korea's relations with both South Korea and the USA have not been realized, the situation in 2020 reflected a return to no worse than the previous status quo—an assessment that is broadly in line with the overview of other geopolitical hotspots in the year.

Climate change

In the background, as in previous years, are the looming and growing risks associated with the impact of climate change. While in some quarters it remains controversial whether climate change has an impact on security issues, awareness of the linkages is steadily increasing. UN peace operations in both Mali and Somalia, for example, are mandated to address the

---

[55] Sinh, H. and Smith, J., 'North Korea destroys inter-Korean liaison office in "terrific explosion"', Reuters, 16 June 2020.

[56] Berlinger, J., Kwon, J. and Seo, Y., 'North Korea blows up liaison office in Kaesong used for talks with South', CNN, 16 June 2020; Davies, G. T. and Tong, Z., 'Expert commentary on current tensions following the destruction of the Inter-Korean Liaison Office', One Earth Future, [June 2020]; and Snyder, S. A., 'North Korea's loyalty test and the demolition of inter-Korean relations', Council on Foreign Relations Blog, 18 June 2020.

[57] Bae, G. and Kwon, J., 'South Korea official shot dead by North Korean troops after crossing border: Seoul', CNN, 24 Sep. 2020; and Kwon, J., 'Kim Jong Un apologizes in letter to Seoul for shooting of South Korean official', CNN, 25 Sep. 2020.

linkages.[58] The UN Peacebuilding Commission and Peacebuilding Fund have likewise begun to address the linkages in recent years.[59] The African Union and the European Union (EU) are also both actively engaged in addressing the linkages.[60] There remain discussions about which exactly are the best policy forums in which to address the linkages—whether, for example, the UN Security Council is appropriate to the task. But recent research on both contemporaneous and historical cases is making clear that the environment and natural resources have never been divorced from violent conflict or from politics, both local and global.[61] It is inevitable that problems generated by the knock-on consequences of climate change for instability and insecurity will eventually end up on the Security Council's agenda. Better to be prepared and able to analyse the risks than not. Disputing the reality of the nexus on the basis that climate change alone does not cause violent conflict carries little weight, not least because violent conflict is generally not a subject of mono-causality but rather the result of several factors interacting. The argument about climate change and insecurity is not that it is the only issue at stake, nor that it is relevant in every case of instability and violence, but rather that there are many cases in which it is a background factor. There is abundant evidence that the impact of climate change figures in a variety of pathways towards violent conflict.[62] It is not the whole explanation but leaving it out would mean the explanation is often incomplete.

According to a combination of datasets put together by the World Meteorological Organization, 2020 was the equal warmest year for which

[58] Eklöw, K. and Krampe, F., *Climate-related Security Risks and Peacebuilding in Somalia*, SIPRI Policy Paper no. 53 (SIPRI: Stockholm, Oct. 2019); and Hegazi, F., Krampe, F. and Smith, E. S., *Climate-related Security Risks and Peacebuilding in Mali*, SIPRI Policy Paper no. 60 (SIPRI: Stockholm, Apr. 2021).

[59] Krampe, F. and Sherman, J., 'The Peacebuilding Commission and climate-related security risks: A more favourable political environment?', SIPRI–IPI Insights on Peace and Security no. 2020/9, Sep. 2020.

[60] Aminga, V., 'Policy responses to climate-related security risks: The African Union', SIPRI Background Paper, May 2020; Aminga, V. and Krampe, F., 'Climate-related security risks and the African Union', SIPRI Policy Brief, May 2020; Bremberg, N., 'EU foreign and security policy on climate-related security risks', SIPRI Policy Brief, Nov. 2019; and Remling, E. and Barnhoorn, A., 'A reassessment of the European Union's response to climate- related security risks', SIPRI Insights on Peace and Security no. 2021/2, 19 Mar. 2021.

[61] Krampe, F., Hegazi, F., and VanDeveer, S. D., 'Sustaining peace through better governance: Three potential mechanisms for environmental peacebuilding', *World Development*, vol. 144 (Aug. 2021).

[62] Van Balen, S. and Mobjörk, M., 'Climate change and violent conflict in East Africa: Integrating qualitative and quantitative research to probe the mechanisms', *International Studies Review*, vol. 20, no. 4 (Dec. 2018); and Mobjörk, M., Krampe, F. and Tarif, K., 'Pathways of climate insecurity: Guidance for policymakers', SIPRI Policy Brief, Nov. 2020.

temperatures have been recorded going as far back as 1850, tying with 2016.[63] The seven warmest years on record are those from 2014 through 2020. A study published in February 2020, based on climate data through 2018, forecasts a greater than 99 per cent probability that most of the years from 2019 through 2028 will rank among what will, by the end of 2028, be the 10 warmest years on record.[64] In short, climate change, driven by the warming of the atmosphere, driven in turn by the release of greenhouse gases—especially carbon dioxide and methane—is continuing apace. The consequences have been felt in a series of extreme weather events throughout 2020, including particularly violent wildfires in Australia, and also in California and Siberia, and unprecedentedly warm temperatures in both the Arctic and the Antarctic.[65] Without remedial action addressing the drivers of climate change in the long term and its impact in the shorter term, further consequences will be felt in the realm of security. It remains the case that, without action and a change of course, the security agenda of the late 2020s and the 2030s risks being essentially unmanageable in some countries and regions.

II. The Covid-19 pandemic

This challenging global security environment is part of the international political background against which to consider the Covid-19 pandemic. By the end of 2020, some 82 million people were recorded as having contracted the disease, and recorded deaths numbered approximately 1.8 million.[66] There were grounds for regarding these figures as major underestimates, including both the many imperfections of testing schemes and data systems in different countries, as well as the diverse ways in which deaths are recorded. One estimate suggested that, compared to recorded data, an additional 500 million people may have been infected and additional deaths may number in multiple hundreds of thousands.[67]

---

[63] World Meteorological Organization (WMO), '2020 was one of three warmest years on record', Press release, 15 Jan. 2021; note that some of the data identifies 2020 as marginally cooler than 2016. See also the US National Aeronautics and Space Administration (NASA), '2020 tied for warmest year on record, NASA analysis shows', Press release no. 21-005, 14 Jan. 2021. Note that while the WMO takes 1850 as the base year for temperature data, NASA takes 1880: see 'Why does the temperature record shown on your "Vital Signs" page begin at 1880?', NASA Global Climate Change: Vital Signs of the Planet, [n.d.].

[64] National Centers for Environmental Information, 'More near-record warm years are likely on horizon', News, 14 Feb. 2020 (updated 29 Jan. 2021).

[65] Watts, J., 'Floods, storms and searing heat: 2020 in extreme weather', *The Guardian*, 30 Dec. 2020.

[66] World Health Organization (WHO), 'Covid-19 weekly epidemiological update—29 Dec. 2020', Emergency Situational Update, 29 Dec. 2020; and WHO, 'WHO coronavirus disease (Covid-19) dashboard', [n.d.]. For details of the unfolding Covid-19 pandemic and key milestones in 2020 see chapter 12, section I, and annex C in this volume.

[67] 'The year when everything changed', *The Economist*, 19 Dec. 2020.

The pandemic is an experience that has been shared in one form or another all around the globe. The speed with which the infection spread was a shock for most people and many governments. At the G20 virtual summit in March 2020, UN Secretary-General Guterres noted that it took three months to reach 100 000 confirmed cases of infection, but the next 100 000 cases were registered in the next 12 days, a further 100 000 in the following 4 days, and the fourth 100 000 in just 36 hours.[68] Understanding the exponential increase in infections perhaps makes it possible to appreciate the pressure decision makers were under and to acknowledge the likelihood of errors of judgement. However, not all countries experienced exponential growth in infections.[69]

Other serious consequences of the pandemic included increases in psychological stress and domestic violence. The pandemic disrupted the delivery of mental health services in 93 per cent of all countries, while the demand for those services increased.[70] Research on the impact of Covid-19 in low- and middle-income countries reported that it caused high rates of psychological distress and signs of an increase in mental health disorders.[71] A US study found that just over 40 per cent of adults in the USA reported symptoms of anxiety or depression during the pandemic, almost four times as many as in the first half of 2019, attributing the increase to the effect of the pandemic and the resulting economic recession.[72] The stress of the pandemic on daily life has also been reflected in reports of increased domestic and gender-based violence in countries as different as Argentina, Canada, Cyprus, Colombia, France, Germany, Kenya, Singapore, South Africa, the United Kingdom, the USA and Zimbabwe.[73] The range of increase varied from 25 per cent in Argentina to over 200 per cent in Bogotá, Colombia, and parts of Kenya. It is unlikely these are the only countries with that experience.

As noted above, SIPRI's overview reveals limited direct impact of Covid-19 on the conduct of conflicts in 2020. The pandemic nonetheless held important

---

[68] UN Secretary-General, 'Remarks at G20 virtual summit on the Covid-19 pandemic', Speech, 26 Mar. 2020.

[69] Komarova, N. L., Schang, L. M. and Wodarz, D., 'Patterns of the Covid-19 pandemic spread around the world: Exponential versus power laws', *Journal of the Royal Society Interface*, vol. 17, no. 170 (30 Sep. 2020).

[70] World Health Organization (WHO), 'Covid-19 disrupting mental health services in most countries, WHO survey', WHO News, 5 Oct. 2020.

[71] Kola, L. et al., 'Covid-19 mental health impact and responses in low-income and middle-income countries: Re-imagining global mental health', *Lancet Psychiatry*, 24 Feb. 2021.

[72] Panchal, N. et al., 'The implications of Covid-19 for mental health and substance use', Kaiser Family Foundation (KFF) Issue Brief, 10 Feb. 2021.

[73] UN Women, 'Covid-19 and ending violence against women and girls', EVAW Covid-19 Brief, 2020; Taub, A., 'A new Covid-19 crisis: Domestic abuse rises worldwide', *New York Times*, 6 Apr. 2020; Janetsky, M., 'Violence against women up amid Latin America Covid-19 lockdowns', *Al Jazeera*, 20 Apr. 2020; and Mlambo, N., 'Africa: Triple threat—conflict, gender-based violence and Covid-19', allAfrica, 26 Apr. 2020.

implications for conflict, peace and security. The most obvious link lies in the heavier impact of Covid-19 in countries already burdened by violent conflict. In Yemen, non-governmental organizations (NGOs) reported how Covid-19 exacerbated what was already a severe humanitarian crisis.[74] Libya, likewise, is reported to face exacerbated Covid-19 effects because violent conflict has degraded the country's once impressive health system.[75] The same can be expected in Syria for the same reason.[76] Comparative research leaves little doubt about the obvious point that violent conflict reduces the effectiveness and comprehensiveness of health services for the general population.[77] In short, violent conflict can be expected to worsen the impact of Covid-19.

The pandemic has also had a major economic effect, which in turn will have a social and human effect and possible security consequences. In 2020, the global economy shrank; economic output declined in all except 20 countries, including all major national economies except China.[78] Employment, consumption, and both collective and individual behaviour changed as lockdowns and lesser restrictions shaped daily life, reduced travel even locally, partially or wholly closed schools and universities, and shut down theatres, sports stadiums and other focal points of cultural life. The pandemic depressed wages, either slowing their increase or forcing them down, in two thirds of countries for which official data is available.[79] It is estimated to have driven approximately 120 million people into extreme poverty in the course of 2020, reversing three decades of progress in poverty reduction.[80] Initial estimates for 2021 suggested a continued, albeit significantly smaller, spread of extreme poverty in the pandemic's second year.[81]

There will, however, also be winners. The pandemic has accelerated corporate absorption of digitalization. One analysis identified several years' worth of change unfolding in a matter of months.[82] For nimble companies,

[74] 'A tipping point for Yemen's health system: The impact of Covid-19 in a fragile state', ReliefWeb, 23 July 2020.

[75] 'ONE UN supporting Libya to tackle Covid-19', ReliefWeb, 2 Dec. 2020.

[76] Li, G., 'Hospital bombings destroy Syria's health system', Health and Human Rights Journal Blog, 11 May 2017.

[77] Chöl, C., Cumming, R. G. and Negin, J., 'The impact of war on health systems and maternal mortality in sub-Saharan Africa: A quantitative analysis of 49 countries', Unpublished paper, ResearchGate, July 2019.

[78] Jones, L., Palumbo, D. and Brown, D., 'Coronavirus: How the pandemic has changed the world economy', BBC News, 24 Jan. 2020.

[79] International Labour Organization (ILO), Global Wage Report 2020–21: Wages and Minimum Wages in the Time of Covid-19, ILO Flagship Report (ILO: Geneva, Feb. 2020), chapter 3.

[80] Lakner, C. et al., 'Updated estimates of the impact of Covid-19 on global poverty: Looking back at 2020 and the outlook for 2021', Data Blog, World Bank, 11 Jan. 2021; and Beaumont, P., 'Decades of progress on extreme poverty now in reverse due to COVID', The Guardian, 3 Feb. 2021.

[81] Lakner et al. (note 80).

[82] McKinsey & Company, 'How Covid-19 has pushed companies over the technology tipping point and transformed business forever', Survey, 5 Oct. 2020.

able to recruit technology-literate talent and adjust their management models and interactions with clients and customers, this offers large opportunities for commercial exploitation and shareholders' profit. The prospects were not so bright for everybody, however. Covid-19 could be slow to dissipate and the fear of another pandemic will linger; one analysis pointed out that companies would adjust around that risk, so some activities, goods and services would be costlier and regarded as riskier, accelerating the existing trend of automating low-skilled work and person-to-person services.[83] These labour market effects would feed already rising economic and social inequalities in many countries.

There has been considerable back and forth among academic researchers for at least the last two decades about whether and how inequality contributes to armed conflict and which of vertical (social class) and horizontal (social group, such as ethnic) inequalities contribute more.[84] Part of the problem here is that there is neither a neat nor a comprehensive explanation of the role of any such factor—inequality, poverty, access to land, climate change, governance—in conflict causality.[85] The real issue is whether and how each individual factor interacts with others to create a background conducive to armed conflict, within which groups and their leaders opt to pursue political ends with violent means. How this happens differs from case to case.[86] Seen in this light, the trend of increasing inequality generates persistent conflict risk. This risk has been intensified by the economic knock-on effects of the pandemic, whose pressures are in turn exacerbated by the impact of climate change.

There has been a similar debate in research on the relationship between democracy and armed conflict. It remains a well-established finding that consolidated democracies are internally more peaceful than autocracies, semi-democracies and transitional states alike.[87] Recognizing that the condition of democracy is a significant factor in conflict causation, though not the sole determinant, the reported deterioration in the quality of democracy

---

[83] Stiglitz, J., 'Conquering the great divide', *Finance and Development*, Sep. 2020.

[84] See e.g. Baghat, K. et al., *Inequality and Armed Conflict: Evidence and Data*, Peace Research Institute Oslo (PRIO) Background Report (PRIO: Oslo, 12 Apr. 2017).

[85] For a useful survey of contending causal concepts, among others in the research literature, that emphasizes the importance of a multicausal approach, see Herbert, S., *Conflict Analysis*, GSDRC Topic Guide (GSDRC, University of Birmingham: Birmingham, May 2017).

[86] See e.g. Bartusevicius, H., 'The inequality–conflict nexus re-examined: Income, education and popular rebellions', *Journal of Peace Research*, vol. 51, no. 1 (2014).

[87] For a review of the literature nearly 2 decades ago that supports this conclusion see e.g. Söderberg, M. and Ohlson, T., *Democratisation and Armed Conflicts* (Sida: Stockholm, Apr. 2003); for a more recent review with effectively the same conclusion, see Hegre, H., 'Democracy and armed conflict', *Journal of Peace Research*, vol. 51, no. 2 (2014).

in 2020, all too often justified as part of the response to the pandemic, is of concern.[88]

Through reasonably well-established and well-understood channels of conflict causality—rising inequality and declining democratic quality—the pandemic forces itself into the field of vision for analysing peace, conflict and security. The number of armed conflicts tends to increase some two to three years after a major economic disruption. Examples include the oil price shock of the early to mid 1970s, the Asian financial crisis of 1997, and the global economic crisis of 2008–2009.[89] The increase in armed conflicts in the early 1990s is in part traceable to similar disruption—the fall of the Soviet Union—but the picture is complicated by other influences including broader aspects of the end of the cold war and the acceleration of attempted democratization in many parts of the world. There are, accordingly, firm grounds for concluding that the erosion of human well-being driven not just by the pandemic, but also by deficient governmental and international responses to it, is a challenge to security broadly defined.

Such deficiencies were visible in denialism, as represented vividly at different times by Presidents Bolsonaro and Magufuli of Brazil and Tanzania respectively, and the systematic downplaying of risk and promotion of non-remedies by US President Trump.[90] They were also visible in a lack of preparedness. Comparing the initial responses of South Korea and the USA is instructive, as both countries recorded their first cases of Covid-19 on 20 January 2020.[91] Within a week, the South Korean authorities engaged 20 commercial companies in fast-track development of a test for the virus, backed up by systematic tracing of infections and quarantining of individuals. By contrast, the US Government took a further six weeks to begin developing a test; by then, the infection had taken hold.

There was considerable criticism in the USA that the Global Health Security and Biodefense unit in the National Security Council (NSC) had been closed down. Established by the Obama administration as a result of its assessment of the implications of the Ebola epidemic, the unit was closed and much of its staff merged into a larger unit in 2018. Partisan disputes broke out over whether the change left the USA less prepared for

---

[88] 'Global democracy has a very bad year: The pandemic caused an unprecedented rollback of democratic freedoms in 2020', *The Economist*, 2 Feb. 2021; and V-Dem Institute, *Autocratization Turns Viral: Democracy Report 2021* (V-Dem Institute, University of Gothenburg: Gothenburg, 2021).

[89] See the conflict trends recorded by the Uppsala Conflict Data Program (note 8).

[90] Watson, K., 'Coronavirus: Brazil's Bolsonaro in denial and out on a limb', BBC News, 29 Mar. 2020; Duncan, E. S., 'Tanzania's layered COVID denialism', *Reinventing Peace*, 11 Sep. 2020; and Hamblin, J., 'Trump's pathology is now clear', *The Atlantic*, 31 Oct. 2020.

[91] Pilkington, E. and McCarthy, T., 'The missing six weeks: How Trump failed the biggest test of his life', *The Guardian*, 28 Mar. 2020.

a pandemic.[92] The evidence on whether the reorganization had a negative effect on readiness is not clear but the US administration's performance in 2020 would seem to confirm the conclusion of a November 2019 report that the USA was 'woefully ill-prepared' for a pandemic.[93] The US Government was by no means alone in giving the impression of wilfully avoiding planning for a pandemic. In the UK, for example, a 2016 exercise involving all national government departments, the National Health Service and local authorities revealed large gaps in the UK's planning for resilience but nothing was done to address them.[94]

There will doubtless be more controversies about responses to the pandemic and preparations against the next one. The record in 2020 makes clear that resilience in the face of a pandemic is a matter of human security.[95] Pandemic risk and response must be addressed through that policy lens as well as through medical, vaccination and public health policy. Among the early decisions of the incoming Biden administration in January 2021 was acknowledgement of that reality, with a national security memorandum on the topic and the appointment of the previous leader of the biodefence unit in the NSC to lead a reformed unit.[96]

III. The US election

The 2020 US presidential election result brought to an end a US administration that had systematically challenged multiple features of the international system which previous administrations of both parties had helped build, and which have benefited the USA and its successive governments for several decades. Among other actions, the Trump administration withdrew from bilateral and multilateral treaties, suspended funding to the WHO, abandoned Pacific trade negotiations, and weakened the World Trade

---

[92] Dozier, K. and Bergengruen, V., 'Under fire for coronavirus response, Trump officials defend disbanding pandemic team', *TIME*, 19 Mar. 2020; 'Partly false claim: Trump fired entire pandemic response team in 2018', Reuters, 25 Mar. 2020; and Heinrichs, R. L., 'The truth about the National Security Council's pandemic team', Hudson Institute, 1 Apr. 2020.

[93] Morrison, J. S., Ayotte, K. and Gerberding, J., *Ending the Cycle of Crisis and Complacency in US Global Health Security*, Center for Strategic & International Studies (CSIS) Commission Report (CSIS: Washington, DC, 20 Nov. 2019).

[94] Sinclair, I. and Read, R., '"A national scandal": A timeline of the UK Government's woeful response to the coronavirus crisis', *Byline Times*, 11 Apr. 2020.

[95] United Nations, Trust Fund for Human Security, 'What is human security?', [n.d.].

[96] White House, 'United States global leadership to strengthen the international Covid-19 response and to advance global health security and biological preparedness', National Security Memorandum no. 1, 21 Jan. 2021; and Hunnicutt, T., 'Biden names pandemic official to new national security team', Reuters, 8 Jan. 2021.

Organization (WTO) by withholding approvals of key positions.[97] It has been a particularity of the international system in recent years that none of the three great powers—China, Russia and the USA—was committed to the international status quo.[98] Each has taken an opportunistic and pragmatic approach to norms, commitments and participation in international institutions. This has been associated with rising insecurity and risk amid increasingly toxic geopolitical relations. The international significance of the election result and change of administration, accordingly, is greater than the norm.

Assessing the likely significance of the replacement of the Trump administration by the internationalist Biden administration, however, needs careful nuance for several reasons. The primary reason concerns the scale of the tasks involved. The Biden administration will have to devote considerable time, energy, resources and political capital to a complex and troubling domestic agenda. It includes post-pandemic economics, education and health provision, the USA's deep social fractures, and policies on immigration. In addition, the new administration must address international issues including preparation against the next pandemic, climate change, international development, trade and the refurbishment of the architecture of arms control. With a narrow majority in the House of Representatives and a split Senate, this is a heavy agenda for the administration to enact, even before unexpected events and crises emerge to distract its attention and blur its focus. The implication must surely be that other governments must step up their active engagement in international institutions. These have continued to operate with perhaps surprising degrees of efficacy but repair is necessary in several places. The USA cannot successfully undertake this by itself, nor, in any case, would it be healthy for the international system if it does so. Leadership of the effort must be shared or success will be limited.

The USA is not today the sole superpower that it was in the 1990s. China's economic growth over the four decades since 1980 makes it the number one trading partner of more countries than the USA.[99] China's economic weight is accompanied by increasingly strong armed forces along with growing political and diplomatic weight. Its diplomacy with African states, for example, is increasingly effective. China has not only invested in Africa but provided development assistance on a scale that makes it Africa's third

[97] Amirfar, C. and Singh, A., 'The Trump administration and the "unmaking" of international agreements', *Harvard International Law Journal*, vol. 59, no. 2 (summer 2018); Council on Foreign Relations, 'Trump's foreign policy moments, 2017–2020', [n.d.]; and Swanson, A., 'Trump cripples WTO as trade war rages', *New York Times*, 8 Dec. 2019.

[98] Smith, D., 'Introduction: International security and human stability in 2018', *SIPRI Yearbook 2019*, pp. 17–20; and Smith (note 5), pp. 19–23.

[99] 'How to deal with China', *The Economist*, 7 Jan. 2021.

largest donor after the USA and the EU.[100] In 2020, it successfully convened a summit meeting with 13 African leaders on the pandemic, while the EU was having difficulties preparing its own summit with African leaders.[101] The return to the international stage of an internationalist USA will not restore the status quo as it was before Trump because the world has changed—and will continue to change—in other ways. Neither the Biden administration, nor the USA's allies, nor its critics can behave any more as if the USA is the hegemon it was in the 1990s.

There is little reason to think global politics will swiftly become less confrontational.[102] In the USA, distrust of China's ambitions became a bipartisan view during the Trump years. In relation to Russia, a Democrat administration is likely to be more critical and abrasive than the Trump administration was, because of the evidence of Russian influence in the 2016 US presidential election.[103] Moreover, the Biden administration's approach includes strengthening US alliances and undoing divisions sown by the Trump administration's policies and rhetoric. China and Russia will likely contest that approach in both direct and indirect ways. For straightforward reasons of policy, both prefer to face fragmentation in the Western alliance system. Thus, while the Biden administration can be expected to seek cooperative solutions to major international problems to a far greater extent than the Trump administration did, it will continue to face (and generate) attitudes in the other two great powers and their allies that are not conducive to working together.

Perhaps the most important reason for noting that there are limits to the significance of the 2020 US presidential election result is that the departure of the Trump administration is not a death knell for its policies and attitudes. What to observers outside (and many inside) the USA has appeared paradoxical—spurning an international system that favoured the USA—is to many American voters simply the assertion of legitimate US interests. Distrust of alliances has a long history in the USA. Warnings against 'permanent alliance with any portion of the foreign world' by President George Washington and against 'entangling alliances' by President Thomas Jefferson were respected for 165 years after the War of Independence.[104] During that time, apart from its treaty with France during the revolutionary

[100] Calabrese, L. et al., 'FOCAC 2018: Top takeaways from the China–Africa summit', ODI, 6 Sep. 2018.

[101] Bilal, S. and Tadesse, L., 'The China–Africa summit on Covid-19: Geopolitical and economic considerations', ECDPM Blog, 22 June 2020.

[102] Wright, R., 'Biden faces more aggressive rivals and a fraying world order', *New Yorker*, 18 Jan. 2021.

[103] Mueller, R. S., *Report on the Investigation into Russian Interference in the 2016 Presidential Election* (US Department of Justice: Washington, DC, Mar. 2019).

[104] Fromkin, D., 'Entangling alliances', *Foreign Affairs*, vol. 48, no. 4 (July 1970).

war, the USA formed no international alliances.[105] By the time of the Trump administration, the USA had alliances with 54 other states.[106] Nostalgia for non-entanglement is never far from the surface of US politics and one analyst has identified a shift in 'the center of political gravity' away from the post-1945 norm of engaged internationalism 'toward something closer to isolationism'.[107]

While the election result was clear, its meaning is not. The facts, though strongly contested within the USA, are not in doubt. What happened once the voting was over has absorbed so much attention that some of the implications of the result have passed many commentators by. That is hardly surprising in view of the unedifying theatre of the then-incumbent pre-emptively complaining about electoral fraud, crowds gathering at vote-counting stations to influence the result, a series of baseless legal challenges, all cheered on by many senior legislators, culminating in the events of 6 January 2021 when a semi-organized mob, audibly urged on by the soon-to-depart president, stormed the US Capitol Building to disrupt the Senate's ratification of the result.

Both candidates in the 2020 presidential election won more votes than any previous presidential candidates. Joe Biden won with a 7 million vote majority; he received 51.3 per cent of the vote compared to Trump's 46.9 per cent—a clear margin but not overwhelming.[108] In the Electoral College, Biden's majority was 306 to 232, only marginally different from the 304 to 227 majority Trump gained in 2016.[109] Just as in Trump's win in 2016, Biden's success in 2020 came down to a handful of narrow victories in 'battleground states', some of them much against expectations on both sides.[110] Biden's win, in short, was far from comfortable. The electoral system will not change, Trump's broad politics and approach still have currency, and a candidate representing them could win a future presidential election.

The Trump presidency will cast a long shadow over a new administration with, on the international stage, antithetical approaches on many issues. Among the USA's international interlocutors, among allies as well as those less friendly to the USA, questions persist about the stability of US policy and the reliability of its word and its commitments. Much changed when Joe Biden was confirmed as president but the tasks are great, the capacity is

---

[105] Beckley, M., 'The myth of entangling alliances', War on the Rocks, 9 June 2015.

[106] US Department of State, 'US collective defense arrangements', [n.d.].

[107] Kirshner, J., 'Gone but not forgotten: Trump's long shadow and the end of American credibility', *Foreign Affairs*, vol. 100, no. 2 (Mar./Apr. 2021).

[108] Lindsay, J. M., 'The 2020 election by the numbers', Council for Foreign Relations Blog, 15 Dec. 2020.

[109] National Archives, '2020 Electoral College results' (updated 16 Apr. 2021); and National Archives, '2016 Electoral College Results' (updated 11 Jan. 2021).

[110] Allen, J. and Parnes, A., *Lucky: How Joe Biden Barely Won the Presidency* (Random House: New York, 2021), chapter 20.

constrained and the politics are volatile. These uncertainties only serve to emphasize the importance of stepping up international cooperation.

IV. International cooperation

On 21 September 2020, the UN General Assembly marked the UN's 75th anniversary with a declaration that, while acknowledging 'moments of disappointment', amounted to an endorsement of and re-commitment to the UN's fundamental goals and norms.[111] Despite vicissitudes during the past half-decade, many institutions of international cooperation remained vibrant, offering a framework for international relations to stay as peaceful and as conducive to human well-being as possible. That framework has not been used to the full for several years but has not suffered irretrievable damage. In September 2015, the UN adopted Agenda 2030 with its 17 Sustainable Development Goals (SDGs).[112] Agenda 2030 remains an important expression of ambition for human progress and, with 169 specific targets, it offers criteria by which to assess economic and social development, including in the sphere of security and peace. There was limited progress on most of the goals up to 2020, when the Covid-19 pandemic hit and made the task much more difficult.[113] But with Agenda 2030 and the SDGs, a global conversation on what path to take as countries come out of the Covid-19 pandemic at least has a shared starting point.

The Paris Agreement, reached in December 2015 at the climate change summit—formally the 21st Conference of Parties (COP) of the United Nations Framework Convention on Climate Change (UNFCCC)—is at least equally important.[114] It established a framework for action to reduce greenhouse gas emissions and adapt to the inevitable impacts of climate change resulting from past emissions. Progress towards these targets, even though they are set by individual national decision, as nationally determined contributions (NDCs), has been limited. Under the Paris Agreement, the targets in the NDCs are to be periodically enhanced—that is, made more demanding. The Climate Ambition Summit, held in December 2020 as something of a substitute for COP26 which was postponed due to the Covid-19 pandemic, convened 75 heads of government. It was the occasion for announcing enhanced targets in a number of NDCs. At or just before the meeting, some 27 governments announced enhanced NDC targets, while the EU announced a collective NDC with enhanced targets for its member states. The UNFCCC secretariat calculated that these commitments, together with

---

[111] UN General Assembly Resolution 75/1, 21 Sep. 2020.

[112] United Nations, Sustainable Development Goals, 'The sustainable development agenda', [n.d.].

[113] United Nations, Sustainable Development Goals, 'Sustainable Development Goals report', [n.d.].

[114] United Nations, Framework Convention on Climate Change (UNFCCC), 'COP 21', [n.d.].

others expected in early 2021, meant countries representing around 65 per cent of global carbon emissions, and 70 per cent of the world's economy, were committed to achieving net zero carbon emissions at a future date.[115] According to an independent analysis, targets and pledges announced so far will not suffice to meet the aim of restricting global warming to 2°C, while current policies are still less adequate for that goal.[116]

A year that began with international attention seized by widespread wildfires in Australia finished with continuing difficulties in achieving a sustainable and actionable international awareness of the urgency of the climate crisis. But the institutional framework for governments to work towards appropriately ambitious goals still stood.

Similarly in arms control and in handling the most combustible of the world's potential flashpoints, the institutional framework of the UN, the Security Council, its key offices and agencies remained active and available for use. The tasks, it is true, have become steadily more complex, in arms control because of the forward momentum of technological development as well as the pressures of rivalry and manoeuvring for advantage, and in crisis management and conflict mediation because it is inevitably harder to address antagonisms that have been left to fester.

Perhaps what is most important at the start of 2021 is to strengthen and re-energize routines of international cooperation in and with key international organizations such as the WHO and the WTO. The ways in which governments relate to each other and how inter-governmental organizations work during normal times do much to determine whether and how they can work together in crisis. The political disputes that festered throughout 2020 about responsibility for the origin of the novel coronavirus that spread the Covid-19 disease were symptoms of an ailing international body politic that requires care and attention. Whatever issue of international concern is in focus, a healthier body politic with strong norms of cooperation is a prerequisite for effective action.

---

[115] UNFCCC, 'Climate Ambition Summit builds momentum for COP26', Press release, 12 Dec. 2020.
[116] Climate Action Tracker, 'New momentum reduces emissions gap, but huge gap remains—analysis', Press release, 23 Apr. 2021.

Part I. Armed conflict and conflict management, 2020

Chapter 2. Global developments in armed conflict, peace processes and peace operations

Chapter 3. Armed conflict and peace processes in the Americas

Chapter 4. Armed conflict and peace processes in Asia and Oceania

Chapter 5. Armed conflict and peace processes in Europe

Chapter 6. Armed conflict and peace processes in the Middle East and North Africa

Chapter 7. Armed conflict and peace processes in sub-Saharan Africa

2. Global developments in armed conflict, peace processes and peace operations

Overview

This chapter describes general developments in 2020 in armed conflicts and peace processes (for detailed regional coverage see chapters 3–7) and global and regional trends and developments in multilateral peace operations.

Section I explores definitions and some of the main features and consequences of the active armed conflicts that occurred in at least 39 states in 2020 (5 more than in 2019): 2 in the Americas, 7 in Asia and Oceania, 3 in Europe, 7 in the Middle East and North Africa (MENA) and 20 in sub-Saharan Africa. As in preceding years most took place within a single country (intrastate), between government forces and one or more armed non-state group(s). Two were major armed conflicts (with more than 10 000 conflict-related deaths in the year)— in Afghanistan and Yemen—and 16 were high-intensity armed conflicts (with 1000–9999 conflict-related deaths)—in Mexico (8400), Syria (8000), Nigeria (7800), the Democratic Republic of the Congo (5800), Ethiopia (3600), Somalia (3100), Mali (2800), Iraq (2700), South Sudan (2400), Burkina Faso (2300), Mozambique (1800), Cameroon (1600), Libya (1500), the Philippines (1400), India (1300) and Niger (1100). Only two armed conflicts were fought between states: the ongoing border clashes between India and Pakistan, and the border conflict between Armenia and Azerbaijan (the latter was also a high-intensity armed conflict with an estimated 6700 conflict-related fatalities). Two other armed conflicts were fought between state forces and armed groups that aspired to statehood (between Israel and the Palestinians and between Turkey and the Kurds). Both major armed conflicts and most of the high-intensity armed conflicts were internationalized.

For at least the second consecutive year the total estimated number of conflict-related fatalities decreased; to about 120 000 in 2020, a 30 per cent reduction since 2018. The decrease in 2020 was driven by further reductions in Asia and Oceania and MENA; estimated conflict-related fatalities were halved in Afghanistan. Two regions bucked this trend: Europe, because of the armed conflict between Armenia and Azerbaijan; and sub-Saharan Africa, where 18 of the 20 armed conflicts had higher estimated conflict-related fatalities in 2020 than in 2019—and the net increase was about 41 per cent. The region also overtook MENA in 2020 as having the most conflict-related fatalities.

While conflict-related fatalities have declined in recent years, other impacts of armed conflict (sometimes in combination with other factors) appear to have increased, including population displacement, food insecurity, humanitarian needs and violations of international humanitarian law. While many peace processes either stalled or suffered serious setbacks during 2020, important advances were made in the peace talks in Afghanistan, and ceasefires in Libya and Syria suggested both of those conflicts might be open to some form of resolution soon. A Russian-brokered ceasefire ended the fighting in Nagorno-Karabakh. However, in sub-Saharan Africa, the peace process in Sudan was the only one to make substantive progress in 2020.

The impact of Covid-19 on armed conflicts in 2020 was mixed: there were some temporary declines in armed violence, but mostly armed conflict levels persisted or sometimes increased. The United Nations secretary-general's call in March 2020 for a global ceasefire had a minimal impact on these conflicts.

Section II describes the trends in multilateral peace operations. With 62 active operations in 2020, there was an increase of 1 compared to the previous year. Three ended in 2020—the Economic Community of West African States Mission in Guinea-Bissau, the African Union (AU)–UN Hybrid Operation in Darfur and the UN Integrated Peacebuilding Office in Guinea-Bissau—and three started—the AU Military Observers Mission to the Central African Republic (CAR), the European Union (EU) Common Security and Defence Policy Advisory Mission in the CAR and the AU Mission in Libya.

Despite this slight increase in the number of multilateral peace operations, the number of personnel deployed in them decreased by 7.7 per cent during 2020 to 127 124 on 31 December 2020—mainly driven by reductions in a number of large multilateral peace operations, especially the Resolute Support Mission in Afghanistan. The UN remained the leading organization in the field, responsible for about one third of all multilateral peace operations and two thirds of all personnel. Multilateral peace operations in sub-Saharan Africa continued to account for most personnel deployed in multilateral peace operations globally.

Despite further force reductions, the AU Mission in Somalia remained the largest multilateral peace operation in 2020. Ethiopia remained the top troop contributor, followed by Uganda and Bangladesh. In 2020 the annual fatality rate for hostile deaths of uniformed personnel in UN peace operations was the lowest in the 2011–20 period. However, the fatality rate for deaths due to all causes was higher than in previous years, as the number of deaths due to illness, including Covid-19, increased significantly. The trend of increasing multilateral operations activity in the grey areas outside the scope of the SIPRI definition of a multilateral peace operation also continued in 2020, with three new deployments: a Russian 'peacekeeping contingent' in Nagorno-Karabakh; the EU Naval Force Mediterranean Operation Irini to implement the UN arms embargo on Libya; and the European multinational Task Force Takuba under the command of the French-led Operation Barkhane in the Sahel. The table in section III provides further details on the different multilateral peace operations and the organizations deploying them.

IAN DAVIS AND JAÏR VAN DER LIJN

I. Tracking armed conflicts and peace processes

IAN DAVIS

In 2020 active armed conflicts occurred in at least 39 states (5 more than in 2019): 2 in the Americas, 7 in Asia and Oceania, 3 in Europe (2 more than in 2019), 7 in the Middle East and North Africa (MENA) and 20 in sub-Saharan Africa (3 more than in 2019)—see chapters 3–7, respectively.[1] As in preceding years most took place within a single country (intrastate), between government forces and one or more armed non-state groups. Only two were fought between states (the border clashes between India and Pakistan and the border conflict between Armenia and Azerbaijan for control of Nagorno-Karabakh), and two were fought between state forces and armed groups that aspired to statehood, with the fighting sometimes spilling outside the recognized state borders (between Israel and the Palestinians and between Turkey and the Kurds).

Of the intrastate conflicts, two were major armed conflicts (with more than 10 000 conflict-related deaths in the year)—in Afghanistan (approximately 21 000 reported fatalities) and Yemen (19 800)—and 16 were high-intensity armed conflicts (with 1000–9999 conflict-related deaths in the year)—in Mexico (8400), Syria (8000), Nigeria (7800), the Democratic Republic of the Congo (DRC; 5800), Ethiopia (3600), Somalia (3100), Mali (2800), Iraq (2700), South Sudan (2400), Burkina Faso (2300), Mozambique (1800), Cameroon (1600), Libya (1500), the Philippines (1400), India (1300) and Niger (1100)—see figure 2.1. The interstate border conflict between Armenia and Azerbaijan was also a high-intensity armed conflict with an estimated 6700 conflict-related fatalities. However, these categorizations should be considered tentative as fatality information is unreliable.[2] Both major armed conflicts and most of the high-intensity armed conflicts were internationalized; that is, they involved foreign elements that may have led to the conflict being prolonged or exacerbated.

This section discusses the definitions of 'armed conflict' and related terms used in chapters 2–7, and then highlights salient (and largely continuing) features of the armed conflicts and some of their main consequences in 2020, as well as key developments in peace processes during the year. The section concludes with a discussion of the impact of the United Nations secretary-general's call for a global Covid-19-related ceasefire.

---

[1] For the definitions of 'armed conflict' and related terms used in chapters 2–7 see the subsection 'Defining armed conflict' and box 2.1 below.

[2] Armed Conflict Location & Event Data Project (ACLED), 'FAQs: ACLED fatality methodology', 27 Jan. 2020. On casualty counting see also Giger, A., 'Casualty recording in armed conflict: Methods and normative issues', *SIPRI Yearbook 2016*, pp. 247–61; and Delgado, C., 'Why it is important to register violent deaths', SIPRI Commentary, 30 Mar. 2020.

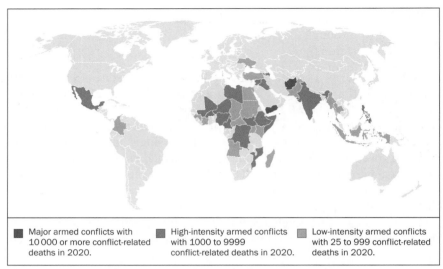

| ■ Major armed conflicts with 10 000 or more conflict-related deaths in 2020. | ■ High-intensity armed conflicts with 1000 to 9999 conflict-related deaths in 2020. | ■ Low-intensity armed conflicts with 25 to 999 conflict-related deaths in 2020. |

Figure 2.1. Armed conflict, by number of conflict-related deaths, 2020

Defining armed conflict

Armed conflicts are often complex and multifaceted, with multiple actors that have diverse and changeable objectives. This complexity can be a major challenge for the conceptual and legal categorization of armed conflict, as well as thinking on peacebuilding and conflict prevention.[3] Determining the existence of an 'armed conflict' within the framework of international law, for example, differs according to whether the conflict occurs between states (interstate or international armed conflict) or between a state and one or more non-state groups or among two or more non-state groups (intrastate armed conflict, or 'non-international armed conflict' under international humanitarian law).[4] Qualifying the situation as an 'armed conflict' and further defining the nature of the armed conflict—international or non-international—is also crucial for determining the level of protection that shall be granted to non-combatants, for defining the status of a combatant and for determining the level of obligations towards captured adversaries.

[3] The complexity is captured in United Nations and World Bank, *Pathways for Peace: Inclusive Approaches to Preventing Violent Conflict* (International Bank for Reconstruction and Development/ World Bank: Washington, DC, 2018).

[4] For primary sources on the definition of armed conflicts see the 1949 Geneva Conventions common Article 2 and 1977 Additional Protocol I, Article 1 (international), and 1949 Geneva Conventions common Article 3 and Additional Protocol II, Article 1 (non-international)—'Treaties, states parties and commentaries', International Committee of the Red Cross, [n.d.]. Also see e.g. International Committee of the Red Cross, 'How is the term "armed conflict" defined in international humanitarian law?', Opinion Paper, Mar. 2008; and International Committee of the Red Cross, *International Humanitarian Law and the Challenges of Contemporary Armed Conflicts* (International Committee of the Red Cross: Geneva, Oct. 2019), pp. 50–52, 58–59, 75–76.

Not every situation of armed violence amounts to an armed conflict. For example, although criminal violence can threaten the authority and capability of a state as much as an armed conflict, law enforcement activities unconnected to an armed conflict fall outside the scope of international humanitarian law (even if a state's military is involved). However, if the criminal violence meets the threshold of a non-international armed conflict—as was the case in 2020 for the three armed conflicts in Mexico between the Government of Mexico and the Jalisco New Generation Cartel (Cártel Jalisco Nueva Generación) and the Sinaloa Cartel, and between those two cartels (see chapter 3, section III)—then international humanitarian law applies.

In 2020 most armed conflicts occurred within states. While there can be complications in classifying an international armed conflict—for example, intervention of foreign or multinational forces in armed conflicts not otherwise of an international character or extraterritorial uses of force by a state—it is usually more complex with non-international armed conflicts. There is often no clear dividing line between intrastate armed conflicts and usually smaller-scale incidents of internal violence, such as riots and organized crime gangs. The threshold for an intrastate armed conflict must be evaluated on a case-by-case basis by weighing up a range of indicative data. The two key thresholds relevant to the classification of a non-international armed conflict are: (a) protracted armed violence and (b) one or more organized armed group(s). This evaluation might include whether explicit political goals are stated by the actors, the duration of the conflict, the frequency and intensity of the acts of violence and military operations and the degree of continuity between them, the nature of the weapons used, the displacement of civilians, the territorial control by opposition forces and the number of victims (including the dead, wounded and displaced people).[5] In the Americas in 2020 it was particularly difficult to distinguish between high levels of political violence and armed conflict (see chapter 3).

This complexity in defining an armed conflict also contributes in part to the differences among the main data sets on violence and conflict—including the one that is predominantly used in chapters 2–7 of this Yearbook, the Armed Conflict Location & Event Data Project (ACLED)—each of which has its own definitions and methodology.[6] This part of the Yearbook offers a primarily descriptive (rather than quantitative) synopsis of trends

---

[5] Vité, S., 'Typology of armed conflicts in international humanitarian law: Legal concepts and actual situations', *International Review of the Red Cross*, vol. 91, no. 873 (Mar. 2009), pp. 69–94.

[6] For an overview of the major advances in the collection and availability of armed conflict data see Brzoska, M., 'Progress in the collection of quantitative data on collective violence', *SIPRI Yearbook 2016*, pp. 191–200. On the role of media bias in conflict data sets see Dietrich, N. and Eck, K., 'Known unknowns: Media bias in the reporting of political violence', *International Interactions*, vol. 46, no. 6 (2020), pp. 1043–60.

Box 2.1. Definitions and types of armed conflict

Armed conflict involves the use of armed force between two or more states or non-state organized armed groups. For the purpose of Part I of this Yearbook , there is a threshold of battle-related violence causing 25 or more deaths in a given year. With the caveat that data on conflict deaths is often imprecise and tentative, the chapters categorize such conflicts, based on the number of conflict-related deaths in the current year, as *major* (10 000 or more deaths), *high intensity* (1000–9999 deaths) or *low intensity* (25–999 deaths).

Armed conflict can be further categorized as follows:

Interstate (international) armed conflict, the use of armed force by one or more states against another state or states, is now rare and mostly occurs at lower intensities or shorter durations. While territorial, border and other disputes persist among states, they are unlikely to escalate to armed conflict.

Intrastate (non-international) armed conflict is the most common form of armed conflict today and usually involves sustained violence between a state and one or more non-state groups fighting with explicitly political goals (e.g. taking control of the state or part of the territory of the state)—although the question of goals is not relevant to the legal classification. It can also be classified as follows:

- *Subnational armed conflict* is typically confined to particular areas within a sovereign state, with economic and social activities in the rest of the country proceeding relatively normally. This kind of conflict often takes place in stable, middle-income countries with relatively strong state institutions and capable security forces. Sometimes it takes place in a troubled border region in a large country that expanded geographically in the past or has arbitrarily drawn borders.

- *Civil war* involves most of the country and results in at least 1000 conflict-related deaths in a given year.

- Either type of conflict is considered *internationalized* if there is significant involvement of a foreign entity (excluding United Nations peace operations) that is clearly prolonging or exacerbating the conflict—such as armed intervention in support of, or provision of significant levels of weapons or military training to, one or more of the conflict parties by a foreign government or foreign non-state actor.

Extrastate armed conflict occurs between a state and a political entity that is not widely recognized as a state but has long-standing aspirations of statehood (e.g. the Israeli–Palestinian conflict). Such conflicts, which are rare, may take place inside and outside of the state boundaries recognized by the international community.

Note: These definitions are used indicatively and not as legal conclusions. Thus, the conflict situations discussed in chapters 2–7 of this Yearbook may be characterized differently under international humanitarian law.

---

and events in 2020 affecting key armed conflicts.[7] It characterizes and distinguishes armed conflicts within three major categories: interstate (i.e. an international armed conflict), intrastate (i.e. a non-international armed conflict) and extrastate (see box 2.1). It also differentiates them from other kinds of organized group violence (such as criminal violence). To define a

---

[7] For more on events in 2020 related to armaments, disarmament and international security see annex C in this volume.

series of violent events as an armed conflict, a threshold of 25 battle-related deaths in a year is used.

Significant features of armed conflicts in 2020

Most armed conflicts since the cold war are fought by regular armies and also militias and armed civilians. Fighting is often intermittent with a wide range of intensities and brief ceasefires, and rarely occurs on well-defined battlefields. The nature of most armed conflicts is context specific; this subsection highlights some of the most significant features of several armed conflicts in 2020.

Non-state armed groups were active in most of the armed conflicts around the world in 2020. An estimated 60–70 million people reside in areas under the control of non-state armed groups.[8] In 2020 ACLED noted a 46 per cent increase in identity militias (armed groups organized around a collective, common feature such as community, ethnicity, religion or livelihood) as compared to 2019. There is also a growing tendency for armed groups, as well as states, to fight in coalitions (such as in Libya, the Sahel and Syria). This sometimes involves state militaries partnering with domestic armed groups, or external states supporting armed groups as proxy agents.[9] At least seven states in 2020 were involved in armed conflicts that were being shaped by proxy elements (Afghanistan, Burkina Faso, Iraq, Libya, Syria, Ukraine and Yemen), as well as the conflict in Kashmir. Despite the growing numbers of non-state armed groups, state forces remained the most powerful and violent actors in 2020, participating in 52 per cent of all political violence.[10]

Most armed conflicts were fought in 2020 along traditional lines with conventional arms. Armed drones were increasingly used to conduct attacks in many situations of armed conflict, including in Libya, Nagorno-Karabakh, Syria, Ukraine and Yemen.[11] In particular, many analysts attributed Azerbaijan's success in its short war with Armenia over Nagorno-Karabakh (see chapter 5, section II) to its technological edge in armed drones.[12] Drone technology has proliferated greatly in recent years, with over 100 states currently operating military drones, while several armed non-state groups

---

[8] Fidelis-Tzourou, M. and Sjöberg, A., 'Forgotten freedoms: The right to free expression in areas controlled by non-state armed groups', Armed Groups and International Law, 23 Oct. 2020.

[9] Rauta, V., 'Proxy warfare and the future of conflict: Take two', *RUSI Journal*, vol. 165, no. 2 (2020), pp. 1–10.

[10] Kishi, R. et al., *ACLED 2020: The Year in Review* (ACLED: Mar. 2021), pp. 15–17.

[11] Bakeer, A., 'The fight for Syria's skies: Turkey challenges Russia with new drone doctrine', Middle East Institute, 26 Mar. 2020; and Zwijnenburg, W. and Jansen, A., 'Violent skies: How lethal drone technology is shaping contemporary warfare', PAX, Aug. 2020.

[12] Brimelow, B., 'A brief, bloody war in a corner of Asia is a warning about why the tank's days of dominance may be over', Insider, 25 Nov. 2020.

Table 2.1. Estimated conflict-related fatalities by region, 2018–20

Region	2018	2019	2020
Americas	21 461	20 150	17 349
Asia and Oceania	49 469	48 715	25 785
Europe	1 092	480	7 304
Middle East and North Africa	76 340	52 805	33 683
Sub-Saharan Africa	26 072	26 063	36 750
Total	**174 434**	**148 213**	**120 871**

Note: Fatality figures are collated from four event types: battles; explosions/remote violence; protests, riots and strategic developments; and violence against civilians—see Armed Conflict Location & Event Data Project (ACLED), 'ACLED definitions of political violence and protest', 11 Apr. 2019.

Source: ACLED, Dashboard, accessed 10 Apr. 2021.

have used commercial drones equipped with explosives.[13] The UN secretary-general called for the 'authority of international law' to be applied to the use of armed drones.[14]

The forced recruitment and use of child soldiers and sexual violence are widely perpetrated in armed conflict. In 2019 (the last year for which data is available) Somalia remained the country with the highest number of cases of recruitment and use of children (1495 out of a total of 7747 children recruited and used as soldiers in that year).[15] In an annual report on conflict-related sexual violence, the UN secretary-general described 19 countries of concern and an updated list of 54 parties to conflict that were credibly suspected of having committed or instigated sexual violence in 2019 (the year covered by the report).[16]

During many of the armed conflicts, especially the major and high-intensity conflicts, other international humanitarian law violations were also committed, including the use of starvation to achieve military ends, the denial of humanitarian aid, forced displacement, and attacks on aid and health workers, hospitals and schools. Such violations appear to be on the increase—the rules that are meant to protect civilians in war are being broken regularly and systematically.[17] In remarks to the UN Security

---

[13] Gettinger, D., 'Drone databook update, March 2020', Center for the Study of the Drone, Mar. 2020; and Hambling, D., 'Mexican drug cartel carries out "drone strikes" in gang war', *Forbes*, 24 Aug. 2020.

[14] UN Secretary-General, 'Secretary-general's remarks to the Security Council open debate on the protection of civilians in armed conflict', 23 May 2020.

[15] United Nations, General Assembly and Security Council, 'Children and armed conflict', Report of the Secretary-General, A/74/845–S/2020/525, 9 June 2020, pp. 2, 19.

[16] United Nations, Security Council, 'Conflict-related sexual violence', Report of the Secretary-General, S/2020/487, 3 June 2020.

[17] See e.g. United Nations, Security Council, 'Protection of civilians in armed conflict', Report of the Secretary-General, S/2020/366, 6 May 2020; and Metcalfe-Hough, V., 'Advocating for humanity? Securing better protection of civilians affected by armed conflict', Humanitarian Policy Group Briefing note, Nov. 2020.

Council on his latest report on the protection of civilians in armed conflict, the UN secretary-general said it showed 'little progress on the protection of civilians, and on compliance with international law, in 2019'.[18]

The latest efforts within the UN system to enhance protection of civilians affected by armed conflict was a 'call to action for human rights' launched by the UN secretary-general in February 2020 to coincide with the 75th anniversary of the UN. Echoing previous calls for a protection agenda for the UN system, the call to action sets out seven key areas for action, including engagement with the Security Council and to 'creatively use the full spectrum of other tools and channels . . . to raise awareness, prevent crisis and protect people effectively'.[19]

Consequences of armed conflicts in 2020

Armed conflicts result in loss of life and life-changing injuries, displacement of civilian populations and destruction of infrastructure and institutions. They also have long-term economic, developmental, political, environmental, health and social consequences.

In 2020 the total estimated number of conflict-related fatalities decreased for at least the second consecutive year (see table 2.1).[20] Overall, conflict-related fatalities have reduced by over 30 per cent since 2018. The decrease in 2020 was driven by further reductions in MENA, where all the armed conflicts had fewer fatalities than in 2019, and in Asia and Oceania, which saw a 47 per cent reduction in 2020, mostly as a result of estimated conflict-related fatalities being halved in Afghanistan. Two regions bucked this trend: in Europe the outbreak of armed conflict between Armenia and Azerbaijan led to a surge in conflict-related fatalities, while in sub-Saharan Africa 18 of the 20 armed conflicts had higher estimated conflict-related fatalities in 2020 than in 2019. For sub-Saharan Africa as a whole, the increase was about 41 per cent, and it overtook MENA in 2020 as the region with the most conflict-related fatalities. Battle-related fatalities decreased by about 10 per cent in 2020 compared to 2019, while fatalities from explosions/remote violence declined by 50 per cent. However, in other ACLED categories of political violence, there was a small increase in fatalities from violence against civilians, while the number of protest-related events rose by over

---

[18] UN Secretary-General (note 14).

[19] Guterres, A., 'The highest aspiration: A call to action for human rights', United Nations, Feb. 2020, p. 6.

[20] This assessment is based on ACLED data. For comparison, the Uppsala Conflict Data Program (UCDP) reported total deaths from organized violence reaching a 15-year high in 2014 with about 103 000 deaths and generally declining since then. UCDP's most recent data for 2019 showed almost 75 600 deaths, a decrease for the fifth successive year. Pettersson, T. and Öberg, M., 'Organized violence, 1989–2019', *Journal of Peace Research*, vol. 57, no. 4 (2020), pp. 597–613.

Table 2.2. Categories of global political violence, 2019–20

Event type	No. of events 2019	2020	Percentage change (2019–20)	Fatalities 2019	2020	Percentage change (2019–20)
Battles	45 398	35 523	−22%	78 619	70 309	−10.6%
Explosions/remote violence	36 197	24 252	−33%	37 832	18 683	−50.6%
Protests, riots and strategic developments	108 413	166 875	54%	3 559	3 107	−12.7%
Violence against civilians	24 091	23 889	−0.8%	28 203	28 772	2.0%
Total	**214 099**	**250 539**		**148 213**	**120 871**	

Note: For definitions of event types, see Armed Conflict Location & Event Data Project (ACLED), 'ACLED definitions of political violence and protest', 11 Apr. 2019.

Source: ACLED, Dashboard, accessed 10 Apr. 2021.

50 per cent, even though fatalities under that category decreased (see table 2.2).

Separate data on global trends and patterns in terrorism also showed a downward trend in deaths and in the impact of terrorism. The *Global Terrorism Index 2020* reported that the number of terrorism-related deaths worldwide fell by 59 per cent in the period from 2014 to 2019 (the latest period for which data was available), while over 96 per cent of deaths from terrorism in 2019 occurred in countries already in conflict, such as Afghanistan and Syria.[21]

However, while conflict-related fatalities have declined in recent years, other impacts of armed conflict (sometimes in combination with other factors) appear to have increased, including population displacement, food insecurity, humanitarian needs and violations of international humanitarian law. Armed conflict is also a major driver of displacement. For example, one study estimated that 37 million people were displaced in eight war-affected countries involving United States military intervention since the terrorist attacks on the USA of 11 September 2001.[22]

At the beginning of 2020, 1 per cent of humanity were living in forced exile, and in the last 10 years the number of people forcibly displaced almost doubled to 80 million, including 46 million internally displaced refugees in their own countries.[23] These record numbers continued into the first six months of 2020, with conflict and violence triggering a further 4.8 million

[21] Institute for Economics & Peace (IEP), *Global Terrorism Index 2020: Measuring the Impact of Terrorism* (IEP: Sydney, Jan. 2021).

[22] Vine, D. et al., 'Creating refugees: Displacement caused by the United States' post-9/11 wars', Costs of War Project, Brown University, 21 Sep. 2020.

[23] UN High Commissioner for Refugees (UNHCR), 'Briefing to the United Nations Security Council', 18 June 2020. Also see 'Global trends: Forced displacement in 2019', UNHCR, June 2020.

internal displacements, mainly in MENA and sub-Saharan Africa. The half-year figures for Cameroon, Mozambique, Niger and Somalia were already higher than those for the whole of 2019, while the highest number of new displacements were in Syria (1.47 million), the DRC (1.43 million) and Burkina Faso (0.42 million).[24] In the second half of 2020 new displacements were created by outbreaks of armed conflicts in Tigray (Ethiopia) and Nagorno-Karabakh (Armenia and Azerbaijan). Protracted displacement crises continued in many other places, including Afghanistan, the Central African Republic, Mali, Myanmar, Nigeria, South Sudan, Sudan, Venezuela and Yemen.[25]

Armed conflict also continued to be one of the main drivers of food insecurity in 2020, with conflict-induced increases in acute food insecurity particularly prevalent in West and Central Africa, and parts of the Middle East.[26] Famine and famine-like conditions were observed during 2020 in areas of Burkina Faso, South Sudan and Yemen. The World Food Programme estimated that at the end of 2020, 270 million people were in acute food insecurity or at risk, across 79 countries, as a result of the triple impact of conflict, climate shocks and the socio-economic consequences of the Covid-19 pandemic (an 82 per cent increase from pre-pandemic levels).[27] Other UN data suggests the situation will likely deteriorate further in 2021: while 168 million people needed humanitarian assistance in 2020 (following year-on-year increases since 2012 when the figure was 62 million), this is projected to rise to 235 million people in 2021—largely driven by anticipated increases in extreme poverty and food insecurity arising from the Covid-19 pandemic.[28]

Large numbers of children suffer the consequences of armed conflicts: in 2019 (the latest year for which figures are available), 426 million children, almost one fifth of children worldwide, were living in areas affected by armed conflict (2 per cent more children than in 2018).[29] In addition to fatalities through direct injury, children suffer indirect effects of conflict, including malnutrition, disease and human rights violations. The UN sec-

[24] 'Internal displacement 2020: Mid-year update', Internal Displacement Monitoring Centre, 15 Sep. 2020.

[25] UN Office for the Coordination of Humanitarian Affairs (OCHA), *Global Humanitarian Overview 2021* (UN OCHA: Geneva, Dec. 2020).

[26] UN OCHA (note 25), p. 32. On food insecurity, also see Zho, J. et al., 'The geopolitics of food security: Barriers to the sustainable development goal of zero hunger', SIPRI Insights on Peace and Security no. 2020/11, Nov. 2020.

[27] World Food Programme, 'WFP global operational response plan 2021', Update 1, Feb. 2021, pp. 4–5.

[28] UN OCHA (note 25), p. 66.

[29] Østby, G. et al., 'Children affected by armed conflict, 1990–2019', Conflict Trends no. 6, Peace Research Institute Oslo, 2020. For an overview of the literature on the use of children in armed conflict see Haer, R., 'Children and armed conflict: Looking at the future and learning from the past', *Third World Quarterly*, vol. 40, no. 1 (2019), pp. 74–91.

retary-general's annual report on children and armed conflict documented more than 25 000 incidents of 'grave violations' against children in conflicts around the world in 2019 (the same as in 2018), more than half committed by non-state actors, and a third by government and international actors. The six categories of grave violations covered in the report are: killing and maiming of children, recruitment and use of children as soldiers, sexual violence against children, abduction of children, attacks on schools and hospitals, and denial of humanitarian access.[30]

Armed conflict also imposes substantial economic costs on society. While calculating the economic costs of violence is extremely difficult, one study estimated the global cost to be $14.4 trillion in 2019, or 11 per cent of the global gross domestic product (GDP). This was a slight improvement on the 2018 calculation, mainly due to significant reductions in armed conflict and terrorism in 2019. The economic impact of violence in the 10 most affected countries in 2019 ranged from 24 to 59 per cent of their GDP; in comparison, the economic costs of violence in the 10 most peaceful countries averaged 3.9 per cent of GDP. The single largest component in the model was global military expenditure (41 per cent of the total), followed by internal security spending (34 per cent) and homicide (7.4 per cent).[31]

Finally, armed conflict also contributes to the deteriorating condition of the global environment, with consequences for sustainable development, human security and ecosystems—vulnerabilities that are being amplified by increasingly unpredictable climate patterns.[32] Climate change poses multidimensional challenges to peace. In 2020 climate-related shocks continued to amplify drivers of violence in a number of countries. Four interrelated pathways from climate change to violent conflict have been identified: livelihoods, migration and mobility, armed group tactics and elite exploitation.[33] For example, worsening livelihood conditions for herders and farmers in West and East Africa in 2020 contributed to communal conflicts (see chapter 7, sections II and IV, respectively, in this volume).

---

[30] United Nations, A/74/845–S/2020/525 (note 15), p. 2. Also see 'Open letter to the UN secretary-general on children and armed conflict', Human Rights Watch, 22 June 2020.

[31] IEP, *Economic Value of Peace 2021: Measuring the Global Economic Impact of Violence and Conflict* (IEP: Sydney, Jan. 2021), p. 2. On global military expenditure in 2020 see chapter 8 in this volume.

[32] Schaar, J., 'A confluence of crises: On water, climate and security in the Middle East and North Africa', SIPRI Insights on Peace and Security no. 2019/4, July 2019; and Peters, K. et al., 'Climate change, conflict and fragility: An evidence review and recommendations for research and action', Overseas Development Institute, 10 June 2020.

[33] Mobjörk, M., Krampe, F. and Tarif, K., 'Pathways of climate insecurity: Guidance for policymakers', SIPRI Policy Brief, Nov. 2020.

Peace processes in 2020

Like the conflicts they attempt to address, peace processes are also increasingly complex, multidimensional and highly internationalized, with a wide range of actors, activities and outcomes.[34] In addition, there is a growing number of peace agreement databases and collections.[35] Peacebuilding efforts typically include: ceasefire negotiations; signing of peace agreements; multilateral peace operations; disarmament, demobilization and reintegration (DDR) of former combatants (often supported as part of UN peace operations); power-sharing arrangements; and state-building measures. These are all designed to bring about sustainable peace among parties to a conflict.[36] Despite increased efforts in recent years to make peace processes more inclusive, women, community and grassroots organizations continue to be under-represented in the political–military hierarchies at the centre of most peace negotiations.[37] Efforts at increasing women's participation in peace operations and in improving gender training for peacekeepers have had similarly limited results.[38]

Not all peace processes lead to sustainable peace. Inconclusive political settlements, failure to address the root causes of a conflict, and ongoing insecurity and tensions have often led to non-compliance, violations and a recurrence of armed conflict. Many contemporary peace processes are long,

[34] Wolff, S., 'The making of peace: Processes and agreements', *Armed Conflict Survey*, vol. 4, no. 1 (2018), pp. 65–80.

[35] Examples include: UN Peacemaker, 'Peace agreements database', <https://peacemaker.un.org/document-search>; UN Peacemaker and University of Cambridge, 'Language of peace database', <https://www.languageofpeace.org/#/>; University of Edinburgh, Political Settlements Research Programme, 'PA-X peace agreements database', <https://www.peaceagreements.org/search>; University of Notre Dame, Kroc Institute for International Peace Studies, 'Peace accords matrix', <https://peaceaccords.nd.edu>; and UCDP, 'UCDP peace agreement dataset', <https://ucdp.uu.se/downloads/>.

[36] On multilateral peace operations see section II in this chapter, and in relation to DDR see 'Disarmament, demobilization and reintegration', UN Peacekeeping, [n.d.]. On various interpretations of the term 'peace' as well as other tools for realizing peace see Caparini, M. and Milante, G., 'Sustaining peace and sustainable development in dangerous places', *SIPRI Yearbook 2017*, pp. 211–52; and Caplan, R., *Measuring Peace: Principles, Practices, and Politics* (Oxford University Press: Oxford, 2019).

[37] Caparini, M. and Cóbar, J. F. A., 'Overcoming barriers to grassroots inclusion in peace processes', SIPRI Commentary, 18 Feb. 2021; Ertürk, Y., 'The political economy of peace processes and the women, peace and security agenda', *Conflict, Security & Development*, vol. 20, no. 4 (2020), pp. 419–39; Wise, L., Forster, R. and Bell, C., 'Local peace processes: Opportunities and challenges for women's engagement', PA-X Spotlight, University of Edinburgh, 2019; and Forster, R. and Bell, C., 'Gender mainstreaming in ceasefires: Comparative data and examples', PA-X Spotlight, University of Edinburgh, 2019.

[38] Ferrari, S. S., 'Is the United Nations uniformed gender parity strategy on track to reach its goals', SIPRI Commentary, 12 Dec. 2019; and Caparini, M., 'Gender training for police peacekeepers: Approaching two decades of United Nations Security Council Resolution 1325', SIPRI Commentary, 31 Oct. 2019.

drawn-out affairs that contain rather than resolve the conflict.[39] Indeed, this may be the best option where resolution of the conflict is not possible. Some peace agreements break down and hostilities resume, whereas others achieve a relatively stable ceasefire but not a sustainable conflict settlement, such as the unresolved armed conflicts in the post-Soviet space. However, even within the latter, there remains the danger of a fresh outbreak of hostilities, as occurred in Nagorno-Karabakh in September 2020 (see chapter 5). Even relatively successful peace agreements, such as the 2016 agreement in Colombia, face continuing challenges (see chapter 3). Since the mid 1990s most armed conflicts have been new outbreaks of old conflicts rather than conflicts over new issues. This indicates that root causes of conflicts are not being sufficiently addressed. Moreover, this blurred boundary between war and peace also makes it difficult to identify and conceptualize the end of an armed conflict.[40]

While many of the armed conflicts in 2020 were being addressed by ongoing or new peace processes, with a few notable exceptions, most were either stalled or suffered serious setbacks. Important advances were made in the peace talks in Afghanistan, including a conditional peace agreement between the Taliban and the USA in February 2020 and the commencement of intra-Afghan peace talks in September 2020.[41] A ceasefire in Idlib province in Syria in March 2020 and a nationwide ceasefire agreed in Libya in October 2020 suggested both of those conflicts might be open to some form of resolution soon.[42] In November 2020 a Japanese-brokered ceasefire between the Arakan Army and Myanmar's military opened up new opportunities for dialogue, while a Russian-brokered ceasefire also in November 2020 ended the fighting in Nagorno-Karabakh.[43] However, in sub-Saharan Africa, the peace process in Sudan was the only one to make substantive progress in 2020.[44]

[39] See e.g. Pospisil, J., *Peace in Political Unsettlement: Beyond Solving Conflict* (Palgrave Macmillan: 2019); and Wittke, C., 'The Minsk Agreements—More than "scraps of paper"?', *East European Politics*, vol. 35, no. 3 (2019), pp. 264–90.

[40] De Franco, C., Engberg-Pedersen, A. and Mennecke, M., 'How do wars end? A multidisciplinary enquiry', *Journal of Strategic Studies*, vol. 42, no. 7 (2019), pp. 889–900. Also see Krause, J., 'How do wars end? A strategic perspective', *Journal of Strategic Studies*, vol. 42, no. 7 (2019), pp. 920–45. On the peace agreement provisions that are consistently associated with successful war-to-peace transitions see Fontana, G., Siewert, M. B. and Yakinthou, C., 'Managing war-to-peace transitions after intra-state conflicts: Configurations of successful peace processes', *Journal of Intervention and Statebuilding*, vol. 15, no. 1 (2020), pp. 25–47.

[41] On the peace process in Afghanistan see chapter 4, section II, in this volume.

[42] On the peace processes in Syria and Libya see chapter 6, sections II and IV, respectively, in this volume.

[43] On the ceasefire in Myanmar see chapter 4, section III, in this volume; on the ceasefire agreement between Armenia and Azerbaijan see chapter 5, section II, in this volume.

[44] On the peace processes in Sudan see chapter 7, section IV, in this volume.

The UN secretary-general's call for a Covid-19-related global ceasefire

On 23 March 2020 UN Secretary-General António Guterres called for an immediate global ceasefire to tackle the threat of Covid-19.[45] By June 2020 at least 171 states, along with religious leaders, regional partners, civil society networks and others, had declared their support for the call.[46] However, attempts to pass a supportive resolution in the UN Security Council were initially stymied by disagreements, especially among the permanent members.[47] It took more than three months after the initial call before the UN Security Council unanimously voted in favour of a resolution backing the call, and called on conflict parties to engage in a 'durable humanitarian pause' to last for at least 90 days.[48] However, military operations against groups designated as terrorist groups by the Security Council, such as the Islamic State, al-Qaeda and al-Nusra Front, were excluded from the UN Security Council ceasefire call. On 22 September 2020 the UN secretary-general renewed his call for a global ceasefire during his speech at the opening of the general debate of the 75th session of the UN General Assembly. He appealed 'for a new push by the international community' to make the global ceasefire a reality by the end of the year.[49]

Despite some armed groups, in addition to governments, initially acknowledging the call and promising to consider it, the reality was that in most of the armed conflicts the conflict parties either simply ignored it or their commitments were largely tokenistic, and the fighting generally continued. Between 23 March 2020 and 31 December 2020 conflict parties declared at least 29 ceasefires in 18 countries, although not all were in response to the secretary-general's appeal (see table 2.3).[50] Most of the ceasefires were unilateral declarations, and many were temporary or conditional; therefore, overall, they were generally only preliminary steps and with minimal material impact on levels of violence. Furthermore, despite often being

[45] Guterres, A., 'The fury of the virus illustrates the folly of war', United Nations, 23 Mar. 2020; and 'Covid-19: UN chief calls for global ceasefire to focus on "the true fight of our lives"', UN News, 23 Mar. 2020. On the Covid-19 pandemic see chapter 12, section I, in this volume.

[46] 'Update on the secretary-general's appeal for a global ceasefire', United Nations, 2 Apr. 2020; and 'Statement of support by 171 UN member states, non-member observer state and observer to the UN secretary-general's appeal for a global ceasefire amid the Covid-19 pandemic', 22 June 2020.

[47] International Rescue Committee, 'UN Security Council fails to support global ceasefire, shows no response to Covid-19', Press release, 19 May 2020; and Gowan, R. and Pradhan, A., 'Is all hope lost for a global cease-fire resolution at the UN?', World Politics Review, 14 May 2020.

[48] UN Security Council Resolution 2532, 1 July 2020.

[49] UN Secretary-General, 'Secretary-general's address to the opening of the general debate of the 75th session of the General Assembly', 22 Sep. 2020.

[50] Also see Wise, L. et al., 'Pandemic pauses: Understanding ceasefires in a time of Covid-19', Political Settlements Research Programme, University of Edinburgh, Mar. 2021; Miller, A., 'Call unanswered: A review of responses to the UN appeal for a global ceasefire', ACLED, 13 May 2020; and Thompson, T. J., 'Searching for Covid-19 ceasefires: Conflict zone impacts, needs, and opportunities', United States Institute of Peace, Special Report no. 480, Sep. 2020.

Table 2.3. Ceasefires during the Covid-19 pandemic, 23 Mar.–31 Dec. 2020

Country	Declaration date (2020)	Parties	Type of ceasefire	Duration/ end date[a]	Recipro- cated?	UN call or Covid-19 related?
Afghanistan	23 Mar.	Taliban	Unilateral	3 days	Yes	No
	28 July	Taliban	Unilateral	3 days	Yes	No
Angola	13 Apr.	FLEC	Unilateral	4 weeks	No	Yes
	4 June	FLEC	Unilateral	..	No	Yes
Armenia/ Azerbaijan	10 Oct. Updated 17 and 25 Oct.	Governments	Bilateral	.. ..	Yes Yes	No No
	9 Nov.	Governments plus Russia	Multilateral	Permanent	Yes	No
Cameroon	25 Mar. Updated 10 and 25 Apr.	SOCADEF	Unilateral	2 weeks ..	No No	Yes Yes
Colombia	29 Mar.	ELN	Unilateral	1 month	No	Yes
India	5 Apr.	CPI	Unilateral	5 days	No	Yes
	23 Dec.	NSCN-K	Unilateral	..	No	No
Indonesia	11 Apr.	OPM and TPNPB	Unilateral	..	No	Yes
Libya	21 Mar.	GNA	Unilateral	..	Yes	Yes
	21 Mar.	LNA	Unilateral	..	Yes	Yes
	6 June	LNA	Unilateral	..	No	No
	21 Aug.	GNA	Unilateral	..	No	No
	23 Oct.	GNA and LNA	Bilateral	..	Yes	No
Myanmar	1 Apr. Updated 3 May	Northern Alliance	Unilateral	1 month 30 May	No No	Yes Yes
	9 May	Myanmar military	Unilateral	31 Aug.	No	Yes
Nigeria	25 Mar.	Regional intercommunal groups	Multilateral	..	No	Yes
Philippines	18 Mar.	Government	Unilateral	15 Apr.	Yes	Yes
	24 Mar. Updated 30 Mar. and 16 Apr.	CPP	Unilateral	15 Apr. 30 Apr.	Yes No	Yes Yes
South Sudan	9 Apr.	SSOMA	Unilateral	..	No	Yes
Sudan	31 Mar. Updated 1 July	SPLM/A–N (al-Hilu)	Unilateral	3 months 31 Jan. 2021	Yes Yes	No No
	31 Mar.	Government	Unilateral	3 months	Yes	No
Syria	24 Mar.	SDF	Unilateral	..	No	Yes
Thailand	3 Apr.	BRN	Unilateral	30 Apr.	No	Yes

Country	Declaration date (2020)	Parties	Type of ceasefire	Duration/ end date[a]	Recipro- cated?	UN call or Covid-19 related?
Ukraine	22 July	Government; Russia; OSCE; CADLR	Multilateral	Permanent	No	No
Yemen	8 Apr. Updated 24 Apr.	Government	Unilateral	23 Apr. 21 May	No No	Yes No
	22 June	Government and STC	Bilateral	..	No	No

.. = not specified; BRN = Patani Malay National Revolutionary Front (Barisan Revolusi Nasional Melayu Patan); CADLR = representatives of certain areas of Donetsk and Luhansk regions; CPI = Communist Party of India; CPP = Communist Party of the Philippines; ELN = National Liberation Army (Ejército de Liberación Nacional); FLEC = Front for the Liberation of the Enclave of Cabinda; GNA = Government of National Accord; LNA = Libyan National Army; NSCN-K = National Socialist Council of Nagaland (K); OPM = Free Papua Movement (Organisasi Papua Merdeka); OSCE = Organization for Security and Co-operation in Europe; SDF = Syrian Democratic Forces; SOCADEF = Southern Cameroons Defence Forces; SPLM/ A–N (al-Hilu) = Sudan People's Liberation Movement/Army–North al-Hilu faction; SSOMA = South Sudan Opposition Movements Alliance; STC = Southern Transitional Council; TPNPB = West Papua National Liberation Army; UN = United Nations.

[a] The duration/end date of the ceasefire refers to the declared length of the ceasefire. The extent to which this was realized (or will be realized for 'permanent' ceasefires) requires a separate assessment in each case.

Source: University of Edinburgh, Political Settlements Research Programme, 'Ceasefires in a time of Covid-19', accessed 5 Apr. 2021.

reported as 'Covid-19' ceasefires, only about 60 per cent of the declared ceasefires included references to the pandemic or humanitarian need.

However, global levels of armed violence did reduce during the early stages of the pandemic and continued to do so throughout 2020. ACLED recorded a decrease in certain types of political violence, such as battles and demonstrations, but increases in others, such as mob violence and state targeting of civilians.[51] Another estimate suggested a 58 per cent decrease globally in civilian victims from explosive violence between April and July 2020, compared to the same four months in 2019, as well as a 30 per cent decline in recorded global explosive weapon incidents during the same period.[52] However, these reductions appeared mostly to be part of the broader trend in declining violence (and the result of individual conflict contexts) rather

[51] Kishi, R. and Wilson, A., 'How the coronavirus crisis is silencing dissent and sparkling repression', *Foreign Policy*, 21 July 2020; and Pavlik, M., 'A great and sudden change: The global political violence landscape before and after the Covid-19 pandemic', ACLED, 4 Aug. 2020.

[52] 'Global explosive violence sharply declines during Covid 19, new data suggests', Action on Armed Violence, 12 Sep. 2020.

than being directly related to either the pandemic itself or as a result of the UN secretary-general's call.

By the end of 2020 it also seemed like most conflict parties had adapted to the pandemic, which now simply formed part of the wider political context of armed conflicts and peace processes. Overall, rather than being game-changing, the impact of Covid-19 on armed conflicts in 2020 was mixed. In a few cases there were temporary declines in armed conflicts, mostly due to decisions by governments or armed opposition groups to account for obstructed logistics and to increase their popular support. However, in many cases armed conflict levels persisted or, in a few cases, even increased as a result of conflict parties exploiting either state weakness or reduced international attention due to the pandemic.[53] The UN secretary-general's call for a global ceasefire had a minimal impact on these conflict dynamics. Some projections based on economic and development data estimate the pandemic may lead to future increases in armed violence in fragile states driven by rising prices and falling incomes.[54]

---

[53] Bell, C., Epple, T. and Pospisil, J., 'The impact of Covid-19 on peace and transition process: Tracking the trends', Political Settlements Research Programme, University of Edinburgh, 2020; and Ide, T., 'Covid-19 and armed conflict', World Development, vol. 140 (Apr. 2021).

[54] Moyer, J. D. and Kaplan, O., 'Will the coronavirus fuel conflict?', Foreign Policy, 6 July 2020.

II. Global and regional trends and developments in multilateral peace operations

TIMO SMIT AND JAÏR VAN DER LIJN

Against the backdrop of two major continuing developments, the main trend of decreasing personnel figures in stable numbers of smaller multilateral peace operations endured in 2020. First, competition and disagreement between the permanent members of the United Nations Security Council, as well as regional powers—particularly in the Middle East and North Africa region and sub-Saharan Africa—have continued, resulting in increased impetus for countries and organizations to show the flag, leading to further fragmentation of conflict management efforts. Second, during its final year, the administration of United States President Donald J. Trump persevered in striving for reduction of the UN peacekeeping budget—and consequently limiting personnel numbers—and the withdrawal of US forces from Afghanistan. In an environment of ongoing need for conflict management, the Covid-19 pandemic was an additional challenge, and many operations and the organizations deploying them struggled to continue their efforts.

Multilateral peace operations in 2020

In 2020 the UN, regional organizations and alliances, and ad hoc coalitions of states carried out 62 multilateral peace operations in 35 countries or territories across the world (see figure 2.2).[1] This was one more than in 2019 and similar to the number of multilateral peace operations that have been active in other years since 2013, when the Central African Republic (CAR) and Mali became hotspots (see figure 2.3).[2] Of the 62 multilateral peace operations that were active in 2020, 22 were in sub-Saharan Africa, 18 in Europe, 14 in the Middle East and North Africa, 5 in Asia and Oceania and 3 in the Americas (see table 2.4).

---

[1] See also table 2.5. The quantitative analysis draws on data collected by SIPRI to examine trends in peace operations. According to SIPRI's definition, a multilateral peace operation must have the stated intention of: (*a*) serving as an instrument to facilitate the implementation of peace agreements already in place, (*b*) supporting a peace process, or (*c*) assisting conflict prevention or peacebuilding efforts. Good offices, fact-finding or electoral assistance missions and missions comprising non-resident individuals or teams of negotiators are not included. Since all SIPRI data is reviewed on a continual basis and adjusted when more accurate information becomes available, the statistics in this chapter may not always fully correspond with data found in previous editions of the SIPRI Yearbook or other SIPRI publications.

[2] See Smit, T., Sacks Ferrari, S. and van der Lijn, J., 'Global trends and developments in multilateral peace operations', *SIPRI Yearbook 2020*, pp. 45–58.

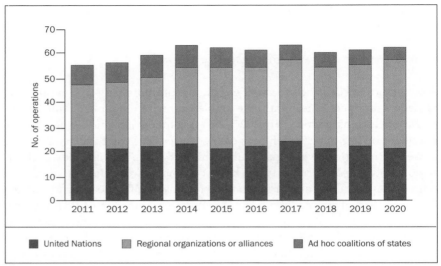

Figure 2.2. Number of multilateral peace operations, by type of conducting organization, 2011–20

New multilateral peace operations

Three multilateral peace operations started in 2020. These were the African Union (AU) Military Observers Mission to the CAR (MOUACA), the European Union (EU) Common Security and Defence Policy (CSDP) Advisory Mission in the CAR (EUAM RCA) and the AU Mission in Libya. While the UN Integrated Transition Assistance Mission in Sudan (UNITAMS) was established in 2020, it did not start until 1 January 2021 and is therefore not included in 2020.

EUAM RCA was established on 9 December 2019 by the Council of the EU and launched on 9 August 2020.[3] The launch date was later than initially expected due to the Covid-19 pandemic and the logistical challenges it imposed on the preparations for the mission. EUAM RCA is mandated to support security sector reform in CAR through the provision of strategic advice at the level of the Ministry of Interior and Public Security and to support development of the internal security forces. The mandate is scalable, which means that the mission can be upgraded to a capacity-building mission, similar to the civilian CSDP EU missions in Mali and Niger. EUAM RCA is the civilian equivalent of the military EU Training Mission in CAR,

---

[3] Council Decision (CFSP) 2019/2110 of 9 Dec. 2019 on the European Union CSDP Advisory Mission in the Central African Republic (EUAM RCA), *Official Journal of the European Union*, L318, 10 Dec. 2019; and Council Decision (CFSP) 2020/1131 of 30 July 2020 launching the European Union CSDP Advisory Mission in the Central African Republic (EUAM RCA), *Official Journal of the European Union*, L247, 31 July 2020.

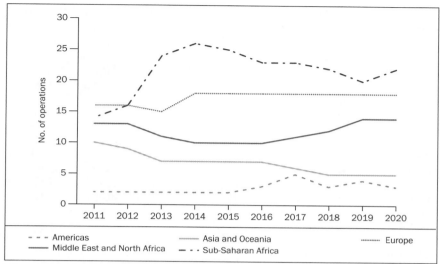

Figure 2.3. Number of multilateral peace operations, by region, 2011–20

which has been training the armed forces of CAR and advising its government on military issues since 2016.

MOUACA was established on 10 July 2020 by the Peace and Security Council of the AU, which on that day authorized the deployment of the mission.[4] MOUACA is mandated to help monitor the implementation of the 2019 Political Agreement for Peace and Reconciliation in the CAR, specifically the provisions on the establishment of three joint security units composed of government forces mixed with reintegrated members of the armed groups that are signatories to the agreement. The deployment of MOUACA was complicated by the Covid-19 pandemic and there has been little information available on its progress. By October 2020, 14 military observers had been deployed out of an authorized strength of 30 military observers and 6 civilian personnel.

The AU Mission in Libya was established on 9 February 2020 by the AU Assembly of Heads of State and Government, which decided on that day to 'Upgrade to the level of mission' the AU Liaison Office in Libya (which did not qualify as a multilateral peace operation). The objective of the decision was to increase the political, diplomatic and military capacity of the AU in Libya 'with a view to ensuring greater contribution and participation of the AU in the efforts aimed at finding a lasting solution to the crisis in Libya'.[5] The decision followed shortly after the January 2020 Berlin Conference on

[4] AU, Communiqué of the 936th meeting of the Peace and Security Council, held on 10 July 2020, on the situation in the Central African Republic, 10 July 2020.
[5] AU Assembly of Heads of State and Government, 'Decision on Libya and the Sahel', 33rd ordinary session of the Assembly of the Union, Assembly/AU/Dec.792(XXXIII), 9–10 Feb. 2020, para. 18(b).

Table 2.4. Number of multilateral peace operations and personnel deployed by region and type of organization, 2020

Conducting organization	Americas	Asia and Oceania	Europe	Middle East and North Africa	Sub-Saharan Africa	World
Operations	3	5	18	14	22	62
United Nations[a]	2	2	2	7	8	21
Regional organization or alliance	1	1	14	6	14	36
Ad hoc coalition	–	2	2	1	–	5
Personnel	304	9 941	8 063	14 615	94 201	127 124
United Nations[a]	274	313	1 020	12 804	72 301	86 712
Regional organization or alliance	30	9 592	5 961	657	21 900	38 140
Ad hoc coalition	–	36	1 082	1 154	–	2 272

– = not applicable.

[a] UN figures include the UN–African Union Hybrid Operation in Darfur.

Notes: Numbers of operations cover the year 2020; personnel figures are as of 31 Dec. 2020.

Source: SIPRI Multilateral Peace Operations Database, accessed 1 Apr. 2021, <http://www.sipri.org/databases/pko/>.

Libya. The AU Peace and Security Council also called for the full engagement of the AU in all efforts to monitor the 23 October 2020 permanent ceasefire agreement, including through the deployment of African civilian and military observers. The establishment of the AU Mission in Libya, along with other initiatives, reflects the wish of the AU to be a more active and credible participant in the Libyan peace process. The AU has been deeply uncomfortable with the military intervention led by the North Atlantic Treaty Organization (NATO) in Libya in 2011 and the extent of foreign interference in the subsequent civil wars in Libya. However, it remains unclear what has been achieved concretely in terms of upgrading the mission. The fact that the AU Peace and Security Council in November 2020 stressed the need to ensure the AU Mission in Libya has enough capacity to carry out its mandate and be more visible suggests progress might have been limited so far.[6] Also, the Libyan parties do not appear to be receptive to all AU involvement. For example, the signatories of the permanent ceasefire agreement have been clear that the request for international observers is strictly limited to unarmed and non-uniformed observers under the auspices of the UN Support Mission in Libya (UNSMIL).[7]

---

[6] AU, Communiqué of the 961st meeting of the Peace and Security Council, held virtually on 3 Nov. 2020, on the situation in Libya, 3 Nov. 2020.

[7] United Nations, Security Council, Letter dated 29 December 2020 from the Secretary-General addressed to the President of the Security Council, S/2020/1309, 30 Dec. 2020.

The three new multilateral peace operations in 2020 follow two trends. First, all three are very small compared to most others. Since the establishment in 2014 of the UN Multidimensional Integrated Stabilization Mission in the CAR (MINUSCA) no large multilateral peace operations have been established. Second, all three are part of complex constellations of other peace operations deployed in the same mission area. EUAM RCA and MOUACA became the fourth and fifth multilateral peace operations that were deployed in parallel in CAR. The AU Mission in Libya is the third concurrent multilateral peace operation in Libya, next to UNSMIL and the EU Border Assistance Mission in Libya.

Closed multilateral peace operations

Three multilateral peace operations ended in 2020. These were the Economic Community of West African States (ECOWAS) Mission in Guinea-Bissau (ECOMIB), which closed on 10 September 2020, and the AU–UN Hybrid Operation in Darfur (UNAMID) and the UN Integrated Peacebuilding Office in Guinea-Bissau (UNIOGBIS), which both ended on 31 December 2020. The two missions in Guinea-Bissau were withdrawn notwithstanding the persistence of significant political instability in the country following a disorderly transition of power in the aftermath of the presidential elections in late 2019. Nonetheless, residual tasks of UNIOGBIS were handed over to the UN country team in Guinea-Bissau, the UN Office for West Africa and the Sahel and other partners.

The closure of UNAMID was a significant milestone. Established in 2007 and once the largest multilateral peace operation, UNAMID was a unique mission for several reasons. The fact that it operated under the joint political authority of the AU and the UN was certainly one of them. The notoriously complicated relationship between the mission and the Sudanese Government under former president Omar al-Bashir was also a defining characteristic. Although the transition of UNAMID had been foreseen, its departure came at a precarious time: amidst a pandemic; while Sudan is undergoing a historic political transition, following the removal of al-Bashir in a coup d'état in 2019; in the wake of the Juba Peace Agreement of 3 October 2020 between the transitional government of Sudan and various Sudanese armed opposition groups; and ongoing and even increasing violence by militia and protection needs, particularly for internally displaced persons.[8]

---

[8] Dessu, M. K., 'Darfur's conflict could return to square one: UNAMID should stay in Darfur to protect civilians until the political transition in Sudan is sustainable', *ISS Today*, Institute for Security Studies, 22 July 2020. On the armed conflict and peace process in Sudan see chapter 7, section IV, in this volume.

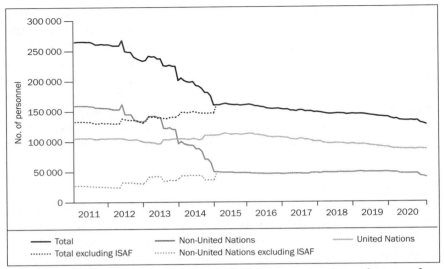

Figure 2.4. Number of personnel in multilateral peace operations, by type of conducting organization, 2011–20

ISAF = International Security Assistance Force.

Personnel deployments

Since 2012 there has been a general downward trend in the number of personnel deployed globally in multilateral peace operations. This can be explained by two main factors. First, the drawdown of troops from Afghanistan, initially the NATO-led International Security Assistance Force (ISAF) and then the Resolute Support Mission (RSM). Second, since 2015 the reduction of personnel deployed in sub-Saharan Africa, and particularly in UN peace operations. Both trends have depended heavily on, but were not limited to, the policies of the US Government, especially the Trump administration.

The number of personnel deployed in multilateral peace operations globally was lower on 31 December 2020 than at any other point in 2011–20. During 2020 it decreased from 137 781 on 31 December 2019 to 127 124 on 31 December 2020 (see figure 2.4).[9] This 7.7 per cent net decrease was thus a continuation of a key trend in the post-ISAF era. Indeed, it was the largest

---

[9] The analyses of personnel levels in this chapter are based on estimates of the number of international personnel (military, police and international civilian staff) deployed at the end of each month in each of the multilateral peace operations that were active in the period Jan. 2011 to Dec. 2020. In previous editions of the SIPRI Yearbook, similar analyses used annual snapshot data on the number of international personnel in multilateral peace operations at the end of each year or, in the case of an operation terminated during a calendar year, on the number at its closure. Consequently, the data in this chapter does not exactly match the data used in previous editions of the SIPRI Yearbook.

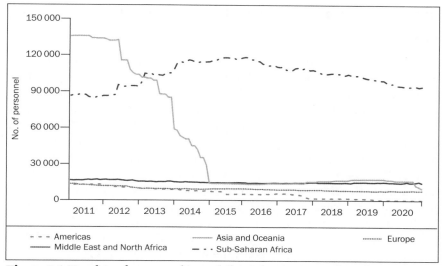

Figure 2.5. Number of personnel in multilateral peace operations, by region, 2011–20

annual decrease in this period, which means that the trend was accelerating. Based on expected future reductions, it is likely to continue.

The net decrease during 2020 was mostly due to reductions in a number of large multilateral peace operations, especially the RSM (see below). The number of personnel deployed in multilateral peace operations on 31 December 2020 included almost 10 000 personnel remaining in the RSM, who are expected to leave Afghanistan by 1 May 2021 as per the February 2020 withdrawal agreement between the Taliban and the USA.[10] Whether this will happen or not will be decided in 2021 and depends primarily on the Afghanistan policy of the new US Government.

Multilateral peace operations in sub-Saharan Africa continued to account for most personnel deployed in multilateral peace operations globally (see figure 2.5). The number of personnel deployed in the region decreased by 3.4 per cent in 2020, from 97 519 on 31 December 2019 to 94 201 on 31 December 2020. It reached the lowest point since December 2012, before the deployment of multilateral peace operations to Mali. The number of personnel deployed in multilateral peace operations in sub-Saharan Africa peaked at almost 120 000 in 2015 and has decreased every year since. The 2020 personnel numbers still include almost 7000 personnel that were part of UNAMID, which ended on 31 December 2020. Had the mission closed earlier, the decrease in 2020 of the number of personnel deployed globally, and in sub-Saharan Africa, would have been much more pronounced.

---

[10] On the armed conflict and peace process in Afghanistan see chapter 4, section II, in this volume.

Organizations conducting multilateral peace operations

United Nations

The UN remains the main organization deploying multilateral peace operations, with about one third of all operations and some two thirds of all personnel. It led 21 multilateral peace operations in 2020. This was one fewer than in 2019. The number of personnel deployed globally in UN peace operations decreased by 2.4 per cent in 2020, from 88 849 on 31 December 2019 to 86 712 on 31 December 2020. Total personnel deployments in UN operations have decreased every year since 2015. This is mainly because several UN peace operations have been drawing down or closing down and because the UN has not established any major or even moderate-sized peace operation since 2014. The last time when there were fewer personnel deployed in UN peace operations than in 2020 was in 2007.

Among the main developments in 2020 were the closure of UNAMID on 31 December 2020 and the establishment of UNITAMS to succeed it, effective as of 1 January 2021. UNAMID is the fourth major UN peacekeeping operation that closed down during 2011–20, after the UN Mission in Liberia in 2018 and the UN Stabilization Mission in Haiti and the UN Operation in Côte d'Ivoire in 2017. The establishment of UNITAMS is the latest example of the trend of small UN peace operations. UNITAMS' budget for 2021 provides for only 21 police and 141 international civilian personnel.[11] Preparations for the build-up of the follow-up mission commenced in Sudan in October 2020.[12] UNITAMS is a UN special political mission rather than a UN peacekeeping operation. Special political missions tend to be small, they do not have a military chain of command and their personnel tend to be unarmed, with the exception of guard units for self-protection.

The UN Organization Stabilization Mission in the Democratic Republic of the Congo (MONUSCO) has also been scaling down since 2015 and could be the next major UN operation in line to close. In December 2020 the UN Security Council endorsed a joint strategy of the mission and the Government of the Democratic Republic of the Congo on the progressive and phased drawdown of MONUSCO and asked the UN secretary-general to prepare a detailed transition plan.[13] According to the joint strategy, maintaining a

---

[11] United Nations, General Assembly, 'Proposed programme budget for 2021', A/75/6 (Sect. 3)/Add. 7, 23 Oct. 2020.

[12] UN Security Council Resolution 2524, 3 June 2020; and United Nations, Security Council, 'Situation in the Sudan and the activities of the United Nations Integrated Transition Assistance Mission in the Sudan', Report of the Secretary-General, S/2020/1155, 1 Dec. 2020.

[13] UN Security Council Resolution 2556, 18 Dec. 2020, paras 49–50.

strong presence of MONUSCO in provinces where fighting continues, such as North Kivu, remains essential in the medium term.[14]

Finally, a highlight for the UN was the role of UNSMIL in facilitating talks that led to a permanent ceasefire agreement between the main rival factions in the Libyan civil war on 23 October 2020.[15] Pursuant to the agreement, the UN is expected to assist in the implementation of a ceasefire monitoring mechanism in Libya.[16] The UN secretary-general has thus recommended to the UN Security Council on 29 December 2020 to establish a monitoring component within UNSMIL.[17]

Regional organizations and alliances

Regional organizations and alliances led 36 multilateral peace operations in 2020, which was 3 more than in 2019. There were three new operations in this category in 2020, two in CAR (EUAM RCA and MOUACA) and one in Libya (the AU Mission in Libya). The number of personnel deployed globally in multilateral peace operations led by regional organizations or alliances decreased by 18 per cent in 2020, from 46 569 on 31 December 2019 to 38 140 on 31 December 2020. This resulted primarily from reductions of the NATO-led RSM in Afghanistan and the AU Mission in Somalia (AMISOM)—by far the two largest multilateral peace operations run by regional actors—and the closure of ECOMIB.

African regional organizations—the AU and the subregional ECOWAS and Intergovernmental Authority on Development (IGAD)—conducted nine multilateral peace operations in 2020, two more than in 2019. The number of personnel in these operations decreased by 7.3 per cent, from 22 114 on 31 December 2019 to 20 496 on 31 December 2020. In addition to AMISOM, the AU Mission in Libya and MOUACA, the AU maintained small political missions in CAR and Mali and a small observer mission in Burundi. The ECOWAS Mission in Gambia, which has been active since January 2017, is the only remaining ECOWAS mission following the closure of ECOMIB. Finally, the IGAD-led Ceasefire and Transitional Security Arrangements Monitoring and Verification Mechanism has been monitoring successive

---

[14] United Nations, Security Council, Letter dated 26 October 2020 from the Secretary-General addressed to the President of the Security Council, S/2020/1041, annex, 27 Oct. 2020. On the armed conflict in the Democratic Republic of the Congo see chapter 7, section III, in this volume.

[15] 'UN salutes new Libya ceasefire agreement that points to "a better, safer, and more peaceful future"', UN News, 23 Oct. 2020. On the ceasefire agreement in Libya see chapter 6, section IV, in this volume.

[16] United Nations, Security Council, Letter dated 27 October 2020 from the Secretary-General addressed to the President of the Security Council, S/2020/1043, 27 Oct. 2020, annex, para. 10.

[17] United Nations, S/2020/1309 (note 7), paras 29–41, 45.

cessation of hostilities and ceasefire agreements in South Sudan under different names since 2014.[18]

Regional organizations and alliances from the northern hemisphere—the EU, NATO and the Organization for Security and Co-operation in Europe (OSCE)—led 26 multilateral peace operations in 2020, one more than in 2019. The number of personnel in these operations decreased by 28 per cent, from 24 426 on 31 December 2019 to 17 614 on 31 December 2020. Whereas the OSCE deploys peace operations in member states only, as most regional organizations do, the EU and NATO conduct peace operations in non-member states only.

The EU led 14 missions and operations in the framework of the EU CSDP that qualified as multilateral peace operations in 2020. This was one more than in 2019. These included: 10 civilian CSDP missions that qualified as a multilateral peace operation, including the new EUAM RCA; a military operation in Bosnia and Herzegovina; and three non-combat military training missions in CAR, Mali and Somalia. The EU Training Mission in Mali (EUTM Mali) has been the largest military peace operation led by the EU since 2018. In 2020 the Council of the EU renewed the mandate of this mission for another four years, until 18 May 2024, and gave it more tasks and a larger budget.[19] In addition to its operations being seriously affected by the Covid-19 pandemic, like all training and capacity-building missions, EUTM Mali temporarily suspended its activities following the August 2020 coup d'état in Mali.[20]

NATO led three multilateral peace operations in 2020: the Kosovo Force (KFOR), the NATO Mission Iraq and the RSM. The partial drawdown of the RSM was one of the main developments of the year. On 29 February 2020 the Taliban and the USA reached an agreement on the conditional withdrawal of all remaining US forces (and all other foreign forces) in Afghanistan within 14 months, that is by 1 May 2021.[21] Since the Taliban–US agreement the Taliban have largely refrained from attacking NATO and US forces in Afghanistan.

---

[18] The mission was named the Monitoring and Verification Mechanism until the entry into force of the 2015 Agreement on the Resolution of the Conflict in South Sudan (ARCSS), after which it was renamed the Ceasefire and Transitional Security Arrangements Mechanism. It was renamed again to its current name following the entry into force of the 2018 Revitalized ARCSS. On the armed conflict and peace process in South Sudan see chapter 7, section IV, in this volume.

[19] Council Decision (CFSP) 2020/434 of 23 Mar. 2020 amending Decision 2013/34/CFSP on a European Union military mission to contribute to the training of the Malian Armed Forces (EUTM Mali), *Official Journal of the European Union*, L89, 24 Mar. 2020.

[20] Emmott, R. and Diallo, T., 'EU freezes Mali training missions after military coup, denies responsibility', Reuters, 26 Aug. 2020. On the armed conflict in Mali see chapter 7, section II, in this volume.

[21] US Department of State, 'Agreement for bringing peace to Afghanistan between the Islamic Emirate of Afghanistan which is not recognized by the United States as a state and is known as the Taliban and the United States of America', 29 Feb. 2020. Also see chapter 4, section II, in this volume.

The OSCE conducted nine field operations that qualified as a multilateral peace operation. With more than 800 international personnel, the OSCE Special Monitoring Mission (SMM) in Ukraine continued to be the largest OSCE field operation by far, and the largest civilian mission in the world.[22] Most of the other OSCE field operations have been active since the 1990s and maintained fewer than 30 international personnel in 2020.

Regional organizations and alliances did not play any meaningful role in the resolution and aftermath of the 2020 Nagorno-Karabakh war.[23]

Ad hoc coalitions

Ad hoc coalitions of states conducted five multilateral peace operations in 2020, one fewer than in 2019. These were the International Monitoring Team in Mindanao, the Philippines, the Office of the High Representative in Bosnia and Herzegovina, the Joint Control Commission (JCC) Joint Peacekeeping Forces in the disputed Trans-Dniester region of Moldova, the Multinational Force and Observers (MFO) in the Sinai Peninsula, and the Neutral Nations Supervisory Commission on the Korean peninsula. The number of personnel deployed in multilateral peace operations in this category decreased by 3.9 per cent in 2020, from 2363 on 31 December 2019 to 2272 on 31 December 2020.

There were some notable ad hoc initiatives in relation to the Nagorno-Karabakh war. However, these did not (yet) qualify as multilateral peace operations. In addition to a Russian 'peacekeeping contingent' (see below), Russia and Turkey signed a memorandum of understanding on 11 November 2020 on the establishment of a joint ceasefire monitoring centre in Azerbaijan to monitor the ceasefire.[24] Turkey's Ministry of National Defence confirmed on 29 December 2020 that it had already dispatched 36 military officers including a general to Azerbaijan, who were on standby to start work as soon as the construction of the joint ceasefire monitoring centre was completed.[25] Russian Government officials, including President Vladimir Putin, have been reported saying that the joint centre will make use of surveillance drones to monitor the situation inside Nagorno-Karabakh and that Turkish monitors would not be physically present there.[26]

---

[22] On the armed conflict in Ukraine see chapter 5, section III, in this volume.

[23] On the armed conflict in Nagorno-Karabakh see chapter 5, section II, in this volume.

[24] 'Russia, Turkey agree creation of Nagorno-Karabakh ceasefire monitoring center', TASS, 11 Nov. 2020.

[25] Turkey's Ministry of National Defence, 'Millî Savunma Bakanı Hulusi Akar: "Personelimiz Azerbaycan'a Gitti, Orada Hazır Bekliyor"' ['Minister of National Defence Hulusi Akar: "Our personnel went to Azerbaijan, they are ready"'], 29 Dec. 2020.

[26] 'Turkey approves sending troops to joint Russian Monitoring center in Azerbaijan', Radio Free Europe/Radio Liberty, 17 Nov. 2020.

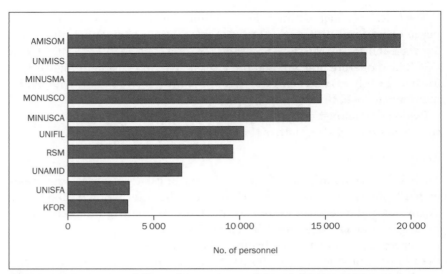

Figure 2.6. Largest multilateral peace operations as of 31 Dec. 2020

AMISOM = African Union (AU) Mission in Somalia; KFOR = Kosovo Force; MINUSCA = United Nations Multidimensional Integrated Stabilization Mission in the Central African Republic; MINUSMA = UN Multidimensional Integrated Stabilization Mission in Mali; MONUSCO = UN Organization Stabilization Mission in the Democratic Republic of the Congo; RSM = Resolute Support Mission; UNAMID = UN–AU Hybrid Operation in Darfur; UNIFIL = UN Interim Force in Lebanon; UNISFA = UN Interim Security Force for Abyei; UNMISS = UN Mission in South Sudan.

The largest multilateral peace operations

AMISOM has been the largest ongoing multilateral peace operation in the world since 2015 (see figure 2.6). The mission maintained this status throughout the year, by some margin even, despite the withdrawal of 1000 troops in February 2020. The reduction was authorized by the UN Security Council and followed similar reductions of AMISOM's military component in 2017 and 2019.[27] AMISOM comprised 19 384 personnel on 31 December 2020. This was the smallest the mission has been since Ethiopia joined it in January 2014.

Among the 10 largest multilateral peace operations in 2020 were 7 UN peacekeeping operations. Most of them decreased in size during the year, especially MONUSCO, which went from 16 179 personnel on 31 December 2019 to 14 754 personnel one year later. UNAMID, once the largest UN operation, was the eighth-largest multilateral peace operation on 31 December 2020, the day on which its mandate ended. The UN Mission in South Sudan (UNMISS) has been the largest UN peace operation since

---

[27] UN Security Council Resolution 2472, 31 May 2019. On the armed conflict in Somalia see chapter 7, section IV, in this volume.

December 2019. The UN Interim Force in Lebanon (UNIFIL) is the only remaining major UN operation outside sub-Saharan Africa. In August 2020 the UN Security Council lowered the maximum authorized strength of UNIFIL for the first time since the end of the 2006 Lebanon War, from 15 000 troops to 13 000 troops.[28] This was mainly a symbolic move, however, as the number of military personnel in UNIFIL has already been well below 13 000 for more than a decade.

The NATO-led KFOR and RSM continued to be among the 10 largest multilateral peace operations. The personnel strength of the RSM decreased from 16 705 personnel on 31 December 2019, when it was the third-largest multilateral peace operation, to 9592 on 31 December 2020. The number of NATO-commanded forces in Afghanistan fell below 10 000 for the first time since 2006.

The total number of personnel deployed in the 10 largest multilateral peace operations decreased by 8.1 per cent during 2020, from 124 274 personnel on 31 December 2019 to 114 182 on 31 December 2020. This equals 90 per cent of all personnel deployed in all multilateral peace operations globally.

The main troop- and police-contributing countries

The 10 main military personnel contributors accounted for 90 per cent of all military personnel deployed globally in multilateral peace operations in 2020. Ethiopia has been the main military personnel contributor to multilateral peace operations since December 2014 (see figure 2.7). Ethiopia maintained this position in 2020 although its contribution decreased for the third year in a row, from 10 727 on 31 December 2019 to 10 124 on 31 December 2020. As a regional power in the Horn of Africa, Ethiopia has been providing troop contingents to all major multilateral peace operations in the region—AMISOM, UNAMID, the UN Interim Security Force for Abyei and UNMISS.

Burundi, Kenya and Uganda were also among the 10 main contributors of military personnel in 2020, thanks to their participation in AMISOM. Their contributions also decreased somewhat during the year due to the withdrawal of 1000 troops from AMISOM, which was divided over the respective national contingents. Political tensions between Kenya and the Federal Government of Somalia escalated when the federal government cut diplomatic relations with Kenya in December 2020.[29] However, this did not immediately affect the participation of Kenya in AMISOM.

Bangladesh, India, Nepal, Pakistan and Rwanda continued to be among the states providing most military personnel thanks to their contributions to UN peace operations. Their contributions remained stable during the

---

[28] UN Security Council Resolution 2539, 28 Aug. 2020, para. 29.
[29] Dahir, A. L., 'Somalia severs diplomatic ties with Kenya', *New York Times*, 15 Dec. 2020.

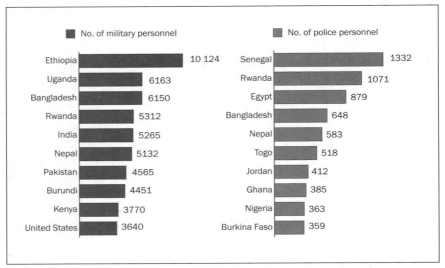

Figure 2.7. Main contributors of military and police personnel as of 31 Dec. 2020

year, although those of Pakistan and Rwanda each included around 1000 troops in UNAMID, which ended on 31 December 2020. Rwanda also dispatched 'several hundred' additional troops to CAR in December 2020, but these were not part of MINUSCA. The deployment was a reaction to a rebel offensive and fears of an attempted coup d'état in CAR ahead of the presidential elections that took place on 27 December 2020. According to the Rwandese Government, the extra troops were sent to protect civilians and Rwandese peacekeepers, and would remain outside MINUSCA so they would not be bound by the UN's rules of engagement.[30]

The US contribution to multilateral peace operations decreased by 60 per cent in 2020, from 9145 military personnel on 31 December 2019 to 3640 on 31 December 2020. This was entirely due to drawdown of US forces in Afghanistan to 2500 military personnel, the lowest level since the start of the US military intervention in 2001. According to NATO, the remaining 2500 US forces were all part of the RSM, although the US Department of Defense has indicated that the parallel US counterterrorism mission in Afghanistan will be its main focus.[31] The USA remained the main contributor of military personnel to the MFO, KFOR and RSM, in addition to remaining the main contributor to the civilian OSCE SMM in Ukraine.

[30] 'Rwanda bolsters force in CAR as rebels "held back"', BBC News, 21 Dec. 2020. On the armed conflict in CAR see chapter 7, section III, in this volume.

[31] US Central Command, 'General Kenneth F. McKenzie Jr. interview on the record media round table—Dec. 20th, 2020', 21 Dec. 2020.

The top 10 of the states providing the most police personnel to multilateral peace operations in 2020 was very similar to that in 2019. Senegal strengthened its position as the main police contributor by deploying an additional formed police unit to MONUSCO in December 2020. The total number of police it contributed increased from 1204 on 31 December 2019 to 1332 on 31 December 2020. Senegal has been the top police contributor to multilateral peace operations since 2016.

Fatalities in United Nations peace operations

Ninety-one international personnel and 32 local staff died while serving in UN peace operations in 2020 (see figure 2.8). This was more than in the previous two years although below the average over 2011–20. Of the 91 international personnel that died, 78 were military or police personnel and 13 were international civilian personnel. The fatality rate for uniformed personnel was 0.9 per 1000 in 2020, based on the average number of uniformed personnel deployed during the year (see figure 2.9).

Deaths of UN peacekeepers can have various causes. Malicious acts, or hostile deaths, tend to receive the most attention. However, UN peace operations suffered 13 hostile deaths in 2020 (less than 15 per cent of the total number of fatalities), which is fewer than in any other year in 2011–20 (see figure 2.8). Twelve of those that died this way were military personnel, while one was civilian. This corresponds to a fatality rate for hostile deaths of 0.15 per 1000 uniformed personnel, which was the lowest rate since 2011 (see figure 2.9). The UN Multidimensional Integrated Stabilization Mission in Mali (MINUSMA), which has been the deadliest UN peace operation since it started in 2013, suffered six hostile deaths during 2020. By comparison, MINUSMA suffered 22 hostile deaths in 2019 alone and 125 in total between 2013 and 2019. The lower number and rate of hostile deaths among UN peacekeepers may be attributed to the Covid-19 pandemic. Measures to prevent infections and the spread of the virus imposed restrictions on the movement of UN peace operations personnel and led to a reduction of patrols and other types of exposure to risks of attacks.

In 2020 there were 54 registered deaths due to illness among international personnel in UN peace operations, twice as many as in 2019. The number of deaths caused by illness among local staff was also much higher in 2020 than in 2019. This increase is explained to a large extent by the Covid-19 pandemic. According to official figures, until 24 January 2021 across all UN field missions, 2486 members of personnel and dependents tested positive for Covid-19, and 24 died as a result of it.[32]

---

[32] United Nations, Security Council, 'Risk of instability, tension growing, amid glaring inequalities in Global Covid-19 recovery, top United Nations officials warn Security Council', SC/14422, 25 Jan. 2021.

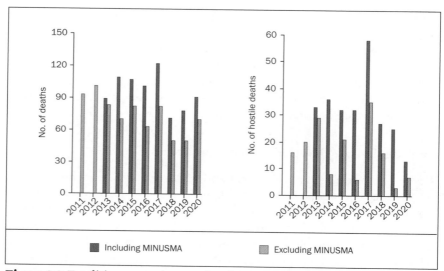

Figure 2.8. Fatalities among international personnel in United Nations peace operations, 2011–20

MINUSMA = UN Multidimensional Integrated Stabilization Mission in Mali.

Other multilateral operations

The trend of increasing multilateral operations activity in the grey areas outside the scope of the SIPRI definition of a multilateral peace operation also continued in 2020. The 10 000-strong Multinational Joint Task Force (MNJTF) in the Lake Chad Basin region and the 5000-strong Joint Force of the Group of Five for the Sahel (G5 Sahel) are two other such multilateral operations.[33] The EU has also been conducting military naval operations in the context of the CSDP, in the Gulf of Aden off the coast of Somalia and in the Mediterranean Sea. There are, however, four noteworthy new initiatives.

First, in the Russian-brokered ceasefire agreement that was reached on 9 November 2020 and entered into force the next day, Armenia and Azerbaijan agreed on the deployment of a Russian 'peacekeeping contingent' of 1960 military personnel along the line of contact inside Nagorno-Karabakh and along the so-called Lachin corridor, which connects the disputed territory with Armenia.[34] The deployment of the Russian peacekeepers commenced immediately. The agreement stipulates that the duration of the deployment will be five years with the possibility of an extension for another five years. The Russian 'peacekeeping contingent' is neither conducted under

---

[33] On the MNJTF and G5 Sahel see chapter 7, section II, in this volume.

[34] President of Russia, 'Statement by the president of the Republic of Azerbaijan, prime minister of the Republic of Armenia and president of the Russian Federation', 10 Nov. 2020. Also see chapter 5, section II, in this volume.

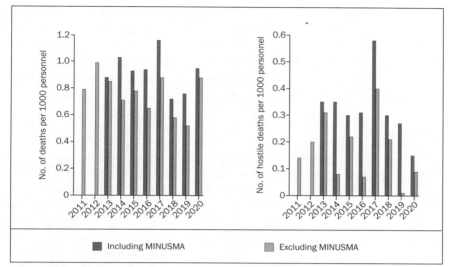

Figure 2.9. Fatality rates for uniformed personnel in United Nations peace operations, 2011–20

MINUSMA = UN Multidimensional Integrated Stabilization Mission in Mali.

the auspices or on behalf of the UN or a regional organization or alliance, nor does it report to a multinational body such as the JCC in Trans-Dniester or the JCC in South Ossetia, which was active from 1992 to 2008. It is therefore not considered to be a multilateral peace operation.

The next two have their origins in Europe. First, is the new EU Naval Force Mediterranean Operation Irini that EU member states established in February 2020 following the January 2020 Berlin Conference on Libya and launched on 31 March 2020. The main task of Operation Irini is to implement the UN arms embargo on Libya.[35] Second, is creation of the European multinational Special Operations Forces Task Force Takuba under the command of the French-led counterterrorism Operation Barkhane in the Sahel. The aim of this force is counterterrorism operations in the Liptako region, at the Burkina Faso–Mali–Niger border.[36]

Lastly, the AU considered increasing its counterterrorism activities in the Sahel. The AU Assembly of Heads of State and Government requested the AU Commission in February 2020 to start planning for a possible deployment of an AU force of 3000 troops to support the Joint Force of the G5 Sahel in order to 'further degrade terrorist groups'.[37] The AU Peace and Security

---

[35] Council Decision (CFSP) 2020/472 of 31 Mar. 2020 on a European Union military operation in the Mediterranean (EUNAVFOR MED IRINI), *Official Journal of the European Union*, L101, 1 Apr. 2020.

[36] On Task Force Takuba see also chapter 7, section II, in this volume.

[37] AU Assembly of Heads of State and Government (note 5), para. 4.

Council endorsed a strategic concept for the force on 30 September 2020 and requested the AU Commission to proceed with the development of a concept of operations, together with ECOWAS and the G5 Sahel.[38] The deployment of the force had not yet been authorized by the end of 2020, and details remained scarce about its mandate, composition, financing and relation to the other military operations in the region.

Conclusions

The continuing competition and disagreement among the permanent members of the UN Security Council and the push of particularly the Trump administration to reduce the UN peacekeeping budget has in recent years resulted in the accelerated drawdown and closure of some of the larger UN peace operations. This trend coincides with the interests of a number of host-country governments and questions raised by some analysts on the effectiveness of large-scale stabilization operations. In 2020 UNAMID was the latest such large UN peacekeeping operation to close. However, the demand for conflict management efforts has continued. The Security Council has only been able to agree on the establishment of smaller specialized political missions, with UNITAMS being the latest addition effectuated at the start of 2021.

Regional organizations and alliances fill this gap to some extent, but often do so in a fragmented manner, resulting in complex constellations of peace operations, such as in Mali, Somalia and particularly CAR—with EUAM RCA and MOUACA as the latest additions in 2020. Also, the establishment of the AU Mission in Libya to increase the AU presence in that country is a case in point. While the number of multilateral peace operations deployed by regional organizations and alliances is increasing, these regional operations are generally smaller in size. As a consequence, the total number of personnel deployed in multilateral peace operations continues to decrease, as the numbers of personnel in newly established operations led by regional organizations do not replace the numbers of personnel reductions in UN peace operations. This is in part because some organizations do not have the capabilities and resources to deploy much more personnel (e.g. the AU), and others have specialized in niche efforts requiring less personnel (e.g. the EU). In fact, the number of personnel in operations deployed by regional organizations and alliances decreased significantly in 2020, as the Trump administration reduced the number of US forces in Afghanistan, and the NATO-led RSM.

---

[38] AU, Communiqué of the 950th meeting of the Peace and Security Council of the African Union on the consideration of the revised draft strategic concept note on planning guidance for the deployment of 3000 troops, 30 Sep. 2020.

Another development in recent years that continued in 2020 is the increasing conflict management activity in the grey areas outside the scope of SIPRI's definition of a multilateral peace operation. On top of ongoing counterterrorism operations, such as the Joint Force of the G5 Sahel and the MNJTF, the European multinational Special Operations Forces Task Force Takuba was set up and the AU was discussing its own force to support the Joint Force. At the same time, the new Russian 'peacekeeping contingent' in the Nagorno-Karabakh conflict cannot be considered multilateral. These operations may be an indication of how peace operations in a more multipolar world may look like: potentially more fragmented, at times unilateral, and sometimes with competing efforts, that are frequently more securitized, and often have the interests of the intervenors higher on the agenda than 'traditional' multilateral peace operations.

The Covid-19 pandemic affected all these efforts in a variety of ways, not least by significantly increasing the number of fatalities due to illness, for example, in UN peace operations. Measures to prevent the further spreading of Covid-19 has meant operations have had to adjust their activities, for example by reducing patrols and ways of working, and troop rotations and the establishment of missions have been delayed. Only some training missions paused their operations for a short period. However, on top of existing challenges many operations faced an additional struggle to sustain their activities due to Covid-19.

III. Table of multilateral peace operations, 2020

TIMO SMIT

Table 2.5 provides data on the 62 multilateral peace operations conducted in 2020, including operations that were either launched or terminated during the year.

The table lists operations conducted under the authority of the United Nations, operations conducted by regional organizations and alliances, and operations conducted by ad hoc coalitions of states. UN operations are divided into three subgroups: (*a*) observer and multidimensional peace-keeping operations run by the Department of Peace Operations, (*b*) special political and peacebuilding missions and (*c*) the joint UN–African Union Hybrid Operation in Darfur.

The table draws on the SIPRI Multilateral Peace Operations Database, <http://www.sipri.org/databases/pko>, which provides information on all UN and non-UN peace operations conducted since 2000, such as location, dates of deployment and operation, mandate, participating countries, number of personnel, budget and fatalities.

Table 2.5. Multilateral peace operations, 2020

Unless otherwise stated, all figures are as of 31 Dec. 2020. Operations that closed in 2020 are shown in italic type and are not included in the aggregate figures.

Operation	Start	Location	Mil.	Pol.	Civ.
UN peacekeeping operations			**67 433**	**6 915**	**3 484**
UNTSO	1948	Middle East	143	–	70
UNMOGIP	1951	India/Pakistan	45	–	21
UNFICYP	1964	Cyprus	809	67	40
UNDOF	1974	Syria (Golan)	1 099	–	43
UNIFIL	1978	Lebanon	10 000	–	239
MINURSO	1991	Western Sahara	218	1	71
MONUSCO	1999	DRC	12 758	1 403	593
UNMIK	1999	Kosovo	8	10	86
UNISFA	2011	Abyei	3 404	24	148
UNMISS	2011	South Sudan	14 869	1 653	852
MINUSMA	2013	Mali	12 623	1 692	735
MINUSCA	2014	CAR	11 457	2 065	586
UN special political missions			**1 170**	**72**	**1 015**
UNAMA	2002	Afghanistan	1	–	246
UNAMI	2003	Iraq	244	–	259
UNIOGBIS	*2010*	*Guinea-Bissau*	–	–	*30*
UNSMIL	2011	Libya	233	–	143
UNSOM	2013	Somalia	630	11	145
UNVMC	2017	Colombia	57	47	112
UNMHA	2019	Yemen	5	1	35
BINUH	2019	Haiti	–	13	45
UN–AU			*3 990*	*2 236*	*397*
UNAMID	*2007*	*Sudan (Darfur)*	*3 990*	*2 236*	*397*
AU			**18 602**	**732**	**75**
AMISOM	2007	Somalia	18 586	732	66
MISAHEL	2013	Mali	–	–	..
MISAC	2014	CAR	–	–	..
AU Observer Mission in Burundi	2015	Burundi	2	–	9
AU Mission in Libya	2020	Libya	..	..	..
MOUACA	2020	CAR	14	–	–
ECOWAS			**875**	**125**	**1**
ECOMIB	*2012*	*Guinea-Bissau*	–	–	–
ECOMIG	2017	Gambia	875	125	1
EU[a]			**1 868**	**–**	**1 124**
EUFOR ALTHEA	2004	Bosnia and Herzegovina	807	–	–
EUBAM Rafah	2005	Palestinian territories	–	–	6
EUPOL COPPS	2005	Palestinian territories	–	–	54
EULEX Kosovo	2008	Kosovo	–	–	273
EUMM Georgia	2008	Georgia	–	–	219
EUTM Somalia	2010	Somalia	130	–	13
EUCAP Sahel Niger	2012	Niger	–	–	118
EUTM Mali	2013	Mali	721	–	5
EUBAM Libya	2013[b]	Libya	–	–	37
EUAM Ukraine	2014	Ukraine	–	–	165
EUCAP Sahel Mali	2015	Mali	–	–	134

Operation	Start	Location	Mil.	Pol.	Civ.
EUTM RCA	2016	CAR	210	–	–
EUAM Iraq	2017	Iraq	–	–	57
EUAM RCA	2020	CAR	–	–	36
NATO			**13 574**	–	–
KFOR	1999	Kosovo	3 482	–	–
RSM	2015	Afghanistan	9 592	–	–
NMI	2018	Iraq	500	–	–
IGAD			–	–	**86**
CTSAMVM	2015	South Sudan	–	–	86
OAS			–	–	**30**
MAPP/OEA	2004	Colombia	–	–	30
OSCE			–	–	**1 062**
OSCE Mission to Skopje	1992	North Macedonia	–	–	37
OSCE Mission to Moldova	1993	Moldova	–	–	12
OSCE PRCIO	1995	Azerbaijan (Nagorno-Karabakh)	–	–	5
OSCE Mission to Bosnia and Herzegovina	1995	Bosnia and Herzegovina	–	–	26
OSCE Presence in Albania	1997	Albania	–	–	20
OMIK	1999	Kosovo	–	–	81
OSCE Mission to Serbia	2001	Serbia	–	–	20
OSCE SMM	2014	Ukraine	–	–	842
OSCE Observer Mission at the Russian checkpoints Gukovo and Donetsk	2014	Russia (Gukovo and Donetsk checkpoints)	–	–	19
Ad hoc coalition of states			**2 254**	**3**	**15**
NNSC	1953	South Korea	10	–	–
MFO	1982	Egypt (Sinai)	1 154	–	..
JCC	1992	Moldova (Trans-Dniester)	1 071	–	–
OHR	1995	Bosnia and Herzegovina	–	–	11
IMT	2004	Philippines (Mindanao)	19	3	4

– = not applicable; . . = information not available; AMISOM = African Union Mission in Somalia; AU = African Union; BINUH = United Nations Integrated Office in Haiti; CAR = Central African Republic; Civ.= international civilian personnel; CTSAMVM = Ceasefire and Transitional Security Arrangements Monitoring and Verification Mechanism; DRC = Democratic Republic of the Congo; ECOMIB = ECOWAS Mission in Guinea-Bissau; ECOMIG = ECOWAS Mission in the Gambia; ECOWAS = Economic Community of West African States; EU = European Union; EUAM Iraq = EU Advisory Mission in Support of Security Sector Reform in Iraq; EUAM RCA = EU Advisory Mission in the CAR; EUAM Ukraine = EU Advisory Mission for Civilian Security Sector Reform Ukraine; EUBAM Libya = EU Integrated Border Management Assistance Mission in Libya; EUBAM Rafah = EU Border Assistance Mission for the Rafah Crossing Point; EUCAP Sahel Mali = EU Common Security and Defence Policy (CSDP) Mission in Mali; EUCAP Sahel Niger = EU CSDP Mission in Niger; EUFOR ALTHEA = EU Military Operation in Bosnia and Herzegovina; EULEX Kosovo = EU Rule of Law Mission in Kosovo; EUMM Georgia = EU Monitoring Mission in Georgia; EUPOL COPPS = EU Police Mission for the Palestinian Territories; EUTM Mali = EU Training Mission Mali; EUTM RCA = EU Training Mission in the CAR; EUTM Somalia = EU Training Mission Somalia; IGAD = Intergovernmental Authority on Development; IMT = International Monitoring Team; JCC = Joint Control Commission Peacekeeping Force; KFOR = Kosovo Force; MAPP/OEA = Organization of American States Mission to Support the Peace Process in Colombia; MFO = Multinational Force and Observers; Mil. = military personnel (troops and military observers); MINURSO = UN Mission for the Referendum in Western Sahara;

MINUSCA = UN Multidimensional Integrated Stabilization Mission in the CAR; MINUSMA = UN Multidimensional Integrated Stabilization Mission in Mali; MISAC = AU Mission for the CAR and Central Africa; MISAHEL = AU Mission for Mali and the Sahel; MONUSCO = UN Organization Stabilization Mission in the DRC; MOUACA = AU Military Observers Mission in the CAR; NATO = North Atlantic Treaty Organization; NMI = NATO Mission Iraq; NNSC = Neutral Nations Supervisory Commission; OAS = Organization of American States; OHR = Office of the High Representative; OMIK = OSCE Mission in Kosovo; OSCE = Organization for Security and Co-operation in Europe; OSCE SMM = OSCE Special Monitoring Mission in Ukraine; Pol. = police; PRCIO = Personal Representative of the Chairman-in-Office on the Conflict Dealt with by the OSCE Minsk Conference; RSM = Resolute Support Mission; UN = United Nations; UNAMA = UN Assistance Mission in Afghanistan; UNAMI = UN Assistance Mission in Iraq; UNAMID = UN–AU Hybrid Operation in Darfur; UNDOF = UN Disengagement Observer Force; UNFICYP = UN Peacekeeping Force in Cyprus; UNIFIL = UN Interim Force in Lebanon; UNIOGBIS = UN Integrated Peacebuilding Office in Guinea-Bissau; UNISFA = UN Interim Security Force for Abyei; UNMHA = UN Mission to Support the Hodeidah Agreement; UNMIK = UN Interim Administration Mission in Kosovo; UNMISS = UN Mission in South Sudan; UNMOGIP = UN Military Observer Group in India and Pakistan; UNSMIL = UN Support Mission in Libya; UNSOM = UN Assistance Mission in Somalia; UNTSO = UN Truce Supervision Organization; UNVMC = UN Verification Mission in Colombia.

[a] Figures on international civilian staff may include uniformed police.

[b] EUBAM Libya was established in 2013 but did not qualify as a multilateral peace operation prior to 1 Jan. 2019.

Source: SIPRI Multilateral Peace Operations Database, accessed 1 Apr. 2021, <http://www.sipri.org/databases/pko/>. Data on multilateral peace operations is obtained from the following categories of open source: (*a*) official information provided by the secretariat of the organization concerned; (*b*) information provided by the operations themselves, either in official publications or in written responses to annual SIPRI questionnaires; and (*c*) information from national governments contributing to the operation under consideration. In some instances, SIPRI researchers may gather additional information on an operation from the conducting organizations or governments of participating states by means of telephone interviews and email correspondence. These primary sources are supplemented by a wide selection of publicly available secondary sources consisting of specialist journals, research reports, news agencies, and international, regional and local newspapers.

3. Armed conflict and peace processes in the Americas

Overview

The Americas presented a complex and mixed picture for peace during 2020, with worsening conflict in certain countries, but less violence in some, partly as a result of Covid-19 pandemic lockdowns. In others armed violence continued at a similar level to that in 2019. Two countries—Colombia and Mexico—had several parallel non-international armed conflicts on their territories.

Implementation of the 2016 peace accord between the Government of Colombia and the Revolutionary Armed Forces of Colombia–People's Army (Fuerzas Armadas Revolucionarias de Colombia–Ejército del Pueblo, FARC–EP) continued to encounter problems. Non-international armed conflicts with other armed non-state groups and paramilitary organizations continued. More FARC–EP dissidents joined armed groups, and violence against civil society actors increased.

In Mexico there were three non-international armed conflicts: between the Government of Mexico and the Jalisco New Generation Cartel (Cártel Jalisco Nueva Generación) and the Sinaloa Cartel, and between those two cartels. Homicides declined slightly in 2020 but remained at a very high level, while government efforts to counter the cartels became increasingly militarized.

The region hosted three multilateral peace operations: the United Nations Verification Mission in Colombia, the Organization of American States Mission to Support the Peace Process in Colombia and the UN Integrated Office in Haiti.

Homicide rates across the region varied significantly. Several countries had some of the highest homicide rates in the world, such as Jamaica, while other countries had significant reductions, including El Salvador, Guatemala, Honduras and Venezuela. Several countries, including Brazil, Colombia, Honduras and Mexico, experienced targeted political violence towards human rights activists and social movement representatives. As a result of Covid-19 lockdowns, 2020 did not bring a repeat of the often-violent mass demonstrations and riots that occurred throughout 2019 in Bolivia, Chile, Colombia and Ecuador, which had been driven by public frustrations with poor economic conditions, growing inequalities and political corruption. Nevertheless, popular protests broke out sporadically in response to political crises in Bolivia, Chile, Colombia, Guatemala, Nicaragua and Peru, and several allegations of harsh public-order policing responses.

MARINA CAPARINI

SIPRI Yearbook 2021: Armaments, Disarmament and International Security
www.sipriyearbook.org

I. Key general developments in the region

MARINA CAPARINI

In 2020 the Americas region experienced varying levels of peace and conflict. According to the global peace index, in 2019 South America experienced the largest decline in peacefulness due to militarization and deterioration of safety and security, while Central America and the Caribbean recorded the second-largest deterioration in peacefulness based on ongoing conflict.[1] In contrast, the trend in violence in 2020 was not as clear—a likely result of the disruptive effects of the Covid-19 pandemic. Non-international armed conflicts continued in two states in the Americas, worsening in Colombia and Mexico. The 2016 peace accord between the Government of Colombia and the Revolutionary Armed Forces of Colombia–People's Army (Fuerzas Armadas Revolucionarias de Colombia–Ejército del Pueblo, FARC–EP), which had brought an end to over 50 years of conflict, experienced continuing implementation problems and delays, while killings of former combatants, activists and community and indigenous leaders persisted (see section II). Criminal gang violence intensified in Mexico, leading international humanitarian law experts to identify a third non-international armed conflict to add to the two already existing (see section III).

The region was host to three multilateral peace operations in 2020, one fewer than in 2019. The United Nations Verification Mission in Colombia verifies the reintegration of former FARC–EP members into political, economic and social life and the security guarantees for former FARC–EP members, their families and communities, and comprehensive security and protection programmes for communities in the territories.[2] The Mission to Support the Peace Process in Colombia (Misión de Apoyo al Proceso de Paz en Colombia) of the Organization of American States is a political and technical mission that assists peace efforts in the areas most affected by internal armed conflict, crime and inequality.[3] In Haiti the UN Integrated Office in Haiti (Bureau Intégré des Nations Unies en Haïti) advises the Government of Haiti on promoting political stability and good governance, preserving and advancing a peaceful and stable environment, and protecting and promoting

---

[1] Institute for Economics & Peace (IEP), *Global Peace Index 2020* (IEP: Sydney, 2020), p. 2. Note most indicators in the global peace index use the measurement period from 16 Mar. 2019 until 15 Mar. 2020; see Appendix B.

[2] UN Security Council Resolution 2366, 10 July 2017; and UN Security Council Resolution 2377, 14 Sep. 2017.

[3] 'Convenio entre el Gobierno de la Republica de Colombia y la Secretaria General de la Organización de los Estados Americanos para el Acompañamiento al proceso de proceso de paz en Colombia' [Agreement between the Government of the Republic of Colombia and the Secretary General of the Organization of American States for accompaniment to the peace process in Colombia], 4 Feb. 2004.

human rights. It is also mandated to advise the Government of Haiti on dialogue and reforms, elections, police professionalism, community violence reduction and gang violence, justice reform, and human rights protection and accountability.[4] The number of personnel in multilateral peace operations in the Americas remained very low compared to the numbers of personnel deployed in other regions. It increased from 275 on 31 December 2019 to 304 on 31 December 2020.

Over the past three decades homicide rates in the Americas have consistently exceeded those in other regions of the world.[5] However, homicide rates across the region have also varied significantly. In 2020 these variations reflected different levels of restrictive measures imposed by governments due to the Covid-19 pandemic, socio-economic conditions, and the varying presence of organized crime, gang violence and illegal armed groups. In contrast, homicides in other global regions were more linked to interpersonal violence.[6] With the highest level of homicides in the region, Jamaica recorded 1301 killings, or a rate of 46.5 per 100 000, a slight decline from the 2019 toll of 1339 killings.[7] High levels of homicides were also seen in Venezuela (45.6), Honduras (37.6), Trinidad and Tobago (28.2), Mexico (27.0), Belize (24.3) and Colombia (24.3) per 100 000.[8] In Colombia and Guatemala homicides dropped significantly by 32 per cent and 26 per cent, respectively, due to the Covid-19 lockdown between March and June, but rebounded afterwards.[9]

Several countries in the Americas experienced targeted political violence towards human rights activists and social movement representatives, including assassinations of indigenous leaders and activists. In Colombia 177 human rights defenders were killed in 2020, far outstripping all other countries globally. Also ranked in the top tier of countries where human rights defenders were killed were Honduras with 20 killed, Mexico with 19, Brazil with 16 and Guatemala with 15.[10]

By early June 2020 the region was heavily affected by the Covid-19 pandemic. Although Argentina and Peru moved quickly to close borders and impose lockdowns, the governments of Brazil and Mexico—the two largest countries in the region—initially downplayed concerns and did not act quickly or effectively to attempt to suppress the rate of contagion. By the

---

[4] UN Security Council Resolution 2476, 25 June 2019.

[5] UN Office on Drugs and Crime (UNODC), *Global Study on Homicide: Homicide Trends, Patterns and Criminal Justice Response* (UN: Vienna, 2019), p. 16.

[6] UNODC, 'Effect of the Covid-19 pandemic and related restrictions on homicide and property crime', Research Brief, 2020, p. 3.

[7] Asmann, P. and Jones, K., 'InSight Crime's 2020 Homicide Round-Up', InSight Crime, 29 Jan. 2021.

[8] Asmann and Jones (note 7).

[9] UNODC (note 6), p. 5.

[10] Front Line Defenders, *Front Line Defenders: Global Analysis 2020* (Front Line Defenders: 2020).

end of 2020 the Latin American countries of the region, accounting for only 8 per cent of the global population, had recorded nearly 20 per cent of global cases and almost 30 per cent of global deaths from Covid-19.[11] Similarly, the region suffered the greatest economic impact of the Covid-19 pandemic globally, resulting in an 8.2 per cent contraction in gross domestic product in 2020. The UN predicted more than 15 million more people would fall into extreme poverty in 2020, bringing the total to over 82 million.[12]

Developments in specific countries

Bolivia

After 14 years as president of Bolivia, Evo Morales resigned and fled the country in November 2019. Mass protests had erupted over allegations of a fraudulent presidential election on 20 October that year in his bid for an unprecedented and unconstitutional fourth term. Police refused to suppress the post-electoral violence in which at least 30 people were killed and over 800 injured.[13] The armed forces withdrew their support and suggested he resign, resulting in Morales' allegations that he was being ousted by a military coup.[14] Bolivia experienced 11 turbulent months under a caretaker government led by Conservative senator and interim president Jeanine Áñez. After the 2019 election was nullified, the planned rerun of the presidential and congressional elections was rescheduled three times due to the Covid-19 pandemic, resulting in nationwide demonstrations, roadblocks and marches by the main workers' union and indigenous and *campesinos* (farmers and farm workers) movements allied to the Movement Toward Socialism.[15] Former members of the Morales administration became the focus of criminal investigations, and Morales was charged with terrorism and terrorist financing by Bolivian prosecutors. This led international human rights groups to allege political interference in judicial investigations and exertion of pressure on judges for political ends.[16] On 18 October 2020 with an 87 per cent electoral turnout, Luis Arce—former finance minister under Morales and his chosen successor in the Movement

---

[11] 'Where the pandemic clobbered economies hardest', *The Economist*, 1 Jan. 2021.

[12] Economic Commission for Latin America and the Caribbean, 'Latin America and the Caribbean and the Covid-19 pandemic: Economic and social effects', Special Report Covid-19 no. 1, Santiago, 3 Apr. 2020, p. 11.

[13] Office of the UN High Commissioner for Human Rights (OHCHR), 'The human rights situation in the aftermath of the 20 October 2019 general elections in Bolivia', [n.d.], p. 5.

[14] 'Was there a coup in Bolivia?', *The Economist*, 14 Nov. 2019.

[15] 'Bolivia delays presidential election due to pandemic', AP News, 23 July 2020; and Blair, L. and Jiménez Bercerra, C., 'Bolivia protesters bring country to standstill over election delays', *The Guardian*, 9 Aug. 2020.

[16] Stott, M., 'Bolivian government accused of hounding ex-president Evo Morales', *Financial Times*, 11 Sep. 2020; and Human Rights Watch, 'Justice as a weapon: Political persecution in Bolivia', 11 Sep. 2020.

Toward Socialism party—won in a landslide victory with 54 per cent of the vote, and the socialists secured a clear mandate with a majority in the senate and congress.[17] One day after Arce was sworn in as president on 10 November Morales ended his exile and returned to Bolivia, although Arce stated Morales would have no role in the new government.[18]

El Salvador

In his first year in office President Nayib Bukele oversaw a dramatic drop in killings in what has been one of the world's most violent countries. He also adopted a confrontational stance to state institutions and political opponents. In February Bukele brought armed police and soldiers into the opposition-controlled Legislative Assembly to pressure it to vote in support of a loan of $109 million to finance his security plan of equipping police and soldiers to combat crime in the country ridden by gang violence.[19] A precipitous decline in homicide rates was seen in El Salvador, with 1332 killings in 2020, a 45 per cent reduction from 2019, constituting a homicide rate of 19.7 per 100 000.[20] The reduction was attributed by the Bukele administration to its new security strategy pairing *mano dura* ('iron fist') law enforcement with violence prevention in low-income communities.[21] However, it appears more likely due to the decision of gangs not to battle with soldiers or among themselves, and to an informal understanding between Bukele and leaders of the Mara Salvatrucha (commonly known as MS-13) gang to reduce violence and gain political support for Bukele's party.[22]

Honduras

Honduras continued to stand out as one of the most violent, corrupt and poverty-afflicted countries of the Americas. It had the highest homicide rate in the subregion of Central America, with 3496 killings for a 2020 homicide rate of 37.6 per 100 000, representing a slight decline compared to 2019.[23] According to the Armed Conflict Location & Event Data Project (ACLED), Honduras experienced 655 fatalities linked to political violence in 2020, a decline from 925 fatalities in 2019.[24] President Juan Orlando Hernández, a key United States ally in the region, was alleged by US federal

---

[17] Segura, R., 'Bolivia's landslide lays to rest the fears of fraud', International Crisis Group, Commentary, 21 Oct. 2020.

[18] Abdalla, J., 'Evo Morales completes triumphant Bolivia return. Now what?', Al Jazeera, 11 Nov. 2020.

[19] 'El Salvador parliament denounces president's "attempted coup"', BBC News, 11 Feb. 2020.

[20] Asmann and Jones (note 7).

[21] Briscoe, I. and Breda, T., 'A bargain worth making? Bukele and the gangs of El Salvador', War on the Rocks, 16 Dec. 2020.

[22] International Crisis Group, 'Miracle or mirage? Gangs and plunging violence in El Salvador', Report no. 81, 8 July 2020.

[23] Asmann and Jones (note 7).

[24] ACLED, Dashboard, accessed 1 Mar. 2021.

prosecutors to have taken bribes from drug traffickers to protect them from law enforcement, and tasked the armed forces with protecting illicit drug production and shipments to the USA.[25] In November two category 4 hurricanes killed at least 94 and displaced hundreds of thousands of people.[26] These disasters exacerbated a longer-running food insecurity crisis driven by droughts induced by climate change and poor environmental practices, setting off new waves of US-bound migrant caravans.[27]

Nicaragua

Nicaragua has been subject to increasingly authoritarian rule since the onset of a political and social crisis that began in March 2018 with mass anti-government uprisings spurred by President Daniel Ortega's social security reforms, and which were suppressed by police and pro-government groups, resulting in over 300 dead. Suppression of dissent continued through 2020, with police abuses against demonstrators and critics of the regime.[28] Persons perceived as opponents of the regime were detained, usually on charges of common crimes.[29] In a move seen as aimed at hindering political opposition in the run-up to the elections in November 2021, legislation was passed in October 2020 banning foreign financing for political purposes, and identifying anyone who receives funding from abroad as a 'foreign agent'.[30] A subsequent cybercrime bill suppressed dissent by regulating what could be published by news outlets and social media, with potential prison sentences for anyone found guilty of publishing information not authorized by the government.[31] The continuing political and social crisis has driven forced displacement. Since the beginning of the crisis in 2018 over 100 000 Nicaraguans have fled the country due to political persecution or human rights abuses, with two thirds seeking asylum in Costa Rica.[32] However, as a result of the Covid-19 pandemic, many of those who had earlier sought refuge in

[25] Torrens, C., 'US motions expand drug claims against Honduras president', AP News, 10 Jan. 2021; and AP News, 'US prosecutors accuse Honduran president of taking drug money', *The Guardian*, 3 Mar. 2020.

[26] 'Hondureños en EEUU envían ayuda humanitaria para damnificados por huracanes' [Hondurans in the US send humanitarian aid for hurricane victims], El Heraldo, 29 Nov. 2020; and Kitroeff, N., '2 hurricanes devastated Central America. Will the ruin spur a migration wave?', *New York Times*, 4 Dec. 2020.

[27] Olson, J., 'Honduran storm survivors form US-bound migrant caravan', New Humanitarian, 11 Dec. 2020.

[28] Human Rights Watch, 'Nicaragua: Events of 2020', World Report 2021.

[29] Bachelet, M., UN High Commissioner for Human Rights, OHCHR, 'Update on the human rights situation in Nicaragua, pursuant to resolution 43/2', 45th session of the Human Rights Council, 14 Sep. 2020.

[30] 'Nicaragua passes controversial "foreign agent" law', Deutsche Welle, 16 Oct. 2020.

[31] Lopez, I., 'Nicaragua passes bill criminalizing what government considers fake news', Reuters, 27 Oct. 2020.

[32] UN High Commissioner for Refugees (UNHCR), 'Two years of political and social crisis in Nicaragua force more than 100,000 to flee', 10 Mar. 2020.

Costa Rica attempted to return to Nicaragua due to lack of employment opportunities in Costa Rica, poverty and increased xenophobia.[33]

Venezuela

Nicolás Maduro's regime in Venezuela withstood a challenge by Juan Guaidó. In 2019 Guaidó was recognized by numerous states including the European Union (EU) and USA as Venezuela's rightful and interim president on account of his role as head of parliament and the allegedly fraudulent election of Maduro in 2018.[34] However Maduro consolidated power in the December 2020 legislative election, when his party won over two thirds of the vote. The election was boycotted by most of the opposition and had a turnout of only 31 per cent. The EU, the USA and over 12 Latin American countries said they would not recognize its results.[35] Maduro entered 2021 with full control of all branches of government. After losing his seat and position as head of the National Assembly, the EU withdrew its support for Guaidó as interim president, although the United Kingdom and the USA continued to declare him the real leader of Venezuela.[36] The humanitarian crisis continued, with over 5.4 million refugees and migrants of an estimated population of around 30 million having left the country between 2014 and the end of 2020 due to violence, political and economic crises, and lack of food and medicine.[37] Due to Covid-19-related lockdowns in neighbouring countries and severe hardship, some 130 000 migrants returned to Venezuela.[38] Ranked the world's second-least peaceful country in 2019 in terms of safety and security, in 2020 there were improvements in some areas and deterioration in others.[39] Homicides dropped by 30 per cent from the extremely high rate in 2019 to 11 891 in 2020, constituting a homicide rate of 45.6 per 100 000.[40] However, there were more than 2000 young people killed between January and August of 2020 in disadvantaged neighbourhoods as a result of state security operations.[41] Furthermore, a fact-finding mission of the UN Human Rights Council in September found state authorities were responsible for atrocities constituting crimes against

---

[33] Dupraz-Dobias, P., 'Nicaraguan asylum seekers face hunger in Costa Rica or dangerous returns', New Humanitarian, 28 Sep. 2020.

[34] 'Venezuela crisis: European states recognise Guaidó as president', BBC News, 4 Feb. 2019.

[35] Sequera, V. and Buitrago, D., 'US, EU say they do not recognize Venezuela parliamentary vote', Reuters, 7 Dec. 2020.

[36] Emmott, R., 'EU states no longer recognise Guaido as Venezuela's interim president', Reuters, 25 Jan. 2021.

[37] UNHCR, 'Venezuela situation', [n.d.].

[38] Human Rights Watch, 'Venezuela', *World Report 2021* (Human Rights Watch: 2021).

[39] IEP (note 1), p. 12.

[40] Asmann and Jones (note 7).

[41] Bachelet, M., UN High Commissioner for Human Rights, OHCHR, 'Oral update on the situation of human rights in the Bolivarian Republic of Venezuela', 45th session of the Human Rights Council, 25 Sep. 2020.

humanity.[42] The desperate humanitarian situation in Venezuela exacerbated by the Covid-19 pandemic resulted in calls for the USA to lift economic and financial sanctions, which went unheeded and also spurred further measures by the Trump administration against individuals, companies and shipping companies transporting Venezuelan oil in violation of sanctions.[43] Sanctions imposed on Venezuela have also contributed to strengthening criminal groups and the informal economy, thus undermining economic recovery and democracy.[44] There was also a continuation of border tensions between Colombia and Venezuela, as well as the low-intensity conflict along the Colombia–Venezuela border (see section II).

[42] Human Rights Council, 'Detailed findings of the independent international fact-finding mission on the Bolivarian Republic of Venezuela', A/HRC/45/CRP.11, 15 Sep. 2020.

[43] Morello, C., 'Pandemic fuels call to lift sanctions as Trump administration imposes more', *Washington Post*, 27 Mar. 2020; and Congressional Research Service, 'Venezuela: Overview of US sanctions', updated 22 Jan. 2021.

[44] Bull, B. and Rosales, A., 'Into the shadows: sanctions, rentierism, and economic informalization in Venezuela', *European Review of Latin America and Caribbean Studies*, no. 109 (2020), pp. 107–33.

II. Armed conflict and the peace process in Colombia

MARINA CAPARINI

The 2016 peace agreement between the Government of Colombia and Colombia's largest guerrilla group—the Revolutionary Armed Forces of Colombia–People's Army (Fuerzas Armadas Revolucionarias de Colombia– Ejército del Pueblo, FARC–EP)—brought an end to a long-running armed conflict. Nevertheless, Colombia continues to experience conflict. Violence by other non-state armed groups and targeted killings of social activists and community leaders, especially in rural areas, persists. Criminal violence has also continued and even increased in some areas as armed and criminal groups have sought to fill the power vacuum in the countryside areas formerly under FARC–EP control and fight to control the drug-trafficking corridors. Colombia experienced 819 fatalities linked to political violence in 2020, an increase from 736 fatalities in 2019.[1]

Non-international armed conflicts between the government and non-state armed groups

The non-state armed group, the National Liberation Army (Ejército de Liberación Nacional, ELN), and a number of criminal organizations continued their conflict with the government. According to the Rule of Law in Armed Conflicts (RULAC) project, in 2020 the Government of Colombia was involved in four parallel and overlapping non-international armed conflicts with: the ELN; the former Eastern Bloc (Bloque Oriental) of FARC– EP; the People's Liberation Army (Ejército Popular de Liberación, EPL); and the Gaitanista Self-Defense Forces of Colombia (Autodefensas Gaitanistas de Colombia, AGC, also known as the Gulf Clan), which is a drug cartel and right-wing paramilitary group considered one of the strongest criminal organizations in Colombia. At the same time non-international armed conflicts were taking place among various non-state armed groups, notably the ELN against the EPL and the AGC.[2]

On 14–17 February 2020 the ELN declared an 'armed strike' across nine Colombian departments, and executed a series of coordinated attacks that brought large parts of the country to a standstill. The 27 attacks included strikes on electrical infrastructure, river transport and ports, national highways and cities, as well as clashes with the Colombian military and a sniper attack. The armed strike was widely seen as a show of force by the

---

[1] Armed Conflict Location & Event Data Project (ACLED), Dashboard, accessed 1 Mar. 2021.
[2] 'Non-international armed conflicts in Colombia', RULAC, 24 Nov. 2020.

ELN.[3] The ELN has grown from 1400 members in 2017 to between 2500 and 3000 members, according to different sources, including FARC–EP members who did not want to lay down their arms to comply with the peace agreement. It has become transnational through its presence in Venezuela and its control of drug trafficking, illegal mining, human trafficking and smuggling in both countries.[4]

However, as the Covid-19 pandemic took hold, a month-long ceasefire was offered on 30 March to the government of Iván Duque Márquez by the ELN. Citing lack of government response, the ELN resumed military operations in May.[5] In response to the call by the United Nations Secretary-General António Guterres for a worldwide ceasefire, the ELN declared a unilateral month-long ceasefire beginning 1 April, and on 7 July the ELN again proposed a bilateral pause in fighting during the pandemic. Duque rejected this. The ELN has accused the Colombian Government of lack of will to carry on with stalled peace talks in Havana, where much of the Central Command of the group has been stranded since Duque ended the peace talks in January 2019 after the group carried out a bomb attack on a police academy in Bogotá. The Cuban Government has refused to extradite the ELN leaders to Colombia to face prosecution.[6] Duque has stated he would restart negotiations only if the ELN released all of its hostages and ended its criminal activity.[7] In June the ELN released 6 hostages, including 2 police officers and 4 civilians, but continued to hold at least 10 more hostages.[8] In July Colombian authorities captured, in a series of raids, eight ELN members who they accused of involvement in the police academy bombing. According to Duque, the raids allegedly provided further proof of the involvement of ELN leadership in the police academy attack, further weakening prospects for renewed peace talks with the ELN since the group's leaders were in Havana at the time of the attack.[9]

Problems continue to plague the implementation of the 2016 peace accord between FARC–EP and the Colombian Government. In its plan for comprehensive rural reform, only 0.08 per cent of 3 million hectares of land promised for distribution had been allocated as part of the Land Fund under

[3] Villalba, J., 'ELN showcases unique ability to paralyze parts of Colombia', InSight Crime, 6 Mar. 2020.

[4] 'ELN', InSight Crime, updated 27 Oct. 2020; and Trejo, M., 'The ELN is prepared to negotiate with the Colombian Government in exchange for a ceasefire', Atalayar, 30 Sep. 2020.

[5] 'Colombia's ELN rebels scrap ceasefire', France 24, 27 Apr. 2020.

[6] Loaiza, L., 'US pressure on Cuba to extradite ELN leaders unlikely to succeed', InSight Crime, 18 May 2020.

[7] Posada, J., 'The ELN's repeated demands for a ceasefire in Colombia', InSight Crime, 15 July 2020.

[8] 'Colombia's ELN rebels free six more hostages amid peace talks plea', BBC News, 15 June 2020.

[9] González, J. C. and Kurmanaev, A., 'Colombia captures guerrillas accused in deadly car bombing', New York Times, 2 July 2020.

Point 1.1.1 of the peace accord.[10] While former FARC–EP combatants have surrendered their weapons, their socio-economic reintegration into civilian life has been slow. According to the UN, only 41 per cent of accredited former combatants have received financial support for productive projects through mechanisms stipulated in the peace agreement.[11] Coca crop eradication continues, but with very slow progress in crop substitution. At the current rate of reparations, it would take 43 years to compensate all victims of the conflict.[12]

Armed and criminal groups have taken advantage of delayed implementation of peace agreement provisions, and social conflict and violence have increased. According to the report of the UN secretary-general on the UN Verification Mission in Colombia, the greatest threat to the peace agreement is the continuing threat of violence against former combatants, conflict-affected communities, and social leaders and human rights defenders.[13] At least 248 former combatants have been killed since the signing of the 2016 peace agreement, 73 during 2020.[14] Illegal armed groups are driving former combatants to flee from training and reintegration areas in several regions, undermining the reintegration process.[15] In October 2020 hundreds of former combatants marched to Bogotá to demand enhanced security guarantees and progress in the reintegration process.[16]

Violence against civilians

Attacks against political candidates, community organizers and local civil society activists also continued in 2020. In February the Office of the UN High Commissioner for Human Rights (OHCHR) criticized Duque for not doing enough to stop the violence against women human rights defenders in particular, which had increased by nearly 50 per cent in 2019 compared to in 2018.[17] Killings of civil society activists continued throughout 2020, and by September had reached 135 according to some sources. This exceeded the number committed during the whole of 2019 (124).[18] Violent protests broke

---

[10] Democracia Abierta, 'Four years later, Colombia's peace agreement advances at a snail's pace', 6 Jan. 2021; and Colombia, *Final Agreement to End the Armed Conflict and Build a Stable and Lasting Peace,* 24 Nov. 2016.

[11] United Nations, Security Council, 'United Nations Verification Mission in Colombia', Report of the Secretary-General, S/2020/1301, 29 Dec. 2020, para. 38.

[12] Democracia Abierta (note 10).

[13] United Nations, S/2020/1301 (note 11), para. 9.

[14] United Nations, S/2020/1301 (note 11), para. 10.

[15] United Nations, S/2020/1301 (note 11), para. 11.

[16] 'Colombia's ex-FARC rebels march in Bogota over killings', Deutsche Welle, 2 Nov. 2020.

[17] United Nations, Human Rights Council, 'Situation of human rights in Colombia', Report of the UN High Commissioner for Human Rights, A/HRC/43/3/Add.3, 26 Feb. 2020, para. 22.

[18] We are Defenders Programme, 'Boletin trimestral SIADDHH julio-septiembre 2020' [SIADDHH Quarterly Bulletin July–September 2020], 26 Nov. 2020.

out in Bogotá over four nights in September, sparked by a video posted on social media of police using a stun gun to lethally shoot a man accused of flouting Covid-19 restrictions. Fourteen people died during the protests. While the initial response to the protests was harsh, authorities subsequently adopted a more conciliatory approach and asked for forgiveness for police brutality.[19]

In mid December the UN High Commissioner for Human Rights called on state authorities to do more to protect the population, noting the increase in violence by non-state armed groups, criminal groups and other elements targeting peasants, indigenous people and Afro-Colombian people. The OHCHR noted 66 massacres in which 255 people had been killed in addition to the killing of 120 human rights defenders between January and mid December.[20]

Between January and June 2020 the International Committee of the Red Cross registered 181 individuals, most of them civilians, who were injured from explosive devices including anti-personnel mines, of which 27 suffered fatal injuries. This represented a 7 per cent decrease over figures from the same period in 2019, a relatively modest decline in view of the severe movement restrictions imposed from March due to the Covid-19 pandemic.[21] The Colombian Government has fallen behind on its pledge as signatory to the 1997 Convention on the Prohibition of the Use, Stockpiling, Production and Transfer of Anti-Personnel Mines and on their Destruction (informally known as the Ottawa Treaty or the Anti-Personnel Mine Ban Convention), to rid the country of landmines by 2021. In March 2020 the government formally requested an extension of the deadline to 31 December 2025.[22]

Forced displacement due to conflict and violence in areas where armed groups are fighting for control of drug production and trafficking routes increased substantially. According to a report on the implementation of the peace accord, issued by senators and members of independent and opposition political parties of the Congress of the Republic of Colombia, 16 190 people were displaced in the first six months of 2020. This was about twice the number over the same period in 2019.[23]

[19] Long, G., 'Bogotá counts costs of fatal police brutality protests', *Financial Times*, 14 Sep. 2020.

[20] OHCHR, 'Bachelet urges Colombia to improve protection amid heightened violence in remote areas', Press release, 15 Dec. 2020.

[21] Sarralde Duque, M., 'Este año, el 69% de víctimas de artefactos explosivos son civiles' [This year, 69% of victims of explosive ordnance are civilians], El Tiempo, 14 July 2020.

[22] Presidencia de la República, *Solicitud de Extensión Colombia 2020* [Presidency of the Republic, *Request for Extension Colombia 2020*] (Presidencia de la República: 31 Mar. 2020).

[23] Colombian Congress, '¿En qué va la paz a 2 años del govierno Duque?' [What is peace about—2 years of the Duque government], 18 Aug. 2020, p. 7.

The border conflict between Colombia and Venezuela

Low-intensity conflict along the 2200 kilometre border between Colombia and Venezuela continued to simmer through 2020. Tensions ratcheted up in 2019 when Colombia accused Venezuela of providing shelter to armed groups seeking safe haven across the border. Nicolás Maduro responded by deploying troops and materiel to the border, leading Duque to invoke the 1947 Inter-American Treaty of Reciprocal Assistance (also known as the Rio Pact), a mutual defence pact. Observers warned further deterioration in bilateral relations or actions by non-state armed groups at the border could result in conflict between the two countries.[24] In March the border was closed to contain the spread of Covid-19, creating chaos for thousands of Venezuelans attempting to return home amid lockdowns in Colombia and other neighbouring countries. Battles among armed groups, drug-trafficking gangs, paramilitary groups and state forces on either side of the border for control of smuggling routes resulted in casualties and displacement of local residents, while traffickers preyed on thousands of Venezuelan migrants desperate to return home.[25]

---

[24] International Crisis Group, 'Containing the border fallout of Colombia's new guerrilla schism', Crisis Group Latin America Briefing no. 40, 20 Sep. 2019.

[25] Collins, J., 'The shadow war on the Venezuela-Colombia border', New Humanitarian, 5 May 2020.

III. Armed conflict in Mexico

MARINA CAPARINI

The Government of Mexico is involved in two parallel non-international armed conflicts, one involving the Jalisco New Generation Cartel (Cartel Jalisco Nueva Generación, CJNG), and the other involving the Sinaloa Cartel. A third non-international armed conflict in Mexico exists between the CJNG and the Sinaloa Cartel.[1] Record high levels of violence in 2019, driven by drug cartels and organized crime, levelled off in 2020, albeit at a very high level. Overall numbers of homicides in 2020 decreased by 0.14 per cent from 2019, with 34 523 homicides recorded by the end of 2020, or 27.01 homicides per 100 000 inhabitants, a decrease of 1.3 per cent compared to in 2019.[2] The Armed Conflict Location & Event Data Project (ACLED) documented 8405 fatalities related to political violence in 2020, down from the 9365 fatalities of 2019.[3]

The powerful drug cartel CJNG has expanded aggressively throughout most states within Mexico and became more brazen in 2020, employing strategic use of violence against state criminal justice officials and publicized displays of firepower. In June the CJNG was implicated in the assassination of a federal judge and his wife in Colima. The judge had presided over several cases involving top CJNG and Sinaloa Cartel leaders, including the extradition of the son of the CJNG leader, Rubén Oseguera González or 'El Menchito', to the United States to face federal drug-trafficking charges.[4] Some judges have subsequently declined presiding over organized crime cases due to concerns for their personal safety.[5] Also in June the CJNG was identified as being behind the first assassination attempt made against a high-ranking security official in the capital Mexico City. The 400-round attack on the armoured vehicle of Mexico City's police chief Omar García Harfuch, who had been cracking down on organized crime and police collusion, wounded him and killed two bodyguards and a bystander.[6] On 17 July the CJNG released a video showing over 20 armoured vehicles and dozens of uniformed gang members with assault weapons celebrating the birthday

---

[1] 'Non-international armed conflicts in Mexico', Rule of Law in Armed Conflicts, 23 Nov. 2020.

[2] 'Mexico sees slight decrease in murders in 2020', France 24, 31 Dec. 2020.

[3] Armed Conflict Location & Event Data Project (ACLED), Dashboard, accessed 1 Mar. 2021.

[4] Goodwin, Z., 'Why one of Mexico's smallest states is also its most violent', InSight Crime, 24 June 2020; and McDonnell, P. J., 'Mexico extradites son of powerful cartel leader to face US charges', Los Angeles Times, 21 Feb. 2020.

[5] Beittel, J. S., Mexico: Organized Crime and Drug Trafficking Organizations, Congressional Research Service (CRS) Report for Congress R41576 (US Congress, CRS: Washington, DC, 28 July 2020), p. 8.

[6] Kitroeff, N., 'Mexico City police chief is wounded in brazen ambush', New York Times, 26 June 2020, updated 12 July 2020; and Kahn, C., 'As Mexico's dominant cartel gains power, the president vows "hugs, not bullets"', NPR, 23 July 2020.

of its leader, Nemesio Oseguera Cervantes or 'El Mencho'. The videotaped show of force was widely spread on social media at the same time as President Andrés Manuel López Obrador was visiting Jalisco, the home territory of the cartel.[7]

Despite the 2019 imprisonment of its leader, Joaquín 'El Chapo' Guzmán, for life in a federal United States super-maximum security prison, the Sinaloa Cartel has maintained a dominant role in the Mexican drug trade, notably the importation of precursor material from China, local production and smuggling of highly lucrative fentanyl into the USA.[8] The incarceration of El Chapo resulted in increased violence as other groups and cartels sought to gain control of Sinaloa production and trafficking routes.[9]

Despite his policy of 'hugs not bullets' and earlier criticism of the militarized 'war on drugs', President López Obrador has increasingly turned to the military as cartel violence increased and security deteriorated throughout the country. Mexico created a National Guard in 2019. The constitutional amendment that created the National Guard, and the 2019 Law on the National Guard passed two months later, established it as a civilian public security institution supervised and subordinate to civilian authorities, and trained according to police doctrine.[10] Having around 100 000 members by 2020, the National Guard is, in practice, based on military police organizational structure and commands, controlled by a military operational command, and largely composed of and trained by military personnel with some federal police using military weapons. When its members are accused of crimes, they are held in military rather than civilian prisons.[11] In May the president issued a decree extending armed forces

---

[7] Duncan, C., 'Mexican drug cartel shows off uniformed troops with military weapons and armoured vehicles in video', *The Independent*, 18 July 2020.

[8] Helmore, E., 'El Chapo: Mexican drug lord sentenced to life in prison', 17 July 2019; and Travère, A. and Giraudat, J., 'Revealed: How Mexico's Sinaloa cartel has created a global network to rule the fentanyl trade', *The Guardian*, 8 Dec. 2020.

[9] Ahmed, A., 'El Chapo's prosecution has fueled the drug war in Mexico', *New York Times*, 17 July 2019.

[10] Mexican Government, 'Decreto por el que se reforman, adicionan y derogan diversas disposiciones de la Constitución Política de los Estados Unidos Mexicanos, en materia de Guardia Nacional' [Decree by which various provisions of the political constitution of the United Mexican States are amended, added and repealed, regarding the National Guard], 26 Mar. 2019; and Mexican Secretary of the Interior,'Decreto por el que se expide la Ley de la Guardia Nacional' [Decree issuing the law of the National Guard], 27 May 2019.

[11] Pérez Correa, C., 'AMLO's broken campaign promise: Demilitarizing Mexico', *Americas Quarterly*, 9 Dec. 2020; and Angel, A., 'Mandos militares controlan a la Guardia Nacional, confirma amparo de Mayor del Ejército' [Military commands control the National Guard, confirms protection of Army Major], Animal Politico, 19 Oct. 2020.

participation in civilian law enforcement for a further four years.[12] In July the president put the military in control of customs at border crossings and ports in an effort to address mismanagement and corruption that enabled the smuggling of precursor chemicals used in the manufacture of synthetic drugs by the cartels.[13]

The CJNG has become the second-most dominant Mexican cartel presence in the USA after the Sinaloa Cartel, and is a major perpetrator of drug trafficking across the border.[14] It is considered by the US Department of Justice to be one of the world's five most dangerous criminal organizations in the world. Since 2018 the USA has placed a $10 million reward for information leading to the arrest of the CJNG leader El Mencho, and a $5 million reward for information leading to the arrest of other high-ranking members of the CJNG.[15]

In addition to armed conflict, corruption scandals affected top figures in the political and economic elite in 2020. Emilio Lozoya Austin, the former chief executive officer of Mexico's state oil company Pemex, was extradited from Spain in July on charges that he had received more than $4 million in bribes from the Brazilian construction firm Odebrecht. In his leaked deposition he accused three former Mexican presidents—his former boss Enrique Peña Nieto, Felipe Calderón and Carlos Salinas de Gortari—as well as numerous legislators and aides of corruption.[16] Retired general Salvador Cienfuegos, a former secretary of defence under President Peña Nieto, was arrested in October in the USA on drug-trafficking and corruption charges. Accused of taking bribes to protect drug cartel leaders, he was released in November at the demand of the Mexican Government, with the promise that he would face justice in Mexico. The Mexican authorities exonerated him shortly afterwards.[17]

---

[12] Mexican Secretary of the Interior, 'Acuerdo por el que se dispone de la Fuerza Armada permanente para llevar a cabo tareas de seguridad pública de manera extraordinaria, regulada, fiscalizada, subordinada y complementaria' [Agreement by which the permanent armed forces are available to carry out public security tasks in an extraordinary, regulated, supervised, subordinate and complementary manner], 11 May 2020; and Stevenson, M., 'Mexico authorizes military policing for 4 more years', AP News, 11 May 2020.

[13] Stevenson, M., 'Mexico puts military in charge of customs operations', *Washington Post*, 17 July 2020.

[14] US Drug Enforcement Administration, *2019 National Drug Threat Assessment* (US Department of Justice: Washington, DC, Dec. 2019), p. 6.

[15] 'US offers $10 million for information leading to Mexican drug lord's arrest', Reuters, 16 Oct. 2018.

[16] Phillips, T. and Agren, D., 'Mexico rocked by claims of corruption against three former presidents', *The Guardian*, 20 Aug. 2020.

[17] Lopez, O., 'Mexico exonerates ex-defense chief who was freed by the USA', *New York Times*, 14 Jan. 2021.

4. Armed conflict and peace processes in Asia and Oceania

Overview

Seven countries in Asia and Oceania experienced active armed conflicts in 2020 (the same as in 2019)—three in South Asia (section II): Afghanistan (major internationalized civil war), India (high-intensity interstate border and subnational armed conflicts) and Pakistan (low-intensity interstate border and subnational armed conflicts); and four low-intensity subnational armed conflicts in South East Asia (section III): Indonesia, Myanmar, the Philippines and Thailand. Total conflict-related fatalities in Asia and Oceania fell by nearly 50 per cent in 2020 (compared to 2019), mostly as a result of conflict-related fatalities being halved in Afghanistan.

However, three emerging trends remained cause for concern in 2020: (a) the growing Chinese–United States rivalry combined with an increasingly assertive Chinese foreign policy, (b) the growing violence related to identity politics, based on ethnic and/or religious polarization, and (c) the increase in transnational violent jihadist groups.

Only a few of the armed conflicts were being addressed in 2020 by ongoing or new peace processes. Important advances were made in the peace talks in Afghanistan, but there was no noticeable peace process between India and Pakistan with regard to their ongoing interstate armed conflict over Kashmir. Despite China and India signing several border agreements since the 1990s, the status quo broke down in 2020 with a significant uptick in violence and tensions over their border dispute. In South East Asia a Japanese-brokered ceasefire opened up new opportunities for dialogue. There were five multilateral peace operations active in Asia and Oceania in 2020. This was the same number as in 2019.

The Covid-19 pandemic appears to have had a minimal impact on the region's armed conflicts in 2020, despite having profound impacts on human security more generally.

The war in Afghanistan remained the deadliest armed conflict in the world, with nearly 21 000 fatalities in 2020—a 50 per cent reduction on 2019. There were grounds for optimism following a conditional peace agreement between the Taliban and the USA in February 2020 and the commencement of intra-Afghan peace talks in September 2020. The Afghan Government reached a preliminary procedural agreement with the Taliban in December 2020, but by the end of the year the talks had faltered and violence continued. With a conditional deadline for complete US and North Atlantic Treaty Organization military withdrawal by May 2021, uncertainty over the incoming Biden administration's approach and the Taliban apparently in the ascendancy, the future of the peace process remained uncertain.

In the territorial conflict between India and Pakistan over Kashmir the situation in 2020 largely reverted to the status quo of relatively low levels of armed violence. This consisted of regular exchanges of artillery fire and other clashes between Indian and Pakistani forces along the line of control, and militant attacks and Indian counter-insurgency operations inside Jammu and Kashmir. However, in June 2020, for the first time in over five decades, the border tensions between China and India in the disputed eastern Ladakh region of Kashmir turned deadly. A violent but gunless confrontation resulted in the deaths of at least 20 Indian soldiers and an unknown number of Chinese soldiers, as well as probable additional Chinese territorial gains.

Some of the most organized Islamist extremist groups were active in South East Asia, most notably in Indonesia, Malaysia and the Philippines. In Myanmar an ongoing peace process made little headway during the year against a backdrop of continuing violence, especially in Rakhine state. However, Japan brokered a diplomatic breakthrough between the Arakan Army and the Myanmar military in November 2020 that included a de facto ceasefire. The agreement has created a vital space for dialogue and the return of several thousand displaced people. However, the voluntary return of almost a million Rohingya people forcibly displaced in 2017 continued to seem unlikely in the short term, despite worsening humanitarian conditions in refugee camps in Bangladesh. Without reforms to address the discrimination and marginalization of ethnic minorities, in Rakhine state and more widely in Myanmar, the prospects for the peace process remained uncertain.

Two long-running insurgencies in the Philippines continued in 2020 at relatively low levels of violence: one in the Muslim-majority areas of the Mindanao region of the southern Philippines and another involving the New People's Army of the Communist Party of the Philippines. However, it was the 'war on drugs' that appeared to produce the most fatalities in the Philippines during the year.

IAN DAVIS

I. Key general developments in the region

IAN DAVIS

Seven countries in Asia and Oceania experienced active armed conflicts in 2020 (the same as in 2019)—three in South Asia: Afghanistan (major internationalized civil war), India (high intensity as a result of combined interstate border and subnational armed conflicts) and Pakistan (low-intensity interstate border and subnational armed conflicts), as discussed in section II; and four low-intensity subnational armed conflicts in South East Asia: Indonesia, Myanmar, the Philippines and Thailand, as discussed in section III.[1] In the Philippines fatalities in the subnational armed conflict were likely surpassed by those arising from the high levels of violence against civilians in a 'war on drugs'. All seven armed conflicts had lower conflict-related fatalities in 2020 than in 2019, and overall the reduction was close to 50 per cent as a result of conflict-related fatalities being halved in Afghanistan (see table 4.1).

Alongside these armed conflicts, parts of Asia and Oceania continued to be affected by instability arising from a variety of causes, with no single unifying trend (other than the Chinese–United States rivalry, discussed below), and important subregional differences.

While Asia, especially East Asia, has experienced a dramatic reduction in armed conflict in the last 40 years, a reversal of this positive trend appears to be under way.[2] Two trends remained cause for concern in 2020: (a) the growing violence related to identity politics, based on ethnic and/ or religious polarization (some of which has long-term roots)—such as the Hindu-nationalist paramilitant group, the Rashtriya Swayamsevak Sangh, in India and Buddhist extremist groups operating in Myanmar, Sri Lanka and Thailand; and (b) the increase in transnational violent jihadist groups— including the presence of actors linked to the Islamic State in Afghanistan, Bangladesh, India, Indonesia, Malaysia, Pakistan, the Philippines and Sri Lanka.[3] In some countries (such as India) Islamic State presence is minimal, while in others (such as Afghanistan) the presence is more entrenched and groups are more capable of carrying out armed attacks.

---

[1] For conflict definitions and typologies see chapter 2, section I, in this volume.

[2] World Bank Group and United Nations, *Pathways for Peace: Inclusive Approaches for Preventing Violent Conflict* (International Bank for Reconstruction and Development/The World Bank: Washington, DC, 2018), pp. 11–12, 19; and Bellamy, A. J., *East Asia's Other Miracle: Explaining the Decline of Mass Atrocities* (Oxford University Press: Oxford, 2017).

[3] Ramachandran, S., 'India: Fanning the flames of extremism and terror at home', *Terrorism Monitor*, vol. 18, no. 1 (14 Jan. 2020), pp. 7–9; Gunasingham, A., 'Buddhist extremism in Sri Lanka and Myanmar: An examination', *Counter Terrorist Trends and Analyses*, vol. 11, no. 3 (Mar. 2019), pp. 1–6; and United Nations, Security Council, 'Eleventh report of the secretary-general on the threat posed by ISIL (Da'esh) to international peace and security and the range of United Nations efforts in support of member states in countering the threat', S/2020/774, 4 Aug. 2020, pp. 6–7.

Table 4.1. Estimated conflict-related fatalities in Asia and Oceania, 2017–20

Country	2017	2018	2019	2020
Afghanistan	36 606	43 278	41 680	20 938
India	1 420	2 100	1 526	1 288
Indonesia	49	167	219	117
Myanmar	1 253	225	1 495	654
Pakistan	1 725	1 226	1 157	813
Philippines	4 088	1 790	1 622	1 448
Thailand	94	231	172	102
Total	**45 235**	**49 017**	**47 871**	**25 360**

Note: Includes only countries with armed conflicts with 25 or more deaths in a given year.

Source: Armed Conflict Location & Event Data Project, 'Data export tool', accessed 23–24 Jan. 2021.

Only a few of the armed conflicts discussed in this chapter were being addressed in 2020 by ongoing or new peace processes. Important advances were made in the peace talks in Afghanistan (see section II), but there was no noticeable peace process between India and Pakistan with regard to their ongoing interstate armed conflict over Kashmir. Despite India and China signing several border agreements since the 1990s, the status quo broke down in 2020 with a significant uptick in violence and tensions over their border dispute (see section II). In South East Asia, a Japanese-brokered ceasefire between Myanmar's military and the Arakan Army opened up new opportunities for dialogue at the end of the year (see section III).

There were five multilateral peace operations in Asia and Oceania in 2020. This was the same number as in 2019. Although none of these operations started or ended during the year, the North Atlantic Treaty Organization (NATO)-led Resolute Support Mission (RSM) is expected to withdraw from Afghanistan in 2021. The number of personnel in multilateral peace operations in Asia and Oceania decreased by 42 per cent in 2020, from 17 086 on 31 December 2019 to 9941 on 31 December 2020. This was mainly due to a partial drawdown of the RSM during the year, which was driven by major reductions of the number of US forces in Afghanistan in accordance with a new agreement between the USA and the Taliban (see section II).

Growing geopolitical tensions in East Asia

In East Asia, North Korea, South Korea and Taiwan are all unrecognized by at least one other East Asian state due to ongoing political tensions in the region, specifically the division of Korea, the political status of Taiwan and developments in the quasi-dependent territory of Hong Kong. These tensions are exacerbated by the geopolitical rivalry between China and the USA, and an increasingly assertive Chinese foreign policy. The latter is a general trend based on domestic developments in China (regime legitimacy) and only partially connected to the relationship with the USA. Nonetheless, a growing number of analysts and officials believe China and the USA are on the edge of a new cold war.[4] These Chinese–US tensions were played out in a 'battle of narratives' in at least four areas: the Covid-19 pandemic response; trade and technology; human rights (especially regarding the treatment of ethnic minorities in the Xinjiang region and the introduction of a new security law in Hong Kong); and military competition in the South China Sea and across the Taiwan Strait.[5] In addition, an alliance to counter China's growing influence—known as the Quadrilateral Initiative, or the Quad—deepened its cooperation during 2020. Consisting of an informal alliance between Australia, India, Japan and the USA, the first Quadrilateral Security Dialogue was held in 2007, but the idea cooled until being revived in 2017. Since then it has met regularly at the working level, and held its second ministerial level meeting in October 2020 but failed to agree on a joint communiqué.[6]

The impact of Covid-19

The Covid-19 pandemic appears to have had a minimal impact on the region's armed conflicts in 2020, despite having profound impacts on human security more generally, although many of these broader consequences were still to be felt or identified. In response to the UN secretary-general's March call for a Covid-19-related global ceasefire, the Communist Party of the Philippines announced a unilateral ceasefire by its armed wing, the New People's Army, until 15 April (see section III) after the government announced a temporary international ceasefire.[7] Although some other armed groups in Indonesia, Myanmar and Thailand also proposed ceasefires, these were largely ignored

---

[4] See e.g. Campbell, K. M. and Wyne, A., 'The growing risk of inadvertent escalation between Washington and Beijing', Lawfare, 16 Aug. 2020; Garton Ash, T., 'China: Lessons for Europe from the cold war', European Council on Foreign Relations, 22 June 2020; and Rachman, G., 'A new cold war: Trump, Xi and the escalating US-China confrontation', *Financial Times*, 5 Oct. 2020. On the different perspectives within the USA on US foreign policy towards China see Sitaraman, G., 'Mapping the China debate', Lawfare, 26 May 2020. Also see the discussion in chapter 1 of this volume.

[5] See e.g. Marquardt, A. and Hansler, J., 'US push to include "Wuhan virus" language in G7 joint statement fractures alliance', CNN, 26 Mar. 2020; Maizland, L. and Chatsky, A., 'Huawei: China's controversial tech giant', Council on Foreign Relations Backgrounder, 6 Aug. 2020; Buckley, C. and Ramzy, A., 'China is erasing mosques and precious shrines in Xinjiang', *New York Times*, 25 Sep. 2020; and Wong, E., 'Hong Kong has lost autonomy, Pompeo says, opening door to US action', *New York Times*, 27 May 2020. On Chinese strategy in the South China Sea see Zhang, F., 'China's long march at sea: Explaining Beijing's South China Sea strategy, 2009–2016', *Pacific Review*, vol. 33, no. 5 (2020), pp. 757–87. On US military strategy towards China see Simón, L., 'Between punishment and denial: Uncertainty, flexibility, and US military strategy toward China', *Contemporary Security Policy*, vol. 41, no. 3 (2020), pp. 361–84. On US arms sales to Taiwan see chapter 9, section III, in this volume.

[6] Madan, T., 'What you need to know about the "Quad," in charts', Brookings, 5 Oct. 2020; Lee, L., 'Assessing the Quad: Prospects and limitations of quadrilateral cooperation for advancing Australia's interests', Lowy Institute, 19 May 2020; and Rich, M., 'Pompeo's message in Japan: Countering China is worth meeting face to face', *New York Times*, 6 Oct. 2020.

[7] On the global ceasefire call by the UN secretary-general see chapter 2, section I, in this volume.

by governments (also see section III). The Myanmar Government declared a ceasefire in May, but military operations continued against some of the major armed groups. In early April 2020 Maoist rebels in India also offered a unilateral ceasefire to enable health workers to address the spread of Covid-19 (see section II).

There is evidence that the pandemic exacerbated some existing identity-based divisions, such as the targeting of Muslims in India and Sri Lanka, fuelled by Covid-19-related hate speech.[8] Regional bodies, namely the Association of Southeast Asian Nations and the South Asian Association for Regional Cooperation, made several commitments to improve cooperation among states in addressing Covid-19-related concerns, but translating such pledges into concrete action often proved difficult.[9] More generally, the pandemic is likely to unravel decades of economic and social progress in some of the more fragile parts of Asia, with the Asian Development Bank predicting the first regional recession in 60 years.[10]

[8] Yadav, K. et al., 'Old hatreds fuel online misinformation about Covid-19 in South Asia', *Bulletin of the Atomic Scientists*, 25 Nov. 2020.

[9] Political Settlements Research Programme, 'Responding to Covid-19: The coming of age of regionalism in Asia?', 4 June 2020.

[10] 'Asia sees first regional recession in 60 years', BBC News, 15 Sep. 2020. Also see Ingram, S., *Lives Upended: How Covid-19 Threatens the Futures of 600 Million South Asian Children* (UNICEF: June 2020); and Perrigo, B. and Bagri, N. T., 'How the pandemic is reshaping India', *TIME*, 19 Aug. 2020.

II. Armed conflict and peace processes in South Asia

IAN DAVIS

The security threats facing the states in South Asia—Afghanistan, Bangladesh, Bhutan, India, Maldives, Nepal, Pakistan and Sri Lanka—are complex and diverse. Security challenges include interstate rivalry, border disputes, nuclear weapon risks, terrorism and internal threats arising from a combination of ethnic, religious and political tensions, which are often exacerbated by oppressive state security forces. Environmental and climate-related challenges include high levels of water stress (floods and droughts) and moderate to severe food insecurity.[1]

This section focuses on the major internationalized civil war in Afghanistan, and the interstate border and subnational armed conflicts in India and Pakistan. The long-running and devastating war in Afghanistan, and the territorial dispute between India and Pakistan over the Kashmir region are crucial barometers for peace and stability in South Asia. In the former, there was renewed optimism following a peace agreement between the Taliban and the United States in February 2020, although subsequent peace talks between the Taliban and the Afghan Government took time to get started and had agreed only procedural rules for further talks by the end of the year. In the latter, after a short but sharp escalation in the conflict in 2019 the situation returned to an uneasy stalemate in 2020. However, there was heightened tension and a short escalation in hostilities on the border between China and India, as discussed below. This China–India border conflict is likely to be an equally important barometer for regional stability in the coming years.

South Asia remains one of the regions most affected by armed conflicts involving non-state groups and state security forces. For example, the *Global Terrorism Index 2020* noted the region recorded more deaths from terrorism in 2019 than any other region (as was also the case in 2018). Afghanistan, India and Pakistan were among the top 10 countries most affected by terrorism worldwide (and have all appeared in the top 10 for over a decade).[2]

Armed conflict in Afghanistan

The war in Afghanistan (2001–present) continued into its 19th year in 2020, although the wider historical conflict in Afghanistan began with the 1979–89 Soviet–Afghan War. It was the deadliest armed conflict in the

[1] Institute for Economics & Peace (IEP), *Ecological Threat Register 2020: Understanding Ecological Threats, Resilience and Peace* (IEP: Sydney, Sep. 2020).

[2] IEP, *Global Terrorism Index 2020: Measuring the Impact of Terrorism* (IEP: Sydney, Nov. 2020), pp. 18, 43.

Table 4.2. Estimated conflict-related fatalities in Afghanistan, 2017–20

Event type	2017	2018	2019	2020
Battles	26 326	31 728	26 510	15 120
Explosions/remote violence	9 587	10 894	14 584	5 187
Protests, riots and strategic developments	259	287	198	167
Violence against civilians	434	369	388	464
Total	**36 606**	**43 278**	**41 680**	**20 938**

Notes: The first available year for data on Afghanistan in the Armed Conflict Location & Event Data Project (ACLED) database is 2017. For definitions of event types, see ACLED, 'ACLED definitions of political violence and protest', 11 Apr. 2019.

Source: ACLED, 'Data export tool', accessed 23 Jan. 2021.

world in 2020 (in terms of conflict-related fatalities), but there was progress in the Afghan peace process. As discussed below, a conditional peace agreement between the Taliban and the USA was signed in February 2020 and intra-Afghan peace talks have been ongoing since September 2020, with a preliminary procedural agreement reached between the Afghan Government and the Taliban in December 2020.

Nonetheless, the humanitarian consequences of the conflict continued to be stark. There were nearly 21 000 estimated fatalities due to the conflict over the course of the year, a 50 per cent reduction from 2019 (see table 4.2).[3] Most of these were combat related and involved Afghan Government forces and the Taliban. Meanwhile, the United Nations Assistance Mission in Afghanistan (UNAMA) continued to document high levels of violence against civilians. It recorded 8820 civilian casualties (3035 fatalities and 5785 injuries) in 2020. While this represents a 15 per cent reduction from 2019 and the lowest number since 2013, total civilian casualties in the past decade (1 January 2011 to 31 December 2020) totalled nearly 100 000 (with more than 33 000 killed and over 64 000 injured).[4]

Food security in Afghanistan has steadily deteriorated over the past five years, with the percentage of food-insecure people doubling (from 37 per cent in September 2015 to 76 per cent in November 2020). The number of people in crisis or emergency levels of food insecurity has increased to 16.9 million people, more than a fivefold increase (from 8 per cent to 42 per cent of the population) over the same period. The spread of Covid-19 throughout Afghanistan—resulting in more than 48 000 confirmed cases and at least

[3] Armed Conflict Location & Event Data Project (ACLED), 'Data export tool', accessed 23 Jan. 2021.
[4] UNAMA, *Afghanistan: Protection of Civilians in Armed Conflict, Annual Report 2020* (UNAMA and UN Human Rights Office of the High Commissioner: Kabul, Feb. 2021).

1900 deaths as of 7 December 2020 (although numbers are likely to be higher due to underreporting)—has exacerbated rising food insecurity.[5]

There have been numerous controversial practices and events associated with the Afghan conflict; at least three more occurred or came to light in 2020. First, in early March 2020 the International Criminal Court (ICC) ruled it could open an investigation into alleged war crimes and crimes against humanity in Afghanistan committed by the Afghan authorities, the Taliban and the US military. This decision was the first from the ICC involving US forces (the USA is not a member state, but Afghanistan is), and led to the US administration applying sanctions against ICC officials in June and September.[6] Second, there were allegations that in 2019 a Russian military intelligence unit secretly offered payments to Taliban-linked militants to kill US and coalition forces. These US allegations were subsequently widened to include Iran. Iran and Russia both denied the allegations.[7] Third, elite Australian soldiers (part of the International Security Assistance Force, led by the North Atlantic Treaty Organization (NATO)) allegedly committed over 36 war crimes, including murder and cruel treatment of non-combatants, in Afghanistan between 2009 and 2013, according to an official report by the Inspector-General of the Australian Defence Force. The report refers to one heavily redacted incident as 'possibly the most disgraceful episode in Australia's military history'.[8]

The Taliban–US peace agreement

During 2019 the Taliban and the USA reached a framework agreement in which the USA would withdraw military forces in exchange for credible assurances from the Taliban that it would prohibit terrorist groups from operating inside the country. The withdrawal of US troops was conditional on the Taliban also agreeing to a ceasefire and holding direct talks with the Afghan Government.[9] Despite these Taliban–US talks being the most

---

[5] UN Office for the Coordination of Humanitarian Affairs (UN OCHA), *Humanitarian Needs Overview: Afghanistan* (UN OCHA: Dec. 2020), p. 6; and Watkins, A., 'Covid-19 in Afghanistan: Compounding crises', International Crisis Group Commentary, 6 May 2020.

[6] ICC, 'Judgment on the appeal against the decision on the authorisation of an investigation into the situation in the Islamic Republic of Afghanistan', 5 Mar. 2020; Deutsch, A. and van den Berg, S., 'International Criminal Court members defend it in face of US sanctions', Reuters, 23 June 2020; and 'International Criminal Court officials sanctioned by US', BBC News, 2 Sep. 2020.

[7] Savage, C., Schmitt, E. and Schwirtz, M., 'Russia secretly offered Afghan militants bounties to kill US troops, intelligence says', *New York Times*, 26 June 2020; 'Afghanistan war: Russia denies paying militants to kill US troops', BBC News, 28 June 2020; and Borger, J., 'Iran reportedly paid bounties to Afghan group for attacks on Americans', *The Guardian*, 17 Aug. 2020.

[8] Commonwealth of Australia, *Inspector-General of the Australian Defence Force Afghanistan Inquiry Report* (Commonwealth of Australia: 2020). For an overview of the inquiry see Elphick, K., 'The Inspector-General of the Australian Defence Force Afghanistan Inquiry (Brereton Inquiry): A quick guide', Australian Parliamentary Library, Research paper series, 3 Sep. 2020.

[9] Mashal, M., 'US and Taliban agree in principle to peace framework, envoy says', *New York Times*, 28 Jan. 2019.

promising of the various strands of a multilevel and multiactor Afghan peace process, they collapsed in September 2019.[10]

However, in December 2019 official Taliban–US talks resumed in Doha, Qatar. These led to a seven-day partial ceasefire that began on 22 February 2020.[11] At the end of the ceasefire period, on 29 February 2020, Zalmay Khalilzad, the US special representative for Afghanistan reconciliation, and Abdul Ghani Baradar, a representative of the Taliban, signed the 2020 Agreement for Bringing Peace to Afghanistan, in Doha.[12] The provisions of the deal reflected the earlier framework agreement. The USA agreed to an initial reduction of its force level from 13 000 to 8600 by July 2020, followed by a full withdrawal within 14 months, conditional on the Taliban meeting its commitments. The agreement received unanimous backing from the UN Security Council and was welcomed by NATO, which was expected to make parallel reductions in its Resolute Support Mission (RSM).[13] At the beginning of 2020 NATO's RSM consisted of about 16 500 troops, including about 8000 from the USA. A further 5000 US troops were deployed in Afghanistan as part of the US counterterrorism operation Freedom's Sentinel.[14]

The resulting intra-Afghan negotiations that were scheduled to begin on 10 March 2020 were delayed due to the disputed outcome of the 2019 Afghan presidential elections (which among other things prevented the formation of the Afghan Government negotiating team) and a stalled prisoner exchange.[15] The February agreement required the release of 5000 Taliban prisoners in exchange for 1000 government soldiers held by the Taliban. The Afghan Government initially rejected the prisoner exchange, but by the end of

[10] For more information on the various international peace processes in Afghanistan see Davis, I., 'Armed conflict and peace processes in Asia and Oceania', *SIPRI Yearbook 2019*, pp. 62–65. For the main developments in 2019 see Davis, I. and Smit, T., 'Armed conflict and peace processes in South Asia', *SIPRI Yearbook 2020*, pp. 92–94.

[11] 'First round of resurrected US-Taliban peace talks open in Qatar', Al Jazeera, 7 Dec. 2019; and Qazi, S., 'US–Taliban truce begins, raising hopes of peace deal', Al Jazeera, 22 Feb. 2020.

[12] 'Agreement for bringing peace to Afghanistan between the Islamic Emirate of Afghanistan which is not recognized by the United States as a state and is known as the Taliban and the United States of America', 29 Feb. 2020; and United Nations, 'Security Council welcomes significant steps towards ending war in Afghanistan, unanimously adopting Resolution 2513 (2020)', 10 Mar. 2020.

[13] 'Security Council resolution endorses moves towards long-sought Afghanistan peace', UN News, 10 Mar. 2020; and NATO, 'Statement by the North Atlantic Council on Afghanistan', Press release, 29 Feb. 2020.

[14] SIPRI Multilateral Peace Operations Database, <https://www.sipri.org/databases/pko>, accessed 1 Apr. 2021; NATO, 'Resolute Support Mission: Key facts and figures', Feb. 2020; and US Department of Defense, *Enhancing Security and Stability in Afghanistan*, Report to Congress (US Department of Defense: Washington, DC, Dec. 2019).

[15] Qazi, S., 'Will the Ghani-Abdullah rivalry undermine Afghan peace process?', Al Jazeera, 9 Mar. 2020.

March it was indicating some prisoners might be released.[16] In the meantime the Taliban resumed military operations against Afghan Government forces, while the USA sought to apply pressure on the Afghan Government to compromise by threatening (but not implementing) a $1 billion cut in US security assistance to the country.[17]

A surge in violence

Although the Taliban stopped conducting attacks against the US-led coalition forces in Afghanistan, attacks against Afghan security forces increased significantly. In the 45 days after the agreement (between 1 March and 15 April 2020) the Taliban conducted more than 4500 attacks, and more than 900 Afghan security forces were killed.[18] US air strikes continued, including against the Taliban, but at a much-reduced tempo.

On 31 March 2020 the first direct talks took place between the Afghan Government and the Taliban on exchanging prisoners, but they quickly collapsed.[19] The cycle of violence continued in May with several insurgent attacks, including on a hospital in Kabul and a suicide bombing in Nangarhar, resulting in more than 100 civilian casualties. Afghan President Ashraf Ghani blamed the Taliban and announced Afghan security forces would drop their defensive posture and resume offensive operations against the group. The Taliban denied responsibility and no other group claimed the attacks, although the USA blamed the Islamic State in the Khorasan Province (IS-KP) for both of them.[20] Afghan security forces arrested two IS-KP leaders in the first half of the year, while the UN estimated that the group had 2200 members in 2020.[21]

On 17 May 2020 President Ghani and his rival Abdullah Abdullah signed a power-sharing deal ending the long-running dispute about the outcome

[16] Sanger, D. E., Schmitt, E. and Gibbons-Neff, T., 'A secret accord with the Taliban: When and how the US would leave Afghanistan', *New York Times*, 8 Mar. 2020; Sediqi, A. Q., 'Taliban rule out taking part in Afghan talks until prisoners freed', Reuters, 2 Mar. 2020; and Sediqi, A. Q. and Shalizi, H., 'Taliban say prisoner release by Afghan government to start by end of March', Reuters, 25 Mar. 2020.

[17] Borger, J., 'US to cut $1bn of Afghanistan aid over failure to agree unity government', *The Guardian*, 24 Mar. 2020; and Mohammed, A., Landay, J. and Ali, I., 'US has not cut Afghan security funds despite Pompeo vow of immediate slash—sources', Reuters, 20 May 2020.

[18] Shalizi, H., Sediqi, A. Q. and Jain, R., 'Taliban step up attacks on Afghan forces since signing US deal: Data', Reuters, 1 May 2020.

[19] 'Afghanistan and Taliban begin direct talks with aim of prisoner swap', BBC News, 1 Apr. 2020; and 'Afghanistan peace deal: Taliban walk out of "fruitless" talks', BBC News, 7 Apr. 2020.

[20] 'Afghanistan: Deadly suicide attack targets funeral in Nangarhar', Al Jazeera, 12 May 2020; and 'US says Islamic State conducted attack on Kabul hospital', Reuters, 15 May 2020.

[21] Mines, A. and Jadoon, A., 'Can the Islamic State's Afghan province survive its leadership losses?', Lawfare, 17 May 2020; and United Nations, Security Council, 'Eleventh report of the secretary-general on the threat posed by ISIL (Da'esh) to international peace and security and the range of United Nations efforts in support of member states in countering the threat', S/2020/774, 4 Aug. 2020, pp. 6–7. On the rivalry between the IS-KP and the Taliban see Semple, M., 'How the Taliban's rivalry with ISIS is shaping the Afghan peace talks', World Politics Review, 22 Dec. 2020.

of the 2019 presidential elections. Abdullah was assigned responsibility for peace negotiations with the Taliban.[22] On 25 May 2020 the Taliban unilaterally declared a three-day ceasefire, and shortly afterwards the Afghan Government agreed to release up to 2000 Taliban prisoners.[23] However, these goodwill gestures did not last. The Taliban carried out a series of attacks on Afghan security forces in June, described by one Afghan official as the 'deadliest' week in Afghanistan's 19 years of conflict.[24]

Despite a continuation of high levels of violence against the Afghan civilian population, including roadside bombs and targeted killings, incremental progress continued to be made in prisoner exchanges.[25] At the beginning of September it was confirmed that all but 7 of the 5000 prisoners on the Taliban list had been released, thus paving the way for intra-Afghan peace talks.[26]

Intra-Afghan negotiations

Talks between representatives from the Afghan Government and the Taliban began in Doha on 12 September 2020. Many of the key negotiators were the children of officials and insurgents who played major roles in the Soviet conflict in Afghanistan in the 1980s.[27] The initial discussions focused on seeking agreement on an agenda and a road map for more detailed talks later. However, reports suggested that both sides were far apart on basic issues such as a ceasefire and women's rights.[28]

Fighting continued despite several rounds of negotiations in Doha. In October the USA carried out air strikes against Taliban fighters in Helmand province, after a major offensive saw insurgents take over government military bases in the region and close in on the provincial capital of Lashkar Gah. The USA renewed diplomatic efforts with the Taliban to try to de-escalate the fighting.[29]

---

[22] 'Afghanistan: Rival leaders Ghani and Abdullah in power-sharing deal', BBC News, 17 May 2020.

[23] Dwyer, C., '3-day truce, prisoner release deal inspire hopes for reconciliation in Afghanistan', NPR, 25 May 2020; and Salizi, H., 'Afghanistan begins freeing 900 Taliban prisoners, urges truce extension', Reuters, 26 May 2020.

[24] 'Afghanistan reports "deadliest" week in its 19 years of conflict', France 24, 23 June 2020.

[25] For details on civilian casualties see UNAMA, 'Afghanistan: Protection of civilians in armed conflict, Midyear report: 1 January–30 June 2020', July 2020.

[26] 'Loya Jirga approves release of 400 Taliban prisoners', Tolo News, 9 Aug. 2020; and Shalizi, H. and Sediqi, A. Q., 'Afghan officials primed for talks with Taliban after deal on prisoners: Sources', Reuters, 3 Sep. 2020.

[27] Mashal, M., 'At Afghan peace talks, hoping to end their fathers' war', New York Times, 5 Oct. 2020. For an assessment of potential Taliban negotiating perspectives see International Crisis Group, *Taking Stock of the Taliban's Perspectives on Peace*, Asia Report no. 311 (International Crisis Group: Brussels, 11 Aug. 2020).

[28] Sediqi, A. Q. and Shalizi, H., 'Afghan peace negotiators far apart on basic issues such as ceasefire, women's rights', Reuters, 21 Sep. 2020; and 'When will the real talks begin? As America draws down its troops, Afghans clear their throats', *The Economist*, 19 Sep. 2020.

[29] 'US air strikes target Taliban fighters advancing on key Afghan city', Reuters, 12 Oct. 2020.

With the peace negotiations stalled and the Taliban increasing attacks near important cities such as Kandahar, in mid November it was reported that the USA was preparing to withdraw troops from Afghanistan (as well as Iraq and Somalia). Under a draft order of the US Department of Defense, the USA would roughly halve the number of soldiers in Afghanistan—from 4500 to 2500—by January 2021.[30] While the Taliban welcomed the US announcement, some NATO allies were concerned that the reductions could undermine the Afghan Government and destabilize the peace talks.[31]

At an international donor conference in Geneva, Switzerland, on 23–24 November 2020 the international community agreed to support Afghanistan with a total of around $12 billion over the next four years. In a new framework agreement for the partnership, the Afghan Government committed to respect democracy, the rule of law, human rights and gender equality, and to take concrete steps against rampant corruption. The conference participants also adopted a communiqué calling for an immediate, permanent and comprehensive ceasefire.[32]

On 2 December 2020 the Afghan Government and the Taliban reached a preliminary agreement—their first written agreement during 19 years of war—to move forward with more detailed negotiations and peace talks, including discussions of a ceasefire.[33] However, by the end of the year the talks had faltered and violence was rising again, with the Taliban seemingly abandoning any initial restraint. An increasing number of casualties appeared to be the result of targeted assassinations.[34]

Conclusions

With neither the Afghan Government nor the Taliban showing much inclination for compromise, the important advances in peace talks made during 2020 remained fragile and could be reversed during 2021. With a conditional deadline for complete US and NATO military withdrawal by May 2021, uncertainty over the incoming Biden administration's approach and the Taliban apparently in the ascendancy, the future of the peace process remained uncertain.[35]

---

[30] Gibbons-Neff, T., Rahim, N. and Faizi, F., 'US troops are packing up, ready or not', *New York Times*, 17 Nov. 2020.

[31] 'Taliban hails US troop drawdown from Afghanistan as "good step"', France 24, 18 Nov. 2020; and 'Guns and poses: As America pulls out of Afghanistan the Taliban fights on', *The Economist*, 18 Nov. 2020.

[32] 'Communiqué', 2020 Afghanistan Conference on Peace Prosperity and Self-Reliance, Geneva, 24 Nov. 2020; 'Afghanistan conference draws donor pledges and calls for lasting ceasefire', UN News, 24 Nov. 2020; and 'Strong support for Afghanistan at the 2020 Afghanistan conference', UNAMA, 24 Nov. 2020.

[33] 'Afghan gov't, Taliban announce breakthrough deal in peace talks', Al Jazeera, 2 Dec. 2020.

[34] Graham-Harrison, E., 'Gunmen shoot dead Afghan journalist and her driver', *The Guardian*, 10 Dec. 2020; and Glinski, S., 'Taliban denies targeting media as 50th journalist dies in Afghanistan', *The Guardian*, 3 Dec. 2020.

[35] International Crisis Group, 'What future for Afghan peace talks under a Biden administration?', Asia Briefing no. 165, 13 Jan. 2021.

Figure 4.1. The disputed territory in Kashmir

Notes: The boundaries, names and designations used here do not imply any endorsement or acceptance by SIPRI of claims or stances in disputes over specific territories. *Aksai Chin:* Both India and China claim the Aksai Chin plateau, which has been administered by China since the 1962 Indo-China War. India considers it part of Ladakh; China considers the plateau a part of its Xinjiang province and Tibet. *Azad Kashmir and Jammu and Kashmir:* These regions are considered to be part of Kashmir by all countries involved. *Gilgit Baltistan:* Pakistan does not consider this region to be part of Kashmir, but India does. *Ladakh:* India does not consider this to be part of Kashmir but Pakistan does. *Shaksgam Valley:* Originally administered by Pakistan, until Pakistan relinquished its claim over to China in 1963. *Siachin Glacier:* India controls two-thirds of this glacier, but both India and Pakistan maintain a military presence.

Source: Ethirajan, A. and Pandey, V., 'China–India border: Why tensions are rising between the neighbours', BBC News, 30 May 2020.

Territorial disputes in Kashmir between China, India and Pakistan

The Kashmir region of some 18 million people has been the subject of a dispute since the independence of British India and the creation of India and Pakistan in 1947 (see figure 4.1). Kashmir is mainly divided between India and Pakistan, but claimed by both in full. India administers the area south of the line of control (LOC), which includes Jammu, Ladakh and the Kashmir Valley. Pakistan administers north-western Kashmir (comprising Gilgit-Baltistan and Azad Kashmir), while China controls a small part of the region (the Shaksgam Valley and Aksai Chin).

The principal conflict has been between India and Pakistan, which have fought three of their four wars over Kashmir (1947–48, 1965 and 1999)—and the other one over Bangladeshi independence (1971)—and have been involved in numerous armed clashes and military stand-offs. In addition to national and territorial contestations, the conflict involves various political demands by religious, linguistic, regional and ethnic groups in both parts of divided Kashmir. There have also been many talks and confidence-building measures over the years that sought to improve the relationship, but no current peace process.[36] There are no accurate cumulative casualty statistics for the conflict. In 2008 the Indian Government stated the death toll since the start of the current phase of the conflict in the late 1980s was over 47 000, while the South Asian Terrorism Portal estimates over 45 000 fatalities from 'terrorist violence' during 1988–2019.[37]

Tensions between India and Pakistan surged again in 2019, especially as a result of the military confrontation across the de facto border in Kashmir in February 2019. In August 2019 the Indian Government dissolved the state of Jammu and Kashmir and formed two union territories ruled by the Indian home ministry: Jammu and Kashmir, and Ladakh. China and Pakistan strongly criticized this move.[38] Early in 2020 (as part of the August 2019 reforms) the Indian Government passed a new residency law, allowing Indian citizens from outside the region who had worked, served or studied in Kashmir for 7–10 years to become permanent residents for the first time. This and other reforms, acts of political repression and harsh counter-insurgency measures appear likely to fuel further militancy.[39]

A further redrawing of the maps in Kashmir by Pakistan and China in the second half of 2020 indicated a new tense phase in the conflict.[40] On 4 August 2020 Pakistan published a new map showing all of Kashmir as part of Pakistan—restricting the disputed territory only to the areas that are 'illegally occupied' by India. In November 2020 Pakistan announced plans to formally integrate the Gilgit-Baltistan region into Pakistan.[41] During the

---

[36] On the history and characteristics of the conflict see e.g. Behera, N. C., 'The Kashmir conflict: Multiple fault lines', *Journal of Asian Security and International Affairs*, vol. 3, no. 1 (2016), pp. 41–63; and Zutshi, C. (ed.), *Kashmir: History, Politics, Representation* (Cambridge University Press: Cambridge, 2017).

[37] 'India revises Kashmir death toll to 47,000', *Hindustan Times*, 21 Nov. 2008; and 'Fatalities in terrorist violence 1988–2019', South Asia Terrorism Portal, [n.d.].

[38] For developments in 2019 see Smith, D., 'Flashpoints', *SIPRI Yearbook 2020*, pp. 8–10; and *SIPRI Yearbook 2020* (note 10), pp. 95–96.

[39] International Crisis Group, *Raising the Stakes in Jammu and Kashmir*, Asia Report no. 310 (International Crisis Group: Brussels, 5 Aug. 2020); and Bhalla, A., 'Kashmir: Big spike in local terror recruitment amid lockdown even as forces killed top commanders', *India Today*, 8 June 2020. On the origins of the militancy in Kashmir see Mehdi, S. E., 'Serving the militant's cause: The role of Indo-Pak state policies in sustaining militancy in Kashmir', *Journal of Asian Security and International Affairs*, vol. 7, no. 2 (2020), pp. 244–55.

[40] Wagner, C. and Stanzel, A., 'Redrawing the maps in Kashmir', SWP Comment no. 52, Nov. 2020.

[41] 'Pakistan affirms claim to IHK with new map', *Dawn*, 5 Aug. 2020; and Farooq, U., 'Pakistani PM says he will upgrade status of part of Kashmir, angering India', Reuters, 1 Nov. 2020.

border conflict with India (see below) the Chinese Government changed the territorial status quo when it declared in September 2020 that it would revert again to the Line of Actual Control (LAC) of 1959.[42]

The Indian–Pakistani conflict

While the situation in 2020 largely reverted to the status quo of relatively low levels of armed violence between India and Pakistan—consisting of: (*a*) regular exchanges of artillery fire and other clashes between Indian and Pakistani forces along the LOC, (*b*) cross-border and cross-LOC infiltration and attacks by militants and (*c*) Indian counter-insurgency operations inside Jammu and Kashmir—the number of these incidents appeared to be rising.[43] There were 431 battle-related fatalities in Jammu and Kashmir in 2020 (compared to 280 in 2019).[44] A new armed group—The Resistance Front—claimed several high-profile attacks on security personnel in April–May 2020.[45] In May Indian Government forces killed one of the leading figures in the region's largest rebel group, Hizbul Mujahideen, which is based in Pakistan-controlled Azad Kashmir.[46] Tensions escalated again in November with several deadly clashes along the LOC.[47]

The Chinese–Indian conflict

In June 2020, for the first time in over five decades, the border tensions between China and India in the disputed eastern Ladakh region of Kashmir turned deadly.[48] Several rounds of talks in the last three decades have failed to resolve the boundary disputes. Both sides have been building infrastructure to support military deployments along the border for about two decades, with Chinese infrastructure projects generally the more advanced. Alleged incursions along this disputed and informal border known as the LAC are common during the summer months, when both sides intensify patrols, but disputes are usually resolved locally through long-standing joint border protocols.[49]

---

[42] Wagner and Stanzel (note 40); and Patranobis, S., 'China makes it official, wants to revert to 1959 LAC India has rejected many times', *ThePrint*, 29 Sep. 2020.

[43] ACLED, *Ten Conflicts to Worry About in 2021* (ACLED: Feb. 2021), pp. 7–10; and Shakil, S., '28 encounter killings in security operations: April most successful month for forces in Kashmir', *Indian Express*, 7 May 2020.

[44] ACLED, 'Data export tool', accessed 24 Jan. 2021.

[45] 'The Resistance Front: New terrorist group in Jammu and Kashmir amplifies attacks on social media', Atlantic Council, 16 July 2020.

[46] AP News, 'Top rebel commander killed by Indian forces in Kashmir', *The Guardian*, 6 May 2020.

[47] International Crisis Group, Conflict tracker, Nov. 2020.

[48] On the China–India rivalry see Paul, V. (ed.), *The China-India Rivalry in the Globalization Era* (Georgetown University Press: Washington, DC, 2018).

[49] Singh, S., 'Line of actual control (LAC): Where it is located, and where India and China differ', *Indian Express*, 1 June 2020.

During May 2020 military stand-offs were being reported in at least three locations—the Galwan Valley, Hot Springs and Pangong Lake (see figure 4.1)—with military reinforcements made by both sides.[50] India accused China of preventing Indian patrols from accessing those contested areas where both sides had previously patrolled. According to some Indian analysts changes to the LAC resulted in Chinese territorial gains of more than 1000 square kilometres, although no additional territorial losses were officially acknowledged by the Indian Government.[51] While attempting to de-escalate the situation, a gunless but brutal confrontation—troops deployed in this sensitive border area follow long-standing protocols that prohibit the use of firearms—in the Galwan Valley on 15 June 2020 resulted in the deaths of at least 20 Indian soldiers and an unknown number of Chinese soldiers (although China later acknowledged that four of its soldiers died), with many others likely injured on both sides.[52]

Drivers for this escalation are contested but are mainly related to domestic and bilateral dynamics on both sides, including recent infrastructure projects.[53] Several rounds of high-level meetings between Chinese and Indian military commanders during June–August and a meeting of defence ministers on 4 September failed to resolve the situation. On 7 September gunshots were fired along the LAC for the first time in 45 years. Both sides blamed each other for the incident.[54] During talks between the countries' foreign ministers in Moscow on 10 September a joint statement called for dialogue and disengagement to ease tensions. 'The two sides also agreed to continue to have dialogue and communication through the Special Representative mechanism on the India-China boundary question', the

[50] Boyd, H. and Nouwens, M., 'Understanding the military build-up on the China-India border', International Institute for Strategic Studies, 18 June 2020; and Topychkanov, P., 'New trends and developments in border tensions between China and India', SIPRI WritePeace Blog, 29 June 2020.

[51] Singh, S., 'What Rajnath left out: PLA blocks access to 900 sq km of Indian territory in Depsang', The Wire, 17 Sep. 2020; Menon, S., 'What China hopes to gain from the standoff with India', The Wire, 3 Dec. 2020; and ANI News, 'China disrupted traditional patrolling pattern of Indian troops in Galwan Valley causing face-off conditions', 15 Sep. 2020.

[52] Singh, S., 'Explained: If soldiers on LAC were carrying arms, why did they not open fire?', Indian Express, 20 June 2020; Griffiths, J. et al., 'Twenty Indian soldiers dead after clash with China along disputed border', CNN, 17 June 2020; Myers, S. L., 'China acknowledges 4 deaths in last year's border clash with India', New York Times, 19 Feb. 2021; and Safi, M., Ellis-Petersen, H. and Davidson, H., 'Soldiers fell to their deaths as India and China's troops fought with rocks', The Guardian, 17 June 2020. On media coverage of the clashes in China and India see Altieri, R., Kannan, V. and Maheshwari, L., 'The days after: A retrospective on Chinese and Indian media coverage of the June 16 border conflict', Lawfare, 8 July 2020. With confirmed fatalities less than 25 it is not treated as an armed conflict within this volume. See definitions in chapter 2, section I, of this volume.

[53] Ethirajan, A. and Pandey, V., 'China–India border: Why tensions are rising between the neighbours', BBC News, 30 May 2020; 'Galwan Valley: Satellite images "show China structures" on India border', BBC News, 25 June 2020; and Topychkanov (note 50).

[54] 'India and China exchange their first border gunfire in 45 years', The Economist, 8 Sep. 2020; and Kaushik, K., 'First time in 45 years, shots fired along LAC as troops foil China's bid to take a key height', Indian Express, 9 Sep. 2020.

statement said.[55] A joint working group to address this boundary question was established in 1989, and by 2019 the special representatives had met 22 times. By mid November 2020 the two sides were discussing a staggered military disengagement from some of the locations.[56]

However, with tensions persisting at the end of 2020, there were fears that the military stand-off on the border could become a permanent feature in the strategic competition between these two nuclear-armed states.[57] Chinese dam projects in Tibet added to these tensions and threatened India's water security.[58] There was also a geostrategic dimension with India's support for the USA being considered as part of wider Chinese–US tensions (see section I).[59]

Conclusions

In 2020 Pakistan and China redrew their maps on Kashmir in reaction to India's move in August 2019, thereby transforming Kashmir into a territorial conflict between three nuclear-armed states. While this configuration was partly there before 2020 it was relatively muted because of the recognized status quo on the western part of the LAC that had existed since the 1990s. With the breakdown of the fragile consensus between China and India the conflict dynamic in Kashmir became even more unpredictable.

India's internal armed conflicts and intercommunal tensions

In addition to the armed conflict zone in Kashmir, in 2020 there was an ongoing non-international armed conflict in India between the Indian Government and the Naxalites (Maoist rebels in rural areas of central and eastern India). The Maoist insurgency started in 1967 and entered its current phase in 2004.[60] On 5 April 2020 the Communist Party of India (Maoist) offered a ceasefire to enable community health workers to address the spread of Covid-19.[61] The Indian Government, which was given five days to respond

---

[55] Government of India, Ministry of External Affairs, 'Joint press statement—Meeting of external affairs minister and the foreign minister of China', 10 Sep. 2020.

[56] 'India, China close in on plan to end months of border standoff', Al Jazeera, 13 Nov. 2020; and Rajagopalan, R. P., 'India-China talks on the standoff: Cautious optimism?', The Diplomat, 12 Nov. 2020.

[57] Purohit, K., 'As India-China border stand-off endures, a fear: Ladakh is the new Kashmir', *South China Morning Post*, 12 Oct. 2020.

[58] Chen, F., 'China's dam plan in Tibet worries downstream India', Asia Times, 1 Dec. 2020.

[59] Myers, S. L., 'China's military provokes its neighbours but the message is for the United States', *New York Times*, 26 June 2020.

[60] On the history of the conflict see Sahoo, N., 'Half a century of India's Maoist insurgency: An appraisal of state response', Observer Research Foundation, Occasional Paper no. 198, June 2019.

[61] Chatterjee, M., 'Days after killing 17 troopers, Maoists offer Covid ceasefire', *Times of India*, 7 Apr. 2020.

to the offer, ignored it and thereafter the levels of activity by the Naxalites appeared to return to normal pre-ceasefire levels.[62]

There were various low-level insurgencies in the north-east of India in 2020, but attacks by insurgent groups were rare. Even the most violent insurgency in Nagaland appeared to be close to a resolution.[63] Peace talks were initiated in 1997 between the Indian Government and the National Socialist Council of Nagaland-Isak-Muivah (NSCN-IM), the main separatist group in Nagaland, and the Naga National Political Groups (NNPGs). A framework agreement was reached in 2015. Talks continued in 2020 and by early October the Indian Government was reported to be close to signing a peace accord with the NNPGs and several civil society organizations, but not the NSCM-IM and several other stakeholders. Two symbolic issues continued to divide the NSCM-IM and the Indian Government: a separate flag and a separate constitution for the Nagas.[64] The situation remained deadlocked at the end of the year.[65]

Finally, intercommunal (mainly Hindu–Muslim) tensions remained a key security issue in India in 2020. Hindu–Muslim communal violence continued following the introduction of a controversial citizenship law in December 2019, which has been criticized for being discriminatory towards Muslims and undermining India's secularism.[66] In India's capital New Delhi in February 2020, for example, intercommunal violence left 53 people dead and hundreds injured.[67] Religious polarization was further heightened in April–May 2020 when Covid-19-related accusations (mainly directed at the Muslim community) fuelled intercommunal attacks, although these were partly tempered by a strict national lockdown to contain the spread of the disease.[68] Overall, conflict-related fatalities in India in 2020 were lower than in 2019 (see table 4.3).

[62] Bhatia, B., 'For red corridor to win Covid war, truce a must', *Deccan Chronicle*, 19 Apr. 2020; and Miller, A., 'Call unanswered: A review of responses to the UN appeal for a global ceasefire', ACLED, 13 May 2020.

[63] 'Insurgency on decline in north east, tri-junction between Assam, Arunachal and north Nagaland arc of violence: Eastern army commander', First Post, 14 Feb. 2020.

[64] Anand, M., 'Naga accord "draft" finalised, demand for separate flag rejected', *Deccan Chronicle*, 7 Oct. 2020; and Chakma, A., 'What is getting in the way of the 3rd round of Indo-Naga peace talks?', *The Diplomat*, 1 Oct. 2020.

[65] Nathanael, M. P., 'The Nagaland deadlock', *Indian Express*, 30 Dec. 2020.

[66] Ellis-Petersen, H., 'Violent clashes continue in India over new citizenship bill', *The Guardian*, 13 Dec. 2019; and Vaid, D., 'One year of India's Citizenship Amendment Act', Deutsche Welle, 11 Dec. 2020.

[67] Ellis-Petersen, H., 'Delhi protests: Death toll climbs amid worst religious violence for decades', *The Guardian*, 26 Feb. 2020; and 'Situation report—3: Delhi violence', Sphere India, 11 Mar. 2020.

[68] Ellis-Petersen, H. and Rahman, S. A., 'How lives were destroyed under cover of lockdown in a small Indian town', *The Guardian*, 8 June 2020; and Saha, T., 'Telinipara riots of West Bengal: A story of human suffering', Times Now News, 14 May 2020.

Table 4.3. Estimated conflict-related fatalities in India, 2016–20

Event type	2016	2017	2018	2019	2020
Battles	1 007	830	1 203	571	658
Explosions/remote violence	69	64	148	114	15
Protests, riots and strategic developments	282	209	224	308	322
Violence against civilians	301	317	525	533	293
Total	1 659	1 420	2 100	1 526	1 288

Notes: The first available year for data on India in the Armed Conflict Location & Event Data Project (ACLED) database is 2016. For definitions of event types, see ACLED, 'ACLED definitions of political violence and protest', 11 Apr. 2019.

Source: ACLED, 'Data export tool', accessed 24 Jan. 2021.

Pakistan's internal armed conflicts and border conflict with Afghanistan

The Government of Pakistan is involved in low-level non-international armed conflicts with various armed groups acting throughout its territory, particularly Taliban-affiliated groups in the north-western Khyber Pakhtunkhwa province and Baloch separatist fighters in the south-western province of Balochistan. Overall battle-related fatalities and deaths in Pakistan have declined considerably since the 2013–15 period (see table 4.4).[69] The UN estimates that more than 6000 Pakistani insurgents are based in Afghanistan, with most belonging to the Pakistan Taliban group, Tehreek-e-Taliban.[70]

The current phase of the Baloch insurgency started in 2003, but it has been at a relatively low level since 2012. The most prominent Baloch nationalist group—the Baloch Liberation Army—attempted an attack on the Pakistan stock exchange building in Karachi in June 2020.[71] There were also several attacks against Pakistani soldiers within Balochistan, where there are a number of high-profile China–Pakistan economic corridor projects.[72] Human rights violations by state security forces in Balochistan also continued to be documented.[73]

---

[69] Also see Pak Institute for Peace Studies, 'Pakistan security report 2020', *Conflict and Peace Studies*, vol. 13, no. 1 (Jan.–June 2021).

[70] United Nations, Security Council, 'Twenty-sixth report of the Analytical Support and Sanctions Monitoring Team submitted pursuant to Resolution 2368 (2017) concerning ISIL (Da'esh), Al-Qaida and associated individuals and entities', S/2020/717, 23 July 2020.

[71] Shah, S., 'Gunmen attack Pakistan stock exchange, citing its links to China', *Wall Street Journal*, 29 June 2020.

[72] 'Pakistan: 7 troops killed in Balochistan insurgent attack', Deutsche Welle, 27 Dec. 2020.

[73] Mir, N. A., 'Abysmal human rights situation in Balochistan', Manohar Parrikar Institute for Defence Studies and Analyses Comment, 30 May 2020.

Table 4.4. Estimated conflict-related fatalities in Pakistan, 2013–20

Event type	2013	2014	2015	2016	2017	2018	2019	2020
Battles	1 532	1 860	1 976	1 173	891	479	630	519
Explosions/remote violence	2 203	2 826	1 956	815	668	410	185	161
Protests, riots and strategic developments	72	53	75	40	16	44	14	39
Violence against civilians	667	639	541	188	150	293	328	94
Total	**4 474**	**5 378**	**4 548**	**2 216**	**1 725**	**1 226**	**1 157**	**813**

Note: For definitions of event types, see Armed Conflict Location & Event Data Project (ACLED), 'ACLED definitions of political violence and protest', 11 Apr. 2019.

Source: ACLED, 'Data export tool', accessed 24 Jan. 2021.

In July the most intense border clashes between Afghan and Pakistani forces in recent years killed at least 23 civilians on the Afghan side in two separate incidents. In a second incident on 30 July 2020 Pakistani forces reportedly fired heavy artillery into civilian areas after protests by communities on both sides, who were demanding the reopening of a border crossing that Pakistan had closed to try to limit the spread of Covid-19.[74]

[74] Shah, T. and Mashal, M., 'Border clashes with Pakistan leaves 15 Afghan civilians dead, officials say', *New York Times*, 31 July 2020. On the impact of Covid-19 in Pakistan see International Crisis Group, 'Pakistan Covid-19 crisis', Asia Briefing no. 162, 7 Aug. 2020.

III. Armed conflict and peace processes in South East Asia

IAN DAVIS

This section focuses on the low-intensity subnational armed conflicts (i.e. less than 1000 deaths) in Indonesia, Myanmar, the Philippines and Thailand. In the Philippines, when fatalities from the 'war on drugs' are added to those from the subnational armed conflict, the number of conflict-related deaths rises to over 1400. Some of Asia's most organized Islamist extremist groups are active in South East Asia, most notably in Indonesia, Malaysia and the Philippines.[1] The many coastal communities in the island-studded region are highly vulnerable to the growing threats from climate change, with sea-level rises predicted to displace millions of people.[2]

Armed conflict in Indonesia

Indonesia faces demands for independence in the two provinces on the island of Papua, where there has been a low-level separatist insurgency since the 1960s.[3] Indonesia has also become one of the main focal points of the Islamic State in South East Asia.[4] However, in 2020 it was the long-running insurgency in Papua that was the focus of most of the combat-related armed violence in the country. Although the Free Papua Movement (Organisasi Papua Merdeka, OPM) offered the Indonesian Government a ceasefire in April 2020 in an effort to contain the spread of Covid-19, it was conditional on the government withdrawing some police and troops from Papua.[5] Although there did not appear to be a government response, there was a pause in the activity of the West Papua National Liberation Army (the armed wing of the OPM) following the ceasefire announcement.[6] At the end of November the Office of the United Nations High Commissioner for Human Rights

---

[1] United Nations, Security Council, 'Twenty-sixth report of the Analytical Support and Sanctions Monitoring Team submitted pursuant to resolution 2368 (2017) concerning ISIL (Da'esh), Al-Qaida and associated individuals and entities', S/2020/717, 23 July 2020, pp. 16–17.

[2] Nordqvist, P. and Krampe, F., 'Climate change and violent conflict: Sparse evidence from South Asia and South East Asia', SIPRI Insights on Peace and Security no. 2018/4, Sep. 2018.

[3] On the origins and recent developments in the conflict see Blades, J., 'West Papua: The issue that won't go away for the Melanesia', Lowy Institute, 1 May 2020; and Sara, S., Worthington, A. and Mambor, V., 'The battle for West Papuan independence from Indonesia has intensified with deadly results', ABC News, 12 May 2020.

[4] United Nations, S/2020/717 (note 1). On Indonesia's counterterrorism policy see Haripin, M., Anindya, C. R. and Priamarizki, A., 'The politics of counter-terrorism in post-authoritarian states: Indonesia's experience, 1998–2018', Defense & Security Analysis, vol. 36, no. 3 (2020), pp. 275–99.

[5] Nirmala, R., 'Indonesian forces kill 2 suspected Papuan rebels', Benar News, 10 Apr. 2020; and Pacific Media Watch, 'OPM proposes West Papua ceasefire to help contain spread of Covid-19', Asia Pacific Report, 11 Apr. 2020.

[6] Miller, A., 'Call unanswered: A review of responses to the UN appeal for a global ceasefire', Armed Conflict Location & Event Data Project (ACLED), 13 May 2020.

warned of escalating violence in the provinces of Papua and West Papua.[7] According to the Armed Conflict Location & Event Data Project (ACLED), there were 117 conflict-related deaths in Indonesia in 2020 (down from 219 in 2019), with 57 of these being related to armed conflict (battles or explosions/remote violence).[8]

Armed conflict in Myanmar

Insurgencies have persisted for much of the past seven decades in Myanmar's Chin, Kachin, Kayin, Mon, Rakhine and Shan states. Various armed insurgent groups have fought the country's armed forces, known as the Tatmadaw, over political control of territory, ethnic minority rights and access to natural resources. All of these decades-old armed conflicts are now structured along complex ethnic and/or religious lines and include about 20 ethnic armed groups and hundreds of armed militias mainly located in the country's border regions.[9]

The armed conflict between government forces and the ethnic Rakhine Arakan Army in western Myanmar was the most serious by far in 2020. At the end of April 2020 the UN special rapporteur on human rights in Myanmar warned of possible war crimes in Chin and Rakhine states, where armed clashes between the Arakan Army and the Tatmadaw escalated, with increasing numbers of civilian casualties.[10] The upsurge in fighting in parts of Rakhine state led to further population displacement (at least 60 000 people by early May 2020) and reduced the already low prospects of voluntary repatriation of the Rohingya from camps in Bangladesh.[11]

A series of unilateral ceasefires in recent years has done little to reduce or stop the fighting. On the same day as the UN appeal on 23 March 2020 for a global Covid-19 ceasefire, the Myanmar Government designated the Arakan Army as a terrorist group and began a crackdown on media reporting of the

[7] Office of the United Nations High Commissioner for Human Rights (OHCHR), 'Comment by UN Human Rights Office spokesperson Ravina Shamdasani on Papua and West Papua, Indonesia', 30 Nov. 2020.

[8] ACLED, 'Data export tool', accessed 24 Jan. 2021.

[9] International Crisis Group, *Identity Crisis: Ethnicity and Conflict in Myanmar*, Asia Report no. 312 (International Crisis Group: Brussels, 28 Aug. 2020). On the rise of Buddhist religious extremism see Subedi, D. B. and Garnett, J., 'De-mystifying Buddhist religious extremism in Myanmar: Confrontation and contestation around religion, development and state-building', *Conflict, Security & Development*, vol. 20, no. 2 (2020), pp. 223–46.

[10] OHCHR, 'Myanmar: "Possible war crimes and crimes against humanity ongoing in Rakhine and Chin states"—UN special rapporteur Yanghee Lee', 29 Apr. 2020; Lian, S. S., 'In southern Chin state, civilians fear bombs more than Covid-19', *Frontier Myanmar*, 17 Apr. 2020; ACLED, 'Coronavirus cover: Myanmar civilians under fire', 6 May 2020; and International Crisis Group, *An Avoidable War: Politics and Armed Conflict in Myanmar's Rakhine State*, Asia Report no. 307 (International Crisis Group: Brussels, 9 June 2020).

[11] International Crisis Group, 'Conflict, health cooperation and Covid-19 in Myanmar', Asia Briefing no. 161, 19 May 2020, p. 3.

Table 4.5. Estimated conflict-related fatalities in Myanmar, 2013–20

Event type	2013	2014	2015	2016	2017	2018	2019	2020
Battles	300	358	1 078	155	196	118	1 248	380
Explosions/remote violence	45	53	27	35	30	31	85	128
Protests, riots and strategic developments	91	9	0	0	9	9	30	8
Violence against civilians	29	84	162	221	1 018	67	132	138
Total	**465**	**504**	**1 267**	**411**	**1 253**	**225**	**1 495**	**654**

Note: For definitions of event types, see Armed Conflict Location & Event Data Project (ACLED), 'ACLED definitions of political violence and protest', 11 Apr. 2019.

Source: ACLED, 'Data export tool', accessed 24 Jan. 2021.

conflict.[12] On 1 April (and again on 3 May) members of three ethnic armed groups known collectively as the Three Brotherhood Alliance—the Arakan Army, the Myanmar National Democratic Alliance Army and the Ta'ang National Liberation Army—extended their own unilateral ceasefire, framing it as a response to the pandemic.[13] Other armed groups in the country also called on the Tatmadaw to announce a ceasefire, which it did from 10 May to 31 August, but it excluded the conflict with the Arakan Army.[14] However a Japanese-brokered ceasefire between the Arakan Army and Myanmar's military in November (discussed below) enabled a resumption of dialogue. According to ACLED, conflict-related deaths in Myanmar declined by 56 per cent in 2020 compared to 2019 (see table 4.5).[15]

The refugee crisis

State-backed systematic persecution in 2017 forcibly displaced more than 700 000 Rohingya people—members of a predominantly Sunni Muslim ethnic group—from Rakhine state.[16] Continuing persecution and the armed conflict with the Arakan Army led to further displacement. At the beginning of 2020 more than 850 000 Rohingya remained in refugee camps in Cox's Bazar in southern Bangladesh—the largest and densest refugee settle-

[12] Lintner, B., 'Covid-19 restores Myanmar military's lost powers', Asia Times, 2 Apr. 2020.

[13] Three Brotherhood Alliance, 'Emergency press release of the Three Brotherhood Alliance in the time of the spread of Covid-19', 1 Apr. 2020.

[14] 'Tatmadaw releases statement on ceasefire and eternal peace', Global New Light of Myanmar, 9 May 2020; and Weng, L., 'Myanmar rebel coalition calls for military to extend ceasefire to Rakhine', The Irrawaddy, 11 May 2020.

[15] On the methodological challenges for the recording of political violence amidst the complexity of the disorder in Myanmar see ACLED, 'ACLED methodology and coding decisions around political violence in Myanmar', Nov. 2019.

[16] On the Rohingya crisis in 2017 see Davis, I., Ghiasy, R. and Su, F., 'Armed conflict in Asia and Oceania', *SIPRI Yearbook 2018*, pp. 49–52. Also see Ahmed, I., 'Special issue on the Rohingya crisis: From the guest editor's desk', *Asian Journal of Comparative Politics*, vol. 5, no. 2 (2020), pp. 85–88; and Nishikawa, Y., 'The reality of protecting the Rohingya: An inherent limitation of the responsibility to protect', *Asian Security*, vol. 16, no. 1 (2020), pp. 90–106.

ment in the world.[17] With no guarantees of citizenship and security if the Rohingya were to return to Myanmar, repatriation plans have been delayed indefinitely.[18] Moreover, conditions in the camps have deteriorated, forcing some Rohingya refugees to seek perilous trafficking routes in search of safer locations in the region. The situation worsened amid the Covid-19 pandemic, with countries such as Malaysia closing their borders to enforce lockdowns.[19] In December 2020 the Bangladeshi Government began transporting several hundred refugees from Cox's Bazar to Bhasan Char, an island in the Bay of Bengal.[20]

Accountability and justice for alleged atrocities committed against the Rohingya people and other ethnic minorities in Myanmar remained elusive in 2020, despite legal efforts pending at the International Criminal Court (ICC) and the International Court of Justice (ICJ).[21] The Government of Myanmar's own Independent Commission of Enquiry, established in August 2018 to investigate the Tatmadaw's conduct, dismissed allegations of genocide against the Rohingya—according to the executive summary of a report published on 21 January 2020.[22] Two days later the ICJ issued an injunction ordering Myanmar to take action to protect the approximately 500 000 Rohingya remaining in the country.[23] In September during video testimony to the ICC two Myanmar soldiers confessed to atrocities carried out against the Rohingya. This first confession of human rights abuses by members of Myanmar's military could prove significant in the ICC case against Myanmar's military leaders.[24]

[17] Ahmed, K., 'Stop ignoring us: Rohingya refugees demand role in running camps', *The Guardian*, 5 Feb. 2020.

[18] International Crisis Group, *A Sustainable Policy for Rohingya Refugees in Bangladesh*, Asia Report no. 303 (International Crisis Group: Brussels, 27 Dec. 2019).

[19] Paul, R. and Das, K. N., 'As other doors close, some Rohingya cling to hope of resettlement', Reuters, 21 Aug. 2020; Ahmed, K., 'Gang violence erupts in Bangladesh Rohingya camps forcing families to flee', *The Guardian*, 9 Oct. 2020; and Mallick, A. H., 'Rohingya refugee repatriation from Bangladesh: A far cry from reality', *Journal of Asian Security and International Affairs*, vol. 7, no. 2 (2020), pp. 202–26.

[20] Regan, H. and Wright, R., 'Fears of forced removals as Bangladesh moves hundreds of Rohingya refugees to remote island', CNN, 8 Dec. 2020; and Thoopkrajae, V., 'Bangladesh moves more Rohingyas to remote island despite rights concerns', *The Guardian*, 28 Dec. 2020.

[21] See Davis, I., 'Armed conflict and peace processes in South East Asia', *SIPRI Yearbook 2020*, pp. 102–104.

[22] Ratcliffe, R., 'Myanmar inquiry into treatment of Rohingya condemned as "cover-up"', *The Guardian*, 22 Jan. 2020; and Office of the President of Myanmar, 'Executive summary of Independent Commission of Enquiry-ICOE' final report', 21 Jan. 2020.

[23] Paddock, R. C., 'UN court order Myanmar to protect Rohingya Muslims', *New York Times*, 23 Jan. 2020.

[24] Beech, H., Nang, S. and Simons, M., '"Kill all you see": In a first, Myanmar soldiers tell of Rohingya slaughter', *New York Times*, 8 Sep. 2020.

The peace process

The Government of Myanmar has been attempting to push forward a complex peace process, the core of which is the 2015 Nationwide Ceasefire Agreement (NCA). The NCA includes a promise for political talks towards the creation of a federal union to guarantee future equality and autonomy for ethic nationalities.[25] China is a major stakeholder in the peace process, not least because of its economic and security interests. In January 2020 President Xi Jinping made a two-day visit to Myanmar, the first by a Chinese president in almost two decades, with the aim of deepening ties between the two countries.[26] The prominent role of the military in politics and government with a set proportion of representation continues to be a major obstacle to constitutional reform.

Eight armed groups signed the NCA in 2015 (and only two more smaller groups since then), leading to a complex, twin-track peace process: negotiations with NCA signatories and bilateral ceasefire discussions with non-signatories. Two further armed groups—the Karen National Union and the Restoration Council of Shan State—returned to the peace process in 2020. Formal meetings with all signatories were convened during the year, and a three-day peace conference took place in August.[27] However, overall the peace process with NCA signatories made little headway in 2020 due to a backdrop of continuing violence and the focus on the country's second general election since the end of full military rule.[28]

Elections and a ceasefire in Rakhine state

Aung San Suu Kyi's National League for Democracy (NLD) was returned to power for another five-year term after achieving a landslide victory in the November 2020 general election. However, voting was cancelled in several areas dominated by ethnic minorities (mainly Rakhine state and some parts of Shan state), ostensibly because of security concerns. This disenfranchised an estimated 1.5 million people (out of a total of about 38 million eligible to vote), in addition to about 1.1 million Rohingya who have long been denied

---

[25] On the history of the 2015 NCA see Bertrand, J., Pelletier, A. and Thawnghmung, A. M., 'First movers, democratization and unilateral concessions: Overcoming commitment problems and negotiating a "nationwide cease-fire" in Myanmar', *Asian Security*, vol. 16, no. 1 (2020), pp. 15–34. On the role of civil society and peace movements in Myanmar see Orjuela, C., 'Countering Buddhist radicalisation: Emerging peace movements in Myanmar and Sri Lanka', *Third World Quarterly*, vol. 41, no. 1 (2020), pp. 133–50.

[26] International Crisis Group, *Commerce and Conflict: Navigating Myanmar's China Relationship*, Asia Report no. 305 (International Crisis Group: Brussels, 30 Mar. 2020).

[27] Nyein, N., 'Myanmar peace conference ends with participants praising "meaningful" principles, post-election plan', The Irrawaddy, 21 Aug. 2020.

[28] International Crisis Group, *Rebooting Myanmar's Stalled Peace Process*, Asia Report no. 308 (International Crisis Group: Brussels, 19 June 2020); and 'Why the stalemate in Myanmar persists', *The Economist*, 18 Aug. 2020.

citizenship and voting rights.[29] However, four days after the election, Japan's special envoy to Myanmar, Yohei Sasakawa, brokered a diplomatic breakthrough, with the Arakan Army and the Tatmadaw agreeing to hold supplementary elections by late January 2021 in areas where they had been cancelled.[30] The agreement also marked the beginning of a de facto ceasefire between the two groups that was holding at the end of 2020.[31] Although the NLD government had still to approve the election, the agreement created a vital space for dialogue and the return of several thousand displaced people. But without reforms to address the discrimination and marginalization of ethnic minorities, in Rakhine state and more widely in Myanmar, the prospects for the peace process remained uncertain.

In addition, the military-backed Union Solidarity and Development Party claimed widespread fraud during the November elections and called for a rerun of the elections with military involvement.[32] The NLD rejected such claims; as a result, civil–military relations remained strained at the end of 2020.

Armed conflict in the Philippines

Two intrastate armed conflicts emerged in the Philippines in the late 1960s: one in the Muslim-majority areas of the Mindanao region of the southern Philippines and another involving the New People's Army (NPA) of the Communist Party of the Philippines.[33] However, as was the case in 2019, it was the war on drugs that appeared to produce the most fatalities during 2020.

The establishment in March 2019 of a new autonomous region—the Bangsamoro Autonomous Region—in the southern Philippines was a major step towards ending the almost 50-year Moro separatist conflict, although many challenges remained.[34] An 80-member Bangsamoro Transition Authority is now responsible for governing the region until 2022 when elections for a Bangsamoro parliament and government are due to take

[29] International Crisis Group, 'Majority rules in Myanmar's second democratic election', Asia Briefing no. 163, 22 Oct. 2020; Ratcliffe, R., 'Aung San Suu Kyi's party returns to power in Myanmar', *The Guardian*, 13 Nov. 2020; and Ratcliffe, R., 'Myanmar minorities, including Rohingya, excluded from voting in election', *The Guardian*, 6 Nov. 2020.

[30] 'Statement no. 41/2020', United League of Arakan/Arakan Army, 12 Nov. 2020; and 'Statement on ceasefire and eternal peace', Office of the Commander-in-Chief of the Defence Services, 12 Nov. 2020.

[31] International Crisis Group, 'From elections to ceasefire in Myanmar's Rakhine state', Asia Briefing no. 164, 23 Dec. 2020.

[32] Strangio, S., 'What's next for Myanmar's military proxy party?', The Diplomat, 26 Nov. 2020.

[33] For background on these two conflicts see Åkebo, M., 'Ceasefire rationales: A comparative study of ceasefires in the Moro and Communist conflicts in the Philippines', *International Peacekeeping*, vol. 28, no. 3 (2020).

[34] On key developments in 2019 see *SIPRI Yearbook 2020* (note 21), pp. 105–107.

Table 4.6. Estimated conflict-related fatalities in the Philippines, 2016–20

Event type	2016	2017	2018	2019	2020
Battles	856	1 955	589	514	537
Explosions/remote violence	67	64	37	48	34
Protests/riots and strategic developments	10	2	0	4	19
Violence against civilians	3 268	2 067	1 164	1 056	858
Total	**4 201**	**4 088**	**1 790**	**1 622**	**1 448**

Notes: The first available year for data on the Philippines in the Armed Conflict Location & Data Project (ACLED) database is 2016. For definitions of event types, see ACLED, 'ACLED definitions of political violence and protest', 11 Apr. 2019.

Source: ACLED, 'Data export tool', accessed 24 Jan. 2021.

place. Nonetheless, tensions in the region remained high, with clan-based politics a principal challenge to the ongoing peace process.[35] A small number of Islamist armed groups outside of the peace process with links to the Islamic State posed the greatest ongoing threat, to state security forces and as potential spoilers of the peace process within local communities.[36] For example, clashes in April and August 2020 in Sulu province in the southern Philippines highlighted the ongoing threat from militant networks.[37] While a large part of the instability in the region was due to the high number of non-state armed groups, there was also a blurring between some of those groups and state actors due to the activities of private militias and clan feuds.[38]

Equally elusive, despite sporadic peace talks, has been the goal of ending the 50-year-old insurgency by the NPA—the armed wing of the Communist Party of the Philippines and its political umbrella organization, the National Democratic Front.[39] Prior to the UN Covid-19 global ceasefire appeal, President Rodrigo Duterte announced a one-month unilateral ceasefire with the NPA on 18 March 2020, to allow government forces time to prioritize the fight against Covid-19. In turn, the NPA enacted its own ceasefire on 26 March.[40] However, the fighting continued despite the ceasefires.[41] On 16 April the NPA extended its ceasefire until the end of the month, but the government allowed its ceasefire to expire, citing continued attacks by the

[35] International Crisis Group, *Southern Philippines: Tackling Clan Politics in the Bangsamoro*, Asia Report no. 306 (International Crisis Group: Brussels, 14 Apr. 2020).
[36] International Crisis Group, *The Philippines: Militancy and the New Bangsamoro*, Asia Report no. 301 (International Crisis Group: Brussels, 27 June 2019), pp. 14–19.
[37] 'Philippine special forces kill Abu Sayyaf militants in Sulu gunbattle', Benar News, 6 Apr. 2020; and Engelbrecht, G., 'Violence in southern Philippines highlights resilience of militant networks', The Strategist, Australian Strategic Policy Institute (ASPI), 16 Sep. 2020.
[38] Herbert, S., 'Conflict analysis of the Philippines', K4D helpdesk service, British Department for International Development, 29 July 2019.
[39] For further details on the peace talks see 'Timeline: The peace talks between the government and the CPP-NPA-NDF, 1986–present', GMA News Online, 6 Dec. 2017.
[40] Central Committee, Communist Party of the Philippines, 'Ceasefire order: 00.00H of 26 March 2020 to 23.59H of 15 April 2020', 24 Mar. 2020; and Gomez, J., 'Philippines: Communist rebels declare ceasefire amid coronavirus pandemic', The Diplomat, 25 Mar. 2020.
[41] Miller, A., 'CDT spotlight: Philippines', ACLED, 2 Apr. 2020.

NPA.[42] By May organized violence between the NPA and government forces had surpassed pre-ceasefire levels, and at the end of 2020 there appeared to be no clear strategy for ending the insurgency.[43]

The war on drugs and contested casualty statistics

While the number of civilians killed in the Philippines in 2020 is uncertain and disputed, indications are that the government's war on drugs, initiated when President Duterte took office in 2016, continued to result in more deaths than the insurgencies (see table 4.6). Concerns about the war on drugs are part of wider concerns about repression of human rights and the targeting of political opponents, activists and journalists.[44] According to the government the estimated death toll in the anti-drugs campaign between 1 July 2016 and 30 September 2020 was 5903. The UN High Commissioner for Human Rights estimated the number of such fatalities at more than 8600, while domestic human rights groups suggest drug-war killings could be up to triple that number.[45] A new Anti-Terrorism Act introduced during the year was also expected to add to political repression and was heavily criticized by human rights groups.[46]

Armed conflict in Thailand

The decades-old non-international armed conflict in the south of Thailand between the military government and various secessionist groups continued in 2020.[47] More than 7000 people have been killed in the conflict since 2004, with little progress in Malaysian-brokered peace talks that started in 2015

---

[42] Gotinga, J. C., 'CPP-NPA extends ceasefire until April 30', Rappler, 16 Apr. 2020; and Hallare, K., 'Palace: Ceasefire extension with reds up to task force, Duterte', Inquirer, 19 Apr. 2020.

[43] Miller (note 6); and Broome, J., 'Inside Duterte's failed response to the Philippine's communist insurgency and the appeal of New People's Army among indigenous peoples', *Terrorism Monitor*, vol. 19, no. 1 (15 Jan. 2021).

[44] ASEAN Parliamentarians for Human Rights, *'In the Crosshairs of the Presidency': Attacks on Opposition Lawmakers in the Philippines* (ASEAN Parliamentarians for Human Rights: June 2019); 'Philippines downgraded as civic freedoms deteriorate', CIVICUS Monitor, 8 Dec. 2020; and Ratcliffe, R., 'Philippines: Mother and son murder by police officer ignites calls for change', *The Guardian*, 22 Dec. 2020.

[45] United Nations, General Assembly, 'Situation of human rights in the Philippines', Report of the United Nations High Commissioner for Human Rights, A/HRC/44/22, 29 June 2020; and Human Rights Watch, *World Report 2021: Events of 2020* (Human Rights Watch: New York, 2021), pp. 541–42. Also see Gallagher, A., Raffle, E. and Maulana, Z., 'Failing to fulfil the responsibility to protect: The war on drugs as crimes against humanity in the Philippines', *Pacific Review*, vol. 33, no. 2 (2020), pp. 247–77; and 'Rodrigo Duterte's lawless war on drugs is widely popular', *The Economist*, 20 Feb. 2020.

[46] Human Rights Watch, 'Philippines: New Anti-Terrorism Act endangers rights', 5 June 2020; and Amnesty International, 'Philippines: Dangerous anti-terror law yet another setback for human rights', 3 July 2020.

[47] See e.g. Quinley, C., 'In Thailand's deep south conflict, a "glimpse of hope", but no momentum to sustain a Covid-19 ceasefire', New Humanitarian, 3 Aug. 2020.

between the government and Mara Patani, an umbrella organization of Thai Malay secessionists groups.[48] Although the most significant insurgent group—the National Revolutionary Front (Barisan Revolusi Nasional, BRN)—had been boycotting the talks, in January 2020 the group met with government officials for the first time in a formal peace dialogue.[49] However, little progress was made in the talks, and on 17 March 2020 a bomb attack on a government meeting to discuss the Covid-19 pandemic was attributed to the BRN.[50] On 3 April the BRN released a statement saying it would cease all hostilities on humanitarian grounds as long as the group was not attacked by government forces, but the Thai military dismissed the offer as 'irrelevant'.[51] Nonetheless, a temporary pause in separatist violence did occur until a further armed clash took place on 30 April.[52] ACLED recorded 102 conflict-related deaths in Thailand in 2020 (down from 172 in 2019), with 60 of these being related to armed conflict (battles or explosions/remote violence).[53]

Abductions and attacks on Thai dissidents also occurred during 2020.[54] The largest pro-democracy demonstration since the 2014 military coup took place in Bangkok in August. The protests escalated in September and October, demanding constitutional and monarchical reform.[55] The introduction of emergency rules and police crackdowns on activists failed to halt the protests, while the emergence of royalist counterdemonstrations added to the risk of greater violence.[56]

[48] Wheeler, M., 'Behind the insurgent attack in southern Thailand', International Crisis Group Q&A, 8 Nov. 2019.

[49] International Crisis Group, *Southern Thailand's Peace Dialogue: Giving Substance to Form*, Asia Report no. 304 (International Crisis Group: Brussels, 21 Jan. 2020).

[50] AP News, 'Bombing of government office in southern Thailand injures 20', ABC News, 17 Mar. 2020.

[51] 'Declaration of BRN's Response to Covid-19', Ceasefires in a time of Covid-19, 3 Apr. 2020; Pathan, D., 'Southern Thai rebels score points with Covid-19 ceasefire', Benar News, 7 Apr. 2020; and Ahmad, M. and Phaicharoen, N., 'Covid-19 pandemic adds hardship to insurgency-hit Thai deep south', Benar News, 16 Apr. 2020.

[52] Ahmad, M., 'Thailand forces kill 3 suspected insurgents in Pattani', Benar News, 30 Apr. 2020.

[53] ACLED (note 8).

[54] Beech, H., 'Thai dissidents are disappearing, and families are fighting for answers', *New York Times*, 26 June 2020.

[55] Tanakasempipat, P. and Thepgumpanat, P., 'Thais defy protest ban in tens of thousands in Bangkok', Reuters, 15 Oct. 2020; and Wheeler, M., 'Behind Bangkok's wave of popular dissent', International Crisis Group, 16 Oct. 2020.

[56] AFP, 'Thai King declares "love" for all after months of pro-democracy protests', Barron's, 1 Nov. 2020; and Wheeler, M., 'Calls to curb the Crown's writ put Thailand on edge', International Crisis Group Commentary, 18 Dec. 2020.

5. Armed conflict and peace processes in Europe

Overview

Two armed conflicts were active in Europe in 2020: the interstate border conflict between Armenia and Azerbaijan for control of Nagorno-Karabakh, which escalated into high-intensity conflict during the year, and the ongoing low-intensity internationalized, subnational armed conflict in Ukraine. Elsewhere in Europe, tensions persisted in largely quiescent but unresolved conflicts in the post-Soviet space, the Western Balkans and Cyprus. There were also persistent tensions between Russia and large parts of the rest of Europe, as well as serious and complex security challenges in Europe's southern flank (see section I).

During the year, three further levels of complexity added to these existing tensions: (a) the Covid-19 pandemic, (b) political protests in Belarus following a disputed presidential election in August 2020 and (c) increased tensions in the eastern Mediterranean, centred on Greece and Turkey but also pulling in other states on both sides. On a more promising note, a modest Kosovo–Serbia détente was mediated by the United States in September. There were 18 multilateral peace operations active in Europe in 2020, the same as in the previous year.

The six weeks of fighting that broke out in 2020 between Armenia and Azerbaijan was the most serious period of fighting since the 1988–94 Nagorno-Karabakh War. Azerbaijan regained control of about one third of Nagorno-Karabakh and most of the adjacent territories (section II). There were an estimated 6700 military and civilian fatalities. A Russian-brokered ceasefire in November ended the fighting, and at the end of the year Russian peacekeepers were helping to maintain an uneasy truce. However, several key issues have still to be clarified, including the future status and governance of Nagorno-Karabakh, how to reconcile potentially competing claims of returning internally displaced persons, Turkey's role in the implementation of the agreement and the future of the Minsk Process of the Organization for Security and Co-operation in Europe.

Ukraine has been the focus of Europe's main territorial conflict since 2014 (section III). In 2020 it was again not possible to bridge the fundamental disagreements among the parties about the nature of the conflict and their involvement in it, as well as the implementation of existing agreements. However, a new ceasefire agreement in July 2020 led to much lower levels of violence and civilian casualties during the year, and the conflict appeared to be heading in the direction of becoming another of Europe's simmering conflicts.

IAN DAVIS

SIPRI Yearbook 2021: Armaments, Disarmament and International Security
www.sipriyearbook.org

I. Key general developments in the region

IAN DAVIS

There were three countries with active armed conflicts on their territory in Europe in 2020: the high-intensity interstate border conflict between Armenia and Azerbaijan for control of Nagorno-Karabakh (see section II) and the ongoing low-intensity internationalized, subnational armed conflict in Ukraine (see section III).[1] The Armenia–Azerbaijan conflict flared up again during the year and involved the most serious fighting since the ceasefire in 1994 that ended the 1988–94 Nagorno-Karabakh War. A Russian-brokered ceasefire, which entered into force on 10 November 2020, ended the 44-day armed conflict in 2020.

Although most of Europe has been relatively peaceful for at least the last two decades, three main areas of tension remain. First, there are persistent tensions between Russia and most of the rest of Europe—over issues as diverse as cyberattacks, Ukraine, the response to Covid-19 and the poisoning of Russian opposition leader Alexei Navalny.[2] These tensions have led to several highly militarized and contested security contexts, within Europe and also further afield (including confrontations in Africa, the Arctic and the Middle East and North Africa (MENA) region). There are competing explanations for this political–military climate of mistrust.[3]

Second, there are several long-standing simmering conflicts (that are mostly frozen but never resolved), especially in the post-Soviet space where five de facto statelets that claimed independence from successor states to the Soviet Union—Abkhazia, Nagorno-Karabakh, South Ossetia, Trans-Dniester and the portions of Ukraine's Donbas now controlled by Russian-backed separatists—remain unrecognized by most states around the world. Similar conditions apply in Cyprus and the Western Balkans.[4]

---

[1] For conflict definitions and typologies see chapter 2, section I, in this volume.

[2] See e.g. Sanger, D. E. and Santora, M., 'US and allies blame Russia for cyberattack on Republic of Georgia', *New York Times*, 20 Feb. 2020; Sanger, D. E. and Perlforth, N., 'Russian criminal group finds new target: Americans working from home', *New York Times*, 25 June 2020; Barnes, J. E. and Sanger, D. E., 'Russian intelligence agencies push disinformation on pandemic', *New York Times*, 28 July 2020; and 'Alexei Navalny blames Vladimir Putin for poisoning him', BBC News, 1 Oct. 2020. On the chemical nerve agent Novichok and its alleged use to poison Navalny see chapter 12, section IV, in this volume.

[3] On the deteriorating relationship between Russia and the USA/Europe see Smith, D., 'International tensions and shifting dynamics of power', *SIPRI Yearbook 2018*, pp. 11–12; Smith, D., 'International tensions and the dynamics of power', *SIPRI Yearbook 2019*, pp. 18–19; and Davis, I., 'Key general developments in the region', *SIPRI Yearbook 2020*, pp. 114–15. Also see Stent, A., *Putin's World: Russia against the West and with the Rest* (Twelve: New York, 2019); and Sakwa, R., 'Greater Russia: Is Moscow out to subvert the West?', *International Politics* (2020).

[4] On the role of identity politics and the dynamics of the Russian–Western geopolitical confrontation on the conflicts in the post-Soviet space see Kazantsev, A. A. et al., 'Russia's policy in the "frozen conflicts" of the post-Soviet space: From ethno-politics to geopolitics', *Caucasus Survey*, vol. 8, no. 2 (2020), pp. 142–62.

Third, there are serious and complex security challenges in Europe's southern neighbourhood and beyond.[5] Two issues at the forefront of European security thinking in recent years—irregular migration and terrorism—both have a strong southern dimension.[6] While Islamist attacks in Europe have been declining since 2017, a spate of attacks in Austria, France and Germany towards the end of the year led to fresh calls for stronger counterterrorism and counter-radicalization efforts.[7]

During the year, two further levels of complexity added to these existing tensions: (*a*) political protests in Belarus following a disputed presidential election in August 2020 and (*b*) increased tensions in the eastern Mediterranean that were centred on Greece and Turkey but also pulled in other states on both sides. On a more promising note, a modest Kosovo–Serbia détente was mediated by the United States in September. These developments are discussed briefly below.

Most of the conflicts in Europe are mediated by the Organization for Security and Co-operation in Europe, but its efforts in 2020 were hampered by reduced mobility due to the Covid-19 pandemic and internal disputes about leadership appointments.[8] More generally, the impact of Covid-19 on armed conflicts in Europe appeared minimal, although the direct and indirect impacts on conflict dynamics and European security more broadly may take years to develop.[9] In addition to large numbers of deaths, the Covid-19 pandemic led to unprecedented peacetime restrictions across most of Europe, including restrictions on freedom of movement, with travel often permitted only for essential work, health reasons or other emergencies.

There were 18 multilateral peace operations in Europe in 2020, all of which had been active in the previous year. The number of personnel deployed in these operations remained stable during 2020, at around 8000 (8063 on 31 December 2020).

Political crisis in Belarus

Against the background of poor political relations between Russia and many other European states, the political crisis in Belarus had a regional and a

[5] On armed conflicts in Afghanistan, MENA and sub-Saharan Africa see respectively, chapter 4, section II, chapter 6 and chapter 7 in this volume.

[6] For details on Europe's response to irregular migration and counterterrorism policy in 2019 see *SIPRI Yearbook 2020* (note 3), pp. 119–21.

[7] Murphy, F., 'Austrian police arrest 14 in manhunt after gunman rampage', Reuters, 2 Nov. 2020; and 'Terrorism in Europe: Despite the horrors in Vienna and Paris, jihadism has declined', *The Economist*, 3 Nov. 2020.

[8] Liechtenstein, S., 'How internal squabbling paralyzed Europe's most vital security organization', World Politics Review, 5 Aug. 2020.

[9] See e.g. Nye, J. S., 'Post pandemic geopolitics', Project Syndicate, 6 Oct. 2020. On the impact of Covid-19 on Russian foreign policy see e.g. Trenin, D., Rumer, E. and Weiss, A. S., 'Steady state: Russian foreign policy after coronavirus', Carnegie Moscow, 8 July 2020.

national significance. Widespread protests erupted in the Belarusian capital Minsk after Aleksander Lukashenko, president since 1994, claimed 80 per cent of the vote in what opposition leaders and many Western governments said was a rigged election on 9 August 2020.[10] The peaceful protests expanded and continued on a weekly basis from September through to December, despite being met with a fierce police crackdown and arrest of opposition leaders.[11]

The internal governance crisis in Belarus has a strong geopolitical dimension.[12] While Belarus is normally a relatively stable junior partner to Russia, President Lukashenko has been pursuing greater autonomy since 2014, leading to growing attention from the West, including visa liberalization with the European Union (EU), military training with the United Kingdom and the resumption of a US ambassadorial appointment.[13] In turn, Russia began to apply pressure to encourage Belarus to return to more Russian-aligned foreign and security policy, and to integrate the two countries more deeply.[14]

After the escalation in protests, Russia, which views Belarus as a close partner and a buffer zone against the North Atlantic Treaty Organization (NATO), offered security assistance to Belarus—including a newly established police force that could be deployed if needed—and also pledged a $1.5 billion loan.[15] In September, as President Lukashenko continued to claim the protests were being driven by the West, Belarus closed its western borders with Poland and Lithuania and placed its army on high alert.[16] Meanwhile, the EU declined to recognize the 'inauguration' of President Lukashenko on 23 September 2020, and imposed sanctions on 40 Belarus officials a week

[10] Makhovsky, A., 'Bloody clashes in Belarus as West condemns crackdown after election', Reuters, 10 Aug. 2020; 'Belarus presidential election results finalized', Belarusian Telegraph Agency, 14 Aug. 2020; 'Joint statement of Nordic-Baltic foreign ministers on recent developments in Belarus', Government Offices of Sweden, 11 Aug. 2020; and Makhovsky, A., 'Thousands stage flower protest as EU weighs sanctions', Reuters, 12 Aug. 2020.

[11] 'Aleksandr Lukashenko is trying to beat protesters into submission', The Economist, 22 Aug. 2020; Walker, S., 'Belarus protests: Nationwide strike looms after "people's ultimatum" rally', The Guardian, 26 Oct. 2020; and 'More than 150 anti-Lukashenka demonstrators detained in Belarus', Radio Free Europe/Radio Liberty, 20 Dec. 2020.

[12] Anthony, I., 'The Belarus election: A challenge to stability and security in Northern Europe', SIPRI Commentary, 19 Aug. 2020.

[13] 'Belarus: EU concludes agreements on visa facilitation and readmission', Council of the European Union, Press release, 27 May 2020; '42 Commando head to Belarus for Exercise Winter Partisan', UK Defence Journal, 1 Mar. 2020; and 'US nominates first Ambassador to Belarus in over a decade', Radio Free Europe/Radio Liberty, 21 Apr. 2020.

[14] Sivitsky, A., 'Belarus–Russia: From a strategic deal to an integration ultimatum', Foreign Policy Research Institute, 2019.

[15] Shotter, J. and Peel, M., 'Russia says it is ready to provide Belarus with military support', Financial Times, 16 Aug. 2020; Tétrault-Farber, G. and Makhovsky, A., 'Putin says Russia has set up force to aid Belarus leader if needed', Reuters, 27 Aug. 2020; and 'Belarus protests: Putin pledges $1.5bn loan at Lukashenko meeting', BBC News, 14 Sep. 2020.

[16] AP News, 'Belarus president closes western borders, puts army on high alert', Al Jazeera, 17 Sep. 2020.

later.[17] Belarus closed its borders with all neighbouring countries (Latvia, Lithuania, Poland and Ukraine) except Russia on 29 October 2020.[18] With protests continuing at the end of the year, there appeared to be no clear way out of the crisis.

US-mediated détente between Kosovo and Serbia

Areas of instability remained in the Western Balkans, including the unresolved dispute between Kosovo and Serbia over Kosovo's independence. Both countries have been at peace with each other since 1999. They have reached some agreements over trade, border management and other common challenges through EU-led mediation. However, despite recent efforts to find a solution, Kosovo remains a contested state, with the governance of Serb-majority communities a particularly problematic issue.[19]

The USA embarked on its own mediation initiative during 2020, apparently with only limited coordination with the EU, which is tasked with facilitating dialogue under Resolution 1739 (2010) of the Parliamentary Assembly of the Council of Europe.[20] In June 2020 US-mediated talks between Kosovan and Serbian leaders aimed at normalizing economic relations were cancelled after a special prosecutor indicted Kosovo's President Hashim Thaçi on charges of war crimes and crimes against humanity relating to Kosovo's 1998–99 conflict.[21] However, the indictment set back efforts to reach a settlement with Serbia by only a few months. On 4 September 2020 the Kosovo and Serbia economic normalization agreements were signed: two documents in which Kosovo and Serbia agreed to normalize economic ties. They also included commitments linked to US peace efforts in the Israeli–Palestinian conflict: Serbia agreed to move its Israeli embassy to Jerusalem (following

---

[17] 'Belarus: Declaration by the high representative on behalf of the European Union on the so-called "inauguration" of Aleksandr Lukashenko', Council of the European Union, Press release, 24 Sep. 2020; and 'Belarus: EU imposes sanctions for repression and election falsification', Council of the European Union, Press release, 2 Oct. 2020.

[18] Balmforth, T., 'Lukashenko shuts borders, shakes up security team to stamp out Belarus protests', Reuters, 29 Oct. 2020. On bilateral tensions between Belarus and Ukraine see Nahaylo, B., 'Alarm bells in Ukraine as Lukashenka calls on Putin to rescue his crumbling regime', Atlantic Council, 17 Aug. 2020.

[19] Kosovo is recognized by about 100 UN member states, but the number fluctuates as some states withdraw their recognition. Key states that do not recognize Kosovo include China, Russia and Serbia, as well as five EU member states (Cyprus, Greece, Romania, Slovakia and Spain). Kartsonaki, A., 'Playing with fire: An assessment of the EU's approach of constructive ambiguity on Kosovo's blended conflict', *Journal of Balkan and Near Eastern Studies*, vol. 22, no. 1 (2020), pp. 103–20; and Turp-Balazs, C., 'Serbia's campaign to reduce the number of countries which recognise Kosovo is working', Emerging Europe, 16 Jan. 2020.

[20] Ushkovska, M., 'The EU's rivalry with the US is complicating Serbia-Kosovo talks', World Politics Review, 9 Nov. 2020; and Council of Europe Parliamentary Assembly, Resolution 1739 (2010), 'The situation in Kosovo and the role of the Council of Europe', 2010.

[21] Kelly, L., 'Trump's Kosovo peace summit postponed amid war crimes allegations', The Hill, 25 June 2020.

the Trump administration's recognition of Jerusalem as Israel's capital in 2017), and Israel and Kosovo mutually recognized each other for the first time.[22] However, the agreements have been criticized for being 'light on substance and heavy on publicity', with little advancement on previous EU initiatives.[23]

Increased tensions in the eastern Mediterranean

A dangerous stand-off developed in the eastern Mediterranean during 2020—pitting Turkey against Cyprus and Greece, but also involving the EU, Egypt, France, and other states with geopolitical and economic interests in the region.[24] Turkish–Western relations have deteriorated over multiple issues, including oil and gas exploration, maritime delimitation, the wars in Libya and Syria, migration and the long-standing Cyprus conflict between Greek Cypriots and Turkish Cypriots.[25] Bilateral Greek–Turkish talks to address some of these underlying issues started in 2002 but broke down in 2016. In 2020 Germany (in the context of its presidency of the Council of the EU) and NATO (in relation to military de-escalation) led diplomatic efforts to prevent a destabilizing conflict.

Competition over hydrocarbon resources and maritime boundaries

Since the signature of commercial exploration contracts in 2018 and the formation of the East Mediterranean Gas Forum in 2019 (by Cyprus, Egypt, Greece, Israel, Italy, Jordan and Palestine), the proprietorship and financial feasibility of the regional gas discoveries have been clouded by uncertainties.[26] In June 2020 the rhetoric between Greece and Turkey over maritime borders and hydrocarbon development became even more heated following Turkey's late-May decision to begin hydrocarbon drilling in areas Greece claimed as its exclusive economic zone.[27] Agreements reached by Greece with Italy (on 9 June 2020) and Egypt (on 6 August 2020) to demarcate their maritime borders further heightened tensions with Turkey (which signed a competing deal with the Government of National Accord in Libya

[22] Wood, V., 'Serbia and Kosovo agree to normalise economic ties in US-brokered deal', *The Independent*, 4 Sep. 2020. On the Israeli–Palestine conflict see chapter 6, section III, in this volume.

[23] Ruge, M., 'Trump's Kosovo show: No big deal', Politico, 8 Sep. 2020.

[24] See e.g. Anthony, I. and Sahlin, M., 'Maritime disputes in the eastern Mediterranean: Why and why now?', SIPRI Commentary, 23 Oct. 2020; 'How to defuse tensions in the eastern Mediterranean', International Crisis Group, 22 Sep. 2020; and 'Angst in the Aegean: A row between Turkey and Greece over gas is raising tensions in the eastern Mediterranean', *The Economist*, 22 Aug. 2020.

[25] On Turkish–Western relations see Daly, G. et al., 'Turkey and the West: Keep the flame burning', German Marshall Fund Policy Paper no. 6, June 2020.

[26] Vesterbye, S. D., 'Keep your friends close and Turkey closer: EU-Turkey relations', Royal United Services Institute Commentary, 22 Sep. 2020.

[27] Antonopoulos, P., 'Greek defence minister: Turkey's behaviour is aggressive but our armed forces are a deterrent', Greek City Times, 5 June 2020.

in November 2019).[28] Although Turkey agreed to temporarily pause energy exploration activities in July following talks brokered by German chancellor Angela Merkel, it later resumed them.[29] On 12 August 2020 a Turkish frigate escorting a survey ship suffered a minor collision with a Greek frigate.[30] Meanwhile, the EU threatened Turkey with fresh sanctions.[31]

In September 2020 the US administration partially lifted an arms embargo imposed on Cyprus in the late 1980s and appeared to provide growing diplomatic support to Greece in its dispute with Turkey.[32] In December the EU agreed to impose sanctions on an unspecified number of Turkish officials and entities, but deferred more significant options (such as trade tariffs or an arms embargo) pending consultations with the new Biden administration.[33]

North Atlantic Treaty Organization 'deconfliction' talks

The regional divisions have also led to intra-NATO tensions, with increased naval deployments and military exercises in the eastern Mediterranean highlighting the risk of a military confrontation among member states, either by accident or by design. A naval incident between French and Turkish ships in June 2020 led to an investigation by NATO, which also initiated 'technical talks' between Greece and Turkey in September.[34] These latter talks led to a military deconfliction mechanism being established at the beginning of October. Deconfliction involves setting up communication links among rival militaries in the same theatre to reduce the risk of military incidents and accidents, as the USA has done with Russia in Syria. In this case, it included the creation of a hotline between Greece and Turkey to facilitate deconfliction at sea or in the air.[35] However, prospects for diplomacy continued to look uncertain at the end of the year.

---

[28] 'Greece, Italy sign deal delimiting maritime zones', Al Jazeera, 9 June 2020; Mourad, M., 'Egypt and Greece sign agreement on exclusive economic zone', Reuters, 6 Aug. 2020; and 'Turkey denounces maritime deal between Greece, Egypt', Al Jazeera, 7 Aug. 2020.

[29] Smith, H. and Henley, J., 'Greek military put on high alert as tensions with Turkey rise', The Guardian, 13 Aug. 2020.

[30] Sharman, J., 'Turkish and Greek warships collide in eastern Mediterranean', The Independent, 14 Aug. 2020.

[31] 'EU warns Turkey of sanctions as east Mediterranean crisis worsens', Al Jazeera, 28 Aug. 2020.

[32] 'Turkey slams US over lifting Cyprus arms embargo, Nicosia welcomes decision', Deutsche Welle, 2 Sep. 2020; and Morello, C., 'Pompeo highlights warmer ties with Greece amid regional tensions with Turkey', Washington Post, 29 Sep. 2020.

[33] Emmott, R., 'After heated debate, EU to prepare new sanctions over Turkish gas drilling', Reuters, 10 Dec. 2020.

[34] Emmott, R., Irish, J. and Gumrukcu, T., 'NATO keeps France-Turkey probe under wraps as tempers flare', Reuters, 17 Sep. 2020; and 'NATO Secretary General statement on technical talks for de-confliction in the eastern Mediterranean', NATO news release, 3 Sep. 2020.

[35] 'Military de-confliction mechanism between Greece and Turkey established at NATO', NATO news release, 1 Oct. 2020. On the conflict in Syria see chapter 6, section II, in this volume.

II. The interstate armed conflict between Armenia and Azerbaijan

IAN DAVIS

The interstate conflict between Armenia and Azerbaijan centres on the disputed territory of Nagorno-Karabakh (see figure 5.1).[1] It was the first secessionist conflict to erupt in the former Soviet Union in 1988 and then became a confrontation between the two sovereign states of Armenia and Azerbaijan when they declared independence in 1991. An estimated 1 million people were displaced by the 1988–94 Nagorno-Karabakh War, and about 30 000 were killed.[2] Following the Russian-brokered 1994 ceasefire, Nagorno-Karabakh and seven other districts (occupied by Armenia after the fighting as a security buffer) remained formally part of Azerbaijan but were de facto controlled by separatist ethnic Armenians whose economy, society and polity were deeply tied to Armenia. The self-proclaimed Republic of Nagorno-Karabakh (referred to as the Republic of Artsakh by Armenia) is not recognized by any United Nations member state, including Armenia.

In 2016–17 the conflict escalated into periodic violence along the 200-kilometre line of contact between Armenian and Azerbaijani forces, but returned to relative calm in 2018–19.[3] Both sides increased their military capabilities in recent years, while a growing internationalization of the conflict (principally due to the greater involvement of Russia and Turkey, as well as Iran) raised concerns that any escalation in fighting could lead to a regional war.[4]

The conflict does not fit neatly into the frame of geopolitical competition between Europe and Russia (discussed in section I). Some Western states provide political support to Azerbaijan (because of its oil wealth and potential as a strategic buffer against Iran and Russia), while others back Armenia (because of the legacy of the Armenian genocide and an active Armenian diaspora). Russia has been similarly conflicted—recognizing the value of Azerbaijan as an ally, but traditionally supportive of Armenia where it has a military base and both are members of the Collective Security Treaty

---

[1] See e.g. Kazantsev et al., 'Russia's policy in the "frozen conflicts" of the post-Soviet space: From ethnopolitics to geopolitics', *Caucasus Survey*, vol. 8, no. 2 (2020), pp. 142–62; and Azimov, A., 'Nagorno-Karabakh conflict in the Caucasus: What documents say?', Modern Diplomacy, 26 July 2020.

[2] Blakemore, E., 'How the Nagorno-Karabakh conflict has been shaped by past empires', *National Geographic*, 16 Oct. 2020.

[3] On developments during 2016–19 see International Crisis Group, *Preventing a Bloody Harvest on the Armenia-Azerbaijan State Border*, Europe Report no. 259 (International Crisis Group: Brussels, 24 July 2020).

[4] On military expenditure in Armenia and Azerbaijan see chapter 8, section II, in this volume.

Figure 5.1. The disputed territory of Nagorno-Karabakh, July 2020

Note: The boundaries, names and designations used here do not imply any endorsement or acceptance by SIPRI of claims or stances in disputes over specific territories.

Source: 'Nagorno-Karabakh conflict in the Caucasus: What documents say?', *Modern Diplomacy*, 26 July 2020.

Organization.[5] Armenia has a historical antipathy towards Turkey, which has close ethnic, religious and cultural ties with Azerbaijan. Iran shares similar ties with Armenia and with Azerbaijan.[6]

Regular peace talks between Armenia and Azerbaijan, mediated by the Organization for Security and Co-operation in Europe (OSCE) Minsk Group and others, have failed to resolve this long-standing conflict.[7] The situation between the 1994 ceasefire and 2019 was characterized by regular low-level incidents and occasional flare-ups (e.g. Russia helped to de-escalate a crisis in 2016), but there was no major escalation until 2020. The six weeks of

[5] Kazantsev et al. (note 1); Popescu, N., 'A captive ally: Why Russia isn't rushing to Armenia's aid', European Council on Foreign Relations Commentary, 8 Oct. 2020; and Sukiasyan, N., 'Appeasement and autonomy: Armenian–Russian relations from revolution to war', European Union Institute for Security Studies, Brief no. 2, Jan. 2021. On membership of the Collective Security Treaty Organization see annex B, section II, in this volume.

[6] Coffey, L., 'Iran the big loser in Nagorno-Karabakh war', Arab News, 13 Nov. 2020; and Motamedi, M., 'Iran's delicate balancing act in the Nagorno-Karabakh conflict', Al Jazeera, 5 Oct. 2020.

[7] For a brief description and list of members of the OSCE Minsk Group see annex B, section II, in this volume. On the history of the Minsk Group process see Remler, P. et al., 'OSCE Minsk Group: Lessons from the past and tasks for the future', OSCE Insights 6, Nomos, 2020. On media framing of the conflict and the role of peace journalism see Atanesyan, A., 'Media framing on armed conflicts: Limits of peace journalism on the Nagorno-Karabakh conflict', *Journal of Intervention and Statebuilding*, vol. 14, no. 4 (2020), pp. 534–50.

fighting that broke out in 2020 was the most serious period of fighting since the Nagorno-Karabakh War. It resulted in Azerbaijan regaining control of about one third of Nagorno-Karabakh and most of the adjacent territories.

The armed conflict in 2020

In March and April 2020 the OSCE Minsk Group called on the two sides to recommit to the 1994 ceasefire for the duration of the Covid-19 health crisis.[8] However, low-level fighting broke out in mid July between Armenian and Azerbaijani forces in the northern section of their border, leaving at least 16 people dead. Reliable detailed information on what occurred on the ground is limited, but officials in both countries blamed each other for starting the fighting.[9] The co-chairs of the Minsk Group (France, Russia and the United States) condemned the violence and called for restraint.[10]

Following heightened tensions in the middle of the year, the speeches of the Armenian and Azerbaijan leaders at the annual general debate of the UN General Assembly in September reflected their hardening positions.[11] A few days later, on 27 September the fighting along the border escalated with the use of major conventional weapons.[12] Azerbaijan is widely believed to have planned and initiated the offensive: having built up its military capacity over some years, it was in a position to try to retake Nagorno-Karabakh.[13] Both countries declared martial law and mobilized for what risked becoming an all-out war. Armenia, France and Russia accused Turkey of sending foreign fighters from Syria to bolster the Azerbaijani armed forces, as well as other military support. Turkey denied these claims.[14] However, it was

---

[8] 'Press statement by the co-chairs of the OSCE Minsk Group', OSCE, 19 Mar. 2020; and 'Joint statement by the foreign ministers of Armenia and Azerbaijan and the co-chairs of the OSCE Minsk Group', OSCE, 21 Apr. 2020.

[9] AP News, 'At least 16 killed in Armenia-Azerbaijan border clashes', *The Guardian*, 14 July 2020; and International Crisis Group (note 3).

[10] 'Press statement by the co-chairs of the OSCE Minsk Group and personal representative of the OSCE chairperson-in-office', OSCE, 24 July 2020.

[11] Ghazanchyan, S., 'People of Nagorno-Karabakh should be able to determine their status without limitation—Armenian PM tells UN General Assembly', Public Radio of Armenia, 25 Sep. 2020; and 'Ilham Aliyev delivered a speech at general debates of 75th session of United Nations General Assembly in a video format', President of the Republic of Azerbaijan, 24 Sep. 2020.

[12] 'Armenia-Azerbaijan conflict: Death toll rises in Nagorno-Karabakh', Deutsche Welle, 28 Sep. 2020; and Kramer, A. E., 'In Nagorno-Karabakh, signs of escalating and widening conflict', *New York Times*, 29 Sep. 2020.

[13] See e.g. Kucera, J., 'New Armenia-Azerbaijan fighting a long time in the making', Eurasianet, 28 Sep. 2020; and 'De-escalating the new Nagorno-Karabakh war', International Crisis Group, 2 Oct. 2020.

[14] Sanders IV, L. and Salameh, K., 'Syrian mercenaries sustain Turkey's foreign policy', Deutsche Welle, 30 Sep. 2020; and McKernan, B., 'Syrian recruit describes role of foreign fighters in Nagorno-Karabakh', *The Guardian*, 2 Oct. 2020.

Table 5.1. Estimated conflict-related fatalities in Armenia and Azerbaijan, 2019–20

Event type	Armenia		Azerbaijan	
	2019	2020	2019	2020
Battles	2	18	12	6 231
Explosions/remote violence	0	8	1	435
Protests, riots and strategic developments	0	0	0	0
Violence against civilians	0	0	1	6
Total	**2**	**26**	**14**	**6 672**

Notes: Figures for Azerbaijan include Nagorno-Karabakh and seven other districts previously occupied by Armenia.

For definitions of event types, see Armed Conflict Location & Event Data Projection (ACLED), 'ACLED definitions of political violence and protest', 11 Apr. 2019.

Source: ACLED, 'Data export tool', accessed 28 Jan. 2021.

reported that Turkey supplied military equipment valued at $123 million to Azerbaijan in the first nine months of 2020.[15]

Despite renewed international calls for restraint—including by the European Union, the OSCE and the UN Security Council (which, in a closed session, addressed the issue for the first time since 1993)—both sides rejected pressure to commence peace talks.[16] The presidents of France, Russia and the USA called for a ceasefire in a joint statement on 1 October 2020, while Turkey vowed to 'do what is necessary' to support Azerbaijan.[17] On 2 October Armenia indicated it would welcome a ceasefire and would be prepared to work with the OSCE to establish peace in the region.[18] Nonetheless, the conflict continued, with both sides accusing each other of targeting civilians.[19]

With about 70 000 people (half of the Nagorno-Karabakh population) displaced by the fighting, a Russian-brokered ceasefire was agreed on

[15] Toksabay, E., 'Turkish arms sales to Azerbaijan surged before Nagorno-Karabakh fighting', Reuters, 14 Oct. 2020.

[16] Bagirova, N. and Hovhannisyan, N., 'Azerbaijan and Armenia reject talks as Karabakh conflict zone spreads', Reuters, 29 Sep. 2020; 'Special meeting of OSCE Permanent Council held on situation in Nagorno-Karabakh context', OSCE, 29 Sep. 2020; 'Nagorno Karabakh: Statement by the high representative/vice president Josep Borrell', European Union External Action Service, 27 Sep. 2020; and 'UN Security Council calls for immediate end to fighting in Nagorno-Karabakh', France 24, 30 Sep. 2020.

[17] 'Statement of the presidents of the Russian Federation, the United States of America and the French Republic on Nagorno-Karabakh', French Ministry of Foreign Affairs, 1 Oct. 2020; 'US, Russia, France condemn fighting in Nagorno-Karabakh', Deutsche Welle, 1 Oct. 2020; and 'Turkey will provide support if Azerbaijan requests it—foreign minister', Reuters, 30 Sep. 2020.

[18] 'Nagorno-Karabakh: Armenia says ready to work towards ceasefire', Al Jazeera, 2 Oct. 2020.

[19] Melikyan, A. et al., 'Missiles, rockets and accusations fly as Nagorno Karabakh flare-up burns into second week', CNN, 5 Oct. 2020.

10 October 2020. However, fighting resumed almost immediately.[20] Reported use of artillery salvos and ballistic missiles by both sides and cluster munitions by Azerbaijani forces added to civilian and military casualties. Hostilities widened to include attacks on Armenian positions, on Nagorno-Karabakh and on Armenian and Azerbaijani cities near the line of conflict.[21] Two further negotiated humanitarian ceasefires—one brokered by Russia on 17 October 2020 and the other by the USA on 25 October 2020—were again broken almost immediately.[22]

Permanent ceasefire agreed

Azerbaijani forces made major gains in the fighting. By early November they were threatening to capture the whole of Nagorno-Karabakh. On 9 November 2020 Armenia, Azerbaijan and Russia signed a peace agreement to end the six-week war, which entered into effect on 10 November.[23] In addition to a full ceasefire the agreement stipulates: (*a*) the phased withdrawal of the Armenian military from territory outside of its internationally recognized borders (Nagorno-Karabakh and three adjacent areas still controlled by Armenia); (*b*) the deployment of 1960 Russian armed peacekeepers to Nagorno-Karabakh, except in those areas now under Azerbaijani control, and to patrol the Lachin corridor connecting Armenia to Stepanakert; (*c*) the deployment of Russian border police to secure a new transit route (running through Armenian territory) between Azerbaijan and its exclave of Nakhichevan (which is surrounded by Armenia, Iran and Turkey); and (*d*) a series of self-renewing five-year time limits for the Russian peacekeeping forces, which can be ended by any party six months prior to a scheduled extension. The agreement also calls for the return of internally displaced persons and refugees to Nagorno-Karabakh and surrounding territories, and for Azerbaijan and Turkey to lift their decades-long blockade of Armenia.[24] Turkey

---

[20] 'Statement by the foreign ministers of the Russian Federation, the Republic of Azerbaijan and the Republic of Armenia', Russian Ministry of Foreign Affairs, 10 Oct. 2020; 'Armenia Azerbaijan: Reports of fresh shelling dent ceasefire hopes', BBC News, 12 Oct. 2020; and Hovhannisyan, N. and Bagirova, N., 'Humanitarian crisis feared as Nagorno-Karabakh ceasefire buckles', Reuters, 13 Oct. 2020.

[21] 'Armenia/Azerbaijan: Civilians must be protected from use of banned cluster bombs', Amnesty International, 5 Oct. 2020; and Troianovski, A., 'At front lines of a brutal war: Death and despair in Nagorno-Karabakh', *New York Times*, 18 Oct. 2020. On international efforts to ban the use of cluster munitions see chapter 13, section I, in this volume.

[22] 'Nagorno-Karabakh: Armenia and Azerbaijan accuse each other of breaking fresh truce', *The Guardian*, 18 Oct. 2020; 'US-Armenia-Azerbaijan joint statement', Armenian Ministry of Foreign Affairs, 25 Oct. 2020; and AP News, 'Azerbaijan and Armenia trade accusations of breaking US-brokered truce', *The Guardian*, 26 Oct. 2020.

[23] President of Russia, [Statement by the president of the Republic of Azerbaijan, the prime minister of the Republic of Armenia and president of the Russian Federation], 10 Nov. 2020 (in Russian).

[24] 'Armenia, Azerbaijan and Russia sign Nagorno-Karabakh peace deal', BBC News, 10 Nov. 2020; and 'Getting from ceasefire to peace in Nagorno-Karabakh', International Crisis Group, 10 Nov. 2020.

and Russia signed a separate accord to establish a joint monitoring centre in Nagorno-Karabakh, and the Turkish Parliament approved the deployment of Turkish peacekeepers to the centre.[25]

With significantly higher estimated losses of military equipment and territory, Armenian leaders said a ceasefire had been unavoidable. Turkey's military and political support, and armed drones purchased from Israel and Turkey, appeared to be central to Azerbaijan's military success.[26] Total military and civilian fatalities were estimated to be about 6700 people (see table 5.1). Other sources suggest there were over 7100 fatalities (including 2400 Armenian troops, 1779 Republic of Artsakh soldiers and 50 civilians, and 2783 Azerbaijani troops and 98 civilians).[27] Human rights organizations allege both sides committed war crimes during the conflict in 2020.[28]

Future outlook

Russian peacekeepers were helping the two sides to maintain an uneasy ceasefire in Nagorno-Karabakh at the end of 2020, despite some minor violations in December.[29] The agreement brokered by Russia on 9 November 2020 is not a comprehensive peace treaty. Several key issues have still to be clarified, including the future status and governance of Nagorno-Karabakh, how to reconcile potentially competing claims by returning Armenians displaced by the fighting in recent months and Azerbaijanis displaced in the early 1990s, Turkey's role in the implementation of the agreement (beyond the deployment of peacekeepers) and the future of the OSCE Minsk Process.[30] Azerbaijan sees itself as the victor, having recaptured most of the territory it lost in the previous war over 30 years ago. Hence, the agreement was celebrated in Azerbaijan, but met with protests in Armenia where it was seen as an imposed peace.[31] A new stalemate—but on different terms to the previous 30-year stalemate—now seems likely.

---

[25] 'Turkish parliament approves troop deployment to Nagorno-Karabakh', Al Jazeera, 18 Nov. 2020.

[26] Dixon, R., 'Azerbaijan's drones owned the battlefield in Nagorno-Karabakh—and showed future of warfare', *Washington Post*, 13 Nov. 2020; and Watling, J. and Kaushal, S., 'The democratisation of precision strike in the Nagorno-Karabakh conflict', Royal United Services Institute Commentary, 22 Oct. 2020.

[27] [Caucasian Knot], [Karabakh: Chronicle of war-2020], 23 Dec. 2020 (in Russian).

[28] 'Armenia: Unlawful rocket, missile strikes on Azerbaijan', Human Rights Watch, 11 Dec. 2020; 'Azerbaijan: Unlawful strikes in Nagorno-Karabakh', Human Rights Watch, 11 Dec. 2020; and 'In the line of fire: Civilian casualties from unlawful strikes in the Armenian-Azerbaijani conflict over Nagorno-Karabakh', Amnesty International, 2021.

[29] Troianovski, A. and Gall, C., 'In Nagorno-Karabakh peace deal, Putin applied a deft new touch', *New York Times*, 1 Dec. 2020; and AP News, 'Nagorno-Karabakh: Both sides blame each other over ceasefire violations', *The Guardian*, 12 Dec. 2020.

[30] 'Improving prospects for peace after the Nagorno-Karabakh war', International Crisis Group, Europe Briefing no. 91, 22 Dec. 2020.

[31] Losh, J. and Roth, A., 'Nagorno-Karabakh peace deal brokered by Moscow prompts anger in Armenia', *The Guardian*, 10 Nov. 2020.

III. Armed conflict and the peace process in Ukraine

IAN DAVIS

Ukraine has been the focus of Europe's main territorial conflict since the annexation of Crimea by Russia in March 2014 and the outbreak of armed conflict in eastern Ukraine shortly thereafter.[1] The conflict in Ukraine is driven by and also helps to drive the wider geopolitical confrontation between Russia and Western powers.[2] The supply of arms and military assistance to the Ukrainian Government (from the United States and other member states of the North Atlantic Treaty Organization) and to the non-state armed groups in eastern Ukraine (backed by Russia) also exemplifies the internationalized nature of the conflict.[3]

The political changes in Ukraine in 2019—the election of Volodymyr Zelensky as president and his newly formed party, Servant of the People, becoming the first party in independent Ukraine to win an outright parliamentary majority—brought renewed expectations that it might be possible to find a peaceful solution to the conflict in eastern Ukraine.[4] However, at the end of 2019 fundamental disagreements endured among the conflict parties (including external state supporters on both sides) about the nature of the conflict and their involvement in it, as well as the implementation of existing agreements.[5] It was not possible to overcome these fundamental disagreements in 2020. However, a new ceasefire agreement in July 2020 led to much lower levels of violence and military and civilian casualties during the year, and the conflict appeared to be heading in the direction of becoming another of Europe's simmering conflicts (see section I).

---

[1] For a discussion on the initial causes of the conflict in Ukraine see Wilson, A., 'External intervention in the Ukraine conflict: Towards a frozen conflict in the Donbas', *SIPRI Yearbook 2016*, pp. 143–57; and Clem, R. S., 'Clearing the fog of war: Public versus official sources and geopolitical storylines in the Russia-Ukraine conflict', *Eurasian Geography and Economics*, vol. 58, no. 6 (2017), pp. 592–612. On the various armed groups fighting in conflict see Galeotti, M., *Armies of Russia's War in Ukraine* (Osprey Publishing: Oxford, 2019). On the economic underpinnings of the conflict see International Crisis Group, *Peace in Ukraine (III): The Costs of War in Donbas*, Europe Report no. 261 (International Crisis Group: Brussels, 3 Sep. 2020).

[2] For a detailed analysis of the roles of external actors in and around Ukraine see Wittke, C. and Rabinovych, M., 'Five years after: The role of international actors in the "Ukraine Crisis"', *East European Politics*, vol. 35, no. 3 (2019), pp. 259–63; and International Crisis Group, *Peace in Ukraine I: A European War*, Europe Report no. 256 (International Crisis Group: Brussels, 28 Apr. 2020). On Russia's political and economic coercive approaches towards Ukraine see Hurak, I. and D'Anieri, P., 'The evolution of Russian political tactics in Ukraine', *Problems of Post-Communism* (2020).

[3] For details of the internationalized nature see Davis, I., 'Armed conflict and the peace process in Ukraine', *SIPRI Yearbook 2020*, pp. 123–25.

[4] 'Hope and fear: Can Volodymyr Zelensky live up to the expectations he has created?', *The Economist*, 26 Sep. 2019.

[5] For developments in the peace process in 2019 see *SIPRI Yearbook 2020* (note 3), pp. 126–28.

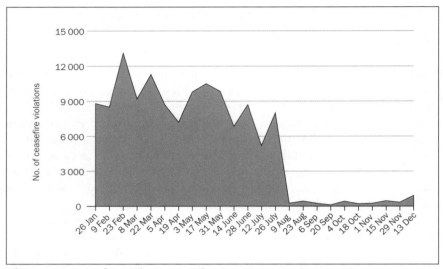

Figure 5.2. Ceasefire violations in Ukraine, 13 Jan.–13 Dec. 2020

Note: Each point represents the end of the corresponding 2-week reporting cycle.

Sources: Various bi-weekly status reports by the Organization for Security and Co-operation in Europe Special Monitoring Mission to Ukraine.

The peace process and a new ceasefire agreement

The 2014–15 Minsk agreements set out steps that the conflict parties (Ukrainian Government, separatist statelets and Russia) needed to take to bring about peace in the Donbas region.[6] These steps were meant to lead to the reintegration of the breakaway areas of Donetsk and Luhansk regions into Ukraine while offering them a measure of autonomy. However, the conflict parties (and, to some extent, their external state supporters) had fundamentally different interpretations of the Minsk agreements and how they should be implemented. This impasse could not be overcome during 2020.[7] Moreover, the disengagement process initiated by the Zelensky administration in 2019 and a proposed prisoner exchange between the Ukrainian Government and separatists also stalled. While the sides had agreed in December 2019 to disengage in three more zones (in addition to the three previously completed in Petriviske, Stanytsia Luhanska and Zolote) by the end of March 2020, they had still not agreed on the next disengagement

---

[6] 'Protocol on the results of consultations of the Trilateral Contact Group with respect to the joint steps aimed at the implementation of the peace plan of the president of Ukraine, P. Poroshenko, and the initiatives of the president of Russia, V. Putin' (Minsk Protocol, or Minsk I Agreement), 5 Sep. 2014; and 'Package of measures for the implementation of the Minsk agreements' (Minsk II Agreement), 12 Feb. 2015.

[7] On diverging positions within the Minsk Process see Druey, C. et al., 'The Minsk Process: Societal perceptions and narratives', OSCE Insights 8, Nomos, 2020.

locations but pledged to continue working towards this goal.[8] In November four new disengagement areas were agreed: near Hryhorivka in the Donetsk region, and Nyzhnoteple, Petrivka and Slovyanoserbsk villages in the Luhansk region.[9] However, the proposed prisoner exchange continued to be blocked.[10]

Ukrainian Government forces and Russian-backed separatist forces remained locked in low-level combat for much of 2020. The United Nations secretary-general's appeal in March for a global ceasefire had little or no impact on the conflict, despite some expressions of local and international support.[11] There have been more than 20 previous ceasefire attempts in the six years of conflict; all have failed to be sustainable, with many being violated almost immediately. However, a new 'comprehensive, sustainable and unlimited ceasefire' was agreed at a videoconference meeting of the Trilateral Contact Group (the Organization for Security and Co-operation in Europe (OSCE), Russia and Ukraine) and representatives from the separatist regions on 22 July 2020, which took effect five days later.[12] The ceasefire largely held, despite initial and continuing low levels of violations being reported by the OSCE Special Monitoring Mission (SMM) to Ukraine (see figure 5.2), although it is difficult to predict whether or how long the ceasefire will remain in effect.[13] Fighting was already beginning to escalate in late December.[14]

Ongoing restrictions on freedom of movement in eastern Ukraine, which were exacerbated by closures of entry–exit checkpoints and other measures to combat the Covid-19 pandemic, made it more difficult for the OSCE SMM to Ukraine—the largest civilian peace operation in Europe—to observe and report on ceasefire violations.[15] These restrictions also hindered

---

[8] On the obstacles that have stood in the way of ceasefires and disengagement see International Crisis Group, *Peace in Ukraine (II): A New Approach to Disengagement*, Europe Report no. 260 (International Crisis Group: Brussels, 3 Aug. 2020).

[9] 'Four new areas for disengagement of forces to appear in Donbass—JFO HQ', 112 Ukraine, 4 Nov. 2020.

[10] Zinets, N., 'Ukraine expects to swap 100 prisoners with Russian-backed separatists within weeks', Reuters, 6 Aug. 2020; 'Ukraine urges Russia, Donbas representatives to unblock prisoner swap', 112 Ukraine, 28 Oct. 2020.

[11] 'Stoltenberg calls for ceasefire to fight Covid-19 crisis in Ukraine's east', *Kyiv Post*, 3 Apr. 2020; and France in the United Kingdom, French Embassy in London, 'Paris and Berlin reiterate UN chief's call for ceasefire in eastern Ukraine', Joint statement by French and German foreign ministers, 30 Mar. 2020. On the UN secretary-general's global ceasefire call see chapter 2, section I, in this volume.

[12] 'Press statement of Special Representative Grau after the regular meeting of Trilateral Contact Group on 22 July 2020', OSCE, 23 July 2020.

[13] The OSCE SMM to Ukraine makes daily and ad hoc reports on the crisis in Ukraine; see <https://www.osce.org/ukrainecrisis>. 'Ukraine ceasefire violated more than 100 times within days: OSCE', Al Jazeera, 29 July 2020.

[14] International Crisis Group, 'CrisisWatch', Conflict tracker, accessed Dec. 2020.

[15] Liechtenstein, S., 'How Covid-19 is impairing the work of the OSCE in eastern Ukraine', Security and Human Rights Monitor, 17 Apr. 2020.

international and humanitarian organizations in providing medical supplies and protective gear, and hindered the population in the Donbas region when seeking medical care in Russia or Ukraine.[16]

The humanitarian impact of the armed conflict

The armed conflict between Ukrainian Government forces and Russian-backed separatists has led to over 13 000 deaths since April 2014, including at least 3367 civilian deaths.[17] However, battle-related deaths and civilian casualties in the Donbas region have been much lower since 2018 than in earlier years: there were an estimated 109 conflict-related deaths in 2020 (down from 403 in 2019 and 893 in 2018).[18] In contrast, there were over 18 000 confirmed Covid-19-related deaths in Ukraine in 2020.[19]

The economic consequences of the conflict have been considerable, resulting in an estimated decrease in Ukraine's per capita gross domestic product over the period 2013–17 of 15 per cent. The decrease in the Donbas regions of Donetsk and Luhansk during 2013–16 is estimated at 47 per cent.[20] In addition, at least 3.4 million people were in need of humanitarian assistance during 2020.[21] At least 1 million people remained internally displaced, while an estimated 1 million refugees have left Donbas for Russia since the conflict began.[22] Eastern Ukraine also has some of the world's worst landmine contamination.[23]

---

[16] Thompson, J. T., 'Searching for Covid-19 ceasefires: Conflict zone impacts, needs, and opportunities', US Institute of Peace special report, 15 Sep. 2020; Abibok, Y., 'Trapped in eastern Ukraine', Institute for War & Peace Reporting, 28 Aug. 2020; and OSCE, 'Checkpoints along the contact line: Challenges civilians face when crossing', Thematic report, SEC.FR/876/20, Dec. 2020.

[17] Office of the UN High Commissioner for Human Rights (OHCHR), *Report on the Human Rights Situation in Ukraine: 16 February–31 July 2020* (OHCHR: 2020), p. 7; and Office of the UN High Commissioner for Human Rights (OHCHR), *Report on the Human Rights Situation in Ukraine: 16 November 2019 to 15 February 2020* (OHCHR: 2020), p. 8.

[18] Armed Conflict Location & Event Data Project, 'Data export tool', accessed 13 Jan. 2021.

[19] 'Covid-19 in Ukraine: Tracking the outbreak', *Kyiv Post*, [n.d.].

[20] Bluszcz, J. and Valente, M., 'The economic costs of hybrid wars: The case of Ukraine', *Defence and Peace Economics* (2020).

[21] UN Office for the Coordination of Humanitarian Affairs (UN OCHA) 'Ukraine, situation report', 19 Oct. 2020.

[22] The Government of Ukraine reports around 1.5 million internally displaced persons, but international organizations estimate the number to be under 1 million. 'Registration of internal displacement', Ukraine Ministry of Social Policy/UN High Commissioner for Refugees, 27 Oct. 2020; US Congressional Research Service (CRS), *Ukraine: Background, Conflict with Russia, and US Policy*, CRS Report for Congress R45008 (US Congress, CRS: Washington, DC, 29 Apr. 2020), p. 17.; and Litvinova, M., [My mother put me on a train to Belgorod, and the next day a shell hit the station building], *Kommersant*, 18 Apr. 2020 (in Russian).

[23] 'Eastern Ukraine one of the areas most contaminated by landmines in the world', UN OCHA, 4 Apr. 2019. On the impact of landmines, also see chapter 13, section I, in this volume.

6. Armed conflict and peace processes in the Middle East and North Africa

Overview

There were seven states with active armed conflicts in the Middle East and North Africa (MENA) in 2020 (the same as in 2017–19): Egypt (low-intensity, subnational armed conflict), Iraq (internationalized civil war), Israel (low-intensity, extrastate armed conflict), Libya (internationalized civil war), Syria (internationalized civil war), Turkey (low-intensity, extrastate and subnational armed conflict) and Yemen (major internationalized civil war). All the armed conflicts had fewer fatalities than in 2019. Overall, conflict-related fatalities have reduced by almost 70 per cent since 2017, and in 2020 Yemen remained the region's only major armed conflict (i.e. with fatalities greater than 10 000 people). Many of these conflicts were interconnected and involved regional and international powers, as well as numerous non-state actors. Tensions between Iran and the United States again threatened to escalate into a more serious interstate military conflict. The Covid-19 pandemic appears to have had minimal impact on the region's armed conflicts, although it clearly added another layer of complexity to the existing humanitarian challenges. Anti-government protests occurred throughout the region, with mass protests in Algeria, Iraq and Lebanon.

A ceasefire in Idlib province in Syria in March 2020 and a nationwide ceasefire agreed in Libya in October 2020 suggested both of those conflicts might be open to some form of resolution soon. However, in Yemen implementation of the 2018 Stockholm Agreement remained stalled. There were 14 multilateral peace operations in the MENA region in 2020, the same as in 2019.

There were complex and interlinked armed conflicts in Iraq, Syria and Turkey (section II). During 2020 the Assad government continued to consolidate its hold in Syria and the March ceasefire in Idlib province led to a further reduction in large-scale hostilities. Iraq remained a fragile, largely post-conflict state with weak institutions and growing protests. Iran remained an influential presence in Iraq and Syria, and Iranian–US tensions spilled over into Iraq. Turkey intensified its military operations in northern Iraq. The Idlib ceasefire brokered by Russia and Turkey cemented their roles as key power brokers in Syria, while US influence in the region continued to wane.

Casualties in the Israeli–Palestinian conflict (section III) in 2020 were at the lowest level in the past decade. A new US 'peace plan', the threatened annexation of parts of the West Bank and a series of normalization agreements between Israel and four states (Bahrain, Morocco, Sudan and the United Arab

Emirates) were key developments in the year. The economic and humanitarian costs to the Palestinian people of the Israeli occupation continued to be severe, and there still appeared to be little prospect of resolving the underlying Israeli– Palestinian territorial dispute.

North Africa (section IV) is undergoing a convergence of crises, with negative spillover onto the stability of neighbouring states in the eastern Mediterranean and sub-Saharan Africa. The 40-year territorial dispute over Sahrawi Arab Democratic Republic (Western Sahara) between Morocco and the Popular Front for the Liberation of Saguia el Hamra and Río de Oro (Polisario Front) erupted again towards the end of the year, while Egypt's low-level Sinai insurgency continued in 2020 with no sign of an end or a decisive outcome. Egypt, Turkey and Russia's deepening roles in the civil war in Libya complicated peace efforts and increased the risk of a direct military confrontation between Turkish and Egyptian/Russian armed forces supporting opposing sides in the armed conflict. An internationally backed ceasefire in Libya in October 2020 offered new grounds for optimism.

Despite attempts mediated by the United Nations to end the civil war in Yemen (section V) the armed conflict continued throughout the year, further exacerbating one of the world's worst humanitarian crises. A UN panel of experts concluded the pattern of armed conflicts in 2020 had predominantly shifted to economic drivers, while in October the UN warned the country was on the brink of a catastrophic food security crisis. At the end of the year the Houthis continued to dominate the Yemeni political, economic and military landscape, controlling one third of the country's territory and two thirds of the population. Agreeing a lasting political settlement remains fraught with difficulty as the Houthis are unlikely to stop fighting until they fully control Marib, Hodeidah and Taiz.

IAN DAVIS

I. Key general developments in the region

IAN DAVIS

There were seven states in the Middle East and North Africa (MENA) with active armed conflicts in 2020 (the same as in 2017–19): Egypt (low-intensity, subnational armed conflict), Iraq (internationalized civil war), Israel (low-intensity, extrastate armed conflict), Libya (internationalized civil war), Syria (internationalized civil war), Turkey (low-intensity, extrastate and subnational armed conflict) and Yemen (major internationalized civil war).[1] All the armed conflicts had lower conflict-related fatalities in 2020 compared with in 2019; overall the reduction was about 35 per cent as a result of fatalities being almost halved in Syria (see table 6.1). Except for Libya, this was the second consecutive yearly reduction in all of the region's conflict fatalities, which have reduced by almost 70 per cent since 2017. With conflict-related fatalities in Syria dropping below 10 000 in 2020, the war in Yemen remained the region's only major armed conflict. Developments in each of the armed conflicts and any related peace processes are covered in subsequent sections: Iraq, Syria and Turkey (section II); the Israeli–Palestinian conflict (section III); Egypt and Libya (section IV); and Yemen (section V).

Many of these conflicts were interconnected and involved regional and international powers, as well as numerous non-state actors. The regional armament dynamic includes the acquisition and growing use of long-range missiles, with 10 countries (Algeria, Bahrain, Egypt, Iran, Israel, Kuwait, Qatar, Saudi Arabia, Turkey and the United Arab Emirates (UAE)) possessing missiles with a range of 250 kilometres or more.[2] Since 2011, 13 United Nations envoys—four in Syria, six in Libya and three in Yemen—have sought to defuse the three main civil wars without success.[3] However, a ceasefire in Idlib province in Syria in March 2020 and a nationwide ceasefire agreed in Libya in October 2020 suggested that both of those conflicts might be open to some form of resolution soon. In Yemen implementation of the 2018 Stockholm Agreement remained stalled.

There were 14 multilateral peace operations in the MENA region in 2020, the same number as in 2019. None of the peace operations that were active in the region in 2020 started or ended during the year. The number of personnel deployed in multilateral peace operations in the MENA region decreased

---

[1] For conflict definitions and typologies see chapter 2, section I, in this volume.

[2] Erästö, T. and Wezeman, P. D., 'Addressing missile threats in the Middle East and North Africa', SIPRI Policy Brief, Nov. 2020. On international arms transfers to the region see chapter 9 in this volume.

[3] 'Frustrated are the peacemakers: Why the United Nations cannot end wars in the Arab world', *The Economist*, 13 Feb. 2020.

Table 6.1. Estimated conflict-related fatalities in the Middle East and North Africa, 2017–20

Country	2017	2018	2019	2020
Egypt	1 544	1 112	1 003	626
Iraq	32 018	5 603	3 701	2 708
Israel–Palestine	131	360	166	38
Libya	1 663	1 188	2 076	1 495
Syria	54 405	30 084	15 301	7 975
Turkey	2 924	1 928	951	541
Yemen	17 618	34 247	28 030	19 757
Total	**110 303**	**74 522**	**51 228**	**33 140**

Note: Includes only countries with armed conflicts with 25 or more battle-related deaths in a given year.

Source: Armed Conflict Location & Event Data Project, 'Data export tool', accessed 26 Jan.– 15 Feb. 2021.

by 3.1 per cent, from 15 082 on 31 December 2019 to 14 615 on 31 December 2020.[4]

Five cross-cutting issues shaped security dilemmas in the region in 2020: (*a*) ongoing regional interstate rivalries with a shifting network of external alliances and interests; (*b*) a new wave of large, sustained protest movements across many states in the region; (*c*) the impact of the Covid-19 pandemic; (*d*) continuing threats from violent jihadist groups; and (*e*) increasing competition over water, and growing climate change impacts.[5] This section examines briefly how these five issues evolved in 2020.

Shifting alliances and rivalries: Continuing Iranian–United States tensions

In the MENA region interstate and intrastate fault lines intersect in complex ways, with shifting alliances and rivalries.[6] The most destabilizing and high-risk interstate rivalries in 2020 continued to be between Iran (and its allies in Iraq, Lebanon, Syria and Yemen) and an ad hoc group of four states: Israel, Saudi Arabia, the UAE and the USA.[7] Saudi Arabia and the UAE (and to a lesser extent some of the other states in the Gulf) have been actively

---

[4] For global and regional trends in multilateral peace operations see chapter 2, section II, in this volume.

[5] For earlier developments in these issues (except the Covid-19 pandemic) see Davis, I., 'Armed conflict and peace processes in the Middle East and North Africa', *SIPRI Yearbook 2019*, pp. 81–87; and Davis, I., 'Key general developments in the region', *SIPRI Yearbook 2020*, pp. 132–36.

[6] Malley, R., 'The unwanted wars: Why the Middle East is more combustible than ever', *Foreign Affairs*, Nov./Dec. 2019.

[7] For further details on the rivalries and their developments in 2018–19 see *SIPRI Yearbook 2019* (note 5), pp. 82–84; and *SIPRI Yearbook 2020* (note 5), pp. 132–34. Also see Tabatabai, A. M., 'Iran's authoritarian playbook: The tactics, doctrine, and objectives behind Iran's influence operation', The Alliance for Securing Democracy and German Marshall Fund, 2020; and Malakoutikhah, Z., 'Iran: Sponsoring or combating terrorism?', *Studies in Conflict & Terrorism*, vol. 43, no. 10 (2020), pp. 913–39.

opposing Iran in Iraq, Lebanon, Syria and Yemen, while Israeli opposition to Iran has been focused on Lebanon and Syria, as well as Iran's nuclear programme. As it did in 2018–19 Israel attacked Iranian and Iranian-aligned targets in Syria on several occasions in 2020, and also continued air strikes against Iranian-backed militias in Iraq and Hezbollah in Lebanon.[8]

Russia and Turkey were influential external actors and rivals in Libya and Syria, where this Russian–Turkish proxy conflict deviated between competition and complicity during the year. It escalated to the brink of a direct military confrontation in Syria in February 2020, before being calmed again by a ceasefire agreed on 5 March 2020 (see section II).

There were also ongoing rifts and political tensions between other groups of states in the region. Egypt, Saudi Arabia and the UAE were in competition with Qatar and Turkey (especially in the Horn of Africa and Libya).[9] The UAE continued to adopt a softer approach towards Iran and became the first Gulf country and only the third Arab state to formally normalize its relationship with Israel (see section III).[10] However, it was the Iranian–US conflict that after worsening during 2019 again threatened to escalate into a regional-wide interstate military conflict in early 2020.[11]

The Iranian–United States conflict

Iranian–US relations have been largely adversarial since the 1979 Islamic Revolution. Despite an improvement in relations during the Obama presidency, they deteriorated in recent years as a result of the US withdrawal from the 2015 multilateral nuclear agreement with Iran (Joint Comprehensive Plan of Action, JCPOA) and the US coercive policy of applying 'maximum pressure' colliding with Iran's policy of 'maximum resistance'.[12] In 2019 this

---

[8] See e.g. 'Syria war: Israel "hits Iran-backed fighters near Damascus"', BBC News, 6 Feb. 2020; 'Hezbollah fighter killed in Israeli strike near Damascus: Death notice', Reuters, 22 July 2020; 'After Covid-19 lull, secret war gets underway again', Intelligence Online, no. 852 (29 Apr. 2020); and Kaye, D. D. and Efron, S., 'Israel's evolving Iran policy', Survival, vol. 62, no. 4 (2020), pp. 7–30.

[9] Milton-Edwards, B., 'The blockade on Qatar: Conflict management failings', International Spectator, vol. 55, no. 2 (2020), pp. 34–48; Başkan, B. and Pala, Ö., 'Making sense of Turkey's reaction to the Qatar crisis', International Spectator, vol. 55, no. 2 (2020), pp. 65–78; and 'Cairo takes steps to establish Arab security front to halt Erdogan's ambitions', Intelligence Online, no. 848 (26 Feb. 2020). On armed conflict in the Horn of Africa see chapter 7, section IV, in this volume.

[10] 'The United Arab Emirates has become a force in the Middle East', The Economist, 20 Aug. 2020.

[11] International Crisis Group, The Middle East between Collective Security and Collective Breakdown, Middle East Report no. 212 (International Crisis Group: Brussels, 27 Apr. 2020).

[12] US Department of State, Office of the Spokesperson, 'Advancing the US maximum pressure campaign on Iran', Fact sheet, 22 Apr. 2019; Geranmayeh, E., 'Reviving the revolutionaries: How Trump's maximum pressure is shifting Iran's domestic politics', European Council on Foreign Relations Policy Brief, June 2020; and Barzegar, K., 'The hard chess puzzle: Trump's "maximum pressure" versus Iran's "maximum resistance"', Al Jazeera, 15 June 2020. On the US withdrawal from the JCPOA see Erästö, T., 'Implementation of the Joint Comprehensive Plan of Action', SIPRI Yearbook 2019, pp. 381–86. On Iran's defence posture and key foreign policy objectives see Ahmadian, H. and Mohseni, P., 'Iran's Syria strategy: The evolution of deterrence', International Affairs, vol. 95, no. 2 (2019), pp. 341–64; and US Congressional Research Service (CRS), Iran's Foreign and Defense Policies, CRS Report for Congress R44017 (US Congress, CRS: Washington, DC, 11 Jan. 2021).

led to a series of serious maritime confrontations in the Strait of Hormuz that raised the risk of a regional conflagration.[13] On 3 January 2020 a US air strike targeted and killed Iranian major general Qasem Soleimani in Baghdad, Iraq. Four other Iranian and five Iraqi nationals were also killed in the air strike.[14] In retaliation Iran carried out a ballistic missile attack on two Iraqi military bases hosting US forces. No serious Iraqi or US casualties were sustained, and US officials regarded the attack as having been calibrated to avoid escalation.[15]

Amidst the heightened tensions on 8 January Iran accidentally shot down a Ukrainian airliner shortly after take-off from Tehran airport killing all 176 people on board. Iranian President Hassan Rouhani promised a thorough investigation into the 'unforgivable error', as anti-government protests started in several Iranian cities linked to economic and political grievances.[16] The Iranian–US rivalry reignited in March 2020 when US forces carried out retaliatory air strikes against the Iran-aligned Kata'ib Hezbollah militia in Iraq after a militia rocket attack killed two US soldiers and one British soldier.[17] This military clash underscored Iraq's centrality as a theatre for Iranian–US tensions (see section II).[18]

The Covid-19 pandemic provided another sphere for Iranian–US tensions, with the USA refusing to lift its sanctions on humanitarian grounds and blocking Iran's request for $5 billion in emergency loans from the International Monetary Fund.[19] Meanwhile, in the Persian Gulf naval clashes between the two countries were narrowly avoided.[20] In late June 2020 Iran issued an arrest warrant for US President Donald J. Trump and 35 other US

---

[13] On developments in 2019 see Smith, D., 'Flashpoints', *SIPRI Yearbook 2020*, pp. 5–8.

[14] 'How Iran can respond to the killing of Qassem Suleimani', *The Economist*, 9 Jan. 2020; and Borger, J. and Chulov, M., 'US kills Iran general Qassem Suleimani in strike ordered by Trump', *The Guardian*, 3 Jan. 2020.

[15] 'US and Iran back away from open conflict', *Wall Street Journal*, 9 Jan. 2020; and Ali, I. and Stewart, P., 'More than 100 US troops diagnosed with brain injuries from Iran attack', Reuters, 10 Feb. 2020.

[16] Hafezi, P. and Dehghanpisheh, B., 'Iran makes arrests in plane shootdown, police crack down on protests', Reuters, 14 Jan. 2020. On the protests in Iran see O' Driscoll, D. et al., *Protest and State–Society Relations in the Middle East and North Africa*, SIPRI Policy Paper no. 56 (SIPRI: Stockholm, Oct. 2020), pp. 17–19.

[17] 'Iraqi religious authorities say US air strike hit civilian airport', Reuters, 13 Mar. 2020; and Schmitt, E. and Gibbons-Neff, T., 'US carries out retaliatory strikes on Iranian-backed militia in Iraq', *New York Times*, 12 Mar. 2020.

[18] Mazzetti, M. and Schmitt, E., 'Pentagon order to plan for escalation in Iraq meets warning from top commander', *New York Times*, 27 Mar. 2020; and Wintour, P., 'Iraq's prime minister says country on tightrope between US and Iran', *The Guardian*, 22 Oct. 2020.

[19] Fassihi, F., 'Iran says US sanctions are taking lives. US officials disagree', *New York Times*, 1 Apr. 2020; and Talley, I. and Faucon, B., 'US to block Iran's request to IMF for $5 billion loan to fight coronavirus', *Wall Street Journal*, 7 Apr. 2020.

[20] Faucon, B. and Said, S., 'Iranian navy temporarily seizes vessel, sparking Persian Gulf alert', *Wall Street Journal*, 14 Apr. 2020; Neuman, S., 'Iranian speedboats conduct "dangerous and provocative" maneuvers near US warship', NPR, 16 Apr. 2020; and Hafezi, P., 'Guards chief: US warships will be destroyed if they threaten Iran in Gulf', Reuters, 23 Apr. 2020.

officials on charges relating to the January killing of Qasem, while the UN special rapporteur on extrajudicial, summary or arbitrary executions called the assassination a violation of international law.[21] Several unexplained incidents in June and July caused significant damage to Iranian nuclear and missile infrastructure, including a large-scale explosion at Natanz, one of Iran's primary nuclear facilities.[22] Iran accused Israel or the USA of sabotage operations against the Natanz nuclear facility, as well as the assassination of a high-ranking Iranian nuclear scientist on 27 November 2020.[23] Neither Israel nor the USA commented officially on these attacks.

For the last quarter of the year most Iranian–US tensions focused on sanctions related to the JCPOA. Despite the US administration seeking to prolong the UN-imposed arms embargo on Iran, it expired in October.[24] In December Iran passed a new nuclear law that could significantly increase its nuclear activities if certain sanction relief measures were not met.[25] At the end of the year, while the incoming Biden administration was expected to engage with Iran and potentially rejoin the JCPOA, the outgoing Trump administration doubled down on its maximum pressure strategy by imposing new sanctions on Iran.[26]

Protest movements

The MENA region has the highest proportion of undemocratic states in the world, and anti-government protests have occurred in many states in the region since 2018.[27] Based on the number, intensity and durability of protests

---

[21] 'Iran issues warrant for Trump over killing of top general', Reuters, 29 June 2020; and Human Rights Council, 'Extrajudicial, summary or arbitrary executions', Report of the Special Rapporteur on extrajudicial, summary or arbitrary executions, A/HRC/44/38, 29 June 2020, annex, pp. 22–39. On the legality of the US drone strike also see Corn, G. S. and Jenks, C., 'Soleimani and the tactical execution of strategic self-defense', Lawfare, 24 Jan. 2020; and Cronin, A. K., 'The age of open assassination', Lawfare, 19 Jan. 2020.

[22] Sanger, D. E., Schmitt, E. and Bergman, R., 'Long-planned and bigger than thought: Strike on Iran's nuclear program', New York Times, 10 July 2020; and 'What to make of a series of odd explosions in Iran', The Economist, 9 July 2020.

[23] Hafezi, P., 'Iran official says sabotage caused fire at Natanz nuclear site—TV', Reuters, 23 Aug. 2020; and Wintour, P. and Holmes, O., 'Iran vows retaliation after top nuclear scientists shot dead near Tehran', The Guardian, 27 Nov. 2020.

[24] Rashad, M., 'Saudi, US officials call for extending UN arms embargo on Iran', Reuters, 29 June 2020; 'Iran nuclear deal: UN rejects US bid to "snapback" Iran sanctions', BBC News, 26 Aug. 2020; and Motamedi, M., 'Arms embargo on Iran expires despite US opposition', Al Jazeera, 18 Oct. 2020. On the UN arms embargo on Iran see chapter 14, section II, in this volume.

[25] Masterson, J. and Davenport, K., 'Iran passes nuclear law', Arms Control Now blog, Arms Control Association, 10 Dec. 2020. On the JCPOA see chapter 11, section II, in this volume.

[26] Schmitt, E. et al., 'Trump sought options for attacking Iran to stop its growing nuclear program', New York Times, 16 Nov. 2020; and Psaledakis, D. and Pamuk, H., 'US imposes sweeping sanctions on Iran, targets Khamenei-linked foundation', Reuters, 18 Nov. 2020.

[27] See e.g. 'Taking stock of regional democratic trends in Africa and the Middle East before and during the Covid-19 pandemic', International Institute for Democracy and Electoral Assistance, The Global State of Democracy in Focus, Special Brief, Jan. 2021.

in this new wave of uprisings, the protests in MENA countries can be divided into four categories: mass protests (Algeria, Iraq and Lebanon), sporadic protests (Egypt, Iran, Israel, Jordan, Morocco, the Palestinian territories and Tunisia), scarce protests (Kuwait, Oman, Qatar and the UAE) and highly suppressed protests (Bahrain and Saudi Arabia).[28] In Lebanon in August, for example, following a massive explosion in the capital Beirut that killed more than 200 people, violent anti-government protests led to resignation of the government.[29]

Key reasons for the protests in the region include extreme levels of inequality, austerity and corruption, as well as calls for broader political and democratic rights. The probable wide-ranging socio-economic consequences of the Covid-19 pandemic are likely to exacerbate these grievances.[30] Government responses have combined repression with compromise in order to maintain the status quo and avoid social and political reforms. External actors in the region, with their focus on mitigating threats to regional and international security, have also contributed to preservation of the status quo.[31]

Impact of Covid-19

The Covid-19 pandemic appears to have had minimal impact on the region's armed conflicts, although it clearly added another layer of complexity to the existing humanitarian challenges. In response to the UN secretary-general's March call for a Covid-19-related global ceasefire, the Kurdish-led Syrian Democratic Forces in north-east Syria supported the call (see section II), as did the main protagonists in Libya. In Yemen the coalition led by Saudi Arabia fighting against the Houthis and their allies declared a two-week ceasefire that was extended on 23 April for another month.[32] However, the fighting in Libya and Yemen continued (see sections IV and V), including attacks against healthcare facilities and personnel.[33]

---

[28] O'Driscoll et al. (note 16), pp. 1–4. On the protests in Iraq see section II in this chapter; on the protests in Israel and Palestinian territories see section III in this chapter; and on the protests in Algeria, Egypt and Morocco see section IV in this chapter.

[29] Qiblawi, T. et al., 'Lebanon's government steps down in wake of Beirut blast', CNN, 11 Aug. 2020; and O'Driscoll et al. (note 16), pp. 13–15.

[30] Assouad, L., 'Inequality and its discontents in the Middle East', Carnegie Middle East Center, 12 Mar. 2020; Bourhrous, A., 'Trust and coercion in times of emergency: Covid-19 and structures of authority in North Africa', SIPRI Commentary, 13 Aug. 2020; and 'The Middle East is fighting a second wave of Covid-19', The Economist, 13 June 2020.

[31] O'Driscoll et al. (note 16), pp. 50–59.

[32] 'SDF calls for humanitarian truce in Syria amid coronavirus crisis', Al-Monitor, 24 Mar. 2020; 'UN welcomes response by Libyan parties to calls for humanitarian pause', UN News, 21 Mar. 2020; and 'Covid-19 in Yemen: Saudi coalition ceasefire declared in bid to contain coronavirus', UN News, 9 Apr. 2020. On the UN global ceasefire call, also see chapter 2, section I, in this volume.

[33] See e.g. 'Aid security and Covid-19', Insecurity Insight Bulletin no. 6, 22 May 2020.

The pace of some armed conflicts was temporarily slowed by the pandemic (e.g. in Syria in March), but over time the violence escalated again, driven more by long-standing conflict dynamics than by Covid-19. In addition, some armed groups appeared to take advantage of the disruption caused by the pandemic to regroup. As the US-led coalition in Iraq scaled back its counterterrorism activities in response to Covid-19, for example, the Islamic State appeared to be slowly recovering and rebuilding in rural Iraq.[34] With infection rates in Iraq reported to be the highest in the Arab world, the pandemic has also added to the growing unrest in the country more generally (see section II).[35] There was cooperation between the Palestinian Authority and Israel in the first months of the pandemic to contain the spread of Covid-19 (see section III), and some states and organizations provided support beyond their borders, such as the UAE supplying Iran with humanitarian aid despite their strained relations.[36]

Violent jihadist groups

The Salafi–jihadist threat in MENA and globally has become fractured and localized, but with the Islamic State and/or al-Qaeda continuing to drive or influence a number of disparate groups.[37] Assessing the size of the remaining jihadi base in the region remains difficult, given its covert nature and a continuing significant component of 'foreign fighters' (individuals that have joined a non-state armed group in an armed conflict abroad). The UN estimated more than 10 000 Islamic State fighters remained active in Iraq and Syria.[38] In Yemen, al-Qaeda in the Arabian Peninsula remained a threat despite being weakened by fragmentation into local factions.[39]

---

[34] Tlozek, E. and Gosh, F. A., 'Islamic State never needed a caliphate to keep menacing the world. Now it's regrouping', ABC News, 10 July 2020. Also see Basit, A., 'Covid-19: A challenge or opportunity for terrorist groups?', *Journal of Policing, Intelligence and Counter Terrorism*, vol. 15, no. 3 (2020), pp. 263–75; and United Nations, Security Council, 'Eleventh report of the secretary-general on the threat posed by ISIL (Da'esh) to international peace and security and the range of United Nations efforts in support of member states in countering the threat', S/2020/774, 4 Aug. 2020.

[35] 'Iraq is too broken to protect itself from Covid-19', *The Economist*, 3 Oct. 2020.

[36] Farmanfarmaian, R., 'Iran, sanctions, and the Covid-19 pandemic', European Leadership Network Commentary, 23 July 2020.

[37] On the future of violent radical Islamism see Clarke, C. P., *After the Caliphate* (Polity Press: Cambridge, 2019). On the Islamic State, its goals, operations and affiliates, and the international military campaign to defeat it see Davis, I., 'The aims, objectives and modus operandi of the Islamic State and the international response', *SIPRI Yearbook 2016*, pp. 22–39; and Davis, I., 'The Islamic State in 2016: A failing "caliphate" but a growing transnational threat', *SIPRI Yearbook 2017*, pp. 89–104.

[38] United Nations, S/2020/774 (note 34). On the Islamic State resurgence in Iraq and Syria also see Knights, M. and Almeida, A., 'Remaining and expanding: The recovery of Islamic State operations in Iraq in 2019–2020', Combating Terrorism Center, *CTC Sentinel*, vol. 13, no. 5 (May 2020); and Pavlik, M. et al., 'A sudden surfacing of strength: Evaluating the possibility of an IS resurgence in Iraq and Syria', ACLED, 24 July 2020.

[39] Johnsen, G. D., 'Khaid Batarfi and the future of AQAP', Lawfare, 22 Mar. 2020.

Water stress and other climate change impacts

Linkages among water scarcity, climate change and insecurity issues in the MENA region are 'complex, diverse and multi-directional'.[40] Most states in the region are facing medium to high exposure to ecological threats, such as food insecurity, water stress and food insecurity.[41] Climate change and water stress have played direct or indirect roles in recent and ongoing conflicts in several cases in the region. For example, all actors in the Syrian conflict have used water systems as a strategic asset to be controlled or targeted by military strikes.[42]

[40] Schaar, J., 'A confluence of crises: On water, climate and security in the Middle East and North Africa', SIPRI Insights on Peace and Security no. 2019/4, July 2019.

[41] Institute for Economics & Peace (IEP), Ecological Threat Register 2020: Understanding Ecological Threats, Resilience and Peace (IEP: Sydney, Sep. 2020).

[42] Daoudy, M., 'Water weaponization in the Syrian conflict: Strategies of domination and cooperation', International Affairs, vol. 96, no. 5 (2020), pp. 1347–66.

II. Armed conflict and peace processes in Iraq, Syria and Turkey

IAN DAVIS AND SHIVAN FAZIL

This section reviews the complex and interlinked armed conflicts in Iraq, Syria and Turkey. During 2020 the government of President Bashar al-Assad continued to consolidate its hold in Syria, and a March ceasefire in Idlib province led to a further reduction in large-scale hostilities. Iraq remained a fragile, largely post-conflict state with weak institutions and growing protests. Iran remained an influential presence in Iraq and Syria, and Iranian–United States tensions spilled over into Iraq. Turkey intensified its military operations in northern Iraq, while the protracted armed conflict in the south-east of Turkey also continued. The Idlib ceasefire brokered by Russia and Turkey cemented their roles as key power brokers in Syria, while US influence in the region continued to wane.

Armed conflict in Iraq

Post-conflict Iraq continues to struggle to resolve its political and security challenges, the crippling economy, endemic corruption and entanglement in the tensions between Iran and the USA.[1] Despite the military defeat of Islamic State in 2017, the country continues to face security threats posed by the remnants of the militant group. Recent assessments indicate a significant increase in the number of Islamic State attacks—especially in the Sunni areas and the Hamrin mountain range (which extends across Diyala, Kirkuk and Salah al-Din provinces)—with its reach and activities almost doubling between the first quarter of 2019 and the first quarter of 2020.[2]

Iraq is facing its worst financial crisis in five years. It was dealt a double blow by plummeting oil prices and Covid-19-induced economic contractions, which the World Bank projected could result in an additional 5.5 million more Iraqis falling into poverty.[3] The spread of Covid-19 has worsened the underlying grievances fuelling protests, especially in the poorer south. In November, after months of struggle between the government and the parliament, the latter approved a deficit law to allow the government to borrow

---

[1] Ibish, H., 'The US and Iran inch toward confrontation in Iraq', Bloomberg, 7 Apr. 2020. Also see section I in this chapter.

[2] Knights, M. and Almeida, A., 'Remaining and expanding: The recovery of Islamic State operations in Iraq in 2019–20', Combating Terrorism Center, *CTC Sentinel*, vol. 13, no. 5 (May 2020); and O'Driscoll, D. and Fazil, S., 'The resurgence of the Islamic State in Iraq: Political and military responses', SIPRI Commentary, 9 June 2020.

[3] World Bank, 'Covid-19 and low oil prices push millions of Iraqis into poverty', 11 Nov. 2020.

Table 6.2. Estimated conflict-related fatalities in Iraq, 2016–20

Event type	2016	2017	2018	2019	2020
Battles	24 595	15 216	2 736	1 735	1 461
Explosions/remote violence	25 645	13 921	2 499	1 257	817
Protests, riots and strategic developments	319	58	57	469	115
Violence against civilians	5 755	2 823	311	240	315
Total	56 314	32 018	5 603	3 701	2 708

Notes: The first available year for data on Iraq in the Armed Conflict Location & Event Data Project (ACLED) database is 2016. For definitions of event types, see ACLED, 'ACLED definitions of political violence and protest', 11 Apr. 2019.

Source: ACLED, 'Data export tool', accessed 15 Feb. 2021.

$10 billion to pay expenses and salaries that had been in arrears for over two months.[4]

In a sign of the growing security challenges, tensions increased among the Popular Mobilization Forces (PMF)—an Iraqi state-sponsored umbrella organization composed of a number of predominantly Shia militias (some supported by Iran)—and smaller militia groups comprising ethno-religious minorities in the country's north. Looking to separate from the Iran-backed divisions after a year-long struggle over allegiance and resources, the PMF shrine factions (20 000 active fighters linked to the shrines of Iraq's twin holy cities of Karbala and Najaf) held a strategic planning meeting during which they emphasized a patriotic 'Iraq-only' discourse.[5] One of the goals of the Iraqi Government has been integrating the PMF into the Iraqi Security Forces (ISF), but progress has been slow.

Turkey's air strikes and ground military incursions against the Kurdistan Workers' Party (Partîya Karkerên Kurdistanê, PKK) in northern Iraq intensified in 2020. Shelling and bombing resulted in civilian casualties and wildfires, and caused the displacement of thousands of people, destroying their livelihoods and fragile ecosystems.[6] In the Kurdistan region of Iraq there were also several skirmishes between PKK fighters and the Peshmerga of the Kurdistan Democratic Party (KDP), heightening fears of an open conflict.[7] There was also a looming armed stand-off between the Peshmerga of the KDP and the Patriotic Union of Kurdistan in April on the demarcation line that split the Kurdish region during the civil war fought in the 1990s between the two ruling Kurdish parties.[8] Nonetheless, Iraq has been described as being in a largely post-conflict period since 2018. The available

---

[4] Saadon, M., 'Iraq increases deficit to pay salaries', Al-Monitor, 23 Nov. 2020.

[5] Malik, H., 'Pro-Sistani "popular mobilization units" break with pro-Iran militias in Iraq', Al-Monitor, 30 Apr. 2020.

[6] 'Violence and wildfires driving people from their lands in Iraqi Kurdistan', PAX, 13 Nov. 2020; and 'Turkey air raids kill 5 civilians in north Iraq: Local officials', AFP, 19 June 2020.

[7] Wali, Z., 'Kurd vs Kurd: Fears of full-scale war rise in northern Iraq', Al Jazeera, 2 Dec. 2020.

[8] Tastekin, F., 'Turkey seeks to exploit claims to Iraqi Kurdish village', Al-Monitor, 23 Apr. 2020.

data indicates a continued decline in combat-related fatalities in 2020 and a marked decline in fatalities as a result of the response to anti-government protests (see table 6.2).

In October the Iraqi Government started closing internally displaced person (IDP) camps across the country, despite concerns their rapid closure could render 100 000 people without shelter during the Covid-19 pandemic and during winter. The government expects IDPs to return to their areas of origin, many of which were destroyed during the war against Islamic State and have not been rebuilt. Many IDPs do not want to return home, fearing reprisal attacks by armed militias.[9] The Iraqi Government and the Kurdistan Regional Government also reached an agreement to normalize the administrative and security situation in Sinjar, the ancestral home town of Yezidis in north-western Iraq. The United Nations Assistance Mission for Iraq hoped the agreement would accelerate the reconstruction process and pave the way for the return of the displaced Yezidis.[10] Nonetheless, the humanitarian situation remained challenging, with more than 1.2 million people internally displaced and 4.1 million people in need of humanitarian assistance, as of December 2020.[11]

Iraq was caught in the middle as tensions between Iran and the USA were heightened following a targeted US drone strike at Baghdad airport in January 2020, which killed the commander of Iran's Islamic Revolutionary Guard Corps Quds Force, Qasem Soleimani, as well as the deputy commander of Iraq's PMF, Abu Mahdi al-Muhandis.[12] Iran responded by launching ballistic missiles at Iraqi bases hosting US troops in Anbar and Erbil provinces, injuring dozens of military personnel.[13] The US air strikes also further strained Iraqi–US relations, with the Iraq Parliament passing a resolution calling on the Iraqi Government to expel foreign troops from the country.[14]

The USA also started decreasing its military footprint in Iraq by handing over several military bases and reducing the number of combat troops in the country.[15] In November the USA announced it would reduce its military presence in Iraq from 3000 to roughly 2500 troops, half of the initially deployed force of 5000.[16] Iraq and the USA held a strategic dialogue, which

---

[9] 'Iraq: Closing camps and repatriating the displaced will put their lives at risk', Euro-Med Monitor, 11 Nov. 2020.

[10] 'UNAMI welcomes agreement on Sinjar: A first and important step in the right direction', Reliefweb, 9 Oct. 2020.

[11] International Organization for Migration, Displacement tracking matrix, Master List Report 119, Nov.–Dec. 2020; and US Agency for International Development, Bureau for Humanitarian Emergency, 'Iraq—complex emergency: Situation at a glance', 16 Dec. 2020.

[12] 'Iran's Qassem Soleimani killed in US air raid at Baghdad airport', Al Jazeera, 3 Jan. 2020.

[13] 'Iran attack: US troops targeted with ballistic missiles', BBC News, 8 Jan. 2020.

[14] 'Iraqi parliament calls for expulsion of foreign troops', Al Jazeera, 5 Jan. 2020.

[15] 'Iraq military bases: US pulling out of three key sites', BBC News, 16 Mar. 2020.

[16] Falk, T. O., 'What the US troop withdrawal means for Iraq', Al Jazeera, 22 Nov. 2020.

took place between June and August, amid heightened tensions over rocket attacks by Iran-backed Iraqi militias targeting the US embassy in Baghdad.[17] During the dialogue, the first between the two countries since 2008, the growing capabilities of the ISF and the success in the fight against Islamic State were cited as enabling the US-led Global Coalition against Daesh to transition to a new phase focused on training, equipping and supporting the ISF.[18] Nonetheless, the ISF remained dependent on the US and global coalition air power to counter the Islamic State resurgence.[19]

Anti-government protests

The major anti-government protests that started in October 2019 gathered pace in early 2020. Undeterred by the forceful response from official and non-official security forces, Iraqis of all backgrounds joined the movement with unprecedented inclusivity across sect, gender and class.[20] The protests constituted the biggest challenge to a government that owed its survival to a fragile compromise between two rival blocs (Bina and Islah) that emerged from the inconclusive 2018 elections.[21] In demanding the overhaul of the Muhasasa Ta'ifia (an ethno-sectarian political apportionment system), pro-testers sought to renegotiate the social contract that had underpinned and strained state–society relations since the toppling of the regime of Saddam Hussein in 2003.[22]

Following the resignation of the former Prime Minister Adil Abdul Mahdi in December 2019, Iraq was left without a functioning government for over five months as successive prime minister-designates struggled to satisfy the protesters and failed to form a government. The incumbent Mustafa al-Khadimi was inaugurated as prime minister on 6 May 2020 and began his mandate by releasing detained protesters, pledging justice and com-pensating relatives of those killed during the protests.[23] He promised to hold early elections and pledged to curb the influence of Iran-backed militias accused of killing protesters and carrying out attacks against foreign troops in the country.[24] While the next general election was initially scheduled for

---

[17] Ibrahim, A., 'US-Iraq talks promise US troop withdrawal, fall short of timeline', Al Jazeera, 12 June 2020.

[18] 'Joint statement on the US-Iraq strategic dialogue', US Embassy in Georgia, 19 Aug. 2020. The Global Coalition against Daesh maintains a website at <https://theglobalcoalition.org/en/>.

[19] Newdick, T., 'The Iraqi air force's F-16 fleet is on the brink of collapse despite showy flybys', The Drive, 7 Jan. 2021; and Williams, K. B., 'Is Iraq's military good enough for US troops to leave?', Defense One, 28 Oct. 2020.

[20] Ali, Z., 'Iraqis demand a country', *Middle East Report*, vol. 292, no. 3 (autumn/winter 2019).

[21] 'Iraq: Adil Abdul Mahdi named prime minister', Al Jazeera, 3 Oct. 2018.

[22] O' Driscoll, D. et al., *Protest and State–Society Relations in the Middle East and North Africa*, SIPRI Policy Paper no. 56 (SIPRI: Stockholm, Oct. 2020).

[23] Ibrahim, A., 'Mustafa al-Kadhimi ends Iraq deadlock but new PM faces hurdles', Al Jazeera, 11 May 2020.

[24] 'US sanctions senior Iraqi official for role in Iran-linked rights abuses', *Wall Street Journal*, 8 Jan. 2021.

6 June 2021, it is likely to be postponed in light of the election commission's demand for more time to complete the necessary preparations.[25]

As demonstrations continued, activists and analysts were plagued by a deliberate campaign of intimidation and terror, highlighting the growing rift between some militias and the government. Notable was the assassination of Hisham al-Hashimi, a prominent security analyst, outside his house on 6 July.[26] A month later in Basra, two prominent activists were killed, while three more survived murder attempts.[27]

Protests also took place in the Kurdistan region of Iraq in December 2020 after a period of relative calm and while anti-government protests gripped much of the rest of Iraq in late 2019 and early 2020. The protests were initially organized by teachers and civil servants demanding the release of their delayed salaries. In the ensuing days the protests expanded to the economically depressed periphery of the region and to midsized towns, and became more violent. Largely led by youth protesting about unemployment, dismal services and endemic corruption, during this second wave, protesters attacked the offices of Kurdish political parties.[28] The protests calmed following a forceful response and curfew, with many teachers and activists being detained in Duhok by Kurdish authorities.[29] Protracted revenue-sharing disputes with the Iraqi Government meant the region's 1.2 million civil servants went unpaid for months. The Iraqi Government had halted budget transfers earlier in April. Revenue sharing has been a contested issue since 2014.

In Iraq as a whole, persistent threats of violence and the Covid-19 pandemic suppressed large protest turnouts for much of 2020, and especially in the first half of the year. However, with their demands unmet, protests resumed again in October in Baghdad and other southern provinces, marking a year since they first erupted.[30] Moreover, Iraq's grim economic outlook looked set to spark further social and political unrest in 2021. Dwindling oil revenues have forced the Iraqi Government to introduce austerity measures, cut spending and devalue its currency by a fifth, thus adding inflation

---

[25] 'Iraq prime minister calls early elections for June 2021', Al Jazeera, 31 July 2020; and 'State media: Iraq to postpone general elections by four months', Voice of America, 19 Jan. 2021.

[26] 'Hisham al-Hashimi: Leading Iraqi security expert shot dead in Baghdad', BBC News, 7 July 2020.

[27] 'Iraq: Prominent female activist killed by unknown gunmen in Basra', Al Jazeera, 20 Aug. 2020.

[28] Loveluck, L. and Salim, M., 'Protests flare in Iraq's Kurdish north, adding new front in national crisis', Washington Post, 12 Dec. 2020.

[29] Wille, B., 'Kurdish authorities clamp down ahead of protests', Human Rights Watch, 19 May 2020; and Abdulla, N., 'Rattled by protests, Iraqi Kurdish leaders punish journalists', Voice of America, 5 Sep. 2020.

[30] Ibrahim, A., 'Demands not met': Anti-government protests resume in Iraq', Al Jazeera, 25 Oct. 2020.

and a significant cost-of-living increase to the list of hardships facing the population.[31]

Armed conflict in Syria

The Syrian civil war is an ongoing multisided armed conflict involving regional and international powers that was initially triggered by the 2011 Arab Spring. Since 2018 there has been a clear de-escalation in the war due to the Syrian Government's consolidation of territorial control and the eventual territorial defeat of the Islamic State in March 2019.[32] In 2020 there was a further relative reduction in large-scale hostilities due to a March ceasefire in Idlib province (see below) and the impact of the Covid-19 pandemic.[33]

At the beginning of 2020 the government of President al-Assad was in control of around 70 per cent of the country, with armed opposition focused on two areas: Idlib province in the north-west, and the north-east partially ruled by Kurds. The armed conflict continued to attract a complex and changing cast of combatants, including regional and global powers: Russia and Turkey in the north-west; and Russia, Turkey and the USA in the north-east.[34] In the south-west Iran retained an entrenched presence, and Israel continued with its campaign of air strikes and other military operations against Iran-allied targets in an attempt to enforce a buffer between itself and the Iranian-backed Syrian Government.[35] Remnants of the Islamic State also remained a threat.[36] In the first quarter of the 2020 there was also a risk of the Syrian conflict being widened, either from an escalation in the conflict in Idlib, where Turkish-backed rebel groups were fighting Russian-

---

[31] Cornish., C., 'Iraq devalues currency by a fifth as oil-price collapse hits', *Financial Times*, 20 Dec. 2020.

[32] On the Syrian conflict in 2016–19 see Smith, D., 'The Middle East and North Africa: 2016 in perspective', *SIPRI Yearbook 2017*, pp. 77–82; Davis, I., 'Armed conflict in the Middle East and North Africa', *SIPRI Yearbook 2018*, pp. 76–79; Davis, I., 'Armed conflict and peace processes in the Middle East and North Africa', *SIPRI Yearbook 2019*, pp. 98–107; and Davis, I. and O'Driscoll, D., 'Armed conflict and peace processes in Iraq, Syria and Turkey', *SIPRI Yearbook 2020*, pp. 140–50. On the nature of the urban warfare in Syria see Hägerdal, N., 'Starvation as siege tactics: Urban warfare in Syria', *Studies in Conflict & Terrorism* (2020). On the roots of the conflict see Lesch, D. W., *Syria* (Polity Press: Cambridge, 2019).

[33] 'Iran's shifting posture in Syria', Cipher Brief, 4 June 2020; 'Russia-Syria cooperation affected by Covid-19', Intelligence Online, no. 852 (29 Apr. 2020); and Mroue, B., 'Hezbollah shifts attention from Syria fight to battle virus', AP News, 1 Apr. 2020.

[34] On the use of Russian military power in Syria see de Haas, M. et al., 'Russia's military action in Syria driven by military reforms', *Journal of Slavic Military Studies*, vol. 33, no. 2 (2020), pp. 292–99. On Turkey's policy in Syria see Aydıntaşbaş, A., 'A new Gaza: Turkey's border policy in northern Syria', European Council on Foreign Relations Policy Brief, May 2020; and Kardaş, Ş., 'Turkey's mission impossible in sustaining Idlib's unstable equilibrium', German Marshall Fund On Turkey, no. 4, Apr. 2020.

[35] Siegal, T., 'IDF special forces carry out covert operation, destroy two Syrian outposts', *Jerusalem Post*, 14 Oct. 2020. On Iran's role in Syria see Juneau, T., 'Iran's costly intervention in Syria: A pyrrhic victory', *Mediterranean Politics*, vol. 25, no. 1 (2020), pp. 26–44.

[36] See e.g. McKernan, B., 'Syria: Dozens killed in Isis bus attack', *The Guardian*, 31 Dec. 2020.

backed government forces, or the broader Iranian–US rivalry (see section I). There were also ongoing concerns about the Syrian Government possessing chemical weapons.[37]

The north-west: Armed conflict and another ceasefire in Idlib

Since the recapture of the Damascus suburbs (eastern Ghouta) and the negotiated surrender of rebels in Homs in 2018, the focus of government forces (backed by Iran and Russia) has been on the remaining rebel-held province of Idlib. It is home to about 3 million civilians (including 1 million IDPs from other parts of Syria) and an estimated 100 000 armed rebels and assorted jihadists.[38] The UN estimated that al-Qaeda affiliates in the province numbered around 15 500–20 000 fighters.[39] Despite efforts within the UN Security Council to seek a cessation of hostilities in Idlib, in November and December 2019 Russian and Syrian forces intensified air strikes and started a ground offensive, taking territory from rebel groups and creating a new wave of refugees.[40]

In January–February 2020 the Russian-backed Syrian Government offensive continued to make incremental gains in Idlib as civilian casualties continued to rise due to indiscriminate attacks against hospitals, schools and other civilian infrastructure.[41] In February clashes between Syrian and Turkish forces (deployed in parts of Idlib to monitor an earlier ceasefire that had since collapsed, see table 6.3) became the focus of a further escalation in the conflict, which displaced nearly a million people. This was the most intense period of displacement since the start of the Syrian civil war.[42] After 33 Turkish soldiers were killed in Idlib on 27 February 2020, Turkey launched a major counteroffensive against Syrian government forces, openly

---

[37] 'OPCW Executive Council adopts decision addressing the possession and use of chemical weapons by the Syrian Arab Republic', Organisation for the Prohibition of Chemical Weapons, 9 July 2020. Also see chapter 12, section III, in this volume.

[38] See Davis, *SIPRI Yearbook 2019* (note 32), pp. 101–102; and Atrache, S., 'A crisis on top of a crisis: Covid-19 looms over war-ravaged Idlib', Refugees International, 28 Apr. 2020.

[39] United Nations, Security Council, Letter dated 20 January 2020 from the Chair of the Security Council Committee pursuant to resolutions 1267 (1999), 1989 (2011) and 2253 (2015) concerning Islamic State in Iraq and the Levant (Da'esh), Al-Qaida and associated individuals, groups, undertakings and entities addressed to the President of the Security Council, S/2020/53, 20 Jan. 2020, p. 7.

[40] Graham-Harrison, E. and Akoush, H., 'More than 235,000 people have fled Idlib region in Syria, says UN', *The Guardian*, 27 Dec. 2019.

[41] United Nations, General Assembly, Report of the Independent International Commission of Inquiry on the Syrian Arab Republic, A/HRC/44/61, 3 Sep. 2020; and McKernan, B., 'Idlib province bombing kills 21 in a single day', *The Guardian*, 26 Feb. 2020.

[42] AP News, '4 Turkish troops, 13 Syrian soldiers killed in north Syria', NBC News, 3 Feb. 2020; UN Office for the Coordination of Humanitarian Affairs, 'Recent developments in northwest Syria', Situation report no. 9, 26 Feb. 2020; and 'Syria war: Alarm after 33 Turkish soldiers killed in attack in Idlib', BBC News, 28 Feb. 2020.

Table 6.3. Ceasefires and other de-escalation measures in Idlib province, Syria, 2017–20

Date	Parties	Details
Jan. 2017	Iran, Russia and Turkey	Parties agreed to enforce a ceasefire between Syria Government and rebels
May 2017	Iran, Russia and Turkey	The 2017 Astana Agreement established four de-escalation zones, including one in Idlib
Sep. 2017	Iran, Russia and Turkey	Parties agreed the de-escalation zone, to cease hostilities and deploy observer force
Oct. 2017	Turkey	Turkey set up observation posts to monitor rebel compliance with agreement
Sep. 2018	Russia and Turkey	The 2018 Sochi Agreement temporarily halted the Russian-backed Syrian Government offensive
Mar. 2020	Russia and Turkey	Ceasefire agreement to be monitored by joint Russian and Turkish patrols

Source: International Crisis Group, *Silencing the Guns in Syria's Idlib*, Middle East Report no. 213 (International Crisis Group: Brussels, 15 May 2020), pp. 12–13.

fighting them for the first time.[43] Turkey also announced it would no longer stop Syrian refugees from reaching Europe, reversing an agreement with the European Union made at the peak of the 2015–16 migration crisis.[44]

On 5 March 2020 the presidents of Russia and Turkey agreed a ceasefire (of an unspecified duration) in Idlib—the latest in several ceasefires and de-escalation initiatives since 2017 (see table 6.3)—as well as joint patrols by Russian and Turkish troops in a 'security corridor' extending six kilometres on each side of the M4 Aleppo–Latakia highway.[45] While the agreement failed to address the future of the main rebel groups operating in Idlib, the ceasefire halted most of the fighting.[46]

Sporadic fighting between pro-government forces and insurgent groups resumed in May and June, and suspected Russian air strikes on rebel groups in October 2020 strained the fragile ceasefire.[47] The USA also continued to carry out occasional air strikes against insurgents affiliated with al-Qaeda.[48]

---

[43] Gumrukcu, T. and Al-Khalidi, S., 'Turkey, Russia face off in Syria as fighting escalates, plane shot down', Reuters, 3 Mar. 2020; and Gall, C., 'Turkey declares major offensive against Syrian Government', *New York Times*, 1 Mar. 2020.

[44] Evans, D. and Coskun, O., 'Turkey says it will let refugees into Europe after its troops killed in Syria', Reuters, 27 Feb. 2020. On the migration crisis in 2015–16 see Grip, L., 'The global refugee crisis and its impact in Europe', *SIPRI Yearbook 2016*, pp. 439–52; and Grip, L., 'United Nations and regional responses to displacement crises', *SIPRI Yearbook 2017*, pp. 280–82.

[45] Higgins, A., 'Putin and Erdogan reach accord to halt fighting in Syria', *New York Times*, 5 Mar. 2020.

[46] 'Fifteen killed in clashes in Syria's Idlib despite ceasefire—monitor', Reuters, 6 Mar. 2020; and United Nations, A/HRC/44/61 (note 41).

[47] United Nations, General Assembly, Report of the Independent International Commission of Inquiry on the Syrian Arab Republic, A/HRC/45/31, 14 Aug. 2020; and 'Air raids in northwest Syria camp kill dozens of rebel fighters', Al Jazeera, 26 Oct. 2020.

[48] Schmitt, E., 'US commandos use secretive missiles to kill Qaeda leaders in Syria', *New York Times*, 24 Sep. 2020; and Schmitt, E., 'Al Qaeda feels losses in Syria and Afghanistan but stays resilient', *New York Times*, 27 Oct. 2020.

At the end of the year the ceasefire continued to hold. However, the truce remained extremely fragile, with Russia and Turkey continuing to have divergent interpretations of their commitments and opposing positions on Idlib's future as well as on how to deal with armed groups operating there.

The north-east: A fragile stalemate endured

In 2019 a protracted, but ultimately partial, withdrawal of US forces from the north-eastern area of Syria led to a new Turkish military offensive in October. The offensive was halted only by a new Russian–Turkish agreement on 22 October 2019, which set out new arrangements for territorial control in north-east Syria.[49] Turkish forces retained seized territory while Russian and Syrian forces were expected to control the remainder of a 'safe zone' on the Syria–Turkey border. Therefore, at the beginning of 2020 a challenging but fragile stalemate had returned to north-eastern Syria. The Syrian Democratic Forces (SDF), led primarily by a Kurdish-dominated armed group—the People's Protection Units (Yekîneyên Parastina Gel, YPG)—was protecting an autonomous administration that continued to govern areas in most of the north-east not held by Turkey or its Syrian allies. On 24 March 2020 the SDF announced it would cease all offensive military activity to facilitate responses to the Covid-19 pandemic, but no other actor indicated a similar commitment.[50] However, the fragile stalemate largely endured until the end of 2020, punctuated by sporadic outbreaks of armed violence among the various parties.[51]

The humanitarian crisis, casualties and war crimes

Despite the territorial focus of the Syrian armed conflict narrowing, it remains one of the most devastating in the world, with around 6.7 million people internally displaced, a further 5.6 million refugees (hosted mainly by Jordan, Lebanon and Turkey) and 11 million in need of humanitarian assistance.[52] During 2020, 9.3 million people (46 per cent of the population) were food insecure (up from 6.6 million in 2019) and a further 2.2 million were at risk of acute food insecurity (2.6 million in 2019).[53] China and Russia attempted to cut UN cross-border humanitarian aid from Turkey to Syria—they argued many areas in Syria could now be reached with humanitarian assistance from within the country. However, on 11 July 2020 after weeks of discussions and on its fourth attempt, the UN Security Council authorized

---

[49] 'Full text of Turkey, Russia agreement on northeast Syria', Al Jazeera, 22 Oct. 2019.

[50] 'SDF calls for humanitarian truce in Syria amid coronavirus crisis', Al-Monitor, 24 Mar. 2020.

[51] See e.g. AFP, 'Fuel truck bomb kills more than 40 in northern Syria', *The Guardian*, 29 Apr. 2020; and 'Syria war: US deploys reinforcements to Syria after Russia clashes', BBC News, 19 Sep. 2020.

[52] Toumeh, V., 'Help needed to meet "urgent humanitarian needs" in Syria, Grandi says', UN High Commissioner for Refugees, News release, 20 Sep. 2020; and World Food Programme, 'Regional Syrian refugee crisis overview', Nov. 2020.

[53] World Food Programme, 'WFP Syria country brief', Nov. 2020.

Table 6.4. Estimated conflict-related fatalities in Syria, 2017–20

Event type	2017	2018	2019	2020
Battles	26 580	16 001	8 299	4 206
Explosions/remote violence	25 245	11 806	5 764	2 751
Protests, riots and strategic developments	222	18	57	21
Violence against civilians	2 358	2 259	1 181	997
Total	**54 405**	**30 084**	**15 301**	**7 975**

Notes: The first available year for data on Syria in the Armed Conflict Location & Event Data Project (ACLED) database is 2017. For definitions of event types, see ACLED, 'ACLED definitions of political violence and protest', 11 Apr. 2019.

Source: ACLED, 'Data export tool', accessed 26 Jan. 2021.

the continuation of cross-border aid into north-west Syria.[54] Syria's economic crisis deepened during the year, leading to a return of street protests in the south of the country where the uprising against President al-Assad started in 2011.[55]

Although there are no reliable casualty statistics, in April 2016 the UN envoy to Syria estimated over 400 000 Syrians had died in the war.[56] Since then the Armed Conflict Location & Event Data Project estimated there have been over 100 000 additional fatalities, including approximately 8000 in 2020 (about half the number of 2019 and 85 per cent less than in 2017, see table 6.4).

Actual or suspected war crimes have been reported at every stage of Syria's civil war, and potential war crimes continued to be committed in 2020 by nearly every conflict actor controlling territory in Syria.[57] Having previously condemned indiscriminate air strikes on civilian targets carried out by Russia in 2019, the Independent International Commission of Inquiry on the Syrian Arab Republic (established by the UN Human Rights Council in 2011) said the Syrian Government and its allies were continuing to use these tactics in Idlib province in 2020.[58] A separate UN investigation into attacks on humanitarian sites in Syria in 2019 concluded the Syrian Govern-

---

[54] Nichols, M., 'Russia fails again at UN ahead of last-ditch vote on Syria cross-border aid', Reuters, 9 July 2020; and United Nations, Security Council, 'After several failed attempts, Security Council authorizes one-year extension of mechanism for cross-border aid delivery into Syria', Press Release SC/14247, 11 July 2020.

[55] Bowen, J., 'Syria war: Assad under pressure as economic crisis spirals', BBC News, 15 June 2020; and McKernan, B. and Akoush, H., 'A second revolution? Syrians take to streets under Russia's watchful eye', *The Guardian*, 13 July 2020.

[56] 'Syria death toll: UN envoy estimates 400,000 killed', Al Jazeera, 23 Apr. 2016. Also see Humud, C. et al., 'Counting casualties in Syria and Iraq: Process and challenges', Congressional Research Service Insight, 12 Apr. 2016.

[57] United Nations, A/HRC/45/31 (note 47).

[58] United Nations, General Assembly, Report of the Independent International Commission of Inquiry on the Syrian Arab Republic, A/HRC/43/57, 28 Jan. 2020 (published 2 Mar. 2020); and United Nations, A/HRC/44/61 (note 41). Also see Human Rights Watch, *'Targeting Life in Idlib': Syrian and Russian Strikes on Civilian Infrastructure* (Human Rights Watch: Oct. 2020).

ment or its allies had committed most of them.[59] In April 2020 the first trial in the world on state torture in Syria began in Koblenz, Germany, where two former Syrian security officers faced charges of crimes against humanity committed in the early days of the civil war.[60]

The Syrian peace processes

The main peace efforts in Syria have included long-standing UN-mediated talks, regular discussions by the Astana Group (Iran, Russia and Turkey), an October 2018 Quartet Meeting (France, Germany, Russia and Turkey) and a fragile patchwork of localized de-escalation agreements and ceasefires.[61] In October 2019, 150 delegates (50 each from the government, opposition and civil society) met in Geneva, Switzerland, for the first time to begin drafting a new Syrian constitution—the first step in a political process expected to lead to UN-supervised elections.[62] However, little progress was made at three subsequent rounds of negotiations (25–29 November 2019, 24–29 August 2020 and 30 November–4 December 2020), although a fifth round was scheduled for 25–29 January 2021 in Geneva.[63]

With the Syrian constitutional committee process seemingly deadlocked, an end to the civil war still seemed some way off. Post-conflict reconstruction and reconciliation among the various conflict parties is likely to be an even longer-term processes.[64] However, as some of the external actors seemed to be adjusting their posture in Syria, to deal with their own domestic eco-

---

[59] UN Secretary-General, 'Summary by the secretary-general of the report of the United Nations Headquarters Board of Inquiry into certain incidents in northwest Syria since 17 September 2018 involving facilities on the United Nations deconfliction list and United Nations supported facilities', 6 Apr. 2020; and Hill, E., 'UN inquiry into Syria bombings is silent on Russia's role', *New York Times*, 6 Apr. 2020.

[60] Hubbard, B., 'Germany takes rare step in putting Syrian officers on trial in torture case', *New York Times*, 23 Apr. 2020.

[61] On the interactions between humanitarian negotiations and international peace negotiations in Syria see Dieckhoff, M., 'Reconsidering the humanitarian space: Complex interdependence between humanitarian and peace negotiations in Syria', *Contemporary Security Policy*, vol. 41, no. 41 (2020), pp. 564–86. On the impact of ceasefires see Karakus, D. C. and Svensson, I., 'Between the bombs: Exploring partial ceasefires in the Syrian civil war, 2011–2017', *Terrorism and Political Violence*, vol. 32, no. 4 (2020), pp. 681–700; and Sosnowski, M., 'Ceasefires as violent state-building: Local truce and reconciliation agreements in the Syrian civil war', *Conflict, Security & Development*, vol. 20, no. 2 (2020), pp. 273–92.

[62] Bibbo, B., 'Long-awaited Syria constitutional committee meets for the first time', Al Jazeera, 30 Oct. 2019; and UN Security Council Resolution 2254, 18 Dec. 2015.

[63] '"Substantive" talks on new constitution bring hope of forging path out of Syria's near decade-long conflict', UN News, 18 Sep. 2020; Shaar, K. and Dasouki, A., 'Syria's Constitutional Committee: The devil in the detail', Middle East Institute, 6 Jan. 2021; United Nations, Security Council, 'Upcoming Constitutional Committee meetings offer hope for advancing Syria peace process, deputy special envoy tells Security Council', 25 Nov. 2020; and 'Syrian opposition document submitted in Geneva calls for establishing a "pluralistic republic"', Asharq Al-Awsat, 6 Dec. 2020.

[64] Asseburg, M., 'Reconstruction in Syria: Challenges and policy options for the EU and its member states', German Institute for International and Security Affairs, Research paper no. 11, July 2020.

Table 6.5. Estimated conflict-related fatalities in Turkey, 2016–20

Event type	2016	2017	2018	2019	2020
Battles	3 648	2 296	1 638	759	402
Explosions/remote violence	1 365	527	254	174	118
Protests, riots and strategic developments	14	4	8	4	1
Violence against civilians	166	97	28	14	20
Total	5 193	2 924	1 928	951	541

Notes: The first available year for data on Turkey in the Armed Conflict Location & Event Data Project (ACLED) database is 2016. For definitions of event types, see ACLED, 'ACLED definitions of political violence and protest', 11 Apr. 2019.

Source: ACLED, 'Data export tool', accessed 29 Jan. 2021.

nomic impacts of the Covid-19 pandemic, a sustained ceasefire that freezes the conflict may have broad appeal.

Armed conflict between Turkey and the Kurds

Turkey's operations in Syria and Iraq are driven by decades-long conflict in the south-east of Turkey between Turkish security forces and the PKK. More recently Turkey's efforts have focused on preventing Syrian Kurds from achieving a degree of political autonomy following their gains in the Syrian conflict. Turkey intensified its military incursions in northern Iraq in 2020. In addition to shelling and bombing, it also set up new bases and outposts.[65] Turkey threatened to carry out a new incursion in northern Syria in October 2020, if the Kurdish forces linked to the YPG did not retreat from the border area. The threat came after a Russian air strike killed a dozen Turkish-backed Failaq al Sham rebels in Idlib, north-western Syria.[66] Despite the established safe zone in north-eastern Syria (see above), Turkish-backed Syrian militias intensified their attacks against US-backed SDF over the flashpoint town of Ain Issa in December 2020.[67]

The armed conflict—almost four decades long—between Turkish security forces and the PKK inside Turkey continued in 2020. Two independent sources tracking the conflict provided different estimates of fatalities in 2020. According to the International Crisis Group, 341 people were killed in 2020 (35 civilians, 265 PKK rebels and 41 state security forces), down from 482 in 2019, with nearly 5229 deaths in the conflict in total since July 2015. ACLED estimated there were 541 conflict-related fatalities in 2020 (indicating a continuous decline in fatalities since 2016, see table 6.5).

---

[65] Coskun, O., 'Turkey plans more military bases in north Iraq after offensive: Official', Reuters, 18 June 2020.

[66] Najjar, F., 'Russian strike on Syria's Idlib fighters a "message" to Turkey', Al Jazeera, 27 Oct. 2020.

[67] Kajjo, S., 'Turkish-backed rebels intensify attacks on Syrian town', Voice of America, 6 Dec. 2020.

Resolving this protracted conflict is intertwined with resumption of the Turkish peace process with the Kurds (also known as the resolution process, which collapsed in July 2015), as well as the creation of peaceful relations between Turkey and the YPG in Syria, which Turkey views as an extension of the PKK. However, neither prospect seems likely soon, with Turkey set to continue its crackdown on the pro-Kurdish Peoples' Democratic Party.[68]

[68] McKernan, B., 'Turkey: The rise and fall of the Kurdish party that threatened Erdoğan', *The Guardian*, 27 Dec. 2020.

III. The Israeli–Palestinian conflict and peace process

IAN DAVIS

The history of Israel's occupation of the Gaza Strip, Golan Heights and West Bank—territories it captured in the 1967 Arab–Israeli War—is well known and much commented on.[1] Israeli settlement expansion in the occupied territories has added to recent instability, especially in the West Bank, where Israel threatened in 2019 to annex parts of the territory with the tacit support of the United States.[2] A new US 'peace plan', the threatened annexation of parts of the West Bank and a series of normalization agreements between Israel and four states—Bahrain, Morocco, Sudan and the United Arab Emirates (UAE)—were the key developments in 2020.[3] The economic and humanitarian costs to the Palestinian people of the Israeli occupation continued to be severe.[4]

Casualties in the conflict in 2020 were at the lowest level in the past decade. Israeli forces killed 30 Palestinians (3 in the Gaza Strip, 24 in the West Bank and 3 'not listed'), with 2751 injured. (A total of 137 Palestinians were killed in 2019, while 299 were killed and more than 29 000 were injured in 2018 by Israeli forces, mostly in protests along the Gaza–Israel border.) In 2020 Palestinians killed 3 Israelis (compared to 10 in 2019) and injured at least 58 others.[5]

A new US peace plan

Intermittent peace discussions have been held since the beginning of the conflict. Since 2003 the basis for an Israeli–Palestinian peace agreement has been a two-state solution: an independent state of Palestine alongside the state of Israel. The latest direct negotiations between the two sides collapsed in 2014.[6] A new US initiative led by President Donald J. Trump's son-in-law and US Middle East peace envoy, Jared Kushner, was partially unveiled in

---

[1] See e.g. Shlaim, A., *The Iron Wall: Israel and the Arab World* (W. W. Norton: New York, 2014); Thrall, N., *The Only Language they Understand: Forcing Compromise in Israel and Palestine* (Metropolitan Books: New York, 2017); Anziska, S., *Preventing Palestine: A Political History from Camp David to Oslo* (Princeton University Press: Princeton, NJ, 2018); and Abdallah, S. L., 'Endless borders: Detaining Palestinians and managing their movements in the occupied territories', *Mediterranean Politics*, vol. 25, no. 3 (2020), pp. 372–93.

[2] AP News, 'Netanyahu vows to annex West Bank settlements if re-elected', Politico, 7 Apr. 2019; and 'America says Israeli settlements in the West Bank are legal', *The Economist*, 21 Nov. 2019.

[3] Israel also established diplomatic relations with Bhutan in 2020 see Ayyub, R., 'Israel and Bhutan establish diplomatic relations', Reuters, 12 Dec. 2020.

[4] United Nations, General Assembly, 'Economic costs of the Israeli occupation for the Palestinian people: The Gaza Strip under closure and restrictions', A/75/310, 13 Aug. 2020.

[5] UN Office for the Coordination of Humanitarian Affairs (UN OCHA), 'Occupied Palestinian territory: Data on casualties', accessed 11 Feb. 2021.

[6] 'Former US envoy explains why Mideast peace talks collapsed in 2014', NPR, 8 June 2017.

June 2019. The economic part of the initiative, which included a pledge of $50 billion worth of investment in Palestine and neighbouring countries after a peace deal, received a mixed reaction.[7]

On 28 January 2020 President Trump unveiled the main US blueprint for a peace agreement between Israel and the Palestinians.[8] In marking a radical departure from past international consensus positions and previous final status parameters, the plan raised widespread concerns about its viability as a sustainable peace plan. For example, the plan would effectively consolidate the Israeli occupation by guaranteeing it control of a unified Jerusalem and allowing it to maintain its settlements in the West Bank. The plan was immediately rejected by Palestinian leaders, and international reaction was largely muted.[9] On 1 February 2020 the Arab League issued a unanimous rejection of the plan, while the European Union's high representative for foreign affairs said it broke with 'internationally agreed parameters'.[10] There was also a surge in violence in the West Bank as Israeli Prime Minister Benjamin Netanyahu said he would move to begin annexing parts of the territory (although this did not happen after US support for the idea cooled, as discussed below).[11]

From April 2020 the US plan was largely overshadowed by the introduction of emergency measures to counter the spread of Covid-19. Israel and the Palestinian Authority cooperated closely in the first months of the pandemic to contain the spread, but at the end of August a new outbreak began and infection rates rose sharply in the occupied Palestinian territories.[12] The pandemic also led to the postponement of a corruption trial against Prime Minister Netanyahu and efforts to form a unity government.[13] After

---

[7] White House, *Peace to Prosperity. The Economic Plan: A New Vision for the Palestinian People* (White House: June 2019); and 'An underwhelming start to the "ultimate" Israel-Palestinian deal', *The Economist*, 27 June 2019. On developments in 2018–19 see Davis, I., 'Armed conflict and peace processes in the Middle East and North Africa', *SIPRI Yearbook 2019*, pp. 90–94; and Davis, I., 'The Israeli–Palestinian conflict and peace process', *SIPRI Yearbook 2020*, pp. 152–55.

[8] White House, *Peace to Prosperity: A Vision to Improve the Lives of the Palestinian and Israeli People* (White House: Washington, DC, Jan. 2020).

[9] Lovatt, H., 'From negotiation to imposition: Trump's Israel-Palestine parameters', European Council on Foreign Relations Commentary, 11 Feb. 2020; Malley, R. and Miller, A. D., 'The real goal of Trump's Middle East plan', Politico, 28 Jan. 2020; AP News, 'Palestinian President Mahmoud Abbas threatens to cut security ties over US Mideast plan', NBC News, 1 Feb. 2020; and Quilliam, N. and Zhelyazkova, R., 'How Donald Trump's peace plan looks to the Gulf and Europe', Chatham House, 19 Feb. 2020.

[10] 'Arab League rejects Trump's Middle East plan: Communique', Reuters, 1 Feb. 2020; and 'EU rejects Trump Middle East peace plan, annexation', Reuters, 4 Feb. 2020.

[11] Halbfinger, D. M. and Kershner, I., 'Trump plan's first result: Israel will claim sovereignty over part of West Bank', *New York Times*, 28 Jan. 2020; and Kershner, I., 'Violence surges in wake of Trump's Mideast plan', *New York Times*, 6 Feb. 2020.

[12] International Crisis Group, 'Gaza's new coronavirus fears', Middle East Briefing no. 78, 9 Sep. 2020; and UN OCHA, 'Occupied Palestinian territory', Covid-19 Emergency Situation Report no. 21, 3 Nov. 2020.

[13] Kershner, I., 'Citing threat to Israeli democracy, Netanyahu opponents take battle to Supreme Court', *New York Times*, 22 Mar. 2020.

12 months of political deadlock and avoiding the need for a fourth general election, on 20 April 2020 Israel formed a unity government with Netanyahu as the prime minister for the first 18 months and his former opponent Benny Gantz as deputy prime minister. They were due to switch roles halfway through the government's three-year term.[14] However, in late December 2020 the Netanyahu–Gantz unity government collapsed, and new elections were scheduled for March 2021.[15]

The threatened annexation of parts of the West Bank

In June 2020, despite opposition from Palestinian leaders, Israel's new unity government began to prepare for the annexation of more of the occupied West Bank in accordance with the US 'peace plan'.[16] At a meeting of the United Nations Security Council on 24 June 2020 UN Secretary-General António Guterres called on the Israeli Government to abandon its annexation plans, which he said 'would constitute a most serious violation of international law, grievously harm the prospect of a two-State solution and undercut the possibilities of a renewal of negotiations'.[17] Israel was reluctant to proceed without the approval of the USA, and in August the Trump administration announced the annexation process would be delayed for 'some time' as the focus shifted to wider regional normalization discussions (see below).[18] Nonetheless, in October Israel approved over 1300 new settler homes in the West Bank, the first since Israel suspended annexation plans in August. In November it carried out further forced displacement activities.[19]

Israel's normalization agreements

On 13 August 2020 President Trump announced a 'historic' deal between Israel and the UAE that would see the two countries, already covert allies in their efforts to counter Iran, open full diplomatic ties—the third Arab country (after Egypt in 1979 and Jordan in 1994) to formally recognize

---

[14] Halbfinger, D. M. and Kershner, I., 'Netanyahu's power is extended as rival accepts Israel unity government', *New York Times*, 20 Apr. 2020.

[15] Wootliff, R., 'Israel calls 4th election in 2 years as Netanyahu-Gantz coalition collapses', *Times of Israel*, 23 Dec. 2020.

[16] 'Israel weighs the future of the West Bank', *The Economist*, 25 June 2020; US Congressional Research Service (CRS), *Israel's Possible Annexation of West Bank Areas: Frequently Asked Questions*, CRS Report for Congress R46433 (US Congress, CRS: Washington, DC, 14 July 2020).; and Halbfinger, D. M. and Rasgon, A., 'Abbas says security cooperation will end, raising stakes for Israeli annexation', *New York Times*, 19 May 2020.

[17] 'UN chief urges Israel to abandon annexation plans', UN News, 24 June 2020.

[18] Williams, D. and Cornwell, A., 'US won't approve Israeli annexations for "some time", Kushner says', Reuters, 17 Aug. 2020.

[19] 'Israel approves first new settler homes since suspending annexation', Reuters, 14 Oct. 2020; and 'UN official: Israel's largest demolition in the occupied West Bank for years', Middle East Monitor, 5 Nov. 2020.

Israel.[20] Notably, Israel also agreed to suspend its annexation plans in the West Bank. A few days later, Sudan announced it would also shortly reach an agreement with Israel, while on 11 September 2020 President Trump announced Bahrain and Israel had also reached an accord.[21] On 15 September 2020 Bahrain and the UAE signed bilateral normalization agreements—the Abraham Accords—with Israel at the White House in Washington, DC.[22] The signatories were motivated by a mixture of domestic politics, shared regional threat perceptions and the prospect of closer trade ties and access to Israeli and US technology.[23] In this regard, in November 2020 the USA approved arms sales to the UAE worth an estimated $23 billion and which included F-35 combat aircraft.[24]

On 23 October 2020 President Trump announced a normalization agreement between Israel and Sudan's transitional government, shortly after agreeing to remove Sudan from the US list of state sponsors of terrorism. This was done in exchange for Sudan paying $335 million to the families of victims of the 1998 al-Qaeda bombings in Dar es Salaam and Nairobi. Removing Sudan from the US terror list was expected to facilitate access to desperately needed international debt relief and loans to combat the country's dire economic crisis.[25] However, in early December the new agreement appeared to be on the point of collapse as Sudan sought immunity from the USA for future terrorism-related lawsuits.[26]

Finally, in December Israel agreed a further normalization agreement with Morocco after the USA became the first state to formally recognize Moroccan sovereignty over the disputed Sahrawi Arab Democratic Republic (Western Sahara) territory.[27]

The four normalization accords further splintered pan-Arab solidarity over Palestine, which had been based on the premise that normal relations

---

[20] Baker, P. et al., 'Israel and United Arab Emirates strike major diplomatic agreement', *New York Times*, 13 Aug. 2020; and AP News, 'Israel and UAE open phone link after historic deal', *The Guardian*, 17 Aug. 2020.

[21] Borger, J., 'Bahrain to normalise ties with Israel, Donald Trump announces', *The Guardian*, 11 Sep. 2020.

[22] White House, 'Abraham Accords peace agreement: Treaty of peace, diplomatic relations and full normalization between the United Arab Emirates and the State of Israel', 15 Sep. 2020; White House, 'Abraham Accords: Declaration of peace, cooperation, and constructive diplomatic and friendly relations, announced by the State of Israel and the Kingdom of Bahrain', 15 Sep. 2020; and 'Trump hails "dawn of new Middle East" with UAE-Bahrain-Israel deals', BBC News, 15 Sep. 2020.

[23] Bianco, C. and Lovatt, H., 'Israel-UAE peace deal: Flipping the regional order of the Middle East', European Council on Foreign Relations Commentary, 14 Aug. 2020.

[24] Reuters, 'US approves $23bn advanced arms sale to UAE: Pompeo', Al Jazeera, 10 Nov. 2020.

[25] Burke, J. and Holmes, O., 'Sudan and Israel agree US-brokered deal on normalising relations', *The Guardian*, 23 Oct. 2020. On the armed conflict and other developments in Sudan see chapter 7, section IV, in this volume.

[26] 'Israel-Sudan normalization at risk over US terror lawsuits law—report', *Times of Israel*, 1 Dec. 2020.

[27] 'Israel, Morocco agree to normalize relations "with minimal delay"', Deutsche Welle, 10 Dec. 2020. On the conflict in Western Sahara see section IV in this chapter.

with Israel would follow but could not precede an Israel–Palestine peace agreement.

Continuing clashes in Gaza

Hamas has been the de facto governing authority of the Gaza Strip since the 2007 Fatah–Hamas conflict resulted in the split of the Palestinian Authority (with Fatah, under Palestinian President Mahmoud Abbas, retaining control of the West Bank). In recent years frequent military exchanges between Hamas and/or the Islamic Jihad Movement in Palestine (rockets fired into Israel) and Israel (air strikes in Gaza) have been punctuated by often short-lived ceasefire arrangements.[28] In February 2020 two days of clashes between Israel and the Islamic Jihad Movement ended in another ceasefire.[29] Clashes escalated again in August 2020, until Israel and Hamas reached a Qatari-mediated de-escalation agreement at the end of the month.[30]

In September 2020 amid ongoing reconciliation talks in Turkey, Fatah and Hamas announced a deal to hold legislative elections for the Palestinian Authority, 15 years after the last elections took place in the occupied territories. It will be followed by Palestinian Authority presidential elections and Palestinian Central Council elections for the Palestinian Liberation Organization.[31] The elections represent an attempt by the Palestinian leadership to counter its marginalization in the aftermath of the US peace plan and the bilateral normalization deals signed by Israel with Bahrain and the UAE.

In November Fatah–Hamas relations soured again after the Palestinian Authority restored ties and security coordination with Israel (having cut them on 19 May 2020 over the Israeli West Bank annexation plan).[32] Further cross-border exchanges of fire between Hamas and Israel took place in November and December.[33]

Conclusions

The developments in 2020—the new US peace plan, the threatened annexation of parts of the West Bank and Israeli normalization agreements with

[28] Al-Mughrabi, N. and Williams, D., 'Islamic Jihad offers Israel truce as Gaza toll hits 26', Reuters, 13 Nov. 2019.

[29] Holmes, O., 'Israeli strikes in Syria and Gaza kill two Islamic Jihad fighters', The Guardian, 24 Feb. 2020.

[30] 'After rocket fire, Israeli airstrikes target Hamas special forces base in Gaza', Times of Israel, 19 Aug. 2020; and 'Hamas says deal reached to end escalation of violence with Israel', Al Jazeera, 31 Aug. 2020.

[31] 'Fatah, Hamas say deal reached on Palestinian elections', Al Jazeera, 24 Sep. 2020.

[32] Melhem, A., 'PA restoring ties with Israel undermining reconciliation, Hamas says', Al-Monitor, 19 Nov. 2020.

[33] AFP, 'Israel strikes Hamas targets in Gaza', The Guardian, 22 Nov. 2020; and AFP, 'Israeli jets strike Gaza after rockets fired across the border', The Guardian, 26 Dec. 2020.

Bahrain, Morocco, Sudan and the UAE—suggested a significant shift in the regional Arab–Israeli conflict. However, despite further marginalization of the Palestinians, the underlying reality in the local Israeli–Palestinian conflict remained largely unchanged. There appeared little prospect of resolving the principal Israeli–Palestinian territorial dispute, including Israel's occupation, in its various forms, or of ending Palestinian political divisions.

IV. Armed conflict and peace processes in North Africa

IAN DAVIS

Almost a decade after the 2011 Arab Spring, North Africa—here comprising Algeria, Egypt, Libya, Morocco and Tunisia—is undergoing a convergence of crises, with negative spillover onto the stability of neighbouring states in sub-Saharan Africa (see chapter 7) and in the eastern Mediterranean (see chapter 5).[1] The lone Arab Spring democracy in Tunisia is also at risk, sandwiched between Libya's civil war and an Algeria in transition (with mass protests demanding extensive constitutional and economic reforms continuing in 2020).[2] This section briefly discusses the non-international armed conflict in Egypt and the growing tensions in Sahrawi Arab Democratic Republic (Western Sahara), but focuses on the civil war in Libya.

Armed conflict in Egypt

In 2020 the Egyptian Government remained involved in a non-international armed conflict against the non-state armed group Wilayat Sinai (also known as Islamic State–Sinai Province) in the Sinai Peninsula. The Sinai insurgency (2011–present) deteriorated in 2014 when Islamist militants in Sinai embraced the Islamic State and carried out large-scale attacks on civilian targets.[3] A state of emergency has existed in northern Sinai since October 2014 and in the country as a whole since April 2017.[4] Human rights groups accuse the government of using counterterrorism measures to silence dissent.[5] The economic fallout from the Covid-19 pandemic led to sporadic protests in parts of Egypt in September 2020 that were violently suppressed.[6]

---

[1] There is no single accepted definition of North Africa. Some definitions include Sudan in North Africa. The conflict in Sudan is discussed in chapter 7, section IV, in this volume.

[2] On the protests in Algeria see O' Driscoll, D. et al., *Protest and State–Society Relations in the Middle East and North Africa*, SIPRI Policy Paper no. 56 (SIPRI: Stockholm, Oct. 2020), pp. 5–7; and 'Algerians back constitutional reforms amid low voter turnout', Al Jazeera, 2 Nov. 2020.

[3] On the historical developments and sociopolitical causes leading to the rise of Sinai province and its military build-up see Ashour, O., 'Sinai's insurgency: Implications of enhanced guerrilla warfare', *Studies in Conflict & Terrorism*, vol. 42, no. 6 (2019), pp. 541–58.

[4] Al-Youm, A., 'President Sisi extends Egypt's state of emergency by 3 months', *Egypt Independent*, 26 Oct. 2020. On developments in Egypt in 2018–19 see Davis, I., 'Armed conflict and peace processes in the Middle East and North Africa', *SIPRI Yearbook 2019*, pp. 87–88; and Davis, I., 'Armed conflict and peace processes in North Africa', *SIPRI Yearbook 2020*, pp. 157–58.

[5] El-Sadany, M., 'Egypt's crackdown on EIPR: Instrumentalizing counterterrorism to silence dissent', Lawfare, 15 Dec. 2020; and Wintour, P., '"Not just Giulio Regeni": Hundreds have died in Egyptian custody, says report', *The Guardian*, 11 Dec. 2020.

[6] Magdi, A., 'Protests still scare Egypt's Government', Human Rights Watch, 13 Oct. 2020; and Amnesty International, 'Egypt: Rare protests met with unlawful force and mass arrests', 2 Oct. 2020.

The low-level armed conflict continued in 2020 with no sign of an end or a decisive outcome.[7] The Egyptian military occasionally provided statements on its operations, claiming in July 2020, for example, that it had killed 18 suspected Islamist militants in northern Sinai.[8] Overall, estimated total conflict-related fatalities in Egypt in 2020 (626 fatalities) fell to their lowest level since 2012.[9]

Armed conflict in Libya

There has been armed conflict in Libya since an armed rebellion, with support of a Western military intervention, deposed Muammar Gaddafi in 2011. Under the 2015 Libyan Political Agreement (LPA) led by the United Nations, a unity government—the Government of National Accord (GNA)—was installed in Tripoli in 2016, headed by Prime Minister Fayez al-Sarraj. The GNA is supported by a loose alliance of militias in the capital and controls what remains of the Libyan state and its institutions in Tripoli. The GNA is opposed by a rival state institution, the Tobruk-based House of Representatives in the east of the country, which has failed to ratify the LPA. Khalifa Haftar, head of the self-styled Libyan National Army (LNA)—a mix of armed groups with a tribal or regional basis—supports the House of Representatives.[10] The Islamic State also remains a threat, especially in southern Libya. The armed conflict has resulted in large-scale forced displacement of civilians, across the border into Tunisia and also within Libya. It has also facilitated migrant smuggling and human trafficking into, through and from Libyan territory.[11] There is a strong economic dimension to the conflict, with competition among internal and external actors for control of key economic levers such as the central bank and oil revenues.[12]

The deepening roles of Egypt, Russia and Turkey in the civil war in 2020 complicated peace efforts and increased the risk of a direct military confrontation between Turkish and Egyptian/Russian armed forces

---

[7] 'Egypt in major standoff with IS after militants occupy Sinai villages', The New Arab, 28 July 2020; al-Anani, K., 'Egypt's counterterrorism strategy in Sinai: Challenges and failures', Arab Center, Washington, DC, 28 Aug. 2020; and 'Shifting militant tactics curb development in Egypt's North Sinai', Reuters, 9 Nov. 2020.

[8] 'Egyptian army says it killed 18 Islamist militants in North Sinai', France 24, 22 July 2020.

[9] Armed Conflict Location & Event Data Project, 'Data export tool', accessed 29 Jan. 2021.

[10] On the Libyan conflict in 2016–19 see Smith, D., 'The Middle East and North Africa: 2016 in perspective', SIPRI Yearbook 2017, pp. 83–84; Davis, I., 'Armed conflict in the Middle East and North Africa', SIPRI Yearbook 2018, pp. 74–75; SIPRI Yearbook 2019 (note 4), pp. 94–98; and SIPRI Yearbook 2020 (note 4), pp. 158–62.

[11] See e.g. United Nations, Security Council, 'Implementation of Resolution 2491 (2019)', Report of the Secretary-General, S/2020/876, 2 Sep. 2020.

[12] Carpenter, S., 'Waging economic war, Libyan strongman wants access to Central Bank cash', Forbes, 31 Jan. 2020.

supporting opposing sides in the armed conflict. An internationally backed ceasefire in Libya in October 2020 offered new grounds for optimism.

Internationalization of the armed conflict and the Berlin Process

Although the armed conflict in Libya started out as a civil war, it quickly became a regional proxy war. In recent years there has been a deepening internationalization of the conflict—with Egypt, France, Russia, Saudi Arabia and the United Arab Emirates (UAE) supporting the LNA, and Qatar and Turkey (and to some extent Italy and the European Union) supporting the GNA, as well as an array of foreign armed groups and mercenaries on both sides.[13] Russian mercenaries joined Haftar's forces in late 2019, while Turkey made a commitment to supply ground troops to the GNA if required.[14] The conflict has also been fuelled by the systematic violation of a UN arms embargo.[15]

In early January 2020 Turkey announced it was deploying military advisers and an estimated 2000 allied Syrian fighters to Libya to counter the LNA offensive on Tripoli and the central coastal city of Sirte.[16] Amid mounting international pressure for a ceasefire, the GNA and LNA agreed to a Russian–Turkish brokered ceasefire on 12 January, but it was sporadically broken almost immediately.[17] Talks between al-Sarraj and Haftar in Moscow on 13 January 2020 failed to achieve a commitment to a permanent ceasefire.[18]

Since September 2019 Germany has been tasked (under the Berlin Process) with cultivating consensus among external parties to the conflict for the three-point peace plan devised by UN Special Representative Ghassan Salamé: a ceasefire, an international meeting to enforce the arms embargo and an intra-Libyan political process of reconciliation under the

---

[13] McKernan, B., 'Gaddafi's prophecy comes true as foreign powers battle for Libya's oil', *The Guardian*, 2 Aug. 2020; Rondeaux, C., 'Libya's expanding proxy war may be the ultimate test of NATO's resilience', World Politics Review, 17 July 2020; and Kausch, K., 'Libya: How Europe failed to end the war', Middle East Eye, 26 May 2020.

[14] 'Foreign powers are piling into Libya', *The Economist*, 12 Dec. 2019; and Wintour, P., 'Turkey renews military pledge to Libya as threat of Mediterranean war grows', *The Guardian*, 15 Dec. 2019.

[15] See e.g. UN Support Mission in Libya (UNSMIL), 'UNSMIL statement on continued violations of arms embargo in Libya', 25 Jan. 2020; United Nations, Security Council, 'Implementation of Resolution 2473 (2019)', Report of the Secretary-General, S/2020/393, 15 May 2020; Walsh, D., 'Waves of Russian and Emirati flights fuel Libyan war, UN finds', *New York Times*, 3 Sep. 2020; Michaelson, R., 'Turkey and UAE openly flouting UN arms embargo to fuel war in Libya', *The Guardian*, 7 Oct. 2020; and chapter 14, section II, in this volume.

[16] McKernan, B. and Akoush, H., 'Exclusive: 2,000 Syrian troops deployed to Libya to support regime', *The Guardian*, 15 Jan. 2020; Reuters, 'Libyan general Khalifa Haftar's forces seize key city of Sirte', *The Guardian*, 6 Jan. 2020; and International Crisis Group, *Turkey Wades into Libya's Troubled Waters*, Europe Report no. 257 (International Crisis Group: Brussels, 30 Apr. 2020).

[17] 'Libya ceasefire: Both sides accuse each other of breaking truce', Deutsche Welle, 12 Jan. 2020; and 'UN envoy to Libya briefs Security Council on violations of ceasefire', *Libya Observer*, 30 Jan. 2020.

[18] 'No breakthrough in Moscow talks for Libya ceasefire deal', Al Jazeera, 14 Jan. 2020.

auspices of the UN.[19] A Berlin Conference on Libya on 19 January 2020, co-chaired by the UN and Germany, therefore adopted a 55-point paper in which the participants committed to refrain from interfering in the armed conflict and to support the work of the UN special representative.[20] More concretely, the GNA and the LNA agreed to appoint five representatives each for a UN-mediated ceasefire dialogue (known as the 5+5 Joint Military Commission), an International Follow-Up Committee of senior officials was tasked with monitoring implementation, and four thematic working groups were established on security, political, economic and international humanitarian law and human rights issues.[21] However, none of the external powers withdrew existing military support, and there remained strong differences of opinion among some of the participating states, especially France and Turkey.[22]

UN Security Council Resolution 2510 (2020), adopted on 12 February 2020, endorsed the outcomes of the Berlin Conference.[23] In addition, on 17 February 2020 European Union foreign ministers agreed to renew a naval mission in the Mediterranean Sea to monitor the UN arms embargo: Operation Irini (a successor to Operation Sophia) was launched on 31 March 2020.[24] The deputy head of the UN Support Mission in Libya (UNSMIL), Stephanie Williams, became UN acting special representative after Salamé resigned in early March 2020 due to ill health.[25]

Renewed hostilities

In March 2020 concerns about the spread of Covid-19 provided added impetus to international efforts to halt the violence. Shortly before the UN global ceasefire appeal, the GNA and LNA welcomed international calls for a humanitarian ceasefire to address the Covid-19 pandemic (on 18 and 21 March 2021, respectively), although neither party agreed to a formal

---

[19] UNSMIL, 'Remarks of SRSG Ghassan Salamé to the United Nations Security Council on the situation in Libya 29 July 2019', 29 July 2019.

[20] German Federal Foreign Office, 'Key to a resolution of the conflict: Libya Conference in Berlin', 20 Jan. 2020. Eleven countries participated—the permanent UN Security Council members (China, France, Russia, the United Kingdom and the United States), regional actors (Egypt, Italy, Turkey and the UAE) and regional mediators (Algeria and the Democratic Republic of the Congo)—as well as representatives from the African Union, Arab League and the European Union.

[21] For the full text see Zaptia, S., 'The Berlin Conference on Libya: Conference conclusions', *Libya Herald*, 19 Jan. 2020. Also see German Federal Foreign Office (note 20).

[22] 'Faltering international steps in Berlin towards peace in Libya', *Libya Herald*, 19 Jan. 2020; 'Views from the capitals: The Libya conference in Berlin', European Council on Foreign Relations, 23 Jan. 2020; and 'Libya civil war: Macron accuses Erdogan of meddling in conflict', BBC News, 29 Jan. 2020.

[23] UN Security Council Resolution 2510, 12 Feb. 2020.

[24] Rankin, J., 'EU agrees to deploy warships to enforce Libyan arms embargo', *The Guardian*, 17 Feb. 2020; and Council of the European Union, 'EU launches Operation Irini to enforce Libya arms embargo', Press release, 31 Mar. 2020.

[25] Wintour, P., 'Libya peace efforts thrown further into chaos as UN envoy quits', *The Guardian*, 2 Mar. 2020.

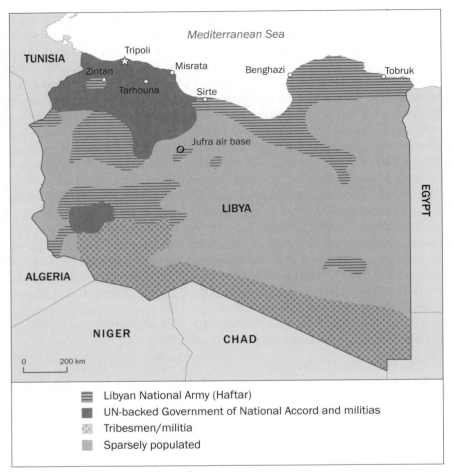

Figure 6.1. Areas of control in Libya, June 2020

Source: 'A warlord retreats: Libya's government regains control of western Libya', *The Economist*, 11 June 2020.

ceasefire.[26] On 24 March 2020 numerous Libyan civil society actors signed a call for national unity to address the Covid-19 pandemic, but with no apparent effect on the armed conflict.[27] At least 39 peace agreements and transition documents were signed in Libya during 2011–19, including national-level agreements (such as the LPA), intercommunal agreements and localized ceasefires. Given this extensive back catalogue of failed peace attempts, it

[26] 'UN welcomes response by Libyan parties to calls for humanitarian pause', UN News, 21 Mar. 2020. On the UN global ceasefire call, also see chapter 2, section I, in this volume.

[27] 'Call for united efforts against the new coronavirus pandemic', Centre for Humanitarian Dialogue, 24 Mar. 2020; and 'A thousand Libyans sign call to unite against the Covid-19 pandemic', Centre for Humanitarian Dialogue, 25 Mar. 2030.

was hardly a surprise when clashes between rival Libyan forces for control of Tripoli escalated in late March, with the reported participation of foreign forces and international arms deliveries to both sides.[28]

The battle for Tripoli intensified in April–June 2020. Following an increase in Turkey's military support for the first time in months, the GNA achieved military successes across western Libya and in areas surrounding Tripoli.[29] Despite these significant military gains, much of eastern and southern Libya remained in the control of the LNA. Overall, the external military support was unable to provide a decisive outcome. A further 30 000 people were displaced in the latest rounds of fighting, bringing the number of internally displaced persons in Libya to over 400 000.[30]

As fighting intensified around Sirte and nearby oil fields Egypt's President Abdel Fattah al-Sisi initiated a new round of ceasefire talks.[31] After al-Sisi's plan for a ceasefire was rebuffed, Egypt threatened direct military intervention in support of Hafter's forces, as a counterweight to Turkey's backing of the GNA.[32] Although these forces were not deployed, the threat further entrenched the sense of a stalemate (see figure 6.1) in the armed conflict, and a de facto halt in the fighting ensued across Libya from August 2020. Total conflict-related fatalities for the year declined by nearly 30 per cent compared to 2019 (see table 6.6). The threat to civilians from explosive remnants of war, including from the suspected use of cluster weapons, was a growing concern, while potential war crimes and other human rights violations by LNA forces continued to be investigated.[33]

Continuing negotiations, protests and a new ceasefire agreement

In June and July UNSMIL resumed separate talks with the GNA and LNA delegations within the framework of the 5+5 Joint Military Commission, but the political position of the parties continued to be determined by military

[28] PA-X, 'Peace agreements database and access tool, version 4', Political Settlements Research Programme, University of Edinburgh, accessed 10 Jan. 2021; Burke, J. and Wintour, P., 'Suspected military supplies pour into Libya as UN flounders', *The Guardian*, 11 Mar. 2020; and Wintour, P., 'Libya fighting intensifies as rival forces defy UN call for global ceasefire', *The Guardian*, 27 Mar. 2020.

[29] McKernan, B., 'Idlib to Tripoli: Turkey moves to dominate eastern Mediterranean', *The Guardian*, 26 May 2020; and 'A warlord retreats: Libya's government regains control of western Libya', *The Economist*, 11 June 2020.

[30] United Nations, Security Council, Letter dated 10 July 2020 from the President of the Security Council addressed to the Secretary-General and the permanent representatives of the members of the Security Council, S/2020/686, 13 July 2020, p. 3.

[31] Graham-Harrison, E., 'Egyptian president announces plan for ceasefire in Libya', *The Guardian*, 6 June 2020.

[32] El Tawil, N., 'Possible Egyptian "direct" intervention in Libya becomes legitimate: President Sisi', *Egypt Today*, 20 June 2020; and 'Averting an Egyptian military intervention in Libya', Statement, International Crisis Group, 27 July 2020.

[33] Ahmed, K., 'Unexploded bombs pose rising threat to civilians in Libya', *The Guardian*, 17 Feb. 2020; and 'Libya: Apparent war crimes in Tripoli', Human Rights Watch, 16 June 2020. On efforts to regulate explosive remnants of war and cluster munitions see chapter 13, section I, in this volume.

Table 6.6. Estimated conflict-related fatalities in Libya, 2011–20

Event type	2011	2012	2013	2014	2015	2016	2017	2018	2019	2020
Battles	2 073	458	197	2 381	1 999	2 207	972	715	1 226	802
Explosions/ remote violence	2 150	27	83	468	647	797	464	350	752	595
Protests, riots and strategic developments	818	21	83	11	19	11	0	0	0	5
Violence against civilians	491	46	76	475	336	250	227	123	98	93
Total	**5 532**	**552**	**439**	**3 335**	**3 001**	**3 265**	**1 663**	**1 188**	**2 076**	**1 495**

Note: For definitions of event types, see Armed Conflict Location & Event Data Project (ACLED), 'ACLED definitions of political violence and protest', 11 Apr. 2019.

Source: ACLED, 'Data export tool', accessed 1 Feb. 2021.

developments and the control of oil resources.[34] Discussions also continued within the International Follow-Up Committee with online meetings on 13 May, 22 June and 23 July 2020, as well as additional virtual discussions within the four thematic working groups in an effort to build consensus.[35] On 21 August 2020 the GNA and LNA, in separate statements, called for a ceasefire across the country, the demilitarization of Sirte, the resumption of oil production and exports, and parliamentary and presidential elections in March 2021.[36] Follow-up meetings took place in Montreux, Switzerland, on 7–9 September and Bouznika, Morocco, on 11 September 2020.[37]

During this period (August–October 2020) protests over corruption and economic austerity broke out in GNA- and LNA-controlled cities, prompting the leader of the GNA (al-Sarraj) to indicate he would step down at the end of October to facilitate a new transitional administration.[38] However, he was later asked by UNSMIL to remain in office for the duration of the negotiations.[39] On 20 September 2020 senior officials from the GNA and LNA reached a Russian-brokered agreement to end the blockade on oil installations and to establish a joint committee to oversee oil revenue disbursement. Oil production resumed across the country from October.[40]

---

[34] UN Secretary-General, 'Remarks to the Security Council on Libya', 8 July 2020; United Nations, S/2020/686 (note 30); and 'UN Libya mission says warring sides have engaged in truce talks', Reuters, 10 June 2020.

[35] United Nations, S/2020/686 (note 30).

[36] United Nations, S/2020/686 (note 30), p. 2; and Walsh, D., 'Libyan rivals call for peace talks. It may be wishful thinking', *New York Times*, 21 Aug. 2020.

[37] UNSMIL, 'Statement on the HD-organised Libyan consultative meeting of 7–9 September 2020 in Montreux, Switzerland', 10 Sep. 2020; and 'Libya rivals reach deal to allocate positions in key institutions', Al Jazeera, 11 Sep. 2020.

[38] Zaptia, S., 'Shooting at Tripoli demonstrations: MoI identifies shooters, will investigate and reveal results', *Libya Herald*, 24 Aug. 2020; 'Anger in Libya's Benghazi over power cuts, living conditions', Al Jazeera, 11 Sep. 2020; and 'Head of Libya's GNA says he wants to quit by end of October', Al Jazeera, 17 Sep. 2020.

[39] German Federal Foreign Office, 'Three milestones along the path to peace in Libya', 10 Nov. 2020.

[40] Cohen, A., 'Libya set for strong comeback to global oil markets', *Forbes*, 2 Oct. 2020.

The intra-Libyan political and military negotiations chaired by UNSMIL also continued, including a successful meeting of police military officers from the GNA and LNA in Egypt in late September.[41] The political track evolved into the Libyan Political Dialogue Forum (LPDF), while the military track led to a 23 October 2020 agreement on a permanent ceasefire covering all areas of Libya.[42] The new agreement required armed groups and military units to return to their respective bases (with some earmarked for demobilization), foreign mercenaries to depart within three months and the creation of a joint military force and a way to monitor violations.[43] The ceasefire was welcomed by the UN Security Council, and UN Secretary-General António Guterres described it as a 'critical step' in reaching a solution to the conflict.[44] At the end of the year the UN was proposing to bring in monitors to oversee the ceasefire.[45]

The first round of talks within the LPDF took place in Tunisia on 7–15 November 2020, and it was agreed to hold elections on 24 December 2021—the 70th anniversary of Libya's independence.[46] However, the November 2020 statement was vague on the exact terms of follow-up actions. Six rounds of online follow-up meetings failed to reach consensus on a legal framework for moving the electoral process forward, while the September agreement on the management of oil revenues also seemed to be unravelling.[47] The sustainability of the fragile consensus for the peace process among external powers and the deep fissures the war has inflicted on Libyan society are additional challenges to a political settlement.

Tensions in Western Sahara

In November 2020 the 40-year territorial dispute over Western Sahara between Morocco and the Popular Front for the Liberation of Saguia el Hamra and Río de Oro (Polisario Front) erupted again when the Polisario

---

[41] UNSMIL, 'Security and military direct talks between Libyan parties in Hurghada, Egypt conclude with important recommendations', 29 Sep. 2020.

[42] 'Agreement for a complete and permanent ceasefire in Libya' (unofficial translation), 23 Oct. 2020; UNSMIL, 'UNSMIL statement on the resumption of intra-Libyan political and military talks', 10 Oct. 2020; and Zaptia, S., 'Immediate and permanent ceasefire agreement throughout Libya signed in Geneva', *Libya Herald*, 23 Oct. 2020.

[43] International Crisis Group, 'Fleshing out the Libya ceasefire agreement', MENA Briefing no. 80, 4 Nov. 2020.

[44] United Nations, Security Council, 'Security Council press statement on Libya', SC/14339, 27 Oct. 2020; and UN Secretary-General, 'Opening remarks at press encounter on Libya', 23 Oct. 2020.

[45] Wintour, P., 'UN to bring in monitors to observe Libya's widely flouted ceasefire', *The Guardian*, 1 Jan. 2021.

[46] British Government, 'Libyan Political Dialogue Forum and the Berlin Conference: Joint statement', Press release, 23 Nov. 2020.

[47] International Crisis Group, 'Negotiations run aground, threatening political and economic stalemate', 11 Dec. 2020; and International Crisis Group, 'Foreign actors drive military build-up amid deadlocked political talks', 24 Dec. 2020.

Front ended a 1991 ceasefire and launched attacks on Moroccan forces. The attacks followed a military operation by Moroccan forces in the buffer zone monitored by the UN Mission for the Referendum in Western Sahara.[48] With the peace process stalled by the end of the year the risk of a military escalation in Western Sahara was growing. A deal brokered by the United States in December to normalize relations between Israel and Morocco (see section III), which included US recognition of Morocco's claim to sovereignty over Western Sahara, added to the tensions.[49]

---

[48] Dahir, A. L., 'Western Sahara independence group ends truce with Morocco', *New York Times*, 14 Nov. 2020.

[49] 'Moroccan Islamist groups reject normalising ties with Israel', *The Guardian*, 13 Dec. 2020.

V. Armed conflict and peace processes in Yemen

IAN DAVIS

The roots of the current multiparty war and humanitarian crisis in Yemen are complex and contested.[1] The Houthi insurgency began in 2004 when Hussein Badreddin al-Houthi, a leader of the Zaidi Shi'a, launched an uprising against the Yemeni Government. Al-Houthi was killed in that uprising, and the insurgents became known as the Houthis (the official name is Ansar Allah). In 2014 after several years of growing violence, the country descended into a new phase of civil war between the internationally recognized government of President Abdrabbuh Mansur Hadi and an uneasy alliance of Iran-backed Houthis and forces loyal to former president Ali Abdallah Saleh that controlled the capital, Sanaa, and large parts of the country.[2] Since March 2015 a coalition led by Saudi Arabia has been intervening militarily on the side of President Hadi, although the coalition itself is divided by conflicts and rivalries. In addition to the United Arab Emirates (UAE) the coalition included Bahrain, Egypt, Jordan, Kuwait, Morocco, Qatar (until 2017), Senegal and Sudan, either supplying ground troops or carrying out air strikes.[3] The coalition has also received substantial international support (including arms transfers) from Canada, France, the United Kingdom and the United States.[4]

Despite attempts mediated by the United Nations to end the civil war—including the 2018 Stockholm Agreement, the 2019 Riyadh Agreement and fresh attempts to broker a nationwide ceasefire in 2020—the armed conflict continued throughout the year, further exacerbating one of the world's worst humanitarian crises.[5] In October 2020 Lise Grande, the UN's humanitarian coordinator for Yemen, warned the country was on the brink of a

[1] See Davis, I., 'Armed conflict in the Middle East and North Africa', *SIPRI Yearbook 2018*, pp. 80–82. See also e.g. Orkaby, A., 'Yemen's humanitarian nightmare: The real roots of the conflict', *Foreign Affairs*, Nov./Dec. 2017; and al-Hamdani, R. and Lackner, H., 'Talking to the Houthis: How Europeans can promote peace in Yemen', European Council on Foreign Relations, Policy Brief, Oct. 2020.

[2] On the national dialogue process in 2014 that failed to avert war see Elayah, M., van Kempen, L. and Schulpen, L., 'Adding to the controversy? Civil society's evaluation of the national conference dialogue in Yemen, *Journal of Intervention and Statebuilding*, vol. 14, no. 3 (2020), pp. 431–58.

[3] On the role of the UAE in Yemen see Juneau, T., 'The UAE and the war in Yemen: From surge to recalibration', *Survival*, vol. 62, no. 4 (2020), pp. 183–208.

[4] Pradhan, P. K., 'Five years of military intervention in Yemen: An assessment', *Strategic Analysis* (2020). On arms transfers to Saudi Arabia and the UAE see also chapter 9, sections II and III, in this volume. On the United Nations arms embargo on Yemen see chapter 14, section II, in this volume.

[5] On the Stockholm and Riyadh agreements and other developments in Yemen in 2018–19, see Davis, I., 'Armed conflict and peace processes in the Middle East and North Africa', *SIPRI Yearbook 2019*, pp. 108–14; and Davis, I., 'Armed conflict and peace processes in Yemen', *SIPRI Yearbook 2020*, pp. 163–70.

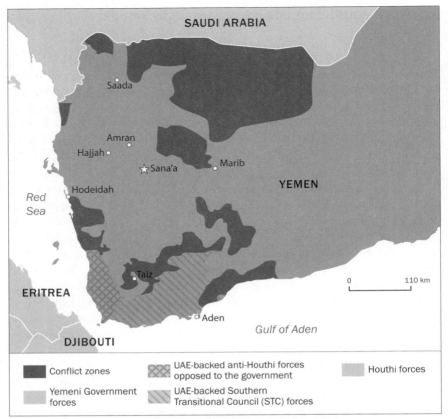

Figure 6.2. Areas of control and conflict in Yemen, May 2020

UAE = United Arab Emirates.

Source: 'Yemen crisis: Why is there a war?', BBC News, 19 June 2020.

catastrophic food security crisis, with almost 100 000 children under the age of five at risk of dying from hunger.[6]

In recent years there have been at least three main conflict zones to this major internationalized civil war in Yemen (see figure 6.2): (*a*) in the north, between the coalition-backed Yemeni Government and Houthi forces, including a Saudi Arabia–Yemen border conflict; (*b*) on the Red Sea coast, between Houthi and UAE-backed forces (that also oppose the Yemeni Government); and (*c*) in the south between the Yemeni Government and the Southern Movement, a fragile coalition of separatist groups operating in Aden, Hadramaut and Shabwa and represented politically by the UAE-backed Southern Transitional Council (STC). Another dimension to the

[6] Ahmed, K., 'Yemen on brink of losing entire generation of children to hunger, UN warns', *The Guardian*, 28 Oct. 2020.

armed conflict is the US-led counterterrorism campaign against radical Islamist groups—mainly al-Qaeda in the Arabian Peninsula (AQAP) and the local affiliate of the rival Islamic State—that have taken advantage of the chaos by carrying out attacks and seizing territory in the south. A UN panel of experts on Yemen concluded: 'The country's many conflicts are interconnected and can no longer be separated by clear divisions between external and internal actors and events'.[7]

Key developments in the three conflict zones in 2020

After a Houthi missile allegedly struck a military compound in Marib governorate on 18 January 2020, killing over 100 soldiers, there was a sudden escalation in the fighting between the Houthis and coalition-led forces on several northern front lines.[8] The Houthis made major territorial gains in Al Jawf governorate between January and March 2020 and threatened an offensive on Marib city and governorate. There was also an upsurge in the Saudi Arabian–Yemeni air war, with Houthi missile strikes targeting cities in Saudi Arabia and retaliatory air strikes of Houthi-controlled areas in Yemen.[9] The UN panel of experts concluded the pattern of conflicts in 2020 had shifted, with economic drivers predominantly motivating all Yemeni conflict parties.[10]

A short-lived Covid-19 ceasefire

On 23 March 2020 UN Secretary-General António Guterres called for a global ceasefire in order to better address the Covid-19 pandemic. In Yemen with Covid-19 threatening to compound an already dire humanitarian crisis, Secretary-General Guterres launched a specific appeal on 25 March for a Yemeni ceasefire. The domestic parties to the conflict and the coalition led by Saudi Arabia backing the UN-recognized government indicated an interest—informal talks between Saudi Arabia and the Houthis towards agreeing a border ceasefire had been taking place since September 2019.[11] While the coalition declared a unilateral two-week ceasefire on 8 April 2020 and then extended it by a month on the 24 April 2020, it was dismissed by

---

[7] United Nations, Security Council, Final report of the panel of experts on Yemen, S/2020/70, 27 Jan. 2020, p. 2.

[8] International Crisis Group, 'Breaking a renewed conflict cycle in Yemen', 24 Jan. 2020.

[9] International Crisis Group (note 8); AFP, 'Yemen airstrikes kill 31 civilians after Saudi jet crash', *The Guardian*, 16 Feb. 2020; and Reuters, 'Houthis launch air attack on Saudi capital', *The Guardian*, 30 Mar. 2020.

[10] United Nations, Security Council, Final report of the panel of experts on Yemen, S/2021/79, 25 Jan. 2021, p. 6.

[11] On the UN global ceasefire call see chapter 2, section I, in this volume. On the Houthi–Saudi talks see Jalal, I., 'Saudi Arabia eyes the exit in Yemen, but Saudi-Houthi talks alone won't resolve the conflict', Middle East Institute, 15 Apr. 2020.

the Houthis for not lifting the blockades on Sanaa and Hodeidah.[12] Fighting continued on multiple old and new fronts, especially around Marib city.[13]

The southern governorates

Meanwhile, in Yemen's fractured south the Riyadh Agreement, signed in November 2019 by the Yemeni Government (backed by Saudi Arabia) and the STC (backed by the UAE), was beginning to unravel.[14] With both sides accusing each other of violating the agreement, on 25 April 2020 the STC declared a state of emergency and the creation of self-rule in the regions under its control.[15] In May tensions flared again in Aden, Abyan and Taiz governorates. Although a ceasefire was agreed in Abyan on 22 June 2020 and coalition ceasefire monitors were deployed two days later, fighting resumed almost immediately with STC forces taking control of the strategic Socotra island.[16] In late July Martin Griffiths, special envoy of the secretary-general for Yemen, reported a reduction in the level of military activity in the southern governorates.[17] On 29 July 2020 the coalition announced the Yemeni Government and STC had renewed their commitment to the Riyadh Agreement, with the STC abandoning its 25 April declaration of self-rule.[18] However, on 25 August 2020 the STC suspended its participation in the consultations to implement the agreement.[19]

In December 2020 there was a breakthrough when the STC agreed to join a newly constituted Hadi government in exchange for allowing the government to move back to Aden. This may eventually unify the southern

[12] 'The Joint Forces Command of the Coalition to Restore Legitimacy in Yemen declares a comprehensive ceasefire in Yemen for a period of two weeks, starting on Thursday, April 9, 2020. at 12:00 KSA time. The two-week period is subject to extension', Saudi Press Agency, 8 Apr. 2020; and 'The Joint Forces Command of the Coalition to Restore Legitimacy in Yemen: Announcing a one-month extension of a comprehensive ceasefire in Yemen', Saudi Press Agency, 24 Apr. 2020.

[13] Salisbury, P., 'Behind the front lines in Yemen's Marib', International Crisis Group, 17 Apr. 2020; Benmansour, M., 'Yemen's Houthis reach Saudi capital with missiles for first time since Covid ceasefire', 23 June 2020; and United Nations, Security Council, 'The situation in the Middle East', S/PV.8757, 15 Sep. 2020, p. 2.

[14] Reuters, 'Yemen's Government signs peace deal with southern rebels', New York Times, 5 Nov. 2019.

[15] International Crisis Group, 'Heading off a renewed struggle for Yemen's south', Commentary, 29 Apr. 2020; and Lackner, H., 'The Yemen conflict: Southern separatism in action', European Council on Foreign Relations, 8 May 2020.

[16] Mukhashaf, M., 'Yemen separatists seize remote Socotra island from Saudi-backed government', Reuters, 21 June 2020; 'Yemen government, southern separatists agree to ceasefire', Al Jazeera, 22 June 2020; and 'Saudi-led coalition in Yemen monitoring cease-fire in Abyan', Al-Monitor, 24 June 2020.

[17] United Nations, Security Council, 'The situation in the Middle East', S/PV.8753, 28 July 2020, p. 3.

[18] 'Official source: Kingdom of Saudi Arabia proposes to Yemeni Government, Southern Transitional Council mechanism to accelerate implementation of Riyadh Agreement', Saudi Press Agency, 29 July 2020; and 'Yemen conflict: Southern separatists give up on self-rule', BBC News, 29 July 2020.

[19] 'Yemen southern separatists pull out of Riyadh agreement talks', Reuters, 25 Aug. 2020.

secessionist groups and the Hadi government against Houthi forces. However, an attack on Aden airport on 30 December 2020—which caused multiple casualties and appeared to target a plane carrying members of the newly formed unity government—reaffirmed the continuing fragility of the situation.[20]

The Red Sea coast

UN Security Council Resolution 2534 (2020) extended the mandate of the UN Mission to Support the Hodeidah Agreement (UNMHA), which was created in January 2019 to lead and support the Redeployment Coordination Committee (RCC)—a Houthi–Hadi working group formed to oversee the Hodeidah ceasefire—until 15 July 2021.[21] Fighting continued intermittently in and around Hodeidah, with multiple ceasefire violations throughout 2020. Accusing the Houthis of violating the agreement and the failure of UNMHA to control the situation, in April the Yemeni Government stated the Stockholm Agreement had collapsed.[22] In July it was reported the RCC and the joint mechanisms to implement the Stockholm Agreement were still not functioning.[23] The wider security situation around Hodeidah deteriorated in October.[24]

Throughout the year there was also an increasing risk of a major oil spill posed by the *Safer* oil tanker, moored off the west coast of Yemen, 60 kilometres north of Hodeidah. With almost no maintenance since 2015, the *Safer*—carrying 1.1 million barrels of oil (four times the amount involved in the *Exxon Valdez* spill in 1989)—risked causing a major oil spill with catastrophic environmental and humanitarian consequences. The UN has been seeking to deploy an expert team to assess the damage and conduct repairs since mid 2019, but has been denied entry by the Houthis who control the territory where the vessel is moored.[25]

The counterterrorism campaign against radical Islamist groups

The USA has been carrying out regular air strikes against AQAP, or its antecedents, in Yemen since at least 2009. The frequency of US air strikes against AQAP has been steadily decreasing, with only three reported (and a further

---

[20] McKernan, B., 'Aden airport blasts kill 26 in attack "directed at Yemen government"', *The Guardian*, 30 Dec. 2020.

[21] UN Security Council Resolution 2534, 14 July 2020.

[22] 'Yemeni Government calls for ending UN's Hodeidah mission', Asharq Al-Awsat, 20 Apr. 2020.

[23] United Nations, S/PV.8753 (note 17), p. 2.

[24] United Nations, S/2021/79 (note 10), p. 10.

[25] United Nations, Security Council, Letter dated 18 August 2020 from the Secretary-General addressed to the President of the Security Council, S/2020/808, 18 Aug. 2020; and United Nations, Security Council, Letter dated 23 September 2020 from the Permanent Representative of Saudi Arabia to the United Nations addressed to the President of the Security Council, S/2020/940, 24 Sep. 2020.

15 suspected air strikes) in 2020.[26] A US air strike in January 2020 killed the leader of AQAP, Qassim al-Rimi.[27] AQAP appeared to be in decline by the end of the year, with its presence mainly focused in Al Bayda governorate.[28]

UN peace talks

UN-brokered negotiations between the Government of Yemen and the Houthis started in March 2020. The negotiations sought to reach agreement on a joint declaration that would include a nationwide ceasefire, economic and humanitarian measures, and the resumption of the political process aimed at comprehensively resolving and ending the conflict. In short, the UN was trying to sequence three distinct tracks—the Stockholm Agreement, the Riyadh Agreement and the Saudi Arabia–Houthi border de-escalation talks—into a single UN-led process to end the war. In mid September Griffiths reported negotiations were continuing on a draft joint declaration.[29]

On 27 September 2020 the two parties agreed to release 1081 prisoners—an important step in the implementation of the Stockholm Agreement and a significant confidence-building measure in the wider peace process.[30] The prisoner exchange—the biggest since the conflict began—took place in October. The Houthis also freed two US hostages, and 200 of their fighters were allowed to return from Oman.[31] However, in Yemen as a whole, by the end of October there were 47 active front lines, as compared to 33 at the beginning of the year.[32]

The humanitarian crisis, fatalities and alleged war crimes

The UN has been describing the humanitarian crisis in Yemen as the worst in the world since 2018. The situation deteriorated further in 2020, driven by escalating conflict, an economic crisis and currency collapse, and exacerbated by heavy rains and flooding, fuel and aid funding shortages, the Covid-19 pandemic, and other diseases such as cholera and poliomyelitis.[33]

---

[26] 'Declared and alleged US actions in Yemen', Airwars, [n.d.].

[27] 'AQAP confirms death of leader Qassim al-Rimi', Al Jazeera, 23 Feb. 2020.

[28] Armed Conflict Location & Event Data Project (ACLED), 'The wartime transformation of AQAP in Yemen', 14 Dec. 2020.

[29] United Nations, S/PV.8757 (note 13), pp. 2–3.

[30] Nebehay, S., 'Yemen's warring parties agree to their largest prisoner swap as UN seeks ceasefire', Reuters, 27 Sep. 2020.

[31] 'Yemen war: Houthis and government complete prisoner exchange', BBC News, 16 Oct. 2020; and Nissenbaum, D., 'Two Americans held hostage by Iran-backed forces in Yemen freed in trade', Wall Street Journal, 14 Oct. 2020.

[32] UN Office for the Coordination of Humanitarian Affairs (UN OCHA), Global Humanitarian Overview 2021 (UN OCHA: 2020), p. 111.

[33] On the impact of Covid-19 in Yemen see 'The invisible outbreak: Covid-19 quietly sweeps across Yemen', The Economist, 4 June 2020; and 'A tipping point for Yemen's health system: The impact of Covid-19 in a fragile state', MedGlobal, Project Hope and The Center for Global Health at the University of Illinois, July 2020.

Six years of armed conflict has contributed to the collapse of critical health and social systems and infrastructure within Yemen.[34] An estimated 80 per cent of the population (24.1 million people) required some form of humanitarian or protection assistance in 2020, with 14.3 million in acute need, and an estimated 3.65 million people displaced, including a further 156 000 in 2020.[35]

By mid 2020 Yemen had returned to high levels of acute food insecurity, in part because the Houthis' systemic interference in relief operations led to a dramatic drop in overall aid as funders refused to continue indirectly financing the Houthi movement.[36] In 2019 the UN received $3.2 billion in aid donations for Yemen, but by May 2020 it had received only $474 million and the aid operation was described as being 'on the verge of collapse'.[37] On 2 June 2020 the UN and Saudi Arabia held a virtual donors' conference that raised $1.35 billion for Yemen, although the UN estimated around $2.4 billion of emergency aid was needed to deal with the worsening situation, including the Covid-19 pandemic.[38] By the end of October 2020 only $1.43 billion of the 2020 financial appeal (for $3.38 billion in total) had been received, forcing 31 of 41 of the UN's major humanitarian programmes in Yemen to close or reduce support.[39]

Armed conflict fatalities

The Armed Conflict Location & Event Data Project estimates approximately 130 000 people have been killed in the Yemeni war since 2015 (including over 13 000 civilian fatalities in direct attacks).[40] Over 19 700 people were killed in 2020 alone (table 6.7)—almost a 30 per cent reduction on 2019 but still the third deadliest year of the war. Moreover, these estimates almost certainly undercount the true extent of casualties, and exclude deaths from disease, malnutrition and other consequences of the crisis.[41]

---

[34] See e.g. McKernan, B., 'Yemen: In a country stalked by disease, Covid barely registers', *The Guardian*, 27 Nov. 2020; and 'Death sentence to civilians: The long-term impact of explosive weapons in populated areas in Yemen', Humanity & Inclusion, May 2020.

[35] UN OCHA, 'Yemen: Situation report', 11 Nov. 2020.

[36] Ahmado, N., 'UN to reduce aid to Houthi-controlled Yemen', Voice of America, 9 Feb. 2020; and Human Rights Watch, *Deadly Consequences: Obstruction of aid in Yemen during Covid-19* (Human Rights Watch: Sep. 2020).

[37] Nichols, M., 'UN seeks $2.4 billion for Yemen, warns aid operation nearly broke', Reuters, 28 May 2020; and United Nations, S/PV.8753 (note 17), p. 5.

[38] Kossaify, E., '$1.35 bn raised for Yemen in virtual donors conference hosted by Saudi Arabia, UN', *Arab News*, 3 June 2020.

[39] UN OCHA (note 35); Slemrod, A. and Parker, B., 'Funding, fuel, and "famine": Unpacking Yemen's overlapping crises', New Humanitarian, 7 Oct. 2020; and United Nations, Office of the Resident Coordinator and Humanitarian Coordinator for Yemen, 'Lack of funding cripples humanitarian operations in Yemen', Press release, 23 Sep. 2020.

[40] Sulz, M. J., 'Yemen: High risk of humanitarian fallout amidst the offensive on Marib', *Ten Conflicts to Worry about in 2021* (ACLED: Feb. 2021), p. 27.

[41] See e.g. Moyer, J. D. et al., *Assessing the Impact of War on Development in Yemen* (UN Development Programme: 2019).

Table 6.7. Estimated conflict-related fatalities in Yemen, 2015–20

Event type	2015	2016	2017	2018	2019	2020
Battles	9 167	8 508	10 857	21 748	16 630	14 761
Explosions/remote violence	8 054	6 895	6 538	12 041	10 887	4 315
Protests, riots and strategic developments	77	14	17	40	174	77
Violence against civilians	228	243	206	418	339	604
Total	17 526	15 660	17 618	34 247	28 030	19 757

Notes: The first available year for data on Yemen in the Armed Conflict Location & Event Data Project (ACLED) database is 2015. For definitions of event types, see ACLED, 'ACLED definitions of political violence and protest', 11 Apr. 2019.

Source: ACLED, 'Data export tool', accessed 5 Feb. 2021.

Allegations of war crimes

All parties to the conflict have faced allegations of crimes under international law over the past five years, including from a UN-established group of experts. Repeated calls by the group for prompt investigations into alleged violations and prosecutions of those responsible have so far had no practical effect.[42]

Conclusions

At the end of 2020 the Houthis continued to dominate the Yemeni political, economic and military landscape, controlling one third of the country's territory and two thirds of the population. With support from Iran, the Houthis have held off a coalition led by Saudi Arabia armed with expensive and sophisticated military technology. The coalition setbacks and stalemated conflict suggest Saudi Arabia may come to believe the costs of involvement in Yemen outweigh the benefits—the UAE reached a similar conclusion in 2019 leading to its partial withdrawal—and will look for a deal with the Houthis to end the crisis with a face-saving exit. However, agreeing a lasting political settlement remains fraught with difficulty as the Houthis are unlikely to stop fighting until they fully control Marib, Hodeidah and Taiz. At the end of the year the prospect of the USA designating the Houthis as a foreign terrorist organization further complicated the peace process and the delivery of humanitarian assistance.[43]

---

[42] United Nations, Human Rights Council, 'Situation of human rights in Yemen, including violations and abuses since September 2014', Report of the group of eminent international and regional experts on Yemen, A/HRC/45/6, 28 Sep. 2020. Also see United Nations, Human Rights Council, 'Situation of human rights in Yemen, including violations and abuses since September 2014', Detailed findings of the group of eminent international and regional experts on Yemen, A/HRC/45/CRP.7, 29 Sep. 2020; and United Nations, S/2021/79 (note 10), pp. 39–46.

[43] Johnsen, G. D., 'The mistake of designating the Houthis as a foreign terrorist organization', Lawfare, 1 Dec. 2020.

7. Armed conflict and peace processes in sub-Saharan Africa

Overview

There were at least 20 states (out of a total of 49 states) with active armed conflicts in sub-Saharan Africa in 2020: Angola, Burkina Faso, Burundi, Cameroon, the Central African Republic (CAR), Chad, Côte d'Ivoire, the Democratic Republic of the Congo (DRC), Ethiopia, Guinea, Kenya, Madagascar, Mali, Mozambique, Niger, Nigeria, Somalia, South Sudan, Sudan and Uganda. Ten were low-intensity, subnational armed conflicts, and 10 were high-intensity armed conflicts. Except for CAR and Somalia, all the other 18 armed conflicts had higher estimated conflict-related fatalities in 2020 than in 2019. For the region as a whole the increase was about 41 per cent. Sub-Saharan Africa also overtook the Middle East and North Africa in 2020 as the region with the most conflict-related fatalities.

Almost all the armed conflicts were internationalized, including as a result of state actors (whether directly or through proxies) and the transnational activities of violent Islamist groups, other armed groups and criminal networks. The conflict dynamics and ethnic and religious tensions were often rooted in a combination of state weakness, corruption, ineffective delivery of basic services, competition over natural resources, inequality and a sense of marginalization. Five other cross-cutting issues (section I) shaped security dilemmas in sub-Saharan Africa in 2020: (a) the presence of militant Islamist groups, other armed groups and criminal networks; (b) the security activities of external actors; (c) election-related violence; (d) the impact of the Covid-19 pandemic; and (e) water insecurity and the growing impact of climate change.

The security situation in West Africa (section II) deteriorated rapidly in 2020, with transnational armed and religious groups extending their grip in the region and a proliferation of community-based militias adding an additional level to the existing violence. The armed conflicts in Burkina Faso, Mali and Niger worsened, especially within the tri-border Liptako-Gourma region. External national and multilateral counterterrorism operations continued (and were expanded by the start of the new European Task Force Takuba, led by France) in the Sahel and Lake Chad regions alongside more traditional multinational United Nations peace operations, but with mixed results. The armed conflicts in Chad and Nigeria also worsened in the context of increasing instability in the Lake Chad region.

In Central Africa (section III) there was a large upsurge in violence in the eastern DRC, as external and Congolese armed groups engaged in multiple armed conflicts with the government, as well as a resurgence of intercommunal violence. Much of this violence was driven by competition for resources, corruption and bad governance. The two unrelated armed conflicts in different regions of Cameroon—the anglophone separatist insurgency and the Boko Haram insurgency—also worsened in 2020.

In East Africa (section IV) the increase in estimated conflict-related fatalities from about 25 600 in 2019 to nearly 36 000 in 2020 was driven by deteriorating situations in Ethiopia, Mozambique and South Sudan, as well as ongoing large-scale violence in Somalia. Six of the nine countries in East Africa involved in armed conflicts in 2020 fell within the regional framework of the Horn of Africa, which contains some of the most fragile states in the world. Disputes over resource allocation and access have also been significant in the region. One of the most high-profile interstate disputes between Egypt, Ethiopia and Sudan over the sharing of the eastern Nile waters remained deadlocked in 2020.

A new armed conflict broke out in the Tigray region of northern Ethiopia in November 2020 between federal government forces and the Tigray People's Liberation Front, which killed thousands and forced more than 46 000 refugees to flee into eastern Sudan. Insecurity also rose in many other areas of Ethiopia in 2020 due to simultaneous armed conflicts and high levels of interethnic violence.

The Islamist insurgency in Cabo Delgado province in the north of Mozambique deepened in 2020. Increased violence against civilians caused the number of internally displaced people to more than quadruple during the year to over 500 000. In Somalia, al-Shabab remained a major threat despite the continued presence of a peace operation led by the African Union and increased United States air strikes.

In South Sudan intercommunal violence fuelled by the proliferation and use of small arms and light weapons rose sharply in 2020, while delays in the implementation of the 2018 peace agreement added to the uncertainty. In Sudan the progress made in the Sudanese peace process in 2019 accelerated during 2020, with further significant peace agreements reached with the main armed groups. These culminated in the Sudanese Government and representatives of several armed groups signing the Juba Peace Agreement on 3 October 2020. This highly complex agreement is a key component of Sudan's larger transition from military to civilian rule. Implementation of the agreement will be difficult amid Sudan's economic problems, as well as ongoing divisions between various actors involved in the political transition and the rejection of the agreement by two armed opposition groups.

The peace process in Sudan was the only one in sub-Saharan Africa to make substantive progress in 2020. There were 22 multilateral peace operations active in sub-Saharan Africa during the year, 2 more than in 2019.

IAN DAVIS

I. Key general developments in the region

IAN DAVIS

There were at least 20 states with active armed conflicts in sub-Saharan Africa in 2020 (see table 7.1). This was three more (Angola, Côte d'Ivoire and Guinea) than in 2019. Ten were low-intensity, subnational armed conflicts (i.e. with fewer than 1000 conflict-related deaths), and 10 were high-intensity armed conflicts (with 1000–9999 deaths). Ethiopia, Mozambique and Niger moved from being low-intensity armed conflicts in 2019 to high-intensity armed conflicts in 2020.[1]

Except for the Central African Republic (CAR) and Somalia, all the other 18 armed conflicts had higher estimated conflict-related fatalities in 2020 than in 2019; for the region as a whole the increase was about 40 per cent. Sub-Saharan Africa also overtook the Middle East and North Africa in 2020 as the region with the most conflict-related fatalities.

Almost all of the armed conflicts were internationalized, and many of them overlapped across states and regions as a result of state actors, whether directly or through proxies, and/or the transnational activities of violent Islamist groups, other armed groups and criminal networks.[2] The conflict dynamics and ethnic and religious tensions were often rooted in a combination of state weakness, corruption, ineffective delivery of basic services, competition over natural resources, inequality and a sense of marginalization. Among the world's economies for which poverty can be measured, 18 of the 20 poorest countries were in sub-Saharan Africa, as were 31 of the 47 least developed countries in 2020.[3] Except for Cameroon, Côte d'Ivoire, Kenya and Nigeria, all the other countries in the region with armed conflicts in 2020 were least developed countries.

Developments in each of the armed conflicts and any related peace processes in 2020 are discussed in more detail in subsequent sections of this chapter. The security situation in West Africa (section II) deteriorated rapidly in 2020, with transnational armed groups extending their grip in the region and a continuing proliferation of community-based militias adding an additional level to the violence. In Central Africa (section III) there was

---

[1] For conflict definitions and typologies see chapter 2, section I, in this volume. For armed conflicts in North Africa see chapter 6 in this volume.

[2] On the extent of cross-border state support to parties involved in intrastate armed conflict and its under-representation in Africa conflict data sets see Twagiramungu, N. et al., 'Re-describing transnational conflict in Africa', *Journal of Modern African Studies*, vol. 57, no. 3 (2019), pp. 377–91.

[3] World Bank, *Poverty and Shared Prosperity: Reversals of Fortune* (International Bank for Reconstruction/World Bank: Washington, DC, Oct. 2020), p. 13; and United Nations, Conference on Trade and Development, *The Least Developed Countries Report 2020* (UN: Geneva, 2020), p. ix. On the factors that influence unrest in the region see Adelaja, A. and George, J., 'Grievances, latent anger and unrest in Africa', *African Security*, vol. 12, no. 1 (2019), pp. 111–40.

Table 7.1. Estimated conflict-related fatalities in sub-Saharan Africa, 2017–20

Country	2017	2018	2019	2020
West Africa				
Burkina Faso	117	303	2 220	2 298
Côte d'Ivoire	43[a]	16[a]	45[a]	132
Guinea	47[a]	39[a]	41[a]	145
Mali	948	1 747	1 875	2 849
Niger	240	506	719	1 114
Nigeria	4 947	6 243	5 431	7 760
Subtotal	**6 342**	**8 854**	**10 331**	**14 298**
Central Africa				
Angola	67	41[a]	23[a]	74
Cameroon	717	1 530	1 232	1 589
Central African Republic	1 829	1 171	573	428
Chad	296	259	567	738
Congo, Democratic Republic of the	3 210	3 189	3 843	5 767
Subtotal	**6 119**	**6 190**	**6 238**	**8 596**
East Africa				
Burundi	285	327	303	329
Ethiopia	1 355	1 565	667	3 553
Kenya	745	407	269	297
Madagascar	210	142	350	354
Mozambique	129	223	663	1 782
Somalia	5 835	5 101	4 031	3 140
South Sudan	4 847	1 700	1 806	2 371
Sudan	1 291	1 054	776	957
Uganda	66	146	159	290
Subtotal	**14 763**	**10 665**	**9 024**	**13 073**
Total	**27 224**	**25 709**	**25 593**	**35 967**

Notes: Fatality figures are collated from four event types: battles; explosions/remote violence; protests, riots and strategic developments; and violence against civilians—see Armed Conflict Location & Event Data Project (ACLED), 'ACLED definitions of political violence and protest', 11 Apr. 2019. A country is treated as being in an armed conflict if there were 25 or more battle-related deaths in a given year—see chapter 2, section I, in this volume.

[a] Battle-related deaths were below 25.

Source: ACLED, 'Data export tool', accessed 22 Feb.–5 Mar. 2021.

a large upsurge in violence in the eastern Democratic Republic of the Congo (DRC), while in East Africa (section IV) the increase in conflict-related fatalities was driven by deteriorating situations in Ethiopia, Mozambique and South Sudan, as well as ongoing large-scale violence in Somalia.

Only one peace process in sub-Saharan Africa made substantive progress in 2020: throughout the year the transitional government of Sudan signed a series of peace agreements with various opposition armed groups, culminating in the Juba Peace Agreement on 3 October 2020 (see section IV). States in sub-Saharan Africa continued to host more multilateral peace operations than in any other region of the world. There were 22 multilateral peace operations active in the region in 2020, 2 more than in 2019.[4] The African Union and the European Union each deployed a new peace operation to CAR in 2020: the African Union Military Observers Mission to the CAR and the European Union Advisory Mission in the CAR.[5] Meanwhile, the number of personnel in multilateral peace operations in sub-Saharan Africa decreased by 3.4 per cent in 2020, from 97 519 on 31 December 2019 to 94 201 on 31 December 2020. The number of deployed personnel in the region decreased for the fifth consecutive year. Nonetheless, the missions deployed in sub-Saharan Africa accounted for almost three quarters of the personnel deployed in all multilateral peace operations globally.[6]

Five cross-cutting issues shaped security challenges in sub-Saharan Africa in 2020: (*a*) the presence of militant Islamist groups, other armed groups and criminal networks; (*b*) the security activities of external actors; (*c*) election-related violence; (*d*) the impact of the Covid-19 pandemic; and (*e*) water insecurity and the growing impact of climate change.[7] The subsections below briefly examine how these five issues evolved in 2020.

Despite these setbacks and persistent problems, significant social, economic and political progress has also been made in the region in the last two decades, with the promise of more to come in the longer term, post Covid-19.[8] Much may depend on the newly created African Continental Free Trade Area (AfCTA) that the World Bank suggested has potential to yield up to $450 billion in regional income and bring millions out of poverty. Headquartered in Accra, Ghana, AfCTA is expected to catalyse market integration, accelerate industrial development and enhance competitiveness.[9]

The growing influence of militant Islamist groups and local 'identity militias'

Many of the countries suffering from armed conflict in sub-Saharan Africa are afflicted by extremist Islamist violence. While this is not new, the epicentre of Islamist violence appears to have moved from the Middle East

[4] The peace operations were deployed across 10 countries see chapter 2, section II, in this volume. On the role of regional organizations in Africa see Coe, B. and Nash, K., 'Peace process protagonism: The role of regional organisations in Africa in conflict management', *Global Change, Peace & Security*, vol. 32, no. 2 (2020), pp. 157–77.

[5] For developments in CAR see section III in this chapter.

[6] For further details see chapter 2, section II, in this volume.

[7] On developments in some of these issues in 2018–19 see Davis, I and Melvin, N., 'Armed conflict and peace processes in sub-Saharan Africa', *SIPRI Yearbook 2019*, pp. 115–21; and Davis, I., 'Key general developments in the region', *SIPRI Yearbook 2020*, pp. 176–79.

[8] See e.g. Rosenthal, J., 'The African century: Africa is changing so rapidly, it is hard to ignore', *The Economist*, 26 Mar. 2020.

[9] Ighobor, K., 'AfCFTA secretariat commissioned in Accra as free trade is set to begin in January 2021', *Africa Renewal*, 17 Aug. 2020; and 'Trade pact could boost Africa's income by as much as $450 billion: World Bank', UN News, 27 July 2020.

and North Africa to sub-Saharan Africa, and is particularly pronounced in Central Sahel and the Lake Chad region (section II) and in the Horn of Africa, from where Islamist and criminal violence has spread into other parts of East Africa (section IV).[10] A range of problems have followed or have been exacerbated by this violence, such as economic fragility, increased poverty, marginalization of certain groups and low resilience to shocks—natural disasters, economic downturns and further outbursts of armed violence. The violence is not just between governments and insurgents, but also includes intra-insurgent violence, especially between supporters and affiliates of al-Qaeda and the Islamic State. Since March 2020, for example, there have been occasional clashes between the Islamic State in the Greater Sahara and the local al-Qaeda-aligned Group to Support Islam and Muslims (Jama'a Nusrat ul-Islam wa al-Muslimin).[11]

The problem of violent extremism has deep societal roots. The increased use of military force (see below) has not prevented the violence spreading to previously unaffected areas. Human rights abuses by state security forces have added to the cycle of violence, and there have been calls for the military response to be backed by a comprehensive political strategy to address the factors driving radicalization.[12]

Militias are another key cause of violence in sub-Saharan Africa and are often formed in response to threats of violent extremism and to counter rival local 'identity militias' (i.e. non-state armed groups that almost exclusively engage in identity-based intercommunity violence in a pattern which is most similar to communal, ethnic or religious groups). According to the Armed Conflict Location & Event Data Project an additional 270 militias became active in Africa in 2020 (an increase of 46 per cent compared to 2019), although sometimes this resulted from the fragmentation of existing

[10] Gardner, F., 'Is Africa overtaking the Middle East as the new jihadist battleground?', BBC News, 3 Dec. 2020; Demuynck, M. and Coleman, J., 'The shifting sands of the Sahel's terrorism landscape', International Centre for Counter-terrorism, 12 Mar. 2020; and 'African militant Islamist groups set record for violent activity', Africa Center for Strategic Studies, 21 July 2020.

[11] United Nations, Security Council, 'Eleventh report of the secretary-general on the threat posed by ISIL (Da'esh) to international peace and security and the range of United Nations efforts in support of member states in countering the threat', S/2020/774, 4 Aug. 2020, p. 4; and Nsaibia, H. and Weiss, C., 'The end of the Sahelian anomaly: How the global conflict between the Islamic State and al-Qa'ida finally came to West Africa', CTC Sentinel, vol. 13, no. 7 (July 2020), pp. 1–14.

[12] On the drivers behind support for and engagement in violent extremism in Mali see e.g. Coleman, J. et al., Dynamics of Support and Engagement: Understanding Malian Youths' Attitudes Towards Violent Extremism (UN Interregional Crime and Justice Research Institute and the International Centre for Counter-Terrorism: Feb. 2021). Also see Nsaibia, H., 'State atrocities in the Sahel: The impetus for counterinsurgency results is fuelling government attacks on civilians', Armed Conflict Location & Event Data Project (ACLED), 20 May 2020; Venturi, B. and Toure, N., 'The great illusion: Security sector reform in the Sahel', International Spectator, vol. 55, no. 4 (2020), pp. 54–68; and Tinti, P., 'How counterinsurgency campaigns are fuelling human rights abuses in the Sahel', World Politics Review, 30 Apr. 2020.

militias. The DRC, Nigeria and South Sudan experienced the greatest rises in the number of active identity militias during 2020.[13]

External actors

Sub-Saharan Africa is increasingly treated as an arena for great power competition. Not only the global powers are involved. In the Horn of Africa for example, there are actors from Asia, Europe, the Middle East and North Africa, and North America—their presence is largely driven by geopolitical, commercial and military competition.[14] The United States and European states in particular are also centrally involved in the fight against transnational jihadist groups in sub-Saharan Africa. In the case of European states this fight also extends to criminal networks and irregular migration, especially in the Sahel. Most Western forces are deployed to train and build capacity in local forces, including the two subregional counterterrorism task forces in the Sahel: the Multinational Joint Task Force in the Lake Chad region and the Joint Force of the Group of Five for the Sahel.[15]

While the aim has been for African partners to gradually take on a larger share of crisis management and counterterrorism activities, the opposite seems to have been the case, with Western forces becoming even more entrenched. France has a long tradition of maintaining a significant military footprint in sub-Saharan Africa, and in 2020 this consisted of about 5100 troops focused on Operation Barkhane in the Sahel, and included command of the new European military task force (Task Force Takuba), launched in March 2020 (see section II). At the annual African Union summit meeting in February 2020 there were calls for stronger African-based joint counterterrorism forces, reflecting growing concerns particularly in the Sahel over this reliance on foreign powers.[16]

While the USA claims to maintain a 'light and relatively low-cost footprint' in Africa as a whole, independent estimates suggest at least 6000 military personnel are deployed across 13 countries in the sub-Saharan Africa region.[17] Since 2018 the USA has been making modest reductions in troop

---

[13] Raleigh, C. and Kishi, R., 'Africa: The only continent where political violence increased in 2020', Mail & Guardian, 1 Feb. 2021; and Kishi, R. et al., 'ACLED 2020: The year in review', Mar. 2021, p. 4.

[14] Melvin, N. J., 'The foreign military presence in the Horn of Africa region', SIPRI Background Paper, Apr. 2019; and Melvin, N. J., 'The new external security politics of the Horn of Africa region', SIPRI Insights on Peace and Security no. 2019/2, Apr. 2019. Also see section IV in this chapter.

[15] Petesch, C., 'US leads training exercises in Africa amid focus on Sahel', ABC News, 22 Feb. 2020; and Hickendorff, A. and Acko, I., 'The European Union Training Mission in the Central African Republic: An assessment', SIPRI Background Paper, Feb. 2021.

[16] Herszenhorn, D. M. and Marks, S., 'African leaders call for home-grown counterterrorism force', Politico, 10 Feb. 2020. Also see chapter 2, section II, in this volume.

[17] Turse, N., 'Pentagon's own map of US bases in Africa contradicts is own claim of "light" footprint', The Intercept, 27 Feb. 2020. Also see Turse, N., Mednick, S. and Sperber, A., 'Inside the secret world of US commandos in Africa', Mail & Guardian, 11 Aug. 2020.

numbers in Africa as part of a reset towards great power competition. In December 2020 President Donald J. Trump announced the withdrawal of all US troops from Somalia (thought to number about 700), but it was expected many of these would be repositioned to neighbouring countries in East Africa.[18]

Russia, China and France were the largest arms exporters to sub-Saharan Africa in 2016–20, accounting for 30, 20 and 9.5 per cent, respectively, of total sub-Saharan arms imports.[19] Russia's military relationships in sub-Saharan Africa are growing and sometimes involve the use of private mercenary groups, as for example in CAR (section III).[20] China's military presence in sub-Saharan Africa is linked to its growing economic presence, as well as its role as a leading supplier of United Nations peacekeepers in the region.[21] Finally, the region has also become a theatre for Middle East and North African power struggles, with Turkey and the Gulf states particularly active in the Horn of Africa (section IV).[22]

Election-related violence

Election transition processes are a major source of instability in sub-Saharan Africa. The causes of electoral instability and violence in the region are multidimensional but broadly fall into two categories: the underlying power structures in new and emerging democracies, and flaws in the electoral process itself.[23]

African governance worsened for the first time in a decade in 2019 due to a broad deterioration in the areas of human rights, security and rule of law, according to the Ibrahim Index of African Governance.[24] This deterioration added to the risk of pre- or post-election violence around several important national and local elections that took place in the region in 2020 (see

---

[18] Cooper, H., 'Trump orders all American troops out of Somalia', *New York Times*, 4 Dec. 2020; and 'Statement from AFRICOM Commander US Army Gen. Stephen Townsend on the activation of Joint Task Force—Quartz', US Africa Command, 19 Dec. 2020.

[19] On arms transfers to sub-Saharan Africa see chapter 9, section III, in this volume.

[20] 'Russia in Africa: What's behind Moscow's push into the continent?', BBC News, 7 May 2020.

[21] Walsh, B., 'China's pervasive yet forgotten regional security role in Africa', *Journal of Contemporary China*, vol. 28, no. 120 (2019), pp. 965–83; and McAllister, P., 'China in Mali and the Sudan: A stepping stone to greater Chinese influence in the UN?', Global Risks Insights, 17 Feb. 2021.

[22] Heibach, J., 'Sub-Saharan Africa: A theater for Middle East power struggles', *Middle East Policy*, vol. 27, no. 2 (summer 2020), pp. 69–80.

[23] Nordic Africa Institute, 'Electoral violence in Africa', Policy Notes no. 2012/3, Sep. 2012; and Kovacs, M. S. and Bjarnesen, J. (eds), *Violence in African Elections: Between Democracy and Big Man Politics* (Nordic Africa Institute and Zed Books: Uppsala and London, 2018). Also see the discussion in *SIPRI Yearbook 2019* (note 7), pp. 117–20. On the linkages between violence and democracy in Africa see Obiagu, U. C., 'A third wave? Creeping autocracy in Africa', *African Studies Quarterly*, vol. 20, no. 1 (Jan. 2021), pp. 114–24.

[24] '2020 Ibrahim Index of African Governance—Index Report', Mo Ibrahim Foundation, Nov. 2020.

table 7.2).[25] While several of the elections were marred by serious irregularities and security clampdowns, the worst electoral violence took place in Cameroon, CAR, Côte d'Ivoire, Guinea, Mali and Tanzania.[26] The Covid-19 pandemic further complicated matters by preventing or restricting oversight by foreign election observers, and led to elections being postponed in Chad and Ethiopia.[27] Elections due to take place in Somalia and Sudan were postponed for other reasons (see section IV).

The impact of Covid-19

The Covid-19 pandemic appears to have had minimal direct impact on most of the region's armed conflicts in 2020. A few armed groups in Angola, Cameroon, South Sudan and Sudan either extended existing ceasefires or declared temporary unilateral ceasefires in response to the UN secretary-general's March call for a Covid-19-related global ceasefire (see sections III and IV). However, the Islamist armed groups operating in sub-Saharan Africa seemingly refused to acknowledge the call and many of them appeared to exploit the disruption caused by the pandemic to recruit new members and carry out attacks.[28]

In the longer term the pandemic is likely to affect many of the key political, social and economic drivers of peace and conflict in the region. For example, the International Monetary Fund estimated that the economy in sub-Saharan Africa contracted by 2.6 per cent in 2020 (after growing by 3.2 per cent in 2019), while the World Bank suggested it would be the second

---

[25] '2020 African election calendar', Electoral Institute for Sustainable Democracy in Africa, Jan. 2021.

[26] 'Cameroon: Election violence in anglophone regions', Human Rights Watch, 12 Feb. 2020; 'Central African Republic election held amid violence', BBC News, 27 Dec. 2020; 'Ivory Coast election violence leaves a "dozen dead"', Deutsche Welle, 1 Nov. 2020; 'Malian parliamentary elections marred by kidnappings, attacks', Al Jazeera, 31 Mar. 2020; 'UN rights chief Bachelet condemns Tanzania election violence', UN News, 10 Nov. 2020; and 'Nearly two dozen dead in Guinea post-election violence: State TV', Al Jazeera, 27 Oct. 2020.

[27] 'Covid-19 helps ballot-dodgers in Africa', The Economist, 16 May 2020. On the impact of Covid-19 on African democracy more broadly see 'Taking stock of regional democratic trends in Africa and the Middle East before and during the Covid-19 pandemic', Special brief, International Institute for Democracy Electoral Assistance, Jan. 2021.

[28] 'Coronavirus: Sudan rebels extend ceasefire', Dabanga, 31 Mar. 2020; 'SSOMA response to UN Secretary General call for immediate global ceasefire in armed conflict countries related to Covid-19', Statement by South Sudan Opposition Movements Alliance, 9 Apr. 2020; Esau, I., 'Insurgents hit second Mozambique town as Islamic State claims earlier attack', Upstream, 25 Mar. 2020; 'Al Shabaab terrorists claim deadly attack in heart of Somalian capital', 23 Mar. 2019, France 24; and Coleman, J., 'The impact of coronavirus on terrorism in the Sahel', International Centre for Counter-Terrorism, 16 Apr. 2020. On the global ceasefire see chapter 2, section I, in this volume.

Table 7.2. Election calendar in sub-Saharan Africa, 2020

Country	Election	Date
Angola	Local	Due 2021 (postponed from 2020)
Benin	Local	Held 17 Apr. 2020
Burkina Faso	President and National Assembly	Held 22 Nov. 2020
Burundi	President	Held 20 May 2020
	Due National Assembly, local, Collines Senate (indirect)	Held 7 June 2020
Cameroon	National Assembly, Senate and local	Held 9 Feb. 2020
Central African Republic	President and National Assembly	Held 27 Dec. 2020 (run-off 14 Feb. 2021)
Chad	National Assembly	Due 2021 (postponed from 2018–20)
Comoros	Parliamentary	Held 19 Jan. 2020 (run-off held 23 Feb. 2020)
Côte d'Ivoire	President and National Assembly	Held 31 Oct. 2020
Ethiopia	House of People's Representatives, regional state councils and local	Due 5 June 2021 (postponed from 29 Aug. 2020)
	House of the Federation (indirect, by regional state councils)	Indirect, after regional state councils 2021
Ghana	President and National Assembly	Held 7 Dec. 2020
Guinea	National Assembly and Referendum	Held 22 Mar. 2020
	Presidential	Held 18 Oct. 2020
Liberia	Senate and Referendum	Held 8 Dec. 2020
Malawi	President	Held 23 June 2020 (rerun)
Mali	National Assembly	Held 29 Mar. 2020 (run-off held 19 Apr. 2020)
Namibia	Regional councils and local	Held 25 Nov. 2020
	National Council (indirect, by regional councils)	Held Nov.–Dec. 2020
Niger	Local	Held 13 Dec. 2020
	President and National Assembly	Held 27 Dec. 2020 (run-off 21 Feb 2021)
Senegal	Local	Due 2021 (postponed from 2020)
Somalia	House of the People (indirect)	Due 2021 (postponed from 10–27 Dec. 2020)
	Senate (indirect)	Due 2021 (postponed from1 Dec. 2020)
Somaliland (autonomous region)	House of Representatives and Senate	Due 2021 (postponed from late 2019 and Mar. 2019)
Seychelles	President and legislative	Held 22–24 Oct. 2020

Country	Election	Date
Sudan	President, legislative, states and local	Due late 2022 (postponed from Feb. 2020)
Tanzania	President, National Assembly, Zanzibar House of Representatives and Zanzibar President and local	Held 28 Oct. 2020
Togo	President	Held 22 Feb. 2020

Source: '2020 African election calendar', Electoral Institute for Sustainable Democracy in Africa, Jan. 2021.

most severely affected region (after South Asia), with 26 million to 40 million more of its people falling into extreme poverty through 2021.[29]

Water insecurity and climate change

Of the 21 countries globally facing the highest risk from the double burden of climate-related factors and political fragility, 12 are in sub-Saharan Africa: Angola, Cameroon, Chad, Côte d'Ivoire, the DRC, Ethiopia, Guinea, Nigeria, Sierra Leone, South Sudan, Sudan and Uganda.[30] Climate-related security risks include 'forced migration and displacement, livelihood insecurity, food and water insecurity, rising levels of intercommunal conflict between pastoralists and farmers, protracted cross-border resource conflicts and unsustainable resource exploitation'.[31] It has been estimated that an additional 86 million people in the region could be displaced by climate change by 2050.[32] In Somalia, for example, climate change has amplified existing challenges, including those faced by peace operations, and strengthened radical groups.[33]

Most countries in sub-Saharan Africa are dependent on rain-fed agriculture, making the region particularly vulnerable to changes in climatic conditions such as seasonal floods and prolonged droughts.[34] For example at the beginning of the year a drought in Lesotho led to increased food insecurity, while in Nigeria's Kebbi state floods in September 2020 destroyed about

[29] 'World Economic Outlook update', International Monetary Fund, Jan. 2021; and World Bank (note 3), p. 15. Also see Nash, K., 'Responses by African intergovernmental organisations to Covid-19', Political Settlements Research Programme, 24 June 2020.

[30] Moran, A. et al., *The Intersection of Global Fragility and Climate Risks* (US Agency for International Development: Sep. 2018), pp. 11–13.

[31] Aminga, V. and Krampe, F., 'Climate-related security risks and the African Union', SIPRI Policy Brief, May 2020.

[32] Institute for Economics & Peace (IEP), *Ecological Threat Register 2020: Understanding Ecological Threats, Resilience and Peace* (IEP: Sydney, Sep. 2020), p. 51.

[33] Eklöw, K. and Krampe, F., *Climate-related Security Risks and Peacebuilding in Somalia*, SIPRI Policy Paper no. 53 (SIPRI: Stockholm, Oct. 2019); and Krampe, F., 'Why United Nations peace operations cannot ignore climate change', SIPRI Commentary, 22 Feb. 2021.

[34] IEP (note 32), p. 16.

90 per cent of the state's crops, putting the country's food security at risk.[35] Accessing safe drinking water is also a challenge for more than 300 million people in rural areas of sub-Saharan Africa.[36] Arguably the highest profile water resource dispute in the region is between Egypt and Ethiopia over the River Nile. These tensions have been exacerbated by Ethiopia's construction of the Grand Ethiopian Renaissance Dam, as well as a shifting regional power struggle that has been playing out in the South Sudan civil war (see section IV).

[35] Charumbira, S., 'Drought leaves tens of thousands in Lesotho "one step from famine"', *The Guardian*, 30 Jan. 2020; and 'Floods, food shortages threaten to push Nigeria into food crisis', Al Jazeera, 14 Sep. 2020.

[36] Food and Agriculture Organization of the UN (FAO), *The State of Food and Agriculture: Overcoming Water Challenges in Agriculture* (FAO: Rome, 2020), p. 21.

II. Armed conflict and peace processes in West Africa

VIRGINIE BAUDAIS AND ANNELIES HICKENDORFF

Six countries experienced armed conflict in West Africa in 2020 (out of a total of 17 states or territories in the subregion, see figure 7.1): Burkina Faso, Côte d'Ivoire, Guinea, Mali, Niger and Nigeria. However, in this section, the focus is on the high-intensity armed conflicts in the Central Sahel (Burkina Faso, Mali and Niger) and the Lake Chad region (Niger and Nigeria, as well as the Central African states of Cameroon and Chad).[1] Burkina Faso, Cameroon, Chad, Mali, Niger and Nigeria were involved in armed conflicts in 2020 that all worsened in terms of conflict-related fatalities (compared with in 2019). In addition, Benin, Côte d'Ivoire and Guinea experienced election-related violence, but only the latter two were classified as armed conflicts in 2020 (with more than 25 battle-related fatalities).[2]

This section is divided into four core discussions: (a) on the key general developments in the region; (b) on the armed conflicts in Burkina Faso, Mali and Niger, within the context of developments within the tri-border Liptako-Gourma region; (c) on the internationalization of counterterrorism activities alongside more traditional multinational United Nations peace operations; and (d) the armed conflict in the Lake Chad region and Nigeria.

Key general developments in the region

Many states in West Africa face severe governance problems linked to state weakness, extreme poverty, economic fragility and growing insecurity—issues compounded in 2020 due to the Covid-19 pandemic. While the exact number of Covid-19 cases and deaths in West Africa in 2020 is uncertain—estimates range between 77 000 and 112 000 fatalities—the border closures and the global slowdown seriously affected socio-economic developments in a region already heavily dependent on foreign aid.[3] On top of this, unequal economic growth and the impact of climate change in a region where more than 80 per cent of the population relies essentially on agriculture and pastoral activities have led to increased food insecurity.[4] Irregular migration, corruption, illicit trafficking and transnational organized crime also flourish, especially where states are challenged by various armed groups.

---

[1] Also see the discussion of armed conflict in Cameroon and Chad in section III of this chapter.

[2] For conflict definitions and typologies see chapter 2, section I, in this volume.

[3] Rougier, A., 'Afrique: le continent résiste à la pandémie de Covid-19' [Africa: The continent resists the Covid-19 pandemic], RFI, 8 Apr. 2021; and 'Coronavirus in Africa tracker', BBC News, 19 Apr. 2021.

[4] 'Food and nutrition crisis 2020: Analyses & responses, maps & facts', no. 3, Sahel and West Africa Club Secretariat and Organisation for Economic Co-operation and Development, Nov. 2020.

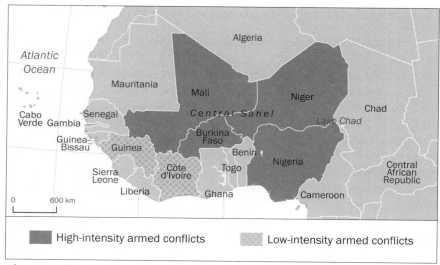

Figure 7.1. West Africa, Central Sahel and Lake Chad

The security situation is aggravated by the strength of transnational armed groups and violent extremist groups such as Boko Haram in the Lake Chad region, and the Group to Support Islam and Muslims (Jama'a Nusrat ul-Islam wa al-Muslimin, JNIM), Islamic State in the Greater Sahara (ISGS), Ansarul Islam and Katiba Serma in the Liptako-Gourma region.[5] Extremist groups are interwoven with local self-defence militias and armed groups, and exacerbate local and community tensions.

Other violence in West Africa was predominantly generated around con-tested elections and the enforcement by national security forces of public health and social measures due to the Covid-19 outbreak.[6] Despite the pandemic, six countries conducted presidential elections (Burkina Faso, Côte d'Ivoire, Ghana, Guinea, Niger and Togo), legislative elections took place in Guinea, Liberia and Mali, and Benin, Cape Verde and Niger held local elections. Following contested constitutional changes, incumbent presidents Alassane Ouattara of Côte d'Ivoire and Alpha Condé of Guinea

---

[5] Eizenga, D. and Williams, W., 'The puzzle of JNIM and militant Islamist groups in the Sahel', Africa Center for Strategic Studies, Africa Security Brief no. 38, 1 Dec. 2020; and International Crisis Group, *Sidelining the Islamic State in Niger's Tillabery*, Africa Report no. 289 (International Crisis Group: Brussels, 3 June 2020). For further details on groups with a Salafist jihadism ideology in the Sahel and Lake Chad regions see Davis, I., 'Armed conflict and peace processes in the Sahel and Lake Chad Region', *SIPRI Yearbook 2020*, p. 181.

[6] United Nations, Security Council, Report of the Secretary-General on the activities of the United Nations Office for West Africa and the Sahel, S/2020/1293, 24 Dec. 2020.

won in the first round of their respective elections in November.[7] In both countries election-related violence resulted in a sharp increase in protest-related fatalities in 2020. In Côte d'Ivoire the number of such fatalities rose from 16 in 2019 to 51 in 2020, while several thousand refugees from the country's west and south-west regions fled to Liberia.[8] In Guinea fatalities increased from 22 in 2019 to 104 in 2020.[9] In Burkina Faso where the out-going president, Roch Marc Christian Kaboré, was also re-elected in the first ballot, elections were dominated by a threat of jihadist violence that prevented people from voting in at least one fifth of the country.[10] In Mali post-legislative election contestation and denunciation of insecurity and bad governance ultimately led to a military coup resulting in the resignation of President Ibrahim Boubacar Keïta on 18 August 2020.[11]

The deteriorating security situation in West Africa was accompanied by a continuous humanitarian crisis: by mid 2020, 31 million people, of whom more than 50 per cent were children, were in need of life-saving assist-ance. This was an increase of 7 million compared with the beginning of the year.[12] As a result of this insecurity, in December 2020 the UN Office for the Coordination of Humanitarian Affairs reported an unprecedented high number of forced displacements in the Sahel with 5 million people, including 4.1 million internally displaced persons and 870 000 refugees.[13]

There were two cross-cutting issues that also contributed to security challenges in West Africa in 2020: (a) the spread of violent extremism and terrorism and (b) the Covid-19 pandemic.

Violent extremism and insecurity

Hotspots of insecurity in West Africa in 2020 were the Liptako-Gourma region of the Sahel (comprising border regions of Burkina Faso, Mali and Niger) and the Lake Chad region, which both confronted violence by extrem-ist religious groups, militias and various armed groups. In the Lake Chad region the main insurgent group, Boko Haram, has spread from Nigeria across the lake-bordering regions in Cameroon, Chad and Niger, causing

---

[7] 'Ivory Coast election: Alassane Ouattara wins amid boycott', BBC News, 3 Nov. 2020; 'Guinea elections: Alpha Condé wins third term amid violent protests', BBC News, 24 Oct. 2020; and 'Côte d'Ivoire: An election delay for dialogue', Africa Briefing no. 161, International Crisis Group, 29 Sep. 2020.

[8] 'Ivorians flee to neighboring countries fearing post-electoral violence', UN High Commissioner for Refugees, 3 Nov. 2020; and Armed Conflict Location & Event Data Project (ACLED), Dashboard, accessed 3 Mar. 2021.

[9] ACLED (note 8).

[10] 'Burkina Faso election takes place amid jihadist threat', BBC News, 23 Nov. 2020; and 'Burkina Faso's Kaboré wins re-election, according to full preliminary results', France 24, 26 Nov. 2020.

[11] Burke, J., 'Mali's president announces resignation after "attempted coup"', The Guardian, 19 Aug. 2020.

[12] United Nations, S/2020/1293 (note 6).

[13] UN Office for the Coordination of Humanitarian Affairs (OCHA), 'West and Central Africa', Global Humanitarian Overview 2021 (UN OCHA: Geneva, 1 Dec. 2020).

a massive humanitarian crisis and increasing internal and cross-border displacements.[14]

In the Liptako-Gourma region, the main violent jihadi groups are: JNIM, which includes al-Qaeda in the Islamic Maghreb, Ansar Eddine, Al-Mourabitoune, Katiba Macina and Katiba Serma; Ansarul Islam; and ISGS.[15] On 9 February 2020 a police station was attacked in Keremou, Benin, at the border with Burkina Faso and Niger; on 11 June 2020 violent extremists believed to be members of JNIM shot around 10 soldiers at a frontier post on Côte d'Ivoire's border with Burkina Faso—the first attack in Côte d'Ivoire since the attack in Grand-Bassam in March 2016.[16] A spillover of the conflict beyond the Sahel to the coastal countries remains a potential risk.[17]

In Central Sahel the presence of armed groups has increased existing vulnerabilities associated with structural fragility and political instability. Burkina Faso, Mali and Niger rank at the bottom of the UN Development Programme's 2020 human development index. According to the World Bank the 2019 poverty rates of these states vary between 40 and 43 per cent.[18] As a result of this protracted crisis, the number of internally displaced people has risen twentyfold since 2018 from 70 000 to 1.5 million.[19] As of 31 December 2020, this number had risen to 1.7 million individuals, of whom 64 per cent were located in Burkina Faso (twice as many as in 2019), while 20 per cent resided in Mali, 12 per cent in Niger and 4 per cent in Mauritania.[20] In Tillabéri and Tahoua regions, the number of internally displaced Nigeriens increased by 77 per cent in 2020 to 138 229.[21]

The impact of Covid-19

Whereas the public health impact of the Covid-19 pandemic was not as devastating in 2020 as initially feared, the restrictions on movement, lockdowns, market closures and barriers to trade had serious political, socio-economic, humanitarian and security impacts.[22] The pandemic has deepened the

---

[14] International Organization for Migration (IOM), 'Central Sahel and Liptako Gourma Crisis— Monthly Dashboard #11', Displacement tracking matrix, 7 Dec. 2020.

[15] Eizenga, D. and Williams, W., 'The puzzle of JNIM and militant Islamist groups in the Sahel', Africa Centre for Strategic Studies, Africa Security Brief no. 38, 1 Dec. 2020; International Crisis Group (note 5); 'The risk of jihadist contagion in West Africa', Africa Briefing no. 149, International Crisis Group, 20 Dec. 2019.

[16] 'Ivory Coast soldiers killed in attack at border post near Burkina Faso', France 24, 11 June 2020.

[17] 'The risk of jihadist contagion in West Africa' (note 15).

[18] '2020 human development index ranking', UN Development Programme, [n.d.]; and 'The World Bank in Africa', World Bank, [n.d.].

[19] UN OCHA (note 13).

[20] UN OCHA, 'Niger update: Sahel situation', Mar. 2021; and IOM (note 14).

[21] UN High Commissioner for Refugees, 'Sahel situation', Mar. 2021.

[22] Economic Community of West African States Commission et al., 'Covid-19 pandemic: Impact of restriction measures in West Africa', Dec. 2020; Eboko, F. and Schlimmer, S., 'Covid-19 in Africa: A continent's response to a global crisis', Politique étrangère, vol. 85, no. 4 (winter 2020–21); and United Nations, Security Council, 'Activities of the United Nations Office for West Africa and the Sahel', Report of the Secretary-General, S/2020/585, 24 Dec. 2020.

pre-existing gender inequalities in West Africa, and women and girls have been disproportionately affected by the consequences of stay-at-home orders and school closures. Increasing domestic and gender-based violence as well as loss of livelihoods have been reported.[23] National security forces in several states used violence to enforce the Covid-19-related restrictions. According to Human Rights Watch the governments in Ghana, Liberia, Niger, Nigeria and Sierra Leone used the pandemic as an excuse to censor the media or limit free speech.[24]

Armed conflict in the Liptako-Gourma region

The 2012 northern Mali crisis has become, over the years, a regionally multidimensional crisis.[25] This subsection focuses on the armed conflicts in Burkina Faso, Mali and Niger with a particular focus on the tri-border Liptako-Gourma region, which includes the provinces of: Boucle du Mouhoun, Centre-Nord, Est, Nord and Sahel (Burkina Faso); Gao, Ménaka and Mopti (Mali); and Tillabéri (Niger). The Liptako-Gourma region struggles with several interconnected layers of conflict, including: (*a*) the presence of jihadist groups; (*b*) intercommunity and intracommunity tensions, farmer–herder competition and land disputes; and (*c*) other sources of violence, such as banditry, illicit trafficking and organized crime.[26]

In 2020 violence in Liptako-Gourma escalated further with over 5000 conflict-related fatalities, most of which occurred in the region's Burkina Faso and Mali provinces (see table 7.3). Violence is directed against civilian populations, local authorities, civil servants and national security forces. Armed groups are kidnapping or killing traditional, religious and community leaders suspected of collaborating with the state. This strategy aims to discourage local populations from cooperating with the state and force them to collaborate with the armed groups, which destroys traditional community ties. The Global Coalition to Protect Education from Attack noted over 85 attacks on schools in Burkina Faso, Mali and Niger between January and July 2020, despite Covid-19-related school closures between late March and May.[27] As of April 2020 more than 135 health centres and

---

[23] 'WHO concerned over Covid-19 impact on women, girls in Africa', World Health Organization, 18 June 2020; and Zara Louan, F., 'Rapid gender analysis—Covid-19: West Africa', CARE, Apr. 2020.

[24] 'Covid-19 triggers wave of free speech abuse', Human Rights Watch, 11 Feb. 2021.

[25] Baudais, V., 'Mali: Fragmented territorial sovereignty and contested political space', SIPRI Commentary, 16 June 2020.

[26] Bodian, M. et al., 'The challenges of governance, development and security in the central regions of Mali', SIPRI Insights on Peace and Security no. 2020/4, Mar. 2020; Tobie, A., 'Central Mali: Violence, local perspectives and diverging narratives', SIPRI Insights on Peace and Security no. 2017/5, Dec. 2017; and Matfess, H., 'What explains the rise of communal violence in Mali, Nigeria and Ethiopia?', World Politics Review, 11 Sep. 2019.

[27] Global Coalition to Protect Education from Attack, 'Supporting safe education in the Central Sahel', Briefing Paper, Sep. 2020.

Table 7.3. Estimated conflict-related fatalities in the Liptako-Gourma region, 2017–20

Provinces (state)	2017	2018	2019	2020 (%)
Boucle du Mouhoun, Centre-Nord, Est, Nord and Sahel (Burkina Faso)	77	266	2 123	2 261 (98)
Gao, Ménaka and Mopti (Mali)	568	1 409	1 658	2 230 (78)
Tillabéri (Niger)	62	170	263	680 (61)
Total	**707**	**1 845**	**4 044**	**5 171**

Note: Percentages are of total national conflict-related fatalities.

Source: Armed Conflict Location & Event Data Project (ACLED), 'Data export tool', accessed 19 Feb. 2021. Data per region is available from 11 Jan. 2017.

2500 schools were closed in Burkina Faso, depriving 338 000 students of access to education and millions of people of access to essential healthcare.[28]

Burkina Faso

Since 2015, the situation in Burkina Faso has deteriorated and the country is under constant pressure from armed groups. The weak state presence has left communities with limited protection and allowed for the proliferation of armed groups and militias, including the Koglweogo groups.[29] To support the fight against terrorism, the government chose to arm civilians and create the civilian defence volunteers' forces (Volontaires pour la défense de la patrie) in January 2020.[30] Arbitrary arrests and executions by national armed forces have led to distrust between the central government and large parts of the population. Human Rights Watch reported that Burkina Faso's state security forces were involved in mass extrajudicial executions[31]

Mali

While the military situation in the north of the country stabilized in 2020, the situation in the centre continued to deteriorate as armed and radicalized groups fuelled old and local intercommunity tensions. The implementation of the 2015 Agreement for Peace and Reconciliation in Mali did not make any major advances in 2020 due to the sociopolitical crisis, the coup d'état and the Covid-19 pandemic.[32]

---

[28] United Nations, S/2020/585 (note 22); and 'Armed group attacks on teachers, students, and schools in Burkina Faso', Human Rights Watch, May 2020.

[29] Da Cunha Dupuy, R. and Quidelleur, T., 'Self-defence movements in Burkina Faso, diffusion and structuration of Koglweogo groups', Noria Research, Nov. 2018.

[30] Zutterling, C., 'Armer les civils : La loi des Volontaires pour la défense de la patrie au Burkina Faso' [Arming civilians: When civilian defence volunteers' forces make the law], GRIP, 30 Oct. 2020.

[31] 'Burkina Faso: Residents' accounts point to mass executions', Human Rights Watch, 8 July 2020.

[32] Carter Center, 'Observations on the implementation of the agreement on peace and reconciliation in Mali, resulting from the Algiers Process', Report of the Independent Observer, Dec. 2020.

Table 7.4. Estimated conflict-related fatalities in Mali, 2013–20

Event type	2013	2014	2015	2016	2017	2018	2019	2020
Battles	547	301	316	210	563	759	831	1 657
Explosions/remote violence	191	39	27	32	144	177	234	262
Protests, riots and strategic developments	7	1	5	7	3	28	4	27
Violence against civilians	138	41	80	71	238	783	806	903
Total	**883**	**382**	**428**	**320**	**948**	**1 747**	**1 875**	**2 849**

Note: For definitions of event types, see Armed Conflict Location & Event Data Project (ACLED), 'ACLED definitions of political violence and protest', 11 Apr. 2019.

Source: ACLED, 'Data export tool', accessed 22 Feb. 2021.

In addition to the persistent insecurity, corruption and bad governance fuelled discontent with the government. After weeks of popular mobilization led by the coalition called 5 June Movement–Rally of Patriotic Forces, a military coup removed President Keïta from power on 18 August 2020. Implementation of the 2015 Bamako Agreement remained the goal of the new transitional authorities and international mediators, and the new Malian authorities expressed their willingness to talk to all groups including those that have not signed the agreement.

To address the situation and support the stabilization of the country, several multinational peace operations and other multilateral operations are operating in the country and in the Liptako-Gourma region (as discussed below). Notwithstanding, the situation worsened in 2020 (see table 7.4).

Niger

The rise in fatalities on a national level from 719 in 2019 to 1114 in 2020 can be explained by the increasing violence in the Liptako-Gourma region, which was responsible for 61 per cent of the total national fatalities (see table 7.3). In Tillabéri, the high number of refugees and displaced people forced authorities to manage the local economy and to avoid the disruption of local dynamics and tensions around natural resources.[33] The crisis also led to a deterioration of the relationship among communities and weakened traditional authorities, which are targeted by armed groups. Although the number of violent events in Diffa increased from 150 in 2019 to 167 in 2020, Niger suffered fewer fatalities involving Boko Haram in 2020 than in 2019 (see table 7.6). Incidents involving Boko Haram in 2020 included an assault

---

[33] Baudais, V., 'The impact of the Malian crisis on the Group of Five Sahel countries: Balancing security and development priorities', SIPRI Commentary, 18 May 2020.

Table 7.5. Active external national and multilateral peace and counterterrorism operations in the Sahel and Lake Chad regions, 2020

Launched or established	Name	Contributing countries/ organizations	Force level (No. of personnel deployed)	Country of deployment
2012	European Union (EU) Capacity Building Mission Sahel Niger	EU member states	123	Niger
2013	Multidimensional Integrated Stabilization Mission in Mali	United Nations (mainly African countries, Bangladesh, China, Egypt and Germany)	15 050	Mali
2013	EU Training Mission in Mali	EU member states	726	Mali
2014[a]	Multinational Joint Task Force	Benin, Cameroon, Chad, Niger and Nigeria	10 620	Cameroon, Chad, Niger and Nigeria
2014[b]	Operation Barkhane	France	5 100	Burkina Faso, Chad, Mali and Niger
2015	EU Capacity Building Mission Sahel Mali	EU member states	152	Mali
2017	Joint Force of the Group of Five for the Sahel	Burkina Faso, Chad, Mali, Mauritania and Niger	5 000	Burkina Faso, Chad, Mali, Mauritania and Niger
2020	Task Force Takuba	France, special forces from European states (Estonia, France)	[. .][c]	Liptako-Gourma region

[a] Initiated as a solely Nigerian force in 1994; expanded to include Chad and Niger in 1998.
[b] Succeeded Operation Serval, which was launched in January 2013 and ended in July 2014.
[c] No estimate for 2020.

Sources: SIPRI Multilateral Peace Operations Database, accessed 1 Apr. 2021; 'G5 Sahel—Pau Summit—statement by the heads of state', French Ministry for Europe and Foreign Affairs, 13 Jan. 2020; van der Lijn, J., 'Multilateral non-peace operations', *SIPRI Yearbook 2018*, pp. 141–42; Dieng, M., 'The Multi-National Joint Task Force and the G5 Sahel Joint Force: The limits of military capacity-building efforts', *Contemporary Security Policy*, vol. 40, no. 4 (2019), pp. 481–501; and French Ministry of Defence, *Operation Barkhane*, Press pack (French Ministry of Defence: Feb. 2020).

in Toumour on the Diffa border, which killed 28 people and injured hundreds more on 13 December, the day of local and regional elections.[34]

---

[34] 'Attack in Niger kills 28, and Boko Haram is blamed', *New York Times*, 14 Dec. 2020; and Boko, H., 'Why Boko Haram's attack on Toumour, Niger is a stark warning to neighbouring states', France 24, 18 Dec. 2020.

Multinational peace and counterterrorism operations

To address insecurities in West Africa, several multinational peace and counterterrorism operations have been deployed, mainly in the Sahel region (see table 7.5). The largest of these is the UN Multidimensional Integrated Stabilization Mission in Mali, which focuses on peacekeeping and stabilization.[35] However, it continued to face enormous difficulties in implementing its protection of civilians mandate in 2020. The United States, the European Union (EU) and several European states are centrally involved in the fight against transnational jihadist and criminal networks in the region, albeit rarely directly: most Western forces train and build capacity in local forces, including the two ad hoc counterterrorism task forces: the Multinational Joint Task Force (MNJTF) in the Lake Chad region and the Group of Five for the Sahel (G5 Sahel) Joint Force.[36] Since March 2020 the EU Training Mission in Mali has been mandated to improve the operational capacity of the Malian army and also to assist the national armed forces of the other G5 Sahel countries.[37] On the civilian side, the EU Capacity Building Mission Sahel Mali and the EU Capacity Building Mission Sahel Niger support the internal security forces (see table 7.5).[38]

At the 13 January 2020 Pau Summit in France, France and the G5 Sahel countries launched the Coalition for the Sahel, a broader coordinating framework. The coalition is based on four pillars: the fight against terrorism, capacity building for Sahelian forces, restoration of state authority and development assistance. The counterterrorism pillar comprises special forces from European states—Task Force Takuba officially launched on 27 March 2020. The European task force is placed under Operation Barkhane's command, and advises, assists and accompanies Malian Armed Forces.[39] An initial operational capability for Task Force Takuba, consisting of French and Estonian units, was in place by the end of 2020, and a 150-troop contingent from Sweden was due to be deployed in early 2021.[40] Belgium, Czechia, Denmark, Greece, Italy, the Netherlands and Portugal have also

[35] United Nations, Security Council, 'Security Council renews Multidimensional Integrated Stabilization Mission in Mali, unanimously adopting Resolution 2531 (2020)', Meetings Coverage and Press Releases, 29 June 2020.

[36] Davis, I., 'Key general developments in the region', SIPRI Yearbook 2020, pp. 176–77.

[37] Council of the European Union, 'EUTM Mali: Council extends training mission with broadened mandate and increased budget', Press release, 23 Mar. 2020.

[38] European External Action Service, 'EUCAP Sahel Mali', [n.d.].

[39] The European signatories of the political statement are Belgium, Czechia, Denmark, Estonia, France, Germany, Mali, Niger, the Netherlands, Norway, Portugal, Sweden and the United Kingdom. Task Force Takuba, 'Political statement by the governments of Belgium, Czech Republic, Denmark, Estonia, France, Germany, Mali, Niger, the Netherlands, Norway, Portugal, Sweden and the United Kingdom', 23 Mar. 2020.

[40] Swedish Armed Forces, 'Mali (Task Force Takuba)', 18 Jan. 2021.

Table 7.6. Estimated conflict-related fatalities in the Lake Chad region, 2017–20

Province (state)	2017	2018	2019	2020 (%)
Far North (Cameroon)	583	322	456	592 (*37*)
Lac (Chad)	217	126	259	441 (*60*)
Diffa (Niger)	147	307	404	338 (*30*)
Adamawa, Borno and Yobe (Nigeria)	3 022	2 591	2 221	3 465 (*45*)
Total	**3 969**	**3 346**	**3 340**	4 836 (*43*)

Note: Percentages are of total national conflict-related fatalities.

Source: Armed Conflict Location & Event Data Project (ACLED), Dashboard, accessed 22 Feb. 2021. Data per region is available from 11 Jan. 2017.

pledged future contributions.[41] France also increased its military personnel under Operation Barkhane from 4500 to 5100 in 2020.[42]

The effectiveness of these peace and counterterrorism operations has been mixed, whether at the military level or in the restoration of state authority, while more needs to be done to differentiate between civilians and combatants in the areas where they operate.[43] From February until April 2020 national and foreign forces intensified their counterterrorism operations in the Liptako-Gourma region, which is reflected in a concurrent peak in battle deaths and in violence against civilians.[44] The involvement of the defence and security forces and international forces in human rights violations committed during military operations in Burkina Faso, Mali and Niger increased in 2020 compared to in 2019.[45] Since late 2019 the crackdown on terrorism by the security forces of Burkina Faso, Mali and Niger has resulted in more than 600 extrajudicial killings of civilians during counterterrorism operations.[46]

Armed conflict in the Lake Chad region

Armed conflict, forced displacement and grave human rights violations, including killings, sexual violence, abduction and recruitment of child soldiers, remained widespread in the Lake Chad region, which includes

[41] See chapter 2, section II, in this volume.

[42] 'France's thankless war against jihadists in the Sahel', *The Economist*, 12 Nov. 2020. On France's military role in Africa more generally see Recchia, S. and Tardy, T., 'French military operations in Africa: Reluctant multilateralism', *Journal of Strategic Studies*, vol. 43, no. 4 (2020), pp. 473–81.

[43] International Crisis Group, *What Role for the Multinational Joint Task Force in Fighting Boko Haram*, Africa Report no. 291 (International Crisis Group: Brussels, 7 July 2020).

[44] ACLED, Dashboard, accessed 22 Feb. 2021; and Amnesty International, *Human Rights Violations by Security Forces in the Sahel* (Amnesty International: London, 2020).

[45] Berger, F., 'Human rights abuses: A threat to security sector reforms in the Sahel', Commentary, Italian Institute for International Political Studies, 3 Mar. 2021; Amnesty International, 'Sahel: Soldiers rampage through villages killing people under guise of anti-terror operations', 10 June 2020.

[46] 'Sahel: End abuses in counterterrorism operations', News release, Human Rights Watch, 13 Feb. 2021.

the provinces of Far North (in Cameroon); Lac (in Chad); Diffa (in Niger); and Adamawa, Borno and Yobe (in Nigeria). Boko Haram, which started its violent uprising in 2009, and the growing influence of the Islamic State West Africa Province (a Boko Haram splinter group) with deepening roots in civilian populations, contributed to a continued humanitarian crisis and increased internal and cross-border displacement of people.[47]

The security situation in the Lake Chad region worsened in 2020, with a sharp increase in conflict-related fatalities of 44 per cent. There were 3340 fatalities in 2019 versus 4836 in 2020 (see table 7.6).[48] The high number can partly be explained by the battles between Boko Haram and Chad's military. Chadian troops claimed to have killed 1000 Boko Haram members around Lake Chad in response to the ambush that killed almost 100 of their soldiers in Boma, Chad, on 23 March 2020.[49]

As of 23 November 2020, 2.7 million people in the region were internally displaced and another 257 000 were refugees in neighbouring countries. An estimated 12.5 million people were in need of humanitarian assistance, of whom 10.6 million were in north-eastern Nigeria where an estimated 4.3 million people faced emergency levels of food insecurity. With increasing attacks on education, 1117 schools in the Lake Chad region remained closed during 2020, of which 934 were in Nigeria.[50]

Chad has been one of the most important regional actors in the fight against jihadist groups in the Sahel. Its troop withdrawals from Borno in Nigeria in January 2020 heightened the risk of attacks in Cameroon, Niger and Nigeria.[51] On 23 March 2020 an estimated force of 400 Boko Haram fighters killed around 100 Chadian soldiers in an unprecedented large attack on a garrison on Bohoma Peninsula, confirming the threat of violent extremism in the country and the region.[52] In response, Chadian troops—mainly outside of the auspices of the MNJTF—claimed to have killed 1000 Boko Haram members during operation Wrath of Boma.[53] This unprecedented attack in Bohoma confirmed the growing threat of violent extremism in the country and the region.

---

[47] International Crisis Group, *Facing the Challenge of the Islamic State in West Africa Province*, Africa Report no. 273 (International Crisis Group: Brussels, 16 May 2019). On the historical processes that produced Boko Haram see MacEachern, S., *Searching for Boko Haram: A History of Violence in Central Africa* (Oxford University Press: Oxford, 2018).

[48] ACLED (note 44).

[49] 'Boko Haram militants kill nearly 100 Chadian soldiers in attack', Reuters, 25 Mar. 2020; and 'Chad's army says 52 soldiers, 1,000 Boko Haram fighters killed in operation', Reuters, 9 Apr. 2020.

[50] UN OCHA, 'Lake Chad Basin: Humanitarian snapshot', 23 Nov. 2020.

[51] Ahmen, K., 'Fears for civilians in Chad after army suffers devastating Boko Haram attack', *The Guardian*, 1 Apr. 2020. Also see the discussion on Chad in section III of this chapter.

[52] 'Boko Haram militants kill nearly 100 Chadian soldiers in attack', Reuters (note 49).

[53] 'Chad's army says 52 soldiers, 1,000 Boko Haram fighters killed in operation', Reuters (note 49); and 'Behind the jihadist attack in Chad', Commentary, International Crisis Group, 6 Apr. 2020.

Table 7.7. Estimated conflict-related fatalities in Nigeria, 2013–20

Event type	2013	2014	2015	2016	2017	2018	2019	2020
Battles	2 326	4 031	3 329	2 191	1 779	2 470	2 475	3 336
Explosions/ remote violence	255	1 311	1 938	681	1 424	759	770	1 900
Protests, riots and strategic developments	66	252	366	138	144	161	111	244
Violence against civilians	2 039	5 794	5 285	1 886	1 600	2 853	2 075	2 280
Total	4 686	11 388	10 918	4 896	4 947	6 243	5 431	7 760

Note: For definitions of event types, see Armed Conflict Location & Event Data Project (ACLED), 'ACLED definitions of political violence and protest', 11 Apr. 2019.

Source: ACLED, 'Data export tool', accessed 22 Feb. 2021.

Nigeria

With 71 per cent of the total conflict-related fatalities in the Lake Chad region, Borno in Nigeria (the birthplace of Boko Haram) continued to be the epicentre of the conflict in 2020 (see table 7.6).[54] In the most violent direct attack on civilians in 2020, at least 110 people were killed near the Borno capital Maiduguri on 28 November 2020.[55] Boko Haram's area of operation also expanded into the north-west region of Nigeria in 2020, where it forged alliances with increasingly overlapping and intertwining bandits and criminal gangs. Banditry, including armed robbery, cattle rustling, murder, kidnapping and sexual violence, surged in 2020: after a lull at the end of 2019, more than 1600 fatalities were recorded in the north-west region between January and June 2020.[56] In mid December 2020 Boko Haram claimed responsibility for the kidnapping of hundreds of students in the state of Katsina, far from its original bases.[57] Some of the kidnapped boys were reportedly released on 17 December 2020.[58]

Aside from the intensifying Boko Haram insurgency in the north-east and the surge in banditry in the north-west, Nigeria experienced additional security challenges in 2020. Against the backdrop of an economic recession due to Covid-19 coupled with a collapse in oil prices, the country faced protests against police brutality, increasing violence between farmers

[54] ACLED (note 44); and 'The Islamic State franchises in Africa: Lessons from Lake Chad', Commentary, International Crisis Group, 29 Oct. 2020.

[55] 'Statement on attack against civilians in Koshobe, Borno', UN OCHA, 29 Nov. 2020; 'At least 110 dead in Nigeria after suspected Boko Haram attack', *The Guardian*, 29 Nov. 2020; and Ewang, A., 'Gruesome Boko Haram killings in northeast Nigeria', Dispatches, 1 Dec. 2020.

[56] Wodu, N., 'Not all violent problems require violent solutions: Banditry in Nigeria's north-west', Council on Foreign Relations, 23 July 2020; and 'Nigeria: Banditry violence and displacement in the northwest', ACAPS, 24 July 2020.

[57] Akinwotu, E., 'Nigerian schoolboys meet president after kidnap ordeal', *The Guardian*, 18 Dec. 2020; and Campbell, J., 'Release of Nigerian school boys: Questions and hypotheses', Council on Foreign Relations, 21 Dec. 2020.

[58] 'Nigeria's Katsina school abduction: Boko Haram says it took the students', BBC News, 15 Dec. 2020; Akinwotu (note 57); and Campbell (note 57).

and herders in the Middle Belt and the north-west, and the long-running militancy in the Niger Delta.[59]

In 2020 Nigeria's conflict-related fatalities were at the highest level since the peak in 2014–15, when the Nigerian armed forces recaptured territory from Boko Haram (see table 7.7).[60] This can partly be explained by the rise in fatalities in the Lake Chad region and banditry in the north-west. Violence by national security forces also contributed to the rise in fatalities: the Nigerian National Human Rights Commission, for instance, reported by mid April that violent enforcing of the lockdown caused almost twice as many fatalities as the officially reported Covid-19 deaths at that time.[61] Nigeria's military spending increased by 29 per cent to reach $2.6 billion in 2020.[62]

---

[59] Lenshie, N. E. et al., 'Desertification, migration, and herder-farmer conflicts in Nigeria: Rethinking the ungoverned spaces thesis', *Small Wars & Insurgencies* (2020); 'Niger Delta annual conflict report: January–December 2020', Linking Partners for Niger Delta Development, 10 Feb. 2021; ACAPS (note 56); and 'Nigeria's #EndSARS protest: De-escalate tensions, start deep police reform', Statement, International Crisis Group, 26 Oct. 2020. For more on Nigeria's economic challenges in 2020 see World Bank, 'World Bank Group to boost Nigeria's efforts to reduce poverty', Press release 2021/072/AFR, 15 Dec. 2020; and 'Finding the balance: Public health and social measures in Nigeria', Africa Centres for Disease Control and Prevention, 19 Aug. 2020.

[60] 'Most territory regained from Boko Haram, Nigeria says', Voice of America, 17 Mar. 2015.

[61] 'Report on human rights violations following the implementation of Covid-19 regulations 2020 and directives issued by federal and state governments from 31st March to 13th April 2020', National Human Rights Commission, 8 July 2020.

[62] On Nigeria's military spending see chapter 8, section II, in this volume.

III. Armed conflict and peace processes in Central Africa

IAN DAVIS

The Central Africa United Nations subregion comprises: Angola, Cameroon, the Central African Republic (CAR), Chad, the Democratic Republic of the Congo (DRC), the Republic of the Congo, Equatorial Guinea, Gabon, and Sao Tome and Principe. Five of the nine Central African states were involved in armed conflicts in 2020—Angola, Cameroon, CAR, Chad and the DRC—and those are the focus of this section. Cameroon and Chad were also discussed briefly in the context of the Lake Chad regional conflict nexus in section II.

Similar to the situation in West Africa (section II), Central Africa contains some of the world's severest and longest crises. Despite most of the countries in the region being resource rich, these natural resources have often been a driver for competition and corruption, leading to high levels of poverty and food insecurity. Rapid population growth and climate change also drive life-threatening levels of vulnerability.[1] Conflict in the region's hotspots in 2020 persisted (in CAR) or worsened (in Cameroon, Chad and especially the DRC).

Angola

In Angola in 2020 battle-related conflict deaths rose above the threshold for an armed conflict for the first time since 2017. The Armed Conflict Location & Event Data Project (ACLED) recorded 74 conflict-related fatalities for the year, of which 27 were battle related.[2] The Cabinda War (1975–present) in Angola was largely ended by a 2006 peace accord, but a low-level separatist insurgency waged by the Front for the Liberation of the Enclave of Cabinda against the government has continued with sporadic fighting. On 30 March 2020 Cabindan militias declared a unilateral ceasefire to help combat the Covid-19 pandemic, but new clashes occurred in June 2020.[3]

Cameroon

The two main unrelated armed conflicts in Cameroon continued in 2020: the anglophone separatist insurgency in the Southwest and Northwest regions and the Boko Haram insurgency in the Far North region (part of the wider

---

[1] UN Office for the Coordination of Humanitarian Affairs (OCHA), *Global Humanitarian Overview 2021* (UN OCHA: Dec. 2020), pp. 141–43.
[2] ACLED, 'Data export tool', accessed 5 Mar. 2021.
[3] 'Angola: Fatal clashes between separatists and military in Cabinda province June 2', Garda World, 4 June 2020; and Organization of Emerging African States, 'More African freedom fighters join Covid-19 ceasefire', ModernGhana, 3 Apr. 2020.

Table 7.8. Estimated conflict-related fatalities in Cameroon, 2013–20

Event type	2013	2014	2015	2016	2017	2018	2019	2020
Battles	17	1 223	959	340	260	996	642	818
Explosions/remote violence	0	33	202	175	223	31	20	62
Protests, riots and strategic developments	1	0	0	11	48	7	2	41
Violence against civilians	14	110	278	195	186	496	568	668
Total	**32**	**1 366**	**1 439**	**721**	**717**	**1 530**	**1 232**	**1 589**

Note: For definitions of event types, see Armed Conflict Location & Event Data Project (ACLED), 'ACLED definitions of political violence and protest', 11 Apr. 2019.

Source: ACLED, 'Data export tool', accessed 22 Feb. 2021.

Lake Chad crisis). Both worsened in 2020, and total conflict-related fatalities in Cameroon were at a slightly higher level than in 2019, with violence against civilians increasing for the third consecutive year (see table 7.8). The number of people requiring humanitarian support in Cameroon increased from 2.7 million in 2016 to 4.4 million in 2020 (out of a total population of 26.5 million).[4]

The conflict in the Lake Chad region

Cameroon remained the country that was second most affected by the Lake Chad crisis (discussed in section II) where, in the Far North region, Boko Haram and other armed groups intensified their attacks. In August 2020, for example, 18 people died and 15 were injured in a Boko Haram attack on a camp for internally displaced persons in the town of Nguetechewe.[5] The number of conflict-related fatalities in the Far North in 2020 increased from 465 in 2019 to 591 in 2020.[6]

The conflict in anglophone Cameroon

The origins of the anglophone crisis are in colonial-era divisions of territory between Britain and France. Today, 5 million people in the Northwest and Southwest regions—about one fifth of the country's population—speak mainly English and have their own legal and educational systems. The anglophone demand for an autonomous republic called Ambazonia, which dates back to at least 1985, turned violent in October 2017.[7] Protests by anglophone teachers and lawyers against the use of French in anglophone schools

[4] UN OCHA (note 1), p. 147.

[5] 'Deadly jihadist attack targets Cameroon village hosting displaced people', France 24, 4 Sep. 2020.

[6] ACLED, Dashboard, accessed 7 Apr. 2021.

[7] International Crisis Group, *Cameroon's Anglophone Crisis at the Crossroads*, Africa Report no. 250 (International Crisis Group: Brussels, 2 Aug. 2017). On developments in 2018 see Davis, I. and Melvin, N., 'Armed conflict and peace processes in sub-Saharan Africa', *SIPRI Yearbook 2019*, pp. 124–25.

and courts were harshly repressed and were transformed into an armed insurgency by separatist militias.

The conflict has now become a significant and complex humanitarian emergency that has displaced more than 700 000 people.[8] In 2020 education facilities continued to be targeted, and attacks on villages and the destruction of homes forced more than 10 000 people to flee in February 2020 alone.[9] There was also a wave of attacks on polling stations during parliamentary elections held on 9 February and again during regional elections in December.[10]

While difficult to estimate, the secessionist forces probably number between 2000 and 4000 armed fighters, largely divided into two rival, so-called Ambazonia interim governments (referred to as IGs): one led by Sisiku Julius Ayuk Tabe, a former university administrator and engineer, who was imprisoned for life in 2019 on terrorism and secession charges, and the other by Samuel Ikome Sako, a former pastor based in the United States. Each IG is an umbrella group for a range of other factions.[11]

On 25 March 2020 one of the IG Sako-aligned groups, the Southern Cameroons Defence Forces (SOCADEF), announced a temporary ceasefire following the UN secretary-general's appeal for a global Covid-19-related ceasefire, but it was not reciprocated by other separatist armed groups nor the Cameroonian Government.[12] Although the largest opposition group (and IG Sisiku aligned) Ambazonia Governing Council (AGC) released a statement in which it supported the global call, it also declared that a ceasefire would be exploited by the government.[13] Nonetheless, in July 2020 tentative peace talks reportedly began between the Cameroonian Government and the leader of IG Sisiku—but it was unclear whether the AGC statement (or the initial ceasefire offer by SOCADEF, which is part of the rival grouping) helped to legitimize these negotiations.[14]

After a national dialogue in October 2019 (that excluded all separatists), in January 2020 the government announced a new 'special status' for the

---

[8] 'Cameroon: North-west and South-west', Situation Report no. 26, UN OCHA, 31 Dec. 2020.

[9] 'Cameroon: North-west and South-west', Situation Report no. 16, UN OCHA, 29 Feb. 2020; and Lay, T., 'Regional overview: Africa, 12–18 July 2020', ACLED, 23 July 2020.

[10] 'Cameroon: Election violence in anglophone regions', Human Rights Watch, 12 Feb. 2020; Amnesty International, 'Cameroon: Rise in killings in anglophone regions ahead of parliamentary elections', 6 Feb. 2020; and UN OCHA (note 8).

[11] On estimates of the number of members attributed to a separatist groups and armed militias see International Crisis Group, *Cameroon's Anglophone Crisis: How to get to Talks?*, Africa Report no. 272 (International Crisis Group: Brussels, 2 May 2019), section IV; and Bone, R. M., 'Ahead of peace talks, a who's who of Cameroon's separatist movements', New Humanitarian, 8 July 2020.

[12] Miller, A., 'Call unanswered: A review of responses to the UN appeal for a global ceasefire', ACLED, 13 May 2020.

[13] Office of the Vice President, Buea Ambazonia Governing Council, 'Declaration of the responsibility to protect the people of Ambazonia during the Covid-19 pandemic', 27 Mar. 2020.

[14] Bone (note 11); and 'Cameroon holds first peace talks with main separatist group', Al Jazeera, 4 July 2020.

two anglophone regions.[15] However, questions remained over the government's commitment to engage in dialogue and grant political concessions to separatist groups. Thus, the ceasefire talks between government representatives and the most important representatives of the separatists (Tabe and another nine imprisoned separatist leaders) in July 2020 came as a surprise—and were condemned by other separatists and downplayed by the government. There were no follow-up talks, and despite a new round of Swiss mediation in August 2020, the security situation in the anglophone regions continued to deteriorate in the remainder of the year.[16]

The Central African Republic

Almost the entire territory of CAR has been affected by conflict and violence among shifting alliances of armed groups since 2013, despite the presence of multinational peace operations—the African Union-led International Support Mission in the CAR (Mission Internationale de Soutien à la Centrafrique sous Conduite Africaine), 2013–14; the UN Multidimensional Integrated Stabilization Mission in the CAR (MINUSCA), 2014 to date and a French military intervention, 2013–16. Elections were held in 2016 and won by President Faustin-Archange Touadéra. A 2019 peace agreement and ceasefire between the government and 14 armed groups (the Political Agreement for Peace and Reconciliation in the Central African Republic, hereafter Political Agreement) curbed some of the violence.[17] Nonetheless, regular attacks against civilian populations, killings and other crimes and violations at the hands of the ex-Seleka and the anti-Balaka armed groups have continued.[18]

In January 2020 the Political Agreement was further strained by clashes between factions of the Popular Front for the Rebirth of the CAR (Front populaire pour la renaissance de la Centrafrique, FPRC) in the eastern town

---

[15] Chimtom, N. K., 'Cameroon's conflict: Will the national dialogue make any difference?', BBC News, 5 Oct. 2019; and Bone, R. M. and Nkwain, A. K., 'Cameroon grants "special status" its restive regions. They don't feel special', African Arguments, 13 Jan. 2020.

[16] Jeune Afrique, 'Cameroon's anglophone crisis: Rivalries hamper peace talks', Africa Report, 11 Aug. 2020; and Reuters, 'Gunmen kill at least six children in attack on Cameroon school', The Guardian, 24 Oct. 2020.

[17] The agreement is annexed to United Nations, Security Council, Letter dated 14 February 2019 from the Secretary-General addressed to the President of the Security Council, S/2019/145, 15 Feb. 2019. On developments in CAR in 2019 see Davis, I., 'Armed conflict and peace processes in Central Africa', SIPRI Yearbook 2020, pp. 196–99.

[18] The Seleka, meaning an 'alliance movement' in Sango, was created in 2012. The anti-Balaka, a collection of 'self-defence' armed groups emerged in 2013. Since 2015 there has been a proliferation of armed groups in CAR as a result of divisions within the ex-Seleka and the anti-Balaka, mainly along ethnic lines and regional origins or based on economic interests. See Vircoulon, T., 'Note Institut Français de Relations Internationales, Écosystème des groupes armés en Centrafrique' [Note French Institute of International Relations, Ecosystem of armed groups in the Central African Republic], Apr. 2020.

Table 7.9. Estimated conflict-related fatalities in the Central African Republic, 2013–20

Event type	2013	2014	2015	2016	2017	2018	2019	2020
Battles	1 223	1 144	191	443	1 250	624	280	322
Explosions/remote violence	4	105	12	1	10	2	3	0
Protests, riots and strategic developments	122	105	56	8	14	25	4	5
Violence against civilians	1 210	2 265	266	287	555	520	286	101
Total	2 559	3 619	525	739	1 829	1 171	573	428

Note: For definitions of event types, see Armed Conflict Location & Event Data Project (ACLED), 'ACLED definitions of political violence and protest', 11 Apr. 2019.

Source: ACLED, 'Data export tool', accessed 3 Mar. 2021.

of Bria that killed over 50 people.[19] While the security situation remained volatile throughout 2020 due to continued threats posed primarily by armed groups against civilians, humanitarian workers, government forces and UN peacekeepers, conflict-related fatalities fell for the third consecutive year (see table 7.9). The political situation also remained fragile, dominated by the preparations for the presidential and legislative elections in December 2020. The security situation deteriorated at the end of the year ahead of those elections.

Over half the population (2.8 million people) required humanitarian assistance and protection at the end of 2020, and approximately 2.3 million people suffered from acute food insecurity.[20] One in four of the population of the country was displaced, either within or outside CAR.[21]

The peace process and the response to the United Nations call for a global ceasefire

Implementation of the Political Agreement stalled in 2020 due to the elections and security context, and there were multiple setbacks in disarmament and demobilization, and in training and operationalization of the mixed security units.[22] The government, with the support of MINUSCA, did have some success with dialogue and reconciliation efforts at the local level.[23] In November 2020 the mandate of MINUSCA was extended for a further 12 months until 15 November 2021.[24] Two small new multilateral peace operations also started in 2020: the African Union Military Observers Mission to the CAR, which is mandated to help monitor the implementation

---

[19] '50 killed in militia clashes in Central African Republic town', TRT World, 28 Jan. 2020.

[20] United Nations, Security Council, 'Central African Republic', Report of the Secretary-General, S/2021/146, 16 Feb. 2021, p. 6.

[21] UN OCHA (note 1), p. 150.

[22] United Nations, Security Council, 'Central African Republic', Report of the Secretary-General, S/2020/545, 16 June 2020, p. 15; and United Nations, S/2021/146 (note 20), p. 4.

[23] United Nations, S/2021/146 (note 20), p. 4.

[24] UN Security Council Resolution 2552, 12 Nov. 2020.

of the Political Agreement and specifically the establishment of mixed security units, and the European Union (EU) Advisory Mission in the CAR, which is mandated to support security sector reform in the country (and will complement the military EU Training Mission in CAR).[25]

On 25 March, two days after the UN secretary-general's Covid-19-related global ceasefire call, the UN secretary-generals' special representative for CAR and head of MINUSCA, Mankeur Ndiaye, called for a national ceasefire in the country. However, although the FPRC, the Democratic Front of the Central African People (Front démocratique du peuple centrafricain) and the Return, Reclamation, Rehabilitation (Retour, réclamation et réhabilitation, known as 3R) armed groups publicly declared their support, this did not translate into adherence on the ground.[26]

In the north-east, violent clashes between rival factions of the FPRC continued; they exacerbated communal tensions in the region and led to mass population displacement. In the north-west, the 3R armed group continued to expand and challenge government forces and MINUSCA. On 15 June MINUSCA launched a military operation to reduce the threat posed by 3R and to encourage the group's compliance with the Political Agreement.[27]

In early December, after CAR's Constitutional Court rejected the candidacy of former president François Bozizé—still influential among anti-Balaka militia groups and the Gbaya community (the country's largest ethnic group)—some armed groups escalated attempts to obstruct the 27 December election.[28] On 17 December several armed groups announced the formation of the Coalition of Patriots for Change (CPC), which Bozizé publicly endorsed on 27 December. The electoral campaigning in December was disrupted by a surge in violence by CPC-affiliated armed groups.[29] At the request of the CAR Government, Russia and Rwanda deployed additional forces to support MINUSCA and government forces.[30] The temporary deployment of 300 Russian military instructors complemented existing Russian private military contractors that have been present in CAR since at least 2018.[31] The CAR and Rwandan governments accused Bozizé of backing the rebels and

[25] See chapter 2, section II, in this volume; and Hickendorff, A. and Acko, I., 'The European Union Training Mission in the Central African Republic: An assessment', SIPRI Background Paper, Feb. 2021.

[26] United Nations, S/2020/545 (note 22), p. 3.

[27] United Nations, Security Council, 'Central African Republic', Report of the Secretary-General, S/2020/994, 12 Oct. 2020, p. 5.

[28] 'Ex-president Bozizé and current president Touadéra seem set on a collision course while elections are in the balance', Africa Confidential, vol. 61, no. 15 (23 July 2020).

[29] United Nations, S/2021/146 (note 20), pp. 1–2.

[30] 'Rwanda bolsters force in CAR as rebels "held back"', BBC News, 21 Dec. 2020.

[31] Schreck, C., 'What are Russian military contractors doing in the Central African Republic?', Radio Free Europe/Radio Liberty, 1 Aug. 2018; and 'Russia sends 300 military instructors to Central African Republic', BBC News, 22 Dec. 2020.

plotting a coup, which he denied—although Ndiaye subsequently confirmed collusion between Bozizé and the CPC.[32]

Only 35 per cent of the 1.85 million registered voters took part in the elections; due to insecurity the vote was not held in roughly 40 per cent of the 140 National Assembly seats. Provisional results for the presidential election confirmed Touadéra as the winner with over 53 per cent of the vote.[33] However, with CPC armed groups likely to continue to carry out attacks in 2021 the political and security situation remained fragile.

Chad

Chad has been one of the most important regional states in the fight against jihadist groups in the Central Sahel and Lake Chad regions (see section II). In 2020 the country was affected by growing insecurity within its borders and within neighbouring countries. In addition to attacks by Boko Haram and Chadian armed groups, intercommunal violence also occurred—particularly in eastern Chad.[34] These conflicts flowed partly from farmer–herder competition, but also from deeper identity-based rivalries over land and political power. There were over 738 conflict-related fatalities in 2020, which is a 30 per cent increase from 2019.[35] Chad is one of the largest refugee host countries in Africa with more than 915 000 refugees, asylum seekers, internally displaced people and Chadian returnees. There were nearly 480 000 refugees in Chad, while food insecurity affected more than 2.3 million people in 2020.[36]

The Democratic Republic of the Congo

The DRC—the second-largest country in Africa with a population of about 80 million—is suffering from one of the longest and most complex crises in the world, where armed conflict, epidemics and natural disasters combine with high levels of poverty and weak public infrastructure and services. Competition over land and mineral resources is among the main drivers of

---

[32] United Nations, Security Council, 'Briefing by the Special Representative of the Secretary-General for the Central African Republic and Head of the United Nations Multidimensional Integrated Stabilization Mission in the Central African Republic, Mankeur Ndiaye', S/2021/76, annex I, 27 Jan. 2021, p. 2.

[33] 'Central African Republic: Respect final results of the election, UN and partners urge', UN News, 5 Jan. 2021; and International Crisis Group, 'Picking up the pieces in the Central African Republic', *Watch List 2021* (International Crisis Group: Brussels, Jan. 2021).

[34] International Crisis Group, *Avoiding the Resurgence of Intercommunal Violence in Eastern Chad*, Africa Report no. 284 (International Crisis Group: Brussels, 30 Dec. 2019).

[35] ACLED, 'Data export tool', accessed 22 Feb. 2021.

[36] 'Chad: New law safeguards 480,000 refugees', UN News, 24 Dec. 2020; and UN OCHA, 'More than 2.3 million people in food insecurity, including 450,000 in severe food insecurity in Chad', 24 Apr. 2020.

the conflict.[37] Since the end of the 1998–2003 Second Congo War, conflict has persisted in the eastern DRC, where there are still dozens of armed groups and a major UN peacekeeping force, the UN Organization Stabilization Mission in the DRC (MONUSCO), has been deployed since 1999.[38] Since 2013 the governments of the DRC and neighbouring states have attempted to collectively address the threat of armed groups through a Peace, Security and Cooperation Framework.[39]

While most of the DRC's 26 provinces were stable in 2020, several of the eastern provinces (particularly Ituri, North Kivu and South Kivu) faced continued instability from external and Congolese armed groups engaged in multiple armed conflicts with the government, as well as a resurgence of intercommunal violence. These armed groups vary in capacity, size and objectives. Some of the most violent clashes were in North Kivu between government forces and the Allied Democratic Forces (ADF), an Islamist armed group that originated in Uganda, with civilians often enduring ADF reprisals.[40] Also in North Kivu there was intense fighting between factions of the Nduma Defence of Congo-Renovated (Nduma défense du Congo-Rénové), which split in July 2020. The Nduma Defence of Congo's former leader, Ntabo Ntaberi 'Sheka', was sentenced to life imprisonment by a military court on 23 November 2020 for war crimes and crimes against humanity.[41] In the north-eastern Ituri province, the Cooperative for Development of Congo (CODECO), a loose association of ethnic Lendu militias, stepped up attacks, especially in the first half of 2020, mainly targeting the Hema community, in a conflict over natural resources and land. On 25 March 2020 CODECO's leader Justin Ngudjolo was killed by government forces, leading to a power struggle and splits within the group.[42] Although CODECO agreed and announced a unilateral ceasefire in August 2020, several factions within the group continued fighting.[43]

[37] For detailed analysis of the armed conflict see the various reports of the group of experts on the DRC, e.g. United Nations, Security Council, 'Final report of the Group of Experts on the Democratic Republic of the Congo', S/2020/482, 2 June 2020.

[38] The UN Organization Mission in the DRC was deployed in 1999 and renamed MONUSCO in 2010. For details of the armed groups see Africa Intelligence, 'Felix Tshisekedi a hostage to armed groups', *West Africa Newsletter*, no. 798 (10 Apr. 2019); and United Nations, S/2020/482 (note 37), pp. 5–12.

[39] 'Peace, security and cooperation framework for the Democratic Republic of the Congo and the region', 24 Feb. 2013.

[40] 'DRC: Attacks by ADF armed group may amount to crimes against humanity and war crimes', UN Human Rights Office of the High Commissioner, 7 July 2020; and Burke, J., 'Militia raids kill dozens as DRC plunges deeper into instability', *The Guardian*, 31 Jan. 2020.

[41] 'Democratic Republic of the Congo', Global Centre for the Responsibility to Protect, 15 Mar. 2021.

[42] International Crisis Group, *DR Congo: Ending the Cycle of Violence in Ituri*, Africa Report no. 292 (International Crisis Group: Brussels, 15 July 2020).

[43] AFP, 'Militias in Eastern DRC agrees to stop attacks', East African, 24 Aug. 2020; and 'Security Council report, Monthly forecast', Security Council Report, Dec. 2020, p. 9.

Table 7.10. Estimated conflict-related fatalities in the Democratic Republic of the Congo, 2013–20

Event type	2013	2014	2015	2016	2017	2018	2019	2020
Battles	1 093	603	748	898	1 364	1 787	1 978	3 254
Explosions/remote violence	77	10	13	4	108	9	15	1
Protests, riots and strategic developments	16	38	65	145	79	63	129	193
Violence against civilians	789	579	936	693	1 659	1 330	1 721	2 319
Total	**1 975**	**1 230**	**1 762**	**1 740**	**3 210**	**3 189**	**3 843**	**5 767**

Note: For definitions of event types, see Armed Conflict Location & Event Data Project (ACLED), 'ACLED definitions of political violence and protest', 11 Apr. 2019.

Source: ACLED, 'Data export tool', accessed 5 Mar. 2021.

The overall scale of violence in the eastern DRC increased in 2020, as reflected in the conflict-related fatalities for the year being the highest recorded in the 2013–20 period (see table 7.10). Serious and widespread violations of human rights and international humanitarian law continued to take place in the eastern DRC, including grave violations committed against children.[44]

As part of an ongoing acute, complex and multilayered humanitarian crisis, 21.8 million people faced acute food insecurity in 2020 (the highest absolute number ever recorded globally), while an estimated 5.2 million people remained internally displaced—the largest internally displaced person population in Africa—including 1.7 million people displacements in 2020.[45] Although the 10th outbreak of Ebola virus disease ended in June 2020 (having killed approximately 2300 people since 2018), a new outbreak began on 1 June 2020 and ended on 18 November 2020, causing a further 55 deaths.[46] The DRC also experienced growing numbers of Covid-19 cases and deaths (308 reported as of the end of October 2020), while measles and cholera remained serious concerns, causing 415 and 184 reported deaths, respectively, in 2020.[47] Attacks on health and humanitarian workers continued to impede efforts to deliver aid, especially in conflict zones in the east of the country.[48]

[44] Bujakera, S., 'UN warns of possible war crimes in northeastern Congo', Reuters, 27 May 2020; United Nations, S/2020/482 (note 37), pp. 24–30; and United Nations, Security Council, 'Children and armed conflict in the Democratic Republic of the Congo', Report of the Secretary-General, S/2020/1030, 19 Oct. 2020.

[45] United Nations, Security Council, 'United Nations Organization Stabilization Mission in the Democratic Republic of the Congo', Report of the Secretary-General, S/2020/1150, 30 Nov. 2020, pp. 6–7; and UN OCHA (note 1), p. 156.

[46] 'New Ebola outbreak detected in northwest Democratic Republic of the Congo; WHO surge team supporting the response', World Health Organization, 1 June 2020; and '11th Ebola outbreak in the Democratic Republic of the Congo declared over', World Health Organization, 18 Nov. 2020.

[47] UN OCHA (note 1), pp. 156–57.

[48] 'Security in the DRC and Yemen: Military conflict, disease outbreak and containment', Oxford Research Group, Nov. 2020.

IV. Armed conflict and peace processes in East Africa

IAN DAVIS

East Africa comprises 22 states or territories and 9 were involved in active armed conflicts in 2020 (see figure 7.2). This section focuses on five of those armed conflicts: in Ethiopia, Mozambique, Somalia, South Sudan and Sudan. There were more than 8.3 million internally displaced people and more than 4.6 million refugees across East Africa, primarily due to conflict and violence in those five countries.[1]

Most East African conflicts are in the Horn of Africa.[2] States in this subregion are particularly fragile for a complex mix of reasons including restricted access to natural resources, intergroup tensions, poverty and inequality, and weak state institutions.[3] Counterterrorism and anti-piracy efforts have been priorities in the Horn of Africa for a growing number of external actors over the last decade. This has created a crowded playing field that includes China, India, the United States and other Western powers (France, Germany, Italy, Japan, Spain and the United Kingdom) and several Middle Eastern countries (Egypt, Qatar, Saudi Arabia, Turkey and the United Arab Emirates)—with growing geopolitical tensions, rivalries and risks of destabilizing proxy conflicts.[4]

Disputes over resource allocation and access have also been significant in the region. For example, the dispute over sharing of the eastern Nile waters, involving Egypt, Ethiopia and Sudan, remained deadlocked in 2020.[5] Many of the region's social, political and economic challenges are compounded by the impacts of climate change, including droughts and floods.[6] From June to October 2020, at least 3.6 million people were affected by floods or landslides

---

[1] UN Office for the Coordination of Humanitarian Affairs (OCHA), *Global Humanitarian Overview 2021* (UN OCHA: Dec. 2020), p. 114.

[2] Geographically, the Horn of Africa is normally understood to comprise Djibouti, Eritrea, Ethiopia and Somalia. There are also broader definitions (as used here) that comprise these four core countries plus all or parts of Kenya, the Seychelles, South Sudan, Sudan and Uganda.

[3] Intergovernmental Authority on Development (IGAD), *IGAD Regional Strategy: Volume 1, The Framework* (IGAD: Djibouti, Jan. 2016), pp. 8–10, 15; and Adeto, Y. A., 'State fragility and conflict nexus: Contemporary security issues in the Horn of Africa', African Centre for the Constructive Resolution of Disputes, 22 July 2019.

[4] See Melvin, N., 'The new external security politics of the Horn of Africa region', SIPRI Insights on Peace and Security no. 2019/2, Apr. 2019; and Melvin, N., 'The foreign military presence in the Horn of Africa region', SIPRI Background Paper, Apr. 2019. On geopolitical tensions in the Middle East and North Africa see chapter 6, section I, in this volume.

[5] 'Nile negotiations break down as Egypt, Sudan accuse Ethiopia of rejecting legally binding agreement', New Arab, 18 June 2020; 'Ethiopia says GERD rising waters "natural" part of construction', Al Jazeera, 15 July 2020; and 'US suspends aid to Ethiopia over Blue Nile dam dispute', Al Jazeera, 3 Sep. 2020.

[6] For a regional analysis of environment, peace and security linkages in the region with specific focus on water security and governance see Krampe, F. et al., *Water Security and Governance in the Horn of Africa*, SIPRI Policy Paper no. 54 (SIPRI: Stockholm, Mar. 2020).

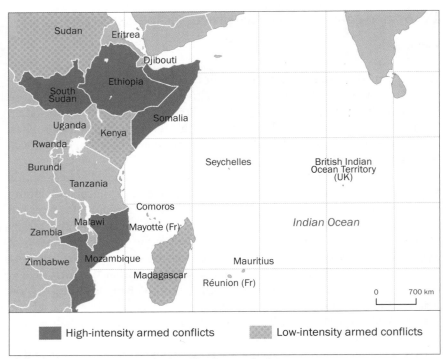

Figure 7.2. East Africa, including the Horn of Africa

across East Africa, many of whom were already suffering due to insecurity and conflict. Problems of food insecurity in the region were heightened by a surge in desert locusts in 2020—the worst in 25 years in Ethiopia and Somalia, and 70 years in Kenya.[7]

Ethiopia

A new armed conflict broke out in the Tigray region of northern Ethiopia in November 2020 between federal government forces and the former administration of the northern Tigray region, the Tigray People's Liberation Front (TPLF), which killed thousands and forced more than 46 000 refugees to flee into eastern Sudan. Insecurity also rose in many other areas of the country in 2020 due to simultaneous armed conflicts and high levels of interethnic violence, including in Konso (in the Southern Nations, Nationalities, and Peoples' Region), Metekel (in Benishangul-Gumuz Region), Guji, Kelam Welega and West Welega (in Oromia Region), and the Oromia–Somalia border area. Most of these proliferating conflicts involved ethnic-based

---

[7] UN OCHA (note 1), pp. 114–15.

armed groups and militias driven by ethno-regional nationalism and the pursuit of self-determination, territory and resources.[8] In particular, Metekel Zone witnessed a series of violent attacks on civilians and a deepening rift between the Amhara and Oromo regional administrations.[9] Tensions were also high between Amhara and Tigray regions.[10]

The killing of a popular ethnic Oromo musician and activist Hachalu Hundessa on 29 June 2020 sparked unrest and ethnic violence in the capital Addis Ababa and the Oromia Region. About 240 people were killed in the unrest. Thousands of local government officials and opposition leaders were later arrested.[11]

In 2020 the number of people in need of humanitarian assistance increased from 8 to 11.7 million people. Conflict, displacement and climate shocks (droughts, floods and locusts) were key drivers of humanitarian needs.[12]

Stalled reforms and tensions related to federal politics

The descent into violence and chaos during 2020 was in contrast to the optimism generated after the relatively peaceful transition of power, the reform agenda of Prime Minister Abiy Ahmed and the signing of a Joint Declaration of Peace and Friendship with Eritrea in 2018.[13] However, with the opening up of the political space, competition increased among the 10 semi-autonomous ethnically based regional states that make up Ethiopia.[14] When Sidama voted to become Ethiopia's 10th regional state in November 2019, after protests and a successful referendum, there were fears it might fuel similar demands by other ethnic regions, particularly those of Tigray and Wolayta.[15] Thus, during 2020 societal tensions in Ethiopia remained high

[8] Raleigh, C. and Fuller, B., 'Ethiopia: At risk of multiplying conflicts stretching the capacity of the state', eds E. Bynum et al., *Ten Conflicts to Worry about in 2021* (Armed Conflict Location & Event Data Project: Feb. 2021), pp. 3–5. On the contribution of the illegal weapons trade to insecurity in Ethiopia see Cochrane, L. and Hadis, S., 'Farmers buying guns: The impact of uncertainty and insecurity in rural Ethiopia', *African Studies Quarterly*, vol. 20, no. 1 (Jan. 2021), pp. 101–13.

[9] 'Ethiopia attack death toll reaches 207, state rights watchdog says', Africa News, 26 Dec. 2020.

[10] 'Bridging the divide in Ethiopia's north', Africa Briefing no. 156, International Crisis Group, 12 June 2020.

[11] AFP, 'Ethiopia violence death toll rises to 239', East African, 8 July 2020; and Tekle, T.-A., 'Ethiopia arrests 1,700 officials over deadly unrest', East African, 13 Aug. 2020.

[12] UN OCHA (note 1), pp. 121–22.

[13] On developments within Ethiopia in 2018–19 and the Eritrea–Ethiopia peace agreement see Davis, I. and Melvin, N., 'Armed conflict and peace processes in sub-Saharan Africa', *SIPRI Yearbook 2019*, pp. 134–37; Davis, I., 'Armed conflict and peace processes in the Horn of Africa', *SIPRI Yearbook 2020*, pp. 203–205; and Addis, A. K. et al., 'The recent political situation in Ethiopia and rapprochement with Eritrea', *African Security Review*, vol. 29, no. 2 (2020), pp. 105–24.

[14] 'Abiy Ahmed's reforms in Ethiopia lift the lid on ethnic tensions', BBC News, 29 June 2019; '67 killed in days of unrest in Ethiopia, police say', AP News, 26 Oct. 2019; and International Crisis Group, *Keeping Ethiopia's Transition on the Rails*, Africa Report no. 283 (International Crisis Group: Brussels, 16 Dec. 2019).

[15] Sileshi, E., 'Sidama becomes Ethiopia's 10th regional state', *Addis Standard*, 23 Nov. 2019; and Temare, G. G., 'The Republic of Tigray? Aydeln, yekenyeley!', Ethiopia Insight, 28 Sep. 2019.

Table 7.11. Estimated conflict-related fatalities in Ethiopia, 2013–20

Event type	2013	2014	2015	2016	2017	2018	2019	2020
Battles	418	237	566	999	877	730	193	1 634
Explosions/remote violence	48	2	16	15	2	22	17	85
Protests, riots and strategic developments	33	53	177	749	131	241	170	225
Violence against civilians	85	43	52	752	345	572	287	1 609
Total	**584**	**335**	**811**	**2 515**	**1 355**	**1 565**	**667**	**3 553**

Note: For definitions of event types, see Armed Conflict Location & Event Data Project (ACLED), 'ACLED definitions of political violence and protest', 11 Apr. 2019.

Source: ACLED, 'Data export tool', accessed 5 Mar. 2021.

as the country continued its political transition. In particular, its system of ethnic federalism was at risk of increased fragmentation.[16] The proliferation of regional 'special forces' (similar to paramilitary forces) also risked exacerbating tensions.[17]

The armed conflict in Tigray

In the second half of 2020 Ethiopia's federal government and the Tigray region—located in the north-west corner of Ethiopia, bordering Eritrea and Sudan, and with a population of about 7 million people (out of a total Ethiopian population of 110 million)—edged towards confrontation. The tensions partly reflected a power struggle between Prime Minister Abiy and Tigrayan elites who once dominated Ethiopia's military and ruling coalition.[18] Regional elections were another source of tensions: the federal government (having decided in June to postpone all elections until 2021 due to the Covid-19 pandemic) declared the September Tigray regional election illegal. In October the federal government moved to divert funding from the TPLF towards lower levels of the regional administration. Tigray responded by threatening to withhold tax revenues it collected on behalf of the federal government.[19]

On 3 November 2020, fearing (it is alleged) an imminent attack by federal forces, Tigray's forces in alliance with some of the Tigrayan officers in the national army, forcibly took control of some of the federal units stationed in the region. The next day, federal forces began an offensive against Tigray with support from Amhara Region forces and militias, and (it is suspected

---

[16] Mosley, J., 'Ethiopia's transition: Implications for the Horn of Africa and Red Sea region', SIPRI Insights on Peace and Security no. 2020/5, Mar. 2020.

[17] Abdu, B., 'Regional special forces: Threats or safeties?', The Reporter, 2 Jan. 2021.

[18] Gardner, T., 'How Abiy's effort to redefine Ethiopia led to war in Tigray', World Politics Review, 8 Dec. 2020; and Burke, J., 'Rise and fall of Ethiopia's TPLF—from rebels to rulers and back', *The Guardian*, 25 Nov. 2020.

[19] 'Steering Ethiopia's Tigray crisis away from conflict', Africa Briefing no. 162, International Crisis Group, 30 Oct. 2020.

but denied by both governments) Eritrean forces.[20] The United Nations warned of a 'full-scale humanitarian crisis' as thousands of Ethiopian refugees fled to nearby Eritrea and Sudan.[21] On 26 November the focus of the offensive moved to Tigray's capital Mekelle after the federal government's 72-hour ultimatum for Tigrayan forces to surrender expired.[22] The federal forces captured Mekelle on 28 November 2020 and declared victory over the TPLF, which vowed to carry on a guerrilla-style resistance and continued to fire rockets into Eritrea.[23]

Thousands of people died in the fighting, as shown in the upsurge in estimated conflict-related fatalities in 2020 (table 7.11). All sides are accused of atrocities and human rights abuses.[24] More than 46 000 people fled into neighbouring eastern Sudan, and up to 2 million people were internally displaced. With the federal government restricting access to the region, the UN warned that the crisis was 'spiralling out of control'.[25] A protracted crisis in Tigray seemed likely at the close of 2020. Border tensions between Ethiopia and Sudan also escalated in late December 2020; relations between the two countries were already strained due to the dispute over the Grand Ethiopian Renaissance Dam on the River Nile.[26]

Mozambique

The Islamist insurgency in Cabo Delgado province in the north of Mozambique deepened in 2020. Increased violence against civilians caused the number of internally displaced people to more than quadruple to over 500 000, while an estimated 1.3 million people in the region were in need of urgent humanitarian assistance.[27] Overall, estimated conflict-related fatalities in Mozambique increased almost threefold in 2020 compared to 2019 (see table 7.12).

While attacks by local Islamist groups have occurred sporadically since late 2017 they escalated sharply in 2020. The main insurgent group is Ansar al-Sunna, although locals call it 'al-Shabab' (there is no connection to the

[20] Beaumont, P., 'Diplomats back claims Eritrean troops have joined Ethiopia conflict', *The Guardian*, 8 Dec. 2020; 'Ethiopia sees war ending, EU complains of partisan aid access', Reuters, 4 Dec. 2020; and Fröhlich, S., 'Once enemies, Ethiopia and Eritrea ally against Tigray', Deutsche Welle, 29 Nov. 2020.

[21] Paravicini, G., 'Ethiopia says its troops marching on Tigrayan capitol', Reuters, 17 Nov. 2020.

[22] Burke, J., 'Ethiopia's military to begin "final offensive" against Tigray capital', *The Guardian*, 26 Nov. 2020.

[23] Anna, C., 'UN: Ethiopia's victory claim doesn't mean war is finished', AP News, 29 Nov. 2020; and 'Rockets hit Eritrea capital after Ethiopia declares victory', Al Jazeera, 29 Nov. 2020.

[24] AFP, '"Terrified" survivors recount attacks on civilians in Tigray', France 24, 15 Dec. 2020; and 'Ethiopia: Investigation reveals evidence that scores of civilians were killed in massacre in Tigray state', Amnesty International, 12 Nov. 2020.

[25] Anna, C., 'UN: Ethiopia's conflict has "appalling" impact on civilians', AP News, 9 Dec. 2020.

[26] De Waal, A., 'Viewpoint: Why Ethiopia and Sudan have fallen out over al-Fashaga', BBC News, 3 Jan. 2021.

[27] UN OCHA (note 1), p. 125.

Table 7.12. Estimated conflict-related fatalities in Mozambique, 2013–20

Event type	2013	2014	2015	2016	2017	2018	2019	2020
Battles	116	43	41	45	40	39	268	885
Explosions/remote violence	3	0	0	0	0	0	8	73
Protests, riots and strategic developments	3	3	3	2	71	5	20	19
Violence against civilians	22	11	4	58	18	179	367	805
Total	**144**	**57**	**48**	**105**	**129**	**223**	**663**	**1 782**

Note: For definitions of event types, see Armed Conflict Location & Event Data Project (ACLED), 'ACLED definitions of political violence and protest', 11 Apr. 2019.

Source: ACLED, 'Data export tool', accessed 5 Mar. 2021.

group of the same name in Somalia). During 2019 the group reportedly pledged allegiance to the Islamic State and analysts now refer to it as being part of the Islamic State Central Africa Province.[28] However, the extent of the group's fragmentation and links to Islamic State is difficult to discern.[29]

During 2020 Islamist militant groups took temporary control of key transport routes, waterways and strategic towns in the region, including the north-eastern port of Mocímboa da Praia in mid August 2020—close to Africa's largest-ever energy project in the Rovuma basin.[30] They also carried out cross-border attacks in southern Tanzania. With Mozambique state forces stretched by the conflict, local communities formed self-defence militias. The government also increasingly relied on military assistance from private security contractors from Russia and South Africa.[31] The armed violence in a region rich in natural resources was underpinned by poverty and inequality, as well as corruption and poor governance.[32] There were allegations of serious human rights abuses by Islamist groups and Mozambique security forces.[33]

At the end of the year additional external assistance or intervention was under consideration by neighbouring states, as well as by other states already involved in counterterrorism operations in sub-Saharan Africa.[34]

---

[28] On the origins of Islamist groups in northern Mozambique see Habibe, S., Forquilha, S. and Pereira, J., 'Islamic radicalization in northern Mozambique', Cadernos IESE no. 17/2019, Sep. 2019.

[29] 'Mozambique's mysterious conflict is intensifying', *The Economist*, 2 Apr. 2020; and Hamming, T. R., 'The Islamic State in Mozambique', Lawfare, 24 Jan. 2021.

[30] 'Mocimboa da Praia: Key Mozambique port "seized by IS"', BBC News, 12 Aug. 2020.

[31] 'Frelimo's belated cry for help', *Africa Confidential*, vol. 16, no. 13 (25 June 2020); 'Paramount and Lionel Dyck massively boost Nyusi's firepower', Africa Intelligence, 10 Dec. 2020; and Cenola, T. and Kleinfeld, P., 'Mozambique's Cabo Delgado: Militants advance as aid access shrinks', New Humanitarian, 21 Dec. 2020.

[32] 'Mozambique's jihadists and the "curse" of gas and rubies', BBC News, 18 Sep. 2020.

[33] 'Mozambique police: Islamists behead 50 people in troubled province', Deutsche Welle, 9 Nov. 2020.

[34] 'Cabo Delgado: President says Mozambique is open to receiving "any type of support"', Club of Mozambique, 19 Nov. 2020.

Somalia

Since 2012 the main armed conflict in Somalia has been between the Somali Government, backed by the African Union Mission in Somalia (AMISOM) and US forces, and al-Shabab insurgents. The Armed Conflict Location & Event Data Project (ACLED) recorded a 33 per cent increase in the activity of al-Shabab in 2020 compared to in 2019, although a UN panel of experts report indicates that these were mainly smaller-scale attacks using improvised explosive devices, suicide bombings and indirect fire attacks.[35] Government forces struggled to mount a cohesive response, partly due to ongoing political factionalism in Somalia. In addition, Somalia's rural populations continued to suffer from clan-based violence, with weak state security forces unable to prevent clashes over water and pasture resources.[36]

This armed violence has contributed to a prolonged humanitarian crisis in Somalia, which is also characterized by climate shocks including floods (that displaced 840 000 people in the first 10 months of 2020), drought, disease outbreaks (including the Covid-19 pandemic in 2020) and weak social protection. A desert locust infestation caused severe crop damage and added to food insecurity. The number of people in need of humanitarian assistance increased from 4.2 million in 2019 to 5.2 million in 2020, while the number of displaced people rose from 770 000 in 2019 to 1.2 million in 2020.[37]

The fight against al-Shabab

In 2018 AMISOM adopted a security transition plan for the gradual transfer of security responsibilities to Somali forces, with final withdrawal of the mission by the end of 2021.[38] AMISOM has been the largest ongoing multilateral peace operation in the world since 2015, and remained so in 2020, despite the further withdrawal of 1000 troops in February 2020.[39] Despite continued AMISOM operations and increased US air strikes, al-Shabab

---

[35] Kishi, R. et al., 'ACLED 2020: The Year in Review', Mar. 2021, p. 16; and United Nations, Security Council, Letter dated 28 September 2020 from the Panel of Experts on Somalia addressed to the Chair of the Security Council Committee pursuant to Resolution 751 (1992) concerning Somalia, S/2020/949, 28 Sep. 2020, p. 15.

[36] Felbab-Brown, V., 'The problem with militias in Somalia: Almost everyone wants them despite their dangers', Brookings, 14 Apr. 2020.

[37] UN OCHA (note 1), pp. 128–29. On the impact of climate-related change in livelihood options and migration, as well as peacebuilding in Somalia see also Eklöw, K. and Krampe, F., *Climate-related Security Risks and Peacebuilding in Somalia*, SIPRI Policy Paper no. 53 (SIPRI: Stockholm, Oct. 2019). On the impact of Covid-19 on Somalia see 'Covid-19 in Somalia: A public health emergency in an electoral minefield', Africa Briefing no. 155, International Crisis Group, 8 May 2020.

[38] Oluoch, F., 'AMISOM ready to withdraw', East African, 10 Nov. 2018. On developments within AMISOM in 2018 see Smit, T., 'Regional trends and developments in peace operations', *SIPRI Yearbook 2019*, pp. 169–71.

[39] On the force strength of AMISOM see chapter 2, section II, in this volume. On friction with AMISOM and the pursuit of national interests by some of the troop contributing countries see Albrecht, P. and Cold-Ravnkilde, S., 'National interests as friction: Peacekeeping in Somalia and Mali', *Journal of Intervention and Statebuilding*, vol. 14, no. 2 (2020), pp. 204–20.

Table 7.13. Estimated conflict-related fatalities in Somalia, 2013–20

Event type	2013	2014	2015	2016	2017	2018	2019	2020
Battles	1 985	2 893	2 786	3 729	2 686	3 034	2 154	1 890
Explosions/remote violence	529	953	750	1 215	2 188	1 446	1 214	761
Protests, riots and strategic developments	15	19	8	27	74	48	23	24
Violence against civilians	628	602	561	676	887	573	640	465
Total	**3 157**	**4 467**	**4 105**	**5 647**	**5 835**	**5 101**	**4 031**	**3 140**

Note: For definitions of event types, see Armed Conflict Location & Event Data Project (ACLED), 'ACLED definitions of political violence and protest', 11 Apr. 2019.

Source: ACLED, 'Data export tool', accessed 5 Mar. 2021.

remained a major threat. The threat extended beyond conventional military action and asymmetric warfare 'to include sophisticated extortion and "taxation" systems, child recruitment practices and an effective propaganda machine', especially in areas under its control in southern and central Somalia.[40] Although al-Shabab was generally unable to carry out large-scale complex attacks in 2020, a notable exception was the attack on the Elite Hotel in Mogadishu on 16 August 2020.[41] Overall, estimated conflict-related fatalities in 2020 were the lowest in the last eight years, but still remained above 3100 (see table 7.13).

The USA continued its engagement in Somalia—conducting 54 air strikes in 2020 (compared to 61 in 2019), while an independent assessment recorded 72 incidents in 2020 (and 93 in 2019).[42] The USA has been carrying out air strikes against the al-Shabab group in Somalia since 2007 and from a US airbase in Niger since 2019. The USA has also sponsored the creation of an elite Somalian counterterrorism force: the Danab Brigade.[43] In December 2020 President Donald J. Trump announced the withdrawal of all US troops from Somalia (thought to number about 700), but it was expected that many of these would be repositioned to neighbouring countries in East Africa.[44]

[40] United Nations, S/2020/949 (note 35), pp. 3, 7–13. Also see 'A losing game: Countering Al-Shabab's financial system', Hiraal Institute, Oct. 2020. On the group's recruitment strategy see Ingiriis, M. H., 'The anthropology of al-Shabaab: The salient factors for the insurgency movement's recruitment project', *Small Wars & Insurgencies*, vol. 31, no. 2 (2020), pp. 359–80.

[41] Nor, O., 'Somali forces kill attackers to end siege at popular Mogadishu hotel', CNN, 16 Aug. 2020.

[42] 'Declared and alleged US actions in Somalia', Airwars, [n.d.]; and Ahmed, K., 'Zero accountability": US accused a failure to report civilian deaths', *The Guardian*, 2 Apr. 2020.

[43] Sperber, A., 'The Danab Brigade: Somalia's elite, US-sponsored special ops force', Pulitzer Center, 11 Aug. 2020.

[44] Cooper, H., 'Trump orders all American troops out of Somalia', *New York Times*, 4 Dec. 2020; and 'Statement from AFRICOM Commander US Army Gen. Stephen Townsend on the activation of Joint Task Force—Quartz', 19 Dec. 2020.

Political fragmentation and Somalia's federalism

Political relations between the federal government and some of the federal member states (especially Galmudug, Jubaland and Puntland) remained volatile in 2020.[45] Electoral processes were the primary source of the tensions, especially in the aftermath of disputed regional elections in Jubaland in August 2019 and Galmudug, and in the preparations for national parliamentary and presidential elections. In Jubaland this led to a military stand-off between federal and regional forces.[46] Power-sharing arrangements along clan lines are common at all levels of Somali governance. A road map for inclusive politics was agreed in 2018, paving the way for a change from indirect voting, whereby clan leaders select electoral college delegates, to a one-person, one-vote system for the first time in 2020. However, in September 2020, after an impasse in the electoral process, agreement was reached to maintain the indirect voting system, albeit slightly modified. Nonetheless, parliamentary elections that were due to take place in mid December 2020 were pushed back until January 2021, while preparations for presidential elections scheduled for February 2021 were also lagging and the process was still being contested by opposition parties. With al-Shabab also threatening to disrupt the vote it remained unclear at the end of 2020 whether these pivotal elections would take place.[47]

South Sudan

South Sudan gained independence from Sudan on 9 July 2011 after a 2005 agreement that ended one of Africa's longest-running civil wars. A UN peacekeeping mission—the UN Mission in South Sudan (UNMISS)—was established on 8 July 2011. Although a post-independence civil war (2013–15) was curtailed by a 2015 peace agreement, the legacy of violence continued in the form of an armed conflict waged primarily between two groups: the Government of South Sudan and its allies, led by President Salva Kiir (an ethnic Dinka), and the Sudan People's Liberation Army-in-Opposition and the Nuer White Army, led by Vice President Riek Machar (an ethnic Nuer). Although the main division in the subsequent conflict has been between the Dinka and Nuer ethnic groups, underlying conflict dynamics are primarily

---

[45] United Nations, S/2020/949 (note 35), pp. 20–22.

[46] 'Jubaland demands for withdrawal of SNA from Gedo ahead of election', Garowe Online, 7 Oct. 2020; and 'Ending the dangerous standoff in southern Somalia', Africa Briefing no. 158, International Crisis Group, 14 July 2020.

[47] 'Who wants an election?', *Africa Confidential*, vol. 61, no. 10 (14 May 2020); 'Staving off violence around Somalia's elections', Africa Briefing no. 163, International Crisis Group, 10 Nov. 2020; and 'Blunting al-Shabaab's impact on Somalia's elections', Africa Briefing no. 165, International Crisis Group, 31 Dec. 2020.

Table 7.14. Estimated conflict-related fatalities in South Sudan, 2013–20

Event type	2013	2014	2015	2016	2017	2018	2019	2020
Battles	1 300	4 473	2 309	2 541	3 409	1 133	822	1 698
Explosions/remote violence	18	61	61	46	18	30	10	10
Protests, riots and strategic developments	0	11	24	1	4	5	4	7
Violence against civilians	3 077	1 849	1 208	960	1 416	532	970	656
Total	4 395	6 394	3 602	3 548	4 847	1 700	1 806	2 371

Note: For definitions of event types, see Armed Conflict Location & Event Data Project (ACLED), 'ACLED definitions of political violence and protest', 11 Apr. 2019.

Source: ACLED, 'Data export tool', accessed 5 Mar. 2021.

political and vary considerably across the country. Opposition groups have become more fractured and localized.

Kiir and Machar signed a new peace deal in September 2018—the Revitalized Agreement on the Resolution of the Conflict in the Republic of South Sudan—but since then implementation has been contested, partial and subject to delays.[48] In particular, further negotiations to form a unity government, transitional security arrangements and a unified national army stalled during 2019. There was also inconsistent support for the agreement among the Intergovernmental Authority on Development states and neighbouring states.[49]

Implementation of the 2018 peace agreement and ongoing conflict

In February 2020 the deadlock was broken after Kiir and Machar agreed to form the long-awaited unity government, as well changes to the number and boundaries of regional states (reducing the number of such states from 32 to 10).[50] However, the implementation of other aspects of the 2018 peace agreement was further slowed during 2020 in part by Covid-19-response measures that, among other things, delayed the registration and training of former combatants who were due to be integrated into new unified national forces.[51] In particular, the failure to agree on local power-sharing jeopardized the unity government and left large parts of the country 'in a governance and

[48] IGAD, *Revitalised Agreement on the Resolution of the Conflict in the Republic of South Sudan* (IGAD: Addis Ababa, 12 Sep. 2018).

[49] On developments in South Sudan in 2017–19 see Davis, I. et al., 'Armed conflict in sub-Saharan Africa', *SIPRI Yearbook 2018*, pp. 99–100; *SIPRI Yearbook 2019* (note 13), pp. 140–43; and *SIPRI Yearbook 2020* (note 13), pp. 208–11.

[50] 'A major step toward ending South Sudan's civil war', Statement, International Crisis Group, 25 Feb. 2020.

[51] Joshi, M. et al., 'The effect of Covid-19 on peace agreement implementation: The cases of Colombia, South Sudan, and the Philippines', PRIO Paper, 2020; and United Nations, Security Council, 'Interim report of the Panel of Experts on South Sudan submitted pursuant to Resolution 2521 (2020)', S/2020/1141, 25 Nov. 2020, pp. 7–8.

security vacuum', which led to further intercommunal violence.[52] There was also no progress in establishing any of the transitional justice mechanisms.[53]

While violence directly attributable to the conflict parties to the civil war continued to ebb as a result of the 2017 ceasefire, intercommunal violence fuelled by the proliferation and use of small arms and light weapons rose sharply in 2020—as reflected in the higher estimated conflict-related fatalities in 2020 (see table 7.14). UNMISS documented more than 1197 incidents of subnational armed violence in 2020—an increase of 146 per cent in comparison to 2019—that resulted in the deaths of 2421 civilians (compared to 1131 civilian deaths from armed violence in 2019).[54] The most devastating localized conflicts involved allied Dinka and Nuer militias and Murle pastoralist militias in central and southern Jonglei State and the lowland, oil-rich Greater Pibor Administrative Area.[55] On 12 August 2020 Kiir declared a three-month state of emergency for those two areas.[56] Efforts to disarm local communities in August led to at least 81 people being killed.[57]

In addition, signatories and non-signatories continued to violate the 2017 ceasefire. Clashes involving the National Salvation Front (a non-signatory to the revitalized agreement), the Sudan People's Liberation Army-in-Opposition, the South Sudan People's Defence Forces and local militias persisted in 2020, especially in Central and Western Equatoria.[58]

All the parties to these conflicts were accused of engaging in gross human rights violations and serious violations of international humanitarian law, including sexual and gender-based violence.[59] In March 2020 the UN Security Council extended the mandate of UNMISS until 15 March 2021, maintaining an authorized strength of 17 000 military personnel and 2101 police.[60] However, as was the case in 2019, UNMISS did not achieve this strength in 2020: as of 31 December 2020 UNMISS deployed 14 869 military personnel and 1653 police officers.[61] An independent strategic review of UNMISS concluded that its mandate remained valid, but among a number of

---

[52] United Nations, Human Rights Council, Report of the Commission on Human Rights in South Sudan, A/HRC/46/53, 4 Feb. 2021, p. 3.

[53] United Nations, A/HRC/46/53 (note 52), pp. 14–15.

[54] Human Rights Division, UN Mission in South Sudan, 'Annual brief on violence affecting civilians, January–December 2020', Mar. 2021.

[55] United Nations, A/HRC/46/53 (note 52), pp. 6–8.

[56] Emmanuel, O., 'Kiir imposes state of emergency to contain greater Jonglei conflict', Eye Radio, 13 Aug. 2020.

[57] Dahir, A. L., 'Efforts to disarm communities in South Sudan fuels deadly clashes', New York Times, 11 Aug. 2020; and United Nations, A/HRC/46/53 (note 52), pp. 8–9.

[58] United Nations, A/HRC/46/53 (note 52), pp. 4–6. For a record of the violations see South Sudan Peace Monitoring, 'CTSAMVM violation reports', 2020.

[59] United Nations, A/HRC/46/53 (note 52), pp. 13–14.

[60] UN Security Council Resolution 2514, 12 Mar. 2020.

[61] SIPRI Multilateral Peace Operations Database, accessed 1 Apr. 2021, <http://www.sipri.org/databases/pko/>. On developments within peace operations more generally see chapter 2, section II, in this volume.

proposed reforms, the review recommended a reduction in the authorized military strength to 15 000 military personnel.[62] On 29 May 2020 the UN Security Council agreed to extend an arms embargo on South Sudan along with individual travel bans and financial sanctions. China, Russia and South Africa abstained from the vote.[63]

The humanitarian situation

As a result of years of persistent armed conflict, enduring vulnerabilities and weak basic services, humanitarian needs in South Sudan remained exceptionally high in 2020. About two thirds of the population (7.5 million people) were in need of humanitarian assistance, while at least 6.5 million people were acutely food insecure—with the risk of famine in Jonglei State. Flooding affected 856 000 people and temporarily displaced nearly 400 000 persons during July–December 2020, while violence and insecurity continued to displace large numbers of people. Overall, some 1.6 million people in South Sudan were internally displaced during 2020.[64]

At the end of 2020 continued delays in the full implementation of the peace agreement and concern over the potential recurrence of even higher levels of violence meant that South Sudan remained at a critical juncture.

Sudan

A major transition of power occurred in Sudan in 2019 following the removal of President Omar al-Bashir by the Sudanese army. Under a subsequent power-sharing agreement reached between the Sudanese Transitional Military Council and a coalition of opposition and protest groups, Sudan is scheduled to hold elections following a 39-month period of shared rule between the military and civilian groups.[65] The new transitional administration inherited a deepening economic and humanitarian crisis, as well as a legacy of armed conflict. At the beginning of 2020 long-standing insurgencies remained extant mainly in Darfur and in the southern border states of Blue Nile and South Kordofan, involving a fragmented mosaic of non-state armed groups (see table 7.15). Some of these armed groups from Darfur were also present in Libya and South Sudan. The progress made in the Sudanese

---

[62] United Nations, Security Council, 'Report on the independent strategic review of the United Nations Mission in South Sudan pursuant to Security Council Resolution 2514 (2020)', S/2020/1224, 15 Dec. 2020, annex.

[63] UN Security Council Resolution 2521, 29 May 2020. On disagreements within the UN Security Council about the arms embargo on South Sudan see chapter 14, section II, in this volume.

[64] UN OCHA (note 1), pp. 131–32.

[65] Burke, J. and Salih, Z. M., 'Sudanese military and protesters sign power-sharing accord', The Guardian, 17 July 2019.

peace process in 2019 accelerated during 2020, with further significant peace agreements reached with the main armed groups.[66]

The Sudanese peace process

The August 2019 deal called for the newly established Sudanese transitional government to reach a peace agreement with the armed groups in Darfur and other states within six months. The peace negotiations were classified into parallel tracks in five geographical regions (see table 7.15).[67] Most of the negotiations took place in the South Sudanese capital Juba. Initial agreements with some of the armed groups were reached during negotiations between October 2019 and February 2020.

Negotiations continued during the Covid-19 pandemic that reached Sudan in early 2020. In response to the UN secretary-general's March call for a Covid-19-related global ceasefire, on 30 March 2020 the Sudan Liberation Movement/Army–Abdel Wahid (SLM/A–AW) stated it would continue to exercise a de facto ceasefire in Darfur but reiterated its rejection to join the peace process in Juba. A day later the Sudan People's Liberation Movement/Army–North (al-Hilu) (SPLM/A–N (al-Hilu)) announced an extension of its pre-Covid-19 ceasefire for a further three months (and on 1 May 2020 extended it until 31 January 2021), and the Sudanese Government recommitted to its own pre-Covid-19 nationwide ceasefire.[68]

On 4 June 2020 the UN Security Council approved Resolution 2524 (2020), which mandated a UN Integrated Transition Assistance Mission in Sudan. This mission started on 1 January 2021 and succeeds the joint UN–African Union Hybrid Operation in Darfur (UNAMID) that closed on 31 December 2020, having been deployed since 2007.[69]

On 31 August 2020 a comprehensive series of peace agreements was reached between the Sudan Revolutionary Front coalition and the government. The agreements covered key issues such as land ownership, security and power-sharing.[70] However, two of the groups in the coalition—the SLM/A–AW and the SPLM–N (al-Hilu)—rejected the agreements. On 4 September the

---

[66] On developments in Sudan in 2019 see *SIPRI Yearbook 2020* (note 13), pp. 211–14.

[67] 'Rebel movement denies suspension of peace negotiations', Radio Dabanga, 18 Dec. 2019.

[68] 'Coronavirus: Sudan rebels extend ceasefire', Radio Dabanga, 31 Mar. 2020; and Wise, L. et al., *Pandemic Pauses: Understanding Ceasefires in a Time of Covid-19*, Political Settlements Research Programme (University of Edinburgh: Edinburgh, 2021), pp. 11–12; and 'Ceasefires in a time of Covid-19', Open access tool, Political Settlements Research Programme, University of Edinburgh, accessed 24 Mar. 2021, <https://pax.peaceagreements.org/static/covid19ceasefires/>. On the UN secretary-general's global ceasefire call see chapter 2, section I, in this volume.

[69] UN Security Council Resolution 2524, 3 June 2020. On the closure of UNAMID see chapter 2, section II, in this volume.

[70] 'Sudan signs peace deal with rebel groups from Darfur', Al Jazeera, 31 Aug. 2020.

Table 7.15. Peace agreements between the Sudanese transitional government and key armed opposition groups, 2019–20

Region	Date of agreement	Type or status	Armed opposition group(s) signees
Darfur	21 Oct. 2019	Political, ceasefire and humanitarian	SRF
	28 Dec. 2019	Framework	JEM, SLM/A–MM, SLM/A–TC, SLFA
	31 Aug. 2020	Preliminary	SRF (incl. SLM/A–MM, JEM, SLM/A–TC)
	3 Oct. 2020	Juba Peace Agreement	SRF (incl. SPLM/A–N (Agar), SLM/A–MM, SLM/A–TC, JEM)
Two Areas (Blue Nile and South Kordofan)	18 Oct. 2019	Political, security and humanitarian	SPLM/A–N (al-Hilu)
	17 Dec. 2019	Ceasefire and humanitarian	SPLM/A–N (Agar)
	24 Jan. 2020	Framework	SPLM/A–N (Agar)
	17 Aug. 2020	Security	SRF
	31 Aug. 2020	Preliminary	SRF (incl. SPLM/A–N (Agar))
	3 Sep. 2020	Declaration of Principles	SPLM/A–N (al-Hilu)
	3 Oct. 2020	Juba Peace Agreement	SRF (incl. SPLM/A–N (Agar), SLM/A–MM, SLM/A–TC, JEM)
Northern	26 Jan. 2020	Final	KLM
Central	24 Dec. 2019	Final	SRF
Eastern	21 Feb. 2020	Final	SRF

JEM = Justice and Equality Movement; KLM = Kush Liberation Movement; SLFA = Sudan Liberation Forces Alliance; SLM/A–AW = Sudan Liberation Movement/Army–Abdel Wahid; SLM/A–MM = Sudan Liberation Movement/Army–Minni Minnawi; SLM/A–TC = Sudan Liberation Movement/Army–Transitional Council; SPLM/A–N = Sudan People's Liberation Movement/Army–North; and SRF = Sudan Revolutionary Front.

Notes: The SRF is an umbrella organization that was founded in 2011. Five major armed groups operating in Sudan were part of the SRF in 2020: (a) SPLM/A–N; (b) SLM/A–AW; (c) SLM/A–MM; (d) JEM; and (e)SLM/A–TC, which is a splinter group from the SLM/A–AW. In 2017 the SPLM/A–N split into two factions: SPLM/A–N (al-Hilu) and SPLM/A–N (Agar). The SLFA is another splinter group created in 2017. The KLM is a minor armed group founded in 1969.

Sources: United Nations, Security Council, 'Final report of the Panel of Experts on the Sudan', S/2020/36, 14 Jan. 2020, pp. 15–28; 'Human security baseline assessment for Sudan and South Sudan, Darfur's Armed Groups', Small Arms Survey, [n.d.]; 'SRF rebels, Sudan govt sign agreement in Juba', Radio Dabanga, 21 Oct. 2019; 'Rebel movement denies suspension of peace negotiations', Radio Dabanga, 18 Dec. 2019; 'Juba peace talks: "Breakthrough accord" on central Sudan track', Radio Dabanga, 25 Dec. 2019; 'Sudan rebels, govt. sign framework agreement in Juba', Radio Dabanga, 26 Jan. 2020; 'Peace agreement on Sudan's northern track', Radio Dabanga, 27 Jan. 2020; 'Sudan peace talks: Agreement on eastern track finalised', Radio Dabanga, 23 Feb. 2020; 'SPLM-N Malik Agar rebels, Sudan govt initial "historic and important" protocol', Radio Dabanga, 18 Aug. 2020; 'Sudan signs peace deal with rebel groups from Darfur', Al Jazeera, 31 Aug. 2020; Atit, M., 'Sudan's government agrees to separate religion and state', Voice of America, 4 Sep. 2020; and Dumo, D., 'Sudan and main rebel groups formalise peace deal', Reuters, 3 Oct. 2020.

Table 7.16. Estimated conflict-related fatalities in Sudan, 2013–20

Event type	2013	2014	2015	2016	2017	2018	2019	2020
Battles	5 595	3 049	2 440	2 939	851	700	321	565
Explosions/remote violence	479	263	263	294	33	28	17	13
Protests, riots and strategic developments	342	15	9	27	34	37	213	34
Violence against civilians	380	831	756	639	373	289	225	345
Total	**6 796**	**4 158**	**3 468**	**3 899**	**1 291**	**1 054**	**776**	**957**

Note: For definitions of event types, see Armed Conflict Location & Event Data Project (ACLED), 'ACLED definitions of political violence and protest', 11 Apr. 2019.

Source: ACLED, 'Data export tool', accessed 5 Mar. 2021.

government signed a separate 'declaration of principles' agreement with SPLM–N (al-Hilu).[71]

On 3 October 2020 the Sudanese Government and representatives of several armed groups (mostly members of the SRF coalition) signed the Juba Agreement for Peace in Sudan.[72] The two armed opposition groups that did not sign the August agreements also remained outside of this one. It is a highly complex agreement that brought together and expanded the individual agreements signed in August 2020. It consists of 10 different chapters—including 6 chapters of bilateral agreements with the different armed groups—and also sets out in considerable detail the future federal system, establishes a complicated web of transnational justice mechanisms and extensive transitional security arrangements, as well as implementation deadlines for many of these issues.[73] While there was positive support for the Juba Peace Agreement in many parts of Sudan, eastern Sudan became the epicentre of demonstrations against it.[74]

Conflict and humanitarian needs

Conflict remained lower than the levels of 2018 and earlier, but conflict-related fatalities increased in 2020 compared to in 2019 (see table 7.16). These were the result of mainly localized security incidents in Darfur and other conflict-affected regions in 2020. Intercommunal clashes and related attacks on civilians by Arab militias increased sharply, in frequency and in

[71] Atit, M., 'Sudan's government agrees to separate religion and state', Voice of America, 4 Sep. 2020.

[72] 'Juba Agreement for Peace in Sudan between the Transitional Government of Sudan and the Parties to the Peace Process', Official English version, 3 Oct. 2020.

[73] Al-Ali, Z., 'The Juba Agreement for Peace in Sudan: Summary and analysis', International IDEA, 2021.

[74] United Nations, Security Council, 'Final report of the Panel of Experts on the Sudan', S/2021/40, 13 Jan. 2021, pp. 7, 11–12; and 'Eastern Sudan rocked by protests and calls for independence', Middle East Eye, 7 Oct. 2020.

scale, particularly in South Darfur and West Darfur in July and August 2020.[75] Sudan's security forces were often accused of negligence and complicity in some of the attacks. Sexual and gender-based violence remained endemic in Darfur.[76]

Humanitarian needs in Sudan continued to rise in 2020: 7.5 million people needed humanitarian assistance, up from 5.7 million in 2019, and this was expected to rise to 13.4 million people in 2021. These emergency levels were driven by an economic crisis, Covid-19, the worst floods in decades, localized conflict and disease outbreaks. The military escalation in the Tigray region of Ethiopia in November 2020 resulted in over 40 000 refugees crossing the border into Sudan.[77]

Efforts to address the economic crisis in 2020 included a virtual international partnership conference on 25 June 2020 that secured pledges of $1.8 billion in financial support, a new International Monetary Fund programme to support economic reforms, and the US Government's announcement on 14 December 2020 of its intention to remove Sudan from its State Sponsors of Terrorism List, an impediment to securing debt relief and international finance.[78] The latter was the result of a normalization agreement between Israel and Sudan, facilitated by the USA.[79]

Future outlook

After the USA removed Sudan from its State Sponsors of Terrorism List, Sudanese Prime Minister Abdalla Hamdok said his country 'officially' rejoined the world community as 'a peaceful nation supporting global stability'.[80] The peace agreements reached in 2020 were key components of Sudan's larger transition from military to civilian rule. Implementation of the Juba Peace Agreement will be difficult amid Sudan's economic problems, as well as ongoing divisions among various actors involved in the political transition. The rejection of the agreement by the SLM/A–AW, the only armed movement with a substantial area of control in Darfur, may also hinder implementation of the security arrangements.

---

[75] United Nations, S/2021/40 (note 74), pp. 32–33; Salih, Z. M., 'In Darfur, civilians pay price in new wave of deadly violence', Al Jazeera, 9 Aug. 2020; and Walsh, D., 'The dictator who waged war on Darfur is gone, but the killing goes on', *New York Times*, 30 July 2020.

[76] United Nations, S/2021/40 (note 74), pp. 27–30.

[77] UN OCHA (note 1), pp. 134–35; Food and Agriculture Organization of the UN and World Food Programme, 'FAO-WFP early warning analysis of acute food insecurity hotspots', Oct. 2020, p. 7; and Salih, Z. M., '"We had to eat our seeds for planting": 10 million in Sudan facing food shortages', *The Guardian*, 28 July 2020. On the economic crisis see 'Financing the revival of Sudan's troubled transition', Africa Briefing no. 157, International Crisis Group, 23 June 2020.

[78] 'Sudan partnership conference', Berlin, 25 June 2020, Final communiqué, 2020.

[79] Burke, J. and Holmes, O., 'US removes Sudan from terrorism blacklist in return for $335m', *The Guardian*, 19 Oct. 2020. On the normalization agreement with Israel see chapter 6, section III, in this volume.

[80] Cited in Magdy, S., 'US embassy says Sudan no longer on list of terror sponsors', AP News, 14 Dec. 2020.

Part II. Military spending and armaments, 2020

Chapter 8. Military expenditure

Chapter 9. International arms transfers and developments in arms production

Chapter 10. World nuclear forces

8. Military expenditure

Overview

World military expenditure is estimated to have been US$1981 billion in 2020, which is equivalent to around $254 per person. Total spending was 2.6 per cent higher than in 2019 and 9.3 per cent higher than in 2011 (see section I). The global military burden—world military expenditure as a share of world gross domestic product (GDP)—rose by 0.2 percentage points in 2020, to 2.4 per cent. This was the biggest increase in military burden since the 2009 global financial and economic crisis.

Military spending increased in 2020 in each of the four regions for which SIPRI can provide an estimate (see section II). The rate of increase was highest in Africa, where spending rose by 5.1 per cent to $43.2 billion. This was followed by Europe, with growth of 4.0 per cent to $378 billion in 2020. Spending by countries in the Americas rose by 3.9 per cent to $853 billion and by those in Asia and Oceania by 2.5 per cent to $528 billion. No regional estimate can be made for the Middle East due to missing data from two known large spenders in the region (Qatar and the United Arab Emirates) and two countries affected by conflict (Syria and Yemen). The combined military spending in the 11 countries in the Middle East for which data was available decreased by 6.5 per cent in 2020.

While the Covid-19 pandemic will have a clearer impact on military spending in the coming years, four general points can already be made about its impact in 2020. First, several countries (e.g. Angola, Brazil, Chile, Kuwait, Russia and South Korea) are known to have reduced or diverted military spending to address the pandemic. Second, one country—Hungary—took the opposite course and increased its military spending in 2020 as part of a financial stimulus package in response to the pandemic. Arguments linking higher military spending and economic recovery are likely to be made in more countries. Third, the military burden in a majority of states increased in 2020. Fourth, most countries have used military assets, especially personnel, to help with the outbreak of Covid-19 and to contain its spread.

The military expenditure of the United States in 2020 totalled an estimated $778 billion, a 4.4 per cent increase since 2019 but a 10 per cent decrease since 2011. The 2020 financial year marked the third consecutive year of growth in US military spending, following continuous real-terms declines between 2010—when US spending peaked—and 2017. Budget items that contributed to this recent episode of growth in the USA's military spending include research and development, upgrading its nuclear arsenal and large-scale arms acquisitions.

Looking ahead, the incoming administration of Joe Biden is unlikely to propose any major cuts to the defence budget.

China's military expenditure is estimated to have totalled $252 billion in 2020, representing an increase of 1.9 per cent since 2019 and of 76 per cent since 2011. Chinese spending has risen for 26 consecutive years—the longest streak of uninterrupted increases by any country in the SIPRI Military Expenditure Database. The Chinese economy managed to rebound fairly quickly from pandemic-related restrictions. This suggests that China is likely to be one of the few countries that is able to fund a continued increase in military spending in the future without an increase in its military burden.

India, with spending of $72.9 billion, was the third highest spender in the world. It increased its military spending by a moderate 2.1 per cent in 2020. Russia's total military spending was $61.7 billion. This was 2.5 per cent higher than in 2019, but 6.6 per cent lower than the initial budget for 2020, reflecting the far-reaching economic consequences of Covid-19. The gap in spending included a shortfall of around $1 billion probably linked to the State Armament Programme. The fifth biggest spender, the United Kingdom, raised its military expenditure by 2.9 per cent in 2020. This was the second highest growth rate in a decade, which until 2017 was characterized by military spending cuts.

The accuracy of the above figures depends on government transparency in military expenditure. Transparency also fulfils a number of other functions: it is a key element of good governance, adequate management and government accountability. Most countries included in the SIPRI Military Expenditure Database provide data on military spending in official government reports. However, information is sometimes difficult to access and the reporting in government publications varies widely in many aspects of transparency.

One possible factor influencing transparency is the quality of democratic institutions, as demonstrated by the case of South East Asia (see section III). Basic indicators of national transparency—accessibility, availability, classification, comprehensiveness, disaggregation and the stage of the budgeting process at which reporting takes place—show that overall transparency in government reporting on military spending in this subregion is fairly good. Five countries (Indonesia, Malaysia, the Philippines, Thailand and Timor-Leste) are transparent, three countries (Cambodia, Myanmar and Singapore) have partial transparency, and only Brunei Darussalam, Laos and Viet Nam are judged to have limited or no transparency. The five most transparent countries are also among those that rank highest in terms of measures of democracy in the subregion.

NAN TIAN

I. Global developments in military expenditure, 2020

NAN TIAN, DIEGO LOPES DA SILVA AND ALEXANDRA MARKSTEINER

World military expenditure is estimated to have been US$1981 billion in 2020, the highest level since 1988—the earliest year for which SIPRI has a consistent estimate for total global military expenditure.[1] Global military spending was 2.6 per cent higher in real terms than in 2019 and 9.3 per cent higher than in 2011 (see table 8.1, below).[2] Military spending thus rose for the sixth straight year, following three years of decreases in 2012–14 and nearly unchanged spending in 2011. The global military burden—world military expenditure as a share of world gross domestic product (GDP)—rose by 0.2 percentage points in 2020, to 2.4 per cent. This was the biggest increase in military burden since the 2009 global financial and economic crisis. Military spending per capita also increased in 2020, up to $254 from $247 in 2019, as the growth in military spending continued to surpass world population growth (1.1 per cent).[3] This was the highest level since SIPRI began estimating per capita spending in 1995.

In all four regions for which SIPRI can provide an estimate, military expenditure increased in 2020 (see figure 8.1; for a breakdown and details on regional developments, see section II). The rate of increase was highest in Africa, at 5.1 per cent, taking the estimated regional total to $43.2 billion. This was followed by Europe, with an increase of 4.0 per cent to $378 billion, the Americas, with growth of 3.9 per cent to $853 billion, and Asia and Oceania, with a rise of 2.5 per cent to $528 billion. For the Middle East, no regional estimate can be made, due to missing data from two known large spenders in the region (Qatar and the United Arab Emirates) and two countries affected by conflict (Syria and Yemen).[4] Spending fell in 7 of the 11 countries in the region for which data is available. The combined military spending of the 11 countries decreased by 6.5 per cent between 2019 and 2020, to $143 billion.

---

[1] Of the 168 countries for which SIPRI attempted to estimate military expenditure in 2020, relevant data was found for 151. See box 8.1 for SIPRI's definition of military expenditure and the notes in table 8.1 for more detail on estimates in world and regional totals. The estimate of total world military expenditure includes a rough estimate of total spending in the Middle East.

[2] All figures for spending in 2020 are quoted in current 2020 US dollars. Except where otherwise stated, figures for increases or decreases in military spending are expressed in constant 2019 US dollars, often described as changes in 'real terms' or adjusted for inflation. All SIPRI's military expenditure data is freely available in the SIPRI Military Expenditure Database, <http://www.sipri.org/databases/milex>. The sources and methods used to produce the data discussed here are summarized in boxes 8.2–8.3 and are presented in full on the SIPRI website, <https://www.sipri.org/databases/milex/sources-and-methods>.

[3] United Nations, Department of Economic and Social Affairs, Population Division, 'World population prospects 2019', Aug. 2019.

[4] The estimate of total world military expenditure includes a rough estimate of total spending in the Middle East.

Box 8.1. The SIPRI definition of military expenditure

The main purpose of the data on military expenditure is to provide an identifiable measure of the scale of financial resources absorbed by the military.

Although the lack of sufficiently detailed data makes it difficult to apply a common definition of military expenditure consistently to all countries, SIPRI has adopted a definition as a guideline. Where possible, SIPRI military expenditure data includes all current and capital expenditure on (*a*) the armed forces, including peacekeeping forces; (*b*) defence ministries and other government agencies engaged in defence projects; (*c*) paramilitary forces, when judged to be trained and equipped for military operations; and (*d*) military space activities. This should include expenditure on personnel, including salaries of military and civil personnel, pensions of military personnel, and social services for personnel; operations and maintenance; procurement; military research and development; and military aid (in the military expenditure of the donor country). Civil defence and current expenditure on previous military activities, such as veterans' benefits, demobilization, conversion, weapon destruction and military involvement in non-military activities (e.g. policing) are not included.

In practice, it is not possible to apply this definition for all countries, and in many cases SIPRI is confined to using the national data provided. Priority is then given to the choice of a uniform definition for each country in order to achieve consistency over time, rather than to adjusting the figures for single years according to a common definition. In the light of these difficulties, military expenditure data is most appropriately used for comparisons over time and may be less suitable for close comparison between individual countries.

This section continues by providing a preliminary assessment of the impact of the Covid-19 pandemic on military expenditure in 2020, followed by a description of the global trends in military expenditure over the period 2011–20. The section then identifies the 15 countries with the highest military spending in 2020, focusing specifically on the two largest spenders: the United States and China. Regional and subregional trends and the spending of other individual countries are discussed in section II.

The impact of the Covid-19 pandemic

The general impact of the pandemic on military expenditure cannot yet be accurately measured and will only become evident in future years. Most military spending figures for 2020 are based on pre-pandemic budgets or an initial revision. However, more updated data is available for the largest military spenders. Based on an analysis of these figures, it is possible to conclude with some certainty that Covid-19 did not have a significant impact on global military spending in 2020.

The Covid-19 pandemic has highlighted an important issue regarding the use and interpretation of military expenditure data for the most recent year, or in some cases, years: the difference between budgeted and actual spending (see box 8.3). While the difference is usually minor, it is likely to be more pronounced for 2020 due to the effect of the pandemic. Likewise, the difference between projected (estimated) and final economic data will be greater than usual.

Box 8.2. Sources and methods for SIPRI military expenditure

The SIPRI military expenditure figures are presented on a calendar-year basis, calculated on the assumption of an even rate of expenditure throughout the financial year. The only exception is the United States, for which data is reported on a financial-year basis.

Military expenditure information in 2020 may include activities related to the Covid-19 pandemic performed by the armed forces that would usually not be counted as military spending. However, due to a lack of disaggregated information on these expenditure items, such spending cannot be subtracted from the total military spending figure.

Sources of information

SIPRI data reflects the official data reported by national governments. Such data is obtained from official publications such as budget documents, public finance statistics, reports of national audit agencies and government responses to questionnaires sent out by SIPRI. Such data is also available in reports published by the United Nations, the International Monetary Fund (IMF) and the North Atlantic Treaty Organization (NATO) to which states submit data about their national military spending. In a few cases the original government documents are not available to SIPRI, for example because they are not published, but the content of these documents may be reported in newspapers.

As a general rule, SIPRI takes national data to be accurate until there is convincing information to the contrary. Estimates are made primarily when the coverage of official data does not correspond to the SIPRI definition or when no consistent time series is available that covers the entire period covered by the data.

Military spending and military capability

Military spending measures the current level of resources devoted to renewing, replacing, expanding and maintaining military capability. Military spending does not reflect the stock of capabilities represented by factors such as weapons, training or knowledge. National military spending data is converted using market exchange rates. This means that the cost of a basic military capability can vary. For instance, the salaries of soldiers vary from country to country—largely depending on general wage levels—even when they have received a similar length of training of a similar quality.

Efforts to estimate military expenditure using methods that reflect the purchasing power of military spending rather than using market exchange rates for conversion into US dollars (the common currency used by SIPRI) suffer from major data deficits as well as conceptual problems.[a] For these reasons, SIPRI does not use purchasing power parity rates to calculate military expenditure figures in US dollars.

Caution must thus be exercised in drawing a relation between military expenditure and military power or capability. However, SIPRI military expenditure data can be directly used for comparisons of the national allocation of financial resources, for instance comparing it with spending on health services or education.

[a] See e.g. Ward, M., 'International comparisons of military expenditures: Issues and challenges of using purchasing power parities', *SIPRI Yearbook 2006*.

The data published and analysed here thus represents an initial assessment of the spending developments in a year heavily affected by the Covid-19 pandemic. Comprehensive information on the resources dedicated to the military in 2020 will become available over the course of 2021. Revised or actual spending information will be available for around 65 per cent of the countries in the SIPRI Military Expenditure Database, including major military spenders, in time for inclusion in *SIPRI Yearbook 2022*.

Box 8.3. The accuracy of financial data for recent years

Data on military expenditure is generally available in three forms: the initial budget, a revised budget and actual expenditure. The initial budget is adopted prior to the start of the new financial year. It indicates the resources that a government plans to allocate to each governmental sector. A revised budget is released during the course of the financial year, showing changes in the government's priorities and financial position. The budget can be revised several times during the course of the year. Accounts of actual expenditure are published after the end of the financial year, to detail how much money has actually been spent.

In the SIPRI Military Expenditure Database, data for the most recent year is most often available in the form of an initial or revised budget. Only a handful of countries will have published an actual expenditure figure for the previous year by mid February each year (when the SIPRI Military Expenditure Database is closed for further changes and updates). Thus, data for the most recent year should always be analysed with caution as further spending revisions are likely to occur. Such revisions would only be reflected in the following edition of the SIPRI Yearbook and the SIPRI Military Expenditure Database.[a]

Similarly, data provided by the International Monetary Fund (IMF) for the most recent year is explicitly identified as a projection. Actual economic data is only provided for years prior to the most recent year. This generates another type of uncertainty in figures for military spending: the calculated figures for military expenditure in dollar terms and as a share of gross domestic product (GDP) are provisional.

[a] Tian, N., 'A cautionary tale of military expenditure transparency during the great lockdown', WritePeace Blog, SIPRI, 23 June 2020.

While the final data for 2020 will show a greater difference than usual with the data published in this edition of the SIPRI Yearbook, four general points can already be made about the types of impact that the Covid-19 pandemic is likely to have on military spending in 2020.

First, numerous countries (e.g. Angola, Brazil, Chile, South Korea, Kuwait and Russia) are known to have reduced or diverted military spending in response to the Covid-19 pandemic. There will be pressure—especially from civil society and other groups that have historically questioned the need for increased military spending—for more countries to divert military spending in 2021 and beyond into post-pandemic economic recovery spending.[5] This is likely to be resisted by many within national and transnational defence establishments.[6] This debate is already taking place in the USA, Central and Western Europe, and the North Atlantic Treaty Organization (NATO).[7]

Second, one country—Hungary—has been identified as taking the opposite course by increasing its military spending in 2020 as part of a financial

---

[5] E.g. Sanders, B., 'A 10% cut to the US military budget would help support struggling Americans', *The Guardian*, 30 June 2020; and Smithberger, M., 'It's a pandemic. Military spending hikes should be off the table', Foreign Policy in Focus, 16 Sep. 2020.

[6] E.g. Marcos, P., 'Toward a new "lost decade"? Covid-19 and defense spending in Europe', Center for Strategic and International Studies (CSIS) Briefs, Oct. 2020; and Barigazzi, J., 'Low defense spending puts strategic autonomy at risk, EU review says', Politico, 20 Nov. 2020.

[7] Cook, L., 'NATO chief urges joint spending as budget debate rolls on', AP News, 17 Feb. 2021.

stimulus package in response to the pandemic. Similar arguments linking higher military spending and economic recovery are likely to be made in other countries by lobby groups, defence ministries and defence establishments.[8]

Third, the military burden in a majority of states increased in 2020 as GDP fell. This trend will have manifested itself in two ways: either military spending rose while GDP fell; or military spending fell at a slower rate than GDP. Irrespective of the precise mechanism, the consequence is that the burden of the military on national economies was much greater in 2020 than in recent years.

Fourth, most countries have used military assets, especially personnel, to help with the outbreak of Covid-19 and to contain its spread (e.g. China, South Africa and Sri Lanka).[9] It is often difficult to quantify these costs, and any additional costs to the military are likely to be marginal.

Trends in military expenditure, 2011–20

The 2.6 per cent increase in global military spending in 2020 continues the trend of annual increases in spending since 2015. Over the period 2011–20, spending rose by 9.3 per cent but with two different trends across the 10-year period. Between 2012 and 2014 spending was on a decreasing trend, falling 2.2 per cent. Thereafter, spending rose considerably, up 13 per cent in real terms.

The USA and China together spent over $1 trillion in 2020 and have accounted for more than half of the world's military spending in recent years. A change in spending by either the USA or China therefore has a substantial effect on the trend in global military expenditure. Other major spenders— such as India, Russia, the United Kingdom and Saudi Arabia, which together accounted for 13 per cent of the global total in 2020—have also affected changes in world military spending, albeit to a lesser extent.

Cuts in US spending over the period 2011–14 contributed significantly to the fall in global military spending. The fall in world spending between 2011 and 2014 was roughly one-third of the drop in US spending. This decrease in world spending would have been far greater if the US fall had not been offset by increases by other major spenders such as China, India, Russia and Saudi Arabia. Likewise, the slowdown in the rate of decrease in US spending by 2015 coupled with substantial increases in spending by China, India, Russia

[8] Chuter, A., 'UK to boost defense budget by $21.9 billion. Here's who benefits—and loses out', *Defense News*, 19 Nov. 2020; and Brustlein, C. (ed.), *Collective Collapse or Resilience? European Defense Priorities in the Pandemic Era*, Focus stratégique no. 103 (Institut Français des Relations Internationales (IFRI): Paris, Feb. 2021), p. 53.

[9] Xinhua, 'Over 10,000 military medics working at front line in COVID-19 fight', China.org.cn, 2 Mar. 2020; 'Extra military deployment for 73 000 for coronavirus campaign', defenceWeb, 22 Apr. 2020; and Srinivasan, M., 'COVID-19: Sri Lanka military is helping the country fight the pandemic', *The Hindu*, 15 Apr. 2020.

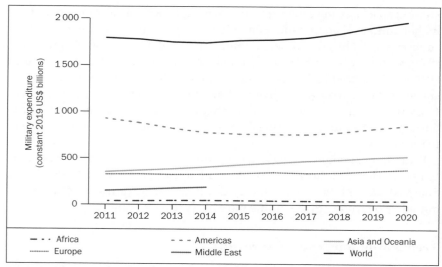

Figure 8.1. Military expenditure, by region, 2011–20

Note: Missing data means that no regional estimate can be made for the Middle East for 2015–20.

Source: SIPRI Military Expenditure Database, Apr. 2021.

and Saudi Arabia reversed the falling trend in global military spending in the second half of the decade. The return to increases in military spending by the USA from 2018 pushed global spending to the highest levels since 1988, the earliest year for which SIPRI has a consistent estimate for total world military expenditure.

Between 2011 and 2020, regional spending decreased only in the Americas (–8.4 per cent), while the highest increase was in Asia and Oceania (47 per cent), followed by Europe (16 per cent), Africa (11 per cent) and for the countries in the Middle East for which data was available (12 per cent). Among the 13 subregions, spending fell over the decade only in two: sub-Saharan Africa (–13 per cent) and North America (–9.6 per cent). The five largest subregional increases were in Central Europe (74 per cent), East Asia (53 per cent), Central Asia (47 per cent), North Africa (42 per cent), and Central America and the Caribbean (40 per cent).

The decline in military spending in sub-Saharan Africa since 2011 was the result of spending decreases by three of the five countries with the largest military expenditure in the subregion at the time: Angola, South Sudan and Sudan. In North America (i.e. Canada and the USA), the decrease was the result solely of spending changes by the USA. After reaching a spending peak in 2010, the USA cut military spending for seven consecutive years between 2011 and 2017. Despite a resumption in spending increases since 2018, US military spending in 2020 remained 10 per cent lower than in 2011.

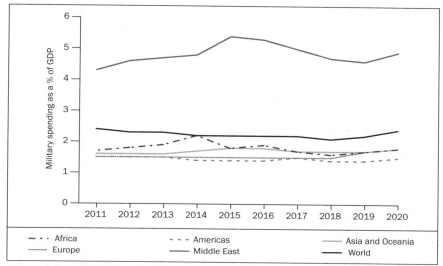

Figure 8.2. Military burden, by region, 2011–20

Note: The military burden is military expenditure as a share of gross domestic product (GDP). The military burden of a region is the average military burden of the countries in the region for which data is available.

Source: SIPRI Military Expenditure Database, Apr. 2021.

In contrast, the growth in spending between 2011 and 2020 in Central Europe was the result of higher spending by all five of the largest spenders in the region: Poland, Romania, Czechia, Hungary and Slovakia. In large part, this was due to higher threat perception in relation to Russia, arms modernization programmes, and pressure from the USA and NATO for these countries to reach NATO's military spending guideline of 2 per cent of GDP.[10] In East Asia, Central Asia and North Africa spending increased in all countries in the subregion.[11] In Central America and the Caribbean the increase was dominated by increases in Mexico (by far the largest spender in the subregion), affected by the ongoing war on drugs.[12]

At 2.4 per cent, the world military burden in 2020 was 0.2 percentage points higher than in 2019 but equal to the level of 2011 (see figure 8.2). The world military burden followed a shallow U-shaped trend over the period 2011–20. Initially at 2.4 per cent of GDP, the military burden fell to 2.1 per

[10] Tian, N., Lopes da Silva, D. and Wezeman, P. D., 'Spending on military equipment by European members of the North Atlantic Treaty Organization', *SIPRI Yearbook 2020*, pp. 255–57; and Defenseworld.net, 'Poland details $49.8 billion military modernization plan 2026', 4 Mar. 2019.

[11] No data was available for North Korea in East Asia; Turkmenistan and Uzbekistan in Central Asia; or Libya in North Africa. An estimate of Libya's spending is included in the subregional and regional totals.

[12] Tian, N. et al., 'Regional developments in military expenditure, 2019', *SIPRI Yearbook 2020*, pp. 238–39.

Table 8.2. The 15 countries with the highest military expenditure in 2020

Expenditure figures and GDP are in US$, at current prices and exchange rates. Changes are in real terms, based on constant (2019) US dollars.

Rank			Military expenditure,	Change (%)		Military expenditure as a share of GDP (%)[b]		Share of world military expenditure,
2020	2019[a]	Country	2020 ($ b.)	2019–20	2011–20	2020	2011	2020 (%)
1	1	United States	778	4.4	–10	3.7	4.8	39
2	2	China	[252]	1.9	76	[1.7]	[1.7]	[13]
3	3	India	72.9	2.1	34	2.9	2.7	3.7
4	4	Russia	61.7	2.5	26	4.3	3.4	3.1
5	6	United Kingdom	59.2	2.9	–4.2	2.2	2.5	3.0
Subtotal top 5			1 224	..	..	..	..	62
6	5	Saudi Arabia	[57.5]	–10	2.3	[8.4]	7.2	[2.9]
7	8	Germany	52.8	5.2	28	1.4	1.2	2.7
8	7	France	52.7	2.9	9.8	2.1	1.9	2.7
9	9	Japan	49.1	1.2	2.4	1.0	1.0	2.5
10	10	South Korea	45.7	4.9	41	2.8	2.5	2.3
Subtotal top 10			1 482	..	..	..	..	75
11	11	Italy	28.9	7.5	–3.3	1.6	1.5	1.5
12	12	Australia	27.5	5.9	33	2.1	1.8	1.4
13	14	Canada	22.8	2.9	26	1.4	1.2	1.1
14	16	Israel	21.7	2.7	32	5.6	5.8	1.1
15	13	Brazil	19.7	–3.1	2.1	1.4	1.4	1.0
Subtotal top 15			1 603	..	..	..	..	81
World			**1 981**	**2.6**	**9.3**	**2.4**	**2.4**	**100**

.. = data not available or not applicable; [ ] = estimated figure; GDP = gross domestic product.

[a] Rankings for 2019 are based on updated military expenditure figures for 2019 in the current edition of the SIPRI Military Expenditure Database. They may therefore differ from the rankings for 2019 given in *SIPRI Yearbook 2020* and in other SIPRI publications in 2020.

[b] These figures are based on GDP estimates from International Monetary Fund, World Economic Outlook Database, Oct. 2020; and International Monetary Fund (IMF), International Financial Statistics Database, Oct. 2020.

Source: SIPRI Military Expenditure Database, Apr. 2021.

cent in 2018, the lowest point since the end of the cold war, before increasing again in 2019 and 2020.

In 2020 the average military burden increased in all five regions. States in the Americas had the lowest military burden, at 1.5 per cent of GDP. For states in Africa, Asia and Oceania, and Europe, the average was slightly higher, at 1.8 per cent of GDP. By far the highest average, 4.9 per cent, was for the Middle East based on countries for which data is available. The jump in the global and regional military burdens in 2020 was the effect of the divergence in the rates of change of military spending and GDP.

The largest military spenders in 2020

Military spending by the top 15 countries reached $1603 billion in 2020, accounting for 81 per cent of global expenditure. There were some changes in the composition and rank order of the top 15 between 2019 and 2020 (see table 8.2).[13] Most notably, Israel entered the top 15 in place of Turkey, and the UK moved above Saudi Arabia—whose military spending fell by 10 per cent—to become the fifth largest spender in 2020.

The USA (accounting for 39 per cent of world military spending in 2020) and China (13 per cent) remained the two largest spenders. The gap between the military spending of China and that of the USA increased for the third consecutive year. It was also the second straight year that the increase in US military spending (of 4.4 per cent) was higher than the increase in Chinese spending (of 1.9 per cent). The biggest fall in ranking was by Brazil, where spending dropped by 3.1 per cent in 2020, the second consecutive decrease, and it moved from 13th place to 15th.

All but three countries in the top 15 had higher military expenditure in 2020 than in 2011. The exceptions were the USA (–10 per cent), the UK (–4.2 per cent) and Italy (–3.3 per cent). China's increase (76 per cent) was by far the largest among the top 15. This was followed by South Korea (41 per cent), India (34 per cent), Australia (33 per cent) and Israel (32 per cent). Japan increased its spending in a gradual but minor manner, up 2.4 per cent over the decade. Brazil (2.1 per cent) and Saudi Arabia (2.3 per cent) also recorded minor overall increases, but the spending of both countries had large annual fluctuations.

The military burdens of all but one of the top 15 military spenders increased in 2020—the exception being China. The Covid-19-related decline in GDP resulted in some sharp climbs in military burden irrespective of whether military spending increased or decreased. Most notably, Saudi Arabia's military burden increased by 0.6 percentage points despite the 10 per cent decrease in spending. There were also notable increases in the military burdens of Russia (0.5 percentage points), Israel (0.4 percentage points) and the USA (0.3 percentage points).

Among the top 15 military spenders in 2020, Saudi Arabia had the highest military burden, 8.4 per cent. Those of Israel (5.6 per cent), Russia (4.3 per cent), the USA (3.7 per cent), India (2.9 per cent) and South Korea (2.8 per cent) were also higher than the average global military burden of 2.4 per cent. Japan had the lowest military burden: it devoted only 1.0 per cent of its GDP to military expenditure.

---

[13] The United Arab Emirates (UAE) would probably rank as one of the 15 largest spenders, most likely within the ranks 11–15, but a lack of data since 2014 means that no reasonable estimate of its military spending can be made and thus it has been omitted from the top 15 ranking.

Table 8.3. Components of US military expenditure, financial years 2016–20

Figures are in US$ b. at current prices unless otherwise stated. Years are US financial years, which start on 1 Oct. of the previous year.

	2016	2017	2018	2019	2020^a
Department of Defense	565	569	601	654	690
Military personnel	148	145	146	156	162
Operations and maintenance	243	245	257	272	284
Procurement	103	104	113	125	135
Research, development, testing and evaluation	65	68	77	89	98
Other (construction, housing etc.)	6.7	6.8	8.6	12	11
Department of Energy	28	29	31	32	34
Atomic energy defence-related activities	19	20	21	23	25
Other defence-related activities	8.6	9.3	9.5	9.3	9.4
National Intelligence Program, military-related	[40]	[41]	[45]	[45]	[47]
Department of State, international security assistance^b	6.7	7.1	6.8	6.8	6.7
Transfers to fund construction of border wall	..	..	..	−3.6	..
Total	**640**	**647**	**682**	**734**	**778**
Military expenditure as a share of GDP (%)	*3.4*	*3.3*	*3.3*	*3.4*	*3.7*

.. = data not available or not applicable; [ ] = estimated figure; GDP = gross domestic product.

^{a} Figures for financial year 2020 are estimates.

^{b} This category captures spending on peacekeeping operations, international military education and training, and foreign military financing.

Sources: SIPRI Military Expenditure Database, Apr. 2021; US Office of Budget and Management (OMB), *Historical Tables* (OMB: Washington, DC, 2020), table 3.2, 'Outlays by function and sub-function: 1962–2025'; Federation of American Scientists (FAS), Intelligence Resource Program, 'Intelligence budget data'; and US Department of State, *Congressional Budget Justification: Department of State, Foreign Operations and Related Programs Fiscal Year 2021* (Department of State: Washington, DC, 10 Feb. 2020).

The United States

US military expenditure in 2020 amounted to an estimated $778 billion, 4.4 per cent more than in 2019 but 10 per cent less than in 2011. The USA remained by far the largest military spender, as has been the case every year for which SIPRI has military expenditure data. The 2020 financial year marked the third consecutive year of growth in US military spending, following continuous real-terms declines between 2010—when US spending peaked—and 2017.[14]

The US military burden also increased between 2019 and 2020, from 3.4 per cent of GDP to 3.7 per cent. This was due in part to the economic fallout of the Covid-19 pandemic and the resulting decline in US economic output. The military burden in 2020 was still 1.2 percentage points lower than in 2010, the year in which US military expenditure peaked following a troop surge in Iraq and Afghanistan.

[14] The SIPRI military expenditure figures are generally presented on a calendar-year basis, calculated on the assumption of an even rate of expenditure throughout the financial year. The only exception is the USA, for which data is reported on a financial-year basis. The US financial year runs for 12 months from 1 Oct. of the year preceding the named year.

The groundwork for the recent increase in US military spending was laid towards the end of the presidency of Barack Obama.[15] It was not until the 2017–21 administration of his successor, President Donald J. Trump, that these plans took shape. During the 2016 presidential campaign, Trump promised to rebuild what he saw as the 'depleted' US military.[16] Within a few months of taking office, Trump added $15 billion to the 2017 budget of the US Department of Defense (DOD), which had originally been passed under President Obama.[17] In the two subsequent years, US military expenditure increased by 3.0 per cent and 5.7 per cent, respectively, in real terms. This trend continued in 2020.

Many budget items have driven this recent episode of growth in US military spending, but a few stand out: research and development (R&D), the nuclear arsenal, modernization of conventional capabilities, operations and maintenance, and military personnel.

R&D received notable investment in the hopes of modernizing key capabilities. Funds directed towards R&D increased by 44 per cent between 2017 and 2020 (see table 8.3). This is in line with the 2018 National Defense Strategy, which notes that '[the USA] cannot expect success fighting tomorrow's conflicts with yesterday's weapons or equipment'.[18]

The USA has simultaneously embarked on an extensive upgrade of its nuclear arsenal.[19] The US Congressional Budget Office projects the annual cost of maintaining and modernizing the country's nuclear arsenal to be roughly $50 billion until 2028.[20] In total, this programme is estimated to cost more than $1.2 trillion.[21]

The DOD also plans to modernize its conventional capabilities. With the aim of expanding the US military force structure, procurement spending was raised by 31 per cent during the Trump presidency. Despite this, several large-scale acquisition targets—such as the 350-ship naval fleet called for by President Trump—were not met.[22]

Operations and maintenance remained the largest category within the DOD budget, accounting for 41 per cent of the total. Despite a partial

---

[15] Zakheim, D. S., 'The great reversal: Obama's military buildup', *National Interest*, 9 Feb. 2016.

[16] Vitali, A., 'Trump calls for increased defense spending, more military might', NBC News, 7 Sep. 2016.

[17] Herb, J., 'Trump gets a $15 billion defense boost', CNN, 1 May 2017.

[18] US Department of Defense (DOD), *Summary of the 2018 National Defense Strategy of the United States of America: Sharpening the American Military's Competitive Edge* (DOD: Arlington, VA, 2018), p. 6.

[19] On the modernization plans see chapter 10, section I, in this volume.

[20] Bennett, M. et al., 'Projected costs of US nuclear forces, 2019 to 2028', US Congress, Congressional Budget Office (CBO), Jan. 2019.

[21] 'US nuclear arsenal to cost $1.2 trillion over next 30 years: CBO', Reuters, 31 Oct. 2017; and Bennett, M. et al., *Approaches for Managing the Costs of US Nuclear Forces, 2017 to 2046* (US Congress, Congressional Budget Office: Washington, DC, Oct. 2017).

[22] Larter, D. B., 'Trump called for a 350-ship fleet, but his budget falls short of even Obama-era goals', *Defense News*, 25 Feb. 2020.

Table 8.4. Components of China's military expenditure, 2016–20

Figures are in b. yuan at current prices unless otherwise stated.

	2016	2017	2018	2019	2020
Official Chinese figures					
National defence (central and local)	977	1 044	1 128	1 213	1 292
Additional items included in SIPRI's estimate of					
China's total military expenditure					
People's Armed Police (central and local)	105	113	123	124	131
China Coast Guard	[6.9]	[8.1]	[9.2]	[11.1]	[11.8]
Payments to demobilized and retired soldiers	98.4	118	124	140	149
Additional military RDT&E spending[a]	[132]	[139]	[153]	[173]	[157]
Additional military construction spending[a]	0.2	0.2	0.1	0.1	0.1
Arms imports[b]	[1.7]	[1.3]	[0.9]	[0.5]	–
Total (yuan b.)	1 320	1 424	1 538	1 660	1 742
Total (US$ b. at current prices)	199	210	233	240	252
Military expenditure as a share of GDP (%)	*1.8*	*1.7*	*1.7*	*1.7*	*1.7*

– = nil or a negligible value; [] = estimated figure; GDP = gross domestic product; RDT&E = research, development, testing and evaluation.

[a] Some spending on military RDT&E and military construction is also included in the main national defence budget.

[b] By 2020 all arms imports are estimated to be paid for by the equipment expenditure reported in the official defence budget.

Sources: SIPRI Military Expenditure Database, Apr. 2021; and Chinese Ministry of Finance, Budget Division.

reduction in overseas military deployments, spending in this category actually increased. This can be partly attributed to fuel costs and higher maintenance costs linked to longer lifetimes of equipment.[23] Operations and maintenance also includes spending on benefits for service members, which were improved in 2020.

Military salaries are determined by a fixed formula. They rose between 2017 and 2020 at the same time as the total number of US military personnel increased from 2.1 million to 2.2 million.[24]

Looking ahead, the incoming administration of Joe Biden is unlikely to propose any major cuts to the military budget, citing potential threats from challengers such as Russia and China.[25] However, in the future there may be pressure from members of the US Congress to reduce military spending levels in order to free up resources to fund the post-pandemic recovery and reduce the fiscal deficit.[26] That said, Biden plans to re-focus spending away

[23] Harrison, T. and Daniels, S. P., *Analysis of the FY 2020 Defense Budget and Its Implications for 2021 and Beyond* (Center for Strategic and International Studies (CSIS): Washington, DC, Feb. 2020).

[24] US Office of the Undersecretary of Defense (Comptroller), *National Defense Budget Estimates for FY 2021* (Department of Defense: Arlington, VA, Apr. 2020); and Shane, L., 'Biggest military pay raise in years takes effect Jan. 1', *Military Times*, 26 Dec. 2019.

[25] Beynon, S., 'Biden says US must maintain small force in Middle East, has no plans for major defense cuts', *Stars and Stripes*, 10 Sep. 2020.

[26] O'Brien, C., 'On defense spending, a Democratic brawl is brewing', Politico, 28 Oct. 2020.

from legacy systems towards defence innovation and modernization.[27] In public statements, Biden has prioritized investment in unmanned capabilities, cyberwarfare tools and information technology (IT) infrastructure.[28]

China

In 2020 China's military expenditure is estimated to have totalled $252 billion (1742 billion yuan), representing a real-terms increase of 1.9 per cent compared with 2019 and of 76 per cent compared with 2011 (see table 8.4). Among the major economies and military spenders, only China's GDP was projected to grow in 2020, by 1.9 per cent.[29] Moreover, China was one of the few countries whose military burden did not increase in 2020. Its military spending has increased for 26 consecutive years, despite going through at least three financial or economic crises (in 1997, 2009 and 2020). This is the longest streak of uninterrupted increases by any country in the SIPRI Military Expenditure Database.

The Chinese economy managed to rebound fairly quickly from pandemic-related restrictions. The government had begun to implement strict containment measures by mid January 2020 and by mid February had started to reopen the economy.[30] China's economy resumed growth in the second quarter of 2020 (by 3.2 per cent year on year), while the rest of the world was still scrambling with lockdown measures and public health responses.[31]

As a result of the Covid-19 pandemic, China delayed the release of its 2020 budget plans by two months, to May 2020. Its long-term ambition for military development, modernization and expansion remains an important factor behind the continued increase in its military spending.[32] The 2020 budget plans also highlighted perceived threats to its national security as a reason to allocate more resources to its military. This includes what the government broadly terms 'hegemonism' and 'power politics', which is generally interpreted as referring to tensions with the USA.[33] The Chinese

---

[27] Daniels, S. P., 'Defense budget priorities for the Biden administration', Defense360, Center for Strategic and International Studies (CSIS), Feb. 2021.

[28] Gould, J., 'Biden not planning any defense cuts, but they may come anyway', *Defense News*, 11 Sep. 2020.

[29] International Monetary Fund (IMF), International Financial Statistics Database, Oct. 2020, <http://data.imf.org/IFS>.

[30] World Health Organization (WHO), 'Coronavirus disease 2019 (COVID-19)', Situation Report no. 94, 23 Apr. 2020; Murphy, F., 'Inside China's response to COVID', *Nature*, 3 Dec. 2020; International Monetary Fund (IMF), 'Policy responses to COVID-19: China, People's Republic of', 4 Mar. 2021; and Mallapaty, S., 'Where did COVID come from? WHO investigation begins but faces challenges', *Nature*, 19 Nov. 2020.

[31] 'China's Q2 GDP grows 3.2%, beats expectations', Reuters, 16 July 2020.

[32] Chinese State Council, *China's National Defense in the New Era* (Foreign Languages Press: Beijing, July 2019).

[33] Chinese Ministry of National Defense, 'China's moderate and steady defense budget increase reasonable and necessary', 26 May 2020.

Government also noted a potential declaration of independence by Taiwan as a specific 'domestic' threat facing China.[34]

SIPRI's military expenditure figures for China differ from the official national defence budget. SIPRI's estimate for 2020 is around one-third or $65 billion (450 billion yuan) higher than the figure that the Chinese Government published in its national defence budget.[35] SIPRI's estimate of Chinese military expenditure includes the costs of some military-related activities for which China budgets, fully or partially, outside the official national defence budget.

In 2020 SIPRI revised its estimates of China's military expenditure to take account of recent changes in its military-related activities and budgetary practices.[36] At $252 billion, the new estimate of Chinese spending in 2020 is about 8 per cent lower than the old SIPRI estimate. The new estimate is comprised of seven components. Official information is available for four: national defence, the People's Armed Police, payments to demobilized and retired soldiers, and additional military construction spending. Together, these four categories accounted for 91 per cent of total spending in 2020. Estimates must be made for the remaining three components, representing 9 per cent of the total: the China Coast Guard, additional funding for military research, development, testing and evaluation (RDT&E), and arms imports paid for outside the national defence budget.[37]

---

[34] 'China: Reunification "inevitable" as Taiwan's Tsai starts second term in office', Deutsche Welle, 20 May 2020; and Chinese Ministry of National Defense (note 33).
[35] Chinese Ministry of National Defense, 'China further lowers defense budget growth to 6.6 pct', 22 May 2020.
[36] Tian, N. and Su, F., *A New Estimate of China's Military Expenditure* (SIPRI: Stockholm, Jan. 2021).
[37] Tian and Su (note 36), pp. 6–13.

Table 8.1. Military expenditure and the military burden, by region, 2011–20

Figures for 2011–20 are in US$ b. at constant (2019) prices and exchange rates. Figures for 2020 in the right-most column, marked *, are in current US$ b. Figures do not always add up to totals because of the conventions of rounding.

	2011	2012	2013	2014	2015	2016	2017	2018	2019	2020	2020*
World total	1793	1779	1748	1740	1767	1774	1796	1842	1909	1960	1981
Africa	(38.6)	(39.7)	44.2	45.6	44.0	(42.6)	(41.5)	(40.5)	(40.9)	(43.0)	(43.2)
North Africa	(17.4)	(18.9)	22.2	23.0	23.3	(23.2)	(22.6)	(22.1)	(23.1)	(24.6)	(24.7)
Sub-Saharan Africa	(21.2)	(20.8)	(21.9)	22.7	20.7	19.4	18.9	18.4	17.8	18.4	18.5
Americas	927	881	820	775	761	757	756	779	817	849	853
Central America and the Caribbean	6.6	7.0	7.4	7.7	7.4	8.2	7.7	8.4	9.2	9.2	8.6
North America	873	825	761	716	702	700	697	717	757	789	801
South America	47.7	49.0	50.9	51.5	50.9	48.6	51.4	52.7	51.8	50.7	43.5
Asia and Oceania	352	368	384	404	428	449	470	484	506	519	528
Central Asia	1.3	1.6	1.8	1.8	1.8	1.6	1.5	1.7	2.1	2.0	1.9
East Asia	229	244	257	272	288	300	313	328	343	351	359
Oceania	22.8	22.1	21.9	23.7	25.9	28.3	28.4	28.0	29.2	30.8	30.7
South Asia	65.8	65.9	65.8	69.4	70.5	76.7	82.6	85.8	88.6	89.7	90.1
South East Asia	33.5	34.7	38.2	37.9	41.6	42.2	43.8	40.8	43.4	45.6	45.5
Europe	325	328	323	327	336	348	339	346	363	378	378
Central Europe	19.0	18.7	18.5	19.7	22.3	22.6	24.4	27.5	31.1	33.0	33.6
Eastern Europe	58.6	67.5	70.6	76.2	82.4	87.0	71.9	70.5	74.3	76.8	71.7
Western Europe	247	242	234	231	231	239	243	248	258	268	273
Middle East	150	162	176	188	..	..	..	..	..	..	..

	2011	2012	2013	2014	2015	2016	2017	2018	2019	2020	2020*
World military spending per capita[a]	248	245	242	239	229	226	233	240	247	254	
Military burden[b]											
Africa	1.7	1.8	1.9	2.2	1.8	1.9	1.7	1.6	1.7	1.8	
Americas	1.5	1.5	1.5	1.4	1.4	1.4	1.5	1.4	1.4	1.5	
Asia and Oceania	1.6	1.6	1.6	1.7	1.8	1.8	1.7	1.7	1.7	1.8	
Europe	1.5	1.5	1.5	1.5	1.5	1.5	1.5	1.5	1.7	1.8	
Middle East	4.3	4.6	4.7	4.8	5.4	5.3	5.0	4.7	4.6	4.9	
World total[c]	2.4	2.3	2.3	2.2	2.2	2.2	2.2	2.1	2.2	2.4	

.. = estimate not provided due to unusually high levels of uncertainty and missing data; ( ) = total based on country data accounting for less than 90% of the regional total.

Notes: The totals for the world and regions are estimates based on data from the SIPRI Military Expenditure Database. When military expenditure data for a country is missing for a few years, estimates are made, most often on the assumption that the rate of change in that country's military expenditure is the same as that for the region to which it belongs. When no estimates can be made, countries are excluded from the totals. The countries excluded from all totals here are Cuba, Djibouti, Eritrea, North Korea, Somalia, Syria, Turkmenistan and Uzbekistan. Totals for regions cover the same groups of countries for all years. Rough estimates for the Middle East are included in the world totals for 2015–20. The SIPRI military expenditure figures are presented on a calendar-year basis, calculated on the assumption of an even rate of expenditure throughout the financial year. Further detail on sources and methods can be found in box 8.2 and on the SIPRI website.

[a] World military spending per capita calculated in current US$.

[b] The military burden of a region is the average military burden for countries in the region for which data is available.

[c] World military spending calculated as a % of world gross domestic product, both measured in current US$.

Sources: SIPRI Military Expenditure Database, Apr. 2021; International Monetary Fund, World Economic Outlook Database, Oct. 2020; International Monetary Fund (IMF), International Financial Statistics Database, Sep. 2020; and United Nations, Department of Economic and Social Affairs, Population Division, 'World population prospects 2019', Aug. 2019.

II. Regional developments in military expenditure, 2020

NAN TIAN, LUCIE BÉRAUD-SUDREAU, DIEGO LOPES DA SILVA
AND ALEXANDRA MARKSTEINER

The global total military expenditure of US$1981 billion in 2020 was heavily skewed towards two of the world's five regions.[1] The Americas (43 per cent) and Asia and Oceania (27 per cent) together account for more than two-thirds of the world total. Europe was the region with the third highest spending in 2020, with 19 per cent of the total. Africa accounted for the smallest share, with only 2.2 per cent of global military expenditure. The Middle East is estimated to have accounted for roughly 9.0 per cent of the total.

This section reviews military expenditure developments in each of the world's five regions over the period 2011–20. It also describes how specific circumstances affected individual countries' spending decisions and which of these affect the subregional and regional trends. On global trends and the top spenders, see section I.

Africa

Military expenditure in Africa is estimated to have totalled $43.2 billion in 2020, a real-terms increase of 5.1 per cent since 2019 (see table 8.5).[2] Over the period 2011–20, spending by countries in Africa followed three distinct trends. It first increased in 2011–14, followed by decreases in 2015–18 and then two consecutive years of increase to give an overall growth of 11 per cent.

North Africa

Spending by countries in North Africa rose by 6.4 per cent to $24.7 billion in 2020, representing 57 per cent of total spending in Africa.[3] Since 2011, spending in the subregion has followed an increasing trend, with seven years of increase (2011–15 and 2019–20) and three years of minor decrease (2016–18) to give an overall increase of 42 per cent (see figure 8.3). This upward trend has been underpinned by the long-standing tensions between

---

[1] All figures for spending in 2020 are quoted in current 2020 US dollars. Except where otherwise stated, figures for increases or decreases in military spending are expressed in constant 2019 US dollars, often described as changes in 'real terms' or adjusted for inflation.

All SIPRI's military expenditure data is freely available in the SIPRI Military Expenditure Database, <http://www.sipri.org/databases/milex>. The sources and methods used to produce the data discussed here are summarized in boxes 8.1–8.3 in section I and are presented in full on the SIPRI website, <https://www.sipri.org/databases/milex/sources-and-methods>.

[2] This total excludes Djibouti, Eritrea and Somalia, for which it was impossible to make a reliable series of estimates for inclusion in the regional total.

[3] No information on Libya's military spending since 2015 could be found. An estimate of Libya's spending is included in the subregional and regional totals.

Table 8.5. Key military expenditure statistics by region and subregion, 2020

Expenditure figures are in US$, at current prices and exchange rates. Changes are in real terms, based on constant (2019) US dollars.

Region/ subregion	Military expenditure, 2020 (US$ b.)	Change (%)		Major changes, 2019–20 (%)[a]			
		2019–20	2011–20	Increases		Decreases	
World	**1 981**	**2.6**	**9.3**				
Africa[b]	(43.2)	*5.1*	*11*				
North Africa	(24.7)	*6.4*	*42*	Uganda	*46*	Sudan	*–37*
Sub-Saharan Africa[b]	18.5	*3.4*	*–13*	Chad	*31*	Togo	*–34*
				Nigeria	*29*	Mozambique	*–24*
				Mauritania	*23*	Burundi	*–23*
Americas[c]	853	*3.9*	*–8.4*				
Central America and the Caribbean[c]	8.6	*–0.2*	*40*	El Salvador	*17*	Trinidad and Tobago	*–8.8*
North America	801	*4.3*	*–9.6*	Uruguay	*9.1*	Jamaica	*–6.9*
South America	43.5	*–2.1*	*6.2*	USA	*4.4*	Ecuador	*–6.5*
				Paraguay	*3.9*	Honduras	*–3.7*
Asia and Oceania[d]	528	*2.5*	*47*				
Central Asia[e]	1.9	*–8.4*	*47*	Myanmar	*41*	Kazakhstan	*–9.2*
East Asia[f]	359	*2.3*	*53*	Afghanistan	*16*	Sri Lanka	*–8.2*
Oceania	30.7	*5.6*	*35*	Mongolia	*7.3*	Pakistan	*–2.8*
South Asia	90.1	*1.3*	*36*	Cambodia	*6.6*	Nepal	*–0.9*
South East Asia	45.5	*5.2*	*36*				
Europe	378	*4.0*	*16*				
Central Europe	33.6	*6.0*	*74*	Montenegro	*29*	Bulgaria	*–44*
Eastern Europe	71.7	*3.4*	*31*	Romania	*21*	Serbia	*–5.0*
Western Europe	273	*3.9*	*8.5*	Hungary	*20*	Greece	*–4.3*
				Azerbaijan	*17*	Armenia	*–2.6*
Middle East[g]	..	..	..				
				Egypt	*7.3*	Saudi Arabia	*–10*
				Israel	*2.7*	Iraq	*–9.8*
				Jordan	*2.5*	Bahrain	*–7.9*

.. = data not available; ( ) = uncertain estimate.

[a] These lists show the countries with the largest increases or decreases for each region as a whole, rather than by subregion. Countries with a military expenditure in 2020 of less than $100 million, or $50 million in Africa, are excluded.

[b] Figures exclude Djibouti, Eritrea and Somalia.

[c] Figures exclude Cuba.

[d] Figures exclude North Korea, Turkmenistan and Uzbekistan.

[e] Figures exclude Turkmenistan and Uzbekistan.

[f] Figures exclude North Korea.

[g] No SIPRI estimates for the Middle East are available for 2015–20. A rough estimate for the Middle East (excluding Syria) is included in the world total.

Source: SIPRI Military Expenditure Database, Apr. 2021.

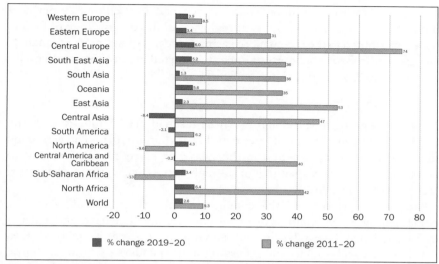

Figure 8.3. Changes in military expenditure by subregion, 2011–20 and 2019–20

Note: No estimate of change in military expenditure in the Middle East is given since data for 2015–20 is highly uncertain. However, an estimate for the Middle East is included in the estimated world total.

Source: SIPRI Military Expenditure Database, Apr. 2021.

Algeria and Morocco, along with their ongoing expansion of military capabilities and Morocco's conflict with the Polisario Front in Western Sahara.[4]

With a total of $9.7 billion in 2020, Algeria's spending was 3.4 per cent lower than in 2019, but it remained by far the largest spender in North Africa and in Africa, accounting for 39 per cent of the subregional total and 22 per cent of the regional total. Algeria's military spending rose almost continuously over the past two decades, and particularly in the period 2004–16 when it rose to an all-time high. Since 2016 the fall in oil prices has had a substantial impact on its military spending.[5] Between 2016 and 2020, Algeria's spending fell in every year except 2019 and fell overall by 5.3 per cent. The large fall in gross domestic product (GDP) related to the Covid-19 pandemic resulted in an increase in Algeria's military burden by 0.7 percentage points to 6.7 per cent of GDP, the highest in Africa and the third highest in the world.

---

[4] On developments in Western Sahara see chapter 6, section IV, in this volume. See also Baudais, V., Bourhrous, A. and O'Driscoll, D., *Conflict Mediation and Peacebuilding in the Sahel*, SIPRI Policy Paper no. 58 (SIPRI: Stockholm, Jan. 2021), pp. 3–4; and North African Post, 'Morocco maintains army modernisation plan', 3 June 2020.

[5] International Monetary Fund (IMF), *Algeria: Staff Report for the 2018 Article IV Consultation* (IMF: Washington, DC, 15 May 2018).

In 2020 Morocco's military spending reached $4.8 billion, 29 per cent more than in 2019 and 54 per cent higher than in 2011. A range of factors have contributed to the recent increase in Morocco's spending; these include a large arms procurement programme that started in 2017, the conflict with the Polisario Front and regional tensions.[6]

Sub-Saharan Africa

Military spending in sub-Saharan Africa reached $18.5 billion in 2020, up 3.4 per cent from 2019, but 13 per cent lower than in 2011.[7] The estimated increase in 2020 was the first in the subregion since 2014. In contrast to North Africa, military spending in sub-Saharan Africa was on a downward trend over the decade 2011–20.

The general trend and the changes in subregional spending can be explained by a combination of underlying factors that have affected the established major spenders in sub-Saharan Africa (i.e. Angola, Nigeria, South Africa and Sudan) and emerging high spenders (e.g. Chad, Kenya, Tanzania and Uganda).

For countries such as Chad, Kenya, Nigeria, Sudan and Uganda, armed conflict, counterterrorism measures and the fight against Islamist extremism (e.g. al-Shabab in Kenya and Boko Haram in Chad and Nigeria) have been persistent challenges over the past 10 years.[8] These types of security concern have had a profound impact in driving up military expenditure. For example, as Uganda continued to fight an insurgency by the Allied Democratic Forces (ADF), it increased its military spending by 53 per cent in 2019 and by 46 per cent in 2020.[9] A similar pattern can be seen in Kenya, where the threat of al-Shabab has led to an increase in spending on military procurement.[10] Although Kenya's military spending was down 1.8 per cent in real terms in 2020, it was 17 per cent higher than in 2011.

---

[6] Lebovich, A., 'Why the Western Sahara dispute could escalate conflicts across North Africa and the Sahel', Commentary, European Council of Foreign Relations, 17 Dec. 2020. See also chapter 6, section IV, in this volume.

[7] The total for sub-Saharan Africa excludes the Comoros and Sao Tome and Principe, which are not in the SIPRI Military Expenditure Database and are assumed to have low expenditure, and Djibouti, Eritrea and Somalia (see note 2).

[8] See e.g. Tian, N. et al., 'Regional developments in military expenditure, 2019', *SIPRI Yearbook 2020*, pp. 236–38. On the armed conflicts in sub-Saharan Africa see chapter 7 in this volume.

[9] Kyeyune, M., 'Defence plans to spend Shs 3 trillion from June', *Daily Monitor* (Kampala), 31 Mar. 2020; and Republic of Uganda, *Approved Estimates of Revenue and Expenditure (Recurrent and Development) FY 2020/21*, vol. 1, *Central Government Votes for the Year Ending on the 30th June 2021* (Republic of Uganda: Kampala, [2020]), pp. 137–49.

[10] Otieno, B., 'KDF gets Sh24bn to buy weapons in EA arms race', *Business Daily* (Nairobi), 14 May 2019.

The economic impact of violent conflicts generated by Islamist extremism can also constrain military spending.[11] For example, Chad's military expenditure totalled $323 million in 2020. While this was 31 per cent higher than in 2019, it was still 46 per cent lower than in 2011. The effects of the armed conflict around the Lake Chad Basin mean that Chad's economy was extremely unstable over the period 2011–20, with four years of economic contraction and six years of economic growth.[12] This volatility is reflected in the country's military expenditure, with five years of decrease and five years of increase since 2011.

Other external factors may affect the spending allocations of sub-Saharan African countries, such as fluctuations in commodity markets. Many countries in the subregion are heavily reliant on exports of natural resources. The boom and bust of these resources, often linked to the global economy and demand, has shaped the level and dynamic of many countries' military expenditure. Two of the major spenders in the subregion—Angola and Nigeria—have been particularly affected by this.

In 2020 Angola's military spending fell for the sixth consecutive year. At $994 million, its spending in 2020 was 12 per cent lower than in 2019, 58 per cent lower than in 2011 and 73 per cent below its peak in 2014. Angola encapsulates the typical relationship between government spending, which includes military expenditure, and an economy driven by natural resource revenue.[13] Over the period 2011–14 its military spending rose by 53 per cent and it became sub-Saharan Africa's largest spender. After reaching a peak of $108 per barrel in June 2014, oil prices plunged to $44 per barrel by January 2015.[14] The military budget of Angola declined by 41 per cent in 2015, largely coinciding with the lower oil price.[15] Since the 2014 oil price shock, oil prices have generally remained low and Angola's economy has failed to recover. This has had an effect on government spending, including on the military, and has been further exacerbated by the Covid-19 pandemic.

[11] Novta, N. and Pugacheva, E., 'The macroeconomic costs of conflict', *Journal of Macroeconomics*, vol. 68 (June 2021), p. 4; and Adhvaryu, A. et al., 'Resources, conflict, and economic development in Africa', *Journal of Development Economics*, vol. 149 (Mar. 2021), p. 3.

[12] Chad's GDP, as estimated by the IMF, rose in 2011–14, 2018 and 2019 and fell in 2015–17 and 2020. International Monetary Fund (IMF), International Financial Statistics Database, Oct. 2020, <http://data.imf.org/IFS>. On the armed conflict in the Lake Chad region see chapter 7, section II, in this volume.

[13] Da Costa António, A. E. and Rodriguez-Gil, A., 'Oil shocks and fiscal policy procyclicality in Angola: Assessing the role of asymmetries and institutions', *Review of Development Economics*, vol. 24, no. 1 (Feb. 2020), pp. 212–13.

[14] Maed, D. and Stiger, P., 'The 2014 plunge in import petroleum prices: What happened?', *Beyond the Numbers* (US Bureau of Labour Statistics), vol. 4, no. 5 (May 2015), p. 5.

[15] On this phenomenon see Tian, N. and Lopes da Silva, D., 'Debt, oil price and military expenditure', *SIPRI Yearbook 2018*.

Amid continued conflict and insecurities in and around Nigeria, its military spending rose by 29 per cent to reach $2.6 billion in 2020.[16] This increase was the highest relative and absolute increase since 2001 and was entirely due to a substantial increase (80 per cent) in recurrent expenditure, rather than capital spending on equipment.[17] Disaggregated information shows this increase to be mostly for the Nigerian Army, which received 105 per cent more funding in 2020 than in 2019.[18] A specific increase for the Nigerian Army was the near threefold increase in 'non regular allowances'. Despite the impacts of Covid-19 and low oil prices on the Nigerian economy, the government did not reduce its 2020 military budget when it had the opportunity to do so in July 2020.[19] Moreover, Nigeria's budget for 2021 includes an estimated 9.4 per cent increase in the military budget.[20]

The Americas

In its third consecutive year of growth, military expenditure in the Americas reached $853 billion in 2020—3.9 per cent higher than in 2019.[21] Three of the top 15 global spenders in 2020 are in the Americas: the United States (rank 1), Canada (rank 13) and Brazil (rank 15).

North American countries (i.e. the USA and Canada) slightly increased their share of total regional spending, reaching 94 per cent, while South America's share shrank from 6.3 per cent in 2019 to 5.1 per cent in 2020. This is mainly the result of changes in the USA, which has increased military spending for the past three years, and in Brazil, which cut military spending in 2020 largely due to the Covid-19 pandemic. The share of total regional spending of Central America and the Caribbean remained nearly unchanged, at 1.0 per cent.

North America

North America's military expenditure grew by 4.3 per cent in 2020, reaching $801 billion. Global military spending is very responsive to fluctuations in this subregion, as North America's military expenditure accounted

---

[16] Africa Research Bulletin, 'Nigeria: Threats have changed and multiplied', *Africa Research Bulletin: Political, Social and Cultural Series*, 22 Jan. 2020.

[17] Federal Republic of Nigeria, '2020 Appropriation Amendment', 2020, pp. 116–23.

[18] Federal Republic of Nigeria, '2019 Appropriation Act', 2019, pp. 23–29; and Federal Republic of Nigeria (note 17), pp. 116–23.

[19] Nigerian Federal Budget Office, 'Revised Appropriation Bill 2020', 14 July 2020, pp. 3–6; and Onuah, F., 'Nigeria set to keep record 2020 budget to fight coronavirus despite earlier cut', Reuters, 13 May 2020.

[20] Federal Republic of Nigeria, '2021 Appropriation Act', Federal Office of the Federation of Nigeria, 31 Dec. 2020, pp. 9–12; and 'Nigeria's Buhari agrees record 2021 budget amid COVID-hit economy', Africanews, 31 Dec. 2020.

[21] This total excludes Cuba, for which it was impossible to make a reliable series of estimates for inclusion in the regional total.

for 40 per cent of the world total in 2020. Despite rising since 2017, North America's military expenditure in 2020 was still 9.6 per cent lower than in 2011. The USA accounted for 99 per cent of the subregion's spending.

Central America and the Caribbean

Following a relatively high increase in 2019, military expenditure in Central America and the Caribbean remained almost unchanged in 2020, with a minor 0.2 per cent decrease to $8.6 billion.[22]

Mexico's military spending accounted for 71 per cent of the subregional total in 2020. About 3 per cent of the $6.1 billion that Mexico spent on its military in 2020 was allocated to the National Guard, a police force created in 2019 to curb the growing criminal activity in the country.[23] The National Guard is a de facto paramilitary force, heavily equipped with military-grade weaponry and military personnel. The government plans to raise the National Guard's budget by 22 per cent in 2021.[24]

Military spending in Guatemala, El Salvador and Honduras is also driven by criminal violence. These countries form Central America's Northern Triangle, the region with the highest homicide rates in the world outside war zones.[25] All three countries have used some form of military engagement to deal with the issue of criminal violence.[26] In El Salvador, the military have been fighting criminal gangs since the early 2000s. In 2020 President Nayib Bukele announced a further expansion of the armed forces' role in public security tasks.[27] El Salvador's military spending grew by 17 per cent in 2020, the fourth consecutive year of growth. The increase came amid heightened tensions between the Legislative Assembly and the president. In early 2020 Bukele pushed legislators to agree to a $109 million loan to help to equip the military and the police in defence against organized crime. In an attempt to pressurize the Assembly for approval, the president entered the Legislative Palace with a group of armed soldiers.[28] The use of the armed forces to intimidate lawmakers raised serious concerns over El Salvador's democratic institutions.[29]

[22] The total for Central America and the Caribbean excludes Cuba (see note 21) and the small Caribbean states (e.g. Antigua and Barbuda, Grenada, and Saint Lucia), which are not in the SIPRI Military Expenditure Database and are assumed to have low expenditure.

[23] Tian et al. (note 8), pp. 238–39.

[24] *El Financiero*, 'Gobierno de AMLO pide 22% más presupuesto para la Guardia Nacional en 2021' [AMLO's government asks for 22% increase to the National Guard budget in 2021], 8 Sep. 2020.

[25] Cheatham, A., 'Central America's turbulent northern triangle', Backgrounder, Council on Foreign Relations, 1 Oct. 2019.

[26] Flores-Macías, G. A. and Zarkin, J., 'The militarization of law enforcement: Evidence from Latin America', *Perspectives on Politics*, published online 27 Dec. 2019.

[27] 'El Salvador: Bukele vuelve a rodearse de militares para criticar a congresistas' [El Salvador: Bukele again surrounds himself with military to criticize congressmen], Deutsche Welle, 19 Feb. 2020.

[28] Renteria, N., 'El Salvador president's power play stokes democracy concerns', Reuters, 11 Feb. 2020.

[29] 'El Salvador's president summons the army to bully congress', *The Economist*, 15 Feb. 2020.

South America

Military expenditure in South America fell by 2.1 per cent in 2020, to $43.5 billion, but this was still 6.2 per cent higher than in 2011.

Brazilian military expenditure remained the third largest in the Americas notwithstanding a 3.1 per cent reduction. While the budget of the Brazilian Ministry of Defence (MOD) was 6.7 per cent higher than in 2019, the actual expenditure was much lower: only 88 per cent ($19.7 billion) of the MOD budget was spent in 2020. In comparison, the MOD executed 94 per cent of its budget in 2019 and 92 per cent in 2018. Military spending seems set to rebound in 2021, with a budget proposal for a 4.8 per cent increase on the 2020 budget.[30] The request for an increase in 2021 comes amid continuous lobbying efforts from the armed forces to secure more resources for arms modernization.[31] In July 2020 the MOD submitted to the Congress a revised version of the National Defence Strategy that proposed raising Brazil's military burden to 2 per cent from the level of 1.4 per cent in 2020.[32]

Chile's initial military budget for 2020 totalled $4.6 billion. This was a 2.8 per cent reduction on its military spending in 2019. In April 2020 the National Congress adjusted its initial budget to reallocate $936 million intended to finance the modernization of Chile's fleet of F-16 combat aircraft to cover costs associated with the Covid-19 pandemic.[33]

Argentina's military spending remained relatively unaltered in 2020, at $2.9 billion, but there was an important change in the funding mechanism. In September 2020 the National Congress approved the creation of a National Defence Fund (Fondef) to finance arms acquisitions for the armed forces.[34] The fund is independent of the MOD budget and will receive a separate share of the state budget. Allocations will start at 0.5 per cent of the total state budget in 2021, increasing to 0.8 per cent from 2023 onwards.[35] The

---

[30] Sassine, V., 'Governo aumenta investimentos para projetos das Forças Armadas em 2021' [Government increases investment for armed forces projects in 2021], *O Globo*, 4 Sep. 2020.

[31] Sassine (note 30).

[32] Sant'Anna, L., 'Militares querem destinar 2% do PIB à Defesa' [The military wants 2% of GDP allocated to defence], CNN Brasil, 16 July 2020; and Brazilian Ministry of Defence (MOD), *Política Nacional de Defesa e Estratégia Nacional de Defesa* [National Defence Policy and National Defence Strategy] (MOD: Brasilia, 22 July 2020).

[33] Squella, P., 'La actualización de los F-16 de la Fuerza Aérea de Chile está suspendida por el momento' [The upgrade of the Chilean Air Force's F-16s is suspended for the time being], defensa. com, 27 July 2020; and Squella, P., 'Crisis Coronavirus en : Expertos sugieren redestinar recursos de compras de armamento militar' [Coronavirus crisis in Chile: Experts suggest redirecting resources from military arms procurement], defensa.com, 27 Mar. 2020.

[34] Fondo Nacional de la Defensa [National Defence Fund], Argentine Law no. 27 565, of 1 Oct. 2020.

[35] Piscetta, J., 'El Senado avanza con la aprobación de un fondo de $30 mil millones para reequipar a las Fuerzas Armadas' [Senate moves ahead with $30 billion fund to re-equip the armed forces], Infobae, 16 Sep. 2020.

mechanism aims to address the historically low levels of military spending in the country since the end of the military dictatorship, in 1983.[36]

Asia and Oceania

Military spending in Asia and Oceania totalled $528 billion in 2020. Five of the top 15 global spenders in 2020 are in Asia and Oceania: China (rank 2), India (rank 3), Japan (rank 9), the Republic of Korea (South Korea, rank 10) and Australia (rank 12).

Military spending by states in Asia and Oceania was 2.5 per cent higher in 2020 than in 2019, continuing an uninterrupted upwards trend dating back to at least 1989. Asia and Oceania is the only region that has had continuous growth since 1989; and the growth of 47 per cent over the decade 2011–20 was by far the largest of any region.[37] The increase was due primarily to the military spending increases of China and India; in 2020, these together accounted for 62 per cent of total spending in the region, up from 48 per cent in 2011.

While spending increased in four of the five subregions in 2020, it fell by 8.4 per cent in Central Asia. Over the period 2011–20, there were substantial increases in all five subregions of Asia and Oceania, ranging from 35 per cent in Oceania up to 53 per cent in East Asia.

Only 6 of the 31 states in Asia and Oceania for which data was available reduced their military spending in 2020. The largest relative decrease was recorded by Kazakhstan (–9.2 per cent), followed by Sri Lanka (–8.2 per cent) and Pakistan (–2.8 per cent).

Central Asia

Data is available for three of the five countries in Central Asia: Kazakhstan, Kyrgyzstan and Tajikistan.[38] At $1.9 billion, their spending accounted for only 0.4 per cent of total spending in Asia and Oceania. Spending by these three countries was down by 8.4 per cent in 2020 but was 47 per cent higher than in 2011.

Kazakhstan was the largest spender in Central Asia in 2020: its expenditure of $1.7 billion was 89 per cent of the subregional total. The fall

---

[36] Battaglino, J., 'The politics of defense revival in Argentina', *Defense and Security Analysis*, vol. 29, no. 1 (2013); and Pardo, D., 'Por qué Argentina es el país que menos gasta en defensa en Sudamérica y cómo pudo eso afectar al submarino desaparecido ARA San Juan' [Why Argentina is the country that spends the least on defence in South America and how this may have affected the missing submarine ARA San Juan], BBC Mundo, 28 Nov. 2017.

[37] No data is available for North Korea, Turkmenistan or Uzbekistan for 2010–19 and they are not included in the totals for Asia and Oceania. Data for Myanmar and Viet Nam is included in the regional totals but is uncertain.

[38] No military spending information has been publicly available for Turkmenistan since 1999 and for Uzbekistan since 2003.

of 9.2 per cent in 2020 followed a year of exceptionally high spending in 2019, which was 29 per cent higher than in 2018.[39] Future spending plans announced in the 2020–22 multiyear budget include efforts to 'optimise' Kazakhstan's military spending by reducing personnel costs and modernize the weaponry of its armed forces.[40]

East Asia

Military spending in East Asia rose by 2.3 per cent in 2020 to reach $359 billion, continuing the consistent trend of growth since 1995. Over the decade 2011–20 spending increased by 53 per cent. China accounted for 70 per cent of the spending in East Asia in 2020, but Japan (14 per cent) and South Korea (13 per cent) are also large spenders in the subregion.

Military spending in Japan was $49.1 billion in 2020, 1.2 per cent higher than in 2019.[41] Its growth rate of 2.4 per cent since 2011 was the lowest in both East Asia and Asia and Oceania. Japan's military burden was 1.0 per cent in 2020 up 0.1 percentage points since 2019. Despite the contraction in the country's GDP, Japan's military burden has not exceeded the threshold of 1 per cent of GDP that has been a policy or guideline since 1976.[42] On 21 December 2020 the Japanese Government presented a draft budget for the 2021 financial year which included a 4.3 per cent nominal increase in military spending.[43]

The Japanese Government's annual defence white paper for 2020 highlights the perceived threats from China and the Democratic People's Republic of Korea (DPRK, or North Korea) as the main drivers for a need to expand military capabilities.[44] Japan's perceived threat from Russia is generally much lower than those from China or North Korea, although, with specifically crafted wording, the white paper refers to the need for 'close scrutiny'.[45]

[39] Altynbayev, K., 'Eyeing "plenty of threats", Kazakhstan ramps up defence spending', Caravanserai, 15 May 2019.

[40] Ashimov, A., 'Kazakhstan to modernise armed forces' weaponry in defence-spending plan', Caravanserai, 14 Feb. 2020; and Kazinform, 'Defense spending to fall in Kazakhstan in 2020', Strategy 2050, 5 Feb. 2020.

[41] The SIPRI figures for Japan do not include spending by the MOD on the large coastguard, which is considered a civilian police force.

[42] Pryor, C. and Le, T., 'Looking beyond 1 percent: Japan's security expenditures', The Diplomat, 3 Apr. 2018; and Jiji Press, 'Japan's record GDP drop seen even worse than preliminary 27.8%', Japan Times, 2 Sep. 2020.

[43] Japanese Ministry of Defense (MOD), Defense Programs and Budget of Japan: Overview of FY2021 Budget Request (MOD: Tokyo, Sep. 2020), p. 2; and Kaneko, R., 'Japan approves record defense budget for fiscal 2021 amid China threats', Japan Times, 21 Dec. 2020.

[44] Japanese Ministry of Defense (MOD), 2020 Defense of Japan (MOD: Tokyo, 2020), chapter 2, sections 2–3.

[45] Japanese Ministry of Defense (note 44), chapter 2, section 4, p. 120; and Oren, E. and Brummer, M., 'How Japan talks about security threats', The Diplomat, 14 Aug. 2020.

After two downward revisions to alleviate some of the adverse economic effects of the Covid-19 pandemic, South Korea's military spending in 2020 was $45.7 billion. South Korea was one of the first countries to officially revise its military spending due to the impact of the pandemic and to support the country's economic relief effort, the Emergency Disaster Assistance Plan.[46] The plan drew finances from the education, industry, agriculture and environment ministries, among others, but the cut to the military budget was the largest.[47]

Despite the two reductions, South Korea's military spending still increased by 4.9 per cent in 2020, although the rate of increase was lower than originally planned and lower than in 2018 and 2019. Between 2011 and 2020, spending grew by 41 per cent. Indeed, against the backdrop of a nuclear-armed rival in North Korea, South Korea's spending has increased for 21 consecutive years since 2000.[48] The 2021 national budget, passed by the National Assembly in December 2020, includes a 5.4 per cent nominal increase in the official defence budget.[49] The planned increase was justified by the perceived need to adequately prepare for both traditional threats and non-traditional threats such as nuclear weapons and infectious disease.[50]

Oceania

At $30.7 billion, military spending in Oceania rose by 5.6 per cent in 2020 and was 35 per cent higher than in 2011.

The increases were principally the result of changes in Australia's spending, which accounted for 90 per cent of the subregion's spending in 2020. Its spending of $27.5 billion was 5.9 per cent higher than in 2019 and 33 per cent higher than in 2011. In recent years Australia's defence strategy has revolved around perceived heightened military threats in its neighbourhood and countering the rise of China.[51] The 2020 Defence Strategic Update and 2020 Force Structure Plan provide an outline of the country's military priorities in the next two decades.[52] In particular, they provide a 10-year funding

---

[46] Grevatt, J., 'Covid-19: South Korea cuts defence budget in response to pandemic', Janes, 16 Apr. 2020; and Darling, D., 'Due to COVID-19, South Korea plans fresh cut to 2020 defense budget', Defense and Security Monitor, Forecast International, 3 June 2020.

[47] Grevatt (note 46).

[48] Beomchul, S., 'South Korea's military readiness under Moon', Carnegie Endowment for International Peace, 18 Mar. 2020.

[49] Grevatt, J. and MacDonald, A., 'South Korea increases defence budget for 2021', Janes, 3 Dec. 2020.

[50] Grevatt and MacDonald (note 49).

[51] Macmillan, J. and Green, A., 'Australia to spend $270b building larger military to prepare for "poorer, more dangerous" world and rise of China', ABC News, 30 June 2020; Reynolds, L., Australian Minister for Defence, '2019 ministerial statement on defence operations', Australian Department of Defence, 5 Dec. 2019; and Packham, B., 'Out-of-date strategies in defence white paper', *The Australian*, 8 Oct. 2019.

[52] Australian Department of Defence (DOD), *2020 Defence Strategic Update* (DOD: Canberra, 2020); and Australian Department of Defence (DOD), *2020 Force Structure Plan* (DOD: Canberra, 2020).

model to deliver on the strategy set out in the 2016 Defence White Paper.[53] Under the 2020 Defence Strategic Update, the Australian Government plans to allocate a total of US$400 billion to the military over the period 2021–30, with annual spending projected to increase to around US$51 billion in nominal terms by 2030.[54] The distribution of spending is also expected to change: more focus will be given to military procurement while personnel spending as a share of total spending is projected to decline.

South Asia

Military spending in South Asia increased by 36 per cent between 2011 and 2020, including an increase of 1.3 per cent in 2020, to reach $90.1 billion.

India is the world's third largest spender, behind the USA and China. It accounted for 81 per cent of South Asia's subregional total in 2020. At $72.9 billion, India's military spending was 2.1 per cent higher in 2020 than in 2019 and 34 per cent higher compared with 2011. The rate of increase in spending in 2020 was the lowest since 2015, which could be partially the result of the Covid-19 pandemic.[55] India's military burden rose for the second consecutive year in 2020. As its GDP contracted by an estimated 11 per cent, the military burden reached 2.9 per cent of GDP, back to a level not seen since 2010 after the 2009 global financial and economic crisis.

About one-quarter of India's total military budget is allocated to capital outlays.[56] The majority (61 per cent in 2020) is spent on personnel expenses such as salaries and military pensions. A relatively large proportion is represented by spending on the paramilitary forces under the Ministry of Home Affairs—11 per cent in 2020. While this expenditure item is common in many large spenders, India's spending on its paramilitary as a proportion of its total military expenditure is by far the largest of the major spenders. The closest to India's share of 11 per cent in 2020 was Russia (9.0 per cent), followed by China (7.6 per cent) and France (0.4 per cent).

The Indian MOD has argued that the recent increase in India's spending is needed as a result of continued conflict with Pakistan over Kashmir, renewed border tensions with China, and a general rivalry with China as the main regional power.[57] In June 2020, tensions between China and India

---

[53] Australian Department of Defence (DOD), 'Defence budget', Fact sheet, May 2020; and Australian Department of Defence (DOD), *2016 Defence White Paper* (DOD: Canberra, 2016).

[54] Australian Department of Defence, *2020 Defence Strategic Update* (note 52), p. 7.

[55] Sen, S. R., 'India's military sees small budget rise despite China standoff', Bloomberg, 1 Feb. 2021.

[56] Indian Ministry of Finance (MOF), Budget Division, *Expenditure Profile 2021–2022* (MOF: New Delhi, Feb. 2021).

[57] US Congressional Research Service (CRS), *China–India Great Power Competition in the Indian Ocean Region: Issues for Congress*, CRS Report for Congress R45194 (US Congress, CRS: Washington, DC, 20 Apr. 2018); Nouwens, M., 'China and India: Competition for Indian Ocean dominance?', Military Balance Blog, 24 Apr. 2018; and Bellman, E. and Roy, R., 'India–China border tensions: What you need to know', *Wall Street Journal*, 25 Jan. 2021. On the India–Pakistan conflict over Kashmir see chapter 4, section II, in this volume.

worsened, with limited clashes in the Galwan Valley over an ill-defined and long-disputed border; both states moved more troops into the area.[58]

At $10.4 billion, Pakistan's military spending in 2020 was 2.8 per cent lower than in 2019, but 55 per cent higher than 2011. The increases in spending over the past decade have occurred in the context of a fragile economy that has been worsened by the Covid-19 pandemic. At 4.0 per cent of GDP, Pakistan's military burden was the second highest in Asia and Oceania, behind only Brunei Darussalam (at 4.1 per cent of GDP).

South East Asia

Military spending in South East Asia increased by 5.2 per cent in 2020 to reach $45.5 billion. Over the decade 2011–20 spending increased by 36 per cent. The largest spenders in 2020 were Singapore ($10.9 billion), Indonesia ($9.4 billion) and Thailand ($7.3 billion).

The nine South East Asian states for which SIPRI has data for 2020 all increased their military spending. The economies of all countries in the subregion except for Brunei Darussalam and Myanmar are predicted to have contracted in 2020. The worst affected states were Malaysia (with a 6.0 per cent decline in GDP), the Philippines (8.3 per cent decline) and Thailand (7.1 per cent decline).[59] As a result, the military burden rose in all countries except for Timor-Leste, where it remained unchanged.

China's continued assertiveness and numerous territorial claimants in the South China Sea is one of the possible factors that has driven recent increases in military spending in the subregion. It has led some of the states to expand their naval capabilities.[60]

Europe

Total military spending in Europe (including Russia) in 2020 amounted to $378 billion. This was 4.0 per cent higher than in 2019 and 16 per cent higher than in 2011. Five of the world's 15 largest military spenders in 2020 are in Europe: Russia (rank 4), the United Kingdom (rank 5), Germany (rank 7), France (rank 8) and Italy (rank 11).

---

[58] Ellis-Petersen, H., 'China and India move troops as border tensions escalate', *The Guardian*, 27 May 2020; and Mazumdaru, S., 'India–China border standoff raises military tensions', Deutsche Welle, 2 June 2020. On the China–India border conflict see chapter 4, section II, in this volume.

[59] Stuart, A. et al., *Navigating the Pandemic: A Multispeed Recovery in Asia*, Regional Economic Outlook: Asia and Pacific (International Monetary Fund: Washington, DC, Oct. 2020), p. 5.

[60] Thayer, C., 'COVID-19 masks mischief in the South China Sea', East Asia Forum, 13 Jan. 2021; Manning, R. A. and Cronin, P. M., 'Under cover of pandemic, China steps up brinkmanship in South China Sea', *Foreign Policy*, 14 May 2020; Asia Maritime Transparency Initiative, 'Maritime claims of the Indo-Pacific', Center for Strategic and International Studies (CSIS); Endo, J., 'Southeast Asia building up maritime defenses', Nikkei Asia, 17 May 2017; and Wezeman, S. T., *Arms Flows to South East Asia* (SIPRI: Stockholm, Dec. 2019).

Box 8.4. Revised estimates for the military expenditure of the United Kingdom

In 2020 SIPRI's figures for the United Kingdom's military spending were revised to incorporate military spending items that are not funded through the core allocation to the Ministry of Defence (MOD) and to reflect spending levels more accurately.

To report on British military spending, SIPRI has used the net cash requirement (NCR) figures reported in the MOD's annual reports and accounts since the 2000/2001 financial year. For the years between 1949 and 2000, SIPRI used defence expenditure data provided by the North Atlantic Treaty Organization (NATO).[a] This allowed SIPRI to have a consistent time series following accounting changes implemented around 2000/2001.

The NCR figures were reasonably close to the UK's submissions to the NATO reports on defence expenditure until 2012, when the two data series began to diverge significantly. This discrepancy led SIPRI to review its assessment of British military expenditure to determine whether SIPRI's coverage is missing elements of military spending in budgets other than the MOD's.

According to information received from the British MOD in 2020, six spending items are excluded from the MOD budget but included in the UK's report to NATO: (*a*) elements of the Conflict Stability and Security Fund (CSSF) related to peacekeeping activities; (*b*) expenditure on MOD civil service pensions and the Armed Forces Pensions Scheme (AFPS); (*c*) elements of the Single Intelligence Account related to defence; (*d*) income generated by the MOD; (*e*) the additional cost of military operations funded through the Treasury's special reserve; and (*f*) Joint Security Fund (JSF) spending by other government departments.[b] SIPRI examined these categories in further detail to determine whether they fall under the SIPRI definition of military expenditure; whether they are already included in the MOD's NCR figure; and if a consistent data series could be uncovered.

As a result of this in-depth examination, SIPRI revised its data for the UK's military spending to include four new line items in addition to the NCR: (*a*) elements of the CSSF related to peacekeeping operations; (*b*) estimates of military intelligence expenditure; (*c*) the AFPS; and (*d*) the MOD's external income.[c] The new SIPRI estimate is higher than the old estimate (e.g. the new estimate for 2020 is $59.2 billion, while the old estimate would have been $53.9 billion) but remains slightly lower than the figure in the NATO report ($62.0 billion for 2020). This could be attributed to the fact that SIPRI excludes the JSF and the net additional cost of operations, which the MOD includes in its NATO defence expenditure figure.

Regardless of the comparison with the NATO figure, SIPRI's new estimate takes into consideration more categories that fall under the SIPRI definition of military expenditure and can therefore be seen as an improvement to the SIPRI Military Expenditure Database.

   [a] North Atlantic Treaty Organization (NATO), 'Information on defence expenditures', 16 Mar. 2021.
   [b] British Ministry of Defence, Defence Resources Secretariat, Freedom of Information request no. FOI2020/03865, 20 Apr. 2020.
   [c] Béraud-Sudreau, L. and Tian, N., 'Reassessing SIPRI's military expenditure estimate for the United Kingdom', SIPRI Topical Backgrounder, 9 Feb. 2021.

Western and Central Europe

Nearly all countries in Western and Central Europe cooperate within the military frameworks of the North Atlantic Treaty Organization (NATO) or the European Union (EU). Taken together, the military expenditure of the states in these subregions totalled $307 billion in 2020 ($273 billion for

Western Europe and $33.6 billion for Central Europe). This was up by 4.1 per cent from 2019 and by 13 per cent from 2011. Numerous political leaders, including Josep Borrell, the EU High Representative for Foreign Affairs and Security Policy, cautioned against decreasing military spending in the context of the Covid-19 pandemic.[61] In 2020, 28 of the 36 states in Western and Central Europe increased their military expenditure.

The UK increased its military expenditure by 2.9 per cent in real terms in 2020, to $59.2 billion. This was the UK's second highest annual rate of growth in a decade that, until 2017, was characterized by military spending cuts. The rate of growth in 2019 was even more pronounced, at 5.0 per cent. This can be explained by specific additional expenses that year, such as $893 million to cover the increased costs of employer pension contributions.[62] The military spending increases of 2019 and 2020 far exceeded previous pledges made by the British Government for real-terms annual increases of 0.5 per cent.[63] The upward trend is likely to continue, according to an announcement in late 2020: the MOD budget—the largest component of the UK's total military spending (see box 8.4)—is set to increase by an average of 1.8 per cent per year in real terms until 2024.[64]

Germany's military spending grew even more steeply than the UK's— by 5.2 per cent to $52.8 billion—meaning that it overtook that of France. According to the Federal Ministry of Defence's approved budget covering 2021, Germany's military spending is set to continue to rise.[65] In addition, a total of $4.3 billion will be made available over this period for procurement, research and development, and system digitalization.[66]

At $52.7 billion, France's military spending also increased in 2020, by 2.9 per cent. France is thus on track to implement its Law on Military Planning for 2019–25, which foresaw regular annual spending increases of $1.9 billion in 2019–21 and a further increase of $3.8 billion in 2023.[67] The economic crisis related to the Covid-19 pandemic—which led to a GDP

---

[61] Daventry, M., 'Don't cut back on military spending because of COVID-19, European defence chief warns', Euronews, 17 Nov. 2020; Brzozowski, A., 'Europe's defence budget up in the air amid COVID-19 recovery spending', Euractiv, 13 May 2020; and Barigazzi, J., 'Low defense spending puts strategic autonomy at risk, EU review says', Politico, 20 Nov. 2020.

[62] British Treasury, *Spending Round 2019* (HM Treasury: London, Sep. 2019), p. 13.

[63] British Ministry of Defence (MOD), *SDSR 2015: Defence Fact Sheets* (MOD: London, Jan. 2015), p. 2.

[64] British Treasury, *Spending Review 2020* (HM Treasury: London, Nov. 2020), pp. 67–68.

[65] Bundeswehr (German Armed Forces), 'Die Trendwende Finanzen' [The turnaround in finance], 2021.

[66] German Federal Chancellery, 'Finanzplan des Bundes 2020 bis 2024' [Federal financial plan 2020 to 2024], German Bundesrat, Drucksache no. 517/20, 9 Oct. 2020, p. 15.

[67] Loi relative à la programmation militaire pour les années 2019 à 2025 [Law on Military Planning for the Years 2019 to 2025], French Law no. 2018-607 of 13 July 2018, *Journal Officiel de la République Française*, 14 July 2018, annexed report, section 4.1.1.

contraction of 9.8 per cent in 2020—could upend these plans.[68] During the vote on the Law on Military Planning in 2018, parliamentarians decided that discussions would be held in 2021 on whether there is a need to revise the budget plans.[69] A large part of the increase in spending in 2020 was for expenditure on equipment, which increased by 16 per cent, from $12.4 billion to $14.4 billion.[70] Other budget priorities for 2020 included space and satellite capabilities, intelligence, and cyber capabilities.[71]

The rate of military expenditure growth in the UK, Germany and France, the largest spenders in Western and Central Europe, remained relatively modest compared to some of their neighbours. Seven of the 10 countries with the fastest growing defence budgets in 2020 in Western and Central Europe were in Central Europe: Montenegro (29 per cent rise), Romania (21 per cent), Hungary (20 per cent), Kosovo (17 per cent), Albania (9.7 per cent), Czechia (9.5 per cent) and Poland (8.7 per cent).

Poland's military spending increased to $13.0 billion. Poland's new National Security Strategy, published in 2020, identifies Russia as the foremost threat. While the NATO guideline military burden is 2.0 per cent of GDP, the strategy commits Poland to exceed this, to reach a military burden of 2.5 per cent by 2024.[72] In 2020 it was 2.2 per cent of GDP.

Romania's increase of 21 per cent in 2020 took its military expenditure to $5.7 billion. This boost can be attributed to an increase in capital spending, which jumped by 30 per cent to $1.9 billion.[73] Like Poland, Romania published a National Defence Strategy in 2020 that accuses Russia of 'aggressive actions' and commits the country to being an active member of NATO and the EU.[74] The strategy also commits Romania to spending 2 per

[68] International Monetary Fund (IMF), *World Economic Outlook, October 2020: A Long and Difficult Ascent* (IMF: Washington, DC, Oct. 2020), p. 10.

[69] Guibert, N., 'Le budget des armées toujours en hausse' [Military budget still rising], *Le Monde*, 29 Oct. 2020; and Bauer, A., 'Le président Macron promet de maintenir l'effort budgétaire pour les armées' [President Macron promises to maintain the budgetary support for the armed forces], *Les Echos*, 19 Jan. 2021.

[70] French Ministry of the Armed Forces, 'Les chiffres clés de la Défense 2019' [Key figures for Defence 2019], 28 Aug. 2019, p. 12; and French Ministry of the Armed Forces, 'Les chiffres clés de la Défense 2020' [Key figures for Defence 2020], 21 Sep. 2020, p. 12.

[71] French Ministry of the Armed Forces, 'Promesse tenue pour le budget de la défense' [Defence budget promise kept], 30 Sep. 2019; and French National Assembly, Committee on Foreign Affairs, *Avis sur le Projet de loi de finances pour 2020 (no. 2272)*, vol. IV, *Défense* [Opinion on the Finance Bill for 2020 (no. 2272), vol. 4, Defence] (National Assembly: Paris, 10 Oct. 2019), pp. 11–13.

[72] Polish National Security Bureau (BBN), *National Security Strategy of the Republic of Poland* (BBN: Warsaw, May 2020), pp. 6, 18.

[73] Romanian Ministry of Finance, Ministry of National Defence budget for 2019 (in Romanian), p. 2; and Romanian Ministry of Finance, Ministry of National Defence budget for 2020 (in Romanian), p. 2. See also Tian, N., Lopes da Silva, D. and Wezeman, P. D., 'Spending on military equipment by European members of the North Atlantic Treaty Organization', *SIPRI Yearbook 2020*.

[74] Romanian Presidential Administration, *Strategia Națională de Apărare a Țării pentru perioada 2020–2024* [National Defence Strategy for 2020–2024] (Presidential Administration: Bucharest, July 2020), pp. 6–7, 41.

cent of its GDP on military activities—in line with the NATO guideline—for at least the next 10 years; in 2020 Romania's military burden was 2.3 per cent of GDP.

Hungary's military spending grew for the sixth consecutive year, to $2.4 billion in 2020. Its military spending has increased by 133 per cent since 2014 to cover the costs of an expansion of its military capabilities and the replacement of ageing Soviet-sourced equipment.[75] The growth in spending in 2020 was partly a result of a financial stimulus package implemented in response to the Covid-19 pandemic.[76]

The military expenditure of only a few countries in Western and Central Europe declined in 2020: Bulgaria (–44 per cent), Malta (–6.1 per cent), Serbia (–5.0 per cent), Greece (–4.3 per cent), Slovenia (–1.9 per cent) and Slovakia (–1.4 per cent). The decrease in Bulgaria's spending in 2020 followed a sharp increase (130 per cent) in 2019, which can be attributed to the one-off full payment for eight new combat aircraft.[77] In addition, the spending of Norway (down 0.1 per cent) and Spain (down 0.2 per cent) remained almost unchanged.

So far, the overall impact of the Covid-19 pandemic on military spending in Western and Central Europe in 2020 appears to have been limited, despite a marked recession (with a GDP contraction of 7 per cent). Continued increases in military expenditure in 2020, like other public spending increases to sustain national economies during the crisis, were financed by a heavy reliance on government borrowing. This may lead to fiscal consolidation—that is, efforts to reduce debt and budget deficits—in the short-to-medium term.[78] The economic ramifications of the pandemic for military spending were more apparent at the EU level. For the EU's multi-annual financial framework for 2021–27, the European Commission initially proposed an allocation of $15.0 billion to the European Defence Fund—which is intended to coordinate investment in military research and improve interoperability between national armed forces. The EU member states eventually agreed on $8.3 billion during budgetary negotiations amid the health crisis.[79]

Eastern Europe

In 2020 military expenditure in Eastern Europe, including Russia, totalled $71.7 billion, 3.4 per cent more than in 2019 (see figure 8.3). Excluding

[75] Tian et al. (note 73), pp. 262–63.
[76] Inotai, E., 'Hungarian "militarisation" under Orban stirs concern', Balkan Insight, 29 July 2020.
[77] Tian et al. (note 73).
[78] International Monetary Fund (IMF), *Whatever It Takes: Europe's Response to COVID-19*, Regional Economic Outlook: Europe (IMF: Washington, DC, Oct. 2020), p. 10.
[79] European Parliament, 'Proposal for a regulation establishing the European Defence Fund', Legislative Train, 18 Dec. 2020.

Russia, the spending of the remaining six countries was $10.0 billion, 9.5 per cent more than in 2019.

The largest increases were recorded by Azerbaijan (17 per cent) and Ukraine (11 per cent). Despite also being hit by recession—the GDP of Azerbaijan contracted by 4 per cent and that of Ukraine by 7.2 per cent—military requirements linked to active conflicts are probably responsible for the increases.[80] In contrast, the military spending of Armenia—the other party to the conflict with Azerbaijan over Nagorno-Karabakh—declined in 2020 by 2.6 per cent as its GDP decreased by 4.5 per cent.

Russia

Russia's total military spending in 2020 was $61.7 billion, 2.5 per cent more than in 2019 and 26 per cent higher than in 2011. The increases in Russian spending in 2019 and 2020 followed two years of decrease in 2017 and 2018. Before 2017, Russia's military spending had risen for 18 straight years.[81]

Russia's arms acquisitions are planned through the periodically updated State Armament Programme (Gosudarstvennuyu Programmu Vooruzheniya, GPV). The programme for 2011–20, GPV-2020, was adopted in December 2010.[82] Total funding for GVP-2020 amounted to 20.7 trillion roubles in current prices, with 31 per cent to be spent in 2011–15 and 69 per cent in 2016–20.[83] Implementation of GPV-2020 was severely delayed after Russia's annexation of Crimea in 2014, military action in eastern Ukraine and economic problems. This was primarily due to the loss of Ukrainian inputs into the Russian arms industry and EU and NATO sanctions, including a ban on all sales of weapon systems and components to Russia.[84]

The next version of the programme, GPV-2025, adopted in 2015, took account of the new circumstances.[85] In 2018 Russia approved its most recent

---

[80] On these conflicts see chapter 5, sections II and III, and chapter 9, section III, in this volume.

[81] The increase in 2016 can be attributed to one-off repayments of loans to the arms industry, which accounted for 17% of the total. Excluding the repayments, Russian military spending would have declined by 12% in 2016. See Tian, N. et al., 'Global developments in military expenditure', *SIPRI Yearbook 2017*, pp. 237–38; and Cooper, J., 'Prospects for military spending in Russia in 2017 and beyond', Working paper, University of Birmingham, Centre for Russian, European and Eurasian Studies (CREES), 23 Mar. 2017.

[82] Martynenko, E. V. and Parkhitko, N. P., 'Implementation of the Russian State Armaments Program 2011–2020: Economic and financial analysis', *European Research Studies Journal*, vol. 21, no. 2 (2018).

[83] Cooper, J., *Russia's State Armament Programme to 2020: A Quantitative Assessment of Implementation 2011–15*, Swedish Defence Research Agency (FOI) Report no. FOI-R—4239—SE (FOI: Stockholm, Mar. 2016), pp. 3–42.

[84] Hunter Christie, E., 'Sanctions after Crimea: have they worked?', *NATO Review*, 13 July 2015; Malmlöf, T., 'A case study of Russo-Ukrainian defense industrial cooperation: Russian dilemmas', *Journal of Slavic Military Studies*, vol. 29, no. 1 (2016), pp. 16–17; Russell, M., 'Sanctions over Ukraine: Impact on Russia', Briefing, European Parliamentary Research Service, Mar. 2016, p. 7; and Kirchberger, S., 'The end of a military-industrial triangle: Arms-industrial cooperation between China, Russia and Ukraine after the Crimea crisis', *SIRIUS*, vol. 1, no. 2 (June 2017), p. 15.

[85] Cooper (note 83), pp. 43–45.

State Armament Programme, GPV-2027, which aims to build on the progress made under GPV-2020 and GPV-2025 and emphasizes procurement of high-precision weapons for all three branches of the Russian armed forces.[86] Russia will allocate about 19 trillion roubles to GPV-2027. While this is in line with the funding for GPV-2020, inflation and currency depreciation mean that GPV-2027 is considered less ambitious in real terms than its predecessor.[87]

The far-reaching economic consequences of Covid-19 had an immediate impact on Russia's military spending and GPV-2027.[88] Russia's actual military spending in 2020 ($61.7 billion) was 6.6 per cent lower than the initial budget ($66.1 billion). The biggest gap in spending between the initial budget and actual spending was a shortfall of around $1 billion under a classified category.[89] This spending category is probably linked to the State Armament Programme.[90]

The Middle East

The combined military spending of the 11 Middle Eastern countries for which data was available in 2020 was $143 billion.[91] While the military spending of all four other regions rose in 2020, the spending of these Middle Eastern countries fell by 6.5 per cent. Two countries in the region—Saudi Arabia (rank 6) and Israel (rank 14)—are among the top 15 global spenders in 2020 (see table 8.2 in section I).

Notwithstanding the widespread reductions in these 11 countries, the economic impact of the pandemic was large enough to result in increases in the military burden. Except for Lebanon, whose military burden shrank from 4.7 per cent in 2019 to 3.0 per cent in 2020, all Middle Eastern countries for which data is available either increased or maintained their military burdens in 2020. The largest increase in military burden was Oman's, which rose by 2.3 percentage points to 11 per cent—the highest in the world. Indeed, 5 of the 11 countries with the highest military burden in 2020 were in the

---

[86] Luzin, P., 'Russia's GPV-2027 State Arms Programme', Riddle, 18 Apr. 2018; and Interfax, [Putin announces the adoption of a new 10-year weapon programme], 24 Jan. 2018 (in Russian).

[87] Connolly, R. and Boulègue, M., *Russia's New State Armament Programme: Implications for the Russian Armed Forces and Military Capabilities to 2027* (Royal Institute of International Affairs–Chatham House: London, May 2018).

[88] Malmlöf, T., 'Russia's new armament programme—Leaner and meaner', RUFS Briefing no. 42, Swedish Defence Research Agency (FOI), Mar. 2018.

[89] Cooper, J., 'The implementation of the 2020 federal budget and military expenditure', Unpublished, 9 Feb. 2021.

[90] Cooper, J., 'Military expenditure in the Russian draft Federal Budget for the three years 2019 to 2021', Research note, Changing Character of War Centre, 2018, p. 5.

[91] SIPRI has not provided an estimate for total Middle Eastern military expenditure since 2014 because of a lack of data for Qatar, Syria, the United Arab Emirates (UAE) and Yemen.

Middle East: Oman (11 per cent), Saudi Arabia (8.4 per cent), Kuwait (6.5 per cent), Israel (5.6 per cent) and Jordan (5.0 per cent).

Egypt's military expenditure rose by 7.3 per cent to $4.5 billion in 2020, the highest rate of increase in the Middle East. Nonetheless, Egypt's military burden remained the lowest in the region, at 1.2 per cent of GDP. The growth in spending can be attributed to a combination of Egypt's regional role, involvement in the conflict in Libya and maintaining authoritarian rule at home.[92] A further factor is the continuing military campaign against insurgent Bedouin tribes and terrorist groups in the Sinai Peninsula.[93] President Abdel Fattah el-Sisi had pledged during his 2018 re-election campaign to strengthen the armed forces against these threats.[94]

Egypt's military expenditure fell almost continuously over the decade 2011–20, shrinking by 6.9 per cent. The downward trend was interrupted by two years of growth, in 2014 and 2015, during the initial years of el-Sisi's first term as president. Over the decade, Egypt acquired a significant number of weapon systems and deployed its military in counterterrorist operations in the Sinai Peninsula. The mismatch between Egypt's well-equipped and sizeable military forces—one of the largest in the Middle East—and a shrinking military budget suggests that a considerable part of Egypt's military spending is undeclared.[95]

Israel's military spending totalled $21.7 billion in 2020, a 2.7 per cent increase over 2019. Israel's military budget has maintained a long streak of growth: apart from small cuts in 2003 (–1.6 per cent) and 2009 (–2.0 per cent), Israel's military spending has been on an upward trend over the past two decades, growing by 59 per cent between 2001 and 2020 and by 32 per cent between 2011 and 2020. The 2020 increase came after the announcement of the Momentum Plan in 2019, an ambitious multi-year programme to overhaul Israel's air, ground, sea and cyber capabilities.[96] This followed the 2030 Security Concept, a separate plan announced in 2018, which aims to increase the growth rate of Israel's military spending.[97]

Israeli Prime Minister Benjamin Netanyahu continued to support the plea from the Israel Defense Forces (IDF) to increase military spending even during the economic downturn resulting from the Covid-19 pandemic;

[92] Council on Foreign Relations, 'Instability in Egypt', Global Conflict Tracker, [n.d.]. On Egypt's role in the Libyan civil war see chapter 6, section IV, in this volume.

[93] Council on Foreign Relations (note 92). On the armed conflict in Egypt see chapter 6, section IV, in this volume.

[94] Wuite, C., 'The rationale for Egypt's military spending spree', The Interpreter, Lowy Institute, 4 Apr. 2020.

[95] Kuimova, A., 'Understanding Egyptian military expenditure', SIPRI Background Paper, Oct. 2020.

[96] Gross, J. A., 'The IDF's new plan: From "Waze of War" to a general charged with countering Iran', Times of Israel, 12 Feb. 2020; and Barkat, A., 'Chief of Staff launches plan for "more lethal" IDF', Globes (Tel Aviv), 13 Feb. 2020.

[97] Tian et al. (note 8), p. 251.

he argued for its strategic necessity given various security threats.[98] The combination of a significant (1.7 per cent) drop in GDP with higher military spending meant that Israel's military burden increased from 5.2 per cent of GDP in 2019 to 5.6 per cent in 2020. By the end of 2020, there were concerns about the financial viability of the Momentum Plan.[99]

Turkey's military expenditure decreased in 2020 by 5.0 per cent, to $17.7 billion. The fall was an exception in a decade marked by a continued upward trend, with growth of 77 per cent between 2011 and 2020. Growth became steeper from 2015, coinciding with an increasingly assertive Turkish foreign policy.[100] In the years that followed, Turkey engaged militarily in Syria against both Syrian Government forces and Kurdish forces, and it supported the Government of National Accord (GNA) in Libya with troops and equipment.[101] Turkey also fought Kurdish groups in northern Iraq in 2019 and 2020. More recently, it held joint military exercises with Azerbaijani armed forces and gave political backing to Azerbaijan in the 2020 conflict with Armenia over Nagorno-Karabakh.[102]

Iran's military spending fell by 3.0 per cent in 2020, to $15.8 billion. This continued a downward trend that started in 2018, when the USA reinstated economic sanctions over Iran's nuclear activities.[103] Between 2018 and 2020, Iranian military spending dropped by more than 20 per cent. In contrast to the 3.0 per cent fall in Iran's military spending, the budget of the Islamic Revolutionary Guard Corps increased by 19 per cent in 2020. This corresponded to 34 per cent of Iran's total military spending. The growth in the budget of the Revolutionary Guard reflects its political importance within the regime and represents an important shift in the composition of Iran's military spending.[104] It is likely that available figures are still underestimates: reports suggest that the Revolutionary Guard may receive

[98] Gross, J. A., 'Netanyahu calls for NIS 3.3 billion increase to the defense budget', *Times of Israel*, 22 July 2020.

[99] Lappin, Y., 'IDF budget uncertainty and the Momentum Plan', Perspectives Paper no. 1686, Begin–Sadat Center for Strategic Studies (BESA), 11 Aug. 2020.

[100] Pierini, M., 'Emerging from the pandemic, Turkey rolls out a more assertive foreign policy', Commentary, Carnegie Europe, 3 June 2020; and Demirdas, A., 'Sources of Turkey's current assertive foreign policy in MENA', Inside Arabia, 17 Feb. 2020.

[101] On these conflicts see chapter 6, sections I, II and IV, in this volume.

[102] Gall, C., 'Turkey jumps into another foreign conflict, this time in the Caucasus', *New York Times*, 1 Oct. 2020; and Keddie, P., 'What's Turkey's role in the Nagorno-Karabakh conflict?', Al Jazeera, 30 Oct. 2020. On the conflict in Nagorno-Karabakh see chapter 5, section II, in this volume.

[103] Marcus, J., 'Trump re-imposes Iran sanctions: Now what?', BBC News, 3 Nov. 2018; and Katzman, K., *Iran Sanctions, Congressional Research Service Report*, Congressional Research Service (CRS) Report for Congress RS20871 (US Congress, CRS: Washington, DC, 6 Apr. 2021), pp. 39–45. On Iran's nuclear activities in 2020 see chapter 11, section II, in this volume.

[104] Dagher, M., 'The Iranian Islamic Revolutionary Guard Corps (IRGC) from an Iraqi view—A lost role or a bright future?', Commentary, Center for Strategic and International Studies (CSIS), 30 July 2020.

additional funding from undeclared revenues from the various economic enterprises that it controls.[105]

Saudi Arabia's military expenditure was $57.5 billion in 2020, 10 per cent less than in 2019. In the four years leading up to Saudi Arabia's military intervention in Yemen in 2015, military spending grew by 63 per cent to reach an all-time high. Since the beginning of the conflict, however, military spending has fallen by 37 per cent, largely as a result of a plunge in oil prices. The resulting financial strain has contributed to a shift in Saudi Arabia's stance towards the conflict, making it more receptive to a political solution.[106] In 2020 Saudi Arabia opened direct peace talks with the Houthis and declared a two-week unilateral ceasefire, which was later extended to a month.[107] However, hostilities were ongoing as the year ended.

Kuwait's military expenditure decreased in 2020 for the first time since the oil price collapse in 2014, falling by 5.9 per cent. Despite this spending decrease, the country's military burden rose by 1.0 percentage points to 6.5 per cent of GDP. The increase in Kuwait's military burden came amid the most severe economic predicament since the 2009 global financial and economic crisis. The fall in oil prices as a result of the pandemic-induced decline in the demand for fuel means that the country's GDP is expected to have contracted by 7.9 per cent in 2020 and government revenue to have fallen by almost 50 per cent.[108] As a consequence, in June 2020 the Kuwaiti Government reduced the budget for the ongoing 2020/21 financial year by 20 per cent.[109]

[105] Wezeman, P. and Kuimova, A., 'Military spending and arms imports by Iran, Saudi Arabia, Qatar and the UAE', SIPRI Fact Sheet, May 2019, p. 7.

[106] Guzansky, Y. and Heistein, A., 'Saudi Arabia's war in Yemen has been a disaster', *National Interest*, 25 Mar. 2018; Allen, J. R. and Riedel, B., 'Ending the Yemen war is both a strategic and humanitarian imperative', Order from Chaos, Brookings Institution, 16 Nov. 2020; and Bazzi, M., 'The United States could end the war in Yemen if it wanted to', *The Atlantic*, 30 Sep. 2018.

[107] Hubbard, B. and Al-Batati, S., 'Saudi Arabia declares cease-fire in Yemen, citing fears of coronavirus', *New York Times*, 8 Apr. 2020. On the conflict in Yemen see chapter 6, section V, in this volume.

[108] World Bank, *Macro Poverty Outlook* (World Bank: Washington, DC, Oct. 2020), pp. 160–61; and 'Kuwait's crisis pushes government to cut spending, expand debt', Arab Weekly, 9 Sep. 2020.

[109] Arab Weekly (note 108). Kuwait's financial year starts on 1 Apr. Its military spending in the 2020 calendar year, as reported by SIPRI, thus takes 3 months from the 2019/20 budget and 9 months from the 2020/21 budget.

III. Transparency in government reporting on military expenditure in South East Asia

LUCIE BÉRAUD-SUDREAU AND DIEGO LOPES DA SILVA

Government transparency in military expenditure is a key element of good governance, adequate management and government accountability. Transparency can help to avoid excessive and wasteful spending, assuring efficient and effective use of public resources. Moreover, it is crucial for open and democratic debate about government budget priorities and for the work of the oversight institutions that are responsible for holding governments and military institutions accountable for their use of public resources.

Most countries included in the SIPRI Military Expenditure Database provide data on military spending in official government reports. In the case of South East Asia, all but two states do so. Nonetheless, information is sometimes difficult to access and the reporting in government publications varies widely in comprehensiveness, disaggregation and other aspects of transparency.

This section assesses the degree of transparency in government reporting on military expenditure in the 11 countries of South East Asia. It follows previous SIPRI studies on transparency in Africa and Latin America.[1] The section continues by elaborating on important indicators of transparency beyond data availability. It then assesses these for each of the countries of South East Asia: Brunei Darussalam, Cambodia, Indonesia, Laos, Malaysia, Myanmar, the Philippines, Singapore, Thailand, Timor-Leste and Viet Nam. It goes on to discuss whether the quality of democratic institutions plays a role in explaining differing degrees of transparency across these countries.[2]

Indicators of transparency

Five indicators in addition to availability of data can be used to assess transparency: the stages of the budgeting process at which reporting takes place, comprehensiveness, disaggregation, classification and accessibility.

There are three main stages in the budgeting process at which figures for military expenditure may change. The first is the initial budget, which is adopted prior to the start of a new financial year. The second stage is during

[1] Tian, N., Wezeman, P. and Yun, Y., *Military Expenditure Transparency in Sub-Saharan Africa*, SIPRI Policy Paper no. 48 (SIPRI: Stockholm, Nov. 2018); Bromley, M. and Solmirano, C., *Transparency in Military Expenditure and Arms Acquisition in Latin America and the Caribbean*, SIPRI Policy Paper no. 31 (SIPRI: Stockholm, Jan. 2012); and Omitoogun, W. and Hutchful, E. (eds), SIPRI, *Budgeting for the Military Sector in Africa: The Processes and Mechanism of Control* (Oxford University Press: Oxford, 2006).

[2] On developments in transparency at the international level in 2020 see chapter 13, section VI, in this volume.

the course of the year, when these figures may be revised to better adapt to current financial constraints or other unforeseen events. Finally, accounts of actual military expenditure show what has actually been spent on the military during the previous year. For the sake of transparency, governments should provide information at all stages of this process, and in particular figures on actual expenditure.[3]

The comprehensiveness of figures may differ depending on whether they reflect all the costs incurred by military activities. The existence of off-budget mechanisms is a particular problem in this regard. For example, official figures may understate overall military expenditure if off-budget mechanisms are used to fund the military.[4] Furthermore, sources of funding for the military may appear under different headings of the state budget (e.g. loans and ad hoc allocations), making them difficult to identify.

Total military expenditure can be disaggregated into various budget categories. Most commonly these categories are personnel, operations and maintenance, procurement, construction, and research and development. Aggregate estimates of military spending obscure the specific uses of funds, and so omit relevant information about budgetary allocations.[5] A related issue is when broader budget categories are aggregated together, such as 'defence and security', making it impossible to ascertain how much is devoted to military activities and how much to internal security.

Expenditure can be classified either by institution or function. An institutional classification covers the expenses of the defence ministry or the analogous state institution. A functional classification identifies expenses by purpose instead of by government unit, and thus includes information related to military expenditure outside the institutional scope of the defence ministry.[6] Preferably, both types of classification should be given.

Finally, accessibility is an important aspect of transparency in military expenditure. Public provision of budgets and related documents in a single official platform, with a user-friendly and easy to navigate interface, significantly improves access to information. Ease of access facilitates oversight of the management of military spending and also disseminates information on military spending to a wider audience, both nationally and internationally.

---

[3] Organisation for Economic Co-operation and Development (OECD), *Budget Transparency Toolkit: Practical Steps to Support Openness, Integrity and Accountability in Public Financial Management* (OECD: Paris, 2019).

[4] Perlo-Freeman, S., 'Transparency and accountability in military expenditure', SIPRI Commentary, 3 Aug. 2016; Tian, N. and Lopes da Silva, D., 'Improving South American military expenditure data', SIPRI Topical Backgrounder, 4 Sep. 2017; and Lopes da Silva, D. and Tian, N., 'Ending off-budget military funding: Lessons from Chile', SIPRI Topical Backgrounder, 16 Dec. 2019.

[5] Omitoogun and Hutchful, eds (note 1).

[6] International Monetary Fund (IMF), *Government Finance Statistics Manual 2014* (IMF: Washington, DC, 2014), pp. 4, 19.

Assessing transparency in South East Asia

Based on a combined assessment of the five criteria for transparency in government reporting, South East Asian countries can be grouped according to their degrees of transparency in military expenditure: limited to no transparency; partial transparency; and transparent (see table 8.6, below).

Three countries have limited to no transparency: Brunei Darussalam, Laos and Viet Nam. Brunei Darussalam presents a 'briefing' with a proposed budget for the Ministry of Defence (MOD), but it does not always provide any spending figures. Some Bruneian media outlets report the briefing with an overall budget figure for the MOD. Moreover, it is unclear whether the Gurkha Reserve Unit, a special elite guard force, is included in the MOD budget. The Laotian Ministry of Finance provides a state budget document, but it does not include any figures for military expenditure. Similarly, Viet Nam's state budget does not give information broken down by either ministry or function.[7] The Vietnamese Government released limited information on its military expenditure in a footnote in its 2019 Defence White Paper.[8] This was expressed as a share of gross domestic product (GDP), but only for the years 2010–18 and with no indication as to which data was used for the GDP figures.

Three countries have partial transparency: Cambodia, Myanmar and Singapore. All three provide relatively easily accessible information on military expenditure on official websites. However, the reliability of the data is questionable, and the level of detail remains fairly limited. In Cambodia, there are indications that some arms deals have been partially financed with off-budget funds. For example, the US$20 million used for the acquisition of military vehicles from China in 2020 was, according to the Prime Minister, Hun Sen, from private donations.[9] In Myanmar, off-budget funding for the military is well documented.[10] Singapore provides a formal but limited breakdown of its military expenditure. The category 'operating expenditure' accounts for 96 per cent of the total. Without further disaggregation, it is not possible to determine how much Singapore spends on, for example, arms procurement.

---

[7] Vietnamese Ministry of Finance, 'Ngân sách Nhà nước: Công khai theo quy định của Luật NSNN' [State budget: Disclosure according to the State Budget Law], [n.d.].

[8] Vietnamese Ministry of National Defence, *2019 Viet Nam National Defence* (National Political Publishing House: Hanoi, Oct. 2019), p. 38.

[9] Hutt, D., 'Who actually funds the Cambodian military?', Asia Times, 23 June 2020. See also Sokhean, B., 'Very successful drive: PM held fundraiser to buy Chinese military trucks', *Khmer Times*, 19 June 2020.

[10] Wezeman, P. D. and Wezeman, S. T., 'Transparency in military expenditure', *SIPRI Yearbook 2020*, pp. 267–70; and United Nations, General Assembly, Human Rights Council, Independent International Fact-Finding Mission on Myanmar, 'The economic interests of the Myanmar military', 5 Aug. 2019, A/HRC/42/CRP.3.

Five countries in South East Asia can be classified as transparent: Indonesia, Malaysia, Philippines, Thailand and Timor-Leste. These states all provide easy-to-access and comprehensive data, including detailed disaggregation of spending by either category or programme. Some publish a 'people's budget' or 'citizen's budget', with information on public spending accessible for the layperson. For example, the Philippines and Timor-Leste provide such documents in the several languages spoken in the country, contributing to wider public access.[11]

Explaining the different degrees of transparency in government reporting: Democratic accountability

A possible factor influencing the different degrees of transparency is the quality of democratic institutions.[12] Democracies have mechanisms for political accountability that largely rely on transparency for their effectiveness. Constituents, state institutions such as the legislature and judiciary, and public audit offices need information to hold the executive accountable for its management of resources.[13] The secrecy that often surrounds military expenditure under the label 'national security' creates an environment particularly conducive to corruption.[14] A strong system of checks and balances can help to prevent this. In many countries, the defence minister is required to present a report to the legislature detailing military expenditure. Another form of accountability is the need for the legislature to approve allocations to the military, thereby limiting the discretionary powers of the executive.

This seems to be true in the South East Asian case. The most transparent countries are also among those that rank highest in terms of the quality of their democratic institutions, with the exception of Thailand. Viet Nam, Laos, Cambodia and Brunei Darussalam, which rank the lowest in the subregion, are also among the least transparent when it comes to military expenditure.[15] Singapore's partially transparent military expenditure also

---

[11] E.g. Timor-Leste makes budget and execution documents available through the Timor-Leste Budget Transparency Portal in English, <http://budgettransparency.gov.tl/public/index?&lang=en>, Portuguese, <http://budgettransparency.gov.tl/public/index?&lang=pt>, and Tetum, <http://budgettransparency.gov.tl/public/index?&lang=tl>. While Myanmar also publishes a citizen's budget, its off-budget mechanisms mean that its official figure is likely to be understated.

[12] Hollyer, J. R., Rosendorff, B. P. and Vreeland, J. R., 'Democracy and transparency', *Journal of Politics*, vol. 73, no. 4 (Oct. 2011); Wezeman and Wezeman (note 10), p. 267; and Gurría, A., OECD Secretary-General, 'Openness and transparency—Pillars for democracy, trust and progress', Organisation for Economic Co-operation and Development (OECD), 20 Sep. 2011.

[13] O'Donnell, G. A., 'Horizontal accountability in new democracies', *Journal of Democracy*, vol. 9, no. 3 (July 1998); and Przeworski, A., Stokes, S. C. and Manin, B., *Democracy, Accountability, and Representation* (Cambridge University Press: Cambridge, 1999).

[14] Perlo-Freeman (note 4).

[15] Varieties of Democracy (V-Dem), *Autocratization Surges—Resistance Grows: Democracy Report 2020* (University of Gothenburg, V-Dem Institute: Gothenburg, Mar. 2020).

aligns with what has been called a 'carefully managed democracy', where freedom of expression and political participation are limited.[16]

Thailand is transparent but ranks poorly as a democracy. In this particular case, another explanation could play a role: the nature of the bureaucracy within the state. The Thai Budget Bureau, which is responsible for the budgetary process and reporting, has been described as a powerful institution, capable in the past of resisting strong political pressure.[17] It describes its mission as 'allocating a limited national budget in the best interests of the people and the nation' and 'ensuring that the expenditure of the national budget is as efficient as possible so that it will not be leaked or wasted'.[18] This indicates the institution's attachment to transparency and accountability, and it seems to have been capable of preserving high levels of transparency under military rule between 2014 and 2019 and the military-led government in place since 2019.

Conclusions

This survey shows that transparency in government reporting in South East Asia is fairly good, with 9 of the 11 states providing official information on their military expenditure. There is still room for progress, in particular in those states where off-budget mechanisms are thought to persist. Eight of the states grant access to budgetary information—either partially or fully disaggregated—to their citizens via easy to navigate government websites. The most transparent countries were also those with better democratic institutions. This suggests that mechanisms of political accountability may be associated with transparency in government reporting on military expenditure.

The classification of countries according to their different degrees of transparency was primarily based on scrutiny of official government reports. Figures were deemed to be comprehensive if there was no evident reason to think otherwise. However, other sources of funding, unaccounted for in official reports, could be revealed by a more in-depth analysis. Future research should expand the scope of sources to better qualify the comprehensiveness of official figures. Notwithstanding this shortcoming, the classification provided here is able to identify significant differences in transparency across South East Asia and to indicate future avenues of research.

---

[16] Han, K., 'Opposition victories force a crack in Singapore's carefully managed democracy', *Foreign Policy*, 14 July 2020; and Freedom House, 'Freedom in the World 2020: Singapore', 2020.

[17] Pungprawat, K., 'Thaksin and budget allocation: A study in political compromise', *Asian and African Area Studies*, vol. 11, no. 2 (Mar. 2012); and Dixon, G., 'Thailand's hurdle approach to budget reform', PREM Notes no. 73, World Bank, Aug. 2002.

[18] Thai Budget Bureau, [History and background], 25 Oct. 2017 (in Thai, author translation).

Table 8.6. Transparency in government reporting on military expenditure in South East Asia, 2020

Country	Military expenditure, 2020 (US$ m.)	LDI rank[a]	Indicators of transparency					Overall degree of transparency
			Budgeting stage of reporting	Comprehensiveness[b]	Disaggregation	Classification	Accessibility	
Brunei Darussalam	437	..	Budget	Uncertain	No disaggregation	Institutional	Limited	Limited to no transparency
Cambodia	647	161	Budget	Off-budget undisclosed	Limited disaggregation	Institutional	Good access, easy-to-navigate website	Partial transparency
Indonesia	9 396	65	Budget; revised; actual	Comprehensive	Detailed disaggregation by programme	Institutional and functional	Good access, easy-to-navigate website	Transparent
Laos	..	157	..	..	..	..	..	Limited to no transparency
Malaysia	3 808	98	Budget; revised; actual	Comprehensive	Detailed disaggregation by programme	Institutional and functional	Good access, easy-to-navigate website	Transparent
Myanmar	2 446	119	Budget; revised	Off-budget undisclosed	Limited disaggregation	Institutional	Good access, easy-to-navigate website	Partial transparency
Philippines	3 733	110	Budget; revised; actual	Comprehensive	Detailed disaggregation by programme	Institutional and functional	Good access, easy-to-navigate website	Transparent
Singapore	10 856	92	Budget; revised; actual	Comprehensive	Limited disaggregation	Institutional	Good access, easy-to-navigate website	Partial transparency
Thailand	7 340	139	Budget	Comprehensive	Detailed disaggregation by service and category	Institutional and functional	Good access, easy-to-navigate website	Transparent
Timor-Leste	38.5	58	Budget	Comprehensive	Detailed disaggregation by programme	Institutional and functional	Good access, easy-to-navigate website	Transparent
Viet Nam	..	146	..	..	..	..	..	Limited to no transparency

. . = unknown value or not applicable; LDI = Liberal Democracy Index.

[a] The V-Dem Institute's LDI measures the extent to which the ideal of liberal democracy has been achieved. According to V-Dem, 'the liberal principle of democracy embodies the importance of protecting individual and minority rights against both the tyranny of the state and the tyranny of the majority. . . . This is achieved by strong rule of law and constitutionally protected civil liberties, independent judiciary and strong parliament that are able to hold the executive to account and limit its power'. See Varieties of Democracy (V-Dem), *Autocratization Surges—Resistance Grows: Democracy Report 2020* (University of Gothenburg, V-Dem Institute: Gothenburg, Mar. 2020), p. 34.

[b] Figures are deemed comprehensive if there is no evident reason to think otherwise.

Sources: Official budget documentation; SIPRI Military Expenditure Database, Apr. 2021; and Varieties of Democracy (note a), table 4, pp. 30–31.

9. International arms transfers and developments in arms production

Overview

The volume of international transfers of major arms in 2016–20 was at almost the same level as in 2011–15 and remained at its highest level since the end of the cold war (see section I). However, the volume of transfers in 2016–20 was still 35 per cent lower than the peak reached in 1981–85, at the height of the cold war. Overall, the Covid-19 pandemic of 2020 and the resulting economic crisis appeared to have little effect on arms deliveries in 2020 or on new orders for major arms during the year.

The five largest suppliers in 2016–20—the United States, Russia, France, Germany and China—accounted for 76 per cent of the total volume of exports of major arms (see section II). Since 1950, the USA and Russia (or the Soviet Union before 1992) have consistently been by far the largest suppliers. In 2016–20 US arms exports accounted for 37 per cent of the global total and were 15 per cent higher than in 2011–15. In contrast, Russia's arms exports decreased by 22 per cent and its share of the global total dropped from 26 per cent in 2011–15 to 20 per cent in 2016–20. Arms exports by France (up by 44 per cent) and Germany (up by 21 per cent) grew between 2011–15 and 2016–20, while China's fell by 7.8 per cent. Many of the 65 states identified by SIPRI as exporters of major arms in 2016–20 supply only small volumes of arms. The top 25 arms-supplying states accounted for 99 per cent of total global arms exports. States in North America and Europe (including Russia) accounted for 86 per cent of all arms exports.

SIPRI identified 164 states as importers of major arms in 2016–20. The five largest arms importers were Saudi Arabia, India, Egypt, Australia and China, which together accounted for 36 per cent of total arms imports (see section III). The region that received the largest volume of major arms in 2016–20 was Asia and Oceania, accounting for 42 per cent of the global total, followed by the Middle East, which received 33 per cent. The flow of arms to two regions increased between 2011–15 and 2016–20: the Middle East (by 25 per cent) and Europe (by 12 per cent). Meanwhile, flows to the other three regions decreased: Africa (by 13 per cent), the Americas (by 43 per cent) and Asia and Oceania (by 8.3 per cent).

While SIPRI data on arms transfers does not represent their financial value, many arms-exporting states do publish figures on the financial value of their arms exports (see section IV). Based on this data, SIPRI estimates that the total value of the global arms trade was at least $118 billion in 2019 (the most recent year for which data is available).

In addition to presenting data and analysis of international arms transfers, this chapter provides information on the global arms industry (see section V). The arms sales of the world's 25 largest arms-producing and military services companies totalled $361 billion in 2019 (the most recent year for which data is available)—an increase of 8.5 per cent compared with 2018. The 2019 SIPRI ranking is the first to include data for some Chinese arms companies. The top 25 arms companies in 2019 are concentrated in North America (12 companies) and Europe (8 companies) but the ranking also includes 4 Chinese companies and 1 from the United Arab Emirates. The top five companies are all based in the USA.

For the first time, SIPRI has mapped the international presence of the arms industry, focusing on the 15 largest arms companies in 2019. The data set is made up of 400 foreign entities, defined as branches, subsidiaries and joint ventures registered in a country other than that in which the parent company is headquartered. Taking account of these foreign entities, the reach of the world's 15 largest arms companies extends across at least 49 different countries.

SIEMON T. WEZEMAN

I. Developments in arms transfers, 2016–20

SIEMON T. WEZEMAN, ALEXANDRA KUIMOVA AND PIETER D. WEZEMAN

The volume of international transfers of major arms in 2016–20 was at almost the same level as in 2011–15 (see box 9.1).[1] This meant that the volume remained at its highest level since 1989–93, the period during which the cold war ended. The volume of transfers in 2016–20 was 12 per cent higher than in 2006–10 and 42 per cent higher than in 2001–2005, but was still 35 per cent lower than the peak reached in 1981–85, at the height of the cold war (see figure 9.1).[2]

The five largest exporters of major arms in 2016–20 were the United States, Russia, France, Germany and China (see section II). The five largest importers were Saudi Arabia, India, Egypt, Australia and China (see section III).

The region that received the largest volume of imports of major arms in 2016–20 was Asia and Oceania, accounting for 42 per cent of the global total.[3] However, arms imports by states in Asia and Oceania fell by 8.3 per cent between 2011–15 and 2016–20. Arms imports by states in Africa (–13 per cent) and the Americas (–43 per cent) also fell and their shares of the global total decreased between the two periods. In contrast, the flow of arms to states in the Middle East increased by 25 per cent and the region's share of the global total rose from 26 per cent to 33 per cent. This is a higher share than in any of the seven consecutive five-year periods since 1981–85. Arms imports by states in Europe increased by 12 per cent between 2011–15 and 2016–20, and the region accounted for 12 per cent of the global total.

The Covid-19 pandemic and international arms transfers

Since there can be significant year-on-year fluctuations in deliveries of major arms, SIPRI usually compares consecutive multi-year periods— normally five-year periods. This provides a more stable measure of trends in transfers of major arms. However, the data is recorded by year and SIPRI also publishes information on annual volumes of deliveries (see e.g. figure 9.1). This data shows that the volume of global transfers of major

---

[1] The estimated volume for 2016–20 was 0.5% lower than for 2011–15, but as data on deliveries of major arms is not exact, the difference between the periods is not significant enough to draw conclusions of change.

[2] Except where indicated, the information on the arms deliveries and orders referred to in this section is taken from the SIPRI Arms Transfers Database. For a definition of 'major arms' and a description of how the volume of transfers is measured see box 9.1. The figures here may differ from those in previous editions of the SIPRI Yearbook because the Arms Transfers Database is updated annually.

[3] On SIPRI's regional coverage see the list of conventions in this volume and the SIPRI website.

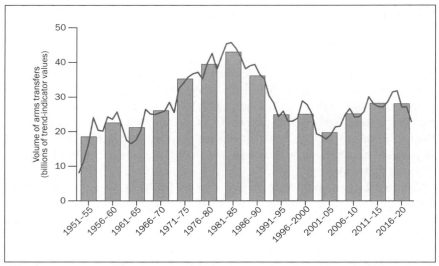

Figure 9.1. The trend in international transfers of major arms, 1950–2020

Note: The bar graph shows the average volume of arms transfers for 5-year periods and the line graph shows the annual totals. See box 9.1 for an explanation of the SIPRI trend-indicator value.

Source: SIPRI Arms Transfers Database, Mar. 2021.

arms in 2020 was exceptionally low—16 per cent lower than in 2019 and 20 per cent below the annual average in 2011–19—and therefore deserves some further discussion.

The drop in arms transfers in 2020 might be partly due to the disruption to arms suppliers' planned production and delivery schedules arising from the Covid-19 pandemic. Many arms-supplying states implemented measures to deal with the impact of the pandemic on the global economy. Some arms-supplying states and arms-producing companies were more negatively affected by the pandemic than others; however, in most cases the effects appeared to be only temporary and, by the end of 2020, most suppliers had managed to mitigate the worst of the disruption caused by the pandemic. The examples below from the three largest arms-supplying states—the USA, Russia and France—show the variation in impact.

In the USA, Lockheed Martin, the world's largest arms-producing company (see section V), announced that, out of a planned total of 141, it had delivered only 120 F-35 combat aircraft to the USA and international customers in 2020.[4] Nonetheless, the company delivered 52 F-35s for export in 2020, compared with 47 in 2019. Some other major US arms-production

---

[4] Jennings, G., 'Update: Lockheed Martin reports reduced F-35 deliveries for 2020 due to Covid-19', *Jane's Defence Weekly*, 3 Feb. 2021.

programmes experienced delays at the start of the pandemic, but most appeared to be back on schedule by the end of 2020, and it seems that major arms export programmes were barely affected.[5] Similarly, the French company Dassault Aviation Group was able to fulfil the planned delivery of 13 Rafale combat aircraft to export customers in 2020, despite some temporary pandemic-induced delays in April that year.[6] In contrast, the disruption to some Russian arms companies' delivery schedules caused by the pandemic appeared to be more significant. According to Russian Deputy Defence Minister Alexander Fomin, in 2020 Russia postponed the delivery of weapon systems to a number of foreign customers due to 'the impossibility of accepting foreign specialists for pre-shipment inspections in Russia and sending Russian representatives to deliver and service military products in the customers' territories'.[7] This seems to have included deliveries of arms to several of Russia's largest arms trade partners, including Algeria, Egypt and India.

While the pandemic-induced global economic crisis may have disrupted some planned arms-production and delivery schedules, it appears to have had a minimal impact during 2020 on future international arms transfers. According to publicly available sources, no major arms export contracts were cancelled or significantly cut in 2020 in response to the economic downturn—although it is possible that in some cases information about such decisions remains outside the public domain. Conversely, many states maintained their pre-pandemic arms-procurement planning and signed new large arms-import contracts in 2020, despite the economic impact of the pandemic. For example, Germany decided on a plan to buy 45 F/A-18E and F/A-18G combat aircraft; Australia started final negotiations for 29 AH-64E combat helicopters; Brazil ordered 4 MEKO-A100 frigates; Egypt ordered 43 AH-64Es and 2 FREMM frigates (of which the first was delivered in 2020); Japan ordered 105 F-35 combat aircraft; Morocco ordered 24 F-16V combat aircraft and 24 AH-64Es; and Poland ordered 32 F-35s.

This suggests that, in general terms, rather than being directly influenced by the pandemic, the overall drop in arms transfers in 2020 may have been related to other supply- and demand-side factors. For example, shifts in national armament procurement cycles are normal and the drop in 2020 could simply reflect this. Other factors could include gaps between deliveries of arms resulting from changes in the relations between suppliers and recipients, and non-pandemic-related economic conditions such as pre-pandemic low oil prices that have led to reductions in income for oil-

---

[5] Metha, A. and Insinna, V., 'Chaos, cash and Covid-19: How the defense industry survived—and thrived—during the pandemic', *Defense News*, 15 Mar. 2021.

[6] Dassault Aviation Group, *2020 Short Form Annual Financial Report* (Dassault Aviation Group: Paris, 4 Mar. 2021), p. 13.

[7] Stepanov, A., [The Red Sea under the keel], *Rossiyskaya Gazeta*, 27 Dec. 2020 (in Russian).

Box 9.1. Definitions and methodology for SIPRI data on international arms transfers

The SIPRI Arms Transfers Database contains information on deliveries of major arms to states, international organizations and non-state armed (i.e. rebel) groups from 1950 to 2020. A new set of data is published annually, replacing the data in earlier editions of the SIPRI Yearbook or other SIPRI publications.

Definitions

SIPRI's definition of 'transfer' includes direct sales, licences for production in the recipient state, aid, gifts, and most loans or leases. The recipient must be the armed forces or paramilitary forces or intelligence agency of another state, a non-state armed group, or an international organization, which use the equipment for military purposes.

The SIPRI Arms Transfers Database only includes 'major arms', which are defined as (*a*) most aircraft, including unmanned aerial vehicles; (*b*) air defence missile systems and larger air defence guns; (*c*) air refuelling systems; (*d*) most armoured vehicles; (*e*) artillery over 100 millimetres in calibre; (*f*) engines for combat-capable aircraft and other larger aircraft, for combat ships and larger support ships, and for armoured vehicles; (*g*) guided munitions (missiles, torpedoes, bombs and shells); (*h*) sensors (radars, sonars and many passive electronic sensors); (*i*) most ships; (*j*) ship-borne weapons (naval guns, missile launch systems and anti-submarine weapons); (*k*) reconnaissance satellites; and (*l*) most gun or missile-armed turrets for armoured vehicles.

In cases where an air refuelling system, engine, sensor, naval gun or other ship-borne system, or turret (items c, f, h, j and l) is fitted on a platform (vehicle, aircraft or ship), the transfer only appears as a separate entry in the database if the item comes from a different supplier from that of the platform.

The SIPRI trend-indicator value

SIPRI has developed a unique system for measuring the volume of transfers of major arms using a common unit, the trend-indicator value (TIV). The TIV is intended to represent the transfer of military resources. Each weapon has its own specific TIV. Second-hand and second-hand but significantly modernized arms are given a reduced TIV. SIPRI calculates the volume of transfers by multiplying the weapon-specific TIV with the number of arms delivered in a given year. SIPRI TIV figures do not represent the financial values of arms transfers.

---

producing states, some of which have been among the largest importers of major arms in recent years.

The uncertainty about the extent to which the pandemic was a cause for the fall in arms transfers in 2020 is also highlighted by the fact that several arms-supplying states that were hit hard by the pandemic had higher levels of arms deliveries in 2020 than in some other years in the period 2011–19. For example, US arms exports were at a higher level in 2020 than in three years in 2011–19 and French arms exports were at a higher level than in five years in that period. Some arms-importing states showed a similar trend. For instance, Australia's volume of arms deliveries in 2020 was higher than in any year in 2011–19.

II. Developments among the suppliers of major arms, 2016–20

SIEMON T. WEZEMAN, ALEXANDRA KUIMOVA AND PIETER D. WEZEMAN

SIPRI has identified 65 states as exporters of major arms in the five-year period 2016–20.[1] The five largest suppliers of arms during that period— the United States, Russia, France, Germany and China—accounted for 76 per cent of all arms exports (see table 9.1). This is slightly higher than in 2011–15 and 2006–10, when the top five accounted for 73 per cent of the global total. France had the highest increase in arms exports among the top five. US and German arms exports also grew, while Russian and Chinese arms exports decreased. The composition of the top five changed between 2011–15 and 2016–20, with Germany replacing the United Kingdom.

The top 25 arms exporters accounted for 99 per cent of global exports of major arms in 2016–20. Of these 25 states, a total of 16 are in Europe and North America, 4 are in Asia and Oceania, 3 are in the Middle East, 1 is in Africa and 1 is in South America (see table 9.1). European and North American (i.e. Canada and the USA) states together accounted for 86 per cent of all arms exports. This concentration of suppliers in the Euro-Atlantic region has been a feature of the entire period covered by the SIPRI Arms Transfers Database (1950–2020). Most of the states listed in the top 25 for 2016–20 have also appeared in this list in previous periods, and there have been very few changes in the top 10 over the years. However, the Republic of Korea (South Korea), which entered the top 10 for the first time in 2015–19, remained in this group in 2016–20 and moved up one place in the ranking to become the 9th largest arms exporter in the world.

This section reviews the arms exports and arms export policies of the world's main arms suppliers in 2016–20. It starts with the two largest suppliers, the USA and Russia, which have dominated the international supply of major arms for decades. Taken together, arms exports by the USA and Russia (including exports by the Soviet Union before 1992) have accounted for more than 50 per cent of the global total for any five-year period since 1950. The section then looks at the arms supplies of members of the European Union (EU), in particular the three largest EU exporters—

---

[1] Except where indicated, the information on the arms deliveries and orders referred to in this section is taken from the SIPRI Arms Transfers Database. For a definition of 'major arms' and a description of how the volume of transfers is measured see box 9.1 in section I. The figures here may differ from those in previous editions of the SIPRI Yearbook because the Arms Transfers Database is updated annually.

Table 9.1. The 40 largest suppliers of major arms and their main recipients, 2016–20

Rank		Exporter[b]	Share of total global exports (%)		Change in volume (%) from 2011–15 to 2016–20	Main recipients (share of exporter's total exports, %), 2016–20		
2016–20	2011–15[a]		2011–15	2016–20		1st	2nd	3rd
1	1	United States	32	37	15	Saudi Arabia (24)	Australia (9.4)	South Korea (6.7)
2	2	Russia	26	20	-22	India (23)	China (18)	Algeria (15)
3	3	France	5.6	8.2	44	India (21)	Egypt (20)	Qatar (18)
4	6	Germany	4.5	5.5	21	South Korea (24)	Algeria (10)	Egypt (8.7)
5	4	China	5.6	5.2	-7.8	Pakistan (38)	Bangladesh (17)	Algeria (8.2)
6	5	United Kingdom	4.6	3.3	-27	Saudi Arabia (32)	Oman (17)	United States (14)
7	7	Spain	3.5	3.2	-8.4	Australia (33)	Singapore (13)	Turkey (9.7)
8	11	Israel	1.9	3.0	59	India (43)	Azerbaijan (17)	Viet Nam (12)
9	15	South Korea	0.9	2.7	210	United Kingdom (14)	Philippines (12)	Thailand (11)
10	8	Italy	2.8	2.2	-22	Turkey (18)	Egypt (17)	Pakistan (7.2)
11	10	Netherlands	2.0	1.9	-6.1	Indonesia (17)	United States (15)	Mexico (10)
12	9	Ukraine	2.6	0.9	-68	China (36)	Russia[c] (20)	Thailand (17)
13	17	Turkey	0.6	0.7	30	Oman (19)	Turkmenistan (19)	Malaysia (11)
14	13	Switzerland	1.1	0.7	-35	Australia (23)	China (13)	Denmark (8.0)
15	12	Sweden	1.5	0.7	-54	United States (25)	Pakistan (11)	Algeria (11)
16	20	Australia	0.3	0.5	81	Chile (31)	United States (27)	Canada (20)
17	14	Canada	0.9	0.5	-45	Saudi Arabia (49)	UAE (17)	Australia (5.0)
18	21	UAE	0.3	0.5	68	Egypt (34)	Jordan (21)	Algeria (14)
19	18	Belarus	0.5	0.3	-34	Viet Nam (26)	Serbia (16)	Sudan (13)
20	29	Brazil	0.1	0.3	147	Afghanistan (26)	France (21)	Chile (10)
21	16	Norway	0.6	0.3	-50	Oman (47)	United States (17)	Poland (13)
22	19	South Africa	0.3	0.3	-16	United States (24)	UAE (17)	India (13)
23	24	Czechia	0.2	0.3	56	Iraq (29)	United States (17)	Ukraine (14)
24	35	India	0.1	0.2	228	Myanmar (52)	Sri Lanka (24)	Mauritius (13)
25	43	Portugal	<0.05	0.2	1 020	Romania (98)	Cabo Verde (1.1)	Colombia (1.1)

26	28	Jordan	0.1	0.2	18	United States (46)	Egypt (35)	Armenia (9.6)
27	53	Indonesia	<0.05	0.1	5 025	Philippines (88)	Nepal (4.4)	Senegal (4.4)
28	22	Finland	0.3	0.1	–54	Poland (46)	United Kingdom (17)	Egypt (11)
29	26	Belgium	0.2	0.1	–30	Saudi Arabia (66)	Indonesia (28)	France (3.3)
30	37	Serbia	0.1	0.1	65	Cyprus (32)	Bangladesh (31)	Saudi Arabia (16)
31	33	Bulgaria	0.1	0.1	–2.5	Iraq (52)	Côte d'Ivoire (15)	Saudi Arabia (14)
32	34	Denmark	0.1	0.1	–30	Portugal (40)	Malaysia (22)	France/Lithuania (9.9)
33	23	Uzbekistan	0.2	<0.05	–72	China (100)	..	..
34	27	Poland	0.1	<0.05	–68	Ukraine (30)	Lithuania (11)	Germany/Nepal (9.4)
35	..	Lithuania	–	<0.05	..	Angola (100)	..	..
36	32	Austria	0.1	<0.05	–58	Latvia (42)	Portugal (21)	Czechia (11)
37	47	Slovakia	<0.05	<0.05	253	Azerbaijan (45)	Senegal (19)	Cameroon (13)
38	31	Singapore	0.1	<0.05	–67	Oman (96)	UAE (4.2)	..
39	..	Greece	–	<0.05	..	Canada (64)	Egypt (36)	..
40	30	Iran	0.1	<0.05	–86	Houthi rebels[d] (80)	Syria (20)	..

.. = data not available or not applicable; – = no deliveries; <0.05 = between 0 and 0.05; UAE = United Arab Emirates.

Note: Percentages below 10 are rounded to 1 decimal place; percentages over 10 are rounded to whole numbers.

[a] The rank order for suppliers in 2011–15 differs from that published in SIPRI Yearbook 2016 because of subsequent revision of figures for these years.
[b] The table lists states, international organizations and non-state armed (i.e. rebel) groups that exported major arms in the 5-year period 2016–20.
[c] This involved transport aircraft produced in Russia until 2018 under licences granted before Ukraine banned arms sales to Russia in 2014.
[d] The Houthi rebels are based in Yemen.

Source: SIPRI Arms Transfers Database, Mar. 2021.

Table 9.2. The 10 largest suppliers of major arms and their recipients, by region, 2016–20

Figures are the percentage shares of the supplier's total volume of exports of major arms delivered to each recipient region in 2016–20.

Recipient region	Supplier									
	USA	Russia	France	Germany	China	UK	Spain	Israel	South Korea	Italy
Africa	2.7	18	4.0	9.6	16	1.0	0.9	1.4	0.2	9.5
Americas	2.6	0.4	6.4	8.2	1.1	18	6.8	11	8.1	6.0
Asia and Oceania	32	55	36	38	76	24	63	63	55	19
Europe	15	5.5	5.3	21	0.4	7.5	4.5	24	23	12
Middle East	47	21	48	23	7.0	50	18	–	14	54

– = no deliveries.

Notes: Figures may not add up to 100% due to the conventions of rounding and because some suppliers exported small volumes of major arms to unidentified recipients or to international organizations that cannot be linked to a particular region. Percentages below 10 are rounded to 1 decimal place; percentages over 10 are rounded to whole numbers.

Source: SIPRI Arms Transfers Database, Mar. 2021.

France, Germany and the UK.[2] It ends by looking at the three largest suppliers outside Europe and North America: China, which is by far the largest, Israel and South Korea.

The United States

The USA's arms exports grew by 15 per cent between 2011–15 and 2016–20, increasing its global share from 32 per cent to 37 per cent. The USA delivered major arms to 96 states in 2016–20, a far higher number of recipients than any other supplier. In 2016–20 the USA's total arms exports were 85 per cent higher than Russia's—the second largest exporter—compared with 24 per cent higher in 2011–15. At the end of 2020, the USA had in place numerous contracts and planned contracts for large deliveries of major arms, with deliveries scheduled from 2021 until at least the end of the decade. This means that the USA will maintain its position as the world's largest exporter of major arms for the foreseeable future.

Almost half of US exports of major arms in 2016–20 went to states in the Middle East (see below and table 9.2). The next highest recipient region was Asia and Oceania. States in Asia and Oceania received 32 per cent of total US arms exports in 2016–20, compared with 34 per cent in 2011–15. Amid the intensifying rivalry between the USA and China, three US allies in the region were among the five largest importers of US arms in 2016–20:

[2] The UK left the EU on 31 Jan. 2020 and the EU's single market and customs union on 31 Dec. 2020. The UK is included in SIPRI's arms transfers data for the EU for 2016–20.

Table 9.3. Deliveries by arms category by the 10 largest suppliers of major arms, 2016–20

Figures are the percentage share of each category of major arms in the exports of the 10 largest suppliers in 2016–20.

Arms category	Supplier										
	USA	Russia	France	Germany	China	UK	Spain	Israel	South Korea	Italy	World[a]
Aircraft	58	49	45	11	30	52	61	3.4	22	47	45
Air defence systems	4.3	7.0	2.2	–	9.9	1.1	–	24	–	–	4.9
Armoured vehicles	12	10	3.3	15	16	0.3	1.4	0.7	1.1	6.5	10
Artillery	0.3	0.2	0.9	1.9	1.8	2.6	0.7	0.9	17	2.2	1.3
Engines	3.0	13	6.0	10	–	12	–	–	–	0.0	5.8
Missiles	19	13	16	9.0	17	10	–	40	–	0.4	14
Naval weapons	0.8	0.6	0.4	–	0.2	–	–	0.4	–	3.9	0.6
Satellites	–	0.2	1.7	–	–	–	–	1.2	–	1.6	0.2
Sensors	2.6	1.2	7.2	6.4	3.2	2.3	2.9	17	–	8.9	4.1
Ships	1.2	5.6	17	46	23	6.8	34	9.8	59	26	13
Other[b]	–	0.5	0.2	–	–	13	–	3.0	–	0.5	0.8

– = no deliveries.

Notes: Figures may not add up to 100% due to the conventions of rounding. Percentages below 10 are rounded to 1 decimal place; percentages over 10 are rounded to whole numbers.

[a] 'World' is the share of each category for all suppliers globally.

[b] 'Other' includes gun turrets for armoured vehicles, and air refuelling systems. On SIPRI's categories of major arms see box 9.1 in section I.

Source: SIPRI Arms Transfers Database, Mar. 2021.

Australia accounted for 9.4 per cent of US arms exports, South Korea for 6.7 per cent and Japan for 5.7 per cent.

States in Europe received 15 per cent of total US arms exports in 2016–20. This was an increase of 79 per cent on 2011–15, which was mainly due to deliveries of combat aircraft that were ordered in 2006–12.

African states accounted for 2.7 per cent of US arms exports in 2016–20, an increase of 6.6 per cent on 2011–15. In 2016–20 Morocco was by far the largest recipient of US arms in Africa, accounting for 77 per cent of US arms exports to the region, followed by Tunisia with 11 per cent.

US arms exports to states in the Americas fell by 48 per cent between 2011–15 and 2016–20, and together these states received 2.6 per cent of US arms exports in 2016–20. Canada (39 per cent) and Mexico (29 per cent) were the main recipients of US arms exports to the Americas.

Aircraft accounted for 58 per cent of US arms exports in 2016–20 (see table 9.3). These transfers included deliveries of a total of 334 combat aircraft, including 177 F-35s.

US arms exports to the Middle East

States in the Middle East received 47 per cent of US arms exports in 2016–20, an increase of 28 per cent on the previous five-year period. There were particularly large increases in US arms exports to three countries in the region between 2011–15 and 2016–20: Israel (335 per cent), Qatar (208 per cent) and Saudi Arabia (175 per cent).

Saudi Arabia was the main recipient of US arms transfers in 2016–20, accounting for 24 per cent of US arms exports. The volume of transfers to Saudi Arabia was especially high in 2016–20 due to the delivery of the first 91 F-15SA combat aircraft, of 152 ordered in 2011. US arms exports to Saudi Arabia came under increased scrutiny from the US Congress after Saudi Arabia launched a controversial military intervention in Yemen in 2015. The US Congress also expressed concerns about the general human rights situation in Saudi Arabia. In 2016 the administration of President Barack Obama imposed restrictions on the delivery of certain major arms to Saudi Arabia, in particular guided bombs. In 2019 the administration of President Donald J. Trump removed the restrictions, despite opposition from many in the US Congress.[3] This resulted in deliveries of large numbers of Paveway guided bombs—estimated to total around 20 000—from the USA to Saudi Arabia during 2019–20.

The delivery of 27 F-35 combat aircraft was the main reason for the large increase in US arms exports to Israel between 2011–15 and 2016–20. The increase in arms exports to Qatar was largely due to the delivery of 9 Patriot surface-to-air missile (SAM) systems and 24 AH-64E combat helicopters in 2016–20, which are part of the recent major expansion of Qatar's armed forces (see section III).

There were notable decreases in US arms exports to the United Arab Emirates (UAE) and to Turkey between 2011–15 and 2016–20. US arms exports to the UAE fell by 36 per cent, making it the fifth largest recipient of US arms in 2016–20, having been the third largest in 2011–15. However, in late 2020 the USA agreed to sell 50 F-35s to the UAE after the UAE improved its relations with Israel through a normalization agreement (see section III).[4]

As part of US efforts to limit Russia's global influence, the US Congress passed the Countering America's Adversaries Through Sanctions Act (CAATSA) in 2017.[5] Among other things, the act gives the US Government

---

[3] Wezeman, S. et al., 'International arms transfers and developments in arms production', *SIPRI Yearbook 2020*, pp. 277–78.

[4] Metha, A., 'US State Dept. approves UAE's purchase of F-35 jets, MQ-9 drones', *Defense News*, 10 Nov. 2020. On the UAE's normalization agreement with Israel see chapter 6, section III, in this volume.

[5] Countering America's Adversaries Through Sanctions Act, US Public Law 115-44, signed into law 2 Aug. 2017.

the authority to deny US arms exports to countries that buy arms from Russia. The act had a considerable impact on US arms exports to Turkey—a long-term ally of the USA and member of the North Atlantic Treaty Organization (NATO)—during 2016–20. US arms exports to Turkey decreased by 81 per cent and it dropped from being the 3rd largest recipient of US arms exports in 2011–15 to the 19th largest in 2016–20. Invoking CAATSA, the USA halted deliveries of F-35 combat aircraft to Turkey in 2019 after Turkey imported S-400 SAM systems from Russia.[6] Had the USA not suspended the contract, the fall in US arms exports to Turkey would not have been as steep.

While CAATSA had a significant impact on US arms exports to Turkey in 2016–20, its influence on US arms trade relations with other importers of major arms in the Middle East remained limited. For example, in 2019 the USA cautioned Egypt that a deal with Russia for Su-35 combat aircraft could trigger sanctions under CAATSA and could be an obstacle to future US arms exports to Egypt.[7] However, although preparations for the delivery of the Su-35s continued throughout 2020, there were no public statements on the issue from the US Government that year. Moreover, the USA continued to supply arms as military aid to Egypt in 2020 and signed a major arms export agreement with the country for 43 AH-64E combat helicopters.

Russia

Russia was the second largest supplier of major arms in 2016–20. It delivered major arms to 45 states and accounted for 20 per cent of total global arms exports in the period. The volume of Russian arms exports in 2016–20 was at a similar level to 2001–2005 and 2006–10, but was 22 per cent lower than in 2011–15, when Russian arms exports peaked.[8] While Russian arms exports in 2016–18 remained at a relatively high level, they fell in both 2019 and 2020. The low volume of transfers in 2020 may be partly explained by the impact of the Covid-19 pandemic, which appears to have affected the delivery schedules for several contracts (see section I).[9] For example, media reports from May 2020 stated that it had not been possible to determine a timeline for the delivery of the first batch of Su-35 combat aircraft to Egypt due to the outbreak of the pandemic.[10] None of the at least 24 Su-35s on order had been delivered to Egypt by the end of the year.

[6] Wezeman et al. (note 3), p. 281.

[7] Sharp, J. M., *Egypt: Background and US Relations*, Congressional Research Service (CRS), Report for Congress RL33003 (US Congress, CRS: Washington, DC, 27 May 2020), pp. 11–12.

[8] Wezeman, S. T. et al., 'International arms transfers', *SIPRI Yearbook 2016*, p. 569.

[9] Stepanov, A., [The Red Sea under the keel], *Rossiyskaya Gazeta*, 27 Dec. 2020 (in Russian).

[10] [Russia started production of Su-35 for Egypt], TASS, 16 May 2020 (in Russian).

While the pandemic may have had some general impact on Russia's arms deliveries in 2020, the overall decrease in its arms exports between 2011–15 and 2016–20 was largely attributable to a 53 per cent drop in its arms exports to India. Despite this, India remained the main recipient of Russian arms in 2016–20, accounting for 23 per cent of total Russian arms exports. Although several large Russian arms deals with India, including for combat aircraft, were completed by 2020, a few remained pending. India placed new orders for a variety of Russian arms in 2019–20, including for a 10-year lease of a Project 971I (Akula class) nuclear-powered attack submarine and for 12 Su-30MK combat aircraft, planned to be produced under licence in India. The ensuing deliveries will probably lead to an increase in Russian arms exports in the coming five years.

In 2016–20 Russia continued to strengthen its arms trade relations with its strategic partners. Russia substantially increased its arms transfers to China (up by 49 per cent compared with 2011–15), Algeria (up by 49 per cent) and Egypt (up by 430 per cent), making these three countries the largest recipients of Russian arms after India. However, these large increases did not offset the fall in Russian arms exports to India.

At the regional level, states in Asia and Oceania accounted for 55 per cent of Russian arms exports in 2016–20, the Middle East for 21 per cent and Africa for 18 per cent. Between 2016–20 and 2011–15, Russian arms exports to Asia and Oceania fell (–36 per cent), while exports to the Middle East and Africa increased by 64 per cent and 23 per cent, respectively.

Aircraft accounted for 49 per cent of Russian arms exports in 2016–20 (see table 9.3). These transfers included deliveries of a total of 231 combat aircraft.

Arms suppliers in the European Union and Western Europe

The combined arms exports of EU member states accounted for 26 per cent of the global total in 2016–20, the same percentage as in 2011–15. The top five West European arms exporters—France, Germany, the UK, Spain and Italy—together accounted for 22 per cent of global arms exports in 2016–20, compared with 21 per cent in 2011–15.

France

French arms exports accounted for 8.2 per cent of the global total after increasing by 44 per cent between 2011–15 and 2016–20. At the regional level, the Middle East accounted for 48 per cent of French arms exports in 2016–20 while Asia and Oceania accounted for 36 per cent. Of the 69 states to which France delivered major arms in 2016–20, the three largest recipients—India, Egypt and Qatar—together received 59 per cent of French arms exports (see table 9.1).

Deliveries of aircraft, which included 97 combat aircraft, made up 45 per cent of French arms exports in 2016–20, while deliveries of ships accounted for 17 per cent.

Germany

German arms exports represented 5.5 per cent of the global total in 2016–20 and were 21 per cent higher than in 2011–15. Germany delivered major arms to 55 states in 2016–20. Deliveries of ships, including 11 submarines, made up 46 per cent of total German arms exports in 2016–20, while deliveries of armoured vehicles accounted for 15 per cent. Deliveries of aircraft represented 11 per cent of German arms exports in 2016–20 (see table 9.3). Germany was the only member of the top five arms exporters that did not export combat aircraft in the period.

A total of 38 per cent of German exports of major arms went to states in Asia and Oceania. South Korea received 64 per cent of German arms exports to the region in 2016–20. Deliveries to South Korea included five Type-214 submarines. States in Europe accounted for 21 per cent of German arms exports in the period.

The Middle East received 23 per cent of German arms exports in 2016–20, making it the second largest recipient of German arms transfers at the regional level. This was mainly due to the delivery of three Type-209 submarines to Egypt, which had not been a major recipient of German arms before 2016. Based on existing contracts, it seems likely that Egypt will remain among the main recipients of German arms in the coming years. At the end of 2020, planned German arms exports to Egypt included deliveries of one Type-209 submarine, four MEKO-A200 frigates and seven IRIS-T SAM systems.

Germany's exports of major arms to the Middle East have regularly caused controversy, which, in a few cases, has led to extensive export restrictions.[11] During 2020, Germany extended its suspension of exports of complete weapons to Saudi Arabia (the world's largest arms importer; see section III), which it first imposed in 2018 based on concerns about the military intervention in Yemen and the alleged involvement of the Saudi Arabian Government in the murder of the journalist Jamal Khashoggi. However, it continued to allow the export of certain components for weapons produced elsewhere for final delivery to Saudi Arabia.[12]

In 2020, in reaction to Turkey's increasingly polarizing approach to its claims on oil and gas resources in the Mediterranean, the German

---

[11] Hüllinghorst, Y. and Roll, S., 'German arms exports and the militarisation of Arab states' foreign policies', SWP Comment no. 6, Stiftung Wissenschaft und Politik (SWP), Jan. 2021; and Wezeman et al. (note 3), pp. 286–87.

[12] 'Stopp für Rüstungsexporte nach Saudi-Arabien verlängert' [Arms export stop to Saudi Arabia extended], Deutsche Welle, 10 Dec. 2020.

parliament discussed the possibility of suspending the permission given in 2009 to export six Type-214 submarines to Turkey. However, the German Government opposed the suspension, thereby allowing the delivery to go ahead as planned over the period 2022–27.[13]

The United Kingdom

The UK was the world's sixth largest arms exporter in 2016–20 and accounted for 3.3 per cent of total arms exports. British arms exports fell by 27 per cent compared with 2011–15, when they peaked due to the delivery to Saudi Arabia of the bulk of an order made in 2007 for 72 Typhoon combat aircraft. The UK exported arms to 39 countries in 2016–20 with its main recipient, Saudi Arabia, receiving 32 per cent of its arms exports in that period. Deliveries included the final batches of Typhoons from the 2007 order, the last of which was delivered in 2017.

The fall in the UK's arms exports between 2011–15 and 2016–20 was due to a sharp drop in deliveries to Saudi Arabia. In 2019–20 the long-standing arms supply relationship between the UK and Saudi Arabia came under increased pressure. In June 2019 the Court of Appeal in London ordered the British Government to re-assess past and future licences for the export of arms to Saudi Arabia. The court's decision was based on concerns that Saudi Arabia had used British-supplied weapons in violations of international humanitarian law in its military intervention in Yemen.[14] As a result, between mid 2019 and mid 2020, the British Government suspended the issuance of new licences for the export of arms to Saudi Arabia that might be used in Yemen. The temporary suspension may have had an impact on Saudi Arabia's planned acquisition of an additional 48 Typhoons, for which it signed a Memorandum of Intent in 2018 with the producer company BAE Systems. As of late 2020, the deal appeared to have stalled.[15]

Spain and Italy

In 2016–20 Spain and Italy—the two other West European states among the top 10 arms exporters—accounted for 3.2 per cent and 2.2 per cent of total

---

[13] Weiland, S., 'FDP-Außenpolitiker gegen U-Boot-Lieferungen in die Türkei' [FDP-foreign policy politician against submarine deliveries to Turkey], *Der Spiegel*, 13 Dec. 2020; and German Federal Ministry for Economic Affairs and Energy, 'Schriftliche Frage an die Bundesregierung im Monat November 2020 Frage Nr. 212' [Written question to the Federal Government in the month November 2020 Question no. 212], 20 Nov. 2020.

[14] Brooke-Holland, L. and Smith, B., *UK Arms Exports to Saudi Arabia: Q&A*, Briefing Paper no. 08425 (House of Commons Library: London, 29 Jan. 2021); and Wezeman et al. (note 3), pp. 287–88.

[15] The Memorandum of Intent was mentioned in BAE Systems' half-yearly report in 2020, but was omitted from its preliminary results report for 2020. BAE Systems, 'Half-yearly report 2020', 29 July 2020, p. 31; and BAE Systems, 'Preliminary announcement 2020', 24 Feb. 2021.

arms exports respectively. Both countries' arms exports decreased between 2011–15 and 2016–20: Spain's by 8.4 per cent and Italy's by 22 per cent.

Spain's exports in 2016–20 included 13 A330 MRTT tanker aircraft and 12 A400M transport aircraft. These aircraft are produced by the trans-European company Airbus, with most of the production taking place outside Spain. The aircraft are finished in Spain and then exported under Spanish export licences. Spain's other main arms transfer in 2016–20 was the delivery of three Hobart frigates to Australia.

Deliveries of aircraft, including 48 A-129 combat helicopters to Turkey, made up the bulk of Italy's arms exports in 2016–20. It also delivered one FREMM frigate to Egypt (see section III).

Both Spain and Italy have several significant export orders with planned deliveries in the coming years. For Spain, these deliveries include 5 Avante-2200 frigates to Saudi Arabia in 2021–22; 1 BPE amphibious assault ship to Turkey in 2021; and 9 A330 MRTTs and 7 A400Ms to various states in 2021–25. Italy plans to deliver another FREMM frigate to Egypt in 2021; 4 frigates and 2 corvettes to Qatar by 2024; and 28 Typhoon combat aircraft to Kuwait in 2021–23.

Arms suppliers outside Europe and North America

Three states outside Europe and North America were among the top 10 arms exporters in 2016–20: China, Israel and South Korea. These three exporters are the focus of this subsection.

China

China was the world's fifth largest arms exporter in 2016–20 and accounted for 5.2 per cent of total arms exports. After an increase of 77 per cent between 2006–10 and 2011–15, Chinese arms exports decreased by 7.8 per cent between 2011–15 and 2016–20. China delivered major arms to 51 states in 2016–20. States in Asia and Oceania (76 per cent) and Africa (16 per cent) received most of China's arms exports in the period. Pakistan remained the main recipient of Chinese arms and accounted for 38 per cent of Chinese arms exports in 2016–20. It was followed by Bangladesh, another long-standing recipient of Chinese arms, which received 17 per cent of total Chinese arms exports in the period.

In 2016–20 China continued to seek new arms export markets in the Middle East. While some states in other regions do not import Chinese arms for political reasons, Middle Eastern states appear less likely to share such concerns. However, China has only been moderately successful in increasing arms sales to the Middle East: exports to the region grew by 71 per cent between 2011–15 and 2016–20 and the region accounted for 7.0 per cent of Chinese arms exports in 2016–20, compared with 3.8 per cent in 2011–15. Despite this increase, China accounted for only 1.1 per cent of all Middle Eastern imports of major arms in 2016–20. The most significant Chinese exports to the Middle East were armed unmanned aerial vehicles (UAVs), with an estimated total of 338 armed UAVs delivered to Egypt, Iraq, Jordan, Saudi Arabia and the UAE in 2016–20. The armed UAVs accounted for 67 per cent of all Chinese exports to the Middle East. While several other states produce armed UAVs, only China and Turkey supplied them to states in the Middle East in 2016–20.

Israel

Israel was the eighth largest arms exporter in 2016–20. Its arms exports represented 3.0 per cent of the global total and were 59 per cent higher than in 2011–15. Israel delivered major arms to 40 states in 2016–20 but its main recipient, India, accounted for 43 per cent of the total. Israel's deliveries to India in 2016–20 included air defence systems. Azerbaijan was the second largest recipient of Israeli arms exports, accounting for 17 per cent of the total (see section III).

South Korea

South Korea was the ninth largest arms exporter in 2016–20, with a 2.7 per cent share of the global total. The volume of its arms exports was 210 per cent higher in 2016–20 than in 2011–15, and 649 per cent higher than in 2001–2005. This rapid growth has mainly been the result of the increased competitiveness of the South Korean arms industry compared with those in more established arms-supplying countries.[16] In 2016–20 Asia and Oceania accounted for 55 per cent of South Korean arms exports, Europe 23 per cent and the Middle East 14 per cent.

---

[16] See also Béraud-Sudreau, L. et al., 'Emerging suppliers in the global arms trade', SIPRI Insights on Peace and Security no. 2020/13, Dec. 2020.

III. Developments among the recipients of major arms, 2016–20

SIEMON T. WEZEMAN, ALEXANDRA KUIMOVA AND PIETER D. WEZEMAN

SIPRI has identified 164 states as importers of major arms in the five-year period 2016–20.[1] The top five arms importers—Saudi Arabia, India, Egypt, Australia and China—received 36 per cent of total arms imports in 2016–20 (see table 9.4). Except for Egypt, which replaced the United Arab Emirates (UAE), the top five were the same as in 2011–15, although there were some changes in rank order. Most notably, Saudi Arabia moved above India to become the world's largest importer of major arms in 2016–20. At the regional level, Asia and Oceania accounted for 42 per cent of arms imports in 2016–20, followed by the Middle East (33 per cent), Europe (12 per cent), Africa (7.3 per cent) and the Americas (5.4 per cent; see table 9.5). This section reviews significant developments among the recipients of arms in each region.

Africa

Between 2011–15 and 2016–20, imports of major arms by African states decreased by 13 per cent. In 2016–20 the three largest arms importers in Africa were Algeria (4.3 per cent of global arms imports), Morocco (0.9 per cent) and Angola (0.5 per cent).

North Africa

The four countries in North Africa (Algeria, Libya, Morocco and Tunisia) accounted for 71 per cent of African arms imports. Their combined arms imports increased by 9.0 per cent between 2011–15 and 2016–20.

Taken together, the arms imports of regional rivals Algeria and Morocco accounted for 70 per cent of total African imports of major arms in 2016–20. Algeria's arms imports were 64 per cent higher in 2016–20 than in 2011–15, making it the sixth largest arms importer in the world. Russia remained the largest arms supplier to Algeria in 2016–20, accounting for 69 per cent of Algeria's arms imports, followed by Germany (12 per cent) and China (9.9 per cent). Russian arms deliveries to Algeria included a total of 16 MiG-29M and Su-30MK combat aircraft, 42 Mi-28N combat helicopters

---

[1] Except where indicated, the information on the arms deliveries and orders referred to in this section is taken from the SIPRI Arms Transfers Database. For a definition of 'major arms' and a description of how the volume of transfers is measured see box 9.1 in section I. The sources and methods used to produce the data discussed here are also presented on the SIPRI website. The figures here may differ from those in previous editions of the SIPRI Yearbook because the Arms Transfers Database is updated annually.

Table 9.4. The 50 largest recipients of major arms and their main suppliers, 2016–20

Rank 2016–20[a]	Rank 2011–15[a]	Importer[b]	Share of total global imports (%) 2011–15	Share of total global imports (%) 2016–20	Change in volume (%) from 2011–15 to 2016–20	Main suppliers (share of importer's total imports, %), 2016–20 1st	2nd	3rd
1	2	Saudi Arabia	7.1	11	61	United States (79)	United Kingdom (9.3)	France (4.0)
2	1	India	14	9.5	–33	Russia (49)	France (18)	Israel (13)
3	13	Egypt	2.4	5.8	136	United States (41)	France (28)	United States (8.7)
4	5	Australia	3.6	5.1	41	United States (69)	Spain (21)	Switzerland (3.4)
5	4	China	4.4	4.7	5.5	Russia (77)	France (9.7)	Ukraine (6.3)
6	11	Algeria	2.6	4.3	64	Russia (69)	Germany (12)	China (9.9)
7	10	South Korea	2.7	4.3	57	United States (58)	Germany (31)	Spain (6.5)
8	32	Qatar	0.8	3.8	361	United States (47)	France (38)	Germany (7.5)
9	3	UAE	4.7	3.0	–37	United States (64)	France (10)	Russia (4.7)
10	7	Pakistan	3.4	2.7	–23	China (74)	Russia (6.6)	Italy (5.9)
11	12	Iraq	2.5	2.5	–0.6	United States (41)	Russia (34)	South Korea (12)
12	28	Japan	1.0	2.2	124	United States (97)	United Kingdom (2.1)	Sweden (1.0)
13	9	United States	2.9	2.1	–30	United Kingdom (22)	Germany (14)	Netherlands (14)
14	20	United Kingdom	1.5	2.1	41	United States (72)	Spain (18)	Germany (4.0)
15	24	Israel	1.2	1.9	65	United States (92)	Germany (5.9)	Italy (2.3)
16	8	Viet Nam	3.0	1.8	–41	Russia (66)	Israel (19)	Belarus/South Korea (4.8)
17	18	Singapore	1.8	1.7	–9.0	United States (36)	Spain (25)	France (17)
18	15	Indonesia	2.0	1.7	–18	United States (23)	Netherlands (19)	South Korea (17)
19	34	Italy	0.7	1.5	120	United States (62)	Germany (26)	Italy (5.9)
20	6	Turkey	3.6	1.5	–59	United States (29)	Italy (27)	Spain (21)
21	35	Norway	0.7	1.3	93	United States (79)	South Korea (12)	Italy (3.3)
22	22	Bangladesh	1.3	1.2	–3.6	China (71)	Russia (16)	United Kingdom (4.1)
23	31	Thailand	0.8	1.2	44	South Korea (26)	China (22)	Ukraine (12)
24	26	Oman	1.0	1.2	12	United Kingdom (47)	United States (14)	Turkey (12)
25	21	Afghanistan	1.3	1.0	–24	United States (89)	Brazil (8.2)	Belarus (1.0)
26	40	Netherlands	0.6	1.0	52	United States (90)	Germany (6.8)	Italy (2.0)

27	42	Kazakhstan	0.6	1.0	62	Russia (89)	Spain (3.6)	China (2.4)
28	39	Jordan	0.6	0.9	38	United States (36)	Netherlands (22)	UAE (11)
29	14	Morocco	2.1	0.9	-60	United States (90)	France (9.2)	United Kingdom (0.3)
30	27	Canada	1.0	0.8	-24	United States (48)	Australia (14)	Israel (12)
31	59	Philippines	0.2	0.8	229	South Korea (42)	Indonesia (17)	United States (17)
32	19	Azerbaijan	1.6	0.7	-56	Israel (69)	Russia (17)	Belarus (4.8)
33	23	Myanmar	1.2	0.7	-40	China (48)	India (16)	Russia (15)
34	16	Taiwan	2.0	0.6	-70	United States (100)	..	..
35	36	Mexico	0.7	0.6	-14	United States (49)	Netherlands (34)	France (10)
36	38	Poland	0.6	0.6	-12	United States (33)	Italy (13)	South Korea (11)
37	29	Brazil	0.9	0.6	-38	France (23)	United States (21)	United Kingdom (20)
38	56	Belarus	0.3	0.5	93	Russia (99)	China (0.5)	..
39	87	Angola	0.1	0.5	843	Russia (64)	China (9.7)	Lithuania (8.1)
40	60	Malaysia	0.2	0.5	114	Spain (32)	Turkey (17)	South Korea (11)
41	33	Greece	0.8	0.4	-45	Germany (49)	United States (28)	France (11)
42	61	France	0.2	0.4	80	United States (43)	Brazil (17)	Switzerland (15)
43	46	Turkmenistan	0.5	0.4	-19	China (46)	Turkey (37)	Russia (6.8)
44	125	NATO[c]	<0.05	0.4	4 691	Spain (61)	United States (35)	Czechia (4.6)
45	74	Romania	0.1	0.4	249	Portugal (54)	United States (29)	Israel (9.5)
46	30	Kuwait	0.9	0.3	-61	United States (52)	France (22)	Switzerland (14)
47	37	Finland	0.7	0.3	-48	United States (41)	Netherlands (36)	Italy (10)
48	44	Chile	0.5	0.3	-37	Australia (53)	United States (14)	Germany (12)
49	70	Iran	0.1	0.3	134	Russia (100)	..	..
50	43	Spain	0.6	0.3	-48	France (74)	United States (17)	Germany (9.1)

.. = data not available or not applicable; <0.05 = between 0 and 0.05; NATO = North Atlantic Treaty Organization; UAE = United Arab Emirates.

Note: Percentages below 10 are rounded to 1 decimal place; percentages over 10 are rounded to whole numbers.

[a] The rank order for recipients in 2011–15 differs from that published in *SIPRI Yearbook 2016* because of subsequent revision of figures for these years.
[b] The table lists states, international organizations and non-state armed (i.e. rebel) groups that imported major arms in the 5-year period 2016–20.
[c] The data is for imports by the organization itself, not the total imports by NATO member states.

Source: SIPRI Arms Transfers Database, Mar. 2021.

Table 9.5. Imports of major arms, by region and subregion, 2011–15 and 2016–20

Figures for volume of imports are SIPRI trend-indicator values (TIV).

Recipient region	Volume of imports (TIV)		Change in volume from 2011–15 to 2016–20 (%)	Share of total imports (%)	
	2011–15	2016–20		2011–15	2016–20
Africa	11 810	10 295	–13	8.4	7.3
North Africa	6 995	7 628	9.0	5.0	5.4
Sub-Saharan Africa	4 809	2 661	–45	3.4	1.9
Americas	13 215	7 548	–43	9.4	5.4
Central America and the Caribbean	1 243	1 065	–14	0.9	0.8
North America	5 571	4 003	–28	4.0	2.9
South America	6 397	2 422	–62	4.5	1.7
Asia and Oceania	63 545	58 254	–8.3	45	42
Central Asia	1 618	2 242	39	1.1	1.6
East Asia	14 457	16 524	14	10	12
Oceania	5 306	7 277	37	3.8	5.2
South Asia	28 357	20 390	–28	20	15
South East Asia	13 808	11 821	–14	9.8	8.4
Europe	15 018	16 779	12	11	12
Central Europe	1 539	2 629	71	1.1	1.9
Eastern Europe	5 656	4 003	–29	4.0	2.9
Western Europe	10 126	11 582	14	7.2	8.3
Middle East	37 201	46 598	25	26	33
Other[a]	134	687	413	0.1	0.5

Notes: The SIPRI TIV is an indicator of the volume of arms transfers and not their financial value. The method for calculating the TIV is described in box 9.1 in section I. Percentages below 10 are rounded to 1 decimal place; percentages over 10 are rounded to whole numbers.

   [a] 'Other' refers to unidentified recipients or to international organizations that cannot be linked to a particular region.

Source: SIPRI Arms Transfers Database, Mar. 2021.

and 2 Project 636 submarines. Other notable deliveries to Algeria included 2 MEKO-A200 frigates from Germany and 2 C-28A frigates from China. In contrast to Algeria, which appears to have been pursuing a policy of diversifying its arms suppliers in recent years, the vast majority (90 per cent) of Morocco's arms imports in 2016–20 came from one main supplier— the United States. Arms imports by Morocco decreased by 60 per cent between 2011–15 and 2016–20, but at the end of 2020 several large planned arms deliveries to Morocco were still pending. These include deliveries of 24 F-16V combat aircraft and 24 AH-64E combat helicopters from the USA.[2]

---

   [2] US Department of State, Bureau of Political–Military Affairs, 'US arms transfers increased by 2.8 percent in FY 2020 to $175.08 billion', Fact sheet, 20 Jan. 2021; and Mebtoul, T., 'US finalizes contract on Morocco's F-16 aircraft purchase', Morocco World News, 19 Aug. 2020.

Morocco's arms imports are likely to increase significantly in the coming five years if these deliveries are implemented as planned.

Libya has two competing governments that have been embroiled in armed conflict with each other since 2014. The internationally recognized Government of National Accord (GNA) controls the western part of the country, while the self-described Libyan National Army (LNA) controls the eastern part.[3] Despite the arms embargo imposed on Libya by the United Nations Security Council in 2011, in 2016–20 both the GNA and the LNA continued to receive major arms. In 2016–20 the LNA received a total of at least 103 armoured vehicles from Jordan and the UAE as well as 2 second-hand Pantsyr-S1 mobile air defence systems from the UAE. During the same period, the GNA received an estimated 13 armoured vehicles and 12 armed unmanned aerial vehicles (UAVs) from Turkey. Turkey and the UAE, which are both generally considered to be emerging arms exporters, were the largest suppliers of major arms to Libya in 2016–20.[4] Turkey and the UAE support opposing sides in Libya and appear to be using their arms exports to the country as a tool for achieving regional influence.[5] While the exports of Turkey and the UAE to Libya represented only a small proportion of the global volume of transfers of major arms in 2016–20, they were highly significant in the context of the civil war there.[6]

Tunisia accounted for 4.3 per cent of North African arms imports. In 2016–20 Tunisia's arms imports increased by 247 per cent compared with 2011–15. The increase occurred against the backdrop of Tunisia's ongoing efforts to combat growing terrorist threats that mainly originate in or are linked to its neighbour Libya.[7] In 2016–20 the USA and the Netherlands were the largest suppliers of major arms to Tunisia, accounting for 48 per cent and 40 per cent of Tunisia's arms imports respectively. In 2016–20 the USA donated major arms to Tunisia to strengthen its border security.[8] The deliveries included 24 second-hand light combat helicopters, 12 light aircraft and 37 light armoured vehicles.

---

[3] On the armed conflict and peace process in Libya see chapter 6, section IV, in this volume.

[4] Béraud-Sudreau, L. et al., 'Emerging suppliers in the global arms trade', SIPRI Insights on Peace and Security no. 2020/13, Dec. 2020.

[5] Wezeman, P. D. and Kuimova, A., 'Military spending and arms imports by Iran, Saudi Arabia, Qatar and the UAE', SIPRI Fact Sheet, May 2019; and Béraud-Sudreau et al. (note 4).

[6] See e.g. UN Security Council, Final report of the Panel of Experts on Libya established pursuant to Security Council Resolution 1973 (2011), S/2019/914, 9 Dec. 2019.

[7] Wehrey, F., *Tunisia's Wake-up Call: How Security Challenges from Libya Are Shaping Defense Reforms*, Working paper (Carnegie Endowment for International Peace: Washington, DC, 18 Mar. 2020).

[8] Amara, T., 'Tunisia gets US planes, jeeps to guard Libyan border', Reuters, 12 May 2016.

Sub-Saharan Africa

In 2016–20 sub-Saharan Africa accounted for 26 per cent of total African arms imports, compared with 41 per cent in 2011–15. The total volume of arms imported by states in the subregion in 2016–20 was 45 per cent lower than in 2011–15 and was at its lowest level since 1996–2000. The five largest arms importers in sub-Saharan Africa in 2016–20—Angola, Nigeria, Sudan, Senegal and Zambia—together accounted for 58 per cent of all arms imports to the subregion.

Angola's arms imports in 2016–20 were nine times higher than in 2011–15 and this was the largest increase among states in the subregion. This sharp rise can largely be attributed to several deliveries from Russia, which accounted for 64 per cent of Angola's arms imports in 2016–20. These deliveries included 12 Su-30 combat aircraft, 12 Mi-24 combat helicopters and 4 Mi-17 transport helicopters.

Despite ongoing external and domestic security challenges, including activities by armed Islamist groups such as Boko Haram, Nigeria's arms imports in 2016–20 were 46 per cent lower than in 2011–15.[9] Sudan's arms imports also decreased between the two periods. Although there were tensions during 2016–20 between Sudan and Ethiopia over the construction of the Grand Ethiopian Renaissance Dam, Sudan's arms imports were 61 per cent lower than in 2011–15.[10] It remains unclear whether these tensions had or will have an impact on arms procurement by the affected states.

Arms imports by Senegal (up by 270 per cent) and Zambia (up by 56 per cent) increased between 2011–15 and 2016–20. Zambia's imports in 2016–20 included 6 L-15Z trainer/combat aircraft from China. Over the same period, Senegal imported 27 Assaulter armoured vehicles from China and a total of 4 Shaldag and Shaldag Mk-5 patrol craft from Israel.

In absolute terms, the volume of arms imports by other sub-Saharan African states remained relatively small in 2016–20. However, armed conflict in the Sahel coincided with increased arms imports by Burkina Faso and Mali, both of which are members of the Joint Force of the Group of Five for the Sahel.[11] Taken together, the deliveries to Burkina Faso and Mali in 2016–20 included a total of 322 light armoured vehicles, 9 combat helicopters and 4 light combat aircraft. Some of these transfers were financed by the European Union or were delivered as military aid by France. In addition, Qatar and the UAE, both of which are seeking to play a bigger international

---

[9] On the armed conflicts in Nigeria see chapter 7, section II, in this volume.

[10] 'Ethiopia warns Sudan it is running out of patience over border dispute', Reuters, 12 Jan. 2021. On the armed conflict in Ethiopia see chapter 7, section IV, in this volume.

[11] On armed conflicts in the Sahel see chapter 7, section II, in this volume.

political role, supplied some of the above-mentioned light armoured vehicles as military aid.[12]

Generally speaking, arms transfers to sub-Saharan Africa reflect the economic, political or security interests of the supplier states. Several major powers are using arms supplies as a foreign policy tool to increase their influence in sub-Saharan Africa, while others have mainly financial motivations. These exports are at least partly driving growing arms supplier competition in the subregion.

Russia delivered arms to 12 sub-Saharan states in 2016–20 and was the largest supplier to the subregion. Its 30 per cent share of total sub-Saharan arms imports was 5 percentage points higher than in 2011–15. Twenty-one sub-Saharan states received major arms from China in 2016–20. China's share of total sub-Saharan arms imports was 20 per cent, as against 24 per cent in 2011–15. France delivered arms to 20 states in the subregion in 2016–20. Its share of total sub-Saharan arms imports was 9.5 per cent, compared with 2.9 per cent in 2011–15. The increase in France's share may be partly due to its continuing military presence in the subregion, especially in the Sahel.[13] Despite its large-scale military involvement in the subregion, the USA was only the fourth largest arms exporter to sub-Saharan Africa in 2016–20. It supplied arms to 17 states and accounted for 5.4 per cent of sub-Saharan arms imports.

The Americas

Arms imports by states in the Americas decreased by 43 per cent between 2011–15 and 2016–20. The region accounted for 5.4 per cent of global arms imports in 2016–20. The USA received 38 per cent of regional arms imports in the period. Its imports included 92 light helicopters from Germany and a total of 89 second-hand combat aircraft. The latter were acquired from several states by US companies to provide training services for the US military.[14] Canada was the second largest arms importer in the region and received 15 per cent of American arms imports in the period.

In 2016–20 Mexico accounted for 11 per cent of the regional total. It was the third largest importer in the Americas and the largest in Central America and the Caribbean. With the notable exception of one SIGMA-105 frigate from the Netherlands, Mexico's arms imports mainly comprised

---

[12] 'Qatar sends 24 armoured vehicles to Mali', Reuters, 26 Dec. 2018; and De Cherisey, E., 'Malian army receives new armour', Janes, 20 Jan. 2020.

[13] Sundberg, A., 'France: A continuing military presence in francophone Africa', ed. K. Gasinska, *Foreign Military Bases and Installations in Africa* (Swedish Defence Research Agency: Stockholm, Aug. 2019). On France's role in the Sahel see also chapter 7, sections I and II, in this volume.

[14] Trevithick, J., 'Air Force hires seven companies in long-awaited mega Adversary Air Support contract', The Drive, 21 Oct. 2019; and Gertler, J., 'Privatized adversary air combat training', In Focus no. IF11612, US Congress, Congressional Research Service, 5 Aug. 2020.

helicopters, fixed-wing aircraft and light armoured vehicles, which appear to be linked to the increasingly violent anti-crime and anti-drug operations performed by Mexico's armed forces.[15] As of the end of 2020, Mexico had no large pending deliveries of major arms.

Imports by states in South America decreased by 62 per cent between 2011–15 and 2016–20. The decrease is probably at least partly due to the low interstate threat perceptions among South American states. The economic situation in some states is another important factor. Venezuela, which dropped from being the 17th largest importer globally in 2011–15 to 65th place in 2016–20, is a notable example of this. Venezuela has been in the grip of a major economic crisis for several years and its arms imports decreased by 93 per cent between 2011–15 and 2016–20. As of the end of 2020, Venezuela's only known planned deliveries of major arms are for a small number of anti-ship missiles.

Unlike Venezuela, some states in South America have large orders with pending deliveries or plans for new orders. Brazil was the fourth largest importer in the Americas in 2016–20, just behind Mexico, and accounted for 11 per cent of the regional total. It is in the process of modernizing and expanding its military capabilities and has several pending deliveries for major arms. These include 35 Gripen-E combat aircraft from Sweden, 5 submarines (4 Scorpenes and 1 SNBR) from France, 4 MEKO-A100 frigates from Germany and over a thousand Guarani armoured personnel carriers (APCs) from Italy. All of these will be partly or fully produced under licence in Brazil.

Asia and Oceania

Arms imports by states in Asia and Oceania decreased by 8.3 per cent between 2011–15 and 2016–20. However, it remained the region with the highest volume of imports, accounting for 42 per cent of the global total. Of the 10 largest importers in 2016–20, 5 are in Asia and Oceania: India, Australia, China, the Republic of Korea (South Korea) and Pakistan. The USA accounted for 29 per cent of arms imports by states in the region, Russia for 27 per cent and China for 9.4 per cent.

India and Pakistan

Between 2011–15 and 2016–20, arms imports by India decreased by 33 per cent. Russia was the largest arms supplier to India in both 2011–15 and 2016–20. However, Russia's deliveries dropped by 53 per cent between the two periods and its share of total Indian arms imports fell from 70 per cent

---

[15] On the armed conflicts in Mexico between the government and drug cartels see chapter 3, section III, in this volume.

to 49 per cent. In 2011–15 the USA was the second largest arms supplier to India, but in 2016–20 India's arms imports from the USA were 46 per cent lower than in the previous five-year period, making the USA the fourth largest supplier to India in 2016–20. France and Israel were the second and third largest arms suppliers to India in 2016–20. India's arms imports from France increased by 709 per cent while those from Israel rose by 82 per cent. Combat aircraft and associated missiles made up more than 50 per cent of Indian arms imports in 2016–20.

The overall drop in India's arms imports between 2011–15 and 2016–20 seems to be mainly a consequence of its complex and lengthy procurement processes, combined with its recent attempts to reduce its reliance on Russian arms by diversifying its network of arms suppliers. This has led to significant delays in new orders for major arms from foreign suppliers over the entire decade 2011–20.[16] As India perceives increasing threats from Pakistan and China (see below) and as its ambitious plans to produce its own major arms have been significantly delayed, it is planning large-scale programmes for arms imports. Based on its planned deliveries of combat aircraft, air defence systems, ships and submarines, India's arms imports are expected to increase over the coming five years.

Tensions between China and India over their common and disputed border have dramatically increased in recent years, heightening India's perception that China is a major and growing threat.[17] India has ordered or plans to order major arms as a response to this perceived threat. Some of these orders are being made as fast-track emergency acquisitions, partly bypassing the slow and far more onerous standard Indian procurement process. In mid 2020 around $2.8 billion was added to the defence budget to fund such fast-track acquisitions.[18] As its tensions with China continued to rise during 2020, India asked Russia to expedite the delivery of an estimated 20 S-400 surface-to-air missile (SAM) systems ordered in 2018—a request to which Russia responded positively.[19]

Based on the new closer, strategic relationship that has developed between the two countries, the USA has offered major arms to India that are alternatives to the weapons on offer to India from Russia. This approach has proved successful in some cases. For example, during 2016–20, India

[16] Singh, A., *Indian Defence Procurement: Righting the Ship*, Observer Research Foundation (ORF) Issue Brief no. 443 (ORF: New Delhi, Feb. 2021); and Das, S. P., *Inordinate Delays in Defence Procurement: An Analysis and Way Forward*, Centre for Land Warfare Studies Issue Brief no. 162 (Centre for Land Warfare Studies: New Delhi, Jan. 2019).

[17] On the China–India and India–Pakistan border tensions see chapter 4, section II, in this volume.

[18] This was in addition to the normal capital outlay of $15.9 billion in the 2020 defence budget. Raghuvanshi, V., 'India releases details of new defense budget', *Defense News*, 2 Feb. 2021.

[19] Chaudhury, D. R., 'India on track to acquire Russian S-400 missile defence system', *Economic Times*, 16 Dec. 2020.

ordered AH-64E combat helicopters from the USA instead of the helicopters offered by Russia. In other cases, most notably with regard to combat aircraft, the competition remains open. The USA has offered F-15EX, F-16V (renamed as F-21) and F/A-18E combat aircraft to India, all for production under licence in India or with major input from the Indian arms industry, but Russian alternatives are still an option for India.[20]

In addition to offering major arms to India, the USA has threatened to invoke the 2017 Countering America's Adversaries Through Sanctions Act (CAATSA).[21] CAATSA allows the US Government to block arms exports to, or apply other sanctions on, states that buy arms from Russia.[22] This perhaps has particular significance for India's order of S-400s from Russia, the first deliveries of which are scheduled for 2021. However, neither the outgoing administration of President Donald J. Trump nor the incoming administration of President Joe Biden has been clear on whether the USA will invoke CAATSA or waive sanctions in this case. It is possible that the USA has chosen not to take a decision until deliveries actually start.[23]

Between 2011–15 and 2016–20, arms imports by Pakistan decreased by 23 per cent. China accounted for 61 per cent of Pakistan's arm imports in 2011–15 and for 74 per cent in 2016–20. Like India, its main regional rival, Pakistan has several large pending orders for major arms. They are scheduled for delivery by 2028 and include 50 JF-17 combat aircraft, 8 Type-041 submarines and 4 Type-054A frigates from China as well as 4 MilGem frigates from Turkey. The ships on order represent the most significant expansion of Pakistan's naval capabilities in the country's history.

East Asia

Arms imports by East Asian states increased by 14 per cent between 2011–15 and 2016–20. China, which received 4.7 per cent of global arms imports in 2016–20, was the largest arms importer in the subregion in both periods. The bulk of its imports came from Russia and these deliveries included S-400 SAM systems and Su-35 combat aircraft, as well as engines for Chinese-designed combat aircraft. However, imports from Russia are likely to decrease in volume once China's own industry manages to consistently produce the types of major arms that it has generally imported from Russia over the years. China currently has no planned orders for SAM systems or

[20] Lockheed Martin, 'F-21', [n.d.]; Grevatt, J., 'Boeing unveils Indian F-15EX and industry plans', Janes, 29 Jan. 2021; and 'India interested in buying MiG-235 jets', DefenseWorld.net, 18 Dec. 2020.

[21] Countering America's Adversaries Through Sanctions Act, US Public Law 115–44, signed into law 2 Aug. 2017. On CAATSA see also section II in this chapter.

[22] Wezeman, S. et al., 'International arms transfers and developments in arms production', *SIPRI Yearbook 2020*, p. 299.

[23] Seligman, L., 'Austin hints India's purchase of Russian missile system could trigger sanctions', *Politico*, 20 Mar. 2021.

combat aircraft and there are strong indications that China has started to produce its own engines for its combat aircraft.[24]

Taiwan's arms imports were 70 per cent lower in 2016–20 than in 2011–15. However, its arms imports will increase in the coming five years based on orders signed in 2019 for 66 F-16V combat aircraft and 108 M-1A2 tanks from the USA as well as planned orders for coastal defence systems with Harpoon anti-ship missiles, also from the USA.[25]

For over a decade up until 2019, the USA had been wary of agreeing to large-scale arms sales to Taiwan due to the damage previous sales had caused to US–Chinese relations. The US arms sales to Taiwan come in the context of increased political and military pressure on Taiwan from China. For example, over the past few years, China has performed naval and amphibious exercises in waters close to Taiwan, incursions by Chinese military aircraft into Taiwanese airspace have increased significantly, and China has issued statements that a military option for 'reunification' remains among the options it is considering.[26] As a result of this pressure, Taiwan's perception of a threat from China has strengthened, which has led to an increase in Taiwanese spending on arms procurement.[27] The USA shares this threat perception in relation to Taiwan, claiming in some recent statements that a Chinese invasion may come within a few years.[28] The US Government also sees China as a growing military threat to the USA itself and to US allies in the region.[29]

Arms imports by Japan, which also perceives China as a growing threat, increased by 124 per cent between 2011–15 and 2016–20.[30] Japan's arms imports will probably continue to rise based on new orders for arms from the USA—including an order placed in 2019 for 105 F-35 combat aircraft. Significantly, 42 of these are F-35B versions that are capable of operating

---

[24] Rupprecht, A. and Ju, J., 'Images suggest China has begun fitting indigenous WS10 engine into J-10C fighters', *Jane's Defence Weekly*, 5 Mar. 2020; and Chan, M., 'China's next-gen J-20 stealth fighter jettisons Russian engine in favour of home-grown technology', *South China Morning Post*, 8 Jan. 2021.

[25] Everington, K., 'Taiwan says new Harpoon missiles will help crush half of Chinese invasion fleet', Taiwan News, 2 Nov. 2020.

[26] Walker, R., 'Taiwan: The threat that the world ignores', Deutsche Welle, 18 Sep. 2020; Tian, Y. L., 'Attack on Taiwan an option to stop independence, top China general says', Reuters, 29 May 2020; and Tu, A. and Hetherington, W., 'Air force costs up amid incursions', *Taipei Times*, 25 Nov. 2020.

[27] Tu and Hetherington (note 26); and Reim, G., 'China to sanction Boeing Defense, Raytheon and Lockheed Martin over Taiwan weapons sale', FlightGlobal, 26 Oct. 2020.

[28] Roy, D., 'Rumors of war in the Taiwan Strait', The Diplomat, 20 Mar. 2021; and Brunnstrom, D., 'US warns China against Taiwan attack, stresses US "ambiguity"', Reuters, 8 Oct. 2020.

[29] US Department of Defense (DOD), Office of the Secretary of Defense, *Military and Security Developments Involving the People's Republic of China 2020*, Annual Report to Congress (DOD: Arlington, VA, Sep. 2020). On China–USA competition and tensions see also chapter 1 and chapter 4, section I, in this volume.

[30] Japanese Ministry of Defense (MOD), *Defense of Japan 2020* (MOD: Tokyo, July 2020); and Mishra, S. K., 'Japan's 2019 defence white paper and the contest for Southeast Asia', East Asia Compass, Institute of Peace and Conflict Studies, 16 Oct. 2019.

from the two amphibious assault ships Japan possesses. This will give Japan additional capabilities for military operations in East Asia or even beyond.[31] The orders from the USA are in addition to those that Japan has placed with its own arms industry.

South Korean arms imports increased by 57 per cent between 2011–15 and 2016–20. This rise was mainly driven by ongoing tensions with the Democratic People's Republic of Korea (DPRK, North Korea) and can largely be attributed to the delivery of 26 F-35 combat aircraft from the USA and 5 Type-214 submarines from Germany. Orders for additional F-35s are planned, including some 20 F-35Bs that South Korea aims to deploy on a locally designed light aircraft carrier by 2031.[32]

Many arms imports by South Korea have involved technology transfers and its arms imports are therefore likely to decrease over the long term. For example, South Korea no longer plans to import submarines, having started domestic production of a type developed by its own arms industry.[33]

Europe

In 2016–20, arms imports by European states were 12 per cent higher than in 2011–15 and represented 12 per cent of the global total. The USA accounted for 47 per cent of the region's arms imports in 2016–20, Germany for 9.7 per cent and Russia for 9.2 per cent.

Western and Central Europe

Arms imports by states in Western and Central Europe rose by 22 per cent between 2011–15 and 2016–20 after a drop of 52 per cent between 2006–10 and 2011–15. The increase was in the context of heightened threat perceptions among West and Central European states relating to Russia and to instability in the Middle East and North Africa.[34] It also coincided with the economic recovery in most of Europe after the 2009 global financial and economic crisis. About 56 per cent of arms imports by states in Western and Central Europe came from the USA in 2016–20. Deliveries of a total of 73 combat aircraft, including 71 F-35s, accounted for just over half of US arms exports to Western and Central Europe in the period.

There is a growing demand for arms in Western and Central Europe, and several states made decisions in 2020 that, if fully implemented, will have a significant effect on the volume of international arm transfers in future

---

[31] Chang, F. K., 'Taking flight: China, Japan and South Korea get aircraft carriers', Foreign Policy Research Institute, 14 Jan. 2021.

[32] Yu, J. and French, E., 'Why South Korea's aircraft carrier makes sense', The Diplomat, 27 Mar. 2021; and Chang (note 31).

[33] Gady, F., 'South Korea KSS-3 submarine program', The Diplomat, 23 Jan. 2018.

[34] On tensions within Europe see chapter 5, section I, in this volume.

years. Among these are the German Government's plan to buy 45 F/A-18E and F/A-18G combat aircraft from the USA, including 30 specifically to maintain Germany's nuclear weapon role within the North Atlantic Treaty Organization (NATO); Poland's order for 32 F-35 combat aircraft from the USA; Greece's order for 18 Rafale combat aircraft from France (see below); and Hungary's order for 218 Lynx infantry fighting vehicles from Germany.

Armenia and Azerbaijan

Prior to the six-week war over the disputed Nagorno-Karabakh region in 2020, both Armenia and Azerbaijan invested in modernizing their armed forces. This included procurement of different types of major arms. The respective arms imports of Azerbaijan and Armenia accounted for only 0.7 per cent and 0.3 per cent of global arms transfers in 2016–20. However, many of the major arms delivered played a key role in the 2020 war between the two states.[35]

In 2016–20 a total of 94 per cent of Armenian arms imports came from Russia. These included air defence systems, combat aircraft, ballistic missiles and artillery. Azerbaijan's arms imports in 2016–20 were more than 2.5 times higher than Armenia's. Israel accounted for 69 per cent and Russia for 17 per cent of Azerbaijan's arms imports in the period. While Russia supplied mainly armoured vehicles and artillery to Azerbaijan, Israeli supplies included UAVs for reconnaissance, ballistic missiles and loitering munitions.

Armenia and Azerbaijan used a variety of older-generation and more advanced weapons—including armoured vehicles, air defence systems and rocket artillery—during the 2020 war.[36] Notably, both countries also deployed either new indigenously produced or recently imported UAVs and loitering munitions, which played a significant role in the fighting.[37] For example, Turkish-produced Bayraktar TB2 armed UAVs were used by Azerbaijan to strike Armenian mobile SAM systems. At least 5 Bayraktar TB2 armed UAVs were transferred to Azerbaijani forces in 2020 along with an estimated 50 MAM-L guided bombs, which media reports suggest Azerbaijan ordered in a bid to increase its military superiority over Armenia.[38]

[35] On the armed conflict in Nagorno-Karabakh see chapter 5, section II, in this volume.

[36] Mitzer, S., 'The fight for Nagorno-Karabakh: Documenting losses on the sides of Armenia and Azerbaijan', Oryx, 27 Sep. 2020; and Shaikh, S. and Rumbaugh, W., 'The air and missile war in Nagorno-Karabakh: Lessons for the future of strike and defense', Center for Strategic and International Studies, 8 Dec. 2020.

[37] Kasapoglu, C., 'Turkey transfers drone warfare capacity to its ally Azerbaijan', Eurasia Daily Monitor, vol. 17, no. 144 (Oct. 2020); and Shaikh and Rumbaugh (note 36).

[38] Bekdil, B. E., 'Azerbaijan to buy armed drones from Turkey', Defense News, 25 June 2020.

The Middle East

Arms imports by states in the Middle East were 25 per cent higher in 2016–20 than in 2011–15. Four of the top 10 arms-importing states in 2016–20 are in the Middle East: Saudi Arabia, Egypt, Qatar and the UAE. The USA accounted for 52 per cent of arms imports by states in the region, while Russia supplied 13 per cent and France 12 per cent.

As well as the large-scale conflicts in Iraq, Syria and Yemen, there were tensions between states across the Middle East in 2016–20, and especially in the Gulf region. Tensions in the eastern Mediterranean, involving several Middle Eastern states as well as two European states (Cyprus and Greece) also increased over the period.[39] In contrast, the relations between two Middle Eastern states, Israel and the UAE, improved dramatically based on a peace accord brokered by the USA in 2020. These developments, discussed in detail below, had significant effects on arms transfer trends in the region in 2016–20.

The Gulf region

Saudi Arabia was the world's largest arms importer in 2016–20 and received 11 per cent of global arms imports. The USA accounted for 79 per cent of Saudi Arabian arms imports in 2016–20, followed by the United Kingdom with 9.3 per cent. In 2016–20 Saudi Arabia strengthened its long-range strike capabilities with 91 F-15SA combat aircraft from the USA and 15 Typhoon combat aircraft from the UK. It also imported 14 Patriot SAM systems from the USA. By the end of 2020, several large deliveries of major arms to Saudi Arabia were pending, including 61 F-15SA combat aircraft, 4 MMSC frigates and 7 THAAD ballistic missile defence systems from the USA as well as 5 Avante-2200 frigates from Spain. If these deliveries are implemented as planned, Saudi Arabia is expected to remain among the world's largest arms importers in the coming five years.

With the aim of increasing its influence in the Middle East, Qatar has vastly expanded its armed forces since around 2013. This process continued in 2016–20 and Qatari arms imports were 361 per cent higher than in the previous five-year period. The increase can mainly be attributed to the delivery of 24 Rafale combat aircraft from France and 10 Patriot PAC-3 SAM systems from the USA. Qatar was the 57th largest arms importer in 2006–10, the 32nd largest in 2011–15 and the 8th largest in 2016–20. Qatar's pending deliveries as at the end of 2020 indicate that its arms imports will increase even further over the coming years and particularly in the period 2021–23. During that period, Qatar is scheduled to receive, among other things, 3 Al Zubarah frigates from Italy and a total of 72 combat aircraft: 36 F-15QAs

---

[39] On the security situation in the Gulf region see chapter 1 and chapter 6, section I, in this volume.

from the USA, 24 Typhoons from the UK and 12 additional Rafales from France.

In 2016–20 Iran's arms imports represented 0.3 per cent of the global total. In 2020 the United Nations lifted its 2010 embargo on exports of most types of major arms to Iran.[40] This led to speculation that Iran would immediately begin to order large volumes of arms. For example, in 2020 US Secretary of State Michael R. Pompeo argued that, following the lifting of the restrictions, Iran would be able to acquire new combat aircraft from China or Russia.[41] In 2020 it was reported that China and Iran had drafted an economic and security partnership that included military cooperation such as joint development of weapon systems.[42] In addition, Russian government sources indicated that Russia will proceed with 'cooperation with Iran in the military–technical sphere', the term used by Russia for arms sales, in a 'calm fashion'.[43] As of the end of 2020, there was no publicly available information to suggest that such military cooperation had resulted in new Iranian contracts for imports of major arms.

The Abraham Accords and arms transfers to Israel and the UAE

In 2020 the USA brokered a formal normalization of the relations between Israel and the UAE—the so-called Abraham Accords.[44] Although the accords may help to reduce the tensions between some Arab states and Israel, they may also trigger a change in US arms export policy that could lead to increases in arms imports by Israel and the UAE.

The UAE has been among the world's top 10 arms importers for each consecutive five-year period since 2001–2005 and was the ninth largest importer in 2016–20. The UAE's arms imports in 2016–20 were 37 per cent lower than in 2011–15, when they peaked. At the end of 2020, the UAE's planned deliveries—including for 2 frigates from France as well as air defence systems and 38 combat helicopters from the USA—indicated that its arms imports will continue to be at a high level in 2021–25.

The USA accounted for 64 per cent of the UAE's arms imports in 2016–20. US deliveries included 2 THAAD ballistic missile defence systems; 552 Patriot PAC-3 and GEM-T air defence missiles; around 3000 APCs, mostly MaxxPros; and around 25 000 guided bombs, mainly GBU-39s, JDAMs and Paveways.

---

[40] On the lifting of the arms embargo on Iran see chapter 14, section II, in this volume.

[41] Katzman, K., 'UN ban on Iran arms transfers and sanctions snapback', In Focus no. IF11429, US Congress, Congressional Research Service, 16 Oct. 2020.

[42] Fassihi, F. and Myers, S. L., 'Defying US, China and Iran near trade and military partnership', *New York Times*, 27 Mar. 2021.

[43] 'Russia has full right to seek technical-military cooperation with Iran: Lavrov', *Tehran Times*, 29 Dec. 2020.

[44] On the series of normalization agreements with Israel in 2020 see chapter 6, section III, in this volume.

The major arms supplied by the USA to the UAE since the late 1990s have included some advanced weapon types. However, the USA has long restricted sales to the UAE of specific advanced weapons that it currently exports to only its closest allies, such as Japan, Israel and NATO member states. This policy is in line with the USA's objective of preserving Israel's military–technical superiority over Arab states. US foreign policy refers to this as Israel's 'Qualitative Military Edge' (QME).[45] As a result, in around 2014 the USA blocked the UAE's attempted acquisition of F-35 combat aircraft, the most advanced US combat aircraft available for export. At that time, the USA considered such a sale to be in contradiction to its QME policy.[46] In late 2019 the US Assistant Secretary of State for Political–Military Affairs, R. Clarke Cooper, again denied any plan to sell F-35 combat aircraft to the UAE.[47] However, the Trump administration in 2020 signalled that the formal normalization of relations between Israel and the UAE might change the USA's stance on the UAE's proposed acquisition.[48] In December 2020 Pompeo announced that the USA had cleared the potential sale of 50 F-35s to the UAE. He stated that the defence against 'heightened threats from Iran' was a key reason for agreeing to the deal and added, referring to the Abraham Accords, that the proposed sale was in recognition of the deepening relations between the USA and the UAE.[49] The actual agreement of sale between the USA and the UAE was signed on 21 January 2021, the day before the end of the Trump administration.[50]

Israel's arms imports were 65 per cent higher in 2016–20 than in 2011–15. In 2016–20 a total of 92 per cent of Israeli arms imports came from the USA and these were in the form of military aid (other suppliers to Israel are discussed below). The increase in Israeli arms imports can be largely attributed to the delivery of 27 (of a total order of 50) F-35 combat aircraft. Some US politicians consider the F-35 to be a central element of Israel's military advantage over neighbouring Arab states and expressed concerns that the possible sale of this type of aircraft to the UAE could jeopardize the Israeli QME.[51] In the past, the USA has attempted to assuage concerns that exports of advanced major arms to Arab states would reduce the Israeli

---

[45] Sharp, J. M. et al., *Israel's Qualitative Military Edge and Possible US Arms Sales to the United Arab Emirates*, Congressional Research Service (CRS), Report for Congress R46580 (US Congress, CRS: Washington, DC, 26 Oct. 2020).

[46] Hoffman, M., 'Israel buys 14 more F-35s as US denies JSF sales to Gulf states', Military.com, 23 Feb. 2015.

[47] Turak, N., 'US defense officials quash rumors of potential F-35 sales to the UAE', CNBC, 22 Nov. 2019.

[48] Sharp et al. (note 45), p. 15.

[49] Metha, A., 'US State Dept. approves UAE's purchase of F-35 jets, MQ-9 drones', *Defense News*, 10 Nov. 2020.

[50] Al Otaiba, Y., 'The UAE and the F-35: Frontline defense for the UAE, US and partners', Embassy of the United Arab Emirates, Washington, DC, 27 Jan. 2021.

[51] Sharp et al. (note 45), p. 14.

QME by increasing its supply of advanced weapons to Israel. In 2020 there were signs that the USA was planning to do the same in this case. In response to requests from Israel, in 2020 the US Government was reportedly putting together a military aid package that would include deliveries of additional F-35s as well as F-15EX combat aircraft, guided bombs and KC-46A tanker aircraft.[52]

The maritime dimension of arms transfers to the eastern Mediterranean

Several states involved in disputes over rights to maritime hydrocarbon resources in the eastern Mediterranean have strengthened their maritime capabilities through arms imports, raising the risk of escalating reactive arms procurement in the region.[53] This process of arms procurement continued in 2016–20 and all the countries discussed below were in negotiations in 2020 for further, and often large, arms deals.

Israel's arms imports and orders over the past few years are partly explained by its decision to include the protection of its developing gas exploration activities in the Mediterranean among the core tasks of its armed forces. Four MEKO PC-IN (Saar-6) frigates, ordered from Germany in 2015 and scheduled for delivery in 2021–22, will be among the main weapon systems used for this task.[54]

Egypt's imports of major arms increased by 136 per cent between 2011–15 and 2016–20, and it became the world's third largest arms importer. It is generally assumed that the recent increases in Egypt's arms procurement are linked to its assessments about a combination of possible threats, including threats to its gas fields in the Mediterranean.[55] Egypt's arms deliveries in 2016–20 appear to be at least partly related to strengthening the protection of these gas fields. Deliveries included 1 FREMM frigate, 2 Mistral amphibious assault ships and 21 Rafale combat aircraft from France; 3 Type-209 submarines from Germany; 1 FREMM frigate from Italy; 50 MiG-29M combat aircraft and 46 Ka-52 ship-borne combat helicopters from Russia; and 1 Po-Hang corvette from South Korea. By the end of 2020, pending deliveries to Egypt included 1 Type-209 submarine and 4 MEKO-200 frigates from Germany, 1 FREMM frigate from Italy, 3 Gowind frigates from France, and 24 Su-35 combat aircraft from Russia.

Turkey's arms imports decreased by 59 per cent between 2011–15 and 2016–20, and it dropped from being the 6th largest arms importer in the

---

[52] Sharp et al. (note 45), p. 17.

[53] On tensions in the eastern Mediterranean see chapter 5, section I, in this volume.

[54] Newdick, T., 'Israel has taken delivery of its most capable warship ever', The Drive, 12 Nov. 2020; and Frantzman, S. J., 'Israel shifts naval doctrine with new Sa'ar 6 warships', Defense News, 5 Nov. 2020.

[55] Springborg, R. and Williams, F. C., The Egyptian Military: A Slumbering Giant Awakes (Carnegie Middle East Centre: Beirut, 28 Feb. 2019). On armed conflict in Egypt see chapter 6, section IV, in this volume.

world to 20th position. This was partly because Turkey increasingly produces its own major arms, including surface ships.[56] Another major reason for the fall in arms imports was that in 2019 the USA halted a planned delivery of F-35 combat aircraft to Turkey (see section II). In addition, Turkey's military intervention in Syria and its claims on hydrocarbon resources in the Mediterranean led to growing political differences with West European arms suppliers during 2016–20 and discussions in some states about placing restrictions on arms exports to Turkey.[57] However, by the end of 2020, Turkey still had pending deliveries for various types of major arms that are of particular relevance for its military presence in the Mediterranean. Planned deliveries include six Type-214 submarines from Germany, five ATR-72MP anti-submarine warfare aircraft from Italy and one BPE amphibious assault ship from Spain.

Greece was the third largest arms importer in the world in 2001–2005. However, Greece's economy has been in crisis for several years, which has led to deep cuts in spending on major arms, and it ranked 41st in 2016–20. Its largest arms import in the period was for 1 Type-214 submarine from Germany. In 2020, as tensions with Turkey over contested waters in the Mediterranean increased, Greece agreed orders with France for the supply of 18 Rafale combat aircraft in 2021–23.

Even Cyprus, whose armed forces are of a much smaller size compared with other states involved in the growing tensions in the eastern Mediterranean, invested in new weapons in 2016–20. Its arms imports included MM-40-3 Exocet anti-ship missiles, delivered by France in 2020, for use with coastal defence systems.

[56] See e.g. Béraud-Sudreau et al. (note 4).
[57] On Turkey's role in the armed conflict in Syria see chapter 6, section II, in this volume. On embargo discussions targeting Turkey see chapter 14, section II, in this volume.

IV. The financial value of states' arms exports

ALEXANDRA MARKSTEINER AND PIETER D. WEZEMAN

Official data on the financial value of states' arms exports in the years 2010–19 is presented in table 9.6. The data is taken from reports by—or direct quotes from—national governments. The stated data coverage reflects the language used by the original source. National practices in this area vary, but the term 'arms exports' generally refers to the financial value of the arms actually delivered; 'arms export licences' generally refers to the financial value of the licences for arms exports issued by the national export licensing authority; and 'arms export agreements' or 'arms export orders' refers to the financial value of contracts or other agreements signed for arms exports.

The arms export data for the states in table 9.6 is based on national definitions and methodologies and is thus not necessarily comparable across countries. There is no internationally agreed definition of what constitutes 'arms' and governments use different lists when collecting and reporting data on the financial value of their arms exports. In addition, there is no standardized methodology concerning the collection and reporting of such data, with some states reporting on export licences issued or used and other states using data collected from customs agencies.

According to the SIPRI Arms Transfers Database, states that produce official data on the financial value of their arms exports accounted for over 90 per cent of the total volume of deliveries of major arms. By adding together the data in table 9.6 it is therefore possible to attain a rough estimate of the financial value of the total global arms trade. However, there are significant limitations in using this data to make such an estimate. First, as noted above, the data sets used are based on different definitions and methodologies and are thus not directly comparable. Second, several states (e.g. the United Kingdom and the United States) do not release data on arms exports but only on arms export agreements and licences, while other states (e.g. China) do not release any data on arms exports, export licences, agreements or orders. Nonetheless, by adding together the data that states have made available on the financial value of their arms exports, as well as estimates for those that only provide data on arms export licences, agreements or orders, it is possible to estimate the rough total value of the global arms trade. The estimate of the financial value of the global arms trade for 2019—the latest year for which relevant data is available—was at least $118 billion.[1] However, the true figure is likely to be higher.

---

[1] For a full description of the methodology used to calculate this figure see the 'Financial value of the global arms trade' page of the SIPRI website.

Table 9.6. The financial value of states' arms exports according to national government and industry sources, 2010–19

Figures are in constant (2019) US$ m. Conversion to constant US dollars is made using the market exchange rates of the reporting year and the US consumer price index (CPI). Years are calendar years unless otherwise stated.

State	2010	2011	2012	2013	2014	2015	2016	2017	2018	2019	Explanation of data
Australia[a]	..	..	..	1 186	1 587	3 409	886	1 271	3 732	3 657	Arms export licences
Austria	579	679	651	766	769	402	753	447	358	381	Arms exports
	2 745	2 579	2 223	3 459	1 294	1 297	4 690	2 359	1 821	1 935	Arms export licences
Belgium	1 557	1 319	1 386	893	6 466	1 334	1 471	871	1 399	3 208	Arms export licences
Bosnia and Herzegovina	16	65	59	57	96	126	123	122	142	..	Arms exports
	43	90	66	163	185	275	359	348	280	..	Arms export licences
Bulgaria	401	365	313	342	578	1 677	1 196	1 433	919	687	Arms exports
	460	352	499	715	1 186	764	1 483	1 633	1 259	959	Arms export licences
Canada[b]	464	728	1 161	726	778	570	577	827	1 625	2 831	Arms exports
Croatia	84	55	73	125	102	47	87	80	118	48	Arms exports
	691	242	341	1 037	691	457	446	533	459	600	Arms export licences
Czechia	337	289	392	420	613	673	812	674	656	693	Arms exports
	700	547	379	478	717	888	405	598	469	619	Arms export licences
Denmark	..	..	..	34	64	92	132	107	99	185	Arms exports
	584	374	318	1 139	210	160	239	241	320	175	Arms export licences
Estonia	3	553	4	4	6	17	11	75	44	12	Arms export licences
Finland	92	153	83	325	319	117	155	123	154	127	Arms exports
	95	291	169	501	325	433	115	230	212	118	Arms export licences
France	5 786	5 977	5 405	4 924	5 796	7 419	8 389	7 914	8 371	11 113	Arms exports
	7 947	10 297	6 892	10 016	11 775	20 243	16 425	8 161	10 957	9 317	Arms export licences
Germany	3 290	2 030	1 353	1 359	2 612	1 860	2 947	3 118	927	923	Arms export licences
	8 526	17 056	12 699	12 152	9 340	15 335	8 137	7 721	5 815	9 542	Arms exports[c]
	458	357	486	..	..	..	..	..	160	113	Arms export licences[d]
Greece	30	28	39	47	48	55	22	52	44	59	Arms exports
Hungary	214	246	386	748	620	1 535	694	687	476	638	Arms export licences

Country	Measure										
India[e]	Arms exports	..	..	96	129	176	346	241	749	1 239	1 295
Ireland	Arms export licences	37	43	67	90	124	51	74	29	40	47
Israel	Arms exports	8 442	>7 000	8 318	7 177	6 112	6 148	6 924	9 596	7 636	7 200
Israel	Arms export agreements	>7 300	..	..	..	..	..	..	..	..	..
Italy	Arms exports	957	1 616	4 306	4 039	4 771	3 845	3 363	3 386	2 953	2 674
Italy	Arms export licences	6 615	8 315	5 952	3 131	3 798	9 430	17 244	11 186	5 743	4 575
Korea, South	Arms exports	5 048	2 707	2 620	3 749	3 901	3 819	2 725	3 254	1 702	1 480
Korea, South	Arms export agreements	1 393	..	..	..	..	..	..	..	..	..
Latvia	Arms exports	12	<1	<1	<1	4	..	<1	105	..	..
Latvia	Arms export licences	12	<1	<1	<1	4	1	<1	105	13	15
Lithuania	Arms exports	23	76	27	23	27	32	48	83	114	58
Lithuania	Arms export licences	36	81	29	32	22	71	108	71	54	55
Montenegro	Arms exports	9	..	4	4	13	5	1	7	10	..
Montenegro	Arms export licences	16	6	7	9	16	13	9	11	22	..
Netherlands	Arms exports	1 050	1 220	1 176	369	359	708	667	782	687	499
Netherlands	Arms export licences	1 418	657	1 346	1 403	2 959	1 044	1 668	946	773	1 033
Norway[f]	Arms exports	712	725	742	616	505	437	454	676	604	504
Pakistan[g]	Arms exports	20	11	14	14	18	65	33	60	..	216
Poland	Arms exports	..	..	..	490	567	504	451	555	585	438
Poland	Arms export licences	710	1 341	906	1 250	1 318	1 518	1 445	1 271	1 871	2 153
Portugal	Arms exports	31	39	44	256	225	228	703	190	252	439
Portugal	Arms export licences	33	49	74	213	365	81	287	69	207	195
Romania	Arms exports	191	207	119	258	228	193	213	227	234	161
Romania	Arms export licences	236	291	256	431	357	263	284	310	245	172
Russia	Arms exports	11 724	15 571	16 926	17 230	16 847	15 640	15 978	>15 000	16 290	>15 000
Russia	Arms export licences	..	..	..	..	..	..	..	..	..	..
Serbia	Arms exports	885	450	499	892	865	874	985	855	793	..
Serbia	Arms export licences	225	197	209	191	338	417	479	288	499	..
Slovakia	Arms exports	23	16	36	45	52	68	71	81	112	76
Slovakia	Arms export licences	90	47	104	178	384	339	245	269	227	210

State	2010	2011	2012	2013	2014	2015	2016	2017	2018	2019	Explanation of data
Slovenia	9	14	6	4	7	13	18	28	14	17	Arms exports
	17	19	13	13	4	37	51	60	78	56	Arms export licences
South Africa	1 334	1 438	1 438	359	297	232	302	269	364	281	Arms export licences
Spain	1 752	3 841	2 794	5 694	4 589	4 450	4 773	5 111	4 472	4 525	Arms exports
	3 475	4 536	11 009	6 296	5 253	12 772	6 538	24 791	13 704	11 296	Arms export licences
Sweden	2 236	2 435	1 604	2 012	1 253	954	1 367	1 370	1 332	1 721	Arms exports
	2 152	1 908	1 304	1 656	705	633	7 695	991	991	1 428	Arms export licences
Switzerland	721	1 117	831	546	665	501	445	474	531	732	Arms exports
Turkey	743	929	1 336	1 525	1 779	1 785	1 787	1 814	2 072	2 741	Arms exports
Ukraine	1 122	1 141	1 140	1 097	..	615	820	..	780	908	Arms exports
United Kingdom	10 560	9 833	15 470	16 814	15 115	12 689	8 480	12 037	19 015	14 031	Arms export orders[h]
	4 405	11 065	3 811	7 624	3 705	9 593	4 654	8 876	3 799	6 511	Arms export licences
United States	21 333	22 210	19 540	22 309	20 976	22 845	22 488	31 877	..	..	Arms exports[i]
	24 859	29 368	69 834	25 770	33 888	48 411	29 310	51 493	..	..	Arms export agreements[j]
									56 667	55 386	Arms export agreements[k]
	39 963	49 866	37 382	22 824	68 072	79 766	53 090	53 795	64 582	55 062	Arms export licences[l]

.. = data not available.

Note: The states included in this table are those that provide official data on the financial value of either 'arms exports', 'contracts signed for arms exports', 'arms export orders placed' or 'licences for arms exports' for at least 6 of the 10 years covered and where the average of the values given in at least one of the data sets exceeds $10 million. The arms export data for the different states in this table is not necessarily comparable and may be based on significantly different definitions and methodologies.

[a] Figures cover the period 1 July–30 June, e.g. the 2019 figure covers the period 1 July 2019–30 June 2020.
[b] Figures exclude exports to the USA.
[c] Figures cover only exports of 'war weapons' as defined by German national legislation.
[d] Figures include arms export licences for international collaborative projects.
[e] Figures for 2013–16 cover the period 1 Apr.–31 Mar., e.g. the figure for 2016 covers the period 1 Apr. 2016–31 Mar. 2017.
[f] Figures exclude dual-use goods and defence-related services.
[g] Figures for 2010–17 cover the period 1 Apr.–31 Mar., e.g. the figure for 2017 covers the period 1 Apr. 2017–31 Mar. 2018. The 2019 figure covers the period 1 Aug. 2018–31 July 2019.

h Figures cover exports of defence equipment and additional aerospace equipment and services.

i Figures include items sold under the government-to-government Foreign Military Sales programme, as well as Direct Commercial Sales by US companies to foreign governments. Figures cover the period 1 Oct.–30 Sep., e.g. the figure for 2017 covers the period 1 Oct. 2016–30 Sep. 2017.

j Figures were calculated by the reporting authority using an old methodology. Arms export agreements are counted as such if the US Government and recipient government signed a Letter of Agreement. Figures only include items sold under the government-to-government Foreign Military Sales programme. They do not include Direct Commercial Sales by US companies to foreign governments. Figures cover the period 1 Oct.–30 Sep., e.g. the figure for 2017 covers the period 1 Oct. 2016–30 Sep. 2017.

k Figures were calculated using a new methodology, which the reporting authority adopted starting in 2020. Arms export agreements are counted as such if the US Government and recipient government signed a Letter of Agreement and an initial payment was made. Figures only include items sold under the government-to-government Foreign Military Sales programme. They do not include Direct Commercial Sales by US companies to foreign governments. Figures cover the period 1 Oct.–30 Sep., e.g. the figure for 2019 covers the period 1 Oct. 2018–30 Sep. 2019.

l Figures only include items sold as Direct Commercial Sales. They do not include sales under the government-to-government Foreign Military Sales programme. Figures are for the period 1 Oct.–30 Sep., e.g. the figure for 2019 covers the period 1 Oct. 2018–30 Sep. 2019.

Sources: Reports by– or direct quotes from–national governments. For a full list of sources and all available financial data on arms exports see the 'Financial value of the global arms trade' page of the SIPRI website.

It is difficult to assess the trend in the value of the global arms trade over time because countries do not always report consistently on their arms export figures each year. For instance, national reporting authorities may change their methodologies, as has been the case with the USA, which is by far the largest arms exporter. This means that comparisons of the value of the global arms trade in different years provide only a very rough indication of trends over time. Nevertheless, the available data suggests a significant real-terms increase over time in the value of the global arms trade, from at least $83 billion in 2010 (in constant 2019 US dollars) to at least $118 billion in 2019. Despite this increase, the estimated value of the global arms trade for 2019 was less than 0.5 per cent of the value of the total global trade of all products and services in 2019.[2]

---

[2] The value of the total global trade in all products and services in 2019 was $24 920 billion. World Trade Organization, 'Trade set to plunge as Covid-19 pandemic upends global economy', Press release, 8 Apr. 2020.

V. Trends in arms production, 2019

ALEXANDRA MARKSTEINER

The 25 largest arms-producing and military services companies, 2019

Table 9.7 ranks the world's 25 largest arms-producing and military services companies ('arms companies' for short) by their arms sales in 2019—the latest year for which relevant data is available (see box 9.2). The arms sales of the top 25 arms companies totalled US$361 billion in 2019. This represents an increase of 8.5 per cent compared with 2018 and 15 per cent compared with 2015. Of the 25 companies included in SIPRI's ranking, 19 recorded higher arms sales in 2019 than in the previous year.[1]

Key developments

For each of the years covered by SIPRI's current data set, the United States was the country with the highest number of companies listed. In 2019 the 12 US companies included in the ranking accounted for 61 per cent of the combined arms sales of the 25 largest arms companies. 2019 was also the second consecutive year in which the top 5 companies were all based in the USA. Lockheed Martin, reporting the largest absolute increase in arms sales of any of the companies listed ($5.9 billion), topped the ranking for the fifth year in a row.

The combined arms sales of the six West European companies in the top 25 made up 18 per cent of the total. Compared with 2018, the arms-related revenue of these six companies grew by 11 per cent. The French producer Dassault Aviation Group more than doubled its arms sales, thereby reporting the largest percentage increase among companies in the top 25.

The 2019 SIPRI ranking is the first to include data for some Chinese arms companies. Four were among the top 25.[2] Together, they accounted for 16 per cent of the total arms sales of the top 25, making China the second largest arms-producing country in the world in 2019. The combined arms-related revenue of the four companies grew by 4.8 per cent since 2018 and by 8.2 per cent since 2015, largely due to the military modernization programmes of the People's Liberation Army.

Russian companies accounted for 3.9 per cent of the total top 25 arms sales in 2019. Both of the Russian companies included in the ranking, Almaz-Antey and United Shipbuilding Corporation, recorded a decrease in revenue.

---

[1] Except where indicated, the information on arms sales of the world's largest arms-producing and military services companies referred to in this section is taken from the SIPRI Arms Industry Database. For a definition of 'arms sales' see box 9.2.

[2] Other Chinese companies might have been among the top 25 arms companies in 2019, but there was insufficient data to include them in the ranking.

Table 9.7. The SIPRI top 25 arms-producing and military services companies, 2019

Rank[a] 2019	Rank[a] 2018	Company[b]	Country[c]	Arms sales, 2019 (US$ m.)	Arms sales, 2018 (constant 2019 US$ m.)[d]	Change in arms sales, 2018–19 (%)	Total sales, 2019 (US$ m.)	Arms sales as a % of total sales, 2019
1	1	Lockheed Martin Corp.	United States	53 230	48 119	11	59 812	89
2	2	Boeing	United States	33 580	32 704	2.7	76 559	44
3	3	Northrop Grumman Corp.	United States	29 220	26 666	9.6	33 841	86
4	4	Raytheon[e]	United States	25 320	23 866	6.1	29 176	87
5	6	General Dynamics Corp.	United States	24 500	22 400	9.4	39 350	62
6	5	AVIC[f]	China	22 470	21 841	2.9	66 846	34
7	7	BAE Systems	United Kingdom	22 240	20 672	7.6	23 378	95
8	9	CETC	China	15 090	13 581	11	32 951	46
9	8	NORINCO	China	14 540	14 580	–0.3	65 929	22
10	–	L3Harris Technologies[g]	United States	13 920	13 460	3.4	18 074	77
11	14	United Technologies Corp.[e]	United States	13 100	9 479	38	77 046	17
12	11	Leonardo	Italy	11 110	9 383	18	15 432	72
13	10	Airbus	Trans-European[h]	11 050	11 197	–1.3	78 905	14
14	13	Thales	France	9 470	9 087	4.2	20 601	46
15	12	Almaz-Antey	Russia	9 420	9 784	–3.7	9 657	98
16	16	Huntington Ingalls Industries	United States	7 740	7 331	5.6	8 899	87
17	38	Dassault Aviation Group	France	5 760	2 812	105	8 219	70
18	18	Honeywell International	United States	5 330	5 529	–3.6	36 709	15
19	19	Leidos	United States	5 330	5 091	4.7	11 094	48
20	22	Booz Allen Hamilton	United States	5 140	4 765	7.9	7 464	69
21	28	General Electric	United States	4 760	3 716	28	95 200	5.0
22	–	EDGE[f]	UAE	4 750	..	..	5 000	95
23	23	Rolls-Royce	United Kingdom	4 710	4 561	3.3	19 732	24
24	25	CSGC	China	4 610	4 125	12	29 065	16
25	21	United Shipbuilding Corp.[f]	Russia	4 500	4 770	–5.7	5 416	83

. . = data not available; – = not ranked in 2018; AVIC = Aviation Industry Corp. of China; CETC = China Electronics Technology Group Corp.; Corp. = corporation; CSGC = China South Industries Group Corp.; NORINCO = China North Industries Group Corp.

Note: Percentages below 10 are rounded to 1 decimal place; percentages over 10 are rounded to whole numbers.

[a] Companies are ranked according to the value of their arms sales at the end of what SIPRI considers to be their financial year. Company names and structures are listed as they were at the end of their financial year. Rankings for 2018 are based on updated figures for arms sales in the SIPRI Arms Industry Database for the years 2015–19. They may differ from those published in any earlier SIPRI publication owing to continual revision of data, most often because of changes reported by the company itself and sometimes because of improved estimations.

[b] Holding and investment companies with no direct operational activities are not treated as arms companies, and companies owned by them are listed and ranked as if they were parent companies.

[c] Country refers to the country in which the ownership and control structures of a company are located, i.e. the location of a company's headquarters.

[d] To allow comparison with arms sales in 2019, figures for arms sales in 2018 are given in constant 2019 US dollars.

[e] Raytheon and United Technologies Corp. merged in 2020.

[f] The arms sales figure for this company is an estimate with a high degree of uncertainty.

[g] L3Harris Technologies is the result of a merger between Harris Corp. and L3 Technologies. Its arms sales figure for 2018 is pro forma, i.e. it is the combined 2018 arms sales of Harris Corp and L3 Technologies.

[h] Trans-European refers to companies whose ownership and control structures are located in more than one European country.

Source: SIPRI Arms Industry Database, Dec. 2020.

Box 9.2. Definitions and methodology for SIPRI data on the top 25 arms-producing and military services companies

The data on the top 25 arms-producing and military services companies is from SIPRI's Arms Industry Database, which is revised annually based on new information. It replaces all data for all years in previous SIPRI publications on arms companies.

'Arms sales' are defined as sales of military goods, services, and research and development to military customers domestically and abroad.

Unless otherwise specified, all changes are expressed in real terms. Comparisons between years are based on the sets of companies included in the ranking in the respective years (i.e. comparison between different sets of 25 companies).

The comparison presented here starts from 2015, as this is the first year for which SIPRI now has sufficient data to include some Chinese companies. The new data set therefore differs from the previous data set produced for the SIPRI Top 100 ranking of arms-producing and military services companies, which does not include Chinese companies.[a]

[a] For further detail see Tian, N. and Su, F., 'Estimating the arms sales of Chinese companies', SIPRI Insights on Peace and Security no. 2020/2, Jan. 2020.

A third Russian company, United Aircraft Corporation, lost $1.3 billion in arms sales and dropped out of the top 25.

The year also marked the rise of a Middle Eastern company into the list of the 25 largest arms companies. EDGE, headquartered in the United Arab Emirates (UAE), was created in 2019 from a merger of more than 25 smaller firms. Ranking at number 22, its arms-related revenue in 2019 is estimated at just under $4.8 billion. Significant investment by the UAE Government into the domestic arms industry contributed to the rapid ascent of these smaller entities, which were then able to import technology to expand their know-how and bolster their production capacity.

Mapping the international presence of the arms industry

A simple survey of the geographical locations of the largest arms companies' headquarters suggests that they operate in only a limited number of states. However, this obscures the fact that the reach of arms companies often extends far beyond the borders of the countries in which they are headquartered, as a result of the internationalization of the arms industry. In order to study the true geographical spread of the arms industry and its activities, SIPRI has built a data set of 400 foreign entities—branches, subsidiaries and joint ventures registered in a country other than that in which the parent company is headquartered—tied to the world's 15 largest arms companies (see box 9.3).

Key findings

When expanding the scope of analysis to include foreign entities, the reach of the world's 15 largest arms companies extends across at least 49 different

---

Box 9.3. Definitions and methodology for SIPRI data mapping the international presence of the arms industry

The SIPRI data set mapping the international presence of the arms industry includes foreign entities tied to the world's 15 largest arms companies. The term 'foreign entity' refers to a branch, subsidiary or joint venture that is registered in a country other than the one in which the ultimate parent company is headquartered. In order to be counted, a foreign entity had to be active for more than six months during 2019 and either manufacture military goods, provide military services or sell to military customers. Entities involved solely in sales, marketing or outreach activities and entities deemed to be holding or investment companies were excluded. Moreover, to be counted, an entity had to be majority-owned and be removed by no more than two levels of ownership from the ultimate parent company.[a]

[a] For more information on definitions, sources and methods see Béraud-Sudreau, L. et al., 'Mapping the international presence of the world's largest arms companies', SIPRI Insights on Peace and Security no. 2020/12, Dec. 2020, p. 2

---

countries, 17 of which are in the Global South.[3] If only the locations of the headquarters were taken into account, the international presence of the same set of companies would span just 8 countries.

Of the 15 companies surveyed, the French producer Thales is the most internationalized, with 67 entities registered in 24 countries across 5 regions (see table 9.8). Airbus, which is categorized as a trans-European company, is also present in 24 countries with a total of 41 entities. Other front-runners include Leonardo (59 entities in 21 countries), Boeing (56 entities in 21 countries) and Lockheed Martin (28 entities in 19 countries).

Chinese and Russian arms companies, by contrast, have a limited international presence. However, open-source data for Chinese and Russian firms is often unavailable. Of the four Chinese and Russian companies included in SIPRI's analysis, Aviation Industry Corporation of China (AVIC) is the only one for which eligible foreign entities were found. AVIC is present in at least six different countries: four are Western industrialized countries—Finland, Spain, the United Kingdom and the USA—and two are in the Global South—Cambodia and Pakistan. The latter two have long participated in military cooperation programmes with China.[4]

There are several reasons why the reach of Chinese and Russian companies may appear less extensive than that of their US and European counterparts. First, both Russia and China focus heavily on domestic arms production and thus may discourage state-owned companies from

---

[3] The 17 countries are Brazil, Cambodia, China, Colombia, Costa Rica, India, Iraq, Jordan, Kazakhstan, Kenya, Malaysia, Mexico, Morocco, Pakistan, South Africa, Thailand and Turkey. 'Global South' here refers to developing countries eligible for official development assistance (ODA). Organisation for Economic Co-operation and Development, Development Co-operation Directorate (DAC), 'DAC list of ODA recipients: Effective for reporting on 2020 flows', 2020.

[4] Phea, K., 'Cambodia–China relations in the new decade', Diplomacy Publication, Konrad Adenauer Stiftung, 26 May 2020; and Gao, C., 'Here's how China made Pakistan into a military powerhouse', *National Interest*, 20 Mar. 2020.

Table 9.8. International presence of the top 15 arms-producing and military services companies, 2019

Parent company	Rank, 2019	Location of headquarters	No. of foreign entities	No. of countries[a]	No. of regions[b]	Entities involved in manufacturing as a % of total foreign entities[c]
Lockheed Martin Corp.	1	United States	28	19	4	50
Boeing	2	United States	56	21	5	9.0
Northrop Grumman Corp.	3	United States	16	9	3	56
Raytheon[d]	4	United States	16	7	4	88
General Dynamics Corp.	5	United States	25	14	4	80
AVIC	6	China	7	6	3	86
BAE Systems	7	United Kingdom	38	18	4	42
CETC	8	China	[0]	[0]	[0]	..
NORINCO	9	China	[0]	[0]	[0]	..
L3Harris Technologies	10	United States	33	15	5	76
United Technologies Corp.[d]	11	United States	14	8	3	93
Leonardo	12	Italy	59	21	5	58
Airbus	13	Trans-European[e]	41	24	5	32
Thales	14	France	67	24	5	73
Almaz-Antey	15	Russia	[0]	[0]	[0]	..

.. = data not available; [0] = estimated number is 0 as no foreign entity matching the research criteria was found; AVIC = Aviation Industry Corp. of China; CETC = China Electronics Technology Group Corp.; Corp. = corporation; NORINCO = China North Industries Group Corp.

Note: Percentages below 10 are rounded to 1 decimal place; percentages over 10 are rounded to whole numbers.

[a] The number of countries in which the parent company's foreign entities are present.

[b] The number of regions (i.e. Africa, the Americas, Asia and Oceania, Europe and the Middle East) in which the parent company's foreign entities are present. On SIPRI's regional coverage see the list of conventions in this volume and the SIPRI website.

[c] The percentage of the parent company's foreign entities that are involved in manufacturing activities.

[d] Raytheon and United Technologies Corp. merged in 2020.

[e] Trans-European refers to companies whose ownership and control structures are located in more than one European country. For this study, Airbus is considered to have headquarters in three European countries: France, Germany and Spain.

Sources: SIPRI Arms Industry Database, Dec. 2020; annual company reports; stock exchange and investment filings; company websites; press statements; media reports; and public company registrars.

establishing a presence abroad.[5] Second, in the case of China, it could be lack of experience in organizing technology transfers that inhibits other forms of industrial cooperation with state customers. Third, efforts by Western governments to regulate foreign direct investment with the aim of thwarting Chinese ambitions to acquire dual-use and emerging technologies may act as a barrier.[6] Fourth, opportunities for Russian arms companies to form partnerships abroad have been affected by European Union and US sanctions.[7]

Of the world's five regions, Europe hosts the highest number of entities (167), followed by Asia and Oceania (91) and the Americas (84). Home to about 56 foreign entities, the UK leads the ranking of host countries, followed by Australia (38), the USA (36), Canada (30) and Germany (29). Beyond North America, Western Europe and Australia, the countries hosting the most entities are: Saudi Arabia (24), India (13), Singapore (11), the UAE (11) and Brazil (10).

The international presence of the world's largest arms companies closely mirrors ties and divisions that exist at the geopolitical level. US companies, for instance, are present in most allied and partnered countries, including Australia, Canada, Israel, Japan, South Korea, Saudi Arabia and Turkey. Transatlantic links are especially prominent. All three European companies surveyed have established themselves in the USA. Notably, the US market accounted for 43 per cent of BAE's total sales in the 2019 financial year.[8] US companies also have an extensive presence in Europe. For example, nearly 79 per cent of United Technologies' foreign entities are located in Europe, as well as more than half of General Dynamics' subsidiaries and joint ventures abroad.

SIPRI's data set also differentiates between entities that manufacture military goods and those that provide military services. The proportion of foreign entities involved in manufacturing varies greatly from company to company. For example, only 9.0 per cent of Boeing's foreign entities are production sites. General Dynamics, on the other hand, has far more significant capabilities abroad, with 80 per cent of its foreign entities involved

---

[5] Cheung, T. M., *Fortifying China: The Struggle to Build a Modern Defense Economy* (Cornell University Press: Ithaca, NY, 2009); and International Institute for Strategic Studies (IISS), 'Defence budgets, defence industry and the State Defence Order', *Russia's Military Modernisation: An Assessment* (Routledge: Abingdon, 2020).

[6] Johnson, K. and Gramer, R., 'The great decoupling', *Foreign Policy*, 14 May 2020.

[7] US Department of the Treasury, 'Announcement of treasury sanctions on entities within the financial services and energy sectors of Russia, against arms or related materiel entities, and those undermining Ukraine's sovereignty', Press release, 16 July 2014; US Department of State, Bureau of International Security and Nonproliferation, 'Section 231 of the Countering America's Adversaries Through Sanctions Act [CAATSA] of 2017', 2017; and Council Regulation (EU) 833/2014 of 31 July 2014 concerning restrictive measures in view of Russia's actions destabilising the situation in Ukraine, *Official Journal of the European Union*, L229, 31 July 2014.

[8] BAE Systems, 'Half year results', 30 July 2020, p. 20.

in military manufacturing. Geographically speaking, the manufacturing capabilities of the largest arms companies remain concentrated in North America, Western Europe and Australia. Together, these locations account for 80 per cent of all surveyed foreign production sites.

Understanding the internationalization of the arms industry

Various factors prompt arms companies to establish entities abroad, both from a supply perspective (company strategies) and a demand perspective (national procurement and arms–industrial policies). For instance, following the contraction of domestic arms procurement markets after the end of the cold war, arms companies in North America and Western Europe had to adapt. By acquiring foreign subsidiaries and partnering with local companies, they successfully gained access to key markets with nascent arms–industrial bases.

The market has also become increasingly competitive. In response, many arms companies have forged new partnerships through mergers, acquisitions and joint ventures. Larger companies are more capable of withstanding, for example, government cuts to military spending because they can leverage economies of scale.[9] Furthermore, by entering into joint ventures, companies pool the risks associated with the development of new weapon programmes. Larger companies can also diversify their portfolios, which makes them less dependent on one single weapon programme.[10]

Moreover, internationalization is driven by national policies aimed at incentivizing investment in the local military–industrial base. For example, Saudi Arabia's Vision 2030 policy sets a target for 50 per cent of arms procurement spending to be localized.[11] In the case of the USA, restrictions on foreign arms imports compel arms companies to acquire USA-based subsidiaries and detach the US operations from their own.[12] Together with the sheer size of the US market, this helps to explain the high number of foreign entities located in the USA.

These strategies are also relevant to many arms companies outside the top 15. Further, the enactment of arms–industrial policies by emerging arms producers will probably continue to encourage foreign arms companies to set up local branches and manufacturing entities in order to gain access to, or expand their presence in, these markets.

---

[9] McKinsey and Company, *The Future of European Defence: Tackling the Productivity Challenge* (McKinsey and Company: May 2013), pp. 24–25.

[10] Devore, M. R., 'Arms production in the global village: Options for adapting to defense-industrial globalization', *Security Studies*, vol. 22, no. 3 (2013), pp. 537–38.

[11] Saudi Arabian Public Investment Fund, 'Saudi Arabian Military Industries', Press release, 17 May 2017.

[12] Manuel, K. M., *The Buy American Act—Preferences for 'Domestic' Supplies: In Brief*, Congressional Research Service (CRS) Report for Congress R43140 (US Congress, CRS: Washington, DC, 26 Apr. 2016); and Perlo-Freeman, S., 'Arms production', *SIPRI Yearbook 2009*, p. 276.

10. World nuclear forces

Overview

At the start of 2021, nine states—the United States, Russia, the United Kingdom, France, China, India, Pakistan, Israel and the Democratic People's Republic of Korea (DPRK, or North Korea)—possessed approximately 13 080 nuclear weapons, of which 3825 were deployed with operational forces (see table 10.1). Approximately 2000 of these are kept in a state of high operational alert.

Overall, the number of nuclear warheads in the world continues to decline. However, this is primarily due to the USA and Russia dismantling retired warheads. Global reductions of operational warheads appear to have stalled, and their numbers may be rising again. At the same time, both the USA and Russia have extensive and expensive programmes under way to replace and modernize their nuclear warheads, missile and aircraft delivery systems, and nuclear weapon production facilities (see sections I and II).

The nuclear arsenals of the other nuclear-armed states are considerably smaller (see sections III–IX), but all are either developing or deploying new weapon systems or have announced their intention to do so. China is in the middle of a significant modernization and expansion of its nuclear arsenal, and India and Pakistan also appear to be increasing the size of their nuclear weapon inventories. North Korea's military nuclear programme remains central to its national security strategy, although in 2020 it did not conduct any tests of nuclear weapons or long-range ballistic missile delivery systems.

The availability of reliable information on the status of the nuclear arsenals and capabilities of the nuclear-armed states varies considerably. The USA, the UK and France have declared some information. Russia refuses to publicly disclose the detailed breakdown of its nuclear forces, even though it shares the information with the USA. China releases little information about force numbers or future development plans. The governments of India and Pakistan make statements about some of their missile tests but provide no information about the status or size of their arsenals. North Korea has acknowledged conducting nuclear weapon and missile tests but provides no information about the size of its nuclear arsenal. Israel has a long-standing policy of not commenting on its nuclear arsenal.

The raw material for nuclear weapons is fissile material, either highly enriched uranium (HEU) or separated plutonium. China, France, Russia, the UK and the USA have produced both HEU and plutonium for use in their nuclear weapons; India and Israel have produced mainly plutonium; and Pakistan has produced mainly HEU but is increasing its ability to produce plutonium.

SIPRI Yearbook 2021: Armaments, Disarmament and International Security
www.sipriyearbook.org

Table 10.1. World nuclear forces, January 2021

All figures are approximate and are estimates based on assessments by the authors. The estimates presented here are based on publicly available information and contain some uncertainties, as reflected in the notes to tables 10.1–10.10.

State	Year of first nuclear test	Deployed warheads[a]	Stored warheads[b]	Other warheads	Total inventory
United States	1945	1 800[c]	2 000[d]	1 750[e]	5 550
Russia	1949	1 625[f]	2 870[g]	1 760[e]	6 255
United Kingdom	1952	120	105	–	225[h]
France	1960	280	10[i]	..	290
China	1964	–	350	–	350
India	1974	–	156	..	156
Pakistan	1998	–	165	..	165
Israel	..	–	90	..	90
North Korea	2006	–	..	[40–50]	[40–50][j]
Total[k]		3 825	5 745	3 510	13 080

.. = not applicable or not available; – = nil or a negligible value; [ ] = uncertain figure.

Note: SIPRI revises its world nuclear forces data each year based on new information and updates to earlier assessments. The data for Jan. 2021 replaces all previously published SIPRI data on world nuclear forces.

[a] These are warheads placed on missiles or located on bases with operational forces.

[b] These are warheads in central storage that would require some preparation (e.g. transport and loading on to launchers) before they could become fully operationally available.

[c] This figure includes approximately 1400 warheads deployed on ballistic missiles and nearly 300 stored at bomber bases in the USA, as well as c. 100 non-strategic (tactical) nuclear bombs deployed outside the USA at North Atlantic Treaty Organization partner bases.

[d] This figure includes c. 130 non-strategic nuclear bombs stored in the USA.

[e] This figure is for retired warheads awaiting dismantlement.

[f] This figure includes approximately 1425 strategic warheads on ballistic missiles and about 200 deployed at heavy bomber bases.

[g] This figure includes c. 960 strategic and c. 1910 non-strategic warheads in central storage.

[h] The British Government declared in 2010 that its nuclear weapon inventory would not exceed 225 warheads. It is estimated here that the inventory remained at that number in Jan. 2021. A planned reduction to an inventory of 180 warheads by the mid 2020s was ended by a government review undertaken in 2020 and published in early 2021. The review introduced a new ceiling of 260 warheads.

[i] The 10 warheads assigned to France's carrier-based aircraft are thought to be kept in central storage and are not normally deployed.

[j] This estimate lists the number of warheads North Korea could potentially build with the amount of fissile material it has produced. There is no publicly available evidence that North Korea has produced an operational nuclear warhead for delivery by an intercontinental-range ballistic missile, but it might have a small number of warheads for medium-range ballistic missiles.

[k] These totals do not include figures for North Korea and are rounded to the nearest 5 warheads.

North Korea has produced plutonium for use in nuclear weapons but may have produced HEU as well. All states with a civilian nuclear industry are capable of producing fissile materials (see section X).

HANS M. KRISTENSEN AND MATT KORDA

I. United States nuclear forces

HANS M. KRISTENSEN AND MATT KORDA

As of January 2021, the United States maintained a military stockpile of approximately 3800 nuclear warheads, roughly the same number as in January 2020. Approximately 1800 of these—consisting of about 1700 strategic and 100 non-strategic (or tactical) warheads—were deployed on aircraft, ballistic missiles and submarines. In addition, about 2000 warheads were held in reserve and around 1750 retired warheads were awaiting dismantlement (250 fewer than the estimate for 2020), giving a total inventory of approximately 5550 nuclear warheads (see table 10.2).

These estimates are based on publicly available information regarding the US nuclear arsenal. In 2010 the USA for the first time declassified the entire history of its nuclear weapon stockpile size, but since 2019 there has been a shift towards a lower level of transparency.[1] This was evidenced by the fact that in 2020, as had been the case in 2019, the US administration of President Donald J. Trump declined to declassify the number of nuclear weapons in the stockpile and the number of retired warheads that had been dismantled over the year.[2] The refusal, which was not explained, provided political cover for other nuclear-armed states to be less transparent and made an accurate independent assessment of the US nuclear arsenal significantly harder.

In 2020 the USA remained in compliance with the final warhead limits prescribed by the 2010 Russian–US Treaty on Measures for the Further Reduction and Limitation of Strategic Offensive Arms (New START), which places a cap on the numbers of US and Russian deployed strategic nuclear forces.[3] The numbers of deployed warheads presented below differ from the numbers reported under New START because the treaty attributes one weapon to each deployed bomber—even though bombers do not carry weapons under normal circumstances—and does not count warheads stored at bomber bases.

The role of nuclear weapons in US military doctrine

According to the 2018 Nuclear Posture Review (NPR), 'The United States would only consider the employment of nuclear weapons in extreme circumstances to defend the vital interests of the United States, its allies, and

---

[1] E.g. US Department of Defense, 'Increasing transparency in the US nuclear weapons stockpile', Fact sheet, 3 May 2010.

[2] Kristensen, H. M., 'Trump administration again refuses to disclose nuclear stockpile size', Federation of American Scientists (FAS) Strategic Security Blog, 3 Dec. 2020.

[3] For a summary and other details of New START see annex A, section III, in this volume. On the negotiation of the renewal of New START see chapter 11, section I, in this volume.

Table 10.2. United States nuclear forces, January 2021

All figures are approximate and some are based on assessments by the authors. Totals for strategic and non-strategic forces are rounded to the nearest 5 warheads.

Type	Designation	No. of launchers	Year first deployed	Range (km)[a]	Warheads x yield	No. of warheads[b]
Strategic nuclear forces						**3 570**
Aircraft (bombers)		107/66[c]				848[d]
B-52H	Stratofortress	87/46	1961	16 000	20 x ALCMs 5–150 kt[e]	528[f]
B-2A	Spirit	20/20	1994	11 000	16 x B61-7,-11, B83-1 bombs[g]	320
Land-based missiles (ICBMs)		400				800[h]
LGM-30G	Minuteman III					
	Mk12A	200	1979	13 000	1–3 x W78 335 kt	600[i]
	Mk21 SERV	200	2006	13 000	1 x W87 300 kt	200[j]
Sea-based missiles (SLBMs)		14/280[k]				1 920[l]
UGM-133A	Trident II (D5/D5LE)					
	Mk4	..	1992	>12 000	1–8 x W76-0 100 kt	–[m]
	Mk4A	..	2008	>12 000	1–8 x W76-1 90 kt	1 511
	Mk4A	..	2019	>12 000	1 x W76-2 8 kt	25[n]
	Mk5	..	1990	>12 000	1–8 x W88 455 kt	384
Non-strategic nuclear forces						230[o]
F-15E	Strike Eagle	..	1988	3 840	5 x B61-3, -4[p]	80
F-16C/D	Falcon	..	1987	3 200[q]	2 x B61-3, -4	70
F-16MLU	Falcon (NATO)	..	1985	3 200	2 x B61-3, -4	40
PA-200	Tornado (NATO)	..	1983	2 400	2 x B61-3, -4	40
Total stockpile						**3 800[r]**
Deployed warheads						1 800[s]
Reserve warheads						2 000
Retired warheads awaiting dismantlement[t]						1 750
Total inventory						**5 550[u]**

.. = not available or not applicable; – = nil or a negligible value; ALCM = air-launched cruise missile; ICBM = intercontinental ballistic missile; kt = kiloton; NATO = North Atlantic Treaty Organization; SERV = security-enhanced re-entry vehicle; SLBM = submarine-launched ballistic missile.

Note: The table lists the total number of warheads estimated to be available for the delivery systems. Only some of these are deployed and the strategic warheads do not necessarily correspond to the data-counting rules of the 2010 Russian–US Treaty on Measures for the Further Reduction and Limitation of Strategic Offensive Arms (New START).

[a] For aircraft, the listed range refers to the maximum unrefuelled range. All nuclear-equipped aircraft can be refuelled in the air. Actual mission range will vary according to flight profile, weapon loading and in-flight refuelling.

[b] These numbers show the total number of warheads estimated to be assigned to nuclear-capable delivery systems. Only some of these warheads are deployed on missiles and at air bases.

[c] The first figure is the total number of bombers in the inventory; the second is the number equipped for nuclear weapons. The USA has declared that it will deploy no more than 60 nuclear bombers at any time but normally only about 50 nuclear bombers are deployed, with the remaining aircraft in overhaul.

[d] Of the c. 848 bomber weapons, c. 300 (200 ALCMs and 100 bombs) are deployed at the bomber bases; all the rest are in central storage. Many of the gravity bombs are no longer fully active and are slated for retirement after the B61-12 is fielded in the early 2020s.

[e] The B-52H is no longer configured to carry nuclear gravity bombs.

[f] In 2006 the Department of Defense decided to reduce the future ALCM fleet to 528 missiles. It is possible the inventory has been reduced slightly since then. Burg., R. (Maj. Gen.), 'ICBMs, helicopters, cruise missiles, bombers and warheads', Statement, US Senate, Armed Services Committee, Strategic Forces Subcommittee, 28. Mar. 2007, p. 7.

[g] Strategic gravity bombs are only assigned to B-2A bombers. The maximum yields of strategic bombs are 360 kt for the B61-7, 400 kt for the B61-11 and 1200 kt for the B83-1. However, all these bombs, except the B-11, have lower-yield options. Most B83-1s have been moved to the inactive stockpile and B-2As rarely exercise with the bomb. The administration of President Barack Obama decided that the B83-1 would be retired once the B61-12 is deployed, but the 2018 Nuclear Posture Review indicates that the B83-1 might be retained for a longer period.

[h] Of the 800 ICBM warheads, only 400 are deployed on the missiles. The remaining warheads are in central storage.

[i] Only 200 of these W78 warheads are deployed; all the rest are in central storage.

[j] SIPRI estimates that another 340 W87 warheads might be in long-term storage outside the stockpile for use in the W78 replacement warhead (W87-1) programme.

[k] The first figure is the total number of nuclear-powered ballistic missile submarines (SSBNs) in the US fleet; the second is the maximum number of missiles that they can carry. However, although the 14 SSBNs can carry up to 280 missiles, 2 vessels are normally undergoing refuelling overhaul at any given time and are not assigned missiles. The remaining 12 SSBNs can carry up to 240 missiles, but 1 or 2 of these vessels are usually undergoing maintenance at any given time and may not be carrying missiles. As of Sep. 2020, the New START aggregate data listed 11 SSBNs deployed with 220 SLBMs.

[l] Of the 1920 SLBM warheads, just over 1000 are deployed on submarines; all the rest are in central storage. Although each D5 missile was counted under the 1991 Strategic Arms Reduction Treaty as carrying 8 warheads and the missile was initially flight tested with 14, the US Navy has downloaded each missile to an average of 4–5 warheads. D5 missiles equipped with the new low-yield W76-2 are estimated to carry only 1 warhead each.

[m] It is assumed here that all W76-0 warheads have been replaced by the W76-1.

[n] According to US military officials, the new low-yield W76-2 warhead will normally be deployed on at least 2 of the SSBNs on patrol in the Atlantic and Pacific oceans.

[o] Approximately 100 of the 230 tactical bombs are thought to be deployed across 6 NATO airbases outside the USA. The remaining bombs are in central storage in the USA. Older B61 versions will be dismantled once the B61-12 is deployed.

[p] The maximum yields of tactical bombs are 170 kt for the B61-3 and 50 kt for the B61-4. All have selective lower yields. The B61-10 was retired in 2016.

[q] Most sources list an unrefuelled ferry range of 2400 km, but Lockheed Martin, which produces the F-16, lists 3200 km.

[r] Of these 3800 weapons, approximately 1800 are deployed on ballistic missiles, at bomber bases in the USA and at 6 NATO airbases outside the USA; all the rest are in central storage.

[s] The deployed warhead number in this table differs from the number declared under New START because the treaty attributes 1 warhead per deployed bomber—even though bombers do not carry warheads under normal circumstances—and does not count warheads stored at bomber bases.

[t] Up until 2018, the US Government published the number of warheads dismantled each year, but the administration of President Donald J. Trump ended this practice. Based on previous performance and the completion of the W76-1 life-extension programme, SIPRI estimates that roughly 250 (but possibly more) retired warheads were dismantled during 2020.

^u In addition to these intact warheads, more than 20 000 plutonium pits are stored at the Pantex Plant, Texas, and perhaps 4000 uranium secondaries are stored at the Y-12 facility at Oak Ridge, Tennessee.

Sources: US Department of Defense, various budget reports and plans, press releases and documents obtained under the Freedom of Information Act; US Department of Energy, various budget reports and plans; US Air Force, US Navy and US Department of Energy, personal communications; *Bulletin of the Atomic Scientists*, 'Nuclear notebook', various issues; and author's estimates.

partners.[4] The NPR further clarifies that the USA reserves the right to use nuclear weapons first in a conflict, and could use nuclear weapons in response to 'significant non-nuclear strategic attacks' on 'the US, allied, or partner civilian population or infrastructure, and attacks on US or allied nuclear forces, their command and control, or warning and attack assessment capabilities'.[5]

The USA continued to implement the 2018 NPR throughout 2020. This included a 25 per cent increase in funding in financial year 2021 for the US National Nuclear Security Administration (NNSA), which, among other things, oversees nuclear warhead research, development and acquisition programmes.[6] The Trump administration continued to implement several large-scale nuclear weapon programmes initiated under the administration of President Barack Obama, including modernization programmes for all three legs of the nuclear triad. The Trump administration also continued to implement several of its own newer non-strategic nuclear weapon programmes. For example, in 2020 the USA completed the deployment of low-yield W76-2 nuclear warheads on its fleet of nuclear-powered ballistic missiles submarines (SSBNs) in the Atlantic and Pacific oceans, and it made progress in its plans to field a new nuclear-armed sea-launched cruise missile (SLCM-N; see below).

The 2018 NPR's justification for the deployment of low-yield warheads and the development of the SLCM-N reflected important doctrinal changes in US nuclear planning. According to the NPR, the W76-2 is intended to provide the USA with a prompt low-yield capability aimed at deterring Russia from escalating to first use of non-strategic nuclear weapons, in the event that Russia perceived it was about to lose a conventional war.[7] However, there is little publicly available evidence of such a shift in Russia's nuclear doc-

---

[4] US Department of Defense (DOD), *Nuclear Posture Review 2018* (DOD: Arlington, VA, Feb. 2018), p. 21.

[5] US Department of Defense (note 4), p. 21.

[6] Woolf, A. F., *Energy and Water Development Appropriations: Nuclear Weapons Activities*, Congressional Research Service (CRS) Report for Congress R44442 (US Congress, CRS: Washington, DC, 22 Dec. 2020), p. i. The US financial year starts on 1 Oct. of the year before the named year and ends on 30 Sep. On US military expenditure see chapter 8, section I, in this volume.

[7] US Department of Defense (note 4), pp. 8, 53–55.

trine.[8] Both the W76-2 and SLCM-N are explicitly intended to restrengthen US non-strategic nuclear weapon operations, which had seemingly reduced in importance for the US military since the end of the cold war. Notably, a 2020 paper by the US Department of Defense (DOD) suggests that the SLCM-N will 'provid[e] additional limited employment capabilities that an adversary will have to consider if contemplating the coercive use of nuclear weapons', and the NPR states that the weapons 'expand the range of credible US options for responding to nuclear or non-nuclear strategic attack'.[9] However, a nuclear attack in response to non-nuclear strategic attacks would constitute first use of nuclear weapons—the very act that the NPR criticizes Russia for including in its presumed doctrine.

Based on the more aggressive nuclear posture set out by the NPR, at the end of 2020 the Trump administration disclosed plans to develop an entirely new nuclear warhead, known as the W93 (see below).[10] This would be the first brand-new warhead developed by the USA since the end of the cold war. The W93 was part of a much broader nuclear weapon modernization plan presented in the NNSA's Nuclear Weapons Stockpile and Management Plan, which doubled the number of new nuclear warhead programmes compared with the previous plan published in 2019.[11]

Strategic nuclear forces

US offensive strategic nuclear forces include heavy bomber aircraft, land-based intercontinental ballistic missiles (ICBMs) and SSBNs. These forces, together known as the triad, changed little during 2020. SIPRI estimates that a total of 3570 nuclear warheads are assigned to the triad, of which an estimated 1700 warheads are deployed on missiles and at bomber bases.

[8] Bruusgaard, K. V., 'Here's why US tactical nukes are a bad idea', *National Interest*, 10 Dec. 2018; Oliker, O. and Baklitskiy, A., 'The Nuclear Posture Review and Russian "de-escalation": A dangerous solution to a nonexistent problem', War on the Rocks, 20 Feb. 2018; and Oliker, O., 'Russia's nuclear doctrine: What we know, what we don't, and what that means', Center for Strategic and International Studies (CSIS), May 2016.

[9] US Office of the Under Secretary of Defense for Policy, *Strengthening Deterrence and Reducing Nuclear Risks*, part II, *The Sea-Launched Cruise Missile-Nuclear (SLCM-N)* (US Department of State, Office of the Under Secretary of State for Arms Control and International Security: Washington, DC, 23 July 2020), p. 3; and US Department of Defense (note 4), p. xiii. For a summary and other details of the Nuclear Posture Review see Kristensen, H. M., 'US nuclear forces', *SIPRI Yearbook 2019*, pp. 289–94.

[10] US Department of Energy, National Nuclear Security Administration (NNSA), *Fiscal Year 2021 Stockpile Stewardship and Management Plan—Biennial Plan Summary*, Report to Congress (NNSA: Washington, DC, Dec. 2020), pp. 2–6. See also Kristensen, H. M., 'NNSA nuclear plan shows more weapons, increasing costs, less transparency', Federation of American Scientists (FAS) Strategic Security Blog, 30 Dec. 2020.

[11] US Department of Energy (note 10).

Aircraft and air-delivered weapons

The US Air Force (USAF) currently operates a fleet of 169 heavy bombers: 62 B-1Bs, 20 B-2As and 87 B-52Hs. Of these, 66 (20 B-2As and 46 B-52Hs) are nuclear-capable. The B-2A can deliver gravity bombs (B61-7, B61-11 and B83-1) and the B-52H can deliver the AGM-86B/W80-1 nuclear air-launched cruise missile (ALCM). SIPRI estimates that almost 850 warheads are assigned to strategic bombers, of which about 300 are deployed at bomber bases and ready for delivery on relatively short notice.

Both the B-2As and B-52Hs are undergoing modernization intended to improve their ability to receive and transmit secure nuclear mission data. This includes the ability to communicate with the Advanced Extreme High Frequency (AEHF) satellite network used by the US president and military leadership to transmit launch orders and manage nuclear operations.[12]

The development of the next-generation long-range strike bomber, known as the B-21 Raider, is well under way and the first two test aircraft are being constructed.[13] The B-21 will be capable of delivering two types of nuclear weapon: the B61-12 guided nuclear gravity bomb, which is nearing full-scale production and will also be deliverable from shorter-range non-strategic aircraft (see below); and the Long-Range Standoff Weapon (LRSO) ALCM, which is in development. The new bomber is scheduled to enter service in the mid 2020s.[14] The B-21 will replace the B-1B and B-2A bombers at Dyess Air Force Base (AFB) in Texas, Ellsworth AFB in South Dakota, and Whiteman AFB in Missouri.[15] The nuclear-capable B-21 will also replace non-nuclear B-1B bombers and entail 'the reintroduction of nuclear mission requirements'.[16] The number of US bomber bases with nuclear weapon storage capability is thus expected to increase from two as of January 2021 to five by the early 2030s.[17] The USAF plans to acquire at least 100 (but possibly as many as 145) B-21 bombers by the mid 2030s.[18] However, the final number will be determined by funding decisions made by the US Congress.

---

[12] US Department of Defense (DOD), *Fiscal Year (FY) 2021 Budget Estimates: Air Force: Justification Book*, vol. 3a, *Research, Development, Test & Evaluation, Air Force*, vol. III, part 1 (DOD: Arlington, VA, Feb. 2020), pp. 109–82, 203–21.

[13] Tirpak, J., 'Second B-21 under construction as bomber moves toward first flight', *Air Force Magazine*, 15 Jan. 2021.

[14] Gertler, J., *Air Force B-21 Raider Long-range Strike Bomber*, Congressional Research Service (CRS) Report for Congress R44463 (US Congress, CRS: Washington, DC, 13 Nov. 2019), p. 10.

[15] US Air Force, Secretary of the Air Force Public Affairs, 'Air force selects locations for B-21 aircraft', 2 May 2018.

[16] Dawkins, J. C., Commander, 8th Air Force and Joint-Global Strike Operations Center, Barksdale AFB, 'B21 General Dawkins intro', YouTube, 19 Mar. 2020, 01:35.

[17] Kristensen, H. M., 'USAF plans to expand nuclear bomber bases', Federation of American Scientists (FAS) Strategic Security Blog, 17 Nov. 2020.

[18] Tirpak, J., 'A new bomber vision', *Air Force Magazine*, 1 June 2020.

Land-based missiles

As of January 2021, the USA deployed 400 Minuteman III ICBMs in 450 silos across three missile wings. The 50 empty silos are kept in a state of readiness and can be reloaded with stored missiles if necessary.[19]

Each Minuteman III ICBM is armed with one warhead: either a 335-kiloton W78 or a 300-kt W87. The W78 warhead is carried in the Mk12A re-entry vehicle and the W87 is carried in the Mk21 re-entry vehicle. Missiles carrying the W78 can be uploaded with up to two more warheads for a maximum of three multiple independently targetable re-entry vehicles (MIRVs). SIPRI estimates that there are 800 warheads assigned to the ICBM force, of which 400 are deployed on the missiles.

The USAF has begun development of a next-generation ICBM, the Ground Based Strategic Deterrent (GBSD). It is scheduled to begin replacing the Minuteman III in 2028, with full replacement by 2036.[20] On 8 December 2020 the USAF awarded a $13.3 billion engineering and manufacturing development contract to Northrop Grumman Corporation—the sole bidder for the GBSD contract. According to the USAF, the GBSD is a 'modular design' with 'evolutionary warfighting effectiveness' that will give the US ICBM force 'increased accuracy, extended range and improved reliability'.[21] It has not yet publicly provided a rationale for why these enhanced capabilities are needed for the ICBM mission.

The projected cost of the programme has continued to increase and the absence of competition in the bidding process for the contract may have eliminated any potential to make savings up front. The total projected cost rose from $62.5 billion in 2015 to $95.8 billion in 2020.[22] For the 10-year period 2019–28 alone, the US Congressional Budget Office (CBO) in 2019 projected that the cost would be $61 billion, $18 billion higher than the 2017 estimate for 2017–26.[23] The cost is likely to increase further, which perhaps calls into question the decision not to extend the life of the existing Minuteman III.

The USAF is also modernizing the nuclear warheads that will be used to arm the GBSD. Initially, some of these will also be used to arm the current Minuteman III for the remainder of its service life. The W87/Mk21 is being

---

[19] Willett, E., 'AF meets New START requirements', US Air Force Global Strike Command, 28 June 2017.

[20] Richard, C. A., Commander, US Strategic Command, Statement, US Senate, Armed Services Committee, 13 Feb. 2020, p. 9.

[21] US Air Force, Secretary of the Air Force Public Affairs, 'Department of the Air Force awards contract for new ICBM that enhances, strengthens US triad', 8 Sep. 2020.

[22] Reif, K., 'New ICBM replacement cost revealed', *Arms Control Today*, vol. 47, no. 2 (Mar. 2017); and Burns, R., 'Pentagon estimates cost of new nuclear missiles at $95.8B', Associated Press, 20 Oct. 2020.

[23] Bennett, M., 'Projected costs of US nuclear forces, 2019 to 2028', US Congressional Budget Office, Jan. 2019, p. 9.

upgraded with a new arming, fusing and firing unit, and the W78/Mk12A will be replaced entirely. The replacement warhead was formerly known as the Interoperable Warhead 1 (IW1), but in 2018 it was given the designation W87-1 to reflect the fact that it will use a plutonium pit similar to that of the W87, with insensitive high explosives (IHE) instead of the conventional high explosives (CHE) used in the W78.[24] The projected cost of the W87-1 programme is between $11.8 billion and $15 billion, but this estimate does not include costs associated with production of plutonium pits for the W87-1.[25]

Sea-based missiles

The US Navy operates a fleet of 14 Ohio-class SSBNs, of which 12 are normally considered to be operational and 2 are typically undergoing refuelling and overhaul at any given time. Eight of the SSBNs are based at Naval Base Kitsap in Washington state and six at Naval Submarine Base Kings Bay in Georgia.

Each Ohio-class SSBN can carry up to 20 Trident II D5 submarine-launched ballistic missiles (SLBMs). To meet the New START limit on deployed launchers, 4 of the 24 initial missile tubes on each submarine were deactivated so that the 12 deployable SSBNs can carry no more than 240 missiles.[26] Around 8 to 10 SSBNs are normally at sea, of which 4 or 5 are on alert in their designated patrol areas and ready to fire their missiles within 15 minutes of receiving the launch order.

The Trident II D5 SLBMs carry two basic warhead types. These are the 455-kt W88 and the W76, which exists in two versions: the 90-kt W76-1 and the low-yield W76-2.[27] The W88 warhead is carried in the Mk5 re-entry body (aeroshell); the W76-1 and W76-2 warheads each use the Mk4A re-entry body. The Mk4A is equipped with a new fuse that improves its damage effectiveness.[28] Each SLBM can carry up to eight warheads but normally carries an average of four to five. SIPRI estimates that around 1920 warheads are assigned to the SSBN fleet, of which about 1000 are currently deployed on missiles.[29]

[24] Padilla, M., 'Sandia on target for first Mk21 Fuze flight test in 2018', *Sandia LabNews*, vol. 70, no. 6 (16 Mar. 2018); and US Department of Energy, National Nuclear Security Administration (NNSA), *W78 Replacement Program (W87-1): Cost Estimates and Use of Insensitive High Explosives*, Report to Congress (NNSA: Washington, DC, Dec. 2018), pp. III, 7.

[25] US Department of Energy (note 10), pp. 5–32, 5–33.

[26] US Navy Office of Information, 'Fleet ballistic missile submarines—SSBN', America's Navy, 29 Jan. 2019.

[27] The older W76-0 version has been, or remains in the process of being, retired.

[28] Kristensen, H. M., McKinzie, M. and Postol, T. A., 'How US nuclear forces modernization is undermining strategic stability: The burst-height compensating super-fuze', *Bulletin of the Atomic Scientists*, 1 Mar. 2017.

[29] US Department of State, Bureau of Arms Control, Verification and Compliance, 'New START Treaty aggregate numbers of strategic offensive arms', Fact sheet, 1 Dec. 2020.

The newest warhead, the low-yield W76-2, was first deployed in late 2019 onboard the USS *Tennessee* (SSBN-734) in the Atlantic Ocean and is now deployed on SSBNs in both the Atlantic and the Pacific.[30] It is a modification of the W76-1 and is estimated to have an explosive yield of about 8 kt.[31] As noted above, the 2018 NPR claims that the warhead is needed to deter Russia from the first use of low-yield non-strategic nuclear weapons, even though the USA already has an estimated 1050 air-delivered weapons with low-yield options in its inventory.[32]

Since 2017, the US Navy has been replacing its Trident II D5 SLBMs with an enhanced version, known as the D5LE (LE for 'life extension'). The upgrade is scheduled to be completed in 2024.[33] The D5LE is equipped with the new Mk6 guidance system. The D5LE will arm Ohio-class SSBNs for the remainder of their service lives (up to 2042) and will be deployed on the United Kingdom's Trident submarines (see section III). A new class of SSBN, the Columbia class, will initially also be armed with the D5LE, but these will eventually be replaced with an upgraded SLBM, the D5LE2, starting in 2039.[34] The first Columbia-class SSBN—the USS *Columbia* (SSBN-826)—is scheduled to start patrols in 2031.

To arm the D5LE2, the NNSA has begun early design development of a new nuclear warhead, known as the W93, to complement the W76 and W88 warheads. The W93 warhead will be housed in a new Mk7 re-entry body (aeroshell) that will also be delivered to the British Royal Navy. According to the DOD, the W93/Mk7 will be lighter than existing SLBM warheads, even though it will use IHE instead of CHE to increase safety. It will 'allow for more efficient targeting by expanding the footprint of targets the warhead can hit, thereby increasing targeting flexibility and efficiency', which will 'improve the SSBN force's ability to hold all targets in current plans at risk'.[35] Production is scheduled to begin in the mid 2030s.[36]

---

[30] Arkin, W. M. and Kristensen, H. M., 'US deploys new low-yield nuclear submarine warhead', Federation of American Scientists (FAS) Strategic Security Blog, 29 Jan. 2020; and US Department of Defense, 'Statement on the fielding of the W76-2 low-yield submarine-launched ballistic missile warhead', Press release, 4 Feb. 2020.

[31] US military officials, Private communications with authors, 2019–20.

[32] US Department of Defense (note 4), pp. 54–55; and Kristensen, H. M., 'The flawed push for new nuclear weapons capabilities', Federation of American Scientists (FAS) Strategic Security Blog, 29 June 2017. This estimate covers strategic and non-strategic weapons but does not include the B61-11, which has a single high-yield option.

[33] Wolfe, J., Director of US Strategic Systems Programs, Statement, US Senate, Armed Services Committee, Strategic Forces Subcommittee, 1 May. 2019, p. 4.

[34] Wolfe, J., Director of US Strategic Systems Programs, 'FY2021 budget request for nuclear forces and atomic energy defense activities', Statement, US House of Representatives, Armed Services Committee, Strategic Forces Subcommittee, 3 Mar. 2020, p. 5.

[35] US Department of Defense, 'W93/Mk7 Navy warhead: Developing modern capabilities to address current and future threats', May 2020, p. 2. Part of this document is available online.

[36] US Department of Defense (note 35), p. 2.

Non-strategic nuclear forces

US non-strategic (tactical) nuclear forces include nuclear bombs delivered by several types of short-range fighter-bomber aircraft, as well as potentially a future nuclear-armed SLCM.

Air force weapons

The USA currently has one basic type of air-delivered non-strategic weapon in its stockpile—the B61 gravity bomb, which exists in two versions: the B61-3 and the B61-4.[37] An estimated 230 tactical B61 bombs remain in the stockpile.

SIPRI estimates that the USA deploys approximately 100 of the bombs for potential use by fighter-bomber aircraft at six airbases in five other member states of the North Atlantic Treaty Organization (NATO): Kleine Brogel in Belgium; Büchel in Germany; Aviano and Ghedi in Italy; Volkel in the Netherlands; and İncirlik in Turkey.[38] The remaining (c. 130) B61 bombs are thought to be stored at Kirtland AFB in New Mexico for potential use by US aircraft in support of allies outside Europe, including in East Asia.[39]

The USA is close to completing the development of the B61-12 guided nuclear bomb, which will replace all existing versions of the B61 (both strategic and non-strategic). Delivery was scheduled to start in 2020 but production problems in 2019 caused delays; delivery is now expected to take place in 2022.[40] The new version is equipped with a guided tail kit that enables it to hit targets more accurately, meaning that it could be used with a lower yield and potentially produce less radioactive fallout.[41]

Operations to integrate the incoming B61-12 on existing USAF and NATO aircraft continued in 2020. The USAF plans to integrate the B61-12 on seven types of US- and allied-operated aircraft: the B-2A, the new B-21, the F-15E, the F-16C/D, the F-16MLU, the F-35A and the PA-200 (Tornado).[42] Germany plans to retire its Tornado aircraft by 2030. In 2020 the German Government stressed the need for Germany to continue to participate in the NATO nuclear strike mission and submitted a proposal to the national parliament

---

[37] A third version, the B61-10, was retired in Sep. 2016. US Department of Energy, National Nuclear Security Administration (NNSA), *Fiscal Year 2018 Stockpile Stewardship and Management Plan*, Report to Congress (NNSA: Washington, DC, Nov. 2017), figure 1-7, pp. 1–13.

[38] For a detailed overview of the dual-capable aircraft programmes of the USA and its NATO allies see Kristensen (note 9), pp. 299–300; and Andreasen, S. et al., *Building a Safe, Secure, and Credible NATO Nuclear Posture* (Nuclear Threat Initiative: Washington, DC, Jan. 2018).

[39] US Department of Defense (note 4), p. 48.

[40] Gould, J. and Mehta, A., 'Nuclear gravity bomb and warhead upgrades face new delays', *Defense News*, 4 Sep. 2019; and Trevithick, J., 'F-15E Strike Eagle first jet cleared to employ Air Force's new B61-12 nuclear bombs', The Drive, 8 June 2020.

[41] Kristensen, H. M. and McKinzie, M., 'Video shows earth-penetrating capability of B61-12 nuclear bomb', Federation of American Scientists (FAS) Strategic Security Blog, 14 Jan. 2016.

[42] US Air Force (USAF), *Acquisition Annual Report Fiscal Year 2018: Cost-effective Modernization* (USAF: Arlington, VA, [n.d.]), p. 24.

to acquire 30 F/A-18E combat aircraft from the USA specifically adapted for delivering the new B61-12 nuclear bomb.[43] The final decision to proceed with the acquisition lies with the parliament and is planned for 2022 or 2023.[44]

Navy weapons

As noted above, the 2018 NPR established a requirement for a new nuclear-armed SLCM—the SLCM-N.[45] In 2019 the US Navy began an 'analysis of alternatives' study for the new weapon. Its Strategic Systems Programs office has been directed to complete the study in time for inclusion in the presidential budget request for financial year 2022.[46]

The USA eliminated all non-strategic naval nuclear weapons after the end of the cold war. Completion of the SLCM-N would therefore mark a significant change in US Navy strategy.[47] If the administration of President Joe Biden continues the programme and the US Congress agrees to fund it, then the new missile could be deployed on attack submarines by the end of the 2020s. This could potentially result in the first increase in the size of the US nuclear weapon stockpile since 1996.

---

[43] German Federal Ministry of Defence, 'Bundeswehr strebt Brückenlösung für Tornado-Nachfolge an' [Bundeswehr strives for a bridge solution for the Tornado successor], 22 Apr. 2020; Wiegold, T., 'Verteidigungsministerium will Boeings F-18 als Brückenlösung' [Defense Ministry wants Boeing's F-18 as a bridge solution], Augengeradeaus.net, 21 Apr. 2020; and Gebauer, M. and von Hammerstein, K., 'Kramp-Karrenbauer sagt Washington Kauf von US-Kampfjets zu' [Kramp-Karrenbauer promises Washington to buy US fighter jets], *Der Spiegel*, 19 Apr. 2020. On Germany's proposed acquisition of F/A-18Es see chapter 9, section III, in this volume.

[44] German Federal Ministry of Defence (note 43).

[45] US Department of Defense (note 4), pp. 54–55.

[46] Wolfe (note 34), p. 8.

[47] Kristensen, H. M., 'Declassified: US nuclear weapons at sea', Federation of American Scientists (FAS) Strategic Security Blog, 3 Feb. 2016.

II. Russian nuclear forces

HANS M. KRISTENSEN AND MATT KORDA

As of January 2021, Russia maintained a military stockpile of approximately 4495 nuclear warheads—around 180 more than the estimate for January 2020. About 2585 of these were offensive strategic warheads, of which roughly 1625 were deployed on land- and sea-based ballistic missiles and at bomber bases. Russia also possessed approximately 1910 non-strategic (tactical) nuclear warheads—a slight increase compared with the estimate for January 2020, largely due to the Russian Navy's fielding of dual-capable non-strategic weapons. All of the non-strategic warheads are thought to be at central storage sites.[1] An estimated additional 1760 retired warheads were awaiting dismantlement (300 fewer than the estimate for 2020), giving a total inventory of approximately 6255 warheads (see table 10.3).

These estimates are based on publicly available information about the Russian nuclear arsenal. Because of a lack of transparency, estimates and analysis of Russia's nuclear weapon developments come with considerable uncertainty, particularly with regard to Russia's sizable stockpile of non-strategic nuclear weapons. However, it is possible to formulate a reasonable assessment of the progress of Russia's nuclear modernization by reviewing satellite imagery and other forms of open-source intelligence, official statements, industry publications and interviews with military officials.

In 2020 Russia remained in compliance with the final warhead limits prescribed by the 2010 Russian–United States Treaty on Measures for the Further Reduction and Limitation of Strategic Offensive Arms (New START).[2] This treaty places a cap on the numbers of Russian and US deployed strategic nuclear forces. The numbers of deployed warheads reported under New START differ from the estimates presented here because the treaty attributes one weapon to each deployed bomber—even though bombers do not carry weapons under normal circumstances—and does not count warheads stored at bomber bases.

---

[1] For an overview of Russia's nuclear weapon storage facilities see Podvig, P. and Serrat, J., *Lock Them Up: Zero-deployed Non-strategic Nuclear Weapons in Europe* (United Nations Institute for Disarmament Research: Geneva, 2017).

[2] US Department of State, Bureau of Arms Control, Verification and Compliance, 'New START Treaty aggregate numbers of strategic offensive arms', Fact sheet, 1 Dec. 2020. For a summary and other details of New START see annex A, section III. On the negotiation of the renewal of New START see chapter 11, section I, in this volume.

The role of nuclear weapons in Russian military doctrine

In June 2020 Russian President Vladimir Putin approved an update to the Basic Principles of State Policy of the Russian Federation on Nuclear Deterrence. Russia's deterrence policy lays out explicit conditions under which it could launch nuclear weapons: to retaliate against an ongoing attack 'against critical governmental or military sites' by ballistic missiles, nuclear weapons or other weapons of mass destruction (WMD), and to retaliate against 'the use of conventional weapons when the very existence of the state is in jeopardy'.[3] This formulation is consistent with previous public iterations of Russian nuclear policy, and the timing of the policy update is probably intended to push back against the claim in the USA's 2018 Nuclear Posture Review that Russia might use nuclear weapons early in a conflict to 'de-escalate' it on favourable terms (see section I).[4]

Strategic nuclear forces

As of January 2021, Russia had an estimated 2585 warheads assigned for potential use by strategic launchers: long-range bombers, land-based intercontinental ballistic missiles (ICBMs), and submarine-launched ballistic missiles (SLBMs). This is an increase of approximately 145 warheads compared with January 2020, due to the fielding of RS-24 Yars (SS-27 Mod 2) ICBMs and the fourth Borei-class nuclear-powered ballistic missile submarine (SSBN).[5]

Aircraft and air-delivered weapons

Russia's Long-Range Aviation command operates a fleet of approximately 13 Tu-160 (Blackjack) and 55 Tu-95MS (Bear) bombers.[6] Not all of these are fully operational and some are undergoing various upgrades. The maximum possible loading on the bombers is nearly 740 nuclear weapons but, since only some of the bombers are fully operational, it is estimated here that the number of assigned weapons is lower—around 580. SIPRI estimates that approximately 200 of these might be deployed and stored at the two strategic bomber bases: Engels in Saratov oblast and Ukrainka in Amur

---

[3] 'Basic principles of state policy of the Russian Federation on nuclear deterrence', Approved by Russian Presidential Executive Order no. 355, 2 June 2020.

[4] US Department of Defense (DOD), *Nuclear Posture Review 2018* (DOD: Arlington, VA, Feb. 2018), p. 30.

[5] For the missiles, aircraft and submarines discussed here, a designation in parentheses (in this case SS-27 Mod 2) following the Russian designation (in this case RS-24 Yars) is that assigned by the North Atlantic Treaty Organization (NATO).

[6] The Tu-95MS exists in 2 versions: the Tu-95MS16 (Bear-H16) and the Tu-95MS6 (Bear-H6).

Table 10.3. Russian nuclear forces, January 2021

All figures are approximate and are estimates based on assessments by the authors. Totals for strategic and non-strategic forces are rounded to the nearest 5 warheads.

Type/ Russian designation (NATO designation)	No. of launchers	Year first deployed	Range (km)[a]	Warheads x yield	No. of warheads[b]
Strategic nuclear forces					2 585[c]
Aircraft (bombers)	68/50[d]				580[e]
Tu-95MS/M (Bear-H)[f]	55/39	1981	6 500– 10 500	6–16 x 200 kt AS-15A or AS-23B ALCMs	448
Tu-160/M (Blackjack)	13/11	1987	10 500– 13 200	12 x 200 kt AS-15B or AS-23B ALCMs, bombs	132
Land-based missiles (ICBMs)	310				1 189[g]
RS-20V (SS-18 Satan)	46	1992	11 000– 15 000	10 x 500–800 kt	460
RS-18 (SS-19 Stiletto)	..	1980	10 000	6 x 400 kt	..[h]
Avangard (SS-19 Mod 4)[i]	4	2019	10 000	1 x HGV [400 kt]	4
RS-12M Topol (SS-25 Sickle)	27	1985	10 500	1 x 800 kt	27
RS-12M2 Topol-M (SS-27 Mod 1/silo)	60	1997	10 500	1 x 800 kt	60
RS-12M1 Topol-M (SS-27 Mod 1/mobile)	18	2006	10 500	1 x [800 kt]	18
RS-24 Yars (SS-27 Mod 2/mobile)	135	2010	10 500	4 x [100 kt]	540
RS-24 Yars (SS-27 Mod 2/silo)	20	2014	10 500	4 x [100 kt]	80
RS-28 Sarmat (SS-X-29)	..	[2021]	>10 000	MIRV [.. kt]	..
Sea-based missiles (SLBMs)	11/176[j]				816[k]
RSM-50 Volna (SS-N-18 M1 Stingray)	1/16	1978	6 500	3 x 50 kt	48
RSM-54 Sineva (SS-N-23 M1)	6/96	1986/ 2007	9 000	4 x 100 kt	384
RSM-56 Bulava (SS-N-32)	4/64	2014	>8 050	6 x [100 kt]	384
Non-strategic nuclear forces					1 910[l]
Air, coastal and missile defence	886				387
53T6 (SH-08, Gazelle)	68	1986	30	1 x 10 kt	68
S-300/400 (SA-20/21)	750[m]	1992/ 2007	..	1 x low kt	290
3M-55 Yakhont (SS-N-26)	60	[2014]	>400	1 x [.. kt]	25
SSC-1B (Sepal)	8	1973	500	1 x 350 kt	4
Air force weapons[n]	260				500
Tu-22M3 (Backfire-C)	60	1974	..	3 x ASMs, bombs	300
Su-24M/M2 (Fencer-D)	70	1974	..	2 x bombs	70[o]
Su-34 (Fullback)	120	2006	..	2 x bombs	120[o]
Su-57 (Felon)	..	[2020]	..	[bombs, ASM]	..
MiG-31K (Foxhound)	10	2018	..	1 x ALBM	10

Type/ Russian designation (NATO designation)	No. of launchers	Year first deployed	Range (km)[a]	Warheads x yield	No. of warheads[b]
Army weapons	164				90
Iskander-M (SS-26 Stone)	144	2005	350[p]	[1 x 10–100 kt]	70[q]
9M729 (SSC-8)	20	2016	2 350	1 x [.. kt]	20
Navy weapons	..				935
Submarines/surface ships/naval aircraft	..		Land-attack cruise missiles, sea-launched cruise missiles, anti-submarine weapons, surface-to-air missiles, depth bombs, torpedoes[r]		
Total stockpile					**4 495**
Deployed warheads					1 625[s]
Reserve warheads					2 870[t]
Retired warheads awaiting dismantlement					**1 760**
Total inventory					**6 255**

.. = not available or not applicable; [ ] = uncertain figure; ALBM = air-launched ballistic missile; ALCM = air-launched cruise missile; ASM = air-to-surface missile; HGV = hypersonic glide vehicle; ICBM = intercontinental ballistic missile; kt = kiloton; MIRV = multiple independently targetable re-entry vehicle; NATO = North Atlantic Treaty Organization; SLBM = submarine-launched ballistic missile.

Note: The table lists the total number of warheads estimated to be available for the delivery systems. Only some of these are deployed and the strategic warheads do not necessarily correspond to the data-counting rules of the 2010 Russian–US Treaty on Measures for the Further Reduction and Limitation of Strategic Offensive Arms (New START).

[a] For aircraft, the listed range is for illustrative purposes only; actual mission range will vary according to flight profile, weapon loading and in-flight refuelling.

[b] These numbers show the total number of warheads estimated to be assigned to nuclear-capable delivery systems. Only some of these warheads are deployed on missiles and at air bases.

[c] Approximately 1625 of these strategic warheads are deployed on land- and sea-based ballistic missiles and at bomber bases. The remaining warheads are in central storage.

[d] The first figure is the total number of bombers in the inventory; the second is the number of bombers estimated to be counted as deployed under New START. Because of ongoing bomber modernization, there is considerable uncertainty about how many bombers are operational.

[e] The maximum possible loading on the bombers is nearly 740 nuclear weapons but, since only some of the bombers are fully operational, SIPRI estimates that only about 580 weapons are assigned to the long-range bomber force, of which approximately 200 might be deployed and stored at the 2 strategic bomber bases. The remaining weapons are thought to be in central storage facilities.

[f] There are 2 types of Tu-95MS aircraft: the Tu-95MS6, which can carry 6 AS-15A missiles internally; and the Tu-95MS16, which can carry an additional 10 AS-15A missiles externally, for a total of 16 missiles. Both types are being modernized. The modernized aircraft (Tu-95MSM) can carry 8 AS-23B missiles externally and possibly 6 internally, for a total of 14 missiles.

[g] These ICBMs can carry a total of 1189 warheads, but it is estimated here that they have been downloaded to carry just over 800 warheads, with the remaining warheads in storage.

[h] It is possible that the remaining RS-18s have been retired.

[i] The missile uses a modified RS-18 ICBM booster with an HGV payload.

[j] The first figure is the total number of nuclear-powered ballistic missile submarines (SSBNs) in the Russian fleet; the second is the maximum number of missiles that they can

carry. Of Russia's 11 operational SSBNs, 1 or 2 are in overhaul at any given time and do not carry their assigned nuclear missiles and warheads.

[k] The warhead loading on SLBMs is thought to have been reduced for Russia to stay below the New START warhead limit. It is estimated here that only about 624 of the 816 SLBM warheads are deployed.

[l] According to the Russian Government, non-strategic nuclear warheads are not deployed with their delivery systems but are kept in storage facilities. Some storage facilities are near operational bases.

[m] There are at least 80 S-300/400 sites across Russia, each with an average of 12 launchers, each with 2–4 interceptors. Each launcher has several reloads.

[n] The subtotal is based on an estimate of the total number of nuclear-capable aircraft. However, only some of them are thought to have nuclear missions. Most can carry more than 1 nuclear weapon. Other potential nuclear-capable aircraft include the Su-25 (Frogfoot) and the Su-30MK.

[o] These estimates assume that half of the aircraft have a nuclear role.

[p] Although many unofficial sources and news media reports state that the Iskander-M has a range of nearly 500 km, the US Air Force's National Air and Space Intelligence Center (NASIC) lists the range as 350 km.

[q] The estimate assumes that around half of the dual-capable launchers have a secondary nuclear role. It is possible that the 9M728 (SSC-7, sometimes called Iskander-K) cruise missile is also nuclear-capable.

[r] Only submarines are assumed to be assigned nuclear torpedoes.

[s] The deployed warhead number in this table differs from the number declared under New START because the treaty attributes 1 warhead per deployed bomber—even though bombers do not carry warheads under normal circumstances—and does not count warheads stored at bomber bases.

[t] Reserve warheads include c. 960 strategic and c. 1910 non-strategic warheads in central storage (see note l).

Sources: Russian Ministry of Defence, various press releases; US Department of State, START Treaty Memoranda of Understanding, 1990–July 2009; New START aggregate data releases, various years; US Air Force, National Air and Space Intelligence Center (NASIC), *Ballistic and Cruise Missile Threat 2020* (NASIC: Wright-Patterson Air Force Base, OH, July 2020); US Department of Defense (DOD), *Nuclear Posture Review 2018* (DOD: Arlington, VA, Feb. 2018); US Department of Defense (DOD), *2019 Missile Defense Review* (DOD: Arlington, VA, 2019); US Office of the Deputy Assistant Secretary of Defense for Nuclear Matters, *Nuclear Matters Handbook 2020* (US Department of Defense: Arlington, VA, Mar. 2020); US Department of Defense, various Congressional testimonies; BBC Monitoring; Russian news media; Russian Strategic Nuclear Forces website; International Institute for Strategic Studies (IISS), *The Military Balance*, various years; Cochran, T. B. et al., *Nuclear Weapons Databook*, vol. 4, *Soviet Nuclear Weapons* (Harper & Row: New York, 1989); IHS *Jane's Strategic Weapon Systems*, various issues; *Proceedings*, US Naval Institute, various issues; *Bulletin of the Atomic Scientists*, 'Nuclear notebook', various issues; and authors' estimates.

oblast.[7] An upgrade of the nuclear weapon storage site at Engels is under way.[8]

Modernization of the bombers, which includes upgrades to their avionics suites, engines and long-range nuclear and conventional cruise missiles, is

[7] Podvig, P., 'Strategic aviation', Russian Strategic Nuclear Forces, 4 Jan. 2020.

[8] Kristensen, H. M. and Korda, M., 'Nuclear upgrade at Russian bomber base and storage site', Federation of American Scientists (FAS) Strategic Security Blog, 25 Feb. 2019.

progressing, but with some delays.[9] The upgraded Tu-95MS is known as the Tu-95MSM and the upgraded Tu-160 is known as the Tu-160M. The upgraded bombers are capable of carrying the new Kh-102 (AS-23B) nuclear air-launched cruise missile. According to the Kremlin, two Tu-160s and five Tu-95MSs were upgraded in 2020.[10] It seems likely that all of the Tu-160s and most of the Tu-95s will be upgraded to maintain a bomber force of perhaps 50–60 operational aircraft. Russia has also resumed production of the Tu-160 airframes to produce up to 50 Tu-160M2 bombers with new engines and advanced communications suites.[11] The first Tu-160M2 is expected to make its maiden flight in late 2021.[12]

The modernized Tu-95MSM, Tu-160M and Tu-160M2 bombers are intended to be only a temporary bridge to Russia's next-generation bomber: the PAK-DA. This is a subsonic aircraft that may look similar to the flying-wing design of the USA's B-2 bomber. The PAK-DA's production has been delayed and final assembly of the first aircraft is now scheduled for 2021, with serial production expected to begin in 2028 or 2029.[13] The PAK-DA will eventually replace all Tu-95s and Tu-160s as well as the Tu-22s that are deployed with non-strategic forces (see below).[14]

Land-based missiles

As of January 2021, Russia's Strategic Rocket Forces (SRF)—the branch of the armed forces that controls land-based ICBMs—consisted of 11 missile divisions grouped into 3 armies, deploying an estimated 310 ICBMs of different types and variations (see table 10.3).[15] These ICBMs can carry a maximum of about 1189 warheads, but it is estimated here that they have been downloaded to carry around 800 warheads to keep Russia below the New START limit for deployed strategic warheads. These represent approximately half of Russia's 1625 deployed strategic warheads.

Russia's ICBM force is most of the way through a significant modernization programme to replace all Soviet-era missiles with new types, albeit not on a one-for-one basis. The modernization, which began in the late 1990s, also involves substantial reconstruction of silos, launch control

---

[9] Trevithick, J., 'Russia rolls out new Tu-160M2, but are Moscow's bomber ambitions realistic?', The Drive, 16. Nov. 2017.

[10] President of Russia, 'Expanded meeting of the Defence Ministry Board', 21 Dec. 2020.

[11] 'Tu-160M2, Tu-22M3M bombers to get communications suite from latest Su-57 fighter', TASS, 12 Aug. 2020.

[12] 'First newly-built Tu-160M to make maiden flight in 4th quarter of 2021', TASS, 30 Dec. 2020.

[13] 'Russia begins construction of the first PAK DA strategic bomber—sources', TASS, 26 May 2020; and Lavrov, A., Kretsul, R. and Ramm, A., [PAKage agreement: The latest bomber assigned a deadline for production], *Izvestia*, 14 Jan. 2020 (in Russian).

[14] 'Russia to test next-generation stealth strategic bomber', TASS, 2 Aug. 2019.

[15] A 12th division, the 40th missile regiment at Yurya, is not nuclear-armed.

centres, garrisons and support facilities.[16] The modernization programme appears to be progressing more slowly than previously envisioned. According to Colonel General Sergey Karakaev, commander of the SRF, over 81 per cent of the ICBM force had been modernized by the end of 2020.[17] This is significantly lower than the goal of 97 per cent announced in 2014 for the end of 2020.[18] In November 2020 the chief designer of the RS-24 suggested that the last Soviet-era ICBM would be phased out by 2024.[19] However, this seems unlikely based on an assessment of the probable time frame for replacing the RS-20V (SS-18; see below).

The bulk of the modernization programme is focused on the RS-24 Yars (SS-27 Mod 2), a version of the RS-12M1/2 Topol-M (SS-27 Mod 1) deployed with multiple independently targetable re-entry vehicles (MIRVs). In December 2020 the Russian Ministry of Defence's television channel declared that approximately 150 mobile and silo-based RS-24 ICBMs had been deployed.[20] Four mobile RS-24 divisions have now been completed (Irkutsk, Nizhniy Tagil, Novosibirsk and Yoshkar-Ola), with two more in progress (Barnaul and Vypolzovo—sometimes referred to as Bologovsky).[21] In addition, one completed mobile division at Teykovo is equipped with single-warhead RS-12M1 Topol-M (SS-27 Mod 1) ICBMs. The first silo-based RS-24s have been installed at Kozelsk, Kaluga oblast; one regiment of 10 silos was completed in 2018, and the second regiment was completed in 2020.[22] In December 2020 Karakaev announced that in 2021 the military would begin to install silo-based RS-24s at a third regiment at Kozelsk; however, given how long the previous silo upgrades took, it is unlikely that the third regiment will be completed by the 2024 target date.[23] It is also possible that some of the former RS-18 (SS-19) silos at Tatishchevo Airbase, Saratov oblast, might eventually be upgraded to the RS-24.

In December 2020 two more RS-18 missiles equipped with the Avangard hypersonic glide vehicle (HGV) system were installed in former RS-20V

---

[16] See e.g. Kristensen, H. M., 'Russian ICBM upgrade at Kozelsk', Federation of American Scientists (FAS) Strategic Security Blog, 5 Sep. 2018.

[17] Andreev, D. and Biryulin, R., [Nuclear missile shield guarantees Russia's sovereignty], *Krasnaya Zvezda*, 16 Dec. 2020 (in Russian).

[18] 'Russian TV show announces new ICBM to enter service soon', TRK Petersburg Channel 5, 21 Apr. 2014, Translation from Russian, BBC Monitoring.

[19] 'Russia to complete rearming Strategic Missile Force with advanced Yars ICBMs by 2024', TASS, 2 Nov. 2020.

[20] Levin, E., [Strategic Rocket Forces commander names the number of Yars complexes entering combat duty], *Krasnaya Zvezda*, 8 Dec. 2020 (in Russian).

[21] Tikhonov, A., [You won't catch them by surprise], *Krasnaya Zvezda*, 28 May 2018 (in Russian); and [The commander of the Strategic Missile Forces announced the completion of the rearmament of the Tagil division], RIA Novosti, 29 Mar. 2018 (in Russian).

[22] [Two regiments of the Strategic Rocket Forces will be re-equipped with 'Yars' missile systems in 2021], TASS, 21 Dec. 2020 (in Russian); and authors' assessment based on observation of satellite imagery.

[23] TASS (note 22).

silos at Dombarovsky Airbase, Orenburg oblast.[24] This missile type has been designated as the SS-19 Mod 4 by the North Atlantic Treaty Organization (NATO).[25] Russia is installing Avangard-equipped missiles at a rate of two per year in upgraded complexes with new facilities and security perimeters. The first Avangard regiment is expected to reach its full complement of six missiles by the end of 2021.[26] Russia plans to install a total of two regiments, each with six missiles, at Dombarovsky by 2027.[27]

Russia is also developing a new 'heavy' liquid-fuelled, silo-based ICBM, known as the RS-28 Sarmat (SS-X-29), as a replacement for the RS-20V. Like its predecessor, the RS-28 is expected to carry a large number of MIRVs (possibly as many as 10), but some might be equipped with one or a few Avangard HGVs. After much delay, full-scale flight testing of the RS-28 is scheduled to begin in mid 2021 at the new proving ground at Severo-Yeniseysky, Krasnoyarsk krai, with serial production expected to begin in 2021—although this would be dependent on a successful flight-test programme.[28] In December 2020 Karakaev announced that the first RS-28 ICBMs would be 'put on combat alert' at the ICBM complex at Uzhur, Krasnoyarsk krai, sometime in 2022.[29]

Russia conducted several large-scale exercises with road-mobile and silo-based ICBMs during 2020. These included combat patrols for road-mobile regiments, simulated launch exercises for silo-based regiments, and participation in command staff exercises.[30]

Sea-based missiles

As of January 2021, the Russian Navy had a fleet of 11 operational nuclear-armed SSBNs. The fleet included 6 Soviet-era Delfin-class or Project 667BDRM (Delta IV) SSBNs, 1 Kalmar-class or Project 667BDR (Delta III) SSBN, and 4 (of a planned total of 10) Borei-class or Project 955 SSBNs.

One of the Borei submarines is of an improved design, known as Borei-A or Project 955A. After delays due to technical issues during sea trials, it

[24] Russian Ministry of Defence, [Installation of the Avangard intercontinental ballistic missile in a silo launcher], YouTube, 16 Dec. 2020 (in Russian).

[25] US Department of Defense (note 4), p. 8; and Kristensen, H. M. and Korda, M., 'Russian nuclear forces, 2019', *Bulletin of the Atomic Scientists*, vol. 75, no. 2 (Mar. 2019), p. 78.

[26] 'Russia's 1st regiment of Avangard hypersonic missiles to assume full strength in 2021', TASS, 23 Dec. 2020.

[27] [Source: The first Avangard complexes will be on duty in 2019], TASS, 29 Oct. 2018 (in Russian).

[28] President of Russia (note 10); and Safronov, I. and Nikolsky, A., [Tests of the latest Russian nuclear missile start at the beginning of the year], *Vedomosti*, 29 Oct. 2019 (in Russian).

[29] Levin (note 20).

[30] Russian Ministry of Defence, [Strategic offensive force management training], YouTube, 9 Dec. 2020 (in Russian).

was accepted into the navy in June 2020.[31] In December 2020 the Russian defence minister, Sergey Shoigu, announced that the navy would receive the next two Borei-A SSBNs in 2021.[32] Two more Borei-As are currently under construction, and the final two boats are expected to be laid down in 2021.[33] Eventually, five Borei SSBNs will be assigned to the Northern Fleet (in the Arctic Ocean) and five will be assigned to the Pacific Fleet.[34]

Assuming that the one remaining Delta III will be retired, the planned deployment of Borei-A SSBNs would bring the number of SSBNs to 12 by the end of 2021. A former Project 941 (Typhoon) SSBN that has been converted to a test-launch platform for SLBMs is not thought to be nuclear-armed.[35]

Each SSBN can be equipped with 16 ballistic missiles and the Russian fleet can carry a total of 816 warheads. However, one or two SSBNs are normally undergoing repairs and maintenance at any given time and are not armed. It is also possible that the warhead loading on some missiles has been reduced to meet the total warhead limit under New START. As a result, it is estimated here that only about 624 of the 816 warheads are deployed.

The Russian Navy is also developing the Poseidon or Status-6 (Kanyon), a long-range, strategic nuclear-powered torpedo. The torpedo is intended for future deployment on two new types of special-purpose submarine: the K-329 *Belgorod* (Project 09852)—a converted Antei-class or Project 949A (Oscar-II) guided-missile submarine (SSGN)—and the Khabarovsk-class or Project 09851 submarine based on the Borei-class SSBN hull.[36] The *Belgorod* was originally scheduled for delivery to the navy by the end of 2020 but has been delayed until 2021.[37] The *Belgorod* and the Khabarovsk submarines will each be capable of carrying up to six Poseidon torpedoes.[38]

Non-strategic nuclear forces

There is no universally accepted definition of 'tactical', 'non-strategic' or 'theatre' nuclear weapons; however, the US Department of Defense describes them as 'nuclear weapons designed to be used on a battlefield in military

[31] Russian Ministry of Defence, [On Russia Day, the newest Borei-A class strategic missile submarine 'Prince Vladimir' was inaugurated into the Navy], 12 June 2020 (in Russian).

[32] President of Russia (note 10).

[33] 'Two Borei-A strategic nuclear subs to be laid down in 2021—Defense Ministry', TASS, 30 Dec. 2020.

[34] [Source: Two more 'Borei-A' strategic submarines will be built at 'Sevmash' by 2028], TASS, 30 Nov. 2020 (in Russian).

[35] Saranov, V., 'Behemoths of the seas: Why Russia is retiring its Akula strategic nuclear subs', Sputnik, 24 Jan. 2018.

[36] Sutton, H. I., 'Khabarovsk-class-submarine', Covert Shores, 20 Nov. 2020; and Sutton, H. I., 'Poseidon torpedo', Covert Shores, 22 Feb. 2019.

[37] ['Poseidon' drone carrier submarine 'Belgorod' to be handed over to the fleet in 2021], TASS, 24 Dec. 2020 (in Russian).

[38] [Second 'Poseidon' carrier submarine planned to be launched in spring-summer 2021], TASS, 6 Nov. 2020 (in Russian).

situations. This is opposed to strategic nuclear weapons, which are designed to be used against enemy cities, factories, and other larger-area targets to damage the enemy's ability to wage war'.[39]

As of January 2021, Russia had an estimated 1910 warheads assigned for potential use by non-strategic forces, a slight increase of about 35 warheads over early 2020, mainly due to the fielding of the Kalibr land-attack sea-launched cruise missile (SLCM). Russia's non-strategic nuclear weapons—most of which are dual-capable, which means that they can also be armed with conventional warheads—are intended for use by ships and submarines, aircraft, air- and missile-defence systems, and army missiles. In February 2020 the commander of US Strategic Command, Admiral Charles A. Richard, suggested that 'Russia's overall nuclear stockpile is likely to grow significantly over the next decade—growth driven primarily by a projected increase in Russia's non-strategic nuclear weapons'.[40]

Russia's non-strategic nuclear weapons chiefly serve to compensate for perceived weaknesses in its conventional forces and to maintain overall parity with the total US nuclear force level. There has been considerable debate about the role that non-strategic nuclear weapons have in Russian nuclear strategy, including potential first use.[41]

Air, coastal and missile defence

The Russian air-, coastal- and missile-defence forces are estimated to have around 387 nuclear warheads. Most are assigned for use by dual-capable S-300 and S-400 air defence forces and the Moscow A-135 missile defence system, and a small number are assigned to coastal defence units. Russia is also developing the S-500 air defence system, which might potentially be dual-capable, but there is no publicly available authoritative information confirming a nuclear role.[42]

Air force weapons

The Russian Air Force is estimated to have approximately 500 nuclear warheads for use by Tu-22M3 (Backfire-C) intermediate-range bombers,

---

[39] US Office of the Deputy Assistant Secretary of Defense for Nuclear Matters, *Nuclear Matters Handbook 2016* (US Department of Defense: Arlington, VA, 2016), p. 17.

[40] Richard, C. A., Commander, US Strategic Command, Statement, US Senate, Armed Services Committee, 13 Feb. 2020, p. 5.

[41] On this debate see e.g. US Department of Defense (note 4), p. 30; Kofman, M. and Fink, A. L., 'Escalation management and nuclear employment in Russian military strategy', War on the Rocks, 23 June 2020; Oliker, O., 'Moscow's nuclear enigma: What is Russia's arsenal really for?', *Foreign Affairs*, vol. 97, no. 6 (Nov./Dec. 2018); Stowe-Thurston, A., Korda, M. and Kristensen, H. M., 'Putin deepens confusion about Russian nuclear policy', Russia Matters, 25 Oct. 2018; Tertrais, B., 'Russia's nuclear policy: Worrying for the wrong reasons', *Survival*, vol. 60, no. 2 (Apr. 2018); and Bruusgaard, K. V., 'The myth of Russia's lowered nuclear threshold', War on the Rocks, 22 Sep. 2017.

[42] Podvig, P., 'Missile defense in Russia', Working paper, Federation of American Scientists (FAS), Project on Nuclear Dynamics in a Multipolar Strategic BMD World, May 2017.

Su-24M (Fencer-D) fighter-bombers, Su-34 (Fullback) fighter-bombers and MiG-31K (Foxhound) attack aircraft.[43] The new Su-57 (Felon) combat aircraft, also known as PAK-FA, is dual-capable. It is currently in production and the first serially built version was delivered to the Russian Air Force in 2020.[44]

The MiG-31K is equipped with the new Kh-47M2 Kinzhal air-launched ballistic missile.[45] Russia is also developing the nuclear-capable Kh-32 air-to-surface missile, an upgrade of the Kh-22N (AS-4) used on the Tu-22M3.[46]

Army weapons

The Russian Army is thought to have approximately 90 warheads to arm Iskander-M (SS-26) short-range ballistic missiles (SRBMs) and 9M729 (SSC-8) ground-launched cruise missiles (GLCMs). The dual-capable Iskander-M has now completely replaced the Tochka (SS-21) SRBM in 12 missile brigades.[47]

The dual-capable 9M729 GLCM was cited by the USA as its main reason for withdrawing from the 1987 Treaty on the Elimination of Intermediate-Range and Shorter-Range Missiles (INF Treaty) in 2019.[48] It is estimated that four or five 9M729 battalions have so far been co-deployed with four or five of the Iskander-M brigades. In October 2020 President Putin declared his willingness to impose a moratorium on future 9M729 deployments in European territory, 'but only provided that NATO countries take reciprocal steps that preclude the deployment in Europe of the weapons earlier prohibited under the INF Treaty'.[49]

There are also rumours that Russia has nuclear artillery and landmines, but the publicly available evidence is conflicting.

---

[43] US Department of Defense (DOD), 'US nuclear deterrence policy', Fact sheet, 1 Apr. 2019, p. 3; International Institute for Strategic Studies (IISS), *The Military Balance 2021* (Routledge: London, 2021); and authors' estimate.

[44] D'Urso, S., 'First serial production Su-57 Felon delivered to the Russian Aerospace Forces', The Aviationist, 30 Dec. 2020; and US Office of the Deputy Assistant Secretary of Defense for Nuclear Matters, *Nuclear Matters Handbook 2020* (US Department of Defense: Arlington, VA, Mar. 2020), p. 3.

[45] [Sources: First Dagger hypersonic missile tests conducted in Arctic], TASS, 30 Nov. 2019 (in Russian).

[46] US Department of Defense (note 4), p. 8.

[47] Authors' assessment based on observation of satellite imagery. It is possible that the 9M728 (SSC-7, sometimes called Iskander-K) cruise missile is also dual-capable.

[48] US Department of State, Bureau of Arms Control, Verification and Compliance, 'INF Treaty at a glance', Fact sheet, 8 Dec. 2017. For a summary and other details of the INF Treaty see annex A, section III, in this volume. See also Topychkanov, P. and Davis, I., 'Russian–US nuclear arms control and disarmament', *SIPRI Yearbook 2020*, pp. 399–405; and Kile, S. N., 'Russian–US nuclear arms control and disarmament', *SIPRI Yearbook 2018*, pp. 321–24.

[49] President of Russia, 'Statement by Vladimir Putin on additional steps to de-escalate the situation in Europe after the termination of the Intermediate-Range Nuclear Forces Treaty (INF Treaty)', 26 Oct. 2020.

Navy weapons

The Russian military service that is assigned the highest number of non-strategic nuclear weapons is the navy, with about 935 warheads for use by land-attack cruise missiles, anti-ship cruise missiles, anti-submarine rockets, depth bombs, and torpedoes delivered by ships, submarines and naval aviation.

The nuclear version of the long-range, land-attack Kalibr SLCM, also known as the 3M-14 (SS-N-30A), is a significant new addition to these weapons.[50] It has been integrated on numerous types of surface ship and attack submarine, including the new Yasen/-M or Project 885/M (Severodvinsk) SSGN. The second boat of this class completed its sea trials in 2020, indicating a potential entry into service in 2021.[51]

Other notable navy weapons include the 3M-55 (SS-N-26) SLCM and the future 3M-22 Tsirkon (SS-NX-33) hypersonic anti-ship missile, which is undergoing final test launches.[52]

[50] There is considerable confusion about the designation of what is commonly referred to as the Kalibr missile. The Kalibr designation actually refers not to a specific missile but to a family of weapons that, in addition to the 3M-14 (SS-N-30/A) land-attack versions, includes the 3M-54 (SS-N-27) anti-ship cruise missile and the 91R anti-submarine missile. For further detail see US Navy, Office of Naval Intelligence (ONI), *The Russian Navy: A Historic Transition* (ONI: Washington, DC, Dec. 2015), pp. 34–35.

[51] US Air Force, National Air and Space Intelligence Center (NASIC), *Ballistic and Cruise Missile Threat 2020* (NASIC: Wright-Patterson Air Force Base, OH, July 2020), p. 36; and 'Newest Russian submarine hits target 1,000 km away with Kalibr cruise missile', TASS, 23 Nov. 2020.

[52] 'Russia plans new trials of Tsirkon hypersonic missile before yearend—source', TASS, 22 Nov. 2019.

III. British nuclear forces

HANS M. KRISTENSEN AND MATT KORDA

As of January 2021, the United Kingdom's nuclear weapon inventory consisted of approximately 225 warheads (see table 10.4).[1] In its 2015 Strategic Defence and Security Review (SDSR), the British Government reaffirmed its intention to cut the size of the nuclear arsenal. By that time, the number of operationally available nuclear warheads had already been reduced from fewer than 160 to no more than 120, and the overall size of the nuclear weapon inventory, including non-deployed warheads, was intended to decrease from no more than 225 in 2010 to no more than 180 by the mid 2020s.[2] These plans changed following the Integrated Review of Security, Defence, Development and Foreign Policy undertaken in 2020 and published in early 2021, which increased the ceiling for the nuclear weapon inventory to 260.[3]

The January 2021 estimate of 225 warheads is based on publicly available information on the British nuclear arsenal, conversations with officials, and assumptions about the scope of the planned reduction. The authors consider the British Government to have been more transparent about its nuclear activities than many other nuclear-armed states—for example by having declared the size of its nuclear inventory in 2010 and the number of warheads it intends to keep in the future. However, the UK has never declassified the history of its inventory or the actual number of warheads it possesses.

The role of nuclear weapons in British military doctrine

The UK remains 'deliberately ambiguous' about the precise conditions under which it would use nuclear weapons; however, the British Government has stated that such weapons would only be used under 'extreme circumstances of self-defence, including the defence of our NATO Allies'.[4]

The UK is the only nuclear-armed state that operates a single nuclear weapon type: the British nuclear deterrent is entirely sea-based. The UK possesses four Vanguard-class nuclear-powered ballistic missile submarines (SSBNs) that carry Trident II D5 submarine-launched ballistic

---

[1] This is a revision of SIPRI's estimate of 215 warheads in *SIPRI Yearbook 2020*.

[2] British Government, *National Security Strategy and Strategic Defence and Security Review 2015: A Secure and Prosperous United Kingdom*, Cm 9161 (HM Stationery Office: London, Nov. 2015), para. 4.66.

[3] British Government, *Global Britain in a Competitive Age: Integrated Review of Security, Defence, Development and Foreign Policy*, CP 403 (HM Stationery Office: London, Mar. 2021). These changes will be discussed in the next edition of the SIPRI Yearbook.

[4] British Government (note 2), para. 4.68.

missiles (SLBMs).[5] In a posture known as Continuous At-Sea Deterrence (CASD), which began in 1969, one British SSBN is on patrol at all times.[6] While the second and third SSBNs remain in port and could be put to sea in a crisis, the fourth would probably be unable to deploy because it would be in the midst of extensive overhaul and maintenance.

Nuclear weapon modernization

The UK's lead SSBN, HMS *Vanguard*, entered service in December 1994, while the last submarine in the class, HMS *Vengeance*, entered service in February 2001, with an expected service life of 25 years.[7] The 2015 SDSR stated the government's intention to replace the Vanguard-class submarines with four new SSBNs.[8] In 2016 the House of Commons, the lower house of the British Parliament, approved a motion supporting the government's decision with cross-party support.[9]

The new Dreadnought-class submarines were originally expected to begin entering into service by 2028, but this has been delayed until the early 2030s. The service life of the Vanguard-class SSBNs has been commensurately extended.[10] The UK is participating in the United States Navy's programme to extend the service life of the Trident II D5 missile (the life-extended version is known as D5LE) to the early 2060s (see section I).[11]

The warhead carried on the Trident II D5 is called the Holbrook. Its nuclear explosive package is thought to be a modified version of the USA's W76 warhead and is contained in the US-produced Mk4 re-entry body. The Atomic Weapons Establishment, the research facility responsible for the design and manufacture of the UK's warheads, is currently upgrading the Holbrook to accommodate the US-produced Mk4A re-entry body, in collaboration with US nuclear laboratories.[12]

In February 2020 the British Government announced its intention to replace the Holbrook with a new warhead.[13] The announcement had been pre-empted by the commander of US Strategic Command, Admiral

---

[5] Mills, C., *Replacing the UK's Strategic Nuclear Deterrent: Progress of the Dreadnought Class*, Briefing Paper no. CBP-8010 (House of Commons Library: London, 17 July 2020), p. 7.

[6] British Ministry of Defence, 'Continuous at sea deterrent 50: What you need to know', 3 May 2019.

[7] Mills (note 5), p. 7.

[8] British Government (note 2), para. 4.73.

[9] British House of Commons, 'UK's nuclear deterrent', *Hansard*, col. 559, vol. 613 (18 July 2016).

[10] British Government (note 2), para. 4.65.

[11] Mills (note 5), p. 7.

[12] British Ministry of Defence, 'The United Kingdom's future nuclear deterrent: 2020 update to Parliament', 17 Dec. 2020; and Kristensen, H. M., 'British submarines to receive upgraded US nuclear warhead', Federation of American Scientists (FAS) Strategic Security Blog, 1 Apr. 2011.

[13] Wallace, B., British Secretary of State for Defence, 'Nuclear deterrent', Written Statement HCWS125, British Parliament, 25 Feb. 2020.

Table 10.4. British nuclear forces, January 2021

All figures are approximate and some are based on assessments by the authors.

Type/designation	No. of launchers	Year first deployed	Range (km)	Warheads x yield	No. of warheads
Sea-based missiles (SLBMs)	4/64[a]				*120*
Trident II D5	48[b]	1994	>10 000[c]	1–8 x 100 kt[d]	120
Total operationally available warheads					**120[e]**
Other stored warheads					105[f]
Total inventory					**225[g]**

kt = kilotons; SLBM = submarine-launched ballistic missile.

[a] The first figure is the total number of nuclear-powered ballistic missile submarines (SSBNs) in the British fleet; the second is the maximum number of missiles that they can carry. However, the total number of missiles carried is lower (see note b). Of the 4 SSBNs, 1 is in overhaul at any given time.

[b] The 3 operational SSBNs can carry a total of 48 Trident SLBMs. The United Kingdom has purchased the right to 58 missiles from a pool shared with the United States Navy.

[c] The Trident II D5 missiles on British SSBNs are identical to the Trident II D5 missiles on US Navy SSBNs, which have demonstrated a range of more than 10 000 km in test flights.

[d] The British warhead is called the Holbrook, a modified version of the USA's W76 warhead, with a potential lower-yield option.

[e] Of the 120 operationally available warheads, 40 are deployed on the single SSBN that is at sea at any given time.

[f] Of the estimated 105 warheads that are not operationally available, it is thought that about half are spares and the other half are undergoing upgrade from the Mk4 to the Mk4A.

[g] The British Government declared in 2010 that its inventory would not exceed 225 warheads. It is estimated here that the inventory remained at that number in Jan. 2021, a revision of SIPRI's estimate of 215 warheads in *SIPRI Yearbook 2020*. A planned reduction to an inventory of 180 warheads by the mid 2020s was ended by the Integrated Review of Security, Defence, Development and Foreign Policy undertaken in 2020 and published in early 2021. The review introduced a new ceiling of 260 warheads.

Sources: British Ministry of Defence, white papers, press releases and website; British House of Commons, *Hansard*, various issues; *Bulletin of the Atomic Scientists*, 'Nuclear notebook', various issues; and authors' estimates.

Charles A. Richard, who reported during testimony to the US Senate that the US W93/Mk7 programme 'will also support a parallel Replacement Warhead Program in the United Kingdom'.[14] In April 2020 Ben Wallace, the British Secretary of State for Defence, sent an unprecedented letter to members of the US Congress, lobbying them in support of the W93 warhead programme and claiming that it is 'critical . . . to the long-term viability of the UK's nuclear deterrent'.[15] This letter and the surprise announcement of the W93 decision have sparked fresh concerns that the UK's nuclear

[14] Richard, C. A., Commander, US Strategic Command, Statement, US Senate, Armed Services Committee, 13 Feb. 2020, p. 13.

[15] Borger, J., 'UK lobbies US to support controversial new nuclear warheads', *The Guardian*, 1 Aug. 2020.

deterrent lacks the appropriate independence and parliamentary scrutiny.[16] The British Ministry of Defence (MOD) acknowledged in 2020 that 'It is not exactly the same warhead, but . . . there is a very close connection, in design terms and production terms.'[17]

The new Dreadnought-class submarines will have 12 launch tubes—a reduction from the 16 carried by the Vanguard class (see below). Technical problems resulted in a delay in the delivery of the missile launch tubes; however, as of January 2021 six tubes—half of the tubes required for the first SSBN in the class (HMS *Dreadnought*)—had been delivered and were in the process of being integrated into the SSBN's pressure hull.[18]

The cost of the Dreadnought programme has been a source of concern and controversy since its inception. In 2015 the MOD estimated the total cost of the programme to be £31 billion ($47.4 billion). It set aside a contingency of £10 billion ($15.3 billion) to cover possible increases, and approximately £800 million of that fund had been allocated by mid 2020.[19] In 2018 the National Audit Office (NAO) reported that the MOD was facing an 'affordability gap' of £2.9 billion ($3.9 billion) in its military nuclear programmes between 2018 and 2028.[20] In its annual update to the parliament in December 2020, the MOD reported that a total of £8.5 billion ($11.8 billion) had been spent on the programme's concept, assessment and delivery phases—an increase of £1.6 billion ($2.2 billion) from the previous financial year.[21]

In 2020 the NAO and the Commons Public Accounts Committee reported that three key nuclear-regulated infrastructure projects in the UK's nuclear weapon programme would be delayed by 1.7–6.3 years, with costs increasing by over £1.3 billion ($1.7 billion) to a forecasted total of £2.5 billion ($3.2 billion).[22] According to these reports, the delays were largely caused by poor management and premature construction. This suggests that the UK's relative inexperience in building new warheads could lead to further delays and cost overruns.

---

[16] Mills, C., 'Replacing the UK's strategic nuclear deterrent: The long-awaited warhead decision', Briefing Paper no. CBP-8941, House of Commons Library, 19 June 2020, p. 1.

[17] Lovegrove, S., Permanent Secretary, Ministry of Defence, Statement, British House of Commons, Defence Committee, 8 Dec. 2020, Q31.

[18] British Ministry of Defence (note 12).

[19] Mills (note 5), pp. 18–19.

[20] British National Audit Office (NAO), *The Defence Nuclear Enterprise: A Landscape Review*, Report by the Comptroller and Auditor General, HC 1003, Session 2017–19 (NAO: London, 22 May 2018). Spending on military nuclear programmes was estimated to account for c. 14% of the total 2018/19 Ministry of Defence budget, and it could rise to 18% or 19% during the peak of recapitalization.

[21] British Ministry of Defence (note 12).

[22] British National Audit Office, *Managing Infrastructure Projects on Nuclear-regulated Sites*, Report by the Comptroller and Auditor General, HC 19, Session 2019–20 (NAO: London, 10 Jan. 2020), pp. 5–6; and British House of Commons, Committee of Public Accounts, *Defence Nuclear Infrastructure*, 2nd report of session 2019–21, HC 86 (House of Commons: London, 13 May 2020).

Sea-based missiles

The Vanguard-class SSBNs can each be armed with up to 16 Trident II D5 SLBMs. Of the four SSBNs, three (with a total of 48 missile tubes) are considered to be operational at any given time, while the fourth SSBN is in overhaul. The UK does not own the missiles, but has purchased the right to 58 Trident SLBMs from a pool shared with the US Navy at the US Strategic Weapons Facility in Kings Bay, Georgia.[23] Under limits set out in the 2010 SDSR and reaffirmed by the 2015 SDSR, when on patrol, the submarines are armed with no more than 8 operational missiles with a total of 40 nuclear warheads.[24] The missiles are kept in a 'detargeted' mode, meaning that target data would need to be loaded into the guidance system before launch. They also have a reduced alert status: several days' notice would be required to fire the missiles.[25]

[23] Allison, G., 'No, America doesn't control Britain's nuclear weapons', UK Defence Journal, 20 July 2017.

[24] British Government, Securing Britain in an Age of Uncertainty: The Strategic Defence and Security Review, Cm 7948 (HM Stationery Office: London, Oct. 2010), pp. 5, 38; and British Government (note 2), para. 4.66.

[25] British Government (note 2), para. 4.78.

IV. French nuclear forces

HANS M. KRISTENSEN AND MATT KORDA

As of January 2021, France's nuclear weapon inventory consisted of about 290 warheads. The warheads are allocated for delivery by 48 submarine-launched ballistic missiles (SLBMs) and approximately 50 air-launched cruise missiles (ALCMs) produced for land- and carrier-based aircraft (see table 10.5). However, the 10 warheads assigned to France's carrier-based aircraft are thought to be kept in central storage and are not normally deployed. The estimate of France's nuclear weapon inventory is based on publicly available information. France is relatively transparent about many of its nuclear weapon activities and has publicly disclosed the size of its stockpile and details of its nuclear-related operations in the past.[1]

The role of nuclear weapons in French military doctrine

France considers all of its nuclear weapons to be strategic and reserved for the defence of France's 'vital interests'.[2] While this concept has appeared in various governmental white papers and presidential speeches for several decades, what constitutes France's 'vital interests' appears to be somewhat vague.

In a speech in February 2020, President Emmanuel Macron suggested that the French nuclear deterrent was intended to deter another state from 'threatening our vital interests, whatever they may be'.[3] Macron also noted that, if deterrence were to fail, 'a unique and one-time-only nuclear warning could be issued to the aggressor State to clearly demonstrate that the nature of the conflict has changed and to re-establish deterrence'.[4] Following that, French nuclear weapons could be used for 'inflicting absolutely unacceptable damages upon that State's centres of power: its political, economic and military nerve centres'.[5]

There is no publicly available evidence to indicate that France has considered incorporating pre-emptive first strikes into its nuclear doctrine.[6] However, the weapons carried by the airborne component of its nuclear

---

[1] Macron, E., French President, Speech on defence and deterrence strategy, École de Guerre, Paris, 7 Feb. 2020 (in French, with English translation).

[2] Tertrais, B., *French Nuclear Deterrence Policy, Forces and Future: A Handbook*, Recherches & Documents no. 04/2020 (Fondation pour la Recherche Stratégique: Paris, Feb. 2020), pp. 25–29, 62–63.

[3] Macron (note 1).

[4] Macron (note 1).

[5] Macron (note 1).

[6] Tertrais (note 2), pp. 25–29, 62–63.

Table 10.5. French nuclear forces, January 2021

All figures are approximate and some are based on assessments by the authors.

Type/designation	No. of launchers	Year first deployed	Range (km)[a]	Warheads x yield	No. of warheads
Land-based aircraft					
Rafale BF3[b]	40	2010–11	2 000	1 x [up to 300 kt] TNA[c]	40
Carrier-based aircraft					
Rafale MF3[b]	10	2010–11	2 000	1 x [up to 300 kt] TNA[c]	10[d]
Sea-based missiles (SLBMs)	4/64[e]				240
M51.2[f]	48[g]	2017	>9 000[h]	4–6 x 100 kt TNO	240
M51.3[i]	–	[2025]	>[9 000]	[up to 6] x [100 kt] TNO	–
Total inventory					**290[j]**

[] = uncertain figure; – = nil or a negligible value; kt = kiloton; SLBM = submarine-launched ballistic missile; TNA = tête nucléaire aéroportée (airborne nuclear warhead); TNO = tête nucléaire océanique (oceanic nuclear warhead).

[a] For aircraft, the listed range is for illustrative purposes only; actual mission range will vary according to flight profile, weapon loading and in-flight refuelling.

[b] The BF3 and MF3 aircraft both carry the ASMP-A (air–sol moyenne portée–améliorée) air-launched cruise missile (ALCM). Most sources report that the ASMP-A has a range of 500–600 km, although some suggest that it might be over 600 km.

[c] The TNA is widely assumed to have a maximum yield of 300 kt, but lower-yield options for this warhead are thought to be available.

[d] The 10 warheads assigned to France's carrier-based aircraft are thought to be kept in central storage and are not normally deployed.

[e] The first figure is the total number of nuclear-powered ballistic missile submarines (SSBNs) in the French fleet; the second is the maximum number of missiles that they can carry. However, the total number of missiles carried is lower (see note g). Of the 4 SSBNs, 1 is in overhaul at any given time.

[f] The last M51.1 missiles were offloaded from *Le Terrible* in late 2020 in preparation for a one-year refuelling overhaul and upgrade to the more advanced M51.2 missile.

[g] France has only produced enough SLBMs to equip the 3 operational SSBNs (48 missiles).

[h] The M51.2 has a 'much greater range' than the M51.1 according to the French Ministry of the Armed Forces.

[i] The M51.3 is under development and has not yet been deployed.

[j] In Feb. 2020 President Emmanuel Macron reaffirmed that the arsenal 'is currently under 300 nuclear weapons'. A small number of the warheads is thought to be undergoing maintenance and surveillance at any given time.

Sources: Macron, E., French President, Speech on defence and deterrence strategy, École de Guerre, Paris, 7 Feb. 2020 (in French); Parly, F., French Minister of the Armed Forces, Speech, ArianeGroup, Les Mureaux, 14 Dec. 2017 (in French); Hollande, F., French President, Speech on nuclear deterrence, Istres Air Base, 19 Feb. 2015 (in French); Sarkozy, N., French President, Speech on the new defence policy, Porte de Versailles, 17 June 2008, (in French); Sarkozy, N., French President, Speech on the white paper on national defence and security, nuclear deterrence and the non-proliferation of nuclear weapons, Cherbourg, 21 Mar. 2008 (in French); Chirac, J., French President, Speech on France's defence policy, Île Longue, Brest, 19 Jan. 2006 (in French); French Ministry of Defence/Ministry of the Armed Forces, various publications; French National Assembly, various defence bills; *Air Actualités*, various issues; *Aviation Week & Space Technology*, various issues; *Bulletin of the Atomic Scientists*, 'Nuclear notebook', various issues; Tertrais, B., *French Nuclear Deterrence Policy, Forces and Future: A Handbook*, Recherches & Documents no. 04/2020 (Fondation pour la Recherche Stratégique: Paris, Feb. 2020); and authors' estimates.

forces have characteristics (i.e. a limited range) that other nuclear-armed states consider to be tactical.

In his 2020 speech, President Macron suggested that 'France's vital interests now have a European dimension', and he offered to open a strategic dialogue with other European countries to discuss 'the role played by France's nuclear deterrence in our collective security'.[7] However, it appears that this proposal only gained support from a few politicians and has not yet been collectively endorsed by European political parties or governments.[8]

Nuclear weapon modernization

President Macron has reaffirmed the French Government's commitment to the long-term modernization of France's air- and sea-based nuclear deterrent forces.[9] Current plans include the modernization of France's nuclear-powered ballistic missile submarines (SSBNs, or sous-marins nucléaires lanceurs d'engins, SNLE), SLBMs and ALCMs (see below). The 2018 Law on Military Planning for 2019–25 allocates €37 billion ($42.2 billion) for maintenance and modernization of France's nuclear forces and infrastructure.[10] This is a significant increase on the €23 billion ($26.2 billion) allocated to nuclear forces and associated infrastructure by the Law on Military Planning for 2014–19.[11]

The 2021 budget of the Ministry of the Armed Forces (France's defence ministry) allocated €5 billion ($5.7 billion) to nuclear weapon-related activity—€0.3 billion ($0.34 billion) more than in the 2020 budget.[12] It also suggests that a total of €25 billion ($28.5 billion) would be spent on nuclear modernization between 2019 and 2023.

---

[7] Macron (note 1).

[8] Berghofer, J., 'An offer postponed: Berlin's silence on Macron's deterrence thinking', Commentary, European Leadership Network, 25 Aug. 2020.

[9] Macron, E., French President, Speech on the challenges and priorities of defence policy, Toulon, 19 Jan. 2018 (in French).

[10] AFP, 'Macron promulgue la loi de programmation militaire 2019–2025' [Macron signs the Law on Military Planning for 2019–2025], Le Figaro, 13 July 2018; Loi relative à la programmation militaire pour les années 2019 à 2025 [Law on Military Planning for the Years 2019 to 2025], French Law no. 2018-607 of 13 July 2018, Journal Officiel de la République Française, 14 July 2018; and AFP, 'France to spend 37 bn euros on upgrading nuclear arsenal', France 24, 8 Feb. 2018. The total defence budget approved for the 7-year period was €295 billion ($336 billion). On France's military expenditure see chapter 8, section II, in this volume.

[11] Loi relative à la programmation militaire pour les années 2014 à 2019 [Law on Military Planning for the Years 2014 to 2019], French Law no. 2013-1168 of 18 Dec. 2013, Journal Officiel de la République Française, 19 Dec. 2013.

[12] French Ministry of the Armed Forces (MAF), Projet de loi de finances: Année 2021 [Finance bill: Year 2021] (MAF: Paris, Sep. 2020), p. 26; Groizeleau, V., 'Dissuasion : 25 milliards en cinq ans pour le renouvellement des deux composantes' [Deterrence: 25 billion in five years for the renewal of the two components], Mer et Marine, 2 Oct. 2019; and Rose, M., 'Amid arms race, Macron offers Europe French nuclear wargames insight', Reuters, 7 Feb. 2020.

Aircraft and air-delivered weapons

The airborne component of the French nuclear forces consists of land- and carrier-based aircraft. The French Air and Space Force has 40 deployed nuclear-capable Rafale BF3 aircraft based at Saint-Dizier Air Base, northeast France. The French Naval Nuclear Air Force (Force aéronavale nucléaire, FANu) consists of a squadron of 10 Rafale MF3 aircraft for deployment on the aircraft carrier *Charles de Gaulle*. The FANu and its nuclear-armed missiles are not permanently deployed but can be rapidly deployed by the French president in support of nuclear operations.[13]

The Rafale aircraft are equipped with medium-range air-to-surface cruise missiles (air–sol moyenne portée–améliorée, ASMP-A), which entered service in 2009. France produced 54 ASMP-As, including test missiles.[14] A midlife refurbishment programme for the ASMP-A that began in 2016 will deliver the first upgraded missiles in 2022 or 2023.[15] The first test of an upgraded ASMP-A took place on 9 December 2020.[16] This will be followed by a qualification firing and subsequent force training firings before the missile's entry into service. The missiles are armed with a nuclear warhead (the tête nucléaire aéroportée, TNA) that has a reported yield of up to 300 kilotons.[17]

The French Ministry of the Armed Forces has initiated research on a successor, fourth-generation air-to-surface nuclear missile (air–sol nucléaire de 4e génération, ASN4G) with enhanced stealth and manoeuvrability to counter potential technological improvements in air defences.[18] The ASN4G is scheduled to replace the ASMP-A in 2035.[19]

---

[13] Pintat, X. et al., 'Rapport d'information fait au nom de la commission des affaires étrangères, de la défense et des forces armées par le groupe de travail "La modernisation de la dissuasion nucléaire"' [Information report made on behalf of the Committee on Foreign Affairs, Defense and the Armed Forces by the working group 'Modernization of nuclear deterrence'], Report of the French Senate no. 560, 23 May 2017.

[14] Hollande, F., French President, Speech on nuclear deterrence, Istres Air Base, 19 Feb. 2015 (in French); and Tertrais (note 2), p. 62.

[15] French Ministry of the Armed Forces, 'Projet de loi de programmation militaire, 2019–2025' [Military Planning Bill, 2019–2025], Press kit, Feb. 2018, p. 42; Medeiros, J., '"Faire FAS" : 55 ans de dissuasion nucléaire aéroportée' ['Go FAS': 55 years of airborne nuclear deterrence], *Air Actualités*, Oct. 2019, pp. 32–37, p. 36; and Tertrais (note 2), p. 60.

[16] French Ministry of the Armed Forces, 'Premier tir d'essai du missile stratégique ASMPA-rénové' [First test firing of the ASMPA-renovated strategic missile], 23 Dec. 2020.

[17] Groizeleau, V., 'Dissuasion : F. Hollande détaille sa vision et l'arsenal français' [Deterrence: F. Hollande outlines his vision and the French arsenal], Mer et Marine, 20 Feb. 2015.

[18] French Ministry of the Armed Forces, 'La dissuasion nucléaire' [Nuclear deterrence], *Actu Défense*, 14 June 2018, p. 1; and Tran, P., 'France studies nuclear missile replacement', *Defense News*, 29 Nov. 2014.

[19] Medeiros (note 15), p. 36.

Sea-based missiles

The main component of France's nuclear forces is the Strategic Oceanic Force (Force océanique stratégique, FOST). It consists of four Triomphant-class SSBNs based on the Île Longue peninsula near Brest, north-west France. Each is capable of carrying 16 SLBMs. However, one SSBN is out of service for overhaul and maintenance work at any given time and is not armed. France has produced only 48 SLBMs, enough to equip the 3 operational SSBNs.

The French Navy maintains a continuous at-sea deterrent posture with one SSBN on patrol at all times. It has conducted more than 500 such patrols since 1972.[20]

France continues to modernize its SLBMs and associated warheads. In June 2020 *Le Téméraire*, which had previously been equipped with the older M45 SLBM, became operational with the newer M51 after a successful test launch of the missile.[21] This was the ninth test of the M51.

The M51 is itself being upgraded. The first version, the M51.1, was capable of carrying up to six TN-75 warheads in multiple independently targetable re-entry vehicles (MIRVs), each with an explosive yield of 100 kt. Over the past several years, the M51.1 has been gradually replaced by an upgraded version, the M51.2, which has greater range and improved accuracy. With the deployment of the M51.2 on *Le Téméraire* in mid 2020, the final SSBN left to receive this upgrade, *Le Terrible*, began its major refit in late 2020.[22] Thus, as of January 2021, the M51.1 had officially been removed from service.

The M51.2 is designed to carry a new, stealthier nuclear warhead (the tête nucléaire océanique, TNO), which has a reported yield of up to 100 kt.[23] The number of warheads on some of the missiles has been reduced in order to improve targeting flexibility.[24] France has also commenced design work on another upgrade, the M51.3, with improved accuracy. The first M51.3

---

[20] French Ministry of the Armed Forces, '500e patrouille d'un sous-marin nucléaire lanceur d'engins' [500th patrol of a nuclear-powered ballistic missile submarine], 12 Oct. 2018.

[21] Parly, F. (@florence_parly), 'Le sous-marin nucléaire lanceur d'engins (SNLE) Le Téméraire a tiré avec succès un missile balistique stratégique M51 au large du Finistère. Cet essai démontre notre excellence technologique et notre attachement à la souveraineté française.' [The nuclear-powered ballistic missile submarine Le Téméraire successfully fired an M51 strategic ballistic missile off the coast of Finistère. This test demonstrates our technological excellence and our commitment to French sovereignty.], Twitter, 12 June 2020.

[22] French Ministry of the Armed Forces and Naval Group, 'Le SNLE *Le Terrible* transféré de l'Île Longue à la base navale de Brest pour son grand carénage' [The SSBN *Le Terrible* transferred from Île Longue to the Brest naval base for its major refit], Press release, 8 Jan. 2021.

[23] Groizeleau (note 12); and Groizeleau (note 17).

[24] Tertrais (note 2), p. 57.

missiles are scheduled to replace their M51.2 predecessors and become operational in 2025.[25]

In the Law on Military Planning for 2019–25, the French Government announced that it would produce a third-generation SSBN, designated the SNLE 3G.[26] The programme was officially launched in early 2021.[27] The SNLE 3G will eventually be equipped with a further modification of the M51 SLBM, the M51.4.[28] The construction of the first of four submarines in the class is scheduled to begin in 2023 and is expected to be completed by 2035. The other three submarines will be delivered on a schedule of one boat every five years.[29]

[25] French Ministry of the Armed Forces, 'Missiles balistiques stratégiques (MSBS)' [Strategic ballistic missiles], 28 Jan. 2020; and Parly, F., French Minister of the Armed Forces, Speech, ArianeGroup, Les Mureaux, 14 Dec. 2017 (in French).

[26] French Ministry of the Armed Forces (note 15), p. 38.

[27] French Ministry of the Armed Forces, 'Florence Parly, ministre des armées, annonce le lancement en réalisation des sous-marins nucléaires lanceurs d'engins de 3e génération (SNLE 3G)' [Florence Parly, minister of the armed forces, announces the launch of the 3rd-generation nuclear-powered ballistic missile submarines (SNLE 3G)], 19 Feb. 2021; and Mackenzie, C., 'France to begin building new ballistic missile subs', *Defense News*, 22 Feb. 2021.

[28] Tertrais (note 2), pp. 56, 60, 65.

[29] French Ministry of the Armed Forces (note 27); Groizeleau (note 12); and Mackenzie (note 27).

V. Chinese nuclear forces

HANS M. KRISTENSEN AND MATT KORDA

As of January 2021, China maintained an estimated total inventory of about 350 nuclear warheads. This is an increase of 30 from the previous year, due largely to the indication that the DF-5B intercontinental ballistic missile (ICBM) can carry more warheads than previously believed.[1] Just over 270 warheads are assigned to China's operational land- and sea-based ballistic missiles and to nuclear-configured aircraft (see table 10.6). The remainder are assigned to non-operational forces, such as new systems in development, operational systems that may increase in number in the future, and reserves.

This estimate relies on publicly available information on the Chinese nuclear arsenal. China has never declared the size of its nuclear arsenal. Occasionally, Chinese officials reference open-source estimates as a means to discuss China's nuclear weapon programme publicly or in diplomatic negotiations.[2] As a result, many of the assessments here rely on data from the United States Department of Defense (DOD) and must therefore be treated with a degree of caution.

The role of nuclear weapons in Chinese military doctrine

The Chinese Government's declared aim is to maintain its nuclear capabilities at the minimum level required for safeguarding national security. The goal is 'deterring other countries from using or threatening to use nuclear weapons against China'.[3] For decades, China did so with a dyad of mainly liquid-fuelled land-based ballistic missiles and a few sea-based ballistic missiles, with a small stockpile of gravity bombs available for bombers as a semi-dormant back-up capacity. China is now building a fully operational triad of nuclear forces with solid-fuelled land-based missiles, six nuclear-powered ballistic missile submarines (SSBNs), and bombers with a full, re-established nuclear mission in order to strengthen its nuclear deterrence and second-strike capabilities in response to what it sees as a growing threat from other countries.[4]

---

[1] US Department of Defense (DOD), *Military and Security Developments Involving the People's Republic of China 2020*, Annual Report to Congress (DOD: Arlington, VA, 21 Aug. 2020), p. 56.

[2] E.g. Chinese Ministry of National Defense, 'China reiterates it will not join so-called China–US–Russia arms control negotiations', 9 July 2020.

[3] Chinese State Council, *China's National Defense in the New Era* (Information Office of the State Council: Beijing, July 2019), chapter 2.

[4] Fabey, M., 'China on faster pace to develop nuclear triad, according to Pentagon, analysts', *Jane's Navy International*, 3 May 2019; and 'Chinese military paper urges increase in nuclear deterrence capabilities', Reuters, 30 Jan. 2018.

Table 10.6. Chinese nuclear forces, January 2021

All figures are approximate and some are based on assessments by the authors.

Type/Chinese designation (US designation)	No. of launchers	Year first deployed	Range (km)[a]	Warheads x yield[b]	No. of warheads[c]
Aircraft	20[d]				20
H-6K (B-6)	20	2009	3 100	1 x bomb	20
H-6N (B-6N)	–	[2022]	..	1 x ALBM	–
H-20 (B-20)	–	[2020s]	..	..	–
Land-based missiles[e]	244				204
DF-4 (CSS-3)	6[f]	1980	5 500	1 x 3.3 Mt	6[f]
DF-5A (CSS-4 Mod 1)	10	1981	>12 000	1 x 4–5 Mt	10
DF-5B (CSS-4 Mod 2)	10	2015	12 000	5 x 200–300 kt MIRV	50
DF-5C (CSS-4 Mod 3)	–	..	..	MIRV	–
DF-21A/E (CSS-5 Mod 2/6)[g]	40	1996/2017	2 100	1 x 200–300 kt	40
DF-26 (CSS-18)	100	2016	>4 000	1 x 200–300 kt	20
DF-31 (CSS-10 Mod 1)	6	2006	>7 000	1 x 200–300 kt	6
DF-31A/AG (CSS-10 Mod 2)	72	2007/2018	>11 200	1 x 200–300 kt	72
DF-41 (CSS-20)	–	[2021][h]	>12 000	3 x 200–300 kt MIRV	–
Sea-based missiles (SLBMs)	4/48[i]				48[j]
JL-2 (CSS-N-14)	48	2016	>7 000	1 x 200–300 kt	48
Total stockpile	312				272
Other stored warheads[k]					[78]
Total inventory	312				[350][k]

.. = not available or not applicable; – = nil or a negligible value; [ ] = uncertain figure; ALBM = air-launched ballistic missile; kt = kiloton; Mt = megaton; MIRV = multiple independently targetable re-entry vehicle; SLBM = submarine-launched ballistic missile.

[a] For aircraft, the listed range is for illustrative purposes only; actual mission range will vary according to flight profile, weapon loading and in-flight refuelling.

[b] Warhead yields are listed for illustrative purposes. Actual yields are not known, except that older missile warheads had Mt yields. Newer long-range missile warheads probably have yields of a few hundred kt.

[c] Figures are based on estimates of 1 warhead per nuclear-capable launcher, except the MIRVed DF-5B, which can carry up to 5 warheads. The DF-26 is a dual-capable launcher. It is thought that its mission is primarily conventional and only a few launchers are assigned nuclear warheads. Only 1 missile load is assumed for nuclear missiles. The warheads are not thought to be deployed on launchers under normal circumstances but kept in storage facilities. All estimates are approximate.

[d] The number of bombers only counts those estimated to be assigned a nuclear role. H-6 bombers were used to deliver nuclear weapons during China's nuclear weapon testing programme (one test used a fighter-bomber) and models of nuclear bombs are exhibited in military museums. It is thought (but uncertain) that a small number of H-6 bombers previously had a secondary contingency mission with nuclear bombs. The US Department of Defense (DOD) reported in 2018 that the People's Liberation Army Air Force has been reassigned a nuclear mission.

[e] China defines missile ranges as short-range, <1000 km; medium-range, 1000–3000 km; long-range, 3000–8000 km; and intercontinental range, >8000 km.

In addition to the nuclear-capable missiles listed in this table, the US Central Intelligence Agency concluded in 1993 that China had 'almost certainly' developed a warhead for the DF-15 (CSS-6), but the warhead does not appear to have been fielded.

[f] Although a few liquid-fuelled DF-4s are still in service, they are thought to be in the process of being retired.

[g] The range of the nuclear-armed DF-21 variants (CSS-5 Mod 2 and Mod 6) is thought to be greater than the 1750 km reported for the original (CSS-5 Mod 1), which has been retired. In 2017 the US Air Force's National Air and Space Intelligence Center (NASIC) reported that China had 'fewer than 50' Mod 2 launchers. The Mod 6 is thought to be a replacement for the Mod 2.

[h] The DF-41 was publicly displayed for the first time in 2019 and is being integrated into training regiments, but as of Jan. 2021 it had not been declared fully operational. The D-41 is thought to be able to carry at least 3 warheads. SIPRI estimates that c. 18 launchers and c. 54 warheads might become operational during or after 2021. See note k.

[i] The first figure is the total number of operational nuclear-powered ballistic missile submarines (SSBNs) in the Chinese fleet; the second is the maximum number of missiles that they can carry. China has 4 operational Type 094 SSBNs, each of which can carry up to 12 SLBMs. Two more Type 094 SSBNs are in development, but were not operational as of Jan. 2021. SIPRI estimates that their armament of 24 additional JL-2 missiles and warheads have probably been produced and might become operational during or after 2021. See note k.

[j] Although Chinese SSBNs conduct patrols, there is no authoritative information suggesting that they have nuclear weapons onboard under normal circumstances.

[k] In addition to the c. 272 warheads estimated to be assigned to operational forces, SIPRI estimates that an additional c. 78 warheads might have been produced to arm China's new DF-41s (c. 54 warheads) and additional JL-2s (c. 24 warheads), for a total estimated inventory of c. 350 warheads. China's inventory is expected to continue to increase.

Sources: US Air Force, National Air and Space Intelligence Center (NASIC), *Ballistic and Cruise Missile Threat*, various years; US Air Force Global Strike Command, various documents; US Central Intelligence Agency, various documents; US Defense Intelligence Agency, various documents; US Department of Defense, *Military and Security Developments Involving the People's Republic of China*, various years; Kristensen, H. M., Norris, R. S. and McKinzie, M. G., *Chinese Nuclear Forces and US Nuclear War Planning* (Federation of American Scientists/ Natural Resources Defense Council: Washington, DC, Nov. 2006); *Bulletin of the Atomic Scientists*, 'Nuclear notebook', various issues; Google Earth; and authors' estimates.

Despite the continuing growth in the sophistication and size of its nuclear arsenal, China's ongoing modernization programme (see below) does not, so far, appear to portend changes to its long-standing core nuclear policies, including its no-first-use policy.[5] Although the Chinese military is working to increase the overall readiness of its missile forces, Chinese nuclear warheads are believed to be de-mated from their delivery vehicles—that is, stored separately and not available for immediate use.[6]

Throughout 2020, US officials asserted that there is 'increasing evidence' that China is moving towards adopting a launch-on-warning posture for its land-based ICBMs, which would necessitate the mating of warheads with delivery vehicles; however, while a fully operational SSBN force would require warheads to be loaded on the missiles (see below), there is

---

[5] US Department of Defense (note 1), p. 86.

[6] Stokes, M. A., *China's Nuclear Warhead Storage and Handling System* (Project 2049 Institute: Arlington, VA, 12 Mar. 2010), p. 8; Li, B., 'China's potential to contribute to multilateral nuclear disarmament', *Arms Control Today*, vol. 41, no. 2 (Mar. 2011); and US Department of Defense (note 1), p. 88.

no publicly available evidence that this has happened yet. Moreover, the evidence of a nascent launch-on-warning posture that US officials have pointed to so far—the development of early-warning systems and new silos for solid-fuelled missiles, in addition to observing the People's Liberation Army Rocket Forces (PLARF) conducting high-alert and combat readiness drills—appears to be relatively circumstantial.[7]

Aircraft and air-delivered weapons

Medium-range combat aircraft were China's earliest means of delivering nuclear weapons and were used to conduct more than 12 atmospheric nuclear tests in the 1960s and 1970s. As of 1993, the US National Security Council stated that 'The [People's Liberation Army Air Force (PLAAF)] has no units whose primary mission is to deliver China's small stockpile of nuclear bombs. Rather, some units may be tasked for nuclear delivery as a contingency mission.'[8]

Before 2018, the US DOD's annual reports on Chinese military developments asserted that PLAAF bombers did not have a nuclear mission. This was probably because China's older bomb-equipped aircraft were unlikely to be useful in the event of a nuclear conflict. This changed in 2018, when the US DOD assessed that 'the PLAAF has been newly re-assigned a nuclear mission'.[9] Throughout this time, SIPRI had continued to assess that China maintained a small inventory of gravity bombs for secondary contingency use by H-6 (B-6) bombers.[10] In its 2020 report, the US DOD concluded that China in 2019 had 'signaled the return of the airborne leg of its nuclear triad after the PLAAF publicly revealed the H-6N (B-6N) as its first nuclear-capable air-to-air refuelable bomber'.[11] Legacy H-6 bombers did not include an air-to-air refuelling probe, which significantly limited their long-range targeting capability.

In 2018 the US Defense Intelligence Agency reported that China was developing two new air-launched ballistic missiles (ALBMs), 'one of which

---

[7] US Department of Defense (note 1), pp. 85–88.

[8] US National Security Council, 'Report to Congress on status of China, India and Pakistan nuclear and ballistic missile programs', 28 July 1993.

[9] US Department of Defense (DOD), *Military and Security Developments Involving the People's Republic of China 2017*, Annual Report to Congress (DOD: Arlington, VA, 15 May 2017), p. 61; and US Department of Defense (DOD), *Military and Security Developments Involving the People's Republic of China 2018*, Annual Report to Congress (DOD: Arlington, VA, 16 May 2018), p. 75.

[10] For the aircraft, missiles and submarines discussed here, a designation in parentheses (in this case B-6) following the Chinese designation (in this case H-6) is that assigned by the USA.

[11] US Department of Defense (note 1), p. 50.

may include a nuclear payload'.[12] The missiles may be variants of the Dong Feng-21, or DF-21 (CSS-5), medium-range ballistic missile (MRBM).[13] The first base to be equipped with this capability might be Neixiang, Henan province.[14] Once deployed, the ALBM 'would provide China for the first time with a viable nuclear triad of delivery systems dispersed across land, sea, and air forces', according to the US DOD.[15] Even so, the 'viability' of the triad would depend on the survivability and capability of each leg.

In addition to the intermediate-range H-6 bomber, the PLAAF is developing its first long-range strategic bomber, known as the H-20 (B-20). The aircraft may have a range of up to 8500 kilometres and a stealthy design. It might be in production within 10 years, according to the US DOD.[16] In its 2020 report, the US DOD also suggested that the H-20 will be able to deliver both conventional and nuclear weapons.[17]

Land-based missiles

China's nuclear-capable land-based ballistic missile arsenal is undergoing gradual modernization as China replaces ageing silo-based, liquid-fuelled missiles with new mobile, solid-fuelled models and increases the number of road-mobile missile launchers. China's shift towards more survivable mobile missiles has been motivated by concerns that the USA's advances in intelligence, surveillance and reconnaissance (ISR) capabilities and in precision-guided conventional weapons pose a pre-emptive threat to fixed missile launch sites and supporting infrastructure.[18]

---

[12] Ashley, R., Director, US Defense Intelligence Agency, 'Worldwide threat assessment', Statement for the record, US Senate, Armed Services Committee, 6 Mar. 2018, p. 8. See also US Department of Defense (DOD), *Military and Security Developments Involving the People's Republic of China 2019*, Annual Report to Congress (DOD: Arlington, VA, 2 May 2019), p. 67; and US Air Force, National Air and Space Intelligence Center (NASIC), *Ballistic and Cruise Missile Threat 2020* (NASIC: Wright-Patterson Air Force Base, OH, July 2020), p. 37.

[13] Wright, T., 'Chinese PLAAF H-6N pictured carrying large missile', International Institute for Strategic Studies (IISS), 23 Oct. 2020; and Panda, A., 'Revealed: China's nuclear-capable air-launched ballistic missile', The Diplomat, 10 Apr. 2018.

[14] Lee, R., 'China's Air Force might be back in the nuclear business', The Diplomat, 9 Sep. 2020.

[15] US Department of Defense (note 1), p. 87.

[16] US Office of the Deputy Assistant Secretary of Defense for Nuclear Matters, *Nuclear Matters Handbook 2020* (US Department of Defense: Arlington, VA, Mar. 2020), figure 1.1, p. 3. See also Yeo, M., 'In first, China confirms "new long-range strategic bomber" designation', *Defense News*, 11 Oct. 2018; and Tate, A., 'Details emerge about requirement for China's new strategic bomber', *Jane's Defence Weekly*, 4 Jan. 2017, p. 4.

[17] US Department of Defense (note 1), p. 80.

[18] O'Connor, S., 'Sharpened Fengs: China's ICBM modernisation alters threat profile', *Jane's Intelligence Review*, vol. 27, no. 12 (Dec. 2015), pp. 44–49; and Eveleth, D., 'China's mobile ICBM brigades: The DF-31 and DF-41', A Boy and His Blog, 2 July 2020.

Intercontinental ballistic missiles

In its 2020 report, the US DOD estimated that China's arsenal includes 100 ICBMs, and that the number of warheads on Chinese ICBMs capable of reaching the USA is expected to grow to 200 by 2025.[19] The silo-based, liquid-fuelled, two-stage DF-5 (CSS-4) family of missiles—which first entered into service in the early 1980s—are currently China's longest-range ICBMs. Along with the road-mobile, solid-fuelled, three-stage DF-31A/AG (CSS-10 Mod 2) ICBM, they are the only operational missiles in China's arsenal capable of targeting all of the continental USA and Europe.[20]

The PLARF has been developing a longer-range ICBM—the road-mobile, solid-fuelled, three-stage DF-41 (CSS-20)—since the late 1990s. The DF-41 has an estimated range in excess of 12 000 km, similar to that of the older DF-5. Rail-mobile and silo-based versions of the missile are believed to be under development.[21] Satellite imagery in 2019 and 2020 indicated that the PLARF was building a significant number of silos—16 so far—at a missile training area near Jilantai, Inner Mongolia, possibly for the DF-41.[22] It also indicated that new silo construction might have started at Sundian, Henan province, in 2017.[23] However, it is unclear whether these silos are intended to achieve an operational capability or if they are just for training; the US DOD assessed in 2020 that Jilantai 'is probably being used to at least develop a concept of operations for silo basing [the DF-41] system'.[24] There have been 11 known flight tests of the DF-41 since 2012. The most recent, in November 2019, was presumably one of the last tests of the system before it becomes operational.[25] The DF-41s are currently being integrated into the first PLARF brigades; and a small number of launchers might reach operational status in 2021.[26]

After many years of research and development, China has modified a small number of ICBMs to deliver nuclear multiple independently target-able re-entry vehicles (MIRVs). This is apparently to improve the penetration capabilities of its warheads in response to advances in US and, to a lesser

---

[19] US Department of Defense (note 1), p. 56.

[20] US Department of Defense (note 1), p. 56.

[21] US Department of Defense (note 1), p. 56.

[22] Kristensen, H. M., 'China's expanding missile training area: More silos, tunnels, and support facilities', Federation of American Scientists (FAS) Strategic Security Blog, 24 Feb. 2021; and Kristensen, H. M., 'New missile silo and DF-41 launchers seen in Chinese nuclear missile training area', FAS Strategic Security Blog, 3 Sep. 2019.

[23] LaFoy, S. and Eveleth, D., 'Possible ICBM modernization underway at Sundian', Arms Control Wonk, 5 Feb. 2020.

[24] US Department of Defense (note 1), p. 89.

[25] Gertz, B., 'Long-range missile test adds to growing Chinese arsenal', *Washington Times*, 25 Nov. 2019.

[26] US Department of Defense (note 16), p. 3; and US Air Force (note 12), p. 29.

extent, Russian and Indian missile defences.[27] The DF-5B (CSS-4 Mod 2) is a MIRVed variant of the DF-5 that can carry up to five MIRVed warheads, two more than previously assumed.[28] A second variant under development, the DF-5C (CSS-4 Mod 3), can reportedly also carry MIRVed warheads. Some US media reports have suggested that it might be capable of carrying up to 10 warheads, but it seems more likely that it will carry a number similar to the DF-5B version.[29] There has been speculation that the DF-41 is able to carry 6–10 MIRVed warheads, but there is significant uncertainty about the actual capability, and it is likely to carry fewer than its maximum capacity in order to maximize range.[30]

Intermediate- and medium-range ballistic missiles

In 2016 the PLARF began the deployment of the new dual-capable DF-26 (CSS-18) intermediate-range ballistic missile.[31] This missile has an esti-mated maximum range exceeding 4000 km and can therefore reach targets all over India and the western Pacific Ocean, including the US strategic base on Guam.[32] The missile is equipped with a manoeuvrable re-entry vehicle (MaRV) that is reportedly capable of precision conventional or nuclear strikes against ground targets, as well as conventional strikes against naval targets.[33] In August 2020 China conducted a flight test of a DF-26B, a variant of the DF-26 that could have an anti-ship mission.[34] China appears to be producing the DF-26 in significant numbers, and might have had an inventory of up to 100 launchers as of the beginning of 2021, with many more in production. There were sightings of the missile at several PLARF brigade bases during 2020.[35]

The PLARF currently deploys an estimated 40 nuclear-capable DF-21 (CSS-5) MRBMs. The DF-21 is a two-stage, solid-fuelled mobile missile. The original DF-21 (CSS-5 Mod 1) was first deployed in 1991 but has since been

[27] US Department of Defense (note 12), p. 65; and Lewis, J. G., 'China's belated embrace of MIRVs', eds M. Krepon, T. Wheeler and S. Mason, *The Lure and Pitfalls of MIRVs: From the First to the Second Nuclear Age* (Stimson Center: Washington, DC, May 2016), pp. 95–99.

[28] US Department of Defense (note 12), p. 44; and US Department of Defense (note 1), p. 56.

[29] Gertz, B., 'China tests missile with 10 warheads', Washington Free Beacon, 31 Jan. 2017.

[30] O'Halloran, J. C. (ed.), *IHS Jane's Weapons: Strategic, 2015–16* (IHS Jane's: Coulsdon, 2015), pp. 21–22; and Gertz, B., 'China flight tests new multiple-warhead missile', Washington Free Beacon, 19 Apr. 2016.

[31] US Department of Defense, *Military and Security Developments Involving the People's Republic of China 2018* (note 9), p. 36; and US Department of Defense (note 12), p. 44.

[32] US Department of Defense (note 1), pp. 59, 81; and Deng, X., 'China deploys Dongfeng-26 ballistic missile with PLA Rocket Force', *Global Times*, 26 Apr. 2018.

[33] Tate, A., 'China touts ASBM capabilities of DF-26', Janes, 28 Jan. 2019; and Deng (note 32).

[34] Huang, K., 'Chinese military fires "aircraft-carrier killer" missile into South China Sea in "warning to the United States"', *South China Morning Post*, 26 Aug. 2020; and Pollack, J. H. and LaFoy, S., 'China's DF-26: A hot-swappable missile?', Arms Control Wonk, 17 May 2020.

[35] Kristensen, H. M., 'China's new DF-26 missile shows up at base in eastern China', Federation of American Scientists (FAS) Strategic Security Blog, 21 Jan. 2020.

retired. An upgraded variant, the DF-21A (CSS-5 Mod 2), was first deployed in 1996 and an enhanced version (CSS-5 Mod 6) was fielded in 2017.[36] Two other versions of the missile (DF-21C and DF-21D) were designed for conventional anti-ship and anti-access/area-denial (A2/AD) missions.[37]

In October 2019 the PLARF paraded 16 new DF-17 (CSS-22) MRBMs carrying hypersonic glide vehicles (HGVs), although the missiles are unlikely to have begun combat deployment as of January 2021.[38] The missile's nuclear capability remains unclear: despite the parade announcer referring to the missiles as conventional, in 2020 the commander of US Strategic Command, Admiral Charles A. Richard, described the DF-17 as a 'strategic nuclear system'.[39] Because of the high level of uncertainty about the status of the DF-17, it is not included in SIPRI's estimate for January 2021.

Sea-based missiles

In 2020 China continued to pursue its long-standing strategic goal from the early 1980s of developing and deploying a sea-based nuclear deterrent. According to the US DOD's 2020 report, the PLA Navy (PLAN) has constructed six Type 094 SSBNs, although the two latest boats—which are believed to be variants of the original design known as Type 094A—are not yet operational.[40] The US DOD report assessed that the four operational Type 094 SSBNs constitute China's 'first credible, sea-based nuclear deterrent'.[41]

China's four Type 094 submarines can each carry up to 12 three-stage, solid-fuelled Julang-2 (JL-2 or CSS-N-14) submarine-launched ballistic missiles (SLBMs). The JL-2 is a sea-based variant of the DF-31 ICBM. It has an estimated maximum range in excess of 7000 km and is believed to carry a single nuclear warhead.[42]

There has been considerable speculation about whether the missiles on China's SSBNs are mated with warheads under normal circumstances; there appear to be no credible reports that nuclear-armed patrols have commenced. The routine deployment of nuclear weapons on China's SSBNs would constitute a significant change to the country's long-held practice of keeping nuclear warheads in central storage in peacetime and would

---

[36] ed. O'Halloran (note 30), pp. 15–17.

[37] US Air Force (note 12), p. 22.

[38] New China TV, 'China holds grand gathering, parade on 70th National Day', YouTube, 1 Oct. 2019.

[39] New China TV (note 38); and Richard, C. A., Commander, US Strategic Command, Statement, US Senate, Armed Services Committee, 13 Feb. 2020, p. 4.

[40] US Department of Defense (note 1), p. 45. The Type 094 SSBN is designated the Jin class by the USA and the North Atlantic Treaty Organization (NATO).

[41] US Department of Defense (note 1), p. 45.

[42] US Department of Defense (note 1), p. 45.

pose operational challenges for its nuclear command-and-control arrangements.[43] During a war, geographic choke points and advanced US antisubmarine warfare capabilities could force China to deploy its nuclear submarines in a protective bastion within the South China Sea, rather than sail them past Japan and out into the Pacific Ocean. These constraints significantly limit Chinese SSBNs from targeting the continental USA.

The PLAN is developing its next-generation SSBN, the Type 096. The US DOD predicted in 2020 that construction would probably begin in the early 2020s.[44] Reports vary widely on the design parameters, but the new submarine is expected to be larger and quieter than the Type 094 and might be equipped with more missile launch tubes. Given the expected lifespans of both the current Type 094 and the next-generation Type 096 submarines, the PLAN will probably operate both types of SSBN concurrently. In 2020 the US DOD assessed that China could have up to eight SSBNs by 2030.[45]

The Type 096 will be armed with a successor to the JL-2: the JL-3 SLBM.[46] The new missile is thought to use technologies from the land-based DF-41 ICBM and have a longer range than the JL-2. The US Air Force's National Air and Space Intelligence Center (NASIC) assesses that the JL-3 will be capable of carrying multiple warheads and have a range of more than 10 000 km.[47]

---

[43] China Power, 'Does China have an effective sea-based nuclear deterrent?', Center for Strategic and International Studies (CSIS), Mar. 2020.

[44] US Department of Defense (note 1), p. 45.

[45] US Department of Defense (note 1), p. 45.

[46] US Department of Defense (note 12), p. 36.

[47] US Air Force (note 12), p. 33.

VI. Indian nuclear forces

HANS M. KRISTENSEN AND MATT KORDA

As of January 2021, India was estimated to have a growing inventory of about 156 nuclear weapons, an increase of roughly 6 from the previous year (see table 10.7). These weapons are assigned to a maturing nuclear triad of aircraft, land-based missiles and ballistic missile submarines. The warhead estimate is based on calculations of India's inventory of weapon-grade plutonium, the number of operational nuclear-capable delivery systems, India's nuclear doctrine, publicly available information on the Indian nuclear arsenal, and private conversations with defence officials. The Indian Government itself does not provide much public information about the status of its nuclear forces, other than occasional parade displays and announcements about missile flight tests. India is expanding the size of its nuclear weapon inventory as well as its infrastructure for producing nuclear warheads.

The role of nuclear weapons in Indian military doctrine

In the past, the limited ranges of many of India's initial nuclear systems meant that their only role was to deter Pakistan. India now appears to place increased emphasis on China, with the development of longer-range missiles capable of targeting all of China. It remains to be seen how this development will affect India's nuclear arsenal and strategy. It also remains to be seen if recent border clashes with China and Pakistan will affect India's nuclear posture.[1]

India has long adhered to a nuclear no-first-use policy; however, this pledge is qualified by a caveat that India could use nuclear forces to retaliate against attacks by non-nuclear weapons of mass destruction (WMD).[2] Remarks in recent years by Indian defence ministers have also created doubts about India's commitment to the no-first-use policy.[3] Recent scholarship and government statements have called that policy into further question, with some analysts suggesting that 'India's NFU [no-first-use]

---

[1] On the border tensions in 2020 between China and India, and between India and Pakistan see chapter 4, section II, in this volume. On the escalation on the India–Pakistan border in 2019 see Smith, D., 'Introduction: International stability and human security in 2019', *SIPRI Yearbook 2020*, pp. 8–12.

[2] Indian Ministry of External Affairs, 'The Cabinet Committee on Security reviews [o]perationalization of India's nuclear doctrine', Press release, 4 Jan. 2003.

[3] E.g. Singh, R., Indian Minister of Defence (@rajnathsingh), 'Pokhran is the area which witnessed Atal Ji's firm resolve to make India a nuclear power and yet remain firmly committed to the doctrine of "No First Use". India has strictly adhered to this doctrine. What happens in future depends on the circumstances.', Twitter, 16 Aug. 2019; and Som, V., 'Defence Minister Manohar Parrikar's nuclear remark stressed as "personal opinion"', NDTV, 10 Nov. 2016.

policy is neither a stable nor a reliable predictor of how the Indian military and political leadership might actually use nuclear weapons'.[4]

In addition, India appears to be taking steps to increase the responsiveness of its arsenal by 'canisterizing' some of its ballistic missiles, initially the Agni-V (see below). This refers to keeping missiles inside a tube to protect them from the elements while being transported. Missiles can also be launched directly from canisters, usually using a 'cold-launch' process that involves using a gas generator to eject the missile from the canister before ignition. Missiles launched from canisters are pre-mated with their warheads to ensure rapid launch. Submarines on deterrence patrol will also have pre-mated warheads; however, it is currently unclear whether India has conducted a true deterrence patrol.

Former senior civilian security officials and former officers of India's Strategic Forces Command (SFC) have reportedly suggested that some portion of India's arsenal, particularly those weapons and capabilities designed for retaliation against Pakistan, 'are now kept at a much higher state of readiness, capable of being operationalized and released within seconds or minutes—not hours, as has been previously assumed'.[5] Whether that means that warheads are mated all the time is unclear; the first canisterized missile (the Agni-V) is not yet deployed. But pre-mating could form the basis of a higher alert posture in the future. Indeed, to provide a credible secure second-strike capability, warheads would have to be mated with missiles on India's nascent fleet of nuclear-powered ballistic missile submarines (SSBNs).

Aircraft and air-delivered weapons

Aircraft are the most mature component of India's nuclear strike capabilities. It is estimated here that approximately 48 nuclear bombs are assigned to aircraft. The Indian Air Force (IAF) has reportedly certified its Mirage 2000H fighter-bombers for delivery of nuclear gravity bombs.[6] It is widely speculated that the IAF's Jaguar IS fighter-bombers may also have a nuclear delivery role.[7]

---

[4] Sundaram, K. and Ramana, M. V., 'India and the policy of no first use of nuclear weapons', *Journal for Peace and Nuclear Disarmament*, vol. 1, no. 1 (2018), p. 153. See also Clary, C. and Narang, V., 'India's counterforce temptations: Strategic dilemmas, doctrine, and capabilities', *International Security*, vol. 43, no. 3 (winter 2018).

[5] Narang, V., 'Five myths about India's nuclear posture', *Washington Quarterly*, vol. 36, no. 3 (summer 2013), p. 149.

[6] Kampani, G., 'New Delhi's long nuclear journey: How secrecy and institutional roadblocks delayed India's weaponization', *International Security*, vol. 38, no. 4 (spring 2014), pp. 94, 97–98.

[7] Cohen, S. and Dasgupta, S., *Arming Without Aiming: India's Military Modernization* (Brookings Institution Press: Washington, DC, 2010), pp. 77–78; and Shukla, A., 'Jaguar fighter gets 20-year lease of life with DARIN-III avionics', *Business Standard*, 24 Nov. 2016.

Table 10.7. Indian nuclear forces, January 2021

All figures are approximate and some are based on assessments by the authors.

Type/designation	No. of launchers	Year first deployed	Range (km)[a]	Warheads x yield[b]	No. of warheads[c]
Aircraft[d]	48				48
Mirage 2000H	32	1985	1 850	1 x 12 kt bomb	32
Jaguar IS	16	1981	1 600	1 x 12 kt bomb	16
Land-based missiles[e]	64				64
Prithvi-II	24	2003	250[f]	1 x 12 kt	24
Agni-I	16	2007	>700	1 x 10–40 kt	16
Agni-II	16	2011	>2 000	1 x 10–40 kt	16
Agni-III	8	2018	>3 200	1 x 10–40 kt	8
Agni-IV	–	[2021]	>3 500	1 x 10–40 kt	–
Agni-V	–	[2025]	>5 000	1 x 10–40 kt	–
Sea-based missiles	3/14[g]				16
Dhanush	2	2013	400	1 x 12 kt	4[h]
K-15 (B-05)[i]	12[j]	2018	700	1 x 12 kt	12
K-4	–[k]	[2025]	3 500	1 x 10–40 kt	–
Total stockpile	**126**				**128**
Other stored warheads[l]					28
Total inventory	**126**				**156**[l]

– = nil or a negligible value; [] = uncertain figure; kt = kiloton.

[a] For aircraft, the listed range is for illustrative purposes only; actual mission range will vary according to flight profile, weapon loading and in-flight refuelling.

[b] The yields of India's nuclear warheads are not known. The 1998 nuclear tests demonstrated yields of up to 12 kt. Since then, it is possible that boosted warheads have been introduced with a higher yield, perhaps up to 40 kt. There is no open-source evidence that India has developed two-stage thermonuclear warheads.

[c] Aircraft and several missile types are dual-capable—that is, they can be armed with either conventional or nuclear warheads. This estimate counts an average of 1 nuclear warhead per launcher. All estimates are approximate.

[d] Other aircraft that could potentially have a secondary nuclear role include the Su-30MKI. India is also in the process of acquiring Rafale aircraft from France, which could potentially be assigned a nuclear role in the future.

[e] In addition to the land-based missiles listed here, an Agni-VI is thought to be in the design phase. With a range of approximately 6000 km, it would be India's first intercontinental ballistic missile.

[f] The Prithvi-II's range is often reported as 350 km. However, the US Air Force's National Air and Space Intelligence Center (NASIC) sets the range at 250 km.

[g] The first figure is the number of operational vessels—2 ships and 1 nuclear-powered ballistic missile submarine (SSBN); the second is the maximum number of missiles that they can carry. India has launched 2 SSBNs, but only 1—INS *Arihant*—is believed to be operational and probably has only a limited operational capability. The other SSBN—INS *Arighat*—is being fitted out and might become operational during or after 2021.

[h] Each Sukanya-class patrol ship equipped with Dhanush missiles is thought to have possibly 1 reload.

[i] Some sources have referred to the K-15 missile as Sagarika, which was the name of the missile development project.

[j] Each SSBN has 4 missile tubes, each of which can carry 3 K-15 submarine-launched ballistic missiles (SLBMs), for a total of 12 missiles per SSBN. SIPRI estimates that an additional

c. 12 K-15 missiles and warheads have been produced and might become operational during or after 2021 (see notes g and l).

[k] Each missile tube will be able to carry 1 K-4 SLBM once it becomes operational.

[l] In addition to the *c*. 128 warheads estimated to be assigned to operational forces, SIPRI estimates that an additional *c*. 28 warheads might have been produced to arm Agni-IV and Agni-V missiles (*c*. 16 warheads) and K-15 missiles (*c*. 12 warheads for INS *Arighat*), for a total estimated inventory of *c*. 156 warheads. India's inventory is expected to continue to increase.

Sources: Indian Ministry of Defence, annual reports, and press releases; International Institute for Strategic Studies, *The Military Balance*, various years; US Air Force, National Air and Space Intelligence Center (NASIC), *Ballistic and Cruise Missile Threat*, various years; Indian news media reports; *Bulletin of the Atomic Scientists*, 'Nuclear notebook', various issues; and authors' estimates.

In addition, India has bought 36 Rafale combat aircraft from France, with delivery starting in July 2020.[8] According to the Indian Ministry of Defence, the 'Rafale will provide IAF the strategic deterrence and requisite capability cum technological edge'.[9] It is unclear whether this language indicates a future nuclear role for the Rafales.

Land-based missiles

The Indian Army's Strategic Forces Command operates four types of mobile nuclear-capable ballistic missile: the short-range Prithvi-II (250 kilometres) and Agni-I (700 km); the medium-range Agni-II (>2000 km); and the intermediate-range Agni-III (>3200 km).[10]

Two new and longer-range land-based ballistic missiles are in development: the Agni-IV (>3500 km) and the Agni-V (>5000 km). A variant with an even longer range, the Agni-VI (6000 km), is in the design stage of development.[11] Unlike the other Agni missiles, the Agni-V is designed to be stored in and launched from a new mobile canister system, which will reduce the time required to place the missiles on alert in a crisis.[12] The Agni-V is currently undergoing final development trials. According to one report, the missile might be handed over to the military (inducted) sometime in the first half of 2021.[13]

India is also developing a land-based, short-range version (750 km) of the K-15 submarine-launched ballistic missile (SLBM)—known as the Shaurya.

[8] 'India: French Rafale jets land amid tensions with China', Deutsche Welle, 29 July 2020.

[9] Indian Ministry of Defence (MOD), *Annual Report 2018–19* (MOD: New Delhi, 2019), p. 43.

[10] The Prithvi-II's range is often reported as 350 km. However, the range is set at 250 km in US Air Force, National Air and Space Intelligence Center (NASIC), *Ballistic and Cruise Missile Threat 2020* (NASIC: Wright-Patterson Air Force Base, OH, July 2020), p. 17.

[11] Vikas, S. V., 'Why India may not test Agni 6 even if DRDO is ready with technology', OneIndia, 10 July 2019.

[12] Aroor, S., 'New chief of India's military research complex reveals brave new mandate', *India Today*, 13 July 2013.

[13] Rout, H. K., 'India plans deployment of nuclear-capable Agni-V this year', *New Indian Express*, 4 Jan. 2021.

Because the K-15 is nuclear-capable, media reports also widely attribute nuclear capability to the Shaurya.[14] No official government statement has confirmed this, however, and with only three or four flight tests, reports about imminent deployment seem premature.[15] The US Air Force's National Air and Space Intelligence Center (NASIC) does not mention the Shaurya in its ballistic and cruise missile reports of 2020 and 2017.[16] Because of the high level of uncertainty about the status of the Shaurya, it is not included in SIPRI's estimate for January 2021.

India reportedly carried out at least five test launches of land-based ballistic missiles in 2020. The known launches included night-time flight tests of four Prithvi-II missiles and one Shaurya missile.[17] An Agni-IV test may have been scheduled for late December; however, it is unclear whether that test took place.

India is reportedly pursuing a technology development programme for multiple independently targetable re-entry vehicles (MIRVs). However, there have been conflicting views among defence planners and officials about how to proceed with the programme, in particular about whether MIRVs should be initially deployed on the intermediate-range Agni-V or on the intercontinental Agni-VI, which will have a heavier payload capacity.[18]

Sea-based missiles

With the aim of creating an assured second-strike capability, India continues to develop the naval component of its nascent nuclear triad and is building a fleet of four to six SSBNs.[19] The first SSBN, the INS *Arihant*, was launched in 2009 and formally commissioned in 2016.[20] It is estimated here

---

[14] Press Trust of India (PTI), 'India successfully test-fires nuclear capable hypersonic missile Shaurya', *Hindustan Times*, 3 Oct. 2020; and Gupta, S., 'Govt okays induction of nuke-capable Shaurya missile amid Ladakh standoff', *Hindustan Times*, 6 Oct. 2020.

[15] Subramanian, T. S. and Mallikarjun, Y., 'India successfully test-fires Shourya missile', *The Hindu*, 24 Sep. 2011; and Press Trust of India (PTI), '"Shaurya" successfully test fired', *The Hindu*, 3 Oct. 2020.

[16] US Air Force (note 10); and US Air Force, National Air and Space Intelligence Center (NASIC), *Ballistic and Cruise Missile Threat 2017* (NASIC: Wright-Patterson Air Force Base, OH, June 2017).

[17] Express News Service, 'Nuke capable Prithvi-II night trial successful', *New Indian Express*, 24 Sep. 2020; Press Trust of India (PTI), 'Successful night trial of nuclear-capable Prithvi-2 missile', *Times of India*, 16 Oct. 2020; Rout, H. J. (@TheHemantRout), '#FirstVisual of Prithvi #missile night trial from ITR off #Odisha coast. #India test fires 2 variants of #Prithvi in quick succession to reconfirm operational readiness. Developed by @DRDO_India, the tactical #nuclear capable weapons can strike targets at a range up to 350 km.', Twitter, 17 Dec. 2020; and Mohanty, D. and Singh, R., 'India successfully tests nuclear-capable Shaurya missile', *Hindustan Times*, 3 Oct. 2020.

[18] Basrur, R. and Sankaran, J., 'India's slow and unstoppable move to MIRV', eds M. Krepon, T. Wheeler and S. Mason, *The Lure and Pitfalls of MIRVs: From the First to the Second Nuclear Age* (Stimson Center: Washington, DC, May 2016).

[19] Davenport, K., 'Indian submarine completes first patrol', *Arms Control Today*, vol. 48, no. 10 (Dec. 2018).

[20] Dinakar, P., 'Now, India has a nuclear triad', *The Hindu*, 18 Oct. 2016.

that 12 nuclear warheads have been delivered for potential deployment by the *Arihant* and another 12 produced for a second SSBN, the INS *Arighat*, which is being fitted out.

In November 2018 the Indian Government announced that the *Arihant* had completed its first 'deterrence patrol'.[21] However, it is doubtful that the submarine's missiles carried nuclear warheads during the patrol.[22] The *Arihant* is assessed here to have only a limited operational capability.

The INS *Arighat* was launched in November 2017 and is expected to be commissioned into the Indian Navy in early 2021.[23] Construction work has reportedly begun on a third and fourth submarine, with expected launch dates in 2021 and 2023, respectively.[24]

Photographs indicate that the *Arihant* and *Arighat* are each equipped with a four-tube vertical-launch system and can carry up to 12 two-stage, 700-km range K-15 SLBMs (which the Indian Ministry of Defence calls the B-05).[25] India's third and fourth submarines are expected to be larger than its first two. They will reportedly have 8 launch tubes to hold up to 24 K-15s or 8 K-4 missiles, which are in development.[26]

The K-4 is a two-stage, 3500-km range SLBM that is being developed by the Defence Research and Development Organisation (DRDO). It will eventually replace the K-15, although only with four or eight missiles per submarine, depending on the number of launch tubes.[27] The DRDO has also started to develop extended-range versions: the K-5 SLBM, which will reportedly have a range in excess of 5000 km, and the K-6, which will have an even longer range.[28] The K-4 was tested twice by the DRDO in January 2020 from a submerged pontoon.[29] With only two successful launches (two

[21] Indian Prime Minister's Office, 'Prime Minister felicitates crew of INS Arihant on completion of Nuclear Triad', Press Information Bureau, 5 Nov. 2018; and Davenport (note 19).

[22] Joshi, Y., 'Angels and dangles: Arihant and the dilemma of India's undersea nuclear weapons', War on the Rocks, 14 Jan. 2019.

[23] Bedi, R., 'India to commission second Arihant-class submarine in 2021', Janes, 22 Dec. 2020. Until its launch, the submarine was assumed to be named INS *Aridhaman*.

[24] Unnithan, S., 'A peek into India's top secret and costliest defence project, nuclear submarines', *India Today*, 10 Dec. 2017.

[25] Indian Defence Research and Development Organisation (DRDO), 'MSS—Achievements', 6 Sep. 2019.

[26] Philip, S. A., 'Ballistic missile submarine Arighat in final stages of trials, to be commissioned early 2021', ThePrint, 16 Dec. 2020; and Kristensen, H. (@nukestrat), 'New submarine cover (17°42'23"N, 83°16'23"E) constructed at Vizag is 40m longer than first one. India's third SSBN will be longer with more missile tubes than the 4 on first two boats. Current missile compartment is ~15m with tubes in row instead of pairs as other navies have.', Twitter, 12 Mar. 2021.

[27] Jha, S., 'India's undersea deterrent', The Diplomat, 30 Mar. 2016; and US Air Force (note 10), p. 30.

[28] Unnithan (note 24).

[29] Peri, D., 'India successfully test-fires 3,500-km range submarine-launched ballistic missile K-4', *The Hindu*, 19 Jan. 2020; and Pandit, R., 'DRDO: Arihant's N-capable missile "ready to roll"', *Times of India*, 25 Jan. 2020.

previous attempts failed), and none from a submarine, the K-4 still seems to be several years from operational capability.

India's first naval nuclear weapon was the Dhanush missile, a version of the dual-capable Prithvi-II that can be launched from a surface ship. Two Sukanya-class offshore patrol vessels based at the Karwar Naval Base on India's west coast have been converted to launch the Dhanush. The missile can reportedly carry a 500-kg warhead to a maximum range of 400 km and is designed to be able to hit both sea- and shore-based targets. Its utility as a second-strike deterrence weapon is limited by its relatively short range, which would make its carrier vessels vulnerable to anti-ship missiles and rapid-response combat aircraft.[30] The Dhanush will probably be retired when the SSBN programme with longer-range missiles matures. The most recent known Dhanush test launch was in November 2018.[31]

Cruise missiles

There are numerous claims in news articles and on private websites that some Indian cruise missiles are nuclear-capable. These claims concern the ground- and air-launched Nirbhay subsonic cruise missile and the supersonic air-, ground-, ship- and submarine-launched BrahMos cruise missile.[32] There is, however, no official or authoritative source that attributes nuclear capability to India's cruise missiles. Therefore, they are not included in SIPRI's estimate for January 2021.

[30] 'Nuke-capable Dhanush and Prithvi-II launched', New Indian Express, 12 Mar. 2011.

[31] Indian Ministry of Defence (note 9), p. 100.

[32] Pandit, R., 'India successfully tests its first nuclear-capable cruise missile', Times of India, 8 Nov. 2017; Gady, F.-S., 'India successfully test fires indigenous nuclear-capable cruise missile', The Diplomat, 8 Nov. 2017; and Mitra, J., 'Nuclear BrahMos: On the anvil?', South Asian Voices, 10 July 2018.

VII. Pakistani nuclear forces

HANS M. KRISTENSEN AND MATT KORDA

It is estimated that Pakistan possessed approximately 165 nuclear warheads as of January 2021, an increase of 5 from the previous year (see table 10.8). The Pakistani Government has never publicly disclosed the size of its nuclear arsenal; the estimate made here is based on analysis of Pakistan's nuclear posture, previous statements by Western officials, and private conversations with officials. Analysing the number and types of Pakistani warheads and delivery vehicles is fraught with uncertainty, due to limited official public data and widespread exaggerated news stories about nuclear weapons. Pakistan's nuclear weapon arsenal and fissile material stockpile are likely to continue expanding over the next decade, although projections vary considerably.[1]

The role of nuclear weapons in Pakistani military doctrine

Pakistan is pursuing the development and deployment of new nuclear weapons and delivery systems as part of its 'full spectrum deterrence posture' in relation to India.[2] According to Pakistan, its full spectrum nuclear weapon posture includes long-range missiles and aircraft as well as several short-range, lower-yield nuclear-capable weapon systems.[3] Pakistan's emphasis on non-strategic nuclear weapons is specifically intended to be a reaction to India's perceived 'Cold Start' doctrine. This alleged doctrine revolves around maintaining the capability to launch large-scale conventional strikes or incursions against Pakistani territory at a level below the threshold at which Pakistan would retaliate with nuclear weapons.[4] In 2015 a retired member of Pakistan's National Command Authority suggested that 'by introducing the variety of tactical nuclear

---

[1] See e.g. Sundaresan, L. and Ashok, K., 'Uranium constraints in Pakistan: How many nuclear weapons does Pakistan have?', *Current Science*, vol. 115, no. 6 (25 Sep. 2018); and Salik, N., 'Pakistan's nuclear force structure in 2025', Regional Insight, Carnegie Endowment for International Peace, 30 June 2016. On Pakistan's fissile material stockpile see Kile, S. N. and Kristensen, H. M., 'Pakistani nuclear forces', *SIPRI Yearbook 2019*, pp. 332–33; and section X of this chapter.

[2] Kidwai, K., Keynote address and discussion session, Workshop on 'South Asian Strategic Stability: Deterrence, Nuclear Weapons and Arms Control', International Institute for Strategic Studies (IISS) and Centre for International Strategic Studies (CISS), 6 Feb. 2020. For a detailed assessment of Pakistan's nuclear posture see Tasleem, S. and Dalton, T., 'Nuclear emulation: Pakistan's nuclear trajectory', *Washington Quarterly*, vol. 41, no. 4 (winter 2019).

[3] Pakistani Inter Services Public Relations, Press Release PR-94/2011-ISPR, 19 Apr. 2011.

[4] Kidwai (note 2). For a US diplomatic assessment of India's 'Cold Start' strategy see Roemer, T., US Ambassador to India, 'Cold Start—A mixture of myth and reality', Cable New Delhi 000295, 16 Feb. 2010.

Table 10.8. Pakistani nuclear forces, January 2021

All figures are approximate and some are based on assessments by the authors.

Type/designation	No. of launchers	Year first deployed	Range (km)[a]	Warheads x yield[b]	No. of warheads[c]
Aircraft[d]	36				36
Mirage III/V	36	1998	2 100	1 x 5–12 kt bomb or Ra'ad ALCM (in development)[e]	36
Land-based missiles	118[f]				118
Abdali (Hatf-2)	10	2015	200	1 x 5–12 kt	10
Ghaznavi (Hatf-3)	16	2004	300	1 x 5–12 kt	16
Shaheen-I (Hatf-4)	16	2003	750	1 x 5–12 kt	16
Shaheen-IA (Hatf-4)[g]	–	..	900	1 x 5–12 kt	–
Shaheen-II (Hatf-6)	16	2014	2 000	1 x 10–40 kt	16
Shaheen-III (Hatf-..)[h]	–	[2022]	2 750	1 x 10–40 kt	–
Ghauri (Hatf-5)	24	2003	1 250	1 x 10–40 kt	24
Nasr (Hatf-9)	24	2013	70	1 x 5–12 kt	24
Ababeel (Hatf-..)	–	..	2 200	MIRV or MRV	–[i]
Babur GLCM (Hatf-7)	12	2014	350[j]	1 x 5–12 kt	12
Babur-2 GLCM (Hatf-..)	–	..[k]	700	1 x 5–12 kt	–
Sea-based missiles					
Babur-3 SLCM (Hatf-..)	–	..[l]	450	1 x 5–12 kt	–
Total stockpile	154				154
Other stored warheads[m]					11
Total inventory	154				165[m]

.. = not available or not applicable; – = nil or a negligible value; [] = uncertain figure; ALCM = air-launched cruise missile; GLCM = ground-launched cruise missile; kt = kiloton; MIRV = multiple independently targetable re-entry vehicle; MRV = multiple re-entry vehicle; SLCM = sea-launched cruise missile.

[a] For aircraft, the listed range is for illustrative purposes only; actual mission range will vary according to flight profile, weapon loading and in-flight refuelling.

[b] The yields of Pakistan's nuclear warheads are not known. The 1998 nuclear tests demonstrated a yield of up to 12 kt. Since then, it is possible that boosted warheads have been introduced with higher yields. There is no open-source evidence that Pakistan has developed two-stage thermonuclear warheads.

[c] Aircraft and several missile types are dual-capable—that is, they can be armed with either conventional or nuclear warheads. Cruise missile launchers (aircraft and land-based and sea-based missiles) can carry more than 1 missile. This estimate counts an average of 1 nuclear warhead per launcher. Warheads are not deployed on launchers but are kept in separate storage facilities.

[d] There are unconfirmed reports that some of the 40 F-16 aircraft procured from the USA in the 1980s were modified by Pakistan for a nuclear weapon delivery role. However, it is assumed here that the nuclear weapons assigned to aircraft are for use by Mirage aircraft. When the Mirage IIIs and Vs are eventually phased out, it is possible that the JF-17 will take over their nuclear role in the Pakistan Air Force.

[e] The Ra'ad (Hatf-8) ALCM has a claimed range of 350 km and an estimated yield of 5–12 kt. However, there is no available evidence to suggest that the Ra'ad has been deployed so it is not included in the operational warhead count. In 2017 the Pakistani military displayed a Ra'ad-II variant with a reported range of 600 km. It was test flown for the first time in 2020 and several additional flights will be needed before it becomes operational.

[f] Some launchers might have 1 or more missile reloads.

[g] It is unclear whether the Shaheen-IA has the same designation as the Shaheen-I.

[h] The designation for the Shaheen-III is unknown.

[i] According to the Pakistani military, the missile is 'capable of delivering multiple warheads, using [MIRV] technology'.

[j] The Pakistani Government claims that the range of the Babur GLCM is 700 km, double the range reported by the United States Air Force's National Air and Space Intelligence Center (NASIC).

[k] The Babur-2, which was first test launched on 14 Dec. 2016, is an improved version of the original Babur GLCM and will probably replace it. A failed test in 2020 indicates additional development is needed before it can be fielded.

[l] The first test launch of a Babur-3 SLCM was carried out from an underwater platform in 2017. A second test occurred in 2018.

[m] In addition to the c. 154 warheads estimated to be assigned to operational forces, a small number of additional warheads (c. 11) are thought to have been produced to arm future Shaheen-III and cruise missiles, for a total estimated inventory of c. 165 warheads. Pakistan's warhead inventory is expected to continue to increase.

Sources: Pakistani Ministry of Defence, various documents; US Air Force, National Air and Space Intelligence Center (NASIC), *Ballistic and Cruise Missile Threat*, various years; International Institute for Strategic Studies (IISS), *The Military Balance*, various years; *Bulletin of the Atomic Scientists*, 'Nuclear notebook', various issues; and authors' estimates.

weapons in Pakistan's inventory . . . , we have blocked the avenues for serious military operations by the other side'.[5]

Aircraft and air-delivered weapons

Pakistan has a small stockpile of gravity bombs. The Ra'ad (Hatf-8) air-launched cruise missile (ALCM) is being developed to supplement this stockpile by providing the Pakistan Air Force (PAF) with a nuclear-capable standoff capability at a range of 350 kilometres. The most recent reported flight test—believed to be the seventh test since 2007—was in 2016.[6] An improved version, the Ra'ad-II, was displayed for the first time in 2017 and is reported to have a range of 600 km due to its more advanced engine.[7] This would theoretically allow Pakistan's aircraft to reach critical targets inside India while remaining within Pakistani airspace. The Ra'ad-II was tested for the first time in February 2020.[8] There is no available evidence to suggest that either version of the Ra'ad ALCM had been deployed as of January 2021.

The aircraft that are most likely to have a nuclear delivery role are the PAF's Mirage III and Mirage V aircraft. The Mirage III has been used for developmental test flights of the nuclear-capable Ra'ad ALCM, while the

[5] Kidwai, K. (Gen.), Conversation transcript, Carnegie Endowment for International Peace, 23 Mar. 2015, p. 5.

[6] Pakistani Inter Services Public Relations, Press Release PR-16/2016-ISPR, 19 Jan. 2016.

[7] Pakistani Inter Services Public Relations, 'Pakistan conducted successful flight test of air launched cruise missile "Ra'ad-II"', Press Release PR-27/2020-ISPR, 18 Feb. 2020.

[8] Pakistani Inter Services Public Relations (note 7).

Mirage V is believed to have been given a strike role with Pakistan's small arsenal of nuclear gravity bombs.[9]

The nuclear capability of Pakistan's F-16 fighter-bombers is uncertain. Many analysts continue to assign a potential nuclear role to these aircraft due to reports in the late 1980s that Pakistan was in the process of modifying them to deliver nuclear weapons.[10] In the light of this uncertainty, Pakistan's F-16s are not identified here as having a dedicated nuclear weapon delivery system (and so are omitted from table 10.8).

Pakistan also operates about 100 JF-17 aircraft, which it has acquired from China. It intends to acquire a total of approximately 150 to replace the ageing Mirage III and Mirage V aircraft.[11] Initial reports from 2016 on upgrades to the JF-17 suggested that the PAF aimed to integrate the dual-capable Ra'ad ALCM onto the aircraft.[12] More recent reporting has not mentioned the weapon, which could indicate that its primary carrier will remain the Mirage III for the foreseeable future. When the Mirage aircraft are eventually phased out, it is possible that the JF-17 will take over their nuclear role in the PAF.[13]

Land-based missiles

Pakistan's current nuclear-capable ballistic missile arsenal comprises short- and medium-range systems.

As of January 2021, Pakistan deployed the Abdali (also designated Hatf-2), Ghaznavi (Hatf-3), Shaheen-I (Hatf-4) and Nasr (Hatf-9) solid-fuelled, road-mobile short-range ballistic missiles. In an important milestone for testing the readiness of Pakistan's nuclear forces, the Ghaznavi was test launched at night in January 2020.[14] The Shaheen-IA, an extended-range version of the Shaheen-I, is still in development.

---

[9] Kerr, P. and Nikitin, M. B. D., *Pakistan's Nuclear Weapons*, Congressional Research Service (CRS) Report for Congress RL34248 (US Congress, CRS: Washington, DC, 1 Aug. 2016), p. 7.

[10] For a more detailed consideration of the role of the F-16s see Kristensen, H. M. and Kile, S. N., 'Pakistani nuclear forces', *SIPRI Yearbook 2020*, p. 370.

[11] Khan, B., 'Pakistan inches closer to inducting the JF-17 Block 3', Quwa Defence News and Analysis Group, 1 July 2019; Waldron, G., 'Paris: JK-17 Block III to have first flight by year-end', FlightGlobal, 20 June 2019; International Institute for Strategic Studies (IISS), *The Military Balance 2019* (Routledge: London, 2019), pp. 298–99; Warnes, A., 'PAC Kamra rolls out final 14 JF-17B fighters for Pakistan Air Force', Janes, 31 Dec. 2020; and 'Pakistan Aeronautical Complex delivers new JF-17B batch', Quwa Defence News and Analysis Group, 2 Jan. 2021.

[12] Fisher, R., 'JF-17 Block II advances with new refuelling probe', *Jane's Defence Weekly*, 27 Jan. 2016.

[13] 'Ra'ad ALCM: The custodian of Pakistan's airborne nuclear deterrence', PakDefense, 6 Dec. 2020.

[14] Pakistani Inter Services Public Relations, 'Pakistan today conducted a successful training launch of surface to surface ballistic missile Ghaznavi, capable of delivering multiple types of warheads up to a range of 290 kilometers', Press Release PR-8/2020-ISPR, 23 Jan. 2020.

The arsenal also included two types of medium-range ballistic missile: the liquid-fuelled, road-mobile Ghauri (Hatf-5), with a range of 1250 km; and the two-stage, solid-fuelled, road-mobile Shaheen-II (Hatf-6), with a range of 2000 km.[15] The Shaheen-II has been test launched seven times since 2004, with the most recent launch taking place in 2019.[16] A longer-range variant, the Shaheen-III, is currently in development but has been test launched only twice—in 2015 and early 2021—and is not yet deployed.[17] This missile has a claimed range of 2750 km, making it the longest-range system to be tested by Pakistan to date. A variant of the Shaheen-III, the Ababeel, is also in development. After the most recent test launch of the Ababeel in 2017, the Pakistani Government claimed that the missile would be 'capable of delivering multiple warheads, using Multiple Independent[ly Targetable] Re-entry Vehicle (MIRV) technology'.[18]

In addition to expanding its arsenal of land-based ballistic missiles, in 2020 Pakistan continued to develop the nuclear-capable Babur (Hatf-7) ground-launched cruise missile. The United States Air Force's National Air and Space Intelligence Center (NASIC) claims the Babur has a range of 350 km.[19] It has been test launched at least 12 times since 2005 and has been used in army field training since 2011, indicating that the system is likely to be operational. An extended-range version, which is known as the Babur-2 and sometimes referred to as Babur Weapon System-1 (B), has a claimed range of 700 km. It was first test launched in 2016 and was subsequently tested in 2018 and 2020, the latter of which failed.[20]

Sea-based missiles

As part of its efforts to achieve a secure second-strike capability, Pakistan is seeking to create a nuclear triad by developing a sea-based nuclear force. The Babur-3 submarine-launched cruise missile (SLCM) is intended to

---

[15] US Air Force, National Air and Space Intelligence Center (NASIC), *Ballistic and Cruise Missile Threat 2020* (NASIC: Wright-Patterson Air Force Base, OH, July 2020), p. 25.

[16] Pakistani Inter Services Public Relations, 'Pakistan conducted successful training launch of surface to surface ballistic missile Shaheen-II', Press Release PR-104/2019-ISPR, 23 May 2019.

[17] Pakistani Inter Services Public Relations, 'Shaheen 3 missile test', Press Release PR-61/2015-ISPR, 9 Mar. 2015; and Jamal, S., 'Pakistan tests nuclear-capable Shaheen-III ballistic missile', *Gulf News*, 20 Jan. 2021.

[18] Pakistani Inter Services Public Relations, Press Release PR-34/2017-ISPR, 24 Jan. 2017. The US National Air and Space Intelligence Center also describes the 2017 test as involving 'the MIRV version of the Ababeel'. US Air Force (note 15), p. 25. On the Ababeel see also Kile and Kristensen (note 1), p. 335.

[19] US Air Force, National Air and Space Intelligence Center (NASIC), *Ballistic and Cruise Missile Threat 2017* (NASIC: Wright-Patterson Air Force Base, OH, June 2017), p. 37.

[20] Pakistan Inter Services Public Relations, 'Pakistan today conducted a successful test of an enhanced range version of the indigenously developed Babur cruise missile', Press Release PR-142/2018-ISPR, 14 Apr. 2018; and Gupta, S., 'Pakistan's effort to launch 750km range missile crashes', *Hindustan Times*, 23 Mar. 2020.

establish a nuclear capability for the Pakistan Navy's Hashmat-class diesel–electric submarines.[21] The Babur-3 was first test launched in 2017 and was tested for a second time in 2018.[22]

Pakistan has ordered eight air-independent propulsion-powered submarines from China, the first of which is expected to be delivered in 2022. It is possible that these Hangor-class submarines might also be given a nuclear role with the Babur-3 SLCM.[23]

[21] Panda, A. and Narang, V., 'Pakistan tests new sub-launched nuclear-capable cruise missile. What now?', The Diplomat, 10 Jan. 2017.

[22] Pakistani Inter Services Public Relations, 'Pakistan conducted another successful test fire of indigenously developed submarine launched cruise missile Babur having a range of 450 kms', Press Release PR-125/2018-ISPR, 29 Mar. 2018. Reports of a ship-launched cruise missile test in 2019 might have been for a different missile. Gady, F.-S., 'Pakistan's navy test fires indigenous anti-ship/land-attack cruise missile', The Diplomat, 24 Apr. 2019.

[23] Khan, B., 'Profile: Pakistan's new Hangor submarine', Quwa Defence News and Analysis Group, 11 Nov. 2019.

VIII. Israeli nuclear forces

HANS M. KRISTENSEN AND MATT KORDA

As of January 2021, Israel was estimated to have an inventory of around 90 nuclear warheads (see table 10.9), the same number as in January 2020. Israel continues to maintain its long-standing policy of nuclear opacity: it neither officially confirms nor denies that it possesses nuclear weapons.[1] Due to Israel's unique lack of transparency, there is significant uncertainty about the size of its nuclear arsenal and associated warhead capabilities. The estimate here is largely based on calculations of Israel's inventory of weapon-grade plutonium and the number of operational nuclear-capable delivery systems. The locations of the storage sites for the warheads, which are thought to be stored partially unassembled, are unknown.

The role of nuclear weapons in Israeli military doctrine

For decades, the Israeli Government has repeated that Israel 'won't be the first to introduce nuclear weapons into the Middle East'.[2] However, the government's interpretation of 'introducing' nuclear weapons appears to have significant caveats, in order to accommodate the high likelihood that Israel in reality possesses a significant nuclear stockpile. Israeli policy-makers have previously suggested that 'introducing' nuclear weapons would necessarily require Israel to test, publicly declare or actually use its nuclear capability, which, according to available open-access sources, it has not yet done.[3] Another caveat may be that the warheads are not fully assembled under normal circumstances.

It is unclear what circumstances would prompt Israel to 'introduce' nuclear weapons into the region under its own narrow definition. It is believed that one such scenario would involve a crisis that poses an existential threat to the State of Israel.

---

[1] On the role of this policy in Israel's national security decision making see Cohen, A., 'Israel', eds H. Born, B. Gill and H. Hänggi, SIPRI, *Governing the Bomb: Civilian Control and Democratic Accountability of Nuclear Weapons* (Oxford University Press: Oxford, 2010).

[2] E.g. Netanyahu, B., Interview, *Piers Morgan Tonight*, CNN, 17 Mar. 2011.

[3] US Department of Defense, Office of the Assistant Secretary of Defense, 'Negotiations with Israel—F-4 and advanced weapons', Memorandum of Conversation, 12 Nov. 1968, via National Security Archive; and Kissinger, H., 'Israeli nuclear program', Memorandum for the President, 19 July 1969, via National Security Archive. For a summary and discussion of available evidence that Israel may have participated in a nuclear test in 1979 see Cohen, A. and Burr, W., 'Revisiting the 1979 VELA mystery: A report on a critical oral history conference', Wilson Center, History and Public Policy Program, Sources and Methods Blog, 31 Aug. 2020.

Table 10.9. Israeli nuclear forces, January 2021

Type/designation	Range (km)^a	Payload (kg)	Status	No. of warheads
Aircraft^b				30
F-16I	1 600	5 400	A small number (1–2 squadrons) of Israel's F-16s is believed to be equipped for nuclear weapon delivery (2 bombs per aircraft).	30
Land-based missiles^c				50
Jericho II	1 500– 1 800	750– 1 000	First deployed in 1990. Being replaced by the Jericho III.	25
Jericho III	>4 000	1 000– 1 300	Became operational in 2011–15 and is gradually replacing the Jericho II.	25
Sea-based missiles				10
..	..	..	Unconfirmed reports suggest that Dolphin- and Dolphin 2-class diesel–electric submarines have been equipped with nuclear-armed SLCMs.	10
Total inventory				**90^d**

.. = not available or not applicable; SLCM = sea-launched cruise missile.

^{a} Aircraft range is for illustrative purposes only; actual range will vary according to flight profile, weapon loading and in-flight refuelling.

^{b} It is possible that some of Israel's F-15 aircraft may also serve a nuclear strike role.

^{c} The Jericho III is gradually replacing the Jericho II, if it has not happened already. A longer-range version of the Jericho ballistic missile with a new rocket motor may be under development.

^{d} SIPRI's estimate is that Israel has c. 90 nuclear warheads that are stored partially assembled. There is significant uncertainty about the size and capabilities of Israel's nuclear arsenal.

Sources: Cohen, A., *The Worst-kept Secret: Israel's Bargain with the Bomb* (Columbia University Press: New York, 2010); Cohen, A. and Burr, W., 'Israel crosses the threshold', *Bulletin of the Atomic Scientists*, vol. 62, no. 3 (May/June 2006); Cohen, A., *Israel and the Bomb* (Columbia University Press: New York, 1998); Albright, D., Berkhout, F. and Walker, W., SIPRI, *Plutonium and Highly Enriched Uranium 1996: World Inventories, Capabilities and Policies* (Oxford University Press: Oxford, 1997); International Institute for Strategic Studies, *The Military Balance*, various years; *IHS Jane's Strategic Weapon Systems*, various issues; Fetter, S., 'Israeli ballistic missile capabilities', *Physics and Society*, vol. 19, no. 3 (July 1990); *Bulletin of the Atomic Scientists*, 'Nuclear notebook', various issues; and authors' estimates.

Military fissile material production

Declassified government documents (mostly from the United States) indicate that Israel began building a stockpile of nuclear weapons in the early 1960s, using plutonium produced by the Israel Research Reactor 2 (IRR-2) at the Negev Nuclear Research Center near Dimona, Southern Israel.[4] This heavy-

---

[4] For a history of Israel's nuclear weapon programme see Cohen, A., *The Worst-kept Secret: Israel's Bargain with the Bomb* (Columbia University Press: New York, 2010); and Burr, W. and Cohen, A., 'Duplicity and self-deception: Israel, the United States, and the Dimona inspections, 1964-65', Briefing Book no. 732, National Security Archive, 10 Nov. 2020.

water reactor, which was commissioned in 1963, is not under International Atomic Energy Agency (IAEA) safeguards. There is little publicly available information about its operating history and power capacity (see section X).[5]

Having produced enough plutonium for Israel to produce some weapons, IRR-2 may now be operated primarily to produce the tritium needed to boost those weapons.[6] Shutdown of the ageing reactor was scheduled for 2003 but has been postponed until at least 2023. The Israel Atomic Energy Commission is reportedly examining ways to extend its service life until the 2040s.[7] Meanwhile, satellite imagery shows that significant construction started at the Negev Nuclear Research Center in late 2018 or early 2019, although the purpose of the construction remains unknown.[8]

Aircraft and air-delivered weapons

Approximately 30 of Israel's nuclear weapons are estimated to be gravity bombs for delivery by F-16I aircraft. Given that the Israeli Air Force refers to its F-15I aircraft as 'strategic', it is possible that some of these aircraft could also play a nuclear role.[9] Nuclear gravity bombs would probably be stored at underground facilities near one or two air force bases, which would contain nuclear-certified aircraft with specially trained crews and unique deployment procedures.

Land-based missiles

Up to 50 warheads are thought to be assigned for delivery by land-based Jericho ballistic missiles. These are believed to be based, along with their mobile transporter-erector-launchers (TELs), in caves at a base near Zekharia, about 25 kilometres west of Jerusalem.[10] The Israeli Government has never publicly confirmed that it possesses the Jericho missiles.

Israel is upgrading its arsenal from the solid-fuelled, two-stage Jericho II medium-range ballistic missile to the Jericho III intermediate-range ballistic missile. The newer and more capable Jericho III is a three-stage missile

---

[5] Glaser, A. and Miller, M., 'Estimating plutonium production at Israel's Dimona reactor', 52nd Annual Meeting of the Institute of Nuclear Materials Management (INMM), 17–21 July 2011.

[6] Kelley, R. and Dewey, K., 'Assessing replacement options for Israel's ageing Dimona reactor', *Jane's Intelligence Review*, 20 Nov. 2018; and International Panel on Fissile Material (IPFM), 'Countries: Israel', 18 May 2020.

[7] Bob, Y. J., 'Experts agree Dimona nuke reactor can exceed original life expectancy', *Jerusalem Post*, 12 July 2019.

[8] International Panel on Fissile Materials (IPFM), 'Significant new construction at the Dimona site', IPFM Blog, 18 Feb. 2021.

[9] Israeli Air Force, 'The F-15I as the IAF's Strategic Aircraft', Defense-Aerospace.com, 19 Jan. 2016.

[10] O'Halloran, J. C. (ed.), 'Jericho missiles', *IHS Jane's Weapons: Strategic, 2015–16* (IHS Jane's: Coulsdon, 2015), p. 53.

with a longer range, exceeding 4000 km. It first became operational in 2011 and might now have replaced the Jericho II.[11] In 2013 Israel tested a Jericho III missile, possibly designated the Jericho IIIA, with a new motor that some sources believe may give the missile an intercontinental range— that is, a range exceeding 5500 km.[12]

On 6 December 2019 the Israeli Ministry of Defense (MOD) announced that it had conducted a test launch of an unspecified rocket propulsion system from a military base in central Israel.[13] It did not identify which missile or military base was used for the test. According to unconfirmed reports, the base was the Palmachim Airbase, which is located on Israel's Mediterranean coast and is used as a test launch site for Jericho missiles.[14] The launch led to renewed speculation that Israel might be developing a new Jericho IV missile.[15] On 31 January 2020 the MOD again acknowledged the test of an unspecified rocket propulsion system, also from a base in central Israel.[16]

Sea-based missiles

Israel operates five German-built Dolphin- and Dolphin 2-class diesel– electric submarines. A sixth boat is being fitted out.[17] Plans to buy three more have been put on hold due to investigations into allegations of corruption.[18] There have been numerous unconfirmed reports that Israel has modified some or all of the submarines to carry indigenously produced nuclear-armed sea-launched cruise missiles (SLCMs), giving it a sea-based nuclear strike capability.[19] In line with Israel's policy of nuclear opacity, Israeli officials have declined to comment publicly on the reports. If they are true, the naval arsenal might include about 10 cruise missile warheads, assuming two warheads per submarine.

---

[11] ed. O'Halloran (note 10).

[12] Ben David, A., 'Israel tests Jericho III missile', *Aviation Week & Space Technology*, 22 July 2013.

[13] Gross, J. A., 'Defense ministry conducts missile test over central Israel', *Times of Israel*, 6 Dec. 2019; and Melman, Y., 'Why would Israel reportedly have missiles that reach beyond Iran', *Haaretz*, 11 Dec. 2019.

[14] Trevithick, J., 'Did Israel just conduct a ballistic missile test from a base on its Mediterranean coast?', The Drive, 6 Dec. 2019.

[15] Ahronheim, A., 'IDF tests rocket propulsion system', *Jerusalem Post*, 7 Dec. 2019.

[16] Israeli Ministry of Defense (@Israel_MOD), 'The Israel Ministry of Defense has completed a test of a rocket propulsion system from a military base in central Israel. The test launch was scheduled in advance and carried out as planned.', Twitter, 31 Jan. 2020.

[17] 'Israel changes name of sixth Dolphin submarine', Naval Today, 11 Jan. 2019.

[18] Bandel, N., 'Gantz agrees to pause commission of inquiry into submarine affair after request by Attorney General', *Haaretz*, 29 Nov. 2020.

[19] See e.g. Cohen (note 4), p. 83; Bergman, R. et al., 'Israel's deployment of nuclear missiles on subs from Germany', *Der Spiegel*, 4 June 2012; and Frantz, D., 'Israel's arsenal is point of contention', *Los Angeles Times*, 12 Oct. 2003.

IX. North Korean nuclear forces

HANS M. KRISTENSEN AND MATT KORDA

The Democratic People's Republic of Korea (DPRK, or North Korea) maintains an active but highly opaque nuclear weapon programme. As of January 2021, it is estimated that North Korea possessed sufficient fissile material for approximately 40–50 nuclear weapons (see table 10.10). This is an increase of 10 from the previous year's estimate due to additional production of fissile material. The estimate is based on calculations of the amount of fissile material—plutonium and highly enriched uranium (HEU)—that North Korea is estimated to have produced for use in nuclear weapons (see section X). It is unknown how much of this material has been used to produce warheads for North Korea's ballistic missiles.[1] Analysing the numbers and types of North Korean warheads and delivery vehicles is fraught with uncertainty due to limited official public data; some of the data presented here is derived from satellite imagery and North Korean media sources, which can be subject to manipulation or exaggeration.

In January 2020 North Korean diplomats stated that the country would no longer observe its self-imposed moratoriums on nuclear explosive tests and flight tests of long-range ballistic missiles.[2] These had been announced by the Supreme Leader of North Korea, Kim Jong Un, in April 2018.[3] Despite this announcement, North Korea did not conduct any such test in 2020. Instead, it conducted multiple tests of short-range ballistic missiles (SRBMs).

The role of nuclear weapons in North Korean military doctrine

In a speech marking the 75th anniversary of the ruling Korean Workers' Party in October 2020, Kim Jong Un reiterated North Korea's pledge not to use nuclear weapons 'preemptively'.[4] This does not constitute a no-first-use policy, however, since Kim made it clear that he could turn to nuclear weapons if 'any forces infringe upon the security of our state'.[5] However, as with other nuclear-armed states, it seems unlikely that North Korea

---

[1] For a discussion of US intelligence and other assessments of North Korea's nuclear warhead status see Kile, S. N. and Kristensen, H. M., 'North Korea's military nuclear capabilities', *SIPRI Yearbook 2020*, pp. 343–44.

[2] Nebehay, S., 'North Korea abandons nuclear freeze pledge, blames "brutal" US sanctions', Reuters, 21 Jan. 2020.

[3] Korean Central News Agency, 'Third plenary meeting of seventh CC, WPK held in presence of Kim Jong Un', 21 Apr. 2018. On North Korea's 6 underground nuclear test explosions in 2006–17 see Fedchencko, V., 'Nuclear explosions, 1945–2017', *SIPRI Yearbook 2018*.

[4] 'Kim Jong Un's October speech: More than missiles', 38 North, 13 Oct. 2020.

[5] 38 North (note 4).

Table 10.10. North Korean forces with potential nuclear capability, January 2021

Type/designation[a]	Range (km)	Payload (kg)	Status	No. of warheads
Land-based missiles				
Hwasong-7 (Nodong)	>1 200	1 000	Single-stage, liquid-fuel ballistic missile. Fewer than 100 launchers; first deployed in 1990.	Some
Hwasong-9 (Scud-ER)	1 000	500	Scud ballistic missile variant, lengthened to carry additional fuel.	Some
Pukguksong-2 (KN15)	>1 000	..	Two-stage, solid-fuel ballistic missile under development. Launched from canister TEL. Land-based version of Pukguksong-1 SLBM. Test launched in 2017.	..
Hwasong-10 (BM-25, Musudan)	>3 000	[1 000]	Single-stage, liquid-fuel ballistic missile under development. Several failed tests in 2016.	..
Hwasong-12 (KN17)	>4 500	1 000	Single-stage, liquid-fuel ballistic missile under development. Tested several times in 2017 with mixed success.	..
Hwasong-13 (KN08)[b]	12 000	..	Three-stage, liquid-fuel ballistic missile with potential intercontinental range under development. No known test launches.	..
Hwasong-14 (KN20)	>10 000	500–1 000	Two-stage, liquid-fuel ballistic missile under development. Tested in 2017.	..
Hwasong-15 (KN22)	>12 000	1 000–1 500	Two-stage, liquid-fuel ballistic missile under development. Two tests in 2017.	..
Hwasong-16 (KN27)	..	..	Two-stage, liquid-fuel ballistic missile under development. First displayed at a parade in Oct. 2020. No known flight tests.	..
Taepodong-2[c]	12 000	..	Under development. Three-stage ballistic space launch vehicle variant placed satellites in orbit in Dec. 2012 and Feb. 2016. ICBM status unclear.	..
Sea-based missiles				
Pukguksong-1 (KN11)	>1 000	..	Two-stage, solid-fuel ballistic missile. Tested several times in 2015 and 2016 with mixed success.	..
Pukguksong-3 (KN-26)	≤1 900	..	Two-stage, solid-fuel SLBM under development. Likely replacing earlier Pukguksong-1 version. First flight tested in Oct. 2019.	..
Pukguksong-4	..	..	Two-stage, solid-fuel SLBM. First displayed at a parade in Oct. 2020. No known flight tests.	..
Total warhead potential				**[40–50]**[d]

.. = not available or not applicable; [] = uncertain figure; ICBM = intercontinental ballistic missile; SLBM = submarine-launched ballistic missile; TEL = transporter-erector-launcher.

[a] This table lists the ballistic missiles that could potentially have a nuclear capability. There is no publicly available evidence that North Korea has produced an operational nuclear warhead for delivery by an ICBM. The first name of each system is the North Korean designation; the second name, in parentheses, is the designation used by the United States Department of Defense.

[b] A two-stage variant, the KN14, may be under development but had not been test launched as of Jan. 2021. It is possible that both the KN08 and KN14 have been abandoned in favour of newer, more advanced ICBM systems.

[c] A two-stage Taepodong-1 missile was unsuccessfully flight tested in 1998.

[d] SIPRI's estimate is that North Korea may have produced enough fissile material to build between 40 and 50 nuclear warheads. It is unknown how many warheads may have been assembled. SIPRI estimates that only a few of these would be hydrogen warheads and nearly all would be lower-yield single-stage fission warheads. See also Hecker, S., 'What do we know about North Korea's nuclear program?', Presentation, Dialogue on DPRK Denuclearization Roadmaps and Verification, Kyung Hee University, Global America Business Institute (GABI) and Natural Resources Defense Council (NRDC), 20 Oct. 2020.

Sources: US Department of Defense (DOD), *2019 Missile Defense Review* (DOD: Arlington, VA, 2019); US Air Force, National Air and Space Intelligence Center (NASIC), *Ballistic and Cruise Missile Threat*, various years; *IHS Jane's Strategic Weapon Systems*, various editions; Hecker, S., Stanford University, Personal communication, 2020; *Bulletin of the Atomic Scientists*, 'Nuclear notebook', various issues; and authors' estimates.

would use its nuclear weapons outside of extreme circumstances when the continued existence of the state and its leadership was in question.

Fissile material and warhead production

North Korea's plutonium production and separation capabilities for manufacturing nuclear weapons are located at the Yongbyon Nuclear Scientific Research Centre (YNSRC) in North Pyongan province.[6] In 2020 some of the nuclear facilities located there appeared not to be operating. In September 2020 the International Atomic Energy Agency (IAEA) reported that there had been no indications of steam or cooling water discharge from the ageing 5-megawatt-electric (MW(e)) graphite-moderated research reactor located at the YNSRC. It therefore concluded, 'it is almost certain that the reactor has remained shut down since early December 2018'.[7] The IAEA also reported that there were no indications that reprocessing activities were under way at the adjacent Radiochemical Laboratory used to separate plutonium from the 5-MW(e) reactor's spent fuel rods, which can be used for

[6] For an assessment of North Korea's nuclear weapon production facilities and infrastructure see Hecker, S. S., Carlin, R. L. and Serbin, E. A., 'A comprehensive history of North Korea's nuclear program: 2018 update', Stanford University, Center for International Security and Cooperation (CISAC), 11 Feb. 2019, p. 3.

[7] International Atomic Energy Agency (IAEA), Board of Governors and General Conference, 'Application of safeguards in the Democratic People's Republic of Korea', Report by the Director General, GOV/2020/42-GC(64)/18, 3 Sep. 2020, para. 12.

the production of nuclear weapons.[8] In October 2020 commercial satellite imagery indicated that activity was increasing at a building used to produce uranium dioxide (UO_2); however, it is unclear whether the observed smoke or vapour emissions are an indication of UO_2 production or a different operation.[9] The IAEA report noted that North Korea may have conducted an infrastructure test at the experimental light water reactor that is under construction at Yongbyon, which is also capable of producing plutonium for nuclear weapons; however, the reactor had not yet commenced operation.[10]

There is considerable uncertainty about North Korea's uranium enrichment capabilities and its stock of HEU. It is widely believed that North Korea has focused on the production of HEU for use in nuclear warheads to overcome its limited capacity to produce weapon-grade plutonium. In 2020 the IAEA assessed that North Korea continued to operate the gas centrifuge enrichment plant located at the Yongbyon complex that it had declared in 2010.[11] Using commercial satellite imagery, several non-governmental researchers have identified a suspected covert uranium enrichment plant located at Kangsong, to the south-west of Pyongyang.[12] However, analysts cautioned that, without access to the plant, it was not possible to confirm the nature and purpose of the activities being conducted on-site.[13] A classified intelligence assessment by the United States in 2018 reportedly concluded that North Korea probably had more than one covert uranium enrichment plant and that the country was seeking to conceal the types and numbers of production facilities in its nuclear weapon programme.[14]

It is unclear how many nuclear weapons North Korea has produced with its fissile material, how many have been deployed on missiles, and what the military characteristics of the weapons are. North Korea has only demonstrated a thermonuclear capability (or a capability with demonstrated thermonuclear yield) once, in 2017.[15] US intelligence sources have not yet confirmed North Korea's capability to deliver a functioning warhead on an intercontinental ballistic missile (ICBM). Moreover, most of North Korea's nuclear tests demonstrated yields in the range 5–15 kilotons. As a result,

---

[8] International Atomic Energy Agency, GOV/2020/42-GC(64)/18 (note 7).

[9] Pabian, F. V., Makowsky, P. and Liu, J., 'North Korea's Yongbyon complex: Activity picks up', 38 North, 30 Oct. 2020.

[10] International Atomic Energy Agency, GOV/2020/42-GC(64)/18 (note 7).

[11] International Atomic Energy Agency, GOV/2020/42-GC(64)/18 (note 7). See also Hecker et al. (note 6), pp. 3–4.

[12] Panda, A., 'Exclusive: Revealing Kangson, North Korea's first covert uranium enrichment site', The Diplomat, 13 July 2018; and Albright, D. with Burkhard, S., 'Revisiting Kangsong: A suspect uranium enrichment plant', Imagery Brief, Institute for Science and International Security, 2 Oct. 2018.

[13] Hecker et al. (note 6), p. 4; and Madden, M., 'Much ado about Kangson', 38 North, 3 Aug. 2018.

[14] Kube, C., Dilanian, K. and Lee, C. E, 'North Korea has increased nuclear production at secret sites, say US officials', NBC News, 1 July 2018; and Nakashima, E. and Warrick, J., 'North Korea working to conceal key aspects of its nuclear program, US officials say', Washington Post, 1 July 2018.

[15] Fedchencko (note 3).

SIPRI estimates that North Korea has used only a small portion of its HEU for thermonuclear weapons and has probably used the majority for a larger number of fission-only or boosted single-stage weapons deliverable by medium-range ballistic missile (MRBM) or possibly by intermediate-range ballistic missile (IRBM). For this reason, SIPRI estimates that North Korea could potentially produce 40–50 nuclear weapons with its current inventory of fissile materials.[16]

Land-based missiles

North Korea is increasing both the size and capability of its ballistic missile force, which consists of indigenously produced missile systems with ranges from a few hundred kilometres to more than 12 000 km.[17] In recent years it has pursued the serial production of several missile systems with progressively longer ranges and increasingly sophisticated delivery capabilities.[18] There is considerable uncertainty about the operational capability of North Korea's long-range ballistic missiles. According to an independent analysis, North Korea has deployed long-range missiles at several missile bases.[19] However, in 2019 the US Department of Defense (DOD) indicated that many of North Korea's newer ballistic missiles (Hwasong-10/12/13/14/15 or Pukguksong-1/2) had not yet been 'fielded'.[20]

It is unclear which of North Korea's missiles would carry nuclear weapons. The available evidence suggests that the longer-range missiles in particular are being developed to fulfil a nuclear role in North Korea's military doctrine. However, North Korea has not yet publicly demonstrated a reliable atmospheric re-entry vehicle or a capability for terminal-stage guidance and warhead activation.[21] As such, it remains unclear whether its missiles would be able to reliably deliver a nuclear warhead to an intercontinental-range target without further development.[22]

[16] For a recent assessment see also Hecker, S., 'What do we know about North Korea's nuclear program?', Presentation, Dialogue on DPRK Denuclearization Roadmaps and Verification, Kyung Hee University, Global America Business Institute (GABI) and Natural Resources Defense Council (NRDC), 20 Oct. 2020, slide 5.

[17] US Air Force, National Air and Space Intelligence Center (NASIC), *Ballistic and Cruise Missile Threat 2020* (NASIC: Wright-Patterson Air Force Base, OH, July 2020).

[18] James Martin Center for Nonproliferation Studies (CNS), The CNS North Korea Missile Test Database, 31 Mar. 2021.

[19] Bermudez, J. and Cha, V., 'Undeclared North Korea: The Yusang-ni missile operating base', Beyond Parallel, Center for Strategic and International Studies (CSIS), 9 May 2019.

[20] US Department of Defense (DOD), *2019 Missile Defense Review* (DOD: Arlington, VA, 2019), p. 7.

[21] Ali, I., 'US general says North Korea not demonstrated all components of ICBM', Reuters, 30 Jan. 2018.

[22] Elleman, M., 'Does size matter? North Korea's newest ICBM', 38 North, 21 Oct. 2020.

Short-range ballistic missiles

North Korea has several types of SRBM, including older systems possibly based on Soviet R-17 Scud missiles and newer missiles with indigenous designs. In 2020 North Korea conducted several initial launches of at least two new types of solid-fuelled SRBM: the KN24 and the KN25.[23] These systems could be nearing or have possibly begun operational deployment.

While older, inaccurate SRBMs might have been developed with dual capability, there is no publicly available, authoritative information confirming a nuclear delivery role for the newer, more accurate SRBMs.[24] Independent assessments suggest that a nuclear device that North Korea displayed in 2017—if, indeed, it was a functional nuclear device—might be too large to fit into these newer SRBMs. However, as North Korea seeks to miniaturize its nuclear warheads, these types of missile could adopt a dual-capable role in the future.[25]

Medium- and intermediate-range ballistic missiles

Assuming that North Korea is able to produce a sufficiently compact warhead, independent assessments indicate that the size, range and operational status of the Hwasong-7 (Nodong or Rodong) MRBM make it the system most likely to be given a nuclear delivery role.[26] Possibly based on a Soviet-era R-17 (Scud) missile design, the Hwasong-7 is a single-stage, liquid-fuelled ballistic missile with an estimated range exceeding 1200 km. In addition, North Korea has developed the single-stage, liquid-fuelled Hwasong-9 (Scud-ER for extended-range), which has an estimated range of 1000 km and may also be a nuclear-capable delivery system. According to the 2020 ballistic and cruise missile report of the US Air Force's National Air and Space Intelligence Center (NASIC), the system has not yet been deployed.[27]

The Hwasong-10 (Musudan or BM-25) is a single-stage, liquid-fuelled missile with an estimated range exceeding 3000 km. It was first unveiled at a military parade in 2010. Flight testing began in 2016, with multiple failures.[28] No flight tests of the Hwasong-10 are known to have been con-

---

[23] Panda, A., 'What was behind North Korea's busy March 2020 missile launches?', The Diplomat, 8 Apr. 2020; and Dempsey, J., 'Assessment of the March 9 KN-25 test launch', 38 North, 10 Mar. 2020.

[24] James Martin Center for Nonproliferation Studies (note 18); and Panda (note 23).

[25] Elleman, M., 'Preliminary assessment of the KN-24 missile launches', 38 North, 25 Mar. 2020.

[26] See e.g. Fitzpatrick, M., 'North Korea nuclear test on hold?', Shangri-La Voices, International Institute for Strategic Studies (IISS), 27 May 2014; and Albright, D., 'North Korean miniaturization', 38 North, 13 Feb. 2013. For the missiles and submarines discussed here, a designation in parentheses (in this case Nodong or Rodong) following the North Korean designation (in this case Hwasong-7) is that assigned by the US Department of Defense (DOD).

[27] US Air Force (note 17), pp. 18, 21, 25.

[28] Savelsberg, R. and Kiessling, J., 'North Korea's Musudan missile: A performance assessment', 38 North, 20 Dec. 2016.

ducted since 2016–17, and the status of the missile's development programme is unclear.

The Hwasong-12 (KN17) is a single-stage IRBM that is believed to have a new liquid-propellant booster engine, as well as design features that may serve as a technology test bed for a future ICBM.[29] NASIC estimated in 2020 that it has a range of more than 4500 km.[30] Some analysts have speculated that the missile carries a small post-boost vehicle that, in addition to increasing its maximum range, can be used to improve warhead accuracy.[31] The missile was last test launched in 2017 but has not been deployed.[32]

North Korea is developing the Pukguksong-2 missile (KN15), which is a land-based variant of the Pukguksong-1 submarine-launched ballistic missile (SLBM). The two-stage, solid-fuelled missile has an estimated range of approximately 1000 km.[33] It was flight tested twice in 2017. Some analysts have noted that North Korea's development of the Pukguksong-2 is probably part of an effort to improve the survivability of its nuclear-capable ballistic missile systems. Solid-fuelled missiles can be fired more quickly than liquid-fuelled systems and require fewer support vehicles that might give away their position to overhead surveillance. In addition, and uniquely for a North Korean missile, the Pukguksong-2 is coupled with a tracked transporter-erector-launcher (TEL). This would allow North Korea to launch it from hidden, off-road sites, whereas other systems use wheeled launchers and thus require paved or relatively smooth roads—a rarity in North Korea's mountainous terrain.[34]

Intercontinental-range ballistic missiles

North Korea is widely believed to have prioritized building and deploying an ICBM that could potentially deliver a nuclear warhead to targets in the continental USA. However, as mentioned above, there remains considerable uncertainty in assessments of North Korea's current long-range missile capabilities, and NASIC does not list any of North Korea's ICBMs as deployed.[35]

[29] Yi, Y., 'Hwasong-12 a stepping-stone in North Korea's ICBM development', *The Hankyoreh*, 16 May 2017; and Savelsberg, R., 'A quick technical analysis of the Hwasong-12 missile', 38 North, 19 May 2017.

[30] US Air Force (note 17), p. 25.

[31] Elleman, M., 'North Korea's Hwasong-12 launch: A disturbing development', 38 North, 30 Aug. 2017.

[32] Panda, A., 'North Korea shows increased operational confidence in the Hwasong-12 IRBM', The Diplomat, 17 Sep. 2017.

[33] US Air Force (note 17), p. 25.

[34] Panda, A., 'It wasn't an ICBM, but North Korea's first missile test of 2017 is a big deal', The Diplomat, 14 Feb. 2017.

[35] Albert, E., 'North Korea's military capabilities', Council on Foreign Relations, 16 Nov. 2020; and US Air Force (note 17), p. 29.

The Hwasong-13 (KN08) was first presented by North Korea as a road-mobile, three-stage missile with intercontinental range at a military parade in April 2012. Some non-governmental analysts have suggested that the missiles displayed were only mock-ups.[36] Estimates of the range and payload capabilities of the missile are highly speculative. As of 2020, it had not been flight tested.

North Korea has twice tested the Hwasong-14 (KN20), a prototype ICBM that first appeared in 2015 at a military parade in Pyongyang.[37] The two-stage missile appears to use the same high-energy liquid-propellant booster engine as the single-stage Hwasong-12 IRBM.[38] In 2020 NASIC assessed that the range of the Hwasong-14 could exceed 10 000 km, putting it in range of most of the continental USA but not Washington, DC, or other targets on the east coast.[39]

North Korea is developing a new two-stage ICBM, the Hwasong-15 (KN22), which has a significantly larger second stage and more powerful booster engines than the Hwasong-14. The first flight test was conducted in 2017, when a Hwasong-15 was launched on an elevated trajectory and flew higher and for a longer duration than any previous North Korean missile.[40] In 2020 NASIC assessed that the range of the Hwasong-15 could exceed 12 000 km, putting it in range of Washington, DC, and other targets on the east coast of the USA.[41] The missile was assessed to be carrying a light payload, however, and the range would be significantly reduced if it were carrying an actual nuclear warhead.[42] Four Hwasong-15 ICBMs were displayed during North Korea's October 2020 military parade.[43]

During the October 2020 parade, North Korea also unveiled four units of a new liquid-fuelled type of ICBM, which has not yet been tested but appears to be the largest road-mobile, liquid-fuelled ICBM on the planet.[44] The new ICBM, which is presumably called the Hwasong-16 in line with North Korea's naming conventions (with likely US DOD designation KN27), would hypothetically be large enough to accommodate multiple warheads; however, such capabilities have not yet been demonstrated.

[36] Schiller, M. and Kelley, R., 'Evolving threat: North Korea's quest for an ICBM', *Jane's Defence Weekly*, 18 Jan. 2017, p. 24.
[37] James Martin Center for Nonproliferation Studies (note 18).
[38] According to one non-governmental analyst, North Korea probably acquired the engine through illicit channels operating in Russia, Ukraine or both. Elleman, M., 'The secret to North Korea's ICBM success', Analysis, International Institute for Strategic Studies (IISS), 14 Aug. 2017.
[39] US Air Force (note 17), pp. 27, 29.
[40] Wright, D., 'North Korea's longest missile test yet', All Things Nuclear, Union of Concerned Scientists, 28 Nov. 2017.
[41] US Air Force (note 17), pp. 27, 29.
[42] Elleman, M., 'North Korea's third ICBM launch', 38 North, 29 Nov. 2017.
[43] 'North Korea military parade 2020—Livestream & analysis', NK News, 10 Oct. 2020.
[44] NK News (note 43).

In 2019 the US DOD indicated that North Korea had deployed one ICBM, the Taepodong-2.[45] However, other official US sources list the missile as a space-launch vehicle that would need reconfiguration to be used as an ICBM.[46]

Sea-based missiles

North Korea continues to pursue the development of a solid-fuelled SLBM system as part of an effort to improve the survivability of its nuclear-capable ballistic missile systems. North Korea's first SLBM, the Pukguksong-1 (KN11), was tested with mixed success throughout 2015 and 2016. A 'new type' of SLBM, called the Pukguksong-3 (KN-26), was tested in October 2019.[47] With an estimated maximum range of more than 1000 km—and per-haps as much as 1900 km—the Pukguksong-3 at that time was the longest-range, solid-fuelled missile that North Korea had displayed.[48] However, during the parade in October 2020, North Korea unveiled yet another new type of SLBM—the Pukguksong-4, that might have a longer range.[49] The two-stage, solid-fuelled missile—which is wider than the Pukguksong-1 and possibly a little shorter than the Pukguksong-3—has not yet been flight tested. Its larger diameter indicates that it could hypothetically carry multiple warheads or penetration aids to overcome US ballistic missile defences.

During 2020, there were indications that North Korea had made progress towards achieving its goal of designing, building and eventually deploying an operational ballistic missile submarine. Currently, North Korea has one Gorae-class (Sinpo) experimental submarine in service, which can hold and launch one SLBM. This is likely to be the Pukguksong-1 until it is replaced by the more advanced SLBMs under development. In November 2020 the National Intelligence Service of the Republic of Korea (South Korea) announced that North Korea was building a new ballistic missile

[45] US Department of Defense (note 20), p. 7.

[46] See e.g. US Defense Intelligence Agency (DIA), *Global Nuclear Landscape 2018* (DIA: Washington, DC, 2018), p. 22.

[47] Ji, D., 'Pukguksong-3 SLBM test-launch is "powerful blow" to hostile forces: Rodong Sinmun', NK News, 4 Oct. 2019.

[48] US Air Force (note 17), p. 33; Panda, A., 'North Korea finally unveils the Pukguksong-3 SLBM: First takeaways', The Diplomat, 3 Oct. 2019; Lee, J., 'North Korea says it successfully tested new submarine-launched ballistic missile', Reuters, 2 Oct. 2019; and Wright, D., 'North Korea's latest missile test', All Things Nuclear, Union of Concerned Scientists, 1 Oct. 2019.

[49] Kuhn, A., 'Kim Jong Un puts new missiles on display at military parade in North Korea', National Public Radio (NPR), 10 Oct. 2020; and Barrie, D. and Dempsey, J., 'What North Korea's latest missile parade tells us, and what it doesn't', Analysis, International Institute for Strategic Studies (IISS), 12 Oct. 2020.

submarine.[50] The vessel, designated Sinpo-C by the US DOD, appears to be based on a modified Project-633 (Romeo) diesel–electric submarine and to be fitted with three missile launch canisters.[51] According to a 2019 report by North Korea's state-run Korean Central News Agency (KCNA), the submarine's operational deployment was 'near at hand'.[52]

[50] Bermudez, J. and Cha, V., 'Sinpo South Shipyard: Construction of a new ballistic missile submarine?', Beyond Parallel, Center for Strategic and International Studies (CSIS), 28 Aug. 2019; and Cha, S., 'North Korea building two submarines, one capable of firing ballistic missiles—lawmaker', Reuters, 3 Nov. 2020.

[51] Hotham, O., 'New North Korean submarine capable of carrying three SLBMs: South Korean MND', NK News, 31 July 2019; and Cha (note 50).

[52] 'NK leader inspects new submarine to be deployed in East Sea: State media', Yonhap News Agency, 23 July 2019.

X. Global stocks and production of fissile materials, 2020

MORITZ KÜTT, ZIA MIAN AND PAVEL PODVIG

INTERNATIONAL PANEL ON FISSILE MATERIALS

Materials that can sustain an explosive fission chain reaction are essential for all types of nuclear explosive, from first-generation fission weapons to advanced thermonuclear weapons. The most common of these fissile materials are highly enriched uranium (HEU) and plutonium. This section gives details of military and civilian stocks, as of the beginning of 2020, of HEU (table 10.11) and separated plutonium (table 10.12), including in weapons. It also provides details of the current capacity to produce these materials (tables 10.13 and 10.14, respectively). The information in the tables is based on estimates prepared for the International Panel on Fissile Materials (IPFM). The most recent annual declarations (INFCIRC/549 declarations) on civilian plutonium and HEU stocks to the International Atomic Energy Agency (IAEA) give data for 31 December 2019.

The production of both HEU and plutonium starts with natural uranium. Natural uranium consists almost entirely of the non-chain-reacting isotope uranium-238 (U-238) and is only about 0.7 per cent uranium-235 (U-235). The concentration of U-235 can be increased through enrichment—typically using gas centrifuges. Uranium that has been enriched to less than 20 per cent U-235 (typically, 3–5 per cent)—known as low-enriched uranium—is suitable for use in power reactors. Uranium that has been enriched to contain at least 20 per cent U-235—known as HEU—is generally taken to be the lowest concentration practicable for use in weapons. However, in order to minimize the mass of the nuclear explosive, weapon-grade uranium is usually enriched to over 90 per cent U-235.

Plutonium is produced in nuclear reactors when U-238 is exposed to neutrons. The plutonium is subsequently chemically separated from spent fuel in a reprocessing operation. Plutonium comes in a variety of isotopic mixtures, most of which are weapon-usable. Weapon designers prefer to work with a mixture that predominantly consists of plutonium-239 (Pu-239) because of its relatively low rate of spontaneous emission of neutrons and gamma rays and the low level of heat generation from radioactive alpha decay. Weapon-grade plutonium typically contains more than 90 per cent of the isotope Pu-239. The plutonium in typical spent fuel from power reactors (reactor-grade plutonium) contains 50–60 per cent Pu-239 but is weapon-usable, even in a first-generation weapon design.

All states that have a civil nuclear industry (i.e. that operate a nuclear reactor or a uranium enrichment plant) have some capability to produce fissile materials that could be used for weapons.

Table 10.11. Global stocks of highly enriched uranium, 2020

State	National stockpile (tonnes)[a]	Production status	Comments
China	14 ± 3	Stopped 1987–89	
France[b]	30 ± 6	Stopped 1996	Includes 5.4 tonnes declared civilian[c]
India[d]	5.2 ± 1.8	Continuing	Includes HEU in naval reactor cores
Israel[e]	0.3	Unknown	
Korea, North[f]	Uncertain	Uncertain	
Pakistan[g]	3.9 ± 0.4	Continuing	
Russia[h]	678 ± 120	Continuing[i]	Includes c. 6 tonnes in use in research applications
UK[j]	22.6	Stopped 1962	Includes HEU in naval reactor cores and 0.7 tonnes declared civilian
USA[k]	562 (83 not available for military purposes)	Stopped 1992	Includes HEU in a naval reserve
Other states[l]	~15		
Total[m]	~1 330		

HEU = highly enriched uranium.

[a] Most of this material is enriched uranium that contains 90–93% uranium-235 (U-235), which is typically considered weapon-grade. The estimates are for the start of 2020. Important exceptions are noted.

[b] The uncertainty in the estimate for France applies only to the military stockpile of c. 25 tonnes and does not apply to the declared civilian stock. A 2014 analysis offers grounds for a significantly lower estimate of the stockpile of weapon-grade HEU (as high as 10 ± 2 tonnes or as low as 6 ± 2 tonnes), based on evidence that the Pierrelatte enrichment plant may have had both a much shorter effective period of operation and a smaller weapon-grade HEU production capacity than previously assumed.

[c] This figure is from France's INFCIRC/549 declaration to the International Atomic Energy Agency (IAEA) for the start of 2020.

[d] It is believed that India is producing HEU (enriched to 30–45%) for use as naval reactor fuel. The estimate is for HEU enriched to 30%.

[e] Israel may have acquired illicitly c. 300 kg of weapon-grade HEU from the USA in or before 1965. Some of this material may have been consumed in the process of producing tritium.

[f] North Korea is known to have a uranium enrichment plant at Yongbyon and possibly others elsewhere. Independent estimates of uranium enrichment capability and possible HEU production extrapolated to the end of 2019 suggest that an accumulated HEU stockpile could be in the range of 230–1180 kg.

[g] This estimate for Pakistan assumes total HEU production of 4 tonnes, of which c. 100 kg was used in nuclear weapon tests.

[h] This estimate is for the amount of 90% enriched uranium that would contain all U-235 in HEU. The actual amount of HEU might be different. It assumes that the Soviet Union stopped all HEU production in 1988. It may therefore understate the amount of HEU in Russia (see also note i). The material in discharged naval cores is not included in the current stock since the enrichment of uranium in these cores is believed to be less than 20% U-235.

[i] The Soviet Union stopped production of HEU for weapons in 1988 but kept producing HEU for civilian and non-weapon military uses. Russia continues this practice.

[j] The estimate for the UK reflects a declaration of 21.9 tonnes of military HEU as of 31 Mar. 2002, the average enrichment of which was not given. As the UK continues to use HEU in

naval reactors, the value contains an increasing fraction of spent naval fuel. In 2018 the UK transferred c. 500 kg of HEU to the USA for downblending into low-enriched uranium.

[k] The amount of US HEU is given in actual tonnes, not 93%-enriched equivalent. In 2016 the USA declared that, as of 30 Sep. 2013, its HEU inventory was 585.6 tonnes, of which 499.4 tonnes was declared to be for 'national security or non-national security programs including nuclear weapons, naval propulsion, nuclear energy, and science'. The remaining 86.2 tonnes was composed of 41.6 tonnes 'available for potential down-blend to low enriched uranium or, if not possible, disposal as low-level waste', and 44.6 tonnes in spent reactor fuel. As of the end of 2019, another 19 tonnes had been downblended or shipped for blending down. The amount available for use had been reduced to c. 480 tonnes, mostly by consumption in naval reactors. The 83 tonnes declared excess includes c. 67 tonnes remaining for downblending as well as 16 tonnes remaining for HEU fuel for research reactors.

[l] The IAEA's 2019 annual report lists 156 significant quantities of HEU under comprehensive safeguards in non-nuclear weapon states as of the end of 2019. In order to reflect the uncertainty in the enrichment levels of this material, mostly in research reactor fuel, a total of 15 tonnes of HEU is assumed. About 10 tonnes of this is in Kazakhstan and has been irradiated; it was initially slightly higher than 20%-enriched fuel. It is possible that this material is no longer HEU.

In INFCIRC/912 (from 2017) more than 20 states committed to reducing civilian HEU stocks and providing regular reports. So far, only 2 countries have reported under this scheme. At the end of 2018 (time of last declaration), Norway held less than 4 kg of HEU for civilian purposes. As of 30 June 2019, Australia held 2.7 kg of HEU for civilian purposes.

[m] Totals are rounded to the nearest 5 tonnes.

Sources: International Panel on Fissile Materials (IPFM), *Global Fissile Material Report 2015: Nuclear Weapon and Fissile Material Stockpiles and Production* (IPFM: Princeton, NJ, 2015). *China*: Zhang, H., *China's Fissile Material Production and Stockpile* (IPFM: Princeton, NJ, 2017). *France*: International Atomic Energy Agency (IAEA), 'Communication received from France concerning its policies regarding the management of plutonium', INFCIRC/549/Add.5/24, 28 Aug. 2020; and Philippe, S. and Glaser, A., 'Nuclear archaeology for gaseous diffusion enrichment plants', *Science & Global Security*, vol. 22, no. 1 (2014), pp. 27–49. *Israel*: Myers, H., 'The real source of Israel's first fissile material', *Arms Control Today*, vol. 37, no. 8 (Oct. 2007), p. 56; and Gilinsky, V. and Mattson, R. J., 'Revisiting the NUMEC affair', *Bulletin of the Atomic Scientists*, vol. 66, no. 2 (Mar./Apr. 2010). *North Korea*: Hecker, S. S., Braun, C. and Lawrence, C., 'North Korea's stockpiles of fissile material', *Korea Observer*, vol 47, no. 4 (winter 2016), pp. 721–49. *Russia*: Podvig, P. (ed.), *The Use of Highly-Enriched Uranium as Fuel in Russia* (IPFM: Washington, DC, 2017). *UK*: British Ministry of Defence, 'Historical accounting for UK defence highly enriched uranium', Mar. 2006; and IAEA, 'Communications received from the United Kingdom of Great Britain and Northern Ireland concerning its policies regarding the management of plutonium', INFCIRC/549/Add.8/23, 11 Jan. 2021. *USA*: US Department of Energy (DOE), National Nuclear Security Administration, *Highly Enriched Uranium, Striking a Balance: A Historical Report on the United States Highly Enriched Uranium Production, Acquisition, and Utilization Activities from 1945 through September 30, 1996* (DOE: Washington, DC, Jan. 2001); White House, 'Transparency in the US highly enriched uranium inventory', Fact sheet, 31 Mar. 2016; US Department of Energy (DOE), *FY 2021 Congressional Budget Request*, vol. 1, *National Nuclear Security Administration* (DOE: Washington, DC, Feb. 2020), p. 593; and US Department of Energy (DOE), *Tritium and Enriched Uranium Management Plan through 2060*, Report to Congress (DOE: Washington, DC, Oct. 2015). *Non-nuclear weapon states*: IAEA, *IAEA Annual Report 2019* (IAEA: Vienna, 2019), Annex, Table A4, p. 113; IAEA, 'Communication Dated 19 July 2019 received From the Permanent Mission of Norway concerning a joint statement on minimising and eliminating the use of highly enriched uranium in civilian applications', INFCIRC/912/Add.3, 15 Aug. 2019; and IAEA, 'Communication dated 23 January 2020 received from the Permanent Mission of Australia concerning the joint statement on minimising and eliminating the use of highly enriched uranium in civilian applications', INFCIRC/912/Add.4, 5 Mar. 2020.

Table 10.12. Global stocks of separated plutonium, 2020

State	Military stocks (tonnes)[a]	Military production status	Civilian stocks (tonnes)[b]
China	2.9 ± 0.6	Stopped in 1991	0.04[c]
France	6 ± 1.0	Stopped in 1992	74.7 (excludes foreign owned)
India[d]	0.62 ± 0.14	Continuing	8.2 ± 4.3 (includes 0.4 under safeguards)
Israel[e]	0.98 ± 0.13	Continuing	–
Japan	–	–	45.5 (includes 36.6 in France and UK)
Korea, North[f]	0.04	Continuing	–
Pakistan[g]	0.41 ± 0.1	Continuing	–
Russia[h]	128 ± 8 (40 not available for weapons)	Stopped in 2010	63
UK	3.2	Stopped in 1995	115.8 (excludes 24.1 foreign owned)
USA[i]	79.7 (41.3 not available for weapons)	Stopped in 1988	8[j]
Other states[k]	–	–	3.0
Total[l]	**~220 (81 not available for weapons)**		**~320**

– = nil or a negligible value.

[a] The estimates are for the start of 2020. Important exceptions are noted.

[b] The data for France, Japan, Russia and the UK is for the end of 2019, reflecting their most recent INFCIRC/549 declaration to the International Atomic Energy Agency (IAEA). Some countries with civilian plutonium stocks do not submit an INFCIRC/549 declaration. Of these countries, Italy, the Netherlands, Spain and Sweden store their plutonium abroad.

[c] These numbers are based on China's INFCIRC/549 declaration to the IAEA for the end of 2016. As of Mar. 2021, this is the most recent declaration.

[d] As part of the 2005 Indian–US Civil Nuclear Cooperation Initiative, India has included in the military sector much of the plutonium separated from its spent power-reactor fuel. While it is labelled civilian here since it is intended for breeder reactor fuel, this plutonium was not placed under safeguards in the 'India-specific' safeguards agreement signed by the Indian Government and the IAEA on 2 Feb. 2009. India does not submit an INFCIRC/549 declaration to the IAEA.

[e] Israel is still operating the Dimona plutonium production reactor but may be using it primarily for tritium production. The estimate is for the end of 2019.

[f] North Korea reportedly declared a plutonium stock of 37 kg in June 2008. It is believed that it subsequently unloaded its 5-MWe reactor 3 additional times, in 2009, 2016 and 2018. The stockpile estimate has been reduced to account for the 6 nuclear tests conducted by the country.

[g] As of the end of 2019, Pakistan was operating 4 plutonium production reactors at its Khushab site. This estimate assumes that Pakistan is separating plutonium from the cooled spent fuel from all 4 reactors.

[h] The 40 tonnes of plutonium not available to Russia for weapons comprises 25 tonnes of weapon-origin plutonium stored at the Mayak Fissile Material Storage Facility and c. 15 tonnes of weapon-grade plutonium produced between 1 Jan. 1995 and 15 Apr. 2010, when the last plutonium production reactor was shut down. The post-1994 plutonium, which is currently stored at Zheleznogorsk, cannot be used for weapon purposes under the terms of a 1997 Russian–US agreement on plutonium production reactors. Russia made a commitment to eliminate 34 tonnes of that material (including all 25 tonnes of plutonium stored at Mayak) as part of the 2000 Russian–US Plutonium Management and Disposition Agreement. Russia does

not include the plutonium that is not available for weapons in its INFCIRC/549 declaration; nor does it make the plutonium it reports as civilian available to IAEA safeguards.

[i] In 2012 the USA declared a government-owned plutonium inventory of 95.4 tonnes as of 30 Sep. 2009. In its 2019 INFCIRC/549 declaration, the most recent submitted, the USA declared 49.3 tonnes of unirradiated plutonium (both separated and in mixed oxide, MOX) as part of the stock that was identified as excess for military purposes (declaration for 31 Dec. 2018). Since most of this material is stored in classified form, it is considered military stock. The USA considers a total of 61.5 tonnes of plutonium to be declared excess to national security needs.

[j] The USA has placed c. 3 tonnes of its excess plutonium, stored at the K-Area Material Storage Facility at the Savannah River Plant, under IAEA safeguards. In addition, it reported that 4.6 tonnes of plutonium was contained in unirradiated MOX fuel, and also declared 0.4 tonnes of plutonium that was brought to the USA in 2016 from Japan, Germany and Switzerland (331 kg, 30 kg and 18 kg, respectively). All this material is considered civilian.

[k] This is estimated by reconciling the amounts of plutonium declared as 'held in locations in other countries' and 'belonging to foreign bodies' in the INFCIRC/549 declarations.

[l] Totals are rounded to the nearest 5 tonnes.

Sources: International Panel on Fissile Materials (IPFM), *Global Fissile Material Report 2015: Nuclear Weapon and Fissile Material Stockpiles and Production* (IPFM: Princeton, NJ, 2015). *Civilian stocks (except for India)*: declarations by countries to the International Atomic Energy Agency (IAEA) under INFCIRC/549. *China*: Zhang, H., *China's Fissile Material Production and Stockpile* (IPFM: Princeton, NJ, 2017). *North Korea*: Kessler, G., 'Message to US preceded nuclear declaration by North Korea', *Washington Post*, 2 July 2008; Hecker, S. S., Braun, C. and Lawrence, C., 'North Korea's stockpiles of fissile material', *Korea Observer*, vol 47, no. 4 (winter 2016), pp. 721–49; and IAEA, Board of Governors and General Conference, 'Application of safeguards in the Democratic People's Republic of Korea', Report by the acting director general, GOV/2019/33-GC(63)/20, 19 Aug. 2019. *Russia*: Russian–US Agreement Concerning the Management and Disposition of Plutonium Designated as No Longer Required for Defense Purposes and Related Cooperation (Plutonium Management and Disposition Agreement), signed 29 Aug. and 1 Sep. 2000, amendment signed 5 Sep. 2006, entered into force 13 July 2011. *USA*: National Nuclear Security Administration (NNSA), *The United States Plutonium Balance, 1944–2009* (NNSA: Washington, DC, June 2012); and Gunter, A., 'K-Area overview/update', US Department of Energy, Savanah River Site, 28 July 2015.

Table 10.13. Significant uranium enrichment facilities and capacity worldwide, 2020

State	Facility name or location	Type	Status	Enrichment process[a]	Capacity (thousands SWU/yr)[b]
Argentina[c]	Pilcaniyeu	Civilian	Uncertain	GD	20
Brazil	Resende	Civilian	Expanding capacity	GC	35
China[d]	Lanzhou	Civilian	Operational	GC	2 600
	Hanzhong (Shaanxi)	Civilian	Operational	GC	2 000
	Emeishan	Civilian	Operational	GC	1 050
	Heping	Dual-use	Operational	GD	230
France	Georges Besse II	Civilian	Operational	GC	7 500
Germany	Urenco Gronau	Civilian	Operational	GC	3 900
India	Rattehalli	Military	Operational	GC	15–30
Iran[e]	Natanz	Civilian	Limited operation	GC	3.5–5
	Qom (Fordow)	Civilian	Limited operation	GC	..
Japan	Rokkasho[f]	Civilian	Resuming operation	GC	75
Korea, North	Yongbyon[g]	Uncertain	Operational	GC	8
Netherlands	Urenco Almelo	Civilian	Operational	GC	5 200
Pakistan	Gadwal	Military	Operational	GC	..
	Kahuta	Military	Operational	GC	15–45
Russia	Angarsk	Civilian	Operational	GC	4 000
	Novouralsk	Civilian	Operational	GC	13 300
	Seversk	Civilian	Operational	GC	3 800
	Zelenogorsk[h]	Civilian	Operational	GC	7 900
UK	Capenhurst	Civilian	Operational	GC	4 600
USA	Urenco Eunice	Civilian	Operational	GC	4 900

[a] The gas centrifuge (GC) is the main isotope-separation technology used to increase the percentage of uranium-235 (U-235) in uranium, but a few facilities continue to use gaseous diffusion (GD).

[b] Separative work units per year (SWU/yr) is a measure of the effort required in an enrichment facility to separate uranium of a given content of U-235 into two components, one with a higher and one with a lower percentage of U-235. Where a range of capacities is shown, the capacity is uncertain or the facility is expanding its capacity.

[c] In Dec. 2015 Argentina announced the reopening of its Pilcaniyeu GD uranium enrichment plant, which was shut down in the 1990s. There is no evidence of actual production.

[d] Assessments of China's enrichment capacity in 2015 and 2017 identified new enrichment sites and suggested a much larger total capacity than had previously been estimated.

[e] In July 2015 Iran agreed the Joint Comprehensive Plan of Action (JCPOA), which ended uranium enrichment at Fordow but kept centrifuges operating and limited the enrichment capacity at Natanz to 5060 IR-1 centrifuges (equivalent to 3500–5000 SWU/yr) for 10 years. In Nov. 2019, following the USA's withdrawal from the JCPOA, Iran announced a limited restart of enrichment at Natanz and Fordow.

[f] The Rokkasho centrifuge plant has been in the process of being refitted with new centrifuge technology since 2011. Production since the start of retrofitting has been negligible.

[g] North Korea revealed its Yongbyon enrichment facility in 2010. It appears to be operational as of 2019. It is believed that North Korea is operating at least one other enrichment facility located elsewhere.

[h] Zelenogorsk operates a cascade for highly enriched uranium production for fast reactor and research reactor fuel.

Sources: Indo-Asian News Service (IANS), 'Argentina president inaugurates enriched uranium plant', *Business Standard*, 1 Dec. 2015; Zhang, H., 'China's uranium enrichment complex', *Science & Global Security*, vol. 23, no. 3 (2015), pp. 171–90; Zhang, H., *China's Fissile Material Production and Stockpile* (IPFM: Princeton, NJ, 2017); Hecker, S. S., Carlin, R. L. and Serbin, E. A., 'A comprehensive history of North Korea's nuclear program', Stanford University, Center for International Security and Cooperation (CISAC), 2018 update; Pabian, F. V., Liu, J. and Town, J., 'North Korea's Yongbyon Nuclear Center: Continuing activity at the uranium enrichment plant', 38 North, 5 June 2019; and Wolgelenter, M. and Sanger, D. E., 'Iran steps further from nuclear deal with move on centrifuges', *New York Times*, 5 Nov. 2019. Enrichment capacity data is based on International Atomic Energy Agency, Integrated Nuclear Fuel Cycle Information Systems (iNFCIS); Urenco, 'Global operations', [n.d.]; and International Panel on Fissile Materials (IPFM), *Global Fissile Material Report 2015: Nuclear Weapon and Fissile Material Stockpiles and Production* (IPFM: Princeton, NJ, 2015).

Table 10.14. Significant reprocessing facilities worldwide, 2020

All facilities process light water reactor (LWR) fuel, except where indicated.

State	Facility name or location	Type	Status	Design capacity (tHM/yr)[a]
China[b]	Jiuquan pilot plant	Civilian	Operational	50
France	La Hague UP2	Civilian	Operational	1 000
	La Hague UP3	Civilian	Operational	1 000
India[c]	Kalpakkam (HWR fuel)	Dual-use	Operational	100
	Tarapur (HWR fuel)	Dual-use	Operational	100
	Tarapur-II (HWR fuel)	Dual-use	Operational	100
	Trombay (HWR fuel)	Military	Operational	50
Israel	Dimona (HWR fuel)	Military	Operational	40–100
Japan	JNC Tokai	Civilian	Reprocessing shut down[d]	(was 200)
	Rokkasho	Civilian	Start planned for 2022	800
Korea, North	Yongbyon (GCR fuel)	Military	Operational	100–150
Pakistan	Chashma (HWR fuel)	Military	Starting up	50–100
	Nilore (HWR fuel)	Military	Operational	20–40
Russia[e]	Mayak RT-1, Ozersk	Civilian	Operational	400
	EDC, Zheleznogorsk	Civilian	Starting up	250
UK	Sellafield B205 (Magnox fuel)	Civilian	To be shut down in 2021	1 500
	Sellafield Thorp	Civilian	Shut down in 2018	(was 1 200)
USA	H-canyon, Savannah River Site	Civilian	Operational	15

HWR = heavy water reactor; GCR = gas cooled reactor.

[a] Design capacity refers to the highest amount of spent fuel the plant is designed to process and is measured in tonnes of heavy metal per year (tHM/yr), tHM being a measure of the amount of heavy metal—uranium in these cases—that is in the spent fuel. Actual throughput is often a small fraction of the design capacity. LWR spent fuel contains c. 1% plutonium, and heavy water- and graphite-moderated reactor fuels contain c. 0.4% plutonium.

[b] China is building a pilot reprocessing facility near Jinta, Gansu province, with a capacity of 200 tHM/yr, to be commissioned in 2025.

[c] As part of the 2005 Indian–US Civil Nuclear Cooperation Initiative, India has decided that none of its reprocessing plants will be opened for International Atomic Energy Agency safeguards inspections.

[d] In 2014 the Japan Atomic Energy Agency announced the planned closure of the head-end of its Tokai reprocessing plant, effectively ending further plutonium separation activity. In 2018 the Japanese Nuclear Regulation Authority approved a plan to decommission the plant.

[e] Russia continues to construct a 250 tHM/yr pilot experimental centre at Zheleznogorsk. A pilot reprocessing line with a capacity of 5 tHM/yr was launched in June 2018. The centre is scheduled to begin operations in 2021.

Sources: Kyodo News, 'Japan approves 70-year plan to scrap nuclear reprocessing plant', 13 June 2018; and RIA Novosti, [Rosatom is ready to start 'green' processing of spent nuclear fuel], 29 May 2018 (in Russian). Data on design capacity is based on International Atomic Energy Agency, Integrated Nuclear Fuel Cycle Information Systems (iNFCIS); and International Panel on Fissile Materials (IPFM), *Global Fissile Material Report 2015: Nuclear Weapon and Fissile Material Stockpiles and Production* (IPFM: Princeton, NJ, 2015).

Part III. Non-proliferation, arms control and disarmament, 2020

11. Nuclear disarmament, arms control and non-proliferation

Overview

Although, on balance, 2020 was a difficult year for nuclear arms control and non-proliferation efforts, it marked an important milestone in the development of international norms on nuclear disarmament: on 24 October 2020 Honduras became the 50th state to ratify or accede to the 2017 Treaty on the Prohibition of Nuclear Weapons (TPNW), triggering its entry into force 90 days later (see section III). The TPNW is the first treaty to establish a comprehensive ban on nuclear weapons, including their development, deployment, possession, use and threat of use. This prohibition has brought to the fore the tension between proponents of nuclear disarmament and nuclear deterrence: while civil society and many non-nuclear weapon states welcomed the entry into force of the treaty, the nuclear weapon states and their allies viewed it as undermining the existing nuclear order based on the 1968 Treaty on the Non-Proliferation of Nuclear Weapons (Non-Proliferation Treaty, NPT).

The Covid-19 pandemic led to the postponement of the 10th Review Conference of the NPT. It would have marked the 50th anniversary of the NPT's entry into force in 1970 and a quarter of a century since the treaty was indefinitely extended in 1995. Many welcomed the postponement as the conference appeared set to fail in the political context that prevailed in 2020—a context shaped mainly by the long-standing failure to make progress on nuclear disarmament.

In keeping with over a decade of diplomatic deadlock in bilateral nuclear arms control between Russia and the United States, little progress was made in their negotiations in 2020 (see section I). In addition to the deterioration in Russian–Western political and security relations, contemporary developments in military technology have also complicated strategic dynamics and contributed to this deadlock. Despite their efforts to address relevant issues in the Strategic Security Dialogue framework, by the end of the year Russia and the USA had still not agreed to extend their last-remaining bilateral nuclear arms control treaty, the 2010 Treaty on Measures for the Further Reduction and Limitation of Strategic Offensive Arms (New START), which was due to expire on 5 February 2021. The fate of New START remained in the balance due to the different approaches and goals of the two sides: Russia focused on preserving the treaty, while the USA sought to convince China—with no success—to join the agreement and to make it more comprehensive in terms of the weapons covered and the verification measures imposed.

SIPRI Yearbook 2021: Armaments, Disarmament and International Security
www.sipriyearbook.org

The future of the 2015 Joint Comprehensive Plan of Action (JCPOA) also remained uncertain in 2020. The JCPOA is an agreement between Iran and six other countries, facilitated by the EU. It is designed to build international confidence about the exclusively peaceful nature of Iran's nuclear programme in return for the lifting of international sanctions (see section II). Iran remained a participant in the JCPOA, although it was no longer observing key provisions of the agreement. Iran had begun to exceed JCPOA limits on its nuclear activities in 2019 in response to the US 'maximum pressure' policy—which, following the US withdrawal from the JCPOA in 2018, included ever harsher sanctions on Iran. Iran continued to maintain that it would return to full compliance as soon as the other participants did the same. The prospects for reviving this ailing nuclear agreement in 2021 were improved by the election of a new US president in late 2020. However, the diplomatic window for Iran and the USA to agree on the terms for returning to their respective JCPOA commitments remained narrow.

In the case of the Democratic People's Republic of Korea (DPRK, North Korea), since the breakdown of the short-lived nuclear diplomacy with the USA in 2018–19 a stalemate has ensued, and this continued throughout 2020. In January, North Korea announced that it would no longer observe its unilateral moratoriums on nuclear test explosions and test flights of long-range ballistic missiles that it had declared in 2018. While it conducted no such tests during the year, it continued development of its shorter-range ballistic missiles (see chapter 10).

Finally, the difficult political context for nuclear arms control was also apparent in relation to the 1996 Comprehensive Nuclear-Test-Ban Treaty (CTBT)—the international treaty that will ban all nuclear test explosions in all environments when it enters into force. In 2020 US officials reportedly discussed the option of conducting a so-called demonstration nuclear explosion, which would have been the first US nuclear explosive test since 1992 (see section III). By the end of the year, given the adverse political reactions, the political changes in the USA after the elections in November, and the technical difficulties involved, such a test seemed unlikely. Meanwhile, as in previous years, the USA questioned whether China and Russia were adhering to their unilateral nuclear testing moratoriums. Both denied the US assertions, which have not been substantiated by publicly available evidence, that they had been carrying out clandestine low-yield nuclear explosions.

TYTTI ERÄSTÖ, VITALY FEDCHENKO AND PETR TOPYCHKANOV

I. Russian–United States nuclear arms control and disarmament

PETR TOPYCHKANOV

In 2020 the Russian–United States nuclear arms control and disarmament agenda seemed to be slowly collapsing and was close to losing its last key pillar. By the end of 2020, Russia and the United States had still not agreed to extend the 2010 Treaty on Measures for the Further Reduction and Limitation of Strategic Offensive Arms (New START), which was due to expire on 5 February 2021. Indeed, negotiations on extending this agreement had not even started. Instead, all the exchanges about this issue were channelled through the Strategic Security Dialogue consultations and in other less formal ways.

The developments of 2020 prolonged the trend of 2019: deterioration of the arms control architecture signified by the collapse of the 1987 Treaty on the Elimination of Intermediate-range and Shorter-range Missiles (INF Treaty) and growing disagreements on New START.[1] Despite mostly positive developments in implementing New START, it was not possible in 2020 to sustain this progress by negotiating deeper reductions in deployed strategic nuclear forces. Russia continued to disagree with the USA's demand to include China in the nuclear arms control framework. China also refused to accept the US invitation. This section describes these developments concerning New START and the Strategic Security Dialogue between Russia and the USA in 2020.

New START implementation and possible extension

Russia and the USA continued to implement the bilateral 2010 New START in 2020. Under the treaty, the two parties agreed to limit the number of their deployed strategic nuclear warheads to 1550 each and to limit the number of their deployed strategic missile launchers and heavy bombers equipped for nuclear armaments to 700 each (see table 11.1).[2] The USA and Russia officially confirmed that they had achieved the New START limits in August 2017 and February 2018, respectively.[3]

---

[1] On developments in 2019 see Topychkanov, P. and Davis, I., 'Russian–United States nuclear arms control and disarmament', *SIPRI Yearbook 2020*, pp. 399–409. For a summary and other details of the INF Treaty see annex A, section III, in this volume.

[2] For a summary and other details of New START see annex A, section III, in this volume.

[3] US Department of State, 'New START Treaty central limits take effect', Press statement, 5 Feb. 2018; and Yermakov, V. I., Head of Russian Delegation, Statement to the First Committee, 73rd session of the United Nations, General Assembly, Russian Ministry of Foreign Affairs, 9 Oct. 2018.

Table 11.1. Russian and United States aggregate numbers of strategic offensive arms under New START, as of 5 February 2011, 1 March and 1 September 2020

Category of data	Treaty limits	Russia			United States		
		Feb. 2011	Mar. 2020	Sep. 2020	Feb. 2011	Mar. 2020	Sep. 2020
Deployed ICBMs, SLBMs and heavy bombers	700	521	485	510	882	655	675
Warheads on deployed ICBMs, SLBMs and heavy bombers[a]	1 550	1 537	1 326	1 447	1 800	1 373[b]	1 457
Deployed and non-deployed launchers of ICBMs, SLBMs and heavy bombers	800	865	754	764	1 124	800	800

ICBM = intercontinental ballistic missile; SLBM = submarine-launched ballistic missile.

Notes: The treaty entered into force on 5 Feb. 2011. The Treaty limits had to be reached by 5 Feb. 2018.

[a] Each heavy bomber, whether equipped with cruise missiles or gravity bombs, is counted as carrying only 1 warhead, even though the aircraft can carry larger weapon payloads.

[b] The figure 1373 appears in the first public release of aggregate data by the US Department of State on 1 Mar. 2020. In subsequent data releases, the figure 1372 appears instead.

Source: US Department of State, Bureau of Arms Control, Verification and Compliance, 'New START Treaty aggregate numbers of strategic offensive arms', Fact sheets, 1 June 2011; 1 July 2020; and 1 Dec. 2020.

New START contains transparency and verification measures—such as biannual data exchanges, notifications and up to 18 on-site inspections annually—that have helped to build mutual confidence between the parties about the size and composition of their respective strategic nuclear forces.

Due to the Covid-19 pandemic, Russia and the USA each conducted only 2 of the 18 on-sight inspections allocated in 2020. In March the Russian deputy foreign minister, Sergey Ryabkov, confirmed that the two countries' mutual decision was to halt the on-sight inspections until 1 May 2020.[4] However, the suspension continued after that date. The Covid-19 pandemic also prevented the Bilateral Consultative Commission (BCC)—which oversees New START implementation—from meeting in 2020 (it had met twice in 2019). However, both sides indicated that these meetings and on-sight inspections would resume once the health risks had been mitigated.[5] They exchanged New START-related information and notifications through regular diplomatic channels instead of BCC meetings.[6] As of 17 December 2020 Russia and the

---

[4] 'Decision on halting inspections under New START made upon mutual agreement—diplomat', TASS, 29 Mar. 2020.

[5] Reif, K. and Bugos, S., 'US shifts arms control strategy with Russia', Arms Control Now blog, Arms Control Association, 17 Sep. 2020.

[6] Schaad, L. and Kimball, D. G., 'Covid-19 delays security meetings, treaty inspections', *Arms Control Today*, vol. 50, no. 3 (Apr. 2020).

USA had exchanged 21 293 notifications over the 10 years since the treaty entered into force.[7]

The biannual treaty data exchanges in March and September 2020 showed that both Russian and US holdings were within the final treaty limits. However, between March and September the combined total number of strategic launchers increased by 45 items and deployed nuclear warheads increased by 205 items. These changes reflected launchers moving in and out of the maintenance or upgrade within the New START limits.[8]

Based on US data from 2019, the USA certified that Russia was in compliance with New START.[9] However, it also raised implementation-related questions through diplomatic channels, especially in relation to new weapons under development in Russia.[10] This issue was discussed in a telephone conversation between the US secretary of state, Michael R. Pompeo, and the Russian foreign minister, Sergey Lavrov, on 17 April 2020, and in other Russian–US communications during 2020. During the exchange, Lavrov confirmed that New START could cover two of Russia's new weapon systems.[11] Ryabkov clarified the same day that these systems were the Sarmat heavy intercontinental ballistic missile (ICBM) and the Avangard hypersonic glide vehicle.[12]

During the conversation with Pompeo, Lavrov also stressed that Russia was interested in extending the agreement for five years and simultaneously ready to discuss a new arms control agreement.[13]

During 2020 Russia also reiterated questions about US compliance that it had previously raised. These included the allegation that the USA continued to exceed the New START aggregate limits for deployed and non-deployed ICBM and submarine-launched ballistic missile (SLBM) launchers and deployed and non-deployed heavy bombers by 101 units.[14]

However, the leading Russian complaint about New START during 2020 was not about US compliance, but rather focused on the lack of US interest

---

[7] US Department of State, 'New START Treaty', 17 Dec. 2020.

[8] Kristensen, H. M., 'At 11th hour, New START data reaffirms importance of extending treaty', Federation of American Scientists, 1 Oct. 2020. On US and Russian nuclear forces see chapter 10, sections I and II, in this volume.

[9] US Department of State, 'Annual report on implementation of the New START treaty', Jan. 2020.

[10] US Department of State (note 9).

[11] Isachenkov, V., 'Top US and Russian diplomats discuss arms control', AP News, 18 Apr. 2020; and Gronlund, L., 'US should extend the New START nuclear weapons treaty to make us all safer', All Things Nuclear, Union of Concerned Scientists, 22 Apr. 2020.

[12] AP News, 'Russia shows willingness to include new nuke, hypersonic weapon in arms control pact', *Defense News*, 17 Apr. 2020.

[13] Russian Ministry of Foreign Affairs, 'Press release on Foreign Minister Sergey Lavrov's telephone conversation with US Secretary of State Mike Pompeo', 17 Apr. 2020.

[14] Russian Ministry of Foreign Affairs, 'Comment by the Information and Press Department on the United States' report on Adherence to and Compliance with Arms Control, Nonproliferation and Disarmament Agreements and Commitments (ACNPD)', 4 July 2020.

in discussing the treaty's extension.[15] The Russian side interpreted the US proposal to have a trilateral arms control agreement with China instead of extending the bilateral New START as a policy designed to end the last Russian–US nuclear arms control agreement.[16]

In sum, Russia and the USA managed to use some of the treaty's verification mechanisms, despite Covid-19 restrictions; both sides were relatively satisfied with each other's compliance, but they could not launch the New START negotiations because of their different approaches towards the document extension. Instead, Russia and the USA used the Strategic Security Dialogue framework to address this particular issue among other strategic challenges of mutual concern, as discussed next.

The Strategic Security Dialogue

Despite the cancellation of the New START BCC meetings due to the Covid-19 pandemic, several rounds of bilateral consultations on strategic issues took place during 2020.

On 16 January 2020 Russian and US delegations met in Vienna to discuss nuclear doctrines and arsenals, crisis and arms race stability, and the future of arms control, including its potential expansion beyond the bilateral format. They agreed to establish working groups to discuss particular issues under the Strategic Security Dialogue, an informal forum for talks between Russia and the USA.[17]

At the following meeting, in Vienna on 22–23 June, the two sides discussed the future of arms control—including extending New START and maintaining stability and predictability after the termination of the INF Treaty in 2019—and other international security problems.[18] They also agreed on the specific working groups for the next round of the Strategic Security Dialogue, including a group on nuclear arsenals and doctrines. Russian and US sources disagreed on the latter group's focus: Russia argued

---

[15] Meyer, H., 'Russia says US shows no readiness to extend key nuclear pact', Bloomberg, 14 May 2020.

[16] Medvedev, D., 'Failing to extend New START could have extremely serious consequences', TASS, 8 Apr. 2020.

[17] Initially established in 1993 as the US-Russian Strategic Stability Group, since 2019 the US State Department has called the forum the Strategic Security Dialogue, while Russia uses various terms to describe it. Talbot, I., 'Unfinished business: Russia and missile defense under Clinton', *Arms Control Today*, vol. 32, no. 5 (June 2002); US Department of State, 'US–Russia Strategic Security Dialogue', Media note, 16 Jan. 2020; and Russian Ministry of Foreign Affairs, 'Press release on Russian–US consultations on strategic matters', 16 Jan. 2020.

[18] US National Nuclear Security Administration (NNSA), 'NNSA hosts special presidential envoy for arms control', 14 Sep. 2020; and Russian Ministry of Foreign Affairs, 'Press release on Russian–US consultations on strategic issues', 22 June 2020.

that it would only cover nuclear doctrines, whereas the USA insisted that nuclear arsenals were also included.[19]

For this June meeting, the US Department of State attempted to convince Chinese representatives to join the dialogue. China declined to attend, noting 'the huge gap between the nuclear arsenal of China and those of the US and Russia'.[20] The USA issued a picture of Chinese flags placed at empty seats around the table, which China dismissed as 'performance art' and Russia as 'staged'.[21] In short, the trilateral dialogue that the USA sought clearly had no chance of success.[22]

Nevertheless, Russia and the USA were relatively satisfied by the outcomes in Vienna, as were some US allies. For example, Jens Stoltenberg, secretary general of the North Atlantic Treaty Organization (NATO), was generally supportive of the 'constructive' June talks. He also stressed the need for China to join Russian–US arms control efforts.[23]

The US representative described the outcomes of the consultations in June as 'very positive' with the potential for agreement at the next bilateral meeting.[24] However, the Vienna discussions included non-strategic nuclear weapons, which are not covered by New START.[25] It was thus unclear whether the US aspiration was for an extension of New START or a broader document to cover a range of weapons never previously included in a single Russian–US agreement. Russia welcomed the affirmation of the mutual

[19] 'Russia, US agree to meeting of experts on military doctrines', TASS, 25 June 2020; and US Department of State, 'Online press briefing with Ambassador Marshall Billingslea, special presidential envoy for arms control, and Lieutenant General Thomas A. Bussiere, deputy commander, United States Strategic Command (USSTRATCOM)', 24 June 2020.

[20] Chinese Ministry of Foreign Affairs, 'Foreign Ministry Spokesperson Hua Chunying's regular press conference on June 9, 2020', 9 June 2020; and Chinese Ministry of Foreign Affairs, 'Department of Arms Control and Disarmament holds briefing for international arms control and disarmament issues', 8 July 2020. On the respective nuclear arsenals see chapter 10, sections I, II and V, in this volume.

[21] Murphy, F., '"Performance art?": China rebukes US envoy for photo stunt at talks with Russia', Reuters, 22 June 2020; and Kostiv, M., [Envoy described the US photo at the consultations with Russia in Vienna as staged], RIA Novosti, 22 June 2020 (in Russian).

[22] For official Chinese, Russian and US reactions and explanations see also Billingslea, M., US Special Presidential Envoy for Arms Control (@USArmsControl), 'Vienna talks about to start. China is a no-show. Beijing still hiding behind #GreatWallofSecrecy on its crash nuclear build-up, and so many other things. We will proceed with #Russia, notwithstanding.', Twitter, 22 June 2020; Chernenko, E., [The third is not superfluous], *Kommersant*, 22 June 2020 (in Russian); US Department of State (note 19); and Chinese Ministry of Foreign Affairs, 'Foreign Ministry spokesperson Zhao Lijian's regular press conference on June 23, 2020', 23 June 2020.

[23] Stoltenberg, J., NATO Secretary General, Remarks at the Brussels Forum, 23 June 2020.

[24] Billingslea, M., US Special Presidential Envoy for Arms Control (@USArmsControl), 'First round of Vienna talks very positive. Detailed discussions on full-range of nuclear topics. Technical working groups launched. Agreement in principle on second round. @MFA_Austria @mfa_russia', Twitter, 22 June 2020.

[25] 'Tactical nuclear arms among issues discussed by Russia, US in Vienna—Pentagon official', TASS, 25 June 2020.

'interest in continuing the security, stability and arms control dialogue', while remaining cautious on the outcomes of the consultations.[26]

The follow-up expert group meeting on 27–30 July, which the USA described as 'trilateral arms control', was a de facto bilateral meeting between Russian and US experts representing various agencies from both sides. The focus of the expert discussions was nuclear doctrines and capabilities, transparency and verification measures. Separately, on 27 July they held a space-related track, titled 'US–Russia Space Security Exchange'.[27] According to official statements from both sides, there were no consultations on the New START extension.[28]

On 17–18 August the Russian and US delegations met again in Vienna. Unlike the previous expert group meeting, this time they discussed the extension of New START. According to the US official statements after the consultations, both sides were ready to reach a consensus on extending New START before the end of 2020.[29] However, US statements also stressed the 'significant verification deficiencies' in New START, as well as the omission of China.[30] Several US officials also expressed the view that it was time for Russia to respond to the US suggestions.[31]

However, the Russian position seemed to remain unchanged: it was ready to agree on the treaty's unconditional extension but not at any price.[32] It also continued to regard the treaty as bilateral despite US pressure to engage China.

As the year progressed, despite these seemingly promising Strategic Security Dialogue discussions, the underlying tensions in the different fundamental positions of the two sides began to resurface. In an interview with a Russian newspaper in September, the US special presidential envoy for arms control, Marshall Billingslea, who had led the US delegation in the discussions, threatened to change the 'price of admission' for Russia to have an arms control agreement with the USA if it did not agree with the

---

[26] Russian Ministry of Foreign Affairs, 'Briefing by Foreign Ministry Spokesperson Maria Zakharova, Moscow, June 25, 2020', 25 June 2020; and Borger, J., 'US–Russia nuclear envoys make guarded comments as talks begin in Vienna', *The Guardian*, 22 June 2020.

[27] US Department of State, 'The United States and Russia hold Space Security exchange', Media note, 28 July 2020.

[28] US Embassy and Consulates in Russia, 'Meeting of US–Russia expert groups on trilateral arms control and for the space security exchange', 24 July 2020; and Russian Ministry of Foreign Affairs, [On the meeting in the framework of the US–Russian strategic dialogue], Press release, 30 July 2020 (in Russian).

[29] '"Ball is in Russia's court" on nuclear arms deal, US says', Reuters, 18 Aug. 2020.

[30] Reif, K. and Bugos, S., 'US modifies arms control aims with Russia', *Arms Control Today*, vol. 50, no. 7 (Sep. 2020).

[31] 'US–Russia non-proliferation talks going well, says Trump', TASS, 5 Sep. 2020.

[32] Ulyanov, M., Russian Permanent Representative to International Organizations in Vienna (@Amb_Ulyanov), 'S. Ryabkov: Russia stands for an extention [sic] of the START Treaty, but is not ready to pay any price for that.', Twitter, 18 Aug. 2020.

US suggestions.[33] The Russian representative at the talks, the deputy foreign minister, Sergey Ryabkov, called on the USA to stop making ultimatums and to start substantial negotiations.[34]

The final round of the Strategic Security Dialogue consultations took place on 5 October in Helsinki, focusing on New START. According to US diplomatic sources, for the first time Russia made constructive suggestions that signalled that a one-year extension of New START might be possible, as well as a nuclear freeze of all strategic stockpiles—not only those covered by New START.[35] However, Russian officials were more guarded, suggesting that the negotiations were relatively close to reaching an agreement, but not on the nuclear freeze issue.[36] Russian President Vladimir Putin also implicitly endorsed the idea of a one-year extension during a meeting of the Russian Security Council on 16 October 2020.[37] However, the USA quickly dismissed this idea as a 'non-starter' without an accompanying nuclear freeze.[38]

Russia relayed Putin's proposal to the USA on the same date but, in the absence of an official response, on 20 October it made a statement repeating the one-year extension suggestion and extending an invitation to the USA to jointly 'undertake a political commitment to "freeze" for the above-mentioned period the number of nuclear warheads that each side possesses'.[39] Russian diplomats highlighted that this proposed political commitment would not involve any additional transparency and verification measures.

Initially, the USA welcomed this statement and began preparing to finalize a verifiable agreement with Russia.[40] However, Russia gave out mixed messages. On the one hand, the Russian president's spokesperson, Dmitry Peskov, confirmed on 23 October that in the coming days the US and Russian expert teams would meet to negotiate the New START extension and the additional suggestions recently made by both sides.[41] On the other hand,

---

[33] Chernenko, E., ['If Russia does not accept our offer before the election, the price of admission will go up'], *Kommersant*, 21 Sep. 2020 (in Russian).

[34] Sonne, P. and Hudson, J., 'US scrambles to do nuclear deal with Russia before election, issuing ultimatum', *Washington Post*, 23 Sep. 2020.

[35] 'Progress in arms control talks with Russian senior diplomat, US representative says', TASS, 6 Oct. 2020; and Gordon, M. R., 'US, Russia move toward outline of nuclear deal, administration says', *Wall Street Journal*, 5 Oct. 2020.

[36] 'No "ironclad" agreements on freezing nuclear arsenals between Russia, US—Kremlin', TASS, 14 Oct. 2020; and 'Russian senior diplomat rejects US proposal to freeze nuclear arsenals, extend New START', TASS, 13 Oct. 2020.

[37] President of Russia, 'Meeting with permanent members of the Security Council', 16 Oct. 2020.

[38] Cohen, Z., Crawford, J. and Atwood, K., 'Trump's national security adviser calls Putin response to arms control talks a "non-starter"', CNN, 16 Oct. 2020.

[39] Russian Ministry of Foreign Affairs, 'Foreign Ministry statement on New START treaty extension', 20 Oct. 2020.

[40] US Department of State, 'Progress on New START', Press statement, 20 Oct. 2020.

[41] 'Russian, US experts to hold talks on extending New START in coming days—Kremlin', TASS, 23 Oct. 2020.

Ryabkov on the same day indicated that there would be no new meetings unless the US side accepted the Russian proposal, as articulated in the statement of 20 October. He also expressed doubts about the US intention to extend New START.[42]

Despite comments in December by Billingslea, the chance for a breakthrough had seemingly passed as the US presidential election took centre stage. He continued to hope for new meetings with his Russian counterparts to 'define what we are freezing' and the capability levels, to start verification talks, and to continue the exchange of documents about the proposals between the two sides.[43] However, by the end of the year, the doubts about the feasibility of reaching agreement in 2020 had become a reality.[44]

Conclusions

The collapse of the Russian–US arms control agenda was linked to changes in the international security environment and military technological developments in recent years and to further deteriorating Russian–Western political and security relations more generally. In 2020, in addition to the lack of progress in Russian–US nuclear arms control consultations, this deterioration encompassed the USA's withdrawal from the 1992 Open Skies Treaty and its deployment of a new low-yield SLBM warhead.[45] The growing capabilities of other nuclear-armed countries—primarily, but not only, China—and technological developments in hypersonic missiles, ballistic missile defence, the militarization of outer space and autonomy in strategic weapons have created new problems for existing nuclear arms control agreements.[46]

The future of the last-remaining Russian–US bilateral nuclear arms control agreement—New START—remained in the balance. Instead of a specific negotiating track for dealing with New START, the issue was combined in the broader framework of the Strategic Security Dialogue, which covered

[42] 'No plans to unilaterally freeze nuclear warhead stockpile, senior Russian diplomat says', TASS, 23 Oct. 2020.

[43] 'US response to Putin may close door to more arms control talks under Trump', Reuters, 17 Dec. 2020; and 'Russia continues dialogue with US on New START extension', TASS, 27 Oct. 2020.

[44] US Embassy and Consulates in Russia, 'Ambassador John J. Sullivan interview with Konstantin Remchukov of Nezavisimaya Gazeta', 18 Dec. 2020; and President of Russia, 'Meeting with senior Defence Ministry officials, heads of federal agencies and defence industry executives', 10 Nov. 2020.

[45] On Russia's relations with the West see chapter 5, section I, in this volume. On the deteriorating international security environment see chapter 1 in this volume. On the US withdrawal from the Open Skies Treaty see chapter 13, section V, in this volume. On the US deployment of a new low-yield SLBM see chapter 10, section I, in this volume.

[46] On the modernization programmes of the nuclear-armed states see chapter 10 in this volume. On militarization of outer space see chapter 13, section IV, in this volume. On autonomy in strategic weapons see Boulanin, V. et al., *Artificial Intelligence, Strategic Stability and Nuclear Risk* (SIPRI: Stockholm, June 2020).

the full spectrum of strategic issues of mutual concern. More importantly, neither side had the same goals for New START-related consultations. Russia focused on preserving the treaty for the next five years, while the USA sought to convince China to join the agreement and make it more comprehensive in terms of the weapons covered and the verification measures imposed.

These differences explained why progress proved to be impossible. The Covid-19 pandemic created additional obstacles for diplomatic efforts, making such negotiation even less feasible.

The incoming US administration of Joe Biden offered a fresh opportunity to preserve the treaty in 2021—the President-elect had indicated that he would support a five-year extension.[47] Russia had also signalled its readiness to negotiate the New START extension with the new US administration, without changing its previously stated conditions.[48]

---

[47] Gordon, M. R., 'Biden to review US nuclear-weapons programs, with eye toward cuts', *Wall Street Journal*, 24 Dec. 2020.

[48] Russian Ministry of Foreign Affairs, 'Foreign Minister Sergey Lavrov's interview with TASS News Agency', 30 Dec. 2020.

II. Implementation of the Joint Comprehensive Plan of Action on Iran's nuclear programme

TYTTI ERÄSTÖ

The Joint Comprehensive Plan of Action (JCPOA) is a landmark agreement concluded on 14 July 2015 by Iran on one side and, on the other, three European states—France, Germany and the United Kingdom (the E3)—and China, Russia and the United States. The agreement appeared to solve the crisis over Iran's nuclear programme that had begun in the early 2000s. The JCPOA, which was facilitated by the European Union (EU), was based on a compromise whereby Iran accepted limits and strict monitoring on its proliferation-sensitive activities in return for the lifting of international sanctions on its nuclear programme.[1]

The JCPOA has been significantly weakened since US President Donald J. Trump withdrew the USA from the agreement in May 2018 and reimposed nuclear-related and other additional sanctions on Iran. As most of the reimposed US sanctions are secondary sanctions aimed at third parties, they also undermined the ability of other JCPOA participants to fulfil their commitments under the agreement. Iran responded by gradually reducing adherence to its commitments under the agreement in May 2019, and by January 2020 it had ceased to observe its operational limits.[2] Iran nevertheless remained a participant in the JCPOA—despite ever harsher US sanctions and growing domestic pressure—and continued to maintain that it would return to full compliance as soon as the other participants did the same.[3]

This section reviews developments related to the JCPOA in 2020. It focuses on Iran's nuclear activities, particularly those that exceeded the JCPOA limits, based on verification reports by the International Atomic Energy Agency (IAEA). It then describes US sanctions and other efforts related to the Trump administration's 'maximum pressure' policy on Iran, as well as the roles of the other JCPOA participants.

---

[1] Joint Comprehensive Plan of Action (JCPOA), 14 July 2015, Vienna, reproduced as annex A of UN Security Council Resolution 2231, 20 July 2015. For background see Rauf, T., 'Resolving concerns about Iran's nuclear programme', *SIPRI Yearbook 2016*, pp. 673–88; Rauf, T., 'Implementation of the Joint Comprehensive Plan of Action in Iran', *SIPRI Yearbook 2017*, pp. 505–10; Erästö, T., 'Implementation of the Joint Comprehensive Plan of Action in Iran', *SIPRI Yearbook 2018*, pp. 337–45; Erästö, T., 'Implementation of the Joint Comprehensive Plan of Action', *SIPRI Yearbook 2019*, pp. 378–86; and Erästö, T., 'Implementation of the Joint Comprehensive Plan of Action', *SIPRI Yearbook 2020*, pp. 418–26.

[2] See Erästö, *SIPRI Yearbook 2020* (note 1).

[3] Islamic Republic News Agency (IRNA), 'Iran takes final step by abandoning JCPOA restrictions', 5 Jan. 2020.

Iran's compliance with its JCPOA commitments

The JCPOA sets limits on Iran's uranium enrichment activities, its stockpiles of enriched uranium, and its production of plutonium in order to prevent it from obtaining weapon-grade fissile materials—highly enriched uranium (HEU) and plutonium. Sensitive materials—excess stockpiles of enriched uranium and heavy water, as well as spent nuclear fuel—were to be shipped abroad under the agreement. Iran also agreed to provisionally apply the Additional Protocol to its Comprehensive Safeguards Agreement with the IAEA pending parliamentary ratification, which Iran would seek by 2023. This meant that Iran would accept additional inspections by the IAEA outside the declared nuclear facilities normally covered under the Safeguards Agreement.[4]

Iran had exceeded most JCPOA limits by January 2020, meaning that it was no longer observing key provisions of the agreement. According to Iran, its actions were in line with articles 26 and 36 of the JCPOA, which state that Iran can 'cease performing its commitments . . . in whole or in part' in response to a reimposition of nuclear-related sanctions.[5] Iran argued that it would return to full compliance once other JCPOA participants did the same by meeting their respective commitments regarding the lifting of sanctions.[6] At the same time, Iran's nuclear activities continued to be closely monitored and verified by the IAEA throughout the year, although there were some disagreements over access to undeclared locations.

Activities related to heavy water and reprocessing

Iran is constructing a new heavy water reactor at Arak, western Iran. As part of the JCPOA, Iran agreed to redesign this reactor to minimize the amount of plutonium in the spent nuclear fuel that it would produce, and to keep its stock of heavy water below 130 tonnes (reduced to 90 tonnes after commissioning).[7] It also agreed not to reprocess spent fuel from any of its reactors, with the sole exception of producing medical and industrial radioisotopes.[8] As in previous years, in 2020 the IAEA reported that Iran had neither pursued the construction of the Arak reactor based on its original design nor carried out activities related to reprocessing at the Tehran

---

[4] Arms Control Association, 'IAEA safeguards agreements at a glance', Fact sheet, June 2020.
[5] JCPOA (note 1), articles 26, 36.
[6] Islamic Republic News Agency (note 3).
[7] JCPOA (note 1), annex I.
[8] JCPOA (note 1), annex I.

Research Reactor (TRR).[9] However, Iran slightly exceeded the heavy water stock limit in February and May, as it had done in November 2019.[10]

Activities related to enrichment and fuel

Under the JCPOA, Iran agreed not to enrich uranium beyond 3.67 per cent of the isotope uranium-235—the minimum level needed for civilian power production. For military use, uranium would need to be enriched up to about 90 per cent.[11] It also agreed to maintain its enriched uranium stockpiles below 300 kilograms and to conduct enrichment activities only at the Fuel Enrichment Plant (FEP) at Natanz, Isfahan province, until 2030. In addition, Iran agreed to keep the number of its operating IR-1 centrifuges at the Natanz FEP below 5060 until 2025, while all non-operational centrifuges would remain in storage. The Fordow Fuel Enrichment Plant (FFEP) at Fordow, Qom province, was to be converted into a nuclear, physics and technology centre.[12]

In 2020 the IAEA reported that Iran continued to enrich uranium up to 4.5 per cent, as it had done since July 2019, and that enrichment activities continued at the FFEP, as had been the case since November 2019.[13] Iran's low enriched uranium stockpile kept growing, from about 1000 kg in February to almost 2500 kg in November.[14]

The number of operating IR-1 centrifuges at the FEP remained below 5060 during 2020. However, from March the IAEA reported that an additional 1057 IR-1 centrifuges had been installed at Fordow, with most of them enriching uranium.[15] In October the IAEA also verified the instalment of the more advanced IR-2 and IR-4 centrifuges at Natanz. In November the agency reported that Iran was using the IR-2 centrifuges to enrich uranium, alongside the IR-1 centrifuges permitted by the JCPOA.[16]

Centrifuge research and development, manufacturing and inventory

While the JCPOA only permits Iran to operationally enrich uranium using first-generation, IR-1 centrifuges, it nevertheless allows limited research

---

[9] IAEA, Board of Governors, 'Verification and monitoring in the Islamic Republic of Iran in light of United Nations Security Council Resolution 2231 (2015)', Report by the Director General, GOV/2020/5, 3 Mar. 2020; GOV/2020/26, 5 June 2020; GOV/2020/41, 4 Sep. 2020; and GOV/2020/51, 11 Nov. 2020.

[10] IAEA, GOV/2020/5 (note 9); and IAEA, GOV/2020/26 (note 9).

[11] On enrichment of uranium and reprocessing of plutonium see chapter 10, section X, in this volume.

[12] JCPOA (note 1), annex I.

[13] IAEA, GOV/2020/5 (note 9); and IAEA, GOV/2020/26 (note 9).

[14] IAEA, GOV/2020/5 (note 9); and IAEA, GOV/2020/51 (note 9).

[15] IAEA, GOV/2020/5 (note 9); IAEA, GOV/2020/26 (note 9); IAEA, GOV/2020/41 (note 9); and IAEA, GOV/2020/51 (note 9).

[16] IAEA, 'Verification and monitoring in the Islamic Republic of Iran in light of United Nations Security Council Resolution 2231 (2015)', Report by the Director General, 17 Nov. 2020, GOV/INF/2020/16.

and development (R&D) activities on more advanced (IR-4, IR-5, IR-6 and IR-8) centrifuges. However, no enriched uranium may be accumulated from these activities. The agreement also allows mechanical testing (typically not involving uranium) on up to two single centrifuges of other types.[17] The limits on centrifuge R&D were intended to be in place until 2025.

In all four quarterly reports of 2020, the IAEA noted that Iran continued to accumulate enriched uranium at the Pilot Fuel Enrichment Plant (PFEP) at Natanz, as it had done since September 2019, using IR-2m, IR-4, IR-5 and IR-6, IR-6s and IR-s centrifuges.[18] The new centrifuge types are more effective than the IR-1 model, which Iran had previously planned to replace only after the expiry of JCPOA limits.[19]

On 2 July a centrifuge-assembly workshop at the Natanz nuclear facility caught fire in what Iranian authorities believed to be an act of sabotage.[20] The incident hindered Iran's ability to produce new centrifuges and prompted the construction of a new underground assembly facility at Natanz.[21] While this development was not discussed in the IAEA reports on implementation of the JCPOA, in a November press briefing the agency's director general, Rafael Grossi, confirmed that Iran had begun operating centrifuges at a new location in Natanz.[22]

Transparency, the Additional Protocol and other issues

The IAEA's quarterly reports reconfirmed that Iran continued to facilitate inspection and monitoring and to apply the Additional Protocol, and that the agency continued to evaluate Iran's declarations under the protocol.[23]

The reports also referred to ongoing interactions related to particles of natural uranium detected in February 2019 at a location that Iran had not formally declared to the IAEA as being associated with its nuclear programme.[24] Separate IAEA reports on Iran's Safeguards Agreement and Additional Protocol shed light on the contentious nature of this issue, which was related to Iran's past nuclear activities and was thus not directly connected with the JCPOA. According to the reports, in July and August 2019

---

[17] See JCPOA (note 1), annex I.

[18] IAEA, GOV/2020/5 (note 9); IAEA, GOV/2020/26 (note 9); IAEA, GOV/2020/41 (note 9); and IAEA, GOV/2020/51 (note 9).

[19] Atomic Energy Organization of Iran (AEOI), 'AEOI deputy elaborates on the JCPOA commitment reduction, third step details', Iran Watch, 21 Sep. 2019; and Hafezi, P., 'Iran launches more advanced machines to speed up nuclear enrichment—official', Reuters, 4 Nov. 2019.

[20] 'Iran nuclear: Fire at Natanz plant "caused by sabotage"', BBC News, 23 Aug. 2020.

[21] 'New building started "in the heart of the mountain" near uranium-enrichment facility in Iran', Radio Free Europe/Radio Liberty, 8 Sep. 2020.

[22] 'IAEA confirms reports that Iran has been operating nuclear centrifuges', Voice of America, 18 Nov. 2020.

[23] IAEA, GOV/2020/5 (note 9); IAEA, GOV/2020/26 (note 9); IAEA, GOV/2020/41 (note 9); and IAEA, GOV/2020/51 (note 9).

[24] IAEA, GOV/2020/41 (note 9). See also Erästö, SIPRI Yearbook 2020 (note 1), p. 422.

the IAEA had first requested clarification on three undeclared locations in Iran suspected of having hosted nuclear material and activities prior to 2003.[25] From January 2020 the agency had also requested access to two of those locations to take environmental samples.[26] The IAEA viewed Iran's initial refusal to grant access as 'adversely affecting' the agency's ability to resolve the relevant questions. This prompted the IAEA Board of Governors to adopt an E3-sponsored resolution on 19 June that called on Iran to 'fully cooperate with the Agency and satisfy the Agency's requests without any further delay'.[27]

Following a high-level meeting between the IAEA and Iranian officials in August, the agency was able to visit the two sites.[28] However, the IAEA found the additional information and explanations provided by Iran in October and November regarding the uranium particles to be 'not technically credible'. In its November report, it argued that 'the presence of multiple uranium particles . . . at a location not declared to the Agency still needs to be fully and promptly explained by Iran'.[29]

The US sanctions on Iran

In 2020 the Trump administration continued to increase sanctions on Iran as part of the 'maximum pressure' policy adopted after the US withdrawal from the JCPOA. The stated objective of the policy was to force Iran to accept a new agreement, with the goal of ending all uranium enrichment in the country and limiting its missile programme and regional activities.[30]

As in 2019, some of the new US sanctions measures directly targeted international nuclear cooperation under the JCPOA. On 29 May 2020 the USA announced that it would revoke the remaining JCPOA-related sanctions waivers, which had enabled international cooperation on redesigning the Arak reactor, the supply of fuel for the TRR, and the export of spent and scrap fuel from that reactor. Two officials of the Atomic Energy Organization of Iran (AEOI) were also added to the Specially Designated Nationals and Blocked Persons List (SDN List) maintained by the US Department of the Treasury.[31]

---

[25] IAEA, GOV/2020/5 (note 9); and IAEA, GOV/2020/26 (note 9).

[26] IAEA, GOV/2020/5 (note 9).

[27] IAEA, Board of Governors, 'NPT safeguards agreement with the Islamic Republic of Iran', Resolution, GOV/2020/34, 19 June 2020, para. 4.

[28] IAEA, 'NPT safeguards agreement with the Islamic Republic of Iran', Report by the Director General, GOV/2020/47, 4 Sep. 2020.

[29] IAEA, GOV/2020/51 (note 9), para. 38.

[30] Erästö, *SIPRI Yearbook 2020* (note 1).

[31] US Department of State, Office of the Spokesperson, 'This week in Iran policy', Fact sheet, 29 May 2020.

Two elements related to UN sanctions on Iran came into play later in the year. UN Security Council resolution 2231, which endorsed the JCPOA and terminated previous UN sanctions related to Iran's nuclear programme, mandated that the conventional arms embargo on Iran would expire on 18 October 2020.[32] In line with the JCPOA, Resolution 2231 also allowed any participant in the agreement, following good-faith efforts to address its compliance concerns, to demand a UN Security Council vote on whether the termination of sanctions on Iran should continue. Given their veto right, in practice this 'snapback clause' meant that any of the five permanent members of the Security Council—China, France, Russia, the UK and the USA (the P5)—could trigger the reimposition of all of the UN sanctions on Iran.[33] In August the Security Council first rejected a resolution drafted by the USA that would have extended the conventional arms embargo on Iran beyond 18 October.[34] In response, on 20 August the USA announced that it would trigger the JCPOA snapback mechanism and claimed that it entered into force one month later, on 20 September.[35]

Reflecting an unprecedented legal controversy within the Security Council, all but one of its other members (the exception being the Dominican Republic) rejected the validity of the US claim on the basis that the snapback mechanism could only be triggered by a JCPOA participant.[36] In a joint statement on 20 September, the E3 argued that the snapback mechanism was 'incapable of having legal effect' as the USA had ceased to be a participant in the JCPOA in 2018.[37] Russia, too, argued that the US measures 'cannot have any effect in terms of international law', stressing that 'Resolution 2231 remains in force, unaltered'.[38] China, for its part, characterized the US claim regarding the sanctions snapback as 'nothing but a political show' that 'receives no support of the Security Council members and no acknowledgment of the international community'.[39] The firm positions of the other JCPOA members arguably contributed to Iran's decision not to respond to

---

[32] Statement by China, France, Germany, Russia, the UK, the USA and the EU, 16 July 2015, annex B of UN Security Council Resolution 2231 (note 1), para. 5. On the arms embargo see also chapter 14, section II, in this volume.

[33] JCPOA (note 1), articles 36–37; and UN Security Council Resolution 2231 (note 1), paras 11–12.

[34] Schwirtz, M., 'UN Security Council rejects US proposal to extend arms embargo on Iran', *New York Times*, 14 Aug. 2020.

[35] Pompeo, M. R., US Secretary of State, 'The return of UN sanctions on the Islamic Republic of Iran', Press statement, US Department of State, 19 Sep. 2020.

[36] 'UN Security Council rejects US demand to "snapback" sanctions on Iran', Deutsche Welle, 26 Aug. 2020.

[37] French Ministry for Europe and Foreign Affairs, 'Iran—JCPOA—Joint statement by the foreign ministers of France, Germany and the United Kingdom', 20 Sep. 2020.

[38] Russian Ministry of Foreign Affairs, 'Foreign Ministry statement on the misleading assertions by the United States on the return of the previously terminated UN Security Council sanctions on Iran', 20 Sep. 2020.

[39] Chinese Permanent Mission to the UN, 'Spokesperson's comment on US demand for snapback on Iran in the Security Council', 20 Aug. 2020.

the US measures. Instead, thanking the other Security Council members for 'supporting Iran', Iran argued that 'the maximum US pressure against the Iranian nation' had 'turned into the maximum isolation of the United States'.[40]

In October the USA imposed sanctions on the remaining 18 Iranian banks which had not previously been so targeted. This prompted European criticism that these measures would further complicate humanitarian trade, which was supposed to be outside the scope of US sanctions.[41]

The role of other JCPOA participants

In 2019 the E3 states established the Instrument in Support of Trade Exchanges (INSTEX) as part of their efforts to save the JCPOA.[42] Its initial objective was to counter US sanctions on Iran's oil exports, but the focus was subsequently reduced to humanitarian trade (e.g. in food and medicine). In principle, humanitarian trade is not covered by US sanctions, but it has nonetheless been affected by them. INSTEX conducted its first pilot transaction in March 2020 but was unable to process further transactions during the year due to US financial sanctions.[43]

While still acknowledging the negative impact of US sanctions on the JCPOA, in 2020 the focus of the E3 increasingly shifted to condemning Iran's breaches of its nuclear commitments. On 14 January the E3 announced that they would trigger the JCPOA dispute resolution mechanism (DRM) in response to Iran's reduced compliance, rejecting the Iranian argument that its actions were in line with the agreement.[44] In July Iran also sought to address through the DRM what it regarded as the E3's failure to implement their JCPOA commitments.[45] Both of these moves were largely symbolic, as the DRM process could ultimately result in the issue being referred to the UN Security Council—an outcome that neither the E3 nor Iran desired since it could have led to a snapback of UN sanctions on Iran.[46] As Russia argued, the DRM 'was created for entirely different purposes', and 'The reasons that led to complications during the implementation of the JCPOA are well-

---

[40] President of Iran, 'President at the cabinet meeting: US' definite defeat in imposing UNSC sanctions made Sep. 20 a memorable day in Iran's diplomacy history', 20 Sep. 2020.

[41] Hudson, J., 'Trump administration imposes crushing sanctions on Iran in defiance of European humanitarian concerns', *Washington Post*, 8 Oct. 2020.

[42] Erästö, *SIPRI Yearbook 2020* (note 1), p. 423.

[43] Norman, L., 'EU ramps up trade system with Iran despite US threats', *Wall Street Journal*, 31 Mar. 2020.

[44] British Government, 'E3 foreign ministers' statement on the JCPoA', Press release, 14 Jan. 2020.

[45] Tasnim News Agency, 'Russia blasts E3 for seeking to launch DRM in Iran deal', 4 July 2020; and Schaart, E., 'EU says Iran has triggered nuclear deal dispute mechanism', Politico, 4 July 2020.

[46] Erästö, T. and Cronberg, T., 'Will Europe's latest move lead to the demise of the Iran nuclear deal?', SIPRI WritePeace Blog, 21 Jan. 2020.

known and are not linked with Iran'.[47] Russia condemned the E3's decisions both to trigger the DRM and to push for the IAEA resolution of 19 June as aggravating the situation.[48] China also criticized these moves by the E3.[49] It stressed that 'the unilateral and bullying practices' of the USA was the root cause of the problem.[50]

In a statement issued on 7 December, the E3 described Iran's plans to install more advanced centrifuges at the Natanz FEP as 'contrary to the JCPOA'.[51] They also expressed concern about a law passed by the Iranian Parliament on 1 December. This law called for further, immediate expansion of Iran's nuclear programme, notably enriching uranium up to 20 per cent, and an end to the implementation of the Additional Protocol within two months if sanctions relief were not provided by then.[52] The legislation had been prompted by the assassination on 27 November of Mohsen Fakhrizadeh, an Iranian nuclear scientist who allegedly played a key role in the country's past nuclear weapon programme.[53]

Looking ahead

The stated intention of the new US president, Joe Biden, to rejoin the JCPOA raised the prospect that the ailing nuclear agreement could still be revived in 2021.[54] The stakes were raised further by growing pressures within Iran to step up its nuclear programme and, more generally, to abandon the moderate policies of Iranian President Hassan Rouhani, which had failed to deliver on promises of sanctions being lifted under the JCPOA. Given the strict deadlines for sanctions relief set by the Iranian Parliament and the Iranian presidential elections scheduled for June 2021, at the end of 2020 there seemed to be only a narrow window of opportunity for Iran and the USA to stop an escalating nuclear crisis by agreeing on the terms for returning to their respective JCPOA commitments.

[47] Russian Ministry of Foreign Affairs, 'Comment by the Information and Press Department on the decision of the United Kingdom, Germany and France to formalize the dispute resolution mechanism under the Joint Comprehensive Plan of Action on the Iranian nuclear programme', 14 Jan. 2020.

[48] Davenport, K., 'IAEA Board presses Iran', *Arms Control Today*, vol. 50, no. 6 (July/Aug. 2020).

[49] 'China regrets Britain, France, Germany's decision to trigger Iran deal dispute mechanism', *Global Times*, 15 Jan. 2020.

[50] Davenport (note 48).

[51] Germany Federal Foreign Office, 'E3 statement on the JCPoA: Response to Iranian plans to expand its nuclear programme and restrict access of IAEA monitoring', Press release, 7 Dec. 2020.

[52] Masterson, J. and Davenport, K., 'Iran passes nuclear law', Arms Control Now blog, Arms Control Association, 10 Dec. 2020; and 'Iran will expel UN nuclear inspectors unless sanctions are lifted: Lawmaker', Reuters, 9 Jan. 2021.

[53] Motamedi, M., 'Iran parliament demands end of nuclear inspections after murder', Al Jazeera, 29 Nov. 2020.

[54] 'Iran Parliament wants nuclear stance hardened after scientist killed', Radio Free Europe/ Radio Liberty, 1 Dec. 2020.

III. Multilateral nuclear arms control, disarmament and non-proliferation treaties and initiatives

TYTTI ERÄSTÖ, SHANNON N. KILE AND VITALY FEDCHENKO

This section reviews the developments that took place in 2020 in three multilateral nuclear arms control, disarmament and non-proliferation treaty frameworks: the 1968 Treaty on the Non-Proliferation of Nuclear Weapons (Non-Proliferation Treaty, NPT), the 2017 Treaty on the Prohibition of Nuclear Weapons (TPNW) and the 1996 Comprehensive Nuclear-Test-Ban Treaty (CTBT). Developments in the Joint Comprehensive Plan of Action (JCPOA) on Iran's nuclear programme are covered in section II. The Covid-19 pandemic complicated procedures during the year, particularly regarding the NPT process. However, it could hardly be blamed for the general deadlock in arms control and disarmament that had persisted for several years.

Postponement of the Non-Proliferation Treaty Review Conference

The states parties of the 1968 Treaty on the Non-Proliferation of Nuclear Weapons meet in quinquennial conferences to review the operation of the treaty.[1] In the years running up to these conferences, a preparatory committee meets to consider procedural and substantive issues and to recommend decisions to the full conference. The 10th Review Conference was initially planned for 27 April–22 May 2020.[2] However, due to the Covid-19 pandemic, the Review Conference was rescheduled, at first until April 2021 and then until August 2021.[3]

The 2020 Review Conference was to have been particularly symbolic, since it would have marked the 50th anniversary of the NPT's entry into force in 1970 and a quarter of a century since the treaty was indefinitely extended in 1995. For the same reason, many welcomed its postponement, as the conference appeared set to fail given the political context that prevailed in 2020.[4] As noted by the president-designate of the 10th Review Conference, Ambassador Gustavo Zlauvinen of Argentina, the NPT was

---

[1] For a summary and other details of the NPT see annex A, section I, in this volume.

[2] On earlier developments see Erästö, T. and Kile, S. N., 'Multilateral nuclear arms control, disarmament and non-proliferation treaties and initiatives', *SIPRI Yearbook 2020*, pp. 427–35.

[3] United Nations, 'Documentation for the NPT Review Conference', ODA-2020-00022, 30 Mar. 2020; and 10th NPT Review Conference, Letter from the president-designate to NPT states parties, 28 Oct. 2020.

[4] Einhorn, B., 'Covid-19 has given the 2020 NPT Review Conference a reprieve. Let's take advantage of it', *Bulletin of the Atomics Scientists*, 13 May 2020; and Pugwash Conferences on Science and World Affairs, 'The postponement of the NPT Review Conference: Antagonisms, conflicts and nuclear risks after the pandemic', 6 May 2020.

facing both internal and external challenges.[5] The former included 'divisions over the pace and scale of nuclear disarmament, and the implementation of commitments given at previous Review Conferences—not least the commitment by nuclear-weapon States to the total elimination of their nuclear arsenals'.[6] As examples of external challenges, Zlauvinen mentioned 'global security conditions defined by poor relations between nuclear-weapon States and the absence of trust and confidence, coupled with the collapse of the nuclear arms control regime and the development of new nuclear weapons systems that are faster, stealthier and more accurate'.[7]

Zlauvinen nevertheless expressed the hope that the hiatus created by the Covid-19 pandemic would provide additional time to find common ground. He sought to facilitate this process by holding consultations with NPT regional groups.[8]

The victory of Joe Biden in the United States presidential election in November raised hopes that the 2010 Russian–US Strategic Arms Reduction Treaty (New START) could still be extended beyond its expiry date in February 2021 and that the JCPOA could be revived (see section II).[9] Many observers believed that preserving these existing agreements would make the political context more favourable for the forthcoming NPT Review Conference. However, at the same time it was recognized that achieving a consensus outcome would likely remain elusive as long as the nuclear weapon states are not seen to be implementing their disarmament commitments under Article VI of the NPT.

Entry into force of the Treaty on the Prohibition of Nuclear Weapons

On 24 October, an important milestone in the development of disarmament norms was reached: Honduras became the 50th state to ratify or accede to the 2017 Treaty on the Prohibition of Nuclear Weapons. As specified by Article 15, this triggered the entry into force of the treaty 90 days later, on 22 January 2021. By 31 December 2020, 51 states had ratified the treaty and an additional 39 states had signed but not yet ratified it.[10]

The TPNW was the result of two rounds of negotiations in 2017 that were based on a United Nations General Assembly decision of December 2016.

---

[5] Zlauvinen, G., President-designate of the 10th NPT Review Conference, Statement at the Oslo Nuclear Forum 2020: Challenges to the NPT, 16 Sep. 2020, p. 3.

[6] Zlauvinen (note 5), p. 3.

[7] Zlauvinen (note 5), p. 4.

[8] Arms Control Association, 'Reviewing the NPT: An interview with Ambassador Gustavo Zlauvinen', *Arms Control Today*, vol. 51, no. 1 (Jan./Feb. 2021).

[9] Council for a Livable World, 'Presidential Candidates: Joe Biden', [n.d.]. For a summary and other details of the 2010 Russian–US Treaty on Measures for the Further Reduction and Limitation of Strategic Offensive Arms (New START) see annex A, section III, in this volume.

[10] For a summary and other details of the TPNW, including lists of the states parties and signatories see annex A, section I, in this volume.

The negotiations built on an initiative that highlighted the catastrophic humanitarian consequences of the use of nuclear weapons and which had gathered pace since the 2010 NPT Review Conference. The TPNW, which draws from existing international law, including humanitarian law, is the first multilateral treaty to establish a comprehensive ban on nuclear weapons, including their development, deployment, possession, use and threat of use.[11]

The TPNW has highlighted the tension between the underlying rationales of nuclear disarmament and deterrence. Its supporters view the TPNW as strengthening Article VI of the NPT and serving the ultimate goal of the complete elimination of nuclear weapons, which they regard as the only guarantee against the unacceptable risk of nuclear weapon use. In contrast, the five NPT-recognized nuclear weapon states (China, France, Russia, the United Kingdom and the USA—the P5) have argued that the TPNW could undermine the NPT as well as international stability based on nuclear deterrence.[12] In line with this view, in December 2020 the members of the North Atlantic Treaty Organization (NATO) issued a joint statement on the TPNW's entry into force. They asserted that they do 'not accept any argument that the ban treaty reflects or in any way contributes to the development of customary international law' and that the 'treaty will not change the legal obligations of our countries with respect to nuclear weapons'.[13]

This controversy has been visible in the voting results of all relevant General Assembly resolutions—including one adopted in December 2020, which calls upon 'all States that have not yet done so to sign, ratify, accept, approve or accede to the [TPNW] at the earliest possible date'.[14] While 130 countries voted in favour of this resolution in November, 42 countries—including all 9 nuclear-armed states and the allies of the USA that rely on its extended nuclear deterrence—cast a negative vote.[15]

The TPNW's entry into force was welcomed by many states and civil society organizations. For example, as he applauded the 50th ratification, the Irish foreign minister, Simon Coveney, argued that 'the support for the Treaty is a clear indication of the will of the majority of countries to add

---

[11] For background see Kile, S. N., 'Treaty on the Prohibition of Nuclear Weapons', *SIPRI Yearbook 2018*, pp. 307–18; and Erästö, T., 'Treaty on the Prohibition of Nuclear Weapons', *SIPRI Yearbook 2019*, pp. 387–90.

[12] Kile (note 11); and Erästö (note 11).

[13] North Atlantic Treaty Organization, 'North Atlantic Council statement as the Treaty on the Prohibition of Nuclear Weapons enters into force', Press release, 15 Dec. 2020, para. 3.

[14] UN General Assembly Resolution 75/40, 'Treaty on the Prohibition of Nuclear Weapons', 7 Dec. 2020, A/RES/75/40, 16 Dec. 2020.

[15] United Nations, 'Treaty on the Prohibition of Nuclear Weapons: Resolution adopted by the General Assembly', Voting data, 7 Dec. 2020; and United Nations, General Assembly, 'General and complete disarmament: Report of the First Committee, Agenda item 103', A/75/399, 16 Nov. 2020.

fresh momentum to achieve the goal of a world free of nuclear weapons'.[16] The president of the International Committee of the Red Cross (ICRC) described the TPNW's entry into force as 'a victory for humanity', arguing that the treaty sets a 'benchmark against which all efforts towards nuclear disarmament and non-proliferation must be judged'.[17] The spokesperson of the UN secretary-general, in turn, characterized the entry into force as 'the culmination of a worldwide movement to draw attention to the catastrophic humanitarian consequences of any use of nuclear weapons'.[18]

While nuclear weapon states continued to oppose the TPNW, some observers detected a slight softening in their tone.[19] Behind the scenes, however, the USA reportedly urged countries that had ratified the treaty to withdraw their ratification, describing it as a 'strategic error'.[20] As before, China seemed more sympathetic to the TPNW than the other nuclear weapon states, arguing that the treaty's objectives were in line with its long-standing nuclear policy.[21] This was despite China's participation in previous joint P5 statements that more clearly opposed the treaty.[22]

The TPNW's role as an established part of international treaty law is likely to inspire further debates about its practical impact. Some observers have argued that the TPNW's comprehensive prohibition of nuclear weapons will eventually become customary international law, even though the five nuclear weapon states that are party to the NPT have explicitly rejected this possibility.[23] As reported by civil society organizations, the treaty has already influenced the behaviour of several financial institutions, which have divested from companies engaged in production of nuclear weapons as a result of the treaty and the related campaigning.[24]

[16] Irish Department of Foreign Affairs, 'Statement by Minister Coveney on the 50th ratification of the Treaty on the Prohibition of Nuclear Weapons', 25 Oct. 2020.

[17] International Committee of the Red Cross (ICRC), 'Statement by ICRC President Peter Maurer on the entry into force of the Treaty on the Prohibition of Nuclear Weapons (TPNW)', 25 Oct. 2020.

[18] United Nations, 'Commending ratification of treaty banning nuclear weapons, secretary-general says entry into force is tribute to test-blast survivors', Press Release, SG/SM/20363, 24 Oct. 2020.

[19] Sauer, T. and Nardon, C., 'The softening rhetoric by nuclear-armed states and NATO allies on the Treaty on the Prohibition of Nuclear Weapons', War on the Rocks, 7 Dec. 2020.

[20] Lederer, E. M., 'US urges countries to withdraw from UN nuke ban treaty', AP News, 22 Oct. 2020.

[21] Kimball, D. G., 'Ban treaty set to enter into force', Arms Control Today, vol. 50, no. 9 (Nov. 2020); and Chinese Mission to the United Nations (@Chinamission2un), 'China has always been advocating complete prohibition and thorough destruction of nuclear weapons, which is fundamentally in line with purposes of #TPNW. China will continuously make relentless efforts towards a nuclear-weapon-free world.', Twitter, 25 Oct. 2020.

[22] E.g. P5 joint statement on the Treaty on the Prohibition of Nuclear Weapons, 24 Oct. 2018.

[23] Rauf, T., 'Does the TPNW contradict or undermine the NPT?', Toda Peace Institute, 22 Nov. 2020.

[24] Snyder, S., 'Nuclear weapons banned, what now for financial institutions?', Don't Bank on the Bomb, PAX, [n.d.].

Controversies related to the Comprehensive Nuclear-Test-Ban Treaty

The 1996 Comprehensive Nuclear-Test-Ban Treaty would prohibit the states parties from conducting 'any nuclear weapon test explosion or any other nuclear explosion' anywhere in the world.[25] Before it can enter into force, the treaty must be ratified by the 44 states named in the treaty's Annex 2, which possessed nuclear power or research reactors when the treaty was negotiated. Eight of these states—China, Egypt, India, Iran, Israel, the Democratic People's Republic of Korea (DPRK, North Korea), Pakistan and the United States—have yet to do so.[26] No new state signed or ratified the treaty in 2020. As of 1 January 2021 the CTBT had been ratified by 168 states and signed by an additional 14 states.

While the CTBT is still not in force, considerable progress has been made on the operational aspects of the treaty by the Preparatory Commission for the Comprehensive Nuclear-Test-Ban Treaty Organization (CTBTO Prep-Com). The CTBTO PrepCom is a plenary body composed of all the treaty's states signatories. It is assisted by a Provisional Technical Secretariat (PTS), which is working to establish the CTBT verification regime. When completed, this will consist of a International Monitoring System (IMS) with 321 seismic, hydroacoustic, infrasound and radionuclide monitoring stations and 16 laboratories around the globe to detect evidence of any nuclear explosion; and an International Data Centre (IDC) to process and analyse the data registered at the monitoring stations and transmit it to member states. As of 1 January 2021, 302 of these 337 facilities were certified operational, a further 9 had been installed, 5 were under construction and 21 were planned.[27] The effectiveness of the IMS has been demonstrated by successful detection of six nuclear tests conducted by North Korea in 2006–17.[28] In addition, the PrepCom continues to develop procedures for on-site inspections (OSIs) to verify whether a nuclear explosion has taken place.[29]

Challenges to multilateralism

Historically, the CTBTO PrepCom's decisions have been taken by consensus. In 2020, however, that consensus was challenged on two occasions, both connected to the elections of the PTS's management.

---

[25] CTBT, Article I(1). For a summary, list of states signatories and other details of the CTBT see annex A, section I, in this volume.

[26] As of 1 Jan. 2021, India, North Korea and Pakistan had not signed the treaty. The other 5 had signed but not ratified the treaty. The most recent Annex 2 state to ratify the treaty was Indonesia, on 6 Feb. 2012.

[27] CTBTO, 'Station profiles', [n.d.].

[28] Fedchenko, V., 'Nuclear explosions, 1945–2017', *SIPRI Yearbook 2018*, 461–69.

[29] E.g. CTBTO, 'Largest-ever CTBT on-site inspection exercise concludes successfully', Press release, 9 Dec. 2014.

The PTS is headed by the executive secretary, who oversees its staff and its annual budget of around US$130 million. The second four-year term of the third executive secretary, Lassina Zerbo of Burkina Faso, was due to end on 31 July 2021. All previous executive secretaries served two consecutive terms: Wolfgang Hoffmann of Germany (1997–2005) and Tibor Tóth of Hungary (2005–13).[30] This corresponds with general good practice across the international organizations of the United Nations system and will be enforced by the CTBT itself when it enters into force.[31]

At the end of the nomination process in October 2020, only one candidate had been nominated: Robert Floyd, director general of the Australian Safeguards and Non-proliferation Office.[32] However, in June 2020 Zerbo had stated that he would be available to serve another term if this were acceptable to the states signatories.[33] This created a controversy among the states signatories, some of which, including Australia, Germany, Italy, Japan, the Netherlands, the United Kingdom and the United States, oppose the third term as a matter of policy. Others, including Russia, consider that a third term could offer continuity during the challenging times of the Covid-19 pandemic and disagreements between nuclear powers.

The states signatories were supposed to discuss the matter on 25–27 November 2020, but the meeting was postponed due to a Covid-19 pandemic-related lockdown in Vienna. No new date for the leadership selection deliberation had been chosen as of December 2020.[34]

The discussions on the choice of executive secretary occurred against the backdrop of another, and possibly more damaging, disagreement in the PrepCom on whether countries with unpaid dues could vote in the election of the executive secretary. According to the resolution establishing the CTBTO PrepCom, states that have not paid their financial contribution within a year of it falling due may not vote in PrepCom decisions.[35] As of July 2020, more than 70 states were in that category, evidently due to the effects of the Covid-19 pandemic. Of these, 29 applied for an exemption due to exceptional circumstances in order to be able to vote in the executive secretary selection

---

[30] Thakur, R., 'Choosing the next overseer of the nuclear-test-ban treaty', The Strategist, Australian Strategic Policy Institute (ASPI), 17 Nov. 2020.

[31] CTBT (note 25), Article 49. After entry into force, the Technical Secretariat of the CTBTO will be headed by a director-general.

[32] Payne, M., Australian Minister for Foreign Affairs, 'Australian candidate nominated to lead the Comprehensive Nuclear-Test Ban Treaty Organisation', Media release, Australian Department of Foreign Affairs and Trade, 18 Sep. 2020.

[33] Kimball, D., 'CTBTO begins leadership selection process', Arms Control Today, vol. 50, no. 8 (Oct. 2020).

[34] Kimball, D., 'Pandemic delays CTBTO leadership vote', Arms Control Today, vol. 50, no. 10 (Dec. 2020).

[35] CTBT Meeting of States Signatories, Resolution establishing the Preparatory Commission for the Comprehensive Nuclear Test-Ban Treaty Organization, adopted 19 Nov. 1996, CTBT/MSS/RES/1, 27 Nov. 1996, para. 5(b).

process. A proposal by the Group of African States that would have allowed all 29 states to vote did not receive the necessary two-thirds majority. A Russian proposal that would have restored voting rights to 15 states that were in partial arrears, had negotiated a payment plan or were engaged in a civil war was opposed by the USA because it would have given voting rights to Iran. The Russian proposal did not receive the necessary majority either, although countries such as France, Germany and Switzerland split from the US position and voted for it. Finally, a Canadian proposal to restore the voting rights of nine states 'dealing with exceptional circumstances' was approved.[36]

This voting process was unique in the 24-year history of the PrepCom, where the decisions are usually taken by consensus. This disunity has been plausibly attributed by commentators to intensifying competition between nuclear powers that has caused an increased politization of discussions in international organizations, including the CTBTO PrepCom.[37]

US allegations of nuclear testing

As in previous years, in 2020 the USA raised questions about whether China and Russia were adhering to their moratoriums on nuclear explosive testing, which is tantamount to questioning their compliance with their commitments under the CTBT.[38] Specifically, a report issued in April by the US Department of State claimed that both countries had engaged in activities that were inconsistent with the 'zero-yield' standard regarding nuclear testing.[39] According to this standard, all nuclear test explosions with any yield exceeding zero are prohibited. It had been established during the negotiation of the CTBT but is not explicitly codified in the treaty itself.[40] Both countries denied the US assertions, which have not been substantiated by publicly available evidence.[41]

---

[36] Kimball, D., 'CTBTO clears path for leadership decision', *Arms Control Today*, vol. 50, no. 9 (Nov. 2020).

[37] Liechtenstein, S., 'Bickering at the nuclear test-ban organization reflects global hardening', PassBlue, 21 Oct. 2020.

[38] On earlier allegations see e.g. Erästö and Kile (note 2), pp. 428–30; and US Department of State, *Adherence to and Compliance with Arms Control, Nonproliferation, and Disarmament Agreements and Commitments* (Department of State: Washington, DC, Aug. 2019), pp. 39–40.

[39] US Department of State, 'Executive summary of findings on adherence to and compliance with arms control, nonproliferation, and disarmament agreements and commitments', Apr. 2020, p. 8. The full report was issued in June. US Department of State, *Adherence to and Compliance with Arms Control, Nonproliferation, and Disarmament Agreements and Commitments* (Department of State: Washington, DC, June 2020), pp. 48–51.

[40] US Department of State, Bureau of Arms Control, Verification, and Compliance, 'Scope of the Comprehensive Nuclear Test-Ban Treaty', Fact sheet, 2013.

[41] Chinese Ministry of Foreign Affairs, 'Foreign Ministry spokesperson Zhao Lijian's regular press conference on April 16, 2020', 16 Apr. 2020; and Russian Ministry of Foreign Affairs, 'Commentary by the Information and Press Department (MFA of Russia) on executive summary of the 2020 Adherence to and Compliance with Arms Control, Nonproliferation, and Disarmament Agreements and Commitments (Compliance Report)—United States Department of State', 23 Apr. 2020.

The US State Department report asserted that certain activities at China's former nuclear testing grounds at Lop Nur 'raise concerns' that China might not be adhering to its nuclear weapon testing moratorium, judged against the zero-yield standard.[42] It mentioned China's 'use of explosive containment chambers' and extensive excavation activities at Lop Nur. It also accused China of 'frequently blocking the flow of data from its [IMS] stations' to the CTBTO IDC.[43] The latter accusation was effectively refuted by the CTBTO.[44] The US report itself concluded that there are 'other, more plausible explanations for China's withholding information from IMS stations' than activities inconsistent with the CTBT.[45]

The US report also repeated the assertion that 'Russia has conducted nuclear weapons experiments that have created nuclear yield and are not consistent with the US "zero-yield" standard'.[46] It did not indicate when or how many low-yield nuclear tests Russia may have carried out, nor did it provide evidence to support the accusation. Some US analysts have concluded that there is probably no evidence that Russia has conducted or is conducting such tests, only that it has long had the capability—along with China and the USA—to do so.[47]

The day after the State Department report was released, the Russian deputy foreign minister, Sergey Ryabkov, responded that 'we repeat once again that we did not take any steps that would include elements of deviation from our obligations stemming from our unilateral moratorium on nuclear testing and from our ratification of the [CTBT]'.[48] Ryabkov stressed that, while Russia had ratified the CTBT in June 2000, the USA had expressed its unwillingness to ratify the treaty and therefore had no right to make accusations on that subject.[49] He also suggested that the latest unsubstantiated allegations from the USA were consistent with repeated US attempts to dismantle existing arms control regimes by accusing Russia

[42] US Department of State, Apr. 2020 (note 39), p. 8.

[43] US Department of State, Apr. 2020 (note 39), p. 8.

[44] Gordon, M. R., 'Possible Chinese nuclear testing stirs US concern', *Wall Street Journal*, 15 Apr. 2020.

[45] US Department of State, June 2020 (note 39), p. 50.

[46] US Department of State, Apr. 2020 (note 39), p. 8.

[47] Borger, J., 'China may have conducted low-level nuclear test, US claims', *The Guardian*, 16 Apr. 2020. See also Sood, R., 'At the edge of a new nuclear arms race', *The Hindu*, 27 Apr. 2020.

[48] 'US may be prepping site in Nevada to test nukes, Russian diplomat warns', TASS, 16 Apr. 2020.

[49] While the USA stated in its 2018 Nuclear Posture Review that it 'will not seek Senate ratification of the [CTBT]', it has made no such formal notification to the treaty depositary and it remains a state signatory. US Department of Defense (DOD), *Nuclear Posture Review* (DOD: Arlington, VA, Feb. 2018), pp. xvii, 63, 72.

and others of violating them, thereby justifying a US withdrawal from the regimes and clearing the way for a US nuclear arms build-up.[50]

In response to the US State Department report, a spokesperson for the Chinese Ministry of Foreign Affairs stated that China fully 'supports the purpose and objective of the treaty, stays committed to the nuclear testing moratorium, and has made important contribution to the work of the [CTBTO]'.[51] He noted that the 'data transmission of the monitoring stations in China has been highly commended by the [CTBTO PTS]' and added that 'In disregard of facts and driven by ulterior motives, the US is leveling irresponsible and groundless allegations against China'.[52]

US consideration of a resumption in nuclear testing

According to a US media report, during an inter-agency meeting in mid May 2020 senior US national security officials had discussed the option of conducting a so-called demonstration nuclear explosion.[53] This would be the first US nuclear explosive test since 1992 and would mark a reversal from a decades-long freeze on such tests. The proposal followed the US allegations that China and Russia had conducted low-yield tests and at a time when the US administration was trying to extend Russian–US arms control negotiations to include China (see section I). Some of the participants in the discussion had reportedly asserted that a US demonstration of the ability to conduct a 'rapid test' could give the USA leverage in these negotiations. The meeting did not conclude with any decision about whether to carry out such a test, with the officials reported to be in serious disagreement over the idea.[54]

The news reports about the discussion elicited criticism and condemnation from governments, civil society groups and international organizations. The CTBTO Group of Eminent Persons issued a statement expressing 'deep concern' about the reports. The group warned that a demonstration nuclear test explosion would, if carried out, 'break the global moratorium on nuclear weapon test explosions and severely undermine the [CTBT] regime'.[55]

From the technical perspective, the process of conducting a 'rapid test' would be slow and difficult. The 1993 presidential directive on the US

[50] TASS (note 48). On the US withdrawal from the Treaty on Open Skies see chapter 13, section V, in this volume. On the US withdrawal from the Intermediate-range Nuclear Forces (INF) Treaty see Topychkanov, P. and Davis, I., 'Russian–United States nuclear arms control and disarmament', *SIPRI Yearbook 2020*, pp. 399–409.

[51] Chinese Ministry of Foreign Affairs (note 41).

[52] Chinese Ministry of Foreign Affairs (note 41).

[53] Hudson, J. and Sonne, P., 'Trump administration discussed conducting first US nuclear test in decades', *Washington Post*, 23 May 2020.

[54] Hudson and Sonne (note 53).

[55] CTBTO, 'Members of CTBTO Group of Eminent Persons warn against any demonstration nuclear test explosion', Press release, 29 May 2020.

nuclear moratorium mandates the US Department of Energy to maintain a capability to conduct a nuclear test within 2–3 years.[56] In June 2020 the US Senate Armed Services Committee approved an amendment to the 2021 budget to authorize $10 million specifically for a potential nuclear test.[57] But, even if the decision to conduct a 'rapid test' were to have been taken in mid 2020, the necessary preparations would likely have taken until 2022 or 2023.

The 1974 Threshold Test-Ban Treaty (TTBT) prohibits the USA from conducting nuclear tests with a yield exceeding 150 kilotons.[58] This limits the choice of warhead designs in the US arsenal available for testing.[59] In addition, under the 1963 Partial Test-Ban Treaty (PTBT), a hypothetical nuclear test could only be conducted underground.[60] In practical terms, this means at the Nevada Test Site (NTS). Experts with direct experience of nuclear weapon testing have pointed out multiple complications associated with testing at the NTS. These include its location in proximity to the Las Vegas metropolitan area, the significantly diminished readiness of the public to tolerate risks of venting of radioactivity into the atmosphere, the increased risks of seismic effects on high-rise buildings, and a failure to preserve knowledge and expertise on nuclear testing.[61]

By the end of the year, it seemed unlikely that the USA would conduct any such a test.

---

[56] White House, 'US policy on stockpile stewardship under an extended moratorium and a comprehensive test ban', Presidential Decision Directive/NSC-15, 3 Nov. 1993, p. 5. See also Nikitin M. B. D. and Woolf, A. F., 'US nuclear weapons tests', In Focus no. IF11662, US Congress, Congressional Research Service, 4 Dec. 2020.

[57] Kimball, D., 'Nuclear testing, never again', *Arms Control Today*, vol. 50, no. 6 (July/Aug. 2020).

[58] For a summary and other details of the 1974 Soviet–US Treaty on the Limitation of Underground Nuclear Weapon Tests (Threshold Test-Ban Treaty, TTBT) see annex A, section III, in this volume.

[59] On the US nuclear weapon stockpile see chapter 10, section I, in this volume.

[60] For a summary and other details of the 1963 Treaty Banning Nuclear Weapon Tests in the Atmosphere, in Outer Space and Under Water (Partial Test-Ban Treaty, PTBT) see annex A, section I, in this volume.

[61] Hopkins, J. C., 'Nuclear test readiness: What is needed? Why?', *National Security Science*, Dec. 2016, pp. 9–15; and Kelley, R., 'Trump and Senator Cotton embrace enhanced testing & face kilotons of surprises', IDN-InDepthNews, 14 July 2020.

12. Chemical and biological security threats

Overview

In 2020 the Covid-19 pandemic changed the world in a way that very few had anticipated. Section I outlines the timeline of the pandemic; the impacts on people's health and on society; competing theories on the origin of the virus; studies into the origins; and its implications for global biosecurity architecture. By the end of 2020, the World Health Organization (WHO) had received reports of over 82 million cases of Covid-19 worldwide, and there had been over 1.8 million recorded deaths. The actual number of infections and recorded deaths were likely to be considerably higher from undiagnosed cases and generally poor Covid-19-related data. The pandemic's global socio-economic impacts were at levels unprecedented since World War II.

According to the state of knowledge at the end of 2020 about Covid-19 and its origin, it was generally thought to be a natural disease outbreak, first detected in Wuhan, China, on the last day of 2019, although very little was known about how, where and when it started circulating. While the 'natural spillover' theory appeared to be the most convincing, a more marginal theory held that the virus could have originated from a research-related incident. Identifying the source of the disease should have been a routine scientific matter; instead it became highly politicized. China in particular made significant attempts to control the pandemic origins narrative, including efforts to stifle the research-related accident theory. In May 2020, the WHO was tasked with trying to establish the origin of the virus, with a WHO-led international mission to be deployed to China in early 2021.

The Covid-19 pandemic, and its public and socio-economic impacts, also threw into sharp relief a problem faced by all governments: how to successfully predict and prepare for biosecurity-related threats to citizens and to national and international security. The biological threat spectrum is complex and evolving, and includes natural disease outbreaks, the unintended consequences of laboratory accidents, the intentional use of disease as a weapon, and now, arguably, biological information warfare.

The pandemic also significantly impacted the functioning of key biological disarmament and non-proliferation activities in 2020, as discussed in section II. Intersessional meetings of experts and the meeting of states parties under the 1972 Biological and Toxin Weapons Convention (BWC) were postponed until 2021. Nonetheless, some significant BWC-related activities and developments still took place during 2020. These included the 45th anniversary of the BWC's entry into force, a United Nations Security Council open debate on pandemics and security in July 2020, and a new controversial UN General Assembly draft resolution on the UN Secretary-General's Mechanism (UNSGM) for investigating allegations of use of chemical and biological weapons.

The introduction of the UNSGM resolution by Russia was consistent with other efforts by a handful of actors, including misinformation and disinformation campaigns, to stop, hinder, undermine and contest the authority and work of investigation teams within the Organisation for the Prohibition of Chemical Weapons (OPCW) and the UN. The Syrian chemical weapons investigations that continued in 2020 (see section III), as well as other experiences, point to investigations becoming more contentious, complex and important. Divisions were also evident in the UN Security Council meetings on Syria and chemical weapons in 2020.

Outside of Syria, there were further developments in 2020 related to toxic chemicals from the novichok group of nerve agents, covered in section IV. These included the entry into force of the technical changes to Schedule 1 of chemicals in the 1993 Chemical Weapons Convention (CWC) and a new instance of alleged use in the poisoning of Alexei Navalny. The OPCW confirmed that a cholinesterase inhibitor from the novichok group was used to poison Navalny, although it was a type not listed in the Schedule.

The pandemic caused the postponement of routine and other inspections by the OPCW Technical Secretariat throughout 2020, as discussed in section V. The main conference of the year, the 25th Session of the Conference of the States Parties (CSP) to the CWC, did go ahead in an adapted format, but with a second part scheduled for 2021. Political divisions were again evident at the CSP and in OPCW Executive Council meetings, especially over the draft programme and budget, as well as efforts to address the threat from chemicals that act on the central nervous system. As of 30 November 2020, 98.3 per cent of declared Category 1 chemical weapons had been destroyed under international verification. The United States remains the only declared possessor state party with chemical weapons yet to be destroyed, but is expected to complete its remaining destruction activities within the current timelines.

FILIPPA LENTZOS AND CAITRÍONA MCLEISH

I. The unfolding Covid-19 pandemic

FILIPPA LENTZOS

Milestones of the pandemic in 2020

On 31 December 2019, the Country Office of the World Health Organization (WHO) in China picked up a media statement on the Wuhan Municipal Health Commission website reporting cases of 'viral pneumonia' in Wuhan. The Country Office notified the International Health Regulations (IHR) focal point in the WHO Western Pacific Regional Office about the media statement. On the same day, the WHO's Epidemic Intelligence from Open Sources (EIOS) platform also picked up a media report on ProMED (a programme of the International Society for Infectious Diseases) about the same cluster of cases in Wuhan. Several health authorities from around the world contacted the WHO seeking additional information. The following day, the WHO requested information on the reported cluster of atypical pneumonia cases from the Chinese authorities. On 2 January 2020, the WHO representative in China wrote to the National Health Commission of China, offering WHO support and repeating the request for further information on the cluster of cases. The WHO also informed its sister United Nations agencies, international organizations, major public health agencies and laboratories, which are all part of its Global Outbreak Alert and Response Network (GOARN), about the atypical pneumonia cases.[1]

On 3 January 2020, Chinese officials confirmed to the WHO that a cluster of cases of 'viral pneumonia of unknown cause' had been identified in Wuhan. The WHO notified its member states about the cluster through the IHR Event Information System and advised them to take precautions to reduce the risk of acute respiratory infections. The WHO issued a web-based Disease Outbreak News report on 5 January 2020 to notify the scientific and public health communities, as well as global media. The report contained information about the number of cases and their clinical status; details about the Wuhan national authority's response measures; and the WHO's risk assessment and advice on public health measures.[2]

On 9 January 2020, the WHO reported that the Chinese authorities had determined the outbreak was caused by a novel coronavirus, and, two days later, the WHO received the genetic sequences of the new virus from the Chinese authorities.[3] The first death from the novel coronavirus was

---

[1] World Health Organization (WHO), 'Listings of WHO's response to Covid-19', News, 29 June 2020, entries 31 Dec. 2019, 1 Jan. 2020 and 2 Jan. 2020.

[2] WHO (note 1), entries 3, 4 and 5 Jan. 2020.

[3] WHO, 'WHO statement regarding cluster of pneumonia cases in Wuhan, China', News, 9 Jan. 2020; and WHO (@WHO), Twitter, 11 Jan. 2020, <https://twitter.com/WHO/status/1216108498188230657>.

reported on 11 January 2020 by Chinese media. The first recorded case of lab-confirmed novel coronavirus from Wuhan outside of China was reported by the Ministry of Public Health in Thailand on 13 January 2020.[4] Human-to-human transmission had initially been denied by Chinese officials, but on 19 January 2020 the WHO Western Pacific Regional Office tweeted that, according to the latest information received and WHO analysis, there was evidence of limited human-to-human transmission.[5]

On 20–21 January 2020, the WHO conducted its first mission to Wuhan. The team met with officials to learn about the public health response to the novel coronavirus cases and visited sites like the Wuhan Tianhe Airport and the Hubei provincial Center for Disease Control in Wuhan (Wuhan CDC). The team concluded that the evidence suggested human-to-human transmission in Wuhan, but that more investigation was needed to understand the full extent of transmission.[6] Chinese authorities placed Wuhan under quarantine on 23 January 2020 and started construction on two new hospitals.[7]

Shortly after, the WHO director-general convened an IHR Emergency Committee comprising 15 independent experts from around the world. The committee was charged with advising the director-general on whether the outbreak constituted a public health emergency of international concern (PHEIC), the WHO's highest level of alarm. When the committee met, on 22 January 2020, it was unable to reach a unanimous conclusion. Several members considered there was simply not enough information available to decide whether the outbreak constituted a PHEIC. The director-general asked the committee to continue its deliberations the next day but it remained equally divided on 23 January 2020, and recommended reconvening within 10 days.[8]

On 27–28 January 2020, a senior WHO delegation led by the director-general arrived in Beijing to meet Chinese leaders, including President Xi Jinping, to learn more about the response in China and to offer technical assistance. The director-general and the Chinese president agreed that an international team of leading scientists should travel to China to better understand the context and the overall response, as well as to exchange information and experiences.[9]

---

[4] WHO, 'WHO statement on novel coronavirus in Thailand', News, 13 Jan. 2020.

[5] WHO Western Pacific Regional Office (@WHOWPRO), Twitter, 19 Jan. 2020, <https://twitter.com/WHOWPRO/status/1218741294291308545>.

[6] WHO, 'Mission summary: WHO field visit to Wuhan, China 20–21 Jan. 2020', News, 22 Jan. 2020.

[7] Chinese National Health Commission, 'Wuhan pulls through the worst, with a tough lockdown', Media release, 24 Mar. 2020; and 'Coronavirus: The hospital built in a matter of days', BBC News, 2 Feb. 2020.

[8] WHO (note 1), entry 22–23 Jan. 2020.

[9] WHO (note 1), entry 27–28 Jan. 2020.

On 30 January 2020, the director-general reconvened the IHR Emergency Committee, which advised the director-general that the outbreak now met the criteria for a PHEIC. The director-general accepted the committee's advice and declared the novel coronavirus outbreak a PHEIC.[10] At that time, there were 98 recorded cases in 18 countries outside China, but no recorded deaths. Four countries (Germany, Japan, the United States and Viet Nam) had evidence (eight cases) of human-to-human transmission outside China.[11]

As the recorded death toll in China surpassed that of the 2002–2003 epidemic of severe acute respiratory syndrome (SARS), and the infections spread to 24 countries, the WHO received final sign-off from China on 9 February 2020 for a WHO–China Joint Mission, and deployed an advance team. The team completed five days of preparation, working with China's National Health Commission, the Chinese Center for Disease Control and Prevention, local partners and related entities, and the WHO China Country Office.[12]

The disease is named Covid-19

The WHO announced on 11 February 2020 that the disease caused by the novel coronavirus would be named coronavirus disease 2019 (Covid-19).[13] The name of the disease was chosen to avoid inaccuracy and stigma, and therefore did not refer to a geographical location, an animal, an individual or a group of people, in accordance with best practice. On the same day, the International Committee on Taxonomy of Viruses announced the name of the new virus to be 'severe acute respiratory syndrome coronavirus 2 (SARS-CoV-2)' to reflect its close genetic relationship to the coronavirus responsible for the SARS outbreak of 2002–2003.[14]

Highlighting the unprecedented prevalence of information—including misinformation and disinformation—surrounding the unfolding pandemic, at the Munich Security Conference on 15 February 2020 the WHO director-general declared: 'We're not just fighting an epidemic; we're fighting an infodemic.'[15] In response the WHO launched a new information platform called WHO Information Network for Epidemics (EPI-WIN), which uses an 'amplification network' to share tailored information with specific target groups.[16]

---

[10] Ghebreyesus, T. A., 'WHO director-general's statement on IHR emergency committee on novel coronavirus', Speech, 30 Jan. 2020.

[11] WHO (note 1), entry 30 Jan. 2020.

[12] WHO (note 1), entry 9 Feb. 2020.

[13] WHO (@WHO), Twitter, 11 Feb. 2020, <https://twitter.com/WHO/status/1227248333871173632>.

[14] WHO, 'Naming the coronavirus disease (Covid-19) and the virus that causes it', WHO Technical Guidance, [n.d.].

[15] WHO Director-General, Speech to the Munich Security Conference, 15 Feb. 2020.

[16] WHO, 'About EPI-WIN', [n.d.].

Teams from the WHO–China Joint Mission initiated on 16 February 2020 completed field visits to Beijing, Guangdong, Sichuan and Wuhan to assess the seriousness of the new disease, its transmission dynamics, and the nature and impact of China's control measures.[17]

On 7 March 2020, the number of confirmed Covid-19 cases surpassed 100 000 globally.[18] On 8 March 2020, Italy placed its 60 million citizens on lockdown. Many more countries followed suit. In April 2020, more than half of the world's population resided in countries enforcing a lockdown, resulting in hugely disruptive impacts on individuals, businesses and entire sectors of society.[19]

The international response: Dealing with a pandemic and an infodemic

On 11 March 2020, the WHO characterized the Covid-19 outbreak as a pandemic.[20] By that time the epicentre of the pandemic was Europe, which had more reported cases and deaths 'than the rest of the world combined, apart from China'.[21] On 13 March 2020, the WHO, the UN Foundation and partners launched the Covid-19 Solidarity Response Fund, raising more than US$70 million in 10 days to assist health workers on the pandemic's frontlines, treat patients, and advance research for treatments and vaccines.[22]

On 23 March 2020, the UN secretary-general appealed for an immediate global ceasefire, in an attempt to reduce the effect of conflict on the pandemic.[23] His call was supported by over 100 governments, as well as regional organizations, leaders, civil society groups and some armed groups.[24]

The UN Global Humanitarian Response Plan was launched on 25 March 2020 by the WHO director-general, the UN secretary-general, the UN under-secretary-general for humanitarian affairs and the executive director of the United Nations International Children's Emergency Fund (UNICEF).[25] By 4 April 2020, over 1 million cases of Covid-19 had been confirmed worldwide, a more than tenfold increase in less than a month.[26] The WHO soon after

---

[17] WHO–China Joint Mission, *Report of the WHO–China Joint Mission on Coronavirus Disease 2019 (Covid-19)* (WHO: Geneva, 16–24 Feb. 2020).

[18] WHO, 'WHO statement on cases of Covid-19 surpassing 100 000', News, 7 Mar. 2020.

[19] Committee for the Coordination of Statistical Activities (CCSA), *How Covid-19 Is Changing the World: A Statistical Perspective* (CCSA: 13 May 2020).

[20] WHO Director-General, 'WHO director-general's opening remarks at the media briefing on Covid-19', Speech, 11 Mar. 2020.

[21] WHO Director-General, 'WHO director-general's opening remarks at the media briefing on Covid-19', Speech, 13 Mar. 2020.

[22] WHO, 'Covid-19 solidarity response fund', [n.d.].

[23] UN Secretary-General, 'Secretary-general's appeal for global ceasefire', Statement, 23 Mar. 2020.

[24] On the call for a global ceasefire see chapter 2, section I, in this volume.

[25] United Nations, Office for the Coordination of Humanitarian Affairs (OCHA), *Global Humanitarian Response Plan: Covid-19* (OCHA: Geneva, 28 Mar. 2020).

[26] WHO, 'Coronavirus disease 2019 (Covid-19)', Situation Report no. 75, 4 Apr. 2020.

convened an ad hoc technical consultation on managing the Covid-19 infodemic, with over 1300 field experts participating in the online webinars held on 7–8 April.[27]

The 73rd World Health Assembly, the first ever to be held virtually, took place on 18–19 May 2020. It generated significant attention, with 14 heads of state participating in the opening and closing sessions. The meeting adopted by consensus a landmark resolution—co-sponsored by more than 130 countries, the largest number on record—to fight the pandemic.[28] Among other actions, the resolution requested the WHO director-general, working with other organizations and countries, 'to identify the zoonotic source of the virus and the route of introduction to the human population'.[29] By the end of June 2020, over 10 million confirmed Covid-19 cases, including over 500 000 deaths, had been reported to the WHO.[30]

On 30 June to 16 July, the WHO hosted its first infodemiology conference, with four objectives: understanding the multidisciplinary nature of infodemic management; identifying current examples and tools to understand, measure and control infodemics; building a public health research agenda to direct focus and investment; and establishing a community of practice and research.[31]

At a side event of the 75th UN General Assembly, held virtually from 15 September to 2 October 2020, the WHO emphasized the need for mitigating the impact of Covid-19 on future generations, stopping the spread of harmful misinformation, and better emergency preparedness.[32] The WHO, the UN, UNICEF, the UN Development Programme, the UN Educational, Scientific and Cultural Organization (UNESCO) and others issued a joint statement on 23 September 2020 that highlighted the Covid-19 infodemic and the need to promote healthy behaviours and mitigate harm from misinformation and disinformation.[33]

By the end of September 2020, global deaths reported to the WHO had passed 1 million.[34]

---

[27] WHO, 'WHO ad-hoc online consultation on managing the Covid-19 infodemic', [n.d.]; and WHO, *Managing the Covid-19 Infodemic: Call for Action* (WHO: Geneva, 15 Sep. 2020).

[28] WHO, 'Historic health assembly ends with global commitment to Covid-19 response', News, 19 May 2020; and 73rd World Health Assembly, 'Covid-19 response', WHA73.1, 19 May 2020.

[29] 73rd World Health Assembly (note 28), para. 9(6).

[30] WHO, 'WHO coronavirus disease (Covid-19) dashboard', [n.d.].

[31] WHO, '1st WHO infodemiology conference', [n.d.].

[32] WHO, 'UNGA virtual high-level side event on mitigating the impact of Covid-19', News, 23 Sep. 2020; WHO, 'Covid-19 pandemic: Countries urged to take stronger action to stop spread of harmful information', News, 23 Sep. 2020; and WHO, 'The best time to prevent the next pandemic is now: Countries join voices for better emergency preparedness', News, 1 Oct. 2020.

[33] WHO et al., 'Managing the Covid-19 infodemic: Promoting healthy behaviours and mitigating the harm from misinformation and disinformation', Joint Statement, 23 Sep. 2020.

[34] WHO (note 30).

Development of a vaccine for Covid-19 began early in 2020, and by the second half of the year, several vaccines were in different stages of clinical trials. By year's end, several countries had started inoculation programmes including Canada, China, Israel, Russia, the United Kingdom, the USA and several European countries.

The worst global crisis since World War II

Health and mortality impacts

By the end of 2020, the WHO had received reports of over 82 million cases of Covid-19 worldwide, with the actual number of infections likely to be considerably higher from undiagnosed cases and generally poor Covid-19-related data. As of 31 December 2020, there were over 35 million reported cases in the Americas, over 27 million in Europe, nearly 12 million in South East Asia, nearly 5 million in the Eastern Mediterranean, nearly 2 million in Africa, and just over 1 million in the Western Pacific. The five countries with the highest cumulative number of cases were, in descending order, the USA, India, Brazil, France and the UK.[35]

As of 31 December 2020, Covid-19 had caused over 1.8 million recorded deaths, with many hundreds of thousands likely to have gone unrecorded. Deaths reported in the Americas numbered over 855 000, in Europe over 579 000, in South East Asia over 183 000, in the Eastern Mediterranean over 120 000, in Africa over 42 000 and in the Western Pacific over 20 000. The five countries with the highest cumulative number of deaths were, again in descending order, the USA, Brazil, India, Mexico and Italy.[36] In the USA, by April 2020 the number of recorded deaths had already outstripped the number of names on the Vietnam War Memorial in Washington, DC.[37] By December, the average daily number of Americans dying of Covid-19 was 2379—comparable to the 2403 who died in Pearl Harbor on 7 December 1941 and the 2977 who died in the terrorist attacks on 11 September 2001.[38]

The impact of Covid-19 goes beyond its high fatality rates: many survivors of the disease have continued to suffer significant health consequences. These lasting health effects, referred to as 'long Covid', are so far poorly understood.[39]

[35] WHO (note 30).
[36] WHO (note 30).
[37] 'The origin of Covid-19: The pieces of the puzzle of Covid-19's origin are coming to light', *The Economist*, 29 Apr. 2020.
[38] Yong, E., 'Where year two of the pandemic will take us', *The Atlantic*, 29 Dec. 2020.
[39] Yong, E., 'Covid-19 can last for several months', *The Atlantic*, 4 June 2020.

Political, social and economic impacts

The pandemic's global socio-economic impacts are at levels unprecedented since the World War II. World economic output was at least 7 per cent lower than it would otherwise have been—the biggest slump since the 1940s.[40] At least 225 million full-time jobs disappeared worldwide because of the pandemic, losses not only significantly worse than those of the global financial crisis in 2009 but also worse than those of the great depression of the 1930s.[41] Among industries, aviation and tourism have been the biggest losers with border closures and quarantine restricting travel. But there were also economic winners. The combined wealth of the world's 10 richest people grew by 57 per cent, to $1.14 trillion, and the MSCI index of world stock markets rose by 11 per cent.[42] The pandemic also exposed and exacerbated long-standing economic, racial and gender divides.[43] Many of these socio-economic effects are highly likely to generate further health effects beyond the direct impacts of Covid-19.

The Covid-19 pandemic also saw unparalleled policies introduced all over the globe of 'locking down' cities and even entire countries, curtailing freedom of movement for millions of people. Technologies combining computing power, algorithms and biological data were used to monitor individuals and control populations at unmatched scales and levels of invasiveness.[44] Technologies adopted by several countries included surveillance cameras with facial recognition to track quarantine evaders or to gauge elevated temperatures of potentially infected individuals in crowds; fine-grained location data transmitted from mobile phones to determine the numbers and identities of people obeying lockdown orders; algorithms to monitor social media posts for signs of disease spread; and contact-tracing apps that centrally stored user interactions to provide 'social graphs' of individuals. A key question in the post Covid-19 world will be whether governments de-escalate their powers of personalized surveillance or keep them in place for 'public protection'.

---

[40] 'The year when everything changed', *The Economist*, 19 Dec. 2020.

[41] International Labour Organization (ILO), ILO Monitor: COVID-19 and the World of Work, Briefing notes, 7th ed. (ILO: Geneva, 25 Jan. 2021), p. 20.

[42] Oxfam International, 'Mega-rich recoup Covid-losses in record-time yet billions will live in poverty for at least a decade', Press release, 25 Jan. 2021; and *The Economist* (note 40).

[43] See e.g. *The Economist* (note 40); Oxfam International, *The Inequality Virus: Bringing Together a World Torn Apart by Coronavirus through a Fair, Just and Sustainable Economy*, Oxfam Briefing Paper (Oxfam GB: Oxford, Jan. 2021); and UN Women, 'The shadow pandemic: Violence against women during Covid-19', [n.d.].

[44] See e.g. Lentzos, F., 'How to protect the world from ultra-targeted biological weapons', *Bulletin of the Atomic Scientists*, 7 Dec. 2020; Xinmei, S., 'Neighborhood sends drone to check people's temperature at their windows', China Tech City, 14 Feb. 2020; Rahim, A. A., 'AR smart glasses can help mitigate Covid-19 resurgence in China', Techwire Asia, 1 Apr. 2020; and Mozus, P., Zhong, R. and Krolik, A., 'In coronavirus fight, China gives citizens a color code, with red flags', *New York Times*, 1 Mar. 2020.

Theories on the origins of SARS-CoV-2

One of the critical questions of the pandemic is where the novel coronavirus came from. Identifying the source of SARS-CoV-2 is essential for ensuring it is not reintroduced to the human population and for reducing the risk of other new virus introductions in the future. However, what should have been a routine science question has instead become politically charged.[45]

The 'natural spillover' theory

At the time of writing very little was known about how, where and when SARS-CoV-2 started circulating in Wuhan. Some evidence can be found in the genetic makeup of the virus, which indicates that it is closely related to coronaviruses isolated from bat populations.[46] However, because there is usually very limited close contact between humans and bats to enable direct transmission, the leading scientific theory was that transmission happened through an intermediate animal host, such as a domestic animal, a wild animal or a domesticated wild animal. As at the end of 2020, however, this host had not been identified.

There is precedent for 'spillover' through intermediate hosts. The first known coronavirus to have caused serious illness in humans, SARS-CoV, likely also had its ecological reservoir in bats, jumping from bats to civet cats (a farmed wild animal), and from there to humans, where it started spreading. The virus caused the SARS outbreak in 2002–2003 and killed over 800 people around the world before it was brought under control.[47] Emerging in 2012, Middle Eastern respiratory syndrome (MERS) was found to be caused by a coronavirus (MERS-CoV) that spread from bats into camels and then humans.[48] By the end of 2020 MERS-CoV had killed over 880 people; it has not yet been eliminated and regularly passes from camels to humans, making it harder to eradicate, but it only spreads in conditions of close proximity, which makes it more manageable.[49]

One of the early theories for SARS-CoV-2 was that pangolins could have served as the intermediate host for the virus. Later susceptibility studies with SARS-CoV-2 showed that domestic cats, ferrets, hamsters and minks are particularly susceptible to infection, and that any one of these could have served as intermediate hosts—or that they could establish reservoirs

---

[45] Huang, Y., 'How the origins of Covid-19 became politicized', Think Global Health, 14 Aug. 2020.

[46] Calisher, C. et al., 'Statement in support of the scientists, public health professionals, and medical professionals of China combatting Covid-19', The Lancet, vol. 395, no. 10226, E42–E43 (7 Mar. 2020); and Andersen, K. G. et al., 'The proximal origin of SARS-CoV-2', Nature Medicine, vol. 26 (2020).

[47] WHO, 'Severe acute respiratory syndrome', [n.d.]; and WHO, 'WHO cumulative number of reported cases of SARS', [n.d.].

[48] WHO, 'Middle East respiratory syndrome coronavirus (MERS-CoV)', [n.d.].

[49] WHO, 'MERS situation update, December 2020', Dec. 2020.

for the virus and provide new sources for 'spillover' events into the human population. No source reservoir had been positively identified by the end of 2020, and there was no evidence to demonstrate the possible route of transmission from a bat reservoir to humans through one or several intermediary animals.[50]

The published genetic sequences of SARS-CoV-2 isolated from early human cases are very similar, suggesting that the start of the outbreak resulted from a single point of introduction in the human population around the time that the virus was first reported in humans in Wuhan.[51] In other words, the evidence suggests the virus jumped from an intermediate species (or, less likely, directly from a bat) only once.

The genetic sequences also indicate that SARS-CoV-2 is genetically stable and already well adapted to human cell receptors, which enables it to invade human cells and easily infect people. Researchers have found that the virus resembles SARS-CoV in the late phase of the 2003 epidemic after SARS-CoV had developed several advantageous adaptations for human transmission.[52] That the virus was already pre-adapted to human transmission was considered 'surprising', particularly since no precursors or intermediate evolutionary versions stemming from a less human-adapted SARS-CoV-2-like virus had been detected.[53] The findings, which were noted in the terms of reference for a joint WHO–China 'global study on the origins of SARS-CoV-2' (described below), suggest the virus could have circulated undetected in people for months while accumulating adaptive mutations.[54] Available evidence suggests this is unlikely, however, leaving only two other possible explanations: that the virus was already highly adept at human transmission while in bats or another animal, or that it had become adapted in human cells or humanized animals—that is, research animals carrying functioning human genes, cells, tissues or organs—in a laboratory.[55]

Epidemiological research on the initial cases of Covid-19 reported in late December 2019 and early January 2020 also provides clues to the origins of the virus. Early work indicated that a large proportion (28/41) of the cases had a direct link to the Huanan Wholesale Seafood Market in Wuhan—a large market with 653 stalls and more than 1180 employees where mainly seafood, but also fresh fruits and vegetables, meat and live animals (farmed,

---

[50] World Organisation for Animal Health (OIE), 'Questions and answers on Covid-19', Updated 22 Jan. 2021.

[51] WHO, 'Origins of SARS-CoV-2', 26 Mar. 2020.

[52] Zhan, S. H., Deverman, B. E. and Chan, Y. A., 'SARS-CoV-2 is well adapted for humans: What does this mean for re-emergence?' (Pre-print article), bioRxiv, 2 May 2020.

[53] Zhan et al. (note 52), p. 9.

[54] WHO, 'WHO-convened global study of the origins of SARS-CoV-2: Terms of references for the China part', 5 Nov. 2020, p. 3.

[55] Ridley, M. and Chan, A., 'Did the Covid-19 virus really escape from a Wuhan lab?', Matt Ridley Blog, 7 Feb. 2021.

wild and domestic) were sold.[56] Many of the initial patients were either stall owners, market employees or regular visitors to the market. Out of 842 environmental samples taken after the market was closed down on 1 January 2020, 69 (8 per cent) tested positive for SARS-CoV-2. Of those, 61 (88 per cent) were from the western wing of the market, with 22 samples from eight different drains and sewage systems. The virus samples collected at the market were 'virtually identical' to the patient samples collected at the same time.[57] However, none of the 336 animal samples collected from the market was positive for SARS-CoV-2. The data suggests either an animal source in the market or an infected human could have introduced the virus to the market, and the virus may then have been amplified in the market environment.[58]

A significant number (13/41, or 32 per cent) of the first cases, however, had no contact whatsoever with the market, including the first recorded person to present with the disease, indicating there might be another, unidentified, source of the outbreak.[59] Reviews by China of possible earlier cases confirmed there were 124 cases presented in December 2019, including 119 from Wuhan and 5 from Hubei or other provinces who had 'travel links to Wuhan during the period of exposure'.[60] That means it is likely these early cases were exposed through contact with other undetected cases as early as November 2019 (incubation time from exposure to symptom onset being up to 14 days). It also seems likely there were early infections which were not serious and which did not reach hospitals, before the first official cases were seen in Wuhan in December. Epidemiological studies into early, unrecognized infections were ongoing at the end of December 2020.

The research-related accident theory

A competing (if still marginal) origin theory to the 'natural spillover' theory is that the source of the initial outbreak could be related to safety lapses in the course of scientific research with coronaviruses. There was, as of December 2020, no solid evidence for this, but the genetic and epidemiological evidence collected so far did not exclude the possibility.

At least two institutions in Wuhan work on coronaviruses: the Wuhan CDC and the Wuhan Institute of Virology (WIV). The WIV houses several laboratory complexes, including the National Biosafety Laboratory, the first biosafety level four (BSL-4) laboratory in mainland China. Conceived following the 2002–2003 SARS outbreak, the laboratory was physically

---

[56] Huang, C. et al., 'Clinical features of patients infected with 2019 novel coronavirus in Wuhan, China', *The Lancet*, vol. 395, no. 10223, E28–E32 (15 Feb. 2020); and WHO (note 54), p. 5.

[57] WHO (note 54), p. 5.

[58] WHO (note 54), pp. 5–6.

[59] Huang et al. (note 56).

[60] WHO (note 54), p. 5.

completed in 2015, in collaboration with the Centre International de Recherche en Infectiologie (CIRI) in France, and became operational in early 2018. The WIV has become a leading authority on bat coronaviruses, having established one of the largest strain collections, including a database of more than 20 000 pathogen samples from wild animals across China.[61] Because most coronaviruses are harmless, and the ones that infect humans generally only cause a cold, they have been classified as relatively low risk, to be studied at biosafety level two (BSL-2) laboratories. Problems arise when new, dangerous coronaviruses unexpectedly appear, as BSL-2 containment only provides minimal protection for workers and the environment. While coronaviruses were studied at BSL-2 at the Wuhan CDC, they were also studied at higher containment levels at the WIV. This work involved high-risk 'gain-of-function' work, where viruses are forced to evolve artificially, and the engineering of chimeric viruses, which contain genetic mixtures of two or more different viruses.[62] Sometimes this work can result in new viruses that are even more dangerous than the parent viruses. For example, this is what happened in 2015 when a team of USA- and WIV-based researchers combined a coronavirus circulating in Chinese horseshoe bats with SARS-CoV.[63]

Research facilities where dangerous viruses and bacteria are stored and studied are designed to protect researchers, the public and the environment from harm. But laboratory design cannot always overcome human error or poor training. With each experiment comes opportunities for accidental exposures and subsequent infections. Incidents of varying severity happen all the time in laboratories around the world.[64] There have already been several documented cases of safety lapses in the course of work specifically with coronaviruses.[65]

At the time of writing there was still no evidence demonstrating a fully natural origin of SARS-CoV-2. Natural spillover, largely based on patterns of previous zoonosis events, was only one of a number of possible origin theories, alongside the research-related accident theory.

Chinese attempts to control the origins narrative

The Chinese Government made significant attempts throughout 2020 to control the pandemic origins narrative, including efforts to stifle the

---

[61] Fan, Y. et al., 'Bat coronaviruses in China', *Viruses*, vol. 11, no. 3 (2019).

[62] National Institutes of Health, Research Portfolio Online Reporting Tool (RePORT), 'Understanding the risk of bat coronavirus emergence', Project Information no. 2R01AI110964-06.

[63] Menachery, V. D. et al., 'A SARS-like cluster of circulating bat coronaviruses shows potential for human emergence', *Nature Medicine*, vol. 21 (9 Nov. 2015).

[64] Furmanski, M., 'Threatened pandemics and laboratory escapes: Self-fulfilling prophecies', *Bulletin of the Atomic Scientists*, 31 Mar. 2013; and Klotz, L., 'Human error in high-biocontainment labs: A likely pandemic threat', *Bulletin of the Atomic Scientists*, 25 Feb. 2019.

[65] Klotz (note 64).

research-related accident theory by diverting attention from scientific research as a possible source of the pandemic.[66] The Chinese Government ordered genomics companies doing some of the early testing of Covid-19 cases to stop releasing their test results and to destroy their samples of the virus.[67] Doctors, investigative journalists and scientists were silenced.[68] The government also placed severe restrictions on the publication of pandemic origins research.[69] Documents were taken down from websites, including from the websites of the WIV and the Wuhan CDC.[70] The WIV's virus database was taken offline at the beginning of 2020 for 'security reasons'.[71] In their publications, scientists at the WIV renamed viruses with sequences closely resembling SARS-CoV-2 in an apparent attempt to obfuscate their previous work with these viruses before the pandemic.[72] The WIV's first Covid-19 papers also failed to mention a significant feature of SARS-CoV-2 (a 'furin cleavage site') that makes the virus more capable of infecting tissues in the human body.[73] The lack of transparency about the WIV's research and the inconsistencies in the information released raised unfortunate but inevitable doubts about the credibility of any Chinese-led origins investigation.

Studies into the origins of SARS-CoV-2

The WHO's first novel coronavirus press conference on 14 January 2020 highlighted the importance of finding the animal source of SARS-CoV-2.[74] The first IHR Emergency Committee of independent scientific experts advising the WHO director-general on the pandemic recommended convening an international multidisciplinary mission, including national experts, to 'review and support efforts to investigate the animal source

---

[66] 'China Covid-19: How state media and censorship took on coronavirus', BBC News, 29 Dec. 2020; and McMullen, J., 'Covid-19: Five days that shaped the outbreak', BBC News, 26 Jan. 2021.

[67] Yu, G. et al., 'How early signs of the coronavirus were spotted, spread and throttled in China', Straits Times, 28 Feb. 2020.

[68] Buckley, C. et al., '25 days that changed the world: How Covid-19 slipped China's grasp', New York Times, 30 Dec. 2020.

[69] Gan, N., Hu, C. and Watson, I., 'Beijing tightens grip over coronavirus research, amid US–China row on virus origin', CNN, 16 Apr. 2020.

[70] Kang, D., Cheng, M. and McNeil, S., 'China clamps down in hidden hunt for coronavirus origins', AP News, 30 Dec. 2020.

[71] Sudworth, J., 'COVID: Wuhan scientist would "welcome" visit probing lab leak theory', BBC News, 21 Dec. 2020.

[72] Zhou, P. et al., 'A pneumonia outbreak associated with a new coronavirus of probable bat origin', Nature, vol. 579, no. 7798 (12 Mar. 2020). An addendum to the paper published online on 17 Nov. 2020 acknowledges the renaming, and links the WIV's pre-Covid-19 research to viruses with genetic sequences closely resembling SARS-CoV-2. Zhou, P. et al., 'Addendum: A pneumonia outbreak associated with a new coronavirus of probable bat origin', Nature, vol. 588, no. 7836 (3 Dec. 2020).

[73] Ridley and Chan (note 55).

[74] WHO, 'Novel coronavirus: Thailand (ex-China)', Disease Outbreak News, 14 Jan. 2020.

of the outbreak'.[75] The WHO director-general directly raised the matter of identifying the virus origins and intermediate hosts with President Xi Jinping during his visit to China in January 2020.[76]

While not its main focus, considering the source of SARS-CoV-2 formed part of the WHO–China Joint Mission in February 2020. Led by a senior adviser to the WHO director-general and the chief expert of the Chinese National Health Commission, the mission team comprised 25 experts from the WHO, China, Germany, Japan, Republic of Korea, Nigeria, Russia, Singapore and the USA.[77] Over nine days beginning on 16 February, the mission team consulted provincial governors, municipal mayors, senior scientists, public health workers and others. They visited hospitals, disease control agencies, transport hubs and emergency supply warehouses in Bejing, Guangdong and Sichuan. They also visited a wet market, though not the one in Wuhan that had been identified as the possible spillover site. Only select team members travelled to Wuhan, where they visited a hospital and a mobile cabin hospital. The mission report concluded that the novel coronavirus was a zoonotic virus, that bats appeared to be the virus reservoir, and that no intermediate hosts had yet been identified.[78] One of the report's recommendations was that 'additional effort should be made to find the animal source, including the natural reservoir and any intermediate amplification host, to prevent any new epidemic foci or resurgence of similar epidemics'.[79] To that end, and in line with the prevailing theory that the spillover event happened at a wet market, the mission report highlighted activities already underway by Chinese authorities to investigate the pandemic's origins. These involved taking environmental samples from the Huanan Wholesale Seafood Market in Wuhan and obtaining records about the wildlife species sold at the market, as well as examining early Covid-19 cases in Wuhan.[80]

The joint mission's call for greater efforts to examine the pandemic's origins was later echoed by the IHR Emergency Committee on the pandemic. Ahead of the annual May meeting of the World Health Assembly, the group advised the WHO to 'work with the World Organisation for Animal Health (OIE), the Food and Agriculture Organization of the United Nations (FAO), and countries to identify the zoonotic source of the virus and the route of introduction to the human population, including the possible

---

[75] WHO, 'Statement on the first meeting of the International Health Regulations (2005) Emergency Committee regarding the outbreak of novel coronavirus (2019-nCoV)', News, 23 Jan. 2020.

[76] WHO, 'How WHO is working to track down the animal reservoir of the SARS-CoV-2 virus', News, 6 Nov. 2020.

[77] Mallapaty, S., 'The scientists investigating the pandemic's origins', Nature, vol. 588, no. 7837 (10 Dec. 2020).

[78] WHO–China Joint Mission (note 17), p. 8.

[79] WHO–China Joint Mission (note 17), p. 39.

[80] WHO–China Joint Mission (note 17), p. 8.

role of intermediate hosts'.[81] In the days before the World Health Assembly meeting, the European Union (EU), Australia and others also called for an international investigation into the origins of the pandemic.[82]

At the opening of the virtual meeting of the 73rd World Health Assembly on 18–19 May 2020, President Xi Jinping, who had previously strongly opposed an international investigation, seemed to reverse his stance and support an international review—albeit a review on his own terms.[83] The World Health Assembly's resolution on the Covid-19 response echoed the IHR Emergency Committee's request to the WHO director-general 'to continue to work closely' with the OIE, the FAO and states on identifying the virus's zoonotic source and path of transmission to humans, 'as part of the One-Health Approach', 'including through efforts such as scientific and collaborative field missions'.[84]

Based on the request, the WHO and China began work to initiate 'a series of studies that will contribute to origin tracing work'.[85] In July, WHO experts travelled to China to define the role of the international investigative team, which was to explore the potential sources of infection among the first reported cases in Wuhan in December 2019, to attempt to identify earlier human cases through sero-epidemiologic studies, and to conduct further animal and environmental studies.[86] The investigative team, agreed by both the WHO and China, was formed in September, but only made public on 20 November 2020. The team included a broad range of expertise with experts from Australia, Denmark, Germany, Japan, the Netherlands, Qatar, Russia, the UK, the USA and Viet Nam, and also included five WHO experts and two OIE representatives—alongside an equal number of scientists (17) from China.[87] Two FAO representatives participated as observers. The first virtual meeting of the international experts with their Chinese counterparts was held on 30 October 2020, and the terms of reference for the Global Study of the Origins of SARS-CoV-2 was published on 5 November 2020.[88]

Adopting a two-phased approach, the joint study aimed in the first instance to explore how the circulation of SARS-CoV-2 might have started, and to gather evidence from the cluster of cases identified in December 2019 for potential links and clues as to its origin. The first phase, scheduled

[81] WHO, 'Statement on the third meeting of the International Health Regulations (2005) Emergency Committee regarding the outbreak of coronavirus disease (Covid-19)', News, 1 May 2020.

[82] Lentzos, F., 'Will the WHO call for an international investigation into the coronavirus's origins?', *Bulletin of the Atomic Scientists*, 18 May 2020.

[83] Niquet, V., 'Decoding Xi Jingping's speech at the World Health Assembly', The Diplomat, 19 May 2020.

[84] 73rd World Health Assembly (note 28), para. 9(6).

[85] WHO (note 54), p. 2.

[86] WHO (note 76).

[87] WHO, 'Origins of the SARS-CoV-2 virus', updated 18 Jan. 2021.

[88] WHO (note 76); and WHO (note 54).

for early 2021, will carry out in-depth reviews of hospital records for cases compatible with Covid-19 before December 2019; review surveillance trends for disease in the months preceding the outbreak; review death registers for specific causes of death compatible with Covid-19; conduct in-depth interviews and reviews of currently identified earlier cases and potentially earlier cases identified during the mission; and undertake serological studies on stored blood/serum samples collected in the weeks and months before December 2019. The results of the first phase will inform a second phase of detailed, longer-term studies, which may include in-depth epidemiologic, virologic, serologic assessments in humans in specific geographic areas or specific settings; and similar studies among animal populations before and after the outbreak in targeted geographic areas. The second phase 'could be conducted elsewhere in China, in neighbouring countries and globally'.[89]

Covid-19 implications for the global biosecurity architecture

The Covid-19 pandemic, and its public and socio-economic impacts, throws into sharp relief a problem faced by all governments: how to successfully predict and prepare for biosecurity-related threats to citizens and to national and international security. The biological threat spectrum is complex and evolving. It includes natural disease outbreaks; the 'slow burn' risk of antimicrobial resistance; the unintended consequences of laboratory accidents; the intentional use of disease as a weapon; and now also, arguably, biological information warfare.

Risks of natural and unintended outbreaks

This pandemic has demonstrated the deep and wide impacts, and the significant national security risks, of pandemics generally and more specifically those involving a novel pathogen like SARS-CoV-2. It has particularly highlighted the need for better national biopreparedness, including (*a*) national strategic leadership on biosecurity efforts; (*b*) annual reporting on the status of national preparations by government and regular scrutiny by parliamentary committees; (*c*) ring-fenced, multi-year funding to support horizon-scanning and stronger preparations for major disruptive events (including biological emergencies); (*d*) increased capabilities to scale up testing, border detection checks, isolation, contact-tracing and hospital care; (*e*) inclusive and regular drills and table-top exercises to test bio-security response capabilities; and (*f*) safeguarding of national capacities to

[89] WHO (note 54), pp. 6–8.

manufacture critical biosecurity and pandemic supplies, including personal protective equipment and vaccines.[90]

But while the pandemic has highlighted threats from natural and emerging diseases, threats from accidental and deliberate biological outbreaks must not be underestimated. Globally, as of December 2020 there were well over 50 high-containment BSL-4 laboratories, either in operation or under construction, spread throughout Africa, Asia, Europe, Russia and the USA. These facilities carry out some of the most dangerous manipulations of pathogens, some of which have pandemic potential. Additionally, as a consequence of Covid-19, many more researchers are now working with coronaviruses—including researchers who may not have previously worked with these viruses and who therefore have less biosafety experience of coronavirus work. That accidents are a regular occurrence in laboratories has been highlighted for years by expert communities, and in 2020 by high profile, in-depth articles from the *New Yorker* and the *South China Morning Post*, as well as by more general media discussion around Covid-19.[91] The increasing potential for accidental biological threats underscores the need to make the global biosecurity architecture more fit for purpose. A key element called for by civil society includes an international body, ideally UN-based, to monitor and inspect high-containment facilities and high-risk biological activities.[92]

Intentional use of disease as a weapon

Deliberate biological threats are also of increasing concern. Should the intent be there, advances in science and technology, and especially in genomic technologies, are significantly facilitating the enhancement of pathogens to make them more deadly; the modification of low-risk pathogens to become high-impact; the engineering of entirely new pathogens; or even the re-creation of extinct, high-impact pathogens like the variola virus that causes smallpox. These possibilities are coming at a time when new delivery mechanisms for transporting pathogens into human bodies are also being developed. In addition to the bombs, missiles, cluster bombs, sprayers and injection devices of past biowarfare programmes, it is now also technically possible to use drones, nano-robots and even insects to deliver pathogens.[93] Moreover, as genomic technologies develop and converge with

---

[90] See e.g. British Parliament, Joint Committee on the National Security Strategy, *Biosecurity and National Security: First Report of Session 2019–21*, Report HC 611/HL 195, 18 Dec. 2020.

[91] See e.g. Furmanski (note 64); Eaves, E., 'The risks of building too many bio labs', *New Yorker*, 18 Mar. 2020; and Baptista, E. et al., 'The labs where monsters live', *South China Morning Post*, 12 Sep. 2020.

[92] Lentzos, F., 'Statement on biological weapons', Speech delivered to the UN General Assembly First Committee, 12 Oct. 2020.

[93] Reeves, R. G., 'Agricultural research, or a new bioweapon system?', *Science*, vol. 362, no. 6410 (5 Oct. 2018).

artificial intelligence, machine learning, automation, affective computing and robotics, an ever more refined record of human biometrics, emotions and behaviours will be captured and analysed.[94] Governments and, increasingly, private companies will be able to sort, categorize, trade and use biological data far more precisely than ever before, creating unprecedented possibilities for social and biological control.[95] Adding computing power to bioinformatics could not only be used to speed up the identification of harmful genes or DNA sequences, but could open up the possibility of ultra-targeted biological warfare.[96]

These developments highlight the need (a) to ensure countries comply with and live up to their obligations under the 1972 Convention on the Prohibition of the Development, Production and Stockpiling of Bacteriological (Biological) and Toxin Weapons and on their Destruction (Biological and Toxin Weapons Convention, BWC); and (b) for a strengthened UN Secretary-General Mechanism for Investigation of Alleged Use of Chemical and Biological Weapons (UNSGM), to conduct independent, in-depth investigations of suspected biological weapons use, as well as for a framework to coordinate an international response following any confirmed use of biological weapons. See section II for discussion of the BWC and the UNSGM.[97]

Biological information warfare

A biological threat that is becoming ever more apparent, and which has significantly increased during the rapidly evolving Covid-19 pandemic, is biological information warfare. A hallmark of the pandemic has been what the WHO called an 'infodemic': the constant production of information, from political, scientific and lay arenas, describing often contradictory findings relating to the natural history, epidemiology and clinical outcomes of Covid-19. The overabundance of information has not only included high levels of scientific reporting and official guidance, but also a vast swathe of media reporting, conflicting statistical interpretations, rumours, theories and fake news. The infodemic has made it difficult to separate truthful and trustworthy sources from false or misleading ones.[98] While misinformation and outbreaks have long coexisted, this phenomenon has been disproportionately amplified in the last decade by a combination of

---

[94] Gleiser, M., 'Biometric data and the rise of digital dictatorship', NPR, 28 Feb. 2018.
[95] Connell, N. et al., 'Driving responsible innovation of AI, life sciences and next generation biotech', *Beyond Standards*, 3 Feb. 2021.
[96] Lentzos (note 44).
[97] For a summary and other details of the Convention on the Prohibition of the Development, Production and Stockpiling of Bacteriological (Biological) and Toxin Weapons and on their Destruction, see annex A, section I, in this volume.
[98] WHO, 'WHO ad-hoc online consultation on managing the Covid-19 infodemic' (note 27).

social media, the normalization of fake news and the delegitimization of scientific expertise.[99]

Bioweapons narratives related to Covid-19 became apparent as early as the second half of January 2020. As the first coronavirus cases outside China were reported, rumours started circulating that linked the developing outbreak to secret Chinese laboratories and alleged bioweapons research. The stories were based on speculation and insinuations but spread quickly on social media and conspiracy theory websites, as well as through mostly minor tabloid news outlets. One prominent article, published on 24 January 2020 in *The Washington Times*, claimed a high-security government facility at the pandemic's initial epicentre in Wuhan could have been researching military applications for the coronavirus and may have been the source of the outbreak. While lacking any evidence, the story spread widely, before the false narrative was exposed a few days later in reputable, high-profile media outlets, most notably in the *Washington Post* and *Foreign Policy*.[100] Yet insinuations and assertions linking the outbreak to biological weapons continued in the ensuing weeks. Elected officials and government representatives with larger outreach platforms became involved. US Senator Tom Cotton, for example, suggested in a Fox News interview on 16 February that the virus was a Chinese military creation.[101] Manish Tewari, a prominent Indian parliamentarian and spokesperson for the Indian National Congress, tweeted to his more than 380 000 followers an article from UK's *Daily Express* tabloid that claimed the coronavirus was a bioweapon leaked from a Chinese research laboratory.[102]

Another version of the bioweapons narrative also surfaced. Pushed most prominently by Iran, Russia and China, including by current and former government officials, the outbreak was portrayed as a biological attack by the US military.[103] Former Iranian president Mahmoud Ahmadinejad sent an open letter to the UN secretary-general asserting that the virus was clearly 'produced in laboratories . . . by the warfare stock houses of biologic war belonging to world hegemonic powers'.[104] Iran's supreme leader issued

[99] Bernard, R. et al., 'Disinformation and epidemics: Anticipating the next phase of biowarfare', *Health Security*, vol. 19, no. 1 (2021).

[100] Taylor, A., 'Experts debunk fringe theory linking China's coronavirus to weapons research', *Washington Post*, 29 Jan. 2020; and Ling, J., 'The Wuhan virus is not a lab-made bioweapon', *Foreign Policy*, 29 Jan. 2020.

[101] Stevenson, A., 'Senator Tom Cotton repeats fringe theory of coronavirus origins', *New York Times*, 17 Feb. 2020.

[102] Tewari, M. (@ManishTewari), Twitter, 13 Mar. 2020, <https://twitter.com/ManishTewari/status/1238299436205236225>; and Hoare, C., 'Coronavirus shock claim: "Smoking gun of Chinese lab leak" exposed by bioweapons expert', *Daily Express*, 12 Mar. 2020.

[103] See e.g. Russia Today, 'Coronavirus may be a product of US "biological attack" aimed at Iran & China, IRGC chief claims', 5 Mar. 2020; and Radio Farda, 'Influential Iran lawmaker says coronavirus is a "bio-terror attack"', 6 Mar. 2020.

[104] Ahmadinejad, M. (@Ahmadinejad1956), Twitter, 9 Mar. 2020, <https://twitter.com/Ahmadinejad1956/status/1237072414841937920>.

an edict on 12 March 2020 endorsing the idea that 'this incident might be a biological attack'.[105]

Russia's state television networks, as well as social media bots and troll farms run by its intelligence services, spread fallacious information.[106] Between 22 January and 19 March 2020, the EU disinformation monitoring team collected over 110 coronavirus-related disinformation cases from Russian sources covering a wide range of narratives, including claims the coronavirus was a biological weapon deployed by China, the US, the UK or even Russia, and that the true origin of the coronavirus is the USA or US-owned laboratories across the world.[107] The report also indicated that a key Russian tactic was to seek to amplify disinformation originating in Iran, China or the US far right, to avoid accusations of Russia creating false content. An updated report in May 2020 stated that the EU team found pro-Russia sources continuing to push narratives linking Covid-19 to biological warfare, and both pro-Kremlin media outlets and Chinese officials and state media falsely portraying high-security public health laboratories in former Soviet republics as involved in covert development of biological weapons.[108] US government officials accused Russia of using thousands of accounts across a variety of social media platforms to promote fake news and conspiracy theories, the most prevalent being that the virus is a US-created bioweapon intended to damage China economically.[109]

China also spread disinformation.[110] Chinese foreign ministry spokesperson Zhao Lijian repeated claims by a prominent Chinese epidemiologist that although the virus was first discovered in China, it may not have originated there—in what became the dominant Beijing narrative by the end of 2020. Zhao later told his 300 000 Twitter followers 'it might be US army who brought the epidemic to Wuhan'.[111] Despite the Chinese ambassador to the USA publicly distancing himself (and his government) from the allegations,

[105] 'Khamenei calls coronavirus "possible biological attack", asks guards to contain it', Radio Farda, 13 Mar. 2020.

[106] Mackinnon, A., 'Russia knows just who to blame for the coronavirus: America', Foreign Policy, 14 Feb. 2020; Anderson, J. and Gamberini, S. J., 'Infodemic: Russian disinformation campaigns, public health, and Covid-19', Inkstick, 25 Mar. 2020; and 'Russian media amplify coronavirus conspiracy theories', BBC Monitoring, 6 Feb. 2020.

[107] EUvsDisinfo, 'EEAS special report: Disinformation on the coronavirus—short assessment of the information environment', 19 Mar. 2020; and EUvsDisinfo, Disinfo Database, <https://euvsdisinfo.eu/disinformation-cases/>.

[108] EUvsDisinfo, 'EEAS special report update: Short assessment of narratives and disinformation around the Covid-19 pandemic (update 23 April–18 May)', 20 May 2020.

[109] Glenza, J., 'Coronavirus: US says Russia behind disinformation campaign', The Guardian, 22 Feb. 2020.

[110] Scott, M., 'Russia and China push "fake news" aimed at weakening Europe: Report', Politico, 1 Apr. 2020.

[111] Myers, S. L., 'China spins tale that the US army started the coronavirus epidemic', New York Times, 13 Mar. 2020.

Zhao's comments fuelled further conspiracy theories online, which were not removed by China's strict internet censors.[112]

The active disinformation campaigns around Covid-19, combined with misinformation spread by social media, likely influenced the course and severity of the pandemic by amplifying mistrust of official reporting and the rejection of scientific evidence by parts of the general public. This has had real health consequences, including people not seeking treatment; stigmatization of those infected; violence against government response facilities or healthcare personnel; and exacerbation of existing political sentiment and movements, such as those opposed to government, foreigners and immigrants.[113]

It has been suggested that the 'consequential nature' of the campaigns means they should be considered as a form of biological threat. By using disinformation campaigns, states can 'produce the consequences of biological terrorism and warfare without deploying a traditional biological agent, and without the technical and regulatory ramifications of their use'.[114] The full potential of this new type of biowarfare is still emerging but some researchers believe 'the necessary conditions for its development' are now in place: (a) the weaponization of far-reaching online fake news campaigns; (b) the potential for these campaigns to have 'significant negative impact on public health'; (c) the 'exacerbating effect' that misinformation and disinformation spread on social media has during an outbreak; and (d) the 'delegitimization of science and mistrust of officials'.[115]

Deliberately propagating false stories is nothing new, but the speed and reach of contemporary campaigns to shape and influence opinions and actions across the globe is unprecedented in history. Biological information warfare aims to undermine sociopolitical and economic systems by weaponizing or virtually escalating natural outbreaks, rather than directly inducing mortality and morbidity in populations through the deployment of harmful biological agents. Such battles of influence are likely to escalate in the future. As 'the lines between reality and deception become blurred', the potential for people, resources and weapons to mobilize on a large scale around false narratives 'creates significant global risks', especially in a pandemic.[116] A biological information warfare capability that could replicate the effects of a biological agent while remaining outside of existing normative frameworks poses significant challenges to disarmament efforts.

---

[112] Swan, J. and Allen-Ebrahimian, B., 'Top Chinese official disowns US military lab coronavirus conspiracy', Axios, 22 Mar. 2020; and Liu, D., Shi, A. and Smith, A., 'Coronavirus: Rumors and misinformation swirl unchecked in China', NBC News, 6 Mar. 2020.

[113] Bernard et al. (note 99), pp. 7–8.

[114] Bernard et al. (note 99), p. 9.

[115] Bernard et al. (note 99), p. 4.

[116] Pauwels, E., *The New Geopolitics of Converging Risks: The UN and Prevention in the Era of AI* (United Nations University Centre for Policy Research: New York, 29 Apr. 2019), p. i.

Improvements in cyber regulations for health and security are crucial to the sustainability and coherence of current frameworks targeting the interface of natural and engineered biological threats.

Conclusions

At the end of 2020, the Covid-19 pandemic was far from over. Its impacts will likely be deep and wide for years to come, including in international security policy.

II. Biological weapon disarmament and non-proliferation

FILIPPA LENTZOS

The principal legal instrument against biological warfare is the 1972 Convention on the Prohibition of the Development, Production and Stockpiling of Bacteriological (Biological) and Toxin Weapons and on their Destruction (Biological and Toxin Weapons Convention, BWC).[1] The treaty has 184 states parties and 4 signatory states. Ten states have neither signed nor ratified the convention. No state joined the treaty in 2020.

Since March 2020, the global Covid-19 pandemic significantly impacted the functioning of the United Nations.[2] UN headquarters in New York and the UN Office at Geneva both locked down for months, cancelling or post-poning in-person meetings and trying, with varying degrees of success, to move certain forums and functions online. The BWC meetings of experts (MXs), originally scheduled for 25 August to 3 September 2020, were postponed to 2021, as was the BWC meeting of states parties, originally scheduled for 8–11 December 2020.[3] A set of 90-minute webinars on each of the MXs ran in October and November 2020, hosted by the BWC Implementation Support Unit and the MX chairs, but held no formal status. Consultations on scheduling the 2021 BWC meetings were still ongoing at the end of 2020.

This section covers states parties' statements marking a milestone of the BWC and in open debate at the UN Security Council; developments in the UN General Assembly with regard to biological weapons; and geopolitical tensions among China, Russia and the United States over biological research activities.

The 45th anniversary of the Biological and Toxin Weapons Convention

On 26 March 2020, the BWC marked its 45th anniversary of entry into force. On the occasion, the UN secretary-general said that the norm against biological weapons remains strong, but that the international community must remain vigilant. He called on states parties to urgently update the treaty's mechanisms for reviewing advances in science and technology,

---

[1] For a summary and other details of the Convention on the Prohibition of the Development, Production and Stockpiling of Bacteriological (Biological) and Toxin Weapons and on their Destruction, see annex A, section I, in this volume.

[2] Nakamitsu, I., 'The Office for Disarmament Affairs remains active and committed—How the Covid-19 pandemic is affecting the work of disarmament', United Nations, Office for Disarmament Affairs, 3 Apr. 2020; and Acheson, R., *Locked Out During Lockdown: An Analysis of the UN System During Covid-19*, Women's International League for Peace & Freedom Report, Sep. 2020.

[3] Kenyan Permanent Mission to the United Nations and Other International Organizations, BWC chair's letters of 28 July 2020 and 23 Nov. 2020.

and to work together to improve biosecurity and biopreparedness so that all countries are equipped to prevent and respond to any potential use of bioweapons. He urged states parties 'to think creatively about the future evolution of the Convention and how to uphold its central role in preventing the misuse of biology for hostile purposes'.[4]

Several states parties issued an anniversary statement. Russia emphasized the BWC's need for 'urgent institutional and operational strengthening' and elaborated its own specific initiatives: 'to resume the work on the legally binding Protocol to the Convention with effective verification mechanism, to establish under the Convention mobile biomedical units and Scientific Advisory Committee and to improve current confidence-building measures'. Russia also emphasized the need for 'multilaterally negotiated decisions agreed upon by the States Parties by consensus' as 'the only way to provide the necessary assurances of compliance and effective deterrent against use or threat of use of biological weapons'.[5]

India, too, used the opportunity to reiterate its call 'for institutional strengthening of the Convention, including negotiation of a comprehensive and legally binding Protocol', for effective BWC implementation, and for full compliance with the treaty 'in letter and spirit'. India also highlighted the challenges posed by developments in science and technology; the need for international cooperation, including institutional strengthening of the World Health Organization (WHO); the bioterrorism threat; and its efforts to establish an Article VII database to deal with biothreats and bio-emergencies.[6]

The USA, communicating via Twitter, reaffirmed the importance of states parties' commitments to preventing biological weapons, and noted that the Covid-19 pandemic highlighted the importance of reducing all biological risks.[7]

The anniversary statement by the European Union (EU) spokesperson for foreign affairs and security policy highlighted some of the EU's international efforts to improve global biosafety and biosecurity, noting that since 2006 it has provided close to €15 million in support of the BWC. The spokesperson said the EU would work towards 'concrete measures to enhance and further develop' the treaty at the Ninth Review Conference of the Biological and

---

[4] UN Secretary-General, 'Secretary-general's message on the forty-fifth anniversary of the entry into force of the Biological Weapons Convention', 26 Mar. 2020.

[5] Russian Ministry of Foreign Affairs, 'Statement of the Ministry of Foreign Affairs of the Russian Federation on the occasion of the 45th anniversary of the BWC entry into force', 26 Mar. 2020.

[6] Indian Ministry of External Affairs, '45th anniversary of entry into force of the Biological and Toxin Weapons Convention (BWC)', 27 Mar. 2020.

[7] US Department of State, Bureau of International Security and Nonproliferation (@StateISN), Twitter, 26 Mar. 2020, <https://twitter.com/StateISN/status/1243146775864709123>.

Toxin Weapons Convention, and urged all states not yet party to the BWC to join without delay.[8]

While the UN and some of its member states made statements marking the 45th anniversary, the statements did not give rise to new initiatives and do not appear to have carried any specific momentum.

United Nations Security Council open debate on pandemics and security

Characterizing global health risks, such as pandemics and epidemics, as a threat to international peace and security, the UN Security Council convened a virtual, high-level open debate on 'Pandemics and Security' on 2 July 2020, chaired by Germany's minister for foreign affairs, Heiko Maas. The aim of the debate was 'to exchange views on the security implications of international health threats, epidemics and pandemics and the corresponding role of the Security Council in maintaining international peace and security'.[9]

Opening the debate, the UN secretary-general focused on the implications of Covid-19 for the maintenance of peace and security, and noted that the pandemic 'has already shown some of the ways in which preparedness might fall short if a disease were to be deliberately manipulated to be more virulent, or intentionally released in multiple places at once'. In considering how to improve global responses to future disease threats, the secretary-general urged states to 'devote serious attention to preventing the deliberate use of diseases as weapons'. He emphasized the need to strengthen the BWC 'by enhancing its role as a forum for the consideration of preventative measures, robust response capacities and effective counter-measures'. He pointed out that 'the best counter to biological weapons is effective action against naturally occurring diseases', and that 'strong public and veterinary health systems are not only an essential tool against Covid-19, but also an effective deterrent against the development of biological weapons'. He continued: 'All of these issues must be on the agenda next year at the Convention's Review Conference.' The secretary-general also noted that the pandemic highlights the risks of bioterrorist attacks and that Security Council Resolution 1540 and its follow-ups remain a key component of the international non-proliferation architecture to prevent bioterrorism.[10]

[8] Battu-Henriksson, V., EU Spokesperson for Foreign Affairs and Security Policy, 'Non-proliferation: Statement by the spokesperson on the 45th anniversary of the entry into force of the Biological and Toxin Weapons Convention', 26 Mar. 2020.

[9] UN Secretary-General, 'Secretary-general's remarks to Security Council open video-teleconference on the maintenance of international peace and security: Implications of Covid-19', 2 July 2020.

[10] UN Secretary-General (note 9); and UN Security Council Resolution 1540, 28 Apr. 2004.

The Security Council debate included over a dozen statements delivered by ministers and representatives, as well as nearly 50 statements submitted in writing.[11] Of particular relevance to biological weapon disarmament and non-proliferation were the statements from Canada and Georgia.

Canada's statement emphasized that 'more work is needed to build capacity to prevent, detect and respond to all manner of infectious disease threats, whether natural, accidental or deliberate in origin'.[12] It welcomed the meeting as an important first step for the Security Council to focus more attention on global health security, and asked it to consider holding additional briefings on the implications for international peace and security of global health security challenges. The statement noted that Canada had recently joined Denmark, Republic of Korea (South Korea), Qatar and Sierra Leone in launching the Group of Friends of Solidarity for Global Health Security, and that the group is ready to support the Security Council in a 'comprehensive consideration of global health security moving forward'. Canada also highlighted its own health security capacity-building efforts that are supporting the global response to Covid-19, including biological laboratories in Africa, the Middle East and the Caribbean, and an infectious disease early warning system in South East Asia delivered through Canada's Weapons Threat Reduction Program.[13]

The Georgian statement drew attention to the deliberate intensification of hybrid warfare tools by Russia against Georgia. It claimed that 'fabricated propaganda myths' were constantly attacking the Richard Lugar Center for Public Health Research, one of the key laboratories in Georgia's response to Covid-19.[14] According to the statement, the disinformation alleges that the Georgian Government has deliberately spread the coronavirus in the occupied Tskhinvali region and collected biological samples from residents in the region. The myths were seen to 'undermine the trust of the local population towards the Government of Georgia' and to create deliberate 'chaos on the ground'. Georgia stressed that the Russian disinformation campaign 'represents an open attack on the health protection of the population and the national security of Georgia'.[15]

Following the 'Pandemics and Security' meeting, Russia circulated a letter to the Security Council raising 'serious concern' about references to the BWC at the debate, since Covid-19 'has no direct relevance to the Convention'. Moreover, Russia did 'not see any reason for the inclusion of this issue

---

[11] United Nations, Security Council, Letter dated 8 July 2020 from the President of the Security Council addressed to the Secretary-General and the Permanent Representatives of the members of the Security Council, S/2020/663, 9 July 2020.

[12] United Nations, S/2020/663 (note 11), annex 22, p. 45.

[13] United Nations, S/2020/663 (note 11), annex 22, pp. 45–46.

[14] United Nations, S/2020/663 (note 11), annex 31, pp. 66–67.

[15] United Nations, S/2020/663 (note 11), annex 31, p. 67.

in the agenda of the Review Conference', and asserted that strengthening public and veterinary health systems should be considered by the WHO, the Food and Agriculture Organization and the World Organisation for Animal Health. The letter also emphasized the need for institutional and operational strengthening of the BWC and, in a nod towards Russia's introduction in the upcoming UN General Assembly of a new resolution on the Secretary-General's Mechanism for Investigation of Alleged Use of Chemical and Biological Weapons (UNSGM), it also noted that 'the principles and procedures of the Secretary-General's Mechanism, established in 1988, should be updated' (see below).[16]

The First Committee of the UN General Assembly

The UN General Assembly committee on disarmament and international security (First Committee) convened virtually from 6 October to 4 November 2020. In the general debate statements, 6 groups of states and 65 individual states referred to biological weapons—an unusually high number, likely reflecting both the Covid-19 pandemic and the upcoming Ninth Review Conference of the BWC.[17] Most of the remarks emphasized the importance of the BWC and expressed support for the treaty. Many highlighted the need to universalize and implement the BWC effectively.

Several states referred to Covid-19's devastating impacts as a stark example of the potential consequences and disruption if biological weapons were ever used. Many, including Australia, Canada, Greece, Finland, France, India, Ireland, Nepal, the Netherlands and the Association of Southeast Asian Nations (ASEAN), said the pandemic underscored the need to strengthen the BWC. China said that 'Covid-19 has sounded the alarm on biosecurity and highlighted the importance and urgency of strengthening global biosecurity governance'.[18]

For Russia and the Non-Aligned Movement (NAM) in particular, but also for others states like Brazil, China, Spain and the Netherlands, strengthening the BWC meant negotiating a legally binding verification mechanism. Many states signalled that this was a main priority for them at the Ninth Review Conference. For other states, strengthening the BWC meant a range of activities, including greater international cooperation, assistance and preparedness; proper and sustained financial support for the treaty;

---

[16] United Nations, Security Council, Letter dated 28 July 2020 from the Permanent Representatives of the Russian Federation to the UN addressed to the President of the Security Council, S/2020/756, 29 July 2020.

[17] Lentzos, F., 'Biological Weapons', *First Committee Monitor*, vol. 18, no. 3 (25 Oct. 2020), p. 9.

[18] Geng, S., China statement at the General Debate of the First Committee of the 75th session of the UN General Assembly, New York, 12 Oct. 2020, p. 7; and Lentzos, F., 'Biological Weapons', *First Committee Monitor*, vol. 18, no. 2 (18 Oct. 2020), p. 11.

more institutional capacity and fostering of synergies between relevant international organizations; establishment of a scientific advisory body; improved implementation of the treaty's confidence-building measures and adoption of additional transparency measures such as peer review; creation of mobile biomedical units to assist in responding to deliberate outbreaks; and development of a voluntary code of conduct for life scientists.[19]

Kazakhstan repeated its 'surprise' proposal (first introduced by the President of Kazakhstan at the 75th General Debate of the General Assembly) to establish an International Agency for Biological Safety as a special multilateral body to strengthen the BWC, but without providing further details.[20]

Several unsupported allegations and insinuations of activities in contravention of the BWC were made during the general debate. Iran said it was 'deeply concerned about the clandestine biological weapon programs pursued by some countries'.[21] Syria said that 'Israel's arsenal of nuclear, chemical and biological weapons remains the greatest threat for peace and security in the Middle East region'.[22] China said: 'The international community is highly concerned with the US military's biological programs. We urge the US to act in an open, transparent and responsible manner and fully clarify its activities in numerous bio-labs overseas.'[23] The USA, one of the three depositary governments of the treaty, spoke of Covid-19 as 'the plague unleashed onto the world by the People's Republic of China' and the need to hold China to account, but did not refer to the BWC in its statement.[24]

Both the First Committee and the General Assembly adopted draft resolution A/C.1/75/L.52 on the BWC without a vote (Resolution 75/88).[25] Changes from last year's version were minimal. Hungary, which following usual practice introduced the resolution, said this was because the pandemic precluded in-person informal consultations being held, and that Hungary's priority was to preserve consensus, something felt to be particularly important in a year preceding a review conference.[26]

[19] Lentzos (note 18), p. 11.

[20] Issetov, A., Kazakhstan statement to the First Committee of the 75th session of the UN General Assembly, New York, 12 Oct. 2020, p. 3; Lentzos (note 18), p. 12; and Zanders, J. P., 'Biological weapons: A surprise proposal from Kazak worth exploring', The Trench, 6 Oct. 2020.

[21] Ravanchi, M. J., Iranian statement to the First Committee of the 75th session of the UN General Assembly, New York, 14 Oct. 2020, p. 2.

[22] Al-Ja'afari, B., Syria statement to the First Committee of the 75th session of the UN General Assembly, New York, 16 Oct. 2020; and Press TV, 'Israel's arsenal of nuclear, chemical warfare poses greats risk to Middle East peace: Syria UN envoy', 17 Oct. 2020.

[23] Geng (note 18), p. 8.

[24] Wood, R., US statement to the First Committee of the 75th session of the UN General Assembly, New York, 9 Oct. 2020.

[25] UN General Assembly Resolution 75/88, 7 Dec. 2020; and Reaching Critical Will, 'Draft resolutions, voting results, and explanations of vote from First Committee 2020', [n.d.].

[26] Balázs, S., Hungary statement to the First Committee of the 75th session of the UN General Assembly, New York, 16 Oct. 2020, p. 4.

The biennial draft resolution A/C.1/75/L.18 on 'Measures to uphold the 1925 Geneva Protocol', which prohibits the use of chemical and biological weapons, was agreed in the First Committee by 179 states.[27] There were three abstentions, from Israel and the USA, who usually abstain on the resolution, and from the Central African Republic. No state voted against. In the General Assembly, 182 states voted for the resolution, including the Central African Republic, with Israel and the USA abstaining.[28] The resolution renewed its previous call to all states 'to observe strictly the principles and objectives of the Protocol'. The resolution also called upon states that continue to maintain reservations to the Geneva Protocol to withdraw these reservations.

A new resolution on the UN Secretary-General's Mechanism

In contrast to the regular resolutions on the BWC and the Geneva Protocol, a new draft resolution (A/C.1/75/L.65/Rev.1) to update the UNSGM generated significant controversy in the First Committee in 2020.[29] Introduced by Russia, the draft resolution encourages states to assess the effectiveness of the UNSGM, and requests the UN secretary-general to seek states' views on the technical guidelines and procedures that operationalize the UNSGM. Russia argued that much has changed in the scientific, technical and diplomatic environment in the 30 years since the guidelines and procedures were agreed on in 1990 and that a review is warranted.[30] The resolution also sought to 'reaffirm the foundational nature of the CWC and the BWC in investigating the alleged use of chemical and biological weapons'.[31]

Several states expressed misgivings that the resolution seems to imply there is a problem with the UNSGM and weakens its credibility and independence. Australia, Switzerland and the United Kingdom in a joint statement, and the EU, Canada, New Zealand and the USA in separate statements, all urged member states to vote against the resolution on the grounds that it was politically motivated and would undermine the UNSGM.[32] They argued that the resolution misrepresented the UNSGM by placing undue emphasis on the link with the BWC and the authority of the UN Security Council, when in

---

[27] United Nations, General Assembly, 'Measures to uphold the authority of the 1925 Geneva Protocol', A/C.1/75/L.18, 6 Oct. 2020; and United Nations, First Committee voting results on A/C.1/75/L.18, 4 Nov. 2020.

[28] United Nations, General Assembly voting results on A/75/399 DR VIII, 7 Dec. 2020.

[29] United Nations, General Assembly, 'Secretary-General's Mechanism for Investigation of Alleged Use of Chemical and Biological Weapons', A/C.1/75/L.65/Rev.1, 22 Oct. 2020.

[30] United Nations, General Assembly, A/C.1/75/L.65/Rev.1 (note 29), paras 6–7.

[31] UN Web TV, 'First Committee, 12th meeting: General Assembly, 75th session' (Video recording), 4 Nov. 2020.

[32] European Union, 'EU Explanation of vote: United Nations 1st Committee: Draft Res L.65 UN Secretary-General's Mechanism for Investigation of Alleged Use of Chemical and Biological Weapons', Statement to the First Committee, 4 Nov. 2020; UN Web TV (note 31); and Lentzos, F., 'Biological weapons', First Committee Monitor, vol. 18, no. 4 (8 Nov. 2020), p. 15.

fact the UNSGM is completely autonomous and the secretary-general does not require UN Security Council approval to initiate the mechanism. Close neighbours to Russia reiterated their support for the UNSGM, with Latvia expressing concern at attempts to 'undermine' the UNSGM and Lithuania saying that 'any attempts to compromise its integrity, independence and efficiency are completely unacceptable'.[33]

The draft resolution initially called for the UN secretary-general to estab-lish a group of governmental experts (GGE), with a proposed membership of up to 15 states, to make consensus recommendations on updating the UNSGM technical guidelines and procedures. However, in light of oppos-ition from a large number of states from different regional groups, Russia abandoned its ambition to create a GGE on this topic and dropped it from the resolution. While this addressed some concerns, many states still considered some language in the resolution as undermining the UNSGM. For example, the resolution stressed the role of the UN Security Council in investigating alleged breaches of the BWC, and that any allegations brought to the UN secretary-general's attention by any state party to the BWC must be con-sidered and addressed within the framework of the BWC.[34] Both aspects are part of Russia's previously articulated position on limiting any BWC-related investigation and compliance-assessment efforts taking place outside of the BWC framework and the UN Security Council.[35]

The draft resolution also called on states parties to strengthen the BWC by 'resuming' multilateral negotiations in order to conclude a non-discriminatory legally binding protocol to the treaty.[36] While many states agree that there is a need for a legally binding mechanism, not all believe this necessitates a return to the protocol negotiations of the 1990s. The verifiability of the BWC has been a divisive topic for many years among its states parties, and the continuing references to it in the draft resolution is another sign that it will be a key topic at the Ninth Review Conference.

The UNSGM resolution is consistent with other efforts, including misinformation and disinformation campaigns, to stop, hinder, undermine and contest the authority and work of investigation teams within the Organisation for the Prohibition of Chemical Weapons and the UN.[37] Syrian chemical weapons investigations, as well as other experiences, point to investigations becoming more contentious, complex and important, and

[33] Pildegovičs, A., Latvian Permanent Representative to the UN, Statement to the First Commit-tee of the 75th session of the UN General Assembly, New York, 15 Oct. 2020; and Lithuania, Statement to the First Committee of the 75th session of the UN General Assembly, New York, 15 Oct. 2020.

[34] United Nations, A/C.1/75/L.65/Rev.1 (note 29), paras 3–4.

[35] Lentzos, F., 'Biological weapon disarmament and non-proliferation', *SIPRI Yearbook 2020*, p. 479.

[36] United Nations, A/C.1/75/L.65/Rev.1 (note 29), p. 2.

[37] Lentzos, F. and Littlewood J., 'How Russia worked to undermine UN bioweapons investigations', *Bulletin of the Atomic Scientists*, 11 Dec. 2020.

suggest that any bioweapons investigations led by the secretary-general would be politically difficult and technically complex. Previous experiences also suggest that if a perpetrator has a supporter on the Security Council, any effort at attribution will be challenged at every level.[38]

The majority of states recognized these problems with the draft UNSGM resolution by overwhelmingly rejecting it in the First Committee on 4 November 2020. Although it was eventually co-sponsored by China, Nicaragua and Venezuela, there were only 31 votes in favour, 63 votes against, and 67 abstentions.[39] In addition, five individual paragraphs were voted on, all of them rejected by similar margins.[40]

The evolving China–Russia–United States relationship

Geopolitical tensions among the USA, China and Russia continued to spill over into the biological field in 2020, with several allegations being aired in public statements. During a regular press briefing by the Chinese Ministry of Foreign Affairs on 4 August 2020, for example, spokesperson Wang Wenbin, in answer to a question about alleged activities in South Korea, accused the USA of conducting activities of 'biological militarization in many countries' that are not transparent, safe or justified.[41] Two days later, the Russian Ministry of Foreign Affairs made similar accusations in a press briefing about the US military conducting biological activities in the post-Soviet space. Ministry spokesperson Alexey Zaytsev suggested that Russia would seek to resolve the issue by activating the consultative mechanism under Article V of the BWC and calling on the USA 'to sit down at the negotiating table and discuss, in a bilateral format, the [Russian] concerns' about the activity.[42]

On 27 August 2020, the US Department of Commerce placed several new entities, including three research facilities of the 48th Central Scientific Research Institute in Kirov, Sergiev Posad and Yekaterinburg—described as Russian 'Ministry of Defense facilities associated with the Russian biological weapons program'—on its list of entities considered to pose a security risk to US interests, making them subject to export control restrictions.[43] The 48th Central Scientific Research Institute, including the Kirov facility, was part

---

[38] Lentzos and Littlewood (note 37).

[39] United Nations, General Assembly, First Committee voting results on A/C.1/75/L.65/Rev.1, 4 Nov. 2020.

[40] Reaching Critical Will (note 25).

[41] Chinese Ministry of Foreign Affairs, 'Foreign Ministry Spokesperson Wang Wenbin's regular press conference on August 4, 2020', Press release, 4 Aug. 2020.

[42] Russian Ministry of Foreign Affairs, 'Briefing by Deputy Director of the Information and Press Department Alexey Zaytsev, Moscow, August 6, 2020', News, 6 Aug. 2020.

[43] US Department of Commerce, Bureau of Industry and Security, 'Addition of entities to the Entity List, and revision of entries on the Entity List', *Federal Register*, vol. 85, no. 167, 27 Aug. 2020.

of Russian efforts to develop and test a coronavirus vaccine, and the listing came within weeks of the Sputnik V vaccine being announced.[44]

The US assistant secretary of state for international security and nonproliferation, Christopher Ford, called attention to these sanctions on 12 November 2020 at the annual conference of the EU Non-Proliferation and Disarmament Consortium, which he said also 'highlighted in public for the first time the fact that there is a Russian biological weapons program'.[45] There is no open-source independent validation of this claim, but scholars have queried the state of Russian compliance with the BWC and the claim is considered to 'colour' how Russia's biotechnology investments should be viewed.[46] The US Government's annual report on treaty compliance noted in June 2020 that 'Russian government entities remained engaged during the reporting period [2019] in dual-use activities, potentially for purposes incompatible with the BWC'.[47] On China, the report noted that it 'continues to develop its biotechnology infrastructure and pursue scientific cooperation with countries of concern', and that 'researchers at Chinese military medical institutes' may be undertaking 'biological activities of a possibly anomalous nature' that have 'potential dual-use applications'.[48]

Conclusions and prospects for the Ninth Review Conference

The Ninth Review Conference of the BWC, originally scheduled for 2021, is likely to be postponed until 2022. While states parties generally recognize the need to strengthen the BWC—especially in light of the pandemic—there are no signs the treaty has attracted high-level political commitment to do so and there are no new initiatives apparent so far. For now, the Review Conference seems destined to divide according to traditional points of contention, most obviously on a legally binding protocol.

---

[44] 'US adds Russian chemical research facilities to sanctions list', UNIAN, 26 Aug. 2020; and Norton, B., 'US sanctions Russian research institute that developed Covid-19 vaccine', Strategic Culture Foundation, 29 Aug. 2020.

[45] Ford, C., Speech to the EU Consortium on Nonproliferation and Disarmament Annual Conference, 12 Nov. 2020.

[46] Zilinskas, R. A. and Mauger, P., *Biosecurity in Putin's Russia* (Lynne Rienner: Boulder, CO, 2018); and Gronvall, G. K. and Bland, B., 'Life-science research and biosecurity concerns in the Russian Federation', *Nonproliferation Review*, Special issue on chemical and biological warfare (forthcoming 2021), online 5 Feb. 2021.

[47] US Government, *Adherence to and Compliance with Arms Control, Non-Proliferation, and Disarmament Agreements and Commitments* (US Department of State: Washington, DC, June 2020), p. 62.

[48] US Government (note 47), p. 57.

III. Allegations of use of chemical weapons in Syria

CAITRÍONA MCLEISH

In 2020 the conflict in Syria entered its ninth year and, as in previous years, the Technical Secretariat of the Organisation for the Prohibition of Chemical Weapons (OPCW) continued to work on issues relating to previous allegations of chemical weapon (CW) use and preparations for use.

The Fact-Finding Mission (FFM) continued its work investigating earlier allegations, including analysing information collected from deployments to Syria in November and December 2019.[1] On its investigation into an allegation made by Russia and Syria regarding toxic chemical use in Aleppo on 24 November 2018, the Secretariat continued to request information collected by a team of Russian chemical, biological, radiological and nuclear (CBRN) weapons specialists.[2] A technical meeting was held in The Hague between the Secretariat and the permanent representatives to the OPCW of Russia and Syria on this matter at the end of May 2020.[3]

At the beginning of October 2020, the Secretariat released two FFM reports, one of which concerned this same allegation of use of toxic chemicals in Aleppo in November 2018.[4] This FFM report noted that the information 'obtained and analysed, the composite summary of the interviews, and the results of the laboratory analyses did not allow [it] to establish whether or not chemicals were used as a weapon in the incident'.[5] On the exchange of correspondence between the Secretariat and Russian and Syrian authorities noted above, the FFM report recorded that 'access to requested information and evidence', including interviews and meetings with the Russian team of CBRN specialists, was denied 'on the basis of military secrecy'.[6] The other FFM report concerned an alleged use of toxic chemicals by Syrian govern-

---

[1] During these deployments, the FFM interviewed witnesses and collected further information regarding incidents that took place in Aleppo on 24 Nov. 2018; Yarmouk, Damascus on 22 Oct. 2017; Khirba Masasinah on 7 July 2017 and 4 Aug. 2017; Qalib Al-Thawr, Al-Salamiyah on 9 Aug. 2017; and Al-Balil, Souran on 8 Nov. 2017. See OPCW, Executive Council, 'Progress in the elimination of the Syrian chemical weapons programme', Note by the Director-General, EC-93/DG.3, 25 Nov. 2019, para. 17; and OPCW, Executive Council, 'Progress in the elimination of the Syrian chemical weapons programme', Note by the Director-General, EC-93/DG.5, 24 Dec. 2019, para. 15.

[2] OPCW, Executive Council, 'Progress in the elimination of the Syrian chemical weapons programme', Report by the Director General, EC-94/DG.12, 24 June 2020, para. 19. In Nov. 2018 the OPCW received a series of notes verbales from Syria that provided information about an incident reported to have occurred in several residential neighbourhoods in Aleppo on 24 Nov. 2018. See McLeish, C., 'Allegations of use of chemical weapons in Syria', *SIPRI Yearbook 2020*, pp. 439–45.

[3] OPCW, EC-94/DG.12 (note 2), para. 19.

[4] OPCW, 'OPCW issues two Fact-Finding Mission reports on chemical weapons use allegations in Aleppo and Saraqib, Syria', News, 2 Oct. 2020.

[5] OPCW, 'Report of the OPCW Fact-Finding Mission in Syria regarding the incident in Aleppo, Syrian Arab Republic, on 24 November 2018', Note by the Technical Secretariat, S/1902/2020, 1 Oct. 2020, para. 8.13.

[6] OPCW, S/1902/2020 (note 5), para. 7.19.

ment forces in Saraqib in August 2016. The FFM reported that it was not able to visit the location of the alleged incident and was also unable to visit the hospital that was reported to have admitted patients, although it did have access to available medical records. The results of the FFM's analysis of 'all available data obtained up until the issuance of this report did not allow the FFM to establish whether or not chemicals were used as a weapon' in this incident.[7]

The OPCW Declaration Assessment Team (DAT) also continued with its efforts to clarify and resolve all of the identified gaps, inconsistencies and discrepancies in the initial declaration submitted by Syria in 2013.[8] On 13 March 2020, the Secretariat informed Syria that in view of the Covid-19 outbreak, all scheduled deployments and missions were postponed until further notice.[9] This included the 23rd round of consultations, which had been scheduled to begin on 15 March; they eventually took place between 22 September and 3 October in Damascus. During the mission, the DAT collected samples to replace those taken during a previous deployment and held discussions on the current status of all outstanding issues.[10] These discussions came after the Syrian National Authority provided further information on eight outstanding issues and made two amendments to their initial declaration.[11] The DAT reported the outcomes of its mission, including that three outstanding issues relating to the initial declaration had been closed during those consultations, to the Executive Council in October 2020.[12] Of the 19 issues still outstanding, one concerned a production facility that had been declared as never having been used for the production of chemical weapons. After a DAT review of all information and other materials gathered since 2014 suggested this not to be the case, and that 'production and/or weaponisation of chemical warfare nerve agents took place' at this facility, the Secretariat requested the Syrian Arab Republic to declare 'the exact types and quantities of chemical agents produced and/or weaponised at the site'.[13]

---

[7] OPCW, 'Report of the OPCW Fact-Finding Mission in Syria regarding the incident of alleged use of chemicals as a weapon in Saraqib, Syrian Arab Republic, on 1 August 2016', Note by the Technical Secretariat, S/1901/2020, 1 Oct. 2020, paras 7.1–7.5.

[8] The OPCW established the Declaration Assessment Team (DAT) in 2014 to engage the relevant Syrian authorities in resolving the identified gaps and inconsistencies in the Syrian declaration. OPCW, 'Declaration Assessment Team', [n.d.].

[9] OPCW, Executive Council, 'Progress in the elimination of the Syrian chemical weapons programme', Note by the Director General, EC-94/DG.1, 24 Mar. 2020, para. 6.

[10] OPCW, Executive Council, 'Progress in the elimination of the Syrian chemical weapons programme', Note by the Director General, EC-96/DG.2, 26 Oct. 2020, para. 11.

[11] OPCW, Executive Council, 'Progress in the elimination of the Syrian chemical weapons programme', Note by the Director General, EC-95/DG.19, 24 Sep. 2020, para. 10.

[12] OPCW, Executive Council, 'Progress in the elimination of the Syrian chemical weapons programme', Note by the Director General, EC-96/DG.3, 24 Nov. 2020, paras 10–11.

[13] OPCW, EC-96/DG.3 (note 12), para. 11.

In December 2020 the OPCW director-general issued the final report for 2020 on progress in eliminating the Syrian chemical weapons programme, which stated: 'the Secretariat assesses that the declaration submitted by the Syrian Arab Republic still cannot be considered accurate and complete'.[14] The 96th Session of the Executive Council will consider the director-general's progress report when it meets in March 2021.

Civil society activities

At the beginning of October, three international human rights non-governmental organizations (NGOs)—the Open Society Justice Initiative, the Syrian Archive and the Syrian Center for Media and Freedom of Expression—jointly lodged a criminal complaint relating to chemical weapons use in Syria, including evidence from a detailed investigation into the sarin attacks on Ghouta in 2013 and Khan Shaykhun in 2017. The complaint, filed with the Office of the German Federal Prosecutor, is the first attempt to hold the Syrian Arab Republic accountable in court for chemical weapons use.[15] Criminal complaints of this type are permitted in Germany because they have universal jurisdiction laws, which provide national prosecutors and courts with the authority to investigate and prosecute international crimes committed on foreign territory by foreign nationals. Reporting on the filing, the German state-owned international broadcaster Deutsche Welle explained that 'key to the criminal complaint is the diverse array of witness testimony', which includes information provided by 'high-ranking military personnel and scientists at Syria's Scientific Studies and Research Center'.[16] The evidence apparently indicates that it was Maher al-Assad, President Bashar al-Assad's younger brother, who gave 'the official order at an operational level' to use sarin in Ghouta, but also that 'deployment of strategic weapons, such as sarin nerve gas' required the president's approval.[17]

Later the same month, on 20 October, the Open Society Justice Initiative and the Syrian Archive also released a report on the Scientific Studies and Research Center (SSCR) in Syria. The report claims to identify SSCR branches responsible for Syria's chemical weapons use: Institute 3000 for producing chemical weapons; Branch 450 for storing, mixing and loading warheads with chemical munitions; and Institute 2000 and Institute 4000

---

[14] OPCW, Executive Council, 'Progress in the elimination of the Syrian chemical weapons programme', Report by the Director General, EC-96/DG.4, 24 Dec. 2020, para. 12.

[15] Open Society Justice Initiative, 'Chemical weapons attacks in Syria', [n.d.]; and Syrian Archive, 'Criminal complaint filed on behalf of sarin attack victims', Press release, 6 Oct. 2020.

[16] Sanders, L., Schülke-Gill, B. and Bayer, J., 'How Germany could indict Syria's Assad for war crimes', Deutsche Welle, 27 Nov. 2020.

[17] Sanders et al. (note 16).

for producing barrel bombs. The two NGOs submitted the report to the OPCW and to the International, Impartial and Independent Mechanism for Syria, as well as to prosecutors in Germany and France 'for use in support of criminal accountability'.[18]

Investigation into possible breaches of confidentiality

In May 2019 an internal document entitled 'Engineering Assessment of Two Cylinders Observed at the Douma Incident: Executive Summary' was disseminated outside of the OPCW and subsequently appeared online. The OPCW launched an investigation into possible breaches of confidentiality, which ended in February 2020 with the release of a report to states parties detailing its findings. A 'modified version' of the report is published on the public website.[19] In a statement accompanying the release of the investigation report, the OPCW director-general explained that the word 'modified' related to the process of anonymization.[20] The public version of the report records the investigators as interviewing 29 individuals, collecting documents, and examining email records and other electronic evidence.[21] The investigation identified two former OPCW officials, designated as 'Inspector A' and 'Inspector B', as being responsible for the breach. With regard to the severity of these breaches, the investigators concluded:

Inspector A's assessment purports to be an official OPCW FFM report that relies upon and contains confidential information. However, it is a personal document created without authorisation through the misuse of incomplete confidential information by a staff member who had ceased to provide support to the FFM seven months prior to the release of the final FFM report on Douma. It was during this seven-month period that the majority of the investigative work was conducted. Inspector A's assessment has thus been misused to call into question the Organisation's competence and credibility. Therefore, the deliberate and premeditated breaches of confidentiality committed by Inspectors A and B are considered to be serious.[22]

In his statement, the director-general told states parties that inspectors A and B were not whistle-blowers but, 'individuals who could not accept that their views were not backed by evidence. When their view could not gain

[18] ArcticWind, 'Syria's Scientific Studies and Research Centre', 21 Oct. 2020.
[19] OPCW, Technical Secretariat, 'Report of the investigation into possible breaches of confidentiality', Note by the Technical Secretariat, S/1839/2020, 6 Feb. 2020; and OPCW, 'Independent investigation into possible breaches of confidentiality report released', News, 6 Feb. 2020.
[20] OPCW Director-General, Statement on the Report of the Investigation into Possible Breaches of Confidentiality, 6 Feb. 2020, p. 1.
[21] OPCW, S/1839/2020 (note 19), paras 4–5.
[22] OPCW, S/1839/2020 (note 19), para. 29.

traction, they took matters into their own hands and committed a breach of their obligations to the Organisation'.[23]

This investigation report was released 17 days after an open UN Security Council Arria-formula meeting on the Douma FFM report.[24] The meeting, held at the request of Russia who held the presidency of the Security Council that month, included a video statement from Ian Henderson, a former Technical Secretariat staff member, in which he described a chronology of events relating to the Douma investigation and report preparation, and gave his own perspective on the report.[25] A written version of the statement was later included as an annex to the Russian summary of the meeting.[26]

Investigation and Identification Team: First report

On 8 April 2020 the Technical Secretariat submitted to the Executive Council the first report of the Investigation and Identification Team (IIT).[27] The IIT report presented findings on the investigation of three incidents where chemical weapons were used in the town of Ltamenah, located within the Hama governorate, on 24, 25 and 30 March 2017 respectively.

In a presentation made a few minutes prior to its release, the OPCW director-general underscored that the mandate of the IIT was 'to establish facts' and that it was 'not a judicial or quasi-judicial body with the authority to assign individual criminal responsibility', nor did it have 'the authority to make final findings on non-compliance with the Convention'; rather, it was for the Executive Council and the Conference of the States Parties to decide the next steps.[28] In summarizing the findings, the IIT coordinator said that the IIT concluded, after considering a range of potential scenarios, that

---

[23] OPCW Director-General, Statement, 6 Feb. 2020 (note 20), p. 8.

[24] United Nations, Security Council, 'Arria-formula meeting—implementation of UNSCR 2118: OPCW FFM Report on Douma', UN Web TV, 20 Jan. 2020. 'Arria-formula' meetings are not formal meetings of the Security Council but are convened at the initiative of a Security Council member or members so that the views of individuals, organizations or institutions on matters within the competence of the Security Council can be heard and engaged with. The first such meeting was in March 1992 and was organized by the then-president of the Security Council, Ambassador Diego Arria (Venezuela). See United Nations, Security Council, 'UN Security Council working methods: Arria-formula meetings', 16 Dec. 2020.

[25] United Nations, Security Council, 'Arria-formula meeting—implementation of UNSCR 2118' (note 24), 0:57:27.

[26] United Nations, General Assembly and Security Council, Identical letters dated 4 February 2020 from the Permanent Representative of the Russian Federation to the United Nations addressed to the Secretary-General and the President of the Security Council, A/74/686–S/2020/96, 13 Feb. 2020, pp. 9–15.

[27] OPCW, Technical Secretariat, 'First report by the OPCW Investigation and Identification Team pursuant to paragraph 10 of Decision C-SS-4/DEC.3 "Addressing the threat from chemical weapons use": Ltamenah (Syrian Arab Republic) 24, 25 and 30 March 2017', Note by the Technical Secretariat, S/1867/2020, 8 Apr. 2020.

[28] Arias, F., 'Director-General's Statement on the First Report by the OPCW Investigation and Identification Team', OPCW Statement, 8 Apr. 2020, p. 4.

'there are reasonable grounds to believe that the perpetrators of use of sarin as a chemical weapon in Ltamenah on 24 and 30 March 2017, and of chlorine as a chemical weapon on 25 March 2017, were individuals belonging to the Syrian Arab Air Force'.[29] More specifically, there were 'reasonable grounds' for each of the following findings:

(a) On 24 March 2017, an Su-22 military airplane belonging to the 50th Brigade of the 22nd Air Division of the Syrian Arab Air Force, departing from Shayrat airbase, dropped an M4000 aerial bomb containing sarin in southern Ltamenah, affecting at least 16 persons.

(b) On 25 March 2017, a helicopter of the Syrian Arab Air Force, departing from Hama airbase, dropped a cylinder on the Ltamenah hospital; the cylinder broke into the hospital through its roof, ruptured, and released chlorine, affecting at least 30 persons.

(c) On 30 March 2017, an Su-22 military airplane belonging to the 50th Brigade of the 22nd Air Division of the Syrian Arab Air Force, departing from Shayrat airbase, dropped an M4000 aerial bomb containing sarin in southern Ltamenah, affecting at least 60 persons.[30]

On the Ltamenah attacks, the report noted that 'a comparison of the results of analysis of samples' collected during these incidents and the 2017 Khan Shaykhun incident show 'significant similarities' and that the analytical results 'are consistent with sarin resulting from a binary process using [difluoride] from the Syrian Arab Republic stockpile'.[31] The report also determines that the 'strategic nature' of these attacks could only have occurred 'pursuant to orders from the highest levels' but that the IIT 'could not . . . draw definitive conclusions to the requisite degree of certainty' regarding the specific chain of command.[32]

Reactions to the release of the first report

Following the release of the first report, a number of states parties submitted statements to the 94th Session of the Executive Council.[33] The Netherlands, the host country, called for the Executive Council to convene 'as soon as is feasible to discuss our response' and further stated:

Until now, the international community, including the Member States of the OPCW, have been unable to take action against Syria, in spite of all the evidence that shows Syria is in non-compliance of the CWC [Chemical Weapons Convention] . . . We, States Parties to the Chemical Weapons Convention, have the obligation to take our commitment to the CWC seriously. Now more than ever is the moment to shake off complacency. If we do not, we jeopardize the integrity and credibility of the global

---

[29] Oñate-Laborde, S., 'IIT Coordinator's remarks on the First Report by the OPCW Investigation and Identification Team', OPCW Statement, 8 Apr. 2020, p. 2.

[30] OPCW, S/1867/2020 (note 27), para. 3.

[31] OPCW, S/1867/2020 (note 27), para. 11.8.

[32] OPCW, S/1867/2020 (note 27), para. 4.

[33] OPCW, 'Ninety-fourth Session of the Executive Council: EC-94' (OPCW EC-94).

Table 12.1. Voting record for Organisation for the Prohibition of Chemical Weapons Executive Council draft decision on 'Addressing the Possession and Use of Chemical Weapons by the Syrian Arab Republic', 9 July 2020

Voting record	State
For the decision (29 votes)	Argentina, Australia, Austria, Belgium, Brazil, Bulgaria, Cameroon, Chile, El Salvador, France, Germany, Ghana, Guatemala, Italy, Japan, Republic of Korea, Lithuania, Mexico, Morocco, Norway, Peru, the Philippines, Poland, Romania, Saudi Arabia, Senegal, Spain, United Kingdom, United States
Against the decision (3 votes)	China, Iran, Russia
Abstentions (9 votes)	Algeria, Bangladesh, India, Kenya, Nigeria, Pakistan, South Africa, Sudan, United Arab Emirates

Source: OPCW, Executive Council, Report of the 94th Session of the Executive Council, EC-94/4, 9 July 2020, para. 6.31.

system of chemical non-proliferation and of the global norm against the use of chemical weapons.[34]

Eight other states parties and the European Union (EU) expressed similar sentiments in the week that followed.[35] However, Russia and Iran questioned the reliability of the report.[36] Syria rejected the report 'in form and in substance' and considered it 'a translation of the desires of the United States of America and its Western allies to target Syria'.[37]

As part of its statement on the issue, the United States, as member of 'a cross-regional group of responsible States Parties seeking to address directly these unconscionable actions of the Syrian regime', suggested that the Executive Council should give the Syrian regime 'a prescribed time frame to take certain actions in order to redress' the non-compliance outlined in

[34] Netherlands Permanent Representative to the OPCW, 'Statement on the First Report by the OPCW Investigation and Identification Team (IIT)', 8 Apr. 2020.

[35] Between 8 and 15 Apr. 2020 the following states parties made statements expressing similar views to the Netherlands: Belgium, Canada, France, Germany, Japan, Switzerland, the UK and the USA. High Representative Josep Borrell also made a statement on behalf of the European Union. See OPCW EC-94 (note 33).

[36] Russian Delegation to the OPCW, 'On the OPCW investigations into incidents of the alleged use of chemical weapons in Ltamenah, Syrian Arab Republic, on 25, 26, and 30 March 2017', OPCW EC-94/NAT.17, 19 June 2020; Shulgin, A. V., Statement of the Russian Permanent Representative to the OPCW at the 94th Session of the Executive Council, OPCW EC-94/NAT.40, 7 July 2020; and Iranian Delegation to the OPCW, 'Statement on the First Report by the OPCW Investigation and Identification Team (IIT)', OPCW EC-94/NAT.3, 15 Apr. 2020, p. 1. See also Russian Ministry of Foreign Affairs, 'Comment by the Information and Press Department on the release of the first report by the OPCW Investigation and Identification Team ("Syrian Chemical Dossier")', 9 Apr. 2020.

[37] Sabbagh, B., 'Statement by the Permanent Representative of the Syrian Arab Republic to the OPCW on the First Report of the OPCW Investigation and Identification Team issued on 8 April 2020', OPCW EC-94/NAT.5, 16 Apr. 2020, p. 1.

the IIT report.[38] Among the actions listed for Syria to take were declarations of facilities which developed, produced, stockpiled and stored for delivery the chemical weapons used in Ltamenah; the declaration of its remaining chemical weapons stockpile and production facilities; and the resolution of all outstanding issues with its initial declarations. In the event that Syria did not complete these measures, the US statement suggested 'the Executive Council should recommend that the Conference of the States Parties take action'.[39]

Forty delegations submitted a draft decision entitled 'Addressing the possession and use of chemical weapons by the Syrian Arab Republic' for consideration by the Executive Council. When states parties were unable to achieve consensus, a vote was taken; the voting record is provided in table 12.1.

With the decision adopted (EC-94/Dec.2), the Executive Council requested Syria to take the following steps within 90 days: (a) declare to the Secretariat the facilities where the chemical weapons, including those used in Ltamenah were developed, produced, stockpiled and operationally stored for delivery; (b) declare to the Secretariat all of the chemical weapons it currently possesses as well as production facilities and other related facilities; and (c) resolve all of the outstanding issues regarding its initial declaration.[40]

Decision EC-94/Dec.2 also directed the OPCW director-general to report to the Executive Council on whether Syria had completed all of those measures within 100 days of the adoption of the decision; and recommended that, if Syria failed to complete the measures within the deadline, the Conference of the States Parties at its next session adopt a decision 'which undertakes appropriate action pursuant to paragraph 2 of Article XII' of the 1993 Chemical Weapons Convention (CWC).[41]

On 20 July, the OPCW director-general sent a letter to the Syrian deputy foreign minister, Dr Faisal Mekdad, to outline Syria's obligations under this decision and to indicate the readiness of the Technical Secretariat to assist Syria in the fulfilment of these obligations.[42]

At the start of the Executive Council's 95th session on 6 October 2020, the director-general informed members that 89 days had passed since the

---

[38] Dinanno, T. G., Statement by the US Deputy Assistant Secretary of State for Defence Policy, Emerging Threats and Outreach at the 94th Session of the Executive Council, OPCW EC-94/NAT.37, 7 July 2020, p. 3.

[39] Dinanno (note 38), p. 3.

[40] OPCW, Executive Council, 'Addressing the possession and use of chemical weapons by the Syrian Arab Republic', Decision, EC-94/Dec.2, 9 July 2020, para. 5.

[41] OPCW, EC-94/Dec.2 (note 40), paras 6–7.

[42] OPCW, Executive Council, 'Implementation of EC-94/DEC.2 on addressing the possession and use of chemical weapons by the Syrian Arab Republic', Report of the Director-General, EC-96/DG.1, 14 Oct. 2020, para. 3. On the CWC see section V in this chapter; and annex A, section I, in this volume.

adoption of the decision and the Technical Secretariat had not yet received any submission from Syria.[43] Eight days later, on 14 October, the director-general informed states parties that the situation remained as previously reported, and that consequently Syria had not fulfilled the requirements of Decision EC-94/Dec.2.[44] The Conference of the States Parties will now consider the 'appropriate action' to be taken under Article XII of the CWC.

Divided views in the United Nations Security Council

The UN Security Council continued its meetings on Syria and chemical weapons during 2020. Its regular meetings on 15 April, 2 June, 14 July and 5 August were in a closed format; its other meetings—on 10 September, 5 October, 5 November and 11 December—were either open or in mixed format and so generated public meeting records.

At the September meeting, the briefing of the UN High Representative for Disarmament Affairs, Izumi Nakamitsu, to Security Council members stressed 'once again' that until outstanding issues on Syria's initial declaration were closed, the international community 'cannot have full confidence' that the Syrian chemical weapons programme has been eliminated.[45] In the debate that followed, delegates roundly condemned the use of chemical weapons 'by any actor', 'under any circumstances'.[46] All but a small number of members also strongly supported the OPCW and the credibility of its investigations, and urged Syria to fully cooperate by providing the requested information. Calls were also made for Security Council unity on efforts to resolve all outstanding issues relating to Syria's initial declaration.

However, long-standing divisions among Security Council members were visible during their meetings. An instance of discord during the meeting on 5 October, on the situation in the Middle East, centred on Russia, as president of the Security Council, proposing to invite the former OPCW director-general, José Bustani, to brief members.[47] Belgium, Estonia, France, Germany, the United Kingdom and the USA objected to this invitation,

---

[43] OPCW, Executive Council, 'Opening statement by the Director-General to the Ninety-fifth Session of the Executive Council (full version)', EC-95/DG.29, 6 Oct. 2020, para. 22.

[44] OPCW, EC-96/DG.1 (note 42), 14 Oct. 2020, paras 4–6.

[45] Nakamitsu, I., Statement by the High Representative for Disarmament Affairs, annex I, p. 2, in United Nations, Security Council, Letter dated 14 September 2020 from the President of the Security Council addressed to the Secretary-General and the Permanent Representatives of the members of the Security Council, S/2020/902, 15 Sep. 2020.

[46] See e.g. statements by China (annex II), South Africa (annex X) and the UK (annex XI), in United Nations, S/2020/902 (note 45). See also United Nations, Security Council, 'Debating Syria's chemical weapons programme, delegates in Security Council roundly condemn use of such armaments by "any actor under any circumstances"', Press release, SC/14298, 10 Sep. 2020.

[47] United Nations, 'The situation in the Middle East (Syria): Security Council, 8674th meeting', UN Web TV, 5 Oct. 2020; and United Nations, Security Council, Provisional minutes of the 8764th meeting, S/PV.8764, 5 Oct. 2020.

arguing that Mr Bustani's tenure as director-general (1997–2002) predated the use of chemical weapons in Syria and so he would not be able to provide members with relevant information. The issue of inviting Mr Bustani to brief the Security Council was eventually put to a vote, with six votes against (Belgium, Estonia, France, Germany, the UK, the USA), three in favour (China, Russia, South Africa) and six abstentions (Dominican Republic, Indonesia, Niger, Saint Vincent and the Grenadines, Tunisia, Viet Nam). As a consequence of the outcome of the vote, the Russian ambassador, speaking in his national capacity, read Mr Bustani's statement to Security Council members, after suggesting that Western governments only wanted to hear confirmations of their allegations.[48]

In December, during the open part of the Security Council briefing on the implementation of Resolution 2118, Director-General Fernando Arias informed the Security Council that he had notified the OPCW Executive Council and other CWC states parties on 14 October that Syria's initial declaration could not be considered accurate or complete, and that Syria had not fulfilled any of the requirements called for in Decision EC-94/Dec.2.[49] The ensuing debate in the public session again displayed division among Security Council members on alleged use of chemical weapons by Syria.

Conclusions

While differing views on the 'Syria file' are highly likely to persist into 2021, the OPCW Technical Secretariat's mandated activities in Syria relating to the full elimination of their chemical weapons programme continue. The second part of the Conference of the States Parties will, among other things, consider 'appropriate action' following Syria's failure to fulfil the requirements of EC-94/Dec.2 and is likely to be a focusing event for states parties in the first quarter of 2021.

[48] United Nations, Security Council, S/PV.8764 (note 47), pp. 7–9.
[49] United Nations, Security Council, 'Middle East (Syria)', S/2020/1152, UN WebTV, 11 Dec. 2020, 00:10:21–00:26:55; United Nations, Security Council, 'Syria's chemical weapons declaration cannot be considered accurate, complete, Director-General tells Security Council', Press release, SC/14380, 11 Dec. 2020; and UN Security Council Resolution 2118, 27 Sep. 2013.

IV. Use of novichok agents

CAITRÍONA MCLEISH

This section focuses on developments related to novichok agents in 2020. It provides a short update on the ongoing investigation into the 2018 poisonings in the United Kingdom; discusses the technical changes made to the Schedule of the 1993 Chemical Weapons Convention (CWC); reviews a new instance of alleged use in the poisoning of Alexei Navalny; and highlights civil society investigations into the Russian novichok programme.[1]

Coronial investigation into Salisbury poisoning

On 17 March 2020, the family of Dawn Sturgess, who died from novichok poisoning linked to the Salisbury attack in 2018, sought a judicial review of the December 2019 coroner's decision not to investigate the responsibility of Russian officials other than the two Russian nationals known by the aliases Alexander Petrov and Ruslan Boshirov for her death, or the source of the novichok.[2] At the hearing held on 14–15 July 2020, counsel for the family argued that the coroner had erred in his reasons for limiting the scope of the inquest and that there was 'acute and obvious public concern not merely at the prima facie evidence that an attempt was made on British soil by Russian agents to assassinate Mr Skripal' but also because this assassination attempt involved 'a prohibited nerve agent exposing the population of Salisbury and Amesbury to lethal risk.'[3] Lord Justice Bean and Mr Justice Lewis found that the claim for judicial review 'must succeed, the ruling must be quashed and the case remitted to the Senior Coroner'.[4]

Technical change to Schedule 1 to the Chemical Weapons Convention

On 7 June 2020, the technical change to the Schedule to the CWC entered into force. This technical change had been adopted by consensus at the 24th Conference of the States Parties (CSP) to the Organisation for the Prohibition of Chemical Weapons (OPCW) in 2019.[5]

---

[1] On the CWC see section V in this chapter; and annex A, section I, in this volume.
[2] *R (GS) v H.M. Senior Coroner for Wiltshire and Swindon*, [2020] EWHC 2007 (Admin), para. 23. On the 2018 novichok attack see McLeish, C., 'The Skripal case: Assassination attempt in the United Kingdom using a toxic chemical', *SIPRI Yearbook 2019*.
[3] *R (GS) v H.M. Senior Coroner for Wiltshire and Swindon* (note 2), para. 88.
[4] *R (GS) v H.M. Senior Coroner for Wiltshire and Swindon* (note 2), para. 84.
[5] OPCW, Conference of the States Parties, 'Technical change to Schedule 1(a) of the Annex on Chemicals to the Chemical Weapons Convention', Decision, C-24/Dec.4, 27 Nov. 2019; and OPCW, Conference of the States Parties, 'Changes to Schedule 1 of the Annex on Chemicals to the Chemical Weapons Convention', Decision, C-24/Dec.5, 27 Nov. 2019.

The addition of the four new entries to Schedule 1—two large families of novichok agents (entry 13 and 14), a single additional novichok agent (entry 15) and two families of carbamate agents (entry 16)—has the effect of subjecting them to the CWC verification regime and declaration requirements. This means, among other things, that any state party operating or intending to operate a single small-scale facility for the production of these chemicals must provide the OPCW Technical Secretariat with a detailed description of the facility and its location, and must also notify the Secretariat of the presence of these newly scheduled chemicals in 'other facilities for protective purposes . . . and other facilities for research, medical or pharmaceutical purposes'. For existing 'other Schedule 1 facilities', initial declarations are to be provided not later than 30 days after entry into force, and inspections under Article VI of the CWC will take place as soon as possible after declarations.[6]

The OPCW director-general told states parties at the 94th Session of the Executive Council that the Secretariat stands ready to assist states parties with implementing these changes and preparing for their initial declarations relating to anticipated annual production for calendar year 2021, which were due by 2 October 2020.[7]

The poisoning of Alexei Navalny

On 20 August 2020, it was reported that Russian opposition figure Alexei Navalny had fallen ill during a flight from the Siberian city of Tomsk to Moscow. The plane made an emergency landing and Navalny was admitted to Omsk Ambulance Hospital No. 1. The following day, French President Emmanuel Macron and German Chancellor Angela Merkel expressed their readiness to provide assistance in terms of healthcare or asylum to Navalny and his family.[8] The Cinema for Peace Foundation, a German non-governmental organization, also announced that it was sending 'an air ambulance with medical equipment and specialists with which Navalny can be brought to Germany'.[9] The European Court of Human Rights also indicated a series of interim measures 'to be enforced without delay' on the treatment Navalny was receiving and his fitness for transfer to Germany.[10]

[6] OPCW, Technical Secretariat, 'Guidance for states parties on Article VI declaration obligations and inspections following entry into force of changes to Schedule 1 of the Annex on Chemicals to the Chemical Weapons Convention', Guidance note, S/1821/2019/Rev.1, 14 Jan. 2020, paras 6 and 24.

[7] OPCW, Executive Council, 'Opening statement by the Director-General to the Ninety-fourth Session of the Executive Council (full version)', EC-94/DG.24, 7 July 2020, paras 58–59.

[8] Didili, Z., 'Merkel, Macron offer asylum, protection to Russia's Navalny', *New Europe*, 21 Aug. 2020.

[9] 'Foundation says it is sending plane for Russia's Navalny', Reuters, 20 Aug. 2020.

[10] European Court of Human Rights, 'The Court grants an interim measure in favour of Aleksey Navalnyy', Press release, ECHR235(2020), 21 Aug. 2020.

The next day, 22 August, the head physician at the hospital in Omsk where Navalny was being treated, Alexander Murakhovsky, announced that a 'working diagnosis' for Navalny's sickness was 'metabolic disorder'; he also indicated that a chemical had been found on the politician's skin and clothing.[11] The Omsk Regional Office of the Russian Ministry of Internal Affairs later expanded on this, explaining that 'a chromatographic study showed the presence of the substance 2-ethylhexyl diphenyl phosphate' (a low toxicity industrial chemical with widespread use).[12] The same day, Navalny was transported to Charité university hospital in Berlin, where he was promptly diagnosed as having been subject to 'poisoning with a substance from the group of cholinesterase inhibitors'.[13] At this time the hospital stated that the specific substance was 'unknown'.[14]

After the announcement by Charité, Chancellor Merkel called on Russia to investigate the poisoning and hold any perpetrators to account.[15] Russia, having conducted pre-investigation checks on 20 August, announced on 27 August that it had found 'no evidence of deliberate criminal actions . . . that would make it possible to qualify this incident under criminal law'.[16] The chief toxicologist of the Omsk Region asserted that Russian medical authorities did not find cholinesterase inhibitors in Navalny's blood.[17]

The following week, on 2 September, Germany announced that testing of samples from Navalny had found 'unequivocal proof' of a novichok nerve agent.[18] These findings were later confirmed by laboratories in France and Sweden.[19] A German Government spokesperson, Steffen Seibert, urged the Russian Government 'to explain itself' and indicated that Germany would 'inform its partners' in the European Union (EU) and the North Atlantic

---

[11] [The main diagnosis of Navalny called metabolic disorder], Interfax, 21 Aug. 2020 (in Russian); and European Chemicals Agency, 'Substance infocard: 2-ethylhexyl diphenyl phosphate', 16 Feb. 2021.

[12] [Industrial chemical found in Navalny's body], Interfax, 21 Aug. 2020 (in Russian).

[13] Charité Universitätsmedizin Berlin, 'Statement by Charité: Clinical findings indicate Alexei Navalny was poisoned', Press release, 24 Aug. 2020.

[14] Charité Universitätsmedizin Berlin (note 13). Navalny remained in a medically induced coma until 7 Sep. and was eventually discharged from hospital on 23 Sep. Charité Universitätsmedizin Berlin, 'Seventh statement by Charité—Universitätsmedizin Berlin: Alexei Navalny discharged from inpatient care', Press release, 23 Sep. 2020.

[15] Nienaber, M. and Nasr, J., 'Merkel tells Russia to investigate suspected poisoning of Kremlin critic', Reuters, 24 Aug. 2020.

[16] 'No elements of crime found during checks into Navalny's hospitalization, says authority', TASS, 27 Aug. 2020.

[17] See e.g. 'No cholinesterase inhibitors found in Navalny's blood in Omsk clinic, says expert', TASS, 24 Aug. 2020; and 'Doctors in Omsk did not use special anti-novichok therapy in Navalny case', TASS, 8 Sep. 2020.

[18] Seibert, S., 'Erklärung der Bundesregierung im Fall Nawalny' [Statement by the Federal Government in the Navalny case], German Cabinet, Press release no. 306, 2 Sep. 2020.

[19] Borrell, J., 'Russia: Poisoning of Alexei Navalny', Speech at the European Parliament plenary session, 15 Sep. 2020. See also Swedish Defence Research Agency (FOI), 'FOI confirms German results on novichok', Press release, 15 Sep. 2020.

Treaty Organization (NATO) of the findings and 'discuss an appropriate joint reaction'.[20] Accordingly, the EU high representative for foreign affairs and security policy, Josep Borrell, stated that the EU condemned the poisoning 'in the strongest possible terms' and that it was 'essential' for Russia to investigate 'thoroughly and in a transparent manner the assassination attempt'.[21] The 27 EU member states issued a declaration the following day.[22] Statements also followed from, among others, the North Atlantic Council and the foreign ministers of the Group of Seven (G7) countries.[23]

Two days later, on 4 September, Germany requested technical assistance from the OPCW under Article VIII subparagraph 38(e).[24] The Technical Assistance Visit (TAV) Team deployed to Germany on 5 September and the next day, 'blood and urine sampling was conducted by the hospital staff under the direct supervision and continuous visual observation of the team members'.[25] On 11 September, and upon receipt of a request from Germany, the samples were sent to two designated laboratories for analysis.[26] The results of the analysis were reported by the Technical Secretariat in a public summary as follows:

The results of the analysis of biomedical samples conducted by the OPCW designated laboratories demonstrate that Mr Navalny was exposed to a toxic chemical acting as a cholinesterase inhibitor. The biomarkers of the cholinesterase inhibitor found in Mr Navalny's blood and urine samples have similar structural characteristics to the toxic chemicals belonging to schedules 1.A.14 and 1.A.15, which were added to the Annex on Chemicals to the Convention at the Twenty-Fourth Session of the Conference of the States Parties in November 2019. This cholinesterase inhibitor is not listed in the Annex on Chemicals to the Convention.[27]

The day before the release of the public summary of the TAV investigation, the OPCW released a statement that it had also received a request from Russia to 'consider' dispatching staff to Russia 'in order to cooperate with Russian experts', and that the OPCW director-general had responded with

---

[20] Seibert (note 18).

[21] Borrell, J., 'Russia: Statement by High Representative/Vice-President Josep Borrell on the poisoning of Alexei Navalny', European External Action Service, Press release, 2 Sep. 2020.

[22] Council of the European Union, 'Russia: Declaration of the High Representative on behalf of the EU on the poisoning of Alexei Navalny', Press release, 3 Sep. 2020.

[23] North Atlantic Treaty Organization, 'Statement by the North Atlantic Council on the poisoning of Alexei Navalny', Press release no. (2020) 071, 4 Sep. 2020; and British Foreign, Commonwealth and Development Office, 'Russia: G7 Foreign Ministers' statement on Navalny poisoning', Press release, 8 Sep. 2020.

[24] OPCW, Technical Secretariat, 'Summary of the report on activities carried out in support of a request for technical assistance by Germany (Technical Assistance Visit–TAV/01/20)', Note by the Technical Secretariat, S/1906/2020, 6 Oct. 2020, para. 1.

[25] OPCW, S/1906/2020 (note 24), paras 2–3.

[26] OPCW, S/1906/2020 (note 24), para. 4.

[27] OPCW, S/1906/2020 (note 24), para. 5 The particular novichok used to poison Navalny was not a scheduled chemical: its chemical structure was different from that of the classes of novichok that had recently been added to Schedule 1.

an assurance of readiness and 'sought further clarification . . . on the type of expertise contemplated'.[28] In December, at the request of Russia, the correspondence between the OPCW Technical Secretariat and the Russian delegation on this matter, dated between 1 October and 21 December, was published on the OPCW's public website.[29] The correspondence included an indication from the Russian delegation on 16 December that they did not wish the requested TAV team to proceed.[30]

Shortly after the OPCW confirmed that Navalny had been exposed to a toxic chemical acting as a cholinesterase inhibitor, the EU imposed travel bans and asset freezes on six Russian individuals and an entity allegedly involved in the poisoning.[31] The sanctions fell under the EU's 2018 sanctions regime that focuses on chemical weapons.[32] The same day, the UK announced that it would also apply the same sanctions through its own 'autonomous UK Chemical Weapons sanctions regime', which would come into force following its departure from the EU.[33]

Civil society activities

At the end of October 2020, Bellingcat—a non-governmental investigative network—released the results of a year-long investigation with partners on the Russian novichok programme. The investigation's main findings include the identification of the St Petersburg State Institute for Experimental Military Medicine of the Russian Ministry of Defence and the Scientific Center Signal as the lead institutes, since 2010, in the continued research, development and weaponization of the Soviet-era novichok programme. Bellingcat claimed that the work of these two institutes had 'stayed out of the focus of Western intelligence services'.[34] The investigation also obtained information suggesting 'close coordination' between these two institutes and 'a secretive sub-unit of Military Unit 29155 of Russia's military intelligence,

---

[28] OPCW, 'OPCW responds to Russian Federation request regarding allegations of chemical weapons use against Alexei Navalny', News, 5 Oct. 2020.

[29] OPCW Technical Secretariat and Russian Permanent Representative to the OPCW, Correspondence, 1 Oct–21 Dec. 2020.

[30] Russian Permanent Representative to the OPCW, Letter to HE Mr Fernando Arias, Director-General of the Technical Secretariat of the OPCW, 16 Dec. 2020, unofficial translation, in Correspondence (note 29), p. 5, para. 7.

[31] Council Implementing Regulation (EU) 2020/1480 of 14 Oct. 2020 implementing Regulation (EU) 2018/1542 concerning restrictive measures against the proliferation and use of chemical weapons, *Official Journal of the European Union*, L341, 15 Oct. 2020.

[32] Council of the European Union, 'Chemical weapons: The Council adopts a new sanctions regime', Press release, 15 Oct. 2018.

[33] British Foreign, Commonwealth and Development Office, 'UK sanctions Alexey Navalny's poisoners', Press release, 15 Oct. 2020.

[34] Bellingcat Investigation Team, 'Russia's clandestine chemical weapons programme and the GRU's Unit 29155', Bellingcat News, 23 Oct. 2020.

the GRU'.[35] Previous Bellingcat investigations had linked members of this unit to the poisoning attempts on Emilian Gebrev in Bulgaria in 2015 and Sergey and Yulia Skripal in the UK in 2018.[36]

In December, Bellingcat also released the results of an investigation with partners CNN, *Der Spiegel* and *The Insider*, which it claims contains data that 'directly links the August 2020 poisoning of Navalny to Russia's domestic security services', that is, to the Federal Security Service (FSB).[37] A timeline of the evidence and note on the investigation's methodology was also released.[38] Findings include that 'FSB operatives from a clandestine unit specialized in working with poisonous substances shadowed Navalny during his trips across Russia' since 2017 and that it is possible that there were earlier attempts to poison him.[39] The report identified seven operatives of this clandestine unit that it said was involved in following Navalny.

A further release from Bellingcat, in late December 2020, concerned validation of key elements of a 49-minute conversation between Alexei Navalny, who was posing as a fictious aide to the head of Russia's Security Council, and Konstantin Kudryavtsev, one of the previously identified members of the FSB clandestine unit that apparently followed him.[40] According to Bellingcat, during the telephone call Kudryavtsev told Navalny a number of important details about the poisoning attempt, including that Alexey Alexandrov and Ivan Osipov were the main perpetrators and that Kudryavtsev had been instructed to travel to Omsk to process Navalny's clothing, including his underwear, which was described as having 'the highest concentration' of poison.[41] The FSB dismissed the telephone call as 'a planned provocation . . . the implementation of which would not have been possible without . . . support of foreign special services'.[42]

[35] Bellingcat Investigation Team (note 34).

[36] Bellingcat Investigation Team, 'The Dreadful Eight: GRU's Unit 29155 and the 2015 poisoning of Emilian Gebrev', Bellingcat News, 23 Nov. 2019; and Bellingcat Investigation Team, 'Third Skripal suspect linked to 2015 Bulgaria poisoning', Bellingcat News, 7 Feb. 2019.

[37] Bellingcat Investigation Team, 'FSB team of chemical weapon experts implicated in Alexey Navalny novichok poisoning', Bellingcat News, 14 Dec. 2020.

[38] See Bellingcat Investigation Team, 'Timeline of movements, phone calls, and actions taken by Team 9 and by Alexey Navalny's team', Dec. 2020; and Bellingcat Investigation Team, 'Hunting the hunters: How we identified Navalny's FSB stalkers', 14 Dec. 2020.

[39] Bellingcat Investigation Team (note 37).

[40] Bellingcat Investigation Team, '"If it hadn't been for the prompt work of the medics": FSB officer inadvertently confesses murder plot to Navalny', Bellingcat News, 21 Dec. 2020.

[41] Bellingcat Investigation Team (note 40).

[42] 'Navalny's so-called investigation into his poisoning a provocation, FSB says', TASS, 22 Dec. 2020.

V. Chemical arms control and disarmament

CAITRÍONA MCLEISH

As of December 2020, there are 193 states parties to the 1993 Chemical Weapons Convention (CWC), the principal international legal instrument against chemical warfare; one state (Israel) has signed but not ratified the treaty; and three states (Egypt, North Korea and South Sudan) have neither signed nor acceded to it.[1]

Organisation for the Prohibition of Chemical Weapons developments

Impact of Covid-19 pandemic on the operations of the OPCW

The Covid-19 pandemic impacted the work of the Technical Secretariat of the Organisation for the Prohibition of Chemical Weapons (OPCW) throughout 2020. Prior to the World Health Organization (WHO) declaring the outbreak a public health emergency of international concern (PHEIC) on 30 January 2020, the OPCW director-general had established an internal task force, chaired by the deputy director-general, to monitor and assess the outbreak as it related to OPCW activities.[2] On 10 March 2020, at the opening of the 93rd Session of the Executive Council (EC-93), the director-general spoke about the measures taken and noted it would be 'challenging' to complete all 241 Article VI inspections that had been planned for calendar year 2020.[3] On the following day the WHO characterized the outbreak as a PHEIC.[4]

Two days later, on 13 March, the OPCW director-general informed states parties of the measures being taken to protect OPCW staff.[5] These included the postponement of all Article VI inspections as well as inspections related to former chemical weapons production facilities, abandoned chemical weapons and old chemical weapons.[6] Only Article IV inspections relating

---

[1] For a summary and other details of the Chemical Weapons Convention see annex A, section I, in this volume.

[2] World Health Organization (WHO), 'Statement on the second meeting of the International Health Regulations (2005) Emergency Committee regarding the outbreak of novel coronavirus (2019-nCoV)', News, 30 Jan. 2020; Ghebreyesus, T. A., 'WHO director-general's statement on IHR emergency committee on novel coronavirus', Speech, 30 Jan. 2020; and OPCW, Executive Council, 'Opening statement by the Director-General to the Ninety-third Session of the Executive Council (full version)', EC-93/DG.18, 10 Mar. 2020, para. 34.

[3] OPCW, EC-93/DG.18 (note 2), para. 34.

[4] WHO, 'WHO director-general's opening remarks at the media briefing on Covid-19', 11 Mar. 2020. On the Covid-19 pandemic see section I in this chapter.

[5] OPCW, Technical Secretariat, 'Impact of the outbreak of the novel coronavirus (Covid-19) on the Organisation for the Prohibition of Chemical Weapons', Note by the Technical Secretariat, S/1863/2020, 20 Mar. 2020, para. 2.

[6] OPCW, S/1863/2020 (note 5), paras 7–11.

to verification of activities at chemical weapons destruction facilities in the United States were to continue. In addition to these changes, the director-general announced the postponement of all non-essential travel worldwide, including for training purposes and relating to capacity-building events, as well as missions to Syria.[7]

As the pandemic evolved the OPCW Technical Secretariat kept states parties up to date on the impact the pandemic was having on its activities and programmes of work.[8] Some activities were significantly impacted—Article VI inspections did not resume until September, so too deployments of the OPCW Declaration Assessment Team (DAT) to Syria. As a result, only 82 out of 241 Article VI inspections were completed in 2020, with those 'not completed' being 'prioritised' for 2021.[9] Planned in-person meetings were generally postponed or cancelled, or pivoted into virtual meetings. The International Cooperation and Assistance Division held capacity-building events online.[10]

Executive Council meetings did take place in person, although with limits on the number of people in the meeting room for health and safety reasons.[11] The 25th Session of the Conference of the States Parties (CSP) likewise went ahead, with adaptations, in the World Forum. The adapted format included splitting the session into two parts (with the first taking place on 30 November to 1 December 2020 and the second scheduled for no later than 30 April 2021) and limiting in-person participation to states parties (with their delegation size reduced) and no in-room general debate. States parties instead uploaded their national statements in written and video formats. International organizations, the chemical industry and non-governmental organizations were similarly offered this option. At the time of writing, OPCW staff continue to work remotely, 'unless work on OPCW premises is absolutely necessary'.[12]

Follow-up to the Fourth Review Conference

Ambassador Agustín Vásquez Gómez of El Salvador, who had been chair of the Fourth Review Conference, and Ambassador I Gusti Agung Wesaka Puja of Indonesia, the former chair of the Open-ended Working Group (OEWG)

---

[7] OPCW, S/1863/2020 (note 5), paras 4, 6, 12 and 14.

[8] The Technical Secretariat sent four Notes in total between Mar. and Aug., all with the same title ('Update on the impact of the outbreak of the novel coronavirus (Covid-19) on the Organisation for the Prohibition of Chemical Weapons'): OPCW, S/1863/2020 (note 5); S/1870/2020, 17 Apr. 2020; S/1876/2020, 3 June 2020; and S/1890/2020, 26 Aug. 2020.

[9] OPCW, Technical Secretariat, 'Update on the impact of the outbreak of the coronavirus disease (Covid-19) on the Organisation for the Prohibition of Chemical Weapons Programme in 2021', Note by the Technical Secretariat, S/1930/2021, 18 Feb. 2021, para. 15.

[10] OPCW, S/1930/2021 (note 9), paras 21–24.

[11] OPCW, S/1876/2020 (note 8), paras 6–7.

[12] OPCW, S/1930/2021 (note 9), para. 2.

Table 12.2. Voting record for the Draft Programme and Budget of the Organisation for the Prohibition of Chemical Weapons for 2021

Voting record	State
For the decision (33 votes)	Argentina, Australia, Austria, Bangladesh, Belgium, Brazil, Bulgaria, Cameroon, Chile, El Salvador, France, Germany, Ghana, Guatemala, Italy, Japan, Republic of Korea, Lithuania, Mexico, Morocco, Nigeria, Norway, Peru, the Philippines, Poland, Romania, Saudi Arabia, Senegal, South Africa, Spain, United Arab Emirates, United Kingdom, United States
Against the decision (3 votes)	China, Iran, Russia
Abstentions (5 votes)	Algeria, India, Kenya, Pakistan, Sudan

Source: OPCW, Executive Council, Report of the 95th Session of the Executive Council, EC-95/4, 9 Oct. 2020, para. 10.33.

for the Preparations for the Fourth Review Conference, continued in their joint role as facilitators on organizational governance issues during 2020.

Ambassadors Gómez and Puja reported to EC-93 that they had held five rounds of facilitation in the run-up to the meeting and had used their 'best judgement' to formulate a set of recommendations in 12 areas around which they had identified a broad convergence of views.[13] The facilitators highlighted a further six areas that would 'especially' benefit from further discussions.[14] The recommendations were relayed to the Executive Council, which expressed 'appreciation' for this work and then 'welcomed' the appointment of the new facilitators on organizational governance issues, Ambassador Matthew Neuhaus of Australia and Ambassador Laura Dupuy Lasserre of Uruguay.[15]

Build-up to the 25th Conference of the States Parties

At EC-93, held on 10–12 March 2020, the OPCW director-general noted that the organization 'will again face the challenge of delivering additional mandated activities under a zero nominal growth budget'.[16] At a general level, he suggested that, should states parties 'continue to maintain' their approach for the 2021 budget, the Secretariat would have to ask them to 'choose among programmatic priorities in order to focus and adapt the Programme and Budget to this reality'.[17] He also noted that some 'critical priorities', such

[13] OPCW, Executive Council, 'Report by HE Ambassador Agustín Vásquez Gómez and H. E. Ambassador I Gusti Agung Wesaka Puja, the co-facilitators on organisational governance issues', EC-93/WP.1, 10 Mar. 2020, paras 4, 6 and 7.

[14] OPCW, EC-93/WP.1 (note 13), paras 7–9.

[15] OPCW, Executive Council, Report of the Ninety-third Session of the Executive Council, EC-93/2, 12 Mar. 2020, para. 4.4.

[16] OPCW, EC-93/DG.18 (note 2), para. 7.

[17] OPCW, EC-93/DG.18 (note 2), para. 7.

as cyber security, 'demand immediate and sustained resources' and that, to be sustainable, the programme would require 'dedicated staff and regular budget funding as soon as 2021'.[18]

The director-general presented states parties with the Draft Programme and Budget on 3 July 2020.[19] When the Executive Council sat four days later for its 94th session, the director-general described the pandemic as further exposing 'the fact that a Budget based on zero nominal growth hinders our ability to adapt to unforeseen circumstances'.[20] He noted, for example, that the information technology (IT) platforms that were required to shift activities online 'proved to be outdated' and that there was insufficient IT infrastructure to support staff working from home.[21]

When Executive Council members sat in October for the 95th session, their reactions to the proposed Draft Programme and Budget were mixed. The publicly available national statements from that session show, for example, Germany considering the proposed budget for 2021 to be 'proportionate and justified' and South Korea considering it to be 'well devised', but Russia as having 'serious complaints' and Iran as dissatisfied with the budget allocation to the International Cooperation and Assistance Programme.[22]

This division meant the proposed Draft Programme and Budget was put to a vote. The result was 33 in favour, 3 against and 5 abstentions (see table 12.2).[23] The Draft Programme and Budget was transmitted to the CSP with a recommendation to approve.

The 25th Conference of the States Parties

The first session of the 25th CSP took place on 30 November and 1 December 2020 with Ambassador José Antonio Zabalgoitia Trejo of Mexico in the chair. The OPCW director-general had previously informed states parties that adaptations to the CSP, including reduced delegation sizes to ensure physical distancing at the meeting, would need to be made so that an in-person

---

[18] OPCW, EC-93/DG.18 (note 2), para. 8.

[19] OPCW, Executive Council, 'Opening statement by the Director-General to the Ninety-fourth Session of the Executive Council (full version)', EC-94/DG.24, 7 July 2020, para. 16. This later appeared on the public website as OPCW, Executive Council, 'Draft Programme and Budget of the OPCW for 2021', Note by the Director-General, EC-95/CRP.1, 3 July 2020.

[20] OPCW, EC-94/DG.24 (note 19), para. 13.

[21] OPCW, EC-94/DG.24 (note 19), paras 13–14.

[22] German Permanent Representative to the OPCW, Statement at the 95th Session of the Executive Council, EC-95/NAT.15, 6 Oct. 2020, p. 3; South Korean Permanent Representative to the OPCW, Statement at the 95th Session of the Executive Council, EC-95/NAT.57, 6 Oct. 2020, p. 2; Russian Permanent Representative to the OPCW, Statement at the 95th Session of the Executive Council, 6 Oct. 2020 (unofficial translation), p. 3; and Iranian Permanent Representative to the OPCW, Statement at the 95th Session of the Executive Council, EC-95/NAT.18, 6 Oct. 2020, p. 3.

[23] OPCW, Executive Council, Report of the Ninety-fifth Session of the Executive Council, EC-95/4, para. 10.3.

meeting could happen.[24] By general agreement, this first part of the CSP only covered issues requiring immediate attention, with the other agenda items to be addressed in a second part of the CSP, to be held in 2021. The issues addressed during this first part were those relating to the Programme and Budget; amendments to the OPCW Financial Regulations and Rules in relation to the new biennial Programme and Budget; scale of assessments for 2021; and the date of submission of the 2021 Financial Statements of the OPCW.[25]

Five delegations took to the floor to detail why they were unable to support the Draft Programme and Budget in the Council: China, Cuba, Russia, Syria and Venezuela. They expressed similar concerns over the use of the cash surplus, using the budget to support the work of the Investigation and Identification Team (IIT) and the 'omnibus format'.[26] Cuba additionally raised concerns that the budget for international cooperation and assistance 'still falls far too short of what we need'.[27]

Taking the floor immediately after the first four of these interventions, Ambassador Paul van den IJssel of the Netherlands described the nature of the objections as not financial or budgetary but 'a principled difference of view on political issues' and requested a roll-call vote.[28] After the required 24 hours had passed, the vote was taken: 103 in favour, 14 against and 13 abstentions.[29] Thirteen delegations took the floor afterward to explain their vote, with the predominant themes being the lack of consensus, the omnibus format and the element of the budget that would support the work of the IIT.[30]

Other developments in 2020

The destruction of chemical weapons

Verification at chemical weapons destruction facilities in the USA continued throughout 2020 despite the pandemic, with modifications to ensure the health and safety of inspectors and personnel on site. The OPCW director-general reported that, as at 30 November 2020, 69 317 metric tonnes or

[24] OPCW, Executive Council, 'Opening statement by the Director-General to the Ninety-fifth Session of the Executive Council (full version)', EC-95/DG.29, 6 Oct. 2020, paras 44–48.

[25] OPCW, Conference of the States Parties, 'Opening Statement by the Director-General to the Conference of the States Parties at its Twenty-fifth Session', C-25/DG.19, 30 Nov. 2020, para. 38.

[26] Omnibus format refers to the packaging together in a single document several issues that may or may not be related. A number of countries object to this format. In this case, reasons for objecting included that the need for a budget was packaged with other financial issues: regular budget matters, funding the IIT following the June 2018 decision, and the allocation of cash surpluses to other purposes, rather than being returned to states parties.

[27] OPCW, CSP-25 Webcast, Day 1, 1:56:28–2:13:47 and 2:17:44–2:22:01.

[28] OPCW, CSP-25 Webcast (note 27), Day 1, 2:14:49–2:17:19.

[29] OPCW, CSP-25 Webcast (note 27), Day 2, 0:45:40–0:46:10.

[30] OPCW, CSP-25 Webcast (note 27), Day 2, 0:46:34–1:26:56.

98.3 per cent of declared Category 1 chemical weapons had been destroyed under verification by the Secretariat.[31]

During the year, the USA reported the completion of the sarin projectile destruction campaign at the main plant in the Blue Grass Chemical Agent-Destruction Pilot Plant and that it continued to be on track to meet the planned completion date of September 2023.[32]

The pandemic put on hold all destruction operations and related activities with regard to chemical weapons abandoned in China at the end of World War II. Accordingly, the number of abandoned chemical weapons in China which were destroyed remained 'at around 57,700 of the 83,650 items declared'.[33]

The OPCW Scientific Advisory Board

In 2020, the OPCW Scientific Advisory Board (SAB) met twice, in a virtual format, and produced two reports. In the report from its 29th session the SAB recommended that the OPCW director-general fully consider the recommendations in the final report of the Temporary Working Group (TWG) on Investigative Science and Technology and particularly those regarding the establishment of one TWG on determining the provenance of chemical samples and another TWG on the analysis of biotoxins. The SAB also recommended the convening of a workshop relating to the newly scheduled chemicals.[34] In his reply, the director-general said that both of the recommended TWGs will be given 'serious consideration', so too the workshop recommendation.[35]

The Centre for Chemistry and Technology

Work continued on the Centre for Chemistry and Technology (ChemTech Centre) project in 2020. The OPCW director-general noted that 'the Centre will be an essential tool to fully address new and emerging chemical weapons threats, as well as to support international cooperation and assistance capacity-building activities'.[36] The director-general also noted that the Technical Secretariat will work with states parties 'to prepare a dossier of potential projects' which 'could encompass activities such as

---

[31] OPCW, C-25/DG.19 (note 25), para. 14.

[32] OPCW, Executive Council, 'Overall progress with respect to the destruction of remaining chemical stockpiles', Report by the Director-General, EC-94/DG.18, 1 July 2020, para. 11.

[33] OPCW, Executive Council, 'Overall progress with respect to the destruction of chemical weapons abandoned by Japan in the People's Republic of China', Report by the Director-General, EC-94/DG.19, 1 July 2020, para. 2.

[34] OPCW, Scientific Advisory Board, 'Report of the Scientific Advisory Board at its Twenty-ninth Session, 1–2 September 2020', SAB-29/1, 2 Sep. 2020, para. 1.4.

[35] OPCW, Executive Council, 'Response to the report of the Twenty-eighth Session of the Scientific Advisory Board, 1–2 September 2020', Note by the Director-General, EC-95/DG.26, 2 Oct. 2020, paras 7a and 7c.

[36] OPCW, C-25/DG.19 (note 25), para. 32.

scientific research programmes, lectures, and visits from academics'.[37] The latest publicly available report on the project noted that the final design of the ChemTech Centre was completed in July 2020 and that the request for expression of interest phase for the main construction contract was completed in August 2020.[38] The Secretariat expects to award the construction contract in the first quarter of 2021.[39] Over the course of the year, 23 states parties made contributions to support the ChemTech Centre, which is expected to be operational by 2022.[40]

OPCW contribution to global antiterrorism efforts

The OPCW continued it efforts to counter the threat of chemical terrorism, including though its participation in the UN Global Counter-Terrorism Coordination Compact and the Compact's Working Group on Emerging Threats and Critical Infrastructure Protection, where the OPCW is a vice-chair.

The OEWG on Terrorism met in March and October of 2020. In March, the group focused on 'strengthening legal frameworks to counter chemical terrorism, as well as effectively monitoring and responding to such incidents', and heard a briefing from the UN Office on Drugs and Crime's Terrorism Prevention Branch, particularly about its work supporting the adoption and implementation of 19 international legal instruments on terrorism.[41] The OEWG also heard from the Secretariat on the Situation Centre and its role as 'the eyes and ears' of the OPCW.[42] In October, the OEWG met under a new chair, Ambassador Vusimuzi Philemon Madonsela of South Africa, and focused on inter-agency capacity-building efforts, particularly the role of the UN and the UN Office of Counter-Terrorism.[43]

The OPCW Technical Secretariat also continued to offer support to states parties in their efforts to prevent acts of terrorism involving the release of toxic chemicals. This support included those states that have yet to adopt national implementing legislation covering all initial measures.[44] Of the

---

[37] OPCW, C-25/DG.19 (note 25), para. 33.

[38] OPCW, Technical Secretariat, 'Progress in the project to upgrade the OPCW Laboratory and Equipment Store to a Centre for Chemistry and Technology', Note by the Technical Secretariat, S/1912/2020, 16 Nov. 2020, paras 6–9.

[39] OPCW, S/1912/2020 (note 38), para. 10.

[40] OPCW, 'News: OPCW Centre for Chemistry and Technology', [n.d.]; and OPCW, S/1912/2020 (note 38), para. 12.

[41] OPCW, Executive Council, 'Report by HE Ambassador Oji Nyimenuate Ngofa Chairperson of the Open-Ended Working Group on Terrorism to the Executive Council at its Ninety-third Session', EC-93/WP.2, 11 Mar. 2020, paras 2 and 4.

[42] OPCW, EC-93/WP.2 (note 41), paras 4 and 6.

[43] OPCW, Executive Council, 'Report by HE Ambassador Mr Vusimuzi Philemon Madonsela, Chairperson of the Open-Ended Working Group on Terrorism to the Executive Council at its Ninety-fifth Session', EC-95/WP.2, 7 Oct. 2020, paras 3 and 5.

[44] OPCW, Executive Council, 'Status of the OPCW's contribution to global anti-terrorism efforts', Note by the Director-General, EC-96/DG.10, 18 Feb. 2021, para. 13.

193 states parties, 74 states parties either have legislation that covers only some of the initial measures or are yet to report on the adoption of any legislation.[45]

The Africa Programme

On 1 January 2020, the OPCW launched the fifth phase of the Programme to Strengthen Cooperation with Africa on the CWC (Africa Programme), a programme of work that promotes the peaceful uses of chemistry for a developed, safe and secure Africa. The objectives assigned to the Africa Programme for 2020–22 were developed through 'a consensual identification of the region's current needs and priorities'.[46] There are three overarching areas for action: advancing CWC implementation; promoting chemical safety and security; and promoting knowledge in peaceful chemistry and applications in support of sustainable development.[47] The OPCW Technical Secretariat is to monitor and evaluate progress and report annually to the Executive Council and the CSP. A steering committee will regularly review and advise on implementation and progress.[48]

Chemicals that act on the central nervous system

At the 93rd Session of the Executive Council in March 2020, Ambassador Kenneth Ward of the USA told council members that it was 'essential' that the threat from chemicals active on the central nervous system (CNS) be addressed and countered 'effectively' in 2020.[49] He described the threat as encompassing 'the repurposing of pharmaceutical compounds, such as anaesthetics—like fentanyl—for military or law enforcement purposes' such that they 'pose a serious risk of further re-emergence of chemical weapons—opening up a backdoor to the Convention'.[50] Recognizing that the use of CNS-acting chemicals in warfare would 'unquestionably be a violation of Article I', Ambassador Ward argued that in aerosol form they could not 'satisfy the "types and quantities" requirement' of the CWC.[51]

A revised draft decision, still entitled 'Understanding Regarding the Aerosolised Use of Central Nervous System-Acting Chemicals for Law Enforcement Purposes', was reissued on 9 March.[52] Further revisions of the proposal were circulated to states parties, along with an explanatory

[45] OPCW, EC-96/DG.10 (note 44), para. 11.

[46] OPCW, Executive Council, 'The fifth phase of the Programme to Strengthen Cooperation with Africa on the Chemical Weapons Convention', EC-93/DG.9, 18 Feb. 2020, para. 8.

[47] OPCW, EC-93/DG.9 (note 46), para. 10.

[48] OPCW, EC-93/DG.9 (note 46), paras 50–52.

[49] US Permanent Representative to the OPCW, Statement at the 93rd Session of the Executive Council, EC-93/NAT.14, 10 Mar. 2020, p. 1.

[50] US Permanent Representative to the OPCW (note 49), pp. 1–2.

[51] US Permanent Representative to the OPCW (note 49), pp. 1–2.

[52] OPCW, EC-93/2 (note 15), para. 13.1.

memorandum, at the end of September.[53] On 5 October 2020, the Technical Secretariat advised that the implication of the revised proposal in terms of additional requirements could be met within existing resources.[54]

Russia, China, Iran and Syria separately submitted working papers on the issue.[55] Russia drew attention to the lack of clarity of the concept and obscurity of basic terms such as 'aerosolized use of CNS-acting chemicals', 'law enforcement purposes', 'riot control agents' and 'temporary incapacitation'; suggested that 'the application of any agents (not only chemical) for law enforcement purposes, are the sovereign and purely internal affair of each State'; and proposed informal consultation or the establishment of a TWG to work through 'the different interpretations that currently exist'.[56] At the time of writing the working papers by China, Iran and Syria were not publicly available. The Executive Council decided to defer the matter for future consideration.[57]

Conclusions and prospects for 2021

As was the case in other international arms control and disarmament forums, the Covid-19 pandemic impacted the work of the OPCW in 2020, yet the states parties and the Technical Secretariat adapted. Some of the latter's adaptations, made to enable continued implementation of its mandate and delivery for states parties, may last beyond the current situation. For example, lessons being learned in the delivery of on-line capacity-building events may optimize future event delivery.[58] At the time of writing, the ongoing global pandemic seems likely to continue impacting the OPCW's work in 2021. Nevertheless, the 2020 Conference of the States Parties will resume not later than 30 April 2021; the regular cycle of Executive Council meetings will also take place in 2021; and states parties will, among other things, consider the Technical Secretariat's first submission of the biennial Programme and Budget.

---

[53] OPCW, EC-95/4 (note 23), para. 16.2.
[54] OPCW, Executive Council, 'Financial, administrative, and programme and budget implications of the proposal for an understanding regarding the aerosolised use of central nervous system-acting chemicals for law enforcement purposes', Report by the Director-General, EC-93/DG.2/Rev.1, 5 Oct. 2020, para. 4.
[55] OPCW, EC-95/4 (note 23), paras 16.4–16.5.
[56] Russian delegation to the OPCW, 'On an understanding regarding the aerosolized use of central nervous system-acting chemicals for law enforcement purposes', Statement submitted to the 93rd Session of the OPCW, EC-93/NAT.6, 6 Mar. 2020, pp. 2 and 4.
[57] OPCW, EC-95/4 (note 23), para. 16.7.
[58] OPCW, C-25/DG.19 (note 25), para. 17.

13. Conventional arms control and regulation of new weapon technologies

Overview

Conventional arms control by states usually falls within one of two broad approaches: limiting or prohibiting weapons considered to be inhumane or indiscriminate; or regulating and managing the procurement, production, transfers and trade of weapons, with a view to preventing their destabilizing accumulation, diversion or misuse. The first category includes the 1981 Certain Conventional Weapons (CCW) Convention, the 1997 Anti-Personnel Mine (APM) Convention and the 2008 Convention on Cluster Munitions (CCM). The second category includes the 2013 Arms Trade Treaty (ATT, see chapter 14). Other categories of weapon are not covered by a specific treaty. In some of these cases, states may consider a new treaty or—as in the case of lethal autonomous weapon systems (LAWS)—extension of the coverage of an existing regime. In cases where this approach has failed, states may consider alternative, less formal approaches—as in the case of explosive weapons in populated areas (EWIPA). In more complex cases—such as the regulation of cyberspace or activity in space—the most appropriate approach may be the subject of intense debate.

International concern is growing over the use of EWIPA (see section I). Little progress has been made on this issue within the CCW Convention in recent years due to the lack of consensus and a handful of states obstructing advances in most of its agenda. In 2020 the difficulties in these negotiations were aggravated by the inability to meet face-to-face due to the Covid-19 pandemic—which had an impact in all the conventional arms control discussions during the year. The lack of progress on EWIPA within the CCW regime has led some states to explore a separate process. Led by Ireland, this process aims to develop a political declaration to address the humanitarian harm arising from the use of EWIPA. Discussion was slowed by the Covid-19 pandemic, but further consultations are expected to lead to the adoption of a declaration in 2021.

While new uses of APMs by states are now extremely rare, use by non-state armed groups in conflicts, and especially of victim-activated improvised explosive devices (IEDs), is a growing problem (see section I). APMs were used by such groups in at least six states between mid 2019 and October 2020: Afghanistan, Colombia, India, Libya, Myanmar and Pakistan. There was also continued use of cluster munitions in Syria in 2019–20.

Efforts to regulate LAWS within the framework of the CCW Convention started in 2014 and, since 2017, have been led by an open-ended group of governmental experts (GGE). In 2020 these discussions largely centred around identifying key areas of convergence in order to inform the Sixth Review Conference of the CCW Convention, scheduled to take place in 2021 (see section II). However, as well as being hampered by pandemic-related restrictions, fundamental disagreements persisted over the outcome and mandate of the GGE, notably between Western delegations, the Non-Aligned Movement (NAM) and Russia. This raised serious questions as to what the GGE will be capable of achieving beyond the 11 guiding principles adopted in 2019.

In the context of ongoing geopolitical tensions around the security of information and communications technology (ICT), dialogue around the governance of ICT and cyber norms has taken place at multiple levels. The main state-driven efforts continued in 2020 within two parallel United Nations processes: an Open-ended Working Group (OEWG) and a GGE (see section III). However, despite changes to the digital landscape caused by the Covid-19 pandemic that have increased the need for action, the differing interests of states and normative preferences have hindered these international efforts to control the malicious use of ICT. In the absence of consensus, a legally binding agreement seems unlikely in the near future.

Despite the growing risk of a conflict in outer space, international discussions on both security and safety aspects of space activities have also remained blocked (see section IV). Destabilizing issues that arose in 2020 included controversial rendezvous and proximity operations and alleged anti-satellite tests by Russia, in addition to the adoption of unilateral policies by the United States. However, in December 2020 the UN General Assembly adopted a promising new initiative proposed by the United Kingdom regarding norms for responsible behaviour in space. It is hoped that this will lead to a return to multilateral regulatory approaches for space security.

As a complement to controlling arms, international security can be improved by states acting to build mutual confidence. This can be through relatively simple multilateral mechanisms for sharing information on arms procurement or military expenditure (see section VI). However, the existing instruments are in urgent need of revitalization as participation is low and the data provided is limited in utility. A more complex confidence-building mechanism is the 1992 Treaty on Open Skies. In May 2020 the USA announced that it would formally withdraw from the treaty, citing the failure of Russia to adhere to the agreement (see section V). Despite international calls for the USA to reconsider, the withdrawal came into effect on 22 November 2020. Although most of the remaining parties to the treaty seemed determined to continue implementing it, at the end of 2020 the longer-term future of the treaty remained uncertain.

LAURA BRUUN, IAN DAVIS, NIVEDITA RAJU, LUKE RICHARDS,
PIETER D. WEZEMAN AND SIEMON T. WEZEMAN

I. Global and regional instruments for conventional arms control

IAN DAVIS

This section reviews the key developments and negotiations that took place in three of the main global instruments for regulating the production, ownership, trade or use of conventional weapons: the 1981 Convention on Prohibitions or Restrictions on the Use of Certain Conventional Weapons which may be Deemed to be Excessively Injurious or to have Indiscriminate Effects (CCW Convention); the 1997 Convention on the Prohibition of the Use, Stockpiling, Production and Transfer of Anti-Personnel Mines and on their Destruction (APM Convention); and the 2008 Convention on Cluster Munitions (CCM). In each case, events related to the weapons themselves—such as their production, use or destruction—are described, as well as procedural developments within the treaty regime in 2020.

Two further such global instruments are the 2001 United Nations Programme of Action to Prevent, Combat and Eradicate the Illicit Trade in Small Arms and Light Weapons in All its Aspects (POA) and the 2013 Arms Trade Treaty (ATT). The seventh biennial meeting of states to consider the implementation of the POA, which was due to take place on 15–19 June 2020, was postponed until 26–30 July 2021 as a result of the Covid-19 pandemic. The ATT is discussed in chapter 14, as are controls on dual-use items and technology more generally—most new and emerging technologies are inherently dual-use and interconnected and require complex regulatory approaches to govern their use in civilian, commercial and military contexts.[1] Other sections in this chapter provide more detailed discussions on efforts to create new global instruments governing lethal autonomous weapon systems (LAWS, section II), cyberspace (section III), and space security (section IV).

At the regional level there are a number of instruments governing various aspects of conventional arms control in Africa, the Americas and Europe (see annex A, section II in this volume). Developments in the Open Skies Treaty in 2020 are discussed in section V of this chapter. Within Africa most of the regional instruments relate to efforts to tackle problems posed by small arms and light weapons (SALW). In August 2020 a revised version of the 2001 Protocol on the Control of Firearms, Ammunition and other related Materials in the Southern African Development Community (SADC) Region was adopted. It became the first regional instrument to take into account

---

[1] On international regulatory frameworks surrounding new and emerging technologies see Boothby, W. H. (ed.), *New Technologies and the Law in War and Peace* (Cambridge University Press: Cambridge, 2019).

Box 13.1. The Certain Conventional Weapons Convention and its protocols

The 1981 Certain Conventional Weapons (CCW) Convention originally contained three protocols: prohibiting the use of weapons that employ fragments not detectable in the human body by X ray (Protocol I); regulating the use of landmines, booby traps and similar devices (Protocol II); and limiting the use of incendiary weapons (Protocol III). In subsequent years, states added two protocols: prohibiting the use and transfer of blinding laser weapons was added in 1995 (Protocol IV); and on explosive remnants of war (ERW)—landmines, unexploded ordnance and abandoned explosive ordnance—in 2003 (Protocol V). In addition, amendments have expanded and strengthened the convention. Amended Protocol II, for example, places further constraints on the use of anti-personnel mines (APMs), while the scope of the convention was expanded in 2001 to situations of intra-state armed conflict. Because Amended Protocol II fell short of a ban on the use of landmines, a parallel process outside of the CCW Convention led to the creation of the 1997 APM Convention. States parties to the CCW Convention are required to ratify at least two of the original, amended or additional protocols, but are not required to sign up to all.

---

the 2016 African Union Roadmap for Silencing the Guns, as well as other updates to reflect contemporary African and global SALW policy.[2]

The Certain Conventional Weapons Convention

The CCW Convention and its five protocols ban or restrict the use of specific types of weapon that are considered to cause unnecessary or unjustifiable suffering to combatants or to affect civilians indiscriminately.[3] It is a so-called umbrella treaty, to which agreements on specific weapon types can be added in the form of protocols (see box 13.1). As of 31 December 2020 there were 125 states parties to the original convention and its protocols. No new states joined the CCW regime in 2020. Not all the states parties have ratified all the amended or additional protocols.[4]

The CCW framework is also important for addressing the challenges posed by the development or use of new types of weapon and their systems with respect to international humanitarian law. Many of the contemporary debates on conventional arms control—such as those seeking to address the use of explosive weapons in populated areas (EWIPA), as discussed below—are shaped by the concept of 'humanitarian disarmament', which prioritizes the protection, security and well-being of people as opposed to states. In particular, this approach strives to increase the protection of civilians by

---

[2] 'Southern Africa's revised firearms protocol is an important step towards ending conflict and violence', Institute for Security Studies, 25 Nov. 2020; and African Union Master Roadmap of Practical Steps to Silence The Guns In Africa By Year 2020, Lusaka Master Roadmap, 2016.

[3] For a summary and other details of the CCW Convention see annex A, section I, in this volume.

[4] For lists of the CCW Convention states parties that have ratified the original, amended and additional protocols see annex A, section I, in this volume.

reducing the human and environmental impacts of arms.[5] In recent years, however, there have been increasing tensions between the prioritization of humanitarian demands and the perceived military needs of certain states, with the result that many of the discussions on the convention have become deadlocked.[6] Over 250 civil society organizations signed an open letter during 2020 calling for humanitarian disarmament as an approach to regulating weapons for an improved post-pandemic world.[7]

Meetings of states parties

The states parties to the CCW Convention meet regularly at annual meetings and quinquennial review conferences. The Sixth Review Conference is scheduled to take place on 13–17 December 2021. These meetings also consider the work of the groups of governmental experts (GGEs) convened since 2001 in various formats. Amended Protocol II and Protocol V have their own implementation processes, which function in parallel with the CCW Convention. Seven CCW-related meetings were scheduled in 2020, but all but three were postponed due to Covid-19 restrictions (see table 13.1).

The Amended Protocol II group of experts meeting in September discussed improvised explosive devices (IEDs), a topic that it has been working on since 2009.[8] The focus remained on voluntary information exchange on national and multilateral measures, and on best practices regarding identification, humanitarian clearance and civilian protection from IEDs. The work of the GGE on LAWS is discussed in section II of this chapter.

In recent years, little progress has been made at these meetings due to the lack of consensus, and a handful of states have obstructed advances in most of the CCW agenda. Problems with the financial sustainability of the convention have also previously led to difficulties in organizing meetings. In 2020 the difficulties in these negotiations were aggravated by the inability to meet face-to-face due to the Covid-19 pandemic.

---

[5] See the discussions on humanitarian disarmament in Anthony, I., 'International humanitarian law: ICRC guidance and its application in urban warfare', *SIPRI Yearbook 2017*, pp. 545–53; and Davis, I. and Verbruggen, M., 'The Convention on Certain Conventional Weapons', *SIPRI Yearbook 2018*, p. 381. See also International Committee of the Red Cross (ICRC), 'International humanitarian law and the challenges of contemporary armed conflicts: Recommitting to protection in armed conflict on the 70th anniversary of the Geneva Conventions', *International Review of the Red Cross*, vol. 101, no. 911 (Aug. 2019), pp. 869–949.

[6] See e.g. the discussion on the 2016 CCW Review Conference in Davis, I. et al., 'Humanitarian arms control regimes: Key developments in 2016', *SIPRI Yearbook 2017*, pp. 554–61; and on developments since then in the 2018–20 editions of the SIPRI Yearbook.

[7] Humanitarian Disarmament, 'Covid-19 and humanitarian disarmament: Open letter from civil society', opened for signature June 2020.

[8] Amended Protocol II to the CCW Convention, 22nd Annual Conference, 'Report on improvised explosive devices', 20 Oct. 2020. Videos of the three sessions of the expert group meeting are available on UN Web TV.

Table 13.1. Meetings of the Certain Conventional Weapons Convention in 2020

Dates	Meeting
21–25 September	GGE on LAWS
28 September	Protocol V meeting of experts
29–30 September	Amended Protocol II group of experts
2–6 November[a]	GGE on LAWS
9 November[a]	14th Annual Conference of the Parties to Protocol V
10 November[a]	22nd Annual Conference of the Parties to Amended Protocol II
11–13 November[a]	CCW annual meeting

GGE = group of governmental experts; LAWS = lethal autonomous weapon systems.

Note: All meetings took place in Geneva and some were conducted in hybrid format to allow participation by those who could not travel to Geneva.

[a] Postponed until 2021 from the scheduled dates due to Covid-19 restrictions.

Towards a political declaration on the use of explosive weapons in populated areas

The use of EWIPA—and especially the use of explosive weapons with a large destructive radius, an inaccurate delivery system or the capacity to deliver multiple munitions over a wide area—has frequently led to situations in which over 90 per cent of casualties in populated areas are civilian rather than combatants.[9] The use of EWIPA also has reverberating effects, with impacts on water, sanitation, ecosystems, healthcare, education and psychological well-being.[10]

The International Network on Explosive Weapons (INEW), a nongovernmental organization (NGO) coalition formed in 2011, was the first to articulate EWIPA as an issue that demanded attention. Its efforts led to calls from an increasing number of states, successive UN secretary-generals, international bodies and other NGOs for measures to provide better protection for civilians and to prevent harm from EWIPA.[11] As a result of this increasing international political pressure, and after many years of

---

[9] Action on Armed Violence (AOAV), *Explosive Violence Monitor 2019* (AOAV: London, 2020), p. 3. See also International Committee of the Red Cross (ICRC), 'Explosive weapons in populated areas', [n.d.]; and International Network on Explosive Weapons (INEW), 'Protecting civilians from the use of explosive weapons in populated areas', May 2020.

[10] Wille, C., *The Implications of the Reverberating Effects of Explosive Weapons Use in Populated Areas for Implementing the Sustainable Development Goals* (United Nations Institute for Disarmament Research: Geneva, 2016); Dathan, J., *Blast Injury: The Reverberating Health Consequences from the Use of Explosive Weapon Use* (Action on Armed Violence: London, 2020); and Dathan, J., *The Broken Land: The Environmental Consequences of Explosive Weapons* (Action on Armed Violence: London, 2020).

[11] See e.g. Austrian Federal Ministry for Europe, Integration and Foreign Affairs, 'Vienna Conference on Protecting Civilians in Urban Warfare: Summary of the conference', Vienna, 1–2 Oct. 2019; and United Nations, 'Joint appeal by the UN secretary-general and the president of the International Committee of the Red Cross on the use of explosive weapons in cities', Press release, SG/2251, 18 Sep. 2019. For a list of 112 states and territories and 9 state groupings that have publicly acknowledged the harm caused by EWIPA in statements see International Network on Explosive Weapons (INEW), 'Political response', [n.d.].

seeking to address EWIPA issues within the CCW framework, a separate process led by the Government of Ireland gathered momentum in late 2019 and early 2020.[12]

The aim of this new process is the development of a political declaration to address the humanitarian harm arising from the use of EWIPA. Such a declaration would aim to establish a new international norm against the use of explosive weapons in towns and cities, which could in turn drive changes in military practice at the policy and operational levels.

Ireland convened a series of open consultations on the proposed declaration. The first rounds of consultations were held in Geneva on 18 November 2019 and 10 February 2020. The Covid-19 pandemic meant that consultations scheduled for 23–24 and 26–27 March 2020 in Geneva and the planned adoption of the declaration on 26 May 2020 in Dublin were abandoned. Instead, the last round of consultations was held online and the adoption of the declaration was postponed. The three rounds of consultations attracted written submissions from a total of at least 36 states (either individually or within a joint submission), 4 international organizations and 16 civil society groups.[13]

During the first consultation, most delegations called for the declaration to acknowledge the humanitarian impact of explosive weapons with wide-area effects. Most also supported the idea of it encouraging the sharing of best practices and policies on the protection of civilians in urban conflict settings and on the provision of victim assistance. Views differed, however, on how the declaration should relate to international humanitarian law and on whether it should seek to prohibit or limit specific types of weapon or uses of weapons.[14]

During the second consultation the Irish Government presented a paper (circulated on 20 January 2020) containing draft elements for the declaration.[15] Several states and civil society organizations welcomed these with reservations. They expressed concern that they did not contain a clear commitment against the use of explosive weapons that have wide-

---

[12] For developments in 2019 see Davis, I., 'Global instruments for conventional arms control', *SIPRI Yearbook 2020*, pp. 485–501.

[13] The submissions are available at Irish Department of Foreign Affairs, 'Written submissions—18 November 2019 consultations', 18 Nov. 2019; Irish Department of Foreign Affairs, 'Written submissions—10 February 2020 consultations', 10 Feb. 2020; and Irish Department of Foreign Affairs, 'Online submissions—Draft political declaration 17 March 2020', 17 Mar. 2020. See also Human Rights Watch and International Human Rights Clinic, 'Key questions and answers on a political declaration on the use of explosive weapons in populated areas', June 2020.

[14] Irish Department of Foreign Affairs, 'Protecting civilians in urban warfare', 2020. For a summary of the issues discussed see Reaching Critical Will, 'Towards a political declaration on the use of explosive weapons in populated areas: States need to ensure that expressed commitments translate into real impacts on the ground', 19 Nov. 2019.

[15] Irish Department of Foreign Affairs, 'Elements of a political declaration to ensure the protection of civilians from humanitarian harm arising from the use of explosive weapons in populated areas', [n.d.].

area effects in populated areas, and that, in parts, they risked normalizing the use of such weapons and weakening existing protection for civilians.[16] There were also suggestions that the political declaration should include language on the arms trade with linkages to the ATT.[17] The African Group, for example, suggested that it include a commitment to prevent diversion of arms, especially to non-state armed groups.[18]

Ireland continued the process online; it circulated a draft of the political declaration on 17 March 2020 and planned to circulate a second draft with a view to holding face-to-face consultations in Geneva as soon as possible.[19] To maintain momentum, Ireland hosted a webinar on 7 September 2020 highlighting the humanitarian harm caused by EWIPA, while in meetings of the First Committee of the UN General Assembly in October and November several states expressed their support for the ongoing political efforts.[20] The humanitarian consequences of the use of EWIPA were also discussed at the margins of the June 2020 humanitarian affairs segment of the UN Economic and Social Council (ECOSOC), an international platform for discussing the coordination of UN humanitarian assistance.[21]

In December 2020, Ireland issued an update on the process, explaining that it would circulate a revised draft political declaration in January 2021, taking into account the submissions received as part of the written consultations and the bilateral feedback it received in 2020. Following this, Ireland planned to schedule an open and informal exchange of views on the revised draft in March 2021, and then a final consultation to conclude the negotiation of the text in mid 2021 (either fully in-person or in a hybrid format, depending on the prevailing public health situation).[22]

---

[16] See e.g. Acheson, R., 'Impacts, not intentionality: The imperative of focusing on the effects of explosive weapons in a political declaration', Reaching Critical Will, 14 Feb. 2020; and Article 36, 'Rejecting calls to address only the "indiscriminate use" of explosive weapons in populated areas', Feb. 2020.

[17] Reaching Critical Will (note 14).

[18] Group of African States, Draft statement at the informal consultations on the political declaration on EWIPA, 10 Feb. 2020.

[19] Irish Department of Foreign Affairs, 'Draft political declaration on strengthening the protection of civilians from humanitarian harm arising from the use of explosive weapons in populated areas', 17 Mar. 2020.

[20] Geyer, K., 'Ireland's webinar on explosive weapons keeps momentum on the process for a political declaration on the protection of civilians', Reaching Critical Will, 9 Sep. 2020; and Boillot, L., 'Explosive weapons', First Committee Monitor, vol. 18, no. 2 (18 Oct. 2020), pp. 16–17.

[21] UN Office for the Coordination of Humanitarian Affairs (OCHA), Inter-Agency Standing Committee, '2020 ECOSOC humanitarian affairs segment', June 2020.

[22] Communiqué from Michael Gaffey, Permanent Representative of Ireland to the United Nations and other International Organisations in Geneva, 17 Feb. 2021.

The Anti-Personnel Mines Convention

The 1997 APM Convention prohibits, among other things, the use, development, production and transfer of APMs.[23] These are mines that detonate on human contact—that is, they are 'victim-activated'—and therefore encompass IEDs that act as APMs, also known as 'improvised mines'.[24] At the Third Review Conference of the convention, in 2014, the states parties set a target of fully eliminating APMs and addressing the consequences of past use by 2025.[25]

While compliance with the APM Convention has generally been good, it continues to be undermined by the refusal of some states, such as China, Iran, Israel, the Democratic People's Republic of Korea (DPRK, North Korea), Russia, Saudi Arabia and the United States, to sign it. As of 31 December 2020 there were 164 states parties to the APM Convention, including all member states of the European Union (EU), every state in sub-Saharan Africa and every state in the Americas apart from Cuba and the USA. Only 33 UN member states remained outside the treaty. No new states joined in 2020.

Production and use of APMs in 2019–20

New use of APMs by states is now extremely rare. According to the International Campaign to Ban Landmines (ICBL), Myanmar (which is not a party to the APM Convention) is the only state to have used APMs in the period mid 2019 to October 2020, and it has been deploying them for the past 20 years.[26]

More than 50 states have produced APMs in the past, but the ICBL identifies only 12 as current producers (and only four as likely active producers: India, Iran, Myanmar and Pakistan).[27] This is an increase of one country—the USA—compared to the previous ICBL report following a change in US landmine policy. In January 2020 the US administration of President Donald J. Trump rescinded a 2014 directive issued by President Barack Obama, which banned production and acquisition of APMs, as well

---

[23] For a summary and other details of the APM Convention see annex A, section I, in this volume.

[24] IEDs are also discussed in the CCW regime (see above) and in the UN General Assembly First Committee, including through the submission of resolutions. See Seddon, B. and Baldo, A. M., *Counter-IED: Capability Maturity Model & Self-assessment Tool* (United Nations Institute for Disarmament Research: Geneva, 2020).

[25] APM Convention, 3rd Review Conference, Final document, APLC/CONF/2014/4, 16 Mar. 2015, annex II, para. 6.

[26] International Campaign to Ban Landmines–Cluster Munition Coalition (ICBL-CMC), *Landmine Monitor 2020* (ICBL-CMC: Geneva, Nov. 2020), pp. 1, 8–11. The report focuses on the calendar year 2019 with information included up to Oct. 2020 where possible.

[27] The other 8 listed producers are China, Cuba, North Korea, South Korea, Russia, Singapore, the USA and Viet Nam. International Campaign to Ban Landmines–Cluster Munition Coalition (note 26), pp. 17–18.

as their use other than in a future conflict on the Korean Peninsula. The new policy allows the USA to again use landmines 'in exceptional circumstances' in conflicts around the world.[28] The US decision was criticized by several European allies, including the EU.[29]

While there is a de facto moratorium on the production and use of the weapon among most states in the world, the use of APMs, including victim-activated IEDs, by non-state armed groups in conflicts is a growing problem.[30] APMs were used by such groups in at least six states between mid 2019 and October 2020: Afghanistan, Colombia, India, Libya, Myanmar and Pakistan. There were also unconfirmed allegations of use by non-state armed groups in 13 other states: Burkina Faso, Cameroon, Chad, Egypt, Mali, Niger, Nigeria, the Philippines, Somalia, Syria, Turkey, Tunisia and Yemen.[31]

In 2019, the most recent year for which comparative data is available, the ICBL recorded 5554 casualties linked to APMs or other ERW (such as cluster munitions), of which at least 2170 were fatal and the vast majority (80 per cent) were civilian.[32] This marked a fifth successive year of high casualties, albeit lower than in 2016–18. The three states with the most casualties in 2019 were Afghanistan (1538), Mali (345) and Ukraine (324).[33] According to another source, APM and ERW casualties in north-east Nigeria worsened in 2020 as a result of conflict involving non-state armed groups, especially Boko Haram.[34]

Clearance and destruction measures

In 2019, $561.3 million was contributed by donors and affected states to international support for mine action, which includes humanitarian demining, risk education, victim assistance, stockpile destruction and threat reduction

---

[28] Esper, M. T., US Secretary of Defense, 'DoD policy on landmines', Memorandum, US Department of Defense, 31 Jan. 2020. See also White House, 'Statement from the Press Secretary', 31 Jan. 2020; and Human Rights Watch, 'US: Trump administration abandons landmine ban', 31 Jan. 2020.

[29] International Campaign to Ban Landmines–Cluster Munition Coalition (note 26), p. 16; and European External Action Service (EEAS), 'Anti-personnel mines: Statement by the Spokesperson on the United States' decision to re-introduce their use', 4 Feb. 2020.

[30] E.g. APM Convention Implementation Support Unit, 'Afghanistan's Chief Executive on growing number of non-state actors using improvised landmines', 27 Feb. 2018; and Luke, D., *Old Issues, New Threats: Mine Action and IEDs in Urban Environments* (LSE Ideas: London, Feb. 2020).

[31] International Campaign to Ban Landmines–Cluster Munition Coalition (note 26), pp. 1, 11–14. On the use of IEDs by the Islamic State in Syria see Anfinson, A. and Al-Dayel, N., 'The threat of the Islamic State's extensive use of improvised explosives', International Centre for Counter-Terrorism, 21 July 2020.

[32] International Campaign to Ban Landmines–Cluster Munition Coalition (note 26), pp. 2, 36–39.

[33] International Campaign to Ban Landmines–Cluster Munition Coalition (note 26), pp. 2, 36–39. In Afghanistan, the problem spans several decades. See Fiederlein, S. and Rzegocki, S., 'The human and financial costs of the explosive remnants of war in Afghanistan', Costs of War project, Brown University, 19 Sep. 2019.

[34] Mines Advisory Group (MAG), *Hidden Scars: The Landmine Crisis in North-East Nigeria* (MAG: Manchester, Dec. 2020). On the armed conflict in Nigeria see chapter 7, section II, in this volume.

advocacy.[35] This was a decline of 13 per cent compared to 2018 and the first time since 2016 that international support fell below $600 million. The top five mine action donors—the USA, the EU, the United Kingdom, Norway and Germany—contributed 72 per cent of all international funding in 2019 (about the same proportion as in 2018).[36]

An estimated 156 square kilometres of land was cleared of APMs in 2019 (compared to 146 km2 in 2018) and more than 123 000 APMs were destroyed (compared to 98 000 in 2018). Since the APM Convention entered into force, 31 states parties have completed clearance of all APMs from their territory, with Chile and the UK doing so in 2020.[37] In November 2020 the UK announced that the Falkland Islands/Malvinas were now clear of nearly all APMs, 38 years on from the war there, and a formal declaration of completion is expected to be submitted in 2021.[38]

In 2020 mine action activities faced additional challenges from the pandemic. Clearance operations were temporarily suspended due to Covid-19-related restrictions in Armenia, Bosnia and Herzegovina, Chad, Colombia, Kosovo, Lebanon, Peru, Senegal, Viet Nam, Western Sahara and Zimbabwe as well as in the Falkland Islands/Malvinas.[39]

The 60 states and other areas that are known to have mine contamination include 33 states parties to the APM Convention. Among them are some of the most mine-affected states in the world: Afghanistan, Bosnia and Herzegovina, Cambodia, Croatia, Ethiopia, Iraq, Thailand, Turkey, Ukraine and Yemen.[40] As of December 2020, 26 of the 33 states parties had deadlines to meet their mine clearance obligations before or during 2025, while seven states parties had deadlines after 2025: Bosnia and Herzegovina (2027), Croatia (2026), Iraq (2028), Palestine (2028), Senegal (2026), South Sudan (2026) and Sri Lanka (2028).[41]

Collectively, states parties have destroyed more than 55 million stockpiled APMs. More than 269 000 were destroyed in 2019 (compared to 1.4 million in 2018). Only three states parties have remaining stockpile destruction obligations: Greece, Sri Lanka and Ukraine. The total remaining global

[35] UN Mine Action Service (UNMAS), *Guide for the Application of International Mine Action Standards (IMAS): IMAS 01.10*, 2nd edn, amendment 9 (UNMAS: New York, Mar. 2018).

[36] International Campaign to Ban Landmines–Cluster Munition Coalition (note 26), pp. 2–3, 85–97.

[37] International Campaign to Ban Landmines–Cluster Munition Coalition (note 26), p. 26, 53–57; and APM Convention Implementation Support Unit, 'Chile ends mine clearance operations: The Americas a step closer to becoming a mine-free region', Press release, 3 Mar. 2020.

[38] Rawlinson, K., 'Falklands cleared of nearly all landmines, 38 years on from war', *The Guardian*, 10 Nov. 2020; and British Foreign and Commonwealth Office, 'Falklands demining programme work plan under Article (5)', 30 Apr. 2020.

[39] International Campaign to Ban Landmines–Cluster Munition Coalition (note 26), pp. 40–42.

[40] International Campaign to Ban Landmines–Cluster Munition Coalition (note 26), pp. 29–33.

[41] International Campaign to Ban Landmines–Cluster Munition Coalition (note 26), pp. 2–4, 26–33, 57–63.

stockpile of APMs is estimated to be less than 50 million, down from about 160 million in 1999. With the exception of Ukraine, the largest stockpilers are non-signatories: Russia (26.5 million), Pakistan (6 million), India (4–5 million), China (5 million), Ukraine (3.3 million) and the USA (3 million).[42]

The 18th meeting of states parties

The 18th meeting of states parties of the APM Convention took place virtually due to Covid-19 restrictions on 16–20 November 2020.[43] It was the first opportunity to assess progress in the Oslo Action Plan adopted at the Fourth Review Conference, in 2019. The plan adopted a gender perspective, advanced mine risk education to prevent new casualties and challenged states parties to increase the pace of mine clearance.[44] Nine states parties requested and were granted extensions to their Article 5 mine clearance obligations: Bosnia and Herzegovina (until 2027), Colombia (2025), the Democratic Republic of the Congo (2022), Mauritania (2022), Niger (2024), Nigeria (2021), Senegal (2026), South Sudan (2026) and Ukraine (2023).[45]

The Convention on Cluster Munitions

The 2008 CCM is an international treaty of more than 100 states, among which are former major producers and users of cluster munitions as well as affected states.[46] The 10th anniversary of the entry into force of the convention fell on 1 August 2020. The convention addresses the humanitarian consequences of, and unacceptable harm to civilians caused by, cluster munitions—air-dropped or ground-launched weapons that release a number of smaller submunitions intended to kill enemy personnel or destroy vehicles. There are three main criticisms of cluster munitions: they disperse large numbers of submunitions imprecisely over an extended area; they frequently fail to detonate and are difficult to detect; and unexploded submunitions can remain explosive hazards for many decades.[47] The CCM establishes an unconditional prohibition and a framework for action. It also requires the destruction of stockpiles within 8 years of entry into force of

---

[42] International Campaign to Ban Landmines–Cluster Munition Coalition (note 26), pp. 4, 19–20.

[43] On the proceedings, documents and statements by states parties see APM Convention, 'Eighteenth meeting of the states parties', 16–20 Nov. 2020.

[44] APM Convention, 4th Review Conference, Final document, part II, APLC/CONF/2019/5/Add.1, 22 Jan. 2020.

[45] For details of each of the requests, additional information submitted by the state party, analysis and decisions see APM Convention, 18th Meeting of the States Parties, Final report, APLC/MSP.18/2020/10, 27 Nov. 2020; and APM Convention (note 44).

[46] For a summary and other details of the CCM see annex A, section I, in this volume.

[47] Feickert, A. and Kerr, P. K., *Cluster Munitions: Background and Issues for Congress*, Congressional Research Service (CRS) Report for Congress RS22907 (US Congress, CRS: Washington, DC, 22 Feb. 2019).

the Convention (Article 3), the clearance of areas contaminated by cluster munition remnants within 10 years (Article 4) and the provision of assistance for victims of such weapons (Article 5).

In 2020 the CCM gained three additional states parties: Sao Tome and Principe, Niue, and Saint Lucia. As of 31 December 2020, the CCM had 110 parties and 13 signatory states. In the UN General Assembly in December 2020, 147 states voted to adopt its sixth resolution supporting the CCM.[48] The resolution provides states outside the CCM an important opportunity to indicate their support for the humanitarian rationale behind the treaty and the objective of its universalization. For the first time, no state voted against the resolution, while 38 states abstained (as was the case in 2019) and 32 non-states parties supported it (1 more than in 2019).[49]

Use and production of cluster munitions in 2019–20

No CCM state party has used cluster munitions since the convention was adopted and most of the states still outside the convention abide de facto by the ban on the use and production of these weapons. Despite international condemnation, however, there was continued use of cluster munitions in Syria in 2019, albeit at decreasing levels. According to the Cluster Munition Coalition, there were at least 11 cluster munition attacks between 1 August 2019 and 31 July 2020 (down from 38 in the previous 12 months), carried out by the armed forces of the Syrian Government with the likely support of Russia, and at least 686 cluster munition attacks by government forces were reported between July 2012 and June 2020.[50] Cluster munition attacks were also documented in Libya during 2019 and unsubstantiated allegations of use in Kashmir in July 2019 and Yemen in June 2020.[51] During 2010–19 at least 4315 cluster munition casualties were identified in 20 countries and other areas. Notably, more than 80 per cent of the global casualties were recorded in Syria.[52]

The most recent use of cluster munitions occurred in the armed conflict in Nagorno-Karabakh between Armenia and Azerbaijan (both non-parties to

---

[48] UN General Assembly Resolution 75/62, 'Implementation of the Convention on Cluster Munitions', 7 Dec. 2019, A/RES/75/62, 15 Dec. 2020.

[49] CCM Implementation Support Unit, 'UNGA adopts 2020 CCM resolution with zero no votes', 8 Dec. 2020. For a summary of the debates on the CCM in the General Assembly First Committee see Mosquera, D. C. P., 'Cluster munitions', *First Committee Monitor*, vol. 18, no. 4 (8 Nov. 2020), p. 17.

[50] International Campaign to Ban Landmines–Cluster Munition Coalition (ICBL-CMC), *Cluster Munition Monitor 2020* (ICBL-CMC: Geneva, Nov. 2020), pp. 1, 16–18. *Cluster Munition Monitor 2020* focuses on the calendar year 2019 with information included to Sep. 2020 where possible. On the armed conflict in Syria see chapter 6, section II, in this volume.

[51] International Campaign to Ban Landmines–Cluster Munition Coalition (note 50), pp. 2, 18–20; and Ahmed, K., 'Unexploded bombs pose rising threat to civilians in Libya', *The Guardian*, 17 Feb. 2020. On the armed conflicts in Libya and Yemen see chapter 6, sections IV and V respectively, in this volume.

[52] International Campaign to Ban Landmines–Cluster Munition Coalition (note 50), pp. 44, 52–56.

the CCM) in October 2020. Two NGOs, Amnesty International and Human Rights Watch, assessed that Azerbaijan had used Israeli-made M095 cluster munitions, while Azerbaijan made counter-allegations of use by Armenia, but without providing any evidence.[53]

Sixteen states, none of which are states parties to the CCM, are listed by the Cluster Munition Coalition as producers of cluster munitions, although a lack of transparency means that it is unclear whether any of them were actively producing such munitions in 2019–20.[54] However, China and Russia were researching and developing new types of cluster munition in 2020.[55]

Destruction and clearance measures

As of November 2020, 36 of the 41 states parties that had declared possession of cluster munitions had completed the destruction of their stockpiles.[56] This destruction of 1.5 million stockpiled cluster munitions containing 178 million submunitions represents the destruction of 99 per cent of all the cluster munitions and submunitions declared as stockpiled under the CCM. Four of the five states parties with remaining cluster munitions stockpiles—Bulgaria, Peru, Slovakia and South Africa—still had a combined total of nearly 11 300 to destroy as of 31 December 2019.[57] The fifth, Guinea-Bissau, was still verifying the existence of cluster munitions within its stocks. During 2020 Bulgaria and Peru requested deadline extensions to complete the destruction of their stockpiles (until 1 October 2022 and 1 April 2024, respectively), and these requests were being considered at the Second Review Conference of the CCM (see below). It is not possible to provide a global estimate of the quantity of cluster munitions currently stockpiled by non-signatories to the CCM as too few have disclosed information on the types and quantities they possess.

An accurate estimate of the total size of the area contaminated by cluster munition remnants is also not possible because the extent of contamination and the progress of clearance are difficult to identify in many states, especially non-signatory states. At least 25 UN member states and 3 other

---

[53] Amnesty International, 'Armenia/Azerbaijan: Civilians must be protected from use of banned cluster bombs', 5 Oct. 2020; and Human Rights Watch, 'Azerbaijan: Cluster munitions used in Nagorno-Karabakh', 23 Oct. 2020. On the armed conflict in Nagorno-Karabakh see chapter 5, section II, in this volume.

[54] The 16 states are Brazil, China, Egypt, Greece, India, Iran, Israel, North Korea, South Korea, Pakistan, Poland, Romania, Russia, Singapore, Turkey and the USA. International Campaign to Ban Landmines–Cluster Munition Coalition (note 50), pp. 20–22.

[55] International Campaign to Ban Landmines–Cluster Munition Coalition (note 50), pp. 9, 21; and Huang, K., 'Chinese state broadcaster reveals details of new airborne weapon Tianlei 500 as tensions simmer with Taiwan', *South China Morning Post*, 18 Aug. 2020.

[56] Convention on Cluster Munitions, 2nd Review Conference, 'Review Document of the Dubrovnik Action Plan', CCM/CONF/2020/13, 1 Oct. 2020, para. 28; and Convention on Cluster Munitions, 2nd Review Conference, Interim report, CCM/CONF/2020/L.1, 10 Dec. 2020, para. 27.

[57] International Campaign to Ban Landmines–Cluster Munition Coalition (note 50), pp. 23–29.

states or areas remain contaminated by cluster munitions.[58] Over the past decade, six state parties have completed clearance of areas contaminated by cluster munition remnants, most recently Croatia and Montenegro in July 2020.[59] Five states parties have requested extensions to their clearance deadlines: Germany and Laos had five-year extensions (to 1 August 2025) granted in 2019; and extension requests by Bosnia and Herzegovina (to 1 September 2022), Chile (to 1 June 2022) and Lebanon (to 1 May 2026) were being considered at the Second Review Conference.[60]

The Second Review Conference

Due to Covid-19-related restrictions, it was agreed to split the Second Review Conference of the CCM into two parts: a virtual meeting (held on 25–27 November 2020) and a hybrid format (scheduled for 4–5 February 2021 but subsequently postponed indefinitely).

The first part of the conference focused on procedural matters, including discussion (but not adoption) of extension requests on stockpile destruction and clearance, and other financial and administrative issues.[61] It also reviewed progress in implementing the convention since the First Review Conference, in 2015, and its adoption of the Dubrovnik Action Plan, which listed concrete steps to implement the CCM in the period 2015–20.[62]

The draft decisions, including recommendations to adopt all of the extension requests, were to be considered at the second part of the Second Review Conference.[63] Substantive discussions were also due to take place on possible measures to address concerns about the financial status of the CCM.[64]

[58] The 10 CCM states parties with cluster munition remnants are Afghanistan, Bosnia and Herzegovina, Chad, Chile, Germany, Iraq, Laos, Lebanon, Mauritania, and Somalia. Two CCM signatory states also have remnants: Angola and the Democratic Republic of the Congo. In addition, there are remnants in 13 non-signatory UN member states—Azerbaijan, Cambodia, Georgia, Iran, Libya, Serbia, South Sudan, Sudan, Syria, Tajikistan, Ukraine, Viet Nam and Yemen—and 3 other states or areas—Kosovo, Nagorno-Karabakh and Western Sahara. International Campaign to Ban Landmines–Cluster Munition Coalition (note 50), pp. 45–52.

[59] The other 4 are Grenada, Mauritania, Mozambique and Norway. International Campaign to Ban Landmines–Cluster Munition Coalition (note 50), p. 45.

[60] Convention on Cluster Munitions, 'Extension requests to be considered at the Second Review Conference (2RC)', 2020.

[61] For videos, documents and decisions of the first part of the conference see CCM Implementation Support Unit, 'First part of the Second Review Conference', 25–27 Nov. 2020.

[62] Convention on Cluster Munitions, 'Dubrovnik Action Plan', adopted 11 Sep. 2015. For an update on progress see Convention on Cluster Munitions, CCM/CONF/2020/13 (note 56).

[63] Convention on Cluster Munitions, CCM/CONF/2020/L.1 (note 56).

[64] Convention on Cluster Munitions, 2nd Review Conference, 'Elements on possible measures to address the financial predictability and sustainability of United Nations assessed contributions', CCM/CONF/2020/11, 28 Sep. 2020.

II. The group of governmental experts on lethal autonomous weapon systems

LAURA BRUUN

The legal, ethical and security challenges posed by lethal autonomous weapon systems (LAWS) have since 2014 been the subject of intergovernmental discussions within the framework of the 1981 Convention on Certain Conventional Weapons (CCW Convention) under the auspices of the United Nations.[1] Since 2017 the discussions have been led by an open-ended group of governmental experts (GGE). The group's mandate is to 'explore and agree on possible recommendations on options related to emerging technologies in the area of LAWS, in the context of the objectives and purposes of the Convention, taking into account all proposals—past, present and future'.[2]

The critical question of whether the challenges posed by LAWS require new regulations—possibly in the form of a new protocol to the CCW Convention—or whether existing law is adequate has divided the GGE from the beginning. However, the group made progress in 2019, with the adoption of 11 guiding principles. These establish, among other things, that international humanitarian law applies to LAWS; that humans, not machines, remain responsible for the use of autonomous weapon systems; and that human–machine interaction should ensure compliance with international law.[3] In 2019 the GGE reached consensus that the principles should be used as a basis for its consensus recommendations on 'the clarification, consideration [and development] of aspects of the normative and operational framework on emerging technologies in the area of lethal autonomous weapons systems'.[4] The guiding principles thus formed the basis of the group's work in 2020. Despite remaining differences of opinion and challenges posed by

---

[1] For a summary and other details of the Convention on Prohibitions or Restrictions on the Use of Certain Conventional Weapons which may be Deemed to be Excessively Injurious or to have Indiscriminate Effects (CCW Convention or 'Inhumane Weapons' Convention) and its protocols see annex A, section I, in this volume. On earlier discussions on the regulation of LAWS see Anthony, I. and Holland, C., 'The governance of autonomous weapon systems', *SIPRI Yearbook 2014*, pp. 423–31; Davis, I. et al., 'Humanitarian arms control regimes: Key development in 2016', *SIPRI Yearbook 2017*, pp. 559–61; Davis, I. and Verbruggen, M., 'The Convention on Certain Conventional Weapons', *SIPRI Yearbook 2018*, pp. 383–86; Boulanin, V., Davis, I. and Verbruggen, M., 'The Convention on Certain Conventional Weapons and lethal autonomous weapon systems', *SIPRI Yearbook 2019*, pp. 452–57; and Peldán Carlsson, M. and Boulanin, V., 'The group of governmental experts on lethal autonomous weapon systems', *SIPRI Yearbook 2020*, pp. 502–12.

[2] CCW Convention, Fifth Review Conference, Report of the 2016 informal meeting of experts on lethal autonomous weapons systems, CCW/CONF.V/2, 10 June 2016, annex, para. 3. The GGE is 'open-ended' in the sense that it is open to participants from all CCW states parties.

[3] CCW Convention, Group of Governmental Experts on Emerging Technologies in the Area of LAWS, Report of the 2019 session, CCW/GGE.1/2019/3, 25 Sep. 2019, annex IV. See also Boulanin et al. (note 1).

[4] CCW Convention, CCW/GGE.1/2019/3 (note 3), para. 26(e).

the Covid-19 pandemic, the GGE was able to continue considering views on legal, technological and military aspects of LAWS.

This section reports on the work of the GGE in 2020. It first discusses how the GGE process was affected by the Covid-19 pandemic. It then outlines areas of convergence identified in the GGE as of 2020. Finally, it reviews the specific issues discussed during the meeting in September 2020, including the way ahead for the GGE on LAWS. While discussions on LAWS also take place in other forums, including the UN General Assembly, this section focuses on the work of the GGE.

The LAWS debate in the midst of a pandemic

The GGE was scheduled to meet twice in 2020; for five days in June and for five days in August. Like all other diplomatic activities, the discussion on LAWS were affected by the Covid-19 pandemic.

The question on how the GGE should continue its work in the context of the pandemic was contentious. The majority of states, including France and the United States, were largely in favour of continuing meetings online and in hybrid formats, stressing the need for flexibility. However, a number of states, such as Pakistan, Russia, South Africa and Venezuela, criticized that proposal, pointing to practical problems such as gaps in technological capacity and time differences. Notably, Russia argued for complete postponement until physical meetings were again possible. The GGE eventually agreed to meet in a hybrid format (with in-person and remote participation) for five days in September and for five days in November. While Russia did not participate in the September meeting, the November meeting was entirely cancelled and postponed until health restrictions in Geneva again would make in-person participation possible.

In an effort to encourage discussions to continue despite the uncertainty around the formal meetings, the chair of the GGE, Ambassador Jānis Kārkliņš of Latvia, invited states to elaborate in writing on their national positions on the guiding principles and their operationalization at the national level. A total of 23 commentaries and working papers were contributed by 26 state parties, the Non-Aligned Movement (NAM) and civil society organizations.[5] Despite the obstacles and delays caused by the pandemic, the GGE was therefore able to engage in some substantive discussions.

---

[5] All commentaries and working papers can be found on the meeting website, UN Office for Disarmament Affairs, Meetings Place. For a brief description and list of member states of NAM see annex B, section I, in this volume.

Identifying areas of convergence

The GGE's work in 2020 centred around identifying key areas of convergence in order to consolidate its work ahead of the Sixth Review Conference of the CCW Convention, scheduled to be held in 2021. To that end, Kārkliņš published a 'commonalities paper' ahead of the September meeting that identified six recurring areas of agreement from states' written contributions: (*a*) international humanitarian law applies to and regulates the use of LAWS; (*b*) the guiding principles are applicable in the entire life cycle of the weapons; (*c*) further work is required to determine the type and extent of human involvement or control necessary to ensure compliance with applicable law; (*d*) national measures are needed in order to ensure that LAWS can be used in compliance with international law; (*e*) states must pay particular attention to the unique characteristics of emerging technologies in the area of LAWS when they conduct the legal reviews required by Article 36 of Additional Protocol I of the Geneva Conventions;[6] and (*f*) the CCW Convention continues to be the appropriate framework to continue work on the topic.[7]

Kārkliņš's paper revealed that states continued to diverge on several issues, including the question of the status and role of the guiding principles. NAM argued that further work is necessary, while Finland and France, for example, argued that the principles are ready to be operationalized at the national level.[8] However, the most divisive (and discussed) issues related to how to ensure compliance with international law; how to prevent an accountability gap; and what type and degree of human–machine interaction are needed in order to develop and use LAWS in compliance with international law. Ultimately, the GGE discussed whether or not new international law is necessary to regulate or prohibit LAWS. The September meeting addressed these issues under its six main agenda items, which are discussed in turn below. Kārkliņš was replaced as chair prior to the September meeting by Ljupčo Jivan Gjorgjinski of North Macedonia, who had chaired the GGE in 2019.

---

[6] For a summary and other details of the 1977 Protocol I Additional to the 1949 Geneva Conventions, and Relating to the Protection of Victims of International Armed Conflicts see annex A, section I, in this volume. See also Boulanin, V. and Verbruggen, M., *Article 36 Reviews: Dealing with the Challenges Posed by Emerging Technologies* (SIPRI: Stockholm, Dec. 2017).

[7] CCW Convention, Group of Governmental Experts on Emerging Technologies in the Area of LAWS, 'Commonalities in national commentaries on guiding principles', Working paper by the Chair, Sep. 2020, para. 21.

[8] All commentaries, statements and working papers related to the Sep. meeting and video recordings of its 10 sessions can be found on the meeting website, UN Office for Disarmament Affairs, Meetings Place.

Potential challenges posed by LAWS to international humanitarian law

While the GGE agreed that international humanitarian law applies to the use of LAWS, states continued to express different views as to whether the existing law is sufficient to address the challenges posed by LAWS, or whether adjustments or new frameworks are needed. Supporters of the former view included Australia, the United Kingdom and the USA, while Brazil and Venezuela, among others, argued that existing provisions are inadequate.

A key point of contention continued to be the question of whether autonomy enhances or undermines the user's ability to make the qualitative assessments that are needed to comply with international humanitarian law. Delegations that voiced concerns, such as Switzerland and the members of NAM, highlighted the impact of autonomy on predictability, particularly on the ability of a weapon's user to reasonably predict the effects of using the weapon. Risk assessments, adequate training and increased use of legal advisors were suggested by Australia, Finland, Sweden and the USA as necessary national measures to deal with predictability issues and to support compliance with international humanitarian law. The conduct of Article 36 legal reviews was also reiterated by most delegations as a critical step to ensure the ability to develop and use emerging technologies in compliance with international humanitarian law.[9] However, significant challenges remain. For example, some states, Chile and Switzerland in particular, highlighted the lack of transparency around national processes and the technical difficulties associated with conducting legal reviews of LAWS, and called for greater information sharing in that area.

Identifying a common understanding on concepts

Reaching a common conceptual understanding of LAWS continued to be an area where progress was difficult. Indeed, the Netherlands pointed out that it was the issue area where the GGE had made least progress.

As in previous years, disagreement centred around whether 'lethality' should be considered a key defining characteristic of LAWS. Germany and Ireland argued that it should not, as lethality lies in the application of the system and not in the system itself. This view was supported by Austria, Pakistan, South Africa and the USA.

States did not agree on a working definition (or whether one was even needed), but their views converged on a number of points: (*a*) autonomy should be considered as a spectrum; (*b*) any definition of LAWS should be guided by elements of human control; and (*c*) any definition should be technology-neutral in order to be applicable to future technological developments.

---

[9] CCW Convention, Working paper by the Chair (note 7), para. 13.

The human element in the use of lethal force

For technical, legal and ethical reasons, the agenda item on the human element in the use of lethal force was considered of primary importance to the GGE. The group agreed that human control should guide the development of a future normative and operational framework.

Overall, as identified in Kārkliņš's commonalities paper or as expressed during the meeting, states agreed that human control (*a*) is not an end it itself but a means through which compliance with international humanitarian law is ensured; (*b*) is highly dependent on context; (*c*) can be implemented at the national level through a variety of steps; and (*d*) should be considered broadly throughout the life cycle of the weapon, as human control is a process, rather than a single action.[10]

However, terminology continued to be a point of disagreement among states.[11] While Brazil and a group of largely European states, for example, preferred the term 'human control', the UK and the USA were in favour of 'human–machine teaming'.

GGE members focused in particular on the elaboration of the type and degree of human control in the two critical functions of LAWS: target selection and engagement.[12] Austria, Brazil, France, Germany, Switzerland, the USA, NAM and the International Committee of the Red Cross (ICRC) suggested types of human control measure (e.g. limits on tasks and targets), temporal and spatial restrictions, and requirements on commanders (ranging across the ability to supervise, intervene, deactivate, modify controls and exercise direct control). In addition, the UK further elaborated on type and degree of human involvement in a separate working paper published following the September discussions.[13]

The need to ensure human responsibility and prevent an accountability gap in the use of LAWS was also discussed under this agenda item. Some, including Brazil, Germany and the USA, suggested that accountability of designers and developers be considered. Rigorous testing and training of users were also mentioned by Germany and the USA as measures to improve accountability mechanisms at the national level.

---

[10] CCW Convention, Working paper by the Chair (note 7), paras 11–12.

[11] For earlier discussions on terminology see CCW Convention, CCW/GGE.1/2019/3 (note 3); and Peldán Carlsson and Boulanin (note 1), p. 508.

[12] International Committee of the Red Cross (ICRC), *Autonomous Weapon Systems: Implications of Increasing Autonomy in the Critical Functions of Weapons*, Expert meeting, Versoix, Switzerland, 15–16 Mar. 2016 (ICRC: Geneva, Aug. 2016), p. 7.

[13] CCW Convention, Group of Governmental Experts on Emerging Technologies in the Area of LAWS, 'United Kingdom expert paper: The human role in autonomous warfare', Working paper by the UK, CCW/GGE.1/2020/WP.6, 18 Nov. 2020.

Review of potential military applications of related technologies

Under the agenda item on review of potential military applications of related technologies, states discussed whether, and under which circumstances, the use of autonomous weapon systems would increase or decrease the risk posed to civilians and the implications for international peace and security.

Views expressed remained similar to previous years. Delegates from NAM warned of the risks of proliferation to non-state actors, hacking and arms races and of the general risk to civilians. The Pakistani delegation noted that 'States that are in possession of LAWS are bound to perceive a distinct military advantage, undeterred by the loss of its soldiers and citizens on the battlefield. This would lower the thresholds for going to war and armed conflicts.'[14] Meanwhile, Australia, France, Israel, Japan and the USA, all of which are working to develop autonomous weapon systems, argued that technologies in the area of LAWS offer military and humanitarian benefits, including improved decision-making capabilities, reduction of human errors, and the ability to operate in hard-to-reach and dangerous environments.

Despite these differences, states could agree on the conclusion that it is the application of autonomous weapon systems—not the technology itself—that should be limited, and thus that the focus should be on developing preventive tools for misuse.

Possible options for addressing challenges to humanitarian and international security

The ultimate outcome of the GGE's work continued to be a subject of disagreement in 2020. NAM and civil society argued that the GGE should work towards the creation of a legally binding instrument or resolution, while Australia, India, Israel, the UK and the USA argued that this would be counterproductive, given the perceived benefits of the use of LAWS. Instead, they argued, the GGE should aim to develop a normative and operational framework guiding the use of LAWS.[15]

Under this agenda item, states also discussed the state of the GGE process and appropriate next steps. Pointing to the compressed time frame, some (e.g. Austria, Chile and Costa Rica) argued that it was time to embark on treaty negotiations. This was contested by others (e.g. France, India, Israel, Japan, the Netherlands and the USA).

---

[14] CCW Convention, Group of Governmental Experts on Emerging Technologies in the Area of LAWS, Statement by Pakistan, 1st session of 2020, 7th meeting, 24 Sep. 2020, UN Web TV, 0:9:44–0:10:06 (author transcription).

[15] CCW Convention, Group of Governmental Experts on Emerging Technologies in the Area of LAWS, Commentary by Campaign to Stop Killer Robots, 5 June 2020.

Consensus recommendations on the normative and operational framework

Under its final agenda item, the GGE made efforts to identify and consolidate areas of convergence on which the normative and operational framework could be based. Chile presented a list of what it identified as core commonalities, including the need for legally binding rules and that the use of LAWS is subject to international humanitarian law, international criminal law, international human rights law and the Martens Clause (i.e. compatibility with 'the principles of humanity and the dictates of the public conscience').[16]

While not all states agreed with the list of commonalities identified by the Chilean delegation, its consensus-seeking approach was welcomed by most states. This indicated a shared political will to drive the process forward, even though the exact direction remained contested. However, Russia's absence from the meeting means that it cannot be assumed to share this view.

In order to support the group in its consideration of consensus recommendations and the elaboration and development of the guiding principles, the GGE chair suggested the creation of three work streams: one legal, one technological and one military. While the work streams did not materialize in 2020, they might be used to guide the work of the GGE in 2021.

The way ahead

Due to the Covid-19 pandemic, the GGE discussion on LAWS in 2020 was, to a large extent, replaced by a discussion on formalities. This may have been wilfully exploited by some states—Russia in particular—to halt the process. Fundamental disagreements over the outcome and mandate of the GGE, notably between Western delegations, NAM and Russia, persist and raise serious questions as to what the group will, in fact, be capable of achieving besides the 11 guiding principles.

While states continued to consider the GGE as the appropriate forum to discuss LAWS, parallel discussions outside the CCW framework may become increasingly relevant in the light of the GGE's limited progress. In a possible sign of developments in this direction, on the day after the GGE session closed, the Austrian foreign minister, speaking to the UN General Assembly, expressed strong concern about giving machines 'the power to decide, who lives and who dies' and invited all states to participate in an international meeting in Vienna in 2021 'to address this urgent issue'.[17]

---

[16] CCW Convention, Group of Governmental Experts on Emerging Technologies in the Area of LAWS, Statement by Chile, 2nd session of 2020, 8th meeting, 24 Sep. 2020, UN Web TV, 0:06:15–0:13:40. A form of the Martens Clause appears in the preamble of the CCW Convention (note 1), among other treaties and conventions.

[17] Schallenberg, A., Austrian Minister for European and International Affairs, Speech at the 75th session of the UN General Assembly, 26 Sep. 2020.

III. Cyberspace and the malicious use of information and communications technology

LUKE RICHARDS

As the cyber landscape develops, so too do cybersecurity threats—both from states and non-state actors such as cybercriminals. Notably, alongside the significant digitalization driven by the Covid-19 pandemic, which led to years of digital adoption being achieved in mere weeks, there was a 600 per cent increase in malicious emails attempting to exploit the growing digital dependency.[1] Computational propaganda—such as the use of cyber-influence operations and the spreading of disinformation—by state and non-state actors also increased around the globe.[2] Growing geopolitical tensions around the security of information and communications technology (ICT) have also led states to increase their scrutiny of ICT supply chains.[3]

As these developments continue, the need to better understand a state's ability to wield its cyber power through the malicious use of ICT grows.[4] Cyber activity often takes place below the threshold of armed conflict. For example, during the final weeks of 2020 the United States Government suffered what appeared to be one of the biggest cybersecurity breaches in its history, the Solar Winds hack, which can be described as an act of espionage rather than war.[5] It was the result of a supply chain vulnerability that also left companies and other governments around the world vulnerable.[6]

International efforts to control the malicious use of ICT were slowed by the Covid-19 pandemic. States' differing interests and normative preferences have also made concrete progress difficult. This section first reviews key developments in cyberspace itself and then describes these efforts to govern it through new global instruments and via multilevel dialogue.

---

[1] Baig, A. et al., 'The Covid-19 recovery will be digital: A plan for the first 90 days', McKinsey Digital, 14 May 2020; and Lederer, E. M., 'Top UN official warns malicious emails on rise in pandemic', AP News, 23 May 2020.

[2] Oxford Internet Institute, Project on Computations Propaganda, 'Industrialized disinformation: 2020 global inventory of organized social media manipulation', University of Oxford, 13 Jan. 2021.

[3] Kuehn, A., 'TechNationalism: Cybersecurity at the intersection of geopolitics', EastWest Institute, 17 Sep. 2020.

[4] On how state cyber power can be measured and an international ranking see Voo, J. et al., *National Cyber Power Index 2020: Methodology and Analytical Considerations* (Belfer Center for Science and International Affairs: Cambridge, MA, Sep. 2020).

[5] Paul, K. and Beckett, L., 'What we know—and still don't—about the worst-ever US Government cyber-attack', *The Guardian*, 18 Dec. 2020.

[6] Smith, B., 'A moment of reckoning: The need for a strong and global cybersecurity response', Microsoft, 17 Dec. 2020.

A divided internet and divided interests

The debate around governing the use of ICT at the international level is not just technical, but also has ideological and strategic aspects.[7] As the competing interests and the use of ICT have grown, the internet's infrastructure has also changed—a trend that continued in 2020.

While seemingly borderless, the internet is not entirely abstract but is bound to an infrastructure with a physical geography.[8] Some states, such as China and Russia, have postulated notions of cyber sovereignty. In 2019 Russia—in emulation of China's closed-off internet and information control—began attempting to cut its internet off from the rest of the world. This process continued in 2020 with a ban on the use of several forms of encryption and plans to replace some of them with Russian alternatives.[9]

Notably, the European Union (EU) is also moving towards a more gated system—that is, towards digital and technological sovereignty. For example, in 2020 the EU began a project to create a European cloud system, GAIA-X, to increase cloud and data services protected by the EU's data laws.[10] Also in 2020 the European Court of Justice invalidated Privacy Shield, a data-exchange agreement between the EU and the USA, in part due to concerns over the surveillance practices of US intelligence agencies and EU data-protection laws.[11]

The USA, too, has tested policies that have had an impact on the internet's infrastructure and development. These include sanctioning Chinese technology companies (e.g. Huawei and ByteDance, the owner of TikTok) and persuading allies not to use Chinese equipment in their telecommunications networks.[12]

[7] Henriksen, A., 'The end of the road for the UN GGE process: The future regulation of cyberspace', *Journal of Cybersecurity*, vol. 5 (2019), tyy009.

[8] Graham, M., 'Geography/internet: Ethereal alternate dimensions of cyberspace or grounded augmented realities?', *Geographical Journal*, vol. 179, no. 2 (June 2013), pp. 177–82.

[9] Weber, V., 'The sinicization of Russia's cyber sovereignty model', Council on Foreign Relations, 1 Apr. 2020; and Kolomychenko, M., 'Russia's Digital Development Ministry wants to ban the latest encryption technologies from the RuNet', 21 Sep. 2020.

[10] Hushes, O., 'What is Gaia-X? A guide to Europe's cloud computing fight-back plan', TechRepublic, 10 June 2020.

[11] Court of Justice of the European Union, *Data Protection Commissioner v Facebook Ireland Limited and Maximillian Schrems*, Case no. C-311/18, Judgment of the Court (Grand Chamber), 16 July 2020. See also Ettari, S. V., 'European Court of Justice invalidates EU–US Privacy Shield framework', Kramer Levin Naftalis & Frankel LLP, 1 Oct. 2020.

[12] On the US response to China see Williams, R. D., 'Beyond Huawei and TikTok: Untangling US concerns over Chinese tech companies and digital security', Working paper, University of Pennsylvania, Penn Project on the Future of US–China Relations, 2020; and Baxendale, H., 'Huawei or our way?: Fissures in the Five Eyes alliance in the face of a rising China', Centre for International Policy Studies, 16 Oct. 2020. On the impact in the EU see Anthony, I. et al., *China–EU Connectivity in an Era of Geopolitical Competition*, SIPRI Policy Paper no. 59 (SIPRI: Stockholm, Mar. 2021).

These examples of states' responses to the shifting cyber landscape and splintering of the internet across 2020 are likely to feed into debates on the governance of ICT in the years ahead.

Governing the malicious use of information and communications technology

Multilevel dialogue

Dialogue around the governance of ICT and cyber norms has taken place at multiple levels. It builds on a raft of measures and initiatives to regulate the use of cyberspace and to develop normative frameworks at a range of levels, from multinational interstate efforts to collaborations by private enterprises.[13] These frameworks have included the Global Commission on Stability in Cyberspace, which was launched in 2017 and reported in 2019; the Paris Call for Trust and Security in Cyberspace of November 2018, which established nine principles on responsible behaviour; and the Cybersecurity Tech Accord, under which 147 technology companies have agreed to protect their customers from malicious threats.[14] This wide proliferation of efforts to create an ecosystem of cyber norms has allowed for the cross-pollination of ideas.

In May 2020 the Oxford Process on International Law Protections in Cyberspace was launched.[15] This partnership between the University of Oxford and Microsoft aims to examine international law as it applies to specific objects of protection, such as within the healthcare sector and electoral processes.

United Nations processes

The main state-driven efforts to govern the malicious use of ICT continued in 2020 within the United Nations. In 2010, 2013 and 2015, groups of governmental experts (GGEs) on this topic had resulted in consensus reports.[16] The process split in 2018 after the adoption by the UN General Assembly of competing resolutions tabled by Russia and the USA which reflected the

---

[13] Ruhl, C. et al., *Cyberspace and Geopolitics: Assessing Global Cybersecurity Norm Processes at a Crossroads*, Working paper (Carnegie Endowment for International Peace: Washington, DC, Feb. 2020), pp. 13–15.

[14] Global Commission on Stability in Cyberspace (GCSC), *Advancing Cyberstability*, Final report (The Hague Centre for Strategic Studies/EastWest Institute: The Hague/New York, Nov. 2019); and Paris Call for Trust and Security in Cyberspace, 12 Nov. 2018.

[15] Oxford Institute for Ethics, Law and Armed Conflict (ELAC), 'The Oxford Process on International Law Protections in Cyberspace', University of Oxford, May 2020.

[16] UN Open-ended Working Group on Developments in the Field of Information and Tele-communications in the Context of International Security, 'International law in the consensus reports of the United Nations groups of governmental experts', Background paper, Feb. 2020.

enduring differences in their approaches to ICT risks.[17] The USA has a narrower focus on cybersecurity and the technical protection of ICT systems and the information that they contain. It sees no need for new international regulation as it considers that international humanitarian law already applies to cyberspace in armed conflicts. Instead, it favours the adoption by states of voluntary and non-binding norms aimed at supporting the security of infrastructure and information in peacetime. Russia meanwhile has a broader perspective that includes risks posed by information itself and reflects its desire to control information within its national borders. It would like to see the development of a legally binding regime with elements that legitimize its view of information security.[18] The US-sponsored resolution established a new GGE on Advancing Responsible State Behaviour in Cyberspace in the Context of International Security.[19] The Russian-sponsored resolution established the Open-ended Working Group (OEWG) on Developments in the Field of Information and Telecommunications in the Context of International Security.[20]

The GGE—the sixth in the series—is comprised of representatives of 25 UN member states. It continued with states sitting for the second substantive session in February 2020. It was unable to sit for a scheduled third session due to the Covid-19 pandemic. Instead, its third and fourth (and final) sessions were rescheduled to convene before May 2021.[21]

The OEWG is the larger of the two processes since it is open to any interested member state. It was unable to meet in person during 2020 for its third and final substantive session and the July deadline for a consensus report. Instead, states met informally over the course of the year. An informal multistakeholder cyber dialogue open to all interested stakeholders also took place in December.[22] The OEWG was engaged through documents produced by states and civil society groups, alongside non-papers and the chair's predrafts of the OEWG report.[23] The chair rescheduled the missed session for March 2021.[24]

---

[17] UN Office for Disarmament Affairs (UNODA), 'Developments in the field of information and telecommunications in the context of international security', [n.d.].

[18] For a thorough discussion on Russia and US differences and how they have shaped the UN process see Tikk, E., 'Cyber arms control and resilience', *SIPRI Yearbook 2019*.

[19] UN General Assembly Resolution 73/266, 'Advancing responsible state behaviour in cyberspace in the context of international security', 22 Dec. 2018, A/RES/73/266, 2 Jan. 2019.

[20] UN General Assembly Resolution 73/27, 'Developments in the field of information and telecommunications in the context of international security', 5 Dec. 2018, A/RES/73/27, 11 Dec. 2018.

[21] United Nations, General Assembly, Decision no. 75/551, 31 Dec. 2020, Official Records, Supplement no. 49, A/75/49 (Vol. II), 2021, p. 23.

[22] Informal Multi-stakeholder Cyber Dialogue, 'Summary report', 4–10 Dec. 2020.

[23] All the documents can be found at UN Office for Disarmament Affairs (UNODA), 'Open-ended working group', [n.d.].

[24] Lauber, J., OEWG Chair, Letter to all permanent representatives and permanent observers from the permanent mission of Switzerland to the United Nations, 9 June 2020.

A group of 47 states suggested a programme of action (POA) as one way to move the debate forward.[25] The proposal suggests the creation of a framework and a political commitment based on recommendations, norms and principles already agreed in previously endorsed GGE reports along with the outcomes of the current GGE and OEWG. The proposed POA would focus on areas such as implementation and capacity building, along with regular monitoring and review of the process itself.[26] Action under the POA would be reported to the UN General Assembly, and it would remain a process of the Assembly's First Committee.

During October 2020, Russia and the USA again proposed competing ways forward, in line with their differing ideological and strategic interests.[27] The USA tabled a draft resolution proposing that future work be decided once the current GGE and OEWG processes had concluded.[28] The following day Russia submitted a draft resolution (later revised) that would establish a new OEWG on Security of and in the Use of Information and Communications Technologies to run in the period 2021–25.[29] The two drafts were both adopted by the General Assembly during plenary sessions on 7 and 31 December.[30] The US proposal to conclude the current processes before deciding what to do next was thus only shortly lived.

The new OEWG is to start its work after the earlier OEWG concludes. The potential POA would thus run concurrently with the new OEWG, rather than acting as a means of bringing the two parallel process into one forum as initially envisioned.

---

[25] UN Open-ended Working Group on Developments in the Field of Information and Telecommunications in the Context of International Security, 'The future of discussions on ICTs and cyberspace at the UN', Submission by France and others, 2 Dec. 2020.

[26] UN Open-ended Working Group on Developments in the Field of Information and Telecommunications in the Context of International Security, 'Concept-note on the organizational aspects of a Programme of Action for advancing responsible state behaviour in cyberspace', Dec. 2020.

[27] Gold, J., 'Competing US–Russia cybersecurity resolutions risk slowing UN progress further', Council on Foreign Relations, 29 Oct. 2020. See also Tikk (note 18).

[28] United Nations, General Assembly, 'Developments in the field of information and telecommunications in the context of international security', Report of the First Committee, A/75/394, 6 Nov. 2020, paras 5–6.

[29] United Nations, A/75/394 (note 28), paras 7–10.

[30] The USA sponsored UN General Assembly Resolution 75/32, 'Advancing responsible state behaviour in cyberspace in the context of international security', 7 Dec. 2020, A/RES/75/32, 16 Dec. 2020. Russia sponsored UN General Assembly Resolution 75/240, 'Developments in the field of information and telecommunications in the context of international security', 31 Dec. 2020, A/RES/75/240, 4 Jan. 2021. On the debate on the competing resolutions see United National, 'First Committee approves 15 draft resolutions, decisions on disarmament measures, including 2 following different paths towards keeping cyberspace safe', Meetings coverage, GA/DIS/3659, 9 Nov. 2020.

Conclusions

Overall, dialogue around cybersecurity and the malicious use of ICT is moving forward, and changes to the digital landscape caused by the Covid-19 pandemic may hasten the need for action. The multilevel approach will probably continue. However, it seems that it will be difficult for states to reach a consensus agreement on the outcomes of the current GGE and OEWG. Looking ahead, the parallel processes will continue through the new OWEG and the POA if the outlined proposal is accepted.

IV. Developments in space security, 2020

NIVEDITA RAJU

The dynamics of space security in 2020 were unsettled by suspicions over state behaviour in outer space. This continued the pattern of 2019, when there was a marked increase in the development and display of counterspace capabilities.[1] Legal ambiguities and an absence of predictability in state behaviour can lead to an increase in militarization and weapon proliferation. This was demonstrated in 2020 by rendezvous and proximity operations (RPOs) and alleged anti-satellite (ASAT) tests.

This section outlines events in 2020 that threatened to undermine international space security. It begins by reviewing RPOs and alleged ASAT tests by Russia and the subsequent responses by other major space powers. It then identifies a growing trend of unilateral policymaking by the United States as a further destabilizing factor due to arbitrary interpretations of international law that are not necessarily equitable. The section concludes with an examination of new initiatives to strengthen space security, recommending a return to multilateral approaches with a reconsideration of traditional institutions through which they may be pursued.

Some of the other defining moments of 2020 each also affected the international space sector. Protests following the murder of George Floyd in the USA led to active steps to improve minority representation in the US space sector.[2] Worsening climate change led to the increased use of space applications for monitoring and mitigation. Some are lobbying for even greater use of such technologies under the new US administration.[3] Space technologies also played a significant role by assisting the health sector in its response to the Covid-19 pandemic by increased use of satellite imagery to track the spread and containment of infections in different locations.[4] Finally, commercial space activity continued to rise, with companies vying to facilitate connectivity through the introduction of multiple megaconstellations of satellites.[5]

---

[1] E.g. Indian Ministry of External Affairs, 'Speech by prime minister on "Mission Shakti", India's anti-satellite missile test conducted on 27 March 2019', 27 Mar. 2019. On developments in 2019 see Porras, D., 'Creeping towards an arms race in outer space', *SIPRI Yearbook 2020*, pp. 513–18.

[2] Werner, D. and Henry, C., 'How the space sector is responding to the killing of George Floyd', *SpaceNews*, 15 July 2020.

[3] Foust, J., 'Biden administration expected to emphasize climate science over lunar exploration at NASA', *SpaceNews*, 9 Nov. 2020.

[4] Lele, A., 'Coronavirus and space technologies: Satellites to fight with Covid-19', *Financial Express* (Delhi), 3 Apr. 2020.

[5] E.g. SpaceX's Starlink; and OneWeb.

Thresholds for rendezvous and proximity operations

In February 2020 the USA claimed that Russian satellite Cosmos-2542 had ejected a subsatellite, Cosmos-2543, with the purpose of spying on a US satellite, USA-245.[6] General John Raymond, chief of operations of US Space Force, labelled the activity as 'unusual and disturbing' and potentially threatening behaviour.[7] These accusations, however, have no legal basis as there is no regulation in international law that defines how such manoeuvres should be conducted. Although USA-245 subsequently moved to create further distance from the Russian satellites, the Russian deputy foreign minister, Sergey Ryabkov, simply stated that 'Moscow will respond' and added that these manoeuvres are 'practices carried out by many countries'.[8]

These manoeuvres fall within the category of rendezvous and proximity operations and they have indeed been frequently conducted by other states, including China, Japan and the USA itself.[9] RPOs are essentially operations in which one space object is intentionally manoeuvred into the vicinity of another at a given time and location, to accomplish specific objectives. RPOs are therefore used in both civil and military activities in space. While RPOs are traditionally perceived as permitting the gathering of intelligence on an adversary's satellite, they are also used in other missions, such as docking capsules on the International Space Station and the on-orbit servicing of satellites.

There is no consensus on what constitutes an unlawful RPO or when conduct would be construed as aggressive. The 1967 Outer Space Treaty grants states the freedom to explore and use outer space, and RPOs can be viewed as a legitimate exercise of this freedom, as long as they comply with other provisions of the treaty, in particular the prohibition on 'potentially harmful interference' with other states' activities.[10] States are also required to conduct their space activities in accordance with general principles of international law, including the United Nations Charter.[11] Whether a manoeuvre amounts to an unlawful threat or use of force under the UN Charter depends on the facts and circumstances of each case. This includes determining whether the countries are on the brink of conflict, and whether the other satellite was capable of damaging a valuable military asset.

---

[6] Hennigan, W. J., 'Strange Russian spacecraft shadowing US spy satellite, general says', *TIME*, 10 Feb. 2020.

[7] Hennigan (note 6).

[8] 'US alleges two Russian satellites are stalking one of its satellites', SpaceWatch.Global, Feb. 2020.

[9] West, J. (ed.), *Space Security Index 2019* (Project Ploughshares: Waterloo, ON, Oct. 2019).

[10] Outer Space Treaty, articles I and IX. For a summary and other details of the Treaty on Principles Governing the Activities of States in the Exploration and Use of Outer Space, Including the Moon and Other Celestial Bodies (Outer Space Treaty) see annex A, section I, in this volume.

[11] Outer Space Treaty (note 10), Article III.

In the absence of any clear thresholds for RPOs, mere manoeuvring by one state of a space object in the vicinity of another state's object cannot be fairly characterized as a threat, especially since many states have routinely engaged in this behaviour. However, actual and planned use of RPOs in the commercial sector, especially for on-orbit servicing and debris removal, is growing, and so appropriate thresholds for RPOs are increasingly desirable.

Accusations of anti-satellite tests

Regulatory gaps in space can cause suspicions to fester, resulting in magnified political tensions. This was evident from three incidents in 2020: in April, when the USA accused Russia of conducting a direct-ascent ASAT test; in July, when the US Space Command claimed that Russia injected a new object into orbit from Cosmos-2543; and in December, when it reported another direct-ascent ASAT test by Russia.[12] General Raymond declared that these constituted evidence of weaponization of space by Russia and put the space assets of the USA and its allies at risk.[13] The head of the United Kingdom's space directorate also voiced concern and stated that the Russian objects had the characteristics of a weapon.[14] Russia responded to the British and US criticism with its own accusation that this was an attempt to present the situation in a 'distorted manner'.[15]

Russia was also accused of hypocrisy by the USA in conducting these tests, given the former's diplomatic efforts to introduce restrictions on specific types of weaponization in space.[16] Indeed, Russia has proposed, jointly with China, a draft treaty banning placement of weapons in space.[17] However, the three tests in 2020 were non-destructive—that is, they avoided the generation of debris, unlike earlier ASAT tests by China, India, Russia and the USA.[18] Thus, the British and US criticism was arguably disproportionate.[19]

Indeed, the response to a perceived threat in space can be more damaging to international security than the original incident. In this case, the

---

[12] US Space Command, 'Russia tests direct-ascent anti-satellite missile', 15 Apr. 2020; US Space Command, 'Russia conducts space-based anti-satellite weapons test', 23 July 2020; and US Space Command, 'Russia tests direct-ascent anti-satellite missile', 16 Dec. 2020.

[13] US Space Command, 16 Dec. 2020 (note 12).

[14] 'Russia satellite: Kremlin accuses US and UK of "distorting" truth', BBC News, 24 July 2020.

[15] BBC News (note 14).

[16] US Space Command, 15 Apr. 2020 (note 12).

[17] Conference on Disarmament, Draft Treaty on the Prevention of the Placement of Weapons in Outer Space, the Threat or Use of Force against Outer Space Objects (PPWT), CD/1985, 12 June 2014.

[18] On past ASAT tests and the debris generated see Porras, D., *Towards ASAT Test Guidelines*, Space Dossier, File no. 2 (UN Institute for Disarmament Research: Geneva, May 2018). On the debris created by India's Mission Shakti in 2019 see McDowell, J., 'Space activities in 2019', Jonathan's Space Report, 12 Jan. 2020.

[19] E.g. O'Flaherty, K., 'Russian spacecraft stalking US spy satellite sparks espionage fears', *Forbes*, 5 Feb. 2020; and Hitchens, T., 'Raymond rips Russian ASAT test, arms control hypocrisy', Breaking Defense, 15 Apr. 2020.

US characterization of this behaviour as 'threatening' contributed to the narrative that outer space is becoming 'weaponized' and encourages states to fortify their own capabilities.

Since space-based assets are frequently used for military purposes, this narrative is not only flawed, but destabilizing in itself; when a state responds to a perceived threat, there is a tendency to not only strengthen its ability to defend assets, but to also develop offensive capabilities.[20] The establishment in December 2019 of the US Space Force and the references to offensive capabilities in the US Space Force Doctrine issued in June 2020 are products of this cycle.[21] Japan also responded to perceived threats of Chinese and Russian activities through the establishment in May 2020 of a dedicated Space Domain Mission Unit for the defence of its satellites against kinetic and non-kinetic threats.[22]

Achieving stability in space security will, in the long term, require regulation that addresses the ambiguities in what is acceptable behaviour in space, while pursuing confidence-building measures among states in the short term to alleviate the impact of this narrative.

A surge in United States unilateralism

During 2020 the USA attempted to further its international space policy through a unilateral approach. This was reflected in three developments. In April President Donald J. Trump issued an executive order that officially rejected space as a global commons.[23] In October the USA and seven other states signed the Artemis Accords, a set of guiding principles for cooperation in civil exploration and use of the Moon and other celestial bodies.[24] In September the USA's space agency, the National Aeronautics and Space Administration (NASA), issued a solicitation for purchase of lunar regolith (soil).[25]

The Artemis Accords

In May 2020 NASA announced the Artemis Accords as a precondition for other countries that wished to collaborate with the USA in Moon exploration.[26] By the end of 2020, nine countries had signed the accords:

---

[20] Grego, L., 'A history of anti-satellite programs', Union of Concerned Scientists, Jan. 2012.

[21] US Space Force, *Spacepower: Doctrine for Space Forces*, Space Capstone Publication (Headquarters US Space Force: Washington, DC, June 2020).

[22] Yamaguchi, M., 'Japan launches new unit to boost defense in space', *Defense News*, 18 May 2020.

[23] White House, 'Encouraging international support for the recovery and use of space resources', Executive Order no. 3914, 6 Apr. 2020.

[24] The Artemis Accords: Principles for Cooperation in the Civil Exploration and Use of the Moon, Mars, Comets and Asteroids for Peaceful Purposes, opened for signature 13 Oct. 2020.

[25] US National Aeronautics and Space Administration (NASA), 'Purchase of lunar regolith and/or rock materials from contractor', 10 Sep. 2020.

[26] Clark, S., 'NASA proposals to allow establishment of lunar "safety zones"', *The Guardian*, 20 May 2020.

Australia, Canada, Italy, Japan, Luxembourg, the United Arab Emirates, the UK and the USA in October and Ukraine in November.

The global response to the accords was mixed. While many welcomed them, many viewed them as a vehicle for arbitrary US influence on international space policy.[27] This apprehension can be attributed to the new terminology and concepts introduced by the accords, including safety zones—areas within which signatories commit to notify and coordinate with relevant actors to avoid harmful interference—and 'deconfliction' on the Moon, as well as the use of space resources. The concept of safety zones in particular raised security concerns, since the Artemis Accords address them only from the perspective of the party implementing the zone. This has been criticized as potentially creating 'de facto "spheres of influence"' that will unfairly empower certain actors (both state and non-state) under the pretext of preventing harmful interference.[28]

Since none of these issues have been clarified in international forums, the Artemis Accords may pave the way for the USA to unilaterally interpret law, rather than taking a consensus-based multilateral approach.

Purchase of lunar regolith

In September 2020 NASA announced that it was soliciting invitations to collect lunar regolith for a fixed price from commercial entities.[29] It claimed that such purchases would be conducted in accordance with international law but, again, the Outer Space Treaty does not expressly discuss the use of space resources.[30] The 1979 Moon Agreement makes references to an international framework for the use of space resources, but the USA, like all but a handful of states, is not a party to this treaty.[31]

NASA's objective in soliciting proposals from both US and foreign companies is most likely to set a precedent for the sale and use of lunar resources. This is an issue that the USA has pursued since it officially recognized that US citizens are entitled to 'obtain' space resources in 2015.[32]

These policies—Trump's executive order, the Artemis Accords and NASA's acquisition of regolith—could erode state relations as they indicate a shift away from the notion that space is for the benefit of all states, and

---

[27] European Space Policy Institute (ESPI), 'Artemis Accords: What implications for Europe?', ESPI Brief no. 46, Nov. 2020.

[28] Wang, G., 'NASA's Artemis Accords: The path to a united space law or a divided one?', Space Review, 24 Aug. 2020.

[29] US National Aeronautics and Space Administration (note 25).

[30] National appropriation of outer space is prohibited by Outer Space Treaty (note 10), Article II.

[31] Agreement Governing the Activities of States on the Moon and Other Celestial Bodies (Moon Agreement), opened for signature 18 Dec. 1979, entered into force 1 July 1984, Article 11. As of 1 Jan. 2020, the Moon Agreement had 18 states parties; the Outer Space Treaty had 110.

[32] Space Resource Exploration and Utilization Act of 2015, Title IV of US Public Law 114–90, signed into law 25 Nov. 2015, section 51 303.

instead suggest that it is becoming exclusionary.[33] When accompanied by US policies that reference 'space superiority', they discourage other states from multilateral engagement and may instead lead them to advance their own military ambitions in space.[34]

The future: Norm-building through inclusive and multilateral approaches

Efforts to address space security issues through the UN—including the Conference on Disarmament (CD), the Group of Governmental Experts (GGE) on Transparency and Confidence-building Measures in Outer Space Activities and the GGE on Further Effective Measures for the Prevention of an Arms Race in Outer Space—have made little progress.[35] However, in December 2020 the UN General Assembly adopted a promising new initiative proposed by the UK regarding norms for responsible behaviour in space.[36] The resolution does not propose specific regulations but instead invites states to submit their views on aspects of space security to the UN secretary-general, for discussion in the 2021 session of the General Assembly.[37] Notably, the resolution departs from the objects-based approach predominant in past multilateral processes (which has resulted in disagreements over defining terms such as 'weapons in space'). Instead, it aims for future dialogue to focus on state behaviour.

Given the legal uncertainty associated with space activities, developing norms for responsible behaviour in space is certainly the current priority. However, political differences and the need for new regulation to sufficiently address non-state actors in space pose complex challenges. The ultimate goal should be a regulatory approach that incorporates an inclusive multilateral process to adequately represent the views of all entities involved. The onus is on space powers to return to multilateral approaches, engage diverse stakeholders and clarify the intent behind future space activities. In the meantime, confidence-building measures, such as the UK's General Assembly resolution, can act as key steps towards alleviating the impact of harmful rhetoric surrounding conflict in space.

[33] Outer Space Treaty (note 10), Article 1.
[34] US Space Force (note 21), pp. 27–30.
[35] United Nations, General Assembly, Report of the Group of Governmental Experts on Transparency and Confidence-building Measures in Outer Space Activities, A/68/189, 29 July 2013; and United Nations, General Assembly, Report of the Group of Governmental Experts on Further Practical Measures for the Prevention of an Arms Race in Outer Space, A/74/77, 9 Apr. 2019, annex II.
[36] UN General Assembly Resolution 75/36, 'Reducing space threats through norms, rules and principles of responsible behaviours', 7 Dec. 2020, A/RES/75/36, 16 Dec. 2020.
[37] UN General Assembly Resolution 75/36 (note 36), para. 6.

V. The withdrawal of the United States from the Treaty on Open Skies

IAN DAVIS

In May 2020 the United States announced that it would formally withdraw from the 1992 Treaty on Open Skies, citing the failure of Russia to adhere to the agreement. It had been threatening to do so since at least October 2019.[1] The US withdrawal came into effect on 22 November 2020 and added to existing tensions between Russia and the USA and its European allies.[2]

The treaty was signed in March 1992, entered into force on 1 January 2002 and, prior to the US withdrawal, had 34 states parties across northern Asia, Europe and North America, with territories stretching 'from Vladivostok to Vancouver'.[3] It established a regime of unarmed aerial observation flights over the entire territory of participating states on a reciprocal basis. It was the only part of the European conventional arms control system to include Canada and the USA within its area of application.

This section first reviews the nature and scope of the outstanding treaty disagreements and allegations of non-compliance. It then discusses the US withdrawal decision and the international reaction to it.

Treaty implementation, disputes and alleged violations

The 97-page Treaty on Open Skies is highly technical. It details how the states parties may fly unarmed fixed-wing observation flights over each other's territory to enhance mutual transparency, build trust and lower potential military tensions. Yearly flight quotas apply. A party can conduct these flights with its own aircraft or it can join the observation mission of another state party. States cannot declare any area or military installation to be off limits—flights can only be restricted or changed for weather or safety reasons.

Russia (jointly with Belarus) and the USA each had an annual quota of 42 observation flights, while the other participating states had quotas of 12 or fewer flights.[4] The treaty is sometimes criticized for its reliance on outdated equipment now that military or commercial reconnaissance

---

[1] Browne, R., 'Trump administration expected to announce exit from "Open Skies" treaty', CNN, 9 Oct. 2019.

[2] US Department of State, 'Treaty on Open Skies', Press statement, 22 Nov. 2020. On these tensions see chapter 5, section I, in this volume.

[3] For a summary and other details of the Treaty on Open Skies see annex A, section II, in this volume.

[4] On the quota system see Graef, A. and Kütt, M., 'Visualizing the Open Skies Treaty', Institute for Peace Research and Security Policy at the University of Hamburg (IFSH), 27 Apr. 2020.

satellites can often provide imagery with comparable or better quality.[5] However, satellites also have limitations (related to fixed orbits, inclinations and cloud formations) and most states parties have limited or no access to them. Moreover, the equipment used under the treaty has been the subject of an ongoing modernization process, with a transition to digital cameras and the acquisition of new dedicated aircraft. Both Germany and Russia have acquired new Open Skies aircraft and, prior to its withdrawal, the USA had budgeted for two new long-range aircraft.[6] For small and medium-sized European states without satellites, Open Skies flights provide an independent tool for collecting intelligence and specific data in particular circumstances.[7]

Since the treaty's entry into force in 2002, the parties have conducted over 1500 surveillance flights.[8] Disagreements about treaty implementation and compliance have been a persistent feature, including debates about flight safety, conflicts over territorial status and national security concerns.[9] Most of these disagreements are normally resolved in the Open Skies Consultative Commission (OSCC). This body holds regular plenary meetings in Vienna and has several informal working groups of experts, mainly to deal with technical issues such as sensors, notification formats, aircraft certification, and rules and procedures.[10] Since at least 2014, however, the USA has raised a number of persistent concerns, principally about Russian restrictions on flights over the Russian exclave of Kaliningrad and an exclusion corridor along Russia's border with Abkhazia and South Ossetia—two regions of Georgia supported and recognized as independent by Russia.

The Georgia–Russia border dispute

The disagreement between Georgia and Russia over implementation of the Open Skies Treaty centres on the status of the disputed territories of

---

[5] Martin, S. and Reynolds, N., 'The Open Skies Treaty and prospects for European confidence-building measures', Commentary, Royal United Services Institute (RUSI), 22 May 2020; and Trevithick, J., 'Air Force is down to one tired old jet to fly Open Skies surveillance flights', The Drive, 28 Apr. 2020.

[6] Spitzer, H., 'Cooperative transparency—Modernization of Open Skies sensors in tense times', eds C. Reuter et al., *Science Peace Security '19: Proceedings of the Interdisciplinary Conference on Technical Peace and Security Research* (TUprints: Darmstadt, 2019), pp. 141–61; and Insinna, V., 'The Air Force cancels its Open Skies recapitalization program after US pulls from treaty', *Defense News*, 16 July 2020.

[7] Reif, K. and Bugos, S., 'Critics question US Open Skies complaints', *Arms Control Today*, vol. 50, no. 6 (July/Aug. 2020). On European perspectives see also Richter, W., 'Attack on the Open Skies Treaty', German Institute for International and Security Affairs (SWP) Comment no. 29, June 2020.

[8] Pifer, S., 'The looming US withdrawal from the Open Skies Treaty', Brookings Institution, 19 Nov. 2020; and Graef and Kütt (note 4).

[9] Graef, A., 'The end of the Open Skies Treaty and the politics of compliance', Lawfare, 6 July 2020.

[10] For a brief description of the OSCC see annex B, section II, in this volume. See also Organization for Security and Co-operation in Europe, 'Open Skies Consultative Commission', [n.d.].

Abkhazia and South Ossetia.[11] Since 2010 Russia has prohibited observation missions over its border area with these two regions, claiming that following the August 2008 Georgia–Russia conflict they are now independent states.[12] To justify this, Russia cites the provision of the treaty that forbids flights over territories within 10 kilometres of a border with a country that is not party to the treaty.[13] The USA and other parties to the treaty have not accepted this interpretation of the status of Abkhazia and South Ossetia.[14]

In order to protect its territorial integrity, since 2012 Georgia has banned all Russian observation flights in Georgian airspace and suspended its own observation flights in Russian airspace.[15] In 2018 Russia indicated that it would be willing to lift the ban on flights within 10 km of its borders with Abkhazia and South Ossetia if Georgia were to accept Open Skies overflights by Russia, but no solution had been agreed by the end of 2020.[16]

Restrictions over Kaliningrad

Kaliningrad Oblast is a relatively small but heavily militarized area that is geographically separate from Russia, lying between Lithuania and Poland. In 2014 Russia limited the total length of observer flights over this region to 500 km. It justified this as a reaction to a Polish overflight in 2014 that allegedly endangered the safety of civil aviation.[17] Other treaty parties maintain that the limit both violates provisions of the treaty and decreases coverage of a militarily significant area.[18]

In February 2020, however, Russia allowed a joint flight by Estonia, Lithuania and the USA with a range of 505 km over the region, the first since it introduced restrictions in 2014.[19] The motives for Russia's apparent policy change are unclear, although it may have been timed to influence public debate over the proposed US withdrawal from the treaty.

---

[11] On the broader territorial dispute between Georgia and Russia see Georgia and Russia see Davis, I., 'Key developments in the region', SIPRI Yearbook 2020, pp. 115–17.

[12] Grigalashvili, M., 'The Treaty on Open Skies and the causes of Russian–Georgian confrontation', Commentary, Georgian Institute of Politics, 19 June 2018.

[13] Treaty on Open Skies (note 3), Article IV(II.2).

[14] Woolf, A. F., US Congressional Research Service, Statement before joint hearing on 'The importance of the Open Skies Treaty', US House of Representatives Committee on Foreign Affairs Subcommittee on Europe, Eurasia, Energy and the Environment and US Commission on Security and Cooperation in Europe, 19 Nov. 2019, p. 6.

[15] Grigalashvili (note 12).

[16] Woolf (note 14), p. 6; and Yermakov, A., 'Darkened skies: The US might withdraw from the Treaty on Open Skies', Russian International Affairs Council (RIAC), 14 Nov. 2019.

[17] Yermakov (note 16); and Kelin, A., 'Open Skies clouded by sham and ambiguity', Commentary, Royal United Services Institute (RUSI), 2 July 2020.

[18] Graef, A., *Saving the Open Skies Treaty: Challenges and Possible Scenarios after the US Withdrawal*, Euro-Atlantic Security Policy Brief (European Leadership Network: London, Sep. 2020), p. 10.

[19] 'US, Estonia, Lithuania observe Russian, Belarusian military sites under Open Skies Treaty', *Baltic Times*, 26 Feb. 2020.

Further Russian and US restrictions

In 2017 the USA announced restrictions of its own, including a limit on the length of Russian observations flights over Hawaii, a US island group in the Pacific Ocean that hosts the US Pacific Fleet among other military facilities, and removal of overnight accommodation at two of the US Air Force bases that Russia used during its missions over the USA.[20] In retaliation, Russia limited the number of its airfields available to US surveillance aircraft within the Open Skies framework.[21]

In 2018, as a result of the Georgian–Russian dispute, the states parties were unable to reach consensus on the annual quota distribution and no regular quota flights took place.[22] Flights resumed in 2019. However, the USA asserted that Russia violated the treaty by refusing to authorize a Canadian–US observation flight over a Russian military exercise.[23] According to Russia this restriction was due to concerns about flight safety and a proposed alternative flight slot was rejected by the USA.[24]

Assessing alleged violations

Assessing compliance with the treaty is difficult and even the annual compliance reports published by the US Department of State acknowledge the normative ambiguity.[25] From 2005 to 2017 the unclassified versions of the reports, while expressing serious concerns about compliance, did not formally find Russia to be 'in violation' of the treaty. This changed in the 2018 report—the first fully drafted by the administration of US President Donald J. Trump.[26] These accusations were repeated in the 2019 and 2020 reports.[27]

The US treaty withdrawal and the international reaction

In a written statement on 21 May 2020, the US Department of State announced that the USA would notify the treaty depositaries of its intention to leave the Open Skies Treaty on 22 November. In the statement the US secretary of state, Michael R. Pompeo, said that the USA could reconsider

[20] US Department of State, *Adherence to and Compliance with Arms Control, Nonproliferation, and Disarmament Agreements and Commitments* (Department of State: Washington, DC, Aug. 2019), p. 52.

[21] US Department of State (note 20), p. 52.

[22] Bell, A. and Wier, A., 'Open Skies Treaty: A quiet legacy under threat', *Arms Control Today*, vol 49, no. 1 (Jan./Feb. 2019).

[23] US Department of State, *Adherence to and Compliance with Arms Control, Nonproliferation, and Disarmament Agreements and Commitments* (Department of State: Washington, DC, June 2020), p. 66.

[24] Kelin (note 17).

[25] See the discussion in Graef (note 9).

[26] US Department of State, *Adherence to and Compliance with Arms Control, Nonproliferation, and Disarmament Agreements and Commitments* (Department of State: Washington, DC, Apr. 2018), pp. 31–34.

[27] US Department of State (note 20); and US Department of State (note 23). See also Graef (note 9).

its withdrawal during the six-month notice period 'should Russia return to full compliance with the Treaty'.[28] Russia denied being in violation of the agreement and none of the other parties indicated that the Russian transgressions were enough to endanger the treaty.[29] President Trump asserted that 'There's a very good chance we'll make a new agreement or do something to put that agreement back together'.[30]

By starting the six-month notice period in May, the Trump administration ensured that the USA would leave the treaty irrespective of the outcome of the US presidential election in November. In so doing, the administration also ignored preconditions for a withdrawal established in US domestic law months earlier.[31]

The Open Skies Treaty was the third arms control agreement that the USA withdrew from during the Trump presidency, after the 2015 Joint Comprehensive Plan of Action (JCPOA, or Iran nuclear deal) in 2018 and the 1987 Intermediate-range Nuclear Forces Treaty (INF Treaty) in 2019.[32] The future of the 2010 Strategic Arms Reduction Treaty (New START) was also in doubt ahead of its last-minute renewal in February 2021.[33]

International reaction

The North Atlantic Treaty Organization (NATO) met at ambassadorial level on 22 May 2020 to discuss the US decision to withdraw from the Open Skies Treaty.[34] In a statement after the meeting, the NATO secretary general, Jens Stoltenberg, blamed Russian 'flight restrictions inconsistent with the treaty' for undermining it.[35] He also noted that the USA would reconsider its withdrawal if Russia respected the treaty's terms and said that NATO members were engaging with Russia to seek its early return to compliance. A number of NATO member states reportedly expressed concerns during the NATO meeting about the planned US withdrawal.[36] In a joint statement

---

[28] Pompeo, M. R., US Secretary of State, 'On the Treaty on Open Skies', Press statement, US Department of State, 21 May 2020.

[29] E.g. German Federal Foreign Office, 'Foreign Minister Maas on America's announcement that it intends to withdraw from the Open Skies Treaty', Press release, 21 May 2020. For a Russian perspective see Kelin (note 17).

[30] Cited in Borger, J., 'Trump to pull US out of third arms control deal', *The Guardian*, 21 May 2020.

[31] National Defense Authorization Act for Fiscal Year 2020, US Public Law 116–92, signed into law 20 Dec. 2019, section 1234. See also Anderson, S. R. and Vaddi, P., 'When can the president withdraw from the Open Skies Treaty?', Lawfare, 22 Apr. 2020.

[32] On developments in the JCPOA see chapter 11, section II, in this volume. On the INF Treaty and the US withdrawal see annex A, section III, in this volume; and Topychkanov, T. and Davis, I., 'Russian–United States nuclear arms control and disarmament', *SIPRI Yearbook 2020*, pp. 399–409.

[33] On developments in Russian–US arms control, including New START, see chapter 11, section I, in this volume. For a brief description of New START see annex A, section III, in this volume.

[34] For a brief description and list of members of NATO see annex B, section II, in this volume.

[35] NATO, 'Statement by the NATO Secretary General on the Open Skies Treaty', Press Release no. (2020) 047, 22 May 2020.

[36] 'European NATO allies voice concern over US plan to quit Open Skies', Reuters, 22 May 2020.

read out during the meeting, 10 NATO member states and 2 NATO partners expressed regret for the USA's intention to withdraw, while sharing 'concerns about implementation of the Treaty clauses by Russia'.[37] Nonetheless, the 12 said that they would 'continue to implement the Open Skies Treaty, which has a clear added value for our conventional arms control architecture and cooperative security'.

The European Union (EU) also urged the USA to reconsider its plan to withdraw.[38] The EU high representative for foreign affairs and security policy, Josep Borrell, said that 'Withdrawing from a treaty is not the solution to address difficulties in its implementation and compliance by another party'.[39] Stanislav Zas, secretary-general of the Collective Security Treaty Organization (CSTO), said the US decision to withdraw was 'deeply regrettable' and would 'cause serious damage not only to the system of control over military activities but also to the entire system of international security'.[40]

In a joint statement on 12 May 2020 a group of 16 retired European military commanders and defence ministers, including a retired NATO military commander and a former head of the Russian Foreign Intelligence Service, also argued in favour of protecting the Open Skies Treaty.[41] They said that the USA leaving the treaty would lead to weaker international arms control and to asymmetry in Russian–US surveillance, since Russia would still be able to oversee US military activities within Europe while the USA could no longer overfly Russia. In the case of a US withdrawal, the group recommended that the remaining member states make a serious effort to persist with the treaty.

Addressing the consequences of the US withdrawal

Preservation of the treaty without US participation depended on finding agreement in three areas: treaty implementation and compliance; quota distribution; and technical challenges, including a shortage of certified aircraft equipped with sensors, the risk of unauthorized data sharing by

---

[37] Statement of the foreign ministries of France, Belgium, Czechia, Finland, Germany, Greece, Italy, Luxemburg, the Netherlands, Portugal, Spain and Sweden, Government Offices of Sweden, 22 May 2020; and Schultz, T., 'NATO allies alarmed, annoyed by US Open Skies exit', Deutsche Welle, 22 May 2020.

[38] For a brief description and list of members of the EU see annex B, section II, in this volume.

[39] Cited in Cook, L., 'EU urges US to reconsider military overflight treaty pullout', AP News, 22 May 2020.

[40] [CSTO secretary general comments on US withdrawal from the Open Skies Treaty], RIA Novosti, 3 June 2020 (in Russian). For a brief description and list of members of the CSTO see annex B, section II, in this volume.

[41] European Leadership Network (ELN), 'Saving the Open Skies Treaty', Group statement, 12 May 2020.

NATO members with the USA, and the loss of US expertise and funding for the OSCC.[42]

Under the terms of the treaty, within 30–60 days of receiving a withdrawal notice, the two depositary states—Canada and Hungary—are required to convene a conference of states parties to review the consequences of the withdrawal.[43] Such a conference was held online (due to the Covid-19 pandemic) on 6 July 2020. According to an OSCC statement issued after the meeting, the representatives of all 34 states parties discussed 'the overall impact on operational functionality of the treaty, the impact on the allocation of observation quotas and on financial arrangements within the treaty, and other potential effects on the treaty'.[44] While the statement gives no indication of any outcomes being agreed, the meeting reportedly agreed to set up a special informal working group chaired by Finland to prepare proposals on the future of the treaty.[45] These were to be considered at the Fourth Review Conference of the treaty, scheduled for October 2020.

Prior to the Review Conference, the states parties successfully agreed a distribution of quotas on 5 October, which included Russia shifting its previously US-bound flights to Europe.[46] The Fourth Review Conference of the treaty, held in Vienna on 7–9 October, was chaired by Belgium.[47] The parties agreed a final document that reportedly emphasized, among other things, that they continue to value the treaty.[48] However, this document was not made public, no official statement was released at the end of the conference and the states parties made few public statements.

Future outlook

A full flight quota distribution was agreed for 2021—effectively compensating for the US withdrawal from flight activity—and the remaining states parties seem determined to continue implementing the treaty, even if the pandemic or a temporary shortfall of aircraft might limit the number of

---

[42] Graef (note 18); and 'Moscow certain NATO will share information about flights over Russia with US—ambassador', TASS, 6 June 2020.

[43] Treaty on Open Skies (note 3), Article XV(3).

[44] Open Skies Consultative Commission (OSCC), 'Conference of States Parties to the Open Skies Treaty discusses US intent to withdraw from Treaty', Press release, 7 July 2020.

[45] Graef (note 18).

[46] Eodmo (@EodLuc), 'Quota allocation 2021 has been successful. [Clapping hands sign]', Twitter, 5 Oct. 2020; Reif, K. and Bugos, S., 'Russia highlights unresolved Open Skies issues', *Arms Control Today*, vol. 50, no. 9 (Nov. 2020); and Graef, A., 'The skies are closing in', Riddle, 20 Jan. 2021.

[47] Belgian Federal Public Service Foreign Affairs, Foreign Trade and Development Cooperation, 'Belgium chairs the Conference of the "Open Skies" treaty, a cornerstone of the European security architecture', 7 Oct. 2020.

[48] Graef, A., Researcher, Institute for Peace Research and Security Policy at the University of Hamburg (IFSH), Correspondence with author, 1 Feb. 2021.

flights. However, at the end of 2020 the longer-term future of the treaty remained uncertain.[49]

In November 2020 the Russian foreign minister, Sergey Lavrov, indicated that Russia required the other states parties 'to legally confirm in writing that . . . they will not prohibit flights over any part of their territory regardless of whether US bases are located there' and to restrict the distribution of treaty data to states parties only.[50] Regarding the latter, Russia submitted a proposal to the OSCC on 11 December to amend the treaty rules concerning data security.[51] In a diplomatic note dated 22 December, the Russian Ministry of Foreign Affairs requested that the other states parties confirm in a legally binding form their acceptance of the draft decision before 1 January 2021, otherwise it would initiate withdrawal procedures. However, on 30 December 2020, 16 European states parties rejected this ultimatum while remaining open to further discussions.[52] An extraordinary OSCC meeting scheduled for 25 January 2021 was expected to be crucial for identifying any potential ways forward and preventing a Russian withdrawal.

Finally, there also remained uncertainty as to whether the USA, under the new US administration of Joe Biden, might rejoin the treaty.[53] The US Congress had indicated that the decision to withdraw from the Open Skies Treaty did not comply with US domestic law and required the US secretaries of State and Defense to submit a report on the security implications of the withdrawal by March 2021.[54] It was conceivable that this report could argue that the USA has been unable to effectively replace imagery and intelligence previously received under the Open Skies Treaty. During the US presidential election, Biden had expressed support for the treaty and condemned the withdrawal decision, although he stopped short of committing to rejoin the agreement once in office. Moreover, any decision to do so would also require the approval of the US Senate by a two-thirds vote.

[49] Gressel, G., 'How a US withdrawal from the Open Skies Treaty would benefit the Kremlin', Commentary, European Council for Foreign Relations, 27 May 2020.

[50] Russian Ministry of Foreign Affairs, 'Foreign Minister Sergey Lavrov's interview with Russian and foreign media on current international issues, Moscow, November 12, 2020', 12 Nov. 2020; and Russian Ministry of Foreign Affairs, 'Foreign Ministry statement on the withdrawal by the United States from the Open Skies Treaty', 22 Nov. 2020.

[51] Gavrilov, K., Head of the Russian Delegation to the Vienna Negotiations on Military Security and Arms Control, Statement at the 4th Plenary meeting of the 83rd Session of the Open Skies Consultative Commission (OSCC), 14 Dec. 2020 (in Russian), English translation: Facebook.

[52] The 16 states parties were Belgium, Croatia, Czechia, Denmark, Finland, France, Germany, Greece, Iceland, Latvia, Luxembourg, the Netherlands, Slovenia, Slovakia, Spain and Sweden. Krüger, P.-A. and Mascolo, G., 'Der Himmel könnte sich schließen' [The sky could close], Süddeutsche Zeitung, 3 Jan. 2021.

[53] Cohen, R. S., 'The US is out of the Open Skies Treaty. What's next?', Air Force Magazine, 23 Nov. 2020; and Gould, J., Insinna, V. and Mehta, A., 'Trump left the Open Skies Treaty, but don't write it off yet', Defense News, 25 Nov. 2020.

[54] National Defense Authorization Act for Fiscal Year 2021, US Public Law 116-283, signed onto law 1 Jan. 2021, section 1232.

VI. International transparency in arms procurement and military expenditure as confidence-building measures

PIETER D. WEZEMAN AND SIEMON T. WEZEMAN

International or multilateral transparency in arms procurement and military spending has long been an important element of conventional arms control and confidence building. Relevant instruments have been created within the United Nations and in several other multilateral organizations, and their perceived utility is regularly reiterated.[1]

This section reviews the status in 2020 of the multilateral instruments to which states report—as a confidence-building measure (CBM)—on several aspects of arms procurement and military spending.[2] It first looks at two that are coordinated by the United Nations: the UN Register of Conventional Arms (UNROCA) and the UN Report on Military Expenditures (UNMILEX). It then describes developments in the transparency mechanisms of the Organization for Security and Co-operation in Europe (OSCE)—the only non-dormant instruments coordinated by a regional organization.[3] The activities under the instruments in 2020 mostly relate to states reporting on arms transfers and military spending in 2019. The section does not discuss multilateral reporting on arms exports within the framework of international and national arms trade regulations.[4]

The United Nations Register of Conventional Arms

UNROCA was established in 1991 by the UN General Assembly. Its main aims are to enhance confidence between states, 'prevent the excessive and destabilizing accumulation of arms', 'encourage restraint' in the transfer

---

[1] E.g. UN Office for Disarmament Affairs (UNODA), *Securing Our Common Future: An Agenda for Disarmament* (United Nations: New York, 2018), p. 44.

[2] The section includes reporting by 31 Dec. 2020. Some states may have submitted reports during 2021 that should have been submitted in 2020.

[3] In the Americas, the states parties of the Inter-American Convention on Transparency in Conventional Weapons Acquisition (Convención Interamericana sobre Transparencia en las Adquisiciones de Armas Convencionales, CITAAC) are required to submit annual reports on arms transfers. However, although they have received annual reminders, including in 2020, there are no public records of states having submitted information to CITAAC since 2015. For a summary and other details of the convention see annex A, section II, in this volume. For the reports submitted up to 2015 see Organization of American States, Committee on Hemispheric Security, 'Inter-American Convention on Transparency in Conventional Weapon Acquisition (CITAAC)', [n.d.].

[4] On multilateral reporting on arms exports under the Arms Trade Treaty see chapter 14, section I, in this volume. On the state of transparency in arms procurement see Wezeman, P. D., Béraud-Sudreau, L. and Wezeman, S. T., 'Transparency in arms procurement: Limitations and opportunities for assessing global armament developments', SIPRI Insights on Peace and Security no. 2020/10, Oct. 2020.

and production of arms, and 'contribute to preventive diplomacy'.[5] However, while UNROCA's objectives relate to armament developments in general, in terms of reporting its focus is on arms transfers.

UN member states are requested to report annually, in a standardized format and on a voluntary basis, information on their exports and imports in the previous year of seven categories of major arms that are deemed to be 'indispensable for offensive operations'.[6] These categories are battle tanks, armoured combat vehicles, large-calibre artillery systems, combat aircraft, attack helicopters, warships, and missiles and missile launchers.

Since 2003, states have also been able to provide background information on transfers of an eighth category: small arms and light weapons (SALW). The discussion and decision to include SALW was largely related to efforts to prevent the illicit trade in these weapons, and not part of UNROCA's function as a CBM between states.[7]

In addition, 'states in a position to do so' are invited to provide—indicating a lower level of commitment—information on their holdings of major arms and procurement of such arms through national production.[8] In 2019 a group of government experts (GGE) that reviewed the operation of UNROCA encouraged states to report this information. This was on the basis that 'countries producing their own weapons should be held to the same standard of transparency as countries that acquire their weaponry abroad'.[9]

Participation

The level of participation in UNROCA has decreased drastically since reporting started in 1993.[10] For example, over 100 states reported on their arms imports and exports annually in the early 2000s and 61 reported for

---

[5] UN General Assembly Resolution 46/36L, 'Transparency in armaments', A/RES/46/36, 6 Dec. 1991, para. 2; and UN Office for Disarmament Affairs, 'UN Register of Conventional Arms'. On the development of UNROCA see United Nations, General Assembly, 'Report on the continuing operation of the United Nations Register of Conventional Arms and its further development', A/74/211, 22 July 2019, paras 6–15.

[6] United Nations, General Assembly, Report on the continuing operation of the United Nations Register of Conventional Arms and its further development, A/71/259, 29 July 2016, para. 61(g).

[7] See e.g. United Nations, General Assembly, Report on the continuing operation of the United Nations Register of Conventional Arms and its further development, A/58/274, 13 July 2003, paras 92–108.

[8] UN General Assembly Resolution 74/53, 'Transparency in armaments', 12 Dec. 2019, A/RES/74/53, 19 Dec. 2019.

[9] United Nations, A/74/211 (note 5), p. 4.

[10] UNROCA submissions are made public in annual reports by the UN secretary-general, available on the website of the UN Office for Disarmament Affairs (note 5); and in the online UNROCA database, <https://www.unroca.org/>.

2013. However, only 43 of the 193 UN member states submitted a report on exports or imports for 2018 and only 39 for 2019.[11]

Most of the states identified by SIPRI as large exporters of major arms in 2016–20 have participated in UNROCA consistently. In particular, the top 10 exporters have all submitted data for almost all of these five years. Of the 10 largest arms exporters in the period 2016–20, only the United States (by far the world's largest exporter of major arms) and the Republic of Korea (South Korea) did not report for 2019.[12] For both countries, this was the first year for which it did not report to UNROCA.[13] Neither has publicly explained the reason for not reporting. Of the 10 largest arms importers in the period 2016–20, seven—Saudi Arabia, Egypt, Algeria, South Korea, Qatar, the United Arab Emirates and Pakistan—did not report to UNROCA for 2019.[14]

Reporting on arms transfers within the framework of the 2013 Arms Trade Treaty (ATT) involves similar reporting templates to those used for UNROCA. However, 56 countries reported to the ATT for 2019, 17 more than to UNROCA.[15] For example, South Korea reported to the ATT but not to UNROCA. Since the templates are similar, a state can simply submit a copy of its ATT report to UNROCA, as Australia and the United Kingdom did for 2019.[16] It is unclear why other countries do not do this.

The level of reporting on military holdings and arms procurement through national production was even lower than on arms transfers. Of the 39 reports for 2019, only 10 included information on military holdings and a further 5 on both military holdings and procurement from national production. For 2018 these numbers were respectively 10 and 2, while further 3 reported only on procurement from national production. Among the major military powers that submitted data for 2019 on arms transfers but did not provide data on holdings or arms procurement through national production were China, France, India and Russia.

---

[11] Figures are according to the public records available on 31 Dec. 2020. Due to technical problems, not all submissions may have been included in the UNROCA database. UN Office for Disarmament Affairs, Communication with authors, 6 May 2020. Information about submissions for 2019 is particularly uncertain because of continuing discrepancies between the two sources that contain submitted reports: the report by the UN secretary-general, which includes all reports submitted by the deadline of 31 May 2020; and the UNROCA database, which should include all submissions but does not include 4 of the 2019 reports included in the secretary-general's report. For more in-depth analysis of participation in the UNROCA reporting on arms transfers see Bromley, M. and Alvarado Cóbar, J. F., *Reporting on Conventional Arms Transfers and Transfer Controls: Improving Coordination and Increasing Engagement* (SIPRI: Stockholm, Aug. 2020); United Nations, A/74/211 (note 5), pp. 4–9; and United Nations, General Assembly, 'United Nations Register of Conventional Arms', Report of the Secretary-General, A/75/152, 9 July 2020.

[12] On the largest exporters in 2016–20 see chapter 9, section II, in this volume.

[13] States were requested to report for 2019 by 31 May 2020. Although it is not uncommon for states to report late, until 2020 the USA and South Korea always reported by the end of the year.

[14] On the largest importers in 2016–20 see chapter 9, section III, in this volume.

[15] On ATT reporting see chapter 14, section I, in this volume.

[16] Arms Trade Treaty Secretariat, 'Annual reports', 16 Dec. 2020.

Data omissions and inaccuracies

Previous research on UNROCA has shown that important information is often omitted from state's submissions.[17] This is particularly clear when an exporting state's UNROCA report does not match the importing state's report. For example, for 2019, exporters reported the supply of 445 'armoured combat vehicles' to 11 states that also reported to UNROCA, while importers reported acquisitions of 100 of the vehicles from 5 exporters that reported to UNROCA.[18] This discrepancy—of hundreds of vehicles—may be due to different national interpretations of the definitions of the seven UNROCA categories of major arms, of what constitutes a transfer and of when a transfer takes place.[19]

In addition, open source information shows that information on arms transfers has not always been included in either of the applicable UNROCA reports because states sometimes want to keep certain arms transfers confidential.[20] Among the transfers in 2019 identified in multiple other sources but not included in any report to UNROCA are deliveries of an estimated 12 combat aircraft and 12 attack helicopters from Russia to Egypt, an estimated 2 combat aircraft from China to Myanmar and an estimated 24 armoured combat vehicles from Germany to Austria.[21]

The United Nations Report on Military Expenditures

In 1980 the UN General Assembly agreed to establish an annual report in which all UN member states could voluntarily provide data on their military expenditure in the previous year.[22] The report, which has been known as the UN Report on Military Expenditures since 2012, aims to enhance transparency in military matters, increase predictability of military activities, reduce the risk of military conflict and raise public awareness of disarmament matters.[23]

---

[17] Wezeman, S. T., 'Reporting to the United Nations Register of Conventional Arms for 2017', SIPRI Background Paper, June 2019.

[18] Items marked in the submissions as being for non-military use have not been included in these figures.

[19] Wezeman (note 17).

[20] Wezeman (note 17), pp. 9–10.

[21] This is based on a comparison between the UNROCA submissions and the SIPRI Arms Transfers Database.

[22] UN General Assembly Resolution 35/142 B, 'Reduction of military budgets', 12 Dec. 1980, A/RES/35/142; and United Nations, General Assembly, Report of the Group of Governmental Experts to Review the Operation and Further Development of the United Nations Report on Military Expenditures, A/72/293, 4 Aug. 2017, paras 2–5. For a detailed description of the history of the instrument see Spies, M., *United Nations Efforts to Reduce Military Expenditures: A Historical Overview*, UN Office for Disarmament Affairs (UNODA) Occasional Papers no. 33 (United Nations: New York, Oct. 2019).

[23] United Nations, A/72/293 (note 22), para. 2.

The highest rate of participation in UNMILEX was reporting for 2001, when 81 states participated.[24] Although questions remain about the reliability of the available public records on reporting (see below), only 30 of the 193 UN member states submitted information on their military spending for 2018, and only 43 did so for 2019.[25] Of the 43 states that reported for 2019, 29 are in Europe, 6 in Asia and Oceania, 5 in the Americas, 2 in the Middle East and 1 in Africa. Five of the 15 states that SIPRI identified as having the highest military spending levels in 2019 did not report to UNMILEX: the USA, China, Saudi Arabia, South Korea and Australia (in order of spending levels). The most significant omissions were the two states with the largest military expenditure: the USA, for which the mostly recent report is for 2015; and China, for which the most recent report is for 2017.

Based on SIPRI military expenditure figures, the 43 states that reported for 2019 accounted for 29 per cent of total world spending in 2019.[26] In contrast to the low level of reporting to UNMILEX, almost all states provide information on their military spending at a national level. Of the 168 states for which SIPRI attempted to estimate military expenditure in 2019, 147 published their military budgets in official sources.[27] These figures are all publicly available in the SIPRI Military Expenditure Database.

The way in which the UN publishes the national reports on military expenditure makes access and use of their contents difficult and hinders the assessment of participation. Reports that are submitted before the deadline of 30 April are included in a report by the UN secretary-general. In addition, there is an online public archive that should include all reports, including those submitted after the deadline.[28] A new version of this database was introduced in 2020.[29] However, by the end of 2020 the database only included reports for 2019 and did not provide reliable information about participation for previous years. Furthermore, 9 of the 41 reports listed for 2019 were

[24] United Nations, Report of the Group of Governmental Experts on the Operation and Further Development of the United Nations Standardized Instrument for Reporting Military Expenditures, A/66/89, 14 June 2011, p. 26.

[25] Tian, N., Lopes da Silva, D. and Wezeman, P. D., 'Transparency in military expenditure', *SIPRI Yearbook 2020*, pp. 264–66; United Nations, General Assembly, 'Objective information on military matters, including transparency of military expenditures', Report of the Secretary-General, A/74/155, 12 July 2019; United Nations, General Assembly, 'Objective information on military matters, including transparency of military expenditures', Report of the Secretary-General, A/75/140, 15 July 2020; and UN Office for Disarmament Affairs (UNODA), 'Military expenditures', [n.d.].

[26] SIPRI Military Expenditure Database, <https://www.sipri.org/databases/milex>.

[27] SIPRI Military Expenditure Database, <https://www.sipri.org/databases/milex>. See also Wezeman, P. D. and Wezeman, S. T., 'Transparency in military expenditure', *SIPRI Yearbook 2020*, pp. 266–67.

[28] Both the reports by the UN secretary-general and the archive are available from UN Office for Disarmament Affairs (note 25).

[29] United Nations, Database on Military Expenditures, <http://www.un-arm.org/Milex/home.aspx>.

inaccessible, while the database omits 2 reports that are mentioned in the UN secretary-general's 2020 report.

Efforts to understand the decline in participation in United Nations transparency

GGEs have suggested a number of causes for the low participation by states in multilateral transparency instruments. These include a lack of understanding as to the purpose and relevance of the reporting, a lack of capacity, a lack of confidence in the reporting, a lack of political will, reporting fatigue and security concerns.[30] In an attempt to better understanding the cause of the decline in participation in the two UN reporting mechanisms, the UN has made several limited efforts to collect explanations by states about their participation or lack thereof. These seem to have been unsuccessful.

In 2016 the General Assembly recognized the need to revitalize UNROCA and tasked the UN Office for Disarmament Affairs (UNODA) with sending to states a questionnaire on the reasons for not reporting and ways to improve reporting. The 2019 GGE on UNROCA concluded that the number of responses to the questionnaires (17) was insufficient to 'substantially inform the Group's understanding of reasons for non-reporting'.[31] Although the questionnaire was circulated again in 2020, the secretary-general's 2020 report on UNROCA does not mention any results from this effort.[32]

In 2017 the General Assembly turned its attention to revitalization of UNMILEX and tasked UNODA with sending a similar questionnaire to states on reporting military expenditure. While 13 states had replied to this questionnaire by 2019, there is no public report that indicates that these replies have led to significant insights.[33] Indeed, the UN secretary-general's 2020 report makes no further reference to the questionnaire, and so the status and outcomes of the effort are unclear.[34]

OSCE transparency mechanisms

As of 2020 the only active regional efforts that aim at multilateral transparency in armaments were the information exchanges within the framework of the Organization for Security and Co-operation in Europe. The OSCE aims to 'contribute to reducing the dangers . . . of misunderstanding or

---

[30] United Nations, A/74/211 (note 5), para. 94; and United Nations, A/72/293 (note 22), para. 23.
[31] United Nations, A/74/211 (note 5), paras 27, 94.
[32] United Nations, A/75/152 (note 11).
[33] United Nations, A/74/155 (note 25), para. 7.
[34] United Nations, A/75/140 (note 25).

miscalculation of military activities which could give rise to apprehension'.[35] Its 57 participating states have agreed a number of CBMs on holdings, procurement and transfers of arms and on military expenditure.

Regarding arms holdings and procurement, the Vienna Document 2011 on Confidence- and Security-Building Measures requires an annual exchange of information on part of the OSCE states' military holdings and procurement of major arms.[36] However, these reports are not made public. In addition, OSCE participating states have agreed to share information on imports and exports of major arms based on the categories and format of UNROCA.[37] These submissions have been publicly available on the OSCE website since 2017.[38] They supplement the information in UNROCA as UNROCA's public records do not contain the equivalent reports in all cases.[39] In 2020, 43 of the 57 states reported on their arms transfers in 2019 to the OSCE.

Concerning military expenditure, the OSCE CBMs include a requirement for participating states to annually exchange information on military budgets.[40] Of the 57 states, 49 reported for 2019, 48 reported for 2018 and 49 for 2017.[41] However, these submissions are not publicly available.

Conclusions

The 2018 UN Agenda for Disarmament concluded that 'In regions of conflict and tension, transparency and confidence-building mechanisms designed to prevent arms competition remain underutilized and underdeveloped'.[42] That conclusion remained valid in 2020. With the partial exception of reporting within the OSCE, the international transparency instruments described above provided a limited contribution to trust and confidence building due to a lack of participation, the limited data reported, inaccuracies in the reporting, and problems with the way the information is made accessible to states and publicly.

---

[35] Conference on Security and Cooperation in Europe Final act, Helsinki, 1 Aug. 1975, p. 10. For a brief description and list of states participating in the OSCE see annex B, section II, in this volume.

[36] Vienna Document 2011, para. 11 and annex III. For a summary and other details of the Vienna Document 2011 see annex A, section II, in this volume. See also OSCE, 'Ensuring military transparency—The Vienna document', [n.d.].

[37] OSCE, Forum for Security Co-operation, 'Further transparency in arms transfers', Decision no. 13/97, FSC.DEC/13/97, 16 July 1997; OSCE, Forum for Security Co-operation, 'Changes in the deadline for the Exchange of Information on Conventional Arms and Equipment Transfers', Decision no. 8/98, FSC.DEC/8/98, 4 Nov. 1998; and OSCE, Forum for Security Co-operation, 'Updating the reporting categories of weapon and equipment systems subject to the Information Exchange on Conventional Arms Transfers', Decision no. 8/08, FSC.DEC/8/08, 16 July 2008.

[38] OSCE, 'Information Exchange on Conventional Arms Transfer'.

[39] See Bromley and Alvarado Cóbar (note 11).

[40] Vienna Document 2011 (note 36), paras 15.3–15.4.

[41] OSCE, Communication with author, 14 Jan. 2021.

[42] UN Office for Disarmament Affairs (note 1), p. 46.

Fewer than one-quarter of UN member states participated in UNROCA or UNMILEX in 2020. A slight increase in participation in UNMILEX was a positive development. This was more than balanced by the fact that, for the first time, the USA reported to neither of these UN instruments. Attempts by the UN to understand the causes for the low participation have not led to tangible outcomes that could help revitalize these instruments.

Only some of the states that participate in UNROCA and UNMILEX provide data that is comprehensive and detailed enough to use as an indicator of key trends in their arms procurements, arms transfers and military spending priorities. In particular, in the case of UNROCA some states only report some of their arms exports, omitting information about other significant arms exports. This risks creation of a false sense of transparency.

At the regional level, only the information-sharing mechanisms within the OSCE framework remained active and had a high, although not stable, level of participation.

14. Dual-use and arms trade controls

Overview

Global, multilateral and regional efforts continued in 2020 to strengthen controls on the trade in conventional arms and in dual-use items connected with conventional, biological, chemical and nuclear weapons and their delivery systems. Membership of the different international and multilateral instruments that seek to establish and promote agreed standards for the trade in arms and dual-use items remained stable. The global Covid-19 pandemic limited in-person meetings for most of the year, testing the resilience of the instruments and the capacity of states to take decisions and address technological and political challenges in such exceptional circumstances. In addition, there were growing signs that the strength of these instruments is being increasingly tested by stretched national resources and broader geopolitical tensions. This could be seen in the shortfalls in compliance with mandatory reporting—coupled with a decline in public reporting—under the 2013 Arms Trade Treaty (ATT); the various reported violations of United Nations arms embargoes; and unilateral efforts by the United States to impose a UN arms embargo on Iran beyond 2020. At the same time, states continued to make progress on reaching agreement on expanding and developing technical aspects of these controls.

The Sixth Conference of States Parties (CSP6) to the ATT was conducted on 17–21 August 2020 through written procedure with no in-person meeting (see section I). The Covid-19 pandemic limited the decision-making capacity of the CSP6, participation and open debate among different stakeholders, and the provision of international assistance to implement the ATT. Some problems that the ATT was already experiencing persisted, particularly a decline in reporting levels and an increase in the submission of reports that are not made public. One of the most significant developments was the establishment of the Diversion Information Exchange Forum, which will allow for 'informal voluntary exchanges between States Parties and signatory States' on 'concrete cases of suspected or detected diversion and for sharing concrete, operational diversion-related information'. A second important development was the accession of China to the ATT.

During 2020, 13 UN embargoes, 21 European Union (EU) embargoes and 1 League of Arab States embargo were in force (see section II). No new multilateral arms embargo was imposed and the UN embargo on the supply of major arms to Iran and exports of any arms from Iran expired, although other aspects of the embargo remained in place. Ten of the EU arms embargoes matched the scope of ones imposed by the UN; three were broader in terms of duration, geographical scope or the types of weapon covered; and eight had no UN counterpart. The single Arab League arms embargo, on Syria, had no UN counterpart. The year 2020 tested multilateral arms embargoes in a quite remarkable way. First, the USA sought to unilaterally extend the UN arms embargo on Iran beyond October 2020. Second, as in previous years, investigations by the UN revealed numerous reported cases of violations. Particular problems were noted in connection with the implementation of the UN arms embargo on Libya, where some states, such as Russia and the United Arab Emirates, pledged to abide by the embargo while reportedly continuing to violate it. Finally, the 2020 combat between Armenia and Azerbaijan in Nagorno-Karabakh raised questions about the implementation and enforcement of the Organization for Security and Co-operation in Europe's voluntary arms embargo on Nagorno-Karabakh.

None of the four multilateral export control regimes—the Australia Group (on chemical and biological weapons), the Missile Technology Control Regime (MTCR), the Nuclear Suppliers Group (NSG) and the Wassenaar Arrangement on Export Controls for Conventional Arms and Dual-use Goods and Technologies—was able to hold its annual plenary due to Covid-19 pandemic restrictions (see section III). The pandemic also severely limited the regimes' ability to take major decisions and discuss political and technical topics, such as amendments to the regimes' control lists. Much of the regimes' work continued through information exchange functions or in smaller groups of states. Several regimes put in place measures or expedited processes to improve resilience in addressing the types of challenges raised by Covid-19. Steps in this direction included upgrading the information-sharing system of the NSG, the launch of an MTCR newsletter, and increased participation of regimes' representatives in virtual meetings organized by third parties. None of the four regimes admitted any new participating states (or partners) during 2020.

To implement these four regimes in its common market, the EU has established a common legal basis for controls on the export, brokering, transit and trans-shipment of dual-use items, software and technology and, to a certain degree, military items (see section IV). The EU is the only regional organization to have developed such a framework. In 2020 the EU reached a provisional agreement on the final text of a new version of the EU dual-use regulation, concluding a review and recast process that started in 2011. Major areas of debate and revision during the recast process included creating greater harmonization of member states' controls, simplifying controls on less sensitive items, strengthening controls on cybersurveillance items, and responding to challenges posed by emerging technologies. The review of the EU common position on arms exports concluded in 2019. In 2020, the EU improved the level of transparency and accessibility of the EU annual report on arms exports, by launching an online database that includes data from the 2013–19 EU annual reports.

ANDREA EDOARDO VARISCO

I. The Arms Trade Treaty

ANDREA EDOARDO VARISCO, GIOVANNA MALETTA AND LUCILE ROBIN

The 2013 Arms Trade Treaty (ATT) is the first legally binding international agreement to establish standards for regulating the international trade in conventional arms and preventing transfers of illicit arms.[1] As of 31 December 2020, 110 states were party to the ATT and 31 had signed but not yet ratified it.[2] Five states—Afghanistan, China, Namibia, Niue, and Sao Tome and Principe— became new states parties in 2020, the same number as in 2019.[3]

The outbreak of the Covid-19 pandemic in 2020 severely impacted the ATT process and ATT-related meetings. The Working Group on Effective Treaty Implementation (WGETI), the Working Group on Transparency and Reporting (WGTR) and the Working Group on Treaty Universalization (WGTU) held only one set of preparatory sessions and meetings this year, in early February. The second set, originally scheduled for April, was cancelled.[4] The Sixth Conference of States Parties (CSP6) to the ATT was held on 17–21 August 2020 under the presidency of Ambassador Federico Villegas of Argentina, and was conducted through written procedure with no in-person meeting.[5] Virtual side events and webinars were also held during the same week. The priority theme for CSP6 was 'transparency and exchange of information: its role in the prevention of diversion'. In all, 102 states and 37 regional and international organizations, non-governmental organizations (NGOs), research institutes, industry associations and national implementing agencies participated in the work of CSP6.[6]

---

[1] For a summary and other details of the Arms Trade Treaty see annex A, section I, in this volume. The 2001 UN Firearms Protocol is also legally binding but only covers controls on the trade in firearms. UN General Assembly Resolution 55/255, Protocol against the Illicit Manufacturing of and Trafficking in Firearms, their Parts and Components and Ammunition, supplementing the UN Convention against Transnational Organized Crime (UN Firearms Protocol), adopted 31 May 2001, entered into force 3 July 2005.

[2] Arms Trade Treaty, 'Treaty status', [n.d.].

[3] Arms Trade Treaty (note 2). Namibia ratified the ATT in Apr. 2020; Afghanistan, China and Sao Tome and Principe in July 2020; and Niue in Aug. 2020. See United Nations, UN Treaty Collection, Status of Treaties, ch. XXVI Disarmament: 8. Arms Trade Treaty.

[4] Arms Trade Treaty, President of the Sixth Conference of States Parties (CSP6), 'Announcement: Cancellation of the working group meetings and 2nd CSP6 informal preparatory meeting: 14–17 April 2020', 18 Mar. 2020. Consultations on the draft documentation arising from the various working groups and to be considered during the second informal preparatory meeting were held during the intersessional period, with stakeholders providing written comments and suggestions on the documentation to the various authors through email exchange. See Arms Trade Treaty, CSP6, Final Report, ATT/CSP6/2020/SEC/635/Conf.FinRep.Rev1, 21 Aug. 2020.

[5] Official CSP6 documents can be found at the Arms Trade Treaty website under 'CSP6 conference documents'. See also Arms Trade Treaty, CSP6 President-designate, 'Announcement on the format of the Sixth Conference of States Parties', 18 July 2020.

[6] CSP6 was attended by 89 states parties of the then 106 states parties and 12 of the then 31 signatories. In addition, China, which by then had acceded to the ATT, also participated in the work of the conference. See Arms Trade Treaty, ATT/CSP6/2020/SEC/635/Conf.FinRep.Rev1 (note 4), paras 11–16.

Under the written procedure for CSP6, stakeholders participated through written interventions and states parties took decisions via the silence procedure, which meant that agreement on draft decisions could be reached only on the basis of consensus.[7] Thus, any state party that broke the silence by requesting an amendment or raising an objection on a decision had de facto power of veto on that decision, as no mechanism for amending a decision was in place. Some NGOs criticized the procedure for the way that it limited participation, open debate and discussion among ATT stakeholders.[8]

The ATT Secretariat circulated 17 draft decisions to be considered for adoption via silence procedure, with a deadline of 17 August 2020, initially only to states parties. Following a series of objections, the decisions were then shared publicly on the ATT Secretariat website. CSP6 adopted 11 of these, including the reappointment of the current head of the ATT Secretariat, Dumisani Dladla, for a second term starting on 1 December 2020.[9] The draft decisions that were not approved will be taken forward during the next ATT cycle.[10] Three such decisions referred to the draft workplans for the sub-working groups of the WGETI (draft decisions 9–11) and one to welcome the CSP6 president's working paper (decision 17). France and the United Kingdom objected to the three WGETI decisions, arguing that the silence procedure should be used 'solely for the adoption of decisions on matters of procedure'.[11] The two other rejected draft decisions referred to issues related to the implementation of states parties' financial obligations (decision 15) and their ability to benefit from the ATT sponsorship programme and the assistance provided by the Voluntary Trust Fund (VTF) (decision 16).[12]

This section summarizes key ATT-related developments and debates during 2020. It first focuses on issues related to transparency and reporting, notably a decline in public reporting and the establishment of the Diversion Information Exchange Forum (DIEF). It then looks at the status of treaty

[7] Arms Trade Treaty, CSP6, Final Report (note 4), para. 5; and Arms Trade Treaty, First Conference of States Parties (CSP1), 'Rules of Procedure', ATT/CSP1/CONF/1, 25 Aug. 2015, Rule 41(3).

[8] Pytlak, A., 'Transparency (still) matters', *ATT Monitor*, vol. 13, no. 3 (14 Aug. 2020); and Pytlak, A., 'One more time for the people in the back—transparency (still) matters!', *ATT Monitor*, vol. 13, no. 4 (27 Aug. 2020).

[9] Arms Trade Treaty, CSP6 President, 'Outcome of CSP6 decision-making process via silence procedure', 19 Aug. 2020; and Arms Trade Treaty, CSP6, Final Report (note 4), Decision 8.

[10] Arms Trade Treaty, CSP6, Final Report (note 4), para. 5; and Arms Trade Treaty, CSP6 President, 'Outcome of CSP6 decision-making process via silence procedure' (note 9), para. 8.

[11] France, Email to the ATT Secretariat, 17 Aug. 2020, and United Kingdom, Email to the ATT Secretariat, 17 Aug. 2020 (see item 6 under 'Objections to CSP6 draft decisions not adopted via silence procedure').

[12] Arms Trade Treaty, CSP6 President-designate, 'Decision 15: Management Committee proposal on the draft elements for a Secretariat's procedure regarding Rule 8(1)D', ATT/CSP6.MC/2020/MC/631/Decision.FinArr8(1)d, 29 July 2020; Arms Trade Treaty, Management Committee, 'Draft elements for a Secretariat's procedure regarding Rule 8(1)d (reference paper)', ATT/CSP6.MC/2020/MC/609/Conf.PropFinArr8(1)d, 17 July 2020; and Arms Trade Treaty, CSP6 President-designate, 'Decision 16: Application of Rule 8(1)d on the ATT Sponsorship Programme and Voluntary Trust Fund', ATT/CSP6.MC/2020/MC/632/Decision.ImpFR8(1)d, 29 July 2020.

universalization and the provision of international assistance. Finally, it analyses issues related to the financial health and functioning of the treaty and concludes with discussion of the prospects for the Seventh Conference of States Parties (CSP7).

Transparency and reporting

A decline in public reporting

States parties to the ATT have two reporting obligations: (*a*) within one year after entry into force at national level, to provide an initial report to the Secretariat of 'measures undertaken in order to implement' the treaty and report 'on any new measures undertaken in order to implement' the treaty;[13] and (*b*) to submit an annual report to the Secretariat on 'authorized or actual exports and imports of conventional arms'.[14]

CSP6 endorsed the mandate for the WGTR for CSP7 to continue work on amending the initial and annual reporting templates.[15] The WGTR also discussed the disaggregation of data in annual reports and the possibility of making 'the information in annual reports available in a searchable database that allows for queries and extracting data'.[16]

Two main trends characterized initial and annual reporting in 2020. The first was a decline in the level of reporting. As of 15 December 2020, 26 out of 105 (25 per cent) states parties that were due to submit an initial report had failed to do so.[17] In addition, the downward trend in annual reporting continued in 2020, with only 56 out of 97 (57 per cent) states fulfilling their annual reporting obligations, the lowest compliance rate of any year so far.[18] This means that, while the number of states parties has increased, there was a proportionate and absolute fall in the number of submitted annual reports on arms transfers (figure 14.1). Among the many possible reasons, challenges and delays due to the global Covid-19 pandemic—such as 'remote work, an inability to access information and data, and competing priorities amidst a health crisis'—might also have contributed to the particularly low levels of reporting in 2020.[19] Reporting practices in the coming years will indicate

---

[13] Arms Trade Treaty (note 1), Article 13(1).

[14] Arms Trade Treaty (note 1), Article 13(3).

[15] Arms Trade Treaty, CSP6, Final Report (note 4), para. 39.

[16] Arms Trade Treaty, CSP6, ATT Working Group on Transparency and Reporting (WGTR), Co-Chairs' draft report to the CSP6, ATT/CSP6.WGTR/2020/CHAIR/607/Conf.Rep, 17 July 2020, p. 6.

[17] ATT Secretariat, 'Initial reports', updated 15 Dec. 2020.

[18] ATT Secretariat, 'Annual reports', updated 16 Dec. 2020. Maldives submitted a report despite not being required to do so. See also Arms Trade Treaty Baseline Assessment Project (ATT-BAP), 'Reporting during a pandemic: Reflections on the Arms Trade Treaty 2019 Annual Reports', Oct. 2020; Maletta, G. and Bromley, M., 'The Arms Trade Treaty', *SIPRI Yearbook 2020*, p. 529; and Bromley, M. and Alvarado, J., *Reporting on Conventional Arms Transfers and Transfer Controls: Improving Coordination and Increasing Engagement* (SIPRI: Stockholm, Aug. 2020).

[19] ATT-BAP (note 18), p. 4.

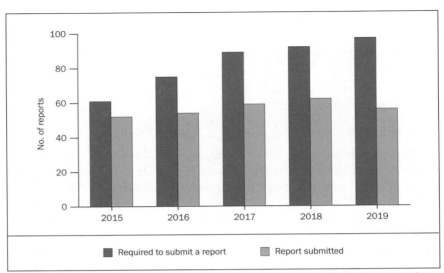

Figure 14.1. Number of Arms Trade Treaty states parties submitting annual reports, 2015–19

Source: Arms Trade Treaty Secretariat, 'Annual reports', as of 31 Dec. 2020.

whether low levels of reporting is a continuing trend or the fall was primarily due to exceptional circumstances in 2020.

A second trend is a decline in public reporting, with a marked increase in reports that are not made public but are only available for states parties and posted on the restricted area of the ATT website. Cameroon, Chile, Kazakhstan and Palestine submitted non-public initial reports in 2020, adding to the 12 non-public initial reports submitted in previous years.[20] In addition, 11 states parties (Albania, Cyprus, Georgia, Greece, Kazakhstan, Lithuania, Maldives, Malta, Mauritius, Palestine and Senegal) submitted a non-public annual report for 2019, and the proportion of non-public reports increased from 2 per cent for 2015 to 21 per cent for 2019.[21] Moreover, 13 states parties indicated in their public annual report that they withheld some commercially sensitive or national security-related information in their annual reports, in accordance with Article 13(3) of the treaty.[22] Although making reports public is not a treaty obligation, this growing tendency goes against one of the treaty's main purposes of promoting transparency in the international arms trade.[23]

[20] These initial reports were due for submission in 2019. ATT Secretariat (note 17).

[21] ATT Secretariat (note 18); ATT-BAP (note 18), p. 9; and ATT Monitor, *ATT Monitor Report 2020* (Control Arms Secretariat: New York, 19 Aug. 2020), p. 39. One state submitted a non-public report even though it did not have to submit an annual report this year.

[22] ATT-BAP (note 18), p. 11; and ATT Secretariat (note 18).

[23] Arms Trade Treaty (note 1), Article 1. See also Arms Trade Treaty, CSP6, ATT WGTR, Co-Chairs' draft report to CSP6 (note 16), p. 5.

A new Diversion Information Exchange Forum

CSP6 adopted decision 13, which establishes the DIEF, a 'sui generis body for informal voluntary exchanges between States Parties and signatory States concerning concrete cases of suspected or detected diversion and for sharing concrete, operational diversion-related information', as a mechanism to facilitate the implementation of articles 11 (diversion) and 15 (international cooperation) of the treaty.[24] Some states have shared this kind of information in similar mechanisms in the contexts of the European Union (EU) and Wassenaar Arrangement on Export Controls for Conventional Arms and Dual-use Goods and Technologies, for many years. The ATT, however, has a broader membership, and the establishment of the DIEF within the ATT will enable a higher number of states, including exporters and importers, to discuss and share information on this issue. The establishment of the DIEF ties in with the theme of CSP6. It is the result of work conducted within the framework of the WGTR and of the attempts made in past CSPs to share information on diversion cases among states parties.[25]

That states parties adopted decision 13 on establishing the DIEF—and decision 12 on the WGTR mandate—stands in contrast to their rejection of other decisions, such as the ones on the adoption of the WGETI sub-working group workplans. Civil society organizations criticized both the procedure and the substance of decision 13, which they argued 'undermines the ATT's purpose of transparency and its historic inclusion of civil society'.[26] In particular, there were questions on the functioning of the DIEF, as participation (including access to draft organizational documents and the terms of reference so far) is limited exclusively to ATT states parties and signatories. Likewise, there were requests for clarification on the process through which states could request non-state experts to participate in the forum and on how this process might challenge the independence of such experts.[27] The DIEF will hold its first formal meeting in 2021 and states parties will review its 'usefulness' at the Eighth Conference of States Parties (CSP8).[28]

---

[24] Arms Trade Treaty, CSP6, WGTR, Co-Chairs' draft report to CSP6 (note 16), p. 7.

[25] Maletta and Bromley (note 18), p. 528.

[26] Control Arms, Statement on draft decision 13, 13 Aug. 2020, p. 1. See also Pytlak, A., 'One more time for the people in the back—transparency (still) matters!' (note 8); and Saferworld, Statement on draft decision 13, Aug. 2020.

[27] Control Arms (note 26), p. 2; Pytlak, A., 'One more time for the people in the back—transparency (still) matters!' (note 8); and Austria, Statement, 17–21 Aug. 2020, p. 2.

[28] Arms Trade Treaty, CSP6 President, 'Decision 13: Establishment of the Diversion Information Exchange Forum', ATT/CSP6.DIEF/2020/CHAIR/629/Decision.DIEFToRs, 29 July 2020, p. 1.

Table 14.1. Arms Trade Treaty numbers of ratifications, accessions and signatories, by region

Region	States	States parties	Signatories	Non-signatories
Africa	53	28	12	13
Americas	35	27	3[a]	5
Asia	29	6	6	17
Europe	48[b]	41	2	5[b]
Middle East	16[c]	2[c]	4	10
Oceania	16[d]	6[e]	3	7[f]
Total	197	110	30	57

Note: The treaty was open for signature until it entered into force in Dec. 2014. Existing signatories may accept, approve or ratify the treaty in order to become a state party. A non-signatory state must now directly accede to the treaty in order to become a state party.

[a] This figure includes the United States. On 18 July 2019, the USA announced its intention not to become a state party to the treaty.
[b] This figure includes the Holy See.
[c] This figure includes Palestine.
[d] This figure includes Niue and the Cook Islands.
[e] This figure includes Niue.
[f] This figure includes the Cook Islands.

Source: United Nations, Treaty Collection, 'Status of treaties—Chapter XXVI: Disarmament, 8. Arms Trade Treaty', endnote 3.

Treaty universalization and international assistance

Treaty universalization

Achieving universalization remains one of the key objectives of the ATT and, as of 31 December 2020, the treaty had 110 states parties.[29] The ATT Secretariat's latest analysis of the trends and pace of ATT universalization confirmed that ATT membership continues to be geographically uneven, with particularly low participation in Asia (table 14.1).[30] For instance, more than half of the states in the Asian region have not yet joined the ATT.[31] In this regard, China's accession to the ATT in 2020 is widely considered as a positive development, and one that could increase interest in the treaty among China's neighbours and other partners in the Global South.[32] In the run-up to and during CSP6, the WGTU continued to discuss ways to promote the universalization of the treaty, and some of these efforts targeted the Asian region specifically. These included South Korea's contribution to support the translation of the 'ATT Universalization Toolkit' and the

---

[29] Arms Trade Treaty, ATT Working Group on Treaty Universalization (WGTU), Co-chairs' draft report to CSP6, ATT/CSP6.WGTU/2020/CHAIR/608/Conf.Rep, 17 July 2020, p. 2.

[30] 'Asia', as defined by the ATT's regional coverage, encompasses 48 states and includes countries (other than Egypt) that SIPRI categorizes as part of the Middle East. For the ATT's regional coverage see Arms Trade Treaty, 'Treaty status'; for SIPRI's geographical regions see p. xxiii, in this volume.

[31] Arms Trade Treaty, ATT/CSP6.WGTU/2020/CHAIR/608/Conf.Rep (note 29), annex A.

[32] Saferworld, 'China's accession to the ATT: Opportunities and challenges', News & Events, 15 July 2020; and Maletta and Bromley (note 18).

'Welcome Pack for New States Parties to the ATT'. Both documents are now available in 10 different Asian languages.[33] Furthermore, the WGTU implemented outreach activities at United Nations or regional meetings, until the escalation of the Covid-19 pandemic made this impossible.[34] The CSP6 president also contributed to universalization outreach efforts by launching a media campaign to raise awareness around the ATT, including an 'ATT outreach video'.[35] The WGTU continued to discuss universalization of the treaty in connection with the ATT VTF, reiterating its importance in promoting ATT participation.[36]

At the end of 2020, the future position of the United States vis-à-vis participation in the ATT remained unclear. In 2019 the USA under President Donald J. Trump announced that it did 'not intend to become a party to the treaty'.[37] However, the new US administration under President Joe Biden may decide not only to reverse this decision but to also push for the ratification of the treaty (although this would require a two-thirds majority in the US Senate).[38]

International assistance

The ATT Secretariat reported to CSP6 on the activities implemented by the VTF over the last year.[39] The latest report confirmed that the VTF continues to have a good financial basis on which to carry out its work. Since its establishment in 2016, the VTF has received over $8.5 million in voluntary contributions from 28 states. These contributions have since then supported, or are still supporting, the implementation of 43 projects aimed at helping states (and mostly African states) to strengthen or build capacity to implement their ATT obligations.[40] As in the case of many other ATT-related activities—and other relevant assistance programmes such as the EU Partner-to-Partner (P2P) ATT Outreach Programme—the outbreak of the Covid-19 pandemic affected the implementation of previously approved VTF

---

[33] Arms Trade Treaty, ATT/CSP6.WGTU/2020/CHAIR/608/Conf.Rep (note 29), para. 8(e). The documents are available at Arms Trade Treaty, 'Tools and guidelines', [n.d.].

[34] Arms Trade Treaty, ATT/CSP6.WGTU/2020/CHAIR/608/Conf.Rep (note 29), pp. 2–3.

[35] Arms Trade Treaty, ATT/CSP6.WGTU/2020/CHAIR/608/Conf.Rep (note 29), para. 8(b); and ATT Secretariat, 'Arms Trade Treaty (ATT): A short video introduction', YouTube, 30 Mar. 2020.

[36] Arms Trade Treaty, ATT/CSP6.WGTU/2020/CHAIR/608/Conf.Rep (note 29), para. 9.

[37] United Nations, UN Treaty Collection (note 3), endnote 3; and Maletta and Bromley (note 18), pp. 523–24.

[38] Democratic National Committee, '2020 Democratic Party Platform', 18 Aug. 2020.

[39] ATT Secretariat, 'Report on the work of the ATT Voluntary Trust Fund (VTF) for the period August 2019 to August 2020' (VTF Report), ATT/VTF/2020/CHAIR/614/Conf.Rep, 17 July 2020.

[40] For a complete list of projects and beneficiaries see ATT Secretariat, ATT/VTF/2020/CHAIR/614/Conf.Rep (note 39), annexes B, D and F.

projects.[41] Specifically, the implementation of projects approved for the 2019 VTF cycle that did not manage to complete their activities was suspended or delayed. However, beneficiaries received an extension to complete related activities by October 2021 at the latest.[42]

In 2020, the Covid-19 pandemic affected not only the implementation of the assistance projects supported by the VTF, but also the work of the VTF itself. For example, the VTF had to postpone the plan to test the 'Guidance for VTF Project Evaluation', approved at the Fifth Conference of States Parties (CSP5) on projects completed in 2019, and reduce the number of planned outreach visits.[43] However, the VTF was still able to implement a few activities aimed at improving its effectiveness and helping states to submit quality applications, such as uploading a 'model' grant application form to the VTF web page.[44]

Other issues related to the functioning of the treaty

The core functions of the Secretariat, as well as the costs of the CSPs and subsidiary bodies, are all supported through the financial contributions that all ATT states parties and signatories, as well as states attending the CSPs as observers, are obliged to provide.[45]

However, the fact that a significant number of states are failing to pay their assessed contributions has raised concerns about the financial health of the ATT and, consequently, the likely impact on its processes and key activities.[46] As of 15 December 2020, 58 out of the 150 states that have been obliged to make contributions since 2015 were behind with their payments, creating an accumulated deficit of $424 405.19.[47] To address the issue of financial liquidity, CSP5 mandated the ATT Management Committee to prepare guidelines on the implementation of Financial Rule 8.1(d), which would entail suspending the voting rights and other prerogatives within CSP bodies for states that have not paid their financial contributions for two or more years.[48]

Since then, the Management Committee has drafted a possible procedure for allowing states in arrears to 'discharge' their financial obligations through

---

[41] E.g. in the case of the EU P2P ATT Outreach Programme, many activities were postponed or moved online in the second half of 2020. See Charatsis, C. et al., *EU P2P Newsletter*, no. N.10 (Oct. 2019–Apr. 2020), pp. 2–3. See also the EU P2P ATT Outreach Programme virtual seminars on the YouTube channel of Expertise France.

[42] ATT Secretariat, ATT/VTF/2020/CHAIR/614/Conf.Rep (note 39), pp. 3–4.

[43] ATT Secretariat, ATT/VTF/2020/CHAIR/614/Conf.Rep (note 39), pp. 4–5.

[44] ATT Secretariat, 'Voluntary Trust Fund (VTF)', [n.d.].

[45] Arms Trade Treaty, CSP1, Financial Rules for the Conferences of States Parties and the Secretariat, ATT/CSP1/CONF/2, 25 Aug. 2015, Rule 6.

[46] Maletta and Bromley (note 18); Bromley, M., Brockmann, K. and Maletta, G., 'The Arms Trade Treaty', *SIPRI Yearbook 2019*, 503–10; and Bromley, M. and Brockmann, K., 'The Arms Trade Treaty', *SIPRI Yearbook 2018*, 405–12.

[47] ATT Secretariat, 'Status of contributions to ATT budgets', 15 Dec. 2020.

[48] Arms Trade Treaty, ATT/CSP1/CONF/2 (note 45).

a multi-year payment plan.[49] However, this proposal (part of decision 15) was rejected as several states parties raised objections, arguing that more time for reflection was needed.[50] Notably, states parties also rejected the adoption of decision 16, which stated that states parties should have not been prejudiced by Financial Rule 8.1(d) in applying for support from the VTF or the Sponsorship Programme.[51] In this case, objecting states' arguments included that decisions on the VTF and the Sponsorship Programme are beyond the scope of Financial Rule 8.1(d). These matters have been deferred to CSP7.[52]

Conclusions and prospects for CSP7

The impact of the Covid-19 pandemic on regular ATT processes in 2020 was severe, reducing the effectiveness of the ATT decision-making processes and the provision of international assistance; limiting opportunities to promote the universalization of the treaty; and limiting civil society participation in ATT-related processes, which negatively affected transparency and the possibility of open debate.

At CSP6, Ambassador Lansana Gberie from Sierra Leone was elected as president of CSP7. He has announced that the focus of his presidency will be on strengthening efforts to eradicate the illicit trade in small arms and light weapons and ensuring efficient stockpile management.[53] The new president will face several tasks, alongside practical challenges related to the ongoing Covid-19 pandemic in 2021. First, the new ATT cycle will need to take forward the draft decisions that were not adopted during CSP6.[54] The non-adoption of decisions 9, 10 and 11 implies that the WGETI sub-working groups do not yet have agreed multi-year workplans Second, developments in 2021 might clarify whether the downward trend in reporting on arms transfers and arms transfer controls and on the ATT will continue, and whether and how the implementation of the DIEF might impact on transparency.[55] Third, the financial situation of the ATT will remain an issue of concern with many states still failing to comply with their financial obligations.

---

[49] Arms Trade Treaty, Management Committee (note 12).

[50] The decision was opposed by Canada, France, Netherlands and the UK in a joint response and separately by Guatemala. See Arms Trade Treaty, 'CSP6 Decisions'; and Arms Trade Treaty, CSP6 President-designate, 'Decision 15: Management Committee Proposal' (note 12).

[51] The decision was opposed by Canada, France, Netherlands and the UK in a joint response and by Costa Rica and Panama in separate responses. See Arms Trade Treaty, 'CSP6 Decisions' (note 50); and Arms Trade Treaty, CSP6 President-designate, 'Decision 16: Application of Rule 8(1)d' (note 12).

[52] Arms Trade Treaty, CSP6, Final Report (note 4), para. 42.

[53] This is in accordance with decisions 3, 6 and 7. Arms Trade Treaty, CSP6, Final Report (note 4), paras 34 and 37. See also Arms Trade Treaty, 'President', [n.d.].

[54] Arms Trade Treaty, CSP6, Final Report (note 4), para. 42.

[55] Bromley and Alvarado (note 18); and Isbister, R., 'Running on the spot: The Sixth Conference of States Parties to the Arms Trade Treaty', Saferworld Blog, 28 Aug. 2020.

II. Multilateral arms embargoes

PIETER D. WEZEMAN

The United Nations Security Council uses its powers under Chapter VII of the UN Charter to impose arms embargoes—that is, restrictions on transfers of arms and related services and, in certain cases, dual-use items—that are binding for all UN member states and which form part of what the UN generally refers to as 'sanctions measures'.[1] During 2020, 13 UN arms embargoes were in force (table 14.2). The European Union (EU) also imposes arms embargoes under its Common Foreign and Security Policy (CFSP) that are binding for EU member states and which form part of what the EU generally refers to as 'restrictive measures'.[2] During 2020, 21 EU arms embargoes were in force. Of these EU embargoes, 10 matched the coverage of a UN arms embargo; 3 (Iran, South Sudan and Sudan) were broader in duration, geographical scope or the types of arms covered; while 8 had no UN counterpart. The Arab League had one arms embargo in place (on Syria) that also had no UN counterpart. In addition, one voluntary multilateral embargo imposed by the Conference on Security and Co-operation in Europe (CSCE, now renamed the Organization for Security and Co-operation in Europe, OSCE) was in force for arms deliveries to forces engaged in combat in the Nagorno-Karabakh area.[3] No new multilateral arms embargo was imposed in 2020.[4] However, most elements of the UN arms embargo on Iran expired. The European Council discussed a possible EU arms embargo on Turkey but did not impose one.

Multilateral arms embargoes varied in coverage (table 14.2). Most covered arms, military materiel and related services. However, the UN and EU arms embargoes on the Democratic People's Republic of Korea (DPRK, North Korea), Iran and Somalia, and the EU arms embargo on Russia, also covered certain exports or imports of dual-use items that can be used both for civilian purposes and to produce, maintain or operate conventional, biological,

---

[1] United Nations, Security Council, 'Sanctions', [n.d.].

[2] These form part of what the EU generally refers to as 'restrictive measures'. European Council, 'Sanctions: How and when the EU adopts restrictive measures', [n.d.].

[3] Conference on Security and Co-operation in Europe, Committee of Senior Officials, Statement, annex 1 to Journal no. 2 of the 7th Meeting of the Committee, Prague, 27–28 Feb. 1992.

[4] The most recent new multilateral arms embargo was that imposed in 2018 by the UN on South Sudan.

chemical or nuclear weapons.[5] Certain EU arms embargoes also covered equipment that might be used for internal repression or certain types of communication surveillance equipment. Multilateral arms embargoes also varied in the types of restrictions imposed and recipients targeted. Some placed a ban on all transfers to the state in question, while others banned transfers to a non-state actor or group of non-state actors. Certain UN arms embargoes were 'partial', in that they allowed transfers to the state in question provided the supplier or recipient state had received permission from, or notified, the relevant UN sanctions committee or the UN Security Council.

During 2020 the various UN investigations on the implementation of UN arms embargoes highlighted issues of varying scope and significance. Unlike the UN, the EU, the Arab League and the OSCE do not have systematic mechanisms in place for monitoring compliance with their arms embargoes.

This section reviews significant developments and implementation challenges in UN, EU and OSCE arms embargoes in 2020. In particular, the section highlights cases where new embargoes or amendments to embargoes were implemented, debated or demanded, and gives examples of actual or alleged violations.

United Nations arms embargoes: Developments and contraventions

During 2020 the UN introduced no new arms embargoes. The UN embargo on the supply of major arms to Iran and exports of any arms by Iran expired, leaving in place only restrictions on exports and imports of certain dual-use items related to nuclear weapons delivery systems and used in the nuclear fuel cycle. No further significant amendments to existing embargoes were made.

This subsection discusses the significant differences among members of the UN Security Council about the arms embargoes on Iran and South Sudan. It also provides a concise overview of the most notable violations of UN arms embargoes in 2020, especially the large-scale violations of the arms embargo on Libya, primarily based on reports by UN panels and groups of experts that monitor UN arms embargoes.

---

[5] The UN and EU embargoes on Iran and North Korea apply to dual-use items on the control lists of the Nuclear Suppliers Group (NSG) and the Missile Technology Control Regime (MTCR). The UN and EU embargoes on Somalia apply to certain dual-use items on the control lists of the Wassenaar Arrangement that can be used to produce, maintain and operate improvised explosive devices. The EU embargo on Russia applies to transfers to military end-users of all items on the EU's dual-use list. For details of the NSG, MTCR and the Wassenaar Arrangement see annex B, section III, in this volume.

Table 14.2. Multilateral arms embargoes in force during 2020

Target (entities or territory covered)[a]	Date embargo first imposed (duration type)	Materiel covered[a]	Key developments, 2020
United Nations arms embargoes			
Afghanistan (Taliban: NGF)	16 Jan. 2002 (OE)	Arms and related materiel and services	
Central African Republic (government: PT; NGF)	5 Dec. 2013 (TL)	Arms and military materiel (small arms exempted for government)	Extended until 31 July 2021
Democratic Republic of the Congo (government: PT; NGF)	28 July 2003 (TL)	Arms and military materiel	Extended until 1 July 2021
Iran (whole country: PT)	23 Dec. 2006 (TL)	Major arms, with some exceptions; Items related to nuclear weapon delivery systems; Items used in the nuclear fuel cycle	Embargo on exports of major arms to Iran and export of any arms by Iran expired on 18 Oct. 2020
Iraq (NGF)	6 Aug. 1990 (OE)	Arms and military materiel	
ISIL (Da'esh), al-Qaeda and associated individuals and entities (NGF)	16 Jan. 2002 (OE)	Arms and military materiel	
Korea, North (whole country)	15 July 2006 (OE)	Arms and military materiel; Items relevant to nuclear, ballistic missiles and other weapons of mass destruction related programmes	
Lebanon (NGF)	11 Aug. 2006 (OE)	Arms and military materiel	
Libya (government: PT; NGF)	26 Feb. 2011 (OE)	Arms and military materiel	
Somalia (government: PT; NGF)	23 Jan. 1992 (TL)	Arms and military materiel; Components for improvised explosive devices	Extended until 15 Nov. 2021
South Sudan (whole country)	13 July 2018 (TL)	Arms and military materiel	Extended until 31 May 2021
Sudan (Darfur: PT)	30 July 2004 (OE)	Arms and military materiel	
Yemen (NGF)	14 Apr. 2015 (OE)	Arms and military materiel	
European Union arms embargoes without UN counterpart or with broader scope than UN embargoes on the same target			
Belarus (whole country)	20 June 2011 (OE)	Arms and military materiel	Extended until 28 Feb. 2021
China[b] (whole country)	27 June 1989 (OE)	Arms	
Egypt[b] (whole country)	21 Aug. 2013 (OE)	Equipment which might be used for internal repression	

Target (entities or territory covered)[a]	Date embargo first imposed (duration type)	Materiel covered[a]	Key developments, 2020
Iran (whole country)	27 Feb. 2007 (TL)	Equipment which might be used for internal repression; Communication surveillance equipment	Extended until 13 April 2021
Myanmar (whole country)	29 July 1991 (TL)	Arms and military materiel; Communication surveillance equipment	Extended until 30 April 2021
Russia (whole country)	31 July 2014 (TL)	Arms and military materiel; Dual-use materiel for military use or military end-user	Extended until 31 Jan. 2021
South Sudan (whole country)	18 July 2011 (OE)	Arms and military materiel	
Sudan (whole country)	15 Mar. 1994 (OE)	Arms and military materiel	
Syria (whole country)	9 May 2011 (OE)	Equipment which might be used for internal repression; Communication surveillance equipment	
Venezuela (whole country)	13 Nov. 2017 (OE)	Arms and equipment which might be used for internal repression; Communication surveillance equipment	Extended until 14 Nov. 2021
Zimbabwe (whole country)	18 Feb. 2002 (OE)	Arms and military materiel	Extended until 20 Feb. 2021

League of Arab States arms embargoes

Syria (whole country)	3 Dec. 2011 (OE)	Arms	

ISIL = Islamic State in Iraq and the Levant; NGF = non-governmental forces; OE = open-ended; PT = partial, i.e. embargo allows transfers to the state in question provided the supplier or recipient state has received permission from, or notified, the relevant United Nations sanctions committee or the UN Security Council; TL = time-limited.

[a] The target, entities and territory, and materiel covered may have changed since the first imposition of the embargo. The target, entities and material stated in this table are as at the end of 2020.

[b] The EU embargoes on China and Egypt are political declarations whereas the other embargoes are legal acts imposed by EU Council decisions and EU Council Regulations.

Sources: UN Security Council, 'Sanctions', [n.d.]; and Council of the European Union, 'EU sanctions map', Updated 18 Feb. 2021. The SIPRI Arms Embargo Archive, <https://www.sipri.org/databases/embargoes>, provides a detailed overview of most multilateral arms embargoes that have been in force since 1950 along with the principle instruments establishing or amending the embargoes.

Disagreement in the UN Security Council about the arms embargo on Iran

Until 18 October 2020 UN sanctions on Iran prohibited transfers of most types of major arms to Iran and the transfer of all arms from Iran. An embargo on the transfer to and from Iran of items that could contribute to the development of nuclear weapon delivery systems, in particular missiles, unless these transfers have been approved in advance by the UN Security Council, remained in force throughout 2020 and is scheduled to expire on 18 October 2023. The UN sanctions also place the same approval requirements on transfers to Iran of items that could contribute to Iran's activities related to uranium enrichment, nuclear fuel reprocessing or heavy water (until 18 October 2025).[6]

The expiration of prohibitions on transfers of major arms to and all arms from Iran on 18 October 2020 had been agreed in the Joint Comprehensive Programme of Action (JCPOA) of 2015, on the condition that Iran would comply with the terms of the agreement.[7] In 2019, after the United States had left the agreement in 2018, Iran began to reduce its commitments under the agreement, which technically could have led to finding Iran in non-compliance with the JCPOA and reimposition of the pre-JCPOA UN sanctions, including a full arms embargo on Iran.[8] However, in 2020 all seven remaining JCPOA participants reconfirmed their determination to preserve the programme.[9]

Several countries heavily opposed ending the UN arms embargo on Iran. In 2020 Bahrain, Israel, Saudi Arabia, the United Arab Emirates (UAE) and Yemen sent formal letters to the UN Security Council before the embargo expired. The letters described Iran as a destabilizing actor in the Middle East; accused Iran of supplying arms to armed groups in the region, in violation of the embargo; and called instead for an extension of the embargo.[10]

The most persistent and far-reaching efforts to extend the embargo came from the USA. In early August 2020, the USA put a draft resolution before the UN Security Council proposing that the existing arms embargo would continue to apply indefinitely, until the UN Security Council decided otherwise. The resolution was only half a page long, without any specific reference to the JCPOA, and argued for maintaining the embargo as 'essential to the maintenance of international peace and security'.[11] The resolution

---

[6] This differs from other UN arms embargoes where responsibility for issuing such approvals devolves to the relevant UN sanctions committee.

[7] UN Security Council Resolution 2231, 20 July 2015, annex A.

[8] By 2020 the JCPOA parties were China, France, Germany, Iran, Russia, the UK and the EU.

[9] On implementation of the JCPOA see chapter 11, section II, in this volume.

[10] United Nations, Security Council, Tenth six-month report of the Facilitator on the implementation of Security Council Resolution 2231 (2015), S/2020/1244, 17 Dec. 2020, paras 13–14 and 17.

[11] United Nations, Security Council, Letter dated 15 Aug. 2020 from the President of the Security Council addressed to the Secretary-General and the Permanent Representatives of the members of the Security Council, S/2020/805, 17 Aug. 2020, p. 3.

was not adopted as only the Dominican Republic supported the USA, while China and Russia voted against it and 11 other UN Security Council members abstained.[12] France, Germany and the United Kingdom were among the abstentions but voiced concerns that allowing the arms embargo on Iran to expire would have 'major implications for regional security and stability', particularly in the light of Iran's violation of the embargo by supplying arms to state and non-state actors in Iraq, Lebanon, Syria and Yemen. However, their abstentions were rooted in the view that the continuation of the JCPOA should not be jeopardized by extending the arms embargo.[13]

This failed effort by the USA to extend the embargo was followed by another in late August. Claiming that it should still legally be considered a participant in the JCPOA, the USA notified the UN Security Council that it considered Iran in 'significant non-performance' of its JCPOA commitments.[14] The USA argued that this initiated a process of reimposition (the so-called snapback mechanism of the JCPOA) of pre-JCPOA UN sanctions, including a full and not time-limited arms embargo.[15] This effort did not succeed either, as all other original signatories of the JCPOA argued that because the USA had unilaterally withdrawn from the agreement in 2018, there was no legal basis for the US claim that it could still initiate the snapback mechanism.[16]

Regardless of the positions of the other UN Security Council members and the remaining JCPOA participants, the US administration declared on 18 October—the same day the UN arms embargo on Iran expired—that the USA considered virtually all pre-JCPOA UN sanctions on Iran to have returned on 19 September, as a result of its initiating the snapback mechanism a month earlier. The statement mentioned, in particular, the return of the original 2007 full UN arms embargo on Iran and underlined that the USA would use its 'domestic authorities' to sanction any individual or entity involved in supplying arms to Iran.[17]

The implementation of the UN arms embargo on Iran has had two contrasting sides. On the one hand, there have been no reports of major violations of the embargo on arms exports to Iran since it was imposed in 2010. On the other hand, there have been persistent allegations that Iran has exported arms in violation of the UN embargo on arms exports from

---

[12] United Nations, S/2020/805 (note 11), p. 1.

[13] United Nations, Security Council, Letter dated 15 Aug. 2020 from the President of the Security Council addressed to the Secretary-General and the Permanent Representatives of the members of the Security Council, S/2020/807, 17 Aug. 2020, pp. 23, 24 and 28.

[14] United Nations, Security Council, Letter dated 20 Aug. 2020 from the Permanent Representative of the United States of America to the United Nations addressed to the President of the Security Council, S/2020/815, 24 Aug. 2020.

[15] United Nations, S/2020/815 (note 14).

[16] United Nations, S/2020/1244 (note 10), paras 19–38.

[17] Pompeo, M. R., US Secretary of State, 'Status of UN arms embargo on Iran', Press statement, US Department of State, 18 Oct. 2020.

Iran, imposed in 2007. In addition, the UN secretary-general and the UN Security Council facilitator for the implementation of Resolution 2231 (2015) issued reports in 2020 that included allegations of Iranian exports of arms that took place before the elements of the UN embargo that prohibited such transfers expired in October 2020. The UN secretary-general's ninth report on the implementation of Resolution 2231 concluded that cruise missiles and unmanned aerial vehicles used in attacks on Saudi oil installations in 2019 were of Iranian origin.[18] However, it drew no conclusions about whether the missiles had been transferred from Iran to another user in violation of the arms embargo or if the missiles had been launched from Iran. The UN Secretariat also analysed two shipments of missiles, small arms and ammunition that had been seized in 2019 and 2020 by the USA on board ships in international waters near Yemen. The report observed that the weapons or their components had characteristics consistent with items produced in Iran and that some components of the weapons had been supplied by another state to Iran.[19] However, the UN Secretariat drew no final conclusions about the involvement of Iran in these shipments. During 2020, the UN Secretariat continued its investigations into possible linkages between Iran and missiles used by Houthi forces in Yemen but again did not reach any final conclusions.[20]

Disagreement in the UN Security Council about the arms embargo on South Sudan

The UN arms embargo on South Sudan prohibits transfers of arms and military materiel to government forces and armed groups in South Sudan. Certain exemptions can be made. Arms and related materiel, as well as technical training and assistance, that are provided solely in support of the implementation of the terms of the peace agreement in South Sudan are allowed if approved in advance by the UN sanctions committee for South Sudan. Under certain conditions foreign armed forces can bring weapons into South Sudan if the sanctions committee is notified in advance.

In May 2020 the embargo was extended for a year when 12 UN Security Council members voted in favour of maintaining an arms embargo against South Sudan in light of the ongoing violence and human rights violations in the country.[21] However, China, Russia and South Africa argued that the continuation of the arms embargo in combination with targeted sanctions on South Sudanese individuals did not take into account progress in the peace

---

[18] United Nations, Security Council, 'Implementation of Security Council Resolution 2231 (2015)', Ninth report of the Secretary-General, S/2020/531, 11 June 2020, paras 32–40.

[19] United Nations, S/2020/531 (note 18), paras 22–31.

[20] United Nations, S/2020/531 (note 18), para. 21.

[21] UN Security Council Resolution 2521, 29 May 2020. On the armed conflict and peace process in South Sudan see chapter 7, section IV, in this volume.

process in South Sudan.[22] These three states abstained on the resolution, as China and Russia had also done on the resolutions that established the arms embargo in 2018 and extended it in 2019. South Africa abstained on the same grounds and stressed that the African Union (AU) and the subregional body, the Intergovernmental Authority on Development, had come to the same conclusion. South Africa mentioned in particular the call from the AU's Peace and Security Council for the lifting of all punitive measures on South Sudan to facilitate the peace process and South Sudanese socio-economic recovery and development.[23]

During 2020 the UN panel of experts on South Sudan reported on two cases of arms embargo violations. It found that in 2019, the South Sudanese National Security Service had received three deliveries of weapons, mainly small arms, from Sudan.[24] It also argued that the presence of the Uganda People's Defence Force in South Sudan was a violation of the embargo as Uganda had not requested any exemptions from the sanctions committee.[25]

Large-scale violations of the United Nations arms embargo on Libya

The UN arms embargo on Libya bans arms transfers and technical assistance related to military activities to non-state armed groups but permits these to the internationally recognized Government of National Accord (GNA), provided that the transfers have been approved in advance by the UN sanctions committee for Libya. In 2020, open conflict continued between forces under the control of the GNA and the main non-state armed group in Libya, the Libyan National Army (LNA, also known as the Haftar Armed Forces).[26] Since the imposition of the embargo in 2011, the associated UN panel of experts has reported on multiple cases of alleged violations.[27] The latest public panel report, published in December 2019, concluded that the GNA and the LNA had 'routinely and sometimes blatantly' received weapons and other military support.[28] In January 2020, 12 countries met at the Berlin Conference on Libya and promised to fully respect and implement the legally

---

[22] United Nations, Security Council, Letter dated 29 May 2020 from the President of the Security Council addressed to the Secretary-General and the Permanent Representatives of the members of the Security Council, S/2020/469, 1 June 2020, pp. 23, 25 and 27.

[23] United Nations, S/2020/469 (note 22), p. 27.

[24] United Nations, Security Council, Final report of the panel of experts on South Sudan submitted pursuant to Resolution 2471 (2019), S/2020/342, 28 Apr. 2020, paras 38–40, 119–21.

[25] United Nations, Security Council, Interim report of the panel of experts on South Sudan submitted pursuant to Resolution 2521 (2020), S/2020/1141, 28 Apr. 2020, para. 83.

[26] On the armed conflict in Libya see chapter 6, section IV, in this volume.

[27] Bromley, M. and Wezeman, P. D., 'Multilateral embargoes on arms and dual-use items', *SIPRI Yearbook 2020*, pp. 539–40. See also equivalent chapters in the 2012–19 editions of the SIPRI Yearbook.

[28] United Nations, Security Council, Final report of the panel of experts on Libya established pursuant to Security Council Resolution 1973 (2011), S/2019/914, 9 Dec. 2019, p. 2.

binding UN arms embargo.[29] Among these 12 countries were Turkey and the UAE, which in 2019 had been assessed by the UN panel as the main arms suppliers to, respectively, the GNA and the LNA.[30]

The UN panel did not publish a report in 2020. However, the overall substance of the panel's findings was summed up by other UN sources. In May 2020, shortly after the Berlin Conference, the head of the UN Support Mission in Libya (UNSMIL) reported on a massive influx of weaponry, equipment and mercenaries to the two sides.[31] In December the head of UNSMIL stated that there were 20 000 'foreign forces and/or mercenaries' in Libya.[32] As mercenaries provide technical assistance related to military activities, their presence in Libya would be a violation of the UN embargo. In the second half of 2020 the chair of the Libya sanctions committee reported that blatant violations of the arms embargo had continued throughout the year.[33]

A combination of remarks by the same chair, reporting by the media on leaked interim reports by the panel, and information from other sources suggested that, during 2020 in particular, Russia, Turkey and the UAE (all three being participants in the Berlin Conference) were involved in embargo violations. The UN panel reportedly estimated that the Wagner Group, a Russian company, had deployed between 800 and 1200 mercenaries and military equipment in Libya as part of a contract with the LNA.[34] The panel reportedly also established that Russia had transferred combat aircraft and other military equipment into Libya.[35] The chair of the Libya sanctions committee confirmed the presence of Wagner Group in Libya.[36] The USA accused Russia of being directly responsible for the activities of the Wagner

[29] French Ministry for Europe and Foreign Affairs, 'The Berlin Conference on Libya: Conference conclusions (19 January 2020)', Libya news, 2020; and United Nations, Security Council, Letter dated 22 Jan. 2020 from the Permanent Representative of Germany to the United Nations addressed to the President of the Security Council, annex I to the letter dated 22 Jan. 2020 from the Permanent Representative of Germany to the United Nations addressed to the President of the Security Council, Berlin Conference on Libya, S/2020/63, 22 Jan. 2020, p. 4.

[30] United Nations, S/2019/914 (note 28), p. 2, paras 60–62.

[31] United Nations, '"Alarming" military build-up underway in Libya, as Covid-19 heightens insecurity', UN News, 19 May 2020.

[32] United Nations Support Mission in Libya (UNSMIL), 'Acting SRSG Stephanie Williams opening remarks during the third virtual meeting of the second round of the LPDF on 2 Dec. 2020', UNSMIL News, 2 Dec. 2020.

[33] Sautter, G., Statement during the UN Security Council VTC Meeting on Libya, 2 Sep. 2020; and Sautter, G., 'Statement as chair of the 1970 Libya sanctions committee in the Security Council VTC briefings by subsidiary organs', 16 Dec. 2020.

[34] Nichols, M., 'Up to 1,200 deployed in Libya by Russian military group: UN report', Reuters, 6 May 2020.

[35] Lederer, E. M., 'Experts: Libya rivals UAE, Russia, Turkey violate UN embargo', AP News, 9 Sep. 2020.

[36] Sautter, Statement, 16 Dec. 2020 (note 33).

Group in Libya and the related supply of arms.[37] However, Russia has denied any involvement in arms supplies to Libya.[38]

According to media reporting, the UN panel concluded in mid 2020 that, since Turkey's and the UAE's 'more direct engagement' in 2019 and January 2020, respectively, 'arms transfers to Libya by those two member states have been extensive, blatant and with complete disregard to the sanctions measures'.[39] The chair of the Libya sanctions committee also mentioned that both Turkey and the UAE had supplied arms to Libya.[40] The panel reportedly found the UAE to be in non-compliance of the arms embargo, because it had deployed military personnel and supplied weapons to the LNA.[41] According to the same media report, the panel concluded that Turkey had sent a variety of arms to Libya.[42] Finally, the leaked reports from the UN panel of experts on Libya purportedly mentioned the recruitment of fighters from Syria by Turkey in support of the GNA.[43]

Interim reports by the UN panel of experts on Libya have not previously been published. However, in September 2020 the German chair of the sanctions committee for Libya, at the request of several other delegations, put the publication of the 2020 interim report on the agenda of the UN Security Council, with the aim of creating 'much needed transparency' and 'naming and shaming' embargo violators. However, China and Russia blocked the report's publication.[44]

None of the allegations about embargo violations led to UN sanctions. However, the EU implemented some limited measures. In July 2020, France, Germany and Italy issued a joint statement in which they urged all foreign actors to fully respect the arms embargo, and indicated that they were ready to consider the possible use of EU sanctions if the breaches of the embargo continued.[45] By the end of 2020 the EU had imposed sanctions on three companies, based in Jordan, Kazakhstan and Turkey, that had been involved

---

[37] US Department of Defense (DOD), 'Russia, Wagner Group continue military involvement in Libya', 24 July 2020; and Lead Inspector General of the DOD, *East Africa Counterterrorism Operation: North and West Africa Counterterrorism Operation*, Report to the US Congress (DOD: Arlington, VA, 1 Apr.–30 June 2020), p. 5.

[38] 'Mike Pompeo's claims of Russian arms shipments to Libya fake, diplomat claims', TASS, 24 Dec. 2020.

[39] Lederer (note 35).

[40] Sautter, Statement, 16 Dec. 2020 (note 33).

[41] Lederer (note 35); and 'UAE delivered weapons to Libya's Haftar despite UN embargo', Middle East Eye, 30 Sep. 2019.

[42] Lederer (note 35).

[43] Security Council Report, 'Libya sanctions: Discussion under "any other business"', 24 Sep. 2020.

[44] Lederer, E. M., 'Russia, China block release of UN report criticizing Russia', AP News, 26 Sep. 2020; and Sautter G., Statement in the Security Council VTC meeting on Libya, 19 Nov. 2020.

[45] 'France, Germany, Italy threaten sanctions over arms for Libya', Reuters, 18 July 2020.

in transporting military material to Libya in 2020.[46] However, the EU did not publicly threaten or impose any sanctions on countries that had been accused of organizing these transports.

Developments in contraventions of other UN arms embargoes

Significant violations of UN arms embargoes in Yemen and Sudan also continued in 2020, whereas violations of the arms embargo on North Korea appeared to be in decline. The UN arms embargo on Yemen prohibits transfers to non-state actors in the country. However, continuous violations of the embargo have been reported since it was imposed in 2015. The UN panel of experts on Yemen concluded that by 2021 there was increasing evidence suggesting that particular individuals and entities within Iran had supplied significant volumes of weapons and components to the Houthi rebels.[47]

The UN panel on Sudan reported that in 2020 the Sudanese Government continued to transfer arms into the Darfur region in violation of the UN arms embargo, which requires such transfers to be approved in advance by the UN sanctions committee for Sudan.[48]

The UN arms embargo on North Korea prohibits transfers to and from North Korea of arms and items relevant to the development of nuclear weapons or ballistic missiles. In 2019, the UN panel on North Korea reported that violations of the embargo on military cooperation with North Korea, many of which had been reported in previous years, appeared to have been declining.[49] Though the panel did not make similar statements in 2020 it only reported in that year on two cases that occurred in previous years.[50] This lack of new cases suggests that the decline in violations had continued.

EU arms embargoes: Developments and implementation challenges

During 2020 the EU made no significant modifications to any existing EU arms embargoes and did not introduce any new embargoes. However, arms embargoes on Saudi Arabia and Turkey continued to be raised as possibilities.

---

[46] Council implementing Regulation (EU) 2020/1309 of 21 Sep. 2020 implementing Article 21(2) of Regulation (EU) 2016/44 concerning restrictive measures in view of the situation in Libya, *Official Journal of the European Union*, L305, 21 Sep. 2020, pp. 3–4.

[47] United Nations, Security Council, Final report of the panel of experts on Yemen, S/2021/79, 25 Jan. 2021, p. 2. On the armed conflict in Yemen see chapter 6, section V, in this volume.

[48] United Nations, Security Council, Final report of the panel of experts on the Sudan, S/2021/40, 13 Jan. 2021, Summary, p. 3. On the armed conflict in Sudan see chapter 7, section IV, in this volume.

[49] United Nations, Security Council, Report of the panel of experts established pursuant to Resolution 1874 (2009), S/2019/691, 30 Aug. 2019, para. 32.

[50] United Nations, Security Council, Report of the panel of experts established pursuant to Resolution 1874 (2009), S/2020/840, 28 Aug. 2020, paras 74–77 and 79; and United Nations, Security Council, Report of the panel of experts established pursuant to Resolution 1874 (2009), S/2020/151, 2 Mar. 2020.

Saudi Arabia

Both within and among EU member states and in the European Parliament there have been continuous discussions since 2015 about the imposition of restrictions on arms supplies to Saudi Arabia in response to concerns about Saudi military operations in Yemen. In February 2016, October 2017 and October 2018 the European Parliament adopted resolutions calling for an EU arms embargo on Saudi Arabia.[51] The European Parliament reiterated this call in a resolution adopted in September 2020.[52]

Turkey

In 2020, for the second time in two years, the possibility of imposing an arms embargo on Turkey was discussed in the EU. The Council of the EU discussed a possible arms embargo on Turkey in 2019 in response to a large Turkish military operation in northern Syria against the armed Kurdish People's Protection Units (YPG).[53] In 2020 Turkish surveying for hydrocarbon deposits in the Eastern Mediterranean, including in Cyprus's Exclusive Economic Zone, led to major tensions between Turkey and the EU.[54] In response Greece called for sanctions against Turkey, including EU restrictions on arms exports to Turkey, arguing there was a risk that Turkey might use military means to reinforce its positions in the Mediterranean.[55] The Netherlands suggested an EU arms embargo against Turkey in response to Turkish involvement in the conflicts in Nagorno-Karabakh, Libya and Syria, and Turkish oil and gas exploration activities in Greek waters.[56] The extent of the support for this suggestion among other EU member states remained unclear from open sources, but it did not find sufficient support during EU Council meetings in 2020. Hence, no arms embargo was imposed. Germany in particular openly opposed restricting arms exports on the grounds of Turkey's role as a NATO partner.[57]

---

[51] Bromley and Wezeman (note 27), p. 543.

[52] European Parliament, 'Arms export: Implementation of Common Position 2008/944/CFSP, 2020/2003(INI)', 17 Sep. 2020, para. 11.

[53] Bromley and Wezeman (note 27), pp. 543–44. On Turkey's military operation in Syria see chapter 6, section II, in this volume.

[54] European Council, European Council meeting (10 and 11 Dec. 2020): Conclusions, EUCO 22/20, 11 Dec. 2020, p. 11. On the tensions in the eastern Mediterranean see chapter 5, section I, in this volume.

[55] Nikas, S., 'Greece seeks arms embargo, halt to EU Turkey customs union', Bloomberg, 20 Oct. 2020; and Brzozowski, A. and Michalopoulos, S., 'EU top diplomat keeps mum over Turkey arms embargo', Euractiv, 8 Dec. 2020.

[56] 'Minister Blok wil met EU praten over wapenembargo Turkije' [Minister Blok wants to talk with EU about arms embargo Turkey], NOS, 13 Nov. 2020.

[57] Maas, H., Statement on arms exports to Turkey, German Federal Foreign Office news, 21 Dec. 2020.

The voluntary OSCE arms embargo related to Nagorno-Karabakh

In 1992 the CSCE (renamed the OSCE) requested that all participating states impose an embargo on arms deliveries to Armenian and Azerbaijani forces engaged in combat in the Nagorno-Karabakh area. The OSCE request has never been repealed. It is a voluntary multilateral arms embargo that OSCE participating states implement in different ways. For example, while Germany does not license the export of military goods to Armenia and Azerbaijan, other OSCE participating states have continued to supply arms to Armenia and Azerbaijan since 1992.[58] In 2020 large-scale fighting erupted between Armenia and Azerbaijan, which was preceded by significant arms supplies from several countries.[59] These included several OSCE participating states, particularly Russia, which supplied arms to both countries; Turkey, which supplied arms to Azerbaijan; and Spain, which supplied radars to Azerbaijan.[60] Russia's role as arms supplier to both countries stood in contrast to its role as co-chair of the Minsk Group, which seeks a peaceful resolution over Nagorno-Karabakh.[61] The apparent lack of interest in strengthening restrictions on arms supplies to Armenia and Azerbaijan was underlined by the fact that there was no public discussion in the OSCE during 2020 about the implementation of the embargo or about changing its status.

Conclusions

In 2020 continuing differences within the UN Security Council about the need for or utility of imposing or extending arms embargoes showed clearly when China and Russia once again abstained in the vote on the extension of the UN arms embargo on South Sudan. However, a new dimension was added in 2020 when the USA became fully isolated from its usual European allies in its efforts to extend the UN arms embargo on Iran. Strong differences in states' views on arms embargoes were also apparent from several OSCE participating states ignoring the voluntary OSCE embargo on the supply of weapons to Armenia and Azerbaijan in the years before and during the large-scale fighting between the two countries in 2020.

Compliance with UN arms embargoes was mixed in 2020 and the UN did not impose sanctions on any of the countries reportedly linked to embargo violations. As in previous years, there were reports of significant and sus-

---

[58] German Customs, 'Länderembargos: Armenien' [Country embargoes: Armenia], [n.d.]; and German Customs, 'Länderembargos: Aserbaidschan' [Country embargoes: Azerbaijan], [n.d.].

[59] On the armed conflict in 2020 see chapter 5, section II, in this volume.

[60] SIPRI arms transfers database, <https://sipri.org/databases/armstransfers>; see also chapter 9 in this volume.

[61] Organization for Security and Co-operation in Europe (OSCE), 'OSCE Minsk Group', [n.d.].

tained violations by several countries of the UN arms embargo on Libya. Of particular concern were allegations that Russia, a permanent member of the UN Security Council, was heavily involved in these violations. There were also reports of significant violations, linked to actors in Iran, of the arms embargo on non-state actors in Yemen. In contrast, violations of the arms embargo on military cooperation with North Korea seemed to have diminished.

III. The multilateral export control regimes

KOLJA BROCKMANN

The four main multilateral export control regimes are the Australia Group (AG), the Missile Technology Control Regime (MTCR), the Nuclear Suppliers Group (NSG) and the Wassenaar Arrangement on Export Controls for Conventional Arms and Dual-use Goods and Technologies (Wassenaar Arrangement, WA).[1] The regimes are informal groups of states which coordinate trade controls and related policies, and exchange information and good practices on trade in goods and technologies that have uses in connection with chemical, biological, nuclear and conventional weapons and their means of delivery (table 14.3). Each of the regimes takes decisions by consensus and their agreed common rules and control lists are politically rather than legally binding. The states participating in a regime implement the regime-prescribed controls through national laws. A large and increasing number of states that are not participating in the regimes adopt regime control lists and adhere to regime guidelines and regime-issued guidance. The regimes thus have an important international norm-setting function beyond their membership.[2] For the participating states, the regimes also serve an important information-exchange function, as they facilitate sharing of information about (*a*) export licence denials, and in some cases licences granted; (*b*) enforcement and prosecution cases; and (*c*) best practices among national policy and licensing officials, technical experts, and enforcement and intelligence officers.

In 2020 the impact of the Covid-19 pandemic was the dominant influence on the work of the regimes—as in almost all areas. The public health situation and the restrictions on international travel and in-person meetings meant that since March 2020 none of the regimes has been able to hold its annual plenary—the main decision-making body—or intersessional meetings. Consequently, no major decisions, such as amendments to the regimes' control lists, could be taken for most of 2020. As in 2019, none of the regimes admitted new participating states or partners, nor did additional states officially declare adherence to either the AG or the MTCR—which both have an official procedure for non-members to declare adherence. The AG is the only one of the four regimes in which participating states agreed to conduct at least some official meetings in virtual formats. The regimes took a range of measures—varying in each one—to address challenges to their work posed

---

[1] For brief descriptions and lists of the participating states in each of these regimes see annex B, section III, in this volume.

[2] Bauer, S., 'Main developments and discussions in the export control regimes', Literature Review for the Policy and Operations Evaluations Department of the Dutch Ministry of Foreign Affairs: Final Report, SIPRI, Aug. 2017, p. 62.

Table 14.3. The four multilateral export control regimes

Regime (year established)	Scope	No. of participants[a]	2020 plenary chair	2020 plenary status
Australia Group (1985)	Equipment, materials, technology and software that could contribute to chemical and biological weapons activities	43	Australia	Cancelled
Missile Technology Control Regime (1987)	Unmanned aerial vehicles capable of delivering weapons of mass destruction	35	Austria	Postponed to 2021
Nuclear Suppliers Group (1974)	Nuclear and nuclear-related materials, software and technology	48[b]	Belgium	Postponed to 2021
Wassenaar Arrangement (1996)	Conventional arms and dual-use items and technologies	42	Croatia	Cancelled

[a] Participant numbers are as of 31 Dec. 2020.

[b] In addition, the European Union and the chair of the Zangger Committee are permanent observers of the Nuclear Suppliers Group.

Sources: Australia Group; Missile Technology Control Regime; Nuclear Suppliers Group; and Wassenaar Arrangement on Export Controls for Conventional Arms and Dual-use Goods and Technologies.

by the pandemic. These included the upgrading of the information-sharing system of the NSG, introduction of a newsletter by the MTCR, and increased participation of regime representatives in virtual meetings organized by third parties.

The Australia Group

The AG participating states coordinate and harmonize their national export controls to reduce the risk of contributing to the proliferation of chemical and biological weapons.[3] The AG was founded in 1985 upon an initiative by Australia in response to the revelation of extensive procurement of precursor chemicals, equipment and materials from Western states that were found by a United Nations investigation to have been used in chemical weapons in the 1980–88 Iran–Iraq War.[4] Since then the AG has significantly expanded its coverage to include equipment, materials and technology relevant to the development, production and use of both chemical weapons and biological weapons.[5] The AG participating states discuss technological developments and emerging technologies to continuously update the control lists defining

[3] Australia Group, 'The Australia Group: An introduction', [n.d.]; and Australia Group, 'Objectives of the Group', [n.d.].

[4] Australia Group, 'The origins of the Australia Group', [n.d.].

[5] Australia Group (note 4).

these items. The AG is permanently chaired by Australia which also runs an informal secretariat situated within the Australian Department of Foreign Affairs and Trade.

The number of participants in the AG has grown from 18 to 43, including the European Union (EU). In 2020, no new participants were admitted, while several applications are still under consideration.[6] The AG encourages states not participating in the regime to make voluntary declarations of adherence to the guidelines and common control lists. Although the AG offers such adherents additional access to information and to assistance from AG participating states with implementing the AG guidelines and control lists, Kazakhstan remains the only state to have submitted the required notification.[7]

The AG held an intersessional meeting on 6 February 2020 in Bratislava, hosted by the Slovak Republic, to continue discussions on the addition of novichok nerve agent precursors to the AG's control lists and on improving the implementation of catch-all controls.[8] In November 2019 the Organisation for the Prohibition of Chemical Weapons had added novichok nerve agents to Schedule 1 of banned substances of the Chemical Weapons Convention. The AG followed and complemented this step by agreeing to add novichok nerve agent precursors to its chemical weapons precursors control list.[9] The AG further agreed to 'continue reviewing other potential chemical precursors that might need to be added to the control list in the future'.[10]

The AG cancelled its annual plenary meeting in Paris and the chair did not conduct any outreach missions in 2020, because of pandemic restrictions. In contrast to the other regimes, the AG managed to find consensus among the participating states on resuming some of its official meetings in a virtual format. Nevertheless, no other changes to the AG control lists were adopted after the February 2020 intersessional meeting.

The Missile Technology Control Regime

The MTCR aims to prevent the proliferation of missiles and other unmanned delivery systems capable of delivering chemical, biological or nuclear (CBN) weapons. The Group of Seven (G7) largest industrialized states founded the MTCR in 1987 with the objective of helping to prevent the proliferation of

---

[6] Australia Group, 'Australia Group participants', [n.d.].

[7] Australia Group, 'Australia Group adherents', [n.d.].

[8] Australia Group, 'Statement by the Australia Group chair: Addition of novichok precursor chemicals to the Australia Group Control List', 28 Feb. 2020.

[9] Brockmann, K., 'The export control regimes', *SIPRI Yearbook 2020*, pp. 547–58. For recent developments on the use of novichok agents, the Chemical Weapons Convention and the work of the Organisation for the Prohibition of Chemical Weapons see chapter 12, sections IV and V, in this volume.

[10] Australia Group (note 8).

nuclear weapons by introducing export controls on goods and technologies related to missiles capable of carrying nuclear weapons.[11] The scope of MTCR controls expanded to include ballistic and cruise missiles, and all unmanned aerial vehicles (UAVs) capable of delivering CBN weapons.[12] The MTCR covers any such missile or UAV 'capable of delivering a payload of at least 500 kg to a range of at least 300 km', or destined to be used to deliver CBN weapons.[13] The number of MTCR participants—referred to as 'the partners'—has grown from 7 to 35 states, but has not increased since the 2016 admission of India despite numerous pending applications—including from nine EU member states.[14] The MTCR has formalized declarations of adherence to the MTCR guidelines since 2014, which offers benefits to adherent states, including invitation to technical outreach meetings, briefings on control list changes, meetings with the MTCR chair and access to some presentations from Licencing and Enforcement Experts Meetings (LEEM).[15] Since its introduction, only three states—Estonia, Kazakhstan and Latvia—have unilaterally declared their adherence by notifying the MTCR Point of Contact in Paris, and no additional states have done so in 2020.

The partners agreed on a provisional postponement of the 2020 plenary to be held in Vienna under the chairship of Austria on 15–19 March 2021—if the circumstances related to the pandemic permit in-person meetings.[16] New Zealand nevertheless handed over the chair to Austria in October 2020, in line with the established chairing periods. Austria will be followed by Russia assuming the chair for the period 2021/22 and by Switzerland for the period 2022/23. Informal consultations among some partners took place in various formats. Proposals and non-papers on topics of discussions continued to be submitted and shared among the participants—for example, on technical topics in the Technical Experts Meeting (TEM).[17] The co-chair of the TEM was taken over by the United Kingdom and Switzerland from the Netherlands and Australia.[18]

The New Zealand chair conducted several outreach activities to engage non-members in late 2019 and early 2020, before in-person outreach had

---

[11] Missile Technology Control Regime, 'Frequently asked questions (FAQs)', [n.d.]. The G7 states are Canada, France, Germany, Italy, Japan, the United Kingdom and the United States.

[12] Missile Technology Control Regime (note 11).

[13] Missile Technology Control Regime, 'MTCR Guidelines and the Equipment, Software and Technology annex', [n.d.].

[14] Missile Technology Control Regime, 'Partners', [n.d.].

[15] Missile Technology Control Regime, 'Adherence policy', [n.d.].

[16] Hajnoczi, T., 'Upcoming chair's introduction', *Missile Technology Control Regime Newsletter*, 3 Sep. 2020, p. 5.

[17] Government senior adviser on export control technical policy, Interview with the author, 16 Dec. 2020.

[18] Horton, A., 'The TEM: Keeping calm and carrying on!', *Missile Technology Control Regime Newsletter*, 3 Sep. 2020, p. 2.

to be suspended due to the pandemic. The chair participated in a training course for UN Security Council Resolution 1540 Points of Contact in the Asia-Pacific Region, which took place in China, and used the opportunity to hold a bilateral meeting with Chinese officials to 'convey the Regime's interest in renewing contact on MTCR issues with China'.[19] China has pursued membership and declared that they would follow the MTCR guidelines in the past, but some partners—most vocally the United States— opposed Chinese membership and pointed to its mixed record on missile non-proliferation and shortcomings in its export control system.[20] The MTCR was also represented at the 27th Asian Export Control Seminar in February 2020 in Tokyo through a presentation and a side event for outreach to Asian countries.[21] The only formal MTCR outreach mission was to Israel in March 2020, continuing the regular engagement with Israel.[22] The MTCR also published its first newsletter in September 2020, which took stock of the outgoing chair's work, the work of the TEM, the Information Exchange Meeting (IEM), and the LEEM. This is a notable step towards more transparency, particularly during the pandemic when public information from the regimes was even more sparse. The newsletter also introduced the incoming chair, thus providing for additional public and official information on the work of the MTCR.[23]

The Hague Code of Conduct against Ballistic Missile Proliferation

The Hague Code of Conduct against Ballistic Missile Proliferation (HCOC) is the only multilateral transparency and confidence-building instrument on ballistic missile non-proliferation.[24] It originated from discussions within the MTCR in 2002 and has since developed into an independent politically binding instrument that complements the MTCR in its goal on missile non-proliferation.[25] Three more states subscribed to the HCOC in 2020—Saint Vincent and the Grenadines (January 2020), Equatorial Guinea (January 2020) and Somalia (February 2020)—bringing the total to 143.[26] Moreover, on 7 December 2020 the UN General Assembly adopted Resolution 75/60

---

[19] Higgie, D., 'MTCR outreach activities', *Missile Technology Control Regime Newsletter*, 3 Sep. 2020, p. 4.

[20] Spector, L. S., 'The Missile Technology Control Regime and shifting proliferation challenges', *Arms Control Today*, vol. 48, no. 3 (Apr. 2018); and Rasmussen, N. A., 'Chinese missile technology control: Regime or no regime?', DIIS Policy Brief, Feb. 2007.

[21] Asian Export Control Seminar Secretariat, 'The 27th Asian Export Control Seminar', [n.d.]; and Sargison, G., 'Missile Technology Control Regime', Presentation to the 27th Asian Export Control Seminar, Tokyo, 12 Feb. 2020.

[22] Missile Technology Control Regime, 'Report by the MTCR Chair: Outreach visit to Israel', News, 23 Mar. 2020.

[23] Missile Technology Control Regime, *Missile Technology Control Regime Newsletter*, 3 Sep. 2020.

[24] Hague Code of Conduct, 'What is HCoC?', Feb. 2020.

[25] Brockmann, K., *Controlling Ballistic Missile Proliferation: Assessing Complementarity between the HCoC, MTCR and UNSCR 1540*, HCOC Research Paper no. 7 (HCOC: Vienna, June 2020).

[26] Hague Code of Conduct, 'List of HCoC subscribing states', Feb. 2020.

in support of the HCOC with 176 votes in favour, 1 against (Iran) and 10 abstentions. This was a considerable increase over the last such biannual resolution in 2018 which had previously held the record for the strongest support received.[27]

In contrast to the export control regimes, which admit participating states by consensus, any state can subscribe to the HCOC by submitting its subscription to the Austrian Ministry for Foreign Affairs, which serves as the Immediate Central Contact for the HCOC. Subscribing states commit to implementing a limited range of transparency and confidence-building measures. In particular, they agree to provide annual declarations about national ballistic missile and space launch programmes and policies, and to exchange pre-launch notifications on launches and test flights of their ballistic missiles and space launch vehicles.[28]

Despite the pandemic circumstances, the 19th annual regular meeting of the HCOC took place in Vienna on 12 October 2020, after being postponed in June.[29] Delegations from 71 of the 143 subscribing states attended—only a small decrease compared to previous regular meetings. On 3 June Switzerland assumed the chair of the HCOC for the 2020/21 period, taking over from Norway. Switzerland stated that it would focus its chairing role on ensuring full compliance by subscribing states and securing the participation of additional states in the HCOC.[30]

Norway carried out several outreach activities on behalf of the HCOC in late 2019 and early 2020. This included providing a presentation on the HCOC during the Asian Export Control Seminar in Tokyo in February 2020.[31] The Swiss chair participated in a range of virtual events, including a virtual side event co-organized with the Foundation for Strategic Research (Fondation pour la recherche stratégique, FRS) on the margins of the UN General Assembly First Committee, a virtual expert mission to Vietnam, and an 'Asian Regional Webinar' on the HCOC co-organized by FRS and the UN Regional Centre for Peace and Disarmament in Asia and the Pacific.[32]

[27] UN General Assembly Resolution 75/60, 7 Dec. 2020; and Maletta, G. et al., 'The export control regimes', *SIPRI Yearbook 2019*, pp. 525–26.

[28] Hague Code of Conduct, 'How to join HCoC', Nov. 2018.

[29] Hague Code of Conduct, '19th regular meeting of the subscribing states to the Hague Code of Conduct against Ballistic Missile Proliferation (HCOC)', Press release, Oct. 2020.

[30] Swiss Federal Department of Foreign Affairs, 'Switzerland seeks to build trust between states to stop the proliferation of delivery systems for weapons of mass destruction', Press release, 3 June 2020.

[31] Nyhamar, I. M. W., 'The Hague Code of Conduct against Ballistic Missile Proliferation (HCoC)', Presentation to the 27th Asian Export Control Seminar, Tokyo, 12 Feb. 2020.

[32] Foundation for Strategic Research and Hague Code of Conduct, 'The state of ballistic missile proliferation today', Virtual side-event organized on the margins on the UN General Assembly First Committee, 29 Oct. 2020; Foundation for Strategic Research, 'Expert mission on the HCoC with Vietnam', 10 Dec. 2020; and Foundation for Strategic Research, 'Asian regional webinar', 18 Dec. 2020.

The Nuclear Suppliers Group

The NSG seeks to prevent the proliferation of nuclear weapons by controlling transfers of nuclear and nuclear-related material, equipment, software and technology. It was established in 1974 in response to India's first nuclear test, the first explosion of a nuclear weapon by a state not recognized as a nuclear-weapon state by the Treaty on the Non-proliferation of Nuclear Weapons (NPT).[33] The number of NSG participating states has grown from 7 to 48, but has not increased since the admission of Serbia in 2013.[34] The NSG continued discussions on several pending requests to participate, but in 2020 there continued to be a lack of consensus for admitting any additional states. In particular, there continues to be no agreement on the long-standing question of whether India and Pakistan, both non-NPT members, should be admitted to the NSG.

The NSG's annual plenary, which was set to take place in Brussels in June, was postponed by a full year to mid 2021.[35] Belgium assumed the chair of the NSG for the period 2020/21, taking over from Kazakhstan. The troika of the previous, current and incoming chairs worked together with the chairs of the subsidiary NSG bodies to implement a regular transition of the NSG chair at the time of the postponed plenary to ensure the functioning of the regime. As a timely measure under the pandemic circumstances, the US National Nuclear Security Administration completed the modernization of the secure NSG Information Sharing System (NISS) in October 2020.[36] The timeliness of the upgrade to the new system highlighted the need for well-functioning and secure electronic communication channels among regime participants and helps build resilience to disruptions to in-person engagement, travel and international meetings.

Despite the pandemic, the Belgian chair announced that he would conduct outreach to 'important players in the nuclear field to promote adherence to the NSG Guidelines' and reiterated the plans for addressing the NPT Review Conference, which was postponed to 2021.[37] The chair acknowledged that while regular NSG activities continue, some of them do so in a 'somewhat adapted format'.[38] Discussions on substantive issues continued among the participating states albeit mainly in smaller groups. The NSG does not disclose topics of discussion or the content of pending proposals regarding the control list and guidance materials. Track 1.5 workshops and

---

[33] Nuclear Suppliers Group, 'About the NSG', [n.d.].

[34] Nuclear Suppliers Group, 'Participants', [n.d.].

[35] Nuclear Suppliers Group, 'Chair's corner', [n.d.].

[36] National Nuclear Security Administration, 'NNSA launches new web platform to support the nonproliferation work of the Nuclear Suppliers Group', 21 Dec. 2020.

[37] For more on the postponed NPT Review Conference see chapter 11, section III, in this volume; and Nuclear Suppliers Group, 'Chair's corner' (note 35).

[38] Nuclear Suppliers Group, 'Chair's corner' (note 35).

conferences continued to focus on emerging technologies, including additive manufacturing, and advanced reactor designs.[39]

The NSG was also represented in several outreach meetings in late 2019 and early 2020, including ones attended by non-participating states. The NSG presented at a training course for UN Security Council Resolution 1540 Points of Contact in the Asia-Pacific Region, hosted by China in October 2019, and presented and conducted a side event at the Asian Export Control Seminar in February 2020.[40]

The Wassenaar Arrangement

The WA was established as the successor to the cold war era Co-ordinating Committee for Multilateral Export Controls (COCOM) in 1996. The WA participating states seek to promote 'transparency and greater responsibility' in the transfers of conventional weapons and dual-use goods and technologies. In doing so they aim to prevent transfers that contribute to 'destabilising accumulations' of such weapons and technologies that could endanger international and regional security and stability, as well as transfers to terrorists. Since its inception, the number of participating states in the WA has expanded from 33 to 42. No additional participating states have been admitted since India in 2017.[41]

The plenary chair was handed over from Croatia to Hungary at the end of 2020, while the USA assumed the chair of the General Working Group and Malta assumed the chair of the Experts Group for 2021. Italy continued chairing the Licensing and Enforcement Officers Meeting in 2021.

Due to the pandemic the participating states did not hold any meetings in 2020 or conduct the usual in-depth technical review of technological developments and potential updates to the WA control lists. The WA participating states nevertheless continued intersessional cooperation and adopted several decisions to ensure the continued implementation of the WA's work programme and the functioning of the WA Secretariat. They also set up a framework to conduct the sixth internal 'Assessment of the Arrangement', which comprises an in-depth review and evaluation of the functioning of the WA to 'improve its effectiveness and efficiency' and will be a key activity in 2021. A 'programme of activities' was agreed to mark the

---

[39] The author participated in several of these meetings as a discussant.

[40] United Nations, 'Security Council Resolution 1540 (2004) points of contact training for states of Asia-Pacific Region', Press release, 30 Oct. 2019; and Nuclear Suppliers Group, 'The Nuclear Suppliers Group and its Guidelines: "A Public Good"', Presentation at the 27th Asian Export Control Seminar, Tokyo, 12 Feb. 2020.

[41] Wassenaar Arrangement, 'About us', updated 17 Dec. 2020.

25th anniversary of the establishment of the WA in 2021, including outreach to non-participating states.[42]

The WA Secretariat participated in several outreach activities in early 2020 before most travel and in-person meetings were suspended. The secretariat participated in the Second Annual Disarmament and International Security Affairs Fellowship Programme in New Delhi in January 2020 and delivered a presentation and organized a side event on the margins of the Asian Export Control Seminar in Tokyo in February.[43]

Conclusions

The impact of the Covid-19 pandemic in 2020 raised serious concerns over the resilience of the multilateral export control regimes and their reliance on annual in-person plenaries as the main decision-making bodies. Most of the regimes' work continued and largely ran through the information-exchange functions or was conducted in smaller groups of participating states. However, the ability to take decisions and continue discussions on difficult and particularly political and technical topics was seriously hampered. The lack of transparency due to reduced participation in public events and fewer public statements and press releases has demonstrated the imperative for the regimes to explore complementary ways of continuing on a trajectory towards more openness. The launch of a new newsletter by the MTCR is an example of a small step in this direction. The modernization of the NSG Information Sharing System is an example of a step that could help ensure a regime's functioning while adding resilience in the face of future disruptions. The volume of proposals and working papers that had to be carried over from 2020 will ensure a significant workload and busy schedule for the regimes in 2021. In addition, many important processes, such as the increased engagement between the regimes, will need to be rekindled as soon as the public health situation permits.

---

[42] Wassenaar Arrangement, 'Statement issued by the plenary chair of the Wassenaar Arrangement on Export Controls for Conventional Arms and Dual-Use Goods and Technologies', Vienna, 17 Dec. 2020.

[43] Griffiths, P., 'The role and relevance of the Wassenaar Arrangement', Presentation to the Second Annual Disarmament and International Security Affairs Fellowship Programme, New Delhi, 17 Jan. 2020; Griffiths, P., 'Wassenaar Arrangement updates', Presentation to the 27th Asian Export Control Seminar, Tokyo, 12 Feb. 2020; and Wassenaar Arrangement, 'Outreach event at the Asian Export Control Seminar', 14 Feb. 2020.

IV. Developments in the European Union's dual-use and arms trade controls

MARK BROMLEY, KOLJA BROCKMANN AND GIOVANNA MALETTA

The European Union (EU) is currently the only regional organization with a common legal framework for controls on the export, brokering, transit and trans-shipment of dual-use items and also, to a certain extent, military items. The key elements of this legal framework are the EU's arms embargoes, dual-use regulation, common position on arms exports, directive on intra-Community transfers, and anti-torture regulation.[1] Developments in EU arms embargoes are addressed in section II of this chapter. This section focuses on developments with regard to the dual-use regulation and the common position. During 2020 the EU reached a provisional agreement on the text of a new version of the dual-use regulation, thereby drawing to a close a long-running process of review and recast that began in 2011. Following a review of the common position that concluded in 2019, the EU also implemented measures to improve the level of transparency and accessibility of the EU annual report on arms exports.

The EU dual-use regulation

The EU dual-use regulation covers controls on the export, re-export, brokering and transit of dual-use goods, software and technology. The regulation is directly applicable law in EU member states but is implemented and enforced via their national control systems. As mandated in Article 25 of the dual-use regulation, the instrument has been under review since 2011. As part of this process, the European Commission published a 'recast' proposal in the form of a new draft version of the regulation in September 2016.[2] The European Parliament published its proposed amendments to the Commission proposal in January 2018 and the Council of the EU published

---

[1] Council Regulation 428/2009 of 5 May 2009 setting up a Community regime for the control of exports, transfer, brokering and transit of dual-use items, *Official Journal of the European Union*, L134, 29 May 2009; Council Common Position 2008/944/CFSP of 8 Dec. 2008 defining common rules governing control of exports of military technology and equipment, *Official Journal of the European Union*, L335, 8 Dec. 2008; Directive 2009/43/EC of the European Parliament and of the Council of 6 May 2009 simplifying terms and conditions of transfers of defence-related products within the Community, *Official Journal of the European Union*, L146, 10 June 2009; and Regulation (EU) 2016/2134 of the European Parliament and of the Council of 23 Nov. 2016 amending Council Regulation (EC) 1236/2005 concerning trade in certain goods which could be used for capital punishment, torture or other cruel, inhuman or degrading treatment or punishment, *Official Journal of the European Union*, L338, 13 Dec. 2016.

[2] European Commission, 'Proposal for a Regulation of the European Parliament and of the Council setting up a Union regime for the control of exports, transfer, brokering, technical assistance and transit of dual-use items (recast)', 12798/16, 28 Sep. 2016. See also Bauer, S. and Bromley, M., 'Developments in EU dual-use and arms trade controls', *SIPRI Yearbook 2017*, 612–15.

its own negotiating mandate in June 2019.[3] In the second half of 2019 the Commission's proposal began to go through a process of 'trilogue' involving the Commission, the Parliament and the Council. Four trilogues were held between October 2019 and September 2020. In November 2020 the Council of the EU—under the presidency of Germany—announced that the Council and the Parliament had reached a provisional political agreement on a revised version of the dual-use regulation in the form of a final compromise text.[4] The new version of the dual-use regulation is expected to be adopted by the Parliament in the first half of 2021 and enter into force in the second half of 2021.[5] The proposal put forward by the Commission sought to revise virtually all aspects of the dual-use regulation, setting the stage for a complex and wide-ranging recast process. However, the length of time needed to adopt a final compromise text was largely due to differences that emerged on certain key points. The most contentious of these was the creation of stronger controls on exports of cybersurveillance items by—among other things— expanding the range and prominence of human rights concerns in the dual-use regulation. Here, the Parliament largely endorsed or expanded on the Commission's proposals. However, member states were initially divided on how to respond and later—through the Council's mandate—pushed back on the Commission and Parliament's proposals.[6]

This section reviews the areas that proved most substantive in terms of the amount of debate generated or the significance of changes made to the dual-use regulation: harmonizing member states' controls; simplifying controls on less sensitive items; and strengthening controls on cybersurveillance items. The section then addresses a fourth area which became increasingly prominent as the review and recast progressed: responding to challenges posed by 'emerging technologies'; and discusses the other initiatives the EU

[3] European Parliament, 'Amendments adopted by the European Parliament on 17 January 2018 on the proposal for a regulation of the European Parliament and of the Council setting up a Union regime for the control of exports, transfer, brokering, technical assistance and transit of dual-use items (recast) (COM(2016)0616–C8–0393/2016–2016/0295(COD))', 17 Jan. 2018; and Council of the European Union, 'Proposal for a for a regulation of the European Parliament and of the Council setting up a Union regime for the control of exports, brokering, technical assistance, transit and transfer of dual-use items (recast)—Mandate for negotiations with the European Parliament (2016/0295(COD))', 5 June 2019.

[4] European Council, 'New rules on trade of dual-use items agreed', Press release, 9 Nov. 2020.

[5] Angersbach, R., 'Stand der EG-Dual-Use-Novelle' [Status of the EU Dual-use Recast], *AW-Prax*, vol. 27, no. 1 (Jan. 2021), pp. 13–16.

[6] Moßbrucker, D., 'Surveillance exports: How EU Member States are compromising new human rights standards', Netzpolitik, 29 Oct. 2018; and Cerulus, L., 'Europe to crack down on surveillance software exports', Politico, 15 Oct. 2020. For a more detailed overview of the Commission's, Parliament's and Council's positions during the review and recast process see Bromley, M. and Maletta G., 'Developments in the European Union's dual-use and arms trade controls', *SIPRI Yearbook 2019*, 532–37; Bromley, M. and Gerharz, P., 'Revising the EU Dual-use Regulation: Challenges and opportunities for the trilogue process', SIPRI Commentary, 7 Oct. 2019; and Immenkamp, B., 'Review of dual-use export controls', European Parliamentary Research Service briefing, 15 Jan. 2021.

engaged in with relation to this area, over and above making changes to the dual-use regulation.

Harmonizing member states' controls

In April 2014 the Commission outlined four priorities for the review of the dual-use regulation. Two of these were focused on creating greater harmonization in the way member states implement dual-use export controls: promoting 'export control convergence and a global level-playing field', and supporting 'effective and consistent export control implementation and enforcement'.[7] During the review and recast, attempts to achieve a more harmonized application of the regulation focused on three key areas: achieving a more uniform interpretation of key concepts; improving intergovernmental information-sharing; and creating new mechanisms in the field of public transparency.

Both the multilateral export control regimes and the dual-use regulation provide limited clarity about how certain key terms associated with dual-use export controls should be interpreted. Areas where there is a lack of common understanding include how the exemptions for 'basic scientific research' and information that is 'in the public domain' should be implemented. This, in turn, contributes to differences in how controls are applied at the national level.[8] The final compromise text makes clear that guidelines are needed and that their development is a joint responsibility of the Council and the Commission.[9] In parallel with the review process, the EU and its member states have taken other steps aimed at promoting a more harmonized implementation of the dual-use regulation, including by publishing guidelines on how to set up and implement internal compliance programmes and developing an additional set of compliance guidelines for the research sector.[10] The final compromise text also seeks to standardize the way in which transfers of knowledge and 'technical assistance' are regulated. In particular, it creates controls on transfers that occur within the national borders of EU member states, such as may happen when a foreign

---

[7] European Commission, 'Ensuring security and competitiveness in a changing world', Communication from the Commission to the Council and the European Parliament on the review of export control policy, COM (2014) 244 final, 24 Apr. 2014.

[8] E.g. Germany and the Belgian region of Flanders recently published guidance material detailing how the exceptions for 'basic scientific research' should be applied, which points to differing views in this area. Flemish Chancellery and Foreign Office, 'Controle op de Handel in Dual-use Items' [Control of trade in dual-use items], 30 Sep. 2017; and German Federal Office for Economic Affairs and Export Control (BAFA), *Export Control and Academia Manual* (BAFA: Eschborn, Feb. 2019).

[9] Council of the European Union, 'Proposal for a Regulation of the European Parliament and of the Council setting up a Union regime for the control of exports, brokering, technical assistance, transit and transfer of dual-use items (recast)', 12798/20, 13 Nov. 2020, p. 47.

[10] Commission Recommendation (EU) 2019/1318 of 30 July 2019 on internal compliance programmes for dual-use trade controls under Council Regulation (EC) No 428/2009, *Official Journal of the European Union*, L205, 5 Aug. 2019; and European Commission, 'EU compliance guidance for research involving dual-use items', Nov. 2020.

citizen enters the EU to attend a university course or participate in industry training, something not covered by the dual-use regulation. However, providing guidance material for how these controls should be applied is the responsibility of member states.[11]

Under the dual-use regulation, member states exchange information on denials of export licences and meet regularly to discuss the implementation of the regulation. However, information exchanges in other areas—particularly on measures taken to enforce controls at the national level and to prosecute violations of export controls—are more limited. The final compromise text makes significant changes in this area, particularly with regard to enforcement issues. Specifically, the Dual-Use Coordination Group—which is chaired by the Commission and brings together officials from EU member states to discuss the application of the dual-use regulation—is tasked with establishing an 'Enforcement Coordination Mechanism'. The new body will bring together member states' licensing authorities and enforcement agencies to exchange information on a range of areas, including 'risk-based audits' and 'the detection and prosecution of unauthorised exports of dual use items'.[12]

In contrast to the common position, the dual-use regulation does not include any requirements for public reporting on issued or denied export licences. Both the Commission and Parliament called for significant advances to be made on this front, while the Council made no reference to the issue in their negotiating mandate. The final compromise text creates an ambitious set of targets on public reporting. Specifically, the annual report which the Commission produces on the implementation of the dual-use regulation will be expanded to include information on export licence 'authorisations', 'denials' and 'prohibitions'. The commitments are most far-reaching for cybersurveillance items. Here, the EU commits itself to publishing annual data on 'the number of applications received by items, the issuing Member State and the destinations concerned by these applications, and on the decisions taken on these applications'.[13] The final compromise text does not specify which data will be collected and published, or when the first report will be produced, but instead tasks the Commission and Council with developing 'guidelines' to address these points.[14] It also notes that member states are obliged to give 'due consideration . . . to legal requirements concerning the protection of personal information, commercial sensitive information or protected defense, foreign policy or national security information' when collecting and submitting data.[15]

---

[11] Council of the European Union, 12798/20 (note 9), p. 47, Article 24(1).
[12] Council of the European Union, 12798/20 (note 9), pp. 46–47, Article 22(2).
[13] Council of the European Union, 12798/20 (note 9), p. 48, Article 24(2).
[14] Council of the European Union, 12798/20 (note 9), p. 48, Article 24(2).
[15] Council of the European Union, 12798/20 (note 9), p. 48, Article 24(3).

Simplifying controls on less sensitive items

The third priority outlined in the April 2014 Commission Communication was to 'develop an effective and competitive EU export control regime'. Many of the Commission's proposals were focused on modernizing EU controls to reduce the regulatory burden they place on both exporters and member states' licensing authorities. Two of the key areas of focus that emerged during the review and recast process were creating additional EU General Export Authorizations (EUGEAs) and facilitating the use of cloud computing services by exporters of dual-use items.[16]

An EUGEA is a type of open licence agreed at the EU level that allows exporters to carry out multiple shipments under a single licence. The dual-use regulation has six EUGEAs and the final compromise text adds two more: one for items that employ cryptography and one for transfers of software and technology to subsidiary and sister companies. The Commission and Parliament had proposed more language on EUGEAs and the Parliament had gone further, particularly on cryptography where it called for a complete lifting of all restrictions.[17] EU member states supported the adoption of new EUGEAs but differed on their precise scope and content due to their particular national economic and security concerns.[18] There was also broad opposition among member states to the Parliament's idea of dropping controls on cryptography completely. Many governments value the controls for their ability to provide oversight of the trade in technologies that are of potential relevance to national security.[19] The coverage of the two new EUGEAs was less ambitious than the Commission and Parliament had proposed and two other EUGEAs—for low-value shipments and 'other dual-use items'—were dropped completely. However, the Commission also received wider powers to amend the coverage of EUGEAs.

For several years, companies and research institutes have pointed to differences in the ways in which EU member states regulate the use of cloud computing services to store and share technical data or software that is subject to dual-use export controls. These differences centre on whether controls take account of the location of the servers where the software or

---

[16] Cloud computing emerged in the early 2000s and can be broadly defined as 'the practice of using a network of remote servers hosted on the Internet to store, manage, and process data, rather than a local server or a personal computer.' Dryfhout, M. and Hewer, S., 'What is cloud computing?', Scout Technology Guides blog, 11 Apr. 2019. For a discussion of cloud computing and export controls see Tauwhare, R., 'Cloud computing, export controls and sanctions', *Journal of Internet Law*, vol. 19, no. 2 (Aug. 2015).

[17] European Parliament, 'Amendments' (note 3), amendments 13 and 15.

[18] Göstl, C., Foreign Trade Administration, Federal Ministry for Digital and Economic Affairs, Austrian Presidency of the Council of the European Union, 'Opening remarks', EU Export Control Forum 2018, Brussels, 13 Dec. 2018.

[19] Bromley, M., Brockmann, K. and Maletta, G., 'Controls on intangible transfers of technology and additive manufacturing', *SIPRI Yearbook 2018*, pp. 437–47.

technology is stored and the steps companies are required to take in order to ensure that technical data or software uploaded to a cloud is kept secure.[20] The final compromise text recommends that member states use 'facilitations in the form of general or global licenses or harmonised interpretation of provisions' for cloud services but leaves the overarching definition of an export intact. This means that member states will remain free to regulate the use of cloud computing according to their own national standards.[21] The Commission had sought to go further by amending the definition of export in a way that would have made clearer that the act of uploading controlled software or technical data to a cloud did not require a licence.[22]

Strengthening controls on cybersurveillance items

The fourth priority provided in the April 2014 Communication was to 'adjust to the evolving security environment and enhance the EU contribution to international security'. Following pressure from the Parliament, the Commission, Council and Parliament committed in 2014 to exploring how to use the dual-use regulation to create stronger controls on the export of cybersurveillance items.[23] Debates about how to achieve this outcome focused on three areas: controlling additional cybersurveillance items through a new 'catch-all control'; controlling additional items through a new 'autonomous' EU control list; and ensuring that fewer exports take place by expanding the range of human rights concerns states would need to consider in their risk assessments.

The list of items subject to licensing requirements under the dual-use regulation is outlined in the EU dual-use list, which is drawn from the control lists produced by the Wassenaar Arrangement and other multi-lateral export control regimes (see section III). The dual-use regulation also includes so-called catch-all controls, which cover items that do not appear on the dual-use list but that may contribute to a programme to develop weapons of mass destruction, have a 'military end use' in an embargoed state, or be used as parts and components in an illegally exported military item. The final compromise text creates a new catch-all control for unlisted cybersurveillance items that may be used for 'internal repression and/or the commission of serious violations of international human rights and international humanitarian law [IHL]'.[24] Exporters are also obliged to inform

---

[20] See Bromley, M. and Maletta, G., *The Challenge of Software and Technology Transfers to Non-proliferation Efforts: Implementing and Complying with Export Controls* (SIPRI: Stockholm, Apr. 2018), pp. 23–24.

[21] Council of the European Union, 12798/20 (note 9), para. 7.

[22] European Commission, 12798/16 (note 2), p. 7.

[23] See Immenkamp (note 6); and 'Joint Statement by the European Parliament, the Council and the Commission on the review of the dual-use export control system', *Official Journal of the European Union*, L173, 12 June 2014.

[24] Council of the European Union, 12798/20 (note 9), p. 23, Article 4a(1).

their national authorities if they are 'aware according to [their] due diligence findings' of any such risks.[25] The creation of a new catch-all control for cybersurveillance items and language on due diligence were supported by the Commission and Parliament but opposed by the Council on the grounds that they risked creating unclear and unnecessary regulatory obligations for governments and exporters.[26] While their inclusion represents a concession by the Council, the final compromise text defines cybersurveillance items more narrowly than the Commission or Parliament proposed—thereby limiting the scope of the catch-all control—and does not create an explicit legal obligation for companies to have due diligence measures.

Between 2012 and 2019 controls on five types of cybersurveillance items were added to the Wassenaar Arrangement dual-use list and—subsequently—the EU dual-use list.[27] However, both the Commission and Parliament saw a need to create an 'autonomous' EU control list for additional cybersurveillance items that did not appear on the Wassenaar Arrangement list. EU member states were initially divided over whether to support the creation of an autonomous EU list but neither the Council's negotiating mandate nor the final compromise text makes any reference to the issue.[28] Instead, the final compromise text states that if an EU member state uses the new catch-all control to regulate an unlisted cybersurveillance item—and if all other EU member states provide their approval—the EU will publish details 'in the C series of the *Official Journal of the European Union*'.[29] EU member states are also required to 'consider' supporting the addition of these items to the 'appropriate' control regime.[30]

The dual-use regulation requires member states 'to take into account' the considerations outlined in the common position when granting an export licence for dual-use items including—by extension—the common position's eight risk assessment criteria. This means that states are obliged to deny an export licence for dual-use items if they 'might be used for internal

[25] Council of the European Union, 12798/20 (note 9), p. 23, Article 4a(2).

[26] See Council of the European Union, General Secretariat, 'EU export control: Recast of the Regulation 428/2009', Working paper WK 1019/2018 INIT, 29 Jan. 2018; and Council of the European Union, 'Paper for discussion: For adoption of an improved EU Export Control Regulation 428/2009 and for cyber-surveillance controls promoting human rights and international humanitarian law', Working paper WK5755/2018 INIT, 15 May 2018.

[27] Controls on 'Mobile telecommunications interception equipment' were added in 2012; controls on 'Internet protocol (IP) network surveillance systems' and 'Intrusion software' were added in 2013; and controls on 'Monitoring centres' and 'Digital forensics' were added in 2019. For more information see Bromley, M., *Export Controls, Human Security and Cyber-surveillance Technology: Examining the Proposed Changes to the EU Dual-use Regulation* (SIPRI: Stockholm, Dec. 2017); and Brockmann, K., 'The multilateral export control regimes', *SIPRI Yearbook 2020*, p. 556.

[28] See Council of the European Union, General Secretariat, WK 1019/2018 INIT (note 26); and Council of the European Union, WK5755/2018 INIT (note 26).

[29] Council of the European Union, 12798/20 (note 9), p. 24, Article 4a(6).

[30] Council of the European Union, 12798/20 (note 9), p. 24, Article 4a(10).

repression' or 'in the commission of serious violations of [IHL]'.[31] The European Parliament's amendments sought to expand the range of human rights concerns covered by the dual-use regulation beyond those covered by 'internal repression'. Specifically, member states and exporters would be obliged to assess the risk of violations of 'the right to privacy, the right to free speech and the freedom of assembly and association' when deciding whether to export cybersurveillance items. The Commission and the Parliament also called for guidance material to inform member states' export licence decision making. The Council's mandate and the final compromise text keep the link with the common position but take out all references to wider human rights concerns and guidance material. However, new language on 'internal repression', 'serious violations of human rights' and IHL have been added to the preamble, noting that these are issues that EU member states should consider when exporting dual-use items—particularly cybersurveillance items.[32] Moreover, the requirements on exports of cybersurveillance items in the section on reporting should provide greater intergovernmental, parliamentary and public oversight of member states' export licensing decision making in this area.

Responding to challenges posed by 'emerging technologies'

One of the central challenges that the review process sought to address was managing and responding to the challenges posed by rapidly developing and spreading dual-use technologies—so-called emerging technologies.[33] The issues mainly in focus in the early stages of the review process related to the increasing foreign availability of strategic technologies reducing the effectiveness of export controls.[34] However, the subsequent focus has expanded to include the increased usage of certain emerging technologies such as cloud computing, additive manufacturing (3D printing) and nanotechnology. The review process also sought to address the difficulties posed by the highly technical discussions on emerging technologies—often lacking technical standards—in the multilateral export control regimes and how some of these technologies could transform the ways in which transfers

[31] 'Internal repression', in turn, is defined as including 'inter alia, torture and other cruel, inhuman and degrading treatment or punishment, summary or arbitrary executions, disappearances, arbitrary detentions and other major violations of human rights and fundamental freedoms as set out in relevant international human rights instruments, including the Universal Declaration of Human Rights and the International Covenant on Civil and Political Rights'. Council of the European Union, Common Position 2008/944/CFSP of 8 Dec. 2008 (note 1).

[32] Council of the European Union, 12798/20 (note 9), p. 4, para. 1a.

[33] European Commission, 'The dual-use export control system of the European Union: Ensuring security and competitiveness in a changing world', Green Paper, COM (2011) 393 final, 30 June 2011; and European Commission, 'Ensuring security and competitiveness in a changing world', Communication from the Commission to the Council and the European Parliament on the review of export control policy, COM (2014) 244 final, 24 Apr. 2014.

[34] European Commission, COM (2011) 393 final (note 33).

of controlled items occur.[35] As the recast process continued, the Commission and an increasing number of EU member states began to pay greater attention to the challenges of creating and agreeing on timely controls on transfers of certain emerging technologies that were not currently or only partially captured by the regimes' control lists. In doing so, the EU further expanded the issues it sought to address in relation to emerging technologies and also responded to steps taken by the United States to create new national controls on exports of emerging technologies. In particular, an advance notice of proposed rule-making issued by the US Department of Commerce in 2018—including a list of emerging technology categories—and increasing discussions on competition with China over the leadership in strategic technologies, spurred the international and European debate on this issue.[36] In this context, the Commission came to view the introduction of an EU autonomous control list—which was initially only considered in the context of cybersurveillance items (see previous subsection)—as a means of also allowing the EU to respond more quickly to risks posed by emerging technologies.

The Council strongly rejected the introduction of an autonomous control list but saw the value of creating an EU export control mechanism to address emerging technologies, particularly in cases where the regimes have yet to reach agreement on new measures, including because of the constraints of the consensus rule.[37] The final compromise text acknowledges the need for coordination mechanisms for the EU to use when 'new risks associated with emerging technologies' are identified.[38] However, it noted that any such controls 'should be followed by initiatives to introduce equivalent controls at the multilateral level', which highlights the primary role of the export control regimes in addressing emerging technologies.[39] The final compromise text introduces transmissible controls whereby one member state can use a national control list entry created by another member state under Article 8 to impose an authorization requirement on a particular transfer.[40] The Commission will compile and publish such national control list entries in a watch list to make them available to all member states. A licensing requirement, however, is not triggered automatically but only if the member state assesses that the items 'are or may be intended . . . for uses of concern with respect to public security, including the prevention of acts of terrorism, or to human rights considerations' and has informed the

---

[35] European Commission, COM (2014) 244 final (note 33).
[36] US Department of Commerce, Bureau of Industry and Security, 'Advance notice of proposed rulemaking: Review of controls for certain emerging technologies', *Federal Register*, vol. 83, no. 223 (19 Nov. 2018).
[37] See recital 6 in Council of the European Union, 5 June 2019 (note 3).
[38] Council of the European Union, 12798/20 (note 9), p. 6, para. 6.
[39] Council of the European Union, 12798/20 (note 9), p. 6, para. 6.
[40] Council of the European Union, 12798/20 (note 9), p. 28.

exporter.[41] While Article 8a is structured similarly to a catch-all control, it notably omits any requirement for exporters to inform national authorities if they have knowledge of a specific end use of concern.

Separately, the EU organized a series of technical workshops on emerging technologies for interested member states, led by the Commission and Germany, which took place between November 2019 and December 2020. The series included workshops on additive manufacturing, quantum computing, semiconductors, biotechnologies, brain–computer interfaces and advanced materials, and a virtual workshop on artificial intelligence. The workshop series resulted in a non-public technical report shared among all member states. Notably, the workshops were limited to member states' delegations and did not include public consultations with experts and stakeholders from science, industry or civil society. While an expansion of the workshops to include public consultation elements was considered, after the outbreak of the Covid-19 pandemic the workshop series was initially put on hold and then concluded with virtual workshops which remained exclusive to the member states.

These measures reflect the EU's continued focus on working through the multilateral export control regimes, rather than replacing regime functions. The EU pursued the creation of forums where member states could obtain the latest information and coordinate views on emerging technologies, which they could then bring to the regimes. At the same time the EU acknowledged the possible need for timely unilateral actions by a member state and enabled other member states to easily uphold and replicate such national controls.

The EU common position on arms exports

In September 2019, almost two years after the initiation of the process, the EU member states completed the second review of the common position.[42] The review resulted in a limited number of amendments to the text of the common position and substantive changes to its accompanying user's guide.[43] Some adjustments sought to increase the level of transparency in EU member states' arms exports. In particular, the text of the common position was amended to include a firm deadline for member states' reporting, with a

[41] Council of the European Union, 12798/20 (note 9), pp. 28–29, Article 8a.

[42] Council of the European Union, 'Control of arms export: Council adopts conclusions, new decision updating the EU's common rules and a revised user's guide', Press release, 16 Sep. 2019.

[43] For an overview of the outcome of the second review process of the EU Common Position see Bromley, M. and Maletta, G., 'Developments in the European Union's dual-use and arms trade controls', *SIPRI Yearbook 2020*, pp. 561–64.

view to limiting the delay in the publication of the EU annual report on Arms exports.[44]

In addition, to increase the accessibility of the annual report—traditionally presented in a several hundred pages-long PDF file—the Council of the EU decided to transform it into a 'searchable online database'.[45] In October 2020, the European External Action Service (EEAS) implemented this decision by launching the Council Working Party on Conventional Arms Exports (COARM) online database.[46] The database does not replace the publication of the annual report or increase the level of detail in the data provided.[47] However, the database allows the data to be easily sorted and aggregated by the categories of the EU military list, the country of export and destination, and year; it also provides a clearer visual representation of the data by means of interactive graphs, charts and maps.[48] As of January 2021 data is available for 2013–19. However, the comprehensiveness and comparability of the information included in both the annual report and database remain limited due to the fact that EU member states use different methodologies to collect and submit data, while several are not able to submit any data on actual exports.[49] In this regard, the Council also tasked COARM with improving the quality of the annual report, including by supporting and encouraging states' efforts to submit information on their actual exports.[50]

The Council also tasked COARM with considering measures to harmonize 'end-user certificates for the export of small arms and light weapons and their ammunition' at the EU level.[51] The issue was discussed in COARM in 2020 and EU member states are reportedly close to agreeing a Council Decision providing common minimum elements for these certificates, but no decision had been taken by the end of the year.

---

[44] Council of the European Union, 'Consolidated text: Council Common Position 2008/944/CFSP of 8 December 2008 defining common rules governing control of exports of military technology and equipment', 17 Sep. 2019.

[45] Council of the European Union, 'Council conclusions on the review of Council Common Position 2008/944/CFSP of 8 Dec. 2008 on the control of arms exports', 12195/19, 16 Sep. 2019, p. 4, para. 7.

[46] European External Action Service (EEAS), 'Arms exports control: Launch of online database increasing transparency on EU arms exports', Press release, 26 Oct. 2020; and EEAS, 'Arms export control', 26 Oct. 2020. COARM handles work concerning export controls for conventional arms.

[47] The EU annual report covers (a) the number of export licences issued and their value; (b) the value of arms exports (where available); and (c) the number of denials and the criteria of the EU Common Position invoked in their support.

[48] COARM Online Database, 'Introduction and guidelines', COARM Public v2.0, 16 Dec. 2020.

[49] European Parliament, 'Arms export: Implementation of Common Position 2008/944/CFSP', P9_TA(2020)0224, 17 Sep. 2020, p. 6; Cops, D., 'Past and future of the review of the EU Common Position on arms exports', Flemish Peace Institute, [n.d.]; and Stewart, I. J. et al., *Recommendations for a Transparent and Detailed Reporting System on Arms Exports within the EU and to Third Countries* (Policy Department, Directorate-General for External Policies, European Parliament: Brussels, May 2020), pp. 13–14.

[50] Council of the European Union, 12195/19 (note 45), p. 4, para. 9.

[51] Council of the European Union, 12195/19 (note 45), p. 5, para. 13.

Conclusions

Reaching an agreed final text of a new version of the dual-use regulation was by no means a foregone conclusion and was only possible to the extent that the Commission, Parliament and Council were willing to make concessions in key areas. The outcome ensures that, in most key respects, the dual-use regulation remains tied to the coverage of the multilateral export control regimes and that all decision making on export licences stays at the national level, both of which were key priorities for EU member states. However, significant changes have been made to the dual-use regulation and many adjustments that the Commission or Parliament proposed—and which member states did not initially support—have been implemented, not least in the field of public transparency. In particular, member states have agreed to an ambitious set of reporting practices that could make detailed information about their exports of dual-use items publicly accessible. This is a significant step given the limited transparency in this area that currently exists among most member states. Developments in the common position show that, in the field of arms export controls, making improvements to public transparency is also the area where the EU and its member states seem able to make the most significant advances.

Annexes

Annex A. Arms control and disarmament agreements

Annex B. International security cooperation bodies

Annex C. Chronology 2020

Annex A. Arms control and disarmament agreements

This annex lists multi- and bilateral treaties, conventions, protocols and agreements relating to arms control and disarmament. Unless otherwise stated, the status of agreements and of their parties and signatories is as of 1 January 2021. On the International security cooperation bodies mentioned here, see annex B.

Notes

1. The agreements are divided into universal treaties (i.e. multilateral treaties open to all states, in section I), regional treaties (i.e. multilateral treaties open to states of a particular region, in section II) and bilateral treaties (in section III). Within each section, the agreements are listed in the order of the date on which they were adopted, signed or opened for signature (multilateral agreements) or signed (bilateral agreements). The date on which they entered into force and the depositary for multilateral treaties are also given.

2. The main source of information is the lists of signatories and parties provided by the depositaries of the treaties. In lists of parties and signatories, states whose name appears in italics ratified, acceded or succeeded to, or signed the agreement during 2020.

3. States and organizations listed as parties had ratified, acceded to or succeeded to the agreements by 1 January 2021. Since many agreements delay the entry into force for a state for a certain period after ratification or accession, when that occurred late in 2020 the agreement may not have fully entered into force for that state by 1 January 2021.

4. Former non-self-governing territories, upon attaining statehood, sometimes make general statements of continuity to all agreements concluded by the former governing power. This annex lists as parties only those new states that have made an uncontested declaration on continuity or have notified the depositary of their succession. The Russian Federation continues the international obligations of the Soviet Union.

5. Unless stated otherwise, the multilateral agreements listed in this annex are open to all states, to all states in the respective zone or region, or to all members of a certain international organization for signature, ratification, accession or succession. Not all the signatories and parties are United Nations members. Taiwan, while not recognized as a sovereign state by many countries, is listed as a party to the agreements that it has ratified.

6. Where possible, the location (in a printed publication or online) of an accurate copy of the treaty text is given. This may be provided by a treaty depositary, an agency or secretariat connected with the treaty, or in the *United Nations Treaty Series* (available online at <https://treaties.un.org/>).

I. Universal treaties

Protocol for the Prohibition of the Use in War of Asphyxiating, Poisonous or Other Gases, and of Bacteriological Methods of Warfare (1925 Geneva Protocol)

Signed at Geneva on 17 June 1925; entered into force on 8 February 1928; depositary French Government

The protocol prohibits the use in war of asphyxiating, poisonous or other gases and of bacteriological methods of warfare. The protocol remains a fundamental basis of the international prohibition against chemical and biological warfare, and its principles, objectives and obligations are explicitly supported by the 1972 Biological and Toxin Weapons Convention and the 1993 Chemical Weapons Convention.

Parties (146): Afghanistan, Albania, Algeria, Angola, Antigua and Barbuda, Argentina, Armenia, Australia, Austria, Bahrain, Bangladesh, Barbados, Belgium, Benin, Bhutan, Bolivia, Brazil, Bulgaria, Burkina Faso, Cabo Verde, Cambodia, Cameroon, Canada, Central African Republic, Chile, China, Colombia, Costa Rica, Côte d'Ivoire, Croatia, Cuba, Cyprus, Czechia, Denmark, Dominican Republic, Ecuador, Egypt, El Salvador, Equatorial Guinea, Estonia, Eswatini, Ethiopia, Fiji, Finland, France, Gambia, Germany, Ghana, Greece, Grenada, Guatemala, Guinea-Bissau, Holy See, Hungary, Iceland, India, Indonesia, Iran, Iraq, Ireland, Israel, Italy, Jamaica, Japan, Jordan, *Kazakhstan*, Kenya, Korea (North), Korea (South), Kuwait, *Kyrgyzstan*, Laos, Latvia, Lebanon, Lesotho, Liberia, Libya, Liechtenstein, Lithuania, Luxembourg, Madagascar, Malawi, Malaysia, Maldives, Malta, Mauritius, Mexico, Moldova, Monaco, Mongolia, Morocco, Nepal, Netherlands, New Zealand, Nicaragua, Niger, Nigeria, North Macedonia, Norway, Pakistan, Palestine, Panama, Papua New Guinea, Paraguay, Peru, Philippines, Poland, Portugal, Qatar, Romania, Russia, Rwanda, Saint Kitts and Nevis, Saint Lucia, Saint Vincent and the Grenadines, Saudi Arabia, Senegal, Serbia, Sierra Leone, Slovakia, Slovenia, Solomon Islands, South Africa, Spain, Sri Lanka, Sudan, Sweden, Switzerland, Syria, Taiwan, Tajikistan, Tanzania, Thailand, Togo, Tonga, Trinidad and Tobago, Tunisia, Turkey, Uganda, UK, Ukraine, Uruguay, USA, Venezuela, Viet Nam, Yemen

Notes: On joining the protocol, some states entered reservations which upheld their right to employ chemical or biological weapons against non-parties to the protocol, against coalitions which included non-parties or in response to the use of these weapons by a violating party. Many of these states have withdrawn these reservations, particularly after the conclusion of the 1972 Biological and Toxin Weapons Convention and the 1993 Chemical Weapons Convention since the reservations are incompatible with their obligation under the conventions.

In addition to these, 'explicit', reservations, a number of states that made a declaration of succession to the protocol on gaining independence inherited 'implicit' reservations from their respective predecessor states. For example, these implicit reservations apply to the states that gained independence from France and the UK before the latter states withdrew or amended their reservations. States that acceded (rather than succeeded) to the protocol did not inherit reservations in this way.

Protocol text: League of Nations, *Treaty Series*, vol. 94 (1929), pp. 65–74, <https://treaties.un.org/doc/Publication/UNTS/LON/Volume 94/v94.pdf>

Convention on the Prevention and Punishment of the Crime of Genocide (Genocide Convention)

Opened for signature at Paris on 9 December 1948; entered into force on 12 January 1951; depositary UN Secretary-General

Under the convention any commission of acts intended to destroy, in whole or in part, a national, ethnic, racial or religious group as such is declared to be a crime punishable under international law.

Parties (152): Afghanistan, Albania*, Algeria*, Andorra, Antigua and Barbuda, Argentina*, Armenia, Australia, Austria, Azerbaijan, Bahamas, Bahrain*, Bangladesh*, Barbados, Belarus*, Belgium, Belize, Benin, Bolivia, Bosnia and Herzegovina, Brazil, Bulgaria*, Burkina Faso, Burundi, Cabo Verde, Cambodia, Canada, Chile, China*, Colombia, Comoros, Congo (Democratic Republic of the), Costa Rica, Côte d'Ivoire, Croatia, Cuba, Cyprus, Czechia, Denmark, Dominica, Ecuador, Egypt, El Salvador, Estonia, Ethiopia, Fiji, Finland, France, Gabon, Gambia, Georgia, Germany, Ghana, Greece, Guatemala, Guinea, Guinea-Bissau, Haiti, Honduras, Hungary*, Iceland, India*, Iran, Iraq, Ireland, Israel, Italy, Jamaica, Jordan, Kazakhstan, Korea (North), Korea (South), Kuwait, Kyrgyzstan, Laos, Latvia, Lebanon, Lesotho, Liberia, Libya, Liechtenstein, Lithuania, Luxembourg, Malawi, Malaysia*, Maldives, Mali, Malta, Mauritius, Mexico, Moldova, Monaco, Mongolia*, Montenegro*, Morocco*, Mozambique, Myanmar*, Namibia, Nepal, Netherlands, New Zealand, Nicaragua, Nigeria, North Macedonia, Norway, Pakistan, Palestine, Panama, Papua New Guinea, Paraguay, Peru, Philippines*, Poland*, Portugal, Romania*, Russia*, Rwanda, Saint Vincent and the Grenadines, San Marino, Saudi Arabia, Senegal, Serbia*, Seychelles, Singapore*, Slovakia, Slovenia, South Africa, Spain, Sri Lanka, Sudan, Sweden, Switzerland, Syria, Tajikistan, Tanzania, Togo, Tonga, Trinidad and Tobago, Tunisia, Turkey, Turkmenistan, Uganda, UK, Ukraine*, United Arab Emirates*, Uruguay, USA*, Uzbekistan, Venezuela*, Viet Nam*, Yemen*, Zimbabwe

* With reservation and/or declaration.

Signed but not ratified (1): Dominican Republic

Convention text: United Nations Treaty Collection, <https://treaties.un.org/doc/Treaties/1951 /01/19510112 08-12 PM/Ch_IV_1p.pdf>

Geneva Convention (IV) Relative to the Protection of Civilian Persons in Time of War

Opened for signature at Geneva on 12 August 1949; entered into force on 21 October 1950; depositary Swiss Federal Council

The Geneva Convention (IV) establishes rules for the protection of civilians in areas covered by war and in occupied territories. Three other conventions were formulated at the same time, at a diplomatic conference held from 21 April to 12 August 1949: Convention (I) for the Amelioration of the Condition of the Wounded and Sick in Armed Forces in the Field; Convention (II) for the Amelioration of the Condition of the Wounded, Sick and Shipwrecked Members of Armed Forces at Sea; and Convention (III) Relative to the Treatment of Prisoners of War.

A party may withdraw from the convention, having given one year's notice. But if the party is involved in an armed conflict at that time, the withdrawal will not take effect until peace has been concluded and that party's obligations under the convention fulfilled.

Parties (196): Afghanistan, Albania*, Algeria, Andorra, Angola*, Antigua and Barbuda, Argentina, Armenia, Australia*, Austria, Azerbaijan, Bahamas, Bahrain, Bangladesh*, Barbados*, Belarus, Belgium, Belize, Benin, Bhutan, Bolivia, Bosnia and Herzegovina, Botswana, Brazil, Brunei Darussalam, Bulgaria, Burkina Faso, Burundi, Cabo Verde, Cambodia, Cameroon, Canada, Central African Republic, Chad, Chile, China*, Colombia, Comoros, Congo (Democratic Republic of the), Congo (Republic of the), Cook Islands, Costa Rica, Côte d'Ivoire, Croatia, Cuba, Cyprus, Czechia*, Denmark, Djibouti, Dominica, Dominican Republic, Ecuador, Egypt, El Salvador, Equatorial Guinea, Estonia, Eritrea, Eswatini, Ethiopia, Fiji, Finland, France, Gabon, Gambia, Georgia, Germany*, Ghana, Greece, Grenada, Guatemala, Guinea, Guinea-Bissau*, Guyana, Haiti, Holy See, Honduras, Hungary, Iceland, India, Indonesia, Iran*, Iraq, Ireland, Israel*, Italy, Jamaica, Japan, Jordan, Kazakhstan, Kenya, Kiribati, Korea (North)*, Korea (South)*, Kuwait*, Kyrgyzstan, Laos, Latvia, Lebanon, Lesotho, Liberia, Libya, Liechtenstein, Lithuania, Luxembourg, Madagascar, Malawi, Malaysia, Maldives, Mali, Malta, Marshall Islands, Mauritania, Mauritius, Mexico, Micronesia, Moldova, Monaco, Mongolia, Montenegro, Morocco, Mozambique, Myanmar, Namibia, Nauru, Nepal, Netherlands, New Zealand*, Nicaragua, Niger, Nigeria, North Macedonia*, Norway, Oman, Pakistan*, Palau, Palestine, Panama, Papua New Guinea, Paraguay, Peru, Philippines, Poland, Portugal*, Qatar, Romania, Russia*, Rwanda, Saint Kitts and Nevis, Saint Lucia, Saint Vincent and the Grenadines, Samoa, San Marino, Sao Tome and Principe, Saudi Arabia, Senegal, Serbia, Seychelles, Sierra Leone, Singapore, Slovakia, Slovenia, Solomon Islands, Somalia, South Africa, South Sudan, Spain, Sri Lanka, Sudan, Suriname*, Sweden, Switzerland, Syria, Tajikistan, Tanzania, Thailand, Timor-Leste, Togo, Tonga, Trinidad and Tobago, Tunisia, Turkey, Turkmenistan, Tuvalu, Uganda, UK*, Ukraine*, United Arab Emirates, Uruguay*, USA*, Uzbekistan, Vanuatu, Venezuela, Viet Nam*, Yemen*, Zambia, Zimbabwe

  * With reservation and/or declaration.

Convention text: Swiss Federal Department of Foreign Affairs, <https://www.fdfa.admin.ch/dam/eda/fr/documents/aussenpolitik/voelkerrecht/geneve/070116-conv4_e.pdf>

Protocol I Additional to the 1949 Geneva Conventions, and Relating to the Protection of Victims of International Armed Conflicts

Protocol II Additional to the 1949 Geneva Conventions, and Relating to the Protection of Victims of Non-International Armed Conflicts

Opened for signature at Bern on 12 December 1977; entered into force on 7 December 1978; depositary Swiss Federal Council

The protocols confirm that the right of parties that are engaged in international or non-international armed conflicts to choose methods or means of warfare is not unlimited and that the use of weapons or means of warfare that cause superfluous injury or unnecessary suffering is prohibited.

Article 36 of Protocol I requires a state party, when developing or acquiring a new weapon, to determine whether its use could be prohibited by international law.

Parties to Protocol I (174) and Protocol II (169): Afghanistan, Albania, Algeria*, Angola*, Antigua and Barbuda, Argentina*, Armenia, Australia*, Austria*, Bahamas,

Bahrain, Bangladesh, Barbados, Belarus*, Belgium*, Belize, Benin, Bolivia*, Bosnia and Herzegovina*, Botswana, Brazil*, Brunei Darussalam, Bulgaria*, Burkina Faso*, Burundi, Cabo Verde*, Cambodia, Cameroon, Canada*, Central African Republic, Chad, Chile*, China*, Colombia*, Comoros, Congo (Democratic Republic of the)*, Congo (Republic of the), Cook Islands*, Costa Rica*, Côte d'Ivoire, Croatia*, Cuba, Cyprus*, Czechia*, Denmark*, Djibouti, Dominica, Dominican Republic, Ecuador, Egypt*, El Salvador, Equatorial Guinea, Estonia*, Eswatini, Ethiopia, Fiji, Finland*, France*, Gabon, Gambia, Georgia, Germany*, Ghana, Greece*, Grenada, Guatemala, Guinea*, Guinea-Bissau, Guyana, Haiti, Holy See*, Honduras, Hungary*, Iceland*, Iraq[1], Ireland*, Italy*, Jamaica, Japan*, Jordan, Kazakhstan, Kenya, Korea (North)[1], Korea (South)*, Kuwait*, Kyrgyzstan, Laos*, Latvia, Lebanon, Lesotho*, Liberia, Libya, Liechtenstein*, Lithuania*, Luxembourg*, Madagascar*, Malawi*, Maldives, Mali*, Malta*, Mauritania, Mauritius*, Mexico[1], Micronesia, Moldova, Monaco*, Mongolia*, Montenegro*, Morocco, Mozambique, Namibia*, Nauru, Netherlands*, New Zealand*, Nicaragua, Niger, Nigeria, North Macedonia*, Norway*, Oman*, Palau, Palestine, Panama*, Paraguay*, Peru, Philippines*, Poland*, Portugal*, Qatar*, Romania*, Russia*, Rwanda*, Saint Kitts and Nevis*, Saint Lucia, Saint Vincent and the Grenadines*, Samoa, San Marino, Sao Tome and Principe, Saudi Arabia*, Senegal, Serbia*, Seychelles*, Sierra Leone, Slovakia*, Slovenia*, Solomon Islands, South Africa, South Sudan, Spain*, Sudan, Suriname, Sweden*, Switzerland*, Syria*[1], Tajikistan*, Tanzania, Timor-Leste, Togo*, Tonga*, Trinidad and Tobago*, Tunisia, Turkmenistan, Uganda, UK*, Ukraine*, United Arab Emirates*, Uruguay*, Uzbekistan, Vanuatu, Venezuela, Viet Nam[1], Yemen, Zambia, Zimbabwe

* With reservation and/or declaration.
[1] Party only to Protocol I.

Signed but not ratified Protocols I and II (3): Iran, Pakistan, USA

Protocol I text: Swiss Federal Department of Foreign Affairs, <https://www.fdfa. admin.ch/dam/eda/fr/documents/aussenpolitik/voelkerrecht/geneve/77prot1_ en.pdf>

Protocol II text: Swiss Federal Department of Foreign Affairs, <https://www.fdfa. admin.ch/dam/eda/fr/documents/aussenpolitik/voelkerrecht/geneve77prot2_ en.pdf>

Antarctic Treaty

Signed by the 12 original parties at Washington, DC, on 1 December 1959; entered into force on 23 June 1961; depositary US Government

The treaty declares the Antarctic an area to be used exclusively for peaceful purposes. It prohibits any measure of a military nature in the Antarctic, such as the establishment of military bases and fortifications, and the carrying out of military manoeuvres or the testing of any type of weapon. The treaty bans any nuclear explosion as well as the disposal of radioactive waste material in Antarctica.

States that demonstrate their interest in Antarctica by conducting substantial scientific research activity there, such as the establishment of a scientific station or the dispatch of a scientific expedition, are entitled to become consultative parties. Consultative parties meet at regular intervals to exchange information and hold consultations on matters pertaining to Antarctica, as well as to recommend to their governments measures in furtherance of the principles and objectives of the treaty. Consultative parties have a right to inspect any station or installation in Antarctica to ensure compliance with the treaty's provisions.

Parties (54): Argentina*, Australia*, Austria, Belarus, Belgium*, Brazil*, Bulgaria*, Canada, Chile*, China*, Colombia, Cuba, Czechia*, Denmark, Ecuador*, Estonia, Finland*, France*, Germany*, Greece, Guatemala, Hungary, Iceland, India*, Italy*, Japan*, Kazakhstan, Korea (North), Korea (South)*, Malaysia, Monaco, Mongolia, Netherlands*, New Zealand*, Norway*, Pakistan, Papua New Guinea, Peru*, Poland*, Portugal, Romania, Russia*, Slovakia, Slovenia, South Africa*, Spain*, Sweden*, Switzerland, Turkey, UK*, Ukraine*, Uruguay*, USA*, Venezuela

* Consultative party (29) under Article IX of the treaty.

Treaty text: Secretariat of the Antarctic Treaty, <https://www.ats.aq/documents/ats/treaty_original.pdf>

The Protocol on Environmental Protection (**1991 Madrid Protocol**) was opened for signature on 4 October 1991 and entered into force on 14 January 1998. It designated Antarctica as a natural reserve, devoted to peace and science.

Protocol text: Secretariat of the Antarctic Treaty, <https://www.ats.aq/documents/recatt/Att006_e.pdf>

Treaty Banning Nuclear Weapon Tests in the Atmosphere, in Outer Space and Under Water (Partial Test-Ban Treaty, PTBT)

Signed by three original parties at Moscow on 5 August 1963 and opened for signature by other states at London, Moscow and Washington, DC, on 8 August 1963; entered into force on 10 October 1963; depositaries British, Russian and US governments

The treaty prohibits the carrying out of any nuclear weapon test explosion or any other nuclear explosion (*a*) in the atmosphere, beyond its limits, including outer space, or under water, including territorial waters or high seas; and (*b*) in any other environment if such explosion causes radioactive debris to be present outside the territorial limits of the state under whose jurisdiction or control the explosion is conducted.

A party may withdraw from the treaty, having given three months' notice, if it decides that its supreme interests have been jeopardized by extraordinary events related to the treaty's subject matter.

Parties (126): Afghanistan, Antigua and Barbuda, Argentina, Armenia, Australia, Austria, Bahamas, Bangladesh, Belarus, Belgium, Benin, Bhutan, Bolivia, Bosnia and Herzegovina, Botswana, Brazil, Bulgaria, Cabo Verde, Canada, Central African Republic, Chad, Chile, Colombia, Congo (Democratic Republic of the), Costa Rica, Côte d'Ivoire, Croatia, Cyprus, Czechia, Denmark, Dominican Republic, Ecuador, Egypt, El Salvador, Equatorial Guinea, Eswatini, Fiji, Finland, Gabon, Gambia, Germany, Ghana, Greece, Guatemala, Guinea-Bissau, Honduras, Hungary, Iceland, India, Indonesia, Iran, Iraq, Ireland, Israel, Italy, Jamaica, Japan, Jordan, Kenya, Korea (South), Kuwait, Laos, Lebanon, Liberia, Libya, Luxembourg, Madagascar, Malawi, Malaysia, Malta, Mauritania, Mauritius, Mexico, Mongolia, Montenegro, Morocco, Myanmar, Nepal, Netherlands, New Zealand, Nicaragua, Niger, Nigeria, Norway, Pakistan, Panama, Papua New Guinea, Peru, Philippines, Poland, Romania, Russia, Rwanda, Samoa, San Marino, Senegal, Serbia, Seychelles, Sierra Leone, Singapore,

Slovakia, Slovenia, South Africa, Spain, Sri Lanka, Sudan, Suriname, Sweden, Switzerland, Syria, Taiwan, Tanzania, Thailand, Togo, Tonga, Trinidad and Tobago, Tunisia, Turkey, Uganda, UK, Ukraine, Uruguay, USA, Venezuela, Yemen, Zambia

Signed but not ratified (10): Algeria, Burkina Faso, Burundi, Cameroon, Ethiopia, Haiti, Mali, Paraguay, Portugal, Somalia

Treaty text: Russian Ministry of Foreign Affairs, <https://mddoc.mid.ru/api/ia/download/?uuid=561590f5-ed1a-4e2a-a04e-f715bccb16ad>

Treaty on Principles Governing the Activities of States in the Exploration and Use of Outer Space, Including the Moon and Other Celestial Bodies (Outer Space Treaty)

Opened for signature at London, Moscow and Washington, DC, on 27 January 1967; entered into force on 10 October 1967; depositaries British, Russian and US governments

The treaty prohibits the placing into orbit around the earth of any object carrying nuclear weapons or any other kind of weapon of mass destruction, the installation of such weapons on celestial bodies, or the stationing of them in outer space in any other manner. The establishment of military bases, installations and fortifications, the testing of any type of weapon and the conducting of military manoeuvres on celestial bodies are also forbidden.

A party may withdraw from the treaty having given one year's notice.

Parties (111): Afghanistan, Algeria, Antigua and Barbuda, Argentina, Armenia, Australia, Austria, Azerbaijan, Bahamas, Bahrain, Bangladesh, Barbados, Belarus, Belgium, Benin, Brazil, Bulgaria, Burkina Faso, Canada, Chile, China, Cuba, Cyprus, Czechia, Denmark, Dominican Republic, Ecuador, Egypt, El Salvador, Equatorial Guinea, Estonia, Fiji, Finland, France, Germany, Greece, Guinea-Bissau, Hungary, Iceland, India, Indonesia, Iraq, Ireland, Israel, Italy, Jamaica, Japan, Kazakhstan, Kenya, Korea (North), Korea (South), Kuwait, Laos, Lebanon, Libya, Lithuania, Luxembourg, Madagascar, Mali, Malta, Mauritius, Mexico, Mongolia, Morocco, Myanmar, Nepal, Netherlands, New Zealand, Nicaragua, Niger, Nigeria, Norway, Pakistan, Papua New Guinea, Paraguay, Peru, Poland, Portugal, Qatar, Romania, Russia, Saint Vincent and the Grenadines, San Marino, Saudi Arabia, Seychelles, Sierra Leone, Singapore, Slovakia, Slovenia, South Africa, Spain, Sri Lanka, Sweden, Switzerland, Syria, Taiwan, Thailand, Togo, Tonga, Tunisia, Turkey, Uganda, UK, Ukraine, United Arab Emirates, Uruguay, USA, Venezuela, Viet Nam, Yemen, Zambia

Signed but not ratified (25): Bolivia, Botswana, Burundi, Cameroon, Central African Republic, Colombia, Congo (Democratic Republic of the), Ethiopia, Gambia, Ghana, Guyana, Haiti, Holy See, Honduras, Iran, Jordan, Lesotho, Malaysia, Montenegro, Panama, Philippines, Rwanda, Serbia, Somalia, Trinidad and Tobago

Treaty text: British Foreign and Commonwealth Office, Treaty Series no. 10 (1968), <https://assets.publishing.service.gov.uk/government/uploads/system/uploads/attachment_data/file/270006/Treaty_Principles_Activities_Outer_Space.pdf>

Treaty on the Non-Proliferation of Nuclear Weapons (Non-Proliferation Treaty, NPT)

Opened for signature at London, Moscow and Washington, DC, on 1 July 1968; entered into force on 5 March 1970; depositaries British, Russian and US governments

The treaty defines a nuclear weapon state to be a state that manufactured and exploded a nuclear weapon or other nuclear explosive device prior to 1 January 1967. According to this definition, there are five nuclear weapon states: China, France, Russia, the United Kingdom and the United States. All other states are defined as non-nuclear weapon states.

The treaty prohibits the nuclear weapon states from transferring nuclear weapons or other nuclear explosive devices or control over them to any recipient and prohibits them from assisting, encouraging or inducing any non-nuclear weapon state to manufacture or otherwise acquire such a weapon or device. It also prohibits non-nuclear weapon states parties from receiving nuclear weapons or other nuclear explosive devices from any source, from manufacturing them, or from acquiring them in any other way.

The parties undertake to facilitate the exchange of equipment, materials, and scientific and technological information for the peaceful uses of nuclear energy and to ensure that potential benefits from peaceful applications of nuclear explosions will be made available to non-nuclear weapon states party to the treaty. They also undertake to pursue negotiations in good faith on effective measures relating to cessation of the nuclear arms race at an early date and to nuclear disarmament, and on a treaty on general and complete disarmament.

Non-nuclear weapon states parties undertake to conclude safeguard agreements with the International Atomic Energy Agency (IAEA) with a view to preventing diversion of nuclear energy from peaceful uses to nuclear weapons or other nuclear explosive devices. A Model Protocol Additional to the Safeguards Agreements, strengthening the measures, was approved in 1997; additional safeguards protocols are signed by states individually with the IAEA.

A review and extension conference, convened in 1995 in accordance with the treaty, decided that the treaty should remain in force indefinitely. A party may withdraw from the treaty, having given three months' notice, if it decides that its supreme interests have been jeopardized by extraordinary events related to the treaty's subject matter.

Parties (192): Afghanistan*, Albania*, Algeria*, Andorra*, Angola*, Antigua and Barbuda*, Argentina*, Armenia*, Australia*, Austria*, Azerbaijan*, Bahamas*, Bahrain*, Bangladesh*, Barbados*, Belarus*, Belgium*, Belize*, Benin*, Bhutan*, Bolivia*, Bosnia and Herzegovina*, Botswana*, Brazil*, Brunei Darussalam*, Bulgaria*, Burkina Faso*, Burundi*, Cabo Verde, Cambodia*, Cameroon*, Canada*, Central African Republic*, Chad*, Chile*, China*†, Colombia*, Comoros*, Congo (Democratic Republic of the)*, Congo (Republic of the)*, Costa Rica*, Côte d'Ivoire*, Croatia*, Cuba*, Cyprus*, Czechia*, Denmark*, Djibouti*, Dominica*, Dominican Republic*, Ecuador*, Egypt*, El Salvador*, Equatorial Guinea, Eritrea, Estonia*, Eswatini*, Ethiopia*, Fiji*, Finland*, France*†, Gabon*, Gambia*, Georgia*, Germany*, Ghana*, Greece*, Grenada*, Guatemala*, Guinea, Guinea-Bissau*, Guyana*, Haiti*, Holy See*, Honduras*, Hungary*, Iceland*, Indonesia*, Iran*, Iraq*, Ireland*, Italy*, Jamaica*, Japan*, Jordan*, Kazakhstan*, Kenya*, Kiribati*, Korea (South)*, Korea (North)‡, Kuwait*,

Kyrgyzstan*, Laos*, Latvia*, Lebanon*, Lesotho*, Liberia*, Libya*, Liechtenstein*, Lithuania*, Luxembourg*, Madagascar*, Malawi*, Malaysia*, Maldives*, Mali*, Malta*, Marshall Islands*, Mauritania*, Mauritius*, Mexico*, Micronesia, Moldova*, Monaco*, Mongolia*, Montenegro*, Morocco*, Mozambique*, Myanmar*, Namibia*, Nauru*, Nepal*, Netherlands*, New Zealand*, Nicaragua*, Niger*, Nigeria*, North Macedonia*, Norway*, Oman*, Palau*, Palestine, Panama*, Papua New Guinea*, Paraguay*, Peru*, Philippines*, Poland*, Portugal*, Qatar*, Romania*, Russia*†, Rwanda*, Saint Kitts and Nevis*, Saint Lucia*, Saint Vincent and the Grenadines*, Samoa*, San Marino*, Sao Tome and Principe, Saudi Arabia*, Senegal*, Serbia*, Seychelles*, Sierra Leone*, Singapore*, Slovakia*, Slovenia*, Solomon Islands*, Somalia, South Africa*, Spain*, Sri Lanka*, Sudan*, Suriname*, Sweden*, Switzerland*, Syria*, Taiwan*, Tajikistan*, Tanzania*, Thailand*, Timor-Leste, Togo*, Tonga*, Trinidad and Tobago*, Tunisia*, Turkey*, Turkmenistan*, Tuvalu*, Uganda*, UK*†, Ukraine*, United Arab Emirates*, Uruguay*, USA*†, Uzbekistan*, Vanuatu*, Venezuela*, Viet Nam*, Yemen*, Zambia*, Zimbabwe*

* Party (181) with safeguards agreements in force with the IAEA, as required by the treaty, or concluded by a nuclear weapon state on a voluntary basis. In addition to these 181 states, as of 1 Jan. 2021 Cabo Verde, Guinea, Guinea-Bissau, Micronesia, Palestine, Timor-Leste had each signed a safeguards agreement that had not yet entered into force.

† Nuclear weapon state as defined by the treaty.

‡ On 12 Mar. 1993 North Korea announced its withdrawal from the NPT with effect from 12 June 1993. It decided to 'suspend' the withdrawal on 11 June. On 10 Jan. 2003 North Korea announced its 'immediate' withdrawal from the NPT. A safeguards agreement was in force at that time. The current status of North Korea is disputed by the other parties.

Treaty text: International Atomic Energy Agency, INFCIRC/140, 22 Apr. 1970, <https://www.iaea.org/sites/default/files/publications/documents/infcircs/1970/infcirc140.pdf>

Additional safeguards protocols in force (137): Afghanistan, Albania, Andorra, Angola, Antigua and Barbuda, Armenia, Australia, Austria, Azerbaijan, Bahrain, Bangladesh, Belgium, Benin, Bosnia and Herzegovina, Botswana, Bulgaria, Burkina Faso, Burundi, Cambodia, Cameroon, Canada, Central African Republic, Chad, Chile, China, Colombia, Comoros, Congo (Democratic Republic of the), Congo (Republic of), Costa Rica, Côte d'Ivoire, Croatia, Cuba, Cyprus, Czechia, Denmark[1], Djibouti, Dominican Republic, Ecuador, El Salvador, Estonia, Eswatini, Ethiopia, Euratom, Fiji, Finland, France, Gabon, Gambia, Georgia, Germany, Ghana, Greece, Guatemala, Haiti, Holy See, Honduras, Hungary, Iceland, India, Indonesia, Iraq, Ireland, Italy, Jamaica, Japan, Jordan, Kazakhstan, Kenya, Korea (South), Kuwait, Kyrgyzstan, Latvia, Lesotho, Liberia, Libya, Liechtenstein, Lithuania, Luxembourg, Madagascar, Malawi, Mali, Malta, Marshall Islands, Mauritania, Mauritius, Mexico, Moldova, Monaco, Mongolia, Montenegro, Morocco, Mozambique, Namibia, Netherlands, New Zealand, Nicaragua, Niger, Nigeria, North Macedonia, Norway, Palau, Panama, Paraguay, Peru, Philippines, Poland, Portugal, Romania, Russia, Rwanda, Saint Kitts and Nevis, Senegal, Serbia, Seychelles, Singapore, Slovakia, Slovenia, South Africa, Spain, Sweden, Switzerland, Tajikistan, Tanzania, Thailand, Togo, Turkey, Turkmenistan, Uganda, UK, Ukraine, United Arab Emirates, Uruguay, USA, Uzbekistan, Vanuatu, Viet Nam

[1] A separate additional protocol is also in force for the Danish territory of Greenland.

Note: Taiwan has agreed to apply the measures contained in the Model Additional Protocol.

Additional safeguards protocols signed but not yet in force (14): Algeria, Belarus, Bolivia, Cabo Verde, Guinea, Guinea-Bissau, Iran*, Kiribati, Laos, Malaysia, Myanmar, Timor-Leste, Tunisia, Zambia

* Iran notified the IAEA that as of 16 Jan. 2016 it would provisionally apply the Additional Protocol that it signed in 2003 but has not yet ratified.

Model Additional Safeguards Protocol text: International Atomic Energy Agency, INFCIRC/540 (corrected), Sep. 1997, <https://www.iaea.org/sites/default/files/infcirc540c.pdf>

Treaty on the Prohibition of the Emplacement of Nuclear Weapons and other Weapons of Mass Destruction on the Seabed and the Ocean Floor and in the Subsoil thereof (Seabed Treaty)

Opened for signature at London, Moscow and Washington, DC, on 11 February 1971; entered into force on 18 May 1972; depositaries British, Russian and US governments

The treaty prohibits implanting or emplacing on the seabed and the ocean floor and in the subsoil thereof beyond the outer limit of a 12-nautical mile (22-kilometre) seabed zone any nuclear weapon or any other type of weapon of mass destruction as well as structures, launching installations or any other facilities specifically designed for storing, testing or using such weapons.

A party may withdraw from the treaty, having given three months' notice, if it decides that its supreme interests have been jeopardized by extraordinary events related to the treaty's subject matter.

Parties (95): Afghanistan, Algeria, Antigua and Barbuda, Argentina, Australia, Austria, Bahamas, Belarus, Belgium, Benin, Bosnia and Herzegovina, Botswana, Brazil*, Bulgaria, Canada*, Cabo Verde, Central African Republic, China, Congo (Republic of the), Côte d'Ivoire, Cuba, Cyprus, Czechia, Denmark, Dominican Republic, Eswatini, Ethiopia, Finland, Germany, Ghana, Greece, Guatemala, Guinea-Bissau, Hungary, Iceland, India*, Iran, Iraq, Ireland, Italy*, Jamaica, Japan, Jordan, Korea (South), Laos, Latvia, Lesotho, Libya, Liechtenstein, Luxembourg, Malaysia, Malta, Mauritius, Mexico*, Mongolia, Montenegro, Morocco, Nepal, Netherlands, New Zealand, Nicaragua, Niger, Norway, Panama, Philippines, Poland, Portugal, Qatar, Romania, Russia, Rwanda, Saint Kitts and Nevis, Saint Vincent and the Grenadines, Sao Tome and Principe, Saudi Arabia, Serbia*, Seychelles, Singapore, Slovakia, Slovenia, Solomon Islands, South Africa, Spain, Sweden, Switzerland, Taiwan, Togo, Tunisia, Turkey*, UK, Ukraine, USA, Viet Nam*, Yemen, Zambia

* With reservation and/or declaration.

Signed but not ratified (21): Bolivia, Burundi, Cambodia, Cameroon, Colombia, Costa Rica, Equatorial Guinea, Gambia, Guinea, Honduras, Lebanon, Liberia, Madagascar, Mali, Myanmar, Paraguay, Senegal, Sierra Leone, Sudan, Tanzania, Uruguay

Treaty text: British Foreign and Commonwealth Office, Treaty Series no. 13 (1973), <https://assets.publishing.service.gov.uk/government/uploads/system/uploads/attachment_data/file/269694/Treaty_Prohib_Nuclear_Sea-Bed.pdf>

Convention on the Prohibition of the Development, Production and Stockpiling of Bacteriological (Biological) and Toxin Weapons and on their Destruction (Biological and Toxin Weapons Convention, BWC)

Opened for signature at London, Moscow and Washington, DC, on 10 April 1972; entered into force on 26 March 1975; depositaries British, Russian and US governments

The convention prohibits the development, production, stockpiling or acquisition by other means or retention of microbial or other biological agents or toxins (whatever their origin or method of production) of types and in quantities that have no justification of prophylactic, protective or other peaceful purposes. It also prohibits weapons, equipment or means of delivery designed to use such agents or toxins for hostile purposes or in armed conflict. The destruction of the agents, toxins, weapons, equipment and means of delivery in the possession of the parties, or their diversion to peaceful purposes, should be completed not later than nine months after the entry into force of the convention for each country.

The parties hold annual political and technical meetings to strengthen implementation of the convention. A three-person Implementation Support Unit (ISU), based in Geneva, was established in 2007 to support the parties in implementing the treaty, including facilitating the collection and distribution of annual confidence-building measures and supporting their efforts to achieve universal membership.

A party may withdraw from the convention, having given three months' notice, if it decides that its supreme interests have been jeopardized by extraordinary events related to the treaty's subject matter.

Parties (184): Afghanistan, Albania, Algeria, Andorra, Angola, Antigua and Barbuda, Argentina, Armenia, Australia, Austria*, Azerbaijan, Bahamas, Bahrain*, Bangladesh, Barbados, Belarus, Belgium, Belize, Benin, Bhutan, Bolivia, Bosnia and Herzegovina, Botswana, Brazil, Brunei Darussalam, Bulgaria, Burkina Faso, Burundi, Cabo Verde, Cambodia, Cameroon, Canada, Central African Republic, Chile, China*, Colombia, Congo (Democratic Republic of the), Congo (Republic of the), Cook Islands, Costa Rica, Côte d'Ivoire, Croatia, Cuba, Cyprus, Czechia*, Denmark, Dominica, Dominican Republic, Ecuador, El Salvador, Equatorial Guinea, Estonia, Eswatini, Ethiopia, Fiji, Finland, France, Gabon, Gambia, Georgia, Germany, Ghana, Greece, Grenada, Guatemala, Guinea, Guinea-Bissau, Guyana, Holy See, Honduras, Hungary, Iceland, India*, Indonesia, Iran, Iraq, Ireland*, Italy, Jamaica, Japan, Jordan, Kazakhstan, Kenya, Korea (North), Korea (South)*, Kuwait*, Kyrgyzstan, Laos, Latvia, Lebanon, Lesotho, Liberia, Libya, Liechtenstein, Lithuania, Luxembourg, Madagascar, Malawi, Malaysia*, Maldives, Mali, Malta, Marshall Islands, Mauritania, Mauritius, Mexico*, Moldova, Monaco, Mongolia, Montenegro, Morocco, Mozambique, Myanmar, Nauru, Nepal, Netherlands, New Zealand, Nicaragua, Niger, Nigeria, Niue, North Macedonia, Norway, Oman, Pakistan, Palau, Palestine, Panama, Papua New Guinea, Paraguay, Peru, Philippines, Poland, Portugal, Qatar, Romania, Russia, Rwanda, Saint Kitts and Nevis, Saint Lucia, Saint Vincent and the Grenadines, Samoa, San Marino, Sao Tome and Principe, Saudi Arabia, Senegal, Serbia, Seychelles, Sierra Leone, Singapore, Slovakia*, Slovenia, Solomon Islands, South Africa, Spain, Sri Lanka, Sudan, Suriname, Sweden, Switzerland*, Taiwan, Tajikistan, Tanzania, Thailand, Timor-Leste, Togo, Tonga, Trinidad and Tobago, Tunisia, Turkey, Turkmenistan, Uganda, UK*, Ukraine, United Arab Emirates, Uruguay, USA, Uzbekistan, Vanuatu, Venezuela, Viet Nam, Yemen, Zambia, Zimbabwe

* With reservation and/or declaration.

Signed but not ratified (4): Egypt, Haiti, Somalia, Syria

Treaty text: British Foreign and Commonwealth Office, Treaty Series no. 11 (1976), <https://assets.publishing.service.gov.uk/government/uploads/system/uploads/attachment_data/file/269698/Convention_Prohibition_Stock_Bacterio.pdf>

Convention on the Prohibition of Military or Any Other Hostile Use of Environmental Modification Techniques (Enmod Convention)

Opened for signature at Geneva on 18 May 1977; entered into force on 5 October 1978; depositary UN Secretary-General

The convention prohibits military or any other hostile use of environmental modification techniques that have widespread, long-lasting or severe effects as the means of destruction, damage or injury to states parties. The term 'environmental modification techniques' refers to any technique for changing—through the deliberate manipulation of natural processes—the dynamics, composition or structure of the earth, including its biota, lithosphere, hydrosphere and atmosphere, or of outer space. Understandings reached during the negotiations, but not written into the convention, define the terms 'widespread', 'long-lasting' and 'severe'.

Parties (78): Afghanistan, Algeria, Antigua and Barbuda, Argentina*, Armenia, Australia, Austria*, Bangladesh, Belarus, Belgium, Benin, Brazil, Bulgaria, Cabo Verde, Cameroon, Canada, Chile, China, Costa Rica, Cuba, Cyprus, Czechia, Denmark, Dominica, Egypt, Estonia, Finland, Germany, Ghana, Greece, Guatemala*, Honduras, Hungary, India, Ireland, Italy, Japan, Kazakhstan, Korea (North), Korea (South)*, Kuwait*, Kyrgyzstan, Lithuania, Laos, Malawi, Mauritius, Mongolia, Netherlands*, New Zealand*, Nicaragua, Niger, Norway, Pakistan, Palestine, Panama, Papua New Guinea, Poland, Romania, Russia, Saint Lucia, Saint Vincent and the Grenadines, Sao Tome and Principe, Slovakia, Slovenia, Solomon Islands, Spain, Sri Lanka, Sweden, Switzerland*, Tajikistan, Tunisia, UK, Ukraine, Uruguay, USA, Uzbekistan, Viet Nam, Yemen

   * With reservation and/or declaration.

Signed but not ratified (16): Bolivia, Congo (Democratic Republic of the), Ethiopia, Holy See, Iceland, Iran, Iraq, Lebanon, Liberia, Luxembourg, Morocco, Portugal, Sierra Leone, Syria, Turkey, Uganda

Convention text: United Nations Treaty Collection, <https://treaties.un.org/doc/Treaties/1978/10/19781005 00-39 AM/Ch_XXVI_01p.pdf>

Convention on the Physical Protection of Nuclear Material and Nuclear Facilities

Original convention opened for signature at New York and Vienna on 3 March 1980; entered into force on 8 February 1987; amendments adopted on 8 July 2005; amended convention entered into force for its ratifying states on 8 May 2016; depositary IAEA Director General

The original convention—named the **Convention on the Physical Protection of Nuclear Material**—obligates its parties to protect nuclear material for peaceful purposes while in international transport.

The convention as amended and renamed also obligates its parties to protect nuclear facilities and material used for peaceful purposes while in storage.

A party may withdraw from the convention, having given 180 days' notice.

Parties to the original convention (162): Afghanistan, Albania, Algeria*, Andorra, *Angola*, Antigua and Barbuda, Argentina*, Armenia, Australia*, Austria*, Azerbaijan*, Bahamas*, Bahrain*, Bangladesh, Belarus*, Belgium*, Benin, Bolivia, Bosnia and Herzegovina, Botswana,

Brazil, Bulgaria, Burkina Faso, Cabo Verde, Cambodia, Cameroon, Canada*, Central African Republic, Chad, Chile, China*, Colombia, Comoros, Congo (Democratic Republic of the), Costa Rica, Côte d'Ivoire, Croatia, Cuba*, Cyprus*, Czechia, Denmark, Djibouti, Dominica, Dominican Republic, Ecuador, El Salvador*, Equatorial Guinea, *Eritrea*, Estonia, Eswatini, Euratom*, Fiji, Finland*, France*, Gabon, Georgia, Germany*, Ghana, Greece*, Grenada, Guatemala*, Guinea, Guinea-Bissau, Guyana, Honduras, Hungary, Iceland, India*, Indonesia*, Iraq, Ireland*, Israel*, Italy*, Jamaica, Japan, Jordan*, Kazakhstan, Kenya, Korea (South)*, Kuwait*, Kyrgyzstan, Laos*, Latvia, Lebanon, Lesotho, Libya, Liechtenstein, Lithuania, Luxembourg*, Madagascar, Malawi, Mali, Malta, Marshall Islands, Mauritania, Mexico, Moldova, Monaco, Mongolia, Montenegro, Morocco, Mozambique*, Myanmar*, Namibia, Nauru, Netherlands*, New Zealand, Nicaragua, Niger, Nigeria, Niue, North Macedonia, Norway*, Oman*, Pakistan*, Palau, Palestine, Panama, Paraguay, Peru*, Philippines, Poland, Portugal*, Qatar*, Romania*, Russia, Rwanda, Saint Kitts and Nevis, Saint Lucia*, San Marino, Saudi Arabia*, Senegal, Serbia, Seychelles, Singapore*, Slovakia, Slovenia, South Africa*, Spain*, Sudan, Sweden*, Switzerland*, Syria*, Tajikistan, Tanzania, Thailand, Togo, Tonga, Trinidad and Tobago, Tunisia, Turkey*, Turkmenistan, Uganda, UK*, Ukraine, United Arab Emirates, Uruguay, USA*, Uzbekistan, Viet Nam*, Yemen, Zambia

* With reservation and/or declaration.

Signed but not ratified (1): Haiti

Convention text: International Atomic Energy Agency, INFCIRC/274, Nov. 1979, <https://www.iaea.org/sites/default/files/infcirc274.pdf>

Parties to the amended convention (125): Albania, Algeria, *Angola*, Antigua and Barbuda, Argentina, Armenia*, Australia, Austria, Azerbaijan*, Bahrain, Bangladesh, Belgium*, Benin, Bolivia, Bosnia and Herzegovina, Botswana, Bulgaria, Burkina Faso, Cameroon, Canada*, Chad, Chile, China*, Colombia, Comoros, Costa Rica, Côte d'Ivoire, Croatia, Cuba, Cyprus, Czechia, Denmark, Djibouti, Dominican Republic, Ecuador, El Salvador, *Eritrea*, Estonia, Eswatini, Euratom*, Fiji, Finland, France, Gabon, Georgia, Germany, Ghana, Greece, Hungary, Iceland, India, Indonesia, Ireland, Israel*, Italy, Jamaica, Japan, Jordan, Kazakhstan, Kenya, Korea (South), Kuwait, Kyrgyzstan, Latvia, Lesotho, Libya, Liechtenstein, Lithuania, Luxembourg, Madagascar, Mali, Malta, Marshall Islands, Mauritania, Mexico, Moldova, Monaco, Montenegro, Morocco, Myanmar*, Namibia, Nauru, Netherlands, New Zealand, Nicaragua, Niger, Nigeria, North Macedonia, Norway, Pakistan*, Palestine, Panama, Paraguay, Peru, Poland, Portugal, Qatar, Romania, Russia, Saint Kitts and Nevis, Saint Lucia, San Marino, Saudi Arabia, Senegal, Serbia, Seychelles, Singapore*, Slovakia, Slovenia, Spain, Sweden, Switzerland, Syria*, Tajikistan, Thailand, Tunisia, Turkey*, Turkmenistan, UK, Ukraine, United Arab Emirates, Uruguay, USA*, Uzbekistan, Viet Nam

* With reservation and/or declaration.

Amendment text and consolidated text of amended convention: International Atomic Energy Agency, INFCIRC/274/Rev.1/Mod.1, 9 May 2016, <https://www.iaea.org/sites/default/files/infcirc274r1m1.pdf>

Convention on Prohibitions or Restrictions on the Use of Certain Conventional Weapons which may be Deemed to be Excessively Injurious or to have Indiscriminate Effects (CCW Convention, or 'Inhumane Weapons' Convention)

Opened for signature with protocols I, II and III at New York on 10 April 1981; entered into force on 2 December 1983; depositary UN Secretary-General

The convention is an 'umbrella treaty', under which specific agreements can be concluded in the form of protocols. In order to become a party to the convention a state must ratify at least two of the protocols.

The convention is an 'umbrella treaty', under which specific agreements can be concluded in the form of protocols. In order to become a party to the convention a state must ratify at least two of the protocols.

The amendment to Article I of the original convention was opened for signature at Geneva on 21 November 2001. It expands the scope of application to non-international armed conflicts. The amended convention entered into force on 18 May 2004.

Protocol I prohibits the use of weapons intended to injure using fragments that are not detectable in the human body by X-rays.

Protocol II prohibits or restricts the use of mines, booby-traps and other devices. *Amended Protocol II*, which entered into force on 3 December 1998, reinforces the constraints regarding anti-personnel mines.

Protocol III restricts the use of incendiary weapons.

Protocol IV, which entered into force on 30 July 1998, prohibits the employment of laser weapons specifically designed to cause permanent blindness to unenhanced vision.

Protocol V, which entered into force on 12 November 2006, recognizes the need for measures of a generic nature to minimize the risks and effects of explosive remnants of war.

A party may withdraw from the convention and its protocols, having given one year's notice. But if the party is involved in an armed conflict or occupation at that time, the withdrawal will not take effect until the conflict or occupation has ended and that party's obligations fulfilled.

Parties to the original convention (125) and protocols I (118), II (95) and III (115): Afghanistan[2], Albania, Algeria[2], Antigua and Barbuda[2], Argentina*, Australia, Austria, Bahrain[5], Bangladesh, Belarus, Belgium, Benin[2], Bolivia, Bosnia and Herzegovina, Brazil, Bulgaria, Burkina Faso, Burundi[4], Cabo Verde, Cambodia, Cameroon[6], Canada*, Chile[2], China*, Colombia, Costa Rica, Côte d'Ivoire[4], Croatia, Cuba, Cyprus*, Czechia, Denmark, Djibouti, Dominican Republic[6], Ecuador, El Salvador, Estonia[2], Finland, France*, Gabon[2], Georgia, Germany, Greece, Grenada[2], Guatemala, Guinea-Bissau, Holy See*, Honduras, Hungary, Iceland, India, Iraq, Ireland, Israel*[1], Italy*, Jamaica[2], Japan, Jordan[2], Kazakhstan[2], Korea (South)[3], Kuwait[2], Laos, Latvia, Lebanon[2], Lesotho, Liberia, Liechtenstein, Lithuania[2], Luxembourg, Madagascar, Maldives[2], Mali, Malta, Mauritius, Mexico, Moldova, Monaco[3], Mongolia, Montenegro, Morocco[4], Nauru, Netherlands*, New Zealand, Nicaragua[2], Niger, North Macedonia, Norway, Pakistan, Palestine[2], Panama, Paraguay, Peru[2], Philippines, Poland, Portugal, Qatar[2], Romania*, Russia, Saint Vincent and the Grenadines[2], Saudi Arabia[2], Senegal[5], Serbia, Seychelles, Sierra Leone[2], Slovakia, Slovenia, South Africa, Spain, Sri Lanka, Sweden, Switzerland, Tajikistan, Togo, Tunisia, Turkey*[3], Turkmenistan[1], Uganda, UK*, Ukraine, United Arab Emirates[2], Uruguay, USA*, Uzbekistan, Venezuela, Zambia

* With reservation and/or declaration.
[1] Party only to 1981 protocols I and II.
[2] Party only to 1981 protocols I and III.
[3] Party only to 1981 Protocol I.
[4] Party only to 1981 Protocol II.
[5] Party only to 1981 Protocol III.
[6] Party to none of the original protocols.

Signed but not ratified the original convention and protocols (4): Egypt, Nigeria, Sudan, Viet Nam

Parties to the amended convention (86): Afghanistan, Algeria, Albania, Argentina, Australia, Austria, Bangladesh, Belarus, Belgium, Benin, Bosnia and Herzegovina, Brazil, Bulgaria, Burkina Faso, Canada, Chile, China, Colombia, Costa Rica, Croatia, Cuba, Czechia, Denmark, Dominican Republic, Ecuador, El Salvador, Estonia, Finland, France, Georgia, Germany, Greece, Grenada, Guatemala, Guinea-Bissau, Holy See*, Hungary, Iceland, India, Iraq, Ireland, Italy, Jamaica, Japan, Korea (South), Kuwait, Latvia, Lebanon, Lesotho, Liberia, Liechtenstein, Lithuania, Luxembourg, Malta, Mexico*, Moldova, Montenegro, Netherlands, New Zealand, Nicaragua, Niger, North Macedonia, Norway, Panama, Paraguay, Peru, Poland, Portugal, Romania, Russia, Serbia, Sierra Leone, Slovakia, Slovenia, South Africa, Spain, Sri Lanka, Sweden, Switzerland, Tunisia, Turkey, UK, Ukraine, Uruguay, USA, Zambia

   * With reservation and/or declaration.

Parties to Amended Protocol II (106): Afghanistan, Albania, Argentina, Australia, Austria*, Bangladesh, Belarus*, Belgium*, Benin, Bolivia, Bosnia and Herzegovina, Brazil, Bulgaria, Burkina Faso, Cabo Verde, Cambodia, Cameroon, Canada*, Chile, China*, Colombia, Costa Rica, Croatia, Cyprus, Czechia, Denmark*, Dominican Republic, Ecuador, El Salvador, Estonia, Finland*, France*, Gabon, Georgia, Germany*, Greece*, Grenada, Guatemala, Guinea-Bissau, Holy See, Honduras, Hungary*, Iceland, India, Iraq, Ireland*, Israel*, Italy*, Jamaica, Japan, Jordan, Korea (South)*, Kuwait, Latvia, Lebanon, Liberia, Liechtenstein*, Lithuania, Luxembourg, Madagascar, Maldives, Mali, Malta, Mauritius, Moldova, Monaco, Montenegro, Morocco, Nauru, Netherlands*, New Zealand, Nicaragua, Niger, North Macedonia, Norway, Pakistan*, Panama, Paraguay, Peru, Philippines, Poland, Portugal, Romania, Russia*, Saint Vincent and the Grenadines, Senegal, Serbia, Seychelles, Sierra Leone, Slovakia, Slovenia, South Africa*, Spain, Sri Lanka, Sweden*, Switzerland*, Tajikistan, Tunisia, Turkey, Turkmenistan, UK*, Ukraine*, Uruguay, USA*, Venezuela, Zambia

   * With reservation and/or declaration

Parties to Protocol IV (109): Afghanistan, Algeria, Albania, Antigua and Barbuda, Argentina, Australia*, Austria*, Bahrain, Bangladesh, Belarus, Belgium*, Benin, Bolivia, Bosnia and Herzegovina, Brazil, Bulgaria, Burkina Faso, Cabo Verde, Cambodia, Cameroon, Canada*, Chile, China, Colombia, Costa Rica, Croatia, Cyprus, Czechia, Denmark, Dominican Republic, Ecuador, El Salvador, Estonia, Finland, France, Gabon, Georgia, Germany*, Greece*, Grenada, Guatemala, Guinea-Bissau, Holy See, Honduras, Hungary, Iceland, India, Iraq, Ireland*, Israel*, Italy*, Jamaica, Japan, Kazakhstan, Kuwait, Latvia, Lesotho, Liberia, Liechtenstein*, Lithuania, Luxembourg, Madagascar, Maldives, Mali, Malta, Mauritius, Mexico, Moldova, Mongolia, Montenegro, Morocco, Nauru, Netherlands*, New Zealand, Nicaragua, Niger, North Macedonia, Norway, Pakistan, Panama, Paraguay, Peru, Philippines, Poland*, Portugal, Qatar, Romania, Russia, Saint Vincent and the Grenadines, Saudi Arabia, Serbia, Seychelles, Sierra Leone, Slovakia, Slovenia, South Africa*, Spain, Sri Lanka, Sweden*, Switzerland*, Tajikistan, Tunisia, Turkey, UK*, Ukraine, Uruguay, USA*, Uzbekistan

   * With reservation and/or declaration.

Parties to Protocol V (96): Afghanistan, Albania, Argentina*, Australia, Austria, Bahrain, Bangladesh, Belarus, Belgium, Benin, Bosnia and Herzegovina, Brazil, Bulgaria, Burkina Faso, Burundi, Cameroon, Canada, Chile, China, Costa Rica, Côte d'Ivoire, Croatia, Cuba,

Cyprus, Czechia, Denmark, Dominican Republic, Ecuador, El Salvador, Estonia, Finland, France, Gabon, Georgia, Germany, Greece, Grenada, Guatemala, Guinea-Bissau, Holy See*, Honduras, Hungary, Iceland, India, Iraq, Ireland, Italy, Jamaica, Korea (South), Kuwait, Laos, Latvia, Lesotho, Liberia, Liechtenstein, Lithuania, Luxembourg, Madagascar, Mali, Malta, Mauritius, Moldova, Montenegro, Netherlands, New Zealand, Nicaragua, North Macedonia, Norway, Pakistan, Palestine, Panama, Paraguay, Peru, Poland, Portugal, Qatar, Romania, Russia, Saint Vincent and the Grenadines, Saudi Arabia, Senegal, Sierra Leone, Slovakia, Slovenia, South Africa, Spain, Sweden, Switzerland, Tajikistan, Tunisia, Turkmenistan, Ukraine, United Arab Emirates, Uruguay, USA*, Zambia

* With reservation and/or declaration.

Original convention and protocol text: United Nations Treaty Collection, <https://treaties.un.org/doc/Treaties/1983/12/19831202 01-19 AM/XXVI-2-revised.pdf>

Convention amendment text: United Nations Treaty Collection, <https://treaties.un.org/doc/Treaties/2001/12/2001122 01-23 AM/Ch_XXVI_02_cp.pdf>

Amended Protocol II text: United Nations Treaty Collection, <https://treaties.un.org/doc/Treaties/1996/05/19960503 01-38 AM/Ch_XXVI_02_bp.pdf>

Protocol IV text: United Nations Treaty Collection, <https://treaties.un.org/doc/Treaties/1995/10/19951013 01-30 AM/Ch_XXVI_02_ap.pdf>

Protocol V text: United Nations Treaty Collection, <https://treaties.un.org/doc/Treaties/2003/11/20031128 01-19 AM/Ch_XXVI_02_dp.pdf>

Convention on the Prohibition of the Development, Production, Stockpiling and Use of Chemical Weapons and on their Destruction (Chemical Weapons Convention, CWC)

Opened for signature at Paris on 13 January 1993; entered into force on 29 April 1997; depositary UN Secretary-General

The convention prohibits the development, production, acquisition, transfer, stockpiling and use of chemical weapons. The CWC regime consists of four 'pillars': disarmament, non-proliferation, assistance and protection against chemical weapons, and international cooperation on the peaceful uses of chemistry. The convention established the Organisation for the Prohibition of Chemical Weapons (OPCW) as its implementing body.

Each party undertook to destroy its chemical weapon stockpiles by 29 April 2012. Of the seven parties that had declared stocks of chemical weapons by that date, three had destroyed them (Albania, India and South Korea). Libya and Russia completed the destruction of their stockpiles in 2017 and Iraq did so in 2018, while the USA continues to destroy its stocks. The stockpile of chemical weapons that Syria declared when it acceded to the CWC in 2013 was destroyed in 2016, although gaps, inconsistencies and discrepancies in the 2013 declaration continue to be investigated. Old and abandoned chemical weapons will continue to be destroyed as they are uncovered from, for example, former battlefields.

A party may withdraw from the convention, having given 90 days' notice, if it decides that its supreme interests have been jeopardized by extraordinary events related to the treaty's subject matter.

Parties (193): Afghanistan, Albania, Algeria, Andorra, Angola, Antigua and Barbuda, Argentina, Armenia, Australia, Austria*, Azerbaijan, Bahamas, Bahrain, Bangladesh, Barbados, Belarus, Belgium*, Belize, Benin, Bhutan, Bolivia, Bosnia and Herzegovina, Botswana, Brazil, Brunei Darussalam, Bulgaria, Burkina Faso, Burundi, Cabo Verde, Cambodia, Cameroon, Canada, Central African Republic, Chad, Chile, China*, Colombia, Comoros, Congo (Democratic Republic of the), Congo (Republic of the), Cook Islands, Costa Rica, Côte d'Ivoire, Croatia, Cuba*, Cyprus, Czechia, Denmark*, Djibouti, Dominica, Dominican Republic, Ecuador, El Salvador, Equatorial Guinea, Eritrea, Estonia, Eswatini, Ethiopia, Fiji, Finland, France*, Gabon, Gambia, Georgia, Germany*, Ghana, Greece*, Grenada, Guatemala, Guinea, Guinea-Bissau, Guyana, Haiti, Holy See*, Honduras, Hungary, Iceland, India, Indonesia, Iran*, Iraq, Ireland*, Italy*, Jamaica, Japan, Jordan, Kazakhstan, Kenya, Kiribati, Korea (South), Kuwait, Kyrgyzstan, Laos, Latvia, Lebanon, Lesotho, Liberia, Libya, Liechtenstein, Lithuania, Luxembourg*, Madagascar, Malawi, Malaysia, Maldives, Mali, Malta, Marshall Islands, Mauritania, Mauritius, Mexico, Micronesia, Moldova, Monaco, Mongolia, Montenegro, Morocco, Mozambique, Myanmar, Namibia, Nauru, Nepal, Netherlands*, New Zealand, Nicaragua, Niger, Nigeria, Niue, North Macedonia, Norway, Oman, Pakistan*, Palau, Palestine, Panama, Papua New Guinea, Paraguay, Peru, Philippines, Poland, Portugal*, Qatar, Romania, Russia, Rwanda, Saint Kitts and Nevis, Saint Lucia, Saint Vincent and the Grenadines, Samoa, San Marino, Sao Tome and Principe, Saudi Arabia, Senegal, Serbia, Seychelles, Sierra Leone, Singapore, Slovakia, Slovenia, Solomon Islands, Somalia, South Africa, Spain*, Sri Lanka, Sudan*, Suriname, Sweden, Switzerland, Syria*, Tajikistan, Tanzania, Thailand, Timor-Leste, Togo, Tonga, Trinidad and Tobago, Tunisia, Turkey, Turkmenistan, Tuvalu, Uganda, UK*, Ukraine, United Arab Emirates, Uruguay, USA*, Uzbekistan, Vanuatu, Venezuela, Viet Nam, Yemen, Zambia, Zimbabwe

* With reservation and/or declaration.

Signed but not ratified (1): Israel

Convention text: United Nations Treaty Collection, <https://treaties.un.org/doc/Treaties/1997/04/19970429 07-52 PM/CTC-XXVI_03_ocred.pdf>

Comprehensive Nuclear-Test-Ban Treaty (CTBT)

Opened for signature at New York on 24 September 1996; not in force; depositary UN Secretary-General

The treaty would prohibit the carrying out of any nuclear weapon test explosion or any other nuclear explosion and urges each party to prevent any such nuclear explosion at any place under its jurisdiction or control and refrain from causing, encouraging or in any way participating in the carrying out of any nuclear weapon test explosion or any other nuclear explosion.

The verification regime established by the treaty will consist of an International Monitoring System (IMS) to detect signs of nuclear explosions, an International Data Centre to collect and distribute data from the IMS, and the right to on-site inspection to determine whether an explosion has taken place. Work under the treaty will be implemented by the Comprehensive Nuclear-Test-Ban Treaty Organization (CTBTO).

The treaty will enter into force 180 days after the date that all of the 44 states listed in an annex to the treaty have deposited their instruments of ratification. All 44 states possess nuclear power reactors or nuclear research reactors. Pending entry into force, a Preparatory Commission is preparing for the treaty's implementation and the establishment of the CTBTO and the IMS.

After entry into force, a party will be able to withdraw from the treaty, having given six months' notice, if it decides that its supreme interests have been jeopardized by extraordinary events related to the treaty's subject matter.

States whose ratification is required for entry into force (44): Algeria, Argentina, Australia, Austria, Bangladesh, Belgium, Brazil, Bulgaria, Canada, Chile, China*, Colombia, Congo (Democratic Republic of the), Egypt*, Finland, France, Germany, Hungary, India*, Indonesia, Iran*, Israel*, Italy, Japan, Korea (North)*, Korea (South), Mexico, Netherlands, Norway, Pakistan*, Peru, Poland, Romania, Russia, Slovakia, South Africa, Spain, Sweden, Switzerland, Turkey, UK, Ukraine, USA*, Viet Nam

   * Has not ratified the treaty.

Ratifications deposited (168): Afghanistan, Albania, Algeria, Andorra, Angola, Antigua and Barbuda, Argentina, Armenia, Australia, Austria, Azerbaijan, Bahamas, Bahrain, Bangladesh, Barbados, Belarus, Belgium, Belize, Benin, Bolivia, Bosnia and Herzegovina, Botswana, Brazil, Brunei Darussalam, Bulgaria, Burkina Faso, Burundi, Cabo Verde, Cambodia, Cameroon, Canada, Central African Republic, Chad, Chile, Colombia, Congo (Democratic Republic of the), Cook Islands, Costa Rica, Côte d'Ivoire, Congo (Republic of the), Croatia, Cyprus, Czechia, Denmark, Djibouti, Dominican Republic, Ecuador, El Salvador, Eritrea, Estonia, Eswatini, Ethiopia, Fiji, Finland, France, Gabon, Georgia, Germany, Ghana, Greece, Grenada, Guatemala, Guinea, Guinea-Bissau, Guyana, Haiti, Holy See, Honduras, Hungary, Iceland, Indonesia, Iraq, Ireland, Italy, Jamaica, Japan, Jordan, Kazakhstan, Kenya, Kiribati, Korea (South), Kuwait, Kyrgyzstan, Laos, Latvia, Lebanon, Lesotho, Liberia, Libya, Liechtenstein, Lithuania, Luxembourg, Madagascar, Malawi, Malaysia, Maldives, Mali, Malta, Marshall Islands, Mauritania, Mexico, Micronesia, Moldova, Monaco, Mongolia, Montenegro, Morocco, Mozambique, Myanmar, Namibia, Nauru, Netherlands, New Zealand, Nicaragua, Niger, Nigeria, Niue, North Macedonia, Norway, Oman, Palau, Panama, Paraguay, Peru, Philippines, Poland, Portugal, Qatar, Romania, Russia, Rwanda, Saint Kitts and Nevis, Saint Lucia, Saint Vincent and the Grenadines, Samoa, San Marino, Senegal, Serbia, Seychelles, Sierra Leone, Singapore, Slovakia, Slovenia, South Africa, Spain, Sudan, Suriname, Sweden, Switzerland, Tajikistan, Tanzania, Thailand, Togo, Trinidad and Tobago, Tunisia, Turkey, Turkmenistan, Uganda, UK, Ukraine, United Arab Emirates, Uruguay, Uzbekistan, Vanuatu, Venezuela, Viet Nam, Zambia, Zimbabwe

Signed but not ratified (16): China, Comoros, Egypt, Equatorial Guinea, Gambia, Iran, Israel, Nepal, Papua New Guinea, Sao Tome and Principe, Solomon Islands, Sri Lanka, Timor-Leste, Tuvalu, USA, Yemen

   Note: In addition to the 168 states that had ratified the treaty as of 1 Jan. 2021, Cuba signed and ratified it on 4 Feb. 2021 and Comoros ratified it on 19 Feb. 2021.

Treaty text: United Nations Treaty Collection, <https://treaties.un.org/doc/Treaties/1997/09/19970910 07-37 AM/Ch_XXVI_04p.pdf>

Convention on the Prohibition of the Use, Stockpiling, Production and Transfer of Anti-Personnel Mines and on their Destruction (APM Convention)

Opened for signature at Ottawa on 3–4 December 1997 and at New York on 5 December 1997; entered into force on 1 March 1999; depositary UN Secretary-General

The convention prohibits anti-personnel mines (APMs), which are defined as mines designed to be exploded by the presence, proximity or contact of a person and which will incapacitate, injure or kill one or more persons.

Each party undertakes to destroy all of its stockpiled APMs as soon as possible but not later than four years after the entry into force of the convention for that state party. Each party also undertakes to destroy all APMs in mined areas under its jurisdiction or control not later than 10 years after the entry into force of the convention for that state party. Of the 164 parties, 161 no longer had stockpiles of APMs and 31 of the 63 parties that reported areas containing APMs had cleared them by 1 January 2021.

A party may withdraw from the convention, having given six months' notice. But if the party is involved in an armed conflict at that time, the withdrawal will not take effect until that conflict has ended.

Parties (164): Afghanistan[‡], Albania, Algeria, Andorra, Angola[‡], Antigua and Barbuda, Argentina[*‡], Australia[*], Austria, Bahamas, Bangladesh, Barbados, Belarus, Belgium, Belize, Benin, Bhutan, Bolivia, Bosnia and Herzegovina[‡], Botswana, Brazil, Brunei Darussalam, Bulgaria, Burkina Faso, Burundi, Cabo Verde, Cambodia[‡], Cameroon, Canada[*], Central African Republic, Chad[‡], Chile[*], Colombia[‡], Comoros, Congo (Democratic Republic of the)[‡], Congo (Republic of the), Cook Islands, Costa Rica, Côte d'Ivoire, Croatia[‡], Cyprus[‡], Czechia[*], Denmark, Djibouti, Dominica, Dominican Republic, Ecuador[‡], El Salvador, Equatorial Guinea, Eritrea[‡], Estonia, Eswatini, Ethiopia[‡], Fiji, Finland, France, Gabon, Gambia, Germany, Ghana, Greece[*†], Grenada, Guatemala, Guinea, Guinea-Bissau, Guyana, Haiti, Holy See, Honduras, Hungary, Iceland, Indonesia, Iraq[‡], Ireland, Italy, Jamaica, Japan, Jordan, Kenya, Kiribati, Kuwait, Latvia, Lesotho, Liberia, Liechtenstein, Lithuania[*], Luxembourg, Madagascar, Malawi, Malaysia, Maldives, Mali, Malta, Mauritania[‡], Mauritius, Mexico, Moldova, Monaco, Montenegro[*], Mozambique, Namibia, Nauru, Netherlands, New Zealand, Nicaragua, Niger[‡], Nigeria[‡], Niue, North Macedonia, Norway, Oman[‡], Palau, Palestine[‡], Panama, Papua New Guinea, Paraguay, Peru[‡], Philippines, Poland[*], Portugal, Qatar, Romania, Rwanda, Saint Kitts and Nevis, Saint Lucia, Saint Vincent and the Grenadines, Samoa, San Marino, Sao Tome and Principe, Senegal[‡], Serbia[*‡], Seychelles, Sierra Leone, Slovakia, Slovenia, Solomon Islands, Somalia[‡], South Africa, South Sudan[‡], Spain, Sri Lanka[†‡], Sudan[‡], Suriname, Sweden, Switzerland, Tajikistan[‡], Tanzania, Thailand[‡], Timor-Leste, Togo, Trinidad and Tobago, Tunisia, Turkey[‡], Turkmenistan, Tuvalu, Uganda, UK[*], Ukraine[†‡], Uruguay, Vanuatu, Venezuela, Yemen[‡], Zambia, Zimbabwe[‡]

[*] With reservation and/or declaration.
[†] Party with remaining APM stockpile.
[‡] Party with areas containing uncleared APMs.

Note: Chile and the UK announced completion of their mine clearance obligations in 2020. In their initial transparency reports, Argentina and the UK both reported areas under their jurisdiction or control to be mine-affected by virtue of their assertions of sovereignty over the Falkland Islands/Malvinas.

Signed but not ratified (1): Marshall Islands

Convention text: United Nations Treaty Collection, <https://treaties.un.org/doc/Treaties/1997/09/19970918 07-53 AM/Ch_XXVI_05p.pdf>

Rome Statute of the International Criminal Court

Opened for signature at Rome on 17 July 1998 and at New York on 18 October 1998; entered into force on 1 July 2002; depositary UN Secretary-General

The Rome Statute established the International Criminal Court (ICC), a permanent international court dealing with accusations of genocide, crimes against humanity, war crimes and the crime of aggression. The ICC can investigate and prosecute an alleged crime that takes place on the territory of a state party, is committed by a state party or is referred to it by the UN Security Council. The ICC may only prosecute a crime if the domestic courts are unwilling or unable to do so.

The *Amendment to Article 8 adopted on 10 June 2010* makes it a war crime to use chemical weapons and expanding bullets in non-international conflicts. A series of *Amendments to Article 8 adopted on 14 December 2017* make it a war crime to use weapons which use microbial or other biological agents, or toxins; weapons the primary effect of which is to injure by fragments undetectable by x-rays in the human body; and blinding laser weapons. The *Amendment to Article 8 adopted on 6 December 2019* makes intentional use of starvation of civilians a war crime. Amendments to Article 8 enter into force for the parties that have accepted them one year after that acceptance.

Amendments adopted on 11 June 2010 define the crime of aggression. The ICC's jurisdiction over the crime of aggression was activated on 17 July 2018. From that date, an apparent act of aggression may be referred to the ICC by the UN Security Council regardless of whether it involves parties or non-parties to the statute.

A state may withdraw from the statute and the ICC by giving 12 months' notice.

Parties to the Rome Statute (123): Afghanistan, Albania, Andorra, Antigua and Barbuda, Argentina*, Australia*, Austria, Bangladesh, Barbados, Belgium, Belize, Benin, Bolivia, Bosnia and Herzegovina, Botswana, Brazil, Bulgaria, Burkina Faso, Cabo Verde, Cambodia, Canada, Central African Republic, Chad, Chile, Colombia*, Comoros, Congo (Democratic Republic of the), Congo (Republic of the), Cook Islands, Costa Rica, Côte d'Ivoire, Croatia, Cyprus, Czechia, Denmark, Djibouti, Dominica, Dominican Republic, Ecuador, El Salvador, Estonia, Fiji, Finland, France*, Gabon, Gambia, Georgia, Germany, Ghana, Greece, Grenada, Guatemala, Guinea, Guyana, Honduras, Hungary, Iceland, Ireland, Italy, Japan, Jordan*, Kenya, Kiribati, Korea (South), Latvia, Lesotho, Liberia, Liechtenstein, Lithuania, Luxembourg, Madagascar, Malawi, Maldives, Mali, Malta*, Marshall Islands, Mauritius, Mexico, Moldova, Mongolia, Montenegro, Namibia, Nauru, Netherlands, New Zealand*, Niger, Nigeria, North Macedonia, Norway, Palestine, Panama, Paraguay, Peru, Poland, Portugal*, Romania, Saint Kitts and Nevis, Saint Lucia, Saint Vincent and the Grenadines, Samoa, San Marino, Senegal, Serbia, Seychelles, Sierra Leone, Slovakia, Slovenia, South Africa, Spain, Suriname, Sweden*, Switzerland, Tajikistan, Tanzania, Timor-Leste, Trinidad and Tobago, Tunisia, Uganda, UK*, Uruguay, Vanuatu, Venezuela, Zambia

* With reservation and/or declaration.

Signed but not ratified (31): Algeria, Angola, Armenia, Bahamas, Bahrain, Cameroon, Egypt, Eritrea, Guinea-Bissau, Haiti, Iran, Israel*, Jamaica, Kuwait, Kyrgyzstan, Monaco, Morocco, Mozambique, Oman, Russia*, Sao Tome and Principe, Solomon Islands, Sudan*, Syria, Thailand, Ukraine†, United Arab Emirates, USA*, Uzbekistan, Yemen, Zimbabwe

* These states have declared that they no longer intend to become parties to the statute.

† Ukraine has accepted the jurisdiction of the ICC with respect to alleged crimes committed on its territory since 21 Nov. 2013.

Notes: Burundi withdrew from the statute and the ICC on 27 Oct. 2017 and the Philippines withdrew on 17 Mar. 2019. Gambia and South Africa, which had declared in 2016 that they would withdraw, rescinded those declarations in 2017.

Parties to the Amendment to Article 8 of 10 June 2010 (39): Andorra, Argentina, Austria, Belgium, Botswana, Chile, Costa Rica, Croatia, Cyprus, Czechia, El Salvador, Estonia, Finland, Georgia, Germany, Guyana, Latvia, Liechtenstein, Lithuania, Luxembourg, Malta, Mauritius, Netherlands, *New Zealand*, North Macedonia, Norway, Palestine, Panama, Paraguay, Poland, Portugal, Samoa, San Marino, Slovakia, Slovenia, Spain, Switzerland, Trinidad and Tobago, Uruguay

Note: In addition to the 39 states that had ratified the amendment as of 1 Jan. 2021, Mongolia ratified it on 18 Jan. 2021.

Parties to the Amendments of 11 June 2010 defining the crime of aggression (40): Andorra, Argentina, Austria, Belgium, *Bolivia*, Botswana, Chile, Costa Rica, Croatia, Cyprus, Czechia, Ecuador, El Salvador, Estonia, Finland, Georgia, Germany, Guyana, Iceland, Ireland, Latvia, Liechtenstein, Lithuania, Luxembourg, Malta, Netherlands, North Macedonia, Palestine, Panama, Paraguay, Poland, Portugal, Samoa, San Marino, Slovakia, Slovenia, Spain, Switzerland, Trinidad and Tobago, Uruguay

Note: In addition to the 40 states that had ratified the amendment as of 1 Jan. 2021, Mongolia ratified it on 18 Jan. 2021.

Parties to the Amendment to Article 8 of 14 December 2017 on weapons which use microbial or other biological agents, or toxins (7): Czechia, *Latvia*, Luxembourg, *Netherlands*, *New Zealand*, Slovakia, *Switzerland*

Note: In addition to the 7 states that had ratified the amendment as of 1 Jan. 2021, Norway ratified it on 22 Mar. 2021.

Parties to the Amendment to Article 8 of 14 December 2017 on weapons the primary effect of which is to injure by fragments undetectable by x-rays in the human body (7): Czechia, *Latvia*, Luxembourg, *Netherlands*, *New Zealand*, Slovakia, *Switzerland*

Note: In addition to the 7 states that had ratified the amendment as of 1 Jan. 2021, Norway ratified it on 22 Mar. 2021.

Parties to the Amendment to Article 8 of 14 December 2017 on blinding laser weapons (7): Czechia, *Latvia*, Luxembourg, *Netherlands*, *New Zealand*, Slovakia, *Switzerland*

Note: In addition to the 7 states that had ratified the amendment as of 1 Jan. 2021, Norway ratified it on 22 Mar. 2021.

Parties to the Amendment to Article 8 of 6 December 2019 on intentional starvation of civilians (3): Andorra, *Netherlands*, *New Zealand*

Note: In addition to the 3 states that had ratified the amendment as of 1 Jan. 2021, Norway ratified it on 22 Mar. 2021.

Statute text: United Nations Treaty Collection, <https://treaties.un.org/doc/Treaties/1998/07/19980717 06-33 PM/Ch_XVIII_10p.pdf>

Text of the Amendment to Article 8 of 10 June 2010: United Nations Treaty Collection, <https://treaties.un.org/doc/Treaties/2010/10/20101011 05-46 PM/CN.533.2010.pdf>

Text of the Amendments of 11 June 2010 defining the crime of aggression: United Nations Treaty Collection, <https://treaties.un.org/doc/Treaties/2010/06/20100611 05-56 PM/CN.651.2010.pdf>

Text of the Amendment to Article 8 of 14 December 2017 on weapons which use microbial or other biological agents or toxins: United Nations Treaty Collection, <https://treaties.un.org/doc/Publication/CN/2018/CN.116.2018-Eng.pdf>

Text of the Amendment to Article 8 of 14 December 2017 on weapons the primary effect of which is to injure by fragments undetectable by x-rays in the human body: United Nations Treaty Collection, <https://treaties.un.org/doc/Publication/CN/2018/CN.125.2018-Eng.pdf>

Text of the Amendment to Article 8 of 14 December 2017 on blinding laser weapons: United Nations Treaty Collection, <https://treaties.un.org/doc/Publication/CN/2018/CN.126.2018-Eng.pdf>

Text of the Amendment to Article 8 of 6 December 2019 on intentional starvation of civilians: United Nations Treaty Collection, <https://treaties.un.org/doc/Publication/CN/2020/CN.394.2020-Eng.pdf>

Convention on Cluster Munitions

Opened for signature at Oslo on 3 December 2008; entered into force on 1 August 2010; depositary UN Secretary-General

The convention's objectives are to prohibit the use, production, transfer and stockpiling of cluster munitions that cause unacceptable harm to civilians. It also establishes a framework for cooperation and assistance to ensure adequate provision of care and rehabilitation for victims, clearance of contaminated areas, risk reduction education and destruction of stockpiles. The convention does not apply to mines.

Each party undertakes to destroy all of its stockpiled cluster munitions as soon as possible but not later than eight years after the entry into force of the convention for that state party. The first deadlines for stockpile destruction were in 2018. Each party also undertakes to clear and destroy all cluster munitions in contaminated areas under its jurisdiction or control not later than 10 years after the entry into force of the convention for that state party. The first deadlines for clearance were in 2020.

A three-person Implementation Support Unit (ISU), based in Geneva, was established in 2015 to, among other things, provide advice and technical support to the parties.

A party may withdraw from the convention, having given six months' notice. But if the party is involved in an armed conflict at that time, the withdrawal will not take effect until that conflict has ended.

Parties (110): Afghanistan, Albania, Andorra, Antigua and Barbuda, Australia, Austria, Belgium, Belize, Benin, Bolivia, Bosnia and Herzegovina, Botswana, Bulgaria, Burkina Faso, Burundi, Cabo Verde, Cameroon, Canada, Chad, Chile, Colombia*, Comoros, Congo (Republic of the), Cook Islands, Costa Rica, Côte d'Ivoire, Croatia, Cuba, Czechia, Denmark, Dominican Republic, Ecuador, El Salvador*, Eswatini, Fiji, France, Gambia, Germany, Ghana, Grenada, Guatemala, Guinea, Guinea-Bissau, Guyana, Holy See*, Honduras, Hungary, Iceland, Iraq, Ireland, Italy, Japan, Laos, Lebanon, Lesotho, Liechtenstein, Lithuania, Luxembourg, Madagascar, Malawi, Maldives, Mali, Malta, Mauritania, Mauritius, Mexico, Moldova, Monaco, Montenegro, Mozambique, Namibia, Nauru, Netherlands, New Zealand, Nicaragua, Niger, *Niue*, North Macedonia, Norway, Palestine, Palau, Panama, Paraguay, Peru, Philippines, Portugal, Rwanda, Saint Kitts and Nevis, *Saint Lucia*, Saint Vincent and the Grenadines, Samoa, San Marino, *Sao Tome and Principe*, Senegal, Seychelles, Sierra Leone, Slovakia, Slovenia, Somalia, South Africa, Spain, Sri Lanka, Sweden, Switzerland, Togo, Trinidad and Tobago, Tunisia, UK, Uruguay, Zambia

* With reservation and/or declaration.

Signed but not ratified (13): Angola, Central African Republic, Congo (Democratic Republic of the), Cyprus, Djibouti, Haiti, Indonesia, Jamaica, Kenya, Liberia, Nigeria, Tanzania, Uganda

Convention text: United Nations Treaty Collection, <https://treaties.un.org/doc/Publication/ CTC/26-6.pdf>

Arms Trade Treaty (ATT)

Opened for signature at New York on 3 June 2013; entered into force on 24 December 2014; depositary UN Secretary-General

The object of the treaty is to establish the highest possible common international standards for regulating the international trade in conventional arms; and to prevent and eradicate the illicit trade in conventional arms and prevent their diversion.

Among other things, the treaty prohibits a state party from authorizing a transfer of arms if they are to be used in the commission of genocide, crimes against humanity or war crimes. The treaty also requires the exporting state to assess the potential for any arms proposed for export to undermine peace and security or be used to commit serious violations of international humanitarian law or international human rights law.

Each party must submit an annual report on its authorized or actual exports and imports of conventional arms.

The treaty established the ATT Secretariat, based in Geneva, to support the parties in its implementation. Among other tasks, it collects the annual reports submitted by each party on imports and exports of conventional arms.

A party may withdraw from the treaty, having given 90 days' notice.

Parties (110): Afghanistan, Albania, Antigua and Barbuda, Argentina, Australia, Austria, Bahamas, Barbados, Belgium, Belize, Benin, Bosnia and Herzegovina, Botswana, Brazil, Bulgaria, Burkina Faso, Cabo Verde, Cameroon, Canada, Central African Republic, Chad, Chile, *China*, Costa Rica, Côte d'Ivoire, Croatia, Cyprus, Czechia, Denmark, Dominica, Dominican Republic, El Salvador, Estonia, Finland, France, Georgia, Germany, Ghana, Greece, Grenada, Guatemala, Guinea, Guinea-Bissau, Guyana, Honduras, Hungary, Iceland, Ireland, Italy, Jamaica, Japan, Kazakhstan*, Korea (South), Latvia, Lebanon, Lesotho, Liberia, Liechtenstein*, Lithuania, Luxembourg, Madagascar, Maldives, Mali, Malta, Mauritania, Mauritius, Mexico, Moldova, Monaco, Montenegro, Mozambique, *Namibia*, Netherlands, New Zealand*, Niger, Nigeria, *Niue*, North Macedonia, Norway, Palau, Palestine, Panama, Paraguay, Peru, Poland, Portugal, Romania, Saint Kitts and Nevis, Saint Lucia, Saint Vincent and the Grenadines, Samoa, San Marino, *Sao Tome and Principe*, Senegal, Serbia, Seychelles, Sierra Leone, Slovakia, Slovenia, South Africa, Spain, Suriname, Sweden, Switzerland*, Togo, Trinidad and Tobago, Tuvalu, UK, Uruguay, Zambia

* With reservation and/or declaration.

Signed but not ratified (31): Andorra, Angola, Bahrain, Bangladesh, Burundi, Cambodia, Colombia, Comoros, Congo (Republic of the), Djibouti, Eswatini, Gabon, Haiti, Israel, Kiribati, Libya, Malawi, Malaysia, Mongolia, Nauru, Philippines, Rwanda, Singapore, Tanzania, Thailand, Turkey, Ukraine, United Arab Emirates, USA*, Vanuatu, Zimbabwe

* This state has declared that it no longer intends to become a party to the treaty.

Treaty text: United Nations Treaty Collection, <https://treaties.un.org/doc/Treaties/2013/ 04/20130410 12-01 PM/Ch_XXVI_08.pdf>

Treaty on the Prohibition of Nuclear Weapons (TPNW)

Opened for signature at New York on 20 September 2017; entered in force on 22 January 2021; depositary UN Secretary-General

In its preamble, the treaty cites the catastrophic humanitarian and environmental consequences of the use of nuclear weapons and invokes the principles of international humanitarian law and the rules of international law applicable in armed conflict. The treaty prohibits parties from developing, testing, producing, manufacturing, acquiring, possessing or stockpiling nuclear weapons or other nuclear explosive devices. Parties are prohibited from using or threatening to use nuclear weapons and other nuclear explosive devices. Finally, parties cannot allow the stationing, installation or deployment of nuclear weapons and other nuclear explosive devices in their territory.

The treaty outlines procedures for eliminating the nuclear weapons of any party that owned, possessed or controlled them after 7 July 2017, to be supervised by a 'competent international authority or authorities' to be designated by the states parties. Each party is required to maintain its existing safeguards agreements with the IAEA and must, at a minimum, conclude and bring into force a comprehensive safeguards agreement with the agency. The treaty also contains provisions on assisting the victims of the testing or use of nuclear weapons and taking necessary and appropriate measures for the environmental remediation of contaminated areas.

Membership of the treaty does not prejudice the parties' other, compatible international obligations (such as the NPT and the CTBT). A party may withdraw from the treaty, having given 12 months' notice, if it decides that its supreme interests have been jeopardized by extraordinary events related to the treaty's subject matter. But if the party is involved in an armed conflict at that time, the withdrawal will not take effect until it is no longer party to an armed conflict.

Ratifications deposited (51): Antigua and Barbuda, Austria, Bangladesh, *Belize, Benin*, Bolivia, *Botswana*, Cook Islands*, Costa Rica, Cuba*, Dominica, Ecuador, El Salvador, *Fiji*, Gambia, Guyana, Holy See, *Honduras, Ireland, Jamaica*, Kazakhstan, Kiribati, Laos, *Lesotho, Malaysia*, Maldives, *Malta*, Mexico, *Namibia, Nauru*, New Zealand, Nicaragua, *Nigeria, Niue*, Palau, Palestine, Panama, *Paraguay, Saint Kitts and Nevis*, Saint Lucia, Saint Vincent and the Grenadines, Samoa, San Marino, South Africa, Thailand, Trinidad and Tobago, *Tuvalu*, Uruguay, Vanuatu, Venezuela, Viet Nam

  * With reservation and/or declaration.

Signed but not ratified (37): Algeria, Angola, Brazil, Brunei Darussalam, Cabo Verde, Cambodia, Central African Republic, Chile, Colombia, Comoros, Congo (Democratic Republic of the), Congo (Republic of the), Côte d'Ivoire, Dominican Republic, Ghana, Grenada, Guatemala, Guinea-Bissau, Indonesia, Libya, Liechtenstein, Madagascar, Malawi, *Mozambique*, Myanmar, Nepal, *Niger*, Peru, Philippines, Sao Tome and Principe, Seychelles, *Sudan*, Tanzania, Timor-Leste, Togo, Zambia, *Zimbabwe*

  Note: In addition to the 51 states that had ratified the treaty as of 1 Jan. 2021, Cambodia ratified it on 22 Jan. 2021, Philippines on 18 Feb. 2021 and Comoros on 19 Feb. 2021.

Treaty text: United Nations Treaty Collection, <https://treaties.un.org/doc/Treaties/2017/07/20170707 03-42 PM/Ch_XXVI_9.pdf>

II. Regional treaties

Treaty for the Prohibition of Nuclear Weapons in Latin America and the Caribbean (Treaty of Tlatelolco)

Original treaty opened for signature at Mexico City on 14 February 1967; entered into force on 22 April 1968; treaty amended in 1990, 1991 and 1992; depositary Mexican Government

The treaty prohibits the testing, use, manufacture, production or acquisition by any means, as well as the receipt, storage, installation, deployment and any form of possession of any nuclear weapons by any country of Latin America and the Caribbean and in the surrounding seas.

The parties should conclude agreements individually with the IAEA for the application of safeguards to their nuclear activities. The IAEA has the exclusive power to carry out special inspections. The treaty also established the Agency for the Prohibition of Nuclear Weapons in Latin America and the Caribbean (Organismo para la Proscripción de las Armas Nucleares en la América Latina y el Caribe, OPANAL) to ensure compliance with the treaty.

The treaty is open for signature by all the independent states of Latin America and the Caribbean. A party may withdraw from the treaty, having given three months' notice, if it decides that its supreme interests or the peace and security of another party or parties have been jeopardized by new circumstances related to the treaty's content.

Under *Additional Protocol I* states with territories within the zone—France, the Netherlands, the UK and the USA—undertake to apply the statute of military denuclearization to these territories.

Under *Additional Protocol II* the recognized nuclear weapon states—China, France, Russia, the UK and the USA—undertake to respect the military denuclearization of Latin America and the Caribbean and not to contribute to acts involving a violation of the treaty, nor to use or threaten to use nuclear weapons against the parties to the treaty.

Parties to the original treaty (33): Antigua and Barbuda[1], Argentina[1], Bahamas, Barbados[1], Belize[2], Bolivia, Brazil[1], Chile[1], Colombia[1], Costa Rica[1], Cuba, Dominica, Dominican Republic[3], Ecuador[1], El Salvador[1], Grenada[1], Guatemala[1], Guyana[3], Haiti, Honduras[1], Jamaica[1], Mexico[1], Nicaragua[3], Panama[1], Paraguay[1], Peru[1], Saint Kitts and Nevis[1], Saint Lucia[1], Saint Vincent and the Grenadines[4], Suriname[1], Trinidad and Tobago[1], Uruguay[1], Venezuela[1]

[1] Has ratified the amendments of 1990, 1991 and 1992.
[2] Has ratified the amendments of 1990 and 1992 only.
[3] Has ratified the amendment of 1992 only.
[4] Has ratified the amendments of 1991 and 1992 only.

Parties to Additional Protocol I (4): France*, Netherlands*, UK*, USA*

Parties to Additional Protocol II (5): China*, France*, Russia*, UK*, USA*

* With reservation and/or declaration.

Original treaty text: *United Nations Treaty Series*, vol. 634 (1968), <https://treaties.un.org/doc/Publication/UNTS/Volume 634/v634.pdf>

Amended treaty text: Agency for the Prohibition of Nuclear Weapons in Latin America and the Caribbean, Inf.11/2018, 5 June 2018, <https://www.opanal.org/wp-content/uploads/2019/10/Inf_11_2018_Treaty_Tlatelolco.pdf>

South Pacific Nuclear Free Zone Treaty (Treaty of Rarotonga)

Opened for signature at Rarotonga on 6 August 1985; entered into force on 11 December 1986; depositary Secretary General of the Pacific Islands Forum Secretariat

The South Pacific Nuclear Free Zone is defined as the area between the zone of application of the Treaty of Tlatelolco in the east and the west coast of Australia and the western border of Papua New Guinea and between the zone of application of the Antarctic Treaty in the south and, approximately, the equator in the north.

The treaty prohibits the manufacture or acquisition of any nuclear explosive device, as well as possession or control over such device by the parties anywhere inside or outside the zone. The parties also undertake not to supply nuclear material or equipment, unless subject to IAEA safeguards, and to prevent the stationing or testing of any nuclear explosive device in their territories and undertake not to dump, and to prevent the dumping of, radioactive waste and other radioactive matter at sea anywhere within the zone. Each party remains free to allow visits, as well as transit, by foreign ships and aircraft.

The treaty is open for signature by the members of the Pacific Islands Forum. If any party violates an essential provision or the spirit of the treaty, every other party may withdraw from the treaty, having given 12 months' notice.

Under *Protocol 1* France, the UK and the USA undertake to apply the treaty prohibitions relating to the manufacture, stationing and testing of nuclear explosive devices in the territories situated within the zone for which they are internationally responsible.

Under *Protocol 2* China, France, Russia, the UK and the USA undertake not to use or threaten to use a nuclear explosive device against the parties to the treaty or against any territory within the zone for which a party to Protocol 1 is internationally responsible.

Under *Protocol 3* China, France, Russia, the UK and the USA undertake not to test any nuclear explosive device anywhere within the zone.

Parties (13): Australia, Cook Islands, Fiji, Kiribati, Nauru, New Zealand, Niue, Papua New Guinea, Samoa, Solomon Islands, Tonga, Tuvalu, Vanuatu

Parties to Protocol 1 (2): France*, UK*; *signed but not ratified (1)*: USA

Parties to Protocol 2 (4): China*, France*, Russia*, UK*; *signed but not ratified (1)*: USA

Parties to Protocol 3 (4): China*, France*, Russia*, UK*; *signed but not ratified (1)*: USA

* With reservation and/or declaration.

Treaty text: Pacific Islands Forum Secretariat, <https://www.forumsec.org/wp-content/uploads/2018/02/South-Pacific-Nuclear-Zone-Treaty-Rarotonga-Treaty-1.pdf>

Protocol texts: Pacific Islands Forum Secretariat, <https://www.forumsec.org/wp-content/uploads/2018/02/South-Pacific-Nuclear-Zone-Treaty-Protocols-1.pdf>

Treaty on Conventional Armed Forces in Europe (CFE Treaty)

Original treaty signed by the 16 member states of the North Atlantic Treaty Organization (NATO) and the 6 member states of the Warsaw Treaty Organization (WTO) at Paris on 19 November 1990; entered into force on 9 November 1992; depositary Dutch Government

The treaty sets ceilings on five categories of treaty-limited equipment (TLE)—battle tanks, armoured combat vehicles, artillery of at least 100-mm calibre, combat aircraft and attack helicopters—in an area stretching from the Atlantic Ocean to the Ural Mountains (the Atlantic-to-the-Urals, ATTU). The treaty established the Joint Consultative Group (JCG) to promote its objectives and implementation.

The treaty was negotiated by the member states of the WTO and NATO within the framework of the Conference on Security and Co-operation in Europe (from 1995 the Organization for Security and Co-operation in Europe, OSCE).

The **1992 Tashkent Agreement**, adopted by the former Soviet republics with territories within the ATTU area of application (with the exception of Estonia, Latvia and Lithuania) and the **1992 Oslo Document** (Final Document of the Extraordinary Conference of the States Parties to the CFE Treaty) introduced modifications to the treaty required because of the emergence of new states after the break-up of the USSR.

A party may withdraw from the treaty, having given 150 days' notice, if it decides that its supreme interests have been jeopardized by extraordinary events related to the treaty's subject matter.

Parties (30): Armenia, Azerbaijan, Belarus, Belgium[2], Bulgaria[2], Canada[2], Czechia[2], Denmark[2], France, Georgia, Germany[2], Greece, Hungary[2], Iceland[2], Italy[2], Kazakhstan, Luxembourg[2], Moldova[2], Netherlands[2], Norway, Poland, Portugal[2], Romania, Russia[1], Slovakia[2], Spain, Turkey[2], UK[2], Ukraine, USA[2]

[1] On 14 July 2007 Russia declared its intention to suspend its participation in the CFE Treaty and associated documents and agreements, which took effect on 12 Dec. 2007. In Mar. 2015 Russia announced that it had decided to completely halt its participation in the treaty, including the JCG.

[2] In Nov.–Dec. 2011 these countries notified the depositary or the JCG that they would cease to perform their obligations under the treaty with regard to Russia.

The first review conference of the CFE Treaty adopted the **1996 Flank Document**, which reorganized the flank areas geographically and numerically, allowing Russia and Ukraine to deploy TLE in a less constraining manner.

Original (1990) treaty text: Dutch Ministry of Foreign Affairs, <https://repository.overheid.nl/frbr/vd/004285/1/pdf/004285_Gewaarmerkt_0.pdf>

Consolidated (1993) treaty text: Dutch Ministry of Foreign Affairs, <https://wetten.overheid.nl/BWBV0002009/>

Flank Document text: Organization for Security and Co-operation in Europe, <https://www.osce.org/library/14099?download=true>, annex A

Concluding Act of the Negotiation on Personnel Strength of Conventional Armed Forces in Europe (CFE-1A Agreement)

Signed by the parties to the CFE Treaty at Helsinki on 10 July 1992; entered into force simultaneously with the CFE Treaty; depositary Dutch Government

This politically binding agreement sets ceilings on the number of personnel of the conventional land-based armed forces of the parties within the ATTU area.

Agreement text: Organization for Security and Co-operation in Europe, <https://www.osce.org/library/14093?download=true>

Agreement on Adaptation of the Treaty on Conventional Armed Forces in Europe

Signed by the parties to the CFE Treaty at Istanbul on 19 November 1999; not in force; depositary Dutch Government

With the dissolution of the WTO and the accession of some former members to NATO, this agreement would have replaced the CFE Treaty's bloc-to-bloc military balance with a regional balance, established individual state limits on TLE holdings, and provided for a new structure of limitations and new military flexibility mechanisms, flank sub-limits and enhanced transparency. It would have opened the CFE regime to all other European states. It would have entered into force when ratified by all of the signatories.

The **1999 Final Act of the Conference of the CFE States Parties**, with annexes, contains politically binding arrangements with regard to Georgia, Moldova and Central Europe and to withdrawals of armed forces from foreign territories (known as the Istanbul commitments). Many signatories of the Agreement on Adaptation made their ratification contingent on the implementation of these political commitments.

Ratifications deposited (3): Belarus, Kazakhstan, Russia*[1]

* With reservation and/or declaration.

Signed but not ratified (27): Armenia, Azerbaijan, Belgium, Bulgaria, Canada, Czechia, Denmark, France, Germany, Georgia, Greece, Hungary, Iceland, Italy, Luxembourg, Moldavia, Netherlands, Norway, Poland, Portugal, Romania, Slovakia, Spain, Turkey, Ukraine[2], UK, USA

[1] On 14 July 2007 Russia declared its intention to suspend its participation in the CFE Treaty and associated documents and agreements, which took effect on 12 Dec. 2007. In Mar. 2015 Russia announced that it had decided to completely halt its participation in the treaty, including the JCG.

[2] Ukraine ratified the Agreement on Adaptation on 21 Sep. 2000 but did not deposit its instrument with the depositary.

Agreement text: Dutch Ministry of Foreign Affairs, <https://repository.overheid.nl/frbr/vd/009241/1/pdf/009241_Gewaarmerkt_0.pdf>

Treaty text as amended by 1999 agreement: SIPRI Yearbook 2000, <https://www.sipri.org/sites/default/files/SIPRI Yearbook 2000.pdf>, appendix 10B, pp. 627–42

Final Act text: Organization for Security and Co-operation in Europe, <https://www.osce.org/library/14114?download=true>

Treaty on Open Skies

Opened for signature at Helsinki on 24 March 1992; entered into force on 1 January 2002; depositaries Canadian and Hungarian governments

The treaty obligates the parties to submit their territories to short-notice unarmed surveillance flights. The area of application stretches from Vancouver, Canada, eastward to Vladivostok, Russia.

The treaty was negotiated between the member states of the WTO and NATO. Since 1 July 2002 any state can apply to accede to the treaty. A party may withdraw from the treaty, having given six months' notice.

Parties (33): Belarus, Belgium, Bosnia and Herzegovina, Bulgaria, Canada*, Croatia, Czechia, Denmark, Estonia, Finland, France, Georgia, Germany, Greece, Hungary, Iceland, Italy, Latvia, Lithuania, Luxembourg, Netherlands, Norway, Poland, Portugal, Romania, Russia, Slovakia, Slovenia, Spain*, Sweden*, Turkey, UK, Ukraine

* With reservation and/or declaration.

Signed but not ratified (1): Kyrgyzstan

Note: The USA withdrew from the treaty on 22 Nov. 2020. On 15 Jan. 2021 Russia announced that it would begin the domestic procedures for its withdrawal from the treaty.

Treaty text: Canada Treaty Information, <https://www.treaty-accord.gc.ca/text-texte.aspx?id=102747>

Treaty on the Southeast Asia Nuclear Weapon-Free Zone (Treaty of Bangkok)

Signed by the 10 member states of the Association of Southeast Asian Nations (ASEAN) at Bangkok on 15 December 1995; entered into force on 27 March 1997; depositary Thai Government

The South East Asia Nuclear Weapon-Free Zone includes the territories, the continental shelves and the exclusive economic zones of the states parties. The treaty prohibits the development, manufacture, acquisition or testing of nuclear weapons inside or outside the zone as well as the stationing and transport of nuclear weapons in or through the zone. Each state party may decide for itself whether to allow visits and transit by foreign ships and aircraft. The parties undertake not to dump at sea or discharge into the atmosphere anywhere within the zone any radioactive material or waste or dispose of radioactive material on land. The parties should conclude an agreement with the IAEA for the application of full-scope safeguards to their peaceful nuclear activities.

The treaty is open for accession by all states of South East Asia. If any party breaches an essential provision of the treaty, every other party may withdraw from the treaty.

Under a *Protocol* to the treaty, China, France, Russia, the UK and the USA are to undertake not to use or threaten to use nuclear weapons against any state party to the treaty. They should further undertake not to use nuclear weapons within the zone. The protocol will enter into force for each state party on the date of its deposit of the instrument of ratification.

Parties (10): Brunei Darussalam, Cambodia, Indonesia, Laos, Malaysia, Myanmar, Philippines, Singapore, Thailand, Viet Nam

Protocol (0): no signatures, no parties

Treaty text: ASEAN Secretariat, <https://asean.org/?static_post=treaty-on-the-southeast-asia-nuclear-weapon-free-zone>

Protocol text: ASEAN Secretariat, <https://asean.org/?static_post=protocol-to-the-treaty-on-the-southeeast-asia-nuclear-weapon-free-zone>

African Nuclear-Weapon-Free Zone Treaty (Treaty of Pelindaba)

Opened for signature at Cairo on 11 April 1996; entered into force on 15 July 2009; depositary Secretary-General of the African Union

The African Nuclear Weapon-Free Zone includes the territory of the continent of Africa, island states members of the African Union (AU) and all islands considered by the AU to be part of Africa.

The treaty prohibits the research, development, manufacture and acquisition of nuclear explosive devices and the testing or stationing of any nuclear explosive device in the zone. Each party remains free to allow visits and transit by foreign ships and aircraft. The treaty also prohibits any attack against nuclear installations. The parties undertake not to dump or permit the dumping of radio-active waste and other radioactive matter anywhere within the zone. Each party should individually conclude an agreement with the IAEA for the application of comprehensive safeguards to their peaceful nuclear activities. The treaty also established the African Commission on Nuclear Energy (AFCONE) to ensure compliance with the treaty.

The treaty is open for accession by all the states of Africa. A party may withdraw from the treaty, having given 12 months' notice, if it decides that its supreme interests have been jeopardized by extraordinary events related to the treaty's subject matter.

Under *Protocol* I China, France, Russia, the UK and the USA undertake not to use or threaten to use a nuclear explosive device against the parties to the treaty.

Under *Protocol II* China, France, Russia, the UK and the USA undertake not to test nuclear explosive devices within the zone.

Under *Protocol III* France and Spain are to undertake to observe certain provisions of the treaty with respect to the territories within the zone for which they are internationally responsible.

Parties (42): Algeria, Angola, Benin, Botswana, Burkina Faso, Burundi, *Cabo Verde*, Cameroon, Chad, Comoros, Congo (Republic of the), Côte d'Ivoire, Equatorial Guinea, Eswatini, Ethiopia, Gabon, Gambia, Ghana, Guinea, Guinea-Bissau, Kenya, Lesotho, Libya, Madagascar, Malawi, Mali, Mauritania, Mauritius, Mozambique, Namibia, Niger, Nigeria, Rwanda, Sahrawi Arab Democratic Republic (Western Sahara), Seychelles, Senegal, South Africa, Tanzania, Togo, Tunisia, Zambia, Zimbabwe

Signed but not ratified (12): Central African Republic, Congo (Democratic Republic of the), Djibouti, Egypt, Eritrea, Liberia, Morocco, Sao Tome and Principe, Sierra Leone, Somalia,

Sudan, Uganda

Parties to Protocol I (4): China, France*, Russia*, UK*; *signed but not ratified (1)*: USA*

Parties to Protocol II (4): China, France*, Russia*, UK*; *signed but not ratified (1)*: USA*

Parties to Protocol III (1): France*

* With reservation and/or declaration.

Treaty text: African Union, <https://au.int/sites/default/files/treaties/37288-treaty-0018_-_ the_african_nuclear-weapon-free_zone_treaty_the_treaty_of_pelindaba_e.pdf>

Agreement on Sub-Regional Arms Control (Florence Agreement)

Adopted by the 5 original parties at Florence and entered into force on 14 June 1996

The agreement was negotiated under the auspices of the OSCE in accordance with the mandate in Article IV of Annex 1-B of the 1995 General Framework Agreement for Peace in Bosnia and Herzegovina (Dayton Agreement). It sets numerical ceilings on armaments of the former warring parties. Five categories of heavy conventional weapons are included: battle tanks, armoured combat vehicles, heavy artillery (75 mm and above), combat aircraft and attack helicopters. The limits were reached by 31 October 1997; by that date 6580 weapon items, or 46 per cent of pre-June 1996 holdings, had been destroyed. By 2014 a further 3489 items had been destroyed voluntarily.

The implementation of the agreement was monitored and assisted by the OSCE's Personal Representative of the Chairman-in-Office and the Contact Group (France, Germany, Italy, Russia, the UK and the USA) and supported by other OSCE states. Under a two-phase action plan agreed in November 2009, responsibility for the implementation of the agreement and mutual inspection was transferred to the parties on 5 December 2014, following the signing of a new set of amendments to the agreement. The Sub-Regional Consultative Commission (SRCC) monitors implementation.

Parties (4): Bosnia and Herzegovina, Croatia, Montenegro, Serbia

Agreement text: RACVIAC–Centre for Security Cooperation, <https://www.racviac.org/ downloads/treaties_agreements/aIV.pdf>

Inter-American Convention Against the Illicit Manufacturing of and Trafficking in Firearms, Ammunition, Explosives, and Other Related Materials (CIFTA)

Opened for signature by the member states of the Organization of American States (OAS) at Washington, DC, on 14 November 1997; entered into force on 1 July 1998; depositary General Secretariat of the OAS

The purpose of the convention is to prevent, combat and eradicate the illicit manufacturing of and the trafficking in firearms, ammunition, explosives and other related materials; and to promote and facilitate cooperation and the exchange of information and experience among the parties. A party may withdraw from the convention, having given six months' notice.

Parties (31): Antigua and Barbuda, Argentina*, Bahamas, Barbados, Belize, Bolivia, Brazil, Chile, Colombia, Costa Rica, Dominica, Dominican Republic, Ecuador, El Salvador, Grenada, Guatemala, Guyana, Haiti, Honduras, Mexico, Nicaragua, Panama, Paraguay, Peru, Saint Kitts and Nevis, Saint Lucia, Saint Vincent and the Grenadines, Suriname, Trinidad and Tobago, Uruguay, Venezuela

* With reservation.

Signed but not ratified (3): Canada, Jamaica, USA

Convention text: OAS, <https://www.oas.org/en/sla/dil/inter_american_treaties_A-63_illicit_manufacturing_trafficking_firearms_ammunition_explosives.asp>

Inter-American Convention on Transparency in Conventional Weapons Acquisitions

Opened for signature by the member states of the OAS at Guatemala City on 7 June 1999; entered into force on 21 November 2002; depositary General Secretariat of the OAS

The objective of the convention is to contribute more fully to regional openness and transparency in the acquisition of conventional weapons by exchanging information regarding such acquisitions, for the purpose of promoting confidence among states in the Americas. A party may withdraw from the convention, having given 12 months' notice.

Parties (17): Argentina, Barbados, Brazil, Canada, Chile, Costa Rica, Dominican Republic, Ecuador, El Salvador, Guatemala, Mexico, Nicaragua, Panama, Paraguay, Peru, Uruguay, Venezuela

Signed but not ratified (6): Bolivia, Colombia, Dominica, Haiti, Honduras, USA

Convention text: OAS, <https://www.oas.org/en/sla/dil/inter_american_treaties_A-64_transparency_conventional_weapons_adquisitions.asp>

Protocol on the Control of Firearms, Ammunition and other related Materials in the Southern African Development Community (SADC) Region

Opened for signature by the members states of SADC at Blantyre on 14 August 2001; entered into force on 8 November 2004; depositary SADC Executive Secretary

The objectives of the protocol include the prevention, combating and eradication of the illicit manufacturing of firearms, ammunition and other related materials, and the prevention of their excessive and destabilizing accumulation, trafficking, possession and use in the region. A party may withdraw from the protocol, having given 12 months' notice.

An agreement amending the protocol was approved by the 40th ordinary SADC summit on 17 August 2020. The agreement broadens the scope of the protocol to include other conventional weapons, aligns it with the ATT and other international and regional conventions, and incorporates contemporary best practices and standards on corruption, tracing and cooperation. It is subject to ratification.

Parties (11): Botswana, Eswatini, Lesotho, Malawi, Mauritius, Mozambique, Namibia, South Africa, Tanzania, Zambia, Zimbabwe

Signed but not ratified (2*): Congo (Democratic Republic of the), Seychelles[†]

* Three member states of SADC—Angola, the Comoros and Madagascar—have neither signed nor ratified the protocol.
[†] Seychelles signed the protocol in 2001 but did not ratify it before withdrawing from SADC in 2004. It rejoined SADC in 2008.

Protocol text: SADC, <https://www.sadc.int/files/8613/5292/8361/Protocol_on_the_Control_of_Firearms_Ammunition2001.pdf>

Nairobi Protocol for the Prevention, Control and Reduction of Small Arms and Light Weapons in the Great Lakes Region and the Horn of Africa

Signed by the 10 member states of the Nairobi Secretariat on Small Arms and Light Weapons and the Seychelles at Nairobi on 21 April 2004; entered into force on 5 May 2006; depositary Regional Centre on Small Arms in the Great Lakes Region, the Horn of Africa and Bordering States (RECSA)

The objectives of the protocol include the prevention, combating and eradication of the illicit manufacture of, trafficking in, possession and use of small arms and light weapons (SALW) in the subregion. Its implementation is overseen by RECSA.

Parties (12): Burundi, Central African Republic, Congo (Democratic Republic of the), Congo (Republic of the), Djibouti, Eritrea, Ethiopia, Kenya, Rwanda, South Sudan, Sudan, Uganda

Signed but not ratified (3*): Seychelles, Somalia, Tanzania

* The accuracy of this list is uncertain. Some or all of these 3 states may have ratified the treaty. They all participate in the implementation activities of RECSA.

Protocol text: RECSA, <https://www.recsasec.org/wp-content/uploads/2018/08/Nairobi-Protocol.pdf>

ECOWAS Convention on Small Arms and Light Weapons, their Ammunition and Other Related Materials

Adopted by the 15 member states of the Economic Community of West African States (ECOWAS) at Abuja, on 14 June 2006; entered into force on 29 September 2009; depositary President of the ECOWAS Commission

The convention obligates the parties to prevent and combat the excessive and destabilizing accumulation of SALW in the ECOWAS member states. The convention bans the transfer of SALW into, through or from the territories of the parties. The ECOWAS member states may, by consensus, grant a party an exemption for national defence and security needs or for use in multilateral peace operations. Possession of light weapons by civilians is banned and their possession of small arms must be regulated. Each party must also control the manufacture of SALW, establish registers of SALW and establish a national commission to implement the convention.

A party may withdraw from the treaty, having given 12 months' notice, if it decides that its supreme interests have been jeopardized by extraordinary events related to the treaty's subject matter.

Parties (14): Benin, Burkina Faso, Cabo Verde, Côte d'Ivoire, Ghana, Guinea, Guinea-Bissau, Liberia, Mali, Niger, Nigeria, Senegal, Sierra Leone, Togo

Signed but not ratified (1): Gambia

Convention text: ECOWAS Commission, <https://documentation.ecowas.int/download/en/legal_documents/protocols/Convention on Small Arms and Light Weapons, their Ammunitions and other Related Matters.pdf>

Treaty on a Nuclear-Weapon-Free Zone in Central Asia (Treaty of Semipalatinsk)

Signed by the 5 Central Asian states at Semipalatinsk on 8 September 2006; entered into force on 21 March 2009; depositary Kyrgyz Government

The Central Asian Nuclear Weapon-Free Zone is defined as the territories of Kazakhstan, Kyrgyzstan, Tajikistan, Turkmenistan, Uzbekistan. The treaty obligates the parties not to conduct research on, develop, manufacture, stockpile or otherwise acquire, possess or have control over nuclear weapons or any other nuclear explosive device by any means anywhere. A party may withdraw from the treaty, having given 12 months' notice, if it decides that its supreme interests have been jeopardized by extraordinary events related to the treaty's subject matter.

Under a *Protocol* China, France, Russia, the UK and the USA undertake not to use or threaten to use a nuclear explosive device against the parties to the treaty.

Parties (5): Kazakhstan, Kyrgyzstan, Tajikistan, Turkmenistan, Uzbekistan

Parties to the protocol (4): China, France*, Russia, UK*; *signed but not ratified (1)*: USA

* With reservations and/or declaration.

Treaty and protocol text: United Nations Treaty Collection, <https://treaties.un.org/doc/Publication/UNTS/No Volume/51633/Part/I-51633-080000028023b006.pdf>

Central African Convention for the Control of Small Arms and Light Weapons, Their Ammunition and All Parts and Components That Can Be Used for Their Manufacture, Repair and Assembly (Kinshasa Convention)

Opened for signature by the 10 member states of the Communauté économique d'États de l'Afrique Centrale (CEEAC, Economic Community of Central African States) and Rwanda at Brazzaville on 19 November 2010; entered into force on 8 March 2017; depositary UN Secretary-General

The objectives of the convention are to prevent, combat and eradicate illicit trade and trafficking in SALW in Central Africa (defined to be the territory of the members of CEEAC and Rwanda); to strengthen the control in the region of the manufacture, trade, transfer and use of SALW; to combat armed violence and ease the human suffering in the region caused by SALW; and to foster cooperation and confidence among the states parties.

A party may withdraw from the treaty, having given 12 months' notice.

Parties (8): Angola, Cameroon, Central African Republic, Chad, Congo (Republic of the), Equatorial Guinea, Gabon, Sao Tome and Principe

Signed but not ratified (3): Burundi, Congo (Democratic Republic of the), Rwanda

Treaty text: United Nations Treaty Collection, <https://treaties.un.org/doc/Treaties/2010/04/20100430 01-12 PM/Ch_xxvi-7.pdf>

Vienna Document 2011 on Confidence- and Security-Building Measures

Adopted by the participating states of the Organization for Security and Co-operation in Europe at Vienna on 30 November 2011; entered into force on 1 December 2011

The Vienna Document 2011 builds on the 1986 Stockholm Document on Confidence- and Security-Building Measures (CSBMs) and Disarmament in Europe and previous Vienna Documents (1990, 1992, 1994 and 1999). The Vienna Document 1990 provided for annual exchange of military information, military budget exchange, risk reduction procedures, a communication network and an annual CSBM implementation assessment. The Vienna Document 1992 and the Vienna Document 1994 extended the area of application and introduced new mechanisms and parameters for military activities, defence planning and military contacts. The Vienna Document 1999 introduced regional measures aimed at increasing transparency and confidence in a bilateral, multilateral and regional context and some improvements, in particular regarding the constraining measures.

The Vienna Document 2011 incorporates revisions on such matters as the timing of verification activities and demonstrations of new types of weapon and equipment system. It also establishes a procedure for updating the Vienna Document every five years. The reissue due in 2016 did not occur.

Participating states of the OSCE (57): See annex B

Document text: Organization for Security and Co-operation in Europe, <https://www.osce.org/files/f/documents/a/4/86597.pdf>

III. Bilateral treaties

Treaty on the Limitation of Anti-Ballistic Missile Systems (ABM Treaty)

Signed by the USA and the USSR at Moscow on 26 May 1972; entered into force on 3 October 1972; not in force from 13 June 2002

The parties—Russia and the USA—undertook not to build nationwide defences against ballistic missile attack and to limit the development and deployment of permitted strategic missile defences. The treaty prohibited the parties from giving air defence missiles, radars or launchers the technical ability to counter strategic ballistic missiles and from testing them in a strategic ABM mode. It also established a standing consultative commission to promote its objectives and implementation. The **1974 Protocol** to the ABM Treaty introduced further numerical restrictions on permitted ballistic missile defences.

In 1997 Belarus, Kazakhstan, Russia, Ukraine and the USA signed a memorandum of understanding that would have made Belarus, Kazakhstan and Ukraine parties to the treaty along with Russia as successor states of the USSR and a set of agreed statements that would specify the demarcation line between strategic missile defences (which are not permitted under the treaty) and non-strategic or theatre missile defences (which are permitted under the treaty). The 1997 agreements were ratified by Russia in April 2000, but the USA did not ratify them and they did not enter into force.

On 13 December 2001 the USA notified Russia that it had decided to withdraw from the treaty, citing the ballistic missile threat to its territory from other states; the withdrawal came into effect six months later, on 13 June 2002.

Treaty text: United Nations Treaty Series, vol. 944 (1974), <https://treaties.un.org/doc/Publication/UNTS/Volume 944/v944.pdf>, pp. 13–17

Protocol text: US Department of State, <https://2009-2017.state.gov/t/avc/trty/101888.htm #protocolabm>

Treaty on the Limitation of Underground Nuclear Weapon Tests (Threshold Test-Ban Treaty, TTBT)

Signed by the USA and the USSR at Moscow on 3 July 1974; entered into force on 11 December 1990

The parties—Russia and the USA—undertake not to carry out any underground nuclear weapon test having a yield exceeding 150 kilotons. The 1974 verification protocol was replaced in 1990 with a new protocol.

Either party may withdraw from the treaty, having given the other 12 months' notice, if it decides that its supreme interests have been jeopardized by extraordinary events related to the treaty's subject matter.

Treaty and protocol texts: United Nations Treaty Series, vol. 1714 (1993), <https://treaties.un.org/doc/Publication/UNTS/Volume 1714/v1714.pdf>, pp. 217–301

Treaty on Underground Nuclear Explosions for Peaceful Purposes (Peaceful Nuclear Explosions Treaty, PNET)

Signed by the USA and the USSR at Moscow and Washington, DC, on 28 May 1976; entered into force simultaneously with the TTBT, on 11 December 1990

The parties—Russia and the USA—undertake not to carry out any individual underground nuclear explosion for peaceful purposes having a yield exceeding 15 kilotons or any group explosion having an aggregate yield exceeding 150 kilotons; and not to carry out any group explosion having an aggregate yield exceeding 1500 kilotons unless the individual explosions in the group could be identified and measured by agreed verification procedures. The treaty established a joint consultative commission to promote its objectives and implementation. The 1976 verification protocol was replaced in 1990 with a new protocol.

The treaty cannot be terminated while the TTBT is in force. If the TTBT is terminated, then either party may withdraw from this treaty at any time.

Treaty and protocol texts: United Nations Treaty Series, vol. 1714 (1993), <https://treaties.un.org/doc/Publication/UNTS/Volume 1714/v1714.pdf>, pp. 432–72

Treaty on the Elimination of Intermediate-Range and Shorter-Range Missiles (INF Treaty)

Signed by the USA and the USSR at Washington, DC, on 8 December 1987; entered into force on 1 June 1988; not in force from 2 August 2019

The treaty obligated the original parties—the USA and the USSR—to destroy all ground-launched ballistic and cruise missiles with a range of 500–5500 kilometres (intermediate-range, 1000–5500 km; and shorter-range, 500–1000 km) and their launchers by 1 June 1991. The treaty established a special verification commission (SVC) to promote its objectives and implementation.

A total of 2692 missiles were eliminated by May 1991. For 10 years after 1 June 1991 on-site inspections were conducted to verify compliance. The use of surveillance satellites for data collection continued after the end of on-site inspections on 31 May 2001.

In 1994 treaty membership was expanded to include Belarus, Kazakhstan and Ukraine in addition to Russia and the USA.

On 2 February 2019 the USA notified the other parties that it would withdraw from the treaty in six months, citing the alleged deployment by Russia of a missile in breach of the treaty's limits. The USA and then Russia also suspended their obligations under the treaty. The withdrawal came into effect on 2 August 2019.

Treaty text: United Nations Treaty Series, vol. 1657 (1991), <https://treaties.un.org/doc/Publication/UNTS/Volume 1657/v1657.pdf>, pp. 4–167

Treaty on the Reduction and Limitation of Strategic Offensive Arms (START I)

Signed by the USA and the USSR at Moscow on 31 July 1991; entered into force on 5 December 1994; expired on 5 December 2009

The treaty obligated the original parties—the USA and the USSR—to make phased reductions in their offensive strategic nuclear forces over a seven-year period. It set numerical limits on deployed strategic nuclear delivery vehicles—intercontinental ballistic missiles (ICBMs), submarine-launched ballistic missiles (SLBMs) and heavy bombers—and the nuclear warheads they carry.

In the Protocol to Facilitate the Implementation of START (**1992 Lisbon Protocol**), which entered into force on 5 December 1994, Belarus, Kazakhstan and Ukraine also assumed the obligations of the former USSR under the treaty alongside Russia.

Treaty and protocol texts: US Department of State, <https://2009-2017.state.gov/t/avc/trty/146007.htm>

Treaty on Further Reduction and Limitation of Strategic Offensive Arms (START II)

Signed by Russia and the USA at Moscow on 3 January 1993; not in force

The treaty would have obligated the parties to eliminate their ICBMs with multiple independently targeted re-entry vehicles (MIRVs) and reduce the number of their deployed strategic nuclear warheads to no more than 3000–3500 each (of which no more than 1750 were to be deployed on SLBMs) by 1 January 2003. On 26 September 1997 the two parties signed a *Protocol* to the treaty providing for the extension until the end of 2007 of the period of implementation of the treaty.

The two signatories ratified the treaty but never exchanged the instruments of ratification. The treaty thus never entered into force. On 14 June 2002, as a response to the taking effect on 13 June of the USA's withdrawal from the ABM Treaty, Russia declared that it would no longer be bound by START II.

Treaty and protocol texts: US Department of State, <https://2009-2017.state.gov/t/avc/trty/102887.htm>

Treaty on Strategic Offensive Reductions (SORT, Moscow Treaty)

Signed by Russia and the USA at Moscow on 24 May 2002; entered into force on 1 June 2003; not in force from 5 February 2011

The treaty obligated the parties to reduce the number of their operationally deployed strategic nuclear warheads so that the aggregate numbers did not exceed 1700–2200 for each party by 31 December 2012. The treaty was superseded by New START on 5 February 2011.

Treaty text: *United Nations Treaty Series*, vol. 2350 (2005), <https://treaties.un.org/doc/Publication/UNTS/Volume 2350/v2350.pdf>

Treaty on Measures for the Further Reduction and Limitation of Strategic Offensive Arms (New START, Prague Treaty)

Signed by Russia and the USA at Prague on 8 April 2010; entered into force on 5 February 2011

The treaty obligates the parties—Russia and the USA—to each reduce their number of (*a*) deployed ICBMs, SLBMs and heavy bombers to 700; (*b*) warheads on deployed ICBMs and SLBMs and warheads counted for deployed heavy bombers to 1550; and (*c*) deployed and non-deployed ICBM launchers, SLBM launchers and heavy bombers to 800. The reductions were achieved by 5 February 2018, as required by the treaty.

The treaty established a bilateral consultative commission (BCC) to resolve questions about compliance and other implementation issues. A protocol to the treaty contains verifications mechanisms.

The treaty followed on from START I and superseded SORT. After being in force for an initial period of 10 years, the treaty was extended on 3 February 2021 for a further period of 5 years, until 5 February 2026. It cannot be extended further but may be superseded by a subsequent agreement. Either party may also withdraw from the treaty, having given the other three months' notice, if it decides that its supreme interests have been jeopardized by extraordinary events related to the treaty's subject matter.

Treaty and protocol texts: US Department of State, <https://2009-2017.state.gov/t/avc/newstart/c44126.htm>

Annex B. International security cooperation bodies

This annex describes the main international organizations, intergovernmental bodies, treaty-implementing bodies and transfer control regimes whose aims include the promotion of security, stability, peace or arms control and lists their members or participants as of 1 January 2021. The bodies are divided into three categories: those with a global focus or membership (section I), those with a regional focus or membership (section II) and those that aim to control strategic trade (section III).

The member states of the United Nations and organs within the UN system are listed first, followed by all other bodies in alphabetical order. Not all members or participants of these bodies are UN member states. States that joined or first participated in the body during 2020 are shown in italics. The address of an internet site with information about each organization is provided where available. On the arms control and disarmament agreements mentioned here, see annex A.

I. Bodies with a global focus or membership

United Nations (UN)

The UN, the world intergovernmental organization, was founded in 1945 through the adoption of its Charter. Its headquarters are in New York, USA. The six principal UN organs are the General Assembly, the Security Council, the Economic and Social Council (ECOSOC), the Trusteeship Council (which suspended operation in 1994), the International Court of Justice (ICJ) and the Secretariat.

The General Assembly has six main committees. The First Committee (Disarmament and International Security Committee) deals with disarmament and related international security questions. The Fourth Committee (Special Political and Decolonization Committee) deals with a variety of subjects including decolonization, Palestinian refugees and human rights, peacekeeping, mine action, outer space, public information, atomic radiation and the University for Peace.

The UN Office for Disarmament Affairs (UNODA), a department of the UN Secretariat, promotes disarmament of nuclear, biological, chemical and conventional weapons. The UN also has a large number of specialized agencies and other autonomous bodies.

UN member states (193) and year of membership

Afghanistan, 1946
Albania, 1955
Algeria, 1962
Andorra, 1993
Angola, 1976
Antigua and Barbuda, 1981
Argentina, 1945
Armenia, 1992
Australia, 1945
Austria, 1955
Azerbaijan, 1992
Bahamas, 1973
Bahrain, 1971
Bangladesh, 1974
Barbados, 1966
Belarus, 1945
Belgium, 1945
Belize, 1981
Benin, 1960
Bhutan, 1971
Bolivia, 1945
Bosnia and Herzegovina, 1992
Botswana, 1966
Brazil, 1945
Brunei Darussalam, 1984
Bulgaria, 1955
Burkina Faso, 1960
Burundi, 1962
Cabo Verde, 1975
Cambodia, 1955
Cameroon, 1960
Canada, 1945
Central African Republic, 1960
Chad, 1960
Chile, 1945
China, 1945
Colombia, 1945
Comoros, 1975
Congo, Democratic Republic of the, 1960
Congo, Republic of the, 1960
Costa Rica, 1945
Côte d'Ivoire, 1960
Croatia, 1992
Cuba, 1945
Cyprus, 1960
Czechia, 1993
Denmark, 1945
Djibouti, 1977
Dominica, 1978
Dominican Republic, 1945

Ecuador, 1945
Egypt, 1945
El Salvador, 1945
Equatorial Guinea, 1968
Eritrea, 1993
Estonia, 1991
Eswatini, 1968
Ethiopia, 1945
Fiji, 1970
Finland, 1955
France, 1945
Gabon, 1960
Gambia, 1965
Georgia, 1992
Germany, 1973
Ghana, 1957
Greece, 1945
Grenada, 1974
Guatemala, 1945
Guinea, 1958
Guinea-Bissau, 1974
Guyana, 1966
Haiti, 1945
Honduras, 1945
Hungary, 1955
Iceland, 1946
India, 1945
Indonesia, 1950
Iran, 1945
Iraq, 1945
Ireland, 1955
Israel, 1949
Italy, 1955
Jamaica, 1962
Japan, 1956
Jordan, 1955
Kazakhstan, 1992
Kenya, 1963
Kiribati, 1999
Korea, Democratic People's Republic of (North Korea), 1991
Korea, Republic of (South Korea), 1991
Kuwait, 1963
Kyrgyzstan, 1992
Laos, 1955
Latvia, 1991
Lebanon, 1945
Lesotho, 1966
Liberia, 1945
Libya, 1955

Liechtenstein, 1990
Lithuania, 1991
Luxembourg, 1945
Madagascar, 1960
Malawi, 1964
Malaysia, 1957
Maldives, 1965
Mali, 1960
Malta, 1964
Marshall Islands, 1991
Mauritania, 1961
Mauritius, 1968
Mexico, 1945
Micronesia, 1991
Moldova, 1992
Monaco, 1993
Mongolia, 1961
Montenegro, 2006
Morocco, 1956
Mozambique, 1975
Myanmar, 1948
Namibia, 1990
Nauru, 1999
Nepal, 1955
Netherlands, 1945
New Zealand, 1945
Nicaragua, 1945
Niger, 1960
Nigeria, 1960
North Macedonia, 1993
Norway, 1945
Oman, 1971
Pakistan, 1947
Palau, 1994
Panama, 1945
Papua New Guinea, 1975
Paraguay, 1945
Peru, 1945
Philippines, 1945
Poland, 1945
Portugal, 1955
Qatar, 1971
Romania, 1955
Russia, 1945
Rwanda, 1962
Saint Kitts and Nevis, 1983
Saint Lucia, 1979
Saint Vincent and the Grenadines, 1980
Samoa, 1976
San Marino, 1992
Sao Tome and Principe, 1975

Saudi Arabia, 1945
Senegal, 1960
Serbia, 2000
Seychelles, 1976
Sierra Leone, 1961
Singapore, 1965
Slovakia, 1993
Slovenia, 1992
Solomon Islands, 1978
Somalia, 1960
South Africa, 1945
South Sudan, 2011
Spain, 1955
Sri Lanka, 1955
Sudan, 1956

Suriname, 1975
Sweden, 1946
Switzerland, 2002
Syria, 1945
Tajikistan, 1992
Tanzania, 1961
Thailand, 1946
Timor-Leste, 2002
Togo, 1960
Tonga, 1999
Trinidad and Tobago, 1962
Tunisia, 1956
Turkey, 1945
Turkmenistan, 1992
Tuvalu, 2000

Uganda, 1962
UK, 1945
Ukraine, 1945
United Arab Emirates, 1971
Uruguay, 1945
USA, 1945
Uzbekistan, 1992
Vanuatu, 1981
Venezuela, 1945
Viet Nam, 1977
Yemen, 1947
Zambia, 1964
Zimbabwe, 1980

Non-member observer states (2): Holy See, Palestine

Website: <https://www.un.org/>

UN Security Council

The Security Council has responsibility for the maintenance of international peace and security. All UN members states must comply with its decisions. It has 5 permanent members, which can each exercise a veto on the Council's decisions, and 10 non-permanent members elected by the UN General Assembly for two-year terms.

Permanent members (the P5): China, France, Russia, UK, USA

Non-permanent members (10): Estonia*, India[†], Ireland[†], Kenya[†], Mexico[†], Niger*, Norway[†], Saint Vincent and the Grenadines*, Tunisia*, Viet Nam*

   * Member in 2020–21.
   [†] Member in 2021–22.

Website: <https://www.un.org/securitycouncil/>

Conference on Disarmament (CD)

The CD is intended to be the single multilateral arms control and disarmament negotiating forum of the international community. It has been enlarged and renamed several times since 1960. It is not a UN body but reports to the UN General Assembly. It is based in Geneva, Switzerland.

Members (65): Algeria, Argentina, Australia, Austria, Bangladesh, Belarus, Belgium, Brazil, Bulgaria, Cameroon, Canada, Chile, China, Colombia, Congo (Democratic Republic of the), Cuba, Ecuador, Egypt, Ethiopia, Finland, France, Germany, Hungary, India, Indonesia, Iran, Iraq, Ireland, Israel, Italy, Japan, Kazakhstan, Kenya, Korea (North), Korea (South), Malaysia, Mexico, Mongolia, Morocco, Myanmar, Netherlands, New Zealand, Nigeria, Norway, Pakistan, Peru, Poland, Romania, Russia, Senegal, Slovakia, South Africa, Spain, Sri Lanka, Sweden, Switzerland, Syria, Tunisia, Turkey, UK, Ukraine, USA, Venezuela, Viet Nam, Zimbabwe

Website: <https://www.un.org/disarmament/conference-on-disarmament/>

UN Disarmament Commission (UNDC)

The UNDC in its original form was established in 1952. After changes of name and format, it became the Conference on Disarmament in 1978. In that year, the UN General Assembly re-established the UNDC in its current form. It meets for three weeks each year in New York to consider a small number of disarmament issues—currently two substantive items per session—and formulate consensus principles, guidelines and recommendations. It was unable to reach agreement on any such outcome in 2000–16, but in 2017 adopted consensus recommendations on 'Practical confidence-building measures in the field of conventional weapons'.

Members (193): The UN member states

Website: <https://www.un.org/disarmament/institutions/disarmament-commission/>

UN Peacebuilding Commission (PBC)

The PBC was established in 2005 by the General Assembly and the Security Council to advise them on post-conflict peacebuilding and recovery, to marshal resources and to propose integrated strategies.

The General Assembly, the Security Council and ECOSOC each elect seven members of the PBC for two-year terms; the remaining members are the top five providers of military personnel and civilian police to UN missions and the top five contributors of funds to the UN. Additional states and organizations participate in country-specific meetings on countries on the PBC agenda.

Members (30): Bangladesh**||, Brazil**†, Canada**#, China**‡, Colombia**§, Costa Rica**†, Egypt**†, Ethiopia**||, France**‡, Germany**#, India**||, Japan**#, Kenya*‡, Korea (South)**§, Lebanon**†, Netherlands**#, Nigeria**§, Norway**§, Pakistan**||, Peru*†, Saint Vincent and the Grenadines*‡, Slovakia*†, Switzerland**§, Thailand**§, Russia**‡, Rwanda**||, South Africa**†, Sweden**#, UK**‡, USA**‡

    * Member until 31 Dec. 2021.
    ** Member until 31 Dec. 2022.
    † Elected by the General Assembly.
    ‡ Elected by the Security Council.
    § Elected by ECOSOC.
    || Top 5 contributor of personnel.
    # Top 5 contributor of funds.

    Note: The full membership of the PBC is 31. One seat elected by ECOSOC was vacant as of 1 Jan. 2021.

Website: <https://www.un.org/peacebuilding/commission/>

International Atomic Energy Agency (IAEA)

The IAEA is an intergovernmental organization within the UN system. It is mandated by its Statute, which entered into force in 1957, to promote the peaceful uses of atomic energy and ensure that nuclear activities are not used to further any military purpose. Under the 1968 Non-Proliferation Treaty and the nuclear weapon-free zone treaties, non-nuclear weapon states must accept IAEA nuclear safeguards to demonstrate the fulfilment of their obligation not to manufacture nuclear weapons. Its headquarters are in Vienna, Austria.

Members (172): Afghanistan, Albania, Algeria, Angola, Antigua and Barbuda, Argentina, Armenia, Australia, Austria, Azerbaijan, Bahamas, Bahrain, Bangladesh, Barbados, Belarus, Belgium, Belize, Benin, Bolivia, Bosnia and Herzegovina, Botswana, Brazil, Brunei Darussalam, Bulgaria, Burkina Faso, Burundi, Cambodia, Cameroon, Canada, Central African Republic, Chad, Chile, China, Colombia, *Comoros*, Congo (Democratic Republic of the), Congo (Republic of the), Costa Rica, Côte d'Ivoire, Croatia, Cuba, Cyprus, Czechia, Denmark, Djibouti, Dominica, Dominican Republic, Ecuador, Egypt, El Salvador, Eritrea, Estonia, Eswatini, Ethiopia, Fiji, Finland, France, Gabon, Georgia, Germany, Ghana, Greece, Grenada, Guatemala, Guyana, Haiti, Holy See, Honduras, Hungary, Iceland, India, Indonesia, Iran, Iraq, Ireland, Israel, Italy, Jamaica, Japan, Jordan, Kazakhstan, Kenya, Korea (South), Kuwait, Kyrgyzstan, Laos, Latvia, Lebanon, Lesotho, Liberia, Libya, Liechtenstein, Lithuania, Luxembourg, Madagascar, Malawi, Malaysia, Mali, Malta, Marshall Islands, Mauritania, Mauritius, Mexico, Moldova, Monaco, Mongolia, Montenegro, Morocco, Mozambique, Myanmar, Namibia, Nepal, Netherlands, New Zealand, Nicaragua, Niger, Nigeria, North Macedonia, Norway, Oman, Pakistan, Palau, Panama, Papua New Guinea, Paraguay, Peru, Philippines, Poland, Portugal, Qatar, Rwanda, Romania, Russia, Saint Lucia, Saint Vincent and the Grenadines, San Marino, Saudi Arabia, Senegal, Serbia, Seychelles, Sierra Leone, Singapore, Slovakia, Slovenia, South Africa, Spain, Sri Lanka, Sudan, Sweden, Switzerland, Syria, Tajikistan, Tanzania, Thailand, Togo, Trinidad and Tobago, Tunisia, Turkey, Turkmenistan, Uganda, UK, Ukraine, United Arab Emirates, Uruguay, USA, Uzbekistan, Vanuatu, Venezuela, Viet Nam, Yemen, Zambia, Zimbabwe

Notes: North Korea was a member of the IAEA until June 1994. In addition to the 172 members as of 1 Jan. 2021, Samoa became a member on 7 Apr. 2021. The IAEA General Conference had also approved the membership of Cabo Verde, Gambia, Guinea and Tonga; each will take effect once the state deposits the necessary legal instruments with the IAEA.

Website: <https://www.iaea.org/>

International Court of Justice (ICJ)

The ICJ was established in 1945 by the UN Charter and is the principal judicial organ of the UN. The court's role is to settle legal disputes submitted to it by states and to give advisory opinions on legal questions referred to it by authorized UN organs and specialized agencies. The Court is composed of 15 judges, who are elected for terms of office of nine years by the UN General Assembly and the Security Council. Its seat is at The Hague, the Netherlands.

Website: <https://www.icj-cij.org/>

Bilateral Consultative Commission (BCC)

The BCC is a forum established under the 2010 Russian–US Treaty on Measures for the Further Reduction and Limitation of Strategic Offensive Arms (New START, Prague Treaty) to discuss issues related to the treaty's implementation. It replaced the joint compliance and inspection commission (JCIC) of the 1991 START treaty. The BCC is required to meet at least twice each year in Geneva, Switzerland, unless the parties agree otherwise. Its work is confidential.

Website: US Department of Defense, Under Secretary of Defense for Acquisition and Sustainment, <https://www.acq.osd.mil/asda/iipm/sdc/tc/nst/NSTtoc.htm>

Commonwealth of Nations

Established in its current form in 1949, the Commonwealth is an organization of developed and developing countries whose aim is to advance democracy, human rights, and sustainable economic and social development within its member states and beyond. It adopted a charter reaffirming its core values and principles in 2012. The members' leaders meet in the biennial Commonwealth Heads of Government Meetings (CHOGMs). Its secretariat is in London, UK.

Members (54): Antigua and Barbuda, Australia, Bahamas, Bangladesh, Barbados, Belize, Botswana, Brunei Darussalam, Cameroon, Canada, Cyprus, Dominica, Eswatini, Fiji, Gambia, Ghana, Grenada, Guyana, India, Jamaica, Kenya, Kiribati, Lesotho, Malawi, Malaysia, *Maldives*, Malta, Mauritius, Mozambique, Namibia, Nauru, New Zealand, Nigeria, Pakistan, Papua New Guinea, Rwanda[†], Saint Kitts and Nevis, Saint Lucia, Saint Vincent and the Grenadines, Samoa, Seychelles, Sierra Leone, Singapore, Solomon Islands, South Africa, Sri Lanka, Tanzania, Tonga, Trinidad and Tobago, Tuvalu, Uganda, UK*, Vanuatu, Zambia

  * CHOGM host in 2018 and Chair-in-Office in 2018–10.
  [†] CHOGM host in 2020 and Chair-in-Office in 2020–23.

Note: Zimbabwe (which withdrew in 2013) applied to rejoin the Commonwealth in May 2018.

Website: <https://www.thecommonwealth.org/>

Comprehensive Nuclear-Test-Ban Treaty Organization (CTBTO)

The CTBTO will become operational when the 1996 Comprehensive Nuclear-Test-Ban Treaty (CTBT) has entered into force. It will resolve questions of compliance with the treaty and act as a forum for consultation and cooperation among the states parties. A Preparatory Commission and provisional Technical Secretariat are preparing for the work of the CTBTO, in particular by establishing the International Monitoring System, consisting of seismic, hydro-acoustic, infrasound and radionuclide stations from which data is transmitted to the CTBTO International Data Centre. Their headquarters are in Vienna, Austria.

Signatories to the CTBT (184): See annex A

Website: <https://www.ctbto.org/>

Financial Action Task Force (FATF)

The FATF is an intergovernmental policymaking body whose purpose is to establish international standards and develop and promote policies, at both national and international levels. It was established in 1989 by the Group of Seven (G7), initially to examine and develop measures to combat money laundering; its mandate was expanded in 2001 to incorporate efforts to combat terrorist financing and again in 2008 to include the financing of weapon of mass destruction (WMD) proliferation efforts. It published revised recommendations in 2012. Its secretariat is in Paris, France.

Members (39): Argentina, Australia, Austria, Belgium, Brazil, Canada, China, Denmark, European Commission, Finland, France, Germany, Greece, Gulf Cooperation Council, Hong Kong (China), Iceland, India, Ireland, Israel, Italy, Japan, Korea (South), Luxembourg, Malaysia, Mexico, Netherlands, New Zealand, Norway, Portugal, Russia, Saudi Arabia, Singapore, South Africa, Spain, Sweden, Switzerland, Turkey, UK, USA

Website: <https://www.fatf-gafi.org/>

Global Initiative to Combat Nuclear Terrorism (GICNT)

The GICNT was established in 2006 as a voluntary international partnership of states and international organizations that are committed to strengthening global capacity to prevent, detect and respond to nuclear terrorism. The GICNT works towards this goal by conducting multilateral activities that strengthen the plans, policies, procedures and interoperability of its partner. The partners meet at biennial plenaries. Russia and the USA act as co-chairs.

Partners (89): Afghanistan, Albania, Algeria, Argentina, Armenia, Australia, Austria, Azerbaijan, Bahrain, Belarus, Belgium, Bosnia and Herzegovina, Bulgaria, Cabo Verde, Cambodia, Canada, Chile, China, Côte d'Ivoire, Croatia, Cyprus, Czechia, Denmark, Estonia, Finland, France, Georgia, Germany, Greece, Hungary, Iceland, India, Iraq, Ireland, Israel, Italy, Japan, Jordan, Kazakhstan, Korea (South), Kyrgyzstan, Latvia, Libya, Lithuania, Luxembourg, Madagascar, Malaysia, Malta, Mauritius, Mexico, Moldova, Montenegro, Morocco, Nepal, Netherlands, New Zealand, Nigeria, North Macedonia, Norway, Pakistan, Palau, Panama, Paraguay, Philippines, Poland, Portugal, Romania, Russia, Saudi Arabia, Serbia, Seychelles, Singapore, Slovakia, Slovenia, Spain, Sri Lanka, Sweden, Switzerland, Tajikistan, Thailand, Turkey, Turkmenistan, UK, Ukraine, United Arab Emirates, USA, Uzbekistan, Viet Nam, Zambia

Official observers (6): European Union, International Atomic Energy Agency, International Criminal Police Organization (INTERPOL), UN Interregional Crime and Justice Research Institute, UN Office on Drugs and Crime, UN Office of Counter-Terrorism

Website: <https://gicnt.org/>

Group of Seven (G7)

The G7 is a group of leading industrialized countries that have met informally, at the level of head of state or government, since the 1970s. The presidents of the European Council and the European Commission represent the European Union at summits.

Between 1997 and 2013 the G7 members and Russia met together as the Group of Eight (G8). Following Russia's annexation of Crimea, the G7 states decided in March 2014 to meet without Russia until further notice.

Members (7): Canada, France, Germany‡, Italy, Japan, UK†, USA*

* G7 presidency in 2020
† G7 presidency and summit host in 2021.
‡ G7 presidency and summit host in 2022.

Website: <https://www.international.gc.ca/world-monde/international_relations-relations_internationales/g7/index.aspx>

Global Partnership against the Spread of Weapons and Materials of Mass Destruction

The Global Partnership was launched in 2002 by the G8 to address non-proliferation, disarmament, counterterrorism and nuclear safety issues. The members meet twice each year, hosted by the state holding the G7 presidency, with the main goal of launching specific projects to tackle the abuse of weapons and materials of mass destruction and reduce chemical, biological, radioactive and nuclear risks. The Global Partnership was extended for an unspecified period in May 2011.

Members (31): Australia, Belgium, Canada, Chile, Czechia, Denmark, European Union, Finland, France, Georgia, Germany, Hungary, Ireland, Italy, Japan, Jordan, Kazakhstan, Korea (South), Mexico, Netherlands, New Zealand, Norway, Philippines, Poland, Portugal, Spain, Sweden, Switzerland, UK, Ukraine, USA

Note: Russia was a founding partner of the Global Partnership, but it ceased to be a partner following its exclusion from the G8.

Website: <https://www.gpwmd.com/>

International Criminal Court (ICC)

The ICC is a permanent international court dealing with the crime of genocide, crimes against humanity, war crimes and the crime of aggression. Its seat is at The Hague, the Netherlands, and it has field offices in the Central African Republic, Côte d'Ivoire, the Democratic Republic of the Congo, Kenya and Uganda. The court has 18 judges and an independent prosecutor, elected by the assembly of states parties for nine-year terms.

The court's powers and jurisdiction are defined by the 1998 Rome Statute and its amendments. While the ICC is independent of the UN, the Rome Statute grants the UN Security Council certain powers of referral and deferral.

Parties to the Rome Statute (123) and its amendments: See annex A

Website: <https://www.icc-cpi.int/>

Non-Aligned Movement (NAM)

NAM was established in 1961 as a forum for non-aligned states to consult on political, economic and arms control issues and coordinate their positions in the UN.

Members (120): Afghanistan, Algeria, Angola, Antigua and Barbuda, Azerbaijan*, Bahamas, Bahrain, Bangladesh, Barbados, Belarus, Belize, Benin, Bhutan, Bolivia, Botswana, Brunei Darussalam, Burkina Faso, Burundi, Cabo Verde, Cambodia, Cameroon, Central African Republic, Chad, Chile, Colombia, Comoros, Congo (Democratic Republic of the), Congo (Republic of the), Côte d'Ivoire, Cuba, Djibouti, Dominica, Dominican Republic, Ecuador, Egypt, Equatorial Guinea, Eritrea, Eswatini, Ethiopia, Fiji, Gabon, Gambia, Ghana, Grenada, Guatemala, Guinea, Guinea-Bissau, Guyana, Haiti, Honduras, India, Indonesia, Iran, Iraq, Jamaica, Jordan, Kenya, Korea (North), Kuwait, Laos, Lebanon, Lesotho, Liberia, Libya, Madagascar, Malawi, Malaysia, Maldives, Mali, Mauritania, Mauritius, Mongolia, Morocco, Mozambique, Myanmar, Namibia, Nepal, Nicaragua, Niger, Nigeria, Oman, Pakistan, Palestine Liberation Organization, Panama, Papua New Guinea, Peru, Philippines, Qatar, Rwanda, Saint Kitts and Nevis, Saint Lucia, Saint Vincent and the Grenadines, Sao Tome and Principe, Saudi Arabia, Senegal, Seychelles, Sierra Leone, Singapore, Somalia, South Africa, Sri Lanka, Sudan, Suriname, Syria, Tanzania, Thailand, Timor-Leste, Togo, Trinidad and Tobago, Tunisia, Turkmenistan, Uganda†, United Arab Emirates, Uzbekistan, Vanuatu, Venezuela, Viet Nam, Yemen, Zambia, Zimbabwe

* NAM chair in 2019–22 and summit host in 2019.
† NAM chair in 2022–25 and summit host in 2022.

Website: <https://www.namazerbaijan.org/>

Organisation for Economic Co-operation and Development (OECD)

Established in 1961, the OECD's objectives are to promote economic and social welfare by coordinating policies among the member states. Its headquarters are in Paris, France.

Members (37): Australia, Austria, Belgium, Canada, Chile, *Colombia*, Czechia, Denmark, Estonia, Finland, France, Germany, Greece, Hungary, Iceland, Ireland, Israel, Italy, Japan, Korea (South), Latvia, Lithuania, Luxembourg, Mexico, Netherlands, New Zealand, Norway, Poland, Portugal, Slovakia, Slovenia, Spain, Sweden, Switzerland, Turkey, UK, USA

Note: In addition to the 37 members as of 1 Jan. 2021, Costa Rica signed an accession agreement with the OECD in May 2020 and will become a member once that agreement has been ratified.

Website: <https://www.oecd.org/>

Organisation for the Prohibition of Chemical Weapons (OPCW)

The OPCW implements the 1993 Chemical Weapons Convention (CWC). Among other things, it oversees the destruction of chemical weapon stockpiles and associated infrastructure, implements a verification regime to ensure that such weapons do not re-emerge, provides assistance and protection to states parties threatened by such weapons, and facilitates and engages in international cooperation to strengthen treaty compliance and to promote the peaceful uses of chemistry. In addition to the responsibility to investigate alleged use of chemical weapons, in 2018 the OPCW gained the power to attribute responsibility for any chemical weapon use on the territory of a member state if requested to do so by that state.

The work of the OPCW and its Technical Secretariat is overseen by the Executive Council, whose 41 members are elected for two-year terms by the Conference of States Parties. It is based in The Hague, the Netherlands.

Parties to the Chemical Weapons Convention (193): See annex A

Website: <https://www.opcw.org/>

Organisation of Islamic Cooperation (OIC)

The OIC (formerly the Organization of the Islamic Conference) was established in 1969 by Islamic states to promote cooperation among the members and to support peace, security and the struggle of the people of Palestine and all Muslim people. Among its organs are the Independent Permanent Human Rights Commission (IPHRC) and the Islamic Development Bank (IDB). Its secretariat is in Jeddah, Saudi Arabia.

Members (57): Afghanistan, Albania, Algeria, Azerbaijan, Bahrain, Bangladesh, Benin, Brunei Darussalam, Burkina Faso, Cameroon, Chad, Comoros, Côte d'Ivoire, Djibouti, Egypt, Gabon, Gambia, Guinea, Guinea-Bissau, Guyana, Indonesia, Iran, Iraq, Jordan, Kazakhstan, Kuwait, Kyrgyzstan, Lebanon, Libya, Malaysia, Maldives, Mali, Mauritania, Morocco, Mozambique, Niger, Nigeria, Oman, Pakistan, Palestine, Qatar, Saudi Arabia, Senegal, Sierra Leone, Somalia, Sudan, Suriname, Syria, Tajikistan, Togo, Tunisia, Turkey, Turkmenistan, Uganda, United Arab Emirates, Uzbekistan, Yemen

Website: <https://www.oic-oci.org/>

II. Bodies with a regional focus or membership

African Commission on Nuclear Energy (AFCONE)

AFCONE was established by the 1996 African Nuclear Weapon Free Zone Treaty (Treaty of Pelindaba) to ensure compliance with the treaty and to advance the peaceful application of nuclear science and technology in Africa. Its seat is in Pretoria, South Africa.

Parties to the Treaty of Pelindaba (41): See annex A

Website: <http://www.afcone.org/>

African Union (AU)

The AU was formally established in 2001 and launched in 2002. It replaced the Organization for African Unity (OAU), which had been established in 1963. Membership is open to all African states. The AU promotes unity, security and conflict resolution, democracy, human rights, and political, social and economic integration in Africa. Its main organs include the Assembly (the supreme body, consisting of heads of state and government), the Executive Council (made up of designated national ministers), the AU Commission (the secretariat), the Pan-African Parliament and the Peace and Security Council. The AU's headquarters are in Addis Ababa, Ethiopia.

Members (55): Algeria, Angola, Benin, Botswana, Burkina Faso, Burundi, Cabo Verde, Cameroon, Central African Republic, Chad, Comoros, Congo (Democratic Republic of the), Congo (Republic of the), Côte d'Ivoire, Djibouti, Egypt, Equatorial Guinea, Eritrea, Eswatini, Ethiopia, Gabon, Gambia, Ghana, Guinea, Guinea-Bissau, Kenya, Lesotho, Liberia, Libya, Madagascar, Malawi, Mali*, Mauritania, Mauritius, Morocco, Mozambique, Namibia, Niger, Nigeria, Rwanda, Sahrawi Arab Democratic Republic (Western Sahara), Sao Tome and Principe, Senegal, Seychelles, Sierra Leone, Somalia, South Africa, South Sudan, Sudan, Tanzania, Togo, Tunisia, Uganda, Zambia, Zimbabwe

* Mali was suspended from the AU on 19 Aug. 2020 following the military coup of 18 Aug. The suspension was lifted on 9 Oct. 2020 after agreement on an 18-month transition to a civilian-led government.

Website: <https://www.au.int/>

Peace and Security Council (PSC)

The PSC is the AU's standing decision-making organ for the prevention, management and resolution of conflicts. Its 15 members are elected by the Executive Council subject to endorsement by the Assembly. It is the main pillar of the African Peace and Security Architecture (APSA).

Members for a 3-year term 1 Apr. 2019–31 Mar. 2022 (5): Algeria, Burundi, Kenya, Lesotho, Nigeria

Members for a 2-year term 1 Apr. 2020–31 Mar. 2022 (10): Benin, Ghana, Cameroon, Chad, Djibouti, Egypt, Ethiopia, Malawi, Mozambique, Senegal

Website: <http://www.peaceau.org/>

Asia–Pacific Economic Cooperation (APEC)

APEC was established in 1989 as a regional economic forum to enhance open trade and economic prosperity in the Asia–Pacific region. Since 2001 the forum has been engaged in helping to protect the economies in the region from terrorism. A task force established in 2003 became the Counter-Terrorism Working Group in 2013. The APEC Secretariat is based in Singapore.

Member economies (21): Australia, Brunei Darussalam, Canada, Chile, China, Hong Kong, Indonesia, Japan, Korea (South), Malaysia*, Mexico, New Zealand[†], Papua New Guinea, Peru, Philippines, Russia, Singapore, Taiwan, Thailand[‡], USA, Viet Nam

* Host of APEC Economic Leaders' Meeting in 2020.
† Host of APEC Economic Leaders' Meeting in 2021.
‡ Host of APEC Economic Leaders' Meeting in 2022.

Website: <https://www.apec.org/>

Association of Southeast Asian Nations (ASEAN)

ASEAN was established in 1967 to promote economic, social and cultural development as well as regional peace and security in South East Asia.

Development of the ASEAN Political–Security Community is one of the three pillars (along with the Economic and Sociocultural communities) of the ASEAN Community, which was launched in 2015. The ASEAN Secretariat is in Jakarta, Indonesia.

Members (10): Brunei Darussalam[†], Cambodia[‡], Indonesia, Laos, Malaysia, Myanmar, Philippines, Singapore, Thailand, Viet Nam[*]

* ASEAN summit host in 2020.
† ASEAN summit host in 2021.
‡ ASEAN summit host in 2022.

Website: <https://www.asean.org/>

ASEAN Regional Forum (ARF)

The ARF was established in 1994 to foster constructive dialogue and consultation on political and security issues and to contribute to confidence-building and preventive diplomacy in the Asia-Pacific region.

Participants (27): The ASEAN member states and Australia, Bangladesh, Canada, China, European Union, India, Japan, Korea (North), Korea (South), Mongolia, New Zealand, Pakistan, Papua New Guinea, Russia, Sri Lanka, Timor-Leste, USA

Website: <https://aseanregionalforum.asean.org/>

ASEAN Plus Three (APT)

The APT cooperation began in 1997, in the wake of the Asian financial crisis, and was institutionalized in 1999. It aims to foster economic, political and security cooperation and financial stability among its participants.

Participants (13): The ASEAN member states and China, Japan, Korea (South)

Website: <https://www.asean.org/asean/external-relations/asean-3>

East Asia Summit (EAS)

The East Asia Summit started in 2005 as a regional forum for dialogue on strategic, political and economic issues with the aim of promoting peace, stability and economic prosperity in East Asia. The annual meetings are held in connection with the ASEAN summits.

Participants (18): The ASEAN member states and Australia, China, India, Japan, Korea (South), New Zealand, Russia, USA

Website: <https://www.asean.org/asean/external-relations/east-asia-summit-eas/>

Collective Security Treaty Organization (CSTO)

The CSTO was formally established in 2002–2003 by six signatories of the 1992 Collective Security Treaty. It aims to promote military and political cooperation among its members. Under Article 4 of the 1992 treaty, aggression against one member state is considered to be aggression against them all. An objective of the CSTO is to provide a more efficient response to strategic problems such as terrorism and narcotics trafficking. Its seat is in Moscow, Russia.

Members (6): Armenia, Belarus, Kazakhstan, Kyrgyzstan, Russia, Tajikistan

Website: <https://odkb-csto.org/>

Commonwealth of Independent States (CIS)

The CIS was established in 1991 as a framework for multilateral cooperation among former republics of the Soviet Union. The institutions of the CIS, including the Council of Defence Ministers, were established by the 1993 Charter. Their headquarters are in Minsk, Belarus.

Members (10): Armenia, Azerbaijan, Belarus, Kazakhstan, Kyrgyzstan, Moldova, Russia, Tajikistan, Turkmenistan*, Uzbekistan

* Turkmenistan has not ratified the 1993 CIS Charter but since 26 Aug. 2005 has participated in CIS activities as an associate member.

> *Note*: Although Ukraine did not ratify the CIS Charter, it was an unofficial associate member from 1993. Ukraine decided to end its participation in CIS institutions in May 2018; it completed the process of withdrawing from the CIS coordination bodies in Feb. 2019. It continues to withdraw from CIS agreements.

Website: <http://www.cis.minsk.by/>

Communauté économique des États de l'Afrique Centrale (CEEAC, Economic Community of Central African States, ECCAS)

CEEAC was established in 1983 to promote political dialogue, create a customs union and establish common policies in Central Africa. It also coordinates activities under the 2010 Central African Convention for the Control of Small Arms and Light Weapons, Their Ammunition and All Parts and Components That Can Be Used for Their Manufacture, Repair and Assembly (Kinshasa Convention). Its secretariat is in Libreville, Gabon.

The **Council for Peace and Security in Central Africa (Conseil de paix et de sécurité de l'Afrique Centrale, COPAX)** is a mechanism for promoting joint political and military strategies for conflict prevention, management and resolution in Central Africa.

Members (11): Angola, Burundi, Cameroon, Central African Republic, Chad, Congo (Democratic Republic of the), Congo (Republic of the), Equatorial Guinea, Gabon, Rwanda, Sao Tome and Principe

Website: <http://www.ceeac-eccas.org/>

Conference on Interaction and Confidence-building Measures in Asia (CICA)

Initiated in 1992, CICA was formally established in 1999 as a forum to enhance security cooperation and confidence-building measures among the member states. It also promotes economic, social and cultural cooperation. Its secretariat is in Astana, Kazakhstan.

Members (27): Afghanistan, Azerbaijan, Bahrain, Bangladesh, Cambodia, China, Egypt, India, Iran, Iraq, Israel, Jordan, Kazakhstan†, Korea (South), Kyrgyzstan, Mongolia, Pakistan, Palestine, Qatar, Russia, Sri Lanka, Tajikistan*, Thailand, Turkey, United Arab Emirates, Uzbekistan, Viet Nam

* Chair in 2018–20.
† Chair from 24 Sep. 2020.

Website: <http://www.s-cica.org/>

Council of Europe (COE)

The Council was established in 1949. Membership is open to all European states that accept the principle of the rule of law and guarantee their citizens' human rights and fundamental freedoms. Its seat is in Strasbourg, France. Among its organs are the Council of Ministers, the Parliamentary Assembly, the European Court of Human Rights and the Council of Europe Development Bank.

Members (47): Albania, Andorra, Armenia, Austria, Azerbaijan, Belgium, Bosnia and Herzegovina, Bulgaria, Croatia, Cyprus, Czechia, Denmark, Estonia, Finland, France, Georgia, Germany, Greece, Hungary, Iceland, Ireland, Italy, Latvia, Liechtenstein, Lithuania, Luxembourg, Malta, Moldova, Monaco, Montenegro, Netherlands, North Macedonia, Norway, Poland, Portugal, Romania, Russia, San Marino, Serbia, Slovakia, Slovenia, Spain, Sweden, Switzerland, Turkey, UK, Ukraine

Website: <https://www.coe.int/>

Council of the Baltic Sea States (CBSS)

The CBSS was established in 1992 as a regional intergovernmental organization for cooperation among the states of the Baltic Sea region. Its secretariat is in Stockholm, Sweden.

Members (12): Denmark, Estonia, European Union, Finland, Germany, Iceland, Latvia, Lithuania, Norway, Poland, Russia, Sweden

Website: <https://www.cbss.org/>

Economic Community of West African States (ECOWAS)

ECOWAS was established in 1975 to promote trade and cooperation and contribute to development in West Africa. In 1981 it adopted the Protocol on Mutual Assistance in Defence Matters. Its Commission, Court of Justice and Parliament are based in Abuja, Nigeria.

Members (15): Benin, Burkina Faso, Cabo Verde, Côte d'Ivoire, Gambia, Ghana, Guinea, Guinea-Bissau, Liberia, Mali*, Niger, Nigeria, Senegal, Sierra Leone, Togo

* Mali was suspended from ECOWAS on 20 Aug. 2020 following the military coup of 18 Aug. The suspension was lifted on 6 Oct. 2020 after agreement on an 18-month transition to a civilian-led government.

Note: In June 2017 ECOWAS agreed in principle to admit Morocco as its 16th member.

Website: <https://www.ecowas.int/>

European Union (EU)

The EU is an organization of European states that cooperate in a wide field, including a single market with free movement of people, goods, services and capital, a common currency (the euro) for some members, and a Common Foreign and Security Policy (CFSP), including a Common Security and Defence Policy (CSDP). The EU's main bodies are the European Council, the Council of the European Union (also known as the Council of Ministers or the Council), the European Commission (the secretariat), the European Parliament and the European Court of Justice.

The CFSP and CSDP are coordinated by the High Representative of the Union for Foreign Affairs and Security Policy, assisted by the European External Action Service (EEAS) and the EU Military Staff.

The principal seat of the EU is in Brussels, Belgium.

Members (27): Austria, Belgium, Bulgaria, Croatia, Cyprus, Czechia, Denmark, Estonia, Finland, France, Germany, Greece, Hungary, Ireland, Italy, Latvia, Lithuania, Luxembourg, Malta, Netherlands, Poland, Portugal, Romania, Slovakia, Slovenia, Spain, Sweden

* The UK withdrew from the EU on 31 Jan. 2020. During a transition period until 31 Dec. 2020, it remained part of the EU's single market but no longer participated in its political institutions.

Website: <https://europa.eu/>

European Atomic Energy Community (Euratom, or EAEC)

Euratom was created by the 1957 Treaty Establishing the European Atomic Energy Community (Euratom Treaty) to promote the development of nuclear energy for peaceful purposes and to administer (in cooperation with the IAEA) the multinational regional safeguards system covering the EU member states. The Euratom Supply Agency, located in Luxembourg, has the task of ensuring a regular and equitable supply of ores, source materials and special fissile materials to EU member states.

Members (27): The EU member states*

* While Euratom is formally independent of the EU, all full members of Euratom must also be members of the EU. The UK withdrew from Euratom on 31 Jan. 2020, although the common rules and arrangements continued to apply until 31 Dec. 2020.

Website: <https://ec.europa.eu/euratom/>

European Defence Agency (EDA)

The EDA is an agency of the EU, under the direction of the Council. It was established in 2004 to help develop European defence capabilities, to promote European armaments cooperation and to work for a strong European defence technological and industrial base. The EDA's decision-making body is the Steering Board, composed of the defence ministers of the participating member states and the EU's High Representative for Foreign Affairs and Security Policy (as head of the agency). The EDA is located in Brussels, Belgium.

Participating member states (26): The EU member states other than Denmark*

* The UK withdrew from the EDA on 31 Jan. 2020.

Note: The EDA has signed administrative arrangements with Norway (2006), Switzerland (2012), Serbia (2013) and Ukraine (2015) that enable these states to participate in its projects and programmes.

Website: <https://eda.europa.eu/>

Permanent Structured Cooperation (PESCO)

The Council of the EU established PESCO in 2017 as a framework to deepen security and defence cooperation between EU member states. Through joint projects, it aims to increase the military capabilities available to EU member states. The EDA and the EEAS jointly act as the PESCO secretariat.

Participating member states (25): The EU member states other than Denmark and Malta

Website: <https://pesco.europa.eu/>

Gulf Cooperation Council (GCC)

Formally called the Cooperation Council for the Arab States of the Gulf, the GCC was created in 1981 to promote regional integration in such areas as economy, finance, trade, administration and legislation and to foster scientific and technical progress. The members also cooperate in areas of foreign policy and military and security matters. The Supreme Council (consisting of the head of each member state) is the highest GCC authority. Its headquarters are in Riyadh, Saudi Arabia.

Members (6): Bahrain, Kuwait, Oman, Qatar, Saudi Arabia, United Arab Emirates

Website: <https://www.gcc-sg.org/>

Intergovernmental Authority on Development (IGAD)

IGAD was established in 1996 to expand regional cooperation and promote peace and stability in the Horn of Africa. It superseded the Intergovernmental Authority on Drought and Development (IGADD), which was established in 1986. Its secretariat is in Djibouti.

Members (8): Djibouti, Eritrea, Ethiopia, Kenya, Somalia, South Sudan, Sudan, Uganda

Website: <https://www.igad.int/>

International Conference on the Great Lakes Region (ICGLR)

The ICGLR, which was initiated in 2004, works to promote peace and security, political and social stability, and growth and development in the Great Lakes region. In 2006 the member states adopted the Pact on Security, Stability and

Development in the Great Lakes Region, which entered into force in 2008. Its executive secretariat is in Bujumbura, Burundi.

The ICGLR Joint Intelligence Fusion Centre (JIFC) was launched in 2012 in Goma, Democratic Republic of the Congo, to collect, analyse and disseminate information on armed groups in the region and recommend action to member states.

Members (12): Angola, Burundi, Central African Republic, Congo (Republic of the), Congo (Democratic Republic of the), Kenya, Rwanda, South Sudan, Sudan, Tanzania, Uganda, Zambia

Website: <http://www.icglr.org/>

League of Arab States

The Arab League was established in 1945 to form closer union among Arab states and foster political and economic cooperation. An agreement for collective defence and economic cooperation among the members was signed in 1950. In 2015 the Arab League agreed to create a joint Arab military force for regional peacekeeping, but no progress in its establishment has been subsequently made. The general secretariat of the Arab League is in Cairo, Egypt

Members (22): Algeria, Bahrain, Comoros, Djibouti, Egypt, Iraq, Jordan, Kuwait, Lebanon, Libya, Mauritania, Morocco, Oman, Palestine, Qatar, Saudi Arabia, Somalia, Sudan, Syria*, Tunisia, United Arab Emirates, Yemen

   * Syria was suspended from the organization on 16 Nov. 2011.

Website: <http://www.leagueofarabstates.net/>

North Atlantic Treaty Organization (NATO)

NATO was established in 1949 by the North Atlantic Treaty (Washington Treaty) as a Western military alliance. Article 5 of the treaty defines the members' commitment to respond to an armed attack against any party to the treaty. Its headquarters are in Brussels, Belgium.

Members (30): Albania, Belgium, Bulgaria, Canada, Croatia, Czechia, Denmark, Estonia, France, Germany, Greece, Hungary, Iceland, Italy, Latvia, Lithuania, Luxembourg, Montenegro, Netherlands, Norway, *North Macedonia*, Poland, Portugal, Romania, Slovakia, Slovenia, Spain, Turkey, UK, USA

Website: <https://www.nato.int/>

Euro-Atlantic Partnership Council (EAPC)

The EAPC brings together NATO and its Partnership for Peace (PFP) partners for dialogue and consultation. It is the overall political framework for the bilateral PFP programme.

Members (50): The NATO member states and Armenia, Austria, Azerbaijan, Belarus, Bosnia and Herzegovina, Finland, Georgia, Ireland, Kazakhstan, Kyrgyzstan, Malta, Moldova, Russia, Serbia, Sweden, Switzerland, Tajikistan, Turkmenistan, Ukraine, Uzbekistan

Website: <https://www.nato.int/cps/en/natohq/topics_49276.htm>

Istanbul Cooperation Initiative (ICI)

The ICI was established in 2004 to contribute to long-term global and regional security by offering practical bilateral security cooperation with NATO to countries of the broader Middle East region.

Participants (34): The NATO member states and Bahrain, Qatar, Kuwait, United Arab Emirates

Website: <https://www.nato.int/cps/en/natohq/topics_58787.htm>

Mediterranean Dialogue

NATO's Mediterranean Dialogue was established in 1994 as a forum for political dialogue and practical cooperation between NATO and countries of the Mediterranean. It reflects NATO's view that security in Europe is closely linked to security and stability in the Mediterranean.

Participants (37): The NATO member states and Algeria, Egypt, Israel, Jordan, Mauritania, Morocco, Tunisia

Website: <https://www.nato.int/cps/en/natohq/topics_60021.htm>

NATO–Georgia Commission (NGC)

The NGC was established in September 2008 to serve as a forum for political consultations and practical cooperation to help Georgia achieve its goal of joining NATO.

Participants (31): The NATO member states and Georgia

Website: <https://www.nato.int/cps/en/natohq/topics_52131.htm>

NATO–Russia Council (NRC)

The NRC was established in 2002 as a mechanism for consultation, consensus building, cooperation, and joint decisions and action on security issues. It focuses on areas of mutual interest identified in the 1997 NATO–Russia Founding Act on Mutual Relations, Cooperation and Security and new areas, such as terrorism, crisis management and non-proliferation.

Participants (31): The NATO member states and Russia

Note: In Apr. 2014, following Russian military intervention in Ukraine, NATO suspended all practical cooperation with Russia, although meetings of the NRC continue at the ambassadorial level or above.

Website: <https://www.nato.int/nrc-website/>

NATO–Ukraine Commission (NUC)

The NUC was established in 1997 for consultations on political and security issues, conflict prevention and resolution, non-proliferation, transfers of arms and technology, and other subjects of common concern.

Participants (31): The NATO member states and Ukraine

Website: <https://www.nato.int/cps/en/natohq/topics_50319.htm>

Organisation Conjointe de Coopération en matière d'Armement (OCCAR, Organisation for Joint Armament Cooperation)

OCCAR was established in 1996, with legal status since 2001, to provide more effective and efficient arrangements for the management of specific collaborative armament programmes. Its headquarters are in Bonn, Germany.

Members (6): Belgium, France, Germany, Italy, Spain, UK

Participants (7): Finland, Lithuania, Luxembourg, Netherlands, Poland, Sweden, Turkey

Website: <https://www.occar.int/>

Organismo para la Proscripción de las Armas Nucleares en la América Latina y el Caribe (OPANAL, Agency for the Prohibition of Nuclear Weapons in Latin America and the Caribbean)

OPANAL was established by the 1967 Treaty of Tlatelolco to resolve, together with the IAEA, questions of compliance with the treaty. Its seat is in Mexico City, Mexico.

Parties to the Treaty of Tlatelolco (33): See annex A

Website: <https://www.opanal.org/>

Organization for Democracy and Economic Development–GUAM

GUAM is a group of four states, established to promote stability and strengthen security, whose history goes back to 1997. The organization was established in 2006. The members cooperate to promote social and economic development and trade in eight working groups. Its secretariat is in Kyiv, Ukraine.

Members (4): Azerbaijan, Georgia, Moldova, Ukraine

Website: <https://guam-organization.org/>

Organization for Security and Co-operation in Europe (OSCE)

The Conference on Security and Co-operation in Europe (CSCE), which had been initiated in 1973, was renamed the OSCE in 1995. It is intended to be the primary instrument of comprehensive and cooperative security for early warning, conflict prevention, crisis management and post-conflict rehabilitation in its area. Its headquarters are in Vienna, Austria, and its other institutions are based elsewhere in Europe.

The OSCE Troika consists of representatives of the states holding the chair in the current year, the previous year and the succeeding year. The Forum for Security Cooperation (FSC) deals with arms control and confidence- and security-building measures.

Participants (57): Albania*, Andorra, Armenia, Austria, Azerbaijan, Belarus, Belgium, Bosnia and Herzegovina, Bulgaria, Canada, Croatia, Cyprus, Czechia, Denmark, Estonia, Finland, France, Georgia, Germany, Greece, Holy See, Hungary, Iceland, Ireland, Italy, Kazakhstan, Kyrgyzstan, Latvia, Liechtenstein, Lithuania, Luxembourg, Malta, Moldova, Monaco, Mongolia, Montenegro, Netherlands, North Macedonia, Norway, Poland‡, Portugal, Romania, Russia, San Marino, Serbia, Slovakia, Slovenia, Spain, Sweden†, Switzerland, Tajikistan, Turkey, Turkmenistan, UK, Ukraine, USA, Uzbekistan

* Chair in 2020.
† Chair in 2021.
‡ Chair in 2022.

Website: <https://www.osce.org/>

Joint Consultative Group (JCG)

The JCG is an OSCE-related body established by the 1990 Treaty on Conventional Armed Forces in Europe (CFE Treaty) to promote the objectives and implementation of the treaty by reconciling ambiguities of interpretation and implementation. Its seat is in Vienna, Austria.

Parties to the CFE Treaty (30): See annex A

Note: In 2007 Russia suspended its participation in the CFE Treaty, and in Mar. 2015 it announced that it had decided to completely halt its participation in the treaty, including the JCG.

Website: <https://www.osce.org/jcg/>

Minsk Group

The Minsk Group supports the Minsk Process, an ongoing forum for negotiations on a peaceful settlement of the conflict in Nagorno-Karabakh.

Members (13): Armenia, Azerbaijan, Belarus, Finland, France*, Germany, Italy, Russia*, Sweden, Turkey, USA*, OSCE Troika (Albania, Poland and Sweden)

* The representatives of these 3 states co-chair the group.

Website: <https://www.osce.org/mg/>

Open Skies Consultative Commission (OSCC)

The OSCC was established by the 1992 Treaty on Open Skies to resolve questions of compliance with the treaty.

Parties to the Open Skies Treaty (33): See annex A

Note: The USA withdrew from the treaty and the OSCC on 22 Nov. 2020. On 15 Jan.

2021 Russia announced that it would begin the domestic procedures for its withdrawal from the treaty.

Website: <https://www.osce.org/oscc/>

Organization of American States (OAS)

The OAS, which adopted its charter in 1948, has the objective of strengthening peace and security in the western hemisphere. Its activities are based on the four pillars of democracy, human rights, security and development. Its general secretariat is in Washington, DC, USA.

Members (35): Antigua and Barbuda, Argentina, Bahamas, Barbados, Belize, Bolivia, Brazil, Canada, Chile, Colombia, Costa Rica, Cuba*, Dominica, Dominican Republic, Ecuador, El Salvador, Grenada, Guatemala, Guyana, Haiti, Honduras, Jamaica, Mexico, Nicaragua, Panama, Paraguay, Peru, Saint Kitts and Nevis, Saint Lucia, Saint Vincent and the Grenadines, Suriname, Trinidad and Tobago, Uruguay, USA, Venezuela

 * By a resolution of 3 June 2009, the 1962 resolution that excluded Cuba from the OAS ceased to have effect; according to the 2009 resolution, Cuba's participation in the organization 'will be the result of a process of dialogue'. Cuba has declined to participate in OAS activities.

Website: <https://www.oas.org/>

Organization of the Black Sea Economic Cooperation (BSEC)

The BSEC initiative was established in 1992 and became a full regional economic organization when its charter entered into force in 1999. Its aims are to ensure peace, stability and prosperity and to promote and develop economic cooperation and progress in the Black Sea region. Its permanent secretariat is in Istanbul, Turkey.

Members (13): Albania, Armenia, Azerbaijan, Bulgaria, Georgia, Greece, Moldova, *North Macedonia*, Romania, Russia, Serbia, Turkey, Ukraine

Website: <http://www.bsec-organization.org/>

Pacific Islands Forum

The forum, which was founded in 1971 as the South Pacific Forum, aims to enhance cooperation in sustainable development, economic growth, governance and security. It also monitors implementation of the 1985 South Pacific Nuclear Free Zone Treaty (Treaty of Rarotonga). Its secretariat is in Suva, Fiji.

Members (18): Australia, Cook Islands, Fiji, French Polynesia, Kiribati, Marshall Islands, Micronesia, Nauru, New Caledonia, New Zealand, Niue, Palau, Papua New Guinea, Samoa, Solomon Islands, Tonga, Tuvalu, Vanuatu

Note: Following a dispute over the appointment of a new secretary-general, in Feb. 2021 Kiribati, Marshall Islands, Micronesia, Nauru and Palau agreed to initiate the formal process of leaving the forum.

Website: <https://www.forumsec.org/>

Regional Centre on Small Arms in the Great Lakes Region, the Horn of Africa and Bordering States (RECSA)

The Nairobi Secretariat on Small Arms and Light Weapons was established to coordinate implementation of the 2000 Nairobi Declaration on the Problem of Illicit Small Arms and Light Weapons in the Great Lakes Region and the Horn of Africa. It was transformed into RECSA in 2005 to oversee the implementation of the 2004 Nairobi Protocol for the Prevention, Control and Reduction of Small Arms and Light Weapons. It is based in Nairobi, Kenya.

Members (15): Burundi, Djibouti, Central African Republic, Congo (Democratic Republic of the), Congo (Republic of the), Eritrea, Ethiopia, Kenya, Rwanda, Seychelles, Somalia, South Sudan, Sudan, Tanzania, Uganda

Website: <https://www.recsasec.org/>

Regional Cooperation Council

The RCC was launched in 2008 as the successor of the Stability Pact for South Eastern Europe that was initiated by the EU at the 1999 Conference on South Eastern Europe. It promotes mutual cooperation and European and Euro-Atlantic integration of states in South Eastern Europe in order to inspire development in the region for the benefit of its people. It focuses on six areas: economic and social development, energy and infrastructure, justice and home affairs, security cooperation, building human capital, and parliamentary cooperation. Its secretariat is in Sarajevo, Bosnia and Herzegovina, and it has a liaison office in Brussels, Belgium.

Participants (46): Albania, Austria, Bosnia and Herzegovina, Bulgaria, Canada, Council of Europe, Council of Europe Development Bank, Croatia, Czechia, Denmark, European Bank for Reconstruction and Development, European Investment Bank, European Union, Germany, Finland, France, Greece, Hungary, International Organization for Migration, Ireland, Italy, Kosovo, Latvia, Moldova, Montenegro, North Atlantic Treaty Organization, North Macedonia, Norway, Organisation for Economic Co-operation and Development, Organization for Security and Cooperation in Europe, Poland, Romania, Serbia, Slovakia, Slovenia, South East European Cooperative Initiative, Spain, Sweden, Switzerland, Turkey, UK, United Nations, UN Economic Commission for Europe, UN Development Programme, USA, World Bank

Website: <https://www.rcc.int/>

Shanghai Cooperation Organisation (SCO)

The SCO's predecessor group, the Shanghai Five, was founded in 1996; it was renamed the SCO in 2001 and opened for membership of all states that support its aims. The member states cooperate on confidence-building measures and regional security and in the economic sphere. Its secretariat is in Beijing, China. The SCO Regional Anti-Terrorist Structure (RATS) is based in Tashkent, Uzbekistan.

Members (8): China, India, Kazakhstan, Kyrgyzstan, Pakistan, Russia, Tajikistan, Uzbekistan

Website: <<http://eng.sectsco.org/>

Sistema de la Integración Centroamericana (SICA, Central American Integration System)

SICA was launched in 1993 on the basis of the 1991 Tegucigalpa Protocol. Its objective is the integration of Central America to constitute a region of peace, freedom, democracy and development, based on respect for and protection and promotion of human rights. The SICA headquarters are in San Salvador, El Salvador.

The **Comisión de Seguridad de Centroamérica (CSC, Central American Security Commission)** was established by the 1995 Framework Treaty on Democratic Security in Central America. Its objectives include following up on proposals on regional security, based on a reasonable balance of forces, strengthening civilian power, and eradicating violence, corruption, terrorism, drug trafficking and arms trafficking.

Members (8): Belize, Costa Rica, Dominican Republic, El Salvador, Guatemala, Honduras, Nicaragua, Panama

Website: <https://www.sica.int/>

Southern African Development Community (SADC)

SADC was established in 1992 to promote regional economic development and the fundamental principles of sovereignty, peace and security, human rights and democracy. It superseded the Southern African Development Coordination Conference (SADCC), established in 1980. Its secretariat is in Gaborone, Botswana.

The **SADC Organ on Politics, Defence and Security Cooperation (OPDS)** is mandated to promote peace and security in the region.

Members (16): Angola, Botswana, Comoros, Congo (Democratic Republic of the), Eswatini, Lesotho, Madagascar, Malawi, Mauritius, Mozambique, Namibia, Seychelles, South Africa, Tanzania, Zambia, Zimbabwe

Website: <https://www.sadc.int/>

Sub-Regional Consultative Commission (SRCC)

The SRCC meets regularly to monitor implementation of the 1996 Agreement on Sub-Regional Arms Control (Florence Agreement) in the former Yugoslavia. Representatives of the Contact Group consisting of France, Italy, Germany, Russia, the UK and the USA also take part in these sessions.

Parties to the Agreement on Sub-Regional Arms Control (4): See annex A

Unión de Naciones Suramericanas (UNASUR, Union of South American Nations)

UNASUR is an intergovernmental organization with the aim of strengthening regional integration, political dialogue, economic development and coordination in defence matters among its member states. Its 2008 Constitutive Treaty entered into force on 11 March 2011 and it was intended to gradually replace the Andean Community and the Mercado Común del Sur (MERCOSUR, Southern Common Market). Its headquarters were in Quito, Ecuador.

The **Consejo de Defensa Suramericano (CDS, South American Defence Council)** met for the first time in March 2009. Its objectives are to consolidate South America as a zone of peace and to create a regional identity and strengthen regional cooperation in defence issues.

Members (5): Bolivia, Guyana, Peru, Suriname, Venezuela

Notes: Argentina, Brazil, Chile, Colombia, Ecuador, Paraguay and Uruguay withdrew from UNASUR during 2019–20. Peru suspended its participation in Apr. 2018. Bolivia suspended its participation in Nov. 2019 but resumed again in Nov. 2020.

At a summit in Santiago, Chile, on 22 Mar. 2019, Argentina, Brazil, Chile, Colombia, Ecuador, Guyana, Paraguay and Peru launched a process to form a new regional group, known as the Forum for the Progress of South America (Foro para el Progreso de América del Sur, PROSUR).

Website: <http://www.unasursg.org/>

III. Strategic trade control regimes

Australia Group (AG)

The AG is an informal group of states and the European Commission formed in 1985. The AG meets annually to exchange views and best practices on strategic trade controls in order to ensure that dual-use material, technology and equipment are not used to support chemical and biological warfare activity or weapon programmes.

Participants (43): Argentina, Australia*, Austria, Belgium, Bulgaria, Canada, Croatia, Cyprus, Czechia, Denmark, Estonia, European Commission, Finland, France, Germany, Greece, Hungary, Iceland, India, Ireland, Italy, Japan, Korea (South), Latvia, Lithuania, Luxembourg, Malta, Mexico, Netherlands, New Zealand, Norway, Poland, Portugal, Romania, Slovakia, Slovenia, Spain, Sweden, Switzerland, Turkey, UK, Ukraine, USA

* Permanent chair.

Website: <https://www.australiagroup.net/>

Hague Code of Conduct against Ballistic Missile Proliferation (HCOC)

The principle of the 2002 HCOC is the need to curb the proliferation of ballistic missile systems capable of delivering WMD. Subscribing states commit to exercise restraint in the development, testing and deployment of such missiles, to issue pre-launch notifications and to provide annual declarations on their policies concerning ballistic missiles and space-launch vehicles. The Ministry for Foreign Affairs of Austria acts as the HCOC Secretariat.

Subscribing states (143): Afghanistan, Albania, Andorra, Antigua and Barbuda, Argentina, Armenia, Australia, Austria, Azerbaijan, Belarus, Belgium, Benin, Bosnia and Herzegovina, Bulgaria, Burkina Faso, Burundi, Cabo Verde, Cambodia, Cameroon, Canada, Central African Republic, Chad, Chile, Colombia, Comoros, Congo (Republic of the), Cook Islands, Costa Rica, Croatia, Cyprus, Czechia, Denmark, Dominica, Dominican Republic, Ecuador, El Salvador, *Equatorial Guinea*, Eritrea, Estonia, Ethiopia, Fiji, Finland, France, Gabon, Gambia,

Georgia, Germany, Ghana, Greece, Guatemala, Guinea, Guinea-Bissau, Guyana, Haiti, Holy See, Honduras, Hungary, Iceland, India, Iraq, Ireland, Italy, Japan, Jordan, Kazakhstan, Kenya, Kiribati, Korea (South), Latvia, Lesotho, Liberia, Libya, Liechtenstein, Lithuania, Luxembourg, Madagascar, Malawi, Maldives, Mali, Malta, Marshall Islands, Mauritania, Micronesia, Moldova, Monaco, Mongolia, Montenegro, Morocco, Mozambique, Netherlands, New Zealand, Nicaragua, Niger, Nigeria, North Macedonia, Norway, Palau, Panama, Papua New Guinea, Paraguay, Peru, Philippines, Poland, Portugal, Romania, Russia, Rwanda, Saint Kitts and Nevis, *Saint Vincent and the Grenadines*, Samoa, San Marino, Senegal, Serbia, Seychelles, Sierra Leone, Singapore, Slovakia, Slovenia, *Somalia*, South Africa, Spain, Sudan, Suriname, Sweden, Switzerland*, Tajikistan, Tanzania, Timor-Leste, Togo, Tonga, Tunisia, Turkey, Turkmenistan, Tuvalu, Uganda, UK, Ukraine, Uruguay, USA, Uzbekistan, Vanuatu, Venezuela, Zambia

* Chair in 2020/21.

Website: <https://www.hcoc.at/>

Missile Technology Control Regime (MTCR)

The MTCR, established in 1987, is an informal group of countries that seeks to coordinate national export licensing efforts aimed at preventing the proliferation of missiles and other delivery systems capable of delivering WMD. The partner countries apply the Guidelines for Sensitive Missile-Relevant Transfers. The MTCR has no secretariat. A point of contact based in the Ministry for Foreign Affairs of France distributes the regime's working papers and hosts regular policy and information-exchange meetings.

Partners (35): Argentina, Australia, Austria[†], Belgium, Brazil, Bulgaria, Canada, Czechia, Denmark, Finland, France, Germany, Greece, Hungary, Iceland, India, Ireland, Italy, Japan, Korea (South), Luxembourg, Netherlands, New Zealand*, Norway, Poland, Portugal, Russia[‡], South Africa, Spain, Sweden, Switzerland, Turkey, UK, Ukraine, USA

* Chair in 2019/20.
† Chair in 2020/21.
‡ Chair in 2021/22.

Website: <https://www.mtcr.info/>

Nuclear Suppliers Group (NSG)

The NSG, formerly also known as the London Club, was established in 1975. It coordinates national transfer controls on nuclear materials according to its Guidelines for Nuclear Transfers (London Guidelines, first agreed in 1978), which contain a 'trigger list' of materials that should trigger IAEA safeguards when they are to be exported for peaceful purposes to any non-nuclear weapon state, and the Guidelines for Transfers of Nuclear-Related Dual-Use Equipment, Materials, Software and Related Technology (Warsaw Guidelines). The NSG Guidelines are implemented by each participating state in accordance with its national laws and practices. The NSG has no secretariat. The Permanent Mission of Japan to the IAEA in Vienna acts as a point of contact and carries out practical support functions.

Participants (48): Argentina, Australia, Austria, Belarus, Belgium*, Brazil, Bulgaria, Canada, China, Croatia, Cyprus, Czechia, Denmark, Estonia, Finland, France, Germany, Greece,

Hungary, Iceland, Ireland, Italy, Japan, Kazakhstan, Korea (South), Latvia, Lithuania, Luxembourg, Malta, Mexico, Netherlands, New Zealand, Norway, Poland, Portugal, Romania, Russia, Serbia, Slovakia, Slovenia, South Africa, Spain, Sweden, Switzerland, Turkey, UK, Ukraine, USA

* NSG chair in 2020–21.

Note: In addition, the European Union and the chair of the Zangger Committee are permanent observers.

Website: <https://www.nuclearsuppliersgroup.org/>

Proliferation Security Initiative (PSI)

Based on a US initiative announced in 2003, the PSI is a multilateral forum focusing on law enforcement cooperation for the interdiction and seizure of illegal WMD, missile technologies and related materials when in transit on land, in the air or at sea. The PSI Statement of Interdiction Principles was issued in 2003. The PSI has no secretariat, but its activities are coordinated by a 21-member Operational Experts Group.

Participants (107): Afghanistan, Albania, Andorra, Angola, Antigua and Barbuda, Argentina*, Armenia, Australia*†, Austria, Azerbaijan, Bahamas, Bahrain, Belarus, Belgium, Belize, Bosnia and Herzegovina, Brunei Darussalam, Bulgaria, Cambodia, Canada*, Chile, Colombia, Croatia†, Cyprus, Czechia†, Denmark*, Djibouti†, Dominica, Dominican Republic, El Salvador, Estonia, Fiji, Finland, France*†, Georgia, Germany*†, Greece*, Holy See, Honduras, Hungary, Iceland, Iraq, Ireland, Israel, Italy*†, Japan*†, Jordan, Kazakhstan, Korea (South)*†, Kyrgyzstan, Kuwait, Latvia, Liberia, Libya, Liechtenstein, Lithuania†, Luxembourg, Malaysia, Malta, Marshall Islands, Micronesia, Moldova, Mongolia, Montenegro, Morocco, Netherlands*†, New Zealand*†, North Macedonia, Norway*†, Oman, Palau, Panama, Papua New Guinea, Paraguay, Philippines, Poland*†, Portugal*†, Qatar†, Romania, Russia*, Saint Lucia, Saint Vincent and the Grenadines, Samoa, San Marino, Saudi Arabia, Serbia, Singapore*†, Slovakia, Slovenia†, Spain*†, Sri Lanka, Sweden, Switzerland, Tajikistan, Thailand, Trinidad and Tobago, Tunisia, Turkey*†, Turkmenistan, UK*†, Ukraine†, United Arab Emirates†, USA*†, Uzbekistan, Vanuatu, Viet Nam, Yemen

* Member of the Operational Experts Group.
† PSI exercise host, 2003–19.

Website: <https://www.psi-online.info>

Wassenaar Arrangement on Export Controls for Conventional Arms and Dual-Use Goods and Technologies (Wassenaar Arrangement, WA)

The Wassenaar Arrangement was formally established in 1996 as the successor to the cold war-era Co-ordinating Committee for Multilateral Export Controls (COCOM). It aims to promote transparency and responsibility in the transfers of conventional weapons and dual-use goods and technologies. Participating states seek to prevent transfers of armaments and sensitive dual-use goods and technologies that contribute to destabilizing accumulations of weapons, as well as transfers to terrorists. The WA Secretariat is located in Vienna, Austria.

Participants (42): Argentina, Australia, Austria, Belgium, Bulgaria, Canada, Croatia*, Czechia, Denmark, Estonia, Finland, France, Germany, Greece, Hungary†, India, Ireland, Italy, Japan, Korea (South), Latvia, Lithuania, Luxembourg, Malta, Mexico, Netherlands, New Zealand,

Norway, Poland, Portugal, Romania, Russia, Slovakia, Slovenia, South Africa, Spain, Sweden, Switzerland, Turkey, UK, Ukraine, USA

  * Chair in 2020.
  † Chair in 2021.

Website: <https://www.wassenaar.org/>

Zangger Committee

Established in 1971–74, the Nuclear Exporters Committee, called the Zangger Committee, is a group of nuclear supplier countries that meets informally twice a year to coordinate transfer controls on nuclear materials according to its regularly updated trigger list of items which, when exported, must be subject to IAEA safeguards. It complements the work of the Nuclear Suppliers Group.

Members (39): Argentina, Australia, Austria, Belarus, Belgium, Bulgaria, Canada, China, Croatia, Czechia, Denmark, Finland, France, Germany, Greece, Hungary, Ireland, Italy, Japan, Kazakhstan, Korea (South), Luxembourg, Netherlands, New Zealand, Norway, Poland, Portugal, Romania, Russia, Slovakia, Slovenia, South Africa, Spain, Sweden, Switzerland, Turkey, UK, Ukraine, USA

Website: <http://www.zanggercommittee.org/>

Annex C. Chronology 2020

This chronology lists the significant events in 2020 related to armaments, disarmament and international security. Keywords are indicated in the right-hand column.

January

1 Jan.	North Korean leader Kim Jong Un announces that North Korea will no longer be 'unilaterally bound' to the moratorium on nuclear and long-range missile tests.	North Korea; nuclear weapons
3 Jan.	China reports over 40 cases to the World Health Organization (WHO) of a viral pneumonia of unknown cause, first identified in Wuhan in Dec. 2019.	China; Covid-19; WHO
3 Jan.	A United States air strike kills General Qasem Soleimani, a senior commander in Iran's Islamic Revolutionary Guards Corps.	Iran; USA
5 Jan.	Turkish troops are deployed to Libya on behalf of Libya's Government of National Accord (GNA), which is backed by the United Nations.	GNA; Libya; Turkey
8 Jan.	Iran launches ballistic missiles at two Iraqi military bases hosting US soldiers, injuring at least 50 of the personnel.	Iran; Iraq; USA
8 Jan.	Ukraine International Airlines Flight 752 is shot down by Iranian forces after taking off from Tehran airport, killing all 176 people on board. On 11 January, the Iranian Government admits that its military mistook the airliner for a cruise missile.	Iran; Ukraine
9 Jan.	Islamic State in the Greater Sahara (ISGS) attacks a Nigerien military base, killing at least 89 soldiers.	ISGS; Niger
9 Jan.	The WHO reports that China has determined the pneumonia outbreak in Wuhan was caused by a novel coronavirus. The first death from it is reported two days later.	China; Covid-19; WHO
13 Jan.	France and the Group of Five for the Sahel (G5 Sahel) countries launch the Coalition for the Sahel, a coordinating framework for counterterrorism, capacity building for Sahelian forces, restoration of state authority and development assistance.	France; G5 Sahel
15 Jan.	The USA and China sign an initial trade deal that seeks to ease their two-year trade dispute.	China; USA
18 Jan.	A missile strike by Houthi forces on a military camp near Marib, Yemen, kills over 100 Yemeni soldiers.	Yemen
23 Jan.	The Chinese city of Wuhan, the suspected epicentre of the initial coronavirus outbreak, is quarantined.	China; Covid-19
28 Jan.	The USA publishes its long-awaited plan to resolve the Israeli–Palestinian conflict, but the plan is rejected by the Palestinian leadership (and by the Arab League on 1 February).	Israel; Palestine; US peace plan

29 Jan.	US President Donald J. Trump signs the US–Mexico–Canada Agreement (USMCA), a trade deal that is set to replace the North American Free Trade Agreement (NAFTA).	Canada; Mexico; NAFTA; USA; USMCA
30 Jan.	The WHO declares the coronavirus outbreak a Public Health Emergency of International Concern.	Covid-19; WHO
31 Jan.	The USA rescinds a 2014 directive banning production and acquisition of anti-personnel mines (APMs), as well as their use, other than in a future conflict on the Korean Peninsula, which allows the USA to again use landmines in exceptional circumstances in global conflicts.	APMs; USA
31 Jan.	The United Kingdom formally withdraws from the European Union (EU) and begins an 11-month transition period.	EU; UK
February		
4 Feb.	The USA announces that it has deployed a new submarine-launched low-yield nuclear warhead.	nuclear weapons; USA
5 Feb.	The US Senate votes to acquit President Trump of two impeachment charges relating to abuse of power and obstruction of Congress.	USA
9 Feb.	The African Union (AU) Assembly of Heads of State and Government upgrades the AU Liaison Office in Libya to the level of a mission.	AU; Libya
10 Feb.	Chinese President Xi Jinping declares a 'People's War' to contain the coronavirus outbreak.	China; Covid-19
11 Feb.	The WHO names the novel coronavirus strain 'Covid-19'.	Covid-19; WHO
16 Feb.	A WHO–China joint mission is initiated to assess the seriousness of Covid-19.	China; Covid-19; WHO
17 Feb.	EU foreign ministers agree to establish a new naval mission in the Mediterranean to monitor the UN arms embargo on Libya. Operation Irini is launched on 31 Mar. 2020.	EU; Libya; UN arms embargo
18 Feb.	Incumbent Afghan President Ashraf Ghani is announced the winner of the 2019 presidential election, after five months of delayed results.	Afghanistan; presidential election
22 Feb.	President Salva Kiir and opposition leader Riek Machar agree to form a long-awaited unity government in South Sudan.	South Sudan
23 Feb.	Following protests over India's new Citizenship Amendment Act, 53 people are killed in Hindu–Muslim communal riots in north-east Delhi.	India
27 Feb.	An attack by Syrian Government forces in the opposition-controlled north-west of Syria kills at least 33 Turkish soldiers.	Syria; Turkey
29 Feb.	The USA and the Taliban sign a conditional peace agreement, which calls for the withdrawal of US troops from Afghanistan within 14 months if the Taliban upholds the terms of the agreement.	Afghanistan; peace agreement; Taliban; USA
March		
1 Mar.	Turkey launches a major counteroffensive in northern Syria against Syrian Government forces, declaring war on the government of President Bashar al-Assad for the first time.	Syria; Turkey

2 Mar.	Armed forces from Somalia's federal government and the regional Jubaland administration, backed by Kenya, clash along the Somali–Kenyan border.	Jubaland conflict; Kenya; Somalia
3 Mar.	Inspectors from the International Atomic Energy Agency (IAEA) report that Iran has increased production of enriched uranium in the wake of the US decision to abandon the 2015 Joint Comprehensive Plan of Action (JCPOA).	IAEA; Iran; JCPOA; nuclear programme
5 Mar.	Turkish President Recep Tayyip Erdogan and Russian President Vladimir Putin agree a cessation of hostilities in Idlib, Syria, after weeks of military clashes between Syrian Government and Turkish forces.	ceasefire; Russia; Syria; Turkey
5 Mar.	The International Criminal Court (ICC) authorizes an inquiry into war crimes in Afghanistan, allowing US forces to be investigated for the first time.	Afghanistan; ICC; USA
6 Mar.	Two gunmen open fire on a crowded event in Kabul, Afghanistan, attended by the Afghan opposition leader Abdullah Abdullah, killing at least 32 people.	Afghanistan
7 Mar.	The number of confirmed cases of Covid-19 worldwide surpasses 100 000. A day later Italy becomes the first country to place its citizens in lockdown.	Covid-19
11 Mar.	The WHO declares Covid-19 a pandemic.	Covid-19; WHO
12 Mar.	The USA launches airstrikes against the Iran-aligned Iraqi militia Kata'ib Hezbollah, after two US soldiers and a British soldier were killed in a rocket attack.	Iran; Iraq; USA
13 Mar.	The WHO, the UN Foundation and numerous partners launch the Covid-19 Solidarity Response Fund to assist health workers, treat patients, and advance research for treatments and vaccines. It raises more than $70 million in 10 days.	Covid-19; humanitarian response; UN; WHO
17 Mar.	The EU's external and Schengen borders are closed for at least 30 days in an attempt to curb the Covid-19 pandemic.	Covid-19; EU
20 Mar.	The number of confirmed cases of Covid-19 worldwide reaches a quarter of a million and the death toll surpasses 10 000.	Covid-19
23 Mar.	UN Secretary-General António Guterres calls for an immediate global ceasefire and for conflict parties to address the challenge of the Covid-19 pandemic.	Covid-19; global ceasefire; UN
23 Mar.	Approximately 100 soldiers are killed in an attack by Boko Haram in Boma, Chad.	Boko Haram; Chad
24 Mar.	Approximately 70 soldiers are killed in an attack by Islamic State West Africa Province (ISWAP) in Niger.	ISWAP; Niger
25 Mar.	The UN Global Humanitarian Response Plan for Covid-19 is launched by the director-general of the WHO, the secretary-general of the UN, the under-secretary-general for humanitarian affairs of the UN and the executive director of the UN International Children's Emergency Fund (UNICEF).	Covid-19; humanitarian response
25 Mar.	An attack by the Islamic State on a Sikh religious complex in Kabul, Afghanistan, kills 25 people.	Afghanistan; Islamic State
26 Mar.	The Biological and Toxin Weapons Convention (BWC) marks its 45th anniversary of entry into force.	BWC
27 Mar.	North Macedonia becomes the 30th country to join the North Atlantic Treaty Organization (NATO).	NATO; North Macedonia

27 Mar.	Several European governments agree to create a military task force to tackle terrorism in the Liptako region of the Sahel. The French-led Task Force Takuba achieves initial operational capacity by the end of 2020.	Sahel; Task Force Takuba
April		
4 Apr.	The number of confirmed cases of Covid-19 worldwide passes 1 million.	Covid-19
8 Apr.	The Saudi Arabian-led coalition declares a unilateral ceasefire in its operations against Houthi forces in Yemen.	ceasefire; Saudi Arabia; Yemen
10 Apr.	The death toll from Covid-19 worldwide exceeds 100 000, a tenfold increase from 20 Mar.	Covid-19
12 Apr.	Oil-producing nations agree the largest production cut ever negotiated in an effort to stabilize oil prices. The plan will cut production by close to 10 per cent of the world's output in May and June.	oil prices
14 Apr.	The USA suspends funding for the WHO, following criticism of its handling of the Covid-19 pandemic.	Covid-19; USA; WHO
15 Apr.	The Group of Twenty (G20) nations agree to suspend debt service payments for the world's poorest states until 2021.	debt relief; G20
15 Apr.	The number of confirmed cases of Covid-19 worldwide passes 2 million.	Covid-19
17 Apr.	The separatist Arakan Army declares a one-month unilateral ceasefire to fight the pandemic, but the Myanmar military rejects the ceasefire.	Arakan Army; Myanmar
20 Apr.	A unity government is formed in Israel, ending more than a year of political deadlock.	Israel
23 Apr.	Two former high-ranking members of the Syrian Army go on trial in Germany for alleged war crimes. It is the first time that Syrian military officials are prosecuted for their roles in the conflict.	Germany; Syria; war crimes
25 Apr.	The Southern Transitional Council (STC) announces a self-rule administration in southern Yemen.	STC; Yemen
28 Apr.	An attack at a market in the northern town of Afrin, Syria, kills at least 40 people. No party claims responsibility, but Turkey, whose forces control the area, blames Kurdish militants.	Syria
May		
3–4 May	Venezuelan dissidents and a US-based private military company unsuccessfully attempt to remove President Nicolás Maduro from office by force.	Venezuela
9 May	Several Chinese and Indian soldiers are injured in a clash at the Nathu La border crossing between India and China.	border dispute; China; India
12 May	An attack on a maternity hospital in Kabul, Afghanistan, kills 24 people, including two newborn babies. In a separate incident in Kuz Kunar, 32 people are killed at a funeral by a suicide bomber. The USA blames the Islamic State for the attacks.	Afghanistan; Islamic State
14 May	The UN warns of a global mental health crisis caused by isolation, fear, uncertainty and economic turmoil due to the Covid-19 pandemic.	Covid-19; mental health; UN
17 May	Afghan President Ghani and his rival Abdullah Abdullah sign a power-sharing deal, ending the long-running dispute about the outcome of the 2019 presidential elections.	Afghanistan

18–19 May	The 73rd World Health Assembly is held virtually and adopts by consensus a resolution to fight the Covid-19 pandemic. It is co-sponsored by more than 130 countries, the largest number on record.	Covid-19; World Health Assembly
19 May	Palestinian President Mahmoud Abbas announces the termination of all agreements with Israel and the USA, including security ones, in response to Israel's plans to annex the West Bank and the Jordan Valley.	Israel; Palestine; USA
21 May	The USA announces that it will withdraw from the Open Skies Treaty within six months, alleging continuous violations by Russia.	Open Skies Treaty; USA
21 May	The number of confirmed cases of Covid-19 worldwide passes 5 million.	Covid-19
25 May	The killing of African-American George Floyd by a police officer in Minneapolis, USA, sparks national and international protests.	USA
25 May	US President Trump announces that the USA will leave the WHO.	USA; WHO
June		
2 June	Estimating that Yemen needs around $2.4 billion in emergency aid, the UN and Saudi Arabia hold a virtual donors conference, but it only raises $1.35 billion.	Yemen
4 June	Libya's GNA says it is in full control of Tripoli, after the Libyan National Army (LNA) retreats following months of intense fighting in the city.	GNA; Libya; LNA
10 June	A naval incident between French and Turkish ships leads to an investigation by NATO.	France; NATO; Turkey
15 June	A border clash between Chinese and Indian armed forces in the Galwan Valley, in the disputed Ladakh region, kills at least 20 Indian soldiers (the extent of Chinese casualties is unclear). These are the first fatalities along the line of actual control in 45 years.	border dispute; China; India
16 June	North Korea destroys the inter-Korean liaison office in the border town of Kaesong.	North Korea; South Korea
17 June	Turkey launches a major attack against Kurdish forces in Iraqi Kurdistan.	Iraq; Kurds; Turkey
22–23 June	Russian–US Strategic Security Dialogue Talks take place in Vienna, Austria. The USA's attempts to get China to join the talks are rebuffed.	nuclear arms control; Russia; USA
25 June– 1 July	Russia holds a constitutional referendum, including a provision that would make it possible for President Putin to serve two further terms in office. According to official results, 79 per cent of voters supported the constitutional reforms.	Russia
29 June	China passes a controversial security law for Hong Kong, seemingly undermining the 'One Country, Two Systems' framework. The law criminalizes acts of secession, subversion, terrorism and collusion with foreign or external forces.	China; Hong Kong
29 June	The killing of a popular ethnic Oromo musician and activist, Hachalu Hundessa, sparks unrest and ethnic violence in Ethiopia's capital, Addis Ababa, and the region of Oromia.	Ethiopia

30 June	The number of confirmed cases of Covid-19 worldwide passes 10 million and the death toll exceeds 500 000.	Covid-19
July		
1 July	The USMCA enters into force, replacing NAFTA.	Canada; Mexico; NAFTA; USA; USMCA
1 July	The UN Security Council passes a resolution supporting Secretary-General Guterres' call in March for a global ceasefire.	Global ceasefire; UN Security Council
2 July	The UN Security Council convenes a virtual, high-level open debate on 'Pandemics and Security'.	International health threats; UN Security Council
8 July	At least 180 bodies are found in mass graves in Djibo, Burkina Faso. Government forces are suspected of being involved in large-scale extrajudicial executions.	Burkina Faso
10 July	The AU Peace and Security Council establishes the AU Military Observers Mission to the Central African Republic (MOUACA).	CAR; MOUACA
14 July	Fighting breaks out between Armenian and Azerbaijani forces in the northern section of the border between the two countries, leaving at least 16 people dead.	Armenia; Azerbaijan
21 July	EU leaders agree to create a €750 billion ($858 billion) recovery fund to rebuild EU economies impacted by the Covid-19 pandemic.	Covid-19; EU
22 July	Ukrainian, Russian and Organization for Security and Co-operation in Europe (OSCE) negotiators reach an agreement for a full ceasefire in eastern Ukraine between government forces and pro-Russian separatists from 27 July.	ceasefire; Ukraine
22 July	The number of confirmed cases of Covid-19 worldwide passes 15 million.	Covid-19
29 July	The STC accepts a Saudi Arabian-brokered peace deal and abandons its aspirations of self-rule in southern Yemen.	STC; Yemen
August		
9 Aug.	The EU Advisory Mission in the Central African Republic (EUAM RCA) is launched, having been established by the Council of the EU in Dec. 2019.	CAR; EUAM RCA
9 Aug.	The presidential election victory of incumbent Belarusian President Alexander Lukashenko sparks widespread protests in Belarus, which continue throughout the year. The EU, among others, subsequently declines to recognize the result.	Belarus; EU; protests; presidential election
10 Aug.	The number of confirmed cases of Covid-19 worldwide passes 20 million.	Covid-19
11 Aug.	Russia announces that it has approved the world's first Covid-19 vaccine.	Covid-19
12 Aug.	Militants linked to the Islamic State seize Mocímboa da Praia, a port in Mozambique, after days of fighting. The port is close to the Rovuma Basin, home to extensive natural gas reserves and Africa's largest-ever energy project.	Islamic State; Mozambique

12 Aug.	Amid increased tensions in the eastern Mediterranean, a Turkish frigate escorting a survey ship suffers a minor collision with a Greek frigate.	Greece; Turkey
13 Aug.	The USA announces it has brokered a deal in which the United Arab Emirates (UAE) and Israel agree to normalize relations.	Israel; UAE; USA
17–18 Aug.	Russian–US Strategic Security Dialogue Talks take place in Vienna, Austria, and discuss extending New START. However, underlying differences in points of view continue during the final round of talks on 5 October.	New START; Russia; USA
17–21 Aug.	The Sixth Conference of States Parties to the Arms Trade Treaty (ATT) is conducted through written procedure only. Among other decisions, it establishes the Diversion Information Exchange Forum, a new body for informal voluntary exchanges between states parties and signatory states on arms diversion.	arms diversion mechanism; ATT
18 Aug.	After months of mass protests, a military coup in Mali forces President Ibrahim Boubacar Keïta to resign. Military leaders propose a three-year timeline to return to civilian rule.	Mali; military coup
20 Aug.	Russian opposition figure Alexei Navalny is poisoned with what is subsequently confirmed to be a novichok nerve agent and hospitalized in a serious condition.	chemical weapons; Russia
21 Aug.	In separate statements, the GNA and the LNA call for a ceasefire across Libya, as well as other measures, including parliamentary and presidential elections in Mar. 2021.	ceasefire; Libya
22 Aug.	The death toll from Covid-19 worldwide exceeds 800 000.	Covid-19
25 Aug.	Africa is declared free of wild polio, the second virus to be eradicated from the continent after smallpox 40 years ago.	Africa; polio
30 Aug.	The number of confirmed cases of Covid-19 worldwide passes 25 million.	Covid-19
31 Aug.	The Sudanese transitional government and the Sudan Revolutionary Front sign a series of peace agreements, as a key part of Sudan's larger transition from military to civilian rule.	peace agreement; Sudan
September		
2 Sep.	UN Secretary-General Guterres notes 'with concern' the imposition by the USA of sanctions against the Chief Prosecutor of the ICC and another senior official.	ICC; USA
4 Sep.	Bahrain and Israel agree to normalize relations.	Bahrain; Israel
4 Sep.	Kosovo and Serbia sign economic normalization agreements, which also include commitments linked to US peace efforts in the Israeli–Palestinian conflict.	Kosovo; Serbia
8 Sep.	Gunshots are fired along the line of actual control between China and India, for the first time in 45 years. Three days later, the Chinese and Indian foreign ministers meet in Moscow, Russia, and agree a joint statement calling for dialogue and disengagement.	border dispute; China; India
12 Sep.	Representatives from the Afghan Government and the Taliban meet in Doha, Qatar, to begin intra-Afghan peace talks. The talks were supposed to immediately follow the US–Taliban peace agreement in February.	Afghanistan; peace talks

15 Sep.	The USA hosts a signing ceremony for the Abraham Accords, in which the UAE and Bahrain recognize Israel.	Bahrain; Israel; UAE; USA
17 Sep.	The number of confirmed cases of Covid-19 worldwide passes 30 million.	Covid-19
21 Sep.	The UN General Assembly marks its 75th anniversary. Due to the Covid-19 pandemic, world leaders address the Assembly via video link.	UN General Assembly
22 Sep.	UN Secretary-General Guterres renews his call for a global ceasefire during his opening speech at the 75th session of the UN General Assembly.	global ceasefire; UN
23 Sep.	The WHO, the UN, UNICEF, the UN Development Programme, the UN Educational, Scientific and Cultural Organization (UNESCO), and others issue a joint statement on 'Managing the Covid-19 infodemic'. It highlights the need to mitigate harm from misinformation and disinformation.	Covid-19; UN; WHO
27 Sep.	Deadly clashes erupt in Nagorno-Karabakh between Armenian and Azerbaijani forces. Armenia, Azerbaijan and Artsakh introduce martial law and mobilize forces.	Armenia; Azerbaijan; Nagorno-Karabakh
30 Sep.	The death toll from Covid-19 worldwide exceeds 1 million.	Covid-19
October		
1 Oct.	Following a series of technical meetings held by NATO between the military representatives of Greece and Turkey, a bilateral military de-confliction mechanism is established to reduce the risk of incidents and accidents in the eastern Mediterranean.	Greece; NATO; Turkey
3 Oct.	The Sudanese transitional government and various armed opposition groups sign the comprehensive Juba Peace Agreement.	Juba Peace Agreement; Sudan
4 Oct.	China becomes a state party of the ATT.	ATT; China
5 Oct.	The number of confirmed cases of Covid-19 worldwide passes 35 million, but the WHO estimates that there may be as many as 760 million cases—roughly one tenth of the global population.	Covid-19; WHO
10 Oct.	Armenia and Azerbaijan agree on a ceasefire in the Nagorno-Karabakh conflict, but fighting continues. Two further ceasefires on 17 and 25 October are also broken almost immediately.	Armenia; Azerbaijan; Nagorno-Karabakh
18 Oct.	UN restrictions on arms transfers to Iran are lifted in line with a timetable set out in the JCPOA.	Iran; JCPOA
19 Oct.	The number of confirmed cases of Covid-19 worldwide passes 40 million.	Covid-19
23 Oct.	Representatives from Libya's GNA and LNA sign a permanent ceasefire agreement during UN-mediated talks in Geneva, Switzerland.	ceasefire; Libya
23 Oct.	At the end of an 11-year demining process, the Falkland Islands/Malvinas are declared free of APMs, 38 years after the 1982 war.	APMs; Falklands/ Malvinas
23 Oct.	Israel and Sudan agree to normalize relations, in a deal brokered by the USA in exchange for Sudan paying $335 million to victims of a 1998 terrorist attack.	Israel; Sudan

24 Oct.	The UN announces that Honduras is the 50th country to ratify the Treaty on the Prohibition of Nuclear Weapons (TPNW), triggering its entry into force in 90 days.	Honduras; TPNW
26 Oct.	At least 56 members of a Turkish-backed armed opposition group are killed in a suspected Russian airstrike in Idlib province in the north-west of Syria.	Russia; Syria; Turkey
29 Oct.	Belarus closes its borders with all neighbouring countries (Latvia, Lithuania, Poland and Ukraine) except Russia, amid continuing protests within the country.	Belarus
30 Oct.	The number of confirmed cases of Covid-19 worldwide passes 45 million.	Covid-19
November		
3–7 Nov.	Joe Biden is elected as the 46th president of the USA.	presidential election; USA
3–4 Nov.	The Tigray People's Liberation Front (TPLF) take control of some of the federal forces in Tigray, Ethiopia. The next day, Ethiopian Prime Minister Abiy Ahmed launches a military offensive in the region against the TPLF.	Ethiopia; Tigray conflict
4 Nov.	The USA formally exits the 2015 Paris Agreement on climate change.	Paris Agreement; USA
5 Nov.	The terms of reference for the WHO Global Study of the Origins of SARS-CoV-2 are published.	Covid-19; WHO
6 Nov.	The UN warns that Burkina Faso, Nigeria, South Sudan and Yemen are at risk of famine, due to conflict, mass displacement, economic crisis, and climate and agricultural problems, as well as Covid-19 related restrictions.	Burkina Faso; famine; Nigeria; South Sudan; UN; Yemen
8 Nov.	The number of confirmed cases of Covid-19 worldwide passes 50 million.	Covid-19
9 Nov.	Armenia and Azerbaijan sign a Russian-brokered ceasefire agreement, which requires Armenia to return much of the Azeri territory surrounding Nagorno-Karabakh. Russian peacekeepers will be deployed along the line of contact in Nagorno-Karabakh and the corridor linking the enclave to Armenia.	Armenia; Azerbaijan; ceasefire; Nagorno-Karabakh; Russia
9 Nov.	The first successful phase III trial of a Covid-19 vaccine is announced by the drug companies Pfizer and BioNTech.	Covid-19; vaccine
9 Nov.	The Council of the EU and the EU Parliament reach a provisional political agreement on a revised version of the Dual-use Regulation, drawing to a close a process of review that began in 2011.	EU Dual-use Regulation
11 Nov.	Russia and Turkey sign a memorandum of understanding on the establishment of a joint ceasefire monitoring centre in Azerbaijan to monitor the ceasefire in Nagorno-Karabakh.	Armenia; Azerbaijan; ceasefire; Russia; Turkey
12 Nov.	A Japanese-brokered ceasefire between the Arakan Army and the Myanmar military opens up new opportunities for dialogue.	Arakan Army; ceasefire; Myanmar
13 Nov.	At least 15 people are killed in cross-border shelling between India and Pakistan, along the line of control in northern Kashmir.	India; Kashmir; Pakistan

15 Nov.	The Regional Comprehensive Economic Partnership (RCEP) is signed by 15 Asia-Pacific countries to form the world's largest free-trade bloc, covering one third of the world's population.	RCEP
17 Nov.	The USA announces plans to reduce the number of US troops in Afghanistan from 4500 to about 2500 by mid January 2021.	Afghanistan; troop withdrawal; USA
17 Nov.	The number of confirmed cases of Covid-19 worldwide passes 55 million, with around 1 million cases recorded on average every two days.	Covid-19
18 Nov.	Iraq and Saudi Arabia open the Arar border crossing for trade, for the first time in three decades.	Iran; Saudi Arabia
19 Nov.	The Brereton Report into Australian war crimes in Afghanistan is released.	Afghanistan; Australia; war crimes
22 Nov.	The USA withdraws from the Open Skies Treaty.	Open Skies Treaty; USA
25 Nov.	The number of confirmed cases of Covid-19 worldwide passes 60 million.	Covid-19
27 Nov.	A senior Iranian nuclear scientist, Mohsen Fakhrizadeh, is assassinated near Tehran.	Iran; nuclear programme
28 Nov.	Ethiopia's federal forces capture Tigray's capital, Mekelle, and declare victory over the TPLF, which vows to carry on a guerrilla-style resistance.	Ethiopia; Tigray conflict
28 Nov.	Boko Haram militants attack a farm in Jere, Nigeria, killing at least 70 people.	Boko Haram; Nigeria
December		
2 Dec.	The Afghan Government and the Taliban reach a preliminary agreement to move forward with more detailed negotiations and peace talks. It is their first written agreement during 19 years of war.	Afghanistan; Taliban
2 Dec.	The UK approves Pfizer-BioNTech's BNT162b2 vaccine, being the first country in the world to do so.	Covid-19; UK; vaccine
4 Dec.	The number of confirmed cases of Covid-19 worldwide passes 65 million and the death toll exceeds 1.5 million.	Covid-19
4 Dec.	President Trump announces the withdrawal of all US troops from Somalia (about 700), although many are likely to be repositioned in neighbouring countries.	Somalia; troop withdrawal; USA
10 Dec.	Israel and Morocco normalize diplomatic relations. Simultaneously, the USA reaffirms its previous recognition of Moroccan sovereignty over Western Sahara.	Israel; Morocco; USA; Western Sahara
12 Dec.	At the Climate Ambition Summit, marking the fifth anniversary of the Paris Agreement, some states commit to further actions to achieve net zero carbon emissions at a future date.	Climate Ambition Summit
12 Dec.	The number of confirmed cases of Covid-19 worldwide passes 70 million.	Covid-19
12 Dec.	Bhutan and Israel normalize diplomatic relations.	Bhutan; Israel
14 Dec.	The USA removes Sudan from its list of state sponsors of terrorism.	Sudan; USA

14 Dec.	The USA applies sanctions on Turkey in retaliation for its purchase of a S-400 missile system from Russia. It is the first time the USA has sanctioned a NATO ally.	sanctions; Turkey; USA
15 Dec.	The ICC accuses the Philippines of crimes against humanity in its war on drugs.	ICC; Philippines
16 Dec.	The UN General Assembly adopts a new initiative proposed by the UK regarding norms for responsible behaviour in space.	space security; UK; UN General Assembly
20 Dec.	A new, highly infectious strain of SARS-CoV-2, which is spreading in Europe and Australia, provokes international border closures.	Covid-19
21 Dec.	In the Chilean Antarctic Territory, 36 cases of Covid-19 are reported, marking the first infections in Antarctica and the last continent to report infections.	Antarctica; Covid-19
24 Dec.	The EU and UK agree a comprehensive free trade agreement, prior to the end of the Brexit transition period.	Brexit; EU; UK
30 Dec.	An attack on Yemen's Aden airport causes multiple casualties and appears to target a plane carrying members of the newly formed unity government.	Yemen
31 Dec.	The joint UN–AU Hybrid Operation in Darfur (UNAMID) officially ends its mission in Sudan.	UNAMID
31 Dec.	The number of confirmed cases of Covid-19 worldwide passes 82 million, with an estimated 1.8 million recorded deaths.	Covid-19

About the authors

Dr Virginie Baudais (France) is a Senior Researcher and the Deputy Director of SIPRI's Sahel/West Africa Programme. Prior to joining SIPRI in August 2019, she worked for two United Nations peacekeeping operations, in Côte d'Ivoire and Mali, as a Political Officer. Prior to her experience with the UN, she worked as a teaching assistant at Toulouse 1 Capitole University. Baudais graduated from Sciences Po Toulouse and holds a PhD in Political Science from Toulouse 1 Capitole University. Her research interests focus on the Sahel, peacebuilding, security, governance and state reform. Her recent publications include *Niger: Armed Force Politics and Counterterrorism* (Oxford Research Encyclopedia, Feb. 2021); and *Conflict Mediation and Peacebuilding in the Sahel: The Role of Maghreb Countries in an African Framework*, SIPRI Policy Paper (Jan. 2021, co-author).

Dr Lucie Béraud-Sudreau (France) is the Director of SIPRI's Arms and Military Expenditure Programme, where her work focuses on the dynamics and implications of global military spending, arms production and transfers. Previously, she was a Research Fellow for Defence Economics and Procurements at the International Institute for Strategic Studies (IISS). Her recent publications include 'Weighing giants: Taking stock of the expansion of China's defence industry', *Defence and Peace Economics* (2021, co-author); *French Arms Exports: The Business of Sovereignty* (Routledge, 2020); 'Mapping the international presence of the world's largest arms companies', SIPRI Insights on Peace and Security (Dec. 2020, co-author); and 'Emerging suppliers in the global arms trade', SIPRI Insights on Peace and Security (Dec. 2020, co-author).

Kolja Brockmann (Germany) is a Researcher in SIPRI's Dual-use and Arms Trade Control Programme. He joined SIPRI in 2017 and conducts research in the fields of export control, non-proliferation and technology governance. He focuses on the multilateral export control regimes, controls on emerging technologies, particularly additive manufacturing, and intangible transfers of technology. Previously, Brockmann did an internship at the German Federal Office for Economic Affairs and Export Control (BAFA). He received his MA with distinction in Non-Proliferation and International Security from King's College London. His recent publications include 'Controlling ballistic missile proliferation: Assessing complementarity between the HCOC, MTCR and UNSCR 1540', HCOC Research Paper (June 2020); and *Responsible Artificial Intelligence Research and Innovation for International Peace and Security*, SIPRI Report (Nov. 2020, co-author).

Mark Bromley (United Kingdom/Sweden) is the Director of SIPRI's Dual-use and Arms Trade Control Programme, where his work focuses on national, regional and international efforts to regulate the international trade in conventional arms and dual-use items. Previously, he was a Policy Analyst for the British American Security Information Council (BASIC). His recent publications include 'Sweden's arms export controls: Balancing support and restraint', in ed. L. Lustgarten, *Law and the Arms Trade: Weapons, Blood and Rules* (Hart Publishing, 2020); *Reporting on Conventional Arms Transfers and Transfer Controls: Improving Coordination and Increasing Engagement*, SIPRI Policy Paper (Aug. 2020, co-author); *Detecting, Investigating and Prosecuting Export Control Violations: European Perspectives on Key Challenges and Good Practices*, SIPRI Report (Dec. 2019, co-author); and 'Measuring illicit arms and financial flows: Improving the assessment of Sustainable Development Goal 16', SIPRI Background Paper (July 2019, co-author).

Laura Brunn (Denmark) is a Research Assistant at SIPRI, working on emerging military and security technologies. Her focus is on how emerging military technologies, notably autonomous weapon systems (AWS), affect compliance with—and interpretation of—international humanitarian law (IHL). She has a background in Middle Eastern Studies and International Security and Law, and wrote her master's thesis on remote warfare's implications for the protection of civilians, by analysing the United States targeting cycle in its aerial campaign against the Islamic State. Before joining SIPRI, Bruun worked at Airwars in London, where she monitored and assessed civilian casualty reports from US and Russian airstrikes in Syria and Iraq. Besides co-authoring a forthcoming SIPRI report on AWS and IHL (June 2021), her recent publications include *Responsible Military Use of Artificial Intelligence: Can the European Union Lead the Way in Developing Best Practice?*, SIPRI Report (Nov. 2020, co-author).

Dr Marina Caparini (Canada) is a Senior Researcher and Director of SIPRI's Governance and Society Programme. Her research focuses on inclusive peacebuilding and the nexus between security and development. She works on security sector governance, policing, stabilization and peace operations, and better aligning the shared outcomes of humanitarian assistance, development aid and peacebuilding. Prior to joining SIPRI in December 2016, Caparini held senior positions at the Norwegian Institute for International Affairs, the International Center for Transitional Justice, and the Geneva Centre for the Democratic Control of Armed Forces. She holds a PhD in War Studies from King's College, University of London.

Dr Ian Davis (United Kingdom) is the Executive Editor of the SIPRI Yearbook and an Associate Senior Fellow within Conflict and Peace at SIPRI. From 2014–16 he was the Director of SIPRI's Editorial, Publications and Library Department. Prior to joining SIPRI, he held several senior positions and worked as an independent human security and arms control consultant. He has a long record of research and publication on international and regional security, and blogs on NATO-related issues. His recent publications include 'Towards an open and accountable NATO', in eds I. Shapiro and A. Tooze, *Charter of NATO* (Yale University Press, 2018); and 'How much does the UK spend on nuclear weapons?', BASIC Research Report (Nov. 2018).

Dr Tytti Erästö (Finland) is a Senior Researcher in SIPRI's Nuclear Disarmament, Arms Control and Non-proliferation Programme. Her research interests include the Iran nuclear deal, the Treaty on the Prohibition of Nuclear Weapons (TPNW), efforts to establish a weapons of mass destruction-free zone in the Middle East, United States–Russian arms control treaties, the USA/NATO–Russia missile defence dispute, and the global disarmament and non-proliferation regime more generally. Previously, she worked at the Ploughshares Fund in Washington, DC; the Belfer Center for Science and International Affairs, Harvard Kennedy School; the Vienna Center for Disarmament and Non-Proliferation; and the Tampere Peace Research Institute in Finland. Her recent publications include *New Technologies and Nuclear Disarmament: Outlining a Way Forward*, SIPRI Report (May 2021); 'Addressing missile threats in the Middle East and North Africa', SIPRI Policy Brief (Nov. 2020, co-author); 'European non-proliferation diplomacy in the shadow of secondary sanctions', SIPRI Policy Brief (Aug. 2020); and 'Towards greater nuclear restraint: Raising the threshold for nuclear weapon use', SIPRI Insights on Peace and Security (May 2020, co-author).

Shivan Fazil (Iraq) is a Researcher in SIPRI's Middle East and North Africa Programme. His work mainly focuses on drivers of conflict, peacebuilding and governance in Iraq, where he has worked for over six years with various organizations, most recently with the United States Institute of Peace. He has also featured in the international media, commenting on Iraq's social, political and security dynamics and the challenges of governance after the military defeat of the Islamic State. Fazil holds an MSc in Middle Eastern Politics from the School of Oriental and African Studies, University of London. He has just co-edited a book on *Youth Identity, Politics and Change in Contemporary Kurdistan*, published by Transnational Press London.

Vitaly Fedchenko (Russia) is a Senior Researcher in SIPRI's European Security Programme, responsible for nuclear security issues and the political, technological and educational dimensions of nuclear arms control and non-proliferation. Previously, he was a visiting researcher at SIPRI and worked at the Center for Policy Studies in Russia and the Institute for Applied International Research in Moscow. He is the author or co-author of several publications on nuclear forensics, nuclear security, international non-proliferation and disarmament assistance, nuclear forces and the international nuclear fuel cycle.

Annelies Hickendorff (Netherlands) is a Research Assistant in SIPRI's Sahel/West Africa Programme. She has been involved in multiple studies contributing to a better understanding of local security perceptions in the region. Her latest project assessed the effectiveness of the European Union Training Mission in the Central African Republic (EUTM RCA). Prior to joining SIPRI, she was a Rotary Peace Fellow in African Peace and Conflict Studies at the University of Bradford, UK, and worked for various international non-governmental organizations and United Nations agencies in Cameroon, Kenya, Mali and Senegal.

Shannon N. Kile (United States) is the Director of SIPRI's Disarmament, Arms Control and Non-proliferation Programme. His principal areas of research are nuclear arms control and non-proliferation, with a special interest in the nuclear programmes of Iran and North Korea. His work also looks at regional security issues related to Iran and the Middle East. He has contributed to numerous SIPRI publications, including chapters on nuclear arms control and nuclear forces and weapon technology for the SIPRI Yearbook since 1994.

Matt Korda (Canada) is an Associate Researcher with SIPRI's Nuclear Disarmament, Arms Control and Non-proliferation Programme and a Research Associate with the Nuclear Information Project at the Federation of American Scientists (FAS). He co-authors the FAS Nuclear Notebook in the *Bulletin of the Atomic Scientists* and has contributed chapters on world nuclear forces to the SIPRI Yearbook. Previously, Korda worked for NATO'S Arms Control, Disarmament and WMD Non-Proliferation Centre in Brussels. He received his MA in International Peace & Security from the Department of War Studies at King's College London, and his research interests and recent publications focus on nuclear deterrence and disarmament, progressive foreign policy, and the nexus between nuclear weapons, climate change and injustice.

Hans M. Kristensen (Denmark) is the Director of the Nuclear Information Project at the Federation of American Scientists (FAS) in Washington, DC, and a SIPRI Associate Senior Fellow. He is a frequent consultant to the news media and institutes on nuclear weapon matters, and is co-author of the FAS Nuclear Notebook in the *Bulletin of the Atomic Scientists*. Prior to joining FAS, Kristensen was a consultant to the nuclear programme at the Natural Resources Defense Council, a programme officer at the Nautilus Institute, and a special adviser to the Danish Ministry of Defence. His recent publications include 'China's strategic systems and programs', in *China's Strategic Arsenal: Worldview, Doctrine, and Systems* (Georgetown University Press, 2021); 'British defense review ends nuclear reduction era' (FAS, Mar. 2021); 'US deploys new low-yield submarine warhead' (FAS, Jan. 2020); and 'Is the Pentagon exaggerating Russia's tactical nuclear weapons?' (Forbes.com, May 2019).

Alexandra Kuimova (Russia) is a Researcher in SIPRI's Arms and Military Expenditure Programme. Her areas of research include the monitoring of arms transfers, military spending and the arms industry, as well as foreign and defence policies, with a particular focus on the Middle East and North Africa, Russia and Eastern Europe. Before joining SIPRI, Kuimova was an intern in the Department of New Challenges and Threats at the Russian Ministry of Foreign Affairs. She has also completed summer internships at Abdelmalek Essaâdi University, Morocco, and Cairo University, Egypt. Her recent publications include 'Arms transfers to conflict zones: The case of Nagorno-Karabakh', SIPRI Topical Backgrounder (Apr. 2021, co-author); 'Mapping the international presence of the world's largest arms companies', SIPRI Insights on Peace and Security (Dec. 2020, co-author); and 'Understanding Egyptian military expenditure', SIPRI Background Paper (Oct. 2020).

Dr Moritz Kütt (Germany) is a Senior Researcher at the Institute for Peace Research and Security Policy at the University of Hamburg, working within the

Arms Control and Emerging Technologies research area. In his research, he develops new approaches and innovative tools for verification of nuclear arms control, non-proliferation and disarmament agreements. These approaches and tools seek, in particular, to enable non-nuclear weapon states to participate effectively in such verification activities. Prior to his time in Hamburg, Moritz was a Postdoctoral Research Associate with the Program on Science and Global Security at Princeton University.

Dr Filippa Lentzos (Norway) is a Senior Lecturer in Science & International Security at the Department of War Studies and Co-Director of the Centre for Science and Security Studies (CSSS) at King's College London. She is also an Associate Senior Researcher within Armament and Disarmament at SIPRI, and a Non-Resident Scholar at the James Martin Center for Nonproliferation Studies (CNS). She serves as a biosecurity columnist at the *Bulletin of the Atomic Scientists*, an editor of the social science journal *BioSocieties*, and as the NGO Coordinator for the Biological and Toxin Weapons Convention. A biologist and social scientist by training, Lentzos has researched and been actively involved in biological disarmament and non-proliferation for nearly 20 years.

Dr Jaïr van der Lijn (Netherlands) is the Director of SIPRI's Peace Operations and Conflict Management Programme. He is also an Associate Fellow at the Radboud University Nijmegen. His research interests include the future of peace operations, their evaluation and factors for success and failure, comprehensive approaches in missions and their relationship with local populations. His recent publications include *Assessing the Effectiveness of the United Nations Mission in Mali (MINUSMA)*, Norwegian Institute of International Affairs Report (2019, lead editor); *Towards Legitimate Stability in CAR and the DRC: External Assumptions and Local Perspective*, SIPRI Policy Report (Sep. 2019, co-author); and 'Multilateral peace operations and the challenges of irregular migration and human trafficking', SIPRI Background Paper (June 2019).

Dr Diego Lopes da Silva (Brazil) is a Researcher in SIPRI's Arms and Military Expenditure Programme. He holds a PhD in Peace, Defence and International Security Studies from São Paulo State University. His publications have addressed the arms trade, arms production and transparency in military expenditure. Prior to SIPRI, he held research positions at the Institute for Public Policy and International Relations (IPPRI) of the São Paulo State University and at the Latin American Network On Defense And Security (RESDAL). His recent publications include 'Military spending and the achievement of the 2030 Agenda for Sustainable Development', in UNODA Occasional Papers no. 35 (United Nations, Apr. 2020, co-author); and 'Trends in world military expenditure, 2020', SIPRI Fact Sheet (Apr. 2021, co-author).

Giovanna Maletta (Italy) is a Researcher in SIPRI's Dual-use and Arms Trade Control Programme. Her research interests include export controls and trade compliance, with a particular focus on the dual-use and arms export control policies of the European Union (EU) and its member states. Her work also involves mapping cooperation and assistance activities in the field of arms transfer and SALW controls and of relevance to the implementation of the Arms Trade Treaty. Further, Maletta coordinates activities related to SIPRI's role in the EU Non-Proliferation and Disarmament Consortium. Her most recent publications include *Supporting Small Arms and Light Weapons Controls through Development Assistance: The Case of sub-Saharan Africa*, SIPRI Report (Feb. 2021, co-author); and 'Seeking a responsible arms trade to reduce human suffering in Yemen', *The International Spectator* (Feb. 2021).

Alexandra Marksteiner (Austria/Germany) is a Research Assistant in SIPRI's Arms and Military Expenditure Programme. In this capacity, she collects and analyses data on military spending and the arms industry. Among her areas of research are the international presence of arms companies and the financial value of arms exports, as well as trends in United States and German military expenditure. Prior to joining SIPRI, Marksteiner interned with the Security and Strategy Team at the Brookings Institution in Washington, DC. She has also worked for the Atlantic Council, the German Federal Foreign Office and the United Nations Department of Peace Operations. During her graduate studies at Johns Hopkins School of Advanced International Studies (SAIS), she focused on the nexus between international security and multilateral cooperation.

Dr Caitríona McLeish (United Kingdom) is a Research Analyst on chemical and biological weapons. At the time of writing, she was a Senior Fellow at the Science Policy Research Unit (SPRU), University of Sussex, and Co-Director of the Harvard Sussex Program on Chemical and Biological Weapons. The main focus of her work there was the governance of dual-use technologies in regard to the effective implementation of the prohibitions under both the Chemical Weapons Convention and the Biological Weapons Convention. This included consideration of how to create effective mechanisms to prevent misuse of legitimate science and technology and examining roles that have and might be played in chemical and biological disarmament efforts by actors outside of government.

Dr Zia Mian (United States) is the Co-Director of the Program on Science and Global Security at Princeton University's School of Public and International Affairs. A physicist, his work focuses on nuclear weapons non-proliferation, arms control and disarmament, and nuclear energy issues. He is co-editor of the journal *Science & Global Security* and co-chair of the International Panel on Fissile Materials. He is also a co-founder and member of the steering committee of the Physicists Coalition for Nuclear Threat Reduction and serves on the board of the Arms Control Association. His recent work has focused on supporting the implementation of the Treaty on the Prohibition of Nuclear Weapons. He has contributed to the SIPRI Yearbook on fissile materials since 2007.

Dr Pavel Podvig (Russia) is a Researcher in the Program on Science and Global Security at Princeton University and a Senior Researcher at the United Nations Institute for Disarmament Research (UNIDIR). He began his work on security issues at the Center for Arms Control Studies at the Moscow Institute of Physics and Technology (MIPT), which was the first independent research organization in Russia dedicated to analysis of technical issues related to arms control and disarmament. Podvig directs his own research project, Russian Nuclear Forces (RussianForces.org). He is also a co-editor of *Science & Global Security* and a member of the International Panel on Fissile Materials.

Nivedita Raju (India) is an Associate Researcher with SIPRI, specializing in space security. Previously, she was a Research Fellow at Open Lunar Foundation and a contributing member of the Manual on International Law Applicable to Military Uses of Outer Space (MILAMOS) Project at McGill University. Raju was also Deputy Representative to the United States Federal Aviation Administration's Center of Excellence for Commercial Space Transportation, where she directed research on regulating cross-border suborbital flights between Canada and the USA. Her recent publications include 'A proposal for a ban on destructive anti-satellite testing: A role for the European Union?', EU Non-Proliferation and Disarmament Consortium (Apr. 2021); and 'Transparency and confidence-building measures for lunar security', Open Lunar Foundation (May 2021).

Luke Richards (United Kingdom) is a Research Assistant at SIPRI, working on emerging military and security technologies. His research interests lie at the intersection of science, technology, innovation, governance and international affairs. Prior to joining SIPRI, he worked on cyber issues at the International Institute for Strategic Studies (IISS), while finishing an MSc in Science and Technology Policy at the Science Policy Research Unit (SPRU), University of Sussex. His recent publications include *Responsible Artificial Intelligence Research and Innovation for International Peace and Security*, SIPRI Report (Nov. 2020, co-author); and *Responsible Military Use of Artificial Intelligence: Can the European Union Lead the Way in Developing Best Practice?*, SIPRI Report (Nov. 2020, co-author).

Lucile Robin (France) is a Research Assistant in SIPRI's Dual-use and Arms Trade Control Programme. Her research is focused on the Arms Trade Treaty (ATT), export controls and small arms and light weapons (SALW) controls. She also contributes to the SIPRI Mapping ATT-Relevant Cooperation and Assistance Activities Database. Her recent publications include *Supporting Small Arms and Light Weapons Controls through Development Assistance: The Case of sub-Saharan Africa*, SIPRI Report (Feb. 2021, co-author); and 'Post-shipment control measures: European approaches to on-site inspections of exported military materiel', SIPRI Background Paper (Dec. 2020, co-author).

Timo Smit (Netherlands/Sweden) is a Researcher in SIPRI's Peace Operations and Conflict Management Programme. He is in charge of SIPRI's database on multilateral peace operations and conducts research on trends in peace operations and various related thematic issues. Before joining SIPRI in 2014, he worked for the European Union Institute for Security Studies (EUISS) and the NATO Parliamentary Assembly. His recent research has focused on, among other things, civilian crisis management and the EU's Common Security and Defence Policy (CSDP).

Dan Smith (Sweden/United Kingdom) is the Director of SIPRI. He has a long record of research and publication on a wide range of conflict and peace issues. His current work focuses on the relationship between climate change and insecurity, on peace and security issues in the Middle East and on global conflict trends. He served four years in the United Nations Peacebuilding Fund Advisory Group, two of which (2010–11) were as the Chair. From 2014 to 2017 he was also a Professor of Peace & Conflict at the University of Manchester. He is the author of successive editions of atlases of politics, war and peace, and the Middle East, and of a blog on international politics.

Dr Nan Tian (South Africa) is a Researcher in SIPRI's Arms and Military Expenditure Programme, where he leads the Military Expenditure Project. His regions of expertise are Africa and China, with research interests focused on the causes and impact of military expenditure and civil conflict, and the issues relating to transparency and accountability in military budgeting, spending and procurement. Previously, he was a Macroeconomics Lecturer at the University of Cape Town. He has published in *Defence and Peace Economics*; *The Economics of Peace and Security Journal*; and *Peace Economics, Peace Science and Public Policy*.

Dr Petr Topychkanov (Russia) is a Senior Researcher in SIPRI's Nuclear Disarmament, Arms Control and Non-proliferation Programme, working on issues related to nuclear non-proliferation, disarmament, arms control and the impact of new technologies on strategic stability. Prior to joining SIPRI in 2018, he held the position of Senior Researcher at the Centre for International Security at the Primakov National Research Institute of World Economy and International Relations, Russian Academy of Sciences. From 2006–17, Topychkanov was a Fellow at the Carnegie Moscow Center's Nonproliferation Program. He received his PhD in History in 2009 from the Institute of Asian and African Studies, Moscow State University.

Dr Andrea Edoardo Varisco (Italy/United Kingdom) is the Acting Director of SIPRI's Dual-use and Arms Trade Control Programme. He has a PhD in Post-war Recovery Studies from the University of York, has worked as Head of Analytics for Conflict Armament Research and has field research experience in conflict-affected countries in the Middle East, South Asia and sub-Saharan Africa. Varisco has authored and co-authored analytical reports on arms control and weapons and ammunition management for national government agencies and security and defence forces in Europe, Africa and Asia. His recent publications include 'Post-shipment control measures: European approaches to on-site inspections of exported military materiel', SIPRI Background Paper (Dec. 2020, co-author).

Pieter D. Wezeman (Netherlands/Sweden) is a Senior Researcher in SIPRI's Arms and Military Expenditure Programme. He has contributed to many SIPRI publications since 1994, including SIPRI's annual reviews of global trends in arms transfers, arms industry, military expenditure and multilateral arms embargoes. Among other things, he has published on transparency in military matters, military expenditure and capabilities in the Middle East, arms flows to Africa, and the European arms industry. In 2003–2006 he also worked as a Senior Analyst on arms proliferation for the Dutch Ministry of Defence, and in 2017 as a Technical Expert for the United Nations Group of Governmental Experts during a review of the UN Report on Military Expenditure.

Siemon T. Wezeman (Netherlands) is a Senior Researcher in SIPRI's Arms and Military Expenditure Programme. His areas of research include the monitoring of arms transfers—with a particular regional focus on the Asia–Pacific, South America, former Soviet regions and South Western Europe—and the use of weapons in conflicts, transparency in arms transfers, and the development of conventional military technologies. His recent publications include 'Transparency in arms procurement', SIPRI Insights on Peace and Security (Oct. 2020, co-author); 'Mapping the international presence of the world's largest arms companies', SIPRI Insights on Peace and Security (Dec. 2020, co-author); *Arms Flows to South East Asia*, SIPRI Report (Dec. 2019); and 'Trends in international arms transfers, 2020', SIPRI Fact Sheet (Mar. 2021, co-author).

Errata

SIPRI Yearbook 2020: Armaments, Disarmament and International Security

Page x, 233   Nan Tian, Pieter D. Wezeman, Diego Lopes da Silva, Siemon T. Wezeman, and Alexandra Kuimova authored 'Regional developments in military expenditure, 2019', section II of chapter 8.

Page 18, footnote 74   *For* 'Some 11 hectares of bush, farmland and towns were affected by the Australian bushfires' *read* 'Some 11 million hectares of bush, farmland and towns were affected by the Australian bushfires'

Page 550   *For* 'the 1992 Chemical Weapons Convention' *read* 'the 1993 Chemical Weapons Convention'

SIPRI Yearbook 2017: Armaments, Disarmament and International Security

Page 144, figure 4.2   *For* the figure's y-axis label 'Constant US$ (2015)' *read* 'No. of deaths'

Errata for this printed version of *SIPRI Yearbook 2021* will appear at <http://www.sipri.org/yearbook/> and in *SIPRI Yearbook 2022*.

Index